54th Annual Meeting of the Association for Computational Linguistics (ACL 2016)

Short Papers

Berlin, Germany
7 – 12 August 2016

ISBN: 978-1-5108-2759-2

The 54th Annual Meeting of the Association for Computational Linguistics

Proceedings of the Conference, Vol. 2 (Short Papers)

August 7-12, 2016
Berlin, Germany

Preface: General Chair

In my welcome to participants in this year's conference handbook, I especially welcomed those for which it was their first ACL. I expressed the hope that the conference fulfilled their expectations and remained in their memory as a great start. Trying to imagine the first experience of a present-day ACL, the magnitude of the whole event may be a bit overwhelming - our field is on an expanding trajectory, and even a selection of the best work fills a great number of parallel sessions over a number of days; plus, there are the workshops and tutorials to quench many topical thirsts. This ACL again promises to be a next peak in a progressive development.

ACL Conferences are the product of many people working together, kindly offering their services to the community at large. ACL-2016 is no exception to this. I would like to thank each and every person who has volunteered their time to make the event possible. I am deeply impressed with the sense of community that organizing an ACL brings about.

Priscilla Rasmussen, the ACL Business Manager, and the 2015 ACL Executive Committee (Chris Manning, Pushpak Bhattacharyya, Joakim Nivre, Graeme Hirst, Dragomir Radev, Gertjan van Nood, Min-Yen Kan, Herman Ney, and Yejin Choi) have been instrumental in setting ACL-2016 in motion and in guiding the ACL-2016 team along the path from concept to execution. Without the collective memory and hands-on guidance of the committee, an ACL conference will never happen.

The ACL-2016 team was formidable in building all the components of the conference and connecting them together in an impressive programme: Katrin Erk and Noah Smith (Programme Committee Chairs); Valia Kordoni, Markus Egg (Local Arrangements Chairs) who brought together a fantastic local organization team; Sabine Schulte im Walde and Jun Zhao (Workshop Chairs), Alexandra Birch and Willem Zuidema (Tutorial Chairs); Hai Zhao, Yusuke Miyao, and Yannick Versley (Publication Chairs); Tao Lei, He He, and Will Roberts (Student Research Workshop Chairs), Yang Liu, Chris Biemann, and Gosse Bouma (Faculty Advisors for the Student Research Workshop), Marianna Apidianaki and Sameer Pradhan (Demonstration Chairs), Barbara Plank (Publicity Chair), Florian Kunneman and Matt Post (Conference Handbook Team), and Yulia Grishina (Student Volunteer Coordinator).

The Program Chairs selected outstanding invited speakers: Mark Steedman (University of Edinburgh) and Amber Boydstun (University of California, Davis).

I am deeply grateful to our sponsors for their generous contributions, allowing the conference not to become prohibitively expensive: Google, Baidu, Amazon (Platinum Sponsors); Bloomberg, Facebook, eBay, Elsevier, Microsoft Research, and Maluuba (Gold Sponsors); Huawei Technologies, Zalando SE (Silver Sponsors); Nuance, Grammarly, Voicebox, Yandex, and Textkernel (Bronze Sponsors).

Finally, I would like to express my deep appreciation for the hard work carried out by all area chairs, workshop organizers, tutorial presenters, and the massive army of reviewers. Kudos to all.

Welcome to ACL-2016!

Antal van den Bosch
General Chair

Preface: Program Committee Co-Chairs

Welcome to the 54th Annual Meeting of the Association for Computational Linguistics! This year, ACL received 825 long paper submissions (a new record) and 463 short paper submissions.[1] Of the long papers, 231 were accepted for presentation at ACL—116 as oral presentations and 115 as poster presentations. 97 short papers were accepted—49 as oral and 48 as poster presentations. In addition, ACL also features 25 presentations of papers accepted in the *Transactions of the Association for Computational Linguistics* (TACL). With 353 paper presentations at the main conference, this is the largest ACL program to date.

In keeping with the tremendous growth of our field, we introduced some changes to the conference. Oral presentations were shortened to fifteen (twelve) minutes for long (short) papers, plus time for questions. While this places a greater demand on speakers to be concise, we believe it is worth the effort, allowing far more work to be presented orally. We also took advantage of the many halls available at Humboldt University and expanded the number of parallel talks during some conference sessions.

We introduced a category of outstanding papers to help recognize the highest quality work in the community this year. The 11 outstanding papers (9 long, 2 short, 0.85% of submissions) represent a broad spectrum of exciting contributions; they are recognized by especially prominent placement in the program. From these, a best paper and an IBM-sponsored best student paper have been selected; those will be announced in the awards session on Wednesday afternoon.

Following other recent ACL conferences, submissions were reviewed under different categories and using different review forms for empirical/data-driven, theoretical, applications/tools, resources/evaluation, and survey papers. We introduced special fields in the paper submission form for authors to explicitly note the release of open-source implementations to enable reproducibility, and to note freely available datasets. We also allowed authors to submit appendices of arbitrary length for details that would enable replication; reviewers were not expected to read this material.

Another innovation we explored during the review period was the scheduling of short paper review before long paper review. While this was planned to make the entire review period more compact (fitting between the constraints of NAACL 2016 and EMNLP 2016 at either end), we found that reviewing short papers first eliminated many of the surprises for the long paper review process.

We sought to follow recently-evolved best practices in planning the poster sessions, so that the many high-quality works presented in that format will be visible and authors and attendees benefit from the interactions during the two poster sessions.

ACL 2016 will have two distinguished invited speakers: Amber Boydstun (Associate Professor of Political Science at the University of California, Davis) and Mark Steedman (Professor of Cognitive Science at the University of Edinburgh). We are grateful that they accepted our invitations and look forward to their presentations.

There are many individuals we wish to thank for their contributions to ACL 2016, some multiple times:

---

[1] These numbers exclude papers that were not reviewed due to formatting, anonymity, or double submission violations (9 short and 21 long papers) or that were withdrawn prior to review (approximately 59 short and 52 long papers).

- The 38 area chairs who recruited reviewers, led the discussion about each paper, carefully assessed each submission, and authored meta-reviews to guide final decisions: Miguel Ballesteros, David Bamman, Steven Bethard, Jonathan Berant, Gemma Boleda, Ming-Wei Chang, Wanxiang Che, Chris Dyer, Ed Grefenstette, Hannaneh Hajishirzi, Minlie Huang, Mans Hulden, Heng Ji, Jing Jiang, Zornitsa Kozareva, Marco Kuhlmann, Yang Liu, Annie Louis, Wei Lu, Marie-Catherine de Marneffe, Gerard de Melo, David Mimno, Meg Mitchell, Daichi Mochihashi, Graham Neubig, Naoaki Okazaki, Simone Ponzetto, Matthew Purver, David Reitter, Nathan Schneider, Hinrich Schuetze, Thamar Solorio, Lucia Specia, Partha Talukdar, Ivan Titov, Lu Wang, Nianwen Xue, and Grace Yang.

- Our full program committee of 884 hard-working individuals who reviewed the conference's 1,288 submissions (including secondary reviewers).

- The ACL coordinating committee members, especially Yejin Choi, Graeme Hirst, Chris Manning, and Shiqi Zhao, who answered many questions as they arose during the year.

- TACL editors-in-chief Mark Johnson, Lillian Lee, and Kristina Toutanova, for coordinating with us on TACL presentations at ACL.

- Ani Nenkova and Owen Rambow, program co-chairs of NAACL 2016, and Michael Strube, program co-chair of ACL 2015, who were generous with advice.

- Yusuke Miyao, Yannick Versley, and Hai Zhao, our well-organized publication chairs, and the responsive team at Softconf led by Rich Gerber.

- Valia Kordoni and the local organization team, especially webmaster Kostadin Cholakov.

- Antal van den Bosch, our general chair, who kept us coordinated with the rest of the ACL 2016 team and offered guidance whenever we needed it.

- Antal van den Bosch, Claire Cardie, Pascale Fung, Ray Mooney, and Joakim Nivre, who carefully reviewed papers under consideration for outstanding and best paper recognition.

- Priscilla Rasmussen, who knows everything about how to make ACL a success.

We hope that you enjoy ACL 2016 in Berlin!

ACL 2016 program co-chairs
Katrin Erk, University of Texas
Noah A. Smith, University of Washington

ACL 2016 Organizing Committee

General Chair

Antal van den Bosch, Radboud University Nijmegen

Program Co-Chairs

Katrin Erk, University of Texas at Austin
Noah A. Smith, University of Washington

Local Organizing Committee

Valia Kordoni (local chair), Humboldt University
Markus Egg (local co-chair), Humboldt University
Kostadin Cholakov, Humboldt University
Maja Popović, Humboldt University
Manfred Stede, University of Potsdam
Anke Lüdeling, Humboldt University
Manfred Krifka, Humboldt University
Ulf Leser, Humboldt University
Yulia Grishina (Student Volunteer Coordinator), University of Potsdam

Workshop Chairs

Jun Zhao, Chinese Academy of Sciences
Sabine Schulte im Walde, IMS Stuttgart

Tutorial Chairs

Alexandra Birch, University of Edinburgh
Willem Zuidema, University of Amsterdam

Publication Chairs

Yannick Versley, Ruprecht-Karls-Universität Heidelberg
Hai Zhao, Shanghai Jiao Tong University
Yusuke Miyao, National Institute of Informatics, Japan

Demonstration Chairs

Sameer Pradhan, Boulder Learning
Marianna Apidianaki, LIMSI-CNRS

Student Research Workshop Chairs

Will Roberts, Humboldt-Universität zu Berlin
Tao Lei, Massachusetts Institute of Technology
He He, University of Maryland

Faculty Advisors to the Student Research Workshop

Yang Liu, Tsinghua University

Chris Biemann, Technische Universität Darmstadt
Gosse Bouma, University of Groningen

Student Volunteer Coordinator

Yulia Grishina, University of Potsdam

Publicity Chair

Barbara Plank, University of Groningen

Conference Handbook Chair

Florian Kunneman, Radboud University Nijmegen

Business Manager

Priscilla Rasmussen, ACL

Professional Conference Organiser

Con gressa GmbH, Berlin

ACL 2016 Program Committee

Omri Abend, Steven Abney, Amjad Abu-Jbara, Heike Adel, Stergos Afantenos, Nitish Aggarwal, Željko Agić, Eneko Agirre, Cem Akkaya, Iñaki Alegria, Laura Alonso Alemany, Enrique Alfonseca, Afra Alishahi, Alexandre Allauzen, David Alvarez-Melis, Waleed Ammar, Jacob Andreas, Ion Androutsopoulos, Gabor Angeli, Masahiro Araki, Ron Artstein, Yoav Artzi, Kristjan Arumae, Nicholas Asher, AiTi Aw,

JinYeong Bak, Collin Baker, Alexandra Balahur, Timothy Baldwin, Borja Balle, Miguel Ballesteros, David Bamman, Srinivas Bangalore, Mohit Bansal, Libby Barak, Marco Baroni, Regina Barzilay, Roberto Basili, David Batista, Timo Baumann, Frederic Bechet, Daniel Beck, Núria Bel, I. Beltagy, Anja Belz, Fabrício Benevenuto, Jonathan Berant, Taylor Berg-Kirkpatrick, Sabine Bergler, Raffaella Bernardi, Robert Berwick, Steven Bethard, Archna Bhatia, Pushpak Bhattacharyya, Klinton Bicknell, Ann Bies, Alexandra Birch, Anders Björkelund, Frédéric Blain, Nate Blaylock, Bernd Bohnet, Ondřej Bojar, Ester Boldrini, Gemma Boleda, Danushka Bollegala, Claire Bonial, Georgeta Bordea, Antoine Bordes, Johan Bos, Samuel R. Bowman, Johan Boye, Kristy Boyer, Cem Bozsahin, S.R.K. Branavan, António Branco, Adrian Brasoveanu, Elia Bruni, Christian Buck, Paul Buitelaar, Harry Bunt, Hendrik Buschmeier,

Aoife Cahill, Lynne Cahill, José Camacho-Collados, Burcu Can, Nicola Cancedda, Hailong Cao, Kris Cao, Yunbo Cao, Claire Cardie, Xavier Carreras, John Carroll, Paula Carvalho, Francisco Casacuberta, Helena Caseli, Tommaso Caselli, Steve Cassidy, Irene Castellon, Giuseppe Castellucci, Asli Celikyilmaz, Özlem Çetinoğlu, Mauro Cettolo, Arun Chaganty, Hou-pong Chan, Jane Chandlee, Angel Chang, Kai-Wei Chang, Ming-Wei Chang, Wanxiang Che, Ciprian Chelba, Berlin Chen, Boxing Chen, Chen Chen, Hsin-Hsi Chen, Kehai Chen, Kuan-Yu Chen, Qian Chen, Wenliang Chen, Xixian Chen, Yun-Nung Chen, Zhiyu Chen, Colin Cherry, Sean Chester, Jackie Chi Kit Cheung, David Chiang, Hai Leong Chieu, Laura Chiticariu, Kyunghyun Cho, Eunsol Choi, Yejin Choi, Janara Christensen, Christos Christodoulopoulos, Grzegorz Chrupała, Alexander Clark, Stephen Clark, Ann Clifton, Maximin Coavoux, Moreno Coco, Trevor Cohn, Sandra Collovini, Miriam Connor, John Conroy, Paul Cook, Ann Copestake, Ryan Cotterell, Benoit Crabbé, Danilo Croce, James Cross, Montse Cuadros, Heriberto Cuayahuitl, Silviu-Petru Cucerzan, Xiaodong Cui, Jennifer Culbertson, Aron Culotta,

Walter Daelemans, Robert Daland, Amitava Das, Dipanjan Das, Hal Daumé III, Brian Davison, Munmun De Choudhury, Adrià de Gispert, Marie-Catherine de Marneffe, Gerard de Melo, Claudio Delli Bovi, Vera Demberg, Pascal Denis, Michael Denkowski, Leon Derczynski, Aliya Deri, Nina Dethlefs, Ann Devitt, Jacob Devlin, Giuseppe Di Fabbrizio, Mona Diab, Brian Dillon, Georgiana Dinu, Dmitriy Dligach, Simon Dobnik, Ellen Dodge, A. Seza Doğruöz, Doug Downey, Eduard Dragut, Mark Dras, Markus Dreyer, Gregory Druck, Lan Du, Kevin Duh, Jesse Dunietz, Long Duong, Nadir Durrani, Greg Durrett, Chris Dyer, Marc Dymetman,

Koji Eguchi, Patrick Ehlen, Vladimir Eidelman, Andreas Eisele, Jacob Eisenstein, Jason Eisner, Michael Elhadad, Micha Elsner, Nikolaos Engonopoulos, Katrin Erk, Miquel Esplà-Gomis, Paula Estrella, Keelan Evanini,

Federico Fancellu, Rui Fang, Manaal Faruqui, Adam Faulkner, Benoit Favre, Anna Feldman, Naomi Feldman, Raquel Fernandez, Daniel Fernández-González, Simone Filice, Katja Filippova, Orhan Firat, Nicholas FitzGerald, Margaret Fleck, Fabian Flöck, Enrique Flores, Evandro Fonseca, Mikel Forcada, Markus Forsberg, George Foster, James Foulds, Bob Frank, Michael Frank, Stefan L. Frank, Stella Frank, Alexander

Fraser, Dayne Freitag, Annemarie Friedrich, Akinori Fujino,

Yarin Gal, Michel Galley, Carlos Gallo, Björn Gambäck, Michael Gamon, Kuzman Ganchev, Kavita Ganesan, Juri Ganitkevitch, Jianfeng Gao, Wei Gao, Miguel A. García-Cumbreras, Claire Gardent, Matt Gardner, Dan Garrette, Milica Gasic, Kallirroi Georgila, Daniel Gildea, Kevin Gimpel, Maite Giménez, Jonathan Ginzburg, Dimitra Gkatzia, Goran Glavaš, Amir Globerson, Yoav Goldberg, Dan Goldwasser, Sharon Goldwater, Carlos Gómez-Rodríguez, Edgar González Pellicer, Matthew R. Gormley, Cyril Goutte, Joao Graca, Yvette Graham, Roger Granada, Edouard Grave, Nancy Green, Spence Green, Ed Grefenstette, Denis Griffis, Tom Griffiths, Liane Guillou, Curry Guinn, James Gung, Jiang Guo, Weiwei Guo, Yuhong Guo, Abhijeet Gupta, Iryna Gurevych, Yoan Gutierrez, Kelvin Guu,

Nizar Habash, Gholamreza Haffari, Hannaneh Hajishirzi, Dilek Hakkani-Tur, John Hale, David Hall, Keith Hall, William L. Hamilton, Michael Hammond, Bo Han, Greg Hanneman, Christian Hardmeier, Sasa Hasan, Helen Hastie, Claudia Hauff, Katsuhiko Hayashi, Daqing He, Luheng He, Xiaodong He, Yifan He, Kenneth Heafield, Carmen Heger, Michael Heilman, James Henderson, Matthew Henderson, Aurélie Herbelot, Karl Moritz Hermann, Daniel Hershcovich, Jack Hessel, Felix Hill, Keikichi Hirose, Graeme Hirst, Julian Hitschler, Anna Hjalmarsson, Kai Hong, Liangjie Hong, Andrea Horbach, Julian Hough, Dirk Hovy, Bo-June (Paul) Hsu, Liang Huang, Minlie Huang, Ruihong Huang, Mans Hulden, Tim Hunter, Jena D. Hwang,

Ignacio Iacobacci, Ryu Iida, Diana Inkpen, Naoya Inoue, Hitoshi Isahara, Hideki Isozaki, Mohit Iyyer,

Cassandra L. Jacobs, Guillaume Jacquet, Evan Jaffe, Jagadeesh Jagarlamudi, Zunaira Jamil, Peter Jansen, Laura Jehl, Yacine Jernite, Heng Ji, Yangfeng Ji, Sittichai Jiampojamarn, Jing Jiang, Wenbin Jiang, Xin Jiang, Salud María Jiménez Zafra, Anders Johannsen, Richard Johansson, Michael Johnston, Kristiina Jokinen, Arne Jonsson, Aditya Joshi, Shafiq Joty, Dan Jurafsky, Filip Jurcicek, David Jurgens,

Mijail Kabadjov, Nobuhiro Kaji, Jaap Kamps, Min-Yen Kan, Hiroshi Kanayama, Mladen Karan, Tatsuya Kawahara, Frank Keller, Casey Kennington, Chloé Kiddon, Douwe Kiela, Jae Won Kim, Joon Kim, Jooyeon Kim, Suin Kim, Sunghwan Kim, Yoon Kim, Young-Bum Kim, Irwin King, Brian Kingsbury, Svetlana Kiritchenko, Julia Kiseleva, Alexandre Klementiev, Sigrid Klerke, Christoph Kling, Julien Kloetzer, Alistair Knott, Tomáš Kočiský, Philipp Koehn, Oskar Kohonen, Prasanth Kolachina, Alexander Koller, Mamoru Komachi, Kazunori Komatani, Rik Koncel-Kedziorski, Lingpeng Kong, Ioannis Konstas, Hahn Koo, Stefan Kopp, Moshe Koppel, Valia Kordoni, Anna Korhonen, Bhushan Kotnis, Zornitsa Kozareva, Julia Kreutzer, Jayant Krishnamurthy, Mark Kroell, Kriste Krstovski, Canasai Kruengkrai, Germán Kruszewski, Lun-Wei Ku, Sicong Kuang, Marco Kuhlmann, Jonas Kuhn, Wu Kui, Shankar Kumar, Nate Kushman, Ilia Kuznetsov, Polina Kuznetsova, Tom Kwiatkowski, Sandra Kübler,

Man Lan, Guy Lapalme, Mirella Lapata, Shalom Lappin, Birger Larsen, Alex Lascarides, Alon Lavie, Angeliki Lazaridou, Phong Le, Joseph Le Roux, Kenton Lee, Moontae Lee, Sungjin Lee, Yoong Keok Lee, Tao Lei, Oliver Lemon, Alessandro Lenci, Lori Levin, Gina-Anne Levow, Omer Levy, Mike Lewis, Chen Li, Fangtao Li, Hang Li, Jing Li, Jiwei Li, Junhui Li, Shoushan Li, Sujian Li, Wenjie Li, Xiaolong Li, Zhenghua Li, Kexin Liao, Xiangwen Liao, Chin-Yew Lin, Hui Lin, Victoria Lin, Wang Ling, Xiao Ling, Christina Lioma, Pierre Lison, Diane Litman, Marina Litvak, Biao Liu, Fei Liu, Jiangming Liu, Jing Liu, Kang Liu, Qun Liu, Yang Liu, Varvara Logacheva, Lucelene Lopes, Adam Lopez, Oier Lopez de Lacalle, Aurelio Lopez-Lopez, Annie Louis, Bin Lu, Jing Lu, Wei Lu, Andy Luecking, Michal Lukasik, Jiaming Luo, Minh-Thang Luong, Franco M. Luque,

Shaoping Ma, Qingsong Ma, Shuming Ma, Wolfgang Macherey, Nitin Madnani, Wolfgang Maier, Prodromos Malakasiotis, Suresh Manandhar, Gideon Mann, Christopher D. Manning, Diego Marcheggiani, Daniel Marcu, Marco Marelli, Eugenio Martínez Cámara, Toni Marti, Patricio Martinez-Barco, Héctor Martínez Alonso, Eugenio Martínez Cámara, Fernando Martínez Santiago, Eugenio Martínez-Cámara, Fernando Javier Martínez Santiago, André F. T. Martins, Vivien Mast, Yuichiro Matsubayashi, Takuya Matsuzaki, Jonathan May, Diana Maynard, Diana McCarthy, David McClosky, Ryan McDonald, Tara McIntosh, Kathy McKeown, Louise McNally, Beata Megyesi, Yashar Mehdad, Oren Melamud, Arul Menezes, Fandong Meng, Helen Meng, Florian Metze, Haitao Mi, Yishu Miao, Tsvetomila Mihaylova, Tomas Mikolov, Timothy Miller, Tristan Miller, David Mimno, Meg Mitchell, Teruhisa Misu, Yusuke Miyao, Ryosuke Miyazaki, Daichi Mochihashi, Ashutosh Modi, Marie-Francine Moens, Samaneh Moghaddam, Saif Mohammad, Karo Moilanen, Luis Gerardo Mojica de la Vega, M. Dolores Molina-González, Manuel Montes, Andres Montoyo, Christof Monz, Taesun Moon, Roser Morante, Silvio Moreira, Alessandro Moschitti, Arjun Mukherjee, Philippe Muller, Yugo Murawaki, Gabriel Murray, Lluís Márquez, Thomas Müller,

Masaaki Nagata, Satoshi Nakamura, Mikio Nakano, Yukiko Nakano, Preslav Nakov, Courtney Napoles, Jason Naradowsky, Karthik Narasimhan, Vivi Nastase, Borja Navarro, Roberto Navigli, Silvia Necsulescu, Mark-Jan Nederhof, Sapna Negi, Matteo Negri, Aida Nematzadeh, Graham Neubig, Jun-Ping Ng, Vincent Ng, Dong Nguyen, Garrett Nicolai, Vlad Niculae, Luis Nieto Piña, Alexandr Nikitin, Zhou Nina, Joakim Nivre,

Brendan O'Connor, Timothy O'Donnell, Stephan Oepen, Kemal Oflazer, Alice Oh, Jong-Hoon Oh, Naoaki Okazaki, Hiroshi G. Okuno, Constantin Orasan, Vicente Ordonez, Miles Osborne, Diarmuid Ó Séaghdha, Mari Ostendorf, Ekaterina Ovchinnikova, Gozde Ozbal,

Sebastian Padó, John Paisley, Alexis Palmer, Martha Palmer, Sinno Jialin Pan, Denis Paperno, Ankur P. Parikh, Cecile Paris, Tommaso Pasini, Peyman Passban, Panupong Pasupat, Siddharth Patwardhan, Michael J. Paul, Adam Pauls, Ellie Pavlick, Bolette Pedersen, Hao Peng, Nanyun Peng, Gerald Penn, Casper Petersen, Slav Petrov, Miriam R. L. Petruck, Hieu Pham, Nghia The Pham, Olivier Pietquin, Mohammad Taher Pilehvar, Manfred Pinkal, Emily Pitler, Paul Piwek, Barbara Plank, Simone Ponzetto, Maja Popović, Fred Popowich, Matt Post, Christopher Potts, Vinod Prabhakaran, Vinodkumar Prabhakaran, Sameer Pradhan, Daniel Preoţiuc-Pietro, Laurent Prévot, Stephen Pulman, Matthew Purver, Sampo Pyysalo,

Xian Qian, Xiuming Qiao, Bing Qin, Guang Qiu, Xipeng Qiu, Chris Quirk,

Alessandro Raganato, Preethi Raghavan, Afshin Rahimi, Altaf Rahman, Jonathan Raiman, Gabriela Ramirez-de-la-Rosa, Ari Rappoport, Mohammad Sadegh Rasooli, Antoine Raux, Sujith Ravi, Marta Recasens, Sravana Reddy, Ines Rehbein, Roi Reichart, Drew Reisinger, David Reitter, Yafeng Ren, Zhaochun Ren, Steve Renals, Evelina Rennes, Corentin Ribeyre, Matthew Richardson, Sebastian Riedel, Jason Riesa, Verena Rieser, Stefan Riezler, German Rigau, Laura Rimell, Alan Ritter, Brian Roark, Molly Roberts, Tim Rocktäschel, Horacio Rodríguez, Stephen Roller, Laurent Romary, Carolyn Rose, Andrew Rosenberg, Sara Rosenthal, Paolo Rosso, Michael Roth, Sascha Rothe, Alexander Rudnicky, Josef Ruppenhofer, Alexander M. Rush,

Mrinmaya Sachan, Mehrnoosh Sadrzadeh, Markus Saers, Kenji Sagae, Horacio Saggion, Benoît Sagot, Magnus Sahlgren, Patrick Saint-Dizier, Avneesh Saluja, Marc Franco Salvador, Felipe Sánchez-Martínez, Germán Sanchis-Trilles, Urko Sanchez Sanz, Anoop Sarkar, Asad Sayeed, Carolina Scarton, David Schlangen,

Allen Schmaltz, Helmut Schmid, Nathan Schneider, Alexandra Schofield, William Schuler, Sabine Schulte im Walde, Sebastian Schuster, Hinrich Schütze, Lane Schwartz, Roy Schwartz, Chun Wei Seah, Djamé Seddah, Wolfgang Seeker, Yohei Seki, Rico Sennrich, Minjoon Seo, Hendra Setiawan, Izhak Shafran, Apurva Shah, Kashif Shah, Shiqi Shen, Chaitanya Shivade, Milad Shokouhi, Szymon Sidor, Avirup Sil, Carina Silberer, Mario J. Silva, Fabrizio Silvestri, Khalil Sima'an, Patrick Simianer, Serra Sinem Tekiroglu, Sameer Singh, Gabriel Skantze, Kevin Small, Noah Smith, Jan Šnajder, Jasper Snoek, Richard Socher, Anders Søgaard, Artem Sokolov, Thamar Solorio, Yan Song, Radu Soricut, Aitor Soroa, Lucia Specia, Caroline Sporleder, Vivek Srikumar, Edward Stabler, Gabriel Stanovsky, Manfred Stede, Mark Steedman, Amanda Stent, Brandon Stewart, Matthew Stone, Svetlana Stoyanchev, Veselin Stoyanov, Carlo Strapparava, Kristina Striegnitz, Markus Strohmaier, Patrick Sturt, Rajen Subba, Katsuhito Sudoh, Weiwei Sun, Xu Sun, Mihai Surdeanu, Jun Suzuki, John Sylak-Glassman, Gabriel Synnaeve, Stan Szpakowicz, Idan Szpektor,

Hiroya Takamura, Partha Talukdar, Akihiro Tamura, Duyu Tang, Jian Tang, Jiliang Tang, Mariona Taulé, Christoph Teichmann, Irina Temnikova, Joel Tetreault, Kapil Thadani, Ran Tian, Jörg Tiedemann, Ivan Titov, Takenobu Tokunaga, Katrin Tomanek, Kentaro Torisawa, David Vilar Torres, Kristina Toutanova, Isabel Trancoso, Harald Trost, Richard Tzong-Han Tsai, Reut Tsarfaty, Kostas Tsioutsiouliklis, Oren Tsur, Yoshimasa Tsuruoka, Yulia Tsvetkov, Gokhan Tur, Marco Turchi, Oscar Täckström,

L. Alfonso Urena Lopez, Olga Uryupina, Masao Utiyama,

Alessandro Valitutti, Lonneke van der Plas, Lucy Vanderwende, David Vandyke, Marten van Schijndel, Paola Velardi, Yannick Versley, Renata Vieira, Esaú Villatoro, Sami Virpioja, Andreas Vlachos, Rob Voigt, Svitlana Volkova, Titus von der Malsburg, Ngoc Thang Vu,

Marilyn Walker, Byron C. Wallace, Stephen Wan, Xiaojun Wan, Chong Wang, Hsin-Min Wang, Lu Wang, Mingxuan Wang, Pidong Wang, Quan Wang, Shaojun Wang, Tong Wang, Wen Wang, Wenya Wang, Yu-Chun Wang, Nigel Ward, Taro Watanabe, Andy Way, Bonnie Webber, Ingmar Weber, Furu Wei, Albert Weichselbraun, Keenon Werling, Michael White, Jason D. Williams, Shuly Wintner, Sam Wiseman, Guillaume Wisniewski, Kam-Fai Wong, Dekai Wu, Hua Wu, Ji Wu, Shumin Wu, Joern Wuebker,

Fei Xia, Rui Xia, Pengtao Xie, Shasha Xie, Wayne Xin Zhao, Chenyan Xiong, Deyi Xiong, Ruifeng Xu, Wang Xuancong, Nianwen Xue,

Yadollah Yaghoobzadeh, Grace Yang, Yi Yang, Zi Yang, Mark Yatskar, Wen-tau Yih, Wenpeng Yin, Anssi Yli-Jyrä, Dani Yogatama, Steve Young, Kai Yu, Xiaotian Yu,

Fabio Massimo Zanzotto, Alessandra Zarcone, Daniel Zeman, Xiaodong Zeng, Luke Zettlemoyer, Deniz Zeyrek, Ke Zhai, Aston Zhang, Chunyue Zhang, Congle Zhang, Hongyi Zhang, Lei Zhang, Meishan Zhang, Min Zhang, Qi Zhang, Sicong Zhang, Yuan Zhang, Yue Zhang, Zhihua Zhang, Chunyue Zhang, Bing Zhao, Kai Zhao, Shenglin Zhao, Tiejun Zhao, Tong Zhao, Guodong Zhou, Qiang Zhou, Xiaodan Zhu, Xiaoning Zhu, Patrick Ziering, Heike Zinsmeister, Willem Zuidema

Table of Contents

Transition-based dependency parsing with topological fields
Daniël de Kok and Erhard Hinrichs 1

Scalable Semi-Supervised Query Classification Using Matrix Sketching
Young-Bum Kim, Karl Stratos and Ruhi Sarikaya 8

Learning Multiview Embeddings of Twitter Users
Adrian Benton, Raman Arora and Mark Dredze 14

Implicit Polarity and Implicit Aspect Recognition in Opinion Mining
Huan-Yuan Chen and Hsin-Hsi Chen 20

A Domain Adaptation Regularization for Denoising Autoencoders
Stephane Clinchant, Gabriela Csurka and Boris Chidlovskii 26

Incremental Parsing with Minimal Features Using Bi-Directional LSTM
James Cross and Liang Huang 32

Improving Statistical Machine Translation Performance by Oracle-BLEU Model Re-estimation
Praveen Dakwale and Christof Monz 38

Sequence-to-Sequence Generation for Spoken Dialogue via Deep Syntax Trees and Strings
Ondřej Dušek and Filip Jurcicek 45

On the Linearity of Semantic Change: Investigating Meaning Variation via Dynamic Graph Models
Steffen Eger and Alexander Mehler 52

Joint Word Segmentation and Phonetic Category Induction
Micha Elsner, Stephanie Antetomaso and Naomi Feldman 59

A Language-Independent Neural Network for Event Detection
Xiaocheng Feng, Lifu Huang, Duyu Tang, Heng Ji, Bing Qin and Ting Liu 66

Improved Parsing for Argument Clusters Coordination
Jessica Ficler and Yoav Goldberg 72

Reference Bias in Monolingual Machine Translation Evaluation
Marina Fomicheva and Lucia Specia 77

Cross-lingual projection for class-based language models
Beat Gfeller, Vlad Schogol and Keith Hall 83

A Fast Approach for Semantic Similar Short Texts Retrieval
Yanhui Gu, Zhenglu Yang, Junsheng Zhou, Weiguang Qu, Jinmao Wei and Xingtian Shi 89

Empty element recovery by spinal parser operations
Katsuhiko Hayashi and Masaaki Nagata 95

Semantic classifications for detection of verb metaphors
Beata Beigman Klebanov, Chee Wee Leong, E. Dario Gutierrez, Ekaterina Shutova and Michael
Flor 101

Recognizing Salient Entities in Shopping Queries
Zornitsa Kozareva, Qi Li, Ke Zhai and Weiwei Guo 107

Leveraging Lexical Resources for Learning Entity Embeddings in Multi-Relational Data
Teng Long, Ryan Lowe, Jackie Chi Kit Cheung and Doina Precup 112

Multiplicative Representations for Unsupervised Semantic Role Induction
Yi Luan, Yangfeng Ji, Hannaneh Hajishirzi and Boyang Li 118

Vocabulary Manipulation for Neural Machine Translation
Haitao Mi, Zhiguo Wang and Abe Ittycheriah 124

Natural Language Inference by Tree-Based Convolution and Heuristic Matching
Lili Mou, Rui Men, Ge Li, Yan Xu, Lu Zhang, Rui Yan and Zhi Jin 130

Improving cross-domain n-gram language modelling with skipgrams
Louis Onrust, Antal van den Bosch and Hugo Van hamme 137

Simple PPDB: A Paraphrase Database for Simplification
Ellie Pavlick and Chris Callison-Burch 143

Improving Named Entity Recognition for Chinese Social Media with Word Segmentation Representation Learning
Nanyun Peng and Mark Dredze 149

How Naked is the Naked Truth? A Multilingual Lexicon of Nominal Compound Compositionality
Carlos Ramisch, Silvio Cordeiro, Leonardo Zilio, Marco Idiart and Aline Villavicencio 156

An Open Web Platform for Rule-Based Speech-to-Sign Translation
Manny Rayner, Pierrette Bouillon, Sarah Ebling, Johanna Gerlach, Irene Strasly and Nikos Tsourakis
162

Word Alignment without NULL Words
Philip Schulz, Wilker Aziz and Khalil Sima'an 169

Unsupervised morph segmentation and statistical language models for vocabulary expansion
Matti Varjokallio and Dietrich Klakow 175

Detecting Mild Cognitive Impairment by Exploiting Linguistic Information from Transcripts
Veronika Vincze, Gábor Gosztolya, László Tóth, Ildikó Hoffmann, Gréta Szatlóczki, Zoltán Bánréti,
Magdolna Pákáski and János Kálmán 181

Multi-Modal Representations for Improved Bilingual Lexicon Learning
Ivan Vulić, Douwe Kiela, Stephen Clark and Marie-Francine Moens 188

Is This Post Persuasive? Ranking Argumentative Comments in Online Forum
Zhongyu Wei, Yang Liu and Yi Li 195

The Value of Semantic Parse Labeling for Knowledge Base Question Answering
Wen-tau Yih, Matthew Richardson, Chris Meek, Ming-Wei Chang and Jina Suh 201

Attention-Based Bidirectional Long Short-Term Memory Networks for Relation Classification
Peng Zhou, Wei Shi, Jun Tian, Zhenyu Qi, Bingchen Li, Hongwei Hao and Bo Xu 207

The red one!: On learning to refer to things based on discriminative properties
Angeliki Lazaridou, Nghia The Pham and Marco Baroni 213

Don't Count, Predict! An Automatic Approach to Learning Sentiment Lexicons for Short Text
Duy Tin Vo and Yue Zhang 219

Dimensional Sentiment Analysis Using a Regional CNN-LSTM Model
Jin Wang, Liang-Chih Yu, K. Robert Lai and Xuejie Zhang 225

Deep multi-task learning with low level tasks supervised at lower layers
Anders Søgaard and Yoav Goldberg 231

Domain Specific Named Entity Recognition Referring to the Real World by Deep Neural Networks
Suzushi Tomori, Takashi Ninomiya and Shinsuke Mori 236

An Entity-Focused Approach to Generating Company Descriptions
Gavin Saldanha, Or Biran, Kathleen McKeown and Alfio Gliozzo 243

Annotating Relation Inference in Context via Question Answering
Omer Levy and Ido Dagan 249

Automatic Semantic Classification of German Preposition Types: Comparing Hard and Soft Clustering Approaches across Features
Maximilian Köper and Sabine Schulte im Walde 256

Natural Language Generation enhances human decision-making with uncertain information
Dimitra Gkatzia, Oliver Lemon and Verena Rieser 264

Tweet2Vec: Character-Based Distributed Representations for Social Media
Bhuwan Dhingra, Zhong Zhou, Dylan Fitzpatrick, Michael Muehl and William Cohen 269

Phrase-Level Combination of SMT and TM Using Constrained Word Lattice
Liangyou Li, Andy Way and Qun Liu 275

A Neural Network based Approach to Automatic Post-Editing
Santanu Pal, Sudip Kumar Naskar, Mihaela Vela and Josef van Genabith 281

An Unsupervised Method for Automatic Translation Memory Cleaning
Masoud Jalili Sabet, Matteo Negri, Marco Turchi and Eduard Barbu 287

Exponentially Decaying Bag-of-Words Input Features for Feed-Forward Neural Network in Statistical Machine Translation
Jan-Thorsten Peter, Weiyue Wang and Hermann Ney 293

Syntactically Guided Neural Machine Translation
Felix Stahlberg, Eva Hasler, Aurelien Waite and Bill Byrne 299

Very quaffable and great fun: Applying NLP to wine reviews
Iris Hendrickx, Els Lefever, Ilja Croijmans, Asifa Majid and Antal van den Bosch 306

Exploring Stylistic Variation with Age and Income on Twitter
Lucie Flekova, Daniel Preoţiuc-Pietro and Lyle Ungar 313

Finding Optimists and Pessimists on Twitter
Xianzhi Ruan, Steven Wilson and Rada Mihalcea 320

Transductive Adaptation of Black Box Predictions
Stephane Clinchant, Boris Chidlovskii and Gabriela Csurka 326

Which Tumblr Post Should I Read Next?
Zornitsa Kozareva and Makoto Yamada 332

Text Simplification as Tree Labeling
Joachim Bingel and Anders Søgaard 337

Bootstrapped Text-level Named Entity Recognition for Literature
Julian Brooke, Adam Hammond and Timothy Baldwin 344

The Enemy in Your Own Camp: How Well Can We Detect Statistically-Generated Fake Reviews – An Adversarial Study
Dirk Hovy 351

Character-based Neural Machine Translation
Marta R. Costa-jussà and José A. R. Fonollosa 357

Learning Monolingual Compositional Representations via Bilingual Supervision
Ahmed Elgohary and Marine Carpuat 362

Event Nugget Detection with Forward-Backward Recurrent Neural Networks
Reza Ghaeini, Xiaoli Fern, Liang Huang and Prasad Tadepalli 369

IBC-C: A Dataset for Armed Conflict Analysis
Andrej Zukov Gregoric, Zhiyuan Luo and Bartal Veyhe 374

A Latent Concept Topic Model for Robust Topic Inference Using Word Embeddings
Weihua Hu and Jun'ichi Tsujii 380

Word Embeddings with Limited Memory
Shaoshi Ling, Yangqiu Song and Dan Roth 387

Hawkes Processes for Continuous Time Sequence Classification: an Application to Rumour Stance Classification in Twitter
Michal Lukasik, P. K. Srijith, Duy Vu, Kalina Bontcheva, Arkaitz Zubiaga and Trevor Cohn . . 393

Hunting for Troll Comments in News Community Forums
Todor Mihaylov and Preslav Nakov 399

Phrase Table Pruning via Submodular Function Maximization
Masaaki Nishino, Jun Suzuki and Masaaki Nagata 406

Multilingual Part-of-Speech Tagging with Bidirectional Long Short-Term Memory Models and Auxiliary Loss
Barbara Plank, Anders Søgaard and Yoav Goldberg 412

Matrix Factorization using Window Sampling and Negative Sampling for Improved Word Representations
Alexandre Salle, Aline Villavicencio and Marco Idiart 419

One model, two languages: training bilingual parsers with harmonized treebanks
David Vilares, Carlos Gómez-Rodríguez and Miguel A. Alonso 425

Using mention accessibility to improve coreference resolution
Kellie Webster and Joel Nothman 432

Exploiting Linguistic Features for Sentence Completion
Aubrie Woods...438

Convergence of Syntactic Complexity in Conversation
Yang Xu and David Reitter...443

User Embedding for Scholarly Microblog Recommendation
Yang Yu, Xiaojun Wan and Xinjie Zhou..449

Integrating Distributional Lexical Contrast into Word Embeddings for Antonym-Synonym Distinction
Kim Anh Nguyen, Sabine Schulte im Walde and Ngoc Thang Vu............................454

Machine Translation Evaluation Meets Community Question Answering
Francisco Guzmán, Lluís Màrquez and Preslav Nakov.....................................460

Science Question Answering using Instructional Materials
Mrinmaya Sachan, Kumar Dubey and Eric Xing..467

Specifying and Annotating Reduced Argument Span Via QA-SRL
Gabriel Stanovsky, Ido Dagan and Meni Adler...474

Improving Argument Overlap for Proposition-Based Summarisation
Yimai Fang and Simone Teufel..479

Machine Comprehension using Rich Semantic Representations
Mrinmaya Sachan and Eric Xing...486

Cross-Lingual Word Representations via Spectral Graph Embeddings
Takamasa Oshikiri, Kazuki Fukui and Hidetoshi Shimodaira.............................493

Semantics-Driven Recognition of Collocations Using Word Embeddings
Sara Rodríguez-Fernández, Luis Espinosa Anke, Roberto Carlini and Leo Wanner...........499

Incorporating Relational Knowledge into Word Representations using Subspace Regularization
Abhishek Kumar and Jun Araki..506

Word Embedding Calculus in Meaningful Ultradense Subspaces
Sascha Rothe and Hinrich Schütze..512

Is "Universal Syntax" Universally Useful for Learning Distributed Word Representations?
Ivan Vulić and Anna Korhonen...518

Claim Synthesis via Predicate Recycling
Yonatan Bilu and Noam Slonim...525

Modelling the Interpretation of Discourse Connectives by Bayesian Pragmatics
Frances Yung, Kevin Duh, Taku Komura and Yuji Matsumoto..............................531

Nonparametric Spherical Topic Modeling with Word Embeddings
Kayhan Batmanghelich, Ardavan Saeedi, Karthik Narasimhan and Sam Gershman...........537

A Novel Measure for Coherence in Statistical Topic Models
Fred Morstatter and Huan Liu...543

Coarse-grained Argumentation Features for Scoring Persuasive Essays
Debanjan Ghosh, Aquila Khanam, Yubo Han and Smaranda Muresan.........................549

Single-Model Encoder-Decoder with Explicit Morphological Representation for Reinflection
Katharina Kann and Hinrich Schütze 555

Joint part-of-speech and dependency projection from multiple sources
Anders Johannsen, Željko Agić and Anders Søgaard 561

Dependency-based Gated Recursive Neural Network for Chinese Word Segmentation
Jingjing Xu and Xu Sun 567

Deep Neural Networks for Syntactic Parsing of Morphologically Rich Languages
Joël Legrand and Ronan Collobert 573

Weakly Supervised Part-of-speech Tagging Using Eye-tracking Data
Maria Barrett, Joachim Bingel, Frank Keller and Anders Søgaard 579

Metrics for Evaluation of Word-level Machine Translation Quality Estimation
Varvara Logacheva, Michal Lukasik and Lucia Specia 585

The Social Impact of Natural Language Processing
Dirk Hovy and Shannon L. Spruit 591

Using Sequence Similarity Networks to Identify Partial Cognates in Multilingual Wordlists
Johann-Mattis List, Philippe Lopez and Eric Bapteste 599

Conference Program

Monday, August 8, 2016

8:45–9:00   *Opening session*

9:00–10:10   *Invited talk I: Amber Boydstun*

10:10–10:40   *Coffee break*

Session 1A: Semantic parsing I

Session 1B: Information extraction

Session 1C: Machine translation I

Session 1D: Word meaning I

Session 1E: Parsing I

10:40–11:00   *Transition-based dependency parsing with topological fields*
Daniël de Kok and Erhard Hinrichs

Monday, August 8, 2016 (continued)

Session 1F: Noncompositionality

12:00–13:40   *Lunch break*

Session 2A: Word vectors I

Session 2B: Events and schemas

Session 2C: Sentiment analysis

Session 2D: Parsing II

Session 2E: Information retrieval

14:40–15:00   *Scalable Semi-Supervised Query Classification Using Matrix Sketching*
Young-Bum Kim, Karl Stratos and Ruhi Sarikaya

Session 2F: Phonology and morphology

15:00–15:30   *Coffee break*

Monday, August 8, 2016 (continued)

       Session 3A: Question answering I

       Session 3B: Sentence vectors

       Session 3C: Parsing III

       Session 3D: Dialog

       Session 3E: Generation

       Session 3F: Entities and coreference

       Session 3G: Topics

18:00–21:00   *Poster and dinner session I (includes SRW)*

       Learning Multiview Embeddings of Twitter Users
       Adrian Benton, Raman Arora and Mark Dredze

       Implicit Polarity and Implicit Aspect Recognition in Opinion Mining
       Huan-Yuan Chen and Hsin-Hsi Chen

       A Domain Adaptation Regularization for Denoising Autoencoders
       Stephane Clinchant, Gabriela Csurka and Boris Chidlovskii

       Incremental Parsing with Minimal Features Using Bi-Directional LSTM
       James Cross and Liang Huang

       Improving Statistical Machine Translation Performance by Oracle-BLEU Model Re-estimation
       Praveen Dakwale and Christof Monz

Sequence-to-Sequence Generation for Spoken Dialogue via Deep Syntax Trees and Strings
Ondřej Dušek and Filip Jurcicek

On the Linearity of Semantic Change: Investigating Meaning Variation via Dynamic Graph Models
Steffen Eger and Alexander Mehler

Joint Word Segmentation and Phonetic Category Induction
Micha Elsner, Stephanie Antetomaso and Naomi Feldman

A Language-Independent Neural Network for Event Detection
Xiaocheng Feng, Lifu Huang, Duyu Tang, Heng Ji, Bing Qin and Ting Liu

Improved Parsing for Argument-Clusters Coordination
Jessica Ficler and Yoav Goldberg

Reference Bias in Monolingual Machine Translation Evaluation
Marina Fomicheva and Lucia Specia

Cross-lingual projection for class-based language models
Beat Gfeller, Vlad Schogol and Keith Hall

A Fast Approach for Semantic Similar Short Texts Retrieval
Yanhui Gu, Zhenglu Yang, Junsheng Zhou, Weiguang Qu, Jinmao Wei and Xingtian Shi

Empty element recovery by spinal parser operations
Katsuhiko Hayashi and Masaaki Nagata

Semantic classifications for detection of verb metaphors
Beata Beigman Klebanov, Chee Wee Leong, E. Dario Gutierrez, Ekaterina Shutova and Michael Flor

Recognizing Salient Entities in Shopping Queries
Zornitsa Kozareva, Qi Li, Ke Zhai and Weiwei Guo

Leveraging Lexical Resources for Learning Entity Embeddings in Multi-Relational Data
Teng Long, Ryan Lowe, Jackie Chi Kit Cheung and Doina Precup

Multiplicative Representations for Unsupervised Semantic Role Induction
Yi Luan, Yangfeng Ji, Hannaneh Hajishirzi and Boyang Li

Vocabulary Manipulation for Neural Machine Translation
Haitao Mi, Zhiguo Wang and Abe Ittycheriah

Natural Language Inference by Tree-Based Convolution and Heuristic Matching
Lili Mou, Rui Men, Ge Li, Yan Xu, Lu Zhang, Rui Yan and Zhi Jin

Improving cross-domain n-gram language modelling with skipgrams
Louis Onrust, Antal van den Bosch and Hugo Van hamme

Simple PPDB: A Paraphrase Database for Simplification
Ellie Pavlick and Chris Callison-Burch

Improving Named Entity Recognition for Chinese Social Media with Word Segmentation Representation Learning
Nanyun Peng and Mark Dredze

How Naked is the Naked Truth? A Multilingual Lexicon of Nominal Compound Compositionality
Carlos Ramisch, Silvio Cordeiro, Leonardo Zilio, Marco Idiart and Aline Villavicencio

An Open Web Platform for Rule-Based Speech-to-Sign Translation
Manny Rayner, Pierrette Bouillon, Sarah Ebling, Johanna Gerlach, Irene Strasly and Nikos Tsourakis

Word Alignment without NULL Words
Philip Schulz, Wilker Aziz and Khalil Sima'an

Unsupervised morph segmentation and statistical language models for vocabulary expansion
Matti Varjokallio and Dietrich Klakow

Detecting Mild Cognitive Impairment by Exploiting Linguistic Information from Transcripts
Veronika Vincze, Gábor Gosztolya, László Tóth, Ildikó Hoffmann, Gréta Szatlóczki, Zoltán Bánréti, Magdolna Pákáski and János Kálmán

Multi-Modal Representations for Improved Bilingual Lexicon Learning
Ivan Vulić, Douwe Kiela, Stephen Clark and Marie-Francine Moens

Is This Post Persuasive? Ranking Argumentative Comments in Online Forum
Zhongyu Wei, Yang Liu and Yi Li

The Value of Semantic Parse Labeling for Knowledge Base Question Answering
Wen-tau Yih, Matthew Richardson, Chris Meek, Ming-Wei Chang and Jina Suh

Monday, August 8, 2016 (continued)

Attention-Based Bidirectional Long Short-Term Memory Networks for Relation Classification
Peng Zhou, Wei Shi, Jun Tian, Zhenyu Qi, Bingchen Li, Hongwei Hao and Bo Xu

Tuesday, August 9, 2016

9:00–10:10   *Invited talk II: Mark Steedman*

10:10–10:40   *Coffee break*

        Session 4A: Relations and knowledge bases

        Session 4B: Semantic parsing II

        Session 4C: Word meaning II

        Session 4D: Tasks and datasets

        Session 4E: Parsing IV

        Session 4F: Document analysis

12:00–13:40   *Lunch break*

Session 5A: Deep learning (short papers)

13:40–13:56   *The red one!: On learning to refer to things based on discriminative properties*
Angeliki Lazaridou, Nghia The Pham and Marco Baroni

13:56–14:12   *Don't Count, Predict! An Automatic Approach to Learning Sentiment Lexicons for Short Text*
Duy Tin Vo and Yue Zhang

14:12–14:28   *Dimensional Sentiment Analysis Using a Regional CNN-LSTM Model*
Jin Wang, Liang-Chih Yu, K. Robert Lai and Xuejie Zhang

14:28–14:44   *Deep multi-task learning with low level tasks supervised at lower layers*
Anders Søgaard and Yoav Goldberg

14:44–15:00   *Domain Specific Named Entity Recognition Referring to the Real World by Deep Neural Networks*
Suzushi Tomori, Takashi Ninomiya and Shinsuke Mori

Session 5B: Semantics and generation (short papers)

13:40–13:56   *An Entity-Focused Approach to Generating Company Descriptions*
Gavin Saldanha, Or Biran, Kathleen McKeown and Alfio Gliozzo

13:56–14:12   *Annotating Relation Inference in Context via Question Answering*
Omer Levy and Ido Dagan

14:12–14:28   *Automatic Semantic Classification of German Preposition Types: Comparing Hard and Soft Clustering Approaches across Features*
Maximilian Köper and Sabine Schulte im Walde

14:28–14:44   *Natural Language Generation enhances human decision-making with uncertain information*
Dimitra Gkatzia, Oliver Lemon and Verena Rieser

14:44–15:00   *Tweet2Vec: Character-Based Distributed Representations for Social Media*
Bhuwan Dhingra, Zhong Zhou, Dylan Fitzpatrick, Michael Muehl and William Cohen

Session 5C: Machine translation II (short papers)

13:40–13:56   *Phrase-Level Combination of SMT and TM Using Constrained Word Lattice*
Liangyou Li, Andy Way and Qun Liu

13:56–14:12   *A Neural Network based Approach to Automatic Post-Editing*
Santanu Pal, Sudip Kumar Naskar, Mihaela Vela and Josef van Genabith

14:12–14:28   *An Unsupervised Method for Automatic Translation Memory Cleaning*
Masoud Jalili Sabet, Matteo Negri, Marco Turchi and Eduard Barbu

14:28–14:44   *Exponentially Decaying Bag-of-Words Input Features for Feed-Forward Neural Network in Statistical Machine Translation*
Jan-Thorsten Peter, Weiyue Wang and Hermann Ney

14:44–15:00   *Syntactically Guided Neural Machine Translation*
Felix Stahlberg, Eva Hasler, Aurelien Waite and Bill Byrne

Session 5D: Text classification (short papers)

13:40–13:56   *Very quaffable and great fun: Applying NLP to wine reviews*
Iris Hendrickx, Els Lefever, Ilja Croijmans, Asifa Majid and Antal van den Bosch

13:56–14:12   *Exploring Stylistic Variation with Age and Income on Twitter*
Lucie Flekova, Daniel Preoţiuc-Pietro and Lyle Ungar

14:12–14:28   *Finding Optimists and Pessimists on Twitter*
Xianzhi Ruan, Steven Wilson and Rada Mihalcea

14:28–14:44   *Transductive Adaptation of Black Box Predictions*
Stephane Clinchant, Boris Chidlovskii and Gabriela Csurka

14:44–15:00   *Which Tumblr Post Should I Read Next?*
Zornitsa Kozareva and Makoto Yamada

Tuesday, August 9, 2016 (continued)

       Session 5E: Potpourri I (short papers)

13:40–13:56   *Text Simplification as Tree Labeling*
Joachim Bingel and Anders Søgaard

13:56–14:12   *Bootstrapped Text-level Named Entity Recognition for Literature*
Julian Brooke, Adam Hammond and Timothy Baldwin

14:12–14:28   *The Enemy in Your Own Camp: How Well Can We Detect Statistically-Generated Fake Reviews – An Adversarial Study*
Dirk Hovy

15:00–15:30   *Coffee break*

       Session 6A: Machine learning

       Session 6B: Word vectors II

       Session 6C: Machine translation III

       Session 6D: Discourse

Session 6E: Language and vision

Session 6F: Summarization

Session 6G: Learner language

17:30–19:00   *Poster and dinner session II*

Character-based Neural Machine Translation
Marta R. Costa-jussà and José A. R. Fonollosa

Learning Monolingual Compositional Representations via Bilingual Supervision
Ahmed Elgohary and Marine Carpuat

Event Nugget Detection with Forward-Backward Recurrent Neural Networks
Reza Ghaeini, Xiaoli Fern, Liang Huang and Prasad Tadepalli

IBC-C: A Dataset for Armed Conflict Analysis
Andrej Zukov Gregoric, Zhiyuan Luo and Bartal Veyhe

A Latent Concept Topic Model for Robust Topic Inference Using Word Embeddings
Weihua Hu and Jun'ichi Tsujii

Word Embeddings with Limited Memory
Shaoshi Ling, Yangqiu Song and Dan Roth

Hawkes Processes for Continuous Time Sequence Classification: an Application to Rumour Stance Classification in Twitter
Michal Lukasik, P. K. Srijith, Duy Vu, Kalina Bontcheva, Arkaitz Zubiaga and Trevor Cohn

Hunting for Troll Comments in News Community Forums
Todor Mihaylov and Preslav Nakov

Phrase Table Pruning via Submodular Function Maximization
Masaaki Nishino, Jun Suzuki and Masaaki Nagata

Multilingual Part-of-Speech Tagging with Bidirectional Long Short-Term Memory Models and Auxiliary Loss
Barbara Plank, Anders Søgaard and Yoav Goldberg

Matrix Factorization using Window Sampling and Negative Sampling for Improved Word Representations
Alexandre Salle, Aline Villavicencio and Marco Idiart

One model, two languages: training bilingual parsers with harmonized treebanks
David Vilares, Carlos Gómez-Rodríguez and Miguel A. Alonso

Using mention accessibility to improve coreference resolution
Kellie Webster and Joel Nothman

Exploiting Linguistic Features for Sentence Completion
Aubrie Woods

Convergence of Syntactic Complexity in Conversation
Yang Xu and David Reitter

User Embedding for Scholarly Microblog Recommendation
Yang Yu, Xiaojun Wan and Xinjie Zhou

20:00   ***Social event***

Wednesday, August 10, 2016

9:00–9:40   ***President's talk***

9:40–10:10   ***Coffee break***

Session 7A: Outstanding papers I

11:30–11:50 *Integrating Distributional Lexical Contrast into Word Embeddings for Antonym-Synonym Distinction*
Kim Anh Nguyen, Sabine Schulte im Walde and Ngoc Thang Vu

Session 7B: Outstanding papers II

11:50–13:30 *Lunch break*

13:30–15:00 *ACL business meeting (open to all)*

15:00–15:30 *Coffee break*

Session 8A: Question answering II (short papers)

15:30–15:46 *Machine Translation Evaluation Meets Community Question Answering*
Francisco Guzmán, Lluís Màrquez and Preslav Nakov

15:46–16:02 *Science Question Answering using Instructional Materials*
Mrinmaya Sachan, Kumar Dubey and Eric Xing

16:02–16:18 *Specifying and Annotating Reduced Argument Span Via QA-SRL*
Gabriel Stanovsky, Ido Dagan and Meni Adler

16:18–16:34 *Improving Argument Overlap for Proposition-Based Summarisation*
Yimai Fang and Simone Teufel

16:34–16:50 *Machine Comprehension using Rich Semantic Representations*
Mrinmaya Sachan and Eric Xing

Wednesday, August 10, 2016 (continued)

Session 8B: Word vectors III (short papers)

15:30–15:46   *Cross-Lingual Word Representations via Spectral Graph Embeddings*
Takamasa Oshikiri, Kazuki Fukui and Hidetoshi Shimodaira

15:46–16:02   *Semantics-Driven Recognition of Collocations Using Word Embeddings*
Sara Rodríguez-Fernández, Luis Espinosa Anke, Roberto Carlini and Leo Wanner

16:02–16:18   *Incorporating Relational Knowledge into Word Representations using Subspace Regularization*
Abhishek Kumar and Jun Araki

16:18–16:34   *Word Embedding Calculus in Meaningful Ultradense Subspaces*
Sascha Rothe and Hinrich Schütze

16:34–16:50   *Is "Universal Syntax" Universally Useful for Learning Distributed Word Representations?*
Ivan Vulić and Anna Korhonen

Session 8C: Topics and discourse (short papers)

15:30–15:46   *Claim Synthesis via Predicate Recycling*
Yonatan Bilu and Noam Slonim

15:46–16:02   *Modelling the Interpretation of Discourse Connectives by Bayesian Pragmatics*
Frances Yung, Kevin Duh, Taku Komura and Yuji Matsumoto

16:02–16:18   *Nonparametric Spherical Topic Modeling with Word Embeddings*
Kayhan Batmanghelich, Ardavan Saeedi, Karthik Narasimhan and Sam Gershman

16:18–16:34   *A Novel Measure for Coherence in Statistical Topic Models*
Fred Morstatter and Huan Liu

16:34–16:50   *Coarse-grained Argumentation Features for Scoring Persuasive Essays*
Debanjan Ghosh, Aquila Khanam, Yubo Han and Smaranda Muresan

Session 8D: Syntax and morphology (short papers)

15:30–15:46   *Single-Model Encoder-Decoder with Explicit Morphological Representation for Reinflection*
Katharina Kann and Hinrich Schütze

15:46–16:02   *Joint part-of-speech and dependency projection from multiple sources*
Anders Johannsen, Željko Agić and Anders Søgaard

16:02–16:18   *Dependency-based Gated Recursive Neural Network for Chinese Word Segmentation*
Jingjing Xu and Xu Sun

16:18–16:34   *Deep Neural Networks for Syntactic Parsing of Morphologically Rich Languages*
Joël Legrand and Ronan Collobert

16:34–16:50   *Weakly Supervised Part-of-speech Tagging Using Eye-tracking Data*
Maria Barrett, Joachim Bingel, Frank Keller and Anders Søgaard

Session 8E: Potpourri II (short papers)

15:30–15:46   *Metrics for Evaluation of Word-level Machine Translation Quality Estimation*
Varvara Logacheva, Michal Lukasik and Lucia Specia

15:46–16:02   *The Social Impact of Natural Language Processing*
Dirk Hovy and Shannon L. Spruit

16:02–16:18   *Using Sequence Similarity Networks to Identify Partial Cognates in Multilingual Wordlists*
Johann-Mattis List, Philippe Lopez and Eric Bapteste

17:00–19:00   ***Awards and closing session***

Transition-based dependency parsing with topological fields

Daniël de Kok and **Erhard Hinrichs**
Seminar für Sprachwissenschaft
Wilhemstraße 19
72072, Tübingen, Germany
{daniel.de-kok,erhard.hinrichs}@uni-tuebingen.de

Abstract

The topological field model is commonly used to describe the regularities in German word order. In this work, we show that topological fields can be predicted reliably using sequence labeling and that the predicted field labels can inform a transition-based dependency parser.

1 Introduction

The topological field model (Herling, 1821; Erdmann, 1886; Drach, 1937; Höhle, 1986) has traditionally been used to account for regularities in word order across different clause types of German. This model assumes that each clause type contains a *left bracket* (*LK*) and a *right bracket* (*RK*), which appear to the left and the right of the *middle field* (*MF*). Additionally, in a verb-second declarative clause, the LK is preceded by the *initial field* (*VF*) with the RK optionally followed by the *final field* (*NF*).[1] Table 1 gives examples of topological fields in verb-second declarative (MC) and verb-final relative (RC) clauses.

Certain syntactic restrictions can be described in terms of topological fields. For instance, only a single constituent is typically allowed in the VF, while multiple constituents are allowed in the MF and the NF. Many ordering preferences can also be stated using the model. For example, in a main clause, placing the subject in the VF and the direct object in the MF is preferred over the opposite order.

In parsing, topological field analysis is often seen as a task that is embedded in parsing itself. For instance, Kübler (2005), Maier (2006), and Cheung and Penn (2009) train PCFG parsers on

---

[1] The abbreviations are derived from the German terms *linke Klammer*, *rechte Klammer*, *Mittelfeld*, *Vorfeld*, and *Nachfeld*.

treebanks that annotate topological fields as interior nodes. It is perhaps not surprising that this approach works effectively for phrase structure parsing, because topological fields favor annotations that do not rely on crossing or discontinuous dependencies (Telljohann et al., 2006).

However, the possible role of topological fields in statistical dependency parsing (Kübler et al., 2009) has not been explored much. We will show that statistical dependency parsing of German can benefit from knowledge of clause structure as provided by the topological field model.

2 Motivation and corpus analysis

Transition-based dependency parsers (Nivre, 2003; Kübler et al., 2009) typically use two transitions (LEFT_ARC and RIGHT_ARC) to introduce a dependency relation between the token that is on top of the processing stack and the next token on the buffer of unprocessed tokens. The decision to make an attachment, the direction of attachment, and the label of the attachment is made by a classifier. Consequently, a good classifier is tasked to learn syntactic constraints, ordering preferences, and selectional preferences.

Since transition-based dependency parsers process sentences in one deterministic linear-time left-to-right sweep, the classifier typically has little global information. One popular approach for reducing the effect of early attachment errors is to retain some competition between alternative parses using a globally optimized model with beam search (Zhang and Clark, 2008). Beam search presents a trade-off between speed (smaller beam) and higher accuracy (larger beam). More recently, Dyer et al. (2015) have proposed to use *Long short-term memory networks* (*LSTMs*) to maintain (unbounded) representations of the buffer of unprocessed words, previous parsing ac-

1

Proceedings of the 54th Annual Meeting of the Association for Computational Linguistics, pages 1–7,
Berlin, Germany, August 7-12, 2016. ©2016 Association for Computational Linguistics

	VF	LK	MF	RK	NF
MC:	In Tansania	ist	das Rad mehr	verbreitet	als in Uganda
	In Tansania	is	the bike more	common	than in Uganda
RC:		der	fünfmal mehr nach Bremerhaven	liefert	als Daewoo
		who	five-times more to Bremerhaven	delivers	than Daewoo

Table 1: Topological fields of a verb-second clause and a verb-final clause.

tions, and constructed tree fragments.

We believe that in the case of German, the topological field model can provide a linguistically-motivated approach for providing the parser with more global knowledge of the sentence structure. More concretely, if we give the transition classifier access to topological field annotations, it can learn regularities with respect to the fields wherein the head and dependent of a particular dependency relations lie.

In the remainder of this section, we provide a short (data-driven) exploration of such regularities. Since there is a myriad of possible triples[2] consisting of *relation*, *head field*, and *dependent field*, we will focus on dependency relations that virtually never cross a field and relations that nearly always cross a field.

Table 2 lists the five dependency relation that cross fields the least often in the TüBa-D/Z treebank (Telljohann et al., 2006; Versley, 2005) of German newspaper text. Using these statistics, a classifier could learn hard constraints with regard to these dependency relations — they should never be used to attach heads and dependents that are in different fields.

Dependency label	Cross-field (%)
Particles	0.00
Determiner	0.03
Adjective or attr. pronoun	0.04
Prepositional complement	0.04
Genetive attribute	0.07

Table 2: The five dependency relations that most rarely cross fields in the TüBa-D/Z.

Table 3 lists the five dependency relations that cross fields most frequently.[3] These relations (virtually) always cross fields because they are verbal attachments and verbs typically form the LK and RK. This information is somewhat informative,

since a classifier should clearly avoid to attach tokens within the same field using one of these relations. However, we can gain more interesting insights by looking at the dependents' fields.

Dependency label	Cross-field (%)
Expletive *es*	100.00
Separated verb prefix	100.00
Subject	100.00
Prepositional object	99.80
Direct object	99.51

Table 3: The five dependency relations that most frequently cross fields in the TüBa-D/Z.

Table 4 enumerates the three (where applicable) most frequent head and dependent field combinations of the five relations that always cross fields. As expected, the head is always in the LK or RK. Moreover, the dependents are in VF or MF in the far majority of cases. The actual distributions provides some insights with respect to these dependency relations. We will discuss the *direct object*, *prepositional object*, and *separated verb prefix* relations in some more detail.

Direct objects In German, direct objects can be put in the VF. However, we can see that direct object fronting only happens very rarely in the TüBa-D/Z. This is in line with earlier observations in corpus-based studies (c.f. Weber and Müller (2004)). Since the probability of having a subject in the VF is much higher, the parser should attach the head of a noun phrase in the VF as a subject, unless there is overwhelming evidence to the contrary, such as case markers, verb agreement, or other cues (Uszkoreit, 1984; Müller, 1999).

Prepositional objects The dependency annotation scheme used by the TüBa-D/Z makes a distinction between prepositional phrases that are a required complement of a verb (*prepositional objects*) and other prepositional phrases. Since a statistical dependency parser does not typically have access to a valency dictionary, it has difficulty de-

---

[2]335 in the TüBa-D/Z treebank.

[3]Dependency relations that connect two clauses are excluded.

Dependency label	Head	Dep	%
Expletive *es*	RK	MF	44.23
	RK	VF	32.99
	LK	VF	13.43
Separated verb prefix	LK	RK	99.95
	RK	RK	00.05
Subject	LK	VF	36.40
	LK	MF	35.10
	RK	MF	20.11
Prepositional object	RK	MF	51.04
	LK	MF	39.81
	LK	VF	04.11
Direct object	RK	MF	54.84
	LK	MF	35.64
	RK	LK	03.38

Table 4: The three most frequent head-dependent field combinations of the five relations that always cross fields.

ciding whether a prepositional phrase is a prepositional object or not. Topological field information can complement verb-preposition co-occurrence statistics in deciding between these two different relations. The prepositional object mainly occurs in MF, while a prepositional phrase headed by the LK is almost as likely to be in the VF as in the MF (42.12% and 55.70% respectively).

Separated verb prefixes Some verbs in German have separable prefixes. A complicating factor in parsing is that such prefixes are often words that can also be used by themselves. For example, in (1-a) *fest* is a separated prefix of *bindet* (present tense third person of *festbinden*), while in (1-b) *fest* is an optional adverbial modifier of *gebunden* (the past participle of *binden*).

(1)   a.   Sie bindet das Pferd fest .
               She ties   the horse tight .

        b.   Das Buch ist fest   gebunden .
               The book is tightly bound   .

Similarly to prepositional objects, a statistical parser is handicapped by not having an extensive lexicon. Again, topological fields can complement co-occurence statistics. In (1-a), *fest* is in the RK. As we can see in Table 4, the separated verb prefix is always in the RK. In contrast, an adverbial modifier as in (1-b) is rarely in the RK (0.35% of the adverbs cases in the TüBa-D/Z).

3 Predicting fields

As mentioned in Section 1, topological field annotation has often been performed as a part of phrase structure parsing. In order to test our hypothesis that topological field annotation could inform dependency parsing, it would be more appropriate to use a syntax-less approach. Several shallow approaches have been tried in the past. For instance, Veenstra et al., (2002) compare three different chunkers (finite state, PCFG, and classification using memory-based learning). Becker and Frank (2002) predict topological fields using a PCFG specifically tailored towards topological fields. Finally, Liepert (2003) proposes a chunker that uses support vector machines.

In the present work, we will treat the topological field annotation as a sequence labeling task. This is more useful in the context of dependency parsing because it allows us to treat the topological field as any other property of a token.

Topological field projection In order to obtain data for training, validation, and evaluation, we use the TüBa-D/Z treebank. Topological fields are only annotated in the constituency version of the TüBa-D/Z, where the fields are represented as special constituent nodes. To obtain token-level field annotations for the dependency version of the treebank, we project the topological fields of the constituency trees on the tokens. The recursive projection function for projection is provided in Appendix B. The function is initially called with the root of the tree and a special unknown field marker, so that tokens that are not dominated by a topological field node (typically punctuation) also receive the topological field feature.

We should point out that our current projection method results in a loss of information when a sentence contains multiple clauses. For instance, an embedded clause is in a topological field of the main clause, but also has its own topological structure. In our projection method, the topological field features of tokens in the embedded clause reflect the topological structure of the embedded clause.

Model Our topological field labeler uses a recurrent neural network. The inputs consist of concatenated word and part-of-speech embeddings. The embeddings are fed to a bidirectional LSTM (Graves and Schmidhuber, 2005), on which we stack a regular LSTM (Hochreiter and Schmidhuber, 1997), and finally an output layer with the softmax activation function. The use of a recurrent model is motivated by the necessity to have long-distance memory. For example, (2-a) consists of a main clause with the LK *wird* and RK *begrünt* and an embedded clause *wie geplant* with its own clausal structure. When the labeler encounters *jetzt*, it needs to 'remember' that it was in the MF field of the main clause.

(2) a. Die neue Strecke wird , wie geplant ,
        The new stretch is   , as   planned ,
        jetzt begrünt   .
        now being-greened .

Moreover, the use of a bidirectional LSTM is motivated by the need for backwards-flowing information to make some labeling decisions. For instance, *die Siegerin* is in the VF of the verb-second clause (3-a), while it is in the MF of the verb-final clause (3-b). The labeller can only make such choices by knowing the position of the finite verb.

(3) a. die Siegerin wurde disqualifiziert
        die winner   was   disqualified
    b. die Siegerin zu disqualifizieren
        the winner   to disqualify

4 Parsing with topological fields

To evaluate the effectiveness of adding topological fields to the input, we use the publicly available neural network parser described by De Kok (2015). This parser uses an architecture that is similar to that of Chen and Manning (2014). However, it learns morphological analysis as an embedded task of parsing. Since most inflectional information that can be relevant for parsing German is available in the prefix or suffix, this parser learns morphological representations over character embeddings of prefixes and suffixes.

We use the same parser configuration as that of De Kok (2015), with the addition of topological field annotations. We encode the topological fields as one-hot vectors in the input of the parser. This information is included for the four tokens on top of the stack and the next three tokens on the buffer.

5 Evaluation and results

To evaluate the proposed topological field model, we use the same partitioning of TüBa-D/Z and the word and tag embeddings as De Kok (2015). For training, validation, and evaluation of the parser, we use these splits as-is. Since we want to test the parser with non-gold topological field annotations as well, we swapped the training and validation data for training our topological field predictor.

The parser was trained using the same hyperparameters and embeddings as in De Kok (2015). Our topological field predictor is trained using Keras (Chollet, 2015).[4] The hyperparameters that we use are summarized in Appendix A. The topological field predictor uses the same word and tag embeddings as the parser.

In Table 5, we show the accuracy of the topological field labeler. The use of a bi-directional LSTM is clearly justified, since it outperforms the stacked unidirectional LSTM by a wide margin.

Parser	Accuracy (%)
LSTM + LSTM	93.33
Bidirectional LSTM + LSTM	97.24

Table 5: Topological field labeling accuracies. The addition of backward flowing information improves accuracy considerably.

Table 6 shows the labeled attachment scores (LAS) for parsing with topological fields. As we can see, adding gold topological field annotations provides a marked improvement over parsing without topological fields. Although the parser does not achieve quite the same performance with the output of the LSTM-based sequence labeler, it is still a relatively large improvement over the parser of De Kok (2015). All differences are significant at $p < 0.0001$.[5]

Parser	LAS	UAS
De Kok (2015)	89.49	91.88
Neural net + TFs	90.00	92.36
Neural net + gold TFs	90.42	92.76

Table 6: Parse results with topological fields and gold topological fields. Parsers that use topological field information outperform parsers without access to such information.

6 Result analysis

Our motivation for introducing topological fields in dependency parsing is to provide the parser with

---

[4]The software is available from: https://github.com/danieldk/toponn

[5]Using paired approximate randomization tests (Noreen, 1989).

a more global view of sentence structure (Section 2). If this is indeed the case, we expect the parser to improve especially for longer-distance relations. Figure 1 shows the improvement in LAS as a result of adding gold-standard topological fields. We see a strong relation between the relation length and the improvement in accuracy. The introduction of topological fields clearly benefits the attachment of longer-distance dependents.

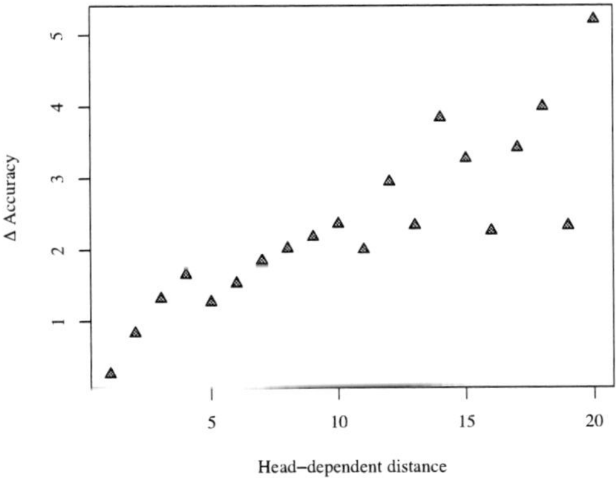

Figure 1: The improvement in labeled attachment score as a result of adding gold topological fields to the parser by dependency length.

Since the introduction of topological fields has very little impact on short-distance relations, the differences in the attachment of relations that virtually never cross fields (Table 2) turn out to be negligible. However, for the relations that cross fields frequently, we see a marked improvements (Table 7) for every relation except the *prepositional object*. In hindsight, this difference should not be surprising — the relations that never cross fields are usually very local, while those that almost always cross fields tend to have longer distances and/or are subject to relatively free ordering.

Dependency label	LAS Δ
Expletive *es*	2.71
Separated verb prefix	1.64
Subject	1.22
Prepositional object	-0.29
Direct object	1.59

Table 7: The LAS Δ of the parser with access to gold standard topological fields compared to the De Kok (2015) parser for the relations of Table 4.

Dependency label	LAS Δ
Coordinating conjunction (clausal)	11.48
Parenthesis	8.31
Dependent clause	3.49
Conjunct	3.38
Sentence root[7]	2.92
Expletive *es*	2.71
Sentence	2.64
Comparative	1.87
Separated verb prefix	1.64
Direct object	1.59

Table 8: The ten dependency relations with the highest LAS Δ of the parser with access to gold topological fields compared to the (de Kok, 2015) parser.

The ten dependency relations with the highest overall improvement in LAS are shown in Table 8. Many of these relations are special when it comes to topological field structure and were not discussed in Section 2. The relations *parenthesis, dependent clause*, and *sentence* link two clauses; the *sentence root* marks the root of the dependency tree; and the *coordinating conjunction (clausal)* relation attaches a token that is always in its own field.[6] This confirms that the addition of topological fields also improves the analysis of the overall clausal structure.

7 Conclusion and outlook

In this paper, we have argued and shown that access to topological field information can improve the accuracy of transition-based dependency parsers. In future, we plan to see how competitive the bidirectional LSTM-based sequence labeling approach is compared to existing approaches. Moreover, we plan to evaluate the use of topological fields in the architecture proposed by Dyer et al., (2015) to see how many of these regularities that approach captures.

Acknowledgments

The authors gratefully acknowledge the financial support of their research by the German Ministry for Education and Research (BMBF) as part of the CLARIN-D research infrastructure grant given to the University of Tübingen. Furthermore, we would like to thank Jianqiang Ma for his extensive comments on an early draft of this paper.

---

[6]The *KOORD* field, see Telljohan et al. (2006).

References

Markus Becker and Anette Frank. 2002. A stochastic topological parser for German. In *Proceedings of the 19th international conference on Computational linguistics-Volume 1*, pages 1–7. Association for Computational Linguistics.

Danqi Chen and Christopher D Manning. 2014. A fast and accurate dependency parser using neural networks. In *Proceedings of the 2014 Conference on Empirical Methods in Natural Language Processing (EMNLP)*, volume 1, pages 740–750.

Jackie Chi Kit Cheung and Gerald Penn. 2009. Topological field parsing of German. In *Proceedings of the Joint Conference of the 47th Annual Meeting of the ACL and the 4th International Joint Conference on Natural Language Processing of the AFNLP: Volume 1-Volume 1*, pages 64–72. Association for Computational Linguistics.

François Chollet. 2015. Keras. `https://github.com/fchollet/keras`.

Daniël de Kok. 2015. A poor man's morphology for German transition-based dependency parsing. In *International Workshop on Treebanks and Linguistic Theories (TLT14)*.

Erich Drach. 1937. *Grundgedanken der Deutschen Satzlehre*. Frankfurt/Main.

Chris Dyer, Miguel Ballesteros, Wang Ling, Austin Matthews, and Noah A. Smith. 2015. Transition-based dependency parsing with stack long short-term memory. In *Proceedings of the 53rd Annual Meeting of the Association for Computational Linguistics and the 7th International Joint Conference on Natural Language Processing (Volume 1: Long Papers)*, pages 334–343, Beijing, China, July. Association for Computational Linguistics.

Oskar Erdmann. 1886. *Grundzüge der deutschen Syntax nach ihrer geschichtlichen Entwicklung dargestellt*. Stuttgart: Cotta. Erste Abteilung.

Alex Graves and Jürgen Schmidhuber. 2005. Framewise phoneme classification with bidirectional lstm and other neural network architectures. *Neural Networks*, 18(5):602–610.

Simon Herling. 1821. Über die Topik der deutschen Sprache. In *Abhandlungen des frankfurterischen Gelehrtenvereins für deutsche Sprache*, pages 296–362, 394. Frankfurt/Main. Drittes Stück.

Sepp Hochreiter and Jürgen Schmidhuber. 1997. Long short-term memory. *Neural computation*, 9(8):1735–1780.

Tilman Höhle. 1986. Der Begriff 'Mittelfeld'. Anmerkungen über die Theorie der topologischen Felder. In A. Schöne, editor, *Kontroversen alte und neue. Akten des 7. Internationalen Germanistenkongresses Göttingen*, pages 329–340. Tübingen: Niemeyer.

Sandra Kübler, Ryan McDonald, and Joakim Nivre. 2009. Dependency parsing. *Synthesis Lectures on Human Language Technologies*, 1(1):1–127.

Sandra Kübler. 2005. How do treebank annotation schemes influence parsing results? or how not to compare apples and oranges. *Proceedings of RANLP 2005*.

Martina Liepert. 2003. Topological fields chunking for German with SVM's: Optimizing SVM-parameters with GA's. In *Proceedings of the International Conference on Recent Advances in Natural Language Processing*.

Wolfgang Maier. 2006. Annotation schemes and their influence on parsing results. In *Proceedings of the 21st International Conference on computational Linguistics and 44th Annual Meeting of the Association for Computational Linguistics: Student Research Workshop*, pages 19–24. Association for Computational Linguistics.

Gereon Müller. 1999. Optimality, markedness, and word order in German. *Linguistics*, 37(5):777–818.

Joakim Nivre. 2003. An efficient algorithm for projective dependency parsing. In *Proceedings of the 8th International Workshop on Parsing Technologies (IWPT)*, pages 149–160.

Eric W Noreen. 1989. Computer intensive methods for hypothesis testing: An introduction.

Nitish Srivastava, Geoffrey Hinton, Alex Krizhevsky, Ilya Sutskever, and Ruslan Salakhutdinov. 2014. Dropout: A simple way to prevent neural networks from overfitting. *The Journal of Machine Learning Research*, 15(1):1929–1958.

Heike Telljohann, Erhard W Hinrichs, Sandra Kübler, Heike Zinsmeister, and Kathrin Beck. 2006. Stylebook for the tübingen treebank of written German (TüBa-D/Z). In *Seminar fur Sprachwissenschaft, Universität Tubingen, Tübingen, Germany*.

Hans Uszkoreit. 1984. *Word order and constituent structure in German*. CSLI Publications.

Jorn Veenstra, Frank Henrik Müller, and Tylman Ule. 2002. Topological field chunking for German. In *Proceedings of the 6th Conference on Natural Language Learning - Volume 20*, COLING-02, pages 1–7, Stroudsburg, PA, USA. Association for Computational Linguistics.

Yannick Versley. 2005. Parser evaluation across text types. In *Proceedings of the Fourth Workshop on Treebanks and Linguistic Theories (TLT 2005)*.

Andrea Weber and Karin Müller. 2004. Word order variation in German main clauses: A corpus analysis. In *Proceedings of the 20th International conference on Computational Linguistics*, pages 71–77.

Yue Zhang and Stephen Clark. 2008. A tale of two parsers: investigating and combining graph-based and transition-based dependency parsing using beam-search. In *Proceedings of the Conference on Empirical Methods in Natural Language Processing*, pages 562–571. Association for Computational Linguistics.

A Hyperparameters

The topological field labeler was trained using Keras (Chollet, 2015). Here, we provide a short overview the hyperparameters that we used:

- **Solver:** *rmsprop*, this solver is recommended by the Keras documentation for recurrent neural networks. The solver is used with its default parameters.

- **Learning rate:** the learning rate was determined by the function $0.01(1 + 0.02^i)^{-2}$, where i is the epoch. The intuition was to start with some epochs with a high learning rate, dropping the learning rate quickly. The results were not drastically different when using a constant learning rate of 0.001.

- **Epochs:** The models was trained for 200 epochs, then we picked the model of the epoch with the highest performance on the validation data (27 epochs for the unidirectional LSTM, 124 epochs for the bidirectional LSTM).

- **LSTM layers:** all LSTM layers were trained with 50 output dimensions. Increasing the number of output dimensions did not provide an improvement.

- **Regularization:** 10% dropout (Srivastava et al., 2014) was used after each LSTM layer for regularization. A stronger dropout did not provide better performance.

B Topological field projection algorithm

Algorithm 1 Topological field projection.

```
function PROJECT(node,field)
    if IS_TERMINAL_NODE(node) then
        node.field ← field
    else
        if IS_TOPO_NODE(node) then
            field ← node.field
        end if
        for child ∈ node do
            PROJECT(child,field)
        end for
    end if
end function
```

Scalable Semi-Supervised Query Classification Using Matrix Sketching

Young-Bum Kim[†]　　　**Karl Stratos**[‡]　　　**Ruhi Sarikaya**[†]

[†]Microsoft Corporation, Redmond, WA
[‡]Columbia University, New York, NY
{ybkim, ruhi.sarikaya}@microsoft.com
stratos@cs.columbia.edu

Abstract

The enormous scale of unlabeled text available today necessitates scalable schemes for representation learning in natural language processing. For instance, in this paper we are interested in classifying the intent of a user query. While our labeled data is quite limited, we have access to virtually an unlimited amount of unlabeled queries, which could be used to induce useful representations: for instance by principal component analysis (PCA). However, it is prohibitive to even store the data in memory due to its sheer size, let alone apply conventional batch algorithms. In this work, we apply the recently proposed *matrix sketching* algorithm to entirely obviate the problem with scalability (Liberty, 2013). This algorithm approximates the data within a specified memory bound while preserving the covariance structure necessary for PCA. Using matrix sketching, we significantly improve the user intent classification accuracy by leveraging large amounts of unlabeled queries.

1　Introduction

The large amount of high quality unlabeled data available today provides an opportunity to improve performance in tasks with limited supervision through a semi-supervised framework: learn useful representations from the unlabeled data and use them to augment supervised models. Unfortunately, conventional exact methods are no longer feasible on such data due to scalability is-

sues. Even algorithms that are considered relatively scalable (e.g., the Lanczos algorithm (Cullum and Willoughby, 2002) for computing eigenvalue decomposition of large sparse matrices) fall apart in this scenario, since the data cannot be stored in the memory of a single machine. Consequently, approximate methods are needed.

In this paper, we are interested in improving the performance for sentence classification task by leveraging unlabeled data. For this task, supervision is precious but the amount of unlabeled sentences is essentially unlimited. We aim to learn sentence representations from as many unlabeled queries as possible via principal component analysis (PCA): specifically, learn a projection matrix for embedding a bag-of-words vector into a low-dimensional dense feature vector. However, it is not clear how we can compute an effective PCA when we are unable to even store the data in the memory.

Recently, Liberty (2013) proposed a scheme, called *matrix sketching*, for approximating a matrix while preserving its covariance structure. This algorithm, given a memory budget, deterministically processes a stream of data points while never exceeding the memory bound. It does so by occasionally computing singular value decomposition (SVD) on a small matrix. Importantly, the algorithm has a theoretical guarantee on the accuracy of the approximated matrix in terms of its covariance structure, which is the key quantity in PCA calculation.

We propose to combine the matrix sketching algorithm with random hashing to completely remove limitations on data sizes. In experiments, we significantly improve the intent classification accuracy by learning sentence representations from

8

huge amounts of unlabeled sentences, outperforming a strong baseline based on word embeddings trained on 840 billion tokens (Pennington et al., 2014).

2 Deterministic Matrix Sketching

PCA is typically performed to reduce the dimension of each data point. Let $X \in \mathbb{R}^{n \times d}$ be a data matrix whose n rows correspond to n data points in $\mathbb{R}^d$. For simplicity, assume that X is preprocessed to have zero column means. The key quantity in PCA is the empirical covariance matrix $X^\top X \in \mathbb{R}^{d \times d}$ (up to harmless scaling). It is well-known that the m length-normalized eigenvectors $u_1 \ldots u_m \in \mathbb{R}^d$ of $X^\top X$ corresponding to the largest eigenvalues are orthogonal directions along which the variance of the data is maximized. Then if $\Pi \in \mathbb{R}^{d \times m}$ be a matrix whose i-th column is u_i, the PCA representation of X is given by $X\Pi$. PCA has been a workhorse in representation learning, e.g., inducing features for face recognition (Turk et al., 1991).

Frequently, however, the number of samples n is simply too large to work with. As n tends to billions and trillions, storing the entire matrix X in memory is practically impossible. Processing large datasets often require larger memory than the capacity of a typical single enterprise server. Clusters may enable a aggregating many boxes of memory on different machines, to build distributed memory systems achieving large memory capacity. However, building and maintaining these industry grade clusters is not trivial and thus not accessible to everyone. It is critical to have techniques that can process large data within a limited memory budget available in most typical enterprise servers.

One solution is to approximate the matrix with some $Y \in \mathbb{R}^{l \times d}$ where $l \ll n$. Many matrix approximation techniques have been proposed, such as random projection (Papadimitriou et al., 1998; Vempala, 2005), sampling (Drineas and Kannan, 2003; Rudelson and Vershynin, 2007; Kim and Snyder, 2013; Kim et al., 2015b), and hashing (Weinberger et al., 2009). Most of these techniques involve randomness, which can be undesirable in certain situations (e.g., when experiments need to be exactly reproducible). Moreover, many are not designed directly for the objective that we care about: namely, ensuring that the covariance matrices $X^\top X$ and $Y^\top Y$ remain "similar".

Input: data stream $x_1 \ldots x_n \in \mathbb{R}^d$, sketch size l

1. Initialize zero-valued $Y \in 0^{l \times d}$.

2. For $i = 1 \ldots n$,

    (a) Insert x_i to the first zero-valued row of Y.

    (b) If Y has no zero-valued row,

       i. Compute SVD of $Y = U\Sigma V^\top$ where $\Sigma = \mathrm{diag}(\sigma_1 \ldots \sigma_l)$ with $\sigma_1 \geq \cdots \geq \sigma_l$.

       ii. Compute a diagonal matrix $\bar{\Sigma}$ with at least $\lceil l/2 \rceil$ zeros by setting

$$\bar{\Sigma}_{j,j} = \sqrt{\max\left(\Sigma_{j,j}^2 - \sigma_{\lfloor l/2 \rfloor}^2, 0\right)}$$

       iii. Set $Y = \bar{\Sigma} V^\top$.

Output: $Y \in \mathbb{R}^{l \times d}$ s.t. $\left\| X^\top X - Y^\top Y \right\|_2 \leq 2 \left\| X \right\|_F^2 / l$

Figure 1: Matrix sketching algorithm by Liberty (2013). In the output, $X \in \mathbb{R}^{n \times d}$ denotes the data matrix with rows $x_1 \ldots x_n$.

A recent result by Liberty (2013) gives a *deterministic* matrix sketching algorithm that tightly preserves the covariance structure needed for PCA. Specifically, given a sketch size l, the algorithm computes $Y \in \mathbb{R}^{l \times d}$ such that

$$\left\| X^\top X - Y^\top Y \right\|_2 \leq 2 \left\| X \right\|_F^2 / l \qquad (1)$$

This result guarantees that the error decreases in $O(1/l)$; in contrast, other approximation techniques have a significantly worse convergence bound of $O(1/\sqrt{l})$.

The algorithm is pleasantly simple and is given in Figure 1 for completeness. It processes one data point at a time to update the sketch Y in an online fashion. Once the sketch is "full", its SVD is computed and the rows that fall below a threshold given by the median singular value are eliminated. This operation ensures that every time SVD is performed at least a half of the rows are discarded. Consequently, we perform no more than $O(2n/l)$ SVDs on a small matrix $Y \in \mathbb{R}^{l \times d}$. The analysis of the bound (1) is an extension of the "median trick" for count sketching and is also surprisingly elementary; we refer to Liberty (2013) for details.

3 Matrix Sketching for Sentence Representations

Our goal is to leverage enormous quantities of unlabeled sentences to augment supervised training for intent classification. We do so by learning a PCA projection matrix Π from the unlabeled data and applying it on both training and test sentences. The matrix sketching algorithm in Figure 1 enables us to compute Π on arbitrarily large data.

There are many design considerations for using the sketching algorithm for our task.

3.1 Original sentence representations

We use a bag-of-words vector to represent a sentence. Specifically, each sentence is a d-dimensional vector $x \in \mathbb{R}^d$ where d is the size of the vocabulary and x_i is the count of an n-gram i in the sentence (we use up to $n = 3$ in experiments); we denote this representation by SENT. In experiments, we also use a modification of this representation, denoted by SENT+, in which we explicitly define features over the first two words in a query and also use intent predictions made by a supervised model.

3.2 Random hashing

When we process an enormous corpus, it can be computationally expensive just to obtain the vocabulary size d in the corpus. We propose using random hashing to avoid this problem. Specifically, we pre-define the hash size H we want, and then on encountering any word w we map $w \to \{1 \ldots H\}$ using a fixed hash function. This allows us to compute a bag-of-words vector for any sentence without knowing the vocabulary size. See Weinberger et al. (2009) for a justification of the hashing trick for kernel methods (applicable in our setting since PCA has a kernel (dual) interpretation).

3.3 Parallelization

The sketching algorithm works in a sequential manner, processing each sentence at a time. While it leaves a small memory footprint, it can take prohibitively long time to process a large corpus. Liberty (2013) shows it is trivial to parallelize the algorithm: one can compute several sketches in parallel and then sketch the conjoined sketches. The theory guarantees that such layered sketches does not degrade the bound (1). We implement this parallelization to obtain an order of magnitude speedup.

3.4 Final sentence representation:

Once we learn a PCA projection matrix Π, we use it in both training and test times to obtain a dense feature vector of a bag-of-words sentence representation. Specifically, if x is the original bag-of-words sentence vector, the new representation is given by

$$x_{\text{new}} = \frac{x}{||x||} \oplus \frac{x\Pi}{||x\Pi||} \tag{2}$$

where $\oplus$ is the vector concatenation operation. This representational scheme is shown to be effective in previous work (e.g., see Stratos and Collins (2015)).

3.5 Experiment

To test our proposed method, we conduct intent classification experiments (Hakkani-Tür et al., 2013; Celikyilmaz et al., 2011; Ji et al., 2014; El-Kahky et al., 2014; Chen et al., 2016) across a suite of 22 domains shown in Table 1. An intent is defined as the type of content the user is seeking. This task is part of the spoken language understanding problem (Li et al., 2009; Tur and De Mori, 2011; Kim et al., 2015c; Mesnil et al., 2015; Kim et al., 2015a; Xu and Sarikaya, 2014; Kim et al., 2015b; Kim et al., 2015d).

The amount of training data we used ranges from 12k to 120k (in number of queries) across different domains, the test data was from 2k to 20k. The number of intents ranges from 5 to 39 per domains. To learn a PCA projection matrix from the unlabeled data, we collected around 17 billion unlabeled queries from search logs, which give the original data matrix whose columns are bag-of-n-grams vector (up to trigrams) and has dimensions approximately 17 billions by 41 billions, more specifically,

$$X \in \mathbb{R}^{17,032,086,719 \times 40,986,835,008}$$

We use a much smaller sketching matrix $Y \in \mathbb{R}^{1,000,000 \times 1,000,000}$ to approximate X. Note that column size is hashing size. We parallelized the sketching computation over 1,000 machines; we will call the number of machines parallelized over "batch". In all our experiments, we train a linear multi-class SVM (Crammer and Singer, 2002).

3.6 Results of Intent Classification Task

Table 1 shows the performance of intent classification across domains. For the baseline, SVM without embedding (w/o Embed) achieved 91.99% accuracy, which is already very competitive. However, the models with word embedding trained on

	w/o Embed	6B-50d	840B-300d	SENT	SENT+
alarm	97.25	97.68	97.5	97.68	97.74
apps	89.16	91.07	92.52	94.24	94.3
calendar	91.34	92.43	92.32	92.53	92.43
communication	99.1	99.13	99.08	99.08	99.12
finance	90.44	90.84	90.72	90.76	90.82
flights	94.19	92.99	93.99	94.59	94.59
games	90.16	91.79	92.09	93.08	92.92
hotel	93.23	94.21	93.97	94.7	94.78
livemovie	90.88	92.64	92.8	93.28	93.37
livetv	83.14	85.02	84.67	85.41	85.86
movies	93.27	94.01	93.97	94.75	95.16
music	87.87	90.37	90.9	91.75	91.33
mystuff	94.2	94.4	94.51	94.51	94.95
note	97.62	98.36	98.36	98.49	98.52
ondevice	97.51	97.77	97.6	97.77	97.84
places	97.29	97.68	97.68	98.01	97.75
reminder	98.72	98.96	98.94	98.96	98.96
sports	76.96	78.53	78.38	78.7	79.44
timer	91.1	91.79	91.33	92.33	92.61
travel	81.58	82.57	82.43	83.64	82.81
tv	91.42	94.11	94.91	95.19	95.47
weather	97.31	97.33	97.4	97.4	97.47
Average	91.99	92.89	93.00	93.49	93.56

Table 1: Performance comparison between different embeddings style.

6 billion tokens (6B-50d) and 840 billion tokens (840B-300d) (Pennington et al., 2014) achieved 92.89% and 93.00%, respectively. 50d and 300d denote size of embedding dimension. To use word embeddings as a sentence representation, we simply use averaged word vectors over a sentence, normalized and conjoined with the original representation as in (2). Surprisingly, when we use sentence representation (SENT) induced from the sketching method with our data set, we can boost the performance up to 93.49%, corresponding to a 18.78% decrease in error relative to a SVM without representation. Also, we see that the extended sentence representation (SENT+) can get additional gains.

As in Table 2 , we also measured performance of our method (SENT+) as a function of the percentage of unlabeled data we used from total unlabeled sentences. The overall trend is clear: as the number of sentences are added to the data for inducing sentence representation, the test performance improves because of both better coverage and better quality of embedding. We believe that if we consume more data, we can boost up the performance even more.

3.7 Results of Parallelization

Table 3 shows the sketching results for various batch size. To evaluate parallelization, we first randomly generate a matrix $\mathbb{R}^{1,000,000 \times 100}$ and it is sketched to $\mathbb{R}^{100 \times 100}$. And then we sketch run with different batch size. The results show that as the number of batch increases, we can speed up dramatically, keeping residual value $||X^\top X - Y^\top Y||_2$. It indeed satisfies the bound value, $||X||_F^2 / l$, which was 100014503.16.

4 Conclusion

We introduced how to use *matrix sketching* algorithm of (Liberty, 2013) for scalable semi-supervised sentence classification. This algorithm approximates the data within a specified memory bound while preserving the covariance structure necessary for PCA. Using matrix sketching, we significantly improved the classification accuracy by leveraging very large amounts of unlabeled sentences.

	0	10%	20%	30%	40%	50%	60%	70%	80%	90%	100%
apps	89.16	89.83	90.04	90.26	90.88	91.9	92.41	92.41	92.95	93.72	94.3
music	87.87	89.12	89.61	90.4	90.83	91.26	91.31	91.33	91.38	91.33	91.33
tv	91.42	92.28	92.83	93.61	93.96	94.67	94.91	95.12	95.34	95.44	95.47

Table 2: Performance for selected domains as the number of unlabeled data increases.

Batch Size	$\lVert X^\top X - Y^\top Y \rVert_2$	time
1	1019779.69	100.21
2	1019758.22	50.31
4	1019714.19	26.50
5	1019713.43	21.67
8	1019679.67	14.53
10	1019692.67	12.13
16	1019686.35	8.53
20	1019709.03	7.35
25	1019650.51	6.40
40	1019703.24	4.97
50	1019689.33	4.48

Table 3: Results for corresponding batch size. Second column indicates the norm of gap between original and sketching matrix. Time represents the running time for sketching methods, measured in seconds.

References

Asli Celikyilmaz, Dilek Hakkani-Tür, and Gokhan Tür. 2011. Leveraging web query logs to learn user intent via bayesian discrete latent variable model. ICML.

Yun-Nung Chen, Dilek Hakkani-Tür, and Xiaodong He. 2016. Zero-shot learning of intent embeddings for expansion by convolutional deep structured semantic models. In *Proc. of ICASSP*.

Koby Crammer and Yoram Singer. 2002. On the learnability and design of output codes for multiclass problems. *Machine Learning*, 47(2-3):201–233.

Jane K Cullum and Ralph A Willoughby. 2002. *Lanczos Algorithms for Large Symmetric Eigenvalue Computations: Vol. 1: Theory*, volume 41. SIAM.

Petros Drineas and Ravi Kannan. 2003. Pass efficient algorithms for approximating large matrices. In *SODA*, volume 3, pages 223–232.

Ali El-Kahky, Xiaohu Liu, Ruhi Sarikaya, Gokhan Tur, Dilek Hakkani-Tur, and Larry Heck. 2014. Extending domain coverage of language understanding systems via intent transfer between domains using knowledge graphs and search query click logs. In *Acoustics, Speech and Signal Processing (ICASSP), 2014 IEEE International Conference on*, pages 4067–4071. IEEE.

Dilek Hakkani-Tür, Asli Celikyilmaz, Larry P Heck, and Gökhan Tür. 2013. A weakly-supervised approach for discovering new user intents from search query logs. In *INTERSPEECH*, pages 3780–3784.

Yangfeng Ji, Dilek Hakkani-Tur, Asli Celikyilmaz, Larry Heck, and Gokhan Tur. 2014. A variational bayesian model for user intent detection. In *Acoustics, Speech and Signal Processing (ICASSP), 2014 IEEE International Conference on*, pages 4072–4076. IEEE.

Young-Bum Kim and Benjamin Snyder. 2013. Optimal data set selection: An application to grapheme-to-phoneme conversion. In *HLT-NAACL*, pages 1196–1205.

Young-Bum Kim, Minwoo Jeong, Karl Stratos, and Ruhi Sarikaya. 2015a. Weakly supervised slot tagging with partially labeled sequences from web search click logs. In *Proc. of the Conference on the North American Chapter of the Association for Computational Linguistics - Human Language Technologies*, pages 84–92.

Young-Bum Kim, Karl Stratos, Xiaohu Liu, and Ruhi Sarikaya. 2015b. Compact lexicon selection with spectral methods. In *Proc. of Annual Meeting of the Association for Computational Linguistics: Human Language Technologies*.

Young-Bum Kim, Karl Stratos, and Ruhi Sarikaya. 2015c. Pre-training of hidden-unit crfs. In *Proc. of Annual Meeting of the Association for Computational Linguistics: Human Language Technologies*, pages 192–198.

Young-Bum Kim, Karl Stratos, Ruhi Sarikaya, and Minwoo Jeong. 2015d. New transfer learning techniques for disparate label sets. In *Proc. of Annual Meeting of the Association for Computational Linguistics: Human Language Technologies*.

Xiao Li, Ye-Yi Wang, and Alex Acero. 2009. Extracting structured information from user queries with semi-supervised conditional random fields. In *Proceedings of the 32nd international ACM SIGIR conference on Research and development in information retrieval*.

Edo Liberty. 2013. Simple and deterministic matrix sketching. In *Proceedings of the 19th ACM SIGKDD international conference on Knowledge discovery and data mining*, pages 581–588. ACM.

Grégoire Mesnil, Yann Dauphin, Kaisheng Yao, Yoshua Bengio, Li Deng, Dilek Hakkani-Tur, Xiaodong He, Larry Heck, Gokhan Tur, Dong Yu, et al. 2015. Using recurrent neural networks for slot filling in spoken language understanding. *Audio, Speech, and Language Processing, IEEE/ACM Transactions on*, 23(3):530–539.

Christos H Papadimitriou, Hisao Tamaki, Prabhakar Raghavan, and Santosh Vempala. 1998. Latent semantic indexing: A probabilistic analysis. In *Proceedings of the seventeenth ACM SIGACT-SIGMOD-SIGART symposium on Principles of database systems*, pages 159–168. ACM.

Jeffrey Pennington, Richard Socher, and Christopher D Manning. 2014. Glove: Global vectors for word representation. *Proceedings of the Empiricial Methods in Natural Language Processing (EMNLP 2014)*, 12:1532–1543.

Mark Rudelson and Roman Vershynin. 2007. Sampling from large matrices: An approach through geometric functional analysis. *Journal of the ACM (JACM)*, 54(4):21.

Karl Stratos and Michael Collins. 2015. Simple semi-supervised pos tagging. In *Proceedings of NAACL-HLT*, pages 79–87.

Gokhan Tur and Renato De Mori. 2011. *Spoken language understanding: Systems for extracting semantic information from speech*. John Wiley & Sons.

Matthew Turk, Alex P Pentland, et al. 1991. Face recognition using eigenfaces. In *Computer Vision and Pattern Recognition, 1991. Proceedings CVPR'91., IEEE Computer Society Conference on*, pages 586–591. IEEE.

Santosh S Vempala. 2005. *The random projection method*, volume 65. American Mathematical Soc.

Kilian Weinberger, Anirban Dasgupta, John Langford, Alex Smola, and Josh Attenberg. 2009. Feature hashing for large scale multitask learning. In *Proceedings of the 26th Annual International Conference on Machine Learning*, pages 1113–1120. ACM.

Puyang Xu and Ruhi Sarikaya. 2014. Contextual domain classification in spoken language understanding systems using recurrent neural network. In *Acoustics, Speech and Signal Processing (ICASSP), 2014 IEEE International Conference on*, pages 136–140. IEEE.

Learning Multiview Embeddings of Twitter Users

Adrian Benton[*] **Raman Arora**[*] **Mark Dredze**[*†]

adrian@cs.jhu.edu   arora@cs.jhu.edu   mdredze@cs.jhu.edu

[*]Human Language Technology Center of Excellence
Center for Language and Speech Processing, Johns Hopkins University
Baltimore, MD 21218 USA
[†]Bloomberg LP, New York, NY 10022

Abstract

Low-dimensional vector representations are widely used as stand-ins for the text of words, sentences, and entire documents. These embeddings are used to identify similar words or make predictions about documents. In this work, we consider embeddings for social media users and demonstrate that these can be used to identify users who behave similarly or to predict attributes of users. In order to capture information from all aspects of a user's online life, we take a multiview approach, applying a weighted variant of Generalized Canonical Correlation Analysis (GCCA) to a collection of over 100,000 Twitter users. We demonstrate the utility of these multiview embeddings on three downstream tasks: user engagement, friend selection, and demographic attribute prediction.

1 Introduction

Dense, low-dimensional vector representations (embeddings) have a long history in NLP, and recent work on neural models have provided new and popular algorithms for training representations for word types (Mikolov et al., 2013; Faruqui and Dyer, 2014), sentences (Kiros et al., 2015), and entire documents (Le and Mikolov, 2014). These embeddings often have nice properties, such as capturing some aspects of syntax or semantics and outperforming their sparse counterparts at downstream tasks.

While there are many approaches to generating embeddings of *text*, it is not clear how to learn embeddings for social media *users*. There are several different types of data (views) we can use to build user representations: the text of messages they post, neighbors in their local network, articles they link to, images they upload, etc. We propose unsupervised learning of representations of users with a variant of Generalized Canonical Correlation Analysis (*GCCA*) (Carroll, 1968; Van De Velden and Bijmolt, 2006; Arora and Livescu, 2014; Rastogi et al., 2015), a multiview technique that learns a single, low-dimensional vector for each user best capturing information from each of their views. We believe this

is more appropriate for learning user embeddings than concatenating views into a single vector, since views may correspond to different modalities (image vs. text data) or have very different distributional properties. Treating all features as equal in this concatenated vector is not appropriate.

We offer two main contributions: (1) an application of *GCCA* to learning vector representations of social media users that best accounts for all aspects of a user's online life, and (2) an evaluation of these vector representations for a set of Twitter users at three different tasks: user engagement, friend, and demographic attribute prediction.

2 Twitter User Data

We begin with a description of our dataset, which is necessary for understanding the data available to our multiview model. We uniformly sampled 200,000 users from a stream of publicly available tweets from the 1% Twitter stream from April 2015. To include typical, English speaking users we removed users with verified accounts, more than 10,000 followers, or non-English profiles[1]. For each user we collected their 1,000 most recent tweets, and then filtered out non-English tweets. Users without English tweets in January or February 2015 were omitted, yielding a total of 102,328 users. Although limiting tweets to only these two months restricted the number of tweets we were able to work with, it also ensured that our data are drawn from a narrow time window, controlling for differences in user activity over time. This allows us to learn distinctions between users, and not temporal distinctions of content. We will use this set of users to learn representations for the remainder of this paper.

Next, we expand the information available about these users by collecting information about their social networks. Specifically, for each user mentioned in a tweet by one of the 102,328 users, we collect up to the 200 most recent English tweets for these users from January and February 2015. Similarly, we collected the 5,000 most recently added friends and followers of each of the 102,328 users. We then sampled 10 friends and 10 followers for each user and collected

---

[1]Identified with `langid` (Lui and Baldwin, 2012).

Proceedings of the 54th Annual Meeting of the Association for Computational Linguistics, pages 14–19,
Berlin, Germany, August 7-12, 2016. ©2016 Association for Computational Linguistics

up to the 200 most recent English tweets for these users from January and February 2015. Limits on the number of users and tweets per user were imposed so that we could operate within Twitter's API limits. This data supports several of our prediction tasks, as well as the four sources for each user: their tweets, tweets of mentioned users, friends and followers.

3 User Views

Our user dataset provides several sources of information on which we can build user views: text posted by the user (*ego*) and people that are mentioned, friended or followed by the user and their posted text.

For each text source we can aggregate the many tweets into a single document, e.g. all tweets written by accounts mentioned by a user. We represent this document as a bag-of-words (*BOW*) in a vector space model with a vocabulary of the 20,000 most frequent word types after stopword removal. We will consider both count and TF-IDF weighted vectors.

A common problem with these high dimensional representations is that they suffer from the curse of dimensionality. A natural solution is to apply a dimensionality reduction technique to find a compact representation that captures as much information as possible from the original input. Here, we consider principal components analysis (PCA), a ubiquitous linear dimensionality reduction technique, as well as word2vec (Mikolov et al., 2013), a technique to learn nonlinear word representations.

We consider the following views for each user.

***BOW*:** We take the bag-of-words (both count and TF-IDF weighted) representation of all tweets made by users in that view (ego, mention, friend, or follower) following the above pre-processing.

***BOW-PCA*:** We run PCA and extract the top principal components for each of the above views. We also consider *all* possible combinations of views obtained by concatenating views before applying PCA, and concatenating PCA-projected views. By considering all possible concatenation of views, we ensure that this method has access to the same information as multiview methods. Both the raw *BOW* and *BOW-PCA* representations have been explored in previous work for demographic prediction (Volkova et al., 2014; Al Zamal et al., 2012) and recommendation systems (Abel et al., 2011; Zangerle et al., 2013).

***Word2Vec*:** *BOW-PCA* is limited to linear representations of *BOW* features. Modern neural network based approaches to learning word embeddings, including word2vec continuous bag of words and skipgram models, can learn nonlinear representations that also capture local context around each word (Mikolov et al., 2013). We represent each view as the simple average of the word embeddings for all tokens within that view (e.g., all words written by the ego user). Word embeddings are learned on a sample of 87,755,398 tweets and profiles uniformly sampled from the 1% Twitter

stream in April 2015 along with all the tweets/profiles collected for our set of users – a total of over a billion tokens. We use the word2vec tool, select either skipgram or continuous bag-of-words embeddings on dev data for each prediction task, and train for 50 epochs. We use the default settings for all other parameters.

***NetSim*:** An alternative to text based representations is to use the social network of users as a representation. We encode a user's social network as a vector by treating the users as a vocabulary, where users with similar social networks have similar vector representations (*NetSim*). An n-dimensional vector then encodes the user's social network as a bag-of-words over this user vocabulary. In other words, a user is represented by a summation of the one-hot encodings of each neighboring user in their social network. In this representation, the number of friends two users have in common is equal to the dot product between their social network vectors. We define the social network may be as one's followers, friends, or the union of both. The motivation behind this representation is that users who have similar networks may behave in similar ways. Such network features are commonly used to construct user representations as well as to make user recommendations (Lu et al., 2012; Kywe et al., 2012).

***NetSim-PCA*:** The PCA-projected representations for each *NetSim* vector. This may be important for computing similarity, since users are now represented as dense vectors capturing linear correlations in the friends/followers a user has. *NetSim-PCA* is to *NetSim* as *BOW-PCA* is to *BOW*– we apply PCA directly to the user's social network as opposed to the *BOW* representations of users in that network.

Each of these views can be treated independently as a user representation. However, different downstream tasks may favor different views. For example, the friend network is useful at recommending new friends, whereas the ego tweet view may be better at predicting what content a user will post in the future. Picking a single view may ignore valuable information as views may contain complementary information, so using multiple views improves on a single view. One approach is to concatenate multiple views together, but this further increases the size of the user embeddings. In the next section, we propose an alternate approach for learning a single embedding from multiple views.

4 Learning Multiview User Embeddings

We use Generalized Canonical Correlation Analysis (*GCCA*) (Carroll, 1968) to learn a single embedding from multiple views. *GCCA* finds G, U_i that minimize:

$$\arg\min_{G, U_i} \sum_i \|G - X_i U_i\|_F^2 \qquad \text{s.t. } G'G = I \qquad (1)$$

where $X_i \in \mathbb{R}^{n \times d_i}$ corresponds to the data matrix for the ith view, $U_i \in \mathbb{R}^{d_i \times k}$ maps from the latent space to observed view i, and $G \in \mathbb{R}^{n \times k}$ contains all user representations (Van De Velden and Bijmolt, 2006).

Since each view may be more or less helpful for a downstream task, we do not want to treat each view equally in learning a single embedding. Instead, we weigh each view differently in the objective:

$$\arg\min_{G,U_i}\sum_i w_i\|G - X_iU_i\|_F^2 \text{ s.t. } G'G = I, w_i \geq 0 \quad (2)$$

where w_i explicitly expresses the importance of the ith view in determining the joint embedding. The columns of G are the eigenvectors of $\sum_i w_iX_i(X_i'X_i)^{-1}X_i'$, and the solution for $U_i = (X_i'X_i)^{-1}X_i'G$. In our experiments, we use the approach of Rastogi et al. (2015) to learn G and U_i, since it is more memory-efficient than decomposing the sum of projection matrices.

GCCA embeddings were learned over combinations of the views in §3. When available, we also consider *GCCA-net*, where in addition to the four text views, we also include the follower and friend network views used by *NetSim-PCA*. For computational efficiency, each of these views was first reduced in dimensionality by projecting its *BOW* TF-IDF-weighted representation to a 1000-dimensional vector through PCA.[2] We add an identity matrix scaled by a small amount of regularization, 10^{-8}, to the per-view covariance matrices before inverting, for numerical stability, and use the formulation of *GCCA* reported in Van De Velden and Bijmolt (2006), which ignores rows with missing data (some users had no data in the mention tweet view and some users accounts were private). We tune the weighting of each view i, $w_i \in \{0.0, 0.25, 1.0\}$, discriminatively for each task, although the *GCCA* objective is unsupervised once the w_i are fixed.

We also consider a minor modification of *GCCA*, where G is scaled by the square-root of the singular values of $\sum_i w_iX_iX_i'$, *GCCA-sv*. This is inspired by previous work showing that scaling each feature of multiview embeddings by the singular values of the data matrix can improve performance at downstream tasks such as image or caption retrieval (Mroueh et al., 2015). Note that if we only consider a single view, X_1, with weight $w_1 = 1$, then the solution to *GCCA-sv* is identical to the PCA solution for data matrix X_1, without mean-centering.

When we compare representations in the following tasks, we sweep over embedding width in $\{10, 20, 50, 100, 200, 300, 400, 500, 1000\}$ for all methods. This applies to *GCCA*, *BOW-PCA*, *NetSim-PCA*, and *Word2Vec*. We also consider concatenations of vectors for every possible subset of views: singletons, pairs, triples, and all views. We tried applying PCA directly to the concatenation of all 1000-dimensional *BOW-PCA* views, but this did not perform competitively in our experiments.

---

[2] We excluded count vectors from the *GCCA* experiments for computational efficiency since they performed similarly to TF-IDF representations in initial experiments.

5 Experimental Setup

We selected three user prediction tasks to demonstrate the effectiveness of the multi-view embeddings: user engagement prediction, friend recommendation and demographic characteristics inference. Our focus is to show the performance of multiview embeddings compared to other representations, not on building the best system for a given task.

User Engagement Prediction The goal of user engagement prediction is to determine which topics a user will likely tweet about, using hashtag as a proxy. This task is similar to hashtag recommendation for a tweet based on its contents (Kywe et al., 2012; She and Chen, 2014; Zangerle et al., 2013). Purohit et al. (2011) presented a supervised task to predict if a hashtag would appear in a tweet using features from the user's network, previous tweets, and the tweet's content.

We selected the 400 most frequently used hashtags in messages authored by our users and which first appeared in March 2015, randomly and evenly dividing them into dev and test sets. We held out the first 10 users who tweeted each hashtag as exemplars of users that would use the hashtag in the future. We ranked all other users by the cosine distance of their embedding to the average embedding of these 10 users. Since embeddings are learned on data pre-March 2015, the hashtags cannot impact the learned representations. Performance is measured using precision and recall at k, as well as mean reciprocal rank (MRR), where a user is marked as correct if they used the hashtag. Note that this task is different than that reported in Purohit et al. (2011), since we are making recommendations at the level of users, not tweets.

Friend Recommendation The goal of friend recommendation/link prediction is to recommend/predict other accounts for a user to follow (Liben-Nowell and Kleinberg, 2007).

We selected the 500 most popular accounts – which we call celebrities – followed by our users, randomly, and evenly divided them into dev and test sets. We randomly select 10 users who follow each celebrity and rank all other users by cosine distance to the average of these 10 representations. The tweets of selected celebrities are removed during embedding training so as not to influence the learned representations. We use the same evaluation as user engagement prediction, where a user is marked as correct if they follow the given celebrity.

For both user engagement prediction and friend recommendation we z-score normalize each feature, subtracting off the mean and scaling each feature independently to have unit variance, before computing cosine similarity. We select the approach and whether to z-score normalize based on the development set performance.

Demographic Characteristics Inference Our final task is to infer the demographic characteristics of a user (Al Zamal et al., 2012; Chen et al., 2015).

Model	Dim	P@1000	R@1000	MRR
BOW	20000	0.009/0.005	0.241/0.157	0.006/0.006
BOW-PCA	500	0.011/0.008	0.312/0.29	0.007/0.009
NetSim	NA	0.006/0.006	0.159/0.201	0.004/0.004
NetSim-PCA	300	0.010/0.008	0.293/0.299	0.006/0.006
Word2Vec	100	0.009/0.007	0.254/0.217	0.005/0.004
GCCA	100	0.012/0.009	0.357/0.325	0.011/0.008
GCCA-sv	500	**0.012/0.010**	0.359/0.334	**0.010/0.011**
GCCA-net	200	0.013/0.009	**0.360/0.346**	**0.011/0.011**
NetSize	NA	0.001/0.001	0.012/0.012	0.000/0.000
Random	NA	0.000/0.000	0.002/0.008	0.000/0.000

Table 1: Macro performance at user engagement prediction on dev/test. Ranking of model performance was consistent across metrics. Precision is low since few users tweet a given hashtag. Values bolded by best test performance per metric. Baselines (bottom): *NetSize*: a ranking of users by the size of their local network; *Random* randomly ranks users.

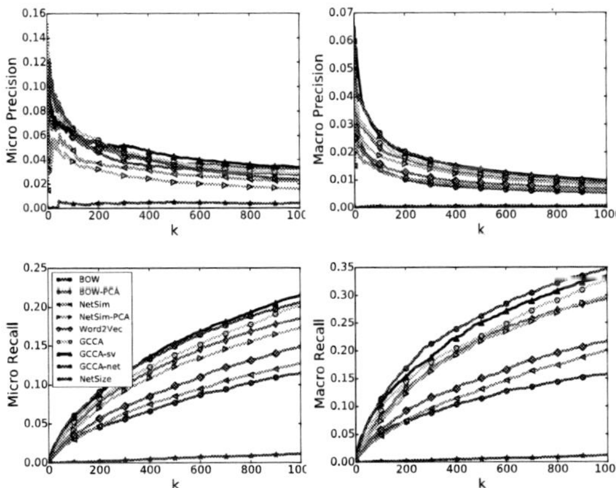

Figure 1: The best-performing approaches on user engagement prediction as a function of k (number of recommendations). The ordering of methods is consistent across k.

We use the dataset from Volkova et al. (2014; Volkova (2015) which annotates 383 users for age (old/young), 383 for gender (male/female), and 396 political affiliation (republican/democrat), with balanced classes. Predicting each characteristic is a binary supervised prediction task. Each set is partitioned into 10 folds, with two folds held out for test, and the other eight for tuning via cross-fold validation. The provided dataset contained tweets from each user, mentioned users, friends and follower networks. It did not contain the actual social networks for these users, so we did not evaluate *NetSim*, *NetSim-PCA*, or *GCCA-net* at these prediction tasks.

Each feature was z-score normalized before being passed to a linear-kernel SVM where we swept over $10^{-4}, \dots, 10^4$ for the penalty on the error term, C.

6 Results

User Engagement Prediction Table 1 shows results for user engagement prediction and Figure 1 the precision and recall curves as a function of number of recommendations. *GCCA* outperforms other methods for precision and recall at 1000, and does close to the best in terms of MRR. Including network views (*GCCA-*

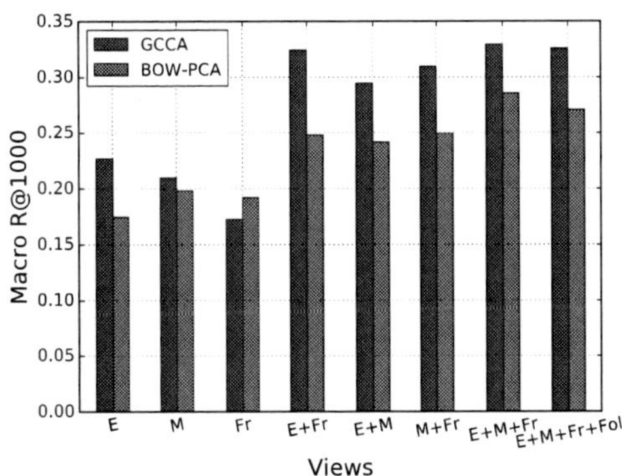

Figure 2: Macro recall@1000 on user engagement prediction for different combinations of text views. Each bar shows the best-performing model swept over dimensionality. *E*: ego, *M*: mention, *Fr*: friend, *Fol*: followertweet views.

Model	Dim	P@1000	R@1000	MRR
BOW	20000	0.133/0.153	0.043/0.048	0.000/0.001
BOW-PCA	20	0.311/0.314	0.101/0.102	0.001/0.001
NetSim	NA	0.406/0.420	0.131/0.132	**0.002/0.002**
NetSim-PCA	500	**0.445/0.439**	**0.149/0.147**	**0.002/0.002**
Word2Vec	200	0.260/0.249	0.084/0.080	0.001/0.001
GCCA	50	0.269/0.276	0.089/0.091	0.001/0.001
GCCA-sv	500	**0.445/0.439**	**0.149/0.147**	**0.002/0.002**
GCCA-net	20	0.376/0.364	0.123/0.120	0.001/0.001
NetSize	NA	0.033/0.035	0.009/0.010	0.000/0.000
Random	NA	0.034/0.036	0.010/0.010	0.000/0.000

Table 2: Macro performance for friend recommendation. Performance of *NetSim-PCA* and *GCCA-sv* are identical since the view weighting for *GCCA-sv* only selected solely the friend view. Thus, these methods learned identical user embeddings.

Model	age	gender	politics
BOW	0.771/0.740	0.723/0.662	0.934/0.975
BOW-PCA	0.784/0.649	0.719/0.662	0.908/0.900
BOW-PCA + BOW	0.767/0.688	0.660/0.714	**0.937/0.9875**
GCCA	0.725/0.740	0.742/0.714	0.899/0.8125
GCCA + BOW	0.764/0.727	0.657/0.701	0.940/0.9625
GCCA-sv	0.709/0.636	0.699/0.714	0.871/0.850
GCCA-sv + BOW	0.761/0.688	0.647/0.675	0.937/0.9625
Word2Vec	**0.790/0.753**	**0.777/0.766**	0.927/0.938

Table 3: Average CV/test accuracy for inferring demographic characteristics.

net and *GCCA-sv*) improves the performance further. The best performing *GCCA* setting placed weight 1 on the ego tweet view, mention view, and friend view, while *BOW-PCA* concatenated these views, suggesting that these were the three most important views but that *GCCA* was able to learn a better representation. Figure 2 compares performance of different view subsets for *GCCA* and *BOW-PCA*, showing that *GCCA* uses information from multiple views more effectively for predicting user engagement.

Friend Recommendation Table 2 shows results for friend prediction and Figure 3 similarly shows that performance differences between approaches are consistent across k (number of recommendations.) Adding network views to *GCCA*, *GCCA-net*, improves performance, although it cannot contend with *NetSim* or

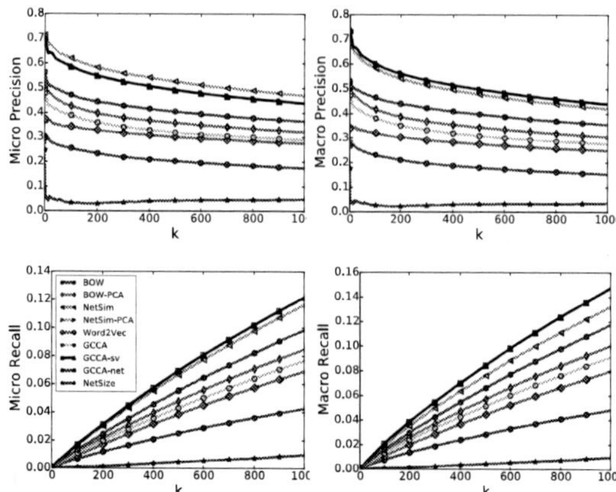

Figure 3: Performance on friend recommendation varying k.

NetSim-PCA, although *GCCA-sv* is able to meet the performance of *NetSim-PCA*. The best *GCCA* placed non-zero weight on the friend tweets view, and *GCCA-net* only places weight on the friend network view; the other views were not informative. *BOW-PCA* and *Word2Vec* only used the friend tweet view. This suggests that the friend view is the most important for this task, and multiview techniques cannot exploit additional views to improve performance. *GCCA-sv* performs identically to *GCCA-net*, since it only placed weight on the friend network view, learning identical embeddings to *GCCA-net*.

Demographic Characteristics Prediction Table 3 shows the average cross-fold validation and test accuracy on the demographic prediction task. *GCCA + BOW* and *BOW-PCA + BOW* are the concatenation of *BOW* features with *GCCA* and *BOW-PCA*, respectively. The wide variation in performance is due to the small size of the datasets, thus it's hard to draw many conclusions other than that *GCCA* seems to perform well compared to other linear methods. *Word2Vec* surpasses other representations in two out of three datasets.

It is difficult to compare the performance of the methods we evaluate here to that reported in previous work, (Al Zamal et al., 2012). This is because they report cross-fold validation accuracy (not test), they consider a wider range of hand-engineered features, different subsets of networks, radial basis function kernels for SVM, and find that accuracy varies wildly across different feature sets. They report cross-fold validation accuracy ranging from 0.619 to 0.805 for predicting age, 0.560 to 0.802 for gender, and 0.725 to 0.932 for politics.

7 Conclusion

We have proposed several representations of Twitter users, as well as a multiview approach that combines these views into a single embedding. Our multiview embeddings achieve promising results on three different prediction tasks, making use of both what a user writes as well as the social network. We found that each task relied on different information, which our method successfully combined into a single representation.

We plan to consider other means for learning user representations, including comparing nonlinear dimensionality reduction techniques such as kernel PCA (Schölkopf et al., 1997) and deep canonical correlation analysis (Andrew et al., 2013; Wang et al., 2015). Recent work on learning user representations with multitask deep learning techniques (Li et al., 2015), suggests that learning a nonlinear mapping from observed views to the latent space can learn high quality user representations. One issue with *GCCA* is scalability: solving for G relies on an SVD of a large matrix that must be loaded into memory. Online variants of *GCCA* would allow this method to scale to larger training sets and incrementally update representations. The PCA-reduced views for all 102,328 Twitter users can be found here: http://www.dredze.com/datasets/multiview_embeddings/.

Acknowledgements

This research was supported in part by NSF BIGDATA grant IIS-1546482 and a gift from Bloomberg LP.

References

Fabian Abel, Qi Gao, Geert-Jan Houben, and Ke Tao. 2011. Analyzing user modeling on twitter for personalized news recommendations. In *User Modeling, Adaption and Personalization - 19th International Conference, UMAP 2011, Girona, Spain, July 11-15, 2011. Proceedings*, pages 1–12.

Faiyaz Al Zamal, Wendy Liu, and Derek Ruths. 2012. Homophily and latent attribute inference: Inferring latent attributes of twitter users from neighbors. In *Internation Conference on Weblogs and Social Media (ICWSM)*.

Galen Andrew, Raman Arora, Jeff Bilmes, and Karen Livescu. 2013. Deep canonical correlation analysis. In *International Conference on Machine Learning (ICML)*, pages 1247–1255.

Raman Arora and Karen Livescu. 2014. Multi-view learning with supervision for transformed bottleneck features. In *Acoustics, Speech and Signal Processing (ICASSP), 2014 IEEE International Conference on*, pages 2499–2503. IEEE.

J Douglas Carroll. 1968. Generalization of canonical correlation analysis to three or more sets of variables. In *Convention of the American Psychological Association*, volume 3, pages 227–228.

Xin Chen, Yu Wang, Eugene Agichtein, and Fusheng Wang. 2015. A comparative study of demographic attribute inference in twitter. In *Conference on Weblogs and Social Media (ICWSM)*.

Manaal Faruqui and Chris Dyer. 2014. Improving vector space word representations using multilingual correlation. In *Proceedings of the 14th Conference of the European Chapter of the Association for Computational Linguistics, EACL 2014, April 26-30, 2014, Gothenburg, Sweden*, pages 462–471.

Ryan Kiros, Yukun Zhu, Ruslan Salakhutdinov, Richard S. Zemel, Antonio Torralba, Raquel Urtasun, and Sanja Fidler. 2015. Skip-thought vectors. *CoRR*, abs/1506.06726.

Su Mon Kywe, Tuan-Anh Hoang, Ee-Peng Lim, and Feida Zhu. 2012. On recommending hashtags in twitter networks. In *Social Informatics - 4th International Conference, SocInfo 2012, Lausanne, Switzerland, December 5-7, 2012. Proceedings*, pages 337–350.

Quoc V Le and Tomas Mikolov. 2014. Distributed representations of sentences and documents. In *Internation Conference on Machine Learning (ICML)*.

Jiwei Li, Alan Ritter, and Dan Jurafsky. 2015. Learning multi-faceted representations of individuals from heterogeneous evidence using neural networks. *arXiv preprint arXiv:1510.05198*.

David Liben-Nowell and Jon Kleinberg. 2007. The link-prediction problem for social networks. *Journal of the American society for information science and technology*, 58(7):1019–1031.

Chunliang Lu, Wai Lam, and Yingxiao Zhang. 2012. Twitter user modeling and tweets recommendation based on wikipedia concept graph. In *IJCAI Workshop on Intelligent Techniques for Web Personalization and Recommender Systems*.

Marco Lui and Timothy Baldwin. 2012. langid. py: An off-the-shelf language identification tool. In *Association for Computational Linguistics (ACL): system demonstrations*, pages 25–30.

Tomas Mikolov, Ilya Sutskever, Kai Chen, Greg S Corrado, and Jeff Dean. 2013. Distributed representations of words and phrases and their compositionality. In *Advances in neural information processing systems (NIPS)*, pages 3111–3119.

Youssef Mroueh, Etienne Marcheret, and Vaibhava Goel. 2015. Asymmetrically weighted cca and hierarchical kernel sentence embedding for multimodal retrieval. *arXiv preprint arXiv:1511.06267*.

Hemant Purohit, Yiye Ruan, Amruta Joshi, Srinivasan Parthasarathy, and Amit Sheth. 2011. Understanding user-community engagement by multi-faceted features: A case study on twitter. In *WWW Workshop on Social Media Engagement (SoME)*.

Pushpendre Rastogi, Benjamin Van Durme, and Raman Arora. 2015. Multiview lsa: Representation learning via generalized cca. In *North American Association for Computational Linguistics (NAACL)*.

Bernhard Schölkopf, Alexander J. Smola, and Klaus-Robert Müller. 1997. Kernel principal component analysis. In *Artificial Neural Networks - ICANN '97, 7th International Conference, Lausanne, Switzerland, October 8-10, 1997, Proceedings*, pages 583–588.

Jieying She and Lei Chen. 2014. Tomoha: Topic model-based hashtag recommendation on twitter. In *International conference on World wide web (WWW)*, pages 371–372. International World Wide Web Conferences Steering Committee.

Michel Van De Velden and Tammo HA Bijmolt. 2006. Generalized canonical correlation analysis of matrices with missing rows: a simulation study. *Psychometrika*, 71(2):323–331.

Svitlana Volkova, Glen Coppersmith, and Benjamin Van Durme. 2014. Inferring user political preferences from streaming communications. In *Association for Computational Linguistics (ACL)*, pages 186–196.

Svitlana Volkova. 2015. *Predicting Demographics and Affect in Social Networks*. Ph.D. thesis, Johns Hopkins University, October.

Weiran Wang, Raman Arora, Karen Livescu, and Jeff Bilmes. 2015. On deep multi-view representation learning. In *Proceedings of the 32nd International Conference on Machine Learning (ICML-15)*, pages 1083–1092.

Eva Zangerle, Wolfgang Gassler, and Günther Specht. 2013. On the impact of text similarity functions on hashtag recommendations in microblogging environments. *Social Network Analysis and Mining*, 3(4):889–898.

Implicit Polarity and Implicit Aspect Recognition in Opinion Mining

Huan-Yuan Chen and Hsin-Hsi Chen
Department of Computer Science and Information Engineering
National Taiwan University, Taipei, Taiwan
`r04922009@ntu.edu.tw; hhchen@ntu.edu.tw`

Abstract

This paper deals with a double-implicit problem in opinion mining and sentiment analysis. We aim at identifying aspects and polarities of opinionated statements not consisting of opinion words and aspect terms. As a case study, opinion words and aspect terms are first extracted from Chinese hotel reviews, and then grouped into positive (negative) clusters and aspect term clusters. We observe that an implicit opinion and its neighbor explicit opinion tend to have the same aspect and polarity. Under the observation, we construct an implicit opinions corpus annotated with aspect class labels and polarity automatically. Aspect and polarity classifiers trained by using this corpus is used to recognize aspect and polarity of implicit opinions.

1 Introduction

Opinions are classified into explicit and implicit ones depending on the subjectivity and objectivity (Liu, 2012; Zhang and Liu, 2014). It is more challenging to detect implicit opinions than explicit ones due to the lack of explicit opinion words in the sentences. Aspects refer to facets of the target entities in opinions. They are also categorized into explicit and implicit ones depending on the occurrences of aspect terms. Recognizing implicit aspects in implicit opinions is much more challenging because both opinion words and aspect terms are absent in opinionated statements.

Implicit opinions often describe the situations at which persons concern in their reviews. (S1) and (S2) are two examples selected from positive and negative rating rows respectively in hotel reviews. They do not mention any explicit opinion words and aspect terms. The situation of "many restaurants nearby" infers the convenience for eating, while the situation of "a lot of ants" infers the dirtiness of a room. The implicit opinion describes not only the situation at which customers feel, but also infers the reason why they have such feelings. Implicit opinions are positive in (S1) and negative in (S2), and the implied aspects are location and cleanness.

(S1) 附近有很多餐廳。(There are many restaurants nearby.)

(S2) 房間裡有很多螞蟻。(There are a lot of ants in the room.)

The implicit opinions may be subjective in some cases. For example, (S1) may be placed in negative rating row in a hotel review. Its implicit interpretation will become "There are many restaurants nearby, and thus the air pollution is severe and the smell of the air is very bad."

People may describe a situation first, and then reveal their attitudes and judgments. (S3) is an example. The first clause (only ten meters to the subway entrance) describes a situation, while the second clause (the location is good) is an explicit opinion. In Chinese review, an explicit opinion can also be specified before a situation description. (S4) is an example. In both cases, the polarity and the aspect of the situation are consistent with those of the explicit opinions.

(S3) 到地鐵出入口僅十米，地段好。(Only ten meters to the subway entrance, good location.)

(S4) 地點不錯，可步行至周圍三個捷運站。(Location is good, within walking distance of three MRTs around.)

This paper aims at extracting implicit opinions and identifying their implicit aspects and polarity. We will extract opinions from Chinese hotel reviews, then transfer polarity and aspect from explicit expressions to the corresponding implicit opinions, and train aspect and polarity classifiers. We evaluate the performance of polarity and aspect recognition on implicit opinions.

Almost all previous approaches identify implicit aspects in explicit opinions. They extract opinion words from opinionated sentences, regard them as

Proceedings of the 54th Annual Meeting of the Association for Computational Linguistics, pages 20–25,
Berlin, Germany, August 7-12, 2016. ©2016 Association for Computational Linguistics

implicit aspect clues, and find aspects through opinion word-aspect term mapping. The lack of opinion words in implicit opinions results in no indicators in mapping. To the best of our knowledge, this paper is the first one to resolve a double-implicit problem in opinion mining and sentiment analysis.

This paper is organized as follows. Section 2 gives a survey on implicit aspect recognition in opinion mining and sentiment analysis. Section 3 constructs an implicit opinions corpus labelled with aspect classes and polarity automatically. Section 4 presents classifiers for implicit polarity and implicit aspect recognition. Section 5 shows and discusses the experimental results.

2 Related Work

Hu and Liu (2004) present the first feature-based opinion summarization system. They point out explicit and implicit product features, and extract explicit features by using association miner and pruning strategies. The opinionated sentences along with their polarity are listed under individual product features. Popescu and Etzioni (2005) introduce an opinion extraction system OPINE. OPINE extracts explicit product features based on Point-wise Mutual Information. This work does not discuss the implicit feature generation. Liu et al. (2005) present an association mining approach to extract both explicit and implicit features in their opinion observer, but the implicit features discussed occur explicitly in an overt form, e.g., [MB] indicates a product feature <memory>.

Su et al. (2008) define an implicit feature as the product feature which does not occur explicitly, but can be inferred from the surrounding opinion word. They propose a mutual reinforcement approach to cluster product features and opinion words simultaneously, and extract implicit features based on opinion words. In the subsequent work, different methodologies are proposed to identify the association between opinion words and aspect terms (called also product features), thus implicit aspects are inferred from opinion word-aspect term mapping (Bagheri et al., 2013).

Zhen et al. (2011) propose a two-phase co-occurrence association rule mining approach. Yu et al. (2011) generate a review hierarchy based on aspects. Implicit aspect of a review can be determined by the cosine similarity of the review vector and the vector for each aspect node in the review hierarchy. Zeng and Li (2013) regard identification of implicit features as a classification problem, and consider reviews for each clustered opinion-pair as training set. Wang et al. (2013) employ five collocation methods including frequency, PMI, frequency/PMI, t-test and chi-square test to measure the association between opinion words and aspect terms.

Cruz et al. (2014) manually annotate implicit aspects and implicit aspect indicators (IAI) on the customer review datasets in Hu and Liu (2004), and employ Conditional Random Fields to recognize IAI. Poria et al. (2014) identify implicit aspect clues (IACs) in a document. Both approaches establish IAI (IAC) and aspect mapping.

Mukherjee and Liu (2012) propose two statistical models to deal with aspect categorization problem. They use hotel reviews from tripadvisor.com, and point out categorizing aspects is a subjective task. Total 9 major aspects based on commonsense knowledge, including Dining, Staff, Maintenance, Check In, Cleanliness, Comfort, Amenities, Location and Value for Money, are considered. Kim et al. (2013) further analyze general aspects and specific aspects, and discuss how aspect structure is helpful. Zhao et al. (2015) present a fine-grained corpus for sentiment analysis.

Our work is different from the previous ones in two-fold: (1) opinion is implicit, so that no opinion words can be used as clues; and (2) aspect is implicit, so that no aspect terms can be found. The direct opinion word and aspect mapping is not feasible in implicit polarity and implicit aspect recognition. We focus on the construction of an implicit opinions corpus for double-implicit recognition. The aspect categorization is not the major concern.

3 Constructing Implicit Opinions Corpus

This section first defines the implicit opinions, collects a Chinese hotel dataset, identifies opinion and aspect clusters from the dataset, and constructs implicit opinion corpus labelled with aspect class and polarity.

3.1 Definitions of Implicit Opinions

A sentence in a review can be partitioned into several segments separated by punctuation marks. The following show four possible types of segments based on the occurrences of opinion words and aspect terms, where + and - denote occurrence and non-occurrence. Segments of types (T1) and (T2) contain explicit opinion words, while segments of types (T3) and (T4) contain no opinion words. They appear together with and without aspect terms.

- (T1) (+opinion word, +aspect term)
    - e.g., 地點不錯 (location is good)
- (T2) (+opinion word, -aspect term)
    - e.g., 很便宜 (very cheap)
- (T3) (-opinion word, +aspect term)
    - e.g., 地理位置 (location)
- (T4) (-opinion word,-aspect term)
    - e.g., 到油麻地地鐵站只要兩分鐘 (Just two minutes to Yau Ma Tei MRT Station)

Segments of either type can not only appear individually, but also can be combined with other types of segments to form a sentence. Segments of types (T1) and (T2) are opinionated. Segments of type (T3) are opinionated implicitly when they appear in positive/negative rating row. Segments of type (T4) can be opinionated or non-opinionated. It is interpreted as an opinionated segment clearly when it is placed in rating row individually.

(S5) is a sentence consisting of 5 segments of types T3, T2, T1, T4 and T3, respectively. The 4th segment, i.e., feeling a little like shanty towns, is a double-implicit opinion. Its polarity and aspect (negative and environment) can be inferred from the 3rd segment, i.e., the surrounding environment is really bad.

(S5) [T3 旅館在小巷子裡]，[T2 安全沒有問題]，[T1 但附近環境確實不好]，[T4 有點棚戶區的感覺]，[T3 周圍沒有飯店]。([T3 hotel in the alley]，[T2 security is no problem]，[T1 but the surrounding environment is really bad]，[T4 feeling a little like shanty towns]，[T3 no hotels around])

In this paper, we deal with opinionated segments of type (T4). On the one hand, we extract pairs of segments of types T1-T4 or T4-T1 from a Chinese hotel review dataset. The segments of type T4 will be annotated with opinion words and aspect terms extracted from their paired segments of type T1. The segments of type T4 along with their annotations form a training corpus. On the other hand, the test segments of types (T4) will be labelled with polarity and aspect by polarity and aspect classifiers.

At first glance, we do not need to perform the classification task on T4 segments since we can directly use polarity and aspect of T1 segments. The scenario is just for test purpose because we do not have large-scale manually-labelled data. In the latter experiments, we will also consider the cases of T4 segments existing individually in rating rows. That will reflect the real situations.

3.2 Extraction of Implicit Opinions

Opinion words and aspect terms are the indicators to define the four types (T1)-(T4). As a case study, we collect a Chinese hotel review dataset from booking.com. It consists of 144,158 positive reviews and 113,844 negative reviews about 20,973 hotels from 49 international cities. Here only Chinese reviews are kept. We use Stanford NLP tools to segment, POS tag, and parse all the reviews.

At first, we construct an opinion dictionary from this dataset. Words of POS tags VA, VV, AD, and JJ are candidates of opinion words. We adopt Chi-square test and point-wise mutual information to filter out less confident words from the candidate set, respectively. We examine the union of the remaining words manually and construct an opinion dictionary consisting of 374 positive and 408 negative opinion words.

Then, we construct an aspect dictionary based on opinion words. A word meeting the following four conditions is regarded as an aspect term candidate: (1) its POS is NN, (2) it occurs at least 100 times, (3) it is accompanied with an opinion word within the same segment, and (4) their dependency is nsubj. We examine 183 proposed candidates manually and construct an aspect dictionary consisting of 153 aspect terms.

In an extreme case, a review does not contain any opinion words and aspect terms. It may be a single segment or multiple segments of type T4. Reviews are listed under positive and negative rating rows, so we know their polarity, but not aspect. Table 1 shows the statistics of such kinds of reviews in the hotel dataset. Interestingly, 2.07% of positive reviews are pure T4, and 7.29% of negative reviews are pure T4. That demonstrates double-implicit is a practical issue and customers tend to express negative opinions implicitly. The pure

	single	multiple	total
# pure T4 (positive reviews)	2,266	717	2,983
# pure T4 (negative reviews)	5,847	2,451	8,298

Table 1: Statistics of pure T4 reviews.

	T1	T2	T3	T4
total	192,353	161,863	257,831	303,357
ratio	21.01%	17.68%	28.17%	33.14%

Table 2: Statistics of segment types.

T4 reviews set consisting of single segments only is called PT4S hereafter.

Table 2 shows the statistics of segments of types T1, T2, T3, and T4. Only 21.01% of segments contain both opinion words and aspect terms, and 33.14% of segments do not contain any opinion words and aspect terms. We further examine the type combinations of two successive segments. There are 103 possible punctuation marks between any two segments, including common ones like " , ", " 。 ", "?", and "!", and some special ones like "~~~". To avoid misinterpretation of the special marks, we considers only those segment pairs linked by commas. Moreover, to obtain an automatically labelled dataset, the ambiguous sequence of segments, X-T4-Y, where X and Y of types T1, T2, or T3, are removed. Total 31,136 T4-T1/T1-T4 segment pairs remain. They are used to derive an implicit opinions corpus for learning and testing polarity classifier and aspect classifiers. This data set is called T41 hereafter.

In most of the cases we observed, segment of type T2 or T3 does not pass its aspect or opinion to nearby segments of type T4. (S6) is an example of a triple of segments of type T1-T4-T3, which introduces ambiguity between aspect and opinion assignment. The aspect of segment of type T1, i.e., *the equipment*, competes with that of segment of type T3, *the toilet*. In this case, *the safety deposit box*, which is the undetected aspect of the segment of type T4, and *the toilet* are two sub-aspects of *the equipment*. The latter two clauses are supplementary description of the first clause.

(S6) 設施比較舊，保險箱不好使，馬桶上水時有故障 (The equipment is old, the safety deposit box is hard to use, and the toilet sometimes stucks while refilling.)

This work bases on the postulation – say, an implicit opinion and its neighbor explicit opinion tending to have the same aspect and polarity, to construct a training corpus automatically. We randomly sampled 1% of pairs of segments of type T1-T4 or T4-T1 in a training corpus (see Section 4) to verify whether our assumption holds. In this setup, we discard clauses that contain parsing errors and those are too short to represent both aspects and opinions. The result is promising. On average, 70.46% of the pairs follow the observation. In particular, the pairs keep the property more often (i.e., 74.51%) when the polarity of T1 is negative.

4 Double-Implicit Opinion Analysis

We assign polarity and aspect of a T4-type segment in T41 dataset based on the information from its paired T1-type segment. Negation in the T1-type segment will reverse the polarity. To avoid data sparseness, 153 aspect terms are partitioned into 10 aspect classes based on common sense knowledge, including food, hotel, price, room, internet, staff, services, facilities, neighborhood, and general. The criterion in the selection of the category of aspects is not the major concern in this paper. For example, facilities and services may be merged into the same aspect category. The 31,136 labelled T4-type segments in T41 dataset are divided into training and test sets consisting of 23,352 and 7,784 segments, respectively.

Figure 1 shows the segment length distribution of T41-train, T41-test, T41, and PT4S datasets. The length is measured by number of Chinese words in a segment. X-axis and Y-axis denote length of segments and ratio, respectively. Segments in PT4S dataset are shorter than those in T41 dataset. Segments of 2 and 3 words occupy 48.61%. Table 3 shows the polarity distribution in these datasets. Because T41 dataset is divided into T41-train and T41-test datasets uniformly, their polarity distribution is the same, i.e., positive:

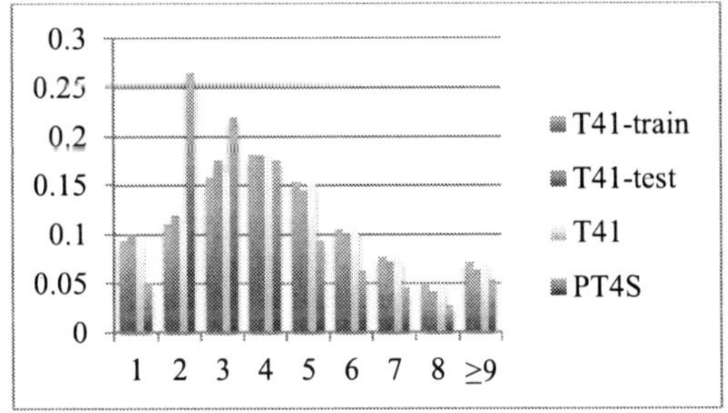

Figure 1: Length distribution in experimental datasets.

	T41	T41-train	T41-test	PT4S
positive	79.64%	79.63%	79.68%	27.93%
negative	20.36%	20.37%	20.32%	72.07%

Table 3: Polarity distribution in experimental datasets.

(%)	BOW linear	W2V linear	BOW RBF	W2V RBF	W2V CNN
T41-test (p)	78.55	73.67	81.54	79.76	**85.04**
PT4S (p)	**77.30**	77.64	72.01	72.22	67.96
MicroAvg	**77.91**	75.69	76.67	75.91	76.32
T41-test (a)	43.25	41.50	46.35	46.13	**55.90**

Table 4: Accuracy of implicit polarity and aspect recognition.

negative=4:1. Comparatively, positive:negative= 1:2.58 in PT4S dataset. The two test sets bias toward different polarities.

We employ T41-train dataset to train binary polarity classifier and 10-way aspect classifiers, and test on T41-test dataset. We also explore T41 dataset to train polarity classifier, and test on PT4S dataset. T41-testing evaluates both implicit polarity and implicit aspect recognition. Note the ground truth is generated automatically. PT4S-testing evaluates implicit polarity only based on the human-annotated ground truth.

We consider bag of words (BOW) and word vectors generated by word2vec (W2V) as features, where word vectors are pre-trained by using the part-of-tagged Chinese sentences extracted from the ClueWeb09 dataset (CMU, 2009; Yu et al., 2012). Moreover, we adopt SVM with linear kernel and SVM with RBF kernel learning algorithms in Scikit-Learn library (Pedregosa et al., 2011), and run cross-validation multiple times on the training set to facilitate a grid search on hyperparameters with F-measure as the metric to optimize.

Besides, we also explore Convolutional Neural Networks (CNN) (Kim, 2014). Table 4 summarizes the accuracy of implicit polarity and implicit aspect recognition, where (p) and (a) after dataset denote polarity and aspect performance of that dataset, respectively. CNN achieves the best implicit polarity and aspect recognition in T41-test dataset. However, its implicit polarity accuracy is decreased to 67.96%. It may be due to overfitting in small amount of training data. Different dropout rates (Srivastava et al., 2014) can be explored. SVM with linear kernel (BOW) gets the best micro average accuracy (77.91%) in implicit polarity recognition.

Figure 2 shows the accuracies of the implicit polarity recognition on segments of different lengths.

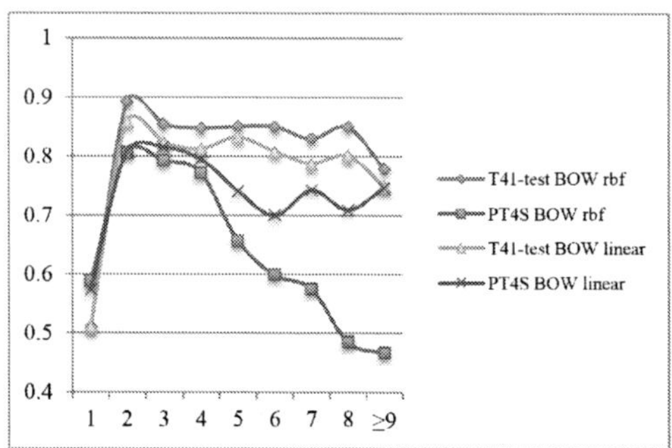

Figure 2: Accuracies of segments of different lengths.

It is challenging to predict the implicit polarity and aspect for segments of very short length. Figure 1 depicts one-word segments occupy 5%-10%. One word segment like "旺角" (Mong Kok) is ambiguous. If we neglect such segments, the micro average accuracy in implicit polarity recognition using SVM with linear kernel (BOW) is increased to 79.94%, and the accuracy in implicit aspect recognition (10-way classification) becomes 46.01%.

5 Conclusion and Future Work

In this paper, we address the double-implicit issue in opinion mining and sentiment analysis, and propose a protocol to derive a labelled corpus for implicit polarity and implicit aspect analysis. SVM with linear kernel (BOW) is robust in implicit polarity recognition. Ten-way classification for implicit aspect recognition still has space to improve.

This work bases on the aspect-and-polarity-transfer postulation to construct a training corpus automatically. We randomly sample T4 segments from T4-T1 or T1-T4 pairs and check them manually. We find that 70.46% of the pairs follow the observation. The experimental setup is reasonable for evaluation with PT4S dataset because it is labelled by users themselves. To derive a more reliable training set, distinguishing if T4 is non-opinionated needs to be investigated further.

Moreover, we neglect the cases T4-X (X-T4), where X is either T2 or T3, in the selection of training set. It is also challenging when either opinion word or aspect term is absent from the cue segment. In this paper, we provide some case studies of these scenarios, but how to utilize the partial information in implicit polarity and implicit aspect recognition is a future work.

Acknowledgments

This research was partially supported by Ministry of Science and Technology, Taiwan, under grant MOST-102-2221-E-002-103-MY3. We thank the anonymous reviewers for their constructive comments to revise this paper.

References

Arjun Mukherjee and Bing Liu. 2012. Aspect Extraction through Semi-Supervised Modeling, *Proceedings of the 50th Annual Meeting of the Association for Computational Linguistics*, pages 339–348.

Ayoub Bagheria, Mohamad Saraeeb, and Franciska de Jong. 2013. Care More about Customers: Unsupervised Domain-independent Aspect Detection for Sentiment Analysis of Customer Reviews, *Knowledge-Based Systems*, 52:201–213.

CMU. 2009. ClueWeb09, http://lemurproject.org/clueweb09.php/.

Ivan Cruz, Alexander Gelbukh, and Grigori Sidorov. 2014. Implicit Aspect Indicator Extraction for Aspect-based Opinion Mining, *International Journal of Computational Linguistics and Applications*, 5(2):135-152.

Minqing Hu and Bing Liu. 2004. Mining and Summarizing Customer Reviews, *Proceedings of the ACM SIGKDD International Conference on Knowledge Discovery and Data Mining*, pages 168–177.

Yoon Kim. 2014. Convolutional Neural Networks for Sentence Classification, *Proceedings of the 2014 Conference on Empirical Methods in Natural Language Processing (EMNLP)*, pages 1746–1751.

Suin Kim, Jianwen Zhang, Zheng Chen, Alice Oh, and Shixia Liu. 2013. A Hierarchical Aspect-Sentiment Model for Online Reviews, *Proceedings of the Twenty-Seventh AAAI Conference on Artificial Intelligence*, pages 526–533.

Bing Liu. 2012. *Sentiment Analysis and Opinion Mining*. Morgan & Claypool Publishers.

Bing Liu, Minqing Hu, and Junsheng Cheng. 2005. Opinion Observer: Analyzing and Comparing Opinions, *Proceedings of the 14th International Conference on World Wide Web*, pages 1024–1025.

Fabian Pedregosa, Gael Varoquaux, Alexandre Gramfort, Vincent Michel, Bertrand Thirion, Olivier Grisel, Mathieu Blondel, Peter Prettenhofer, Ron Weiss, Vincent Dubourg, Jake Vanderplas, Alexandre Passos, David Cournapeau, Matthieu Brucher, Matthieu Perrot, and Edouard Duchesnay. 2011. Scikitlearn: Machine learning in Python. *Journal of Machine Learning Research*, 12:2825–2830.

Ana-Maria Popescu and Oren Etzioni. 2005. Extracting Product Features and Opinions from Reviews, *Proceedings of Conference on Empirical Methods in Natural Language Processing*, pages 3–28.

Soujanya Poria, Erik Cambria, Lun-Wei Ku, Chen Gui and Alexander Gelbukh. 2014. A Rule-Based Approach to Aspect Extraction from Product Reviews, *Proceedings of the Second Workshop on Natural Language Processing for Social Media (SocialNLP)*, pages 28–37.

Nitish Srivastava, Georey Hinton, Alex Krizhevsky, Ilya Sutskever, and Ruslan Salakhutdinov. 2014. Dropout: A Simple Way to Prevent Neural Networks from Overfitting, Journal of Machine Learning Research, 15, pages, 1929–1958.

Qi Su, Xinying Xu, Honglei Guo, Zhili Guo, Xian Wu, Xiaoxun Zhang, Bin Swen, and Zhong Su. 2008. Hidden Sentiment Association in Chinese Web Opinion Mining, *Proceedings of International Conference on World Wide Web*, pages 959–968.

Wei Wang, Hua Xu, and Wei Wan. 2013. Implicit Feature Identification via Hybrid Association Rule Mining, *Expert Systems with Applications*, 40(9): 3518–3531.

Jianxing Yu, Zheng-Jun Zha, Meng Wang, Kai Wang, and Tat-Seng Chua. 2011. Domain-Assisted Product Aspect Hierarchy Generation: Towards Hierarchical Organization of Unstructured Consumer Reviews, *Proceedings of the Conference on Empirical Methods in Natural Language Processing*, pages 140–150.

Lingwei Zeng and Fang Li. 2013. A Classification-Based Approach for Implicit Feature Identification, *Proceedings of the China National Conference on Computational Linguistics*, LNAI 8202, pages 190–202.

Lei Zhang and Bing Liu. 2014. Aspect and Entity Extraction for Opinion Mining, *Data Mining and Knowledge Discovery for Big Data*, Studies in Big Data, 1, pages 1-40.

Yanyan Zhao, Bing Qin, and Ting Liu. 2015. Creating a Fine-Grained Corpus for Chinese Sentiment Analysis, *IEEE Intelligent Systems*, 30(1),36–43.

Chi-Hsin Yu, Yi-jie Tang, and Hsin-Hsi Chen. 2012. Development of a Web-Scale Chinese Word N-gram Corpus with Parts of Speech Information, *Proceedings of 8th International Conference on Language Resources and Evaluation*, pages 320–324.

Hai Zhen, Kuiyu Chang, and Jung-jae Kim. 2011. Implicit Feature Identification via Co-occurrence Association Rule Mining, *Proceedings of 12th International Conference on Computational Linguistics and Intelligent Text Processing*, pages 393–404.

A Domain Adaptation Regularization for Denoising Autoencoders

Stéphane Clinchant, Gabriela Csurka and Boris Chidlovskii
Xerox Research Centre Europe
6 chemin Maupertuis, Meylan, France
`Firstname.Lastname@xrce.xerox.com`

Abstract

Finding domain invariant features is critical for successful domain adaptation and transfer learning. However, in the case of unsupervised adaptation, there is a significant risk of overfitting on source training data. Recently, a regularization for domain adaptation was proposed for deep models by (Ganin and Lempitsky, 2015). We build on their work by suggesting a more appropriate regularization for denoising autoencoders. Our model remains unsupervised and can be computed in a closed form. On standard text classification adaptation tasks, our approach yields the state of the art results, with an important reduction of the learning cost.

1 Introduction

Domain Adaptation problem arises each time when we need to leverage labeled data in one or more related *source* domains, to learn a classifier for unseen data in a *target* domain. It has been studied for more than a decade, with applications in statistical machine translation, opinion mining, part of speech tagging, named entity recognition and document ranking (Daumé and Marcu, 2006; Pan and Yang, 2010; Zhou and Chang, 2014).

The idea of finding domain invariant features underpins numerous works in domain adaptation. A shared representation eases prediction tasks, and theoretical analyses uphold such hypotheses (Ben-David et al., 2007). For instance, (Daumé and Marcu, 2006; Daumé, 2009) have shown that replicating features in three main subspaces (source, common and target) yields improved accuracy as the classifier can subsequently pick the most relevant common features. With the pivoting technique (Blitzer et al., 2006; Pan

et al., 2010), the bag of words features are projected on a subspace that captures the relations between some central *pivot* features and the remaining words. Similarly, there are several extensions of topic models and matrix factorization techniques where the latent factors are shared by source and target collections (Chen and Liu, 2014; Chen et al., 2013).

More recently, deep learning has been proposed as a generic solution to domain adaptation and transfer learning problems by demonstrating their ability to learn invariant features. On one hand, unsupervised models such as *denoising autoencoders* (Glorot et al., 2011) or models built on word embeddings (Bollegala et al., 2015) are shown to be effective for domain adaptation. On the other hand, supervised deep models (Long et al., 2015) can be designed to select an appropriate feature space for classification. Adaptation to a new domain can also be performed by fine tuning the neural network on the target task (Chopra et al., 2013). While such solutions perform relatively well, the refinement may require a significant amount of new labeled data. Recent work by (Ganin and Lempitsky, 2015) has proposed a better strategy; they proposed to regularize intermediate layers with a domain prediction task, i.e. deciding whether an object comes from the source or target domain.

This paper proposes to combine the domain prediction regularization idea of (Ganin and Lempitsky, 2015) with the denoising autoencoders. More precisely, we build on *stacked Marginalized Denoising Autoencoders* (sMDA) (Chen et al., 2012), which can be learned efficiently with a closed form solution. We show that such domain adaptation regularization keeps the benefits of the sMDA and yields results competitive to the state of the art results of (Ganin and Lempitsky, 2015).

Proceedings of the 54th Annual Meeting of the Association for Computational Linguistics, pages 26–31,
Berlin, Germany, August 7-12, 2016. ©2016 Association for Computational Linguistics

2 Target Regularized MDA

Stacked Denoising Autoencoders (sDA) (Vincent et al., 2008) are multi-layer neural networks trained to reconstruct input data from partial random corruption. The random corruption, called blank-out noise or *dropout*, consists in randomly setting to zero some input nodes with probability p; it has been shown to act as a regularizer (Wager et al., 2013). The sDA is composed of a set of stacked one-layer linear denoising autoencoder components, which consider a set of N input documents (represented by d-dimensional features $\mathbf{x}_n$) to be corrupted M times by random feature dropout and then reconstructed with a linear mapping $\mathbf{W} \in \mathbb{R}^{d \times d}$ by minimizing the squared reconstruction loss:

$$\mathcal{L}(\mathbf{W}) = \sum_{n=1}^{N} \sum_{m=1}^{M} ||\mathbf{x}_n - \tilde{\mathbf{x}}_{nm}\mathbf{W}||^2. \qquad (1)$$

As explicit corruption comes at a high computational cost, (Chen et al., 2012) propose to *marginalize* the loss (1) by considering the limiting case when $M \to \infty$ and reducing *de facto* the learning cost. The main advantage of this method is a closed form solution for $\mathbf{W}$, which depends only on the uncorrupted inputs ($\mathbf{x}_n$) and the dropout probability. Several Marginalized Denoising Autoencoders (MDA) can be then stacked together to create a deep architecture where the representations of the $(l-1)^{th}$ layer serves as inputs to the lth layer[1].

In the case of domain adaptation, the idea is to apply MDA (or sMDA) to the union of unlabeled source $\mathbf{X}^s$ and target $\mathbf{X}^t$ examples. Then, a standard learning algorithm such as SVM or Logistic Regression is trained on the labeled source data using the new feature representations ($\mathbf{x}_n^s\mathbf{W}$) which captures better the correlation between the source and target data.

In Figure 1, we illustrate the effect of the MDA, it shows the relation between the word log document frequency (x-axes) and the *expansion mass* defined as the total mass of words transformed into word i by MDA and represented by $\sum_j W_{ji}$. We can see that the mapping $\mathbf{W}$ learned by MDA is heavily influenced by frequent words. In fact, MDA behaves similarly to document expansion on text documents: it adds new words with a

---

[1]Between layers, in general, a non linear function such as *tanh* or *ReLU* is applied.

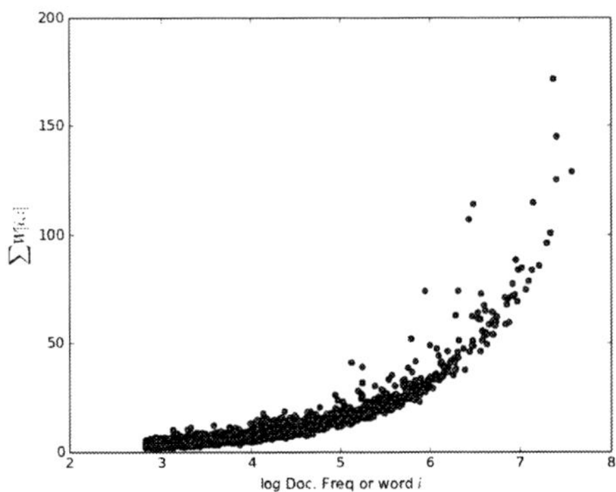

Figure 1: Relation between log document frequency and expansion mass. One dot represents one word.

very small frequency and sometimes words with a small negative weight. As the figure shows, MDA promotes common words (despite the use of tf-idf weighting scheme) that are frequent both in source and target domains and hence aims to be domain invariant.

This is in line with the work of (Ganin et al., 2015). To strengthen the invariance effect, they suggested a deep neural architecture which embeds a domain prediction task in intermediate layers, in order to capture domain invariant features. In this paper we go a step further and refine this argument by claiming that *we want to be domain invariant* but also to be *as close as possible to the target domain distribution*. We want to match the target feature distribution because it is where the classification takes place.

We therefore propose a regularization for the denoising autoencoders, in particular for MDA, with the aim to make *source data resemble the target data* and hence to ease the adaptation.

We describe here the case of two domains, but it can be easily generalized to multiple domains. Let $\mathbf{D}$ be the vector of size N indicating for each document its domain, *e.g.* taking values of '-1' for source and '$+1$' for target examples. Let $\mathbf{c}$ be a linear classifier represented as a d dimensional vector trained to distinguish between source and target, *e.g.* a ridge classifier that minimizes the loss $\mathcal{R}(\mathbf{c}, \alpha) = ||\mathbf{D} - \mathbf{X}\mathbf{c}^\top||^2 + \alpha||\mathbf{c}||^2$.

We guide the mapping $\mathbf{W}$ in such a way that the denoised data points $\mathbf{x}\mathbf{W}$ go towards the target side, *i.e.* $\mathbf{x}\mathbf{W}\mathbf{c}^\top = 1$ for both source and target samples. Hence, we can extend each term of the loss (1) as follows:

$$||\mathbf{x}_n - \tilde{\mathbf{x}}_{nm}\mathbf{W}||^2 + \lambda||\mathbf{1} - \tilde{\mathbf{x}}_{nm}\mathbf{W}\mathbf{c}^\top||^2. \quad (2)$$

The first term here represents the reconstruction loss of the original input, like in MDA. In the second term, $\tilde{\mathbf{x}}_{mn}\mathbf{W}\mathbf{c}^\top$ is the domain classifier prediction for the denoised objects forced to be close to 1, the target domain indicator, and $\lambda > 0$.

Let $\bar{\mathbf{X}}$ be the concatenation of M replicated version of the original data $\mathbf{X}$, and $\tilde{\mathbf{X}}$ be the matrix representation of the M corrupted versions. Taking into account the domain prediction term, the loss can be written as:

$$\mathcal{L}_{\mathcal{R}}(\mathbf{W}) = ||\bar{\mathbf{X}} - \tilde{\mathbf{X}}\mathbf{W}||^2 + \lambda||\bar{\mathbf{R}} - \tilde{\mathbf{X}}\mathbf{W}\mathbf{c}^\top||^2, \quad (3)$$

where $\mathbf{R}$ is a vector of size N, indicating a desired regularization objective, and $\bar{\mathbf{R}}$ its M-replicated version. Loss (3) represents a generic form to capture three different ideas:

- If $\mathbf{R} = \mathbf{1}$, the model incites the reconstructed features moving towards target specific features.

- If $\mathbf{R} = -\mathbf{D}$, the model aims to promote domain invariant features as in (Ganin et al., 2015).

- If $\mathbf{R} = [\mathbf{0}; \mathbf{1}]$, where $\mathbf{0}$ values are used for source data, the model penalizes the source specific features.

Learning the mapping W. (Chen et al., 2012) observed that the random corruption from equation (1) could be *marginalized out* from the reconstruction loss, yielding a unique and optimal solution. Furthermore, the mapping $\mathbf{W}$ can be expressed in closed form as $\mathbf{W} = \mathbf{P}\mathbf{Q}^{-1}$, with:

$$\mathbf{Q}_{ij} = \begin{cases} \mathbf{S}_{ij}q_i q_j, & \text{if} \quad i \neq j, \\ \mathbf{S}_{ij}q_i, & \text{if} \quad i = j, \end{cases}$$
$$\mathbf{P}_{ij} = \mathbf{S}_{ij}q_j, \quad (4)$$

where[2] $q = [1 - p, \ldots, 1 - p] \in \mathbb{R}^d$, p is the dropout probability, and $\mathbf{S} = \mathbf{X}\mathbf{X}^T$ is the covariance matrix of the uncorrupted data $\mathbf{X}$.

The domain regularization term in (3) is quadratic in $\mathbf{W}$, the random corruption can still be

---

[2]In contrast to (Chen et al., 2012), we do not add a bias feature so that the domain and MDA have the same dimensionality. Experiments shown no impact on the performance.

marginalized out and the expectations obtained in closed form. Indeed, the mapping $\mathbf{W}$ which minimizes the expectation of $\frac{1}{M}\mathcal{L}_{\mathcal{R}}(\mathbf{W})$ is the solution of the following linear system[3]:

$$(\mathbf{P} + \lambda(1 - p)\mathbf{X}^\top\mathbf{R}\mathbf{c}^\top)(I + \lambda\mathbf{c}\mathbf{c}^\top)^{-1} = \mathbf{Q}\mathbf{W}. \quad (5)$$

In (5), parameter λ controls the effect of the proposed target regularization in the MDA and the regularization on $\mathbf{c}$ is controlled by parameter α. This approach preserves the good properties of MDA, *i.e.* the model is unsupervised and can be computed in closed form. In addition, we can easily stack several layers together and add non-linearities between layers.

3 Experiments

We conduct unsupervised domain adaptation experiments on two standard collections: the Amazon reviews (Blitzer et al., 2011) and the 20Newsgroup (Pan and Yang, 2010) datasets.

From the Amazon dataset we consider the four most used domains: *dvd (D), books (B), electronics (E) and kitchen (K)*, and adopt the settings of (Ganin et al., 2015) with the 5000 most frequent common features selected for each adaptation task and a tf-idf weighting. We then use the Logistic Regression (LR) to classify the reviews.

Our previous experiments with MDA revealed that the MDA noise probability p needs to be set to high values (*e.g.* 0.9). A possible explanation is that document representations are already sparse and adding low noise has no effect on the features already equal to zero. Figure 2 shows the average accuracy for the twelve Amazon tasks, when we vary the noise probability p.

In addition, we observed that a *single layer* with a *tanh* activation function is sufficient to achieve top performance; stacking several layers and/or concatenating the outputs with the original features yields no improvement but increases the computational time.

The dropout probability p is fixed to 0.9 in all experiments, for both the MDA baseline and our model; we test the performance with a single layer and a *tanh* activation function. Stacking several layers is left for future experiments. Parameters α and λ are tuned on a grid of values[4] by cross validation on the source data. In other words, we

---

[3]The derivation is not included due to space limitation.
[4]$\alpha \in [.1, 1, 50, 100, 150, 200, 300]$, $\lambda \in [.01, .1, 1, 10]$.

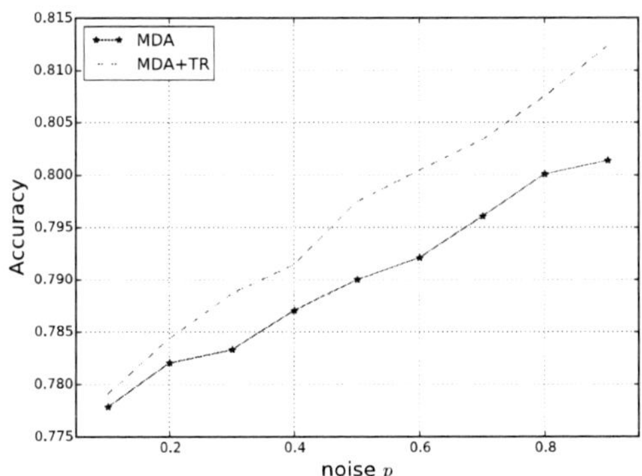

S	T	MDA	MDA+TR	G-sMDA	DA_NN
D	B	81.1	<u>81.4</u>	82.6	**82.5**
D	K	84.1	**<u>85.3</u>**	84.2	84.9
D	E	76.0	**<u>81.1</u>**	73.9	80.9
B	D	82.7	81.7	**83.0**	82.9
B	K	79.8	<u>81.8</u>	82.1	**84.3**
B	E	75.9	<u>79.3</u>	76.6	**80.4**
K	D	78.5	**<u>79.0</u>**	78.8	**78.9**
K	B	**77.0**	77.0	76.9	71.8
K	E	87.2	**<u>87.4</u>**	86.1	85.6
E	D	**78.5**	78.3	77.0	78.1
E	B	73.3	<u>75.1</u>	76.2	**77.4**
E	K	87.7	**<u>88.2</u>**	84.7	**88.1**
Avg		80.15	<u>81.27</u>	80.18	**81.32**

Table 1: Accuracies of MDA, MDA+TR, G-sMDA and DA_NN on the Amazon review dataset. Underline indicates improvement over the baseline MDA, bold indicates the highest value.

Figure 2: Impact of the noise parameter p on the average accuracy for the 12 Amazon adaptation tasks. Both MDA and its extension with the regularization (MDA+TR) perform better with a high dropout-out noise. Here MDA+TR is run with fixed parameters $\alpha = 100$ and $\lambda = 1$.

select the LR parameters and the parameters α, λ by cross validating the classification results using only the "reconstructed" source data; for estimating $\mathbf{W}$ we used the source with an unlabeled target set (excluded at test time). This corresponds to the setting used in (Ganin et al., 2015), with the difference that they use SVM and *reverse cross-validation*[5].

Table 3 shows the results for twelve adaptation tasks on the Amazon review dataset for the four following methods. Columns 1 and 2 show the LR classification results on the target set for the single layer MDA and the proposed target regularized MDA (MDA+TR). Column 3 reports the SVM result on the target from (Ganin et al., 2015). They used a 5 layers sMDA where the 5 outputs are concatenated with input to generate 30,000 features, on which the SVM is then trained and tested (G-sMDA). Finally, column 4 shows the current state of the art results obtained with Domain-Adversarial Training of Neural Networks (DA_NN) instead of SVM (Ganin et al., 2015)

Despite a single layer and LR trained on the source only, the MDA baseline (80.15% on average) is very close to the G-sMDA results obtained with 5 layer sMDA and 6 times larger feature set (80.18%). Furthermore, adding the target regularization allows to significantly outperform in many cases the baseline and the state of the art DA_NN. We note that our method has a much lower cost, as it uses *the closed form solution* for the reconstruction and a *simple LR on the reconstructed source data*, instead of domain-adversarial training of deep neural networks.

We also look at the difference between the previously introduced expansion mass for the MDA and MDA+TR. In the adaptation task from *dvd* (D) to *electronics* (E), the words for which the mass changed the most are the following[6]: *worked, to_use, speakers, i_have, work, mouse, bought, cable, works, quality, unit, ipod, price, _number_, sound, card, phone, use, product, my*. These words are mostly target specific and the results confirm that they get promoted by the new model.

Our model favors features which are more likely to appear in target examples, while DA_NN seeks domain invariant features. Despite this difference, the two approaches achieve similar results. It is surprising, and we argue that eventually both approaches penalize *source specific features*. To test this hypothesis, we use MDA with $\mathbf{R} = [0; 1]$ (case 3) that penalizes source specific features and we obtain again similar performances.

Finally, we test our approach on the 20Newsgroup adaptation tasks described in (Pan and Yang, 2010). We first filter out rare words and keep at most 10,000 features. Then, we apply both MDA and MDA+TR as above. Table 3 shows results for ten adaptation tasks. As we can see, in all cases the target regularization (MDA+TR) helps improve the classification accuracy.

---

[5]It consists in using self training on the target validation set and calibrating parameters on a validation set from the source labeled data.

[6]In ascending order of the differences.

Task	MDA	MDA+TR
comp vs sci	73.69	73.38
sci vs comp	69.39	69.92
rec vs talk	72.54	85.10
talk vs rec	72.30	76.22
rec vs sci	77.25	82.70
sci vs rec	79.95	80.00
sci vs talk	78.94	79.26
talk vs sci	77.17	77.91
comp vs rec	89.84	89.66
rec vs comp	89.92	90.29
Avg	78.1	80.40

Table 2: Accuracies of MDA and MDA+TR on 20Newsgroup adaptation tasks.

4 Conclusion

This paper proposes a domain adaptation regularization for denoising autoencoders, in particular for marginalized ones. One limitation of our model is the linearity assumption for the domain classifier, but for textual data, linear classifiers are the state of the art technique. As new words and expressions become more frequent in a new domain, the idea of using the dropout regularization that forces the reconstruction of initial objects to resemble target domain objects is rewarding. The main advantage of the new model is in the closed form solution. It is also unsupervised, as it does not require labeled target examples and yields performance results comparable with the current state of the art.

References

Shai Ben-David, John Blitzer, Koby Crammer, and Fernando Pereira. 2007. Analysis of representations for domain adaptation. In *Advances in Neural Information Processing Systems, NIPS Conference Proceedings, Vancouver, British Columbia, Canada, December 4-7, 2006.*, volume 19.

John Blitzer, Ryan McDonald, and Fernando Pereira. 2006. Domain adaptation with structural correspondence learning. In *Proceedings of Conference on Empirical Methods in Natural Language Processing, EMNLP, 22-23 July 2006, Sydney, Australia.*

John Blitzer, Sham Kakade, and Dean P. Foster. 2011. Domain adaptation with coupled subspaces. In *Proceedings of the Fourteenth International Conference on Artificial Intelligence and Statistics, AISTATS, Fort Lauderdale, USA, April 11-13, 2011.*

Danushka Bollegala, Takanori Maehara, and Ken-ichi Kawarabayashi. 2015. Unsupervised cross-domain word representation learning. In *Proceedings of the 53rd Annual Meeting of the Association for Computational Linguistics, ACL, July 26-31, 2015, Beijing, China*, volume 1.

Zhiyuan Chen and Bing Liu. 2014. Topic modeling using topics from many domains, lifelong learning and big data. In *Proceedings of the 31st International Conference on Machine Learning, ICML Bejing, 21-16 June 2014.*

M. Chen, Z. Xu, K. Q. Weinberger, and F. Sha. 2012. Marginalized denoising autoencoders for domain adaptation. *ICML*, arXiv:1206.4683.

Zhiyuan Chen, Arjun Mukherjee, Bing Liu, Meichun Hsu, Malu Castellanos, and Riddhiman Ghosh. 2013. Leveraging multi-domain prior knowledge in topic models. In *Proceedings of the Twenty-Third International Joint Conference on Artificial Intelligence*, IJCAI '13, pages 2071–2077. AAAI Press.

S. Chopra, S. Balakrishnan, and R. Gopalan. 2013. DLID: Deep learning for domain adaptation by interpolating between domains. In *Proceedings of the 30th International Conference on Machine Learning, ICML, Atlanta, USA, 16-21 June 2013.*

H. Daumé and D. Marcu. 2006. Domain adaptation for statistical classifiers. *JAIR*, 26:101–126.

H. Daumé. 2009. Frustratingly easy domain adaptation. *CoRR*, arXiv:0907.1815.

Yaroslav Ganin and Victor S. Lempitsky. 2015. Unsupervised domain adaptation by backpropagation. In *Proceedings of the 32nd International Conference on Machine Learning, ICML, Lille, France, 6-11 July 2015*, pages 1180–1189.

Yaroslav Ganin, Evgeniya Ustinova, Hana Ajakan, Pascal Germain, Hugo Larochelle, François Laviolette, Mario Marchand, and Victor S. Lempitsky. 2015. Domain-adversarial training of neural networks. *CoRR*, abs/1505.07818.

X. Glorot, A. Bordes, and Y. Bengio. 2011. Domain adaptation for large-scale sentiment classification: A deep learning approach. In *Proceedings of the 28th International Conference on Machine Learning, ICML, Bellevue, Washington, USA, June 28-July 2, 2011.*

M. Long, Y. Cao, , J. Wang, and M. Jordan. 2015. Learning transferable features with deep adaptation networks. In *Proceedings of the 32nd International Conference on Machine Learning, ICML 2015, Lille, France, 6-11 July 2015.*

S. J. Pan and Q. Yang. 2010. A survey on transfer learning. *Knowledge and Data Engineering, IEEE Transactions on*, 22(10):1345–1359.

Sinno Jialin Pan, Xiaochuan Ni, Jian-Tao Sun, Qiang Yang, and Zheng Chen. 2010. Cross-domain sentiment classification via spectral feature alignment. In *Proceedings of the 19th International Conference on World Wide Web*, WWW, New York, NY, USA. ACM.

P. Vincent, H. Larochelle, Y. Bengio, and P.-A. Manzagol. 2008. Extracting and composing robust features with denoising autoencoders. In *Proceedings of the 25nd International Conference on Machine Learning, ICML, Helsinki, Finland on July 5-9, 2008*.

Stefan Wager, Sida I. Wang, and Percy Liang. 2013. Dropout training as adaptive regularization. In 26, editor, *Advances in Neural Information Processing Systems, NIPS Conference Proceedings, Lake Tahoe, Nevada, United States, December 5-8, 2013*.

Mianwei Zhou and Kevin C. Chang. 2014. Unifying learning to rank and domain adaptation: Enabling cross-task document scoring. In *Proceedings of the 20th ACM SIGKDD International Conference on Knowledge Discovery and Data Mining*, KDD '14, pages 781–790, New York, NY, USA. ACM.

Incremental Parsing with Minimal Features Using Bi-Directional LSTM

James Cross and **Liang Huang**
School of Electrical Engineering and Computer Science
Oregon State University
Corvallis, Oregon, USA
{crossj,liang.huang}@oregonstate.edu

Abstract

Recently, neural network approaches for parsing have largely automated the combination of individual features, but still rely on (often a larger number of) atomic features created from human linguistic intuition, and potentially omitting important global context. To further reduce feature engineering to the bare minimum, we use bi-directional LSTM sentence representations to model a parser state with only three sentence positions, which automatically identifies important aspects of the entire sentence. This model achieves state-of-the-art results among greedy dependency parsers for English. We also introduce a novel transition system for constituency parsing which does not require binarization, and together with the above architecture, achieves state-of-the-art results among greedy parsers for both English and Chinese.

1 Introduction

Recently, neural network-based parsers have become popular, with the promise of reducing the burden of manual feature engineering. For example, Chen and Manning (2014) and subsequent work replace the huge amount of manual feature combinations in non-neural network efforts (Nivre et al., 2006; Zhang and Nivre, 2011) by vector embeddings of the atomic features. However, this approach has two related limitations. First, it still depends on a large number of carefully designed atomic features. For example, Chen and Manning (2014) and subsequent work such as Weiss et al. (2015) use 48 atomic features from Zhang and Nivre (2011), including select third-order dependencies. More importantly, this approach inevitably leaves out some nonlocal information which could be useful. In particular,

though such a model can exploit similarities between words and other embedded categories, and learn interactions among those atomic features, it cannot exploit any other details of the text.

We aim to reduce the need for manual induction of atomic features to the bare minimum, by using bi-directional recurrent neural networks to automatically learn context-sensitive representations for each word in the sentence. This approach allows the model to learn arbitrary patterns from the entire sentence, effectively extending the generalization power of embedding individual words to longer sequences. Since such a feature representation is less dependent on earlier parser decisions, it is also more resilient to local mistakes.

With just three positional features we can build a greedy shift-reduce dependency parser that is on par with the most accurate parser in the published literature for English Treebank. This effort is similar in motivation to the stack-LSTM of Dyer et al. (2015), but uses a much simpler architecture.

We also extend this model to predict phrase-structure trees with a novel shift-promote-adjoin system tailored to greedy constituency parsing, and with just two more positional features (defining tree span) and nonterminal label embeddings we achieve the most accurate greedy constituency parser for both English and Chinese.

2 LSTM Position Features

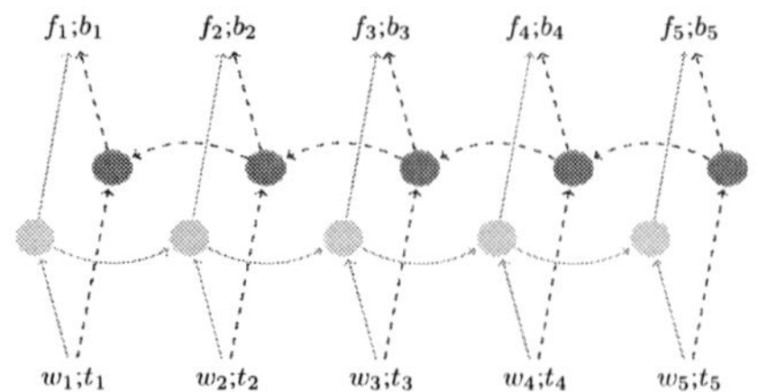

Figure 1: The sentence is modeled with an LSTM in each direction whose input vectors at each time step are word and part-of-speech tag embeddings.

Proceedings of the 54th Annual Meeting of the Association for Computational Linguistics, pages 32–37,
Berlin, Germany, August 7-12, 2016. ©2016 Association for Computational Linguistics

The central idea behind this approach is exploiting the power of recurrent neural networks to let the model decide what apsects of sentence context are important to making parsing decisions, rather than relying on fallible linguistic information (which moreover requires leaving out information which could be useful). In particular, we model an input sentence using Long Short-Term Memory networks (LSTM), which have made a recent resurgence after being initially formulated by Hochreiter and Schmidhuber (1997).

The input at each time step is simply a vector representing the word, in this case an embedding for the word form and one for the part-of-speech tag. These embeddings are learned from random initialization together with other network parameters in this work. In our initial experiments, we used one LSTM layer in each direction (forward and backward), and then concatenate the output at each time step to represent that sentence position: that word in the entire context of the sentence. This network is illustrated in Figure 1.

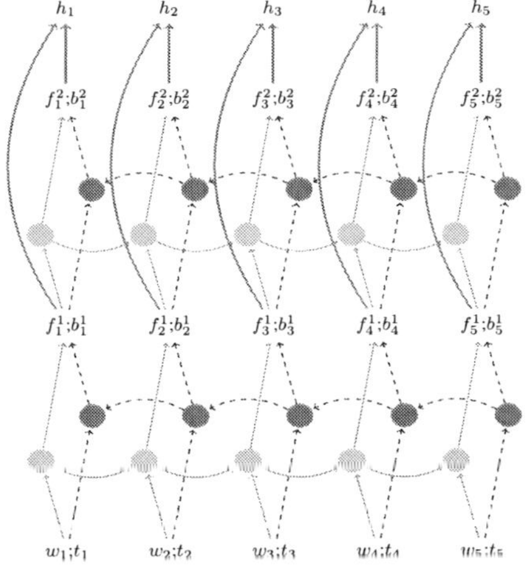

Figure 2: In the 2-Layer architecture, the output of each LSTM layer is concatenated to create the positional feature vector.

It is also common to stack multiple such LSTM layers, where the output of the forward and backward networks at one layer are concatenated to form the input to the next. We found that parsing performance could be improved by using two bidirectional LSTM layers in this manner, and concatenating the output of both layers as the positional feature representation, which becomes the input to the fully-connected layer. This architec-

input: $w_0 \ldots w_{n-1}$

axiom $\langle \epsilon,\ 0 \rangle : \emptyset$

shift $\dfrac{\langle S,\ j \rangle\ :\ A}{\langle S|j,\ j+1 \rangle\ :\ A}\ j < n$

re$_\frown$ $\dfrac{\langle S|s_1|s_0,\ j \rangle\ :\ A}{\langle S|s_0,\ j \rangle\ :\ A \cup \{s_1 {}^\frown s_0\}}$

goal $\langle s_0,\ n \rangle : A$

Figure 3: The arc-standard dependency parsing system (Nivre, 2008) (re$_\frown$ omitted). Stack S is a list of heads, j is the start index of the queue, and s_0 and s_1 are the top two head indices on S.

	dependency	constituency
positional	s_1, s_0, q_0	$s_1, s_0, q_0, s_1.\text{left}, s_0.\text{left}$
labels	-	$s_0.\{\text{left}, \text{right}, \text{root}, \text{head}\}$
		$s_1.\{\text{left}, \text{right}, \text{root}, \text{head}\}$

Table 1: Feature templates. Note that, remarkably, even though we do labeled dependency parsing, we do *not* include arc label as features.

ture is shown in Figure 2.

Intuitively, this represents the sentence position by the word in the context of the sentence up to that point and the sentence after that point in the first layer, as well as modeling the "higher-order" interactions between parts of the sentence in the second layer. In Section 5 we report results using only one LSTM layer ("Bi-LSTM") as well as with two layers where output from each layer is used as part of the positional feature ("2-Layer Bi-LSTM").

3   Shift-Reduce Dependency Parsing

We use the arc standard system for dependency parsing (see Figure 4). By exploiting the LSTM architecture to encode context, we found that we were able to achieve competitive results using only three sentence-position features to model parser state: the head word of each of the top two trees on the stack (s_0 and s_1), and the next word on the queue (q_0); see Table 1.

The usefulness of the head words on the stack is clear enough, since those are the two words that are linked by a dependency when taking a reduce action. The next incoming word on the queue is also important because the top tree on the stack should not be reduced if it still has children which have not yet been shifted. That feature thus allows

$$
\begin{array}{ll}
\text{input:} & w_0 \dots w_{n-1} \\[4pt]
\text{axiom} & \langle \epsilon,\, 0 \rangle : \emptyset \\[8pt]
\text{shift} & \dfrac{\langle S,\, j \rangle}{\langle S \mid j,\, j+1 \rangle} \quad j < n \\[12pt]
\text{pro}(X) & \dfrac{\langle S \mid t,\, j \rangle}{\langle S \mid X(t),\, j \rangle} \\[12pt]
\text{adj}_\frown & \dfrac{\langle S \mid t \mid X(t_1 \dots t_k),\, j \rangle}{\langle S \mid X(t, t_1 \dots t_k),\, j \rangle} \\[12pt]
\text{goal} & \langle s_0,\, n \rangle
\end{array}
$$

Figure 4: Our shift-promote-adjoin system for constituency parsing ($\text{adj}_\curvearrowright$ omitted).

the model to learn to delay a right-reduce until the top tree on the stack is fully formed, shifting instead.

3.1 Hierarchical Classification

The structure of our network model after computing positional features is fairly straightforward and similar to previous neural-network parsing approaches such as Chen and Manning (2014) and Weiss et al. (2015). It consists of a multilayer perceptron using a single ReLU hidden layer followed by a linear classifier over the action space, with the training objective being negative log softmax.

We found that performance could be improved, however, by factoring out the decision over structural actions (i.e., shift, left-reduce, or right-reduce) and the decision of which arc label to assign upon a reduce. We therefore use separate classifiers for those decisions, each with its own fully-connected hidden and output layers but sharing the underlying recurrent architecture. This structure was used for the results reported in Section 5, and it is referred to as "Hierarchical Actions" when compared against a single action classifier in Table 3.

4 Shift-Promote-Adjoin Constituency Parsing

To further demonstrate the advantage of our idea of minimal features with bidirectional sentence representations, we extend our work from dependency parsing to constituency parsing. However, the latter is significantly more challenging than the former under the shift-reduce paradigm because:

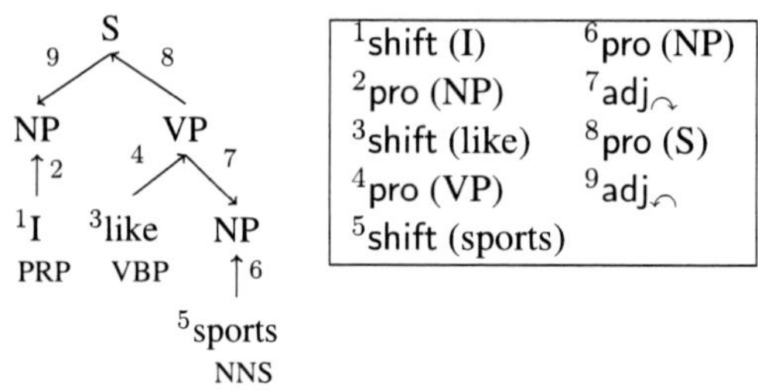

Figure 5: Shift-Promote-Adjoin parsing example. Upward and downward arrows indicate promote and (sister-)adjunction actions, respectively.

- we also need to predict the nonterminal labels

- the tree is not binarized (with many unary rules and more than binary branching rules)

While most previous work binarizes the constituency tree in a preprocessing step (Zhu et al., 2013; Wang and Xue, 2014; Mi and Huang, 2015), we propose a novel "Shift-Promote-Adjoin" paradigm which does not require any binariziation or transformation of constituency trees (see Figure 5). Note in particular that, in our case only the Promote action produces a new tree node (with a non-terminal label), while the Adjoin action is the linguistically-motivated "sister-adjunction" operation, i.e., attachment (Chiang, 2000; Henderson, 2003). By comparison, in previous work, both Unary-X and Reduce-L/R-X actions produce new labeled nodes (some of which are auxiliary nodes due to binarization). Thus our paradigm has two advantages:

- it dramatically reduces the number of possible actions, from $3X + 1$ or more in previous work to $3 + X$, where X is the number of nonterminal labels, which we argue would simplify learning;

- it does not require binarization (Zhu et al., 2013; Wang and Xue, 2014) or compression of unary chains (Mi and Huang, 2015)

There is, however, a more closely-related "shift-project-attach" paradigm by Henderson (2003). For the example in Figure 5 he would use the following actions:

shift(I), project(NP), project(S), shift(like), project(VP), shift(sports), project(NP), attach, attach.

The differences are twofold: first, our Promote action is head-driven, which means we only promote the head child (e.g., VP to S) whereas his Project action promotes the *first* child (e.g., NP to S); and secondly, as a result, his Attach action is always right-attach whereas our Adjoin action could be either left or right. The advantage of our method is its close resemblance to shift-reduce dependency parsing, which means that our constituency parser is jointly performing both tasks and can produce both kinds of trees. This also means that we use head rules to determine the correct order of gold actions.

We found that in this setting, we did need slightly more input features. As mentioned, node labels are necessary to distinguish whether a tree has been sufficiently promoted, and are helpful in any case. We used 8 labels: the current and immediate predecessor label of each of the top two stacks on the tree, as well as the label of the left- and rightmost adjoined child for each tree. We also found it helped to add positional features for the leftmost word in the span for each of those trees, bringing the total number of positional features to five. See Table 1 for details.

5 Experimental Results

We report both dependency and constituency parsing results on both English and Chinese.

All experiments were conducted with minimal hyperparameter tuning. The settings used for the reported results are summarized in Table 6. Networks parameters were updated using gradient backpropagation, including backpropagation through time for the recurrent components, using ADADELTA for learning rate scheduling (Zeiler, 2012). We also applied dropout (Hinton et al., 2012) (with $p = 0.5$) to the output of each LSTM layer (separately for each connection in the case of the two-layer network).

We tested both types of parser on the Penn Treebank (PTB) and Penn Chinese Treebank (CTB-5), with the standard splits for each of training, development, and test sets. Automatically predicted part of speech tags with 10-way jackknifing were used as inputs for all tasks except for Chinese dependency parsing, where we used gold tags, following the traditions in literature.

5.1 Dependency Parsing: English & Chinese

Table 2 shows results for English Penn Treebank using Stanford dependencies. Despite the minimally designed feature representation, relatively few training iterations, and lack of precomputed embeddings, the parser performed on par with state-of-the-art incremental dependency parsers, and slightly outperformed the state-of-the-art greedy parser.

The ablation experiments shown in the Table 3 indicate that both forward and backward contexts for each word are very important to obtain strong results. Using only word forms and no part-of-speech input similarly degraded performance.

Parser	Dev		Test	
	UAS	LAS	UAS	LAS
C & M 2014	92.0	89.7	91.8	89.6
Dyer et al. 2015	93.2	90.9	93.1	90.9
Weiss et al. 2015	-	-	93.19	91.18
+ Percept./Beam	-	-	93.99	92.05
Bi-LSTM	93.31	91.01	93.21	91.16
2-Layer Bi-LSTM	93.67	91.48	93.42	91.36

Table 2: Development and test set results for shift-reduce dependency parser on Penn Treebank using only (s_1, s_0, q_0) positional features.

Parser	UAS	LAS
Bi-LSTM Hierarchical[†]	93.31	91.01
† - Hierarchical Actions	92.94	90.96
† - Backward-LSTM	91.12	88.72
† - Forward-LSTM	91.85	88.39
† tag embeddings	92.46	89.81

Table 3: Ablation studies on PTB dev set (wsj 22). Forward and backward context, and part-of-speech input were all critical to strong performace.

Figure 6 compares our parser with that of Chen and Manning (2014) in terms of arc recall for various arc lengths. While the two parsers perform similarly on short arcs, ours significantly outpeforms theirs on longer arcs, and more interestingly our accuracy does not degrade much after length 6. This confirms the benefit of having a global sentence repesentation in our model.

Table 4 summarizes the Chinese dependency parsing results. Again, our work is competitive with the state-of-the-art greedy parsers.

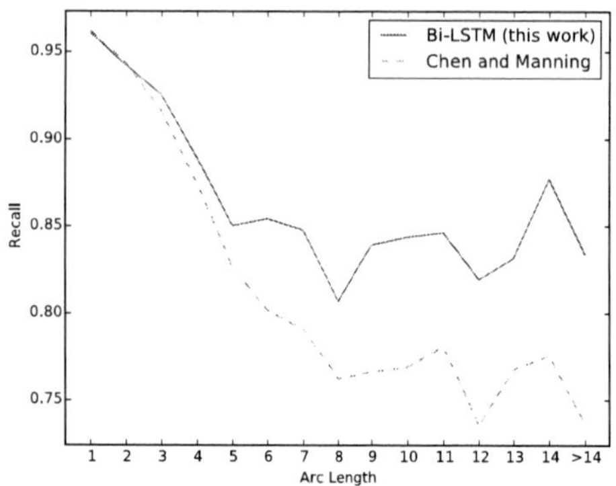

Figure 6: Recall on dependency arcs of various lengths in PTB dev set. The Bi-LSTM parser is particularly good at predicting longer arcs.

Parser	Dev		Test	
	UAS	LAS	UAS	LAS
C & M 2014	84.0	82.4	83.9	82.4
Dyer et al. 2015	87.2	85.9	87.2	85.7
Bi-LSTM	85.84	85.24	85.53	84.89
2-Layer Bi-LSTM	86.13	85.51	86.35	85.71

Table 4: Development and test set results for shift-reduce dependency parser on Penn Chinese Treebank (CTB-5) using only (s_1, s_0, q_0) position features (trained and tested with gold POS tags).

5.2 Constituency Parsing: English & Chinese

Table 5 compares our constituency parsing results with state-of-the-art incremental parsers. Although our work are definitely less accurate than those beam-search parsers, we achieve the highest accuracy among greedy parsers, for both English and Chinese.[1,2]

Parser	b	English		Chinese	
		greedy	beam	greedy	beam
Zhu et al. (2013)	16	86.08	90.4	75.99	85.6
Mi & Huang (05)	32	84.95	90.8	75.61	83.9
Vinyals et al. (05)	10	-	90.5	-	-
Bi-LSTM	-	89.75	-	79.44	-
2-Layer Bi-LSTM	-	**89.95**	-	**80.13**	-

Table 5: Test F-scores for constituency parsing on Penn Treebank and CTB-5.

---

[1] The greedy accuracies for Mi and Huang (2015) are from Haitao Mi, and greedy results for Zhu et al. (2013) come from duplicating experiments with code provided by those authors.

[2] The parser of Vinyals et al. (2015) does not use an explicit transition system, but is similar in spirit since generating a right bracket can be viewed as a reduce action.

	Dependency	Constituency
Embeddings		
Word (dims)	50	100
Tags (dims)	20	100
Nonterminals (dims)	-	100
Pretrained	No	No
Network details		
LSTM units (each direction)	200	200
ReLU hidden units	200 / decision	1000
Training		
Training epochs	10	10
Minibatch size (sentences)	10	10
Dropout (LSTM output only)	0.5	0.5
L2 penalty (all weights)	none	1×10^{-8}
ADADELTA ρ	0.99	0.99
ADADELTA ϵ	1×10^{-7}	1×10^{-7}

Table 6: Hyperparameters and training settings.

6 Related Work

Because recurrent networks are such a natural fit for modeling languages (given the sequential nature of the latter), bi-directional LSTM networks are becoming increasingly common in all sorts of linguistic tasks, for example event detection in Ghaeini et al. (2016). In fact, we discovered after submission that Kiperwasser and Goldberg (2016) have concurrently developed an extremely similar approach to our dependency parser. Instead of extending it to constituency parsing, they also apply the same idea to graph-based dependency parsing.

7 Conclusions

We have presented a simple bi-directional LSTM sentence representation model for minimal features in both incremental dependency and incremental constituency parsing, the latter using a novel shift-promote-adjoint algorithm. Experiments show that our method are competitive with the state-of-the-art greedy parsers on both parsing tasks and on both English and Chinese.

Acknowledgments

We thank the anonymous reviewers for comments. We also thank Taro Watanabe, Muhua Zhu, and Yue Zhang for sharing their code, Haitao Mi for producing greedy results from his parser, and Ashish Vaswani and Yoav Goldberg for discussions. The authors were supported in part by DARPA FA8750-13-2-0041 (DEFT), NSF IIS-1449278, and a Google Faculty Research Award.

References

Danqi Chen and Christopher D Manning. 2014. A fast and accurate dependency parser using neural networks. In *Empirical Methods in Natural Language Processing (EMNLP)*.

David Chiang. 2000. Statistical parsing with an automatically-extracted tree-adjoining grammar. In *Proc. of ACL*.

Chris Dyer, Miguel Ballesteros, Wang Ling, Austin Matthews, and Noah A Smith. 2015. Transition-based dependency parsing with stack long short-term memory. *arXiv preprint arXiv:1505.08075*.

Reza Ghaeini, Xiaoli Z. Fern, Liang Huang, and Prasad Tadepalli. 2016. Event nugget detection with forward-backward recurrent neural networks. In *Proc. of ACL*.

James Henderson. 2003. Inducing history representations for broad coverage statistical parsing. In *Proceedings of NAACL*.

Geoffrey E. Hinton, Nitish Srivastava, Alex Krizhevsky, Ilya Sutskever, and Ruslan Salakhutdinov. 2012. Improving neural networks by preventing co-adaptation of feature detectors. *CoRR*, abs/1207.0580.

Sepp Hochreiter and Jürgen Schmidhuber. 1997. Long short-term memory. *Neural computation*, 9(8):1735–1780.

Eliyahu Kiperwasser and Yoav Goldberg. 2016. Simple and accurate dependency parsing using bidirectional LSTM feature representations. *CoRR*, abs/1603.04351.

Haitao Mi and Liang Huang. 2015. Shift-reduce constituency parsing with dynamic programming and pos tag lattice. In *Proceedings of the 2015 Conference of the North American Chapter of the Association for Computational Linguistics: Human Language Technologies*.

Joakim Nivre, Johan Hall, and Jens Nilsson. 2006. Maltparser: A data-driven parser-generator for dependency parsing. In *Proc. of LREC*.

Joakim Nivre. 2008. Algorithms for deterministic in cremental dependency parsing. *Computational Linguistics*, 34(4):513–553.

Oriol Vinyals, Łukasz Kaiser, Terry Koo, Slav Petrov, Ilya Sutskever, and Geoffrey Hinton. 2015. Grammar as a foreign language. In *Advances in Neural Information Processing Systems*, pages 2755–2763.

Zhiguo Wang and Nianwen Xue. 2014. Joint pos tagging and transition-based constituent parsing in chinese with non-local features. In *Proceedings of ACL*.

David Weiss, Chris Alberti, Michael Collins, and Slav Petrov. 2015. Structured training for neural network transition-based parsing. In *Proceedings of ACL*.

Matthew D. Zeiler. 2012. ADADELTA: an adaptive learning rate method. *CoRR*, abs/1212.5701.

Yue Zhang and Joakim Nivre. 2011. Transition-based dependency parsing with rich non-local features. In *Proceedings of ACL*, pages 188–193.

Muhua Zhu, Yue Zhang, Wenliang Chen, Min Zhang, and Jingbo Zhu. 2013. Fast and accurate shift-reduce constituent parsing. In *Proceedings of ACL 2013*.

Improving Statistical Machine Translation Performance
by Oracle-BLEU Model Re-estimation

Praveen Dakwale
Informatics Institute
University of Amsterdam
`p.dakwale@uva.nl`

Christof Monz
Informatics Institute
University of Amsterdam
`c.monz@uva.nl`

Abstract

We present a novel technique for training translation models for statistical machine translation by aligning source sentences to their oracle-BLEU translations. In contrast to previous approaches which are constrained to phrase training, our method also allows the re-estimation of re-ordering models along with the translation model. Experiments show an improvement of up to 0.8 BLEU for our approach over a competitive Arabic-English baseline trained directly on the word-aligned bitext using heuristic extraction. As an additional benefit, the phrase table size is reduced dramatically to only 3% of the original size.

1 Introduction

In phrase-based SMT, the phrase pairs in the translation model are traditionally trained by applying a heuristic extraction method (Och and Ney, 2000) which extracts phrase pairs based on consistency of word alignments from a word-aligned bilingual training data. The probabilities of the translation model are then calculated based on the relative frequencies of the extracted phrase pairs.

A notable shortcoming of this approach is that the translation model probabilities thus calculated from the training bitext can be unintuitive and unreliable (Marcu and Wong, 2002; Foster et al., 2006) as they reflect only the distribution over the phrase pairs observed in the training data.

However, from an SMT perspective it is important that the models reflect probability distributions which are preferred by the decoding process, i.e., phrase translations which are likely to be used frequently to achieve better translations should get higher scores and phrases which are less likely to be used should get low scores. In addition, the heuristic extraction algorithm generates all possible, consistent phrases including overlapping phrases. This means that translation probabilities are distributed over a very large number of phrase translation candidates most of which never lead to the best possible translation of a sentence.

In this paper, we propose a novel solution which is to re-estimate the models from the best BLEU translation of each source sentence in the bitext. An important contribution of our approach is that unlike previous approaches such as forced alignment (Wuebker et al., 2010), reordering and language models can also be re-estimated.

2 Related Work

The forced alignment technique of Wuebker et al. (2010) forms the main motivation for our work. In forced alignment, given a sentence pair (F, E), a decoder determines the best phrase segmentation and alignment which will result in a translation of F into E. The best segmentation is defined as the one which maximizes the probability of translating the source sentence into the given target sentence. At the end, the phrase table is re-estimated using the phrase pair segmentations obtained from forced decoding. Thus forced alignment is a re-estimation technique where translation probabilities are calculated based on their frequency in best-scoring hypotheses instead of the frequencies of all possible phrase pairs in the bitext. However, one limitation of forced alignment is that only the phrase translation model can be re-estimated since it is restricted to align the source sentence to the given target reference, thus fixing the choice of re-ordering decisions.

A similar line of work is proposed by Lambert et al. (2011) and Schwenk et al. (2011) who use a self-enhancing strategy to utilize additional mono-

Proceedings of the 54th Annual Meeting of the Association for Computational Linguistics, pages 38–44,
Berlin, Germany, August 7-12, 2016. ©2016 Association for Computational Linguistics

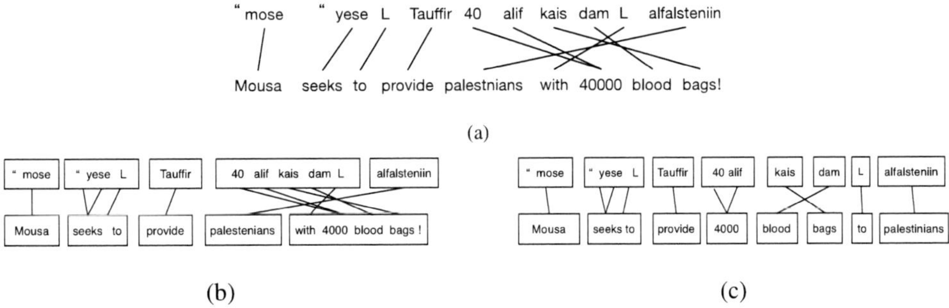

(a)

(b)   (c)

Figure 1: (a) : Word alignment from EM training for Arabic (transliterated) -English sentence pair. (b): Phrase segmentations and alignments from forced decoding. (c): Phrase segmentations and alignments from oracle BLEU re-estimation. Blocks represent phrase boundaries.

lingual source language data by aligning it to its target language translation obtained by using an SMT system to rank sentence translation probabilities. However, the main focus of their work is translation model adaptation by augmenting the bitext with additional training data and not the re-estimation of the translation models trained on the parallel data.

In this work, we propose that aligning source sentences to their oracle BLEU translations provides a more realistic estimate of the models from the decoding perspective instead of aligning them to high quality human translations as in forced decoding.

Another relevant line of research relates tuning (weight optimisation), where our work lies between forced decoding (Wuebker et al., 2010) and the bold updating approach of (Liang et al., 2006). However, our approach specifically proposes a novel method for training models using oracle BLEU translations.

3 Model Re-estimation

The idea of our approach is to re-estimate the models with n-best oracle-BLEU translations and sentence alignments resulting from decoding the source sentence. Given a source and its reference translation, the oracle-BLEU translation is defined as the translation output with highest BLEU score. Oracle BLEU translations have been previously used for different analytical purposes in SMT (Srivastava et al., 2011; Dreyer et al., 2007; Wisniewski et al., 2010).

Figure 1 shows example of word alignment obtained from EM training, segmentations and alignment obtained from forced decoding and oracle-BLEU re-estimation.

3.1 Oracle BLEU

Ideally, one would like to re-estimate translation models directly from the n-best BLEU translations. However there are two problems in calculating BLEU for individual sentence: First, as discussed in (Chiang et al., 2008), BLEU is not designed to be used for sentences in isolation where it can exhibit rather volatile behavior. Hence, following their work and (Watanabe et al., 2007), we calculate BLEU for a sentence in the context of a exponentially-weighted moving average of previous translations. We briefly discuss the computation from (Chiang et al., 2008) as follows: Given a source sentence $\mathbf{f}$, and its reference translation $\mathbf{r}$, for an n-best translation e^*, let c(e) be defined as the vector of target length $|e|$, source length $|f|$, reference length $|r|$, and the number of n-gram matches between $\mathbf{e}$ and $\mathbf{r}$, then two pseudo document parameters $\mathbf{O}$ and $\mathbf{O}_f$ are defined as:

$$\mathbf{O} \leftarrow 0.9 \cdot (\mathbf{O} + c(e^*)), \mathbf{O}_f \leftarrow 0.9 \cdot (\mathbf{O}_f + |f|) \quad (1)$$

$\mathbf{O}$ is an exponentially-weighted moving average of the vectors from previous sentences and $\mathbf{O}_f$ is the correction of source length with respect to the previous sentences. Then the BLEU score for a sentence pairs (f,r) and translation e^* is defined as:

$$\mathbf{B}(e; f, r) = (\mathbf{O}_f + |f|) \cdot BLEU(O + c(e^*; r)) \quad (2)$$

The second problem as discussed in Chiang et al. (2008) is that due to noise in the training data, a high-BLEU translation may contain certain rules which are unlikely to be used by the model. Hence following them, we use a weighted combination of BLEU and model score to select the n-best list:

$$e^* = argmax_e(B(e) - \mu \cdot (B(e) - h(e).w)) \quad (3)$$

where B(e) and h(e) are the BLEU and model scores of the candidate translation and w is the optimised weights for the models, μ controls the preference between BLEU and model scores to determine oracle translations. We set μ=0.5 to balance between BLEU scores almost as high as the max-BLEU translations, while staying close to translations preferred by the model. We also conducted a set of experiments with μ=0 (pure or absolute BLEU) in order to verify the necessity for the optimal combination. The lower scores for this setting as compared to the baseline verified that using only the best BLEU translation indeed degrades the performance of the re-estimated models. This finding for the optimal value of μ has also been established in (Chiang et al., 2008) through a series of experiments.

3.2 Training

For obtaining the oracle-BLEU translations, we first train the translation models from the bitext using the standard pipeline of word alignment and heuristic extraction. Along with the phrase translation and language models, we also train a bilingual language model (BiLM) (Niehues et al., 2011; Garmash and Monz, 2014), as well as lexicalized (Tillman, 2004) and hierarchical re-ordering models (Galley and Manning, 2008). We use a BiLM specifically as an instance of a re-ordering model in order to determine the effect of re-estimating re-ordering decisions from oracle-BLEU translations.

We use the decoder trained on these models to translate the training bitext. Along with the 1-best translation (based on model scores), we also store search graphs or lattices generated during the translations process. Using the target sentences, we convert the translation lattice to an isomorphic oracle-BLEU lattice which has the same set of nodes but the edges represent BLEU score differences corresponding to each transition. Finally, we extract n-best candidate translations from the graphs ranked on BLEU score as defined in Equation (3). Using the word alignments from the initial phrase table, we extract the alignments between each source sentence and each of their n-best oracle-BLEU translations. Finally, we

re-train the phrase translations, re-ordering and BiLM on these translations and alignments.

3.3 Avoiding over-fitting

Re-estimation of the translation models from the n-best translation of the bitext could re-enforce the probabilities of the low frequency phrase pairs in the re-estimated models leading to over-fitting. Within forced decoding, Wuebker et al. (2010) address this problem by using a leave-one-out approach where they modify the phrase translation probabilities for each sentence pair by removing the counts of all phrases that were extracted from that particular sentence. However, in our approach, we do not impose a constraint to produce the exact translation, instead we use the highest BLEU translations which may be very different from the references. Thus it is not strictly necessary to apply leave-one-out in our approach as a solution to over-fitting. Instead, we handle the problem by simply removing all the phrase pairs below a threshold count which in our case is 2,

$$\phi_{init} = \phi_{baseline} - \phi_{C(e,f)<2} \quad (4)$$

therefore removing phrase pairs with high probability but low frequency.

4 Experimental set up

Our experiments are carried out for an Arabic-English parallel corpus of approximately 1 million sentence pairs. We establish a baseline system by training models on this bitext and then compare this to a forced decoding implementation and to oracle-BLEU re-estimation using the same bitext.

4.1 Baseline and forced decoding

The initial training corpus we use is a collection of parallel sentences taken from OpenMT data sources released by the LDC.

Phrase table, distortion models and the lexical BiLM are trained with initial alignments obtained using GIZA++ (Och and Ney, 2003). The English 5-gram target language model is trained with Kneser-Ney smoothing on news data of nearly 1.6B tokens. We use an in-house phrase-based SMT system similar to Moses. For all settings in this paper, weights were optimized on NIST's MT04 data set using pairwise ranked optimization (Hopkins and May, 2011).

For forced alignment we use the existing implementation within the Moses SMT toolkit (Koehn

Baseline	50.1		
	n=1	n=10	n=100
PT_{re}	50.1(0.0)	50.1(0.0)	50.0(-0.1)
PT_{in}	50.7▲(+0.6)	50.5▲(+0.4)	50.0(-0.1)
$BiLM_{re}$ + PT_{in}	50.9▲(+0.8)	50.5▲(+0.4)	49.6(-0.5)

Table 1: Performance of our oracle-BLEU re-estimation with varying size n of n-best lists for the MT09 test set. ▲/▼ indicates a statistically significant gain/drop at p < 0.01 and △/▽ at p < 0.05. Values in brackets show gains over the baseline.

et al., 2007) trained on the baseline phrase translation model. In order to increase the chances of producing the exact reference, we follow Foster and Kuhn (2012) and relax the standard decoding parameters as follows: distortion limit=∞, stack size=2000, beam width=10e-30, and no threshold pruning of the translation model.

4.2 Oracle BLEU re-estimation

To obtain oracle-BLEU translations, we first train an initial SMT system and use it to decode the bitext. This system is identical to the baseline system except for the removal of low-frequency phrase pairs from the baseline phrase table as described in Section 3.3. To obtain the n-best oracle-BLUE translations, we experiment with different values of n, where $n \in \{1, 10, 100\}$. From these oracle-BLEU translations and alignments all phrases that were used in the derivation of these n-best sentences are extracted and the models are re-estimated by re-calculating the translation probabilities. Hierarchical and lexicalized re-ordering models as well as the BiLM are re-trained using the source sentences, oracle-BLEU translations and word alignments. For testing the performance of the re-estimated models, we tune different systems while replacing the baseline models with the corresponding re-estimated models. We also experiment with the interpolation of re-estimated models with the respective baseline models. We evaluate against 4 test sets: MT05, MT06, MT08, and MT09. Case-insensitive 4-gram BLEU (Papineni et al., 2002) is used as evaluation metric. Approximate randomization (Noreen., 1989; Riezler and Maxwell, 2005) is used to detect statistically significant differences.

5 Results

We discuss the experimental results of our oracle-BLEU re-estimation approach for different mod-

els and settings and provide a comparison with the baseline (heuristic training) and forced alignment.

Re-estimated models with three different values of $n \in \{1, 10, 100\}$ were evaluated under three settings: phrase table re-estimation, interpolation, and BiLM re-estimation. The best improvements over the baseline are obtained by using only 1-best (n= 1) alignments as shown in Table 1. Surprisingly, this is in contrast with forced decoding as discussed in Wuebker et al. (2010), where the best improvements are obtained for $n = 100$.

Table 2 provides a comparison between BLEU improvements achieved by forced decoding ($n = 100$ best) and our oracle-BLEU re-estimation approach ($n = 1$ best) over the baseline for different models. One can see in Table 2 that while phrase table re-estimation drops substantially for forced decoding for all test sets (up to -1.4 for MT09), oracle-BLEU phrase table re-estimation shows either slight improvements or negligible drops compared to the baseline. For the linear interpolation of the re-estimated phrase table with the baseline, forced decoding shows only a slight improvement for MT06, MT08 and MT09 and still suffers from a substantial drop for MT05. On the other hand, oracle-BLEU re-estimation shows consistent improvements for all test sets with a maximum gain of up to +0.7 for MT06. It is important to note here that although linear interpolation extinguishes the advantage of a smaller phrase table size obtained by re-estimation, the improvement achieved by interpolation for oracle-BLEU re-estimation are significantly higher as compared to forced decoding.

An important novelty of oracle-BLEU re-estimation is that it also allows for re-training of other models alongside the phrase table. Here we provide the results for the re-estimation of a BiLM. For all test sets, BiLM re-estimation provides additional improvements over simple phrase table interpolation, demonstrating that re-estimation of re-ordering models can further improve translation performance. The last row of Table 2 shows that the re-estimated BiLM on its own adds BLEU improvement of up to +0.5 (for MT09). The highest BLEU improvement of +0.8 is achieved by using a re-estimated BiLM and an interpolated phrase table. Note that re-estimation of BiLM or re-ordering models is not possible for forced decoding due to the constraint of having to match the exact reference. For an additional anal-

	MT05		MT06		MT08		MT09	
Baseline	58.5		47.9		47.3		50.1	
	FD	OB	FD	OB	FD	OB	FD	OB
PT_{re}	57.4▼(-1.1)	58.7△(+0.2)	46.3(-0.7)	47.8▼(-0.1)	46.1▼(-1.2)	47.4△(+0.1)	48.7▼(-1.4)	50.1(0.0)
PT_{in}	58.2▽(-0.3)	58.8▲(+0.3)	48.0(+0.1)	**48.6▲(+0.7)**	47.5(+0.2)	47.7▲(+0.4)	50.4△(+0.3)	50.7▲(+0.6)
PT_{in}+ $BiLM_{re}$	-	**59.2▲(+0.7)**	-	48.5▲(+0.6)	-	**47.7▲(+0.4)**	-	**50.9▲(+0.8)**
PT_{base} + $BiLM_{re}$	-	58.6(+0.1)	-	48.2(+0.3)	-	47.2▼(-0.1)	-	50.6(+0.5)

Table 2: BLEU scores for Forced decoding and Oracle BLEU re-estimation. $PT_{re/in}$ = Phrase table re-estimation/interpolation/baseline, PT_{base} = Baseline Phrase table, $BiLM_{re}$ = BiLM re-estimation, FD=Forced decoding, OB=oracle-BLEU.

	TEST	
Baseline	51.0	
	FD_{LO}	OB
PT_{re}	50.7▽(-0.3)	51.0 (0.0)
PT_{in}	51.5▲(+0.5)	51.5▲(+0.5)
PT_{in} + $BiLM_{re}$	-	**51.6▲(+0.6)**

Table 3: BLEU scores for Oracle-Bleu and Forced decoding with leave-one-out against concatenation of MT03, MT05-MT09.

	(% of baseline)
OB_{100}	5.07
OB_{10}	4.16
OB_{1}	**3.28**
FD	27.71
FD_{LO}	7.6

Table 4: Phrase table sizes compared to baseline for Oracle-BLUE re-estimation and Forced decoding for different n-best list sizes, FD_{LO} = Forced decoding with leave-one-out.

ysis, we experimented with the interpolation of both the re-estimated phrase table (forced decoding and oracle-BLEU) with the baseline. However, improvements achieved with this interpolation did not surpass the best result obtained for the oracle-BLEU re-estimation.

Additionally, we also compare oracle-BLEU re-estimation to forced decoding with leave-one-out (Wuebker et al., 2010) by evaluating both on a concatenation of 5 test sets (MT03, MT05-MT09). As shown in Table 3, even with leave-one-out, forced decoding performance drops below the baseline by -0.3 BLEU. In contrast, phrase tables re-estimated from oracle-BLEU translation achieves the same performance as the baseline. When interpolated with the baseline phrase table, both approaches show significant improvements over the baseline. This implies that only in combination with the original phrase table does forced-decoding with leave-one-out outperform the baseline. On the other hand, oracle-BLEU re-estimation by its own not only performs better than forced decoding, but also gives a performance equal to forced decoding with leave-one-out when interpolated with baseline phrase table. In addition to the BLEU improvements, our approach also results in a re-estimated phrase table with a significantly reduced size as compared to the baseline. As shown in Table 4, out of all the settings, the minimum phrase table size after oracle-BLEU re-estimation is only 3.28% of baseline (i.e., a reduction of 96.72%) while it is 7.6% for forced decoding.

6 Conclusions

In this paper, we proposed a novel technique for improving the reliability of SMT models by model re-estimation from oracle-BLEU translations of the source sentences in the bitext. Our experimental results show BLEU score improvements of up to +0.8 points for oracle-BLEU re-estimation over a strong baseline along with a substantially reduced size of the re-estimated phrase table (3.3% of the baseline). An important novelty of our approach is that it also allows for the re-estimation of re-ordering models which can yield further improvements in SMT performance as demonstrated by the re-estimation of a BiLM.

Acknowledgments

This research was funded in part by the Netherlands Organization for Scientific Research (NWO) under project numbers 639.022.213 and 612.001.218. We thank Arianna Bisazza and the anonymous reviewers for their comments.

References

David Chiang, Yuval Marton, and Philip Resnik. 2008. Online large-margin training of syntactic and structural translation features. In *Proceedings of the Conference on Empirical Methods in Natural Language Processing*. Association for Computational Linguistics.

Markus Dreyer, Keith Hall, and Sanjeev Khudanpur. 2007. Comparing reordering constraints for smt using efficient BLEU oracle computation. In *Proceedings of 2007 Workshop on Syntax and Structure in Statistical Trans- lation*.

George Foster and Roland Kuhn. 2012. Forced decoding for phrase extraction. Technical report, University of Montreal.

George Foster, Roland Kuhn, and Howard Johnson. 2006. Phrasetable smoothing for statistical machine translation. In *Proceedings of the 2006 Conference on Empirical Methods in Natural Language Processing*. Association for Computational Linguistics.

Michel Galley and Christopher D. Manning. 2008. A simple and effective hierarchical phrase reordering model. In *Proceedings of the Conference on Empirical Methods in Natural Language Processing*. Association for Computational Linguistics.

Ekaterina Garmash and Christof Monz. 2014. Dependency-based bilingual language models for reordering in statistical machine translation. In *Proceedings of the 2014 Conference on Empirical Methods in Natural Language Processing (EMNLP)*, pages 1689–1700.

Mark Hopkins and Jonathan May. 2011. Tuning as ranking. In *Proceedings of the 2011 Conference on Empirical Methods in Natural Language Processing*. Association for Computational Linguistics.

Philipp Koehn, Hieu Hoang, Alexandra Birch, Chris Callison-Burch, Marcello Federico, Nicola Bertoldi, Brooke Cowan, Wade Shen, Christine Moran, Richard Zens, Chris Dyer, Ondřej Bojar, Alexandra Constantin, and Evan Herbst. 2007. Moses: Open source toolkit for statistical machine translation. In *Proceedings of the 45th Annual Meeting of the ACL on Interactive Poster and Demonstration Sessions*. Association for Computational Linguistics.

Patrik Lambert, Holger Schwenk, Christophe Servan, and Sadaf Abdul-Rauf. 2011. Investigations on translation model adaptation using monolingual data. In *Proceedings of the Sixth Workshop on Statistical Machine Translation*. Association for Computational Linguistics.

Percy Liang, Alexandre Bouchard-Côté, Dan Klein, and Ben Taskar. 2006. An end-to-end discriminative approach to machine translation. In *Proceedings of the 21st International Conference on Computational Linguistics and 44th Annual Meeting of the Association for Computational Linguistics*. Association for Computational Linguistics, July.

Daniel Marcu and William Wong. 2002. A phrase-based, joint probability model for statistical machine translation. In *Proceedings of the ACL-02 Conference on Empirical Methods in Natural Language Processing*. Association for Computational Linguistics.

Jan Niehues, Teresa Herrmann, Stephan Vogel, and Alex Waibel. 2011. Wider context by using bilingual language models in machine translation. In *Proceedings of the Sixth Workshop on Statistical Machine Translation*. Association for Computational Linguistics.

Eric W. Noreen. 1989. *Computer Intensive Methods for Testing Hypotheses. An Introduction*. Wiley-Interscience.

Franz Josef Och and Hermann Ney. 2000. Improved statistical alignment models. In *Proceedings of the 38th Annual Meeting on Association for Computational Linguistics*. Association for Computational Linguistics.

Franz Josef Och and Hermann Ney. 2003. A systematic comparison of various statistical alignment models. *Computational Linguistics*, 29.

Kishore Papineni, Salim Roukos, Todd Ward, and Wei-Jing Zhu. 2002. Bleu: a method for automatic evaluation of machine translation. In *Proceedings of 40th Annual Meeting of the Association for Computational Linguistics*. Association for Computational Linguistics.

Stefan Riezler and John T. Maxwell. 2005. On some pitfalls in automatic evaluation and significance testing for MT. In *Proceedings of the ACL Workshop on Intrinsic and Extrinsic Evaluation Measures for Machine Translation and/or Summarization*.

Holger Schwenk, Patrik Lambert, Loïc Barrault, Christophe Servan, Haithem Afli, Sadaf Abdul-Rauf, and Kashif Shah. 2011. LIUM's SMT machine translation systems for WMT 2011. In *Proceedings of the Sixth Workshop on Statistical Machine Translation*. Association for Computational Linguistics.

Ankit K. Srivastava, Yanjun Ma, and Andy Way. 2011. Oracle-based training for phrase-based statistical machine translation. In *Proceedings of the 15th annual meeting of the European Association for Machine Translation*.

Christoph Tillman. 2004. A unigram orientation model for statistical machine translation. In *Proceedings of HLT-NAACL*. Association for Computational Linguistics.

Taro Watanabe, Jun Suzuki, Hajime Tsukada, and Hideki Isozaki. 2007. Online large-margin training for statistical machine translation. In *Proceedings of the 2007 Joint Conference on Empirical Methods in Natural Language Processing and Computational

Natural Language Learning (EMNLP-CoNLL). Association for Computational Linguistics.

Guillaume Wisniewski, Alexandre Allauzen, and François Yvon. 2010. Assessing phrase-based translation models with oracle decoding. In *Proceedings of the 2010 Conference on Empirical Methods in Natural Language Processing*. Association for Computational Linguistics.

Joern Wuebker, Arne Mauser, and Hermann Ney. 2010. Training phrase translation models with leaving-one-out. In *Proceedings of the Annual Meeting of the Association for Computational Linguistics*. Association for Computational Linguistics, July.

Sequence-to-Sequence Generation for Spoken Dialogue via Deep Syntax Trees and Strings

Ondřej Dušek and **Filip Jurčíček**
Charles University in Prague, Faculty of Mathematics and Physics
Institute of Formal and Applied Linguistics
Malostranské náměstí 25, CZ-11800 Prague, Czech Republic
{odusek,jurcicek}@ufal.mff.cuni.cz

Abstract

We present a natural language generator based on the sequence-to-sequence approach that can be trained to produce natural language strings as well as deep syntax dependency trees from input dialogue acts, and we use it to directly compare two-step generation with separate sentence planning and surface realization stages to a joint, one-step approach.

We were able to train both setups successfully using very little training data. The joint setup offers better performance, surpassing state-of-the-art with regards to n-gram-based scores while providing more relevant outputs.

1 Introduction

In spoken dialogue systems (SDS), the task of natural language generation (NLG) is to convert a meaning representation (MR) produced by the dialogue manager into one or more sentences in a natural language. It is traditionally divided into two subtasks: *sentence planning*, which decides on the overall sentence structure, and *surface realization*, determining the exact word forms and linearizing the structure into a string (Reiter and Dale, 2000). While some generators keep this division and use a two-step pipeline (Walker et al., 2001; Rieser et al., 2010; Dethlefs et al., 2013), others apply a joint model for both tasks (Wong and Mooney, 2007; Konstas and Lapata, 2013).

We present a new, conceptually simple NLG system for SDS that is able to operate in both modes: it either produces natural language strings or generates deep syntax dependency trees, which are subsequently processed by an external surface realizer (Dušek et al., 2015). This allows us to show a direct comparison of two-step generation, where sentence planning and surface realization are separated, with a joint, one-step approach.

Our generator is based on the sequence-to-sequence (seq2seq) generation technique (Cho et al., 2014; Sutskever et al., 2014), combined with beam search and an n-best list reranker to suppress irrelevant information in the outputs. Unlike most previous NLG systems for SDS (e.g., (Stent et al., 2004; Raux et al., 2005; Mairesse et al., 2010)), it is trainable from unaligned pairs of MR and sentences alone. We experiment with using much less training data than recent systems based on recurrent neural networks (RNN) (Wen et al., 2015b; Mei et al., 2015), and we find that our generator learns successfully to produce both strings and deep syntax trees on the BAGEL restaurant information dataset (Mairesse et al., 2010). It is able to surpass n-gram-based scores achieved previously by Dušek and Jurčíček (2015), offering a simpler setup and more relevant outputs.

We introduce the generation setting in Section 2 and describe our generator architecture in Section 3. Section 4 details our experiments, Section 5 analyzes the results. We summarize related work in Section 6 and offer conclusions in Section 7.

2 Generator Setting

The input to our generator are *dialogue acts* (DA) (Young et al., 2010) representing an action, such as *inform* or *request*, along with one or more attributes (*slots*) and their values. Our generator operates in two modes, producing either deep syntax trees (Dušek et al., 2012) or natural language strings (see Fig. 1). The first mode corresponds to the sentence planning NLG stage as it decides the syntactic shape of the output sentence; the resulting deep syntax tree involves content words (lemmas) and their syntactic form (formemes, purple in Fig. 1). The trees are linearized to strings using a

Proceedings of the 54th Annual Meeting of the Association for Computational Linguistics, pages 45–51,
Berlin, Germany, August 7-12, 2016. ©2016 Association for Computational Linguistics

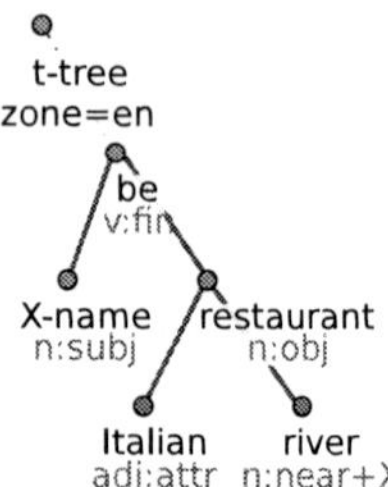

Figure 1: Example DA (top) with the corresponding deep syntax tree (middle) and natural language string (bottom)

surface realizer from the TectoMT translation system (Dušek et al., 2015). The second generator mode joins sentence planning and surface realization into one step, producing natural language sentences directly.

Both modes offer their advantages: The two-step mode simplifies generation by abstracting away from complex surface syntax and morphology, which can be handled by a handcrafted, domain-independent module to ensure grammatical correctness at all times (Dušek and Jurčíček, 2015), and the joint mode does not need to model structure explicitly and avoids accumulating errors along the pipeline (Konstas and Lapata, 2013).

3 The Seq2seq Generation Model

Our generator is based on the seq2seq approach (Cho et al., 2014; Sutskever et al., 2014), a type of an encoder-decoder RNN architecture operating on variable-length sequences of tokens. We address the necessary conversion of input DA and output trees/sentences into sequences in Section 3.1 and then describe the main seq2seq component in Section 3.2. It is supplemented by a reranker, as explained in Section 3.3.

3.1 Sequence Representation of DA, Trees, and Sentences

We represent DA, deep syntax trees, and sentences as sequences of tokens to enable their usage in the sequence-based RNN components of our generator (see Sections 3.2 and 3.3). Each token is represented by its embedding – a vector of floating-point numbers (Bengio et al., 2003).

To form a sequence representation of a DA, we create a triple of the structure "DA type, slot, value" for each slot in the DA and concatenate

the triples (see Fig. 3). The deep syntax tree output from the seq2seq generator is represented in a bracketed notation similar to the one used by Vinyals et al. (2015, see Fig. 2). The inputs to the reranker are always a sequence of tokens; structure is disregarded in trees, resulting in a list of lemma-formeme pairs (see Fig. 2).

3.2 Seq2seq Generator

Our seq2seq generator with attention (Bahdanau et al., 2015, see Fig. 3)[1] starts with the encoder stage, which uses an RNN to encode an input sequence $\mathbf{x} = \{x_1, \ldots, x_n\}$ into a sequence of encoder outputs and hidden states $\mathbf{h} = \{h_1, \ldots, h_n\}$, where $h_t = \mathrm{lstm}(x_t, h_{t-1})$, a non-linear function represented by the long-short-term memory (LSTM) cell (Graves, 2013).

The decoder stage then uses the hidden states to generate a sequence $\mathbf{y} = \{y_1, \ldots, y_m\}$ with a second LSTM-based RNN. The probability of each output token is defined as:

$$p(y_t|y_1, \ldots, y_{t-1}, \mathbf{x}) = \mathrm{softmax}((s_t \circ c_t)W_Y)$$

Here, s_t is the decoder state where $s_0 = h_n$ and $s_t = \mathrm{lstm}((y_{t-1} \circ c_t)W_S, s_{t-1})$, i.e., the decoder is initialized by the last hidden state and uses the previous output token at each step. W_Y and W_S are learned linear projection matrices and "$\circ$" denotes concatenation. c_t is the *context vector* – a weighted sum of the encoder hidden states $c_t = \sum_{i=1}^{n} \alpha_{ti} h_i$, where α_{ti} corresponds to an *alignment model*, represented by a feed-forward network with a single tanh hidden layer.

On top of this basic seq2seq model, we implemented a simple beam search for decoding (Sutskever et al., 2014; Bahdanau et al., 2015). It proceeds left-to-right and keeps track of log probabilities of top n possible output sequences, expanding them one token at a time.

3.3 Reranker

To ensure that the output trees/strings correspond semantically to the input DA, we implemented a classifier to rerank the n-best beam search outputs and penalize those missing required information and/or adding irrelevant one. Similarly to Wen et al. (2015a), the classifier provides a binary decision for an output tree/string on the presence of all dialogue act types and slot-value combinations seen in the training data, producing a 1-hot vector.

---

[1] We use the implementation in the TensorFlow framework (Abadi et al., 2015).

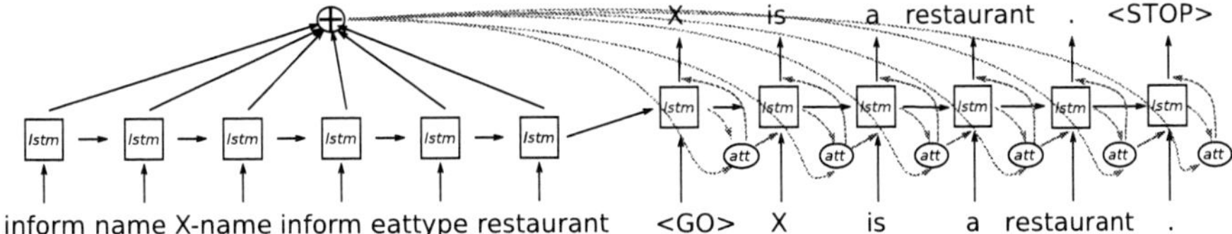

Figure 2: Trees encoded as sequences for the seq2seq generator (top) and the reranker (bottom)

Figure 3: Seq2seq generator with attention

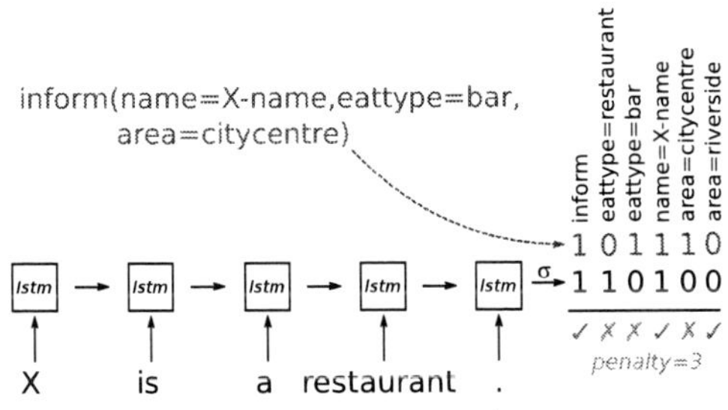

Figure 4: The reranker

The input DA is converted to a similar 1-hot vector and the reranking penalty of the sentence is the Hamming distance between the two vectors (see Fig. 4). Weighted penalties for all sentences are subtracted from their n-best list log probabilities.

We employ a similar architecture for the classifier as in our seq2seq generator encoder (see Section 3.2), with an RNN encoder operating on the output trees/strings and a single logistic layer for classification over the last encoder hidden state. Given an output sequence representing a string or a tree $\mathbf{y} = \{y_1, \ldots, y_n\}$ (cf. Section 3.1), the encoder again produces a sequence of hidden states $\mathbf{h} = \{h_1, \ldots, h_n\}$ where $h_t = \mathrm{lstm}(y_t, h_{t-1})$. The output binary vector o is computed as:

$$o_i = \mathrm{sigmoid}((h_n \cdot W_R + h)_i)$$

Here, W_R is a learned projection matrix and b is a corresponding bias term.

4 Experiments

We perform our experiments on the BAGEL data set of Mairesse et al. (2010), which contains 202 DA from the restaurant information domain with two natural language paraphrases each, describing restaurant locations, price ranges, food types etc. Some properties such as restaurant names or phone numbers are delexicalized (replaced with "X" symbols) to avoid data sparsity.[2] Unlike Mairesse et al. (2010), we do not use

manually annotated alignment of slots and values in the input DA to target words and phrases and let the generator learn it from data, which simplifies training data preparation but makes our task harder. We lowercase the data and treat plural -s as separate tokens for generating into strings, and we apply automatic analysis from the Treex NLP toolkit (Popel and Žabokrtský, 2010) to obtain deep syntax trees for training tree-based generator setups.[3] Same as Mairesse et al. (2010), we apply 10-fold cross-validation, with 181 training DA and 21 testing DA. In addition, we reserve 10 DA from the training set for validation.[4]

To train our seq2seq generator, we use the Adam optimizer (Kingma and Ba, 2015) to minimize unweighted sequence cross-entropy.[5] We perform 10 runs with different random initialization of the network and up to 1,000 passes over the training data,[6] validating after each pass and selecting the parameters that yield the highest BLEU score on the validation set. Neither beam search nor the reranker are used for validation.

We use the Adam optimizer minimizing cross-entropy to train the reranker as well.[7] We perform a single run of up to 100 passes over the data, and we also validate after each pass and select the parameters giving minimal Hamming distance on both validation and training set.[8]

---

[2] We adopt the delexicalization scenario used by Mairesse et al. (2010) and Dušek and Jurčíček (2015).

[3] The input vocabulary size is around 45 (DA types, slots, and values added up) and output vocabulary sizes are around 170 for string generation and 180 for tree generation (45 formemes and 135 lemmas).

[4] We treat the two paraphrases for the same DA as separate instances in the training set but use them together as two references to measure BLEU and NIST scores (Papineni et al., 2002; Doddington, 2002) on the validation and test sets.

[5] Based on a few preliminary experiments, the learning rate is set to 0.001, embedding size 50, LSTM cell size 128, and batch size 20. Reranking penalty for decoding is 100.

[6] Training is terminated early if the top 10 so far achieved validation BLEU scores do not change for 100 passes.

[7] We use the same settings as with the seq2seq generator.

[8] The validation set is given 10 times more importance.

Setup	BLEU	NIST	ERR
Mairesse et al. (2010)*	~67	-	0
Dušek and Jurčíček (2015)	59.89	5.231	30
Greedy with trees	55.29	5.144	20
+ Beam search (b. size 100)	58.59	5.293	28
+ Reranker (beam size 5)	60.77	5.487	24
(beam size 10)	60.93	5.510	25
(beam size 100)	60.44	5.514	19
Greedy into strings	52.54	5.052	37
+ Beam search (b. size 100)	55.84	5.228	32
+ Reranker (beam size 5)	61.18	5.507	27
(beam size 10)	62.40	5.614	21
(beam size 100)	62.76	5.669	19

Table 1: Results on the BAGEL data set

NIST, BLEU, and semantic errors in a sample of the output. *Mairesse et al. (2010) use manual alignments in their work, so their result is not directly comparable to ours. The zero semantic error is implied by the manual alignments and the architecture of their system.

5 Results

The results of our experiments and a comparison to previous works on this dataset are shown in Table 1. We include BLEU and NIST scores and the number of semantic errors (incorrect, missing, and repeated information), which we assessed manually on a sample of 42 output sentences (outputs of two randomly selected cross-validation runs).

The outputs of direct string generation show that the models learn to produce fluent sentences in the domain style;[9] incoherent sentences are rare, but semantic errors are very frequent in the greedy search. Most errors involve confusion of semantically close items, e.g., *Italian* instead of *French* or *riverside area* instead of *city centre* (see Table 2); items occurring more frequently are preferred regardless of their relevance. The beam search brings a BLEU improvement but keeps most semantic errors in place. The reranker is able to reduce the number of semantic errors while increasing automatic scores considerably. Using a larger beam increases the effect of the reranker as expected, resulting in slightly improved outputs.

Models generating deep syntax trees are also able to learn the domain style, and they have virtually no problems producing valid trees.[10] The surface realizer works almost flawlessly on this lim-

ited domain (Dušek and Jurčíček, 2015), leaving the seq2seq generator as the major error source. The syntax-generating models tend to make different kinds of errors than the string-based models: Some outputs are valid trees but not entirely syntactically fluent; missing, incorrect, or repeated information is more frequent than a confusion of semantically similar items (see Table 2). Semantic error rates of greedy and beam-search decoding are lower than for string-based models, partly because confusion of two similar items counts as two errors. The beam search brings an increase in BLEU but also in the number of semantic errors. The reranker is able to reduce the number of errors and improve automatic scores slightly. A larger beam leads to a small BLEU decrease even though the sentences contain less errors; here, NIST reflects the situation more accurately.

A comparison of the two approaches goes in favor of the joint setup: Without the reranker, models generating trees produce less semantic errors and gain higher BLEU/NIST scores. However, with the reranker, the string-based model is able to reduce the number of semantic errors while producing outputs significantly better in terms of BLEU/NIST.[11] In addition, the joint setup does not need an external surface realizer. The best results of both setups surpass the best results on this dataset using training data without manual alignments (Dušek and Jurčíček, 2015) in both automatic metrics[12] and the number of semantic errors.

6 Related Work

While most recent NLG systems attempt to learn generation from data, the choice of a particular approach – pipeline or joint – is often arbitrary and depends on system architecture or particular generation domain. Works using the pipeline approach in SDS tend to focus on sentence planning, improving a handcrafted generator (Walker et al., 2001; Stent et al., 2004; Paiva and Evans, 2005) or using perceptron-guided A* search (Dušek and Jurčíček, 2015). Generators taking the joint approach employ various methods, e.g., factored language models (Mairesse et al., 2010), inverted parsing (Wong and Mooney, 2007; Konstas and Lapata, 2013), or a pipeline of discriminative classifiers (Angeli et al., 2010). Unlike most previous

---

[9]The average sentence length is around 13 tokens.

[10]The generated sequences are longer, but have a very rigid structure, i.e., less uncertainty per generation step. The average output length is around 36 tokens in the generated sequence or 9 tree nodes; surface realizer outputs have a similar length as the sentences produced in direct string generation.

[11]The difference is statistically significant at 99% level according to pairwise bootstrap resampling test (Koehn, 2004).

[12]The BLEU/NIST differences are statistically significant.

Input DA	inform(name=X-name, type=placetoeat, eattype=restaurant, area=citycentre, near=X-near, food="Chinese takeaway", food=Japanese)
Reference	X is a Chinese takeaway and Japanese restaurant in the city centre near X.
Greedy with trees	X is a restaurant offering chinese takeaway in the centre of town near X. [Japanese]
+ Beam search	X is a restaurant and japanese food and chinese takeaway.
+ Reranker	X is a restaurant serving japanese food in the centre of the city that offers chinese takeaway.
Greedy into strings	X is a restaurant offering italian and indian takeaway in the city centre area near X. [Japanese, Chinese]
+ Beam search	X is a restaurant that serves fusion chinese takeaway in the riverside area near X. [Japanese, citycentre]
+ Reranker	X is a japanese restaurant in the city centre near X providing chinese food. [takeaway]
Input DA	inform(name=X-name, type=placetoeat, eattype=restaurant, area=riverside, food=French)
Reference	X is a French restaurant on the riverside.
Greedy with trees	X is a restaurant providing french and continental and by the river.
+ Beam search	X is a restaurant that serves french takeaway. [riverside]
+ Reranker	X is a french restaurant in the riverside area.
Greedy into strings	X is a restaurant in the riverside that serves italian food. [French]
+ Beam search	X is a restaurant in the riverside that serves italian food. [French]
+ Reranker	X is a restaurant in the riverside area that serves french food.
Input DA	inform(name=X-name, type=placetoeat, eattype=restaurant, near=X-near, food=Continental, food=French)
Reference	X is a French and Continental restaurant near X.
Greedy with trees	X is a french restaurant that serves french food and near X. [Continental]
+ Beam search	X is a french restaurant that serves french food and near X. [Continental]
+ Reranker	X is a restaurant serving french and continental food near X.
Greedy into strings	X is a french and continental style restaurant near X.
+ Beam search	X is a french and continental style restaurant near X.
+ Reranker	X is a restaurant providing french and continental food, near X.

Table 2: Example outputs of different generator setups (beam size 100 is used). Errors are marked in color (missing, superfluous, repeated information, disfluency).

NLG systems, our generator is trainable from unaligned pairs of MR and sentences alone.

Recent RNN-based generators are most similar to our work. Wen et al. (2015a) combined two RNN with a convolutional network reranker; Wen et al. (2015b) later replaced basic sigmoid cells with an LSTM. Mei et al. (2015) present the only seq2seq-based NLG system known to us. We extend the previous works by generating deep syntax trees as well as strings and directly comparing pipeline and joint generation. In addition, we experiment with an order-of-magnitude smaller dataset than other RNN based systems.

7 Conclusions and Future Work

We have presented a direct comparison of two-step generation via deep syntax trees with a direct generation into strings, both using the same NLG system based on the seq2seq approach. While both approaches offer decent performance, their outputs are quite different. The results show the direct approach as more favorable, with significantly higher n-gram based scores and a similar number of semantic errors in the output.

We also showed that our generator can learn to produce meaningful utterances using a much smaller amount of training data than what is typically used for RNN-based approaches. The resulting models had virtually no problems with producing fluent, coherent sentences or with generating valid structure of bracketed deep syntax trees. Our generator was able to surpass the best BLEU/NIST scores on the same dataset previously achieved by a perceptron-based generator of Dušek and Jurčíček (2015) while reducing the amount of irrelevant information on the output.

Our generator is released on GitHub at the following URL:

```
https://github.com/UFAL-DSG/tgen
```

We intend to apply it to other datasets for a broader comparison, and we plan further improvements, such as enhancing the reranker or including a bidirectional encoder (Bahdanau et al., 2015; Mei et al., 2015; Jean et al., 2015) and sequence level training (Ranzato et al., 2015).

Acknowledgments

This work was funded by the Ministry of Education, Youth and Sports of the Czech Republic under the grant agreement LK11221 and core research funding, SVV project 260 333, and GAUK grant 2058214 of Charles University in Prague. It used language resources stored and distributed by the LINDAT/CLARIN project of the Ministry of Education, Youth and Sports of the Czech Republic (project LM2015071). We thank our colleagues and the anonymous reviewers for helpful comments.

References

M. Abadi, A. Agarwal, P. Barham, E. Brevdo, Z. Chen, C. Citro, G. S. Corrado, A. Davis, J. Dean, M. Devin, S. Ghemawat, I. Goodfellow, A. Harp, G. Irving, M. Isard, Y. Jia, R. Jozefowicz, L. Kaiser, M. Kudlur, J. Levenberg, D. Mané, R. Monga, S. Moore, D. Murray, C. Olah, M. Schuster, J. Shlens, B. Steiner, I. Sutskever, K. Talwar, P. Tucker, V. Vanhoucke, V. Vasudevan, F. Viégas, O. Vinyals, P. Warden, M. Wattenberg, M. Wicke, Y. Yu, and X. Zheng. 2015. TensorFlow: Large-scale machine learning on heterogeneous systems. Software available from tensorflow.org.

G. Angeli, P. Liang, and D. Klein. 2010. A simple domain-independent probabilistic approach to generation. In *Proceedings of the 2010 Conference on Empirical Methods in Natural Language Processing*, pages 502–512.

D. Bahdanau, K. Cho, and Y. Bengio. 2015. Neural Machine Translation by Jointly Learning to Align and Translate. arXiv:1409.0473.

Y. Bengio, R. Ducharme, P. Vincent, and C. Jauvin. 2003. A Neural Probabilistic Language Model. *Journal of Machine Learning Research*, 3:1137–1155.

K. Cho, B. van Merrienboer, C. Gulcehre, D. Bahdanau, F. Bougares, H. Schwenk, and Y. Bengio. 2014. Learning Phrase Representations using RNN Encoder-Decoder for Statistical Machine Translation. In *Proceedings of the 2014 Conference on Empirical Methods in Natural Language Processing (EMNLP)*, pages 1724–1734, Doha, Qatar. arXiv:1406.1078.

N. Dethlefs, H. Hastie, H. Cuayáhuitl, and O. Lemon. 2013. Conditional Random Fields for Responsive Surface Realisation using Global Features. In *Proceedings of ACL*, Sofia.

G. Doddington. 2002. Automatic Evaluation of Machine Translation Quality Using N-gram Co-occurrence Statistics. In *Proceedings of the Second International Conference on Human Language Technology Research*, pages 138–145, San Francisco, CA, USA. Morgan Kaufmann Publishers Inc.

O. Dušek and F. Jurčíček. 2015. Training a Natural Language Generator From Unaligned Data. In *Proceedings of the 53rd Annual Meeting of the Association for Computational Linguistics and the 7th International Joint Conference on Natural Language Processing*, pages 451–461, Beijing, China. Association for Computational Linguistics.

Ondřej Dušek, Zdeněk Žabokrtský, Martin Popel, Martin Majliš, Michal Novák, and David Mareček. 2012. Formemes in English-Czech Deep Syntactic MT. In *Proceedings of the Seventh Workshop on Statistical Machine Translation*, pages 267–274, Montréal, Canada. Association for Computational Linguistics.

O. Dušek, L. Gomes, M. Novák, M. Popel, and R. Rosa. 2015. New Language Pairs in TectoMT. In *Proceedings of the 10th Workshop on Machine Translation*, pages 98–104, Lisbon, Portugal. Association for Computational Linguistics.

A. Graves. 2013. Generating Sequences With Recurrent Neural Networks. *arXiv:1308.0850 [cs]*, August.

S. Jean, K. Cho, R. Memisevic, and Y. Bengio. 2015. On Using Very Large Target Vocabulary for Neural Machine Translation. In *Proceedings of the 53rd Annual Meeting of the Association for Computational Linguistics and the 7th International Joint Conference on Natural Language Processing (Volume 1: Long Papers)*, pages 1–10, Beijing, China. Association for Computational Linguistics.

D. Kingma and J. Ba. 2015. Adam: A Method for Stochastic Optimization. In *International Conference on Learning Representations*. arXiv:1412.6980.

P. Koehn. 2004. Statistical significance tests for machine translation evaluation. In *Proceedings of EMNLP*, pages 388–395.

I. Konstas and M. Lapata. 2013. A Global Model for Concept-to-Text Generation. *Journal of Artificial Intelligence Research*, 48:305–346.

F. Mairesse, M. Gašić, F. Jurčíček, S. Keizer, B. Thomson, K. Yu, and S. Young. 2010. Phrase-based statistical language generation using graphical models and active learning. In *Proceedings of the 48th Annual Meeting of the Association for Computational Linguistics*, pages 1552–1561.

H. Mei, M. Bansal, and M. R. Walter. 2015. What to talk about and how? Selective Generation using LSTMs with Coarse-to-Fine Alignment. *arXiv:1509.00838 [cs]*, September.

D. S. Paiva and R. Evans. 2005. Empirically-based control of natural language generation. In *Proceedings of the 43rd Annual Meeting on Association for Computational Linguistics*, ACL '05, pages 58–65, Stroudsburg, PA, USA. Association for Computational Linguistics.

K. Papineni, S. Roukos, T. Ward, and W.-J. Zhu. 2002. BLEU: a method for automatic evaluation of machine translation. In *Proceedings of the 40th annual meeting of the Association for Computational Linguistics*, pages 311–318.

M. Popel and Z. Žabokrtský. 2010. TectoMT: modular NLP framework. In *Proceedings of IceTAL, 7th International Conference on Natural Language Processing,*, pages 293–304, Reykjavík.

M. Ranzato, S. Chopra, M. Auli, and W. Zaremba. 2015. Sequence Level Training with Recurrent Neural Networks. *arXiv:1511.06732 [cs]*, November.

A. Raux, B. Langner, D. Bohus, A. W. Black, and M. Eskenazi. 2005. Let's go public! taking a spoken dialog system to the real world. In *in Proc. of Interspeech 2005*. Citeseer.

E. Reiter and R. Dale. 2000. *Building Natural Language Generation Systems*. Cambridge University Press, studies in natural language processing edition.

V. Rieser, O. Lemon, and X. Liu. 2010. Optimising information presentation for spoken dialogue systems. In *Proceedings of the 48th Annual Meeting of the Association for Computational Linguistics*, pages 1009–1018.

A. Stent, R. Prasad, and M. Walker. 2004. Trainable sentence planning for complex information presentation in spoken dialog systems. In *Proceedings of the 42nd Annual Meeting on Association for Computational Linguistics*, pages 79–86.

I. Sutskever, O. Vinyals, and Q. V V Le. 2014. Sequence to sequence learning with neural networks. In *Advances in Neural Information Processing Systems*, pages 3104–3112. arXiv:1409.3215.

O. Vinyals, Ł. Kaiser, T. Koo, S. Petrov, I. Sutskever, and G. Hinton. 2015. Grammar as a Foreign Language. In C. Cortes, N. D. Lawrence, D. D. Lee, M. Sugiyama, R. Garnett, and R. Garnett, editors, *Advances in Neural Information Processing Systems 28*, pages 2755–2763.

M. A. Walker, O. Rambow, and M. Rogati. 2001. SPoT: a trainable sentence planner. In *Proceedings of the second meeting of the North American Chapter of the Association for Computational Linguistics on Language technologies*, pages 1–8, Stroudsburg, PA, USA. Association for Computational Linguistics.

T.-H. Wen, M. Gasic, D. Kim, N. Mrksic, P.-H. Su, D. Vandyke, and S. Young. 2015a. Stochastic Language Generation in Dialogue using Recurrent Neural Networks with Convolutional Sentence Reranking. In *Proceedings of the 16th Annual Meeting of the Special Interest Group on Discourse and Dialogue*, pages 275–284, Prague, Czech Republic, September. Association for Computational Linguistics.

T.-H. Wen, M. Gasic, N. Mrkšić, P.-H. Su, D. Vandyke, and S. Young. 2015b. Semantically Conditioned LSTM-based Natural Language Generation for Spoken Dialogue Systems. In *Proceedings of the 2015 Conference on Empirical Methods in Natural Language Processing*, pages 1711–1721, Lisbon, Portugal. Association for Computational Linguistics.

Y. W. Wong and R. J. Mooney. 2007. Generation by inverting a semantic parser that uses statistical machine translation. In *Proceedings of Human Language Technologies: The Conference of the North American Chapter of the Association for Computational Linguistics (NAACL-HLT-07)*, pages 172–179.

S. Young, M. Gašić, S. Keizer, F. Mairesse, J. Schatzmann, B. Thomson, and K. Yu. 2010. The Hidden Information State model: A practical framework for POMDP-based spoken dialogue management. *Computer Speech & Language*, 24(2):150–174, April.

On the Linearity of Semantic Change: Investigating Meaning Variation via Dynamic Graph Models

Steffen Eger
Ubiquitous Knowledge Processing Lab
Department of Computer Science
Technische Universität Darmstadt

Alexander Mehler
Text Technology Lab
Department of Computer Science
Goethe-Universität Frankfurt am Main

Abstract

We consider two graph models of semantic change. The first is a time-series model that relates embedding vectors from one time period to embedding vectors of previous time periods. In the second, we construct one graph for each word: nodes in this graph correspond to time points and edge weights to the similarity of the word's meaning across two time points. We apply our two models to corpora across three different languages. We find that semantic change is *linear* in two senses. Firstly, today's embedding vectors (= meaning) of words can be derived as linear combinations of embedding vectors of their neighbors in previous time periods. Secondly, self-similarity of words decays linearly in time. We consider both findings as new laws/hypotheses of semantic change.

1 Introduction

Meaning is not uniform, neither across space, nor across time. Across space, different languages tend to exhibit different polysemous associations for corresponding terms (Eger et al., 2015; Kulkarni et al., 2015b). Across time, several well-known examples of meaning change in English have been documented. For example, the word *gay*'s meaning has shifted, during the 1970s, from an adjectival meaning of *cheerful* at the beginning of the 20th century to its present meaning of *homosexual* (Kulkarni et al., 2015a). Similarly, technological progress has led to semantic broadening of terms such as *transmission, mouse,* or *apple.*

In this work, we consider two graph models of semantic change. Our **first** model is a *dynamic* model in that the underlying paradigm is a (time-)series of graphs. Each node in the series of graphs corresponds to one word, associated with which is a semantic embedding vector. We then ask how the embedding vectors in one time period (graph) can be predicted from the embedding vectors of neighbor words in previous time periods. In particular, we postulate that there is a linear functional relationship that couples a word's today's meaning with its neighbor's meanings in the past. When estimating the coefficients of this model, we find that the linear form appears indeed very plausible. This functional form then allows us to address further questions, such as negative relationships between words — which indicate semantic differentiation over time — as well as projections into the future. We call our **second** graph model *time-indexed self-similarity graphs*. In these graphs, each node corresponds to a time point and the link between two time points indicates the semantic similarity of a specific word across the two time points under consideration. The analysis of these graphs reveals that most words obey a law of linear semantic 'decay': semantic self-similarity decreases linearly over time.

In our work, we capture semantics by means of word embeddings derived from context-predicting neural network architectures, which have become the state-of-the-art in distributional semantics modeling (Baroni et al., 2014). Our approach and results are partly independent of this representation, however, in that we take a structuralist approach: we derive new, 'second-order embeddings' by modeling the meaning of words by

Proceedings of the 54th Annual Meeting of the Association for Computational Linguistics, pages 52–58,
Berlin, Germany, August 7-12, 2016. ©2016 Association for Computational Linguistics

means of their semantic similarity relations to all other words in the vocabulary (de Saussure, 1916; Rieger, 2003). Thus, future research may in principle substitute the deep-learning architectures for semantics considered here by any other method capable of producing semantic similarity values between lexical units.

This work is structured as follows. In §2, we discuss related work. In §3.1 and 3.2, respectively, we formally introduce the two graph models outlined. In §4, we detail our experiments and in §5, we conclude.

2   Related work

Broadly speaking, one can distinguish two recent NLP approaches to meaning change analysis. On the one hand, *coarse-grained* trend analyses compare the semantics of a word in one time period with the meaning of the word in the preceding time period (Jatowt and Duh, 2014; Kulkarni et al., 2015a). Such coarse-grained models, by themselves, do not specify *in which respects* a word has changed (e.g., semantic broadening or narrowing), but just aim at capturing whether meaning change has occurred. In contrast, more fine-grained analyses typically sense-label word occurrences in corpora and then investigate changes in the corresponding meaning distributions (Rohrdantz et al., 2011; Mitra et al., 2014; Plitz et al., 2015; Zhang et al., 2015). Sense-labeling may be achieved by clustering of the context vectors of words (Huang et al., 2012; Chen et al., 2014; Neelakantan et al., 2014) or by applying LDA-based techniques where word contexts take the roles of documents and word senses take the roles of topics (Rohrdantz et al., 2011; Lau et al., 2012). Finally, there are studies that test particular meaning change hypotheses such as whether similar words tend to diverge in meaning over time (according to the 'law of differentiation') (Xu and Kemp, 2015) and papers that intend to detect corresponding terms across time (words with similar meanings/roles in two time periods but potentially different lexical forms) (Zhang et al., 2015).

3   Graph models

Let $V = \{w_1, \ldots, w_{|V|}\}$ be the common vocabulary (intersection) of all words in all time periods $t \in \mathcal{T}$. Here, $\mathcal{T}$ is a set of time indices. Denote an embedding of a word w_i at time period t as $\mathbf{w}_i(t) \in \mathbb{R}^d$. Since embeddings $\mathbf{w}_i(s), \mathbf{w}_i(t)$ for two different time periods s, t are generally not comparable, as they may lie in different coordinate systems, we consider the vectors $\tilde{\mathbf{w}}_i(t) =$

$$(\mathrm{sim}(\mathbf{w}_i(t), \mathbf{w}_1(t)), \ldots, \mathrm{sim}(\mathbf{w}_i(t), \mathbf{w}_{|V|}(t))), \quad (1)$$

each of which lies in $\mathbb{R}^{|V|}$ and where sim is a similarity function such as the cosine. We note that our structuralist definition of $\tilde{\mathbf{w}}_i(t)$ is not unproblematic, since the vectors $\mathbf{w}_1(t), \ldots, \mathbf{w}_{|V|}(t)$ tend to be different across t, by our very postulate, so that there is non-identity of these 'reference points' over time. However, as we may assume that the meanings of at least a few words are stable over time, we strongly expect the vectors $\tilde{\mathbf{w}}_i(t)$ to be suitable for our task of analysis of meaning changes.[1] For the remainder of this work, for convenience, we do not distinguish, in terms of notation, between $\mathbf{w}_i(t)$ and $\tilde{\mathbf{w}}_i(t)$.

3.1   A linear model of semantic change

We postulate, and subsequently test, the following model of meaning dynamics which describes meaning change over time for words w_i:

$$\mathbf{w}_i(t) = \sum_{n=1}^{p} \sum_{w_j \in V \cap N(w_i)} \alpha_{w_j}^n \mathbf{w}_j(t - n) \quad (2)$$

where $\alpha_{w_j}^n \in \mathbb{R}$, for $n = 1, \ldots, p$, are coefficients of meaning vectors $\mathbf{w}_j(t - n)$ and $p \geq 1$ is the *order* of the model. The set $N(w_i) \subseteq V$ denotes a set of 'neighbors' of word w_i.[2] This model says that the meaning of a word w_i at some time t is determined by reference to the meanings of its 'neighbors' in previous time periods, and that the underlying functional relationship is *linear*.

We remark that the model described by Eq. (2) is a time-series model, and, in particular, a vector-autoregressive (VAR) model with special

---

[1] An alternative to our second-order embeddings is to project vectors from different time periods in a common space (Mikolov et al., 2013a; Faruqui and Dyer, 2014), which requires to find corresponding terms across time. Further, one could also consider a 'core' vocabulary of semantically stable words, e.g., in the spirit of Swadesh (1952), instead of using all vocabulary words as reference.

[2] We also constrain the vectors $\mathbf{w}_i(t)$, for all $w_i \in V$, to contain non-zero entries only for words in $N(w_i)$.

structure. The model may also be seen in the socio-economic context of so-called "opinion dynamic models" (Golub and Jackson, 2010; Acemoglu and Ozdaglar, 2011; Eger, 2016). There it is assumed that agents are situated in network structures and continuously update their opinions/beliefs/actions according to their ties with other agents. Model (2) substitutes multi-dimensional embedding vectors for one-dimensional opinions.

3.2 Time-indexed self-similarity graphs

We track meaning change by considering a fully connected graph $G(w)$ for each word w in V. The nodes of $G(w)$ are the time indices $\mathcal{T}$, and there is an undirected link between any two $s, t \in \mathcal{T}$ whose weight is given by $\text{sim}(\mathbf{w}(s), \mathbf{w}(t))$. We call the graphs $G(w)$ *time-indexed self-similarity (TISS) graphs* because they indicate the (semantic) similarity of a given word with itself across different time periods. Particular interest may lie in *weak links* in these graphs as they indicate low similarity between two different time periods, i.e., semantic change across time.

4 Experiments

Data As corpus for English, we use the Corpus of Historical American (COHA).[3] This covers texts from the time period 1810 to 2000. We extract two slices: the years 1900-2000 and 1810-2000. For both slices, each time period t is one decade, e.g., $\mathcal{T} = \{1810, 1820, 1830, \ldots\}$.[4] For each slice, we only keep words associated to the word classes nouns, adjectives, and verbs. For computational and estimation purposes, we also only consider words that occur at least 100 times in each time period. To induce word embeddings $\mathbf{w} \in \mathbb{R}^d$ for each word $w \in V$, we use word2vec (Mikolov et al., 2013b) with default parametrizations. We do so for each time period $t \in \mathcal{T}$ independently. We then use these embeddings to derive the new embeddings as in Eq. (1). Throughout, we use cosine similarity as sim measure. For German, we consider a proprietary dataset of the German newspaper *SZ*[5] for which $\mathcal{T} = \{1994, 1995, \ldots, 2003\}$.

We lemmatize and POS tag the data and likewise only consider nouns, verbs and adjectives, making the same frequency constraints as in English. Finally, we use the PL (Migne, 1855) as data set for Latin. Here, $\mathcal{T} = \{300, 400, \ldots, 1300\}$. We use the same preprocessing, frequency, and word class constraints as for English and German.

Throughout, our datasets are well-balanced in terms of size. For example, the English COHA datasets contain about 24M-30M tokens for each decade from 1900 to 2000, where the decades 1990 and 2000 contain slighly more data than the earlier decades. The pre-1900 decades contain 18-24M tokens, with only the decades 1810 and 1820 containing very little data (1M and 7M tokens, respectively). The corpora are also balanced by genre.

4.1 TISS graphs

We start with investigating the TISS graphs. Let D_{t_0} represent how semantically similar a word is across two time periods, on average, when the distance between time periods is t_0: $D_{t_0} = \frac{1}{C} \sum_{w \in V} \sum_{|s-t|=t_0} \text{sim}(\mathbf{w}(s), \mathbf{w}(t))$, where $C = |V| \cdot |\{(s,t) \,|\, |s-t| = t_0\}|$ is a normalizer. Figure 1 plots the values D_{t_0} for the time slice from 1810 to 2000, for the English data. We notice a clear trend: self-similarity of a word tends to (almost perfectly) linearly decrease with time distance. In

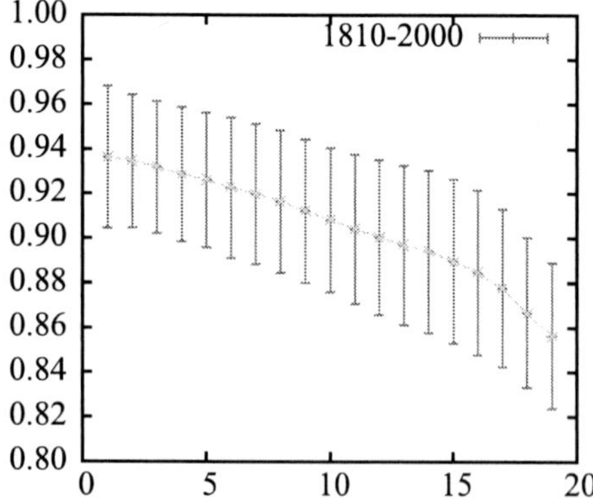

Figure 1: D_{t_0} (y-axis) as a function of t_0 (x-axis), values of D_{t_0} (in green) and error-bars.

fact, Table 1 below indicates that this trend holds across all our corpora, i.e., for different time scales and different languages: the linear 'decay' model

---

[3]http://corpus.byu.edu/coha/.
[4]Each time period contains texts that were written in that decade.
[5]http://www.sueddeutsche.de/

fits the D_{t_0} curves very well, with adjusted R^2 values substantially above 90% and consistently and significantly negative coefficients. We believe that this finding may be considered a new statistical law of semantic change.

Corpus	Lang.	Time interval	Years	Coeff.	R^2
COHA	English	Decade	1900-2000	-0.425	98.63
			1810-2000	-0.405	96.03
SZ	German	Year	1994-2003	-0.678	98.64
PL	Latin	Century	400-1300	-0.228	92.28

Table 1: Coefficients (%) in regression of D_{t_0} on t_0, and adjusted R^2 values (%).

The values D_{t_0} as a function of t_0 are averages over all words. Thus, it might be possible that the average word's meaning decays linearly in time, while the semantic behavior, over time, of a large fraction of words follows different trends. To investigate this, we consider the distribution of $D_{t_0}(w) = \frac{1}{C'} \sum_{|s-t|=t_0} \mathrm{sim}(\mathbf{w}(s), \mathbf{w}(t))$ over fixed words w. Here $C' = |\{(s,t) \,|\, |s - t| = t_0\}|$. We consider the regression models

$$D_{t_0}(w) = \alpha \cdot t_0 + \mathrm{const.}$$

for each word w independently and assess the distribution of coefficients α as well as the goodness-of-fit values. Figure 2 shows — exemplarily for the English 1900-2000 COHA data — that the coefficients α are negative for almost all words. In fact, the distribution is left-skewed with a mean of around -0.4%. Moreover, the linear model is always a good to very good fit of the data in that R^2 values are centered around 85% and rarely fall below 75%. We find similar patterns for all other datasets considered here. This shows that not only the average word's meaning decays linearly, but almost all words' (whose frequency mass exceeds a particular threshold) semantics behaves this way.

Next, we use our TISS graphs for the task of finding words that have undergone meaning change. To this end, we sort the graphs $G(w)$ by the ratios $R_{G(w)} = \frac{\mathrm{maxlink}}{\mathrm{minlink}}$, where maxlink denotes maximal weight of a link in graph $G(w)$ and minlink is the minimal weight of a link in graph $G(w)$. We note that weak links may indicate semantic change, but the stated ratio requires that 'weakness' is seen relative to the strongest semantic links in the TISS graphs. Table 2 presents

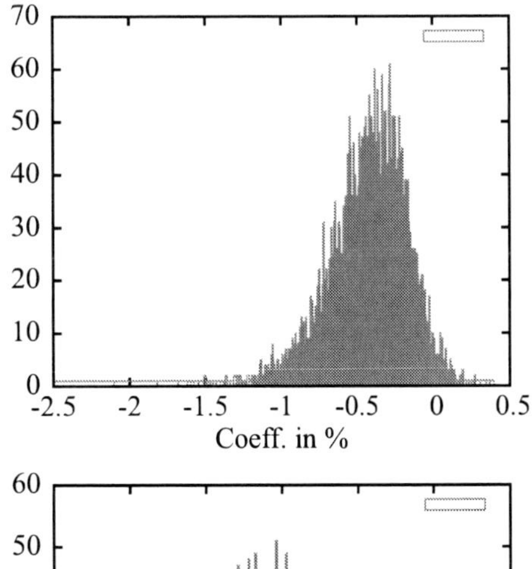
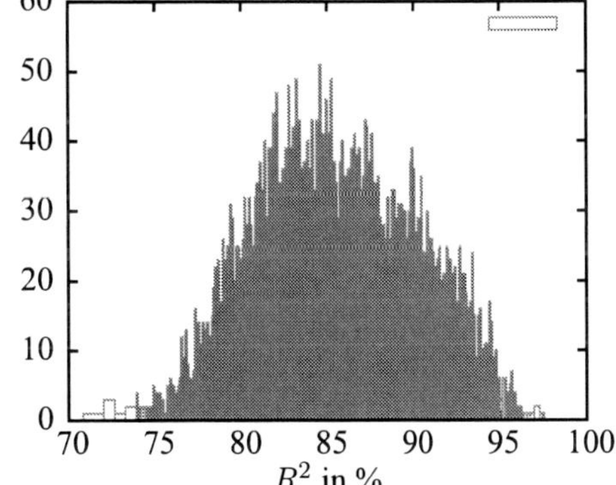

Figure 2: Distribution of Coefficients α (top) and R^2 values (bottom) in regression of values $D_{t_0}(w)$ on t_0. The plots are histograms: y-axes are frequencies.

selected words that have highest values $R_{G(w)}$.[6] We omit a fine-grained semantic change analysis,

bush (1), web (2), alan (3), implement (4) jeff (5), gay (6), program (7), film (8), focus (9), terrific (16), axis (36)

Table 2: Selected words with highest values $R_{G(w)}$ in COHA for the time period 1900-2000. In brackets are the ranks of words, i.e., *bush* has the highest value $R_{G(w)}$, *web* the 2nd highest, etc.

which could be conducted via the methods outlined in §2, but notice a few cases. 'Terrific' has a large semantic discrepancy between the 1900s and

---

[6]The top ten words with the lowest values $R_{G(w)}$ are *one, write, have, who, come, only, even, know, hat, fact.*

the 1970s, when the word probably (had) changed from a negative to a more positive meaning. The largest discrepancy for 'web' is between the 1940s and the 2000s, when it probably came to be massively used in the context of the Internet. The high $R_{G(w)}$ value for $w =$ 'axis' derives from comparing its use in the 1900s with its use in the 1940s, when it probably came to be used in the context of Nazi Germany and its allies. We notice that the presented method can account for gradual, accumulating change, which is not possible for models that compare two succeeding time points such as the model of Kulkarni et al. (2015a).

4.2 Meaning dynamics network models

Finally, we estimate meaning dynamics models as in Eq. (2), i.e., we estimate the coefficients $\alpha_{w_j}^n$ from our data sources. We let the neighbors $N(w)$ of a word w as in Eq. (2) be the union (w.r.t. t) over sets $N_t(w; n)$ denoting the $n \geq 1$ semantically most similar words (estimated by cosine similarity on the original word2vec vectors) of word w in time period $t \in \mathcal{T}$.[7] In Table 3, we indicate two measures: adjusted R^2, which indicates the goodness-of-fit of a model, and prediction error. By prediction error, we measure the average Euclidean distance between the true semantic vector of a word in the *final* time period t_N vs. the predicted semantic vector, via the linear model in Eq. (2), estimated on the data excluding the final period. The indicated prediction error is the average over all words. We note the following: R^2 values are high (typically above 95%), indicating that the linear semantic change model we have suggested fits the data well. Moreover, R^2 values slightly increase between order $p = 1$ and $p = 2$; however, for prediction error this trend is reversed.[8] We also include a strong baseline that claims that word meanings do not change in the final period t_N but are the same as in t_{N-1}. We note that the order $p = 1$ model consistently improves upon this baseline, by as much as 18%, depending upon parameter settings.

Negative relationships Another very interest-

---

[7]We exclude word w from $N_t(w; n)$. We found that including w did not improve performance results.

[8]We experimented with orders $p \geq 3$, but found them to be inadequate. Typically, coefficients for lagged-3 variables are either zero or model predictions are way off, possibly indicating multi-collinearity.

n	p	Adjusted-R^2	Pred. Error	Baseline
5	1	95.68± 2.80	0.402±.234	0.447±.232
	2	96.13± 1.83	0.549±.333	
10	1	95.24± 2.78	0.378±.169	0.445±.187
	2	95.75± 2.67	0.515±.247	
20	1	94.72± 2.85	0.362±.127	0.442±.156
	2	95.27± 2.74	0.493±.190	

Table 3: English data, 1900-2000. R^2 and prediction error in %.

ing aspect of the model in Eq. (2) is that it allows for detecting words w_j whose embeddings have negative coefficients α_{w_j} for a target word w_i (we consider $p = 1$ in the remainder). Such negative coefficients may be seen as instantiations of the 'law of differentiation': the two words' meanings move, over time, in opposite directions in semantic space. We find significantly negative relationships between the following words, among others: summit $\leftrightarrow$ foot, boy $\leftrightarrow$ woman, vow $\leftrightarrow$ belief, negro $\leftrightarrow$ black. Instead of a detailed analysis, we mention that the Wikipedia entry for the last pair indicates that the meanings of 'negro' and 'black' switched roles between the early and late 20th century. While 'negro' was once the "neutral" term for the colored population in the US, it acquired negative connotations after the 1960s; and vice versa for 'black'.

5 Concluding remarks

We suggested two novel models of semantic change. First, TISS graphs allow for detecting gradual, non-consecutive meaning change. They enable to detect statistical trends of a possibly general nature. Second, our time-series models allow for investigating negative trends in meaning change ('law of differentiation') as well as forecasting into the future, which we leave for future work. Both models hint at a linear behavior of semantic change, which deserves further investigation. We note that this linearity concerns the *core* vocabulary of languages (in our case, words that occurred at least 100 times in each time period), and, in the case of TISS graphs, is an *average* result; particular words may have drastic, non-linear meaning changes across time (e.g., proper names referring to entirely different entities). However, our analysis also finds that most core words' meanings decay linearly in time.

References

Daron Acemoglu and Asuman Ozdaglar. 2011. Opinion dynamics and learning in social networks. *Dynamic Games and Applications*, 1(1):3–49.

Marco Baroni, Georgiana Dinu, and Germán Kruszewski. 2014. Don't count, predict! a systematic comparison of context-counting vs. context-predicting semantic vectors. In *Proceedings of the 52nd Annual Meeting of the Association for Computational Linguistics (Volume 1: Long Papers)*, pages 238–247, Baltimore, Maryland, June. Association for Computational Linguistics.

Xinxiong Chen, Zhiyuan Liu, and Maosong Sun. 2014. A unified model for word sense representation and disambiguation. In *Proceedings of the 2014 Conference on Empirical Methods in Natural Language Processing, EMNLP 2014, October 25-29, 2014, Doha, Qatar, A meeting of SIGDAT, a Special Interest Group of the ACL*, pages 1025–1035.

Ferdinand de Saussure. 1916. *Cours de linguistique générale*. Payot, Lausanne/Paris.

Steffen Eger, Niko Schenk, and Alexander Mehler. 2015. Towards semantic language classification: Inducing and clustering semantic association networks from europarl. In *Proceedings of the Fourth Joint Conference on Lexical and Computational Semantics*, pages 127–136, Denver, Colorado, June. Association for Computational Linguistics.

Steffen Eger. 2016. Opinion dynamics and wisdom under out-group discrimination. *Mathematical Social Sciences*, 80(C):97–107.

Manaal Faruqui and Chris Dyer. 2014. Improving vector space word representations using multilingual correlation. In *Proceedings of EACL*.

Benjamin Golub and Matthew O. Jackson. 2010. Nave learning in social networks and the wisdom of crowds. *American Economic Journal: Microeconomics*, 2(1):112–49, February.

Eric H. Huang, Richard Socher, Christopher D. Manning, and Andrew Y. Ng. 2012. Improving word representations via global context and multiple word prototypes. In *Proceedings of the 50th Annual Meeting of the Association for Computational Linguistics: Long Papers - Volume 1*, ACL '12, pages 873–882, Stroudsburg, PA, USA. Association for Computational Linguistics.

Adam Jatowt and Kevin Duh. 2014. A framework for analyzing semantic change of words across time. In *Proceedings of the Joint JCDL/TPDL Digital Libraries Conference*.

Vivek Kulkarni, Rami Al-Rfou, Bryan Perozzi, and Steven Skiena. 2015a. Statistically significant detection of linguistic change. In *Proceedings of the 24th International Conference on World Wide Web*, WWW '15, pages 625–635, Republic and Canton of Geneva, Switzerland. International World Wide Web Conferences Steering Committee.

Vivek Kulkarni, Bryan Perozzi, and Steven Skiena. 2015b. Freshman or fresher? quantifying the geographic variation of internet language. *CoRR*, abs/1510.06786.

Jey Han Lau, Paul Cook, Diana McCarthy, David Newman, and Timothy Baldwin. 2012. Word sense induction for novel sense detection. In *Proceedings of the 13th Conference of the European Chapter of the Association for Computational Linguistics*, EACL '12, pages 591–601, Stroudsburg, PA, USA. Association for Computational Linguistics.

Jacques-Paul Migne, editor. 1855. *Patrologiae cursus completus: Series latina*. 1–221. Chadwyck-Healey, Cambridge.

Tomas Mikolov, Quoc V. Le, and Ilya Sutskever. 2013a. Exploiting similarities among languages for machine translation. *CoRR*, abs/1309.4168.

Tomas Mikolov, Ilya Sutskever, Kai Chen, Greg S Corrado, and Jeff Dean. 2013b. Distributed representations of words and phrases and their compositionality. In C.J.C. Burges, L. Bottou, M. Welling, Z. Ghahramani, and K.Q. Weinberger, editors, *Advances in Neural Information Processing Systems 26*, pages 3111–3119. Curran Associates, Inc.

Sunny Mitra, Ritwik Mitra, Martin Riedl, Chris Biemann, Animesh Mukherjee, and Pawan Goyal. 2014. That's sick dude!: Automatic identification of word sense change across different timescales. In *Proceedings of the 52nd Annual Meeting of the Association for Computational Linguistics, ACL 2014, June 22-27, 2014, Baltimore, MD, USA, Volume 1: Long Papers*, pages 1020–1029.

Arvind Neelakantan, Jeevan Shankar, Alexandre Passos, and Andrew McCallum. 2014. Efficient non-parametric estimation of multiple embeddings per word in vector space. In *Proceedings of the 2014 Conference on Empirical Methods in Natural Language Processing, EMNLP 2014, October 25-29, 2014, Doha, Qatar, A meeting of SIGDAT, a Special Interest Group of the ACL*, pages 1059–1069.

Christian Plitz, Thomas Bartz, Katharina Morik, and Angelika Strrer. 2015. Investigation of word senses over time using linguistic corpora. In Pavel Krl and Vclav Matouek, editors, *Text, Speech, and Dialogue*, volume 9302 of *Lecture Notes in Computer Science*, pages 191–198. Springer International Publishing.

Burghard B. Rieger. 2003. Semiotic cognitive information processing: Learning to understand discourse. A systemic model of meaning constitution.

In R. Kühn, R. Menzel, W. Menzel, U. Ratsch, M. M. Richter, and I. O. Stamatescu, editors, *Adaptivity and Learning. An Interdisciplinary Debate*, pages 347–403. Springer, Berlin.

Christian Rohrdantz, Annette Hautli, Thomas Mayer, Miriam Butt, Daniel A. Keim, and Frans Plank. 2011. Towards tracking semantic change by visual analytics. In *The 49th Annual Meeting of the Association for Computational Linguistics: Human Language Technologies, Proceedings of the Conference, 19-24 June, 2011, Portland, Oregon, USA - Short Papers*, pages 305–310.

Morris Swadesh. 1952. Lexico-statistic dating of prehistoric ethnic contacts. *Proceedings of the American Philosophical Society*, 96(4):452463.

Y. Xu and C. Kemp. 2015. A computational evaluation of two laws of semantic change. In *Proceedings of the 37th Annual Conference of the Cognitive Science Society*.

Yating Zhang, Adam Jatowt, Sourav S. Bhowmick, and Katsumi Tanaka. 2015. Omnia mutantur, nihil interit: Connecting past with present by finding corresponding terms across time. In *Proceedings of the 53rd Annual Meeting of the Association for Computational Linguistics and the 7th International Joint Conference on Natural Language Processing of the Asian Federation of Natural Language Processing, ACL 2015, July 26-31, 2015, Beijing, China, Volume 1: Long Papers*, pages 645–655.

Joint Word Segmentation and Phonetic Category Induction

Micha Elsner
Dept. of Linguistics
The Ohio State University
`melsner0@gmail`

Stephanie Antetomaso
Dept. of Linguistics
The Ohio State University
`antetomaso.2@osu.edu`

Naomi H. Feldman
Dept. of Linguistics and UMIACS
University of Maryland
`nhf@umd.edu`

Abstract

We describe a model which jointly performs word segmentation and induces vowel categories from formant values. Vowel induction performance improves slightly over a baseline model which does not segment; segmentation performance decreases slightly from a baseline using entirely symbolic input. Our high joint performance in this idealized setting implies that problems in unsupervised speech recognition reflect the phonetic variability of real speech sounds in context.

1 Introduction

In learning to speak their native language, a developing infant must acquire two related pieces of information: a set of lexical items (along with the contexts in which they are likely to occur), and a set of phonetic categories. For instance, an English-learning infant must learn that [i] and [$ɪ$] are different segments, differentiating between words like *beat* and *bit*, while for a Spanish-learning infant, [i] and [$ɪ$]-like tokens represent realizations of the same category. It is clear that these two tasks are intimately related, and that models of language acquisition must solve both together— but how?

This problem has inspired much recent work in low-resource speech recognition (Lee et al., 2015; Lee and Glass, 2012; Jansen and Church, 2011; Varadarajan et al., 2008), with impressive results. Nonetheless, many of these researchers conclude that their systems learn too many phonetic categories, a problem they attribute to the presence of contextual variants (allophones) of the different sounds. For instance, the [a] in *dog* is likely longer than the [a] in *dock* (Ladefoged and Johnson, 2010), but this difference is not phonologically meaningful in English— it cannot differentiate any pair of words on its own. Many unsupervised systems are claimed to erroneously learn these kinds of differences as categorical ones.

Here, we attempt to model the problem in a more controlled setting by extending work in cognitive modeling of language acquisition. We present a system which jointly acquires vowel categories and lexical items from a mixed symbolic/acoustic representation of the input. As is traditional in cognitive models of vowel acquisition, it uses a single-point formant representation of the vowel acoustics, and is tested on a simulated corpus in which vowel acoustics are unaffected by context. We find that, under these circumstances, vowel categories and lexical items can be learned jointly with relatively little decrease in accuracy from learning either alone. Thus, our results support the hypothesis that the more realistic problem is hard because of contextual variability. As a secondary point, we show that the results reflect problems with local minima in the popular framework of hierarchical Bayesian modeling.

2 Related work

This work aims to induce both a set of phonetic vowel categories and a lexical representation from unlabeled data. It extends the closely related model of Feldman et al. (2013a), which performs the same task, but with known word boundaries; this requirement is a significant limitation on the model's cognitive plausibility. Our model infers a latent word segmentation. Another extension, Frank et al. (2014), uses semantic information to disambiguate words, but still with known word boundaries.

A few models learn a lexicon while categorizing all sounds, instead of just vowels. Lee et al. (2015) and Lee and Glass (2012) use hierarchical Bayesian models to induce word and subword units. These models are mathematically very similar to

Proceedings of the 54th Annual Meeting of the Association for Computational Linguistics, pages 59–65,
Berlin, Germany, August 7-12, 2016. ©2016 Association for Computational Linguistics

our own, differing primarily using more complex acoustic representations and inducing categories for all sounds instead of just vowels. Jansen and Church (2011) learns whole-word Markov models, then clusters their states into phone-like units using a spectral algorithm. Their system still learns multiple allophonic categories for most sounds.

In the segmentation literature, several previous systems learn lexical items from variable input (Elsner et al., 2013; Daland and Pierrehumbert, 2011; Rytting et al., 2010; Neubig et al., 2010; Fleck, 2008). However, these models use pre-processed representations of the acoustics (phonetic transcription or posterior probabilities from a phone recognizer) rather than inducing an acoustic category structure directly. Elsner et al. (2013) and Neubig et al. (2010) use Bayesian models and sampling schemes similar to those presented here.

Acquisition models like Elsner et al. (2013),Rytting et al. (2010) and Fleck (2008) are designed to handle *phonological* variability. In particular, they are designed to cope with words which have multiple transcribed pronunciations (*[wan]* and *[want]* for "want"); this kind of alternation can insert or delete whole segments, or change a vowel sound from one perceptual category to another. Such variability is common in spoken English (Pitt et al., 2005) and presents a challenge for speech recognition (McAllaster et al., 1998).

In contrast, the system presented here models *phonetic* variability within a single category. It uses an untranscribed, continuous-valued representation for vowel sounds, so that different tokens within a single category may differ from one another. But it does so within an idealized dataset which lacks phonological variants. Moreover, although the phonetic input to the system is variable, the variation is not predictable; tokens within the category differ at random, independently from their environment.

Several other models also learn phonetic categories from continuous input, either from real or idealized datasets, without learning a lexicon. Varadarajan et al. (2008) learn subword units by incrementally splitting an HMM model of the data to maximize likelihood. Badino et al. (2014) perform k-means clustering on the acoustic representation learned by an autoencoder. Cognitive models using formant values as input are common, many using mixture of Gaussians (Vallabha et al., 2007; de Boer and Kuhl, 2003). Because they lack a lexicon,

these models have particular difficulty distinguishing meaningful from allophonic variability.

3 Dataset and model

Our dataset replicates the previous idealized setting for vowel category induction in cognitive modeling, but in a corpus of unsegmented utterances rather than a wordlist. We adapt a standard word segmentation corpus of child-directed speech (Brent, 1999), which consists of 8000 utterances from Bernstein-Ratner (1987), orthographically transcribed and then phonetically transcribed using a pronunciation dictionary.

We add simulated acoustics (without contextual variation) to each vowel in the Brent corpus. Following previous cognitive models of category induction (Feldman et al., 2013b), we use the vowel dataset given by Hillenbrand et al. (1995), which gives formants for English vowels read in the context *h_d*. We estimate a multivariate Gaussian distribution for each vowel, and, whenever a monophthongal vowel occurs in the Brent corpus, we replace it with a pair of formants (f_1, f_2) drawn from the appropriate Gaussian. The ARPABET diphthongs "oy, aw, ay, em, en", and all the consonants, retain their discrete values. The first three words of the dataset, orthographically "you want to", are rendered: *y[380.53 1251.69] w[811.88 1431.96]n t[532.91 1094.14]*.

3.1 Model

Our model merges the Feldman et al. (2013a) vowel category learner with the Elsner et al. (2013) noisy-channel framework for word segmentation, which is in turn based on the segmentation model of Goldwater et al. (2009). In generative terms, it defines a sequential process for sampling a dataset. The observations will be surface strings S, which are divided into (latent) words $X_{i=1:n}$. We denote the j-th character of word i as S_{ij}. When S_{ij} is a vowel, the observed value is a real-valued formant pair (f_1, f_2); when it is a consonant, it is observed directly.

1. Draw a distribution over vowel categories, $\pi_v \sim DP(\alpha_v)$
2. Sample parameters for each category, $\mu_v, \Sigma_v \sim NIW(\mu_0, \Lambda, \nu)$
3. Draw a distribution over word strings, $G_0 \sim DP(\alpha_0, CV(\pi_v, p_c, p_{stop}))$
4. Draw bigram transition distributions, $G_x \sim DP(\alpha_1, G_0)$

5. Sample word sequences, $X_i \sim G_{X_{i-1}}$

6. Realize each vowel token in the surface string, $S_{ij} \sim Normal(\mu_{X_{ij}}, \Sigma_{X_{ij}})$

The initial prior over word forms, $CV(\pi_v, p_c, p_{stop})$ is the following: sample a word length ≥ 1 from $Geom(p_{stop})$; for each character in the word, choose to sample a consonant with probability p_c or a vowel otherwise; sample all consonants uniformly, and all vowels according to the (possibly-infinite) probability vector π_v.[1] In practice, we integrate out π_v, yielding a Chinese restaurant process in which the distribution over vowels in a new word depend on those used in already-seen words. Vowels which occur in many word types are more likely to recur (Goldwater et al., 2006; Teh et al., 2006).

The hyperparameters for the model are α_0 and α_1 (which control the size of the unigram and bigram vocabularies), α_v (which weakly affects the number of vowel categories), μ_0, n, Λ and ν (which affect the average location and dispersion of vowel categories in formant space), and p_c and p_{stop} (which weakly affect the length and composition of words). We set α_0 and α_1 to their optimal values for word segmentation (3000 and 100 (Goldwater et al., 2009)) and α_v to .001. In practice, no value of α_v we tried would produce a useful number of vowels and so we fix the maximum number of vowels (non-probabilistically) to n_v; we explore a variety of values of this parameter below. The mean vector for the vowel category parameters is set to $[500, 1500]$ and the inverse precision matrix to $500I$, biasing vowel categories to be near the center of the vowel space and have variances on the order of hundreds of hertz. We set the prior degrees of freedom ν to 2.001. Since ν can be interpreted as a pseudocount determining the prior strength, this means the prior influence is relatively weak for reasonably-sized vowel categories. We set $p_c = .5$ and $p_{stop} = .5$; based on Goldwater et al. (2009), we do not expect these parameters to be influential.

These hyperparameter values were mostly taken from previous work. The vowel inverse precision and degrees of freedom differ from those in Feldman et al. (2013a), since our approach requires us to sample from the prior, but the uninformative prior used there was too poor a fit for the data. We chose a variance with units on the order of the overall data variance, but did not tune it.

<hr>

[1]Feldman et al. (2013a) assumes a more complex distribution over consonants, while Goldwater et al. (2009) assumes uniformity over all sounds.

3.2 Inference

We conduct inference by Gibbs sampling, including three sampling moves: block sampling of the analyses of a single utterance, table label relabeling of a lexical item (Johnson and Goldwater, 2009) and resampling of the vowel category parameters μ_v and Σ_v. We run 1000 iterations of utterance resampling, with table relabeling every 10 iterations.[2] Following previous work, we integrate out the mixing weight distributions G_0, G_1 and π_v, resulting in Chinese restaurant process distributions for unigrams, bigrams and vowel categories in the lexicon (Teh et al., 2006). Unlike Feldman et al. (2013a) and many other variants of the Infinite Mixture of Gaussians (Rasmussen, 1999), we do not integrate out μ_v and Σ_v, since this would create long-distance dependencies between different tokens of the same vowel category within an utterance and thus complicate the implementation of a whole-utterance block sampling scheme.

To block sample the analyses of a single utterance, we use beam sampling (Van Gael et al., 2008; Huggins and Wood, 2014), an auxiliary-variable sampling scheme in which we encode the model as an (infeasibly large) finite-state transducer, then sample cutoff variables which restrict our algorithm to a finite subset of the transducer and sample a trajectory within it. We then use a Metropolis-Hastings acceptance test to correct for the discrepancy between our finite-state encoding and the actual model probability caused by repetitions of a lexical item within the same utterance.

Specifically, for each vowel s_{ij}, we sample a cutoff $c_{ij} \sim U[0, P(s_{ij}|X_{ij})]$. This cutoff indicates the least probable category assignment we will permit for the surface symbol s_{ij}. This cutoff constrains us to consider only a finite number of vowels at each point; if there are not enough, we can instantiate unseen vowels by sampling their μ and Σ from the prior. We then construct the lattice of possible word segmentations in which s_{ij} is allowed to correspond to any vowel in any lexical entry, as long as all the consonants match up and the vowel assignment density $P(s_{ij}|x_{ij})$ is greater than the cutoff. We then propose a new trajectory by sampling from this lattice. See Mochihashi et al.

<hr>

[2]Annealing is applied linearly, with inverse temperature scaling from .1 to 1 for 800 iterations, then linearly from 1.0 to 2.0 to encourage a MAP solution. The Gaussian densities for acoustic token emissions are annealed to inverse temperature .3, to keep them comparable to the LM probabilities (Bahl et al., 1980).

61

(2009) for details of the finite-state construction.

As in Feldman et al. (2013a), we use a table relabeling move (Johnson and Goldwater, 2009) which changes the word type for a single table in the unigram Chinese restaurant process by changing one of the vowels. This recategorizes a large number of tokens which share the same type (though not necessarily all, since there may be multiple unigram tables for the same word type). The implementation is tricky because of the bigram dependencies between adjacent words, some of which may be tokens of the same lexical item. Nonetheless, this move is necessary because token-level sampling has insufficient mobility to change the representation of a whole word type: if the sampler has incorrectly assigned many tokens to the non-word *hav*, moving any single token to the correct *hæv* will raise the transducer probability but also catastrophically lower the lexical probability by creating a singleton lexical item.

Finally, because μ_v and Σ_v are explicitly represented rather than integrated out, their values must be resampled given the set of formant values associated with each vowel cluster. The use of a conjugate (Normal-Inverse Wishart) prior makes this simple, applying equations 250-254 in Murphy (2007).

4 Results

Despite using multiple block moves, mobility is a severe issue for the sampler; the inference procedure fails to merge together redundant vowel categories even when doing so would raise the posterior probability significantly. We demonstrate this by running the sampler with various numbers of vowel categories n_v. Posterior probabilities peak around the true value of 12, but models with extra categories always use the entire set.

With n_v set to 11 or 12 categories, quantitative performance is relatively good, although segmentation is not as good as the Goldwater et al. (2009) segmenter without any acoustics. In fact, the system slightly outperforms the Feldman et al. (2013a) lexical-distributional model with gold-standard segmentation. Results are shown in Table 1.

Word tokens are correctly segmented (both boundaries correct) with an F-score of 67%[3] (versus 74% in (Goldwater et al., 2009). Individual boundaries are detected with an F-score of 82%

System	Seg P	R	F	Vow P	R	F
Goldwater	76	72	74	-	-	-
Feldman	-	-	-	-	-	76
joint, n_v=12	64	69	67	87	80	83
joint, n_v=11	65	70	67	85	84	85

Table 1: Segmentation and vowel clustering scores.

versus 87%. We also evaluate the lexical items, checking whether words are correctly grouped as well as segmented (for example, whether tokens of "is" and "as" are separated). Feldman et al. (2013a) evaluates the lexicon by computing a pairwise F-score on tokens (positive class: clustered together). Under this metric, their highest lexicon score for English words is 93%. We compute this metric on the subset of words for which the segmentation system performs correctly (it is not clear how to count "misses" and "false alarms" for tokens which were mis-segmented). On this subset, this metric scores our system with $n_v = 12$ at 91%, which indicates that we correctly identify most of the correctly segmented items.

We evaluate our phonetic clustering by computing the same pairwise F-score on pairs of vowel tokens. Our score is 83%; the Feldman et al. (2013a) model scores 76%. We conjecture that the improvement results from the use of bigram context information to disambiguate between homophones. Confusion between vowels (attached as supplemental material) is mostly reasonable. We find cross-clusters for *ah,ao*, *ey,ih*, and *uh,uw*. The model's successful learning of the vowel categories demonstrates that the high performance of cognitive models in this domain is not due solely to their access to gold-standard word boundaries (see also Martin et al. (2013)). We believe that the idealized acoustic values (sampled from stationary Gaussians reflecting laboratory production) are critical in allowing these models to outperform those which use natural speech.

Though solving the two tasks together is harder than tackling either alone, these results nonetheless demonstrate comparable performance to other models which have to cope with variability while segmenting. Fleck (2008) reports only 44% segmentation scores on transcribed English text including phonological variability; the noisy channel model of Elsner et al. (2013) yields a segmentation token score of 67%.[4]

Besides generic task difficulty, we attribute the

---

[3]The joint model scores are averaged over two sampler runs.

[4]Word segmentation scores from Lee et al. (2015), learning directly on acoustics, range between 16 and 20.

low scores to the model's inability to mix, which prevents it from merging similar vowel classes. Because table relabeling does not merge tables in the CRP hierarchy, even if it replaces an uncommon word with a more common one, the configurational probability does not change. Thus the model's sparsity preference cannot encourage such moves. The prior on vowel categories, $DP(p_v)$, does encourage changes which reduce the number of lexical types using a rare vowel, but relabeling a table can rearrange at most a single sample from this prior distribution and is easily outweighed by the likelihood.

A hand analysis of one sampler run in which $/\textsc{i}/$ was split into two categories showed clear mixing problems. Many common words, such as "it" and "this", appeared as duplicate lexical entries (e.g. $[\textsc{i}_1 t]$ and $[\textsc{i}_2 t]$). These presumably captured some chance variation within the category, but not an actual linguistic feature.

We suspect that this mobility problem is also a likely issue with models like Lee and Glass (2012) which use deep Bayesian hierarchies and relatively local inference moves. Since the problem occurs even in this idealized setting, we expect it to exacerbate the problems caused by contextual variability in more realistic experiments.

Some errors did result from the joint nature of the task itself. We looked for reanalyses involving both a mis-segmentation and a vowel category mistake. For instance, the model is capable of misanalyzing the word "milk" as "me" followed by the phonotactically implausible sequence "lk". Mistakes like these, in which the misanalysis creates a word, are relatively rare as a proportion of the total. The most common words created are "say", "and", "shoe", "it" and "a". More commonly, misanalyses of this type segment out single vowels or nonwords like *[luk]*, *[eŋ]*, and *[mɔ]*. Some such errors could be corrected by incorporating phonotactics into the model (Johnson and Goldwater, 2009). In general, the error patterns are neither particularly interpretable nor cognitively very plausible. This stands in contrast to the effects on word boundary detection found in a model of phonological variation (Elsner et al., 2013).

5 Conclusion

The main result of our work is that joint word segmentation and vowel clustering is possible, with relatively high effectiveness, by merging models known to be successful in each setting independently. The finding that success of this kind is possible in an idealized setting reinforces an argument made in previous work: that much of the difficulty in category acquisition is due to contextual variation.

Both phonological and phonetic variability probably contribute to the difficulty of the real task. Phonological processes such as reduction create variant versions of words, splitting real lexical items and creating misleading minimal pairs. Phonetic processes like coarticulation and compensatory lengthening create predictable variation within a category, encouraging the model to split the category into allophones. In future work, we hope to quantify the contributions of these sources of error and work to address them explicitly within the same model.

Acknowledgements

This research was funded by NSF grants 1422987 and 1421695. We are grateful for the advice of three anonymous reviewers, and to Sharon Goldwater for distributing the baseline DPSeg system.

References

Leonardo Badino, Claudia Canevari, Luciano Fadiga, and Giorgio Metta. 2014. An auto-encoder based approach to unsupervised learning of subword units. In *Acoustics, Speech and Signal Processing (ICASSP), 2014 IEEE International Conference on*, pages 7634–7638. IEEE.

Lalit Bahl, Raimo Bakis, Frederick Jelinek, and Robert Mercer. 1980. Language model/acoustic channel model balance mechanism. Technical disclosure bulletin Vol. 23, No. 7b, IBM, December.

Nan Bernstein-Ratner. 1987. The phonology of parent-child speech. In K. Nelson and A. van Kleeck, editors, *Children's Language*, volume 6. Erlbaum, Hillsdale, NJ.

Michael R. Brent. 1999. An efficient, probabilistically sound algorithm for segmentation and word discovery. *Machine Learning*, 34:71–105, February.

Robert Daland and Janet B. Pierrehumbert. 2011. Learning diphone-based segmentation. *Cognitive Science*, 35(1):119–155.

Bart de Boer and Patricia Kuhl. 2003. Investigating the role of infant-directed speech with a computer model. *Acoustic Research Letters On-Line*, 4:129–134.

Micha Elsner, Sharon Goldwater, Naomi Feldman, and Frank Wood. 2013. A joint learning model of word segmentation, lexical acquisition, and phonetic variability. In *Proceedings of the 2013 Conference on Empirical Methods in Natural Language Processing*, pages 42–54, Seattle, Washington, USA, October. Association for Computational Linguistics.

Naomi H. Feldman, Thomas L. Griffiths, Sharon Goldwater, and James L. Morgan. 2013a. A role for the developing lexicon in phonetic category acquisition. *Psychological Review*, 4:751–778.

Naomi H. Feldman, Emily B. Myers, Katherine S. White, Thomas L. Griffiths, and James L. Morgan. 2013b. Word-level information influences phonetic learning in adults and infants. *Cognition*, 127(3):427–438.

Margaret M. Fleck. 2008. Lexicalized phonotactic word segmentation. In *Proceedings of ACL-08: HLT*, pages 130–138, Columbus, Ohio, June. Association for Computational Linguistics.

Stella Frank, Naomi Feldman, and Sharon Goldwater. 2014. Weak semantic context helps phonetic learning in a model of infant language acquisition. In *ACL (1)*, pages 1073–1083.

Sharon Goldwater, Thomas L. Griffiths, and Mark Johnson. 2006. Contextual dependencies in unsupervised word segmentation. In *Proceedings of the 21st International Conference on Computational Linguistics and 44th Annual Meeting of the Association for Computational Linguistics*, pages 673–680, Sydney, Australia, July. Association for Computational Linguistics.

Sharon Goldwater, Thomas L. Griffiths, and Mark Johnson. 2009. A Bayesian framework for word segmentation: Exploring the effects of context. *Cognition*, 112(1):21–54.

James Hillenbrand, Laura A. Getty, Michael J. Clark, and Kimberlee Wheeler. 1995. Acoustic characteristics of American English vowels. *The Journal of the Acoustical society of America*, 97:3099.

Jonathan Huggins and Frank Wood. 2014. Infinite structured hidden semi-Markov models. *arXiv preprint arXiv:1407.0044*, June.

Aren Jansen and Kenneth Church. 2011. Towards unsupervised training of speaker independent acoustic models. In *INTERSPEECH*, pages 1693–1692.

Mark Johnson and Sharon Goldwater. 2009. Improving nonparametric Bayesian inference: Experiments on unsupervised word segmentation with adaptor grammars. In *Proceedings of Human Language Technologies: The 2009 Annual Conference of the North American Chapter of the Association for Computational Linguistics*, Boulder, Colorado.

Peter Ladefoged and Keith Johnson. 2010. *A course in phonetics*. Wadsworth Publishing.

Chia-ying Lee and James Glass. 2012. A nonparametric Bayesian approach to acoustic model discovery. In *Proceedings of the 50th Annual Meeting of the Association for Computational Linguistics (Volume 1: Long Papers)*, pages 40–49, Jeju Island, Korea, July. Association for Computational Linguistics.

Chia-ying Lee, Timothy J O'Donnell, and James Glass. 2015. Unsupervised lexicon discovery from acoustic input. *Transactions of the Association for Computational Linguistics*, 3:389–403.

Andrew Martin, Sharon Peperkamp, and Emmanuel Dupoux. 2013. Learning phonemes with a proto-lexicon. *Cognitive Science*, 37:103–124.

Don McAllaster, Lawrence Gillick, Francesco Scattone, and Michael Newman. 1998. Fabricating conversational speech data with acoustic models: a program to examine model-data mismatch. In *ICSLP*.

Daichi Mochihashi, Takeshi Yamada, and Naonori Ueda. 2009. Bayesian unsupervised word segmentation with nested pitman-yor language modeling. In *Proceedings of the Joint Conference of the 47th Annual Meeting of the ACL and the 4th International Joint Conference on Natural Language Processing of the AFNLP*, pages 100–108, Suntec, Singapore, August. Association for Computational Linguistics.

Kevin Murphy. 2007. Conjugate Bayesian analysis of the gaussian distribution. Technical report, University of British Columbia.

Graham Neubig, Masato Mimura, Shinsuke Mori, and Tatsuya Kawahara. 2010. Learning a language model from continuous speech. In *11th Annual Conference of the International Speech Communication Association (InterSpeech 2010)*, pages 1053–1056, Makuhari, Japan, 9.

Mark A. Pitt, Keith Johnson, Elizabeth Hume, Scott Kiesling, and William Raymond. 2005. The Buckeye corpus of conversational speech: labeling conventions and a test of transcriber reliability. *Speech Communication*, 45(1):89–95.

Carl Edward Rasmussen. 1999. The infinite Gaussian mixture model. In *NIPS*, volume 12, pages 554–560.

Anton Rytting, Chris Brew, and Eric Fosler-Lussier. 2010. Segmenting words from natural speech: subsegmental variation in segmental cues. *Journal of Child Language*, 37(3):513–543.

Y. W. Teh, M. I. Jordan, M. J. Beal, and D. M. Blei. 2006. Hierarchical Dirichlet processes. *Journal of the American Statistical Association*, 101(476):1566–1581.

Gautam K. Vallabha, James L. McClelland, Ferran Pons, Janet F. Werker, and Shigeaki Amano. 2007. Unsupervised learning of vowel categories from infant-directed speech. *Proceedings of the National Academy of Sciences*, 104(33):13273–13278.

Jurgen Van Gael, Yunus Saatci, Yee Whye Teh, and Zoubin Ghahramani. 2008. Beam sampling for the infinite Hidden Markov model. In *Proceedings of the 25th International Conference on Machine learning*, ICML '08, pages 1088–1095, New York, NY, USA. ACM.

Balakrishnan Varadarajan, Sanjeev Khudanpur, and Emmanuel Dupoux. 2008. Unsupervised learning of acoustic sub-word units. In *Proceedings of the Association for Computational Linguistics: Short Papers*, pages 165–168.

A Language-Independent Neural Network for Event Detection

Xiaocheng Feng[1], Lifu Huang[2], Duyu Tang[1], Bing Qin[1], Heng Ji[2], Ting Liu[1]
[1] Harbin Institute of Technology, Harbin, China
{$xcfeng, dytang, qinb, tliu$}@ir.hit.edu.cn
[2] Rensselaer Polytechnic Institute, Troy, USA
{$huangl7, jih$}@rpi.edu

Abstract

Event detection remains a challenge due to the difficulty at encoding the word semantics in various contexts. Previous approaches heavily depend on language-specific knowledge and pre-existing natural language processing (NLP) tools. However, compared to English, not all languages have such resources and tools available. A more promising approach is to automatically learn effective features from data, without relying on language-specific resources. In this paper, we develop a hybrid neural network to capture both sequence and chunk information from specific contexts, and use them to train an event detector for multiple languages without any manually encoded features. Experiments show that our approach can achieve robust, efficient and accurate results for multiple languages (English, Chinese and Spanish).

1 Introduction

Event detection aims to extract event triggers (most often a single verb or noun) and classify them into specific types precisely. It is a crucial and quite challenging sub-task of event extraction, because the same event might appear in the form of various trigger expressions and an expression might represent different event types in different contexts. Figure 1 shows two examples. In S1, *"release"* is a verb concept and a trigger for *"Transfer-Money"* event, while in S2, *"release"* is a noun concept and a trigger for *"Release-Parole"* event.

Most of previous methods (Ji et al., 2008; Liao et al., 2010; Hong et al., 2011; Li et al., 2013; Li et al., 2015b) considered event detection as a classi-

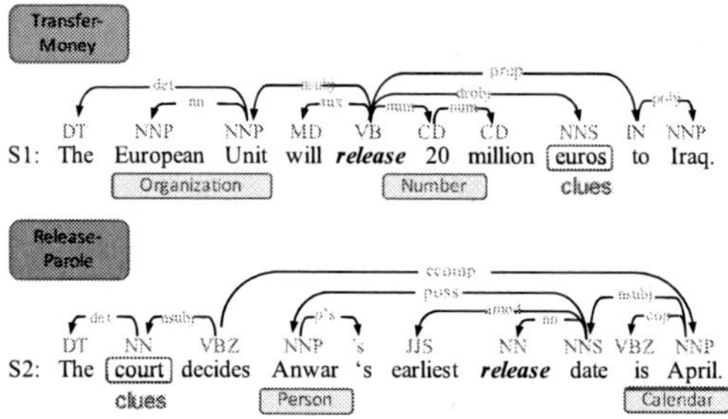

Figure 1: Event type and syntactic parser results of an example sentence.

fication problem and designed a lot of lexical and syntactic features. Although such approaches perform reasonably well, features are often derived from language-specific resources and the output of pre-existing natural language processing toolkits (e,g., name tagger and dependency parser), which makes these methods difficult to be applied to different languages. Sequence and chunk are two types of meaningful language-independent structures for event detection. For example, in S2, when predicting the type of a trigger candidate " *release*", the forward sequence information such as "court" can help the classifier label *"release"* as a trigger of a *"Release-Parole"* event. However, for feature engineering methods, it is hard to establish a relation between "court" and "release", because there is no direct dependency path between them. In addition, considering S1, "European Union" and "20 million euros" are two chunks, which indicate that this sentence is related to an organization and financial activities. These cluese are very helpful to infer *"release"* as a trigger of a *"Transfer-Money"* event. However, chunkers and parsers are only available for a few high-resource languages and their performance varies a lot.

Proceedings of the 54th Annual Meeting of the Association for Computational Linguistics, pages 66–71,
Berlin, Germany, August 7-12, 2016. ©2016 Association for Computational Linguistics

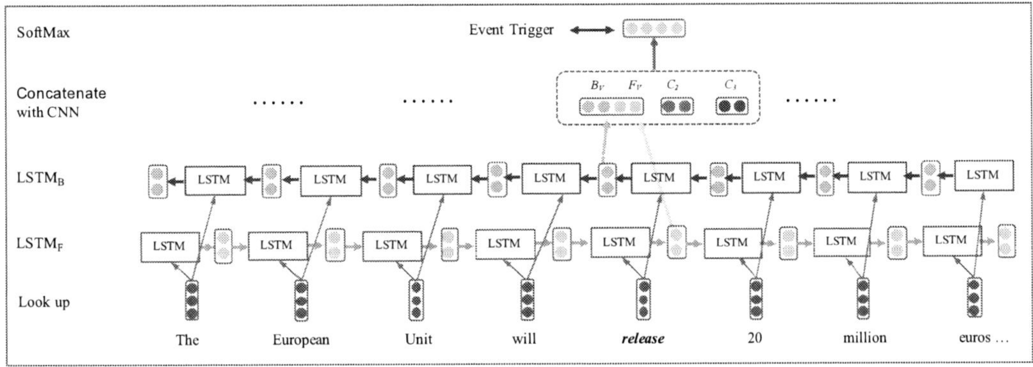

Figure 2: An illustration of our model for event trigger extraction (here the trigger candidate is "*release*"). F_v and B_v are the output of Bi-LSTM and C_2, C_3 are the output of CNN with convolutional filters with widths of 2 and 3.

Recently, deep learning techniques have been widely used in modeling complex structures and proven effective for many NLP tasks, such as machine translation (Bahdanau et al., 2014), relation extraction (Zeng et al., 2014) and sentiment analysis (Tang et al., 2015a). Bi-directional long short-term memory (Bi-LSTM) model (Schuster et al., 1997) is a two-way recurrent neural network (RNN) (Mikolov et al., 2010) which can capture both the preceding and following context information of each word. Convolutional neural network (CNN) (LeCun et al., 1995) is another effective model for extracting semantic representations and capturing salient features in a flat structure (Liu et al., 2015), such as chunks. In this work, we develop a hybrid neural network incorporating two types of neural networks: Bi-LSTM and CNN, to model both sequence and chunk information from specific contexts. Taking advantage of word semantic representation, our model can get rid of hand-crafted features and thus be easily adapted to multiple languages.

We evaluate our system on the event detection task for various languages for which ground-truth event detection annotations are available. In English event detection task, our approach achieved 73.4% F-score with average 3.0% absolute improvement compared to state-of-the-art. For Chinese and Spanish, the experiment results are also competitive. We demonstrate that our combined model outperforms traditional feature-based methods with respect to generalization performance across languages due to: (i) its capacity to model semantic representations of each word by capturing both sequence and chunk information. (ii) the use of word embeddings to induce a more general representation for trigger candidates.

2 Our Approach

In this section, we introduce a hybrid neural networks, which combines Bi-directional LSTM (Bi-LSTM) and convolutional neural networks to learn a continuous representation for each word in a sentence. This representation is used to predict whether the word is an event trigger or not. Specifically, we first use a Bi-LSTM to encode semantics of each word with its preceding and following information. Then, we add a convolutional neural network to capture structure information from local contexts.

2.1 Bi-LSTM

In this section we describe a Bidirectional LSTM model for event detection. Bi-LSTM is a type of bidirectional recurrent neural networks (RNN), which can simultaneously model word representation with its preceding and following information. Word representations can be naturally considered as features to detect triggers and their event types. As show in (Chen et al., 2015), we take all the words of the whole sentence as the input and each token is transformed by looking up word embeddings. Specifically, we use the Skip-Gram model to pre-train the word embeddings to represent each word (Mikolov et al., 2013; Bahdanau et al., 2014).

We present the details of Bi-LSTM for event trigger extraction in Figure 2. We can see that Bi-LSTM is composed of two LSTM neural networks, a forward LSTM$_F$ to model the preced-

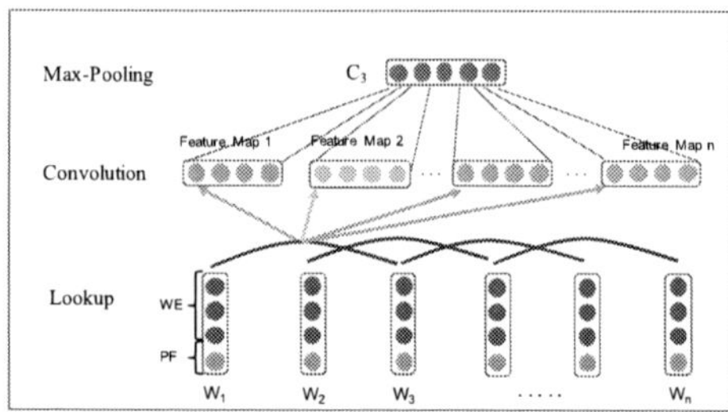

Figure 3: CNN structure.

ing contexts, and a backward LSTM_B to model the following contexts respectively. The input of LSTM_F is the preceding contexts along with the word as trigger candidate, and the input of LSTM_B is the following contexts plus the word as trigger candidate. We run LSTM_F from the beginning to the end of a sentence, and run LSTM_B from the end to the beginning of a sentence. Afterwards, we concatenate the output F_v of LSTM_F and B_v of LSTM_B as the output of Bi-LSTM. One could also try averaging or summing the last hidden vectors of LSTM_F and LSTM_B as alternatives.

2.2 Convolution Neural Network

As the convolutional neural network (CNN) is good at capturing salient features from a sequence of objects (Liu et al., 2015), we design a CNN to capture some local chunks. This approach has been used for event detection in previous studies (Nguyen and Grishman, 2015; Chen et al., 2015). Specifically, we use multiple convolutional filters with different widths to produce local context representation. The reason is that they are capable of capturing local semantics of n-grams of various granularities, which are proven powerful for event detection. In our work, multiple convolutional filters with widths of 2 and 3 encode the semantics of bigrams and trigrams in a sentence. This local information can also help our model fix some errors due to lexical ambiguity.

An illustration of CNN with three convolutional filters is given in Figure 3. Let us denote a sentence consisting of n words as $\{w_1, w_2, ...w_i, ...w_n\}$, and each word w_i is mapped to its embedding representation $e_i \in \mathbb{R}^d$. In addition, we add a position feature (PF), which is defined as the relative distance between the current word and the trigger candidate. A convolutional filter is a list of linear layers with shared parameters. We feed the output of a convolutional filter to a MaxPooling layer and obtain an output

vector with fixed length.

2.3 Output

At the end, we concatenate the bidirectional sequence features: F and B, which are learned from the Bi-LSTM, and local context features: C_2 and C_3, which are the output of CNN with convolutional filters with width of 2 and 3, as a single vector $O = [F, B, C_2, C_3]$. Then, we exploit a softmax approach to identify trigger candidates and classify each trigger candidate as a specific event type.

2.4 Training

In our model, the loss function is the cross-entropy error of event trigger identification and trigger classification. We initialize all parameters to form a uniform distribution $U(-0.01, 0.01)$. We set the widths of convolutional filters as 2 and 3. The number of feature maps is 300 and the dimension of the PF is 5. Table 1 illustrates the setting parameters used for three languages in our experiments (Zeiler, 2012).

3 Experiments

In this section, we will describe the detailed experimental settings and discuss the results. We evaluate the proposed approach on various languages (English, Chinese and Spanish) with Precision (P), Recall (R) and F-measure (F). Table 1 shows the detailed description of the data sets used in our experiments. We abbreviate our model as HNN (Hybrid Neural Networks).

3.1 Baseline Methods

We compare our approach with the following baseline methods.

(1) *MaxEnt*, a basesline feature-based method, which trains a Maximum Entropy classifier with some lexical and syntactic features (Ji et al., 2008).

(2) *Cross-Event* (Liao et al., 2010), using document-level information to improve the performance of ACE event extraction.

(3) *Cross-Entity* (Hong et al., 2011), extracting events using cross-entity inference.

(4) *Joint Model* (Li and Ji, 2014), a joint structured perception approach, incorporating multi-level linguistic features to extract event triggers and arguments at the same time so that local predictions can be mutually improved.

Language	Word Embedding		Gradient Learning Method		Data Sets			
	corpus	dim	method	parameters	Corpus	Train	Dev	Test
English	NYT	300	SGD	learning rate $r = 0.03$	ACE2005	529	30	40
Chinese	Gigaword	300	Adadelta	$p = 0.95, \delta = 1e^{-6}$	ACE2005	513	60	60
Spanish	Gigaword	300	Adadelta	$p = 0.95, \delta = 1e^{-6}$	ERE	93	12	12

Table 1: Hyperparameters and # of documents used in our experiments on three languages.

Model	Trigger Identification			Trigger Classification		
	P	R	F	P	R	F
MaxEnt	76.2	60.5	67.4	74.5	59.1	65.9
Cross-Event	N/A	N/A	N/A	68.7	68.9	68.8
Cross-Entity	N/A	N/A	N/A	72.9	64.3	68.3
Joint Model	76.9	65.0	70.4	73.7	62.3	67.5
PR	N/A	N/A	N/A	68.9	**72.0**	70.4
CNN	80.4	67.7	73.5	75.6	63.6	69.1
RNN	73.2	63.5	67.4	67.3	59.9	64.2
LSTM	78.6	67.4	72.6	74.5	60.7	66.9
Bi-LSTM	80.1	69.4	74.3	81.6	62.3	70.6
HNN	**80.8**	**71.5**	**75.9**	**84.6**	64.9	**73.4**

Table 2: Comparison of different methods on English event detection.

(5) *Pattern Recognition* (Miao and Grishman, 2015), using a pattern expansion technique to extract event triggers.

(6) *Convolutional Neural Network* (Chen et al., 2015), which exploits a dynamic multi-pooling convolutional neural network for event trigger detection.

3.2 Comparison On English

Table 2 shows the overall performance of all methods on the ACE2005 English corpus. We can see that our approach significantly outperforms all previous methods. The better performance of HNN can be further explained by the following reasons: (1) Compared with feature based methods, such as *MaxEnt*, *Cross-Event*, *Cross-Entity*, and *Joint Model*, neural network based methods (including *CNN*, *Bi-LSTM*, *HNN*) performs better because they can make better use of word semantic information and avoid the errors propagated from NLP tools which may hinder the performance for event detection. (2) Moreover, *Bi-LSTM* can capture both preceding and following sequence information, which is much richer than dependency path. For example, in S2, the semantic of "court" can be delivered to release by a forward sequence in our approach. It is an important clue which can help to predict "release" as a trigger for "*Release-Parole*". For explicit feature based methods, they can not establish a relation between "court" and "release", because they belong to different clauses,

and there is no direct dependency path between them. While in our approach, the semantics of "court" can be delivered to release by a forward sequence. (3) *Cross-entity* system achieves higher recall because it uses not only sentence-level information but also document-level information. It utilizes event concordance to predict a local trigger's event type based on cross-sentence inference. For example, an "attack" event is more likely to occur with "killed" or "die" event rather than "marry" event. However, this method heavily relies on lexical and syntactic features, thus the precision is lower than neural network based methods. (4) *RNN* and *LSTM* perform slightly worse than Bi-LSTM. An obvious reason is that *RNN* and *LSTM* only consider the preceding sequence information of the trigger, which may miss some important following clues. Considering S1 again, when extracting the trigger "*releases*", both models will miss the following sequence "20 million euros to Iraq". This may seriously hinder the performance of RNN and LSTM for event detection.

3.3 Comparison on Chinese

For Chinese, we follow previous work (Chen et al., 2012) and employ Language Technology Platform (Liu et al., 2011) to do word segmentation.

Table 3 shows the comparison results between our model and the state-of-the-art methods (Li et al., 2013; Chen et al., 2012). *MaxEnt* (Li et al., 2013) is a pipeline model, which employs human-designed lexical and syntactic features. *Rich-C* is developed by Chen et al. (2012), which also incorporates Chinese-specific features to improve Chinese event detection. We can see that our method outperforms methods based on human designed features for event trigger identification and achieves comparable F-score for event classification.

3.4 Spanish Extraction

Table 4 presents the performance of our method on the Spanish ERE corpus. The results show that

Model	Trigger Identification			Trigger Classification		
	P	R	F	P	R	F
MaxEnt	50.0	**77.0**	60.6	47.5	73.1	57.6
Rich-C	62.2	71.9	66.7	58.9	**68.1**	**63.2**
HNN	**74.2**	63.1	**68.2**	**77.1**	53.1	63.0

Table 3: Results on Chinese event detection.

HNN approach performed better than LSTM and Bi-LSTM. It indicates that our proposed model could achieve the best performance in multiple languages than other neural network methods. We did not compare our system with other systems (Tanev et al., 2009), because they reported the results on a non-standard data set .

Model	Trigger Identification			Trigger Classification		
	P	R	F	P	R	F
LSTM	62.2	52.9	57.2	56.9	32.6	41.6
Bi-LSTM	76.2	63.1	68.7	61.5	42.2	50.1
HNN	**81.4**	**65.2**	**71.6**	**66.3**	**47.8**	**55.5**

Table 4: Results on Spanish event detection.

4 Related Work

Event detection is a fundamental problem in information extraction and natural language processing (Li et al., 2013; Chen et al., 2015), which aims at detecting the event trigger of a sentence (Ji et al., 2008). The majority of existing methods regard this problem as a classification task, and use machine learning methods with hand-crafted features, such as lexical features (e.g., full word, pos tag), syntactic features (e.g., dependency features) and external knowledge features (WordNet). There also exists some studies leveraging richer evidences like cross-document (Ji et al., 2008), cross-entity (Hong et al., 2011) and joint inference (Li and Ji, 2014).

Despite the effectiveness of feature-based methods, we argue that manually designing feature templates is typically labor intensive. Besides, feature engineering requires expert knowledge and rich external resources, which is not always available for some low-resource languages. Furthermore, a desirable approach should have the ability to automatically learn informative representations from data, so that it could be easily adapted to different languages. Recently, neural network emerges as a powerful way to learn text representation automatically from data and has obtained promising performances in a variety of NLP tasks.

For event detection, two recent studies (Nguyen and Grishman, 2015; Chen et al., 2015) explore neural network to learn continuous word representation and regard it as the feature to infer whether a word is a trigger or not. Nguyen (2015) presented a convolutional neural network with entity type information and word position information as extra features. However, their system limits the context to a fixed window size which leads the loss of word semantic representation for long sentences.

We introduce a hybrid neural network to learn continuous word representation. Compared with feature-based approaches, the method here does not require feature engineering and could be directly applied to different languages. Compared with previous neural models, we keep the advantage of convolutional neural network (Nguyen and Grishman, 2015) in capturing local contexts. Besides, we also incorporate a Bi-directional LSTM to model the preceding and following information of a word as it has been commonly accepted that LSTM is good at capturing long-term dependencies in a sequence (Tang et al., 2015b; Li et al., 2015a).

5 Conclusions

In this work, We introduce a hybrid neural network model, which incorporates both bidirectional LSTMs and convolutional neural networks to capture sequence and structure semantic information from specific contexts, for event detection. Compared with traditional event detection methods, our approach does not rely on any linguistic resources, thus can be easily applied to any languages. We conduct experiments on various languages (English, Chinese and Spanish. Empirical results show our approach achieved state-of-the-art performance in English and competitive results in Chinese. We also find that bi-directional LSTM is powerful for trigger extraction in capturing preceding and following contexts in long distance.

6 Acknowledgments

The authors give great thanks to Ying Lin (RPI) and Shen Liu for (HIT) the fruitful discussions. We also would like to thank three anonymous reviewers for their valuable comments and suggestions. RPI co-authors were supported by the U.S. DARPA LORELEI Program No. HR0011-15-C-0115, DARPA DEFT Program No. FA8750-13-2-0041 and NSF CAREER Award IIS-1523198.

References

Dzmitry Bahdanau, Kyunghyun Cho, and Yoshua Bengio. 2014. Neural machine translation by jointly learning to align and translate. *arXiv preprint arXiv:1409.0473*.

Chen Chen, V Incent Ng, and et al. 2012. Joint modeling for chinese event extraction with rich linguistic features. In *In COLING*. Citeseer.

Yubo Chen, Liheng Xu, Kang Liu, Daojian Zeng, and Jun Zhao. 2015. Event extraction via dynamic multi-pooling convolutional neural networks. In *Proceedings of the 53rd Annual Meeting of the Association for Computational Linguistics and the 7th International Joint Conference on Natural Language Processing*, volume 1, pages 167–176.

Yu Hong, Jianfeng Zhang, Bin Ma, Jianmin Yao, Guodong Zhou, and Qiaoming Zhu. 2011. Using cross-entity inference to improve event extraction. In *Proceedings of the 49th Annual Meeting of the Association for Computational Linguistics: Human Language Technologies-Volume 1*, pages 1127–1136. Association for Computational Linguistics.

Heng Ji, Ralph Grishman, and et al. 2008. Refining event extraction through cross-document inference. In *ACL*, pages 254–262.

Yann LeCun, Yoshua Bengio, and et al. 1995. Convolutional networks for images, speech, and time series. *The handbook of brain theory and neural networks*, 3361(10).

Qi Li and Heng Ji. 2014. Incremental joint extraction of entity mentions and relations. In *Proceedings of the Association for Computational Linguistics*.

Qi Li, Heng Ji, and Liang Huang. 2013. Joint event extraction via structured prediction with global features. In *ACL (1)*, pages 73–82.

Jiwei Li, Dan Jurafsky, and Eudard Hovy. 2015a. When are tree structures necessary for deep learning of representations? *arXiv preprint arXiv:1503.00185*.

Jiwei Li, Minh-Thang Luong, and Dan Jurafsky. 2015b. A hierarchical neural autoencoder for paragraphs and documents. *arXiv preprint arXiv:1506.01057*.

Shasha Liao, Ralph Grishman, and et al. 2010. Using document level cross-event inference to improve event extraction. In *Proceedings of the 48th Annual Meeting of the Association for Computational Linguistics*, pages 789–797. Association for Computational Linguistics.

Ting Liu, Wanxiang Che, and Zhenghua Li. 2011. Language technology platform. *Journal of Chinese Information Processing*, 25(6):53–62.

Yang Liu, Furu Wei, Sujian Li, Heng Ji, Ming Zhou, and Houfeng Wang. 2015. A dependency-based neural network for relation classification. *arXiv preprint arXiv:1507.04646*.

Fan Miao and Ralph Grishman. 2015. Improving event detection with active learning. In *EMNLP*.

Tomas Mikolov, Martin Karafiát, Lukas Burget, Jan Cernocký, and Sanjeev Khudanpur. 2010. Recurrent neural network based language model. In *INTERSPEECH*, volume 2, page 3.

Tomas Mikolov, Ilya Sutskever, Kai Chen, Greg S Corrado, and Jeff Dean. 2013. Distributed representations of words and phrases and their compositionality. In *Advances in neural information processing systems*, pages 3111–3119.

Thien Huu Nguyen and Ralph Grishman. 2015. Event detection and domain adaptation with convolutional neural networks. *Volume 2: Short Papers*, page 365.

Mike Schuster, Kuldip K Paliwal, and et al. 1997. Bidirectional recurrent neural networks. *Signal Processing, IEEE Transactions on*, 45(11):2673–2681.

Hristo Tanev, Vanni Zavarella, Jens Linge, Mijail Kabadjov, Jakub Piskorski, Martin Atkinson, and Ralf Steinberger. 2009. Exploiting machine learning techniques to build an event extraction system for portuguese and spanish. *Linguamática*, 1(2):55–66.

Duyu Tang, Bing Qin, and Ting Liu. 2015a. Document modeling with gated recurrent neural network for sentiment classification. EMNLP.

Duyu Tang, Bing Qin, and Ting Liu. 2015b. Document modeling with gated recurrent neural network for sentiment classification. In *Proceedings of the 2015 Conference on Empirical Methods in Natural Language Processing*, pages 1422–1432.

Matthew D Zeiler. 2012. Adadelta: an adaptive learning rate method. *arXiv preprint arXiv:1212.5701*.

Daojian Zeng, Kang Liu, Siwei Lai, Guangyou Zhou, Jun Zhao, et al. 2014. Relation classification via convolutional deep neural network. In *COLING*, pages 2335–2344.

Improved Parsing for Argument-Clusters Coordination

Jessica Ficler
Computer Science Department
Bar-Ilan University
Israel
jessica.ficler@gmail.com

Yoav Goldberg
Computer Science Department
Bar-Ilan University
Israel
yoav.goldbreg@gmail.com

Abstract

Syntactic parsers perform poorly in prediction of Argument-Cluster Coordination (ACC). We change the PTB representation of ACC to be more suitable for learning by a statistical PCFG parser, affecting 125 trees in the training set. Training on the modified trees yields a slight improvement in EVALB scores on sections 22 and 23. The main evaluation is on a corpus of 4th grade science exams, in which ACC structures are prevalent. On this corpus, we obtain an impressive $\times 2.7$ improvement in recovering ACC structures compared to a parser trained on the original PTB trees.

1 Introduction

Many natural language processing systems make use of syntactic representations of sentences. These representations are produced by parsers, which often produce incorrect analyses. Many of the mistakes are in coordination structures, and structures involving non-constituent coordination, such as Argument Cluster Coordination, Right Node-Raising and Gapping (Dowty, 1988), are especially hard.

Coordination is a common syntactic phenomena and work has been done to improve coordination structures predication in the general case (Hogan, 2007; Hara et al., 2009; Shimbo and Hara, 2007; Okuma et al., 2009). In this work we focus on one particular coordination structure: Argument Cluster Coordination (ACC). While ACC are not common in the Penn TreeBank (Marcus et al., 1993), they commonly appear in other corpora. For example, in a dataset of questions from the Regents 4th grade science exam (the Aristo Challenge), 14% of the sentences include ACC.

ACC is characterized by non-constituent sequences that are parallel in structure. For instance, in *"I bought John a microphone on Monday and Richie a guitar on Saturday"*, the conjunction is between *"John a microphone on Monday"* and *"Richie a guitar on Saturday"* which are both non-constituents and include parallel arguments: the NPs *"John"* and *"Richie"*; the NPs *"a microphone"* and *"a guitar"*; and the PPs *"on Monday"* and *"on Saturday"*.

Previous NLP research on the Argument Clusters Coordination (Mouret, 2006) as well as the Penn TreeBank annotation guidelines (Marcus et al., 1993; Bies et al., 1995) focused mainly on providing representation schemes capable of expressing the linguistic nuances that may appear in such coordinations. The resulting representations are relatively complex, and are not easily learnable by current day parsers, including parsers that refine the grammar by learning latent annotations (Petrov et al., 2006), which are thought to be more agnostic to the annotations scheme of the trees. In this work, we suggest an alternative, simpler representation scheme which is capable of representing most of the Argument Cluster coordination cases in the Penn Treebank, and is better suited for training a parser. We show that by changing the annotation of 125 trees, we get a parser which is substantially better at handling ACC structures, and is also marginally better at parsing general sentences.

2 Arguments Cluster Coordination in the Penn Tree Bank

Argument Cluster Coordinations are represented in the PTB with two or more conjoined VPs, where the first VP contains a verb and indexed arguments, and the rest of the VPs lack a verb and include arguments with indices corresponding to

Proceedings of the 54th Annual Meeting of the Association for Computational Linguistics, pages 72–76,
Berlin, Germany, August 7-12, 2016. ©2016 Association for Computational Linguistics

those of the first conjoined VP. For example, consider the PTB representation of *"The Q ratio was only 65% in 1987 and 68.9% in 1988"*:

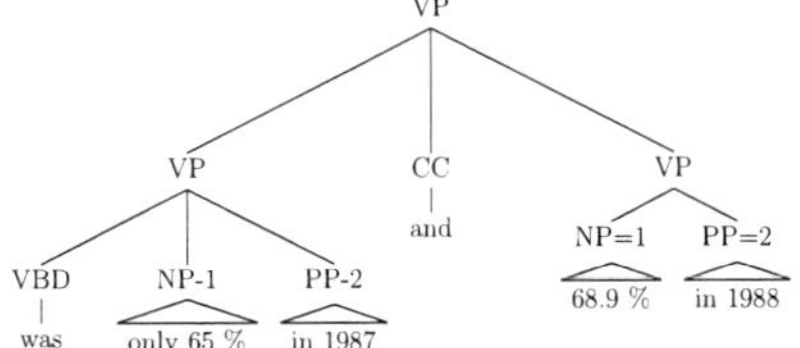

The main VP includes two conjoined VPs. The first VP includes the verb *was* and two indexed arguments: *"only 65%"* (1) and *"in 1987"* (2). The second VP does not include a verb, but only two arguments, that are co-indexed with the parallel argument at the first conjoined VP.

ACC structures in the PTB may include modifiers that are annotated under the main VP, and the conjoined VPs may includes arguments that are not part of the cluster. These are annotated with no index, i.e. *"insurance costs"* in [1a].

ACC structures are not common in the PTB. The training set includes only 141 ACC structures of which are conjoined by *and* or *or*. Some of them are complex but most (78%) have the following pattern (NT is used to denote non-terminals):

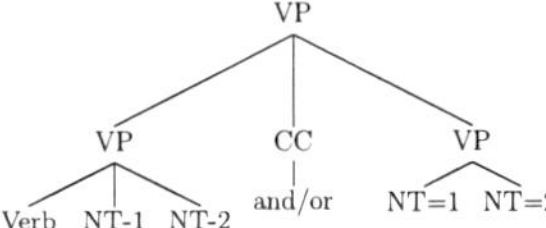

These structures can be characterized as follows: (1) the first token of the first conjoined VP is a verb; (2) the indexed arguments are direct children of the conjoined VPs; (3) the number of the indexed arguments is the same for each conjoined VP.

Almost all of these cases (98%) are symmetric: each of the conjoined VPs has the same types of indexed arguments. Non-symmetric clusters (e.g. "He made [these gestures]$_{NP}^1$ [to the red group]$_{PP}^2$ and [for us]$_{PP}^2$ [nothing]$_{NP}^1$") exist but are less common.

We argue that while the PTB representation for ACC gives a clear structure and covers all the ACC forms, it is not a good representation for learning PCFG parsers from. The arguments in the clusters are linked via co-indexation, breaking the context-free assumptions that PCFG parsers rely on. PCFG parsers ignore the indexes, essentially losing all the information about the ACC construction. Moreover, ignoring the indexes result

in "weird" CFG rules such as VP → NP PP. Not only that the RHS of these rules do not include a verbal component, it is also a very common structure for NPs. This makes the parser very likely to either mis-analyze the argument cluster as a noun-phrase, or to analyze some NPs as (supposedly ACC) VPs. The parallel nature of the construction is also lost. To improve the parser performance for ACC structures prediction, we suggest an alternative constituency representation for ACC phrases which is easier to learn.

3 Alternative Representation for ACC

Our proposed representation for ACC respects the context-free nature of the parser. In order to avoid incorrect syntactic derivations and derivations that allows conjoining of clusters with other phrases, as well as to express the symmetry that occur in many ACC phrases, we change the PTB representation for ACC as follows: (1) we move the verb and non-indexed elements out of the first argument cluster to under the main VP; (2) each argument cluster is treated as a phrase, with new non-terminal symbols specific to argument clusters; (3) the conjunction of clusters also receives a dedicated phrase level. For example see comparison between the original and new representations:

[1]

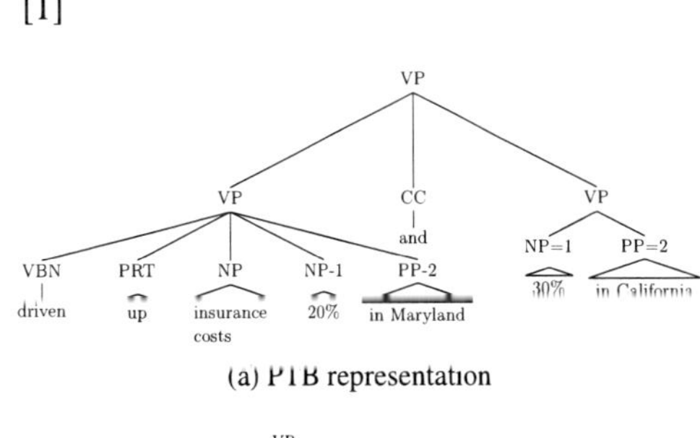

(a) PTB representation

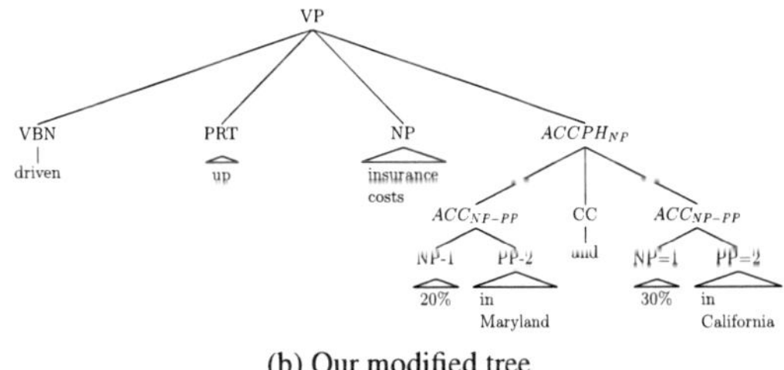

(b) Our modified tree

The main verb *driven* as well as the particle *up* and the non-indexed argument *insurance costs* are moved to the external VP. The two argument clusters (formerly VPs) receive dedicated phrase labels ACC_X, where X reflects the syntactic types of the indexed elements (e.g. ACC_{NP-PP} for the first cluster in [1b] above). The most common cases are ACC_{NP-PP} which appears in 41.6% of the clusters, $ACC_{ADJP-PP}$ with 21.2% of the clusters and ACC_{PP-PP} with 5.3% of the clusters.

Finally, we introduce a new phrase type ($ACCPH_X$) for the coordination of the two clusters. Here X denotes the main element in the clusters, determined heuristically by taking the first of the following types that appear in any of the clusters: NP, PP, ADJP, SBAR. Cases where the clusters contains an ADVP element are usually special (e.g. the following structure is missing "people" in the second cluster: ((NP 8000 people) (in Spain)) and ((NP 2000) (ADVP abroad))). For such cases, we add "ADVP" to the $ACCPH$ level label. Table 1 lists the $ACCPH$ level labels and their number of the appearances in the 125 modified trees.[1]

The representation is capable of representing common cases of ACC where the cluster elements are siblings. We similarly handle also some of the more complex cases, in which an extra layer appears between an indexed argument and the conjoined VP to host an empty element, such as in the following case with an extra S layer above *single-B-3*:

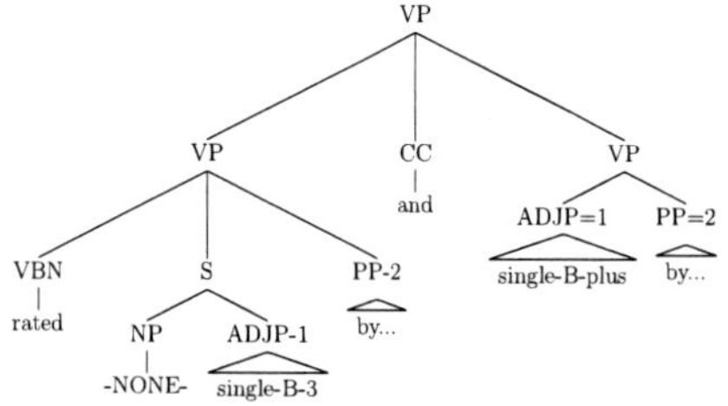

in which we remove the empty NP as well as the extra S layer:

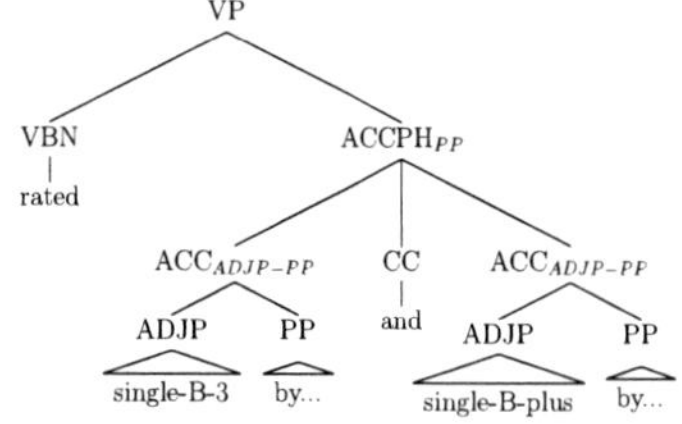

___

[1]Parsers that apply latent annotations to the grammar, such as the Berkeley Parser (Petrov et al., 2006) we use in our experiments, can potentially learn some of our proposed refinements on their own. However, as we show in the experiments section, the performance of the Berkeley Parser on ACC structures significantly improve when applying our transformations prior to training.

Label	#	Label	#
$ACCPH_{NP}$	69	$ACCPH_{NP-ADVP}$	6
$ACCPH_{PP}$	36	$ACCPH_{PP-ADVP}$	11
$ACCPH_{ADJP}$	2	$ACCPH_{SBAR-ADVP}$	1

Table 1: The labels for the new level in the ACC trees. #: number of occurrences.

Limitations Our representation is similar to the representation that was suggested for ACC by Huddleston et al. (2002) in their comprehensive linguistic description of the English grammar. However, while it is capable of representing the common cases of ACC, it does not cover some complex and rare cases encountered in the PTB: (1) Argument-Cluster structures that include errors such as missing indexed argument and a wrong POS tag for the main verb; (2) ACC constructions where the main verb is between the indexed arguments such as the following: "([About half]$_1$ invested [in government bonds]$_2$) and ([about 10%]$_1$ [in cash]$_2$)"; (3) Argument-Cluster structures that include an indexed phrase which is not a direct child of the cluster head and has non-empty siblings, such as in the following case that includes an indexed argument (*8%*) which is not directly under the conjoined VP and has non-empty sibling (*of*): "see a raise [[of] [8%]$_{NP-1}$]$_{PP}$ in the first year] and [7%]$_{NP=1}$ in each of the following two years".

Our changes are local and appear in small number of trees (0.003% of the PTB train set). We also ignore more complex cases of ACC. Yet, training the parser with the modified trees significantly improves the parser results on ACC structures.

4 Experiments

We converted 125 trees with ACC structures in the training sets (sections 2-21) of the PTB to the new representation, and trained the Berkeley parser (Petrov et al., 2006) with its default settings.

As the PTB test and dev sets have only 12 ACC structures that are coordinated by *and* or *or*, we evaluate the parser on Regents, a dataset in which ACC structures are prevalent (details below). As Regents does not include syntactic structures, we focus on the ACC phenomena and evaluate the parsers' ability to correctly identify the spans of the clusters and the arguments in them.

To verify that the new representation does not harm general parsing performance, we also eval-

Dataset		R	P	F1
Dev	PTB Trees	90.88	90.89	90.88
	Modified Trees	90.97	91.21	91.09
Test	PTB Trees	90.36	90.79	90.57
	Modified Trees	90.62	91.06	90.84

Table 2: Parsing results (EVALB) on PTB Sections 22 (DEV) and 23 (TEST).

	PTB Trees	Modified Trees
ACC_{PTB}	13.0	-
ACC_{OUR}	24.1	64.8

Table 3: The parser Recall score in recovering ACC conjunct spans on the Regents dataset. ACC_{PTB}: the set is annotated with the verb inside the first cluster. ACC_{OUR}: the set is annotated following our approach.

uate the parer on the traditional development and test sets (sections 22 and 23). As can be seen in Table 2, the parser results are slightly better when trained with the modified trees.[2]

4.1 Regents data-set

Regents – a dataset of questions from the Regents 4th grade science exam (the Aristo Challenge),[3] includes 281 sentences with coordination phrases, where 54 of them include Argument Cluster coordination. We manually annotated the sentences by marking the conjuncts spans for the constituent coordination phrases, e.g.:

Wendy (ran 19 miles) and (walked 9 miles)

as well as the spans of each component of the argument-cluster coordinations, including the inner span of each argument:

Mary paid ([$11.08] [for berries]), ([$14.33] [for apples]), and ([$9.31] [for peaches])

The bracketing in this set follow our proposed ACC bracketing, and we refer to it as ACC_{OUR}.

We also created a version in which the bracketing follow the PTB scheme, with the verb included in span of the first cluster, e.g.:

Mary ([paid] [$11.08] [for berries]), ([$14.33] [for apples]), and ([$9.31] [for peaches])

We refer to this dataset as ACC_{PTB}.

We evaluate the parsers' ability to correctly recover the components of the coordination structures by computing the percentage of gold annotated phrases where the number of predicted conjunct is correct and all conjuncts spans (round brackets) are predicted correctly (Recall). For example, consider the following gold annotated phrase:

A restaurant served (9 pizzas during lunch) and (6 during dinner) today

A prediction of ("*9 pizzas during lunch*", "*6 during dinner today*") is considered as incorrect because the second conjunct boundaries are not matched to the gold annotation.

We compare the Recall score that the parser achieves when it is trained on the modified trees to the score when the parser is trained on the PTB trees.

When evaluated on all coordination cases in the Regents dataset (both ACC and other cases of constituent coordination), the parser trained on the modified trees was successful in recovering 54.3% of the spans, compared to only 47% when trained on the original PTB trees.

We now focus on specifically on the ACC cases (Table 3). When evaluating the PTB-trained parser on ACC_{PTB}, it correctly recovers only 13% of the ACC boundaries. Somewhat surprisingly, the PTB-trained parser performs *better* when evaluated against ACC_{OUR}, correctly recovering 24.1% of the structures. This highlights how unnatural the original ACC representation is for the parser: it predicts the alternative representation more often than it predicts the one it was trained on. When the parser is trained on the modified trees, results on ACC_{OUR} jump to 64.8%, correctly recovering ×2.7 more structures.

The previous results were on recovering the spans of the coordinated elements (the round brackets in the examples above). When measuring the Recall in recovering any of the arguments themselves (the elements surrounded by square brackets), the parser trained on the modified trees recovers 72.46% of the arguments in clusters, compared to only 58.29% recovery by the PTB-trained parser. We also measure in what percentage of the cases in which both the cluster boundaries (round brackets) were recovered correctly, all the internal structure (square brackets) was recovered correctly as well. The score is 80% when the parser trained on the modified trees com-

---

[2]The same trend holds also if we exclude the 12 modified trees from the evaluation sets.

[3]http://allenai.org/content/data/Regents.zip

pared to 61.5% when it is trained on the PTB-trees.

Overall, the parser trained on the modified trees significantly outperforms the one trained on the original trees in all the evaluation scenarios.

Another interesting evaluation is the ability of the parser that is trained on the modified trees to determine whether a coordination is of Argument Clusters type (that is, whether the predicted coordination spans are marked with the ACCPH label).[4] The results are a Recall of 57.4% and Precision of 83.78%. When we further require that both the head be marked as ACCPH and the internal structure be correct, the results are 48.14% Recall and 70.27% Precision.

5 Conclusions

By focusing on the details of a single and relatively rare syntactic construction, argument clusters coordination, we have been able to significantly improve parsing results for this construction, while also slightly improving general parsing results. More broadly, while most current research efforts in natural language processing and in syntactic parsing in particular is devoted to the design of general-purpose, data-agnostic techniques, such methods work on the common phenomena while often neglecting the very long tail of important constructions. This work shows that there are gains to be had also from focusing on the details of particular linguistic phenomena, and changing the data such that it is easier for a "data agnostic" system to learn.

Acknowledgments

This work was supported by The Allen Institute for Artificial Intelligence as well as the German Research Foundation via the German-Israeli Project Cooperation (DIP, grant DA 1600/1-1).

References

Ann Bies, Mark Ferguson, Karen Katz, Robert MacIntyre, Victoria Tredinnick, Grace Kim, Mary Ann Marcinkiewicz, and Britta Schasberger. 1995. Bracketing guidelines for treebank ii style penn treebank project. *University of Pennsylvania*, 97:100.

David Dowty. 1988. Type raising, functional composition, and non-constituent conjunction. In *Categorial grammars and natural language structures*, pages 153–197. Springer.

Kazuo Hara, Masashi Shimbo, Hideharu Okuma, and Yuji Matsumoto. 2009. Coordinate structure analysis with global structural constraints and alignment-based local features. In *Proceedings of the Joint Conference of the 47th Annual Meeting of the ACL and the 4th International Joint Conference on Natural Language Processing of the AFNLP: Volume 2-Volume 2*, pages 967–975. Association for Computational Linguistics.

Deirdre Hogan. 2007. Coordinate noun phrase disambiguation in a generative parsing model. Association for Computational Linguistics.

Rodney Huddleston, Geoffrey K Pullum, et al. 2002. The cambridge grammar of english. *Language. Cambridge: Cambridge University Press*, pages 1273–1362.

Mitchell P Marcus, Mary Ann Marcinkiewicz, and Beatrice Santorini. 1993. Building a large annotated corpus of english: The penn treebank. *Computational linguistics*, 19(2):313–330.

François Mouret. 2006. A phrase structure approach to argument cluster coordination. In *Proceedings of the HPSG06 Conference*, pages 247–267. CSLI online Publications.

Hideharu Okuma, Kazuo Hara, Masashi Shimbo, and Yuji Matsumoto. 2009. Bypassed alignment graph for learning coordination in japanese sentences. In *Proceedings of the ACL-IJCNLP 2009 Conference Short Papers*, pages 5–8. Association for Computational Linguistics.

Slav Petrov, Leon Barrett, Romain Thibaux, and Dan Klein. 2006. Learning accurate, compact, and interpretable tree annotation. In *Proceedings of the 21st International Conference on Computational Linguistics and the 44th annual meeting of the Association for Computational Linguistics*, pages 433–440. Association for Computational Linguistics.

Masashi Shimbo and Kazuo Hara. 2007. A discriminative learning model for coordinate conjunctions. In *EMNLP-CoNLL*, pages 610–619.

---

[4]This measurement is relevant only when parsing based on our proposed annotation, and cannot be measured for parse trees based the original PTB annotation.

Reference Bias in Monolingual Machine Translation Evaluation

Marina Fomicheva
Institute for Applied Linguistics
Pompeu Fabra University, Spain
`marina.fomicheva@upf.edu`

Lucia Specia
Department of Computer Science
University of Sheffield, UK
`l.specia@sheffield.ac.uk`

Abstract

In the translation industry, human translations are assessed by comparison with the source texts. In the Machine Translation (MT) research community, however, it is a common practice to perform quality assessment using a reference translation instead of the source text. In this paper we show that this practice has a serious issue – annotators are strongly biased by the reference translation provided, and this can have a negative impact on the assessment of MT quality.

1 Introduction

Equivalence to the source text is the defining characteristic of translation. One of the fundamental aspects of translation quality is, therefore, its semantic adequacy, which reflects to what extent the meaning of the original text is preserved in the translation. In the field of Machine Translation (MT), on the other hand, it has recently become common practice to perform quality assessment using a human reference translation instead of the source text. Reference-based evaluation is an attractive practical solution since it does not require bilingual speakers.

However, we believe this approach has a strong conceptual flaw: the assumption that the task of translation has a single correct solution. In reality, except for very short sentences or very specific technical domains, the same source sentence may be correctly translated in many different ways. Depending on a broad textual and real-world context, the translation can differ from the source text at any linguistic level – lexical, syntactic, semantic or even discourse – and still be considered perfectly correct. Therefore, using a single translation as a proxy for the original text may be unreliable.

In the monolingual, reference-based evaluation scenario, human judges are expected to recognize acceptable variations between translation options and assign a high score to a good MT, even if it happens to be different from a particular human reference provided. In this paper we argue that, contrary to this expectation, annotators are strongly biased by the reference. They inadvertently favor machine translations (MTs) that make similar choices to the ones present in the reference translation. To test this hypothesis, we perform an experiment where the same set of MT outputs is manually assessed using different reference translations and analyze the discrepancies between the resulting quality scores.

The results confirm that annotators are indeed heavily influenced by the particular human translation that was used for evaluation. We discuss the implications of this finding on the reliability of current practices in manual quality assessment. Our general recommendation is that, in order to avoid reference bias, the assessment should be performed by comparing the MT output to the original text, rather than to a reference.

The rest of this paper is organized as follows. In Section 2 we present related work. In Section 3 we describe our experimental settings. In Section 4 we focus on the effect of reference bias on MT evaluation. In Section 5 we examine the impact of the fatigue factor on the results of our experiments.

2 Related Work

It has become widely acceptable in the MT community to use human translation instead of (or along with) the source segment for MT evaluation. In most major evaluation campaigns (ARPA (White et al., 1994), 2008 NIST Metrics for Machine Translation Challenge (Przybocki et al., 2008), and annual Workshops on Statistical Ma-

Proceedings of the 54th Annual Meeting of the Association for Computational Linguistics, pages 77–82,
Berlin, Germany, August 7-12, 2016. ©2016 Association for Computational Linguistics

chine Translation (Callison-Burch et al., 2007; Bojar et al., 2015)), manual assessment is expected to consider both MT fluency and adequacy, with a human (reference) translation commonly used as a proxy for the source text to allow for adequacy judgement by monolingual judges.

The reference bias problem has been extensively discussed in the context of automatic MT evaluation. Evaluation systems based on string-level comparison, such as the well known BLEU metric (Papineni et al., 2002) heavily penalize potentially acceptable variations between MT and human reference. A variety of methods have been proposed to address this issue, from using multiple references (Dreyer and Marcu, 2012) to reference-free evaluation (Specia et al., 2010).

Research in manual evaluation has focused on overcoming annotator bias, i.e. the preferences and expectations of individual annotators with respect to translation quality that lead to low levels of inter-annotator agreement (Cohn and Specia, 2013; Denkowski and Lavie, 2010; Graham et al., 2013; Guzmán et al., 2015). The problem of reference bias, however, has not been examined in previous work. By contrast to automatic MT evaluation, monolingual quality assessment is considered unproblematic, since human annotators are supposed to recognize meaning-preserving variations between the MT output and a given human reference. However, as will be shown in what follows, manual evaluation is also strongly affected by biases due to specific reference translations.

3 Settings

To show that monolingual quality assessment depends on the human translation used as gold-standard, we devised an evaluation task where annotators were asked to assess the same set of MT outputs using different references. As control groups, we have annotators assessing MT using the same reference, and using the source segments.

3.1 Dataset

MT data with multiple references is rare. We used MTC-P4 Chinese-English dataset, produced by Linguistic Data Consortium (LDC2006T04). The dataset contains 919 source sentences from news domain, 4 reference translations and MT outputs generated by 10 translation systems. Human translations were produced by four teams of professional translators and included editor's proofread-

ing. All teams used the same translation guidelines, which emphasize faithfulness to the source sentence as one of the main requirements.

We note that even in such a scenario, human translations differ from each other. We measured the average similarity between the four references in the dataset using the Meteor evaluation metric (Denkowski and Lavie, 2014). Meteor scores range between 0 and 1 and reflect the proportion of similar words occurring in similar order. This metric is normally used to compare the MT output with a human reference, but it can also be applied to measure similarity between any two translations. We computed Meteor for all possible combinations between the four available references and took the average score. Even though Meteor covers certain amount of acceptable linguistic variation by allowing for synonym and paraphrase matching, the resulting score is only 0.33, which shows that, not surprisingly, human translations vary substantially.

To make the annotation process feasible given the resources available, we selected a subset of 100 source sentences for the experiment. To ensure variable levels of similarity between the MT and each of the references, we computed sentence-level Meteor scores for the MT outputs using each of the references and selected the sentences with the highest standard deviation between the scores.

3.2 Method

We developed a simple online interface to collect human judgments. Our evaluation task was based on the adequacy criterion. Specifically, judges were asked to estimate how much of the meaning of the human translation was expressed in the MT output (see Figure 1). The responses were interpreted on a five-point scale, with the labels in Figure 1 corresponding to numbers from 1 ("None") to 5 ("All").

For the main task, judgments were collected using English native speakers who volunteered to participate. They were either professional translators or researchers with a degree in Computational Linguistics, English or Translation Studies. 20 annotators participated in this monolingual task. Each of them evaluated the same set of 100 MT outputs. Our estimates showed that the task could be completed in approximately one hour. The annotators were divided into four groups, corresponding to the four available refer-

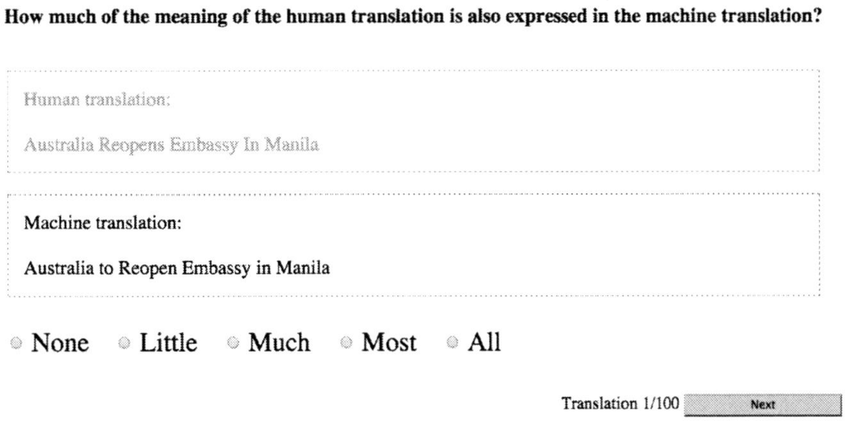

Figure 1: Evaluation Interface

ences. Each group contained five annotators independently evaluating the same set of sentences. Having multiple annotators in each group allowed us to minimize the effect of individual annotators' biases, preferences and expectations.

As a control group, five annotators (native speakers of English, fluent in Chinese or bilingual speakers) performed a bilingual evaluation task for the same MT outputs. In the bilingual task, annotators were presented with an MT output and its corresponding source sentence and asked how much of the meaning of the source sentence was expressed in the MT.

In total, we collected 2,500 judgments. Both the data and the tool for collecting human judgments are available at https://github.com/mfomicheva/tradopad.git.

4 Reference Bias

The goal of the experiment is to show that depending on the reference translation used for evaluation, the quality of the same MT output will be perceived differently. However, we are aware that MT evaluation is a subjective task. Certain discrepancies between evaluation scores produced by different raters are expected simply because of their backgrounds, individual perceptions and expectations regarding translation quality.

To show that some differences are related to reference bias and not to the bias introduced by individual annotators, we compare the agreement between annotators evaluating with the same and with different references. First, we randomly se-

lect from the data 20 pairs of annotators who used the same reference translations and 20 pairs of annotators who used different reference translations. The agreement is then computed for each pair. Next, we calculate the average agreement for the same-reference and different-reference groups. We repeat the experiment 100 times and report the corresponding averages and confidence intervals.

Table 1 shows the results in terms of standard (Cohen, 1960) and linearly weighted (Cohen, 1968) Kappa coefficient (k).[1] We also report one-off version of weighted k, which discards the disagreements unless they are larger than one category.

Kappa	Diff. ref.	Same ref.	Source
Standard	.163±.01	.197±.01	0.190±.02
Weighted	.330⊥.01	.373⊥.01	0.336⊥.02
One-off	.597±.01	.662±.01	0.643+.02

Table 1: Inter-annotator agreement for different-references (Diff. ref.), same-reference (Same ref.) and source-based evaluation (Source)

As shown in Table 1, the agreement is consistently lower for annotators using different references. In other words, the same MT outputs systematically receive different scores when differ-

---

[1] In MT evaluation, agreement is usually computed using standard k both for ranking different translations and for scoring translations on an interval-level scale. We note, however, that weighted k is more appropriate for scoring, since it allows the use of weights to describe the closeness of the agreement between categories (Artstein and Poesio, 2008).

ent human translations are used for their evaluation. Here and in what follows, the differences between the results for the same-reference annotator group and different-reference annotator group were found to be statistically significant with p-value < 0.01.

The agreement between annotators using the source sentences is slightly lower than in the monolingual, same-reference scenario, but it is higher than in the case of the different-reference group. This may be an indication that reference-based evaluation is an easier task for annotators, perhaps because in this case they are not required to shift between languages. Nevertheless, the fact that given a different reference, the same MT outputs receive different scores, undermines the reliability of this type of evaluation.

	Human score	BLEU score
Reference 1	1.980	0.1649
Reference 2	2.342	0.1369
Reference 3	2.562	0.1680
Reference 4	2.740	0.1058

Table 2: Average human scores for the groups of annotators using different references and BLEU scores calculated with the corresponding references. Human scores range from 1 to 5, while BLEU scores range from 0 to 1.

In Table 2 we computed average evaluation scores for each group of annotators. Average scores vary considerably across groups of annotators. This shows that MT quality is perceived differently depending on the human translation used as gold-standard. For the sake of comparison, we also present the scores from the widely used automatic evaluation metric BLEU. Not surprisingly, BLEU scores are also strongly affected by the reference bias. Below we give an example of linguistic variation in professional human translations and its effect on reference-based MT evaluation.

Src: 不过这一切都由不得你[2]
MT: But all this is beyond the control of you.
R1: But all this is beyond your control.
R2: However, you cannot choose yourself.
R3: However, not everything is up to you to decide.

---

[2]Literally: "However these all totally beyond the control of you."

R4: But you can't choose that.

Although all the references carry the same message, the linguistic means used by the translators are very different. Most of these references are high-level paraphrases of what we would consider a close version of the source sentence. Annotators are expected to recognize meaning-preserving variation between the MT and any of the references. However, the average score for this sentence was 3.4 in case of Reference 1, and 2.0, 2.0 and 2.8 in case of the other three references, respectively, which illustrates the bias introduced by the reference translation.

5 Time Effect

It is well known that the reliability and consistency of human annotation tasks is affected by fatigue (Llorà et al., 2005). In this section we examine how this factor may gave influenced the evaluation on the impact of reference bias and thus the reliability of our experiment.

We measured inter-annotator agreement for the same-reference and different-reference annotators at different stages of the evaluation process. We divided the dataset in five sets of sentences based on the chronological order in which they were annotated (0-20, 20-40, ..., 80-100). For each slice of the data we repeated the procedure reported in Section 4. Figure 2 shows the results.

First, we note that the agreement is always higher in the case of same-reference annotators. Second, in the intermediate stages of the task we observe the highest inter-annotator agreement (sentences 20-40) and the smallest difference between the same-reference and different-reference annotators (sentences 40-60). This seems to indicate that the effect of reference bias is minimal half-way through the evaluation process. In other words, when the annotators are already acquainted with the task but not yet tired, they are able to better recognize meaning-preserving variation between different translation options.

To further investigate how fatigue affects the evaluation process, we tested the variability of human scores in different (chronological) slices of the data. We again divided the data in five sets of sentences and calculated standard deviation between the scores in each set. We repeated this procedure for each annotator and averaged the results. As can be seen in Figure 3, the variation between

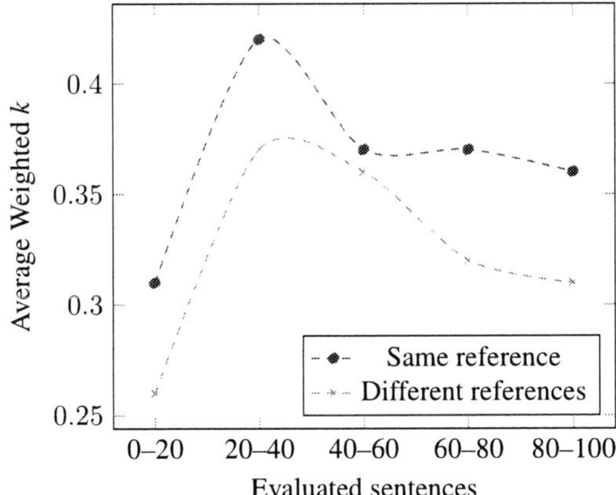

Figure 2: Inter-annotator agreement at different stages of evaluation process

the scores is lower in the last stages of the evaluation process. This could mean that towards the end of the task the annotators tend to indiscriminately give similar scores to any translation, making the evaluation less informative.

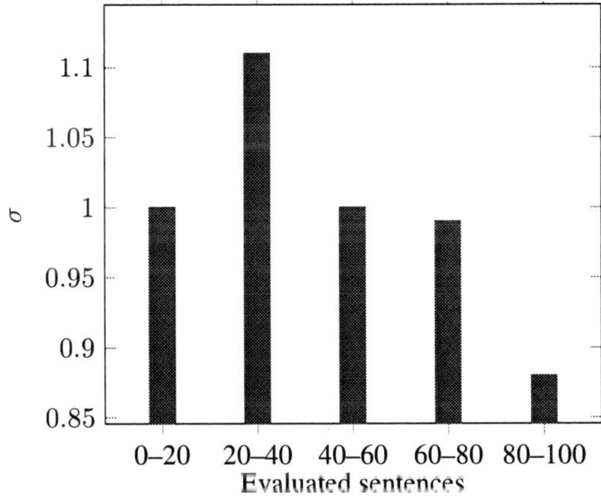

Figure 3: Average standard deviations between human scores for all annotators at different stages of evaluation process

6 Conclusions

In this work we examined the effect of reference bias on monolingual MT evaluation. We compared the agreement between the annotators who used the same human reference translation and those who used different reference translations. We were able to show that in addition to the inevitable bias introduced by different annotators, monolingual evaluation is systematically affected by the reference provided. Annotators consistently assign different scores to the same MT outputs when a different human translation is used as gold-standard. The MTs that are correct but happen to be different from a particular human translation are inadvertently penalized during evaluation.

We also analyzed the relation between reference bias and annotation at different times throughout the process. The results suggest that annotators are less influenced by specific translation choices present in the reference in the intermediate stages of the evaluation process, when they have already familiarized themselves with the task but are not yet fatigued by it. To reduce the fatigue effect, the task may be done in smaller batches over time. Regarding the lack of experience, annotators should receive previous training.

Quality assessment is instrumental in the development and deployment of MT systems. If evaluation is to be objective and informative, its purpose must be clearly defined. The same sentence can be translated in many different ways. Using a human reference as a proxy for the source sentence, we evaluate the similarity of the MT to a particular reference, which does not necessarily reflect how well the contents of the original is expressed in the MT or how suitable it is for a given purpose. Therefore, monolingual evaluation undermines the reliability of quality assessment. We recommend that unless the evaluation is aimed for a very specific translation task, where the number of possible translations is indeed limited, the assessment should be performed by comparing MT to the original text.

Acknowledgments

Marina Fomicheva was supported by funding from IULA (UPF) and the FI-DGR grant program of the Generalitat de Catalunya. Lucia Specia was supported by the QT21 project (H2020 No. 645452). The authors would also like to thank the three anonymous reviewers for their helpful comments and suggestions.

References

Ron Artstein and Massimo Poesio. 2008. Inter-coder Agreement for Computational Linguistics. *Computational Linguistics*, 34(4):555–596.

Ondřej Bojar, Rajen Chatterjee, Christian Federmann, Barry Haddow, Matthias Huck, Chris Hokamp, Philipp Koehn, Varvara Logacheva, Christof Monz,

Matteo Negri, Matt Post, Carolina Scarton, Lucia Specia, and Marco Turchi. 2015. Findings of the 2015 Workshop on Statistical Machine Translation. In *Proceedings of the Tenth Workshop on Statistical Machine Translation*, pages 1–46, Lisboa, Portugal.

Chris Callison-Burch, Cameron Fordyce, Philipp Koehn, Christof Monz, and Josh Schroeder. 2007. (meta-) evaluation of machine translation. In *Proceedings of the Second Workshop on Statistical Machine Translation*, pages 136–158.

Jacob Cohen. 1960. A Coefficient of Agreement for Nominal Scales. *Educational and Psychological Measurement*, 20:37–46.

Jacob Cohen. 1968. Weighted Kappa: Nominal Scale Agreement Provision for Scaled Disagreement or Partial Credit. *Psychological bulletin*, 70(4):213–220.

Trevor Cohn and Lucia Specia. 2013. Modelling Annotator Bias with Multi-task Gaussian Processes: An Application to Machine Translation Quality Estimation. In *Proceedings of 51st Annual Meeting of the Association for Computational Linguistics*, pages 32–42.

Michael Denkowski and Alon Lavie. 2010. Choosing the Right Evaluation for Machine Translation: an Examination of Annotator and Automatic Metric Performance on Human Judgment Tasks. In *Proceedings of the Ninth Biennal Conference of the Association for Machine Translation in the Americas.*

Michael Denkowski and Alon Lavie. 2014. Meteor Universal: Language Specific Translation Evaluation for Any Target Language. In *Proceedings of the EACL 2014 Workshop on Statistical Machine Translation*, pages 376–380.

Markus Dreyer and Daniel Marcu. 2012. HyTER: Meaning-equivalent Semantics for Translation Evaluation. In *Proceedings of 2012 Conference of the North American Chapter of the Association for Computational Linguistics: Human Language Technologies*, pages 162–171.

Yvette Graham, Timothy Baldwin, Alistair Moffat, and Justin Zobel. 2013. Continuous Measurement Scales in Human Evaluation of Machine Translation. In *Proceedings 7th Linguistic Annotation Workshop and Interoperability with Discourse*, pages 33–41.

Francisco Guzmán, Ahmed Abdelali, Irina Temnikova, Hassan Sajjad, and Stephan Vogel. 2015. How do Humans Evaluate Machine Translation. In *Proceedings of the Tenth Workshop on Statistical Machine Translation*, pages 457–466.

Xavier Llorà, Kumara Sastry, David E Goldberg, Abhimanyu Gupta, and Lalitha Lakshmi. 2005. Combating User Fatigue in iGAs: Partial Ordering, Support Vector Machines, and Synthetic Fitness. In *Proceedings of the 7th Annual Conference on Genetic and Evolutionary Computation*, pages 1363–1370.

Kishore Papineni, Salim Roukos, Todd Ward, and Wei-Jing Zhu. 2002. BLEU: a Method for Automatic Evaluation of Machine Translation. In *Proceedings of the 40th Annual Meeting of the ACL*, pages 311–318.

Mark Przybocki, Kay Peterson, and Sebastian Bronsart. 2008. Official Results of the NIST 2008 "Metrics for MAchine TRanslation" Challenge (Metrics-MATR08). In *Proceedings of the AMTA-2008 Workshop on Metrics for Machine Translation*, Honolulu, Hawaii, USA.

Lucia Specia, Dhwaj Raj, and Marco Turchi. 2010. Machine Translation Evaluation versus Quality Estimation. *Machine Translation*, 24(1):39–50.

John White, Theresa O'Connell, and Francis O'Mara. 1994. The ARPA MT Evaluation Methodologies: Evolution, Lessons, and Future Approaches. In *Proceedings of the Association for Machine Translation in the Americas Conference*, pages 193–205, Columbia, Maryland, USA.

Cross-lingual projection for class-based language models

Beat Gfeller and **Vlad Schogol** and **Keith Hall**
Google Inc.
{beatg,vlads,kbhall}@google.com

Abstract

This paper presents a cross-lingual projection technique for training class-based language models. We borrow from previous success in projecting POS tags and NER mentions to that of a trained class-based language model. We use a CRF to train a model to predict when a sequence of words is a member of a given class and use this to label our language model training data. We show that we can successfully project the contextual cues for these classes across pairs of languages and retain a high quality class model in languages with no supervised class data. We present empirical results that show the quality of the projected models as well as their effect on the down-stream speech recognition objective. We are able to achieve over 70% of the WER reduction when using the projected class models as compared to models trained on human annotations.

1 Introduction

Class-based language modeling has a long history of being used to improve the quality of speech recognition systems (Brown et al., 1992; Knesser and Ney, 1993). Recent work on class-based models has exploited named entity recognition (NER) approaches to label language model training data with class labels (Levit et al., 2014; Vasserman et al., 2015), providing a means to assign words and phrases to classes based on their context. These contextually assigned classes have been shown to improve speech recognition significantly over grammar-based, deterministic class assignments.

In this work, we address the problem of labeling training data in order to build a class se-

quence tagger. We borrow from the successes of previous cross-lingual projection experiments for labeling tasks (Yarowsky et al., 2001; Yarowsky and Ngai, 2001; Burkett et al., 2010; Padó and Lapata, 2009). We focus on *numeric* classes (e.g., address numbers, dates, currencies, times, etc.) as the sequence-based labeling approach has been shown to be effective for identifying them. Given a model trained from human-labeled data in one language (we refer to this as the high-resource language), we label translations of sentences from another language (referred to as the low-resource language). We show that we can project the numeric entity boundaries and labels across the aligned translations with a phrase-based translation model. Furthermore, we show that if we train a class labeling model on the projected low-resource language and then use that to build a class-based speech recognition system, we achieve between 70% and 85% of the error reduction as we would have achieved with human-labeled examples in the low-resource language.

We present empirical results projecting numeric entity labels from English to Russian, Indonesian, and Italian. We present full speech recognition results for using human annotated data (the ideal performance) and projected data with various sizes of training data.

2 Related work

There is an increasingly large body of work based on exploiting alignments between translations of sentences in multiple languages (Yarowsky et al., 2001; Yarowsky and Ngai, 2001; Burkett et al., 2010; Das and Petrov, 2011). In this work we employ the simple approach of projecting annotations across alignments of translated sentences. Our cross-lingual approach is closely related to other NER projection approaches (Huang et al.,

Proceedings of the 54th Annual Meeting of the Association for Computational Linguistics, pages 83–88,
Berlin, Germany, August 7-12, 2016. ©2016 Association for Computational Linguistics

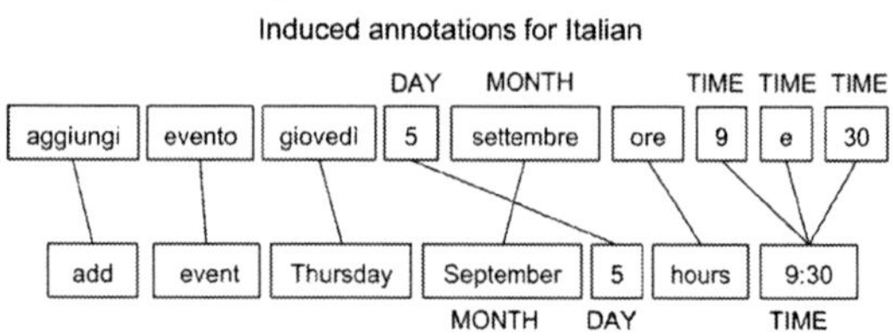

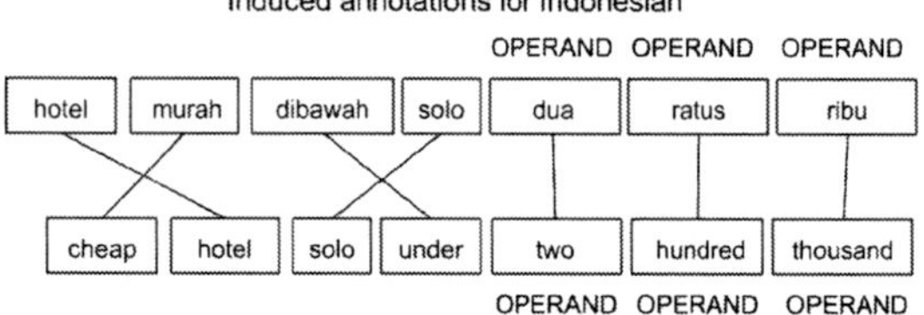

Figure 1: Examples of cross-lingual projection for numeric entities.

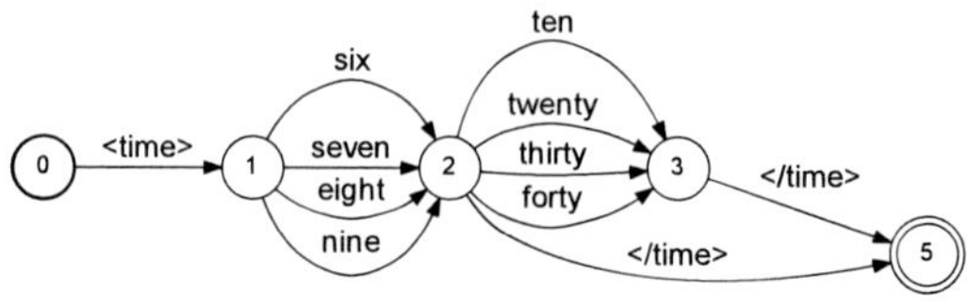

Figure 2: This FST is a small excerpt of the full grammar for *TIME*. Arc weights are not shown.

2003; Moore, 2003); however, we have focused on a limited class of entities which may explain why the simple approach works reasonably well.

Our projection approach is most closely related to that presented in (Yarowsky et al., 2001) and (Padó and Lapata, 2009). In each of these, labels over sequences of words are projected across alignments directly from one language to the other. While we follow a similar approach, our goal is not necessarily to get the exact projection, but to get a projection which allows us to learn contextual cues for the classes we are labeling. Additionally, we focus on the case where we are generating the translated data rather that identifying existing parallel data. Similar to (Yarowsky and Ngai, 2001), we filter out poor alignments (details are described in Section 3.2).

3 Methodology

3.1 Training class taggers for language modeling

We use a statistical sequence tagger to identify and replace class instances in raw text with their label. For example, the tokens *10 thousand dollars* in the raw training text may be replaced with a placeholder class symbol. The decision is context-dependent: the tagger is able to resolve ambiguities among possible labels, or even leave the text unchanged. Next, this modified text is used to train a standard n-gram language model. Fi-

nally, all placeholders become non-terminals in the language model and are expanded either statically or dynamically with stochastic finite-state class grammars (see Figure 2 for an example). Decorator tokens inside the grammars are used to mark class instances in the word lattice so that they can be converted (after recognition) to the desired written forms using deterministic spoken-to-written text-normalization rules.

3.2 Cross-lingual Projection Techniques

The starting point for cross-lingual projection is to train a statistical sentence tagger of high quality in a high-resource language, i.e., a language where both a lot of training data and human annotators are readily available. We use English in our experiments.

To obtain annotated sentences in a low-resource language, we translate unlabeled sentences into the high-resource language. We use an in-house phrase-based statistical machine translation system (Koehn et al., 2003) which is trained with parallel texts extracted from web pages; described in detail in Section 4.1 of (Nakagawa, 2015). The translation system we use provides token-by-token alignments as part of the output. This is achieved by keeping alignments along with phrase-pairs during the phrase extraction stage of training the alignment system.

The high quality sentence tagger is applied to the translated sentences. Then, using the alignments between the translated sentences, we map class tags back to the low-resource language. See Figure 1 for examples of actual mappings produced by this procedure.

With this approach, we can produce arbitrarily large in-domain annotated training sets for the low-resource language. These annotated sentences are then used to train a class tagger for the low-resource language. The main question is whether the resulting class tagger is of sufficient quality for our down-stream objective.

For the goal of training a class-based language model in a low-resource language, one may consider a different approach than the one just described: instead of training a tagger in the low-resource language, each sentence in the language model training data could be translated to the high-resource language, tagged using the statistical tagger, and projected back to the low-resource language. The primary reason for not pursuing this approach is the size of the language model training data (tens of billions of sentences). Translating a corpus this large is prohibitive. As the high-resource language tagger is trained on approximately 150K tokens, we believe that we have covered a large number of the predictive cues for the set of classes.

Alignment details

When projecting the class labels back from a translated sentence to the original sentence, various subtle issues arise. We describe these and our solutions for each in this section.

To tag a token in the low-resource language, we see which tokens in the high-resource language are aligned to it in the translation, and look at their class tags. If all of these tokens have the same class tag, we assign the same tag to the low-resource language token. Otherwise, we use the following rules:

- If some tokens have no class tag but others have some class tag, we still assign the class tag to the original token.

- If multiple tokens with different class tags map to the original token, we consider the tagging ambiguous. In such a case, we simply skip the sentence and do not use it for training the low-resource tagger. We can afford to do so because there is no shortage of unlabeled training sentences.

In a number of cases, we ignore sentence pairs which may have contained alignments allowing us to project labels, but also contained noise (e.g., spurious many-to-one alignments). We rejected poor alignments 2%, 31% and 14% of the time for Indonesian, Russian and Italian respectively. Date and time expressions were often affected by these noisy alignments.

4 Empirical evaluation

4.1 Data

We trained an English conditional random field (CRF) (Lafferty et al., 2001) tagger to be used in all experiments in order to provide labels for the sentences produced by translation. To train this tagger we obtained a data set of 24,503 manually labeled sentences (150K tokens) sampled from a corpus of British English language model training material. Each token is labeled with one of 17 possible tags. About 95% of the tokens are labeled with a 'none' tag, meaning that the token is not in any of the pre-determined non-lexical classes.

Separately, we obtained similar training sets to create Italian, Indonesian and Russian taggers. The models trained from these labeled data sets were used only to create baseline systems for comparison with the cross-lingual systems.

To provide input into our cross-lingual projection procedure, we also sampled datasets of unlabeled sentences of varying sizes for each evaluation language, using the same sampling procedure as used for the human-labeled sets.

Note that these tagger training sets have inconsistent sizes across languages (see Table 2) due to the nature of the sampling procedure: Each training source is searched for sentences matching an extensive list of patterns of numeric entities. Sentences from each training source are collected up to a source-specific maximum number (which may not always be reached). We also apply a flattening step to increase diversity of the sample.

4.2 CRF model

Our CRF tagger model was trained online using a variant of the MIRA algorithm (Crammer and Singer, 2003). Our feature set includes isolated features (for word identity w_i, word type d_i, and word cluster c_i) as well as features for neighboring words $w_{i-2}, w_{i-1}, w_{i+1}, w_{i+2}, w_{i+3}$, neighboring clusters $c_{i-2}, c_{i-1}, c_{i+1}, c_{i+2}, c_{i+3}$, pair features $(w_i, d_{i-1}), (w_i, d_{i+1}), (d_i, d_{i-1}), (d_i, d_{i+1})$, and domain-specific features (indicators for tokens within a given numeric range, or tokens that end in a certain number of zero digits). We also include class bias features, which capture the class prior distribution found in the training set.

4.3 Metrics

We use two manually transcribed test sets to evaluate the performance of our approach in the con-

Test Set	Utts	Words	% Numeric words
NUM ID	9,744	60,781	19%
NUM RU	10,988	59,933	22%
NUM IT	8,685	48,195	18%
VS ID	9,841	36,276	2%
VS RU	12,467	49,403	3%
VS IT	12,625	47,867	2%

Table 1: *NUM* refers to the NUMERIC entities test set and *VS* refers to the VOICE-SEARCH test set.

text of numeric transcription. The first test set VOICE-SEARCH (approximately 48K words for Italian and Russian, and approximately 36K words for Indonesian) is a sample from general voice-search traffic, and tracks any regressions that appear as a result of biasing too heavily toward the selected classes. The other test set NUMERIC (approximately 48K words for Italian, and approximately 60K for Russian and Indonesian) contains utterances we expect to benefit from class-based modeling of numeric entities. See Table 1 for details on these test sets.

We report word-error-rate (WER) on each test set for each model evaluated, including two baseline systems (one built without classes at all and another that has classes identified by a tagger trained on human-labeled data). We also report a labeled-bracket F1 score to show the performance of the tagger independent of the speech-recognition task. For each language, the test set used for labeled-bracket F1 is a human-labeled corpus of approximately 2K sentences that were held out from the human-labeled corpora for the baseline systems.

4.4 Results

The results in Table 2 show that all class-based systems outperform the baseline in WER on the NUMERIC test set, while performance on the VOICE-SEARCH test set was mostly flat. The flat performance on VOICE-SEARCH is expected: as seen in Table 1 this test set has a very low proportion of words that are numeric in form. We provide results on this test set in order to confirm that our approach does not harm general voice-search queries. As for performance on the NUMERIC test set, larger cross-lingual data sets led to better performance for Russian and Italian, but caused a slight regression for Indonesian. The translation system we use for these experiments has been optimized for a general-purpose web search

		NUM	*VS*
Model	F1	WER	WER
ID Baseline (no classes)	-	20.0	10.1
ID Cross-lingual 15K	0.64	19.3	10.1
ID Cross-lingual 37K	0.65	19.4	10.1
ID Cross-lingual 77K	0.64	19.5	10.1
ID Human-labeled	0.83	19.1	10.1
RU Baseline (no classes)	-	28.7	17.1
RU Cross-lingual 16K	0.37	26.4	17.0
RU Cross-lingual 98K	0.39	26.2	17.1
RU Human-labeled	0.87	25.3	16.8
IT Baseline (no classes)	-	23.0	14.8
IT Cross-lingual 18K	0.55	19.7	14.8
IT Cross-lingual 104K	0.57	19.6	14.8
IT Human-labeled	0.88	19.0	14.8

Table 2: *NUM* refers to the NUMERIC entities test set and *VS* refers to the VOICE-SEARCH test set. All *NUM* WER results are statistically significant ($p < 0.1\%$) using a paired random permutation significance test.

translation task rather than for an academic task. When evaluated on a test set matched to the translation task, performance for Russian-to-English was considerably worse than for Indonesian-to-English or Italian-to-English.

For Indonesian (ID), the human-labeled system achieved a 4.5% relative WER reduction on NUMERIC, while the best cross-lingual system achieved a 3.5% relative reduction.

For Russian (RU), the human-labeled system improved more, achieving an 11.8% relative reduction on NUMERIC, while the best cross-lingual system achieved an 8.7% relative reduction.

Finally, for Italian (IT), the human-labeled system gave an impressive 17.4% relative reduction on NUMERIC, while the best cross-lingual system achieved a 14.8% relative reduction on the same test set.

Across the three languages, the cross-lingual systems achieved relative error reductions on the NUMERIC test set that were between 70% and 85% of the reduction achieved when using only human-labeled data for training the class tagger.

4.5 Error Analysis

We noticed that the Russian cross-lingual-derived training set was of lower quality than those of the other languages, as seen in the labeled-bracket F1 metric in Table 2. Looking more closely, we noticed that the per-class F1 scores tended to be lower for labels used for dates and times. This observation also concides with the observation that the alignment procedure frequently ran into ambiguity issues when aligning month, day and year tokens between Russian and English, thus significantly reducing the coverage of these labels in the induced cross-lingual training set.

5 Conclusion

We presented a cross-lingual projection technique for training class-based language models. We extend a previously successful sequence-modeling-based class labeling approach for identifying contextually-dependent class assignments by projecting labels from a high-resource language to a low-resources language. This allows us to build class-based language models in low-resource languages with no annotated data. Our empirical results show that we are able to achieve between 70% and 85% of the error reduction that we would have obtained had we used human-labeled data.

While cross-lingual projection for sequence-labeling techniques are well known in the community, our approach exploits the fact that we are generating training data from the projection rather than using the projected result directly. Furthermore, noise in the class-labeling system does not cripple the language model as it learns a distribution over labels (including no label).

In future work, we will experiment with alternative projection approaches including projecting the training data and translating from the high-resource language to the low-resource language. We also plan to experiment with different projection approaches to address the ambiguity issues we observed when aligning time and date expressions.

6 Acknowledgments

We would like to thank the anonymous reviewers for their detailed reviews and suggestions.

References

Peter F. Brown, Peter V. deSouza, Robert L. Mercer, Vincent J. Della Pietra, and Jenifer C. Lai. 1992. Class-based n-gram models of natural language. *Computational Linguistics*, 18:467–479.

David Burkett, Slav Petrov, John Blitzer, and Dan Klein. 2010. Learning better monolingual models with unannotated bilingual text. In *Proceedings of the Fourteenth Conference on Computational Natural Language Learning*, CoNLL '10, pages 46–54. Association for Computational Linguistics.

Koby Crammer and Yoram Singer. 2003. Ultraconservative online algorithms for multiclass problems. *J. Mach. Learn. Res.*, 3:951–991, March.

Dipanjan Das and Slav Petrov. 2011. Unsupervised part-of-speech tagging with bilingual graph-based projections. In *Proceedings of the 49th Annual Meeting of the Association for Computational Linguistics: Human Language Technologies - Volume 1*, HLT '11, pages 600–609. Association for Computational Linguistics.

Fei Huang, Stephan Vogel, and Alex Waibel. 2003. Automatic extraction of named entity translingual equivalence based on multi-feature cost minimization. In *Proceedings of the ACL 2003 Workshop on Multilingual and Mixed-language Named Entity Recognition - Volume 15*, MultiNER '03, pages 9–16. Association for Computational Linguistics.

Reinhard Knesser and Hermann Ney. 1993. Improved clustering techniques for class-based statistical language modelling. In *Proc. Eurospeech*. ISCA - International Speech Communication Association, September.

Philipp Koehn, Franz Josef Och, and Daniel Marcu. 2003. Statistical phrase-based translation. In *Proceedings of the 2003 Conference of the North American Chapter of the Association for Computational Linguistics on Human Language Technology*, volume 1 of *NAACL '03*, pages 48–54. Association for Computational Linguistics.

John D. Lafferty, Andrew McCallum, and Fernando C. N. Pereira. 2001. Conditional random fields: Probabilistic models for segmenting and labeling sequence data. In *Proceedings of the Eighteenth International Conference on Machine Learning*, ICML '01, pages 282–289, San Francisco, CA, USA. Morgan Kaufmann Publishers Inc.

Michael Levit, Sarangarajan Parthasarathy, Shuangyu Chang, Andreas Stolcke, and Benoit Dumoulin. 2014. Word-phrase-entity language models: Getting more mileage out of n-grams. In *Proc. Interspeech*. ISCA - International Speech Communication Association, September.

Robert C. Moore. 2003. Learning translations of named-entity phrases from parallel corpora. In *Proceedings of the Tenth Conference on European*

Chapter of the Association for Computational Linguistics - Volume 1, EACL '03, pages 259–266. Association for Computational Linguistics.

Tetsuji Nakagawa. 2015. Efficient top-down BTG parsing for machine translation preordering. In *Proceedings of the 53rd Annual Meeting of the Association for Computational Linguistics, ACL 2015, Volume 1: Long Papers*, pages 208–218.

Sebastian Padó and Mirella Lapata. 2009. Cross-lingual annotation projection of semantic roles. *Journal of Artificial Intelligence Research*, 36(1):307–340, September.

Lucy Vasserman, Vlad Schogol, and Keith Hall. 2015. Sequence-based class tagging for robust transcription in asr. In *Proc. Interspeech*. ISCA - International Speech Communication Association, September.

David Yarowsky and Grace Ngai. 2001. Inducing multilingual pos taggers and np bracketers via robust projection across aligned corpora. In *Proceedings of the Second Meeting of the North American Chapter of the Association for Computational Linguistics on Language Technologies*, NAACL '01, pages 1–8. Association for Computational Linguistics.

David Yarowsky, Grace Ngai, and Richard Wicentowski. 2001. Inducing multilingual text analysis tools via robust projection across aligned corpora. In *Proceedings of the First International Conference on Human Language Technology Research*, HLT '01, pages 1–8. Association for Computational Linguistics.

A Fast Approach for Semantic Similar Short Texts Retrieval

Yanhui Gu[1] Zhenglu Yang[2]* Junsheng Zhou[1]
Weiguang Qu[1] Jinmao Wei[2] Xingtian Shi[3]
[1]School of Computer Science and Technology, Nanjing Normal University, China
{gu,zhoujs,wgqu}@njnu.edu.cn
[2]CCCE&CS, Nankai University, Tianjin, China
{yangzl,weijm}@nankai.edu.cn
[3]SAP Labs China, Shanghai, China
{xingtian.shi}@sap.com

Abstract

Retrieving semantic similar short texts is a crucial issue to many applications, e.g., web search, ads matching, question-answer system, and so forth. Most of the traditional methods concentrate on how to improve the precision of the similarity measurement, while current real applications need to efficiently explore the top similar short texts semantically related to the query one. We address the efficiency issue in this paper by investigating the similarity strategies and incorporating them into the **FAST** framework (efficient **FrA**mework for semantic similar **S**hort **T**exts retrieval). We conduct comprehensive performance evaluation on real-life data which shows that our proposed method outperforms the state-of-the-art techniques.

1 Introduction

In this paper, we investigate the fast approach of short texts retrieval, which is important to many applications, e.g., web search, ads matching, question-answer system, etc. (Yu et al., 2016; Wang et al., 2015; Hua et al., 2015; Yang et al., 2015; Wang et al., 2010; Wei et al., 2008; Cui et al., 2005; Metzler et al., 2007; Ceccarelli et al., 2011; Radlinski et al., 2008). The setting of the problem is that users always ask for those most semantically related to their queries from a huge text collection. A common solution is applying the state-of-the-art short texts similarity measurement techniques (Islam and Inkpen, 2008; Li et al., 2006; Mihalcea et al., 2006; Sahami and Heilman, 2006; Tsatsaronis et al., 2010; Mohler et al., 2011; Wang et al., 2015), and then return the top-k ones

by sorting them with regard to the similarity score. After surveying the previous approaches, we find that almost all the methods concentrate on how to improve the precision, i.e., effectiveness issue. In addition, the data collections which they conducted are rather small. However, the scale of the problem has dramatically increased and the current short texts similarity measurement techniques could not handle when the data collection size becomes enormous. In this paper, we aim to address the efficiency issue in the literature while keeping their high precision. Moreover, we focus on the top-k issue because users commonly do not care about the individual similarity score but only the sorted results. Furthermore, most of the previous studies (Islam and Inkpen, 2008; Li et al., 2006; Tsatsaronis et al., 2010; Wang et al., 2015) need to set predefined threshold to filter out those dissimilar texts which is rather difficult to determine by users.

Different from long texts, short texts cannot always observe the syntax of a written language and usually do not possess sufficient information to support statistical based text processing techniques, e.g., TF-IDF. This indicates that the traditional NLP techniques for long texts may not be always appropriate to apply to short texts. The related works on short texts similarity measurement can be classified into the following major categories, i.e., (1) inner resource based strategy (Li et al., 2006; Islam and Inkpen, 2008); (2) outer resource based strategy (Tsatsaronis et al., 2010; Mihalcea et al., 2006; Islam and Inkpen, 2008; Wang et al., 2015); and (3) hybrid based strategy (Islam and Inkpen, 2008; Li et al., 2006; Wang et al., 2015).

Naively testing the candidate short texts for top-k similar short texts retrieval is inefficient when directly using these strategies. To tackle the efficiency problem, we propose an efficient strategy

---

* Corresponding author.

Proceedings of the 54th Annual Meeting of the Association for Computational Linguistics, pages 89–94,
Berlin, Germany, August 7-12, 2016. ©2016 Association for Computational Linguistics

to evaluate as few candidates as possible. Moreover, our fast algorithm aims to output the results progressively, i.e., the top-1 should be obtained instantly. This scheme meets the demand of the real world applications, especially for big data environment. We list our contribution of this paper as follows: we propose a fast approach to tackle the efficiency problem for retrieving top-k semantic similar short texts; we present the optimized techniques and improve the efficiency which minimizes the candidate number to be evaluated in our framework. The results of four different settings demonstrate that the efficiency of our fast approach outperforms the state-of-the-art methods while keeping effectiveness.

2 Preliminaries

Formally, for a given query short text q, retrieving a set of k short texts T_s in a data collection D_s which are most semantically similar to q, i.e., $\forall t \in T_s$ and $\forall r \in (D_s - T_s)$ will yield $sim(q, t) \geq sim(q, r)$. To obtain the similarity score $sim(q, t)$ between two short texts, we can apply the current state-of-the-art strategies (Tsatsaronis et al., 2010; Mihalcea et al., 2006; Islam and Inkpen, 2008; Wang et al., 2015). In this paper, we judiciously select some similarity metrics which are assembled into a general framework to tackle the efficiency problem. Most of the existing strategies of evaluating the similarity between short texts are based on word similarity, because of the intuitive idea that short text is composed of words. As a result, we introduce the representative word similarity in the next section.

2.1 Selected Representative Similarity Measurement Strategies

There are a number of semantic similarity strategies having been developed in the previous decades which are useful in some specific applications of NLP tasks. Recently, outer resources are indispensable for short texts similarity measurement (Tsatsaronis et al., 2010; Mihalcea et al., 2006; Islam and Inkpen, 2008; Wang et al., 2015; Hua et al., 2015). After extensively investigating a number of similarity measurement strategies, we judiciously explore two representative word similarity measurement strategies which obtain the best performance compared with human judges.

Knowledge based Strategy

Knowledge based strategy determines whether two words are semantically similar by measuring their shortest path in the predefined taxonomy. The path between them can be calculated by applying word thesauri, e.g., WordNet. In this paper, we take one representative metric which has been proposed in (Leacock and Chodorow, 1998). Let's take two words w_i, w_j as an example, the similarity is as follows:

$$Sim_k(w_i, w_j) = -ln\frac{path_s(w_i, w_j)}{2 * D}$$

where $path_s(w_i, w_j)$ is the shortest path between two word concepts by using related strategy, e.g., node-counting strategy. D is the maximum depth of such taxonomy (D is with different size in either noun taxonomy or verb taxonomy).

Corpus based Strategy

Different from knowledge based strategy, corpus based strategy cannot form a new entity which means we can only apply statistical information to determine the similarity between two words. There are a few corpus based similarity measurement strategies, e.g., PMI, LSA, HAL, and so forth. In this paper, we select a representative strategy which applies Wiki encyclopedia to map Wiki texts into appropriate topics. Each Wiki topic is represented as an attribute vector. The words in the vector occur in the corresponding articles. Entries of these vectors are assigned weight which quantifies the association between words and each Wiki topic after applying vector based scheme, e.g., TF-IDF. The similarity can be evaluated by aggregating each word distributing on these topics. In addition, a short text is a vector based on topics with weight of each topic T_i formulated as: $\sum_{w_i \in T_s} v_i \cdot d_j$, where v_i is TF-IDF weight of w_i and d_j which quantifies the degree of association of word w_i with Wiki topic T_j. Here, the Wiki topic could be concepts or topics generated by other techniques, e.g., LDA, LSA, etc.

2.2 Semantic Similarity Measurement between Two Short Texts

Semantic similarity between two short texts can be measured by combining the words similarity in a general framework. Therefore, the method of combining the words similarities into a framework may affect the efficiency and effectiveness of the similarity score. In this paper, we integrate different similarity strategies linearly and this method has been proved that it has high precision by comparing with human judges (Li et al., 2006; Islam and Inkpen, 2008). The scheme measures each word pair of short texts and then constructs a similarity score matrix. Finally, the similarity score between two short texts is recursively executed by aggregating the representative words.

3   A Fast Approach for Semantic Similar Short Texts Retrieval

We propose a fast approach for retrieving the top-k semantic similar short texts to a given query q in this section. The key idea of this scheme is to access a rather small size of candidates in the whole data collection. The scheme is conducted by building appropriate indices in offline procedure, i.e., preprocessing procedure. We illustrate the whole framework in Figure 1. The figure tells us, to efficiently retrieve top-k similar short texts, our proposed strategy only accesses as small as possible part of candidates which are filled in grey color.

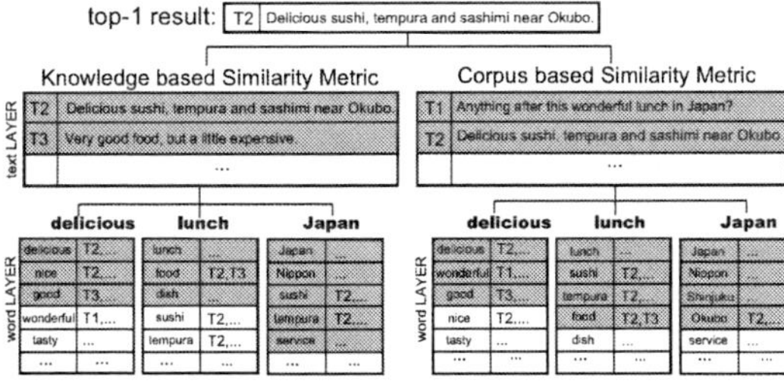

Figure 1: The framework of proposed fast approach

3.1   Efficiently Aggregate Similarity Metrics

In this section, we present an efficient assembling strategy to hasten the process of retrieving top-k similar short texts (Fagin et al., 2001). A concrete example to illustrate our proposal is presented in Figure 1. For example, let the query short text is: "Delicious lunch in Japan". After preprocessing (stemming and removing the stopwords), the query is: delicious lunch Japan. From Figure 1, we can see that there is a hierarchical structure in our framework. Suppose that if we want to retrieve top-1 short text from the whole data, the ranked list (i.e., order list) of knowledge based similarity and corpus based similarity are needed respectively. From the analysis on the property of threshold algorithm, the top-1 short text comes from these two

ranked lists instantly. However, we cannot know such ranking directly because these two lists are texts layer but each list has its sub layer, i.e., word layer. In this paper, we apply two kinds of similarity metrics. Therefore, there are two assembling tasks, i.e., (1)assembling knowledge based and corpus based similarities; and (2)assembling words to texts. The words are query words and each query word corresponds to a list which can be found in Figure 1. Figure 1 also tells us for each word, it has the corresponding list in which all the words have been ranked based on the relatedness with such word. Since each word may occur in several short texts, the proposed method here should take the ID of each short text into consideration (e.g., word "delicious" occurs T2, etc.). We apply threshold algorithm to obtain the top short texts based on each query word. Therefore, the top-1 result comes from these two ranked lists based on threshold algorithm. In this example, T2 is finally outputted as the top-1 value.

3.2   Ranking list on Similarity Strategies

From the description in Section 3.1, we can see that the ranked list is crucial for using threshold algorithm to retrieve top-k short texts. In this section, we introduce the optimized method on each similarity metric.

Ranking on Knowledge based strategy

Since WordNet is a representative knowledge base, we apply the Leacock and Chodorow strategy as a WordNet evaluator which optimized as an efficient technique (Yang and Kitsuregawa, 2011).

Lemma 1 (Ordering in WordNet) *Let q be the query. Let P and S be two candidates that exist in the same taxonomy of q, that is, T_P and T_q. The shortest path between q and P (or S) is L_P in T_P (or L_S in T_S). The maximum depth of T_P is D_P (or D_S of T_S). P is more similar to Q compared with S. Thus, we have $\frac{D_P}{L_P} > \frac{D_S}{L_S}$.*

The lemma tells us that the similarity ordering between candidates in WordNet depends on the integration of the shortest path and the maximum depth of the taxonomy. We access the related synonyms set between two taxonomies successively based on the value of $\frac{D}{L}$ and obtain the top-k results in a progressive manner.

Ranking on Corpus based Strategy

We measure the similarity between short texts

by aggregating each word distribution on topics. A short text is a valued vector based on topics, where the weight of each topic T_i calculated as: $\sum_{w_i \in T_s} v_i \cdot k_j$, where v_i is TF-IDF weight of w_i and k_j which quantifies the strength of association of word w_i with Wiki topic T_j. Different from the traditional approaches, we first calculate all the similarity scores between each word in Wiki and that between topics in the data collection to obtain a set of lists during preprocessing. The topic could be generated either by ESA or by LDA. After that, we build a weighted inverted list where each list presents a word with sorted corresponding short texts according to the similarity score. Therefore, for a given query text q, each word in q corresponds to a list of short texts. As that, we apply the threshold algorithm retrieve the top-k results by using this manner. This manner accesses a small size of components of the data without necessity to evaluate every candidate short text.

After obtaining all the ranking lists, we can apply the threshold algorithm aforementioned to efficiently retrieve the top-k semantic similar short texts either by equal weight scheme or weight tuning strategy.

4 Experimental Evaluation

In this section, we conduct on three different datasets to evaluate the performance of our approach. To evaluate the effectiveness, we test the dataset which was used in (Li et al., 2006). For efficiency evaluation, we apply the BNC and MSC datasets which are extracted from British National Corpus and Microsoft Research Paraphrase Corpus respectively. The baseline strategy is implemented according to the state-of-the-art (linear assembling strategy as (Islam and Inkpen, 2008)). In our proposed strategy, we take four different settings: (1) $\mathbf{FAST}_E$ is the one that we apply the ESA topic strategy; (2) $\mathbf{FAST}_L$ employs the LDA topic strategy in corpus based similarity with equal weight; and (3) $\mathbf{FAST}_{Ew}$ and $\mathbf{FAST}_{Lw}$ are implemented based on the former two ones, respectively, with the tuned combinational weights.

4.1 Efficiency Evaluation

We evaluate the efficiency by using two real-life datasets which have been denoted as BNC and MSC. To test the effect of size of data collection, we select different size of these two datasets. Firstly, we conducted experiments on the fixed size of data collection by using 4 settings of our proposed approach. The results show that comparing with the baseline strategy, $\mathbf{FAST}_E$, $\mathbf{FAST}_L$, $\mathbf{FAST}_{Ew}$ and $\mathbf{FAST}_{Lw}$ have promotion at 75.34%, 74.68%, 75.31% and 74.59% respectively. The four settings have similar results which indicates that the weight is not the crucial factor in our proposed strategy. Table. 1 tells us the number of candidates accessed. Our evaluation has been conducted on different data collection size to test the scalability of our proposed strategy. Since the baseline strategy should access all the short texts in each size of data collection, which means in 1k size of BNC data collection, the baseline strategy access all these 1k candidates. However, our proposed strategies under different settings only access small size candidates to obtain the results. From the table, we can see that, our proposed strategy can largely reduce the number of candidates accessed in both data collections. In addition, the number of candidates accessed has increases not quickly which indicate our proposed approach scales well. Therefore, the proposed strategy is efficient than the baseline strategy.

Strategies	BNC (#Candidates accessed)			
	1k	5k	10k	20k
$\mathbf{FAST}_E$	215	1,368	1,559	1,974
$\mathbf{FAST}_L$	217	1,478	1,551	2,001
$\mathbf{FAST}_{Ew}$	225	1,511	1,621	2,043
$\mathbf{FAST}_{Lw}$	225	1,521	1,603	2,025

Strategies	MSC (#Candidates accessed)			
	10%	20%	50%	100%
$\mathbf{FAST}_E$	74	304	712	1,253
$\mathbf{FAST}_L$	85	313	705	1,128
$\mathbf{FAST}_{Ew}$	87	308	725	1,135
$\mathbf{FAST}_{Lw}$	81	309	712	1,076

Table 1: Number of candidates accessed in efficiency evaluation

We also evaluate the effect of k which is an important factor for evaluating the efficiency of an algorithm. The experiments conducted on a fixed size of data collection which show that the top-1 value has been outputted instantly by apply our proposed strategy while baseline strategy should access all candidates. For the query time of $\mathbf{FAST}_E$ setting costs only 19.12s while baseline strategy costs 897.5s for obtaining the top-1 value. $\mathbf{FAST}_L$, $\mathbf{FAST}_{Es}$ and $\mathbf{FAST}_{Lw}$ cost 20.13s, 21.21s and 20.32s respectively which confirms that combinational weight is not an important factor in our proposed strategy.

4.2 Effectiveness Evaluation

We illustrate the results of the correlation coefficient with human ratings in Table. 2. Note here, the baseline strategy is composed by knowledge based strategy and corpus based strategy (ESA method) with equal weight. From the table we can see that, the $\mathbf{FAST}_E$ has the same precision as the baseline because our proposed strategy only changes the order of the evaluated short texts but not the similarity strategy. $\mathbf{FAST}_L$ has better precision than $\mathbf{FAST}_E$ because we select the best LDA topic size to form Wiki topic. $\mathbf{FAST}_{Ew}$ and $\mathbf{FAST}_{Lw}$ have dynamically changed the combinational weights and therefore, the performance of them has been improved.

Baseline	Proposed Strategies			
	$\mathbf{FAST}_E$	$\mathbf{FAST}_L$	$\mathbf{FAST}_{Ew}$	$\mathbf{FAST}_{Lw}$
0.72162	0.72162	0.73333	0.74788	0.74941

Table 2: Effectiveness evaluation on different strategies

5 Conclusion

In this paper, we propose a fast approach to tackle the efficiency problem of retrieving top-k similar short texts which has not been extensively studied before. We select two representative similarity metrics, i.e., knowledge based and corpus based similarity. Efficient strategies are introduced to test as few candidates as possible in the querying process. Four different settings have been proposed to improve the effectiveness. The comprehensive experiments demonstrate the efficiency of the proposed techniques while keeping the high precision. In the future, we will investigate new methods to tackle efficiency issue and take effect semantic similarity strategies to obtain high performance.

Acknowledgment. We would like to thank the anonymous reviewers for their insightful comments. This work is partially supported by Chinese National Fund of Natural Science under Grant 61272221, 61472191, 61070089, 11431006, Jiangsu Province Fund of Social Science under Grant 12YYA002, the Natural Science Research of Jiangsu Higher Education Institutions of China under Grant 14KJB520022, and the Science Foundation of TianJin under grant 14JCYBJC15700.

References

Diego Ceccarelli, Claudio Lucchese, Salvatore Orlando, Raffaele Perego, and Fabrizio Silvestri. 2011. Caching query-biased snippets for efficient retrieval. In *Proceedings of the International Conference on Extending Database Technology*, EDBT/ICDT '11, pages 93–104.

Hang Cui, Renxu Sun, Keya Li, Min-Yen Kan, and Tat-Seng Chua. 2005. Question answering passage retrieval using dependency relations. In *Proceedings of the International ACM SIGIR Conference on Research and Development in Information Retrieval*, SIGIR '05, pages 400–407.

Ronald Fagin, Amnon Lotem, and Moni Naor. 2001. Optimal aggregation algorithms for middleware. In *Proceedings of the ACM SIGMOD symposium on Principles of Database Systems*, PODS '01, pages 102–113.

Wen Hua, Zhongyuan Wang, Haixun Wang, Kai Zheng, and Xiaofang Zhou. 2015. Short text understanding through lexical-semantic analysis In *31st IEEE International Conference on Data Engineering*, ICDE'15, pages 495–506.

Aminul Islam and Diana Inkpen. 2008. Semantic text similarity using corpus-based word similarity and string similarity. *ACM Transactions on Knowledge Discovery from Data*, 2(2):1–25.

C. Leacock and M. Chodorow. 1998. Combining local context and wordnet similarity for word sense identification. In *WordNet: An Electronic Lexical Database*, pages 305–332. In C. Fellbaum (Ed.), MIT Press.

Yuhua Li, David McLean, Zuhair Bandar, James O'Shea, and Keeley A. Crockett. 2006. Sentence similarity based on semantic nets and corpus statistics. *IEEE Transactions on Knowledge and Data Engineering*, 18(8):1138–1150.

Donald Metzler, Susan T. Dumais, and Christopher Meek. 2007. Similarity measures for short segments of text. In *Proceedings of the European Conference on Information Retrieval*, ECIR '07, pages 16–27.

Rada Mihalcea, Courtney Corley, and Carlo Strapparava. 2006. Corpus-based and knowledge-based measures of text semantic similarity. In *Proceedings of the AAAI Conference on Artificial Intelligence*, AAAI'06, pages 775–780.

Michael Mohler, Razvan C. Bunescu, and Rada Mihalcea. 2011. Learning to grade short answer questions using semantic similarity measures and dependency graph alignments. In *Proceedings of the 49th Annual Meeting of the Association for Computational Linguistics: Human Language Technologies, Proceedings of the Conference*, ACL'11, pages 752–762.

Filip Radlinski, Andrei Broder, Peter Ciccolo, Evgeniy Gabrilovich, Vanja Josifovski, and Lance Riedel. 2008. Optimizing relevance and revenue in ad search: a query substitution approach. In *Proceedings of the International ACM SIGIR Conference on Research and Development in Information Retrieval*, SIGIR '08, pages 403–410.

Mehran Sahami and Timothy D. Heilman. 2006. A web-based kernel function for measuring the similarity of short text snippets. In *Proceedings of the International Conference on World Wide Web*, WWW '06.

George Tsatsaronis, Iraklis Varlamis, and Michalis Vazirgiannis. 2010. Text relatedness based on a word thesaurus. *Journal of Artificial Intelligence Research*, 37:1–39.

Kai Wang, Zhao-Yan Ming, Xia Hu, and Tat-Seng Chua. 2010. Segmentation of multi-sentence questions: towards effective question retrieval in cqa services. In *Proceedings of the International ACM SIGIR Conference on Research and Development in Information Retrieval*, SIGIR '10, pages 387–394.

Peng Wang, Jiaming Xu, Bo Xu, Cheng-Lin Liu, Heng Zhang, Fangyuan Wang, and Hongwei Hao. 2015. Semantic clustering and convolutional neural network for short text categorization. In *Proceedings of the 53rd Annual Meeting of the Association for Computational Linguistics and the 7th International Joint Conference on Natural Language Processing of the Asian Federation of Natural Language Processing*, ACL '15, pages 352–357.

Furu Wei, Wenjie Li, Qin Lu, and Yanxiang He. 2008. Query-sensitive mutual reinforcement chain and its application in query-oriented multi-document summarization. In *Proceedings of the International ACM SIGIR Conference on Research and Development in Information Retrieval*, SIGIR '08, pages 283–290.

Zhenglu Yang and Masaru Kitsuregawa. 2011. Efficient searching top-k semantic similar words. In *Proceedings of the International Joint Conference on Artificial Intelligence*, IJCAI'11, pages 2373–2378.

Shansong Yang, Weiming Lu, Dezhi Yang, Liang Yao, and Baogang Wei. 2015. Short text understanding by leveraging knowledge into topic model. In *The 2015 Conference of the North American Chapter of the Association for Computational Linguistics: Human Language Technologies*, NAACL/HLT'15, pages 1232–1237.

Zheng Yu, Haixun Wang, Xuemin Lin, and Min Wang. 2016. Understanding short texts through semantic enrichment and hashing. *IEEE Trans. Knowl. Data Eng.*, 28(2):566–579.

Empty element recovery by spinal parser operations

Katsuhiko Hayashi and **Masaaki Nagata**

NTT Communication Science Laboratories, NTT Corporation
2-4 Hikaridai, Seika-cho, Soraku-gun, Kyoto, 619-0237 Japan
{hayashi.katsuhiko, nagata.masaaki}@lab.ntt.co.jp

Abstract

This paper presents a spinal parsing algorithm that can jointly detect empty elements. This method achieves state-of-the-art performance on English and Japanese empty element recovery problems.

1 Introduction

Empty categories, which are used in Penn Treebank style annotations to represent complex syntactic phenomena like constituent movement and discontinuous constituents, provide important information for understanding the semantic structure of sentences. Previous studies attempt empty element recovery by casting it as linear tagging (Dienes and Dubey, 2003), PCFG parsing (Schmid, 2006; Cai et al., 2011) or post-processing of syntactic parsing (Johnson, 2002; Gabbard et al., 2006). To the best of our knowledge, the results reported by (Cai et al., 2011) are the best yet reported, so we pursue a method that uses syntactic parsing to jointly solve the empty element recovery problem.

Our proposal uses the spinal Tree Adjoining Grammar (TAG) formalism of (Carreras et al., 2008). The spinal TAG has a set of elementary trees, called spines, each consisting of a lexical anchor with a series of unary projections. Figure 1 displays (a) a head-annotated constituent tree and (b) spines extracted from the tree. This paper presents a transition-based algorithm together with several operations to combine spines for constructing full parse trees with empty elements. Compared with the PCFG parsing approaches, one advantage of our method is its flexible feature representations, which allow the incorporation of constituency-, dependency- and spine-based features. Of particular interest, the motivation for our spinal TAG-based approach comes from the

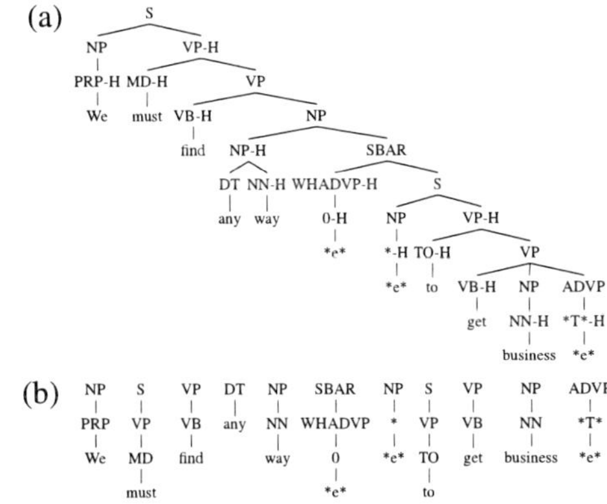

Figure 1: (a) an example of a constituent tree with head annotations denoted by -H; (b) spinal elementary trees extracted from the parse tree (a).

intuition that features extracted from spines can be expected to be useful for empty element recovery in the same way as constituency-based vertical higher-order conjunctive features are used in recent post-processing methods (Xiang et al., 2013; Takeno et al., 2015). Experiments on English and Japanese datasets empirically show that our system outperforms existing alternatives.

2 Spinal Tree Adjoining Grammars

We define here the spinal TAG $G = (N, PT, T, LS)$ where N is a set of nonterminal symbols, PT is a set of pre-terminal symbols (or part-of-speech tags), T is a set of terminal symbols (or words), and LS is a set of **lexical spines**. Each spine, s, has the form $n_0 \rightarrow n_1 \rightarrow \cdots \rightarrow n_{k-1} \rightarrow n_k$ $(k \in \mathbb{N})$ which satisfies the conditions:

- $n_0 \in T$ and $n_1 \in PT$,

- $\forall i \in [2, k], n_i \in N$.

The **height** of spine s is $ht(s) = k + 1$ and for some position $i \in [0, k]$, the **label** at i is $s(i) = n_i$. Tak-

Proceedings of the 54th Annual Meeting of the Association for Computational Linguistics, pages 95–100,
Berlin, Germany, August 7-12, 2016. ©2016 Association for Computational Linguistics

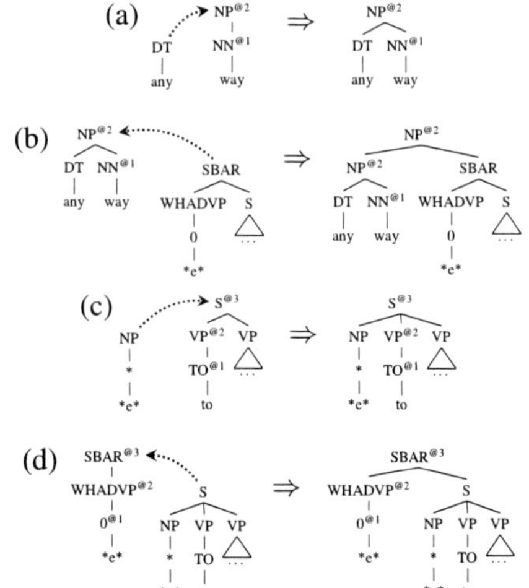

Figure 2: An example of parser operations: (a) sister adjunction left (b) regular adjunction right (c) insert left (d) combine right.

ing the leftmost spine $s = \text{We} \rightarrow \text{PRP} \rightarrow \text{NP}$ in Figure 1 (b), $ht(s) = 3$ and $s(1) = \text{PRP}$.

The spinal TAG uses two operations, **sister** and **regular** adjunctions, to combine spines. Both adjunctions also have **left** and **right** types. Figures 2 (a) and (b) show examples of sister adjunction left and regular adjunction right operations. We use @# to illustrate node position on a spine, explicitly. After a regular adjunction, the resulting tree has an additional node level which has a copy of its original node at position @x, while a sister adjunction simply inserts a spine into some node of another spine. If adjunction left (or right) inserts spine s_1 into some node at @x on spine s_2, we call s_2 the **head spine** of s_1 and s_1 the **left** (or **right**) **child spine** of s_2[1]. This paper denotes sister adjunction left and right as $s_1 \bigominus^x s_2$, $s_2 \bigominus^x s_1$, regular adjunction left and right as $s_1 \bigomoon^x s_2$, $s_2 \bigomoon^x s_1$, respectively.

3 Arc-Standard Shift-Reduce Spinal TAG Parsing

There are three algorithms for spinal TAG parsing, (1) Eisner-Satta CKY (Carreras et al., 2008), (2) arc-eager shift-reduce (Ballesteros and Carreras, 2015) and (3) arc-standard shift-reduce (Hayashi et al., 2016) algorithms. This paper uses the arc-

standard shift-reduce algorithm since it provides a more simple implementation.

A **transition system** for spinal TAG parsing is the tuple $S = (C, T, I, C_t)$, where C is a set of configurations, T is a set of transitions, which are partial functions $t : C \rightharpoonup C$, I is a total initialization function mapping each input string to a unique configuration, and $C_t \subseteq C$ is a set of terminal configurations. A **configuration** is the tuple (α, β, A) where α is a **stack** of stack elements, β is a **buffer** of elements from an input, and A is a set of parser operations. A **stack element** s is a pair (s, j) where s is a spine and j is a node index of s. We refer to s and j of s as $s.s$ and $s.j$, respectively.

Let $\mathbf{x} = \langle w_1/t_1, \ldots, w_n/t_n \rangle$ ($\forall i \in [1, n]$, $w_i \in T$ and $t_i \in PT$) be a pos-tagged input sentence. The **arc-standard transition system** by Hayashi et al. (2016) can be defined as follows: its initialization function is $I(\mathbf{x}) = ([], [w_1/t_1, \ldots, w_n/t_n], \emptyset)$, its set of terminal configurations is $C_t = ([], [], A)$, and it has the following transitions:

1. for each $s \in LS$ with $s(0) = w_i$ and $s(1) = t_i$, a shift transition of the form $(\alpha, w_i/t_i|\beta, A) \vdash (\alpha|s_1, \beta, A)$ where $s_1 = (s, 2)$[2];

2-3. for each j with $s_1.j \leq j < ht(s_1.s)$, a sister adjunction left transition of the form

$$(\sigma|s_2|s_1, \beta, A) \vdash (\sigma|s_1', \beta, A \cup \{s_2.s \bigominus^j s_1.s\})$$

and a regular adjunction left transition of the form

$$(\sigma|s_2|s_1, \beta, A) \vdash (\sigma|s_1', \beta, A \cup \{s_2.s \bigomoon^j s_1.s\})$$

where $s_1' = (s_1.s, j)$;

4-5. for each j with $s_2.j \leq j < ht(s_2.s)$, a sister adjunction right transition of the form

$$(\sigma|s_2|s_1, \beta, A) \vdash (\sigma|s_1', \beta, A \cup \{s_2.s \bigominus^j s_1.s\})$$

and a regular adjunction right transition of the form

$$(\sigma|s_2|s_1, \beta, A) \vdash (\sigma|s_1', \beta, A \cup \{s_2.s \bigomoon^j s_1.s\})$$

where $s_1' = (s_2.s, j)$;

6. a finish transition of the form $([s], [], A) \vdash ([], [], A)$.

---

[1] After adjunctions, the result forms a phrase consisting of several spines. If a phrasal spine is also used in adjunction operations as Figure 2 (b), we treat it as a lexical spine by referring to its head spine.

[2] To construct a full parse tree from A, our actual implementation attaches index i to spine s after shift transition.

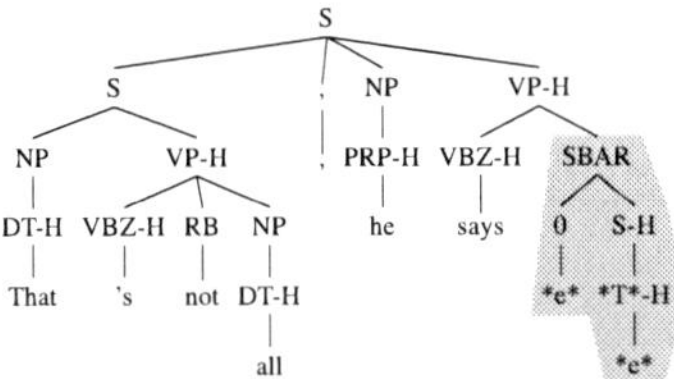

Figure 3: A phrasal empty spine shown on the shaded region.

To reduce search errors, Hayashi et al. (2016) employed beam search with Dynamic Programming of (Huang and Sagae, 2010). For experiments, we also use this technique and discriminative modeling of (Hayashi et al., 2016).

4 Empty Element Recovery

4.1 Spinal TAG with Empty Elements

In this paper, we redefine the spinal TAG as $G = (N, PT, T, LS, *e*, ET, ES)$, where $*e*$ is a special word, ET is a set of empty categories, and ES is a set of empty spines. An **empty spine** $s = n_0 \rightarrow n_1 \rightarrow \cdots \rightarrow n_{k-1} \rightarrow n_k$ ($k \in \mathbb{N}$) has the same form as lexical spines, but $n_0 = *e*$ and $n_1 \in ET$. The height and label definitions are also the same as those of lexical spines. For example, the rightmost spine $s = *e* \rightarrow *T* \rightarrow ADVP$ in Figure 1 (b) is an empty spine with $ht(s) = 3$ and $s(1) = *T*$.

This paper extends empty spines to allow the use of phrasal constituents that consist of only empty elements, as a single spine. A **phrasal empty spine** is a tuple (t, h), where t is a sequence of (phrasal) empty spines specifying some sister adjunctions between these spines and h is a head spine in t. The phrasal empty spine in Figure 3 consists of two empty spines $*e* \rightarrow 0$ and $*e* \rightarrow *T* \rightarrow S \rightarrow SBAR$, where a sister adjunction left is performed at the SBAR node of the latter spine, which is a head spine in the phrase. To apply parser operations to a phrasal empty spine, we use its head spine rather than itself. This paper defines the height and label of a phrasal empty spine as those of its head spine.

To recover empty elements, this paper introduces two additional operations, **insert** and **combine**, both of which have **left** and **right** types. Figures 2 (c) and (d) show insert left and combine right operations. These operations are similar to sister adjunctions in that the former simply inserts some phrasal empty spine into some node of another spine and the latter also inserts a spine into

some node of a phrasal empty spine.

4.2 New Transitions

To handle empty spines in parsing process, we add the following five transitions to the arc-standard transition system of (Hayashi et al., 2016):

7-8. for each $s \in ES$ and each j with $s_1.j \leq j < ht(s_1.s)$, an insert left transition of the form

$$(\sigma|s_1, \beta, A) \vdash (\sigma|s_1', \beta, A \cup \{s \oslash^j s_1.s\})$$

and an insert right transition of the form

$$(\sigma|s_1, \beta, A) \vdash (\sigma|s_1', \beta, A \cup \{s_1.s \oslash^j s\})$$

where $s_1' = (s_1.s, j)$;

9-10. for each $s \in ES$ and each j with $2 \leq j < ht(s)$, a combine left transition of the form

$$(\sigma|s_1, \beta, A) \vdash (\sigma|s_1', \beta, A \cup \{s_1.s \oslash^j s\})$$

and a combine right transition of the form

$$(\sigma|s_1, \beta, A) \vdash (\sigma|s_1', \beta, A \cup \{s \oslash^j s_1.s\})$$

where $s_1' = (s, j)$;

11. an idle transition of the form $(\sigma|s_1, \beta, A) \vdash (\sigma|s_1, \beta, A)$;

Like **unary** and **idle** rules in shift-reduce CFG parsing (Zhu et al., 2013), our current system prohibits $> b$ consecutive actions consisting of only insert, combine and idle operations. Given an input sentence with length n, after performing n shift, $n - 1$ adjunction, $b \cdot (2n - 1)$ {insert, combine or idle} actions, the system triggers the finish action and terminates. For training, we make oracle derivations using the stack-shortest strategy.

5 Related Work

To realize empty element recovery, other lexicalized TAG formalisms (Chen and Shanker, 2004; Shen et al., 2008) attach some or all empty elements directly to surface word lexicons. Our framework, however, uses spinal TAG parser operations as they provide more efficient parsing and more compact sets of lexicons. It is remarkable that this paper is the first study to present a shift-reduce spinal TAG parsing algorithm to recover empty elements.

Recent work has shown that empty element recovery can be effectively solved in conjunction

	Tagger		Lattice		Proposed		
	M	O	M	O	M	O	Gold
ICH	2	5	2	2	31	43	78
RNR	0	3	0	4	4	5	6
EXP	10	12	0	0	19	26	30

Table 2: Result Analysis: M denotes the number of matches of system outputs (O) with the gold.

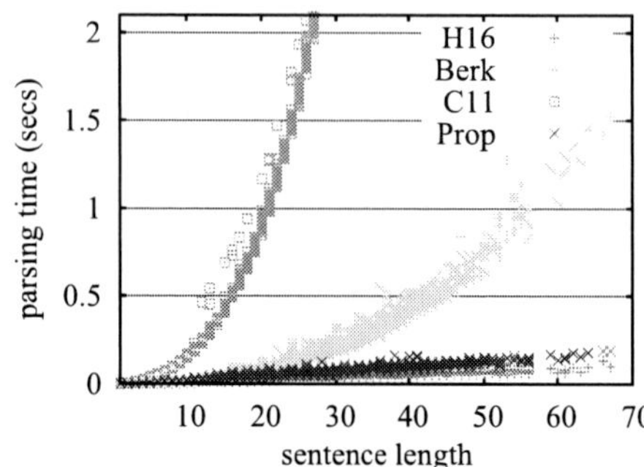

Figure 4: Scatter plot of parsing time against sentence length, comparing with Hayashi16, Berkeley and Cai11 parsers.

with parsing (Schmid, 2006; Cai et al., 2011). Schmid (2006) annotated a constituent tree with slash features to recover a direct path from a filler node to its trace. Cai et al. (2011) successfully integrated empty element recovery into lattice parsing for latent PCFGs. Compared with PCFG parsing, the spinal TAG parser provides a more flexible feature representation.

6 Experiments

6.1 Experiments on the English Penn Treebank

We used the Wall Street Journal (WSJ) part of the English Penn Treebank: Sections 02–21 were used for training, Section 22 for development, and Section 23 for testing. We annotated trees with heads by **treep** (Chiang and Bikel, 2002)[3] with the application of Collins's head rules. The 78524 lexical and 115 phrasal empty spine types were obtained from the training data[4]. The set of phrasal empty spines covered all phrasal empty spines extracted from the development data.

We used the Stanford part-of-speech tagger to tag development and test data. To train the proposed parsing model, we used the violation–fixing

---

	Typed-empty (t,i,i)			All Brackets		
	P	R	F1	P	R	F1
Rule	57.4	50.5	53.7	–	–	–
Takeno15	60.4	50.6	55.1	–	–	–
Tagger	63.1	34.7	44.8	72.9	68.6	70.7
Lattice	64.1	52.2	57.5	73.7	70.6	72.1
Proposed	**65.3**	**57.6**	**61.2**	**74.3**	**72.8**	**73.6**

Table 3: Results on the Japanese Keyaki Treebank.

perceptron algorithm (Huang et al., 2012). For training and testing, we set beam size to 16 and max count b, introduced in Section 4.2, to 2. For comparison with other systems in our environment, we also implemented two systems:

- **Lattice** is a method by Cai et al. (2011). We also used **blatt**[5], which is an extension of the Berkeley parser, to parse word lattices in which the special word *e* is encoded as described in (Cai et al., 2011).

- **Tagger** decides whether some empty category is inserted at the front of a word or not, with regularized logistic regression. To simplify point-wise linear tagging, we combined empty categories, those that appeared in the same position of a sentence, into a single category: thus the original 10 empty types increased to 63.

Table 1 shows final results on Section 23. To evaluate the accuracy of empty element recovery, we calculated precision, recall and F1 scores for (1) Labeled Empty Bracket (X/t,i,i), (2) Labeled Empty Element (t,i,i), and (3) All Brackets, where $X \in NT$, $t \in ET$ and i is a position of the empty element, using **eevalb**[6]. The results clearly show that our proposed method significantly outperforms the other systems. Table 2 shows the main reason for the improvement achieved by our method. The *ICH*, *RNR* and *EXP* empty types are used to show the relation between non-adjacent constituents, caused by syntactic phenomena like Extraposition and Conjunction. Our method captures such complex relations better with the help of the syntactic feature richness.

Table 1 reports the scores for non-empty brackets to examine whether the joint method improves the standard PARSEVAL scores. While the Lattice

---

[3] http://www3.nd.edu/~dchiang/software/treep/treep.html

[4] Excluding words from lexical spines, there were 1080 lexical spine types.

[5] http://www.cs.bgu.ac.il/~yoavg/software/blatt/

[6] http://www3.nd.edu/~dchiang/software/eevalb.py

	Johnson (X/t,i,i)			Typed-empty (t,i,i)			All Brackets			Non-empty Brackets		
	P	R	F1	P	R	F1	P	R	F1	P	R	F1
Schmid06	–	–	–	87.9	83.0	85.4	–	–	–	–	–	–
Cai11	90.1	79.5	84.5	92.3	80.9	86.2	90.1	88.5	89.3	–	–	–
Tagger	89.7	69.3	78.1	90.7	70.1	79.0	87.8	85.5	86.7	87.8	86.8	87.3
Lattice (Cai11)	89.8	79.2	84.2	91.4	80.6	85.7	90.2	88.7	89.5	90.2	89.5	89.8
Proposed	**90.3**	**81.7**	**85.8**	**91.8**	**83.2**	**87.3**	**90.8**	**89.7**	**90.3**	90.8	90.3	90.6
Berkeley	–	–	–	–	–	–	–	–	–	89.9	90.3	90.1
Hayashi16	–	–	–	–	–	–	–	–	–	**90.9**	**90.4**	**90.7**

Table 1: Results on the English Penn Treebank (Section 23): to calculate the scores for Tagger, we obtained a parse tree by supplying the 1-best Tagger output with the Berkeley parser trained on Sections 02-21 including empty elements (using the option "-useGoldPOS").

method was less accurate than the vanilla Berkeley parser, the performance of our method could be maintained with little loss in parsing accuracy. Figure 4 shows the parse time in seconds for each test sentence and that our empty element recovery parser works in reasonable time.

6.2 Experiments on the Japanese Keyaki Treebank

Finally, to show that our method works well on other languages, we conduct experiments on the Japanese Keyaki Treebank (Butler et al., 2012). For this data, we modified blatt to keep function labels And, in order to consider segmentation errors, we also modified eevalb to calculate not word but character span in a sentence. We follow the experiments in (Takeno et al., 2015) and show the results in Table 3. Our method significantly outperforms the state-of-the-art post-processing method in Japanese.

7 Conclusion and Future Work

Using spinal parsing for the joint recovery of empty elements achieves state-of-the-art performance in standard English and Japanese datasets. We plan to extend our work to recover trace-filler and frame semantic structures using the PropBank data.

Acknowledgments

The authors would like to thank the anonymous reviewers for their valuable comments and suggestions to improve the quality of the paper. This work was supported in part by JSPS KAKENHI Grant Number 26730126.

References

M. Ballesteros and X. Carreras. 2015. Transition-based spinal parsing. In *Proc. of CoNLL*.

A. Butler, Z. Hong, T. Hotta, R. Otomo, K. Yoshimoto, and Z. Zhou. 2012. Keyaki treebank: phrase structure with functional information for japanese. In *Proc. of Text Annotation Workshop*.

S. Cai, D. Chiang, and Y. Goldberg. 2011. Language-independent parsing with empty elements. In *Proc. of ACL-HLT*, pages 212–216.

X. Carreras, M. Collins, and T. Koo. 2008. TAG, dynamic programming, and the perceptron for efficient, feature-rich parsing. In *Proc. of CoNLL*, pages 9–16.

J. Chen and V. K. Shanker. 2004. Automated extraction of tags from the penn treebank. In *New developments in parsing technology*, pages 73–89. Springer.

D. Chiang and D. M. Bikel. 2002. Recovering latent information in treebanks. In *Proc. of COLING*, pages 1–7.

P. Dienes and A. Dubey. 2003. Deep syntactic processing by combining shallow methods. In *Proc. of ACL*, pages 431–438.

R. Gabbard, M. Marcus, and S. Kulick. 2006. Fully parsing the penn treebank. In *Proc. of NAACL-HLT*, pages 184–191.

K. Hayashi, J. Suzuki, and M. Nagata. 2016. Shift-reduce spinal tag parsing with dynamic programming. *Transactions of the Japanese Society for Artificial Intelligence*, 31(2).

L. Huang and K. Sagae. 2010. Dynamic programming for linear-time incremental parsing. In *Proc. of ACL*, pages 1077–1086.

L. Huang, S. Fayong, and Y. Guo. 2012. Structured perceptron with inexact search. In *Proc. of NAACL*, pages 142–151.

M. Johnson. 2002. A simple pattern-matching algorithm for recovering empty nodes and their antecedents. In *Proc. of ACL*, pages 136–143.

H. Schmid. 2006. Trace prediction and recovery with unlexicalized pcfgs and slash features. In *Proc. of COLING-ACL*, pages 177–184.

L. Shen, L. Champollion, and A. K. Joshi. 2008. Ltag-spinal and the treebank. *Language Resources and Evaluation*, 42(1):1–19.

S. Takeno, M. Nagata, and K. Yamamoto. 2015. Empty category detection using path features and distributed case frames. In *Proc. of EMNLP*, pages 1335–1340.

B. Xiang, X. Luo, and B. Zhou. 2013. Enlisting the ghost: modeling empty categories for machine translation. In *Proc. of ACL*, pages 822–831.

M. Zhu, Y. Zhang, W. Chen, M. Zhang, and J. Zhu. 2013. Fast and accurate shift-reduce constituent parsing. In *Proc. of ACL*, pages 434–443.

Semantic classifications for detection of verb metaphors

Beata Beigman Klebanov[1] and **Chee Wee Leong**[1] and **Elkin Dario Gutierrez**[2]
and **Ekaterina Shutova**[3] and **Michael Flor**[1]
[1] Educational Testing Service
[2] University of California, San Diego
[3] University of Cambridge
{bbeigmanklebanov,cleong,mflor}@ets.org
edg@icsi.berkeley.edu,ekaterina.shutova@cl.cam.ac.uk

Abstract

We investigate the effectiveness of semantic generalizations/classifications for capturing the regularities of the behavior of verbs in terms of their metaphoricity. Starting from orthographic word unigrams, we experiment with various ways of defining semantic classes for verbs (grammatical, resource-based, distributional) and measure the effectiveness of these classes for classifying all verbs in a running text as metaphor or non metaphor.

1 Introduction

According to the Conceptual Metaphor theory (Lakoff and Johnson, 1980), metaphoricity is a property of concepts in a particular context of use, not of specific words. The notion of a concept is a fluid one, however. While *write* and *wrote* would likely constitute instances of the same concept according to any definition, it is less clear whether *eat* and *gobble* would. Furthermore, the Conceptual Metaphor theory typically operates with whole semantic domains that certainly generalize beyond narrowly-conceived concepts; thus, *save* and *waste* share a very general semantic feature of applying to finite resources – it is this meaning element that accounts for the observation that they tend to be used metaphorically in similar contexts.

In this paper, we investigate which kinds of generalizations are the most effective for capturing regularities of metaphor usage.

2 Related Work

Most previous supervised approaches to verb metaphor classification evaluated their systems on selected examples or in small-scale experiments (Tsvetkov et al., 2014; Heintz et al., 2013; Turney et al., 2011; Birke and Sarkar, 2007; Gedigan et al., 2006), rather than using naturally occurring continuous text, as done here. Beigman Klebanov et al. (2014) and Beigman Klebanov et al. (2015) are the exceptions, used as a baseline in the current paper.

Features that have been used so far in supervised metaphor classification address concreteness and abstractness, topic models, orthographic unigrams, sensorial features, semantic classifications using WordNet, among others (Beigman Klebanov et al., 2015; Tekiroglu et al., 2015; Tsvetkov et al., 2014; Dunn, 2014; Heintz et al., 2013; Turney et al., 2011). Of the feature sets presented in this paper, all but WordNet features are novel.

3 Semantic Classifications

In the following subsections, we describe the different types of semantic classifications; Table 1 summarizes the feature sets.

Name	Description	#Features
U	orthographic unigram	*varies*
UL	lemma unigram	*varies*
VN-Raw	VN frames	270
VN-Pred	VN predicate	145
VN-Role	VN thematic role	30
VN-RoRe	VN them. role filler	128
WordNet	WN lexicographer files	15
Corpus	distributional clustering	150

Table 1: Summary of feature sets. All features are binary features indicating class membership.

3.1 Grammar-based

The most minimal level of semantic generalization is that of putting together verbs that share the same lemma (lemma unigrams, **UL**). We use NLTK (Bird et al., 2009) for identifying verb lemmas.

Proceedings of the 54th Annual Meeting of the Association for Computational Linguistics, pages 101–106,
Berlin, Germany, August 7-12, 2016. ©2016 Association for Computational Linguistics

3.2 Resource-based

VerbNet: The VerbNet database (Kipper et al., 2006) provides a classification of verbs according to their participation in *frames* – syntactic patterns with semantic components, based on Levin's classes (Levin, 1993). Each verb class is annotated with its member verb lemmas, syntactic constructions in which these participate (such as transitive, intransitive, diathesis alternations), semantic predicates expressed by the verbs in the class (such as motion or contact), thematic roles (such as agent, patient, instrument), and restrictions on the fillers of these semantic roles (such as pointed instrument).

VerbNet can thus be thought of as providing a number of different classifications over the same set of nearly 4,000 English verb lemmas. The main classification is based on syntactic frames, as enacted in VerbNet classes. We will refer to them as **VN-Raw** classes. An alternative classification is based on the predicative meaning of the verbs; for example, the verbs *assemble* and *introduce* are in different classes based on their syntactic behavior, but both have the meaning component of *together*, marked in VerbNet as a possible value of the Predicate variable. Similarly, *shiver* and *faint* belong to different VerbNet classes in terms of syntactic behavior, but both have the meaning element of describing an *involuntary* action. Using the different values of the Predicate variable, we created a set of **VN-Pred** classes. We note that the same verb lemma can occur in multiple classes, since different senses of the same lemma can have different meanings, and even a single sense can express more than one predicate. For example, the verb *stew* participates in the following classes of various degrees of granularity: *cause* (shared with 2,912 other verbs), *use* (with 700 other verbs), *apply heat* (with 49 other verbs), *cooked* (with 49 other verbs).

Each VerbNet class is marked with the thematic roles its members take, such as *agent* or *beneficiary*. Here again, verbs that differ in syntactic behavior and in the predicate they express could share thematic roles. For example, *stew* and *prick* belong to different VerbNet classes and share only the most general predicative meanings of *cause* and *use*, yet both share a thematic role of *instrument*. We create a class for each thematic role (**VN-Role**).

Finally, VerbNet provides annotations of the restrictions that apply to fillers of various thematic roles. For example, verbs that have a thematic role of *instrument* can have the filler restricted to being inanimate, body part, concrete, pointy, solid, and others. Across the various VerbNet classes, there are 128 restricted roles (such as *instrument_pointy*). We used those to generate **VN-RoRe** classes.

WordNet: We use lexicographer files to classify verbs into 15 classes based on their general meaning, such as verbs of communication, consumption, weather, and so on.

3.3 Corpus-based

We also experimented with automatically-generated verb clusters as semantic classes. We clustered VerbNet verbs using a spectral clustering algorithm and lexico-syntactic features. We selected the verbs that occur more than 150 times in the British National Corpus, 1,610 in total, and clustered them into 150 clusters (**Corpus**).

We used verb subcategorization frames (SCF) and the verb's nominal arguments as features for clustering, as they have proved successful in previous verb classification experiments (Shutova et al., 2010). We extracted our features from the Gigaword corpus (Graff et al., 2003) using the SCF classification system of Preiss et al. (2007) to identify verb SCFs and the RASP parser (Briscoe et al., 2006) to extract the verb's nominal arguments.

Spectral clustering partitions the data relying on a similarity matrix that records similarities between all pairs of data points. We use *Jensen-Shannon divergence* (d_{JS}) to measure similarity between feature vectors for two verbs, v_i and v_j, and construct a similarity matrix S_{ij}:

$$S_{ij} = \exp(-d_{\mathrm{JS}}(v_i, v_j)) \qquad (1)$$

The matrix S encodes a similarity graph G over our verbs. The clustering problem can then be defined as identifying the optimal partition, or *cut*, of the graph into clusters. We use the multiway normalized cut (MNCut) algorithm of Meila and Shi (2001) for this purpose. The algorithm transforms S into a stochastic matrix P containing transition probabilities between the vertices in the graph as $P = D^{-1}S$, where the degree matrix D is a diagonal matrix with $D_{ii} = \sum_{j=1}^{N} S_{ij}$. It then computes the K leading eigenvectors of P, where K is the desired number of clusters. The graph is partitioned by finding approximately equal elements in the eigenvectors using a simpler clustering algorithm, such as *k-means*. Meila and Shi (2001) have shown that the partition I derived in this way minimizes the MNCut criterion:

$$\text{MNCut}(I) = \sum_{k=1}^{K} [1 - P(I_k \rightarrow I_k | I_k)], \quad (2)$$

which is the sum of transition probabilities across different clusters. Since k-means starts from a random cluster assignment, we ran the algorithm multiple times and used the partition that minimizes the cluster distortion, that is, distances to cluster centroid.

We tried expanding the coverage of VerbNet verbs and the number of clusters using grid search on the training data, with coverage grid ={2,500; 3,000; 4,000} and #clusters grid = {200; 250; 300; 350; 400}, but obtained no improvement in performance over our original setting.

4 Experiment setup

4.1 Data

We use the VU Amsterdam Metaphor Corpus (Steen et al., 2010).[1] The corpus contains annotations of all tokens in running text as metaphor or non metaphor, according to a protocol similar to MIP (Pragglejaz, 2007). The data come from the BNC, across 4 genres: news (**N**), academic writing (**A**), fiction (**F**), and conversation (**C**). We address each genre separately. We consider all verbs apart from *have*, *be*, and *do*.

We use the same training and testing partitions as Beigman Klebanov et al. (2015). Table 2 summarizes the data. [2]

Data	Training			Testing	
	#T	#I	%M	#T	#I
News	49	3,513	42%	14	1,230
Fict.	11	4,651	25%	3	1,386
Acad.	12	4,905	31%	6	1,260
Conv.	18	4,181	15%	4	2,002

Table 2: Summary of the data. #T = # of texts; #I = # of instances; %M = percentage of metaphors.

4.2 Machine Learning Methods

Our setting is that of supervised machine learning for binary classification. We experimented with a number of classifiers using VU-News training data, including those used in relevant prior work: Logistic Regression (Beigman Klebanov et

al., 2015), Random Forest (Tsvetkov et al., 2014), Linear Support Vector Classifier. We found that Logistic Regression was better for unigram features, Random Forest was better for features using WordNet and VerbNet classifications, whereas the corpus-based features yielded similar performance across classifiers. We therefore ran all evaluations with both Logistic Regression and Random Forest classifiers. We use the skll and scikit-learn toolkits (Blanchard et al., 2013; Pedregosa et al., 2011). During training, each class is weighted in inverse proportion to its frequency. The optimization function is F1 (metaphor).

5 Results

We first consider the performance of each type of semantic classification separately as well as various combinations using cross-validation on the training set. Table 3 shows the results with the classifier that yields the best performance for the given feature set.

Name	N	F	A	C	Av.
U	.64	.51	.55	.39	.52
UL	.65	.51	.61	.39	.54
VN-Raw	.64	.49	.60	.38	.53
VN-Pred	.62	.47	.58	.39	.52
VN-Role	.61	.46	.55	.40	.50
VN-RoRe	.59	.47	.54	.36	.49
WN	.64	.50	.60	.38	.53
Corpus	.59	.49	.53	.36	.49
VN-RawToCorpus	.63	.49	.59	.38	.53
UL+WN	.67	.52	.63	.40	.56
UL+Corpus	.66	.53	.62	.39	.55

Table 3: Performance (F1) of each of the feature sets, xval on training data. U = unigram baseline.

Of all types of semantic classification, only the grammatical one (lemma unigrams, UL) shows an overall improvement over the unigram baseline with no detriment for any of the genres.VN-Raw and WordNet show improved performance for Academic but lower performance on Fiction than the unigram baseline. Other versions of VerbNet-based semantic classifications are generally worse than VN-Raw, with some exceptions for the Conversation genre. Distributional clusters (Corpus) generally perform worse than the resource-based classifications, even when the resource is restricted to the exact same set of verbs as that covered in the Corpus clusters (compare Corpus to VN-RawToCorpus).

The distributional features are, however, about as effective as WordNet features when combined

---

[1] available at http://metaphorlab.org/metcor/search/

[2] Data and features will be made available at https://github.com/EducationalTestingService/metaphor.

with the lemma unigrams (UL); the combinations improve the performance over UL alone for every genre. We also note that the better performance for these combinations is generally attained by the Logistic Regression classifier. We experimented with additional combinations of feature sets, but observed no further improvements.

To assess the consistency of metaphoricity behavior of semantic classes across genres, we calculated correlations between the weights assigned by the UL+WN model to the 15 WordNet features. All pairwise correlations between News, Academic, and Fiction were strong ($r > 0.7$), while Conversation had low to negative correlation with other genres. The low correlations with Conversation was largely due to a highly discrepant behavior of verbs of weather[3] – these are consistently used metaphorically in all genres apart from Conversation. This discrepancy, however, is not so much due to genre-specific differences in behavior of the same verbs as to the difference in the identity of the weather verbs that occur in the data from the different genres. While *burn*, *pour*, *reflect*, *fall* are common in the other genres, the most common weather verb in Conversation is *rain*, and none of its occurrences is metaphoric; its single occurrence in the other genres is likewise not metaphoric. More than a difference across genres, this case underscores the complementarity of lemma-based and semantic class-based information – it is possible for weather verbs to tend towards metaphoricity as a class, yet some verbs might not share the tendency – verb-specific information can help correct the class-based pattern.

5.1 Blind Test Benchmark

To compare the results against state-of-art, we show the performance of Beigman Klebanov et al. (2015) system (**SOA'15**) on the test data (see Table 2 for the sizes of the test sets per genre). Their system uses Logistic Regression classifier and a set of features that includes orthographic unigrams, part of speech tags, concreteness, and difference in concreteness between the verb and its direct object. Against this benchmark, we evaluate the performance of the best combination identified during the cross-validation runs, namely, UL+WN feature set using Logistic Regression classifier. We also show the performance of the resource-lean model, UL+Corpus. The top three rows of Table 4 show the results. The UL+WN model outperforms the state of art for every genre; the improvement is statistically significant ($p<0.05$).[4] The improvement of UL+Corpus over SOA'15 is not significant.

Following the observation of the similarity between weights of semantic class features across genres, we also trained the three systems on all the available training data across all genres (all data in the Train column in Table 2), and tested on test data for the specific genre. This resulted in performance improvements for all systems in all genres, including Conversation (see the bottom 3 rows in Table 4). The significance of the improvement of UL+WN over SOA'15 was preserved; UL+Corpus now significantly outperformed SOA'15.

	Feature Set	N	F	A	C	Av.
Train	SOA'15	.64	.47	.71	.43	.56
in	UL+WN	.68	.49	.72	.44	.58
genre	UL+Corpus	.65	.49	.71	.43	.57
Train	SOA'15	.66	.48	.74	.44	.58
on all	UL+WN	.69	.50	.77	.45	.60
genres	UL+Corpus	.67	.51	.76	.45	.60

Table 4: Benchmark performance, F1 score.

6 Conclusion

The goal of this paper was to investigate the effectiveness of semantic generalizations/classifications for metaphoricity classification of verbs. We found that generalization from orthographic unigrams to lemmas is effective. Further, lemma unigrams and semantic class features based on WordNet combine effectively, producing a significant improvement over the state of the art. We observed that semantic class features were weighted largely consistently across genres; adding training data from other genres is helpful. Finally, we found that a resource-lean model where lemma unigram features were combined with clusters generated automatically using a large corpus yielded a competitive performance. This latter result is encouraging, as the knowledge-lean system is relatively easy to adapt to a new domain or language.

---

[3]Removing verbs of weather propelled the correlations with Conversation to a moderate range, $r = 0.25$-0.45 across genres.

[4]We used McNemar's test of significance of difference between correlated proportions (McNemar, 1947), 2-tailed. We combined data from all genres into on a 2X2 matrix: both SOA'15 and UL+WN correct in (1,1), both wrong (0,0), SOA'15 correct UL+WN wrong (0,1), UL+WN correct SOA'15 wrong (1,0)).

Acknowledgment

We are grateful to the ACL reviewers for their helpful feedback. Ekaterina Shutova's research is supported by the Leverhulme Trust Early Career Fellowship.

References

Beata Beigman Klebanov, Chee Wee Leong, Michael Heilman, and Michael Flor. 2014. Different texts, same metaphors: Unigrams and beyond. In *Proceedings of the Second Workshop on Metaphor in NLP*, pages 11–17, Baltimore, MD, June. Association for Computational Linguistics.

Beata Beigman Klebanov, Chee Wee Leong, and Michael Flor. 2015. Supervised word-level metaphor detection: Experiments with concreteness and reweighting of examples. In *Proceedings of the Third Workshop on Metaphor in NLP*, pages 11–20, Denver, Colorado, June. Association for Computational Linguistics.

Steven Bird, Edward Loper, and Ewan Klein. 2009. *Natural Language Processing with Python*. OReilly Media Inc.

Julia Birke and Anoop Sarkar. 2007. Active learning for the identification of nonliteral language. In *Proceedings of the Workshop on Computational Approaches to Figurative Language*, pages 21–28, Rochester, New York.

Daniel Blanchard, Michael Heilman, and Nitin Madnani. 2013. *SciKit-Learn Laboratory*. GitHub repository, https://github.com/EducationalTestingService/skll.

E. Briscoe, J. Carroll, and R. Watson. 2006. The second release of the rasp system. In *Proceedings of the COLING/ACL on Interactive presentation sessions*, pages 77–80.

Jonathan Dunn. 2014. Multi-dimensional abstractness in cross-domain mappings. In *Proceedings of the Second Workshop on Metaphor in NLP*, pages 27–32, Baltimore, MD, June. Association for Computational Linguistics.

M. Gedigan, J. Bryant, S. Narayanan, and B. Ciric. 2006. Catching metaphors. In *PProceedings of the 3rd Workshop on Scalable Natural Language Understanding*, pages 41–48, New York.

D. Graff, J. Kong, K. Chen, and K. Maeda. 2003. English Gigaword. *Linguistic Data Consortium, Philadelphia*.

Ilana Heintz, Ryan Gabbard, Mahesh Srivastava, Dave Barner, Donald Black, Majorie Friedman, and Ralph Weischedel. 2013. Automatic Extraction of Linguistic Metaphors with LDA Topic Modeling. In *Proceedings of the First Workshop on Metaphor in NLP*, pages 58–66, Atlanta, Georgia, June. Association for Computational Linguistics.

Karin Kipper, Anna Korhonen, Neville Ryant, and Martha Palmer. 2006. Extensive classifications of english verbs. In *Proceedings of the 12th EURALEX International Congress*, Turin, Italy, September.

George Lakoff and Mark Johnson. 1980. *Metaphors we live by*. University of Chicago Press, Chicago.

Beth Levin. 1993. *English Verb Classes and Alternations: A Preliminary Investigation*. Chicago, IL: University of Chicago Press.

Quinn McNemar. 1947. Note on the sampling error of the difference between correlated proportions or percentages. *Psychometrika*, 12(2).

M. Meila and J. Shi. 2001. A random walks view of spectral segmentation. In *Proceedings of AISTATS*.

F. Pedregosa, G. Varoquaux, A. Gramfort, V. Michel, B. Thirion, O. Grisel, M. Blondel, P. Prettenhofer, R. Weiss, V. Dubourg, J. Vanderplas, A. Passos, D. Cournapeau, M. Brucher, M. Perrot, and E. Duchesnay. 2011. Scikit-learn: Machine Learning in Python. *Journal of Machine Learning Research*, 12:2825–2830.

Group Pragglejaz. 2007. MIP: A Method for Identifying Metaphorically Used Words in Discourse. *Metaphor and Symbol*, 22(1):1–39.

Judita Preiss, Ted Briscoe, and Anna Korhonen. 2007. A system for large-scale acquisition of verbal, nominal and adjectival subcategorization frames from corpora. In *Proceedings of the 45th Annual Meeting of the Association of Computational Linguistics*, pages 912–919, Prague, Czech Republic, June. Association for Computational Linguistics.

Ekaterina Shutova, Lin Sun, and Anna Korhonen. 2010. Metaphor identification using verb and noun clustering. In *Proceedings of the 23rd International Conference on Computational Linguistics (COLING)*, pages 1002–1010.

Gerard Steen, Aletta Dorst, Berenike Herrmann, Anna Kaal, Tina Krennmayr, and Trijntje Pasma. 2010. *A Method for Linguistic Metaphor Identification*. Amsterdam: John Benjamins.

Serra Sinem Tekiroglu, Gözde Özbal, and Carlo Strapparava. 2015. Exploring sensorial features for metaphor identification. In *Proceedings of the Third Workshop on Metaphor in NLP*, pages 31–39, Denver, Colorado, June. Association for Computational Linguistics.

Yulia Tsvetkov, Leonid Boytsov, Anatole Gershman, Eric Nyberg, and Chris Dyer. 2014. Metaphor detection with cross-lingual model transfer. In *Proceedings of the 52nd Annual Meeting of the Association for Computational Linguistics (Volume 1: Long Papers)*, pages 248–258, Baltimore, Maryland, June. Association for Computational Linguistics.

Peter Turney, Yair Neuman, Dan Assaf, and Yohai Cohen. 2011. Literal and metaphorical sense identification through concrete and abstract context. In *Proceedings of the Conference on Empirical Methods in Natural Language Processing*, pages 680–690, Stroudsburg, PA, USA. Association for Computational Linguistics.

Recognizing Salient Entities in Shopping Queries

Zornitsa Kozareva, Qi Li, Ke Zhai and Weiwei Guo
Yahoo!
701 First Avenue
Sunnyvale, CA 94089
`zornitsa@kozareva.com`
`{lqi|kzhai}@yahoo-inc.com`
`weiwei@cs.columbia.edu`

Abstract

Over the past decade, e-Commerce has rapidly grown enabling customers to purchase products with the click of a button. But to be able to do so, one has to understand the semantics of a user query and identify that in *digital lifestyle tv*, *digital lifestyle* is a brand and *tv* is a product.

In this paper, we develop a series of structured prediction algorithms for semantic tagging of shopping queries with the *product*, *brand*, *model* and *product family* types. We model wide variety of features and show an alternative way to capture knowledge base information using embeddings. We conduct an extensive study over $37,000$ manually annotated queries and report performance of 90.92 F_1 independent of the query length.

1   Introduction

Recent study shows that yearly e-Commerce sales in the U.S. top 100 Billion (Fulgoni, 2014). This leads to substantially increased interest in building semantic taggers that can accurately recognize *product*, *brand*, *model* and *product family* types in shopping queries to better understand and match the needs of online shoppers.

Despite the necessity for semantic understanding, yet most widely used approaches for product retrieval categorize the query and the offer (Kozareva, 2015) into a shopping taxonomy and use the predicted category as a proxy for retrieving the relevant products. Unfortunately, such procedure falls short and leads to inaccurate product retrieval. Recent efforts (Manshadi and Li, 2009; Li, 2010) focused on building CRF taggers that recognize basic entity types in shopping query such as *brands*, *types* and *models*. (Li, 2010) conducted

a study over 4000 shopping queries and showed promising results when huge knowledge bases are present. (Paşca and Van Durme, 2008; Kozareva et al., 2008; Kozareva and Hovy, 2010) focused on using Hearst patterns (Hearst, 1992) to learn semantic lexicons. While such methods are promising, they cannot be used to recognize all product entities in a query. In parallel to the semantic query understanding task, there have been semantic tagging efforts on the product offer side. (Putthividhya and Hu, 2011) recognize *brand*, *size* and *color* entities in eBay product offers, while (Kannan et al., 2011) recognized similar fields in Bing product catalogs.

Despite these efforts, to date there are three important questions, which have not been answered, but we address in our work. (1) *What is an alternative method when product knowledge bases are not present?* (2) *Is the performance of the semantic taggers agnostic to the query length?* (3) *Can we minimize manual feature engineering for shopping query log tagging using neural networks?*

The main contributions of the paper are:

- Building semantic tagging framework for shopping queries.

- Leveraging missing knowledge base entries through word embeddings learned on large amount of unlabeled query logs.

- Annotating $37,000$ shopping queries with *product*, *brand*, *model* and *product family* entity types.

- Conducting a comparative and efficiency study of multiple structured prediction algorithms and settings.

- Showing that long short-term memory networks reaches the best performance of 90.92 F_1 and is agnostic to query length.

Proceedings of the 54th Annual Meeting of the Association for Computational Linguistics, pages 107–111,
Berlin, Germany, August 7-12, 2016. ©2016 Association for Computational Linguistics

2 Problem Formulation and Modeling

2.1 Task Definition

We define our task as given a shopping query identify and classify all segments that are *product*, *brand*, *product family* and *model*, where:

-**Product** is generic term(s) for goods not specific to a particular manufacturer (e.g. *shirts*).

-**Brand** is the actual name of the product manufacturer (e.g. *Calvin Klein*).

-**Product Family** is a brand-specific grouping of products sharing the same product (e.g. Samsung *Galaxy*).

-**Model** is used by manufacturer to distinguish variations (e.g. for the brand Lexus has *IS* product family, which has model *200t* and *300 F Sport*).

For modeling, we denote with $\mathcal{T} = \{\perp, t_1, t_2, \ldots, t_K\}$ the whole *label space*, where $\perp$ indicates a word that is not a part of an entity and t_i stands for an entity category. The tagging models have to recognize the following types *product, brand, model, product family* and $\perp$ (other) using the BIO schema (Tjong Kim Sang, 2002).

We denote as $\mathbf{x} = (x_1, x_2, \ldots, x_M)$ a shopping query of length M. The objective is to find the best configuration $\hat{\mathbf{y}}$ such that:

$$\hat{\mathbf{y}} = \arg\max_{\mathbf{y}} p(\mathbf{y}|\mathbf{x}),$$

where $\mathbf{y}=(y_1, y_2, \ldots, y_N)$ $(N \leq M)$ are the shopping query segments labeled with their corresponding entity category. Each segment y_i corresponds to a triple $\langle b_i, e_i, t_i \rangle$ indicating the start index b_i and end index e_i of the sequence followed by the entity category $t_i \in \mathcal{T}$. When $t_i = \perp$, the segment contains only one word.

2.2 Structured Prediction Models

To tackle the shopping tagging problem of query logs, we use Conditional Random Fields (Lafferty et al., 2001, CRF)[1], learning to search (Daumé III et al., 2009, SEARN)[2], structured perceptron (Collins, 2002, STRUCTPERCEPTRON) and a long short-term memory networks extended by CRF layer (Hochreiter and Schmidhuber, 1997; Graves, 2012, LSTM-CRF).

CRF: is a popular algorithms for sequence tagging tasks (Lafferty et al., 2001). The objective is

to find the label sequence $\mathbf{y} = (y_1, ..., y_M)$ that maximizes

$$p(\mathbf{y}|\mathbf{x}) = \tfrac{1}{Z_\lambda(\mathbf{x})} \exp\{\boldsymbol{\lambda} \cdot \boldsymbol{f}(\mathbf{y}, \mathbf{x})\},$$

where $Z_\lambda(\mathbf{x})$ is the normalization factor, $\boldsymbol{\lambda}$ is the weight vector and $\boldsymbol{f}(\mathbf{y}, \mathbf{x})$ is the extracted feature vector for the observed sequence $\mathbf{x}$.

SEARN is a powerful structured prediction algorithm, which formulates the sequence labeling problem as a search process. The objective is to find the label sequence $\boldsymbol{y} = (y_1, ..., y_M)$ that maximizes

$$p(\mathbf{y}|\mathbf{x}) \propto \textstyle\sum_{m=1}^{M} \mathbb{I}_{[C(\mathbf{x}, y_1, ..., y_{m-1}) = \hat{y}_m]},$$

where $C(\bullet)$ is a cost sensitive multiclass classifier and $\hat{\mathbf{y}}$ are the ground-truth labels.

STRUCTPERCEPTRON is an extension of the standard perceptron. In our setting we model a segment-based search algorithm, where each unit is a segment of $\mathbf{x}$ (e.g., $\langle b_i, e_i \rangle$), rather than a single word (e.g., x_i). The objective is to find the label sequence $\boldsymbol{y} = (y_1, ..., y_M)$ that maximizes

$$p(\mathbf{y}|\mathbf{x}) \propto \mathbf{w}^\top \cdot \boldsymbol{f}(\mathbf{x}, \mathbf{y}),$$

where $\boldsymbol{f}(\mathbf{x}, \mathbf{y})$ represents the feature vector for instance $\mathbf{x}$ along with the configuration $\mathbf{y}$ and $\mathbf{w}$ is updated as $\mathbf{w} \leftarrow \mathbf{w} + \boldsymbol{f}(\mathbf{x}, \hat{\mathbf{y}}) - \boldsymbol{f}(\mathbf{x}, \mathbf{y})$.

LSTM-CRF The above algorithms heavily rely on manually-crafted features to perform sequence tagging. We decided to alleviate that by using long short-term memory networks with a CRF layer. Our model is similar to R-CRF (Mesnil et al., 2015), but for the hidden recurrent layer we use LSTM (Hochreiter and Schmidhuber, 1997; Graves, 2012). We denote with h_i the hidden vector produced by the LSTM cell at i-th token. Then the conditional probability of $\mathbf{y}$ given a query $\mathbf{x}$ becomes:

$$p(\mathbf{y}|\mathbf{x}) = \tfrac{1}{Z(h)} \exp\{\textstyle\sum_i (W_{y_i}^h h_i + W_{y_i, y_{i-1}}^t)\},$$

where $W_{y_i}^h$ is the weight vector corresponding to label y_i, and $W_{y_i, y_{i-1}}^t$ is the transition score corresponding to y_i and y_{i-1}. During training, the values of W^h, W^t, the LSTM layer and the input word embeddings are updated through the standard back-propagation with AdaGrad algorithm. We also concatenate pre-trained word embedding and randomly initialized embedding (50-d) for the knowledge-base types of each token and use this information in the input layer. In our experiments, we set the learning rate to 0.05 and take each query as a mini-batch and run 5 epochs to finish training.

---

[1] taku910.github.io/crfpp/

[2] github.com/JohnLangford/vowpal_wabbit

Features	CRF			SEARN			STRUCTPERCEPTRON		
	P (%)	R (%)	F_1	P (%)	R (%)	F_1	P (%)	R (%)	F_1
POS	39.86	35.51	37.56	34.97	33.55	34.25	33.03	24.70	28.27
KB	51.64	41.08	45.76	41.96	37.26	39.47	35.70	35.97	35.84
WE	65.31	61.02	63.11	67.58	67.00	67.29	71.29	68.12	69.67
LEX+ORTO+PSTNL + POS + KB	86.49	83.84	**85.15**	84.19	84.30	**84.24**	88.88	86.87	**87.87**
LEX+ORTO+PSTNL + POS + WE	88.30	85.74	**87.00**	84.32	84.15	**84.24**	87.85	85.69	**86.76**
LEX+ORTO+PSTNL + POS + KB + WE	88.86	86.29	87.55	84.30	84.50	84.40	89.18	87.10	**88.13**

Table 1: Results from feature study.

2.3 Features

Lexical (LEX): are widely used N-gram features. We use unigrams of the current w_0, previous w_{-1} and next w_{+1} words, and bigrams $w_{-1}w_0$ and w_0w_{+1}.

Orthographic (ORTO): are binary mutually non-exclusive features that check if w_0, w_{-1} and w_{+1} contain *all-digits, any-digit, start-with-digit-end-in-letter* and *start-with-letter-end-in-digit*. They are designed to capture model names like *hero3* and *m560*.

Positional (PSTNL): are discrete features modeling the position of the words in the query. They capture the way people tend to write products and brands in the query.

Part-of-Speech (POS): capture nouns and proper names to better recognize *products* and *brands*. We use Stanford tagger (Toutanova et al., 2003).

Knowledgebase (KB): are powerful semantic features (Tjong Kim Sang, 2002; Carreras et al., 2002; Passos et al., 2014). We automatically collected and manually validated $200K$ brands, products, models and product families items extracted from Macy's and Amazon websites.

WordEmbeddings (WE): While external knowledge bases are great resource, they are expensive to create and time-consuming to maintain. We use word embeddings (Mikolov et al., 2013) [3] as a cheap low-maintenance alternative for knowledge base construction. We train the embeddings over 2.5M unlabeled shopping queries. For each token in the query, we use as features the 200 dimensional embeddings of the top 5 most similar terms returned by cosine similarity.

3 Experiments and Results

Data Set To the best of our knowledge, there is no publicly available shopping query data annotated with *product, brand, model, product family* and *other* categories. To conduct our experiments, we collect 2.5M shopping queries through click logs (Hua et al., 2013). We randomly sampled $37,000$ unique queries from the head, torso and tail of a commercial web search engine and asked two independent annotators to tag the data. We measured the Kappa agreement of the editors and found .92 agreement, which is sufficient to warrant the goodness of the annotations.

We randomly split the data into 80% for training and 20% for testing. Table 2 shows the distribution of the entity categories in the data.

	Product	Brand	Model	Prod. Family	$\perp$
Train	21,688	10,417	4,394	6,697	47,517
Test	5,413	2,659	1,099	1,716	11,780

Table 2: Entity category distribution.

We tune all parameters on the training set using 5-fold cross validation and report performance on the test set. All results are calculated with the CoNLL evaluation script[4].

Performance w.r.t. Features Table 1 shows the performance of the different models and feature combinations. We use the individual features as a baseline. The obtained results show that these are insufficient to solve such a complex task. We compared the performance of the KB and WE features when combined with (LEX+ORTO+PSTNL) information. As we can see, both KB and WE reach comparable performance. This study shows that training embeddings on large in-domain data of shopping queries is a reliable and cheap source for knowledge base construction, when such information is not present. In our study the best performance is reached when all features are combined. Among all machine learning classifiers for which we manually designed features, structured perception reaches the best performance of 88.13 F_1 score.

In addition to the feature combination and model comparison, we also study in Figure 1 the training time of each model in log scale against its F_1 score. SEARN is the fastest algorithm to train,

[3] https://code.google.com/p/word2vec/

[4] cnts.ua.ac.be/conll2000/chunking/
conlleval.txt

Category	CRF			SEARN			STRUCTPERCEPTRON			LSTM-CRF		
	P (%)	R (%)	F_1	P (%)	R (%)	F_1	P (%)	R (%)	F_1	P (%)	R (%)	F_1
brand	91.79	87.93	89.82	89.3	89.3	89.3	93.99	91.20	92.57	95.15	92.29	93.70
model	86.28	80.71	83.40	80.7	78.9	79.8	85.56	80.89	83.16	87.25	85.90	86.57
product	87.85	88.16	88.00	83.4	85.0	84.2	87.90	87.92	87.91	91.94	90.98	91.46
product family	89.27	81.41	85.16	81.4	79.0	80.2	88.12	82.17	85.04	87.98	87.47	87.73
Overall	88.86	86.29	87.55	84.3	84.5	84.4	89.18	87.10	88.13	**91.61**	**90.24**	**90.92**

Table 3: Per category performance.

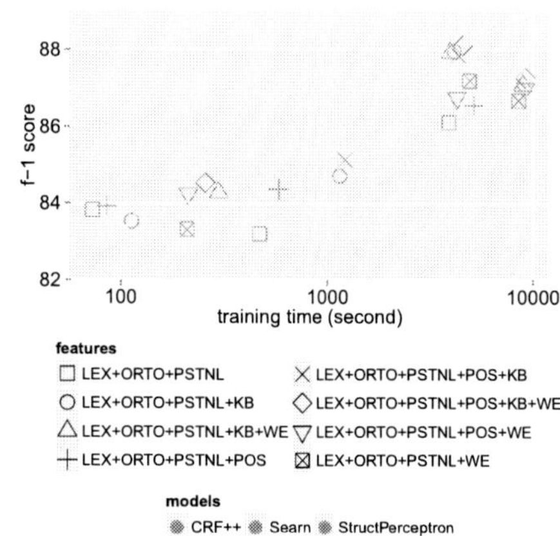

Figure 1: Training time vs F_1 performance.

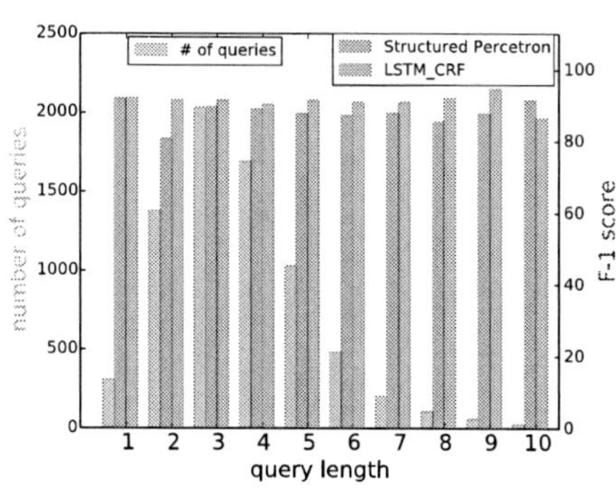

Figure 2: F_1 performance with varying query length.

while CRF takes the longest time to train. Among all STRUCTPERCEPTRON offers the best balance between efficiency and performance in a real time setting.

Performance w.r.t. Entity Category Table 3 shows the performance of the algorithms with the manually designed features against the automatically induced ones with LSTM-CRF. We show the performance of each individual product entity category. Compared to all models and settings, LSTM-CRF reaches the best performance of 90.92 F_1 score. The most challenging entity types are *product family* and *model*, due to their "wild" and irregular nature.

Performance w.r.t. Query Length Finally, we also study the performance of our approach with respect to the different query length. Figure 2 shows the F_1 score of the two best performing algorithms LSTM-CRF and STRUCTPERCEPTRON against the different query length in the test set. Around 83% of the queries have length between 2 to 5 words, the rest are either very short or very long ones. As it can be seen in Figure 2, independent of the query length, our models reach the same performance for short and long queries. This shows that the models are robust and agnostic to the query length.

4 Conclusions and Future Work

In this work, we have defined the task of product entity recognition in shopping queries. We have studied the performance of multiple structured prediction algorithms to automatically recognize *product, brand, model* and *product family* entities. Our comprehensive experimental study and analysis showed that combining lexical, positional, orthographic, POS, knowledge base and word embedding features leads to the best performance. We showed that word embeddings trained on large amount of unlabeled queries could substitute knowledge bases when they are missing for specialized domains. Among all manually designed feature classifiers STRUCTPERCEPTRON reached the best performance. While among all algorithms LSTM-CRF achieved the highest performance of 90.92 F1 score. Our analysis showed that our models reach robust performance independent of the query length. In the future we plan to tackle attribute identification to better understand queries like "*diamond shape emerald ring*", where *diamond shape* is a cut and *emerald* is a gemstone type. Such fine-grained information could further enrich online shopping experience.

References

Xavier Carreras, Lluís Màrques, and Lluís Padró. 2002. Named entity extraction using adaboost. In *Proceedings of CoNLL-2002*, pages 167–170.

Michael Collins. 2002. Discriminative training methods for hidden markov models: Theory and experiments with perceptron algorithms. In *Proc. EMNLP*, pages 1–8.

Hal Daumé III, John Langford, and Daniel Marcu. 2009. Search-based structured prediction. *Machine Learning*, 75(3):297–325.

Gian Fulgoni. 2014. State of the US retail economy in q1 2014. In *Comscore, Technical Report*.

Alex Graves. 2012. *Supervised Sequence Labelling with Recurrent Neural Networks*, volume 385 of *Studies in Computational Intelligence*. Springer.

Marti Hearst. 1992. Automatic acquisition of hyponyms from large text corpora. In *Proc. of the 14th conference on Computational linguistics*, pages 539–545.

Sepp Hochreiter and Jürgen Schmidhuber. 1997. Long short-term memory. *Neural Computation*, 9(8):1735–1780.

Xian-Sheng Hua, Linjun Yang, Jingdong Wang, Jing Wang, Ming Ye, Kuansan Wang, Yong Rui, and Jin Li. 2013. Clickage: Towards bridging semantic and intent gaps via mining click logs of search engines. In *Proceedings of the 21st ACM International Conference on Multimedia*, MM '13, pages 243–252.

Anitha Kannan, Inmar E. Givoni, Rakesh Agrawal, and Ariel Fuxman. 2011. Matching unstructured product offers to structured product specifications. In *Proceedings of the 17th ACM SIGKDD International Conference on Knowledge Discovery and Data Mining*, KDD '11, pages 404–412.

Zornitsa Kozareva and Eduard Hovy. 2010. Learning arguments and supertypes of semantic relations using recursive patterns. In *Proceedings of the 48th Annual Meeting of the Association for Computational Linguistics*, pages 1482–1491.

Zornitsa Kozareva, Ellen Riloff, and Eduard Hovy. 2008. Semantic class learning from the web with hyponym pattern linkage graphs. In *Proceedings of ACL-08: HLT*, pages 1048–1056.

Zornitsa Kozareva. 2015. Everyone likes shopping! multi-class product categorization for e-commerce. In *Proceedings of the 2015 Conference of the North American Chapter of the Association for Computational Linguistics: Human Language Technologies*, pages 1329–1333.

John D. Lafferty, Andrew McCallum, and Fernando C. N. Pereira. 2001. Conditional random fields: Probabilistic models for segmenting and labeling sequence data. In *icml*, pages 282–289.

Xiao Li. 2010. Understanding the semantic structure of noun phrase queries. In *Proceedings of the 48th Annual Meeting of the Association for Computational Linguistics*, pages 1337–1345.

Mehdi Manshadi and Xiao Li. 2009. Semantic tagging of web search queries. In *Proceedings of the Joint Conference of the 47th Annual Meeting of the ACL and the 4th International Joint Conference on Natural Language Processing of the AFNLP: Volume 2 - Volume 2*, pages 861–869.

Grégoire Mesnil, Yann Dauphin, Kaisheng Yao, Yoshua Bengio, Li Deng, Dilek Z. Hakkani-Tür, Xiaodong He, Larry P. Heck, Gökhan Tür, Dong Yu, and Geoffrey Zweig. 2015. Using recurrent neural networks for slot filling in spoken language understanding. *IEEE/ACM Transactions on Audio, Speech & Language Processing*, 23(3):530–539.

Tomas Mikolov, Ilya Sutskever, Kai Chen, Greg Corrado, and Jeffrey Dean. 2013. Distributed representations of words and phrases and their compositionality. volume abs/1310.4546, pages 3111–3119.

Marius Paşca and Benjamin Van Durme. 2008. Weakly-supervised acquisition of open-domain classes and class attributes from web documents and query logs. In *Proceedings of ACL-08: HLT*, pages 19–27.

Alexandre Passos, Vineet Kumar, and Andrew McCallum. 2014. Lexicon infused phrase embeddings for named entity resolution. *CoRR*, abs/1404.5367.

Duangmanee (Pew) Putthividhya and Junling Hu. 2011. Bootstrapped named entity recognition for product attribute extraction. In *Proceedings of the 2011 Conference on Empirical Methods in Natural Language Processing*, pages 1557–1567.

Erik F. Tjong Kim Sang. 2002. Introduction to the conll-2002 shared task: Language-independent named entity recognition. In *Proceedings of CoNLL-2002*, pages 155–158.

Kristina Toutanova, Dan Klein, Christopher D Manning, and Yoram Singer. 2003. Feature-rich part-of-speech tagging with a cyclic dependency network. In *Proceedings of the 2003 Conference of the North American Chapter of the Association for Computational Linguistics on Human Language Technology - Volume 1*, pages 173–180.

Leveraging Lexical Resources for Learning Entity Embeddings in Multi-Relational Data

Teng Long, Ryan Lowe, Jackie Chi Kit Cheung & Doina Precup
School of Computer Science
McGill University
`teng.long@mail.mcgill.ca`
`{ryan.lowe,jcheung,dprecup}@cs.mcgill.ca`

Abstract

Recent work in learning vector-space embeddings for multi-relational data has focused on combining relational information derived from knowledge bases with distributional information derived from large text corpora. We propose a simple approach that leverages the descriptions of entities or phrases available in lexical resources, in conjunction with distributional semantics, in order to derive a better initialization for training relational models. Applying this initialization to the TransE model results in significant new state-of-the-art performances on the WordNet dataset, decreasing the mean rank from the previous best of 212 to 51. It also results in faster convergence of the entity representations. We find that there is a trade-off between improving the mean rank and the hits@10 with this approach. This illustrates that much remains to be understood regarding performance improvements in relational models.

1 Introduction

A surprising result of work on vector-space word embeddings is that word representations that are learned from a large training corpus display semantic regularities in the form of linear vector translations. For example, Mikolov et al. (2013b) show that using their induced word vector representations, $king - man + woman \approx queen$. Such a structure is appealing because it provides an interpretation to the distributional vector space through lexical-semantic analogical inferences.

Concurrent to that work, Bordes et al. (2013) proposed *translating embeddings* (TransE), which takes a pre-existing semantic hierarchy as in-

Dataset	Total	W2V found %	GloVe found %
WN	40943	9.7%	51.3%
FB15k	14951	4.0%	20.3%

Table 1: The percentage of WN and FB15k entities that can be found in the pre-trained word2vec (W2V) and GloVe vectors. This does not include the W2V embeddings trained with the FB15k vocabulary[2], which covers 93% of the FB15k entities.

put and embeds its structure into a vector space. In their model, the linear relationship between two entities that are in some semantic relation to each other is an explicit part of the model's objective function. For example, given a relation such as *won*(*Germany, FIFA Worldcup*), the TransE model learns vector representations for *won*, *Germany*, and *FIFA Worldcup* such that *Germany* + *won* $\approx$ *FIFA Worldcup*.

A natural next step is to attempt to integrate the two approaches in order to develop a representation that is informed by both unstructured text and a structured knowledge base (Faruqui et al., 2015; Xu et al., 2014; Fried and Duh, 2015; Yang et al., 2015). However, existing work makes a crucial assumption—that reliable distributional vectors are available for all of the entities in the hierarchy being modeled. Unfortunately, this assumption does not hold in practice; when moving to a new domain with a new knowledge base, for example, there will likely be many entities or phrases for which there is no distributional information in

---

[2]This means that word2vec was trained in the usual way on a large textual corpus, but the vocabulary was truncated to include as many entities from Freebase as possible. Indeed, this is the reason for the small overlap between W2V, GloVe, and the relational databases: after training the word embeddings, the vocabulary must be truncated to a reasonable size, which leaves out many entities from these datasets.

Proceedings of the 54th Annual Meeting of the Association for Computational Linguistics, pages 112–117,
Berlin, Germany, August 7-12, 2016. ©2016 Association for Computational Linguistics

the training corpus. This important problem is illustrated in Table 1, where most of the entities from WordNet and Freebase are seen to be missing from the distributional vectors derived using Word2Vec and GloVe trained on the Google News corpus. Even when the entities are found, they may not have occurred enough times in the training corpus for their vector representation to be reliable. What is needed is a method to derive entity representations that works well for both common and rare entities.

Fortunately, knowledge bases typically contain a short description or definition for each of the entities or phrases they contain. For example, in a medical dataset with many technical words, the Wikipedia pages, dictionary definitions, or medical descriptions via a site such as `medilexicon.com` could be leveraged as lexical resources. Similarly, when building language models for social media, resources such as `urbandictionary.com` could be used for information about slang words. For the WordNet and Freebase datasets, we use *entity descriptions* which are readily available (see Table 2).

In this paper, we propose a simple and efficient procedure to convert these short descriptions into a vector space representation, with the help of existing word embedding models. These vectors are then used as the input to further training with the TransE model, in order to incorporate structural information. Our method provides a better initialization for the TransE model, not just for the entities that do not appear in the data, but in fact for *all* entities. This is demonstrated by achieving state-of-the-art mean rank on an entity ranking task on two very different data sets: WordNet synsets with lexical semantic relations (Miller, 1995), and Freebase named entities with general semantic relations (Bollacker et al., 2008).

2 Related Work

Dictionary definitions were the core component of early methods in word sense disambiguation (WSD), such as the Lesk algorithm (1986). Chen et al. (2014) build on the use of synset glosses for WSD by leveraging lexical resources. Our work goes further to tie these glosses together with relational semantics, a connection that has not been drawn in the literature before. The integration of lexical resources into distributional semantics has been studied in other lexical semantic tasks,

WordNet Descriptions	
photography#3	*the occupation of taking and printing photographs or making movies*
transmutation#2	*a qualitative change*
Freebase Descriptions	
Stephen Harper	*Stephen Joseph Harper is a Canadian politician who is the 22nd and current Prime Minister of Canada and the Leader of the Conservative Party...*
El Paso	*El Paso is the county seat of El Paso County, Texas, United States, and lies in far West Texas...*

Table 2: Sample entity descriptions from WordNet and Freebase. As Freebase descriptions are lengthy paragraphs, only the first sentence is shown.

such as synonym expansion (Sinha and Mihalcea, 2009), relation extraction (Kambhatla, 2004), and calculating the semantic distance between concepts (Mohammad, 2008; Marton et al., 2009). We aim to combine lexical resources and other semantic knowledge, but we do so in the context of neural network-based word embeddings, rather than in specific lexical semantic tasks.

Bordes et al. (2011) propose the Structured Embeddings (SE) model, which embeds entities into vectors and relations into matrices. The relation connection between two entities is modeled by the projection of their embeddings into a different vector space. Rothe and Schütze (2015) use Wordnet as a lexical resource to learn embeddings for synsets and lexemes. Perhaps most related to our work are previous relational models that initialize their embeddings via distributional semantics calculated from a larger corpus. Socher et al. (2013) propose the Neural Tensor Network (NTN), and Yang et al. (2015) the Bilinear model using this technique. Other approaches modify the objective function or change the structure of the model in order to integrate distributional and relational information (Xu et al., 2014; Fried and Duh, 2015; Toutanova and Chen, 2015). Faruqui et al. (2015) retrofit word vectors *after* they are trained according to distributional criteria. We propose a method that does not necessitate post-processing of the embeddings, and can be applied orthogonally to the previously mentioned improvements.

3 Architecture of the Approach

3.1 The TransE Model

The Translating Embedding (TransE) model (Bordes et al., 2013) has become one of the most popular multi-relational models due to its relative simplicity, scalability to large datasets, and (until recently) state-of-the-art results. It assumes a simple additive interaction between vector representations of entities and relations. More precisely, assume a given relationship triplet (h, l, t) is valid; then, the embedding of the object t should be very close to the embedding of the subject h plus some vector in $\mathbb{R}^k$ that depends on the relation l[3].

For each positive triplet $(h, l, t) \in S$, a negative triplet $(h', l, t') \in S'$ is constructed by randomly sampling an entity from E to replace either the subject h or the object t of the relationship. The training objective of TransE is to minimize the dissimilarity measure $d(h + l, t)$ of a positive triplet while ensuring that $d(h' + l, t')$ for the corrupted triplet remains large. This is accomplished by minimizing the hinge loss over the training set:

$$L = \sum_{(h,l,t) \in S} \sum_{(h',l,t') \in S'} [\gamma + d(h+l, t) - d(h'+l, t')]_+$$

where γ is the hinge loss margin and $[x]_+$ represents the positive portion of x. There is an additional constraint that the L_2-norm of entity embeddings (but not relation embeddings) must be 1, which prevents the training process to trivially minimize L by artificially increasing the norms of entity embeddings.

3.2 Initializing Representations with Entity Descriptions

We propose to leverage some external lexical resource to improve the quality of the entity vector representations. In general, this could consist of product descriptions in a product database, or information from a web resource. For the WordNet and Freebase datasets, we use *entity descriptions* which are readily available.

Although there are many ways to incorporate this, we propose a simple method whereby the entity descriptions are used to *initialize* the entity representations of the model, which we show to have empirical benefits. In particular, we first decompose the description of a given entity into a sequence of word vectors, and combine them into a single embedding by averaging. We then reduce the dimensionality using principle component analysis (PCA), which we found

---

[3]Note that we use $h, l, t \in \mathbb{R}^k$ to denote both the entities and relations, in addition to the vector representations of the entities and relations

experimentally to reduce overfitting. We obtain these word vectors using distributed representations computed using word2vec (Mikolov et al., 2013a) and GloVe (Pennington et al., 2014). Approximating compositionality by averaging vector representations is simple, yet has some theoretical justification (Tian et al., 2015) and can work well in practice (Wieting et al., 2015).

Additional decisions need to be made concerning which parts of the entity description to include. In particular, if an entity description or word definition is longer than several sentences, using the entire description could cause a 'dilution' of the desired embedding, as not all sentences will be equally pertinent. We solve this by only considering the first sentence of any entity description, which is often the most relevant one. This is necessary for Freebase, where the description length can be several paragraphs.

4 Experiments

4.1 Training and Testing Setup

We perform experiments on the WordNet (WN) (Miller, 1995) and Freebase (FB15k) (Bollacker et al., 2008) datasets used by the original TransE model. TransE hyperparameters include the learning rate λ for stochastic gradient descent, the margin γ for the hinge loss, the dimension of the embeddings k, and the dissimilarity metric d. For the TransE model with random initialization, we use the optimal hyperparameters from (Bordes et al., 2013): for WN, $\lambda = 0.01$, $\gamma = 2$, $k = 20$, and $d = L_1$-norm; for FB15k, $\lambda = 0.01$, $\gamma = 0.5$, $k = 50$, and $d = L_2$-norm. The values of k were further tested to ensure that $k = 20$ and $k = 50$ were optimal. For the TransE model with strategic initialization, we used different embedding dimensions. The distributional vectors used in the entity descriptions are of dimension 1000 for the word2vec vectors with Freebase vocabulary, and dimension 300 in all other cases. Dimensionality reduction with PCA was then applied to reduce this to $k = 30$ for WN, and $k = 55$ for FB15k, which were empirically found to be optimal. PCA was necessary in this case as pre-trained vectors from word2vec and GloVe are not available for all dimension values.

We use the same train/test/validation split and evaluation procedure as (Bordes et al., 2013): for each test triplet (h, l, t), we remove entity h and t in turn, and rank each entity in the dictionary

		WN					FB15k			
		k	Mean rank		Hits@10		k	Mean rank		Hits@10	
			Raw	Filt	Raw	Filt		Raw	Filt	Raw	Filt
Prev. models	SE (Bordes et al., 2011)	—	1,011	985	68.5%	80.5%	—	273	162	28.8%	39.8%
	TransD (unif) (Ji et al., 2015)	—	242	229	79.2%	**92.5%**	—	211	**67**	49.4%	74.2%
	TransD (bern) (Ji et al., 2015)	—	224	212	**79.6%**	92.2%	—	194	91	**53.4%**	**77.3%**
	TransE random init.	20	266	254	76.1%	89.2%	50	195	92	41.2%	55.2%
	TransE Freebase W2V init.	—	—	—	—	—	50	195	91	41.3%	55.4%
Our models	TransE W2V entity defs. (NS)	30	210	192	78.5%	92.1%	55	195	91	41.6%	55.7%
	TransE GloVe entity defs. (NS)	30	**63**	**51**	64.6%	73.2%	55	194	90	41.7%	55.8%
	TransE W2V entity defs.	30	191	179	77.8%	91.6%	55	195	91	41.6%	55.6%
	TransE GloVe entity defs.	30	71	59	75.3%	88.0%	55	**193**	90	41.8%	55.8%

Table 3: Comparison between random initialization and using the entity descriptions. 'NS' tag indicates stopword removal from the entity descriptions 'TransE Freebase W2V init' model uses word2vec pretrained with the Freebase vocabulary, and thus was not tested on WN.

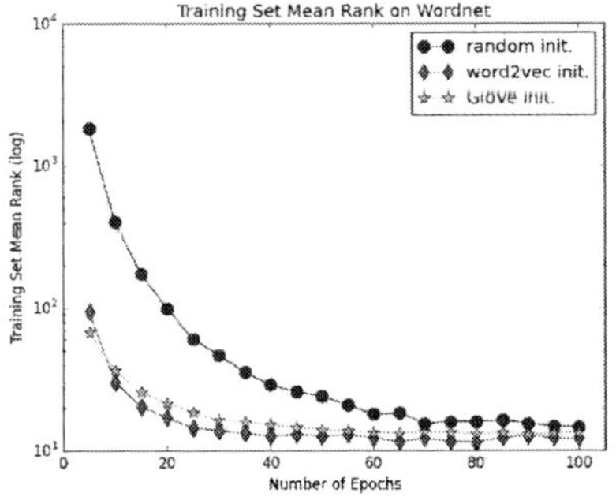

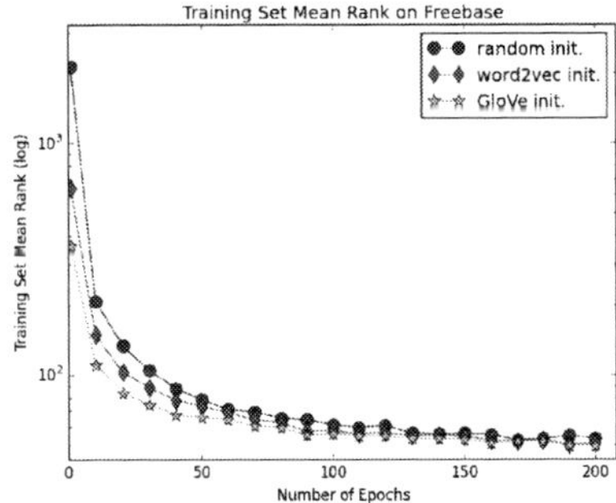

Figure 1: Learning curves for the mean ranks on the training set for WordNet (left) and Freebase (right).

by similarity according to the model. We evaluate using the original and most common metrics for relational models: *i)* the *mean* of the predicted ranks, and *ii) hits@10*, which represents the percentage of correct entities found in the top 10 list; however, other metrics are possible, such as mean reciprocal rank (MRR). We evaluate in both the filtered setting, where other correct responses are removed from the lists ranked by the model, and the raw setting, where no changes are made.

We compare against the TransE model with random initialization, and the SE model (Bordes et al., 2011). We also compare against the state-of-the-art TransD model (Ji et al., 2015). This model uses two vectors to represent each entity and relation; one to represent the meaning of the entity, and one to construct a mapping matrix dynamically. This allows for the representation of more diverse entities.

4.2 Results and Analysis

Table 3 summarizes the experimental results, compared to baseline and state-of-the-art relational models. We see that the mean rank is greatly im-

proved for the TransE model with strategic initialization over random initialization. More surprisingly, all of our models achieve state-of-the-art performance for both raw and filtered data, compared to the recently developed TransD model. These results are highly significant with $p < 10^{-3}$ according to the Mann-Whitney U test. Thus, even though our method is simple and straightforward to apply, it can still beat all attempts at more complicated structural modifications to the TransE model on this dataset. Further, the fact that our optimal embedding dimensions are larger (30 and 55 vs. 20 and 50) suggests that our initialization approach helps avoid overfitting.

For Freebase, our models slightly outperform the TransE model with random initialization, with p-values of 0.173 and 0.410 for initialization with descriptions (including stopwords) using GloVe and word2vec, respectively. We also see improvements over the case of direct initialization with word2vec. Further, we set a new state-of-the-art for mean rank on the raw data, though the improvement is marginal.

WordNet Relations		
_hyponym		
_derivationally_related_form		
_member_holonym		
Freebase Relations		
/award/award_nominee/award_nominations./award/ award_nomination/nominated_for		
/broadcast/radio_station_owner/ radio_stations		
/medicine/disease/notable_people_with _this_condition		

Table 4: Sample relations from WordNet and Freebase. The relations from Freebase are clearly much more specific as they relate named entities.

Finally, we see in Figure 1 that the TransE model converges more quickly during training when initialized with our approach, compared to random initialization. This is particularly true on WordNet.

Mean rank and hits@10 discrepancy   It is interesting to note the relationship between the mean rank and hits@10. By changing our model, we are able to increase one at the expense of the other. For example, using word2vec without stopwords gives similar hits@10 to TransD with better mean rank, while using GloVe further improves the mean rank at a cost to hits@10. The exact nature of this trade-off isn't clear, and is an interesting avenue for future work.

However, there are potential reasons for the results discrepancy betweeen mean rank and hits@10. We conjecture that our model helps avoid 'disasters' where some correct entities are ranked very low. For TransE with random initialization, these disasters cause a large decrease in mean rank, which is significantly improved by our model. On the other hand, reducing the number of correct entities that are poorly ranked may not significantly affect the hits@10, since this only considers entities near the top of the ranking.

Note also that using hits@10 to evaluate relational models is not ideal; a model can rank reasonable alternative entities highly, but be penalized because the target entity is not in the top 10. For example, given "rabbit IS-A", both "animal" and "mammal" fit as target entities. This is alleviated by filtering, but is not completely eliminated due to the sparsity of relations in the dataset (which is the reason we require the link prediction task). Thus, we believe the mean rank is a more accurate measure of the performance of a model, particularly on raw data.

Dataset differences   It is also interesting to note the discrepancy between the results on the WordNet and Freebase datasets. Although using the entity descriptions leads to a significantly lower mean rank for the WordNet dataset, it only results in a faster convergence rate for Freebase. However, the relations presented in these two datasets are significantly different: WordNet relations are quite general and are meant to provide links between concepts, while the Freebase relations are very specific, and denote relationships between named entities. This is shown in Table 4. It seems that incorporating the definition of these named entities does not improve the ability of the algorithm to answer very specific relation questions. This would be the case if the optimization landscape for the TransE model had fewer local minima for Freebase than for WordNet, thus rendering it less sensitive to the initial condition. It is also possible that the TransE model is simply not powerful enough to achieve a filtered mean rank lower than 90, no matter the initialization strategy.

5   Conclusion and Future Work

We have shown that leveraging external lexical resources, along with distributional semantics, can lead to both a significantly improved optimum and a faster rate of convergence when applied with the TransE model for relational data. We established new state-of-the-art results on WordNet, and obtain small improvements to the state-of-the-art on raw relational data for Freebase. Our method is quite simple and could be applied in a straightforward manner to other models that take entity vector representations as input. Further research is needed to investigate whether performance on other NLP tasks can be improved by leveraging available lexical resources in a similar manner.

More complex methods initialization methods could easily be devised, e.g. by using inverse document frequency (idf) weighted averaging, or by applying the work of Le et al. (2014) on paragraph vectors. Alternatively, distributional semantics could be used as a regularizer, similar to (Labutov and Lipson, 2013), with learned embeddings being penalized for how far they stray from the pre-trained GloVe embeddings. However, *even with intuitive and straightforward methodology*, leveraging lexical resources can have a significant impact on the results of models for multi-relational data.

References

Kurt Bollacker, Colin Evans, Praveen Paritosh, Tim Sturge, and Jamie Taylor. 2008. Freebase: a collaboratively created graph database for structuring human knowledge. In *Proceedings of SIGMOD*.

Antoine Bordes, Jason Weston, Ronan Collobert, and Yoshua Bengio. 2011. Learning structured embeddings of knowledge bases. In *Proceedings of AAAI*.

Antoine Bordes, Nicolas Usunier, Alberto Garcia-Duran, Jason Weston, and Oksana Yakhnenko. 2013. Translating embeddings for modeling multi-relational data. In *Proceedings of NIPS*.

Xinxiong Chen, Zhiyuan Liu, and Maosong Sun. 2014. A unified model for word sense representation and disambiguation. In *EMNLP*, pages 1025–1035. Citeseer.

Manaal Faruqui, Jesse Dodge, Sujay K Jauhar, Chris Dyer, Eduard Hovy, and Noah A Smith. 2015. Retrofitting word vectors to semantic lexicons. In *Proceedings of NAACL*.

Daniel Fried and Kevin Duh. 2015. Incorporating both distributional and relational semantics in word representations. In *In Proceedings of ICLR*.

Guoliang Ji, Shizhu He, Liheng Xu, Kang Liu, and Jun Zhao. 2015. Knowledge graph embedding via dynamic mapping matrix. In *Proceedings of ACL*.

Nanda Kambhatla. 2004. Combining lexical, syntactic, and semantic features with maximum entropy models for extracting relations. In *Proceedings of ACL on Interactive Poster and Demonstration Sessions*.

Igor Labutov and Hod Lipson. 2013. Re-embedding words. In *Proceedings of ACL*.

Quoc V Le and Tomas Mikolov. 2014. Distributed representations of sentences and documents. In *Proceedings of ICML*.

Michael Lesk. 1986. Automatic sense disambiguation using machine readable dictionaries: How to tell a pine cone from an ice cream cone. In *Proceedings of SIGDOC*.

Yuval Marton, Saif Mohammad, and Philip Resnik. 2009. Estimating semantic distance using soft semantic constraints in knowledge-source-corpus hybrid models. In *Proceedings of EMNLP*.

Tomas Mikolov, Kai Chen, Greg Corrado, and Jeffrey Dean. 2013a. Efficient estimation of word representations in vector space. In *Proceedings of ICLR*.

Tomas Mikolov, Wen-tau Yih, and Geoffrey Zweig. 2013b. Linguistic regularities in continuous space word representations. In *Proceedings of NAACL-HLT*.

George A Miller. 1995. Wordnet: a lexical database for english. *Communications of the ACM*, 38(11):39–41.

Saif Mohammad. 2008. *Measuring semantic distance using distributional profiles of concepts*. Ph.D. thesis, University of Toronto.

Jeffrey Pennington, Richard Socher, and Christopher D Manning. 2014. Glove: Global vectors for word representation. In *Proceedings of EMNLP*.

Sascha Rothe and Hinrich Schütze. 2015. Autoextend: Extending word embeddings to embeddings for synsets and lexemes. *Proceedings of ACL*.

Ravi Sinha and Rada Mihalcea. 2009. Combining lexical resources for contextual synonym expansion. In *Proceedings of RANLP*.

Richard Socher, Danqi Chen, Christopher D Manning, and Andrew Ng. 2013. Reasoning with neural tensor networks for knowledge base completion. In *Proceedings of NIPS*.

Ran Tian, Naoaki Okazaki, and Kentaro Inui. 2015. The mechanism of additive composition. *arXiv preprint arXiv:1511.08407*.

Kristina Toutanova and Danqi Chen. 2015. Observed versus latent features for knowledge base and text inference. In *Proceedings of the 3rd Workshop on Continuous Vector Space Models and their Compositionality*.

John Wieting, Mohit Bansal, Kevin Gimpel, and Karen Livescu. 2015. Towards universal paraphrastic sentence embeddings. *arXiv preprint arXiv:1511.08198*.

Chang Xu, Yalong Bai, Jiang Bian, Bin Gao, Gang Wang, Xiaoguang Liu, and Tie-Yan Liu. 2014. Rc-net: A general framework for incorporating knowledge into word representations. In *Proceedings of CIKM*.

Bishan Yang, Wen-tau Yih, Xiaodong He, Jianfeng Gao, and Li Deng. 2015. Embedding entities and relations for learning and inference in knowledge bases. In *Proceedings of ICLR*.

Multiplicative Representations for Unsupervised Semantic Role Induction

Yi Luan[†♣]   **Yangfeng Ji**[◇]   **Hannaneh Hajishirzi**[†]   **Boyang Li**[♣]

[†]Department of Electrical Engineering, University of Washington
[◇]School of Interactive Computing, Georgia Institute of Technology
[♣]Disney Research

{luanyi,hannaneh}@uw.edu, jiyfeng@gatech.edu, boyang.li@disney.com

Abstract

In unsupervised semantic role labeling, identifying the role of an argument is usually informed by its dependency relation with the predicate. In this work, we propose a neural model to learn argument embeddings from the context by explicitly incorporating dependency relations as multiplicative factors, which bias argument embeddings according to their dependency roles. Our model outperforms existing state-of-the-art embeddings in unsupervised semantic role induction on the CoNLL 2008 dataset and the SimLex999 word similarity task. Qualitative results demonstrate our model can effectively bias argument embeddings based on their dependency role.

1   Introduction

Semantic role labeling (SRL) aims to identify predicate-argument structures of a sentence. The following example shows the arguments labeled with the roles A0 (typically the agent of an action) and A1 (typically the patient of an action), as well as the predicate in bold.

[Little Willy $_{A0}$] **broke** [a window $_{A1}$].

As manual annotations are expensive and time-consuming, supervised approaches (Gildea and Jurafsky, 2002; Xue and Palmer, 2004; Pradhan et al., 2005; Punyakanok et al., 2008; Das et al., 2010; Das et al., 2014) to this problem are held back by limited coverage of available gold annotations (Palmer and Sporleder, 2010). SRL performance decreases remarkably when applied to out-of-domain data (Pradhan et al., 2008).

Unsupervised SRL offer a promising alternative (Lang and Lapata, 2011; Titov and Klementiev,

2012; Garg and Henderson, 2012; Lang and Lapata, 2014; Titov and Khoddam, 2015). It is commonly formalized as a clustering problem, where each cluster represents an induced semantic role. Such clustering is usually performed through manually defined semantic and syntactic features defined over argument instances. However, the representation based on these features are usually sparse and difficult to generalize.

Inspired by the recent success of distributed word representations (Mikolov et al., 2013; Levy and Goldberg, 2014; Pennington et al., 2014), we introduce two unsupervised models that learn embeddings of arguments, predicates, and syntactic dependency relations between them. The embeddings are learned by predicting each argument from its context, which includes the predicate and other arguments in the same sentence. Driven by the importance of syntactic dependency relations in SRL, we explicitly model dependencies as multiplicative factors in neural networks, yielding more succinct models than existing representation learning methods employing dependencies (Levy and Goldberg, 2014; Woodsend and Lapata, 2015). The learned argument embeddings are then clustered and are evaluated by the clusters' agreement with ground truth labels.

On unsupervised SRL, our models outperform the state of the art by Woodsend and Lapata (2015) on gold parses and Titov and Khoddam (2015) on automatic parses. Qualitative results suggest our model is effective in biasing argument embeddings toward a specific dependency relation.

2   Related Work

There has been growing interest in using neural networks and representation learning for supervised and unsupervised SRL (Collobert et al., 2011; Hermann et al., 2014; Zhou and Xu, 2015;

Proceedings of the 54th Annual Meeting of the Association for Computational Linguistics, pages 118–123,
Berlin, Germany, August 7-12, 2016. ©2016 Association for Computational Linguistics

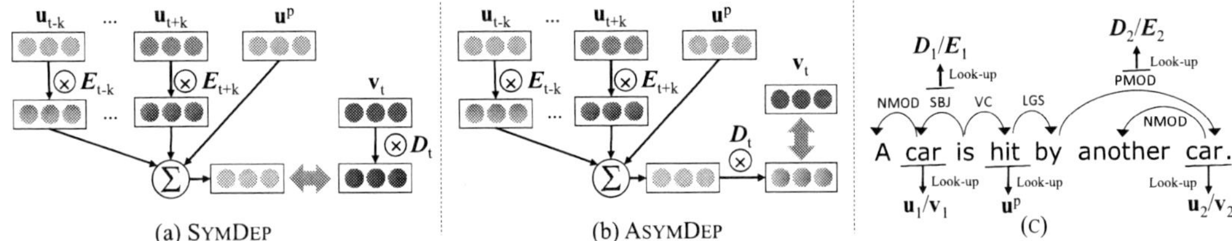

Figure 1: (a): The SYMDEP model. (b): The ASYMDEP model. (c): An example of how embeddings relate to the parse tree. In SYMDEP, the biasing of dependency is uniformly applied to all argument embeddings. In ASYMDEP, they are concentrated on one side of the dot product.

FitzGerald et al., 2015). Closely related to our work, Woodsend and Lapata (2015) concatenate one hot features of dependency, POS-tag and a distributed representation for head word and project the concatenation onto a dense feature vector space. Instead of using dependency relations as one-hot vectors, we explicitly model the multiplicative compositionality between arguments and dependencies, and investigate two different compositionality configurations.

Our model is related to Levy and Goldberg (2014) who use dependency relations in learning word embeddings. In comparison, our models separate the representation of dependency relations and arguments, thereby allow the same word in different relations to share weights in order to reduce model parameters and data sparsity.

3 Approach

Most unsupervised approaches to SRL perform the following two steps: (1) identifying the arguments of the predicate and (2) assigning arguments to unlabeled roles, such as argument clusters. Step (1) can be usually tackled with heuristic rules (Lang and Lapata, 2014). In this paper, we focus on tackling step (2) by creating clusters of arguments that belongs to the same semantic role. As we assume PropBank-style roles (Kingsbury and Palmer, 2002), our models allocate a separate set of role clusters for each predicate and assign its arguments to the clusters. We evaluate the results by the overlapping between the induced clusters and PropBank-style gold labels.

The example below suggests that SRL requires more than just lexical embeddings.

[A car $_{A1}$] is **hit** by [another car $_{A0}$].

The A0 and A1 roles are very similar lexically, but their dependency relations to the predicate differ. To allow the same lexical embedding to shift ac-

cording to different relations to the predicate, we propose the following models.

3.1 Models

Following the framework of CBOW (Mikolov et al., 2013), our models predict an argument by its context, which includes surrounding arguments and the predicate.

Let v_t be the embedding of the tth argument in a sentence, and u_t the embedding of the argument when it is part of the context. Let u^p be the embedding of the predicate. $u^c = \{u_{t-k}, \ldots, u_{t-1}, u_{t+1}, \ldots, u_{t+k}\}$ are the vectors surrounding the tth argument with a window of size k.[1] The prediction of the tth argument is:

$$p(v_t|u^p, u^c) \propto \exp(f(v_t)^{\mathsf{T}} g(u^p, u^c)) \quad (1)$$

where $f(\cdot)$ and $g(\cdot)$ are two transformation functions of the target argument embedding and context vectors respectively.

We further associate a dependency relation with each argument (explained in more details in §4.1). Let matrix D_t encode the biasing effect of the dependency relation between the tth argument and its predicate, and E_t be the corresponding dependency matrix for the tth argument if it is used as a context. We define a $\otimes$ operator:

$$\begin{aligned} v_t \otimes D_t &\triangleq \tanh\left(D_t v_t\right) \\ u_t \otimes E_t &\triangleq \tanh\left(E_t u_t\right), \end{aligned} \quad (2)$$

where $\tanh(\cdot)$ is the element-wise tanh function. Eq. 2 composes an argument and its dependency with a multiplicative nonlinear operation. The multiplicative formulation encourages the decoupling of dependencies and arguments, which is

---

[1] To be precise, the embeddings are indexed by the arguments, which are then indexed by their positions, like $u_{w(t)}$. Here we omit w. The same convention applies to dependency matrices, which are indexed by the dependency label first.

useful in learning representations tightly focused on lexical and relational semantics, respectively.

Symmetric-Dependency. In our first model, we apply the dependency multiplication to all arguments. We have

$$\boldsymbol{f}_1(\boldsymbol{v}_t) = \boldsymbol{v}_t \otimes \boldsymbol{D}_t \tag{3}$$

$$\boldsymbol{g}_1(\boldsymbol{u}^p, \boldsymbol{u}_c) = \boldsymbol{u}^p \otimes \boldsymbol{E}^p + \sum_{\boldsymbol{u}_i \in \boldsymbol{u}^c} \boldsymbol{u}_i \otimes \boldsymbol{E}_i \tag{4}$$

This model is named Symmetric-Dependency (SYMDEP) for the symmetric use of $\otimes$. Since the predicate does not have an dependency with itself, we let $\boldsymbol{E}^p = \boldsymbol{I}$. Generally, $\forall i, \boldsymbol{E}_i \neq \boldsymbol{I}$.

Asymmetric-Dependency. An alternative model is to concentrate the dependency relations' effects by shifting the dependency of the predicted argument from $\boldsymbol{f}(\cdot)$ to $\boldsymbol{g}(\cdot)$, thereby move all $\otimes$ operations to construct context vector:

$$\boldsymbol{g}_2(\boldsymbol{u}^p, \boldsymbol{u}^c) = (\boldsymbol{u}^p \otimes \boldsymbol{E}^p + \sum_{\boldsymbol{u}_i \in \boldsymbol{u}^c} \boldsymbol{u}_i \otimes \boldsymbol{E}_i) \otimes \boldsymbol{D}_t \tag{5}$$

$$\boldsymbol{f}_2(\boldsymbol{v}_t) = \boldsymbol{v}_t \tag{6}$$

This model is named Asymmetric-Dependency or ASYMDEP. Figure 1 shows the two models side by side. Note that Eq. 5 actually defines a feed-forward neural network structure $\boldsymbol{g}_2(\boldsymbol{u}^p, \boldsymbol{u}^c)$ for predicting arguments. Consider the prediction function defined in Eq. 1, these two models will be equivalent if we eliminate all nonlinearities introduced by $\tanh(\cdot)$.

3.2 Clustering Arguments

In the final step of semantic role induction, we perform agglomerative clustering on the learned embeddings of arguments. We first create a number of seed clusters based on syntactic positions (Lang and Lapata, 2014), which are hierarchically merged. Similar to Lang and Lapata (2011), we define the similarity between clusters as the cosine similarity ($CosSim$) between the centroids with a penalty for clustering two arguments from the same sentence into the same role. Consider two clusters C and C' with the centroids $\boldsymbol{x}$ and $\boldsymbol{y}$ respectively, their similarity is:

$$S(C, C') = CosSim(\boldsymbol{x}, \boldsymbol{y}) - \alpha \cdot pen(C, C') \tag{7}$$

where α is heuristically set to 1.

To compute the penalty, let $V(C, C')$ be the set of arguments $a_i \in C$ such that a_i appears in the same sentence with another argument $a_j \in C'$. We have

$$pen(C, C') = \frac{|V(C, C')| + |V(C', C)|}{|C| + |C'|} \tag{8}$$

where $|\cdot|$ is set cardinality. When this penalty is large, the clusters C and C' will appear dissimilar, so it becomes difficult to merge them into the same cluster, preventing a_i and a_j from appearing in the same cluster.

4 Experiments

We evaluate our models in unsupervised SRL and compare the effectiveness our approach in modeling dependency relations with the previous work.

4.1 Setup

Our models are trained on 24 million tokens and 1 million sentences from the North American News Text corpus (Graff, 1995). We use MATE (Björkelund et al., 2009) to parse the dependency tree and identify predicates and arguments. Embeddings of head words are the only feature we use in clustering. Dependency matrices are restricted to contain only diagonal terms. The vocabulary sizes for arguments and predicates are 10K and 5K respectively. We hand-picked the dimension of embeddings to be 50 for all models.

We take the first dependency relation on the path from an argument's head word to the predicate as its dependency label, considering the dependency's direction. For example, the label for the first *car* in Figure 1(c) is SBJ^{-1}. We use negative sampling (Mikolov et al., 2013) to approximate `softmax` in the objective function. For SYMDEP, we sample both the predicted argument and dependency. For ASYMDEP, we sample only the argument. Models are trained using AdaGrad (Duchi et al., 2011) with L2 regularization. All embeddings are randomly initialized.[2]

Baselines. We compare against several baselines using representation learning: CBOW and Skip-Gram (Mikolov et al., 2013), GloVe (Pennington et al., 2014), L&G (Levy and Goldberg, 2014) and Arg2vec (Woodsend and Lapata, 2015). Similar to ours, L&G and Arg2vec both encode dependency relations in the embeddings. We train all models on the same dataset as ours using publicly avail-

---

[2]Resulted embeddings can be downloaded from `https://bitbucket.org/luanyi/unsupervised-srl`.

able code[3], and then apply the same clustering algorithm. Introduced by Lang and Lapata (2014), SYNTF is a strong baseline that clusters arguments based on purely syntactic cues: voice of the verb, relative position to the predicate, syntactic relations, and realizing prepositions. The window size for Arg2vec and our models are set to 1, while all other embeddings are set to 2. We also employ two state-of-the-art methods from Titov and Klementiev (2012) (T&K12) and Titov and Khoddam (2015) (T&K15).

4.2 SRL Results

Following common practices (Lang and Lapata, 2014), we measure the overlap of induced semantic roles and their gold labels on the CoNLL 2008 training data (Surdeanu et al., 2008). We report purity (PU), collocation (CO), and their harmonic mean (F1) evaluated on gold arguments in two settings of gold parses and automatic parses from the MaltParser (Nivre et al., 2007). Table 1 shows the results.[4]

SYMDEP and ASYMDEP outperform all representation learning baselines for SRL. T&K12 outperforms our models on gold parsing because they use a strong generative clustering method, which shared parameters across verbs in the clustering step. In addition, T&K15 incorporates feature-rich latent structure learning. Nevertheless, our models perform better with automatic parses, indicating the robustness of our models under noise in automatic parsing. Future work involves more sophisticated clutering techniques (Titov and Klementiev, 2012) as well as incorporating feature-rich models (Titov and Khoddam, 2015) to improve performance further

Table 1 shows that including dependency relations (L&G, Arg2vec, SYMDEP, and ASYMDEP) improves performance. Additionally, our models achieve the best performance among those, showing the strength of modelling dependencies as multiplicative factors. Arg2vec learns word embeddings from the context features which are concatenation of syntactic features (dependency reations and POS tags) and word embeddings. L&G treats each word-dependency pair as a separate to-

---

[3]Except that Arg2vec is reimplemented since there is no public code online.

[4]The numbers reported for Arg2vec with gold parsing (80.7) is different from Woodsend and Lapata (2015) (80.9) since we use a different clustering method and different training data.

Model	Gold parses			Automatic parses		
	PU	CO	F1	PU	CO	F1
SYNTF	81.6	78.1	79.8	77.0	71.5	74.1
Skip-Gram	86.6	74.7	80.2	84.3	72.4	77.9
CBOW	84.6	74.9	79.4	84.0	71.5	77.2
GloVe	84.9	74.1	79.2	83.0	70.8	76.5
L&G	87.0	75.6	80.9	86.6	71.3	78.2
Arg2vec	84.0	77.7	80.7	86.9	71.4	78.4
SYMDEP	85.3	77.9	81.4	81.9	76.6	**79.2**
ASYMDEP	85.6	78.3	**81.8**	82.9	75.2	78.9
T&K12	88.7	78.1	**83.0**	86.2	72.7	78.8
T&K15	79.7	86.2	82.8	-	-	-
SYM1DEP	83.8	77.4	80.5	82.3	74.8	78.4

Table 1: Purity, collocation and F1 measures for the CoNLL-2008 data set.

ken, leading to a large vocabulary (142k in our dataset) and potentially data scarcity. In comparison, SYMDEP and ASYMDEP formulate the dependency as the weight matrix of the second non-linear layer, leading to a deeper structure with less parameters compared to previous work.

Qualitative results. Table 2 demonstrates the effectiveness of our models qualitatively. For example, we identify that *car* is usually the subject of *crash* and *unload*, and the object of *sell* and *purchase*. In comparison, CBOW embeddings do not reflect argument-predicate relations.

Ablation Study. To further understand the effects of the multiplicative representation on unsupervised SRL, we create an ablated model SYM1DEP, where we force all dependencies in SYMDEP to use the same matrix. The network has the same structure as SYMDEP, but the dependency information is removed. Its performance on SRL is shown at the bottom of Table 1. SYM1DEP performs slightly worse than Arg2vec. This suggests that the performance gain in SYMDEP can be attributed to the use of dependency information instead of the way of constructing context.

4.3 Word Similarity Results

As a further evaluation of the learned embeddings, we test if similarities between word embeddings agree with human annotation from Sim-Lex999 (Hill et al., 2015). Table 3 shows that SYMDEP outperforms Arg2vec on both nouns and verbs, suggesting multiplicative dependency relations are indeed effective. However, ASYMDEP performs better than SYMDEP on noun similarity but much worse on verb similarity. We explore this further in an ablation study.

Argument	SYMDEP (SBJ)	SYMDEP (OBJ)	CBOW
car	*crash*, roar, capsize, land, lug, *unload*, bounce, ship	*sell*, *purchase*, buy, retrieve, board, haul, lease, unload	train, splash, mail, shelter, jet, ferry, drill, ticket
victim	injure, die, protest, complain, weep, hospitalize, shout, suffer	insult, assault, stalk, avenge, harass, interview, housing, apprehend	void, murder, kidnap, widow, massacre, surge, sentence, defect
teacher	teach, mentor, educate, note, reminisce, say, learn, lecture	hire, bar, recruit, practice, assault, enlist, segregate, encourage	coach, mentor, degree, master, guide, pilot, partner, captain
student	learn, resurface, object, enroll, note, protest, deem, teach	teach, encourage, educate, assault, segregate, enroll, attend, administer	graduate, degree, mortgage, engineer, mentor, pilot, partner, pioneer

Table 2: The 8 most similar predicates to a given argument in a given dependency role.

Model	Nouns	Verbs
L&G	31.4	27.2
Arg2vec	38.2	31.4
SYMDEP	39.2	**36.5**
ASYMDEP	**39.7**	15.3
ASYM1DEP	33.2	24.2

Table 3: A POS-based analysis of the various embeddings. Numbers are the Spearman's ρ scores of each model on nouns and verbs of SimLex999.

Ablation Study. We create an ablated model to explore the reason for ASYMDEP's performance on verb similarity. ASYM1DEP is based on ASYMDEP where we force all dependency relations for the predicted argument v_t to use the same matrix D_i. The aim of this experiment is to check the negative influence of asymmetric dependency matrix to verb embedding. The results are shown at the bottom of Table 3. By keeping D_i dependency independent, performance on verbs is significantly improved with the cost of noun performance.

5 Conclusions

We present a new unsupervised semantic role labeling approach that learns embeddings of arguments by predicting each argument from its context and considering dependency relation as a multiplicative factor. Two proposed neural networks outperform current state-of-the-art embeddings on unsupervised SRL and the SimLex999 word similarity task. As an effective model for dependency relations, our multiplicative argument-dependency factor models encourage the decoupling of argument and dependency representations. Disentangling linguistic factors in similar manners may be worth investigating in similar tasks such as frame semantic parsing and event detection.

References

Anders Björkelund, Love Hafdell, and Pierre Nugues. 2009. Multilingual semantic role labeling. In *Proceedings of the Thirteenth Conference on Computational Natural Language Learning: Shared Task*, pages 43–48.

R. Collobert, J. Weston, L. Bottou, M. Karlen, K. Kavukcuoglu, and P. Kuksa. 2011. Natural language processing (almost) from scratch. *Journal of Machine Learning Research*, 12:2493–2537.

Dipanjan Das, Nathan Schneider, Desai Chen, and Noah A. Smith. 2010. Probabilistic frame-semantic parsing. In *Proceedings of the Human Language Technologies Conference of the North American Chapter of the Associattion for Computational Linguistics*, pages 948–956.

Dipanjan Das, Desai Chen, André FT Martins, Nathan Schneider, and Noah A. Smith. 2014. Frame-semantic parsing. *Computational Linguistics*, 40(1):9–56.

John Duchi, Elad Hazan, and Yoram Singer. 2011. Adaptive subgradient methods for online learning and stochastic optimization. *The Journal of Machine Learning Research*, 12:2121–2159.

Nicholas FitzGerald, Oscar Tckstrm, Kuzman Ganchev, and Dipanjan Das. 2015. Semantic role labeling with neural network factors. In *Proceedings of the 2015 Conference on Empirical Methods in Natural Language Processing*.

Hagen Fürstenau and Mirella Lapata. 2012. Semi-supervised semantic role labeling via structural alignment. *Computational Linguistics*, 38(1):135–171.

Nikhil Garg and James Henderson. 2012. Unsupervised semantic role induction with global role ordering. In *Proceedings of the 50th Annual Meeting of the Association for Computational Linguistics*, pages 145–149.

Daniel Gildea and Daniel Jurafsky. 2002. Automatic labeling of semantic roles. *Computational Linguistics*, 28(9):245–288.

David Graff. 1995. North american news text corpus.

Karl Moritz Hermann, Dipanjan Das, Jason Weston, and Kuzman Ganchev. 2014. Semantic frame identification with distributed word representations. In *Proceedings of the 52nd Annual Meeting of the Association for Computational Linguistics*.

Felix Hill, Roi Reichart, and Anna Korhonen. 2015. Simlex-999: Evaluating semantic models with (genuine) similarity estimation. *Computational Linguistics*.

Paul Kingsbury and Martha Palmer. 2002. From Tree-Bank to PropBank. In *Proceedings of the Third International Conference on Language Resources and Evaluation*, pages 1989–1993. Las Palmas.

Meghana Kshirsagar, Sam Thomson, Nathan Schneider, Jaime Carbonell, Noah A. Smith, and Chris Dyer. 2015. Frame-semantic role labeling with heterogeneous annotations. In *Proceedings of the 53rd Annual Meeting of the Association for Computational Linguistics and the 7th International Joint Conference on Natural Language Processing*, Beijing, China.

Joel Lang and Mirella Lapata. 2011. Unsupervised semantic role induction via split-merge clustering. In *Proceedings of Human Language Technologies Conference of the North American Chapter of the Association for Computational Linguistics*, pages 1117–1126.

Joel Lang and Mirella Lapata. 2014. Similarity-driven semantic role induction via graph partitioning. *Computational Linguistics*, 40(3):633–669.

Omer Levy and Yoav Goldberg. 2014. Dependencybased word embeddings. In *Proceedings of the 52nd Annual Meeting of the Association for Computational Linguistics*, volume 2, pages 302–308.

Tomas Mikolov, Ilya Sutskever, Kai Chen, Greg Corrado, and Jeffrey Dean. 2013. Distributed representations of words and phrases and their compositionality. In *Proceedings of NIPS*.

Joakim Nivre, Johan Hall, Jens Nilsson, Atanas Chanev, Gülsen Eryigit, Sandra Kübler, Svetoslav Marinov, and Erwin Marsi. 2007. Maltparser: A language-independent system for data-driven dependency parsing. *Natural Language Engineering*, 13(2):95–135.

Alexis Palmer and Caroline Sporleder. 2010. Evaluating FrameNet-style semantic parsing: the role of coverage gaps in FrameNet. In *Proceedings of the 23rd International Conference on Computational Linguistics*, pages 928–936.

Jeffrey Pennington, Richard Socher, and Christopher D. Manning. 2014. GloVe: Global vectors for word representation. In *Proceedings of the 2014 Conference on Empirical Methods in Natural Language Processing*, pages 1532–1543.

Sameer Pradhan, Kadri Hacioglu, Wayne Ward, James H. Martin, and Daniel Jurafsky. 2005. Semantic role chunking combining complementary syntactic views. In *Proceedings of the Ninth Conference on Computational Natural Language Learning*, pages 217–220.

Sameer S. Pradhan, Wayne Ward, and James H. Martin. 2008. Towards robust semantic role labeling. *Computational Linguistics*, 34(2):289–310.

Vasin Punyakanok, Dan Roth, and Wen-tau Yih. 2008. The importance of syntactic parsing and inference in semantic role labeling. *Computational Linguistics*, 34(2):257–287.

Mihai Surdeanu, Richard Johansson, Adam Meyers, Lluís Màrquez, and Joakim Nivre. 2008. The conll-2008 shared task on joint parsing of syntactic and semantic dependencies. In *Proceedings of the Twelfth Conference on Computational Natural Language Learning*, CoNLL '08, pages 159–177.

Ivan Titov and Ehsan Khoddam. 2015. Unsupervised induction of semantic roles within a reconstruction-error minimization framework. *Proceedings of the 53rd Annual Meeting of the Association for Computational Linguistics*.

Ivan Titov and Alexandre Klementiev. 2012. A Bayesian approach to unsupervised semantic role induction. In *Proceedings of the 13th Conference of the European Chapter of the Association for Computational Linguistics*, pages 12–22.

Kristian Woodsend and Mirella Lapata. 2015. Distributed representations for unsupervised semantic role labeling. In *Proceedings of the 2015 Conference on Empirical Methods in Natural Language Processing*.

Nianwen Xue and Martha Palmer. 2004. Calibrating features for semantic role labeling. In *Proceedings of the 2004 Conference on Empirical Methods in Natural Language Processing*, pages 88–94.

Jie Zhou and Wei Xu. 2015. End-to-end learning of semantic role labeling using recurrent neural networks. In *Proceedings of the 53rd Conference of the Association for Computational Linguistics*, pages 1127–1137.

Vocabulary Manipulation for Neural Machine Translation

Haitao Mi   **Zhiguo Wang**   **Abe Ittycheriah**
T.J. Watson Research Center
IBM
{hmi, zhigwang, abei}@us.ibm.com

Abstract

In order to capture rich language phenomena, neural machine translation models have to use a large vocabulary size, which requires high computing time and large memory usage. In this paper, we alleviate this issue by introducing a sentence-level or batch-level vocabulary, which is only a very small sub-set of the full output vocabulary. For each sentence or batch, we only predict the target words in its sentence-level or batch-level vocabulary. Thus, we reduce both the computing time and the memory usage. Our method simply takes into account the translation options of each word or phrase in the source sentence, and picks a very small target vocabulary for each sentence based on a word-to-word translation model or a bilingual phrase library learned from a traditional machine translation model. Experimental results on the large-scale English-to-French task show that our method achieves better translation performance by 1 BLEU point over the large vocabulary neural machine translation system of Jean et al. (2015).

1 Introduction

Neural machine translation (NMT) (Bahdanau et al., 2014) has gained popularity in recent two years. But it can only handle a small vocabulary size due to the computational complexity. In order to capture rich language phenomena and have a better word coverage, neural machine translation models have to use a large vocabulary.

Jean et al. (2015) alleviated the large vocabulary issue by proposing an approach that partitions the training corpus and defines a subset of the full target vocabulary for each partition. Thus, they only use a subset vocabulary for each partition in the training procedure without increasing computational complexity. However, there are still some

drawbacks of Jean et al. (2015)'s method. First, the importance sampling is simply based on the sequence of training sentences, which is not linguistically motivated, thus, translation ambiguity may not be captured in the training. Second, the target vocabulary for each training batch is fixed in the whole training procedure. Third, the target vocabulary size for each batch during training still needs to be as large as $30k$, so the computing time is still high.

In this paper, we alleviate the above issues by introducing a sentence-level vocabulary, which is very small compared with the full target vocabulary. In order to capture the translation ambiguity, we generate those sentence-level vocabularies by utilizing word-to-word and phrase-to-phrase translation models which are learned from a traditional phrase-based machine translation system (SMT). Another motivation of this work is to combine the merits of both traditional SMT and NMT, since training an NMT system usually takes several weeks, while the word alignment and rule extraction for SMT are much faster (can be done in one day). Thus, for each training sentence, we build a separate target vocabulary which is the union of following three parts:

- target vocabularies of word and phrase translations that can be applied to the current sentence. (to capture the translation ambiguity)
- top $2k$ most frequent target words. (to cover the unaligned target words)
- target words in the reference of the current sentence. (to make the reference reachable)

As we use mini-batch in the training procedure, we merge the target vocabularies of all the sentences in each batch, and update only those related parameters for each batch. In addition, we also shuffle the training sentences at the beginning of each epoch, so the target vocabulary for a specific sentence varies in each epoch. In the beam search for the development or test set, we apply the similar procedure for each source sentence, except the third bullet (as we do not have

Proceedings of the 54th Annual Meeting of the Association for Computational Linguistics, pages 124–129,
Berlin, Germany, August 7-12, 2016. ©2016 Association for Computational Linguistics

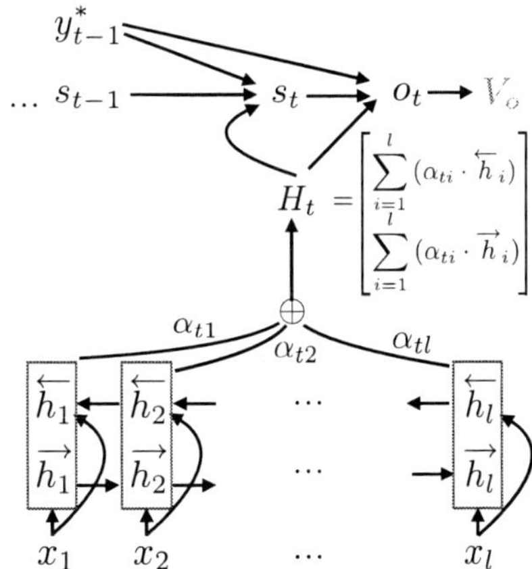

Figure 1: The attention-based NMT architecture. $\overleftarrow{h}_i$ and $\overrightarrow{h}_i$ are bi-directional encoder states. α_{tj} is the attention prob at time t, position j. H_t is the weighted sum of encoding states. s_t is the hidden state. o_t is an intermediate output state. A single feedforward layer projects o_t to a target vocabulary V_o, and applies softmax to predict the probability distribution over the output vocabulary.

the reference) and mini-batch parts. Experimental results on large-scale English-to-French task (Section 5) show that our method achieves significant improvements over the large vocabulary neural machine translation system.

2   Neural Machine Translation

As shown in Figure 1, neural machine translation (Bahdanau et al., 2014) is an encoder-decoder network. The encoder employs a bi-directional recurrent neural network to encode the source sentence $\mathbf{x} = (x_1, ..., x_l)$, where l is the sentence length, into a sequence of hidden states $\mathbf{h} = (h_1, ..., h_l)$, each h_i is a concatenation of a left-to-right $\overrightarrow{h}_i$ and a right-to-left $\overleftarrow{h}_i$,

$$h_i = \begin{bmatrix} \overleftarrow{h}_i \\ \overrightarrow{h}_i \end{bmatrix} = \begin{bmatrix} \overleftarrow{f}(x_i, \overleftarrow{h}_{i+1}) \\ \overrightarrow{f}(x_i, \overrightarrow{h}_{i-1}) \end{bmatrix},$$

where $\overleftarrow{f}$ and $\overrightarrow{f}$ are two gated recurrent units (GRU).

Given $\mathbf{h}$, the decoder predicts the target translation by maximizing the conditional log-probability of the correct translation $\mathbf{y}^* = (y_1^*, ... y_m^*)$, where m is the length of target sentence. At each time t, the probability of each word y_t from a target vocabulary V_y is:

$$p(y_t|\mathbf{h}, y_{t-1}^* .. y_1^*) \propto \exp(g(s_t, y_{t-1}^*, H_t)), \quad (1)$$

where g is a multi layer feed-forward network, which takes the embedding of the previous word y_{t-1}^*, the hidden state s_t, and the context state H_t as input. The output layer of g is a target vocabulary V_o, $y_t \in V_o$ in the training procedure. V_o is originally defined as the full target vocabulary V_y (Cho et al., 2014). We apply the softmax function over the output layer, and get the probability of $p(y_t|\mathbf{h}, y_{t-1}^* .. y_1^*)$. In Section 3, we differentiate V_o from V_y by adding a separate and sentence-dependent V_o for each source sentence. In this way, we enable to maintain a large V_y, and use a small V_o for each sentence.

The s_t is computed as:

$$s_t = q(s_{t-1}, y_{t-1}^*, c_t) \quad (2)$$

$$c_t = \begin{bmatrix} \sum_{i=1}^{l} (\alpha_{ti} \cdot \overleftarrow{h}_i) \\ \sum_{i=1}^{l} (\alpha_{ti} \cdot \overrightarrow{h}_i) \end{bmatrix}, \quad (3)$$

where q is a GRU, c_t is a weighted sum of $\mathbf{h}$, the weights, α, are computed with a feed-forward neural network r:

$$\alpha_{ti} = \frac{\exp\{r(s_{t-1}, h_i, y_{t-1}^*)\}}{\sum_{k=1}^{l} \exp\{r(s_{t-1}, h_k, y_{t-1}^*)\}} \quad (4)$$

3   Target Vocabulary

The output of function g is the probability distribution over the target vocabulary V_o. As V_o is defined as V_y in Cho et al. (2014), the softmax function over V_o requires to compute all the scores for all words in V_o, and results in a high computing complexity. Thus, Bahdanau et al. (2014) only uses top $30k$ most frequent words for both V_o and V_y, and replaces all other words as *unknown words* (UNK).

3.1   Target Vocabulary Manipulation

In this section, we aim to use a large vocabulary of V_y (e.g. $500k$, to have a better word coverage), and, at the same, to reduce the size of V_o as small as possible (in order to reduce the computing time). Our basic idea is to maintain a separate and small vocabulary V_o for each sentence so that we only need to compute the probability distribution of g over a small vocabulary for each sentence. Thus, we introduce a sentence-level vocabulary $V_{\mathbf{x}}$ to be our V_o, which depends on the sentence $\mathbf{x}$. In the following part, we show how we generate the sentence-dependent $V_{\mathbf{x}}$.

The first objective of our method aims to capture the real translation ambiguity for each word, and the target vocabulary of a sentence $V_o = V_{\mathbf{x}}$ is supposed to cover as many as those possible translation candidates. Take the English to Chinese translation for example, the target vocabulary for the English word $bank$ should contain *yínháng* (a financial institution) and *héàn* (sloping land) in Chinese.

So we first use a word-to-word translation dictionary to generate some target vocaularies for $\mathbf{x}$. Given a dictionary $D(x) = [y_1, y_2, ...]$, where x is a source word, $[y_1, y_2, ...]$ is a sorted list of candidate translations, we generate a target vocabulary $V_{\mathbf{x}}^D$ for a sentence $\mathbf{x} = (x_1, ..., x_l)$ by merging all the candidates of all words x in $\mathbf{x}$.

$$V_{\mathbf{x}}^D = \bigcup_{i=1}^{l} D(x_i)$$

As the word-to-word translation dictionary only focuses on the source words, it can not cover the target unaligned functional or content words, where the traditional phrases are designed for this purpose. Thus, in addition to the word dictionary, given a word aligned training corpus, we also extract phrases $P(x_1...x_i) = [y_1, ..., y_j]$, where $x_1...x_i$ is a consecutive source words, and $[y_1, ..., y_j]$ is a list of target words[1]. For each sentence $\mathbf{x}$, we collect all the phrases that can be applied to sentence $\mathbf{x}$, e.g. $x_1...x_i$ is a sub-sequence of sentence $\mathbf{x}$.

$$V_{\mathbf{x}}^P = \bigcup_{\forall x_i...x_j \in subseq(\mathbf{x})} P(x_i...x_j),$$

where $subseq(\mathbf{x})$ is all the possible sub-sequence of $\mathbf{x}$ with a length limit.

In order to cover target un-aligned functional words, we need top n most common target words.

$$V_{\mathbf{x}}^T = T(n).$$

Training: in our training procedure, our optimization objective is to maximize the log-likelihood over the whole training set. In order to make the reference reachable, besides $V_{\mathbf{x}}^D$, $V_{\mathbf{x}}^P$ and $V_{\mathbf{x}}^T$, we also need to include the target words in the reference $\mathbf{y}$,

$$V_{\mathbf{x}}^R = \bigcup_{\forall y_i \in \mathbf{y}} y_i,$$

---

[1] Here we change the definition of a phrase in traditional SMT, where the $[y_1, ...y_j]$ should also be a consecutive target words. But our task in this paper is to get the target vocabulary, so we only care about the target word set, not the order.

where $\mathbf{x}$ and $\mathbf{y}$ are a translation pair. So for each sentence $\mathbf{x}$, we have a target vocabulary $V_{\mathbf{x}}$:

$$V_{\mathbf{x}} = V_{\mathbf{x}}^D \cup V_{\mathbf{x}}^P \cup V_{\mathbf{x}}^T \cup V_{\mathbf{x}}^R$$

Then, we start our mini-batch training by randomly shuffling the training sentences before each epoch. For simplicity, we use the union of all $V_{\mathbf{x}}$ in a batch,

$$V_o = V_{\mathbf{b}} = V_{\mathbf{x_1}} \cup V_{\mathbf{x_2}} \cup ...V_{\mathbf{x_b}},$$

where b is the batch size. This merge gives an advantage that V_b changes dynamically in each epoch, which leads to a better coverage of parameters.

Decoding: different from the training, the target vocabulary for a sentence $\mathbf{x}$ is

$$V_o = V_{\mathbf{x}} = V_{\mathbf{x}}^D \cup V_{\mathbf{x}}^P \cup V_{\mathbf{x}}^T,$$

and we do not use mini-batch in decoding.

4 Related Work

To address the large vocabulary issue in NMT, Jean et al. (2015) propose a method to use different but small sub vocabularies for different partitions of the training corpus. They first partition the training set. Then, for each partition, they create a sub vocabulary V_p, and only predict and apply softmax over the vocabularies in V_p in training procedure. When the training moves to the next partition, they change the sub vocabulary set accordingly.

Noise-contrastive estimation (Gutmann and Hyvarinen, 2010; Mnih and Teh, 2012; Mikolov et al., 2013; Mnih and Kavukcuoglu, 2013) and hierarchical classes (Mnih and Hinton, 2009) are introduced to stochastically approximate the target word probability. But, as suggested by Jean et al. (2015), those methods are only designed to reduce the computational complexity in training, not for decoding.

5 Experiments

5.1 Data Preparation

We run our experiments on English to French (En-Fr) task. The training corpus consists of approximately 12 million sentences, which is identical to the set of Jean et al. (2015) and Sutskever et al. (2014). Our development set is the concatenation of news-test-2012 and news-test-2013, which

set	$V_\mathbf{x}^P$	$V_\mathbf{x}^D$			$V_\mathbf{x}^P \cup V_\mathbf{x}^D$			$V_\mathbf{x}^P \cup V_\mathbf{x}^D \cup V_\mathbf{x}^T$		
		10	20	50	10	20	50	10	20	50
train	73.6	82.1	87.8	93.5	86.6	89.4	93.7	**92.7**	94.2	96.2
development	73.5	80.0	85.5	91.0	86.6	88.4	91.7	**91.7**	92.7	94.3

Table 1: The average reference coverage ratios (in word-level) on the training and development sets. We use fixed top 10 candidates for each phrase when generating $V_\mathbf{x}^P$, and top $2k$ most common words for $V_\mathbf{x}^T$. Then we check various top n (10, 20, and 50) candidates for the word-to-word dictionary for $V_\mathbf{x}^D$.

has 6003 sentences in total. Our test set has 3003 sentences from WMT news-test 2014. We evaluate the translation quality using the case-sensitive BLEU-4 metric (Papineni et al., 2002) with the multi-bleu.perl script.

Same as Jean et al. (2015), our full vocabulary size is $500k$, we use AdaDelta (Zeiler, 2012), and mini-batch size is 80. Given the training set, we first run the 'fast_align' (Dyer et al., 2013) in one direction, and use the translation table as our word-to-word dictionary. Then we run the reverse direction and apply 'grow-diag-final-and' heuristics to get the alignment. The phrase table is extracted with a standard algorithm in Moses (Koehn et al., 2007).

In the decoding procedure, our method is very similar to the 'candidate list' of Jean et al. (2015), except that we also use bilingual phrases and we only include top $2k$ most frequent target words. Following Jean et al. (2015), we dump the alignments for each sentence, and replace UNKs with the word-to-word dictionary or the source word.

5.2 Results

5.2.1 Reference Reachability

The reference coverage or reachability ratio is very important when we limit the target vocabulary for each source sentence, since we do not have the reference in the decoding time, and we do not want to narrow the search space into a bad space. Table 1 shows the average reference coverage ratios (in word-level) on the training and development sets. For each source sentence $\mathbf{x}$, $V_\mathbf{x}^*$ here is a set of target word indexes (the vocabulary size is $500k$, others are mapped to UNK). The average reference vocabulary size $V_\mathbf{x}^R$ for each sentence is 23.7 on the training set (22.6 on the dev. set). The word-to-word dictionary $V_\mathbf{x}^D$ has a better coverage than phrases $V_\mathbf{x}^P$, and when we combine the three sets we can get better coverage ratios. Those statistics suggest that we can not use each of them alone due to the low reference coverage ratios. The last three columns show three combinations,

system	train		dev.
	sentence	mini-batch	sentence
Jean (2015)	$30k$	$30k$	$30k$
Ours	2080	6153	2067

Table 2: Average vocabulary size for each sentence or mini-batch (80 sentences). The full vocabulary is $500k$, all other words are UNKs.

all of which have higher than 90% coverage ratios. As there are many combinations, training an NMT system is time consuming, and we also want to keep the output vocabulary size small (the setting in the last column in Table 1 results in an average $11k$ vocabulary size for mini-batch 80), thus, in the following part, we only run one combination (top 10 candidates for both $V_\mathbf{x}^P$ and $V_\mathbf{x}^D$, and top $2k$ for $V_\mathbf{x}^T$), where the full sentence coverage ratio is 20.7% on the development set.

5.2.2 Average Size of V_o

With the setting shown in **bold** column in Table 1, we list average vocabulary size of Jean et al. (2015) and ours in Table 2. Jean et al. (2015) fix the vocabulary size to $30k$ for each sentence and mini-batch, while our approach reduces the vocabulary size to 2080 for each sentence, and 6153 for each mini-batch. Especially in the decoding time, our vocabulary size for each sentence is about 14.5 times smaller than $30k$.

5.2.3 Translation Results

The red solid line in Figure 2 shows the learning curve of our method on the development set, which picks at epoch 7 with a BLEU score of 30.72. We also fix word embeddings at epoch 5, and continue several more epochs. The corresponding blue dashed line suggests that there is no significant difference between them.

We also run two more experiments: $V_\mathbf{x}^D \cup V_\mathbf{x}^T$ and $V_\mathbf{x}^P \cup V_\mathbf{x}^T$ separately (always have $V_\mathbf{x}^R$ in training). The final results on the test set are 34.20 and 34.23 separately. Those results suggest that we should use both the translation dictionary and phrases in order to get better translation quality.

top n common words	50	200	500	1000	2000	10000
BLEU on dev.	30.61	30.65	30.70	30.70	30.72	30.69
avg. size of $V_o = V_{\mathbf{x}}^P \cup V_{\mathbf{x}}^D \cup V_{\mathbf{x}}^T$	202	324	605	1089	2067	10029

Table 3: Given a trained NMT model, we decode the development set with various top n most common target words. For En-Fr task, the results suggest that we can reduce the n to 50 without losing much in terms of BLEU score. The average size of V_o is reduced to as small as 202, which is significant lower than 2067 (the default setting we use in our training).

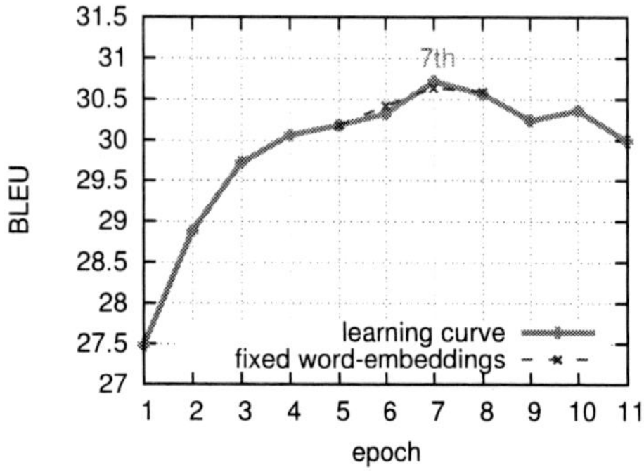

Figure 2: The learning curve on the development set. An epoch means a complete update through the full training set.

single system		dev.	test
Moses from Cho et al. (2014)		N/A	33.30
Jean (2015)	candidate list	29.32	33.36
	+UNK replace	29.98	34.11
Ours	voc. manipulation	30.15	34.45
	+UNK replace	30.72	35.11
best from Durrani et al. (2014)		N/A	37.03

Table 4: Single system results on En-Fr task.

Table 4 shows the single system results on En-Fr task. The standard Moses in Cho et al. (2014) on the test set is 33.3. Our target vocabulary manipulation achieves a BLEU score of 34.45 on the test set, and 35.11 after the UNK replacement. Our approach improves the translation quality by 1.0 BLEU point on the test set over the method of Jean et al. (2015). But our single system is still about 2 points behind of the best phrase-based system (Durrani et al., 2014).

5.2.4 Decoding with Different Top n Most Common Target Words

Another interesting question is what is the performance if we vary the size top n most common target words in $V_{\mathbf{x}}^T$. As the training for NMT is time consuming, we vary the size n only in the decoding time. Table 3 shows the BLEU scores on the development set. When we reduce the n from 2000 to 50, we only loss 0.1 points, and the av-

erage size of sentence level V_o is reduced to 202, which is significant smaller than 2067 (shown in Table 2). But we should notice that we train our NMT model in the condition of the **bold** column in Table 2, and only test different n in our decoding procedure only. Thus there is a mismatch between the training and testing when n is not 2000.

5.2.5 Speed

In terms of speed, as we have different code bases[2] between Jean et al. (2015) and us, it is hard to conduct an apple to apple comparison. So, for simplicity, we run another experiment with our code base, and increase $V_{\mathbf{b}}$ size to $30k$ for each batch (the same size in Jean et al. (2015)). Results show that increasing the $V_{\mathbf{b}}$ to $30k$ slows down the training speed by 1.5 times.

6 Conclusion

In this paper, we address the large vocabulary issue in neural machine translation by proposing to use a sentence-level target vocabulary V_o, which is much smaller than the full target vocabulary V_y. The small size of V_o reduces the computing time of the softmax function in each predict step, while the large vocabulary of V_y enable us to model rich language phenomena. The sentence-level vocabulary V_o is generated with the traditional word-to-word and phrase-to-phrase translation libraries. In this way, we decrease the size of output vocabulary V_o under $3k$ for each sentence, and we speedup and improve the large-vocabulary NMT system.

Acknowledgment

We thank the anonymous reviewers for their comments.

---

[2]Two code bases share the same architecture, initial states, and hyper-parameters. We simulate Jean et al. (2015)'s work with our code base in the both training and test procedures, the final results of our simulation are 29.99 and 34.16 on dev. and test sets respectively. Those scores are very close to Jean et al. (2015).

References

D. Bahdanau, K. Cho, and Y. Bengio. 2014. Neural Machine Translation by Jointly Learning to Align and Translate. *ArXiv e-prints*, September.

Kyunghyun Cho, Bart van Merrienboer, Caglar Gulcehre, Dzmitry Bahdanau, Fethi Bougares, Holger Schwenk, and Yoshua Bengio. 2014. Learning phrase representations using rnn encoder–decoder for statistical machine translation. In *Proceedings of EMNLP*, pages 1724–1734, Doha, Qatar, October.

Nadir Durrani, Barry Haddow, Philipp Koehn, and Kenneth Heafield. 2014. Edinburghs phrase-based machine translation systems for wmt-14. In *Proceedings of WMT*, pages 97–104, Baltimore, Maryland, USA, June.

Chris Dyer, Victor Chahuneau, and Noah A. Smith. 2013. A simple, fast, and effective reparameterization of ibm model 2. In *Proceedings of the 2013 Conference of the North American Chapter of the Association for Computational Linguistics: Human Language Technologies*, pages 644–648, Atlanta, Georgia, June. Association for Computational Linguistics.

Michael Gutmann and Aapo Hyvarinen. 2010. Noise-contrastive estimation: A new estimation principle for unnormalized statistical models. In *Proceedings of AISTATS*.

Sébastien Jean, Kyunghyun Cho, Roland Memisevic, and Yoshua Bengio. 2015. On using very large target vocabulary for neural machine translation. In *Proceedings of ACL*, pages 1–10, Beijing, China, July.

P. Koehn, H. Hoang, A. Birch, C. Callison-Burch, M. Federico, N. Bertoldi, B. Cowan, W. Shen, C. Moran, R. Zens, C. Dyer, O. Bojar, A. Constantin, and E. Herbst. 2007. Moses: open source toolkit for statistical machine translation. In *Proceedings of ACL*.

Tomas Mikolov, Kai Chen, Greg Corrado, and Jeffrey Dean. 2013. Efficient estimation of word representations in vector space. In *International Conference on Learning Representations: Workshops Track*.

Andriy Mnih and Geoffrey Hinton. 2009. A scalable hierarchical distributed language model. In *Advances in Neural Information Processing Systems*, volume 21, pages 1081–1088.

Andriy Mnih and Koray Kavukcuoglu. 2013. Learning word embeddings efficiently with noise-contrastive estimation. In *Proceedings of NIPS*, pages 2265–2273.

Andriy Mnih and Yee Whye Teh. 2012. A fast and simple algorithm for training neural probabilistic language models. In *Proceedings of the 29th International Conference on Machine Learning*, pages 1751–1758.

Kishore Papineni, Salim Roukos, Todd Ward, and Wei-Jing Zhu. 2002. Bleu: a method for automatic evaluation of machine translation. In *Proceedings of ACL*, pages 311–318, Philadephia, USA, July.

Ilya Sutskever, Oriol Vinyals, and Quoc V. Le. 2014. Sequence to sequence learning with neural networks. In *Proceedings of NIPS*, pages 3104–3112, Quebec, Canada, December.

Matthew D. Zeiler. 2012. ADADELTA: an adaptive learning rate method. *CoRR*.

Natural Language Inference by Tree-Based Convolution and Heuristic Matching

Lili Mou,[*][1] **Rui Men,**[*][1] **Ge Li,**[†][1] **Yan Xu,**[1] **Lu Zhang,**[1] **Rui Yan,**[2] **Zhi Jin**[†][1]

[1]Key Laboratory of High Confidence Software Technologies (Peking University),
Ministry of Education, China; Software Institute, Peking University, China
{doublepower.mou,menruimr}@gmail.com
{lige,xuyan14,zhanglu,zhijin}@sei.pku.edu.cn
[2]Baidu Inc., China yanrui02@baidu.com

Abstract

In this paper, we propose the TBCNN-pair model to recognize entailment and contradiction between two sentences. In our model, a tree-based convolutional neural network (TBCNN) captures sentence-level semantics; then heuristic matching layers like concatenation, element-wise product/difference combine the information in individual sentences. Experimental results show that our model outperforms existing sentence encoding-based approaches by a large margin.

1 Introduction

Recognizing entailment and contradiction between two sentences (called a *premise* and a *hypothesis*) is known as *natural language inference* (NLI) in MacCartney (2009). Provided with a premise sentence, the task is to judge whether the hypothesis can be inferred (`entailment`), or the hypothesis cannot be true (`contradiction`). Several examples are illustrated in Table 1.

NLI is in the core of natural language understanding and has wide applications in NLP, e.g., question answering (Harabagiu and Hickl, 2006) and automatic summarization (Lacatusu et al., 2006; Yan et al., 2011a; Yan et al., 2011b). Moreover, NLI is also related to other tasks of sentence pair modeling, including paraphrase detection (Hu et al., 2014), relation recognition of discourse units (Liu et al., 2016), etc.

Traditional approaches to NLI mainly fall into two groups: feature-rich models and formal reasoning methods. Feature-based approaches typically leverage machine learning models, but require intensive human engineering to represent lexical and syntactic information in two sentences

---

Premise	Two men on bicycles competing in a race.	
	People are riding bikes.	E
Hypothesis	Men are riding bicycles on the streets.	C
	A few people are catching fish.	N

Table 1: Examples of relations between a premise and a hypothesis: Entailment, Contradiction, and Neutral (irrelevant).

(MacCartney et al., 2006; Harabagiu et al., 2006). Formal reasoning, on the other hand, converts a sentence into a formal logical representation and uses interpreters to search for a proof. However, such approaches are limited in terms of scope and accuracy (Bos and Markert, 2005).

The renewed prosperity of neural networks has made significant achievements in various NLP applications, including individual sentence modeling (Kalchbrenner et al., 2014; Mou et al., 2015) as well as sentence matching (Hu et al., 2014; Yin and Schütze, 2015). A typical neural architecture to model sentence pairs is the "Siamese" structure (Bromley et al., 1993), which involves an underlying sentence model and a matching layer to determine the relationship between two sentences. Prevailing sentence models include convolutional networks (Kalchbrenner et al., 2014) and recurrent/recursive networks (Socher et al., 2011b). Although they have achieved high performance, they may either fail to fully make use of the syntactical information in sentences or be difficult to train due to the long propagation path. Recently, we propose a novel tree-based convolutional neural network (TBCNN) to alleviate the aforementioned problems and have achieved higher performance in two sentence classification tasks (Mou et al., 2015). However, it is less clear whether TBCNN can be harnessed to model sentence pairs for implicit logical inference, as is in the NLI task.

In this paper, we propose the TBCNN-pair neural model to recognize entailment and contradiction between two sentences. We lever-

---

*Equal contribution. †Corresponding authors.

Proceedings of the 54th Annual Meeting of the Association for Computational Linguistics, pages 130–136,
Berlin, Germany, August 7-12, 2016. ©2016 Association for Computational Linguistics

age our newly proposed TBCNN model to capture structural information in sentences, which is important to NLI. For example, the phrase "riding bicycles on the streets" in Table 1 can be well recognized by TBCNN via the dependency relations `dobj(riding,bicycles)` and `prep_on(riding,street)`. As we can see, TBCNN is more robust than sequential convolution in terms of word order distortion, which may be introduced by determinators, modifiers, etc. A pooling layer then aggregates information along the tree, serving as a way of semantic compositonality. Finally, two sentences' information is combined by several heuristic matching layers, including concatenation, element-wise product and difference; they are effective in capturing relationships between two sentences, but remain low complexity.

To sum up, the main contributions of this paper are two-fold: (1) We are the first to introduce tree-based convolution to sentence pair modeling tasks like NLI; (2) Leveraging additional heuristics further improves the accuracy while remaining low complexity, outperforming existing sentence encoding-based approaches to a large extent, including feature-rich methods and long short term memory (LSTM)-based recurrent networks.[1]

2 Related Work

Entailment recognition can be viewed as a task of sentence pair modeling. Most neural networks in this field involve a sentence-level model, followed by one or a few matching layers. They are sometimes called "Siamese" architectures (Bromley et al., 1993)

Hu et al. (2014) and Yin and Schütze (2015) apply convolutional neural networks (CNNs) as the individual sentence model, where a set of feature detectors over successive words are designed to extract local features. Wan et al. (2015) build sentence pair models upon recurrent neural networks (RNNs) to iteratively integrate information along a sentence. Socher et al. (2011a) dynamically construct tree structures (analogous to parse trees) by recursive autoencoders to detect paraphrase between two sentences. As shown, inherent structural information in sentences is oftentimes important to natural language understanding.

The simplest approach to match two sentences,

perhaps, is to concatenate their vector representations (Zhang et al., 2015; Hu et al., 2014, Arc-I). Concatenation is also applied in our previous work of matching the subject and object in relation classification (Xu et al., 2015; Xu et al., 2016). He et al. (2015) apply additional heuristics, namely Euclidean distance, cosine measure, and element-wise absolute difference. The above methods operate on a fixed-size vector representation of a sentence, categorized as *sentence encoding*-based approaches. Thus the matching complexity is $\mathcal{O}(1)$, i.e., independent of the sentence length. Word-by-word similarity matrices are introduced to enhance interaction. To obtain the similarity matrix, Hu et al. (2014) (Arc-II) concatenate two words' vectors (after convolution), Socher et al. (2011a) compute Euclidean distance, and Wan et al. (2015) apply tensor product. In this way, the complexity is of $\mathcal{O}(n^2)$, where n is the length of a sentence; hence similarity matrices are difficult to scale and less efficient for large datasets.

Recently, Rocktäschel et al. (2016) introduce several context-aware methods for sentence matching. They report that RNNs over a single chain of two sentences are more informative than separate RNNs; a static attention over the first sentence is also useful when modeling the second one. Such context-awareness interweaves the sentence modeling and matching steps. In some scenarios like sentence pair re-ranking (Yan et al., 2016), it is not feasible to pre-calculate the vector representations of sentences, so the matching complexity is of $\mathcal{O}(n)$. Rocktäschel et al. (2016) further develop a word-by-word attention mechanism and obtain a higher accuracy with a complexity order of $\mathcal{O}(n^2)$.

3 Our Approach

We follow the "Siamese" architecture (like most work in Section 2) and adopt a two-step strategy to classify the relation between two sentences. Concretely, our model comprises two parts:

- A tree-based convolutional neural network models each individual sentence (Figure 1a). Notice that, the two sentences, premise and hypothesis, share a same TBCNN model (with same parameters), because this part aims to capture general semantics of sentences.
- A matching layer combines two sentences' information by heuristics (Figure 1b). After individual sentence models, we design a sentence matching layer to aggregate information. We use simple heuristics, including concate-

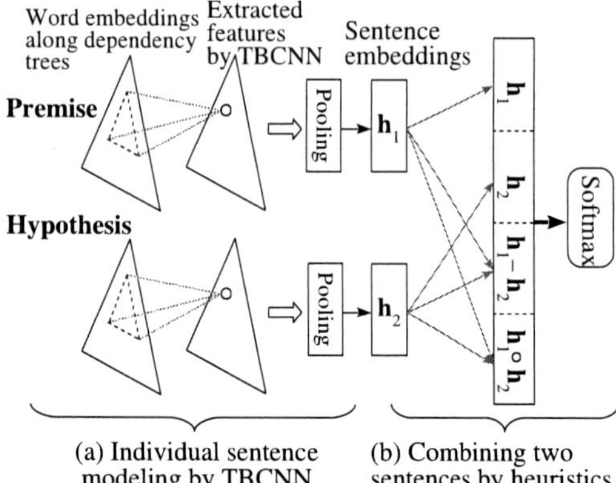

(a) Individual sentence modeling by TBCNN

(b) Combining two sentences by heuristics

Figure 1: TBCNN-pair model. (a) Individual sentence modeling via tree-based convolution. (b) Sentence pair modeling with heuristics, after which a softmax layer is applied for output.

nation, element-wise product and difference, which are effective and efficient.

Finally, we add a softmax layer for output. The training objective is cross-entropy loss, and we adopt mini-batch stochastic gradient descent, computed by back-propagation.

3.1 Tree-Based Convolution

The tree-based convolutoinal neural network (TBCNN) is first proposed in our previous work (Mou et al., 2016)[2] to classify program source code; later, we further propose TBCNN variants to model sentences (Mou et al., 2015). This subsection details the tree-based convolution process.

The basic idea of TBCNN is to design a set of subtree feature detectors sliding over the parse tree of a sentence; either a constituency tree or a dependency tree applies. In this paper, we prefer the dependency tree-based convolution for its efficiency and compact expressiveness.

Concretely, a sentence is first converted to a dependency parse tree.[3] Each node in the dependency tree corresponds to a word in the sentence; an edge $a \rightarrow b$ indicates a is governed by b. Edges are labeled with grammatical relations (e.g., nsubj) between the parent node and its children (de Marneffe et al., 2006). Words are represented by pretrained vector representations, also known as *word embeddings* (Mikolov et al., 2013a).

Now, we consider a set of two-layer subtree feature detectors sliding over the dependency tree. At a position where the parent node is p with child nodes $c_1, \cdots, c_n$, the output of the feature detector, y, is

$$y = f\left(W_p p + \sum_{i=1}^{n} W_{r[c_i]} c_i + b\right)$$

Let us assume word embeddings (p and c_i) are of n_e dimensions; that the convolutional layer y is n_c-dimensional. $W \in \mathbb{R}^{n_c \times n_e}$ is the weight matrix; $b \in \mathbb{R}^{n_c}$ is the bias vector. $r[c_i]$ denotes the dependency relation between p and c_i. f is the non-linear activation function, and we apply ReLU in our experiments.

After tree-based convolution, we obtain a set of feature maps, which are one-one corresponding to original words in the sentence. Therefore, they may vary in size and length. A dynamic pooling layer is applied to aggregate information along different parts of the tree, serving as a way of *semantic compositionality* (Hu et al., 2014). We use the max pooling operation, which takes the maximum value in each dimension.

Then we add a fully-connected hidden layer to further mix the information in a sentence. The obtained vector representation of a sentence is denoted as h (also called a *sentence embedding*). Notice that the same tree-based convolution applies to both the premise and hypothesis.

Tree-based convolution along with pooling enables structural features to reach the output layer with short propagation paths, as opposed to the recursive network (Socher et al., 2011b), which is also structure-sensitive but may suffer from the problem of long propagation path. By contrast, TBCNN is effective and efficient in learning such structural information (Mou et al., 2015).

3.2 Matching Heuristics

In this part, we introduce how vector representations of individual sentences are combined to capture the relation between the premise and hypothesis. As the dataset is large, we prefer $\mathcal{O}(1)$ matching operations because of efficiency concerns. Concretely, we have three matching heuristics:

- Concatenation of the two sentence vectors,
- Element-wise product, and
- Element-wise difference.

The first heuristic follows the most standard procedure of the "Siamese" architectures, while the latter two are certain measures of "similarity" or

---

[2] Preprinted on arXiv on September 2014 (http://arxiv.org/abs/1409.5718v1)

[3] Parsed by the Stanford parser (http://nlp.stanford.edu/software/lex-parser.shtml)

"closeness." These matching layers are further concatenated (Figure 1b), given by

$$m = [h_1; h_2; h_1 - h_2; h_1 \circ h_2]$$

where $h_1 \in \mathbb{R}^{n_c}$ and $h_2 \in \mathbb{R}^{n_c}$ are the sentence vectors of the premise and hypothesis, respectively; "$\circ$" denotes element-wise product; semicolons refer to column vector concatenation. $m \in \mathbb{R}^{4n_c}$ is the output of the matching layer.

We would like to point out that, with subsequent linear transformation, element-wise difference is a special case of concatenation. If we assume the subsequent transformation takes the form of $W[h_1 \ h_2]^\top$, where $W = [W_1 \ W_2]$ is the weights for concatenated sentence representations, then element-wise difference can be viewed as such that $W_0(h_1 - h_2) = [W_0 \ -W_0][h_1 \ h_2]^\top$. ($W_0$ is the weights corresponding to element-wise difference.) Thus, our third heuristic can be absorbed into the first one in terms of model capacity. However, as will be shown in the experiment, explicitly specifying this heuristic significantly improves the performance, indicating that optimization differs, despite the same model capacity. Moreover, word embedding studies show that linear offset of vectors can capture relationships between two words (Mikolov et al., 2013b), but it has not been exploited in sentence-pair relation recognition. Although element-wise distance is used to detect paraphrase in He et al. (2015), it mainly reflects "similarity" information. Our study verifies that vector offset is useful in capturing generic sentence relationships, akin to the word analogy task.

4 Evaluation

4.1 Dataset

To evaluate our TBCNN-pair model, we used the newly published Stanford Natural Language Inference (SNLI) dataset (Bowman et al., 2015).[4] The dataset is constructed by crowdsourced efforts, each sentence written by humans. Moreover, the SNLI dataset is magnitudes of larger than previous resources, and hence is particularly suitable for comparing neural models. The target labels comprise three classes: Entailment, Contradiction, and Neutral (two irrelevant sentences). We applied the standard train/validation/test split, contraining 550k, 10k, and 10k samples, respectively. Figure 2 presents

Statistics	Mean	Std
# nodes	8.59	4.14
Max depth	3.93	1.13
Avg leaf depth	3.13	0.65
Avg node depth	2.60	0.54

Table 2: Statistics of the Stanford Natural Language Inference dataset where each sentence is parsed into a dependency parse tree.

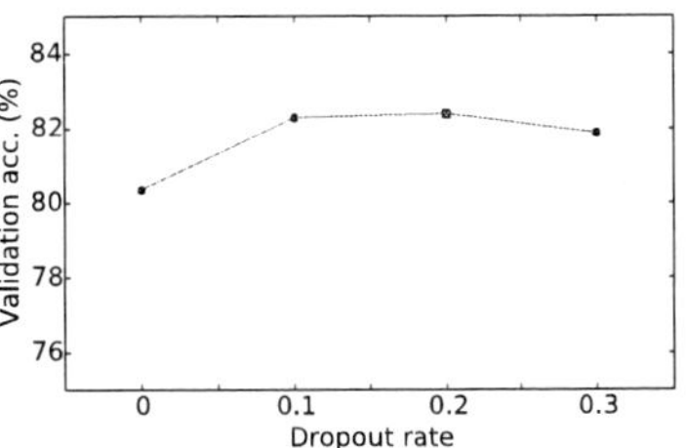

Figure 2: Validation accuracy versus dropout rate (full TBCNN-pair model).

additional dataset statistics, especially those relevant to dependency parse trees.[5]

4.2 Hyperparameter Settings

All our neural layers, including embeddings, were set to 300 dimensions. The model is mostly robust when the dimension is large, e.g., several hundred (Collobert and Weston, 2008). Word embeddings were pretrained ourselves by word2vec on the English Wikipedia corpus and fined tuned during training as a part of model parameters. We applied ℓ_2 penalty of 3×10^{-4}; dropout was chosen by validation with a granularity of 0.1 (Figure 2). We see that a large dropout rate (> 0.3) hurts the performance (and also makes training slow) for such a large dataset as opposed to small datasets in other tasks (Peng et al., 2015). Initial learning rate was set to 1, and a power decay was applied. We used stochastic gradient descent with a batch size of 50.

4.3 Performance

Table 3 compares our model with previous results. As seen, the TBCNN sentence pair model, followed by simple concatenation alone, outperforms existing sentence encoding-based approaches (without pretraining), including a feature-rich method using 6 groups of human-engineered features, long short term memory

---

[4]http://nlp.stanford.edu/projects/snli/

[5]We applied *collapsed* dependency trees, where prepositions and conjunctions are annotated on the dependency relations, but these auxiliary words themselves are removed.

Model	Test acc. (%)	Matching complexity
Unlexicalized features[b]	50.4	
Lexicalized features[b]	78.2	
Vector sum + MLP[b]	75.3	
Vanilla RNN + MLP[b]	72.2	
LSTM RNN + MLP[b]	77.6	$\mathcal{O}(1)$
CNN + cat	77.0	
GRU w/ skip-thought pretraining[v]	81.4	
TBCNN-pair + cat	79.3	
TBCNN-pair + cat,○,-	**82.1**	
Single-chain LSTM RNNs[r]	81.4	$\mathcal{O}(n)$
+ static attention[r]	**82.4**	
LSTM + word-by-word attention[r]	**83.5**	$\mathcal{O}(n^2)$

Table 3: Accuracy of the TBCNN-pair model in comparison with previous results ([b]Bowman et al., 2015; [v]Vendrov et al., 2015; [r]Rocktäschel et al., 2015). "cat" refers to concatenation; "-" and "○" denote element-wise difference and product, resp.

Model Variant	Valid Acc.	Test Acc.
TBCNN+○	73.8	72.5
TBCNN+-	79.9	79.3
TBCNN+cat	80.8	79.3
TBCNN+cat,○	81.6	80.7
TBCNN+cat,-	81.7	81.6
TBCNN+cat,○,-	**82.4**	**82.1**

Table 4: Validation and test accuracies of TBCNN-pair variants (in percentage).

(LSTM)-based RNNs, and traditional CNNs. This verifies the rationale for using tree-based convolution as the sentence-level neural model for NLI.

Table 4 compares different heuristics of matching. We first analyze each heuristic separately: using element-wise product alone is significantly worse than concatenation or element-wise difference; the latter two are comparable to each other.

Combining different matching heuristics improves the result: the TBCNN-pair model with concatenation, element-wise product and difference yields the highest performance of 82.1%. As analyzed in Section 3.2, the element-wise difference matching layer does not add to model complexity and can be absorbed as a special case into simple concatenation. However, explicitly using such heuristic yields an accuracy boost of 1–2%. Further applying element-wise product improves the accuracy by another 0.5%.

The full TBCNN-pair model outperforms all existing sentence encoding-based approaches, in-cluding a 1024d gated recurrent unit (GRU)-based RNN with "skip-thought" pretraining (Vendrov et al., 2015). The results obtained by our model are also comparable to several attention-based LSTMs, which are more computationally intensive than ours in terms of complexity order.

4.4 Complexity Concerns

For most sentence models including TBCNN, the overall complexity is at least $\mathcal{O}(n)$. However, an efficient matching approach is still important, especially to *retrieval-and-reranking* systems (Yan et al., 2016; Li et al., 2016). For example, in a retrieval-based question-answering or conversation system, we can largely reduce response time by performing sentence matching based on pre-computed candidates' embeddings. By contrast, context-aware matching approaches as described in Section 2 involve processing each candidate given a new user-issued query, which is time-consuming in terms of most industrial products.

In our experiments, the matching part (Figure 1b) counts 1.71% of the total time during prediction (single-CPU, C++ implementation), showing the potential applications of our approach in efficient retrieval of semantically related sentences.

5 Conclusion

In this paper, we proposed the TBCNN-pair model for natural language inference. Our model relies on the tree-based convolutional neural network (TBCNN) to capture sentence-level semantics; then two sentences' information is combined by several heuristics including concatenation, element-wise product and difference. Experimental results on a large dataset show a high performance of our TBCNN-pair model while remaining a low complexity order.

Acknowledgments

We thank all anonymous reviewers for their constructive comments, especially those on complexity issues. We also thank Sam Bowman, Edward Grefenstette, and Tim Rocktäschel for their discussion. This research was supported by the National Basic Research Program of China (the 973 Program) under Grant No. 2015CB352201 and the National Natural Science Foundation of China under Grant Nos. 61232015, 61421091, and 61502014.

References

Johan Bos and Katja Markert. 2005. Combining shallow and deep NLP methods for recognizing textual entailment. In *Proceedings of the First PASCAL Challenges Workshop on Recognising Textual Entailment*, pages 65–68.

Samuel R. Bowman, Gabor Angeli, Christopher Potts, and Christopher D. Manning. 2015. A large annotated corpus for learning natural language inference. In *Proceedings of the 2015 Conference on Empirical Methods in Natural Language Processing*, pages 632–642.

Jane Bromley, James W Bentz, Léon Bottou, Isabelle Guyon, Yann LeCun, Cliff Moore, Eduard Säckinger, and Roopak Shah. 1993. Signature verification using a "Siamese" time delay neural network. *International Journal of Pattern Recognition and Artificial Intelligence*, 7(04):669–688.

Ronan Collobert and Jason Weston. 2008. A unified architecture for natural language processing: Deep neural networks with multitask learning. In *Proceedings of the 25th International Conference on Machine learning*, pages 160–167.

Marie-Catherine de Marneffe, Bill MacCartney, and Christopher D Manning. 2006. Generating typed dependency parses from phrase structure parses. In *Proceedings of the Language Resource and Evaluation Conference*, pages 449–454.

Sanda Harabagiu and Andrew Hickl. 2006. Methods for using textual entailment in open-domain question answering. In *Proceedings of the 21st International Conference on Computational Linguistics and the 44th Annual Meeting of the Association for Computational Linguistics*, pages 905–912.

Sanda Harabagiu, Andrew Hickl, and Finley Lacatusu. 2006. Negation, contrast and contradiction in text processing. In *Proceedings of AAAI Conference on Artificial Intelligence*, pages 755–762.

Hua He, Kevin Gimpel, and Jimmy Lin. 2015. Multiperspective sentence similarity modeling with convolutional neural networks. In *Proceedings of the 2015 Conference on Empirical Methods in Natural Language Processing*, pages 17–21.

Baotian Hu, Zhengdong Lu, Hang Li, and Qingcai Chen. 2014. Convolutional neural network architectures for matching natural language sentences. In *Advances in Neural Information Processing Systems*, pages 2042–2050.

Nal Kalchbrenner, Edward Grefenstette, and Phil Blunsom. 2014. A convolutional neural network for modelling sentences. In *Proceedings of the 52nd Annual Meeting of the Association for Computational Linguistics*, pages 655–665.

Finley Lacatusu, Andrew Hickl, Kirk Roberts, Ying Shi, Jeremy Bensley, Bryan Rink, Patrick Wang, and Lara Taylor. 2006. LCCs GISTexter at DUC 2006: Multi-strategy multi-document summarization. In *Proceedings of DUC 2006*.

Xiang Li, Lili Mou, Rui Yan, and Ming Zhang. 2016. StalemateBreaker: A proactive content-introducing approach to automatic human-computer conversation. In *Proceedings of the 25th International Joint Conference on Artificial Intelligence*.

Yang Liu, Sujian Li, Xiaodong Zhang, and Zhifang Sui. 2016. Implicit discourse relation classification via multi-task neural networks. In *Proceedings of the Thirtieth AAAI Conference on Artificial Intelligence*.

Bill MacCartney, Trond Grenager, Marie-Catherine de Marneffe, Daniel Cer, and Christopher D. Manning. 2006. Learning to recognize features of valid textual entailments. In *Proceedings of the Human Language Technology Conference of the NAACL*, pages 41–48.

Bill MacCartney. 2009. *Natural Language Inference*. Ph.D. thesis, Stanford University.

Tomas Mikolov, Ilya Sutskever, Kai Chen, Greg S Corrado, and Jeff Dean. 2013a. Distributed representations of words and phrases and their compositionality. In *Advances in Neural Information Processing Systems*, pages 3111–3119.

Tomas Mikolov, Wen-tau Yih, and Geoffrey Zweig. 2013b. Linguistic regularities in continuous space word representations. In *NAACL-HLT*, pages 746–751.

Lili Mou, Hao Peng, Ge Li, Yan Xu, Lu Zhang, and Zhi Jin. 2015. Discriminative neural sentence modeling by tree-based convolution. In *Proceedings of the 2015 Conference on Empirical Methods in Natural Language Processing*, pages 2315–2325.

Lili Mou, Ge Li, Lu Zhang, Tao Wang, and Zhi Jin. 2016. Convolutional neural networks over tree structures for programming language processing. In *Proceedings of the Thirtieth AAAI Conference on Artificial Intelligence*.

Hao Peng, Lili Mou, Ge Li, Yunchuan Chen, Yangyang Lu, and Zhi Jin. 2015. A comparative study on regularization strategies for embedding-based neural networks. In *Proceedings of the 2015 Conference on Empirical Methods in Natural Language Processing*, pages 2106–2111.

Tim Rocktäschel, Edward Grefenstette, Karl Moritz Hermann, Tomáš Kočiský, and Phil Blunsom. 2016. Reasoning about entailment with neural attention. In *Proceedings of the International Conference on Learning Representations*.

Richard Socher, Eric H Huang, Jeffrey Pennin, Christopher D Manning, and Andrew Y Ng. 2011a. Dynamic pooling and unfolding recursive autoencoders for paraphrase detection. In *Advances in Neural Information Processing Systems*, pages 801–809.

Richard Socher, Jeffrey Pennington, Eric H Huang, Andrew Y Ng, and Christopher D Manning. 2011b. Semi-supervised recursive autoencoders for predicting sentiment distributions. In *Proceedings of the Conference on Empirical Methods in Natural Language Processing*, pages 151–161.

Ivan Vendrov, Ryan Kiros, Sanja Fidler, and Raquel Urtasun. 2015. Order-embeddings of images and language. *arXiv preprint arXiv:1511.06361*.

Shengxian Wan, Yanyan Lan, Jiafeng Guo, Jun Xu, Liang Pang, and Xueqi Cheng. 2015. A deep architecture for semantic matching with multiple positional sentence representations. *arXiv preprint arXiv:1511.08277*.

Yan Xu, Lili Mou, Ge Li, Yunchuan Chen, Hao Peng, and Zhi Jin. 2015. Classifying relations via long short term memory networks along shortest dependency paths. In *Proceedings of Conference on Empirical Methods in Natural Language Processing*, pages 1785–1794.

Yan Xu, Ran Jia, Lili Mou, Ge Li, Yunchuan Chen, Yangyang Lu, and Zhi Jin. 2016. Improved relation classification by deep recurrent neural networks with data augmentation. *arXiv preprint arXiv:1601.03651*.

Rui Yan, Liang Kong, Congrui Huang, Xiaojun Wan, Xiaoming Li, and Yan Zhang. 2011a. Timeline generation through evolutionary trans-temporal summarization. In *Proceedings of the Conference on Empirical Methods in Natural Language Processing*, pages 433–443.

Rui Yan, Xiaojun Wan, Jahna Otterbacher, Liang Kong, Xiaoming Li, and Yan Zhang. 2011b. Evolutionary timeline summarization: A balanced optimization framework via iterative substitution. In *Proceedings of the 34th international ACM SIGIR conference on Research and development in Information Retrieval*, pages 745–754.

Rui Yan, Yiping Song, and Hua Wu. 2016. Learning to respond with deep neural networks for retrieval based human-computer conversation system. In *Proceedings of the 39th International ACM SIGIR Conference on Research and Development in Information Retrieval*.

Wenpeng Yin and Hinrich Schütze. 2015. Convolutional neural network for paraphrase identification. In *Proceedings of the 2015 Conference of the North American Chapter of the Association for Computational Linguistics: Human Language Technologies*, pages 901–911.

Biao Zhang, Jinsong Su, Deyi Xiong, Yaojie Lu, Hong Duan, and Junfeng Yao. 2015. Shallow convolutional neural network for implicit discourse relation recognition. In *Proceedings of the 2015 Conference on Empirical Methods in Natural Language Processing*, pages 2230–2235.

Improving cross-domain n-gram language modelling with skipgrams

Louis Onrust
CLS, Radboud University Nijmegen
ESAT-PSI, KU Leuven
`l.onrust@let.ru.nl`

Antal van den Bosch
CLS, Radboud University Nijmegen
`a.vandenbosch@let.ru.nl`

Hugo Van hamme
ESAT-PSI, KU Leuven
`hugo.vanhamme@esat.kuleuven.be`

Abstract

In this paper we improve over the hierarchical Pitman-Yor processes language model in a cross-domain setting by adding skipgrams as features. We find that adding skipgram features reduces the perplexity. This reduction is substantial when models are trained on a generic corpus and tested on domain-specific corpora. We also find that within-domain testing and cross-domain testing require different backoff strategies. We observe a 30-40% reduction in perplexity in a cross-domain language modelling task, and up to 6% reduction in a within-domain experiment, for both English and Flemish-Dutch.

1   Introduction

Since the seminal paper on hierarchical Bayesian language models based on Pitman-Yor processes (Teh, 2006), Bayesian language modelling has regained an interest. Although Bayesian language models are not new (MacKay and Peto, 1995), previously proposed models were reported to be inferior compared to other smoothing methods. Teh's work was the first to report on improvements over interpolated Kneser-Ney smoothing (Teh, 2006).

To overcome the traditional problems of over-estimating the probabilities of rare occurrences and underestimating the probabilities of unseen events, a range of smoothing algorithms have been proposed in the literature (Goodman, 2001). Most methods take a heuristic-frequentist approach combining n-gram probabilities for various values of n, using back-off schemes or interpolation.

Teh (2006) showed that MacKay and Peto's (1995) research on parametric Bayesian language models with a Dirichlet prior could be extended to give better results, but also that one of the best smoothing methods, interpolated Kneser-Ney (Kneser and Ney, 1995), can be derived as an approximation of the Hierarchical Pitman-Yor process language model (HPYLM).

The success of the Bayesian approach to language modelling is due to the use of statistical distributions such as the Dirichlet distribution, and distributions over distributions, such as the Dirichlet process and its two-parameter generalisation, the Pitman-Yor process. Both are widely studied in the statistics and probability theory communities. Interestingly, language modelling has acquired the status of a "fruit fly" problem in these communities, to benchmark the performance of statistical models. In this paper we approach language modelling from a computational linguistics point of view, and consider the statistical methods to be the tool with the future goal of improving language models for extrinsic tasks such as speech recognition.

We derive our model from Teh (2006), and propose an extension with skipgrams. A frequentist approach to language modelling with skipgrams is described by Pickhardt et al. (2014), who introduce an approach using skip-n-grams which are interpolated using modified Kneser-Ney smoothing. In this paper we show that a Bayesian skip-n-gram approach outperforms a frequentist skip-n-gram model.

2   Method

Traditionally, the most widely used pattern in language modelling is the n-gram, which represents

Proceedings of the 54th Annual Meeting of the Association for Computational Linguistics, pages 137–142,
Berlin, Germany, August 7-12, 2016. ©2016 Association for Computational Linguistics

a pattern of n contiguous words, of which we call the first $(n-1)$ words the history or context, and the nth word the focus word. The motivation for using n-grams can be traced back to the distributional hypothesis of Harris (Harris, 1954; Sahlgren, 2008). Although n-grams are small patterns without any explicit linguistic annotation, they are surprisingly effective in many tasks, such as language modelling in machine translation, automatic speech recognition, and information retrieval.

One of the main limitations of n-grams is their contiguity, because this limits the expressive power to relations between neighboring words. Many patterns in language span a range that is longer than the typical length of n; we call these relations long-distance relations. Other patterns may be within the range of n, but are still non-contiguous; they skip over positions. Both types of relations may be modelled with (syntactic) dependencies, and modelling these explicitly requires a method to derive a parser, e.g. a dependency parser, from linguistically annotated data.

To be able to model long-distance and other non-contiguous relations between words without resorting to explicitly computing syntactic dependencies, we use skipgrams. Skipgrams are a generalisation of n-grams. They consist of n tokens, but now each token may represent a skip of at least one word, where a skip can match any word. Let $\{m\}$ be a skip of length m, then *the $\{1\}$ house* can match "the big house", or "the yellow house", etc. We do not allow skips to be at the beginning or end of the skipgram, so for $n > 2$ skipgrams are a generalisation of n-grams (Goodman, 2001; Shazeer et al., 2015; Pickhardt et al., 2014).

Pitman-Yor Processes (PYP) belong to the family of non-parametric Bayesian models. Let W be a fixed and finite vocabulary of V words. For each word $w \in W$ let $G(w)$ be the probability of w, and $G = [G(w)]_{w \in W}$ be the vector of word probabilities. Since word frequencies generally follow a power-law distribution, we use a Pitman-Yor process, which is a distribution over partitions with power-law distributions. In the context of a language model this means that for a space $P(\mathbf{u})$, with $c(\mathbf{u}\cdot)$ elements (tokens), we want to partition $P(\mathbf{u})$ in V subsets such that the partition is a good approximation of the underlying data, in which $c(\mathbf{u}w)$ is the size of subset w of $P(\mathbf{u})$. We assume that the training data is an sample of the underlying data, and for this reason we seek to find an approximation, rather than using the partitions precisely as found in the training data.

Since we also assume that a power-law distribution on the words in the underlying data, we place a PYP prior on G:

$$G \sim \mathrm{PY}(d, \theta, G_0),$$

with discount parameter $0 \leq d < 1$, a strength parameter $\theta > -d$ and a mean vector $G_0 = [G_0(w)]_{w \in W}$. $G_0(w)$ is the a-priori probability of word w, which we set uniformly: $G_0(w) = 1/V$ for all $w \in W$. In general, there is no known analytic form for the density of $\mathrm{PY}(d, \theta, G_0)$ when the vocabulary is finite. However, we are interested in the distribution over word sequences induced by the PYP, which has a tractable form, and is sufficient for the purpose of language modelling.

Let G and G_0 be distributions over W, and $x_1, x_2, \ldots$ be a sequence of words drawn i.i.d. from G. The PYP is then described in terms of a generative procedure that takes $x_1, x_2, \ldots$ to produce a separate sequence of i.i.d. draws $y_1, y_2, \ldots$ from the mean distribution G_0 as follows. The first word x_1 is assigned the value of the first draw y_1 from G_0. Let t be the current number of draws from G_0, c_k the number of words assigned the value of draw y_k and $c. = \sum_{k=1}^{t} c_k$ the number of draws from G_0. For each subsequent word $x_{c.+1}$, we either assign it the value of a previous draw y_k, with probability $\frac{c_k - d}{\theta + c.}$, or assign it the value of a new draw from G_0 with probability $\frac{\theta + dt}{\theta + c.}$.

For an n-gram language model we use a hierarchical extension of the PYP. The hierarchical extension describes the probabilities over the current word given various contexts consisting of up to $n - 1$ words. Given a context $\mathbf{u}$, let $G_{\mathbf{u}}(w)$ be the probability of the current word taking on value w. A PYP is used as the prior for $G_{\mathbf{u}} = [G_{\mathbf{u}}(w)]_{w \in W}$:

$$G_{\mathbf{u}} \sim \mathrm{PY}(d_{|\mathbf{u}|}, \theta_{|\mathbf{u}|}, G_{\pi(\mathbf{u})}),$$

where $\pi(\mathbf{u})$ is the suffix of $\mathbf{u}$ consisting of all but the first word, and $|\mathbf{u}|$ being the length of $\mathbf{u}$. The priors are recursively placed with parameters $\theta_{|\pi(\mathbf{u})|}, d_{|\pi(\mathbf{u})|}$ and mean vector $G_{\pi(\pi(\mathbf{u}))}$, until we get to $G_\emptyset$:

$$G_\emptyset \sim \mathrm{PY}(d_0, \theta_0, G_0),$$

with G_0 being the uniformly distributed global mean vector for the empty context $\emptyset$.

3 Backoff Strategies

In this paper we investigate three backoff strategies: ngram, limited, and full. ngram is the traditional n-gram backoff method as described by Teh (2006); limited and full are extensions that also incorporate skipgram probabilities. The full backoff strategy is similar to ngram in that it always backs off recursively to the word probabilities, while limited halts as soon as a probability is known for a pattern. The backoff strategies can be formalised as follows. For all strategies, we have that $p(w|\mathbf{u}) = G_0(w)$ if $\mathbf{u} = \emptyset$. For ngram, the other case is defined as:

$$p(w|\mathbf{u}) = \frac{c_{\mathbf{u}w\cdot} - d_{|\mathbf{u}|}t_{\mathbf{u}w\cdot}}{\theta_{|\mathbf{u}|} + c_{\mathbf{u}\cdot\cdot}} + \frac{\theta_{|\mathbf{u}|} + d_{|\mathbf{u}|}t_{\mathbf{u}\cdot\cdot}}{\theta_{|\mathbf{u}|} + c_{\mathbf{u}\cdot\cdot}} p(w|\pi(\mathbf{u}))$$

with $c_{\mathbf{u}w\cdot}$ being the number of $\mathbf{u}w$ tokens, and $c_{\mathbf{u}\cdot\cdot}$ the number of patterns starting with context $\mathbf{u}$. Similarly, $t_{\mathbf{u}wk}$ is 1 if draw the kth from $G_{\mathbf{u}}$ was w, 0 otherwise. $t_{\mathbf{u}w\cdot}$ then denotes if there is a pattern $\mathbf{u}w$, and $t_{\mathbf{u}\cdot\cdot}$ is the number of types following context $\mathbf{u}$.

Now let σ_n be the operator that adds a skip to a pattern $\mathbf{u}$ on the nth position if there is not already a skip. Then $\sigma(\mathbf{u}) = [\sigma_n(\mathbf{u})]_{n=2}^{|\mathbf{u}|}$ is the set of patterns with one skip more than the number of skips currently in $\mathbf{u}$. The number of generated patterns is $\varsigma = |\sigma(\mathbf{u})|$. We also introduce the indicator function S, which for the full backoff strategy always returns its argument: $S_{\mathbf{u}w}(y) = y$. The full backoff strategy is defined as follows, with $\mathbf{u}_x = \sigma_x(\mathbf{u})$, and discount frequency $\delta_{\mathbf{u}} = 1$:

$$\begin{aligned} p(w|\mathbf{u}) = & \\ \sum_{m=1}^{\varsigma} & \left\{ \frac{1}{\varsigma+1} \left[\frac{c_{\mathbf{u}_m w\cdot} - \delta_{\mathbf{u}_m} d_{|\mathbf{u}_m|} t_{\mathbf{u}_m w\cdot}}{\delta_{\mathbf{u}_m}\theta_{|\mathbf{u}_m|} + c_{\mathbf{u}_m\cdot\cdot}} + \right. \right. \\ & \left. \left. S_{\mathbf{u}_m w}\left(\frac{\theta_{|\mathbf{u}_m|} + d_{|\mathbf{u}_m|}t_{\mathbf{u}_m}}{\delta_{\mathbf{u}_m}\theta_{|\mathbf{u}_m|} + c_{\mathbf{u}_m\cdot\cdot}} p(w|\pi(\mathbf{u}_m)) \right) \right] \right\} \\ + & \frac{1}{\varsigma+1} \left[\frac{c_{\mathbf{u}w\cdot} - \delta_{\mathbf{u}} d_{|\mathbf{u}|} t_{\mathbf{u}w\cdot}}{\delta_{\mathbf{u}}\theta_{|\mathbf{u}|} + c_{\mathbf{u}\cdot\cdot}} + \right. \\ & \left. S_{\mathbf{u}w}\left(\frac{\theta_{|\mathbf{u}|} + d_{|\mathbf{u}|}t_{\mathbf{u}\cdot\cdot}}{\delta_{\mathbf{u}}\theta_{|\mathbf{u}|} + c_{\mathbf{u}\cdot\cdot}} p(w|\pi(\mathbf{u})) \right) \right] \end{aligned}$$

The limited backoff strategy is an extension of the full backoff strategy that stops the recursion if a test pattern $\mathbf{u}w$ has already occurred in the training data. This means that the count is not zero, and hence at training time a probability has been assigned to that pattern. S is the indicator function which tells if a pattern has been seen during training: $S_{\mathbf{u}w}(\cdot) = 0$ if $\text{count}(\mathbf{u}w) > 0$, 1 otherwise; and $\delta_{\mathbf{u}} = V - \sum_{w \in W} S_{\mathbf{u}w}(\cdot)$. Setting $S_{\mathbf{u}w}(\cdot) = 0$ stops the recursion.

4 Data

In this section we give an overview of the data sets we use for the English and Flemish-Dutch experiments.

4.1 English Data

For the experiments on English we use four corpora: two large generic mixed-domain corpora and two smaller domain-specific corpora. We train on the largest of the two mixed-domain corpora, and test on all four corpora.

The first generic corpus is the Google 1 billion words shuffled web corpus of 769 million tokens (Chelba et al., 2013). For training we use sets 1 through 100, out of the 101 available training sets; for testing we use all available 50 test sets (8M tokens). The second generic corpus, used as test data, is a Wikipedia snapshot (368M tokens) of November 2013 as used and provided by Pickhardt et al. (2014). The first domain-specific corpus is from JRC-Acquis v3.0 (Steinberger et al., 2006), which contains legislative text of the European Union (8M tokens). The second domain-specific corpus consists of documents from the European Medicines Agency, EMEA (Tiedemann, 2009). We shuffled all sentences, and selected 20% of them as the test set (3M tokens).

Since the HPYLM uses a substantial amount of memory, even with histogram based sampling, we cannot model the complete 1bw data set without thresholding the patterns in the model. We used a high occurrence threshold of 100 on the unigrams, yielding 99,553 types that occur above this threshold. We use all n-grams and skipgrams that occurred at least twice, consisting of the included unigrams as focus words, with UNKs occupying the positions of words not in the vocabulary. Note that because these settings are different from models competing on this benchmark, the results in this paper cannot be compared to those results.

4.2 Flemish-Dutch Data

For the experiments on Flemish-Dutch data, we use the Mediargus corpus as training material. It contains 5 years of newspaper texts from 12 Flemish newspapers and magazines, totaling 1.3 billion words.

For testing we use the Flemish part of the Spoken Dutch Corpus (CGN) (Oostdijk, 2000) (3.2M words), divided over 15 components, ranging from spontaneous speech to books read aloud. CGN also contains two components which are news articles and news, which from a domain perspective are similar to the training data of Mediargus. We report on each component separately.

Similarly to the 1bw models, we used a threshold on the word types, such that we have a similar size of vocabulary (100k types), which we produced with a threshold of 250. We used the same occurrence threshold of 2 on the n- and skipgrams.

5 Experimental Setup

We train 4-gram language model on the two training corpora, the Google 1 billion word benchmark and the Mediargus corpus. We do not perform any preprocessing on the data except tokenisation. The models are trained with a HPYLM. We do not use sentence beginning and end markers. The results for the ngram backoff strategy are obtained by training without skipgrams; for limited and full we added skipgram features during training.

At the core of our experimental framework we use cpyp,[1] which is an existing library for non-parametric Bayesian modelling with PY priors with histogram-based sampling (Blunsom et al., 2009). This library has an example application to showcase its performance with n-gram based language modelling. Limitations of the library, such as not natively supporting skipgrams, and the lack of other functionality such as thresholding and discarding of certain patterns, led us to extend the library with Colibri Core,[2] a pattern modelling library. Colibri Core resolves the limitations, and together the libraries are a complete language model that handles skipgrams: cococpyp.[3]

Each model is run for 50 iterations (without an explicit burn-in phase), with hyperparameters $\theta = 1.0$ and $\gamma = 0.8$. The hyperparameters are resampled every 30 iterations with slice sampling (Walker, 2007). We test each model on different test sets, and we collect their intrinsic performance by means of perplexity. Words in the test set

---

[1] https://github.com/redpony/cpyp
[2] http://proycon.github.io/colibri-core/
[3] https://github.com/naiaden/cococpyp

Test	ngram	limited	↓%	full	↓%
1bw	171	**141**	6	199	-16
jrc	1232	994	19	**728**	**41**
emea	1749	1304	25	**1069**	**39**
wp	724	635	12	**542**	**25**

Table 1: Results of the full and limited backoff systems, trained on 1bw, tested on 1bw (in-domain), and cross-domain sets jrc, emea, and wp. ↓% is the relative reduction in perplexity for the column to its left.

Comp.	ngram	limited	↓%	full	↓%
a	1280	1116	13	**828**	**35**
b	847	785	7	**639**	**24**
c	1501	1272	15	**946**	**37**
d	1535	1306	15	**975**	**36**
f	708	647	9	**572**	**19**
g	479	445	7	**440**	**8**
h	1016	916	10	**718**	**29**
i	1075	990	8	**783**	**27**
j	469	**434**	7	442	6
k	284	**253**	**11**	333	-17
l	726	639	12	**629**	**13**
m	578	538	7	**512**	**11**
n	895	794	11	**664**	**26**
o	1017	887	13	**833**	**18**

Table 2: Results of the full and limited backoff systems, trained on Mediargus, tested on CGN. Components range from spontaneous (a) to non-spontaneous (o), with components j (news reports) and k (news) being in-domain for the training corpus, and the other components being out-of-domain. ↓% is the relative reduction in perplexity for the column to its left.

that were unseen in the training data are ignored in computing the perplexity on test data.

6 Results

The results are reported in terms of perplexity, in Table 1 for English, and in Table 2 for Flemish-Dutch. We computed baseline perplexity scores with SRILM (Stolcke, 2002) for 1bw. We used an interpolated modified Kneser-Ney language model, with Good-Turing discounting to mimic our thresholding options. Although the models are not comparable, this is arguably the closest approximation in SRILM of our HPYLM. For 1bw the baseline is 147; for jrc, emea, and wp, 1391, 1430, and 1403 respectively. In some cases the baseline is better compared to the ngram backoff strategy. With adding skipgrams we always outperform the baseline, especially on the out-of-domain test sets.

We find that with large data sets adding skipgrams lowers the perplexity, for both languages, in both within- and cross-domain experiments. For English, we observe absolute perplexity reductions up to 680 (a relative reduction of 39%) in a cross-domain setting, and absolute perplexity reductions of 10 (relative reduction of 6%) in a within-domain setting. For Flemish-Dutch we observe similar results with absolute reductions up to 560 (relative reduction of 36%) and 31 (relative reduction 11%), respectively.

If we consider the three backoff strategies individually, we can see the following effects on both English and Flemish-Dutch data. In a within-domain experiment limited backoff is the best stratgey. In a cross-domain setting, the full backoff strategy yields the lowest perplexity and largest perplexity reductions. In the first case, stopping the backoff when there is a pattern probability for the word and its context yields a more certain probability than when the probability is diffused by more uncertain backoff probabilities.

Upon inspection of the model sizes, we observe that the skipgram model contains almost five times as many parameters as the n-gram model. This difference is explained by the addition of skipgrams of length 3 and 4, and the bigrams and unigrams derived from these skipgrams. Each 4-gram can be deconstructed into three skipgrams of length 4, and one of these skipgrams yields a skipgram of length 3. Tests with ngram backoff on skipgram models show that the performance is worse compared to ngram backoff in pure n-gram models because of the extra bigrams and unigrams (ngram ignores the skipgrams). Yet, the experimental results also indicate that with sufficient data, skipgram models outperform n-gram models. Because the difference in parameters is only noticeable in terms of memory, and it hardly impacts the run-time, this makes the skipgram model the favourable model.

7 Conclusions

In this paper we showed that by adding skipgrams, a straightforward but powerful generalisation of n-gram word patterns, we can reduce the perplexity of a Bayesian language model, especially in a cross-domain language modelling task. By changing the backoff strategy we can also improve on a within-domain task. We found this effect in two languages.

References

P Blunsom, T Cohn, S Goldwater, and M Johnson. 2009. A note on the implementation of hierarchical Dirichlet processes. In *Proceedings of the ACL-IJCNLP 2009 Conference Short Papers*, pages 337–340. Association for Computational Linguistics.

C Chelba, T Mikolov, M Schuster, Q Ge, T Brants, P Koehn, and T Robinson. 2013. One billion word benchmark for measuring progress in statistical language modeling. Technical Report Google Tech Report 41880.

JT Goodman. 2001. A bit of progress in language modeling. *Computer Speech & Language*, 15(4):403–434.

ZS Harris. 1954. Distributional structure. *Word*.

R Kneser and H Ney. 1995. Improved backing-off for m-gram language modeling. In *In Proceedings of the IEEE International Conference on Acoustics, Speech and Signal Processing*, volume I, pages 181–184, May.

DJC MacKay and LCB Peto. 1995. A hierarchical Dirichlet language model. *Natural language engineering*, 1(3):289–308.

N Oostdijk. 2000. The spoken Dutch corpus. Overview and first evaluation. In *LREC*.

R Pickhardt, T Gottron, M Körner, PG Wagner, T Speicher, and S Staab. 2014. A generalized language model as the combination of skipped n-grams and modified Kneser-Ney smoothing. *arXiv preprint arXiv:1404.3377*.

M Sahlgren. 2008. The distributional hypothesis. *Italian Journal of Linguistics*, 20(1):33–54.

N Shazeer, J Pelemans, and C Chelba. 2015. Sparse non-negative matrix language modeling for skipgrams. In *Proceedings of Interspeech*, pages 1428–1432.

R Steinberger, B Pouliquen, A Widiger, C Ignat, T Erjavec, D Tufis, and D Varga. 2006. The JRC-Acquis: A multilingual aligned parallel corpus with 20+ languages. *Proceedings of the 5th International Conference on Language Resources and Evaluation*.

A Stolcke. 2002. SRILM — an extensible language modeling toolkit. In *Proceedings International Conference on Spoken Language Processing*, pages 257–286, November.

YW Teh. 2006. A hierarchical Bayesian language model based on Pitman-Yor processes. In *Proceedings of the 21st International Conference on Computational Linguistics and the 44th annual meeting of the Association for Computational Linguistics*, pages 985–992. Association for Computational Linguistics.

J Tiedemann. 2009. News from OPUS — A collection of multilingual parallel corpora with tools and interfaces. In *Recent Advances in Natural Language Processing*, volume 5, pages 237–248.

SG Walker. 2007. Sampling the Dirichlet mixture model with slices. *Communications in Statistics — Simulation and Computation*, 36(1):45–54.

Simple PPDB: A Paraphrase Database for Simplification

Ellie Pavlick
University of Pennsylvania
`epavlick@seas.upenn.edu`

Chris Callison-Burch
University of Pennsylvania
`ccb@cis.upenn.edu`

Abstract

We release the Simple Paraphrase Database, a subset of of the Paraphrase Database (PPDB) adapted for the task of text simplification. We train a supervised model to associate simplification scores with each phrase pair, producing rankings competitive with state-of-the-art lexical simplification models. Our new simplification database contains 4.5 million paraphrase rules, making it the largest available resource for lexical simplification.

1 Motivation

Language is complex, and the process of reading and understanding language is difficult for many groups of people. The goal of text simplification is to rewrite text in order to make it easier to understand, for example, by children (De Belder and Moens, 2010), language learners (Petersen and Ostendorf, 2007), people with disabilities (Rello et al., 2013; Evans et al., 2014), and even by machines (Siddharthan et al., 2004). Automatic text simplification (Napoles and Dredze, 2010; Wubben et al., 2012; Xu et al., 2016) has the potential to dramatically increase access to information by making written documents available at all reading levels.

Full text simplification involves many steps, including grammatical restructuring and summarization (Feng, 2008). One of the most basic subtasks is *lexical simplification* (Specia et al., 2012)– replacing complicated words and phrases with simpler paraphrases. While there is active research in the area of lexical simplification (Coster and Kauchak, 2011a; Glavaš and Štajner, 2015; Paetzold, 2015), existing models have been by-and-large limited to single words. Often, how-

medical practitioner	→	doctor
legislative texts	→	laws
hypertension	→	high blood pressure
prevalent	→	very common
significant quantity	→	a lot
impact negatively	→	be bad

Table 1: In lexical simplification, it is often necessary to replace single words with phrases or phrases with single words. The above are examples of such lexical simplifications captured by the Simple PPDB resource.

ever, it is preferable, or even necessary to paraphrase a single complex word with multiple simpler words, or to paraphrase multiple words with a single word. For example, it is difficult to imagine a simple, single-word paraphrase of *hypertension*, but the three-word phrase *high blood pressure* is a very good simplification (Table 1). Such phrasal simplifications are overlooked by current lexical simplification models, and thus are often unavailable to the end-to-end text simplification systems that require them.

Recent research in data-driven paraphrasing has produced enormous resources containing millions of meaning-equivalent phrases (Ganitkevitch et al., 2013). Such resources capture a wide range of language variation, including the types of lexical and phrasal simplifications just described. In this work, we apply state-of-the-art machine learned models for lexical simplification in order to identify phrase pairs from the Paraphrase Database (PPDB) applicable to the task of text simplification. We introduce Simple PPDB,[1] a subset of the Paraphrase Database containing 4.5 million simplifying paraphrase rules. The large scale of Simple PPDB will support research into increasingly advanced methods for text simplification.

---

[1] `http://www.seas.upenn.edu/~nlp/resources/simple-ppdb.tgz`

143

Proceedings of the 54th Annual Meeting of the Association for Computational Linguistics, pages 143–148,
Berlin, Germany, August 7-12, 2016. ©2016 Association for Computational Linguistics

2 Identifying Simplification Rules

2.1 Paraphrase Rules

The Paraphrase Database (PPDB) is currently the largest available collection of paraphrases. Each paraphrase rule in the database has an automatically-assigned quality score between 1 and 5 (Pavlick et al., 2015). In this work, we use the PPDB-TLDR[2] dataset, which contains 14 million high-scoring lexical and phrasal paraphrases, and is intended to give a generally good tradeoff between precision and recall. To preprocess the data, we lemmatize all of the phrases, and remove rules which differ only by morphology, punctuation, or stop words, or which involve phrases longer than 3 words. The resulting list contains 7.5 million paraphrase rules covering 625K unique lemmatized words and phrases.

2.2 Lexical Simplification Model

Our goal is to build a model which can accurately identify paraphrase rules that both 1) simplify the input phrase and 2) preserve its meaning. That is, we want to avoid a model which favors "simple" words (e.g. *the, and*) even when they capture none of the meaning of the input phrase. We therefore train our model to make a three-way distinction between rules which simplify the input, rules which make the input less simple, and rules which generate bad paraphrases.

Data. We collect our training data in two phases. First, we sample 1,000 phrases from the vocabulary of the PPDB. We limit ourselves to words which also appear at least once in the Newsela corpus for text simplifcation (Xu et al., 2015), in order to ensure that we focus our model on the types of words for which the final resource is most likely to be applied. For each of these 1,000 words/phrases, we sample up to 10 candidate paraphrases from PPDB, stratified evenly across paraphrase quality scores. We ask workers on Amazon Mechanical Turk to rate each of the chosen paraphrase rules on a scale from 1 to 5 to indicate how well the paraphrase preserves the meaning of the original phrase. We use the same annotation design used in Pavlick et al. (2015). We have 5 workers judge each pair, omitting workers who do not provide correct answers on the embedded gold-standard pairs which we draw from WordNet. For 62% of the paraphrase rules we had

scored, the average human rating falls below 3, indicating that the meaning of the paraphrase differs substantially from that of the input. We assign all of these rules to the "bad paraphrase" class.

We take the remaining 3,758 meaning-preserving paraphrase rules (scored ≥ 3 in the above annotation task) and feed them into a second annotation task, in which we identify rules that simplify the input. We use the same annotation interface as in Pavlick and Nenkova (2015), which asks workers to choose which of the two phrases is simpler, or to indicate that there is no difference in complexity. We collect 7 judgements per pair and take the majority label, discarding pairs for which the majority opinion was that there was no difference. We include each rule in our training data twice, once as an instance of a "simplifying" rule, and once in the reverse direction as an instance of a "complicating" rule.

In the end, our training dataset contains 11,829 pairs, with the majority class being "bad paraphrase" (47%), and the remaining split evenly between "simplifying" and "complicating" paraphrase rules (26% each).

Features. We use a variety of features that have been shown in prior work to give good signal about phrases' relative complexity. The features we include are as follows: phrase length in words and in characters, frequency according to the Google NGram corpus (Brants and Franz, 2006), number of syllables, the relative frequency of usage in Simple Wikipedia compared to normal Wikipedia (Pavlick and Nenkova, 2015), character unigrams and bigrams, POS tags, and the averaged Word2Vec word embeddings for the words in the phrase (Mikolov et al., 2013). For each phrase pair $\langle e_1, e_2 \rangle$, for each feature f, we include $f(e_1)$, $f(e_2)$ and $f(e_1) - f(e_2)$.[3] We also include the cosine similarity of the averaged word embeddings and the PPDB paraphrase quality score as features.

We train a multi-class logistic regression model[4] to predict if the application of a paraphrase rule will result in 1) simpler output, 2) more complex output, or 3) non-sense output.

Performance. Table 2 shows the performance of the model on cross-validation, compared to several baselines. The full model achieves 60% accuracy,

---

[3] We do not compute the difference $f(e_1) - f(e_2)$ for sparse features, i.e. character ngrams and POS tags.

[4] http://scikit-learn.org/

	Acc	Prec.
Random	47.1%	0.0%
Simple/Regular Wiki. Ratio	49.1%	47.6%
Length in Characters	51.4%	47.3%
Google Ngram Frequency	51.4%	44.2%
Number of Syllables	51.5%	45.3%
Supervised Model, W2V	54.7%	46.3%
Supervised Model, Full	**60.4%**	**52.9%**

Table 2: Accuracy on 10-fold cross-validation, and precision for identifying simplifying rules. Folds are constructed so that train and test vocabularies are disjoint.

5 points higher than the strongest baseline, a supervised model which uses only word embeddings as features.

2.3 Simple PPDB

We run the trained model described above over all 7.5 million paraphrase rules. From the predictions, we construct Simple PPDB: a list of 4.5 million simplifying paraphrase rules. A rule in Simple PPDB is represented as a triple, consisting of a syntactic category, and input phrase, and a simplified output phrase. Each rule is associated with both a paraphrase quality score from 1 to 5 (taken from PPDB 2.0), and simplification confidence score from 0 to 1.0 (our classifier's confidence in the prediction that the rule belongs to the "simplifying" class). Note that ranking via the confidence scores of a classification model has not, to our knowledge, been explored in previous work on lexical simplification. The remainder of this paper evaluates the quality of the simplification ranking. For an evaluation of the paraphrase quality ranking, see Pavlick et al. (2015). Table 3 shows examples of some of the top ranked paraphrases according to Simple PPDB's simplification score for several input phrases.

3 Evaluation

To evaluate Simple PPDB, we apply it in a setting intended to emulate the way it is likely to be used in practice. We use the Newsela Simplification Dataset (Xu et al., 2015), a corpus of manually simplified news articles. This corpus is currently the cleanest available simplification dataset and is likely to be used to train and/or evaluate the simplification systems that we envision benefitting most from Simple PPDB.

We draw a sample of 100 unique word types ("targets") from the corpus for which Simple PPDB has at least one candidate simplification. For each target, we take Simple PPDB's full list of simplification rules which are of high quality according to the PPDB 2.0 paraphrase score[5] and which match the syntactic category of the target. On average, Simple PPDB proposes 8.8 such candidate simplifications per target.

Comparison to existing methods. Our baselines include three existing methods for generating lists of candidates that were proposed in prior work. The methods we test for generating lists of candidate paraphrases for a given target are: the **WordNetGenerator**, which pulls synonyms from WordNet (Devlin and Tait, 1998; Carroll et al., 1999), the **KauchakGenerator**, which generates candidates based on automatic alignments between Simple Wikipedia and normal Wikipedia (Coster and Kauchak, 2011a), and the **GlavasGenerator**, which generates candidates from nearby phrases in vector space (Glavaš and Štajner, 2015) (we use the pre-trained Word2Vec VSM (Mikolov et al., 2013)).

For each generated list, we follow Horn et al. (2014)'s supervised SVM Rank approach to rank the candidates for simplicity. We reimplement the main features of their model: namely, word frequencies according to the Google NGrams corpus (Brants and Franz, 2006) and the Simple Wikipedia corpus, and the alignment probabilities according to automatic word alignments between Wikipedia and Simple Wikipedia sentences (Coster and Kauchak, 2011b). We omit the language modeling features since our evaluation does not consider the context in which the substitution is to be applied.

All of these methods (the three generation methods and the ranker) are implemented as part of the LEXenstein toolkit (Paetzold and Specia, 2015). We use the LEXenstein implementations for the results reported here, using off-the-shelf configurations and treating each method as a black box.

Setup. We use each of the generate-and-rank methods to produce a ranked list of simplification candidates for each of the 100 targets drawn from the Newsela corpus. When a generation method fails to produce any candidates for a given target, we simply ignore that target for that particular method. This is to avoid giving Simple PPDB

---

[5]Heuristically, we define "high quality" as ≥ 3.5 for words and ≥ 4 for phrases.

keenly	omit	employment opportunity	remedied
most strongly	leave out	a new job	set right
deeply	delete it	opportunity	be fixed
strongly	be removed	business opportunity	be corrected
eagerly	forget about it	the job	to be resolved
very	be ignored	labour	be solved

Table 3: Examples of top-ranked simplifications proposed by Simple PPDB for several input words. Often, the best simplification for a single word is a multiword phrase, or vice-versa. These many-to-one mappings are overlooked when systems use only length or frequency as a proxy for simplicity.

an unfair advantage, since, by construction, PPDB will have full coverage of our list of 100 targets. In the end, the GlavasGenerator is evaluated over 95, the WordNetGenerator over 82, and the Kauchak-Generator over 48. The results in Table 4 do not change significantly if we restrict all systems to the 48 targets which the KauchakGenerator is capable of handling. Since the GlavasGenerator is capable of producing an arbitrary number of candidates for each target, we limit the length of each of its candidate lists to be equal to the number of candidates produced by Simple PPDB for that same target.

Human judgments. For each of the proposed rules from all four systems, we collect human judgements on Amazon Mechanical Turk, using the same annotation interface as before. That is, we ask 7 workers to view each pair and indicate which of the two phrases is simpler, or to indicate that there is no difference. We take the majority label to be the true label for each rule. Workers show moderate agreement on the 3-way task ($\kappa = 0.4 \pm 0.03$), with 14% of pairs receiving unanimous agreement and 37% receiving the same label from 6 out of 7 annotators. We note that the κ metric is likely a lower bound, as it punishes low agreement on pairs for which there is little difference in complexity, and thus the "correct" answer is not clear (e.g. for the pair $\langle matter, subject \rangle$, 3 annotators say that *matter* is simpler, 2 say that *subject* is simpler, and 2 say there is no difference).

Results. Table 4 compares the different methods in terms of how well they rank simplifying rules above non-simplifying rules. Simple PPDB's ranking of the relative simplicity achieves an averaged precision of 0.72 (0.77 P@1), compared to 0.70 (0.69 P@1) achieved by the Horn et al. (2014) system– i.e. the KauchakGenerator+SVM Ranker. We hypothesize that the performance difference between these two ranking systems is

	Avg. Prec.	P@1
Glavas+SVR	0.21	0.13
Wordnet+SVR	0.53	0.50
Kauchak+SVR	0.70	0.69
Simple PPDB	**0.72**	**0.77**

Table 4: Precision of relative simplification rankings of three existing lexical simplification methods compared to the Simple PPDB resource in terms of Average Precision and P@1 (both range from 0 to 1 and higher is better). All of the existing methods were evaluated using the implementations as provided in the LEXenstein toolkit.

likely due to a combination of the additional features applied in Simple PPDB's model (e.g. word embeddings) and the difference in training data (Simple PPDB's model was trained on 11K paraphrase pairs with trinary labels, while the Horn et al. (2014) model was trained on 500 words, each with a ranked list of paraphrases). Table 5 provides examples of the top-ranked simplification candidates proposed by each of the methods described.

alarm	
Glavas	**enrage**, perturb, stun
WordNet	horrify, dismay, **alert**, appall, appal
Kauchak	**pure**, **worry**
PPDB	**worry**, **concern**, **alert**

genuine	
Glavas	credible, **sort**, feign, **phoney**, good naturedness, **sincere**, **sincerely**, insincere, bonafide
WordNet	**real**, **actual**, unfeigned, literal, echt, **true**
Kauchak	thermal
PPDB	**true**, **real**, **actual**, **honest**, **sincere**

Table 5: Examples of candidate simplifications proposed by Simple PPDB and by three other generate-and-rank methods. Bold words were rated by humans to be simpler than the target word. Note that these candidates are judged on simplicity, not on their goodness as paraphrases.

In addition, Simple PPDB offers the largest coverage (Table 6). It has a total vocabulary of 624K unique words and phrases, and provides the largest number of potential simplifications for

	Avg. PPs per Input	Total Vocab.
Glavas+SVR	∞	∞
Kauchak+SVR	4.4	127K
Wordnet+SVR	6.7	155K
Simple PPDB	8.8	624K

Table 6: Overall coverage of three existing lexical simplification methods compared to the Simple PPDB resource. Glavas is marked as ∞ since it generates candidates based on nearness in vector space, and in theory could generate as many words/phrases as are in the vocabulary of the vector space.

each target– for the 100 targets drawn from the Newsela corpus, PPDB provided an average of 8.8 candidates per target. The next best generator, the WordNet-based system, produces only 6.7 candidates per target on average, and has a total vocabulary of only 155K words.

4 Conclusion

We have described Simple PPDB, a subset of the Paraphrase Database adapted for the task of text simplification. Simple PPDB is built by applying state-of-the-art machine learned models for lexical simplification to the largest available resource of lexical and phrasal paraphrases, resulting in a web-scale resource capable of supporting research in data-driven methods for text simplification. We have shown that Simple PPDB offers substantially increased coverage of both words and multiword phrases, while maintaining high quality compared to existing methods for lexical simplification. Simple PPDB, along with the human judgements collected as part of its creation, is freely available with the publication of this paper.[6]

Acknowledgments

This research was supported by a Facebook Fellowship, and by gifts from the Alfred P. Sloan Foundation, Google, and Facebook. This material is based in part on research sponsored by the NSF grant under IIS-1249516 and DARPA under number FA8750-13-2-0017 (the DEFT program). The U.S. Government is authorized to reproduce and distribute reprints for Governmental purposes. The views and conclusions contained in this publication are those of the authors and should not be interpreted as representing official policies or endorsements of DARPA and the U.S. Government.

---

[6]http://www.seas.upenn.edu/~nlp/
resources/simple-ppdb.tgz

We would especially like to thank Ani Nenkova for suggesting this line of research and for providing the initial ideas on which this work builds. We would also like to thank Courtney Napoles and Wei Xu for valuable discussions, the anonymous reviewers for thoughtful comments, and the Amazon Mechanical Turk annotators for their contributions.

References

Thorsten Brants and Alex Franz. 2006. Web 1T 5-gram Version 1. *Linguistic Data Consortium, Philadelphia.*

John Carroll, Guido Minnen, Darren Pearce, Yvonne Canning, Siobhan Devlin, and John Tait. 1999. Simplifying text for language-impaired readers. In *Proceedings of EACL*, volume 99, pages 269–270.

Will Coster and David Kauchak. 2011a. Learning to simplify sentences using Wikipedia. In *Proceedings of the Workshop on Monolingual Text-To-Text Generation*, pages 1–9, Portland, Oregon, June. Association for Computational Linguistics.

William Coster and David Kauchak. 2011b. Simple English Wikipedia: A new text simplification task. In *Proceedings of the 49th Annual Meeting of the Association for Computational Linguistics: Human Language Technologies*, pages 665–669, Portland, Oregon, USA, June. Association for Computational Linguistics.

Jan De Belder and Marie-Francine Moens. 2010. Text simplification for children. In *Proceedings of the SIGIR workshop on accessible search systems*, pages 19–26. ACM.

Siobhan Devlin and John Tait. 1998. The use of a psycholinguistic database in the simplification of text for aphasic readers. *Linguistic databases*, pages 161–173.

Richard Evans, Constantin Orasan, and Iustin Dornescu. 2014. An evaluation of syntactic simplification rules for people with autism. In *Proceedings of the 3rd Workshop on Predicting and Improving Text Readability for Target Reader Populations (PITR)*, pages 131–140.

Lijun Feng. 2008. Text simplification: A survey. *The City University of New York, Tech. Rep.*

Juri Ganitkevitch, Benjamin Van Durme, and Chris Callison-Burch. 2013. PPDB: The paraphrase database. In *Proceedings of the 2013 Conference of the North American Chapter of the Association for Computational Linguistics: Human Language Technologies*, pages 758–764, Atlanta, Georgia, June. Association for Computational Linguistics.

Goran Glavaš and Sanja Štajner. 2015. Simplifying lexical simplification: Do we need simplified corpora? In *Proceedings of the 53rd Annual Meeting of the Association for Computational Linguistics and the 7th International Joint Conference on Natural Language Processing (Volume 2: Short Papers)*, pages 63–68, Beijing, China, July. Association for Computational Linguistics.

Colby Horn, Cathryn Manduca, and David Kauchak. 2014. Learning a lexical simplifier using Wikipedia. In *Proceedings of the 52nd Annual Meeting of the Association for Computational Linguistics (Volume 2: Short Papers)*, pages 458–463, Baltimore, Maryland, June. Association for Computational Linguistics.

Tomas Mikolov, Kai Chen, Greg Corrado, and Jeffrey Dean. 2013. Efficient estimation of word representations in vector space. *arXiv preprint arXiv:1301.3781*.

Courtney Napoles and Mark Dredze. 2010. Learning Simple Wikipedia: A cogitation in ascertaining abecedarian language. In *Proceedings of the NAACL HLT 2010 Workshop on Computational Linguistics and Writing: Writing Processes and Authoring Aids*, pages 42–50, Los Angeles, CA, USA, June. Association for Computational Linguistics.

Gustavo Paetzold and Lucia Specia. 2015. LEXenstein: A framework for lexical simplification. In *Proceedings of ACL-IJCNLP 2015 System Demonstrations*, pages 85–90, Beijing, China, July. Association for Computational Linguistics and The Asian Federation of Natural Language Processing.

Gustavo Paetzold. 2015. Reliable lexical simplification for non-native speakers. In *Proceedings of the 2015 Conference of the North American Chapter of the Association for Computational Linguistics: Student Research Workshop*, pages 9–16, Denver, Colorado, June. Association for Computational Linguistics.

Ellie Pavlick and Ani Nenkova. 2015. Inducing lexical style properties for paraphrase and genre differentiation. In *Proceedings of the 2015 Conference of the North American Chapter of the Association for Computational Linguistics: Human Language Technologies*, pages 218–224, Denver, Colorado, May–June. Association for Computational Linguistics.

Ellie Pavlick, Pushpendre Rastogi, Juri Ganitkevitch, Benjamin Van Durme, and Chris Callison-Burch. 2015. PPDB 2.0: Better paraphrase ranking, fine-grained entailment relations, word embeddings, and style classification. In *Proceedings of the 53rd Annual Meeting of the Association for Computational Linguistics and the 7th International Joint Conference on Natural Language Processing (Volume 2: Short Papers)*, pages 425–430, Beijing, China, July. Association for Computational Linguistics.

Sarah E. Petersen and Mari Ostendorf. 2007. Text simplification for language learners: a corpus analysis. In *SLaTE*, pages 69–72. Citeseer.

Luz Rello, Ricardo A. Baeza-Yates, and Horacio Saggion. 2013. The impact of lexical simplification by verbal paraphrases for people with and without dyslexia. In *CICLing (2)*, pages 501–512.

Advaith Siddharthan, Ani Nenkova, and Kathleen McKeown. 2004. Syntactic simplification for improving content selection in multi-document summarization. In *Proceedings of the 20th international conference on Computational Linguistics*, page 896. Association for Computational Linguistics.

Lucia Specia, Sujay Kumar Jauhar, and Rada Mihalcea. 2012. SemEval-2012 task 1: English lexical simplification. In **SEM 2012: The First Joint Conference on Lexical and Computational Semantics – Volume 1: Proceedings of the main conference and the shared task, and Volume 2: Proceedings of the Sixth International Workshop on Semantic Evaluation (SemEval 2012)*, pages 347–355, Montréal, Canada, 7-8 June. Association for Computational Linguistics.

Sander Wubben, Antal Van Den Bosch, and Emiel Krahmer. 2012. Sentence simplification by monolingual machine translation. In *Proceedings of the 50th Annual Meeting of the Association for Computational Linguistics: Long Papers-Volume 1*, pages 1015–1024. Association for Computational Linguistics.

Wei Xu, Chris Callison-Burch, and Courtney Napoles. 2015. Problems in current text simplification research: New data can help. *Transactions of the Association for Computational Linguistics*, 3:283–297.

Wei Xu, Courtney Napoles, Ellie Pavlick, Quanze Chen, and Chris Callison-Burch. 2016. Optimizing statistical machine translation for text simplification. *Transactions of the Association for Computational Linguistics*, 4.

Improving Named Entity Recognition for Chinese Social Media
with Word Segmentation Representation Learning

Nanyun Peng[*] and **Mark Dredze**[*†]
[*] Human Language Technology Center of Excellence
Center for Language and Speech Processing
Johns Hopkins University, Baltimore, MD, 21218
[†]Bloomberg LP, New York, NY 10022
`npeng1@jhu.edu, mdredze@cs.jhu.edu`

Abstract

Named entity recognition, and other information extraction tasks, frequently use linguistic features such as part of speech tags or chunkings. For languages where word boundaries are not readily identified in text, word segmentation is a key first step to generating features for an NER system. While using word boundary tags as features are helpful, the signals that aid in identifying these boundaries may provide richer information for an NER system. New state-of-the-art word segmentation systems use neural models to learn representations for predicting word boundaries. We show that these same representations, jointly trained with an NER system, yield significant improvements in NER for Chinese social media. In our experiments, jointly training NER and word segmentation with an LSTM-CRF model yields nearly 5% absolute improvement over previously published results.

1 Introduction

Entity mention detection, and more specifically named entity recognition (NER) (Collins and Singer, 1999; McCallum and Li, 2003; Nadeau and Sekine, 2007; Jin and Chen, 2008; He et al., 2012), has become a popular task for social media analysis (Finin et al., 2010; Liu et al., 2011; Ritter et al., 2011; Fromreide et al., 2014; Li et al., 2012; Liu et al., 2012a). Many downstream applications that use social media, such as relation extraction (Bunescu and Mooney, 2005) and entity linking (Dredze et al., 2010; Ratinov et al., 2011), rely on first identifying mentions of entities. Not surprisingly, accuracy of NER systems in social media trails state-of-the-art systems for news text and

other formal domains. While this gap is shrinking in English (Ritter et al., 2011; Cherry and Guo, 2015), it remains large in other languages, such as Chinese (Peng and Dredze, 2015; Fu et al., 2015).

One reason for this gap is the lack of robust up-stream NLP systems that provide useful features for NER, such as part-of-speech tagging or chunking. Ritter et al. (2011) annotated Twitter data for these systems to improve a Twitter NER tagger, however, these systems do not exist for social media in most languages. Another approach has been that of Cherry and Guo (2015) and Peng and Dredze (2015), who relied on training unsupervised lexical embeddings in place of these upstream systems and achieved state-of-the-art results for English and Chinese social media, respectively. The same approach was also found helpful for NER in the news domain (Collobert and Weston, 2008; Turian et al., 2010; Passos et al., 2014)

In Asian languages like Chinese, Japanese and Korean, word segmentation is a critical first step for many tasks (Gao et al., 2005; Zhang et al., 2006; Mao et al., 2008). Peng and Dredze (2015) showed the value of word segmentation to Chinese NER in social media by using character positional embeddings, which encoded word segmentation information.

In this paper, we investigate better ways to incorporate word boundary information into an NER system for Chinese social media. We combine the state-of-the-art Chinese word segmentation system (Chen et al., 2015) with the best Chinese social media NER model (Peng and Dredze, 2015). Since both systems used learned representations, we propose an integrated model that allows for joint training learned representations, providing more information to the NER system about hidden representations learned from word segmentation, as compared to features based on segmentation output. Our integrated model achieves nearly

Proceedings of the 54th Annual Meeting of the Association for Computational Linguistics, pages 149–155,
Berlin, Germany, August 7-12, 2016. ©2016 Association for Computational Linguistics

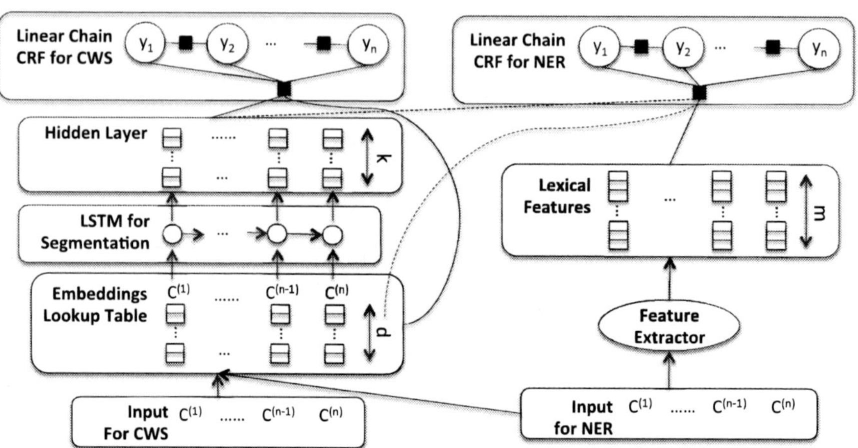

Figure 1: The joint model for Chinese word segmentation and NER. The left hand side is an LSTM module for word segmentation, and the right hand side is a traditional feature-based CRF model for NER. Note that the linear chain CRF for NER has both access to the feature extractor specifically for NER and the representations produced by the LSTM module for word segmentation. The CRF in this version is a log-bilinear CRF, where it treats the embeddings and hidden vectors inputs as variables and modifies them according to the objective function. As a result, it enables propagating the gradients back into the LSTM to adjust the parameters. Therefore, the word segmentation and NER training share all the parameters of the LSTM module. This facilitates the joint training.

a 5% absolute improvement over the previous best results on both NER and nominal mentions for Chinese social media.

2 Model

We propose a model that integrates the best Chinese word segmentation system (Chen et al., 2015) using an LSTM neural model that learns representations, with the best NER model for Chinese social media (Peng and Dredze, 2015), that supports training neural representations by a log-bilinear CRF. We begin with a brief review of each system.

2.1 LSTM for Word Segmentation

Chen et al. (2015) proposed a single layer, left to right LSTM for Chinese word segmentation. An LSTM is a recurrent neural network (RNN) which uses a series of gates (input, forget and output gate) to control how memory is propagated in the hidden states of the model. For the Chinese word segmentation task, each Chinese character is initialized as a d dimensional vector, which the LSTM will modify during its training. For each input character, the model learns a hidden vector h. These vectors are then used with a biased-linear transformation to predict the output labels, which in this case are **Begin**, **Inside**, **End**, and **Singleton**. A prediction for position t is given as:

$$y^{(t)} = W_o h^{(t)} + b_o \qquad (1)$$

where W_o is a matrix for the transformation parameters, b_o is a vector for the bias parameters, and $h^{(t)}$ is the hidden vector at position t. To model the tag dependencies, they introduced the transition score A_{ij} to measure the probability of jumping from tag $i \in T$ to tag $j \in T$.

We used the same model as Chen et al. (2015) trained on the same data (segmented Chinese news article). However, we employed a different training objective. Chen et al. (2015) employed a max-margin objective, however, while they found this objective yielded better results, we observed that maximum-likelihood yielded better segmentation results in our experiments[1]. Additionally, we sought to integrate their model with a log-bilinear CRF, which uses a maximum-likelihood training objective. For consistency, we trained the LSTM with a maximum-likelihood training objective as well. The maximum-likelihood CRF objective function for predicting segmentations is:

---

[1] Chen et al. (2015) preprocessed the data specifically for Chinese word segmentation, such as replacing English characters, symbols, dates and Chinese idioms as special symbols. Our implementation discarded all these preprocessing steps, which while it achieved nearly identical results on development data (as inferred from their published figure), it lagged in test accuracy by 2.4%. However, we found that while these preprocessing steps improved segmentation, they hurt NER results as they resulted in a mis-match between the segmentation and NER input data. Since our focus is on improving NER, we do not use their preprocessing steps in this paper.

$$\mathcal{L}_s(\boldsymbol{y}_s; \boldsymbol{x}_s, \Theta) = \frac{1}{K} \sum_k \Big[\log \frac{1}{Z(\boldsymbol{x}_s)^k}$$
$$+ \sum_i \Big(T_s(y_{i-1}^k, y_i^k) + s(y_i^k; \boldsymbol{x}_s^k, \boldsymbol{\Lambda}_s) \Big) \Big] \quad (2)$$

Example pairs $(\boldsymbol{y}_s, \boldsymbol{x}_s)$ are word segmented sentences, k indexes examples, and i indexes positions in examples. $T_s(y_{i-1}^k, y_i^k)$ are standard transition probabilities learned by the CRF[2]. The LSTM parameters $\boldsymbol{\Lambda}_s$ are used to produce $s(y_i^k; \boldsymbol{x}_s^k, \Lambda_s)$, the emission probability of the label at position i for input sentence k, which is obtained by taking a soft-max over (1). We use a first-order Markov model.

2.2 Log-bilinear CRF for NER

Peng and Dredze (2015) proposed a log-bilinear model for Chinese social media NER. They used standard NER features along with additional features based on lexical embeddings. By fine-tuning these embeddings, and jointly training them with a word2vec (Mikolov et al., 2013) objective, the resulting model is log-bilinear.

Typical lexical embeddings provide a single embedding vector for each word type. However, Chinese text is not word segmented, making the mapping between input to embedding vector unclear. Peng and Dredze (2015) explored several types of representations for Chinese, including pre-segmenting the input to obtain words, using character embeddings, and a combined approach that learned embeddings for characters based on their position in the word. This final representation yielded the largest improvements.

We use the same idea but augmented it with LSTM learned representations, and we enable interaction between the CRF and the LSTM parameters. More details are described in (§2.3).

2.3 Using Segmentation Representations to Improve NER

The improvements provided by character position embeddings demonstrated by Peng and Dredze (2015) indicated that word segmentation information can be helpful for NER. Embeddings aside, a simple way to include this information in an NER system would be to add features to the CRF using the predicted segmentation labels as features.

However, these features alone may overlook useful information from the segmentation model.

Previous work showed that jointly learning different stages of the NLP pipeline helped for Chinese (Liu et al., 2012b; Zheng et al., 2013). We thus seek approaches for deeper interaction between word segmentation and NER models. The LSTM word segmentor learns two different types of representations: 1) embeddings for each character and 2) hidden vectors for predicting segmentation tags. Compressing these rich representations down to a small feature set imposes a bottleneck on using richer word segmentation related information for NER. We thus experiment with including both of these information sources directly into the NER model.

Since the log-bilinear CRF already supports joint training of lexical embeddings, we can also incorporate the LSTM output hidden vectors as dynamic features using a joint objective function.

First, we augment the CRF with the LSTM parameters as follows:

$$\mathcal{L}_n(\boldsymbol{y}_n; \boldsymbol{x}_n, \Theta) = \frac{1}{K} \sum_k \Big[\log \frac{1}{Z(\boldsymbol{x}_n)^k}$$
$$+ \sum_j \Lambda_j F_j(\boldsymbol{y}_n^k, \boldsymbol{x}_n^k, \boldsymbol{e}_w, \boldsymbol{h}_w) \Big], \quad (3)$$

where k indexes instances, j positions, and

$$F_j(\boldsymbol{y}^k, \boldsymbol{x}^k, \boldsymbol{e}_w, \boldsymbol{h}_w) = \sum_{i=1}^{n} f_j(y_{i-1}^k, y_i^k, \boldsymbol{x}^k, \boldsymbol{e}_w, \boldsymbol{h}_w, i)$$

represents the feature functions. These features now depend on the embeddings learned by the LSTM ($\boldsymbol{e}_w$) and the LSTM's output hidden vectors ($\boldsymbol{h}_w$). Note that by including $\boldsymbol{h}_w$ alone we create dependence on all LSTM parameters on which the hidden states depend (i.e. the weight matrices). We experiment with including input embeddings and output hidden vectors independently, as well as both parameters together. An illustration of the integrated model is shown in Figure 1.

Joint Training In our integrated model, the LSTM parameters are used for both predicting word segmentations and NER. Therefore, we consider a joint training scheme. We maximize a (weighted) joint objective:

$$\mathcal{L}_{joint}(\Theta) = \lambda \mathcal{L}_s(\boldsymbol{y}_s; \boldsymbol{x}_s, \Theta) + \mathcal{L}_n(\boldsymbol{y}_n; \boldsymbol{x}_n, \Theta) \quad (4)$$

where λ trades off between better segmentations or better NER, and Θ includes all parameters used in both models. Since we are interested in improving NER we consider settings with $\lambda < 1$.

---

[2]The same functionality as A_{ij} in the model of Chen et al. (2015).

| | | Named Entity | | | | | | Nominal Mention | | | | | |
| | | Dev | | | Test | | | Dev | | | Test | | |
	Method	Precision	Recall	F1	Precision	Recall	F1	Precision	Recall	F1	Precision	Recall	F1
1	CRF with baseline features	60.27	25.43	35.77	57.47	25.77	35.59	72.06	32.56	44.85	59.84	23.55	33.80
2	+ Segment Features	62.34	27.75	38.40	58.06	27.84	37.63	58.50	38.87	46.71	47.43	26.77	34.23
3	P & D best NER model	57.41	35.84	44.13	57.98	35.57	44.09	72.55	36.88	48.90	63.84	29.45	40.38
4	+ Segment Features	47.40	42.20	44.65	48.08	38.66	42.86	76.38	36.54	49.44	63.36	26.77	37.64
5	P & D w/ Char Embeddings	58.76	32.95	42.22	57.89	34.02	42.86	66.88	35.55	46.42	55.15	29.35	38.32
6	+ Segment Features	51.47	40.46	45.31	52.55	37.11	43.50	65.43	40.86	50.31	54.01	32.58	40.64
7	Pipeline Seg. Repr. + NER	64.71	38.14	**48.00**	64.22	36.08	46.20	69.36	39.87	50.63	56.52	33.55	42.11
8	Jointly LSTM w/o feat.	59.22	35.26	44.20	60.00	35.57	44.66	60.10	39.53	47.70	56.90	31.94	40.91
9	Jointly Train Char. Emb.	64.21	35.26	45.52	63.16	37.11	46.75	73.55	37.87	50.00	65.33	31.61	42.61
10	Jointly Train LSTM Hidden	61.86	34.68	44.44	63.03	38.66	47.92	67.23	39.53	49.79	60.00	33.87	43.30
11	Jointly Train LSTM + Emb.	59.29	38.73	46.85	63.33	39.18	**48.41**	61.61	43.19	**50.78**	58.59	37.42	**45.67**

Table 1: NER results for named and nominal mentions on dev and test data.

3 Parameter Estimation

We train all of our models using stochastic gradient descent (SGD.) We train for up to 30 epochs, stopping when NER results converged on dev data. We use a separate learning rate for each part of the joint objective, with a schedule that decays the learning rate by half if dev results do not improve after 5 consecutive epochs. Dropout is introduced in the input layer of LSTM following Chen et al. (2015). We optimize two hyper-parameters using held out dev data: the joint coefficient λ in the interval $[0.5, 1]$ and the dropout rate in the interval $[0, 0.5]$. All other hyper-parameters were set to the values given by Chen et al. (2015) for the LSTM and Peng and Dredze (2015) for the CRF.

We train the joint model using an alternating optimization strategy. Since the segmentation dataset is significantly larger than the NER dataset, we subsample the former at each iteration to be the same size as the NER training data, with different subsamples in each iteration. We found subsampling critical and it significantly reduced training time and allowed us to better explore the hyper-parameter space.

We initialized LSTM input embeddings with pre-trained character-positional embeddings trained on 112,971,734 Weibo messages to initialize the input embeddings for LSTM. We used word2vec (Mikolov et al., 2013) with the same parameter settings as Peng and Dredze (2015) to pre-train the embeddings.

4 Experiments and Analysis

4.1 Datasets

We use the same training, development and test splits as Chen et al. (2015) for word segmentation and Peng and Dredze (2015) for NER.

Word Segmentation The segmentation data is taken from the SIGHAN 2005 shared task. We used the PKU portion, which includes 43,963 word sentences as training and 4,278 sentences as test. We did not apply any special preprocessing.

NER This dataset contains 1,890 Sina Weibo messages annotated with four entity types (person, organization, location and geo-political entity), including named and nominal mentions. We note that the word segmentation dataset is significantly larger than the NER data, which motivates our subsampling during training (§3).

4.2 Results and Analysis

Table 1 shows results for NER in terms of precision, recall and F1 for named (left) and nominal (right) mentions on both dev and test sets. The hyper-parameters are tuned on dev data and then applied on test. We now explain the results.

We begin by establishing a CRF baseline (#1) and show that adding segmentation features helps (#2). However, adding those features to the full model (with embeddings) in Peng and Dredze (2015) (#3) did not improve results (#4). This is probably because the character-positional embeddings already carry segmentation information. Replacing the character-positional embeddings with character embeddings (#5) gets worse results than (#3), but benefits from adding segmentation features (#6). This demonstrates both that word segmentation helps and that character-positional embeddings effectively convey word boundary information.

We now consider our model of jointly training the character embeddings (#9), the LSTM hidden vectors (#10) and both (#11). They all improve over the best published results (#3). Jointly training the LSTM hidden vectors (#10) does better than jointly training the embeddings (#9), probably because they carry richer word boundary information. Using both representations achieves the single best result (#11): 4.3% improvement on named and 5.3% on nominal mentions F1 scores.

Finally, we examine how much of the gain is from joint training versus from pre-trained segmentation representations. We first train an LSTM for word segmentation, then use the trained embeddings and hidden vectors as inputs to the log-bilinear CRF model for NER, and fine tune these representations. This (#7) improved test F1 by 2%, about half of the overall improvements from joint training.

5 Discussion

Huang et al. (2015) first proposed recurrent neural networks stacked with a CRF for sequential tagging tasks, as was applied to POS, chunking and NER tasks. More recent efforts have been made to add character level modeling and explore different types of RNNs (Lample et al., 2016; Ma and Hovy, 2016; Yang et al., 2016). These methods have achieved state-of-the-art results for NER on English news and several other Indo-European languages. However, this work has not considered languages that require word segmentation, nor do they consider social media.

We can view our method as multi-task learning (Caruana, 1997; Ando and Zhang, 2005; Collobert and Weston, 2008), where we are using the same learned representations (embeddings and hidden vectors) for two tasks: segmentation and NER, which use different prediction and decoding layers. Result #8 shows the effect of excluding the additional NER features and just sharing a jointly trained LSTM[3]. While this does not perform as well as adding the additional NER features (#11), it is impressive that this simple architecture achieved similar F1 as the best results in Peng and Dredze (2015). While we may expect both NER and word segmentation results to improve, we found the segmentation performances of the best joint model tuned for NER lose to the stand alone word segmentation model (F1 of 90.7% v.s. 93.3%). This lies in the fact that tuning λ means choosing between the two tasks; no single setting achieved improvements for both, which suggests further work is needed on better model structures and learning.

Second, our segmentation data is from the news domain, whereas the NER data is from social media. While it is well known that segmentation systems trained on news do worse on social media (Duan et al., 2012), we still show large improvements in applying our model to these different domains. It may be that we are able to obtain better results in the case of domain mismatch because we integrate the representations of the LSTM model directly into our CRF, as opposed to only using the predictions of the LSTM segmentation model. We plan to consider expanding our model to explicitly include domain adaptation mechanisms (Yang and Eisenstein, 2015).

References

Rie Kubota Ando and Tong Zhang. 2005. A framework for learning predictive structures from multiple tasks and unlabeled data. *The Journal of Machine Learning Research*, 6:1817–1853.

Razvan C Bunescu and Raymond J Mooney. 2005. A shortest path dependency kernel for relation extraction. In *Empirical Methods in Natural Language Processing (EMNLP)*, pages 724–731.

Rich Caruana. 1997. Multitask learning. *Machine learning*, 28(1):41–75.

Xinchi Chen, Xipeng Qiu, Chenxi Zhu, Pengfei Liu, and Xuanjing Huang. 2015. Long short-term memory neural networks for chinese word segmentation. In *Empirical Methods in Natural Language Processing (EMNLP)*.

Colin Cherry and Hongyu Guo. 2015. The unreasonable effectiveness of word representations for twitter named entity recognition. In *North America Chapter of Association for Computational Linguistics (NAACL)*.

Michael Collins and Yoram Singer. 1999. Unsupervised models for named entity classification. In *Empirical Methods in Natural Language Processing (EMNLP)*, pages 100–110.

Ronan Collobert and Jason Weston. 2008. A unified architecture for natural language processing: Deep neural networks with multitask learning. In *International Conference on Machine Learning (ICML)*, pages 160–167.

Mark Dredze, Paul McNamee, Delip Rao, Adam Gerber, and Tim Finin. 2010. Entity disambiguation for knowledge base population. In *Conference on Computational Linguistics (Coling)*.

---

[3]This reduces to the multi-task setting of Yang et al. (2016).

Huiming Duan, Zhifang Sui, Ye Tian, and Wenjie Li. 2012. The cips-sighan clp 2012 chineseword segmentation onmicroblog corpora bakeoff. In *CIPS-SIGHAN Joint Conference on Chinese Language Processing*, pages 35–40, Tianjin, China, December.

Tim Finin, William Murnane, Anand Karandikar, Nicholas Keller, Justin Martineau, and Mark Dredze. 2010. Annotating named entities in twitter data with crowdsourcing. In *NAACL Workshop on Creating Speech and Language Data With Mechanical Turk*.

Hege Fromreide, Dirk Hovy, and Anders Søgaard. 2014. Crowdsourcing and annotating NER for Twitter# drift. In *Language Resources and Evaluation Conference (LREC)*.

JinLan Fu, Jie Qiu, Yunlong Guo, and Li Li. 2015. Entity linking and name disambiguation using SVM in chinese micro-blogs. In *Conference on Natural Computation*, pages 468–472.

Jianfeng Gao, Mu Li, Andi Wu, and Chang-Ning Huang. 2005. Chinese word segmentation and named entity recognition: A pragmatic approach. *Computational Linguistics*, 31(4):531–574, December.

Zhengyan He, Houfeng Wang, and Sujian Li. 2012. The task 2 of cips-sighan 2012 named entity recognition and disambiguation in chinese bakeoff. In *CIPS-SIGHAN Joint Conference on Chinese Language Processing*, pages 108–114, Tianjin, China, December.

Zhiheng Huang, Wei Xu, and Kai Yu. 2015. Bidirectional lstm-crf models for sequence tagging. *arXiv preprint arXiv:1508.01991*.

Guangjin Jin and Xiao Chen. 2008. The fourth international Chinese language processing bakeoff: Chinese word segmentation, named entity recognition and Chinese pos tagging. In *SIGHAN Workshop on Chinese Language Processing*, page 69.

Guillaume Lample, Miguel Ballesteros, Sandeep Subramanian, Kazuya Kawakami, and Chris Dyer. 2016. Neural architectures for named entity recognition. In *North America Chapter of Association for Computational Linguistics (NAACL)*.

Chenliang Li, Jianshu Weng, Qi He, Yuxia Yao, Anwitaman Datta, Aixin Sun, and Bu-Sung Lee. 2012. Twiner: Named entity recognition in targeted twitter stream. In *Conference on Research and Development in Information Retrieval (SIGIR)*, SIGIR '12, pages 721–730, New York, NY, USA.

Xiaohua Liu, Shaodian Zhang, Furu Wei, and Ming Zhou. 2011. Recognizing named entities in tweets. In *Association for Computational Linguistics (ACL)*, pages 359–367.

Xiaohua Liu, Ming Zhou, Furu Wei, Zhongyang Fu, and Xiangyang Zhou. 2012a. Joint inference of named entity recognition and normalization for tweets. In *Association for Computational Linguistics (ACL)*, pages 526–535.

Xiaohua Liu, Ming Zhou, Furu Wei, Zhongyang Fu, and Xiangyang Zhou. 2012b. Joint inference of named entity recognition and normalization for tweets. In *Association for Computational Linguistics (ACL)*, pages 526–535.

Xuezhe Ma and Eduard H. Hovy. 2016. End-to-end sequence labeling via bi-directional lstm-cnns-crf. *CoRR*, abs/1603.01354.

Xinnian Mao, Yuan Dong, Saike He, Sencheng Bao, and Haila Wang. 2008. Chinese word segmentation and named entity recognition based on conditional random fields. In *International Joint Conference on Natural Language Processing*, pages 90–93.

Andrew McCallum and Wei Li. 2003. Early results for named entity recognition with conditional random fields, feature induction and web-enhanced lexicons. In *North America Chapter of Association for Computational Linguistics (NAACL)*.

Tomas Mikolov, Ilya Sutskever, Kai Chen, Greg S Corrado, and Jeff Dean. 2013. Distributed representations of words and phrases and their compositionality. In *Neural Information Processing Systems (NIPS)*, pages 3111–3119.

David Nadeau and Satoshi Sekine. 2007. A survey of named entity recognition and classification. *Lingvisticae Investigationes*, 30(1):3–26.

Alexandre Passos, Vineet Kumar, and Andrew McCallum. 2014. Lexicon infused phrase embeddings for named entity resolution. *CoRR*, abs/1404.5367.

Nanyun Peng and Mark Dredze. 2015. Named entity recognition for chinese social media with jointly trained embeddings. In *Proceedings of the Conference on Empirical Methods in Natural Language Processing (EMNLP)*.

Lev Ratinov, Dan Roth, Doug Downey, and Mike Anderson. 2011. Local and global algorithms for disambiguation to Wikipedia. In *Association for Computational Linguistics (ACL)*, pages 1375–1384.

Alan Ritter, Sam Clark, Oren Etzioni, et al. 2011. Named entity recognition in tweets: an experimental study. In *Empirical Methods in Natural Language Processing (EMNLP)*, pages 1524–1534.

Joseph Turian, Lev Ratinov, and Yoshua Bengio. 2010. Word representations: a simple and general method for semi-supervised learning. In *Association for Computational Linguistics (ACL)*, pages 384–394.

Yi Yang and Jacob Eisenstein. 2015. Unsupervised multi-domain adaptation with feature embeddings. In *North America Chapter of Association for Computational Linguistics (NAACL)*.

Zhilin Yang, Ruslan Salakhutdinov, and William Cohen. 2016. Multi-task cross-lingual sequence tagging from scratch. *CoRR*, abs/1603.06270.

Suxiang Zhang, Ying Qin, Juan Wen, and Xiaojie
Wang. 2006. Word segmentation and named entity
recognition for sighan bakeoff3. In *SIGHAN Workshop on Chinese Language Processing*, pages 158–
161, Sydney, Australia, July.

Xiaoqing Zheng, Hanyang Chen, and Tianyu Xu.
2013. Deep learning for Chinese word segmentation
and POS tagging. In *Empirical Methods in Natural
Language Processing (EMNLP)*, pages 647–657.

How Naked is the Naked Truth?
A Multilingual Lexicon of Nominal Compound Compositionality

Carlos Ramisch[1], Silvio Cordeiro[1,2], Leonardo Zilio[2]
Marco Idiart[3], Aline Villavicencio[2], Rodrigo Wilkens[2]
[1] Aix Marseille Université, CNRS, LIF UMR 7279 (France)
[2] Institute of Informatics, Federal University of Rio Grande do Sul (Brazil)
[3] Institute of Physics, Federal University of Rio Grande do Sul (Brazil)
silvioricardoc@gmail.com carlos.ramisch@lif.univ-mrs.fr lzilio@inf.ufrgs.br
marco.idiart@gmail.com avillavicencio@inf.ufrgs.br rswilkens@inf.ufrgs.br

Abstract

We introduce a new multilingual resource containing judgments about nominal compound compositionality in English, French and Portuguese. It covers 3 × 180 noun-noun and adjective-noun compounds for which we provide numerical compositionality scores for the head word, for the modifier and for the compound as a whole, along with possible paraphrases. This resource was constructed by native speakers via crowdsourcing. It can serve as basis for evaluating tasks such as lexical substitution and compositionality prediction.

1 Introduction

Multiword expressions (MWEs) are notoriously challenging for NLP, due to their many potential levels of idiosyncrasy, from lexical to semantic and pragmatic to statistical (Sag et al., 2002; Ramisch, 2015). One widely known problem is the semantic interpretation of noun compounds, which in English are noun phrases composed by a sequence of nouns. These MWEs often lack a structure from which to identify implicit semantic relations unambiguously. For instance, there is no indication that a *brick wall* is a wall *made of* bricks, while a *cheese knife* is not a knife *made of* cheese, but rather a knife *for cutting* cheese (Girju et al., 2005).

Noun compounds are often idiomatic or non-compositional. That is, the meaning of the whole does not come directly from the meaning of the parts. For instance, a *black Friday* is not any Friday that is somehow black, but is the day following Thanksgiving Day in the United States. Moreover, the contribution of the semantics of each element for the meaning of the compound may vary considerably (e.g. *police car* vs. *crocodile tears*). Any NLP application that intends to deal with phrasal semantics adequately must be able to distinguish fairly compositional from fully idiomatic compounds. For example, automatically translating *dead end* literally into French (*?fin morte*) or Portuguese (*?fim morto*) would drastically alter the meaning of the original expression. In this paper we introduce a resource with human judgments about the semantics of compounds and their individual elements.

Eliciting quantitative judgments about compositionality from non-linguists may be too abstract, even with accompanying guidelines and training. We propose a more constrained way of obtaining these judgments, with the participation of non-experts through crowdsourcing. We first focus the participants' attention on compound interpretation in context, by requesting paraphrases in example sentences. Then, we inquire about the degree to which the meaning of a given compound arises from each of its elements. The assumption is that if the interpretation of the compound comes from both nouns (e.g. *access road*), then it is fully compositional, whereas if it is unrelated to both nouns (e.g. *nut case*), then it is fully idiomatic. This indirect annotation does not require expert knowledge and provides reliable and stable data.

This paper presents a multilingual resource that models compounds compositionality, including both numerical scores and free paraphrases. Data is currently available for 180 compounds in 3 different languages: English, French and Portuguese. Such resources are extremely valuable, as they enable the development and evaluation of techniques for automatic compositionality prediction and lexical substitution. This paper is structured as follows: §2 discusses related work; §3 discusses the target compounds, the annotation schema and interface; §4 presents the results and §5 the conclusions and future work.

2 Related Work

There are many proposals in the literature to represent the semantics of nominal compounds. Lauer (1995) argues that prepositions (such as *from*, *for*, *in*) provide information about the role of each noun in a compound (e.g. *olive oil* is *oil from olives*). These prepositions are explicitly part of some nominal compounds in Romance languages (e.g. *huile d'olive* in French and *azeite de oliva* in Portuguese). Girju et al. (2005) present and compare several inventories of semantic relations between nouns, from fine-grained to coarse senses. These relations include syntactic and semantic classes such as *subject*, *instrument* and *location*. Free paraphrases have also been used to model noun compound semantics. Nakov (2008) suggests using unsupervised generation of paraphrases combined with web

Proceedings of the 54th Annual Meeting of the Association for Computational Linguistics, pages 156–161,
Berlin, Germany, August 7-12, 2016. ©2016 Association for Computational Linguistics

search engines to classify nominal compounds. This was further extended in SemEval 2013, in a task where free paraphrases were ranked according to their relevance for explicitly describing the underlying semantic relations in the compounds (Hendrickx et al., 2013). For instance, for the MWE *flu virus*, paraphrases involving the verbs *cause, spread* and *create* (*virus that causes/spreads/creates flu*) were in the top of the rank.

Some authors model the meaning of compounds using numerical compositionality scores: low values mean completely idiomatic compounds while high values represent compositional ones. Separate scores can be provided for the amount of meaning provided by each individual word. For instance, *olive oil* could be 80% related to *olives* and 100% related to *oil*, whereas *dead end* is 5% *dead* and 90% an *end*. Some datasets that employ a numerical representation for different types of MWE are:

- Baldwin and Villavicencio (2002): binary type-level judgments for 3,078 English phrasal verbs, from which 14% are considered idiomatic.
- McCarthy et al. (2003): type-based scores on a scale from 0 to 10 provided by three experts for 116 English phrasal verbs.
- Reddy et al. (2011): average of 30 judgments on a scale from 0 to 5 provided by native speakers via crowdsourcing for 90 English noun compounds.
- Gurrutxaga and Alegria (2013): three-way classification (idiom, collocation, free combination) provided by three experts for 1,200 Basque noun-verb expressions.
- Roller et al. (2013): average of around 30 judgments on a scale from 1 to 7 obtained through crowdsourcing for 244 German noun compounds.
- Farahmand et al. (2015): individual binary judgments for non-compositionality and conventionality for 1,042 English noun compounds, annotated by 4 experts.

One possible source of divergence among annotators is that some datasets do not take polysemy into account. Authors ask annotators to think about the most common sense of an MWE without providing context. Some of these datasets address this issue by providing example sentences to attenuate this problem. We also employ this strategy in our questionnaires. The most similar datasets to ours are the ones presented by Reddy et al. (2011) and Hendrickx et al. (2013). Our dataset combines the methodology from both of these, extending it to French and Portuguese.

3 Dataset Construction

Although noun-noun compounds are rare in some languages mainly due to syntactic reasons, these languages present alternatives to this type of configuration. In French (FR) and Brazilian Portuguese (PT), the equivalents of English (EN) compounds of the form N_1 N_2 are usually:

1. N_2 PREP N_1, connecting the nouns through a preposition and optional determiner; e.g. *lung cancer* (EN) → *cancer du poumon* (FR), *câncer de pulmão* (PT).
2. N_2 ADJ$_1$, using a denominal adjective which is derived from N_1; e.g. *cell death* (EN) → *mort cellulaire* (FR), *morte celular* (PT).

We describe the construction of datasets for English, French and Brazilian Portuguese. Given the two syntactic forms above, we focus on N_2 ADJ$_1$ for French and Portuguese, as its simpler structure resembles more closely the English noun-noun compound structure, and also because we have some ADJ$_1$ N_2 compounds in English as well (e.g. *sacred cow*). We collectively call our target constructions *nominal compounds*, as they have nouns as head of the phrase.

For each language, data collection involves the following steps: (1) compound selection; (2) sentence selection; and (3) questionnaire design.

Compound selection The initial set of idiomatic and partially compositional candidates was constructed by introspection, independently for each language, since these may be harder to find in corpora because of lower frequency. This list of compounds was complemented by selecting entries from lists of frequent *adjective+noun* and *noun+noun* pairs. These were automatically extracted through POS-sequence queries using the mwetoolkit (Ramisch, 2015) from ukWaC (Baroni et al., 2009), frWaC and brWaC (Boos et al., 2014). We removed all compounds in which the complement is not an adjective in Portuguese/French (e.g. PT noun-noun *abelha rainha*), those in which the head is not necessarily a noun (e.g. FR *aller simple*, as *aller* is also a verb) and those in which the literal sense is very common in the corpus (e.g. EN *low blow*). For each language, we attempted to select a balanced set of 60 idiomatic, 60 partially compositional and 60 fully compositional compounds by rough manual pre-annotation.[1]

Sentence selection For each compound, we selected 3 sentences from a WaC corpus where the compound is used with the same meaning. These sentences are used during the data collection process (described later) as disambiguating context for the annotators. We sort them by sentence length, in order to favor shorter sentences, and manually select 3 examples that satisfy these criteria:

- The occurrence of the compound must have the same meaning in all sentences.
- A sentence must contain enough context to enable mental disambiguation of the compound.
- Inter-sentence variability can be used to provide more information to the reader.

---

[1] We have not attempted to select equivalent compounds for all three languages. A compound in a given language may correspond to a single word in the other languages. Even when it does translate as a compound, its POS pattern and level of compositionality may be widely different.

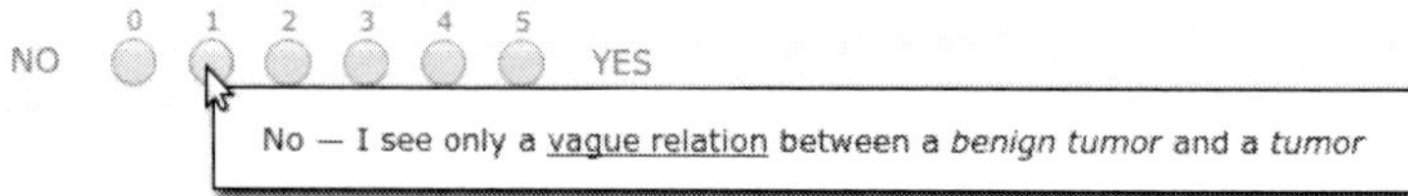

Figure 1: Evaluating compositionality regarding a compounds' head.

Questionnaire design We collect data for each compound through a separate HIT (Human Intelligence Task). Each HIT page contains a list of instructions followed by the questionnaire associated with that compound. In the instructions, we briefly describe the task and require that the users fill in an external identification form, following Reddy et al. (2011). This form provides us with demographics about the annotators, ensuring that they are native speakers of the target language. At the end of the form, they are also given extra example questions with annotated answers for training. After filling in the identification form, users can start working on the task. This section of the HIT is structured in 5 subtasks:

1. Read the compound itself.
2. Read 3 sentences containing the compound.
3. Provide 2 to 3 synonym expressions for the target compound seen in the sentences.
4. Using a Likert scale from 0 to 5, judge how much of the meaning of the compound comes from $word_1$ (mod) and $word_2$ (head) separately, as shown in Figure 1.
5. Using a Likert scale from 0 to 5, judge how much of the meaning of the compound (comp) comes from its components.

We have been consciously careful about requiring answers in an even-numbered scale (0–5 makes for 6 reply categories), as otherwise, undecided annotators would be biased towards the middle score. As an additional help for the annotators, when the mouse hovers over a reply to a multiple-choice question, we present a guiding tooltip, as in Figure 1. We avoid incomplete HITs by making Subtasks 3–5 mandatory.

The order of subtasks has also been taken into account. During a pilot test, we found that presenting the multiple-choice questions (Subtasks 4–5) before asking for synonyms (Subtask 3) yielded lower agreement, as users were often less self-consistent in the multiple-choice questions (e.g. replying "non-compositional" for Subtask 4 but "compositional" for Subtask 5), even if they carefully selected their synonyms in response to Subtask 3. Asking for synonyms prior to the multiple-choice questions helps the user focus on the target meaning for the compound and also have more examples (the synonyms) when considering the semantic contribution of each element of the compound.

For EN and FR, annotators were recruited and paid via Amazon Mechanical Turk. The quality of FR results was manually controlled by only accepting HITs

with reasonable paraphrases. During a pilot, we noticed the lack of qualified PT native speakers on the platform. For PT only, judgments were provided by volunteers through a standalone web interface that simulated the HIT page.

4 Results

For each compound, we have collected judgments from around 15 HITs. The average of these scores, for EN[2], FR and PT, are shown in Figure 2. The compositionality judgments for the compounds confirm that they are balanced with respect to idiomaticity. Moreover, there seems to be a greater agreement between the score for the compound and that of its head (or modifier) for the two extremes (totally idiomatic and fully compositional). For PT and FR, in particular, the compound score seems to be a lower bound to each member word's score.

We also looked at the distribution of each of the scores around the mean in terms of the standard deviation (σ). Ideally, if all the annotators agreed on compositionality, σ should be low. We calculated for each language the number of compounds, heads and modifiers with standard deviations greater than 1.5 (Table 1). The largest variations are for modifiers, which may reflect their potentially accessory role in the meaning of the compound in relation to the head.

	EN	FR	PT
Pearson r head-compound	0.75	0.81	0.80
Pearson r mod-compound	0.74	0.89	0.84
compound $\sigma > 1.5$	22	41	30
head $\sigma > 1.5$	23	44	33
modifier $\sigma > 1.5$	35	55	34

Table 1: Pearson correlation r and number of cases of high standard deviation σ.

Out of all human judges, 3 of them annotated a large subset of 119 compounds in PT. For this subset, we report inter-annotator agreement. Pairwise weighted κ values range from .28 to .58 depending on the question (head, mod or comp) and on the annotator pair. Multi-rater α agreement (Artstein and Poesio, 2008) values are $\alpha = .52$ for head, $\alpha = .36$ for mod and $\alpha = .42$ for comp scores. We have also calculated the α score of an expert annotator with himself, performing the same task a few weeks later. The score ranges from

---

[2]We include the 90 compounds from Reddy et al. (2011), which are compatible with the new dataset.

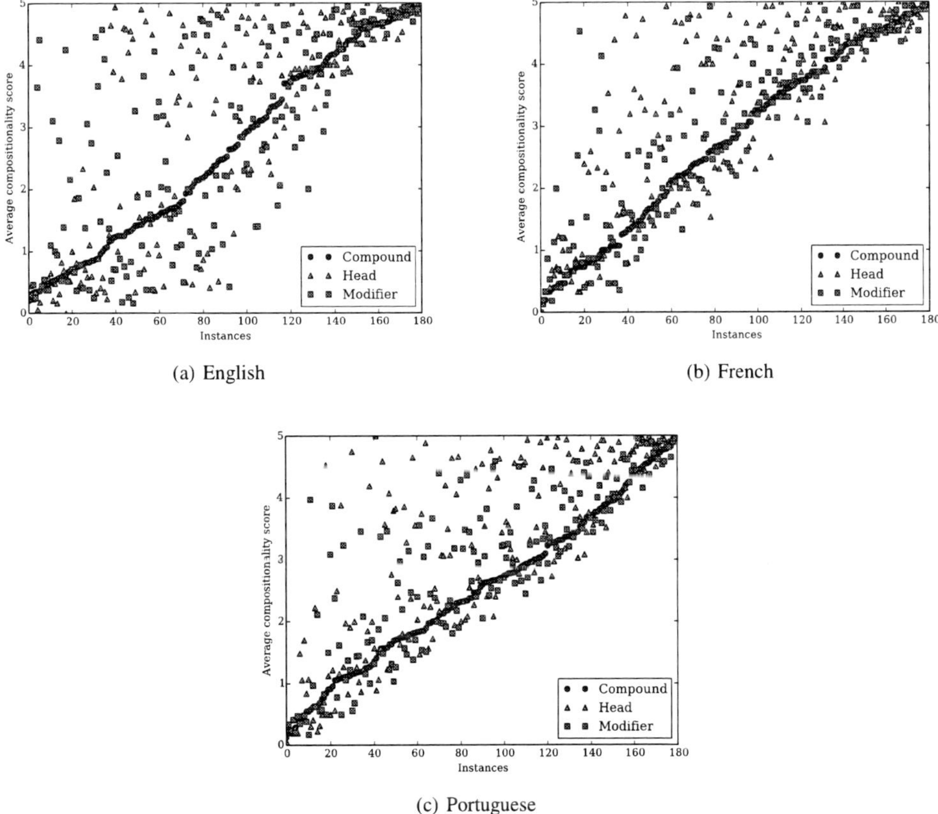

(a) English   (b) French

(c) Portuguese

Figure 2: Average compositionality for compounds, heads and modifiers.

0.59 for modifiers and compounds to 0.69 for heads. This seems to confirm the hypothesis that modifiers are harder to annotate than heads.

Table 2 presents the most controversial compounds, along with the ones that had highest agreement (lowest σ). The most consensual compounds are mostly 100% compositional and sometimes 100% idiomatic. Low σ values are consistent among the three questions, indicating that some compounds are simply easier to judge than others.

There are multiple reasons for divergences in the judgment scores. For some MWEs, our sentences were not enough for disambiguation, e.g. one of the *fish story* sentences talked about a whale and prompted literal interpretations of *fish* for some judges). Other differences have been caused by the interpretation of uncommon words; e.g. the PT noun *olhado* does not appear by itself very often; some judges seem to have interpreted it as an adjective and thus concluded that *mau-olhado* (*evil eye*, lit. *bad-glance*) has a fully non-compositional head. Finally, some differences have been caused by whether speakers had incorporated a new meaning into their lexicon; e.g. EN speakers agreed on the level of head and head+modifier compositionality for *dirty word*, but disagreed when judging the modifier: it is

fully idiomatic for some, while just containing an uncommon sense of *dirty* for others.

5 Conclusions and Future Work

We presented a multilingual dataset of nominal compounds containing human judgments about compositionality. It contains 180 compounds for each of the 3 target languages: English, French and Portuguese. Annotations are collected through crowdsourcing. Since the task is performed by native speakers who may not have a background in linguistics, it needs to be appropriately constrained not to require expert knowledge. The resulting resource can be used for applications and tasks involving some degree of semantic processing, such as lexical substitution and text simplification. For the cases where the numerical judgments alone are not enough for a given task, our dataset also provides sets of paraphrases, which serve as a symbolic counterpart to those scores. The complete resource will be made freely available.[3] As future work, we plan to validate these scores through compositionality prediction (Yaz-

---

[3]`http://pageperso.lif.univ-mrs.`
`fr/~carlos.ramisch/?page=downloads/`
`compounds`

compound	head	mod	comp
brass ring	3.9 ±2.0	3.7 ±1.9	3.7 ±1.8
fish story	4.8 ±0.4	1.5 ±1.8	1.7 ±1.8
tennis elbow	4.3 ±1.3	2.2 ±1.8	2.5 ±1.8
brick wall	3.5 ±1.9	3.2 ±2.2	3.8 ±1.7
dirty word	4.1 ±1.4	2.0 ±1.4	2.5 ±1.7
prison guard	4.8 ±0.4	4.9 ±0.3	4.9 ±0.3
graduate student	5.0 ±0.0	4.7 ±0.5	4.9 ±0.3
engine room	5.0 ±0.0	4.9 ±0.3	4.9 ±0.3
climate change	4.8 ±0.4	4.9 ±0.3	5.0 ±0.2
insurance company	4.9 ±0.5	5.0 ±0.0	5.0 ±0.0
match nul	4.4 ±1.3	2.2 ±2.3	2.5 ±2.1
mort né	4.6 ±1.1	3.5 ±1.8	3.2 ±2.0
carte grise	4.5 ±0.9	3.2 ±2.0	3.1 ±1.9
second degré	1.7 ±1.9	2.4 ±2.1	1.4 ±1.9
grippe aviaire	4.6 ±1.4	3.8 ±1.9	3.6 ±1.9
eau chaude	5.0 ±0.0	5.0 ±0.0	5.0 ±0.0
eau potable	5.0 ±0.0	5.0 ±0.0	5.0 ±0.0
matière grasse	4.8 ±0.4	5.0 ±0.0	5.0 ±0.0
poule mouillée	0.0 ±0.0	0.0 ±0.0	0.0 ±0.0
téléphone portable	4.9 ±0.5	4.9 ±0.3	5.0 ±0.0
pavio curto	1.6 ±1.8	1.1 ±1.9	1.9 ±2.3
sexto sentido	4.0 ±1.4	2.5 ±2.1	2.8 ±2.2
gelo-seco	3.2 ±1.6	3.2 ±1.8	3.0 ±2.1
mau-olhado	1.8 ±1.2	4.2 ±1.5	2.3 ±2.1
câmara fria	3.6 ±2.2	5.0 ±0.0	3.4 ±2.1
núcleo atômico	5.0 ±0.0	4.4 ±1.8	5.0 ±0.0
pão-duro	0.0 ±0.0	1.0 ±1.7	0.0 ±0.0
sentença judicial	5.0 ±0.0	5.0 ±0.0	5.0 ±0.0
tartaruga-marinha	5.0 ±0.0	5.0 ±0.0	5.0 ±0.0
vôo internacional	5.0 ±0.0	5.0 ±0.0	5.0 ±0.0

Table 2: Most polemic and consensual compounds in each language (average$\pm\sigma$ score).

dani et al., 2015; Salehi et al., 2015) and by incorporating the scores and paraphrases into a machine translation system. We also envisage extending the dataset for each of the languages and for additional languages.

Acknowledgments

This work has been partly funded by projects PARSEME-FR (ANR-14-CERA-0001), AIM-WEST (FAPERGS-INRIA 1706- 2551/13-7), CNPq 482520/2012-4, 312114/2015-0, "Simplificação Textual de Expressões Complexas", sponsored by Samsung Eletrônica da Amazônia Ltda. under the terms of Brazilian federal law No. 8.248/91.

References

Ron Artstein and Massimo Poesio. 2008. Inter-coder agreement for computational linguistics. *Computational Linguistics*, 34(4):555–596.

Timothy Baldwin and Aline Villavicencio. 2002. Extracting the unextractable: A case study on verb-particles. In *Proceedings of CoNLL 2002*, COLING-02, pages 1–7. ACL.

Marco Baroni, Silvia Bernardini, Adriano Ferraresi, and Eros Zanchetta. 2009. The wacky wide web: a collection of very large linguistically processed web-crawled corpora. *Language Resources and Evaluation*, 43(3):209–226, September.

Rodrigo Boos, Kassius Prestes, and Aline Villavicencio. 2014. Identification of multiword expressions in the brWaC. In *Proceedings of LREC 2014*, pages 728–735. ELRA, May. ACL Anthology Identifier: L14-1429.

Meghdad Farahmand, Aaron Smith, and Joakim Nivre. 2015. A multiword expression data set: Annotating non-compositionality and conventionalization for english noun compounds. In *Proceedings of NAACL-HLT*, pages 29–33.

Roxana Girju, Dan Moldovan, Marta Tatu, and Daniel Antohe. 2005. On the semantics of noun compounds. *Computer speech & language*, 19(4):479–496.

Antton Gurrutxaga and Iñaki Alegria. 2013. Combining different features of idiomaticity for the automatic classification of noun+verb expressions in Basque. In *Proceedings of the 9th Workshop on Multiword Expressions*, pages 116–125. ACL, June.

Iris Hendrickx, Zornitsa Kozareva, Preslav Nakov, Diarmuid Ó Séaghdha, Stan Szpakowicz, and Tony Veale. 2013. Semeval-2013 task 4: Free paraphrases of noun compounds. In *Proceedings of *SEM 2013, Volume 2 – SemEval*, pages 138–143. ACL, June.

Mark Lauer. 1995. How much is enough?: Data requirements for statistical NLP. *CoRR*, abs/cmp-lg/9509001.

Diana McCarthy, Bill Keller, and John Carroll. 2003. Detecting a continuum of compositionality in phrasal verbs. In *Proceedings of the ACL 2003 Workshop on Multiword Expressions*, MWE '03, pages 73–80. ACL.

Preslav Nakov. 2008. Paraphrasing verbs for noun compound interpretation. In *Proc. of the LREC Workshop Towards a Shared Task for MWEs (MWE 2008)*, pages 46–49.

Carlos Ramisch. 2015. *Multiword Expressions Acquisition - A Generic and Open Framework*. Theory and Applications of Natural Language Processing. Springer.

Siva Reddy, Diana McCarthy, and Suresh Manandhar. 2011. An empirical study on compositionality in compound nouns. In *Proceedings of IJCNLP 2011*, November.

Stephen Roller, Sabine Schulte im Walde, and Silke Scheible. 2013. The (un)expected effects of applying standard cleansing models to human ratings on compositionality. In *Proceedings of the 9th Workshop on Multiword Expressions*, pages 32–41. ACL, June.

I. Sag, T. Baldwin, F. Bond, A. Copestake, and D. Flickinger. 2002. Multiword expressions: A pain in the neck for NLP. In *Proceedings of CICLing-2002*, pages 1–15.

Bahar Salehi, Paul Cook, and Timothy Baldwin. 2015.
A word embedding approach to predicting the compositionality of multiword expressions. In *Proceedings of NAACL-HLT 2015*, pages 977–983. ACL,
May–June.

Majid Yazdani, Meghdad Farahmand, and James Henderson. 2015. Learning semantic composition to detect non-compositionality of multiword expressions.
In *Proceedings of EMNLP 2015*, pages 1733–1742.
ACL, September.

An Open Web Platform for Rule-Based Speech-to-Sign Translation

Manny Rayner, Pierrette Bouillon, Johanna Gerlach, Irene Strasly, Nikos Tsourakis
University of Geneva, FTI/TIM, Switzerland
`{Emmanuel.Rayner,Pierrette.Bouillon,Johanna.Gerlach}@unige.ch`
`{Irene.Strasly,Nikolaos.Tsourakis}@unige.ch`

Sarah Ebling
University of Zurich, Institute of Computational Linguistics, Switzerland
`ebling@ifi.uzh.ch`

Abstract

We present an open web platform for developing, compiling, and running rule-based speech to sign language translation applications. Speech recognition is performed using the Nuance Recognizer 10.2 toolkit, and signed output, including both manual and non-manual components, is rendered using the JASigning avatar system. The platform is designed to make the component technologies readily accessible to sign language experts who are not necessarily computer scientists. Translation grammars are written in a version of Synchronous Context-Free Grammar adapted to the peculiarities of sign language. All processing is carried out on a remote server, with content uploaded and accessed through a web interface. Initial experiences show that simple translation grammars can be implemented on a time-scale of a few hours to a few days and produce signed output readily comprehensible to Deaf informants. Overall, the platform drastically lowers the barrier to entry for researchers interested in building applications that generate high-quality signed language.

1 Introduction

While a considerable amount of linguistic research has been carried out on sign languages to date, work in automatic sign language processing is still in its infancy. Automatic sign language processing comprises applications such as sign language recognition, sign language synthesis, and sign language translation (Sáfár and Glauert, 2012). For all of these applications, drawing on the expertise of native signers, sign language linguists and sign language interpreters is crucial. These different types of sign language experts may exhibit varying degrees of computer literacy. In the past, their contribution to the development of systems that automatically translate into sign language has been restricted mostly to the provision of transcribed and/or annotated sign language data.

In this paper, we report on the development and evaluation of a platform that allows sign language experts with modest computational skills to play a more active role in sign language machine translation. The platform enables these users to independently develop and run applications translating speech into synthesized sign language through a web interface. Synthesized sign language is presented by means of a signing avatar. To the best of our knowledge, our platform is the first to facilitate low-threshold speech-to-sign translation, opening up various possible use cases, e.g. that of communicating with a Deaf customer in a public service setting like a hospital, train station or bank.[1] By pursuing a rule-based translation approach, the platform also offers new possibilities for empirical investigation of sign language linguistics: the linguist can concretely implement a fragment of a hypothesized sign language grammar, sign a range of generated utterances through the avatar, and obtain judgements from Deaf informants.

The remainder of this paper is structured as follows. Section 2 presents background and related work. Section 3 describes the architecture of the speech-to-sign platform. Section 4 reports on a preliminary evaluation of the usability of the platform and of translations produced by the platform. Section 5 offers a conclusion and an outlook on future research questions.

---

[1] We follow the widely recognized convention of using the upper-cased word *Deaf* to describe members of the linguistic community of sign language users and, in contrast, the lower-cased word *deaf* to describe the audiological state of a hearing loss (Morgan and Woll, 2002).

Proceedings of the 54th Annual Meeting of the Association for Computational Linguistics, pages 162–168,
Berlin, Germany, August 7-12, 2016. ©2016 Association for Computational Linguistics

2 Background and related work

There has been surprisingly little work to date on speech to sign language translation. The best-performing system reported in the literature still appears to be TESSA (Cox et al., 2002), which translated English speech into British Sign Language (BSL) in a tightly constrained post office counter service domain, using coverage captured in 370 English phrasal patterns with associated BSL translations. The system was evaluated in a realistic setting in a British post office, with three post office clerks on the hearing side of the dialogues and six Deaf subjects playing the role of customers, and performed creditably. Another substantial project is the one described by San-Segundo et al. (2008), which translated Spanish speech into Spanish Sign Language; this, however, does not appear to have reached the stage of being able to achieve reasonable coverage even of a small domain, and the evaluation described in the paper is restricted to comprehensibility of signs from the manual alphabet.[2]

It is reasonable to ask why so little attention has been devoted to what many people would agree is an important and interesting problem, especially given the early success of TESSA. Our own experiences, and those of other researchers we have talked to, suggest that the critical problem is the high barrier to entry: in order to build a speech-to-sign system, it is necessary to be able to combine components for speech recognition, translation and sign language animation. The first two technologies are now well-understood, and good platforms are readily available. Sign language animation is still, however, a niche subject, and the practical problems involved in obtaining usable sign language animation components are non-trivial. The fact that San-Segundo et al. (2008) chose to develop their own animation component speaks eloquently about the difficulties involved.

There are three approaches to sign language animation: hand-crafted animation, motion capturing and synthesis from form notation (Glauert, 2013). Hand-crafted animation consists of manually modeling and posing an avatar character. This procedure typically yields high-quality results but is very labor-intensive. A signing avatar may also be animated based on information obtained from motion capturing, which involves recording a human's signing. Although sign language animations obtained through motion capturing also tend to be of good quality, the major drawback of this approach is the long calibration time and extensive postprocessing required.

Synthesis from form notation permits construction of a fully-fledged animation system that allows synthesis of any signed form that can be described through the associated notation. Avatar signing synthesized from form notation is the most flexible in that it is able to render dynamic content, e.g. display the sign language output of a machine translation system, present the contents of a sign language wiki or an e-learning application, visualize lexicon entries or present public transportation information (Efthimiou et al., 2012; Kipp et al., 2011). At the same time, this approach to sign language animation typically results in the lowest quality: controlling the appearance of all possible sign forms that may be produced from a given notation is virtually impossible.

The most comprehensive existing sign language animation system based on synthesis from form notation is undoubtedly JASigning (Elliott et al., 2008; Jennings et al., 2010), a distant descendant of the avatar system used in TESSA which was further developed over the course of the eSIGN and DictaSign European Framework projects. JASigning performs synthesis from SiGML (Elliott et al., 2000), an XML-based representation of the physical form of signs based on the well-understood Hamburg Notation System for Sign Languages (HamNoSys) (Prillwitz et al., 1989). HamNoSys can be converted into SiGML in a straightforward fashion. Unfortunately, despite its many good and indeed unique properties, JASigning is a piece of research software that in practice has posed an insurmountable challenge to most linguists without a computer science background.

The basic purpose of the Lite Speech2Sign project can now be summarised in a sentence: we wished to package JASigning together with a state-of-the-art commercial speech recognition platform and a basic machine translation framework in a way that makes the combination easily usable by sign language linguists who are not software engineers. In the rest of the paper, we describe the result.

---

[2] Sign languages make use of a communication form known as the *manual alphabet* (or, *finger alphabet*), in which the letters of a spoken language word are fingerspelled, i.e., dedicated signs are used for each letter of the word.

3   The Lite Speech2Sign platform

The fact that the Lite Speech2Sign platform is intended primarily for use by sign language experts who may only have modest skills in computer science has dictated several key design decisions. In particular, 1) the formalism used is simple and minimal and 2) no software need be installed on the local machine: all processing (compilation, deployment, testing) is performed on a remote server accessed through the web interface.

3.1   Runtime functionality and formalism

At runtime, the basic processing flow is speech $\rightarrow$ source language text $\rightarrow$ "sign table" $\rightarrow$ SiGML $\rightarrow$ signed animation. Input speech, source language text and signed animation have their obvious meanings, and we have already introduced SiGML in the preceding section. At the input end of the pipeline, speech recognition is carried out using the Nuance Recognizer 10.2 platform, equipped with domain-specific language models compiled from the grammar. At the output end, SiGML is converted into signed animation form using the JASigning avatar system.

The "sign table", the level which joins all these pieces together, is an intermediate representation modelled on the diagrams typically used in theoretical sign language linguistics to represent signed utterances. A sign table is, concretely, a matrix whose rows represent the different parallel channels of signed language output (manual activities, gaze, head movements, mouth movements, etc). The only obligatory row is the one for manual activities, which consists of a sequence of "glosses", each gloss referring to one manual activity. There is one column for each gloss/manual activity in the signed utterance.

The usefulness of this representation is dependent on the appropriateness of the assumption that sign language is timed so that each non-manual activity can be assumed synchronous with some manual activity. This has been shown to be true for non-manual activities that serve linguistic functions. Non-manual activities that serve purely affective purposes, e.g., expressing anger or disgust, are known to start slightly earlier than the surrounding manual activities (Reilly and Anderson, 2002; Wilbur, 2000). A restriction imposed by the low-level SiGML representation is that non-manual activities cannot be extended across several manual activities in a straightforward way;

```
include lsf_ch.csv
include visicast.txt

Domain
Name toy1
Client speech2sign_client
SourceLanguage french
TargetLanguages gloss head gaze \
    eyebrows aperture mouthing
EndDomain

Utterance
Source    je m'appelle $$name
Gloss     MOI      S_APPELER $$name
Head      Nod      Neutral   Neutral
Gaze      Neutral Neutral   Neutral
Eyebrows Up       Up        Up
Aperture Wide     Wide      Wide
Mouthing mwe      appel     $$name
EndUtterance

TrPhrase $$name
Source     claude
Gloss      C L A U  D E
Mouthing   C L a u: d e
EndTrPhrase

TrPhrase $$name
Source     marie
Gloss      M  A R I E
Mouthing   L23 a R i e
EndTrPhrase
```

Figure 1: Toy speech2sign application definition.

however, workarounds have been introduced for this (Ebling and Glauert, 2015). Experience with SiGML has shown that it is capable of supporting signed animation of satisfactory quality (Smith and Nolan, 2015).

The core translation formalism is a version of Synchronous Context Free Grammar (SCFG; (Aho and Ullman, 1969; Chiang, 2005)) adapted to the peculiarities of sign language translation. A complete toy application definition is shown in Figure 1. The top-level Utterance rule translates French expressions of the form *Je m'appelle* ⟨*NAME*⟩ ("I am called ⟨NAME⟩") to Swiss French Sign Language (LSF-CH) expressions of a form that can be glossed as *MOI S_APPELER ⟨NAME⟩* together with accompanying non-manual components; for example, the manual activity *MOI* (signed by pointing at one's chest) is here performed together with a head nod, raised eyebrows, widened eyes, and a series of mouth movements approximating the shapes used to say "mwe". The two `TrPhrase` rules translate the names "Claude" and "Marie" into fingerspelled forms with accompanying mouthings.

The mapping between the sign table and SiGML levels is specified using three other types of declarations, defined in the resource lexica listed in the initial `include` lines. 1) Glosses are associated with strings of HamNoSys symbols; in this case, the resource lexicon used is `lsf_ch.csv`, a CSV spreadsheet whose columns are glosses and HNS strings for LSF-CH signs. 2) Symbols in the non-manual rows (`Head`, `Gaze`, etc) are mapped into the set of SiGML tags supported by the avatar, according to the declarations in the sign-language-independent resource file `visicast.txt`. 3) The `Mouthing` line is treated specially. Two types of mouthings are supported: "mouth pictures", approximate mouthings of phonemes, are written as SAMPA (Wells, 1997) strings (e.g. `mwe` is a SAMPA string). It is also possible to use the repertoire of "mouth gestures" (mouth movements not related to spoken language words, produced with teeth, jaw, lips, cheeks, or tongue) supported by the avatar, again using definitions taken from the `visicast.txt` resource file. For example, `L23` denotes pursed lips (Hanke, 2001).

The `Domain` unit at the top defines the name of the translation app, the source language[3] and sign language channels, and the type of web client used to display it.

3.2 Compile- and deploy-time functionality

The compilation process takes application descriptions like the one above as input and transforms them first into SCFG grammars, then into GrXML grammars[4], and finally into runnable Nuance recognition grammars. The compiler also produces tables of metadata listing associations between symbols and HamNoSys, SAMPA, and SiGML constants.

Two main challenges needed to be addressed when designing the compile-time functionality. The first was to make the process of developing, uploading, compiling, and deploying web-based speech applications simple to invoke, so that these operations could be performed without detailed understanding of the underlying technology. The second was to support development on a shared server; here, it is critical to ensure that a developer who uploads bad content is not able to break the system for other users.

At an abstract level, the architecture is as follows. Content is divided into separate "namespaces", with each developer controlling one or more namespaces; a namespace in turn contains one or more translation apps. At the source level, each namespace is a self-contained directory, and each app a self contained subdirectory.

From the developer's point of view, the whole upload/compile/deploy cycle reduces to a simple progression across a dashboard with four tabs labeled "Select", "Compile", "Test", and "Release". The developer starts the upload/compile/deploy cycle by uploading one or more namespace directories over an FTP client and choosing one of them from the "Select" tab.

The platform contains three separate servers, respectively called *compilation*, *staging*, and *deployment*. After selecting the app on the first tab, the developer moves to the second one and presses the "Compile" button to invoke the compilation server. Successful compilation results in a Nuance grammar recognition module and a set of namespace-specific table entries; a separate Nuance recognition grammar is created for each namespace. As part of the compilation process, a set of files is also created which list undefined constants. These can be downloaded over the FTP connection and are structured so as to make it easy for the developer to fill in missing entries and add the new content to the resource files.

When the app has compiled, the developer proceeds to the third, "Staging" tab, and presses the "Test" button. This initiates a process which copies the compiled recognition grammar, table entries and metadata to appropriate places on the staging server and registers the grammar as available for use by the recognition engine, after which the developer can interactively test the application

---

[3] Any recognition language supported by Nuance Recognizer 10.2 can potentially be used as a source language; the current version of the platform is loaded with language packs for English, French, German, Italian, Japanese and Slovenian.

[4] GrXML is an open standard for writing speech recognition grammars.

through the web interface. It is important that only copying actions are performed by the "Staging" server; experience shows that recompiling applications can often lead to problems if the compiler changes after an application is uploaded.

When the developer is satisfied with the application, they move to the fourth tab and press the "Release" button. This carries out a second set of copying operations which transfer the application to the deployment server.

4 Initial experiences with the platform

The Lite Speech2Sign platform is undergoing initial testing; during this process, we have constructed half a dozen toy apps for the translation directions French → LSF-CH and German → Swiss German Sign Language, and one moderately substantial app for French → LSF-CH. Grammars written so far all have a flat structure.

Our central claims regarding the platform are that it greatly simplifies the process of building a speech-to-sign application and allows rapid construction of apps which produce signed language of adequate quality. To give some substance to these statements, we tracked the construction of a small French → LSF-CH medical questionnaire app and performed a short evaluation. The app was built by a sign language expert whose main qualifications are in sign language interpretation. The expert began by discussing the corpus with Deaf native signers, to obtain video-recorded material on which to base development. They then implemented rules and HNS entries, uploaded, debugged, and deployed the content, and used the deployed system to perform the evaluation.

Rule-writing typically required on the order of ten to fifteen minutes per rule, using a method of repeatedly playing the recorded video and entering first the gloss line and then the accompanying non-manual lines. Uploading, debugging, and deployment of the app was completely straightforward and took approximately one hour. The most time-consuming part of the process was implementing HNS entries for signs missing from the current LSF-CH HNS lexicon. The time required per entry varied a great deal depending on the sign's complexity, but was typically on the order of half an hour to two hours. This part of the task will of course become less important as the HNS lexicon resource becomes more complete.

The evaluation was carried out with five Deaf subjects and based on recommendations for sign language animation evaluation studies by Kacorri et al. (2015). Each subject was first given a short demographic questionnaire. Subjects were then asked to watch seven outputs from the app and echo them back, either in signed or mouthed form, to check the comprensibility of the app's signed output. They then answered a second short questionnaire which asked for their overall impressions. The result was encouraging: although none of the subjects felt the signing was truly fluent and human-like (a frequent comment was "artificial"), they all considered it grammatically correct and perfectly comprehensible.

5 Conclusions and further directions

Although the Lite Speech2Sign platform is designed to appear very simple and most of its runtime processing is carried out by the third-party JASigning and Nuance components, it represents a non-trivial engineering effort. The value it adds is that it allows sign language linguists who may have only modest computational skills to build translation applications that produce synthesized signed language, using a tool whose basic functioning can be mastered in two or three weeks. By including speech recognition, these applications can potentially be useful in real situations.

In a research context, the platform opens up new possibilities for investigation of the grammar of signed languages. If the linguist wishes to investigate the productivity of a hypothesized syntactic rule, they can quickly implement a grammar fragment and produce a set of related signed utterances, all signed uniformly using the avatar. Our initial experiences, as described in Section 4, suggest that rendering quality is sufficient to obtain useful signer judgements.

Full documentation for Lite Speech2Sign is available (Rayner, 2016). The platform is currently in alpha testing; we plan to open it up for general use during Q3 2016. People interested in obtaining an account may do so by mailing one of the authors of this paper.

Acknowledgements

We would like to thank John Glauert of the School of Computing Sciences, UEA, for his invaluable help with JASigning, and Nuance Inc for generously making their software available to us for research purposes.

References

Alfred V. Aho and Jeffrey D. Ullman. Properties of syntax directed translations. *Journal of Computer and System Sciences*, 3(3):319–334, 1969.

David Chiang. A hierarchical phrase-based model for statistical machine translation. In *Proceedings of the 43rd Annual Meeting on Association for Computational Linguistics*, pages 263–270. Association for Computational Linguistics, 2005.

Stephen Cox, Michael Lincoln, Judy Tryggvason, Melanie Nakisa, Mark Wells, Marcus Tutt, and Sanja Abbott. Tessa, a system to aid communication with deaf people. In *Proceedings of the fifth international ACM conference on Assistive technologies*, pages 205–212. ACM, 2002.

Sarah Ebling and John Glauert. Building a Swiss German Sign Language avatar with JASigning and evaluating it among the Deaf community. *Universal Access in the Information Society*, pages 1–11, 2015. Retrieved from `http://dx.doi.org/10.1007/s10209-015-0408-1` (last accessed November 20, 2015).

Eleni Efthimiou, Stavroula-Evita Fotinea, Thomas Hanke, John Glauert, Richard Bowden, Annelies Braffort, Christophe Collet, Petros Maragos, and François Lefebvre-Albaret. The Dicta-Sign Wiki: Enabling web communication for the Deaf. In *Proceedings of the 13th International Conference on Computers Helping People with Special Needs (ICCHP)*, pages 205–212, Linz, Austria, 2012.

Ralph Elliott, John RW Glauert, JR Kennaway, and Ian Marshall. The development of language processing support for the ViSiCAST project. In *Proceedings of the fourth international ACM conference on Assistive technologies*, pages 101–108. ACM, 2000.

Ralph Elliott, John RW Glauert, JR Kennaway, Ian Marshall, and Eva Safar. Linguistic modelling and language-processing technologies for avatar-based sign language presentation. *Universal Access in the Information Society*, 6(4): 375–391, 2008.

John Glauert. Animating sign language for Deaf people. Lecture held at the University of Zurich, October 9, 2013 (unpublished), 2013.

Thomas Hanke. ViSiCAST Deliverable D5-1: Interface definitions. Technical report, ViSiCAST project, 2001. Retrieved from `http://www.visicast.cmp.uea.ac.uk/Papers/ViSiCAST_D5-1v017rev2.pdf` (last accessed November 20, 2015).

Vince Jennings, Ralph Elliott, Richard Kennaway, and John Glauert. Requirements for a signing avatar. In *Proceedings of the 4th LREC Workshop on the Representation and Processing of Sign Languages*, pages 133–136, La Valetta, Malta, 2010.

Hernisa Kacorri, Matt Huenerfauth, Sarah Ebling, Kasmira Patel, and Mackenzie Willard. Demographic and experiential factors influencing acceptance of sign language animation by Deaf users. In *Proceedings of the 17th International ACM SIGACCESS Conference on Computers & Accessibility*, pages 147–154. ACM, 2015.

Michael Kipp, Alexis Heloir, and Quan Nguyen. Sign language avatars: Animation and comprehensibility. In *Proceedings of the 11th International Conference on Intelligent Virtual Agents (IVA)*, pages 113–126, Reykjavík, Iceland, 2011.

Gary Morgan and Bencie Woll. The development of complex sentences in British Sign Language. In Gary Morgan and Bencie Woll, editors, *Directions in Sign Language Acquisition: Trends in Language Acquisition Research*, pages 255–276. John Benjamins, Amsterdam, Netherlands, 2002.

Siegmund Prillwitz, Regina Leven, Heiko Zienert, Thomas Hanke, and Ian Henning. *HamNoSys: Version 2.0: An Introductory Guide*. Signum, Hamburg, Germany, 1989.

Manny Rayner. *Using the Regulus Lite Speech2Sign Platform*. `http://www.issco.unige.ch/en/research/projects/Speech2SignDoc/build/html/index.html`, 2016. Online documentation.

J. Reilly and D. Anderson. FACES: The acquisition of non-manual morphology in ASL. In G. Morgan and B. Woll, editors, *Directions in Sign Language Acquisition*, pages 159–181. John Benjamins, Amsterdam, Netherlands, 2002.

Eva Sáfár and John Glauert. Computer modelling. In Roland Pfau, Markus Steinbach, and Bencie

Woll, editors, *Sign Language: An International Handbook*, pages 1075–1101. De Gruyter Mouton, Berlin, Germany, 2012.

Rubén San-Segundo, Juan Manuel Montero, Javier Macías-Guarasa, R Córdoba, Javier Ferreiros, and José Manuel Pardo. Proposing a speech to gesture translation architecture for Spanish deaf people. *Journal of Visual Languages & Computing*, 19(5):523–538, 2008.

Robert Smith and Brian Nolan. Emotional facial expressions in synthesised sign language avatars: A manual evaluation. *Universal Access in the Information Society*, pages 1–10, 2015. Retrieved from `http://dx.doi.org/10.1007/s10209-015-0410-7` (last accessed November 20, 2015).

J.C. Wells. SAMPA computer readable phonetic alphabet. In D. Gibbon, R. Moore, and R. Winski, editors, *Handbook of Standards and Resources for Spoken Language Systems*. De Gruyter Mouton, Berlin, Germany, 1997.

Ronnie B. Wilbur. Phonological and prosodic layering of nonmanuals in American Sign Language. In Karen Emmorey and Harlan Lane, editors, *The Signs of Language Revisited*, pages 215–244. Erlbaum, Mahwah, NJ, 2000.

Word Alignment without NULL Words

Philip Schulz
P.Schulz@uva.nl

Wilker Aziz
W.Aziz@uva.nl

Khalil Sima'an
K.Simaan@uva.nl

ILLC
University of Amsterdam

Abstract

In word alignment certain source words are only needed for fluency reasons and do not have a translation on the target side. Most word alignment models assume a target NULL word from which they generate these untranslatable source words. Hypothesising a target NULL word is not without problems, however. For example, because this NULL word has a position, it interferes with the distribution over alignment jumps. We present a word alignment model that accounts for untranslatable source words by generating them from preceding source words. It thereby removes the need for a target NULL word and only models alignments between word pairs that are actually observed in the data. Translation experiments on English paired with Czech, German, French and Japanese show that the model outperforms its traditional IBM counterparts in terms of BLEU score.

1 Introduction

When the IBM models (Brown et al., 1993) were designed, some way of accounting for words that likely have no translation was needed. The modellers back then decided to introduce a NULL word on the target (generating) side[1]. All words on the source side without a proper target translation would then be generated by that NULL word.

While this solution is technically valid, it neglects that those untranslatable words are required for source fluency. Moreover, the NULL word, although hypothetical in nature, does have a position. It is well-known that this NULL posi-

tion is problematic for distortion-based alignment models. Alignments to NULL demand a special treatment as they would otherwise induce very long jumps that one does not usually observe in distortion-based alignment models. Examples of this can be found in Vogel et al. (1996), who drop the NULL word entirely and thus force all source words to align lexically, and Och and Ney (2003), who choose a *fixed* NULL probability.

In the present work, we introduce a family of IBM-style alignment models that can express dependencies between translated and untranslated source words. The models do not use NULL words and instead allow untranslatable source words to be generated from translated words in their context. This is achieved by modelling source word collocations. From a technical point of view the model can be seen as a mixture of an alignment and a language model.

2 IBM models 1 and 2

Here, we quickly review the IBM alignment models 1 and 2 (Brown et al., 1993). We assume a random variable E over the English (target) vocabulary[2], a variable F over the French (source) vocabulary and a variable A over alignment links[3]. The IBM models assign probabilities to alignment configurations and source sentences given the target side. Under the assumption that all source words are conditionally independent given the alignment links, these probabilities factorise as

$$P(f_1^m, a_1^m | e_0^l) = P(a_1^m) \prod_{j=1}^{m} P(f_j | e_{a_j}) \quad (1)$$

where x_1^k is a vector of outcomes $x_1, \ldots, x_k$ and e_{a_j} denotes the English word that the French word

---

[1] The target side is often identified with English and the source side is usually taken to be French.

[2] Crucially, this vocabulary includes a NULL word.

[3] We denote realisations of random variables by the corresponding lower case letters.

Proceedings of the 54th Annual Meeting of the Association for Computational Linguistics, pages 169–174,
Berlin, Germany, August 7-12, 2016. ©2016 Association for Computational Linguistics

in the jth position (f_j) is aligned to under a_1^m.

In IBM model 1 $P(a_1^m)$ is uniform. In IBM model 2, all alignment links a_j are assumed to be independent and follow a categorical distribution. Here, we choose to parametrise this categorical based on the distance between the two words to be aligned, as has been done by Vogel et al. (1996) and Liang et al. (2006). Thus, in our IBM model 2

$$P(a_1^m) = \prod_{j=1}^{m} P(a_j) = \prod_{j=1}^{m} P\left(i - \left\lfloor \frac{jl}{m} \right\rfloor\right) \quad (2)$$

where i is the position of the English word that a_j links to and the values l and m stand for the target and source sentence lengths. Notice that there is a target position $i = 0$ for the NULL word. Alignment to this NULL position often causes unusually long alignment jumps.

3 Removing the NULL word

3.1 Model description

Our model consists of an alignment model component (which is either IBM model 1 or 2 without NULL words) and a language model component. It also contains a random variable Z that indicates which component to use. If $Z = 0$ we use the alignment model, if $Z = 1$ we instead use the language model. We generate each z_j conditional on f_{j-1}. By making the outcome z_j depend on f_{j-1}, we allow the model to capture the tendency of individual source words to be part of a collocation, i.e. to be followed by a closely related word. A similar strategy has been employed for topic modelling by Griffiths et al. (2007).

When generating the source side, the model does the following for each source word f_j:

1. Depending on the previous source word f_{j-1}, draw z_j.

2. If $z_j = 1$, generate f_j from f_{j-1} and choose a_j according to $P(a_j)$. Otherwise, if $z_j = 0$, generate f_j from the target side and choose a_j according to the probability that it has under the relevant alignment model *without a target NULL word*.

Our model thus induces a joint probability distribution of the form

$$P(f_1^m, a_1^m, z_1^m | e_1^l) \quad (3)$$

$$= P(a_1^m) \prod_{j=1}^{m} P(z_j | f_{j-1}) P(f_j | e_{a_j}, f_{j-1}, z_j)$$

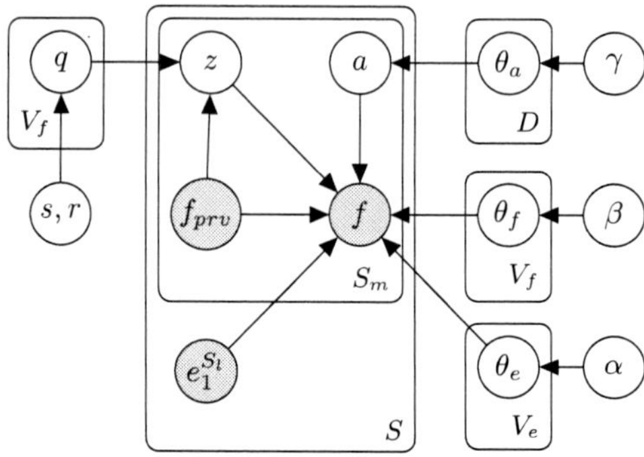

Figure 1: A graphical representation of our model for S sentence pairs. We use $V_{f/e}$ to denote the source/target vocabulary sizes and D to denote the number of possible alignment link configurations. Furthermore, $S_{m/l}$ is the number of source/target words in the current sentence and f_{prv} the source word preceding the one that we currently generate.

where it is crucial to note that there is no E_0 variable, standing for the NULL word, anymore. Therefore, jumps to a NULL position do not need to be modelled. Notice further that the formulation of our model is general enough to be readily extensible to an HMM alignment model (Vogel et al., 1996).

Depending on the value of z_j, F_j is distributed either according to an alignment (4) or a language model[4] (5).

$$P(f_j | e_{a_j}, f_{j-1}, z_j = 0) = P(f_j | e_{a_j}) \quad (4)$$
$$P(f_j | e_{a_j}, f_{j-1}, z_j = 1) = P(f_j | f_{j-1}) \quad (5)$$

3.2 The full model

Our full model is a Bayesian model, meaning that we treat all model parameters as random variables that are drawn from prior distributions. A graphical depiction of the model can be found in Figure 1. We impose Dirichlet priors on the translation (θ_e), language model (θ_f) and distortion parameters (θ_a). This has been done before and improved the standard IBM models.

In order to be able to bias the model against using the language model component (5) too often and instead make it prefer the alignment model component (4), we impose a Beta prior on the Bernoulli distributions over component choices. In effect, the model will only explain a source word with the language model if there is a lot of

---

[4] We use a bigram LM to avoid conditioning Z on longer $(n-1)$-grams.

evidence that this word cannot be translated from the target side. The full model can be summarised as follows:

$$F_j | e, a_j, z_j = 0 \sim Cat(\theta_{e_{aj}}) \qquad \Theta_{e_{aj}} \sim Dir(\alpha)$$
$$F_j | f_{j-1}, z_j = 1 \sim Cat(\theta_{f_{j-1}}) \qquad \Theta_{f_{j-1}} \sim Dir(\beta)$$
$$Z_j | f_{j-1} \sim Bernoulli(q) \qquad Q \sim Beta(s, r) .$$

For IBM model 1, A_j is uniformly distributed whereas for model 2 we have

$$A \sim Cat(\theta_a) \qquad \Theta_a \sim Dir(\gamma) .$$

3.3 Inference

We use a Gibbs sampler to perform inference of the alignment and choice variables. Since our priors are conjugate to the model distributions, we integrate over the model parameters, giving us a collapsed sampler[5]. The sampler alternates between sampling alignment links A and component choices Z.

The predictive posterior probabilities for $Z_j = 0$ and $Z_j = 1$ are given in Equations (6) and (7) (up to proportionality). We use $c(\cdot)$ as a (conditional) count function that counts how often an outcome has been observed in a given context. We furthermore use V_f to denote the French (source) vocabulary size. To ease notation, we also introduce the context set $\mathcal{C}_{-X_j}$ which contains the current values of all variables in our model except X_j and the set $\mathcal{H}$ which simply contains all hyperparameters.

$$P\left(Z_j = 0 | \mathcal{C}_{-Z_j}, \mathcal{H}\right) \propto \tag{6}$$
$$(c(z = 0 | f_{j-1}) + s) \, P(a_j) \frac{c(f_j | e_{a_j}, z = 0) + \alpha}{c(e_{a_j} | z = 0) + \alpha V_f}$$
$$P\left(Z_j = 1 | \mathcal{C}_{-Z_j}, \mathcal{H}\right) \propto \tag{7}$$
$$(c(z = 1 | f_{j-1}) + r) \frac{c(f_j | f_{j-1}, z = 1) + \beta}{c(z = 1 | f_{j-1}) + \beta V_f}$$

When $Z_j = 0$, the predictive probability for alignment link A_j is proportional to Equation (8).

$$P\left(a_j | \mathcal{C}_{-Z_j, -A_j}, Z_j = 0, \mathcal{H}\right) \propto \tag{8}$$
$$P(a_j) \frac{c(f_j | e_{a_j}, z = 0) + \alpha}{c(e_{a_j} | z = 0) + \alpha V_f}$$

When $Z_j = 1$, it is simply proportional to $P(a_j)$. In the case of IBM model 1, $P(a_j)$ is a constant. For IBM model 2, we use

$$P(a_j) \propto c\left(i - \left\lfloor \frac{jl}{m} \right\rfloor\right) + \gamma .$$

where l and m are the target and source sentence lengths. Notice that target positions start at 1 as we do not use a NULL word.

Notice that a naïve implementation of our sampler is unpractically slow. We therefore augment the sampler with an auxiliary variable (Tanner and Wong, 1987) that uniformly chooses only one possible new assignment per sampled link. The sampling complexity, which would normally be linear in the size of the target sentence, thus becomes constant. In practice this speed up the sampler by several orders of magnitude, making our aligner as fast as Giza++. Unfortunately, this strategy also slightly impairs the mobility of our sampler.

3.4 Decoding

Our samples contain assignments of the A and Z variables. If for a word f_j we have $z_j = 1$, we treat the word as not aligned. We then use maximum marginal decoding (Johnson and Goldwater, 2009) over alignment links to generate final word alignments. This means that we align each source word to the target word it has been aligned to most often in the samples. If the word was unaligned in most samples, we leave it unaligned in the output alignment.

4 Experiments and results

We present translation experiments on English paired with German, French, Czech and Japanese, thereby covering four language families. We compare our model and the Bayesian IBM models 1 and 2 of Mermer et al. (2013) against IBM model 2 as a baseline.

4.1 Experiments

Data We use the news commentary data from the WMT 2014 translation task[6] for German, French and Czech paired with English. We use newstest-2013 as development data and we use the newstest-2014 for testing. We use all available monolingual data from WMT 2014 for language modelling. All data are truecased and sentences

---

[5]Derivations of samplers similar to ours can be found in the appendices of Mermer et al. (2013) and Griffiths et al. (2007). We omit the derivation here for space reasons.

[6]`http://statmt.org/wmt14/translation-task.html`

171

Model	En-De	En-Fr	En-Cs	En-Ja	De-En	Fr-En	Cs-En	Ja-En
Brown et al. (model 2)	14.56	27.16	13.74	25.78	18.12	26.69	18.77	23.29
Mermer et al. (model 1)	-0.09	-0.64	+0.38	-0.13	+0.32	-0.92	+0.66	-0.31
Mermer et al. (model 2)	**+1.07**	-0.17	**+1.76**	+0.39	+1.63	-1.04	**+1.63**	-0.21
This work (model 1)	-0.03	-0.79	-0.42	+0.15	+0.29	-1.49	+0.45	-0.65
This work (model 2)	+0.92	**+1.32**	+1.66	**+1.69**	**+1.73**	**+2.01**	+1.42	**+2.24**
Giza	+0.96	+0.23	+1.58	+2.97	+2.27	+2.26	+1.96	+2.73
fastAlign	+0.88	+0.70	+1.47	+1.97	+2.27	+1.90	+1.86	+2.63

(a) Directional: alignments obtained in target-to-source direction.

Model	En-De	En-Fr	En-Cs	En-Ja	De-En	Fr-En	Cs-En	Ja-En
Brown et al. (model 2)	+0.84	+0.77	+1.14	+3.02	+1.80	+1.77	+1.15	+2.95
Mermer et al. (model 1)	+0.52	+0.80	+1.30	+3.19	+1.51	+1.60	+1.77	+2.44
Mermer et al. (model 2)	+0.63	+0.33	+1.94	+3.00	+2.02	+1.22	**+2.34**	+2.48
This work (model 1)	+0.39	+0.23	+1.31	**+3.33**	+1.61	+0.98	+1.87	+2.56
This work (model 2)	**+1.07**	**+1.47**	**+2.08**	+2.65	**+2.30**	**+2.19**	+2.13	**+3.21**
Giza	+1.59	+0.87	+1.70	+4.24	+2.54	+2.08	+2.36	+3.94
fastAlign	+1.39	+1.23	+1.87	+2.47	+2.44	+2.06	+2.21	+3.58

(b) Symmetrised: alignments obtained in both directions independently and heuristically symmetrised (grow-diag-final-and).

Table 1: Translation results from and into English. Alignments in the top (1a) and bottom (1b) tables were obtained in the target-to-source direction and symmetrised, respectively. Differences are computed with respect to the directional IBM model 2 in its original parameterisation (Brown et al., 1993). The best Bayesian model in each column is boldfaced.

with more than 100 words discarded as is standardly done in SMT.

The Japanese training data consist of 200.000 randomly extracted sentence pairs from the NTCIR-8 Patent Translation Task. The full data are used for language modelling. We use the NTCIR-7 dev sets for tuning and the NTCIR-9 test set for testing.[7]

Training The maximum likelihood IBM model 2 is initialized with model 1 parameter estimates and trained for 5 EM iterations. Following Mermer and Saraçlar (2011), we initialize the Gibbs samplers of all Bayesian models with the Viterbi alignment from IBM model 1. We run each sampler for 1000 iterations and take a sample after every 25th iteration. We do not use burn-in.[8]

Hyperparameters All Bayesian models are trained with $\alpha = 0.0001$ and $\beta = 0.0001$ to induce sparse lexical distributions. We also set $s = 1$ and $r = 0.1$ when IBM1 is the alignment component in our model. This has the effect of biasing the model towards using the align-

ment component. For the IBM2 version we even set $r = 0.01$ since IBM2 is a more trustworthy alignment model. For IBM2, we furthermore set $\gamma = 1$ to obtain a flat distortion prior.

Observe that experiments presented here use *the same* fixed hyperparameters for all language pairs. We tried to add another level to our model by imposing Gamma priors on the hyperparameters. The hyperparameters were then inferred using slice sampling after each Gibbs iteration. When run on the German-English and Czech-English data, this strategy increased the posterior probability of the states visited by our sampler but had no effect on BLEU. This may indicate that either the hand-chosen hyperparameters are adequate for the task or that the model generally performs well for a large range of hyperparameters.

Translation We train Moses systems (Koehn et al., 2007) with 5-gram language models with modified Kneser-Ney-smoothing using KenLM (Heafield et al., 2013) and orientation-based lexicalised reordering. We tune the systems with MERT (Och, 2003) on the dev sets. We report the BLEU score (Papineni et al., 2002) for all models averaged over 5 MERT runs.

4.2 Results

We report the translation results in Tables (1a) and (1b). Results of the full Giza++ pipeline and fastAlign (Dyer et al., 2013) are reported as a com-

---

[7]The Japanese data was provided to us by a colleague with the pre-processing steps already performed, with sentences shortened to at most 40 words. Our algorithm can handle sentences of any length and there is actually no need to restrict the sentence lengths.

[8]Burn-in is simply a heuristic that is not guaranteed to improve the samples in any way. See http://users.stat.umn.edu/~geyer/mcmc/burn.html for further details.

parison standard. All symmetrised results were obtained using the `grow-diag-final-and` heuristic.

Using IBM2 as an alignment component, our model mostly outperforms the standard IBM models and their Bayesian variants. Importantly, the improvement that our model 2 achieves over its model 1 variant is much larger than the difference between the corresponding models of Mermer et al. (2013). This indicates that our model makes better use of the distortion distribution that is not altered by NULL alignments. We also observe that our model gains relatively little from symmetrisation, likely because it is a very strong model already. It is interesting that although our model 2 does not use fertility parameters or dependencies between alignment links, it often approaches the performance of Giza which does use these features. Moreover, it also approaches the performance of fastAlign which does not use fertility nor dependencies between alignment links, but has a stronger inductive bias with respect to distortion.

5 Discussion and future work

We have presented an IBM-style word alignment model that does not need to hypothesise a NULL word as it explains untranslatable source words by grouping them with translated words. This also leads to a cleaner handling of distortion probabilities.

In our present work, we have only considered IBM models 1 and 2. As we have mentioned already, our model can easily be extended with the HMM alignment model. We are currently exploring this possibility. Our models also allow symmetrisation (Liang et al., 2006) of *all* translation and distortion parameters where before the NULL distortion parameters had to be fixed. We therefore plan to extend them towards model-based instead of heuristic alignment symmetrisation.

A limitation of our model is that it is only capable of modelling left-to-right linear dependencies in the source language. In languages like German or English, however, where an adjective or determiner is selected by the following noun, this may not be appropriate to model selection biases amongst neighbouring words. An interesting extension to our model is thus to add more structure to it such that it will be able to capture more complex source side dependencies.

Another concern is the inference in our model.

Using the auxiliary variable sampler, inference becomes very fast but may sacrifice performance. This is why we are interested in improving the inference method, e.g. by using a more mobile sampler or by employing a variational Bayes algorithm.

The software used in our experiments can be downloaded from `https://github.com/philschulz/Aligner`.

Acknowledgements

We would like to thank Miloš Stanojević for providing us with the preprocessed Japanese data. We would also like to thank our reviewers for their helpful feedback. This work was supported by the Netherlands Organization for Scientific Research (NWO) VICI Grant nr. 277-89-002.

References

Peter F. Brown, Vincent J.Della Pietra, Stephen A. Della Pietra, and Robert. L. Mercer. 1993. The mathematics of statistical machine translation: Parameter estimation. *Computational Linguistics*, 19:263–311.

Chris Dyer, Victor Chahuneau, and Noah A. Smith. 2013. A simple, fast, and effective reparameterization of IBM model 2. In *In Proceedings of NAACL*.

Thomas L. Griffiths, Mark Steyvers, and Joshua B. Tenenbaum. 2007. Topics in semantic representation. *Psychological review*, 114(2):211–244.

Kenneth Heafield, Ivan Pouzyrevsky, Jonathan H. Clark, and Philipp Koehn. 2013. Scalable modified Kneser-Ney language model estimation. In *Proceedings of the 51st Annual Meeting of the Association for Computational Linguistics*, pages 690–696, Sofia, Bulgaria

Mark Johnson and Sharon Goldwater. 2009. Improving nonparameteric Bayesian inference: Experiments on unsupervised word segmentation with adaptor grammars. NAACL '09, pages 317–325.

Philipp Koehn, Hieu Hoang, Alexandra Birch, Chris Callison-Burch, Marcello Federico, Nicola Bertoldi, Brooke Cowan, Wade Shen, Christine Moran, Richard Zens, Chris Dyer, Ondřej Bojar, Alexandra Constantin, and Evan Herbst. 2007. Moses: Open source toolkit for statistical machine translation. In *Proceedings of the 45th Annual Meeting of the ACL on Interactive Poster and Demonstration Sessions*, ACL '07, pages 177–180.

Percy Liang, Ben Taskar, and Dan Klein. 2006. Alignment by agreement. HLT-NAACL '06, pages 104–111. Association for Computational Linguistics.

Coşkun Mermer and Murat Saraçlar. 2011. Bayesian word alignment for statistical machine translation. In *Proceedings of the 49th Annual Meeting of the Association for Computational Linguistics: Human Language Technologies: Short Papers - Volume 2*, pages 182–187.

Coşkun Mermer, Murat Saraçlar, and Ruhi Sarikaya. 2013. Improving statistical machine translation using Bayesian word alignment and Gibbs sampling. *IEEE Transactions on Audio, Speech & Language Processing*, 21(5):1090–1101.

Franz Josef Och and Hermann Ney. 2003. A systematic comparison of various statistical alignment models. *Computational Linguistics*, 29(1):19–51.

Franz Josef Och. 2003. Minimum error rate training in statistical machine translation. ACL '03, pages 160–167.

Kishore Papineni, Salim Roukos, Todd Ward, and Wei-Jing Zhu. 2002. BLEU: a method for automatic evaluation of machine translation. In *Proceedings of the 40th Annual Meeting on Association for Computational Linguistics*, pages 311–318.

Martin A. Tanner and Wing Hung Wong. 1987. The calculation of posterior distributions by data augmentation. *Journal of the American Statistical Association*, 82(398):528–550.

Stephan Vogel, Hermann Ney, and Christoph Tillmann. 1996. HMM-based word alignment in statistical translation. In *Proceedings of the 16th Conference on Computational Linguistics - Volume 2*, COLING '96, pages 836–841, Stroudsburg, PA, USA. Association for Computational Linguistics.

Unsupervised morph segmentation and statistical language models for vocabulary expansion

Matti Varjokallio [*]
Dept. of Signal Processing and Acoustics
Aalto University
Espoo, Finland
matti.varjokallio@aalto.fi

Dietrich Klakow
Spoken Language Systems
Saarland University
Saarbrücken, Germany
dietrich.klakow@lsv.uni-saarland.de

Abstract

This work explores the use of unsupervised morph segmentation along with statistical language models for the task of vocabulary expansion. Unsupervised vocabulary expansion has large potential for improving vocabulary coverage and performance in different natural language processing tasks, especially in less-resourced settings on morphologically rich languages. We propose a combination of unsupervised morph segmentation and statistical language models and evaluate on languages from the Babel corpus. The method is shown to perform well for all the evaluated languages when compared to the previous work on the task.

1 Introduction

Language modelling for different natural language processing tasks like speech recognition, machine translation or optical character recognition require large training corpora to achieve good language model estimates and high enough vocabulary coverage. Sometimes such resources are not readily available or easily acquirable. This is especially the case for the many less-resourced languages. In the case of morphologically rich languages, these issues are emphasized, as words appear in many forms, thus increasing the required vocabulary size and the data sparsity. Automatic speech recognition of spontaneous speech is a task with some special characteristics, as speech transcriptions are expensive to acquire. Taking all these factors into account, the importance of making the most out of the available resources becomes evident.

Previous work on handling out-of-vocabulary (OOV) words in automatic speech recognition have included explicit OOV word modelling and confidence measures (Hazen and Bazzi, 2001) and hybrid word-subword language modelling for OOV word detection (Yazgan and Saraçlar, 2004). Speech recognition by directly using optimized subword units has also (Kneissler and Klakow, 2001) proven a good approach for speech recognition of a morphologically rich language.

In this work, we study unsupervised vocabulary expansion for conversational speech recognition of morphologically rich languages in a less-resourced setting. We expand the recognition vocabulary, and thus lower the OOV rate, by generating new word forms. Two recent works also target the unsupervised vocabulary expansion.

In (Rasooli et al., 2014), an unsupervised morphological segmentation was inferred from the training corpus using the Morfessor Categories-MAP (Creutz and Lagus, 2007) method. The prefix-stem-suffix structure estimated by the model was then represented as a finite-state-transducer for sampling new word forms. Different reranking schemes using a bigram language model and a letter trigraph language model were evaluated.

The Kaldi speech recognition package (Povey et al., 2011) includes an approach (Trmal et al., 2014) for vocabulary expansion. In this approach, the provided syllable segmented pronunciation lexicon is used as the basis for the expansion. An n-gram model is trained over the syllable segmentation and syllabic words are generated from the model. Finally a phoneme-to-grapheme mapping is performed to obtain the grapheme form for the words.

In our approach, statistical language models are trained over a morph segmentation, which is learned unsupervisedly from the data. Words are

---

[*] This work was done while the author was visiting the Saarland University Spoken Language Systems group

Proceedings of the 54th Annual Meeting of the Association for Computational Linguistics, pages 175–180,
Berlin, Germany, August 7-12, 2016. ©2016 Association for Computational Linguistics

sampled from the language models and ordered according to the probabilities given by the language models. We evaluate the method on seven morphologically rich languages from the Babel (Harper, 2013) corpus and compare to the previously suggested approaches.

2 Suggested method

We present a combination of unsupervised morph segmentation and statistical language models for unsupervised vocabulary expansion. The suggested approach operates in four steps: unsupervised morph segmentation, statistical language model training, sampling of new word types and reranking of the sampled words. The phases are described in more detail in the corresponding subsections.

2.1 Unsupervised morph segmentation

Morfessor Baseline (Creutz and Lagus, 2002) is a method for unsupervised morphological segmentation. The algorithm optimizes a two-part minimum description length code, finding a balance between the cost of encoding the training corpus and the lexicon, as in Formula 1.

$$\arg\min_{\theta} L(x, \theta) = \arg\min L(x|\theta) + L(\theta) \quad (1)$$

The corpus encoding is based on a unigram model. A so-called α-term may be used for fine-tuning the corpus encoding cost. For the experiments in this work, a recent Python implementation Morfessor 2.0 (Smit et al., 2014) was used.

2.2 Statistical language models over morphs

As statistical language models, two state-of-the-art models were selected. These language models were trained on a corpus, where one segmented word was treated as what would in normal language model training be a sentence. The training was done using log-weighted word frequencies, thus some words appearing multiple times in the training corpus. The rationale of the log-weighting was to slightly emphasize the most common words. As a last step, the order of the training words was randomized.

The first model was a trigram model trained with the modified Kneser-Ney smoothing (Kneser and Ney, 1995) using three discounts per order. The discount parameters could normally be optimized on a held-out-set, but here leave-one-out

estimates were used, as it is not clear what would in this case constitute a reasonable held-out set. The model was trained using the VariKN software package (Siivola et al., 2007).

It has recently been shown, that the recurrent neural network language models may efficiently be trained using the backpropagation algorithm (Mikolov et al., 2010), making it also an appealing choice for language modelling. As the second language model, a recurrent neural network language model was trained using the RNNLM toolkit. The words were treated as independent of the preceeding words in both the model training and the word sampling phases.

2.3 Sampling and reranking

The initial set of candidate words was obtained by sampling separately from both the n-gram model and the recurrent neural network language model. These word lists were then merged. It is very important to rerank the obtained word list, as the goal is to improve the OOV rate as much as possible with introducing as little incorrect words as possible to the vocabulary. As the final estimate on the word likelihood, the linear interpolation of these two model scores was used. The linear interpolation was applied morph-wise. The list of the sampled words was sorted in descending order with the linearly interpolated likelihood as the score.

3 Experiments

3.1 Training corpus

The vocabulary expansion experiments were conducted on the Babel corpus (DARPA, 2013). The experiments were run on the following set of languages: Assamese, Bengali, Pashto, Tagalog, Tamil, Turkish and Zulu. The training corpora consist mainly of conversation transcriptions, but also additional scripted data is provided. Including the scripted training data in general helps to lower the OOV rate. The OOV reduction rate reachable by the vocabulary expansion then becomes, with some exceptions, slightly slower. Statistics of the datasets are in the Table 1.

As preprocessing, all special symbols were removed from the texts. Asterisk symbols are used to denote misspellings in cases where the real word was identifiable. Asterisk symbols were removed and the words included in the training corpus. Dash symbols in the beginning and end of

Language	Training data		Development data			
	Types	Tokens	Types	Tokens	Type OOV%	Token OOV%
Assamese	8738	73284	7309	66357	49.75	8.36
Bengali	9507	81564	7844	70724	50.90	8.56
Pashto	7027	115225	6174	108273	44.91	4.26
Tagalog	6370	69791	5614	64506	55.61	8.13
Tamil	16284	76916	14279	70429	65.08	16.89
Turkish	12147	77310	9944	67171	57.25	12.53
Zulu	16008	65821	13848	57217	68.88	21.91

Table 1: Statistics of the datasets used in the experiments. The scripted training corpus is included.

a word are used to indicate hesitations. These words were removed from the training corpus. Only proper names were written in uppercase in the transcriptions, so these words were kept intact.

3.2 Expansion model

As statistical language models, we evaluated a trigram language model, a recurrent neural network language model, and the linear interpolation of these models. 10 million new distinct word types were sampled from both the models separately. These lists were then merged and reranked as explained in the Section 2.3.

The model parameters were optimized on selected languages and these parameters were used in all the experiments. For the recurrent neural network language model, the number of classes was set to 50 and the hidden layer size to 20. These values were reasonably close to optimum for all the languages.

The suitable α-value for the Morfessor Baseline segmentation was studied. With the default value of 1.0, the method seemed to suffer from a slight undersegmentation. To encourage the method to segment more, the α value was set to 0.8. This setting was equal or better for all the evaluated languages.

When evaluating the language models as standalone models, the trigram model provided better generation accuracy for 4 of the in total 7 languages and the recurrent neural network language model for 3 of the languages. Linear interpolation of the models was without exceptions the most accurate model. The linear interpolation weight was set to 0.5.

Figure 1 shows an example of the OOV rate development as a function of the extended vocabulary size for Turkish. The rapid improvement of the OOV rate for small extensions and the superi-

Figure 1: Token-based OOV rate as a function of the extended vocabulary size for Turkish

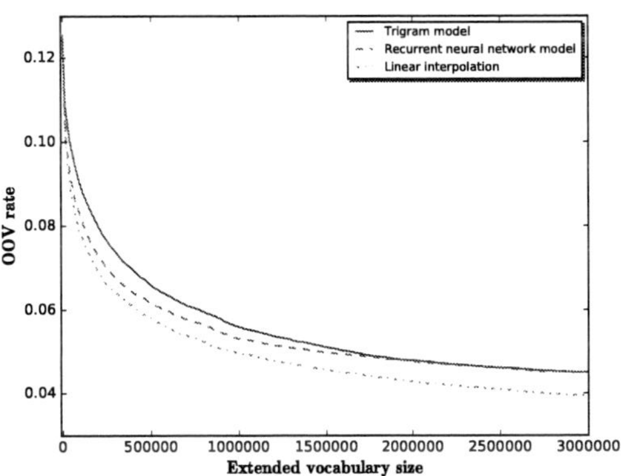

ority of the linearly interpolated model are characteristics shared by all the languages.

3.3 Comparison to the previous work

We compared the approach to the previous results in (Rasooli et al., 2014). They reported the results for a vocabulary expansion of 50k best words. Table 2 compares the type-based expansion results and Table 3 the token-based expansion results. Models for these comparisons were trained with the scripted data included.

Language	Rasooli et al.	Suggested method
Assamese	28.46	31.93
Bengali	24.75	33.20
Pashto	19.43	32.95
Tagalog	16.81	21.27
Tamil	-	16.27
Turkish	14.79	28.32
Zulu	13.87	21.18

Table 2: Type-based OOV reduction rates for the 50k best words

Language	Rasooli et al.	Suggested method
Assamese	29.43	35.17
Bengali	25.61	35.16
Pashto	21.27	35.55
Tagalog	16.88	23.75
Tamil	-	19.24
Turkish	17.82	31.89
Zulu	15.67	23.62

Table 3: Token-based OOV reduction rates for the 50k best words

Language	Vocabulary size	Kaldi	Suggested
Assamese	845k	26.4	21.2
Bengali	834k	27.4	22.0
Pashto	494k	26.7	20.3
Tagalog	581k	37.5	33.2
Tamil	896k	45.2	38.0
Turkish	704k	37.1	28.4
Zulu	818k	40.7	37.0

Table 4: Type-based OOV rate comparison to Kaldi

Language	Vocabulary size	Kaldi	Suggested
Assamese	845k	4.3	3.5
Bengali	834k	4.6	3.6
Pashto	494k	2.4	1.9
Tagalog	581k	5.3	4.6
Tamil	896k	11.2	9.1
Turkish	704k	7.9	6.0
Zulu	818k	12.5	11.4

Table 5: Token-based OOV rate comparison to Kaldi

We ran the Kaldi vocabulary expansion in the limited language pack setting as in (Trmal et al., 2014). In the default setting, around 1M distinct syllabic words are generated and converted by a phoneme-to-grapheme mapping to obtain the graphemic word form. Table 4 compares the type-based expansion results and Table 5 the token-based expansion results for a vocabulary expansion of similar size (in graphemic words). The scripted data was not used in training the models for these comparisons.

3.4 OOV reduction and type to token ratio

The OOV reduction was evaluated as a function of the type/token ratio. This analysis may provide information about the properties of the evaluated languages. The token-based analysis is in the Figure 2 and the type-based analysis in the Figure 3. As the type/token ratio is dependent on the number of tokens, these values are computed on a matched number of tokens (65821) from the training corpus. The plots show that there are similarities, but also big differences between the languages. Most notable exceptions seem to be Tamil and Tagalog. For Tamil, the number of the most frequent words was lower with a slightly more even tail of less frequent words. For Tagalog, the average number of morphs per word as estimated by the Morfessor Baseline algorithm was 2.8, which was the highest value among all the languages. Still, the number of distinct word types in the training set was the lowest. These properties seem to play a role in the different vocabulary expansion characteristics.

Figure 2: Token-based OOV reduction rate for 50k word expansion as a function of type/token ratio

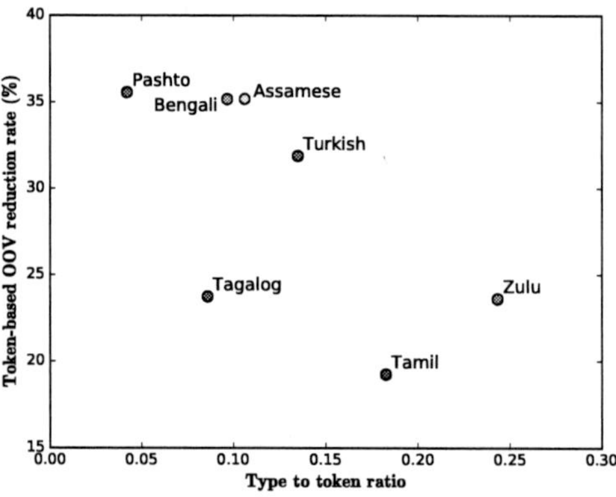

Figure 3: Type-based OOV reduction rate for 50k word expansion as a function of type/token ratio

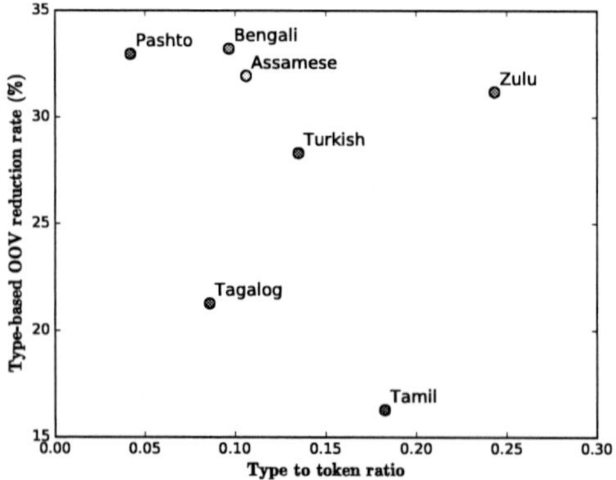

4   Discussion

This work concerned the use of unsupervised morphological segmentation and statistical language models for the task of vocabulary expansion. Unsupervised vocabulary expansion has large potential for reducing OOV-rates and improving results in NLP tasks especially in less-resourced settings for morphologically rich languages.

The suggested method was evaluated on some of the morphologically rich languages of the Babel corpus in the limited language pack condition. The performance of the method was evaluated in terms of the improvement of the OOV-rate on the development set. The suggested combination of segmentation and interpolation of statistical language models provided to our understanding the best results on the task so far. Compared to (Rasooli et al., 2014), our approach differed in that the statistical language models were used directly in the word generation phase. As opposed to (Trmal et al., 2014), our approach operated purely on the grapheme level.

It is perhaps noteworthy, that the methods are not that different from what one would use in a normal language modelling scenario for automatic speech recognition. Morfessor Baseline (Creutz and Lagus, 2002) has been seen to give good results in morph-based speech recognition (Creutz et al., 2007) when used along with standard n-gram models. If a larger training corpus is available, optimizing unigram likelihood more directly may be a good choice (Varjokallio et al., 2013).

Morph segmentations provided by the Morfessor Flatcat (Grönroos and Virpioja, 2014) -method were also evaluated for this work, but Morfessor Baseline was found to perform better. It is possible, that the tradeoff between the lexicon cost and the corpus encoding cost, as given by the Minimum Description Length -principle, is important for the modelling accuracy in this type of a less-resourced scenario. Morfessor Flatcat will in most cases segment more accurately according to the grammatical morph boundaries. This is likely a more valuable property for statistical machine translation than for the present task.

The linear interpolation of an n-gram model and a recurrent neural network language model provides at the moment state-of-the-art modelling accuracy in many statistical language modelling tasks. Some forms of class n-grams were also evaluated for this work. Sampling from a class n-gram provided many complementary word forms, not easily generated by the other models. However, it became successively harder to improve the OOV reduction rates by a combination of three models.

This work concentrated only on methods for expanding the vocabulary. Naturally some language modelling methods are required to utilize these generated words in speech recognition or some other task. One possibility is to extend the unknown symbol and improve the obtained estimates via class n-gram models (Trmal et al., 2014). Morph-based language models may be utilized using a constrained vocabulary as suggested in (Varjokallio and Kurimo, 2014). In this case word-level pronunciation variants may be applied. Performing the vocabulary expansion may also provide insights into unlimited vocabulary speech recognition (Kneissler and Klakow, 2001; Hirsimäki et al., 2006) with morph language models. Finding units with consistent grapheme-to-phoneme mapping may, however, be challenging for some of the Babel languages.

Regarding the type of approaches considered in this work, it is possible that advances in either unsupervised morph segmentation or statistical language models could bring about further improvements in the expansion accuracy. Unsupervised learning of morphological paradigms is also a potential direction when seeking for improvements in the task.

5   Conclusion

Unsupervised vocabulary expansion has great potential for reducing out-of-vocabulary rates and improving results in different natural language processing tasks, including ASR. In this work, an approach comprising of unsupervised morph segmentation and statistical language models was suggested. The model was evaluated on the Babel languages and was shown to give large improvements compared to the previous work on the task.

Acknowledgments

This research was conducted while the first author was visiting the Saarland University Spoken Language Systems group. The work was partially funded by the Saarland University SFB1102 Collaborative Research Center for Information Density and Linguistic Encoding.

References

Mathias Creutz and Krista Lagus. 2002. Unsupervised Discovery of Morphemes. In *Proceedings of the ACL-02 Workshop on Morphological and Phonological Learning - Volume 6*, pages 21–30.

Mathias Creutz and Krista Lagus. 2007. Unsupervised Models for Morpheme Segmentation and Morphology Learning. *ACM Transactions on Speech and Language Processing*, 4(1), January.

Mathias Creutz, Teemu Hirsimäki, Mikko Kurimo, Antti Puurula, Janne Pylkkönen, Vesa Siivola, Matti Varjokallio, Ebru Arisoy, Murat Saraçlar, and Andreas Stolcke. 2007. Morph-based Speech Recognition and Modeling of Out-of-vocabulary Words Across Languages. *ACM Transactions on Speech and Language Processing*, 5(1):3:1–3:29, December.

DARPA, 2013. *IARPA Babel Data Specifications for Performers*.

Stig-Arne Grönroos and Sami Virpioja. 2014. Morfessor FlatCat: An HMM-Based Method for Unsupervised and Semi-Supervised Learning of Morphology. In *Proceedings of the 25th International Conference on Computational Linguistics*, pages 1177–1185, Dublin, Ireland, August.

Mary Harper. 2013. The Babel Program and Low Resource Speech Technology. Automatic Speech Recognition and Understanding Workshop (ASRU), Invited talk.

Timothy J. Hazen and Issam Bazzi. 2001. A Comparison and Combination of Methods for OOV Word Detection and Word Confidence Scoring. In *Proceedings of the 2001 IEEE International Conference on Acoustics, Speech and Signal Processing (ICASSP)*, volume 1, pages 397–400.

Teemu Hirsimäki, Mathias Creutz, Vesa Siivola, Mikko Kurimo, Sami Virpioja, and Janne Pylkkönen. 2006. Unlimited Vocabulary Speech Recognition with Morph Language Models Applied to Finnish. *Computer Speech and Language*, 20(4):515–541.

Jan Kneissler and Dietrich Klakow. 2001. Speech Recognition for Huge Vocabularies by Using Optimized Sub-word Units. In *Proceedings of the 2nd Annual Conference of the International Speech Communication Association (INTER-SPEECH 2001)*, pages 69–72.

Reinhard Kneser and Hermann Ney. 1995. Improved Backing-off for M-gram Language Modeling. In *Proceedings of the 1995 IEEE International Conference on Acoustics, Speech and Signal Processing (ICASSP)*, pages 181–184.

Tomáš Mikolov, Martin Karafiát, Lukáš Burget, Jan Černocký, and Sanjeev Khudanpur. 2010. Recurrent Neural Network Based Language Model. In *Proceedings of the 11th Annual Conference of the International Speech Communication Association (INTERSPEECH 2010)*, pages 1045–1048.

Daniel Povey, Arnab Ghoshal, Gilles Boulianne, Lukas Burget, Ondrej Glembek, Nagendra Goel, Mirko Hannemann, Petr Motlicek, Yanmin Qian, Petr Schwarz, Jan Silovsky, Georg Stemmer, and Karel Vesely. 2011. The Kaldi Speech Recognition Toolkit. In *Proceedings of the IEEE 2011 Workshop on Automatic Speech Recognition and Understanding*, December.

Mohammad Sadegh Rasooli, Thomas Lippincott, Nizar Habash, and Owen Rambow. 2014. Unsupervised Morphology-Based Vocabulary Expansion. In *Proceedings of the 52nd Annual Meeting of the Association for Computational Linguistics (Volume 1: Long Papers)*, pages 1349–1359, Baltimore, Maryland, June.

Vesa Siivola, Teemu Hirsimäki, and Sami Virpioja. 2007. On Growing and Pruning Kneser-Ney Smoothed N-gram Models. *IEEE Transactions on Audio, Speech and Language Processing*, 15(5):1617–1624, July.

Peter Smit, Sami Virpioja, Stig-Arne Grönroos, and Mikko Kurimo. 2014. Morfessor 2.0: Toolkit for Statistical Morphological Segmentation. In *Proceedings of the 14th Conference of the European Chapter of the Association for Computational Linguistics (EACL)*, pages 21–24, Gothenburg, Sweden, April.

Jan Trmal, Guoguo Chen, Daniel Povey, Sanjeev Khudanpur, Pegah Ghahremani, Xiaohui Zhang, Vimal Manohar, Chunxi Liu, Aren Jansen, Dietrich Klakow, David Yarowsky, and Florian Metze. 2014. A Keyword Search System Using Open Source Software. In *Proceedings of the IEEE 2014 Workshop on Spoken Language Technology*, South Lake Tahoe, USA, December.

Matti Varjokallio and Mikko Kurimo. 2014. A Word-Level Token-Passing Decoder for Subword n-gram LVCSR. In *Proceedings of the IEEE 2014 Workshop on Spoken Language Technology*, South Lake Tahoe, USA, December.

Matti Varjokallio, Mikko Kurimo, and Sami Virpioja. 2013. Learning a Subword Vocabulary Based on Unigram Likelihood. In *Proceedings of the IEEE 2013 Workshop on Automatic Speech Recognition and Understanding*, Olomouc, Czech Republic, December.

Ali Yazgan and Murat Saraçlar. 2004. Hybrid Language Models for Out of Vocabulary Word Detection in Large Vocabulary Conversational Speech Recognition. In *Proceedings of the 2004 IEEE International Conference on Acoustics, Speech and Signal Processing (ICASSP)*, volume 1, pages I–745–8.

Detecting Mild Cognitive Impairment
by Exploiting Linguistic Information from Transcripts

Veronika Vincze[1,2], Gábor Gosztolya[1,2], László Tóth[1], Ildikó Hoffmann[3,4],

Gréta Szatlóczki[5], Zoltán Bánréti[4], Magdolna Pákáski[5] and **János Kálmán[5]**

[1] MTA-SZTE Research Group for Artificial Intelligence
[2] University of Szeged, Institute of Informatics
[3] University of Szeged, Department of Linguistics
[4] Research Institute of Linguistics, Hungarian Academy of Sciences
[5] University of Szeged, Department of Psychiatry
`vinczev@inf.u-szeged.hu`

Abstract

Here we seek to automatically identify Hungarian patients suffering from mild cognitive impairment (MCI) based on linguistic features collected from their speech transcripts. Our system uses machine learning techniques and is based on several linguistic features like characteristics of spontaneous speech as well as features exploiting morphological and syntactic parsing. Our results suggest that it is primarily morphological and speech-based features that help distinguish MCI patients from healthy controls.

1 Background

Mild cognitive impairment (MCI) is a heterogeneous set of symptoms that are essential in the early detection of Alzheimer's Disease (AD) (Negash et al., 2007). Symptoms such as language dysfunctions may occur even nine years before the actual diagnosis (APA, 2000). Thus, the language use of the patient may often indicate MCI well before the clinical diagnosis of dementia.

MCI is known to influence the (spontaneous) speech of the patient via three main aspects. First, verbal fluency declines, which results in longer hesitations and a lower speech rate (Roark et al., 2011). Second, the lexical frequency of words and part-of-speech tags may also change significantly as the patient has problems with finding words (Croot et al., 2000). Third, the emotional responsiveness of the patient was also observed to change in many cases (Lopez-de Ipiña et al., 2015).

For many patients, MCI is never recognized as in the early stage of the disease it is not trivial even for experts to detect cognitive impairment: according to Boise et al. (2004), up to 50% of MCI

patients are never diagnosed with MCI. Although there are well known tests such as the Mini Mental Test, they are usually not sensitive enough to reliably filter out MCI in its early stage. Tests on linguistic memory prove more efficient in detecting MCI, but they tend to yield a relatively high number of false positive diagnoses (Roark et al., 2011).

Although language abilities are impaired from an early stage of the disease, evaluating the language capacities of the patients has only received marginal attention when diagnosing AD (Bayles, 1982). However, if diagnosed early, a proper medical treatment may delay the occurrence of other (more severe) symptoms of dementia to the latest extent possible (Kálmán et al., 2013).

Here we seek to automatically identify Hungarian patients suffering from mild cognitive impairment based on their speech transcripts. Our system uses machine learning techniques and is based on several features like linguistic characteristics of spontaneous speech as well as features exploiting morphological and syntactic parsing.

Recently, several studies have reported results on identifying different types of dementia with NLP and speech recognition techniques. For instance, automatic speech recognition tools were employed in detecting aphasia (Fraser et al., 2013b; Fraser et al., 2014; Fraser et al., 2013a) and mild cognitive impairment (Lehr et al., 2012), and Alzheimer's Disease (Baldas et al., 2010; Satt et al., 2014). Jarrold et al. (2014) distinguished four types of dementia on the basis of spontaneous speech samples. Lexical analysis of spontaneous speech may also indicate different types of dementia (Bucks et al., 2000; Holmes and Singh, 1996) and may be exploited in the automatic detection of patients suffering from dementia (Thomas et al.,

Proceedings of the 54th Annual Meeting of the Association for Computational Linguistics, pages 181–187,
Berlin, Germany, August 7-12, 2016. ©2016 Association for Computational Linguistics

2005). As for analyzing written language, changes in the writing style of people may also refer to dementia (Garrard et al., 2005; Hirst and Wei Feng, 2012; Le et al., 2011).

Concerning the automatic detection of MCI in Hungarian subjects, Tóth et al. (2015) experimented with speech recognition techniques. However, to the best of our knowledge, this is the first attempt to identify MCI on the basis of written texts, i.e. speech transcripts for Hungarian.

In the long run, we would like to develop a system that can automatically detect linguistic symptoms of MCI in its early stage, so that the person can get medical treatment as early as possible. It should be noted, however, that our goal cannot be an official diagnosis as diagnosing patients requires medical experience. All we can do is implement a test supported by methods used in artificial intelligence, which indicates whether the patient is at risk and if so, s/he can turn to medical experts who will provide the clinical diagnosis.

2 Data

In our experiments[1], two short animated films were presented to the patients at the memory ambulance of the University of Szeged. Patients were asked to talk about the first film then about their previous day, and lastly, about the second film. Their speech productions were recorded and transcribed by linguists, who explicitly marked speech phenomena like hesitations and pauses in the transcripts. These transcripts formed the basis of our experiments, i.e. we exploited only written information.

All of our 84 subjects were native speakers of Hungarian, a morphologically rich language. For each person, a clinical diagnosis was at our disposal, i.e. it was clinically proved whether the patient suffers from MCI or not. On the basis of these data, subjects were classified as either MCI patient or healthy control at the university memorial. Table 1 shows data on the subjects' gender and diagnosis while Table 2 shows the mean values for age and education (in terms of years attended at school).

Speech transcripts reflect several characteristics of spontaneous speech. On the one hand, they contain several forms of hesitations and silent pauses,

	MCI	Control	Total
Male	16	13	29
Female	32	23	55
Total	48	36	84

Table 1: Subjects' gender and diagnosis.

	MCI	Control	Significance
age	73.08	69.28	0.0124
education	11.42	12.47	

Table 2: Mean values of demographic features and level of statistical significance in terms of p-value.

which are also marked in the transcripts, on the other hand, they abound in phenomena typical of spontaneous Hungarian speech such as phonological deletion (*mer* instead of the standard form *mert* "because" or *ement* instead of the standard form *elment* "(he) left") and lengthening (*utánna* instead of the standard form *utána* "then"). There are duplications (*ez ezt* "this this-ACC") and neologisms created by the speaker (*feltkáva*, which probably means *főtt kávé* "boiled coffee").

Fillers also deserve special attention when studying transcripts. Besides hesitations, we treated words and phrases referring to some kind of uncertainty together with indefinite pronouns as fillers such as *ilyen* "such", *olyan* "such", *izé* "thing, gadget", *és aztán* "and then", *valamilyen* "some kind of", *valahogy* "somehow", *valamerre* "somewhere"[2]. Thus, MCI patients often seem to substitute content words with fillers or indefinite pronouns, moreover, they also appear to use lots of paraphrases, which also indicate uncertainty just like *egy ilyen bagolyszerűség* a such owl-likeness "something similar to an owl" or *az olyan délelőtt volt* that such morning was "that happened some time in the morning".

3 Experiments

In order to determine the status of the subjects, we experimented with machine learning tools. The task was regarded as binary classification, i.e. subjects were classified as either an MCI patient or a healthy control, on the basis of a feature set derived from their transcripts.

At first, transcripts were morphologically and syntactically analysed with magyarlanc, a linguistic preprocessing toolkit developed for Hungarian

---

[2] This words seem to have a lot in common with weasel and hedge words, which refer to uncertainty (Vincze, 2013).

(Zsibrita et al., 2013). For classification, we exploited morphological, syntactic and semantic features extracted from the output of magyarlanc.

Each person was asked to recall three different stories. As MCI is strongly related to memory deficit, we believe that the order of the tasks might also influence performance, hence we opted for processing each transcript separately. Thus, for each person, features to be discussed below were calculated separately for the three transcripts and all of them were exploited in the system.

3.1 Feature set

In our experiments, we employed features of spontaneous speech and morphological and semantic features derived from the transcripts and their automatic linguistic analyses. When defining our features, we took into account the fact that the speech of MCI patients may contain more pauses and hesitations than that of healthy controls (Tóth et al., 2015) and they are also supposed to have a restricted vocabulary due to cognitive deficit, which may affect the choice of words and the frequency of parts of speech (Croot et al., 2000) and might even yield neologisms. We also made use of demographic features that were at our disposal.

Our feature set contained the following features:

Spontaneous speech based features:

number of filled and silent pauses; number and rate of hesitations compared to the number of tokens; number of pauses that follow an article and precede content words as this might reflect that MCI patients may have difficulties with finding the appropriate content words; number of lengthened sounds (which we considered as a special form of hesitation).

Morphological features:

number of tokens and words; number and rate of distinct lemmas; number of punctuation marks; number and rate of nouns, verbs, adjectives, pronouns and conjunctions; number of first person singular verbs as it might also be indicative how often the patient reflects to him/herself; number and rate of unanalyzed words, i.e. those with an "unknown" POS tag, which might indicate neologisms created by the speaker on the spot.

Semantic features:

number and rate of fillers and uncertain words compared to the number of all tokens; number and rate of words/phrases related to memory activity (e.g. *nem emlékszem* not remember-1SG "I

can't remember") as they directly signal problems with memory and recall; number of negation words; number and rate of content words and function words; number of thematic words related to the content of the films, based on manually constructed lists.

Demographic features:

gender; age; education.

The mean values for each feature are reported in Table 3.

3.2 Statistical analysis of features

In order to reveal which features can most effectively distinguish healthy controls from MCI patients, we carried out a statistical analysis of the data (t-tests for each feature and transcript). For most of the features, significant differences were found between the two groups – p-values are listed in Table 3. The age of the patients also indicates significant differences: people who were at least 71 years old were more probable to suffer from MCI than those who were younger at the time of the experiment (p = 0.0124).

According to the data, each group of features has a significant effect in distinguishing controls and MCI patients. It is shown that it is mostly the second transcript (the one including the narratives about the subjects' previous days) where significant differences may be found among MCI patients and the control group. However, significant differences exist for the other two types of texts as well.

3.3 Machine learning experiments

To automatically identify MCI patients, we exploited machine learning techniques, i.e. support vector machines (SVM) (Cortes and Vapnik, 1995) with the default settings of Weka (Hall et al., 2009) and due to the small size of the dataset, we applied leave-one-out cross validation. As a baseline, majority labeling was used. For the evaluation, the accuracy, precision, recall and F-measure metrics were utilized.

In order to examine the effect of certain groups of features, we carried out an ablation study, i.e. we retrained the system without making use of one specific group of features. The results and differences are shown in Table 4.

	T1		T2		T3		Significance		
Feature	MCI	control	MCI	control	MCI	control	T1	T2	T3
token #	141.46	126.31	209.40	129.72	124.21	121.33		0.0017	
sentence #	8.38	8.50	13.42	10.22	8.08	8.11			
token %	22.40	18.42	20.01	16.04	20.19	19.25		0.0015	
word #	115.54	101.53	168.65	101.39	100.27	99.36			
lemma #	68.40	64.31	101.19	70.86	61.85	61.50		0.0017	
lemma %	0.51	0.54	0.54	0.59	0.53	0.53		0.0214	
verb #	21.71	21.31	36.63	24.11	19.56	19.97		0.0033	
verb %	0.19	0.21	0.23	0.25	0.20	0.21	0.0009		
noun #	23.98	25.42	33.23	23.00	21.69	21.97		0.0149	
noun %	0.21	0.25	0.19	0.24	0.22	0.22	0.0004	0.0001	
adjective #	6.13	3.75	9.50	5.47	4.77	5.50	0.0068	0.0051	
adjective %	0.05	0.04	0.06	0.05	0.04	0.05	0.0067	0.0259	
pronoun #	14.29	10.11	15.85	7.67	14.21	13.25	0.0082	0.0001	
pronoun %	0.12	0.10	0.09	0.08	0.14	0.13	0.0053	0.0227	
conjunction #	12.69	9.53	18.19	8.72	10.81	10.14	0.0345	0.0009	
conjunction %	0.10	0.09	0.10	0.08	0.10	0.10		0.0417	
Sg1 verb #	3.42	2.25	18.94	13.36	2.63	2.64	0.0341	0.0224	
punctuation #	25.92	24.78	40.75	28.33	23.94	21.97		0.0062	
unknown word #	0.31	0.19	0.31	0.11	0.08	0.08			
unknown word %	0.21	0.25	0.12	0.10	0.07	0.07			
filled pause #	3.65	2.44	3.92	1.56	2.35	1.44		0.0319	
pause #	12.63	9.11	19.77	9.89	11.15	7.28		0.0008	0.0191
pause after article #	1.40	1.08	1.23	0.72	1.29	0.81			0.0449
lengthened sound #	24.35	20.39	35.44	19.89	19.94	18.22		0.0008	
hesitation #	17.40	12.39	25.92	12.25	14.71	9.25	0.0362	0.0007	0.0047
hesitation %	12.93	9.32	12.67	10.19	12.06	7.55	0.0216		0.0010
uncertain word #	6.44	4.83	7.48	2.81	6.23	5.89		0.0003	
uncertain word %	4.36	3.69	3.15	2.07	4.89	4.89		0.0087	
memory word #	1.23	0.69	0.54	0.17	0.96	1.14	0.0211	0.0166	
memory word %	0.93	0.56	0.28	0.12	0.72	0.83			
film word 1	10.56	12.92	0.21	0.14	4.02	4.75	0.0325		
film word 2	5.75	5.69	0.33	0.28	9.10	11.06			0.0291
content word %	0.60	0.63	0.69	0.72	0.60	0.61	0.0441	0.0042	
function word %	0.39	0.37	0.31	0.28	0.40	0.39	0.0342	0.0041	
negation #	2.42	1.39	3.50	1.47	2.13	2.17	0.0305	0.0034	

Table 3: Mean values of features and level of statistical significance in terms of p-value. #: number, %:ratio, T: transcript.

Features	MCI			Control			Total			
	P	R	F	P	R	F	P	R	F	%
all included	72.0	75.0	73.5	64.7	61.1	62.9	68.9	69.0	68.9	69.1
w/o semantic	75.0	81.3	78.0	71.9	63.9	67.6	73.7	73.8	73.6	73.8
	+3.0	+6.3	+4.5	+7.2	+2.8	+4.7	+4.8	+4.8	+4.7	+4.7
w/o demographic	70.0	72.9	71.4	61.8	58.3	60.0	66.5	66.7	66.5	66.7
	-2.0	-2.1	-2.1	-2.9	-2.8	-2.9	-2.4	-2.3	-2.4	-2.4
w/o speech-based	70.8	70.8	70.8	61.1	61.1	61.1	66.7	66.7	66.7	66.7
	-1.2	-4.2	-2.7	-3.6	0.0	-1.8	-2.2	-2.3	-2.2	-2.4
w/o morphological	72.3	70.8	71.6	62.2	63.9	63.0	68.0	67.9	67.9	67.9
	+0.3	-4.2	-1.9	-2.5	+2.8	+0.1	-0.9	-1.1	-1.0	-1.2
only significant	81.4	72.9	76.9	68.3	77.8	72.7	75.8	75.0	75.1	75.0
	+9.4	-2.1	+3.4	+3.6	+16.7	+9.8	+6.9	+6.0	+6.2	+5.9

Table 4: Results and differences. MCI: mild cognitive impairment, P: precision, R: recall, F: F-measure, %: accuracy.

4 Results and Discussion

Using all the features, our system managed to achieve an accuracy score of 69.1%, that is, 58 out of the 84 patients were correctly diagnosed. 12 patients were falsely diagnosed as healthy and 14 controls were falsely labeled as MCI patients. Our results outperformed the baseline (57.14% in terms of accuracy). The system got a high recall value for MCI patients (75.0) but a lower one for controls (61.1), which is encouraging in the light of the fact that our main goal is to identify the widest possible range of potential MCI patients, who can turn to clinical experts to find out what their clinical diagnosis is.

We also experimented with using only features that displayed statistically significant differences among controls and MCI patients (see Table 3). Somewhat surprisingly, an accuracy of 75% could be achieved in this way, which indicates that some of our original features are superfluous and just confused the system, and this result needs further investigation.

An ablation study was also carried out to analyze the added value of each feature group. Speech-based, demographic and morphological features unequivocally contributed to performance. However, the effect of semantic features seems less obvious as they harm performance taken as a whole but some individual semantic features are useful for the system, as shown by the results achieved with just using significant features.

When investigating the errors made by our system, we found that MCI patients that spoke only a few short sentences were often classified as healthy controls. They had a lower number and rate of hesitations and pauses, moreover, their vocabulary contained fewer fillers and uncertain words, and these features resemble those typical of healthy controls. What is more, healthy subjects who talked more also hesitated more, which might be indicative of MCI. Furthermore, their use of pronouns and conjunctions was also more similar to those of MCI patients, hence the system falsely predicted a positive diagnosis for them.

Due to the specific characteristics of the data and the complexity of data collection – which requires clinical experiments – our dataset can be expanded only step by step. However, we found statistically significant differences among MCI patients and healthy controls concerning several linguistic and speech-based features even in our small dataset, which may be beneficial for our future experiments and might be also exploited by those who study spontaneous speech.

5 Conclusions

In this study, we introduced our system that automatically detects Hungarian patients suffering from mild cognitive impairment on the basis of their speech transcripts. The system is based on features derived from morphological and syntactic analysis as well as characteristics of spontaneous speech. Both statistical and machine learning results revealed that morphological and spontaneous speech-based features have an essential role in distinguishing MCI patients from healthy controls.

In the future, we would like to extend our dataset with new transcripts. Also, we intend to improve our machine learning system and investigate the role of semantic features. Lastly, we would like to integrate features from automatic speech recognition into our system so that tools from both speech technology and natural language processing can contribute to the automatic detection of mild cognitive impairment.

References

APA. 2000. *DSM-IV-TR*. American Psychiatric Association.

Vassilis Baldas, Charalampos Lampiris, Christos N. Capsalis, and Dimitrios Koutsouris. 2010. Early Diagnosis of Alzheimer's Type Dementia Using Continuous Speech Recognition. In James C. Lin and Konstantina S. Nikita, editors, *MobiHealth*, volume 55 of *Lecture Notes of the Institute for Computer Sciences, Social Informatics and Telecommunications Engineering*, pages 105–110. Springer.

Kathryn A Bayles. 1982. Language function in senile dementia. *Brain and Language*, 16(2):265–280.

Linda Boise, Margaret B Neal, and Jeffrey Kaye. 2004. Dementia assessment in primary care: Results from a study in three managed care systems. *The Journals of Gerontology Series A: Biological Sciences and Medical Sciences*, 59(6):M621–M626.

R.S. Bucks, S. Singh, J.M. Cuerden, and G.K. Wilcock. 2000. Analysis of spontaneous, conversational speech in dementia of alzheimer type: evaluation of an objective technique for analysing lexical performance. *Aphasiology*, 14(1):71–91.

Corinna Cortes and Vladimir Vapnik. 1995. Support-vector networks. *Machine Learning*, 20(3):273–297.

Karen Croot, John R. Hodges, John Xuereb, and Karalyn Patterson. 2000. Phonological and articulatory impairment in alzheimer's disease: A case series. *Brain and Language*, 75(2):277 – 309.

Kathleen Fraser, Frank Rudzicz, Naida Graham, and Elizabeth Rochon. 2013a. Automatic speech recognition in the diagnosis of primary progressive aphasia. *Proceedings of the Fourth Workshop on Speech and Language Processing for Assistive Technologies*, pages 47–54.

Kathleen C. Fraser, Frank Rudzicz, and Elizabeth Rochon. 2013b. Using text and acoustic features to diagnose progressive aphasia and its subtypes. In Frdric Bimbot, Christophe Cerisara, Ccile Fougeron, Guillaume Gravier, Lori Lamel, Franois Pellegrino, and Pascal Perrier, editors, *INTERSPEECH*, pages 2177–2181. ISCA.

Kathleen C Fraser, Jed A Meltzer, Naida L Graham, Carol Leonard, Graeme Hirst, Sandra E Black, and Elizabeth Rochon. 2014. Automated classification of primary progressive aphasia subtypes from narrative speech transcripts. *Cortex*, 55:43–60.

Peter Garrard, Lisa M Maloney, John R Hodges, and Karalyn Patterson. 2005. The effects of very early Alzheimer's disease on the characteristics of writing by a renowned author. *Brain*, 128(2):250–260.

Mark Hall, Eibe Frank, Geoffrey Holmes, Bernhard Pfahringer, Peter Reutemann, and Ian H. Witten. 2009. The WEKA data mining software: an update. *SIGKDD Explorations*, 11(1):10–18.

Graeme Hirst and Vanessa Wei Feng. 2012. Changes in style in authors with Alzheimer's disease. *English Studies*, 93(3):357–370.

David I. Holmes and Sameer Singh. 1996. A stylometric analysis of conversational speech of aphasic patients. *Literary and Linguistic Computing*, 11:133–140.

William Jarrold, Bart Peintner, David Wilkins, Dimitra Vergryi, Colleen Richey, Maria L. Gorno-Tempini, and Jennifer Ogar. 2014. Aided diagnosis of dementia type through computer-based analysis of spontaneous speech. In *Proceedings of the Workshop on Computational Linguistics and Clinical Psychology: From Linguistic Signal to Clinical Reality*, pages 27–37, Baltimore, Maryland, USA, June. Association for Computational Linguistics.

János Kálmán, Magdolna Pákáski, Ildikó Hoffmann, Gergely Drótos, Gyöngyi Darvas, Krisztina Boda, Tamás Bencsik, Aliz Gyimesi, Zsófia Gulyás, Magdolna Bálint, Gréta Szatlóczki, and Edina Papp. 2013. Early mental test – developing a screening test for mild cognitive impairment. *Ideggyógyászati szemle*, 66(1-2):43–52.

Xuan Le, Ian Lancashire, Graeme Hirst, and Regina Jokel. 2011. Longitudinal detection of dementia through lexical and syntactic changes in writing: a case study of three British novelists. *Literary and Linguistic Computing*, 26(4):435–461.

Maider Lehr, Emily Tucker Prud'hommeaux, Izhak Shafran, and Brian Roark. 2012. Fully automated neuropsychological assessment for detecting mild cognitive impairment. In *INTERSPEECH*, pages 1039–1042. ISCA.

Karmele Lopez-de Ipiña, Jesús B Alonso, Jordi Solé-Casals, Nora Barroso, Patricia Henriquez, Marcos Faundez-Zanuy, Carlos M Travieso, Miriam Ecay-Torres, Pablo Martinez-Lage, and Harkaitz Eguiraun. 2015. On automatic diagnosis of alzheimers disease based on spontaneous speech analysis and emotional temperature. *Cognitive Computation*, 7(1):44–55.

Selam Negash, Lindsay E Petersen, Yonas E Geda, David S Knopman, Bradley F Boeve, Glenn E Smith, Robert J Ivnik, Darlene V Howard, James H Howard Jr, and Ronald C Petersen. 2007. Effects of ApoE genotype and Mild Cognitive Impairment on implicit learning. *Neurobiology of Aging*, 28(6):885–893.

Brian Roark, Margaret Mitchell, John-Paul Hosom, Kristy Hollingshead, and Jeffrey Kaye. 2011. Spoken language derived measures for detecting mild cognitive impairment. *IEEE Transactions on Audio, Speech, and Language Processing*, 19(7):2081–2090.

Aharon Satt, Ron Hoory, Alexandra König, Pauline Aalten, and Philippe H. Robert. 2014. Speech-based automatic and robust detection of very early dementia. In *15th Annual Conference of the International Speech Communication Association*, pages 2538–2542.

Calvin Thomas, Vlado Kešelj, Nick Cercone, Kenneth Rockwood, and Elissa Asp. 2005. Automatic detection and rating of dementia of Alzheimer type through lexical analysis of spontaneous speech. In *Mechatronics and Automation, 2005 IEEE International Conference*, volume 3, pages 1569–1574. IEEE.

László Tóth, Gábor Gosztolya, Veronika Vincze, Ildikó Hoffmann, Gréta Szatlóczki, Edit Biró, Fruzsina Zsura, Magdolna Pákáski, and János Kálmán. 2015. Automatic detection of mild cognitive impairment from spontaneous speech using ASR. In *16th Annual Conference of the International Speech Communication Association*, pages 2694–2698.

Veronika Vincze. 2013. Weasels, Hedges and Peacocks: Discourse-level Uncertainty in Wikipedia Articles. In *Proceedings of the Sixth International Joint Conference on Natural Language Processing*, pages 383–391, Nagoya, Japan, October. Asian Federation of Natural Language Processing.

János Zsibrita, Veronika Vincze, and Richárd Farkas. 2013. magyarlanc: A toolkit for morphological and dependency parsing of Hungarian. In *Proceedings of RANLP*, pages 763–771.

Multi-Modal Representations for Improved Bilingual Lexicon Learning

Ivan Vulić
Language Technology Lab, DTAL
University of Cambridge
iv250@cam.ac.uk

Douwe Kiela
Computer Laboratory
University of Cambridge
dk427@cam.ac.uk

Stephen Clark
Computer Laboratory
University of Cambridge
sc609@cam.ac.uk

Marie-Francine Moens
Department of Computer Science
KU Leuven
sien.moens@cs.kuleuven.be

Abstract

Recent work has revealed the potential of using visual representations for bilingual lexicon learning (BLL). Such image-based BLL methods, however, still fall short of linguistic approaches. In this paper, we propose a simple yet effective multi-modal approach that learns bilingual semantic representations that fuse linguistic and visual input. These new bilingual multi-modal embeddings display significant performance gains in the BLL task for three language pairs on two benchmarking test sets, outperforming linguistic-only BLL models using three different types of state-of-the-art bilingual word embeddings, as well as visual-only BLL models.

1 Introduction

Bilingual lexicon learning (BLL) is the task of finding words that share a common meaning across different languages. It plays an important role in a variety of fundamental tasks in IR and NLP, e.g. cross-lingual information retrieval and statistical machine translation. The majority of current BLL models aim to learn lexicons from comparable data. These approaches work by (1) mapping language pairs to a *shared cross-lingual vector space (SCLVS)* such that words are close when they have similar meanings; and (2) extracting close lexical items from the induced SCLVS. Bilingual word embedding (BWE) induced models currently hold the state-of-the-art on BLL (Hermann and Blunsom, 2014; Gouws et al., 2015; Vulić and Moens, 2016).

Although methods for learning SCLVSs are predominantly text-based, this space need not be linguistic in nature: Bergsma and van Durme (2011) and Kiela et al. (2015) used labeled images from the Web to learn bilingual lexicons based on *visual* features, with features derived from deep convolutional neural networks (CNNs) leading to the best results (Kiela et al., 2015). However, vision-based BLL does not yet perform at the same level as state-of-the-art linguistic models. Here, we unify the strengths of both approaches into one single multi-modal vision-language SCLVS.

It has been found in multi-modal semantics that linguistic and visual representations are often complementary in terms of the information they encode (Deselaers and Ferrari, 2011; Bruni et al., 2014; Silberer and Lapata, 2014). This is the first work to test the effectiveness of the multi-modal approach in a BLL setting. Our contributions are: We introduce bilingual multi-modal semantic spaces that merge linguistic and visual components to obtain semantically-enriched bilingual multi-modal word representations. These representations display significant improvements for three language pairs on two benchmarking BLL test sets in comparison to three different bilingual linguistic representations (Mikolov et al., 2013; Gouws et al., 2015; Vulić and Moens, 2016), as well as over the uni-modal visual representations from Kiela et al. (2015).

We also propose a weighting technique based on image dispersion (Kiela et al., 2014) that governs the influence of visual information in fused representations, and show that this technique leads to robust multi-modal models which do not require fine tuning of the fusion parameter.

2 Methodology

2.1 Linguistic Representations

We use three representative linguistic BWE models. Given a source and target vocabulary V^S and V^T, BWE models learn a representation of each word $w \in V^S \cup V^T$ as a real-valued vec-

Proceedings of the 54th Annual Meeting of the Association for Computational Linguistics, pages 188–194,
Berlin, Germany, August 7-12, 2016. ©2016 Association for Computational Linguistics

tor: $\mathbf{w}_{ling} = [f_1^{ling}, \ldots, f_{d_l}^{ling}]$, where $f_k^{ling} \in \mathbb{R}$ is the value of the k-th cross-lingual feature for w. Similarity between $w, v \in V^S \cup V^T$ is computed through a similarity function (SF), $sim_{ling}(w, v) = SF(\mathbf{w}_{ling}, \mathbf{v}_{ling})$, e.g., cosine.

Type 1: M-EMB This type of BWE induction model assumes the following setup for learning the SCLVS (Mikolov et al., 2013; Faruqui and Dyer, 2014; Dinu et al., 2015; Lazaridou et al., 2015a): First, two monolingual spaces, $\mathbb{R}^{d_S}$ and $\mathbb{R}^{d_T}$, are induced separately in each language using a standard monolingual embedding model. The bilingual signal is provided in the form of word translation pairs (x_i, y_i), where $x_i \in V^S$, $y_i \in V^T$, and $\mathbf{x_i} \in \mathbb{R}^{d_S}$, $\mathbf{y_i} \in \mathbb{R}^{d_T}$. Training is cast as a multivariate regression problem: it implies learning a function that maps the source language vectors to their corresponding target language vectors. A standard approach (Mikolov et al., 2013; Dinu et al., 2015) is to assume a linear map $\mathbf{W} \in \mathbb{R}^{d_S \times d_T}$, which is learned through an L_2-regularized least-squares error objective. Any previously unseen source language word vector $\mathbf{x_u}$ may be mapped into the target embedding space $\mathbb{R}^{d_T}$ as $\mathbf{Wx_u}$. After mapping all vectors $\mathbf{x}$, $x \in V^S$, the target space $\mathbb{R}^{d_T}$ serves as a SCLVS.

Type 2: G-EMB Another collection of BWE induction models optimizes two monolingual objectives *jointly*, with the cross-lingual objective acting as a cross-lingual regularizer during training (Gouws et al., 2015; Soyer et al., 2015). In a simplified formulation (Luong et al., 2015), the objective is: $\gamma(Mono_S + Mono_T) + \delta Bi$. The monolingual objectives $Mono_S$ and $Mono_T$ ensure that similar words in each language are assigned similar embeddings and aim to capture the semantic structure of each language, whereas the cross-lingual objective Bi ensures that similar words across languages are assigned similar embeddings, and ties the two monolingual spaces together into a SCLVS. Parameters γ and δ govern the influence of the monolingual and bilingual components.[1] The bilingual signal used as the cross-lingual regularizer during the joint training is obtained from sentence-aligned parallel data. We opt for the Bil-

BOWA model from Gouws et al. (2015) as the representative model to be included in the comparisons, due to its solid performance and robustness in the BLL task (Luong et al., 2015), its reduced complexity reflected in fast computations on massive datasets and its public availability.[2]

Type 3: V-EMB The third set of models requires a different bilingual signal to induce a SCLVS: *document alignments*. Vulić and Moens (2016) created a collection of pseudo-bilingual documents by merging every pair of aligned documents in the data, in a way that preserves important local information – which words appeared next to which other words (in the same language), and which words appeared in the same region of the document (in different languages). This collection was then used to train word embeddings with monolingual skip-gram with negative sampling using word2vec. With pseudo-bilingual documents, the "context" of a word is redefined as a mixture of neighboring words (in the original language) and words that appeared in the same region of the document (in the foreign language). Bilingual contexts for each word in each pseudo-bilingual document steer the final model towards constructing a SCLVS.

2.2 Visual Representations

Only a few studies have tried to make use of the intuition that words in different languages denoting the same concepts are similarly grounded in the perceptual system (bicycles resemble each other irrespective of whether we call them *bicyle*, *vélo*, *fiets* or *Fahrrad*, see Fig. 1) (Bergsma and van Durme, 2011; Kiela et al., 2015). Although the idea is promising, such visual methods are still limited in comparison with linguistic ones, especially for more abstract concepts (Kiela et al., 2015). Recent findings in multi-modal semantics suggest that visual representations encode pieces of semantic information complementary to linguistic information derived from text (Deselaers and Ferrari, 2011; Silberer and Lapata, 2014).

We compute visual representations in a similar fashion to Kiela et al. (2015): For each word we retrieve n images from Google image search (see Fig. 1), and for each image we extract the pre-softmax layer of an AlexNet (Krizhevsky et al., 2012) that has been pre-trained on the ImageNet

---

[1] Setting $\gamma = 0$ reduces the model to the bilingual models trained solely on parallel data (Hermann and Blunsom, 2014; Chandar et al., 2014). $\gamma = 1$ results in the models from Gouws et al. (2015) and Soyer et al. (2015). Although they use the same data sources, all G-EMB models differ in the choice of monolingual and cross-lingual objectives.

[2] https://github.com/gouwsmeister/bilbowa

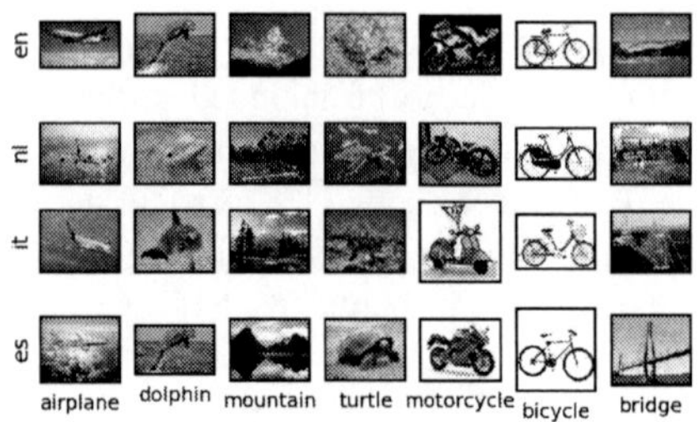

Figure 1: Example images for several languages.

classification task (Deng et al., 2009; Russakovsky et al., 2015) using Caffe (Jia et al., 2014).

Each image is thus represented as a 4096-dimensional feature vector extracted from a convolutional neural network (CNN). We use two methods for computing visual similarity: (1) CNN-MAX produces a single visual vector by taking the pointwise maximum across the n image vector representations from the image set. The representation of each word $w \in V^S \cup V^T$ in a visual SCLVS is now a real-valued vector $\mathbf{w}_{vis} = [f_1^{vis}, \ldots, f_{d_v}^{vis}]$, where $f_k^{vis} \in \mathbb{R}$ denotes the score for the k-th visual cross-lingual feature for w within a d_v-dimensional visual SCLVS ($d_v = 4096$). As before, similarity between two words $w, v \in V^S \cup V^T$ is computed by applying a similarity function on their representations in the visual SCLVS: $sim_{vis}(w, v) = SF(\mathbf{w}_{vis}, \mathbf{v}_{vis})$, e.g. cosine. (2) CNN-AVGMAX: An alternative strategy, introduced by Bergsma and van Durme (2011), is to consider the similarities between individual images from the two sets and take the average of the maximum similarity scores as the final similarity $sim_{vis}(w, v)$.

2.3 Multi-Modal Representations

We experiment with two ways of fusing information stemming from the linguistic and visual modalities. Following recent work in multi-modal semantics (Bruni et al., 2014; Kiela and Bottou, 2014), we construct representations by concatenating the centered and L_2-normalized linguistic and visual feature vectors:

$$\mathbf{w}_{mm} = \alpha \times \mathbf{w}_{ling} \,\|\, (1 - \alpha) \times \mathbf{w}_{vis} \qquad (1)$$

where $\|$ denotes concatenation and α is a parameter governing the contributions of each uni-modal representation. The final similarity may again be computed by applying an SF on the multi-modal representations. We call this method **Early-Fusion**. Note that it is possible only with CNN-MAX. The alternative is not to build a full multi-modal (MM) representation, but instead to combine the individual similarity scores from each uni-modal SCLVS. The similarity $sim(w, v)$ between two words w and v is:

$$\alpha \times sim_{ling}(w, v) + (1 - \alpha) \times sim_{vis}(w, v) =$$
$$= \alpha \times SF(\mathbf{w}_{ling}, \mathbf{v}_{ling}) + (1 - \alpha) \times SF(\mathbf{w}_{vis}, \mathbf{v}_{vis})$$

where α again controls for the importance of the uni-modal scores in the final combined scores. We call this method **Late-Fusion**[3].

3 Experimental Setup

Task: Bilingual Lexicon Learning Given a source language word w_s, the task is to find a target language word w_t closest to w_s in the SCLVS, and the resulting pair (w_s, w_t) is a bilingual lexicon entry. Performance is measured using the BLL standard *Top 1* accuracy (Acc_1) metric (Gaussier et al., 2004; Gouws et al., 2015).

Test Sets We work with three language pairs: English-Spanish/Dutch/Italian (EN-ES/NL/IT), and two benchmarking BLL test sets:
(1) BERGSMA500: consisting of a set of 500 ground truth noun pairs for the three language pairs, it is considered a benchmarking test set in prior work on BLL using vision (Bergsma and van Durme, 2011)[4]. Translation direction in our tests is $EN \rightarrow ES/IT/NL$.
(2) VULIC1000: constructed to measure the general performance of linguistic BLL models from comparable Wikipedia data (Vulić and Moens, 2013), this is considered a benchmarking test set for (linguistic) BLL models from comparable data (Vulić and Moens, 2016)[5]. It comprises $1,000$ nouns in ES, IT, and NL, along with their one-to-one ground-truth word translations in EN compiled semi-automatically. Translation direction is $ES/IT/NL \rightarrow EN$.

Training Data and Setup We used standard training data and suggested settings to learn M/G/V-EMB model representations. M-EMB and G-EMB were trained on the full cleaned and tokenized Wikipedias from the Polyglot website (Al-Rfou et al., 2013). V-EMB was trained on the full tokenized document-aligned Wikipedias from

---

[3]Under the assumption of having the centered and L_2-normalized feature vectors, and *cos* as SF, Early-Fusion may be transformed into Late-Fusion with adapted weighting:
$\alpha^2 \times cos(\mathbf{w}_{ling}, \mathbf{v}_{ling}) + (1 - \alpha)^2 \times cos(\mathbf{w}_{vis}, \mathbf{v}_{vis})$
[4]http://www.clsp.jhu.edu/~sbergsma/LexImg/
[5]http://www.cl.cam.ac.uk/~dk427/bli.html

Pair:	B: EN→ES|V: ES→EN			B: EN→IT|V: IT→EN			B: EN→NL|V: NL→EN		
Models	M-EMB	G-EMB	V-EMB	M-EMB	G-EMB	V-EMB	M-EMB	G-EMB	V-EMB
Linguistic									
$d = 300$	0.71 *0.77*	0.60 *0.73*	0.68 *0.82*	0.77 *0.76*	0.63 *0.71*	0.75 *0.79*	0.77 *0.76*	0.59 *0.75*	0.74 *0.79*
Visual									
CNN-Max	0.51 *0.35*	0.51 *0.35*	0.51 *0.35*	0.54 *0.22*	0.54 *0.22*	0.54 *0.22*	0.56 *0.33*	0.56 *0.33*	0.56 *0.33*
CNN-AvgMax	0.55 *0.38*	0.54 *0.38*	0.54 *0.38*	0.56 *0.25*	0.56 *0.25*	0.56 *0.25*	0.60 *0.34*	0.60 *0.34*	0.60 *0.34*
Multi-modal with global α									
Max-E-0.5	0.76 *0.79*	0.66 ***0.79***	0.71 *0.83*	0.83 *0.75*	0.72 *0.70*	0.80 *0.80*	0.85 *0.80*	0.69 *0.78*	0.80 *0.81*
Max-E-0.7	0.75 *0.80*	0.62 *0.76*	0.70 ***0.85***	0.81 *0.77*	0.66 *0.73*	0.78 *0.82*	0.84 *0.80*	0.61 *0.79*	0.80 *0.82*
Max-L-0.7	0.76 *0.80*	0.64 *0.78*	0.71 ***0.85***	0.82 *0.77*	0.69 *0.73*	0.80 *0.82*	0.85 *0.82*	0.64 *0.79*	0.81 ***0.83***
Avg-L-0.5	**0.77** *0.78*	**0.68** *0.79*	**0.73** *0.83*	**0.84** *0.77*	**0.75** *0.70*	**0.81** *0.79*	**0.86** *0.80*	**0.76** *0.78*	**0.83** *0.81*
Avg-L-0.7	**0.77** *0.81*	0.66 *0.79*	0.72 ***0.85***	0.83 ***0.78***	0.72 ***0.75***	0.80 ***0.83***	**0.86** ***0.83***	0.70 ***0.81***	0.81 ***0.83***
Multi-modal with image dispersion (ID) weighting									
Max-E-ID	0.76 *0.80*	0.66 *0.78*	0.71 *0.84*	0.81 *0.77*	0.69 *0.73*	0.80 *0.81*	0.84 *0.80*	0.64 *0.79*	0.81 *0.82*
Max-L-ID	**0.77** *0.80*	0.66 *0.78*	0.72 ***0.85***	0.82 *0.77*	0.70 *0.73*	0.80 *0.81*	0.84 *0.82*	0.65 *0.79*	0.81 *0.82*
Avg-L-ID	**0.77** ***0.81***	0.67 ***0.79***	**0.73** *0.84*	0.83 ***0.78***	0.74 *0.73*	0.80 ***0.83***	0.85 *0.82*	0.72 *0.80*	0.82 *0.82*

Table 1: Summary of the Acc_1 scores on BERGSMA500 (regular font) and VULIC1000 (*italic*) across all BLL runs. M/G/V-EMB denotes the BWE linguistic model. Other settings are in the form Y-Z-0.W: (1) Y denotes the visual metric, (2) Z denotes the fusion model: E is for Early-Fusion, L is for Late-Fusion, and (3) 0.W denotes the α value. Highest scores per column are in bold.

LinguaTools[6]. The 100K most frequent words were retained for all models.

We followed related work (Mikolov et al., 2013; Lazaridou et al., 2015a) for learning the mapping **W** in M-EMB: starting from the BNC word frequency list (Kilgarriff, 1997), the $6,318$ most frequent EN words were translated to the three other languages using Google Translate. The lists were subsequently cleaned, removing all pairs that contain IT/ES/NL words occurring in the test sets and least frequent pairs, to build the final $3 \times 5K$ training pairs. We trained two monolingual SGNS models, using SGD with a global learning rate of 0.025. For G-EMB, as in the original work (Gouws et al., 2015), the bilingual signal for the cross-lingual regularization was provided in the first 500K sentences from Europarl.v7 (Tiedemann, 2012). We used SGD with a global learning rate 0.15. For V-EMB, monolingual SGNS was trained on pseudo-bilingual documents using SGD with a global learning rate 0.025. All BWEs were trained with $d = 300$.[7] Other parameters are: 15 epochs, 15 negatives, subsampling rate $1e - 4$. We report results with two α standard values: 0.5 and 0.7 (more weight assigned to the linguistic part).

4 Results and Discussion

Table 1 summarizes Acc_1 scores, focusing on interesting comparisons across different dimen-

sions[8]. There is a marked difference in performance on BERGSMA500 and VULIC1000: visual-only BLL models on VULIC1000 perform two times worse than linguistic-only BLL models. This is easily explained by the increased abstractness of test words in VULIC1000 in comparison to BERGSMA500[9], which highlights the need for a multi-modal approach.

Multi-Modal vs. Uni-Modal The multi-modal models outperform both linguistic and visual models across all setups and combinations on BERGSMA500. On VULIC1000 multi-modal models again outperform their uni-modal components in both modalities. In the latter case, improvements are dependent on the amount of visual information included in the model, as governed by α. Since the dataset also contains highly abstract words, the inclusion of visual information may be detrimental to performance. These models outperform the uni-modal models across a wide variety of settings: they outperform the three linguistic-only BLL models that held best reported Acc_1 scores on the evaluation set (Vulić and Moens, 2016). The largest improvements are statistically significant according to McNemar's test, $p < 0.01$. We find improvements on both test sets for all three BWE types.

The relative ranking of the visual metrics intro-

---

[6]http://linguatools.org/tools/corpora/

[7]Similar trends were observed with all models and $d = 64, 500$. We also vary the window size from 4 to 16 in steps of 4, and always report the best scoring linguistic embeddings.

[8]Similar rankings of different models are also visible with more lenient Acc_{10} scores, not reported for brevity.

[9]The average image dispersion value (Kiela et al., 2014), which indicates abstractness, on VULIC1000 is 0.711 compared to 0.642 on BERGSMA500.

duced in Kiela et al. (2015) extends to the MM setting: Late-Fusion with CNN-AVGMAX is the most effective MM BLL model on average, but all other tested MM configurations also yield notable improvements.

Concreteness To measure concreteness, we use an unsupervised data-driven method, shown to closely mirror how concrete a concept is: *image dispersion (ID)* (Kiela et al., 2014). ID is defined as the average pairwise cosine distance between all the image representations/vectors $\{\mathbf{i}_1 \ldots \mathbf{i}_n\}$ in the set of images for a given word w:

$$id(w) = \frac{2}{n(n-1)} \sum_{j < k \leq n} 1 - \frac{\mathbf{i}_j \cdot \mathbf{i}_k}{|\mathbf{i}_j||\mathbf{i}_k|} \qquad (2)$$

Intuitively, more concrete words display more coherent visual representations and consequently lower ID scores (see Footnote 9 again). The lowest improvements on VULIC1000 are reported for the IT-EN language pair, which is incidentally the most abstract test set.

There is some evidence that abstract concepts are also perceptually grounded (Lakoff and Johnson, 1999), albeit in a more complex way, since abstract concepts will relate more varied situations (Barsalou and Wiemer-Hastings, 2005). Consequently, uni-modal visual representations are not powerful enough to capture all the semantic intricacies of such abstract concepts, and the linguistic components are more beneficial in such cases. This explains an improved performance with $\alpha = 0.7$, but also calls for a more intelligent decision mechanism on how much perceptual information to include in the multi-modal models. The decision should be closely related to the degree of a concept's concreteness, e.g., eq. (2).

Image Dispersion Weighting The intuition that the inclusion of visual information may lead to negative effects in MM modeling has been exploited by Kiela et al. (2014) in their work on image-dispersion filtering: Although the filtering method displays some clear benefits, its shortcoming lies in the fact that it performs a binary decision which can potentially discard valuable perceptual information for less concrete concepts. Here, we introduce a weighting scheme where the perceptual information is weighted according to its ID value. Early-Fusion is now computed as:

$$\mathbf{w}_{mm} = \alpha(id) \times \mathbf{w}_{ling} \parallel (1 - \alpha(id)) \times \mathbf{w}_{vis}$$

Late-Fusion model becomes:

$$\alpha(id) \times SF(\mathbf{w}_{ling}, \mathbf{v}_{ling}) + (1 - \alpha(id)) \times SF(\mathbf{w}_{vis}, \mathbf{v}_{vis})$$

$\alpha(id)$ denotes a weight that is proportional to the ID score of the source language word w: we opt for a simple approach and specify $\alpha(id) = id(w)$. Instead of having one global parameter α, the ID weighting adjusts the amount of information locally according to each concept's concreteness.

The results are summarised in Table 1. All multi-modal models with ID-based weighting are outperforming their uni-modal components. The ID-weighted BLL models reach (near-)optimal BLL results across a variety of language-vision combinations without any fine-tuning.

5 Conclusion

We have presented a novel approach to bilingual lexicon learning (BLL) that combines linguistic and visual representations into new bilingual multi-modal (MM) models. Two simple yet effective ways to fuse the linguistic and visual information for BLL have been described. Such MM models outperform their linguistic and visual uni-modal component models on two standard benchmarking BLL test sets for three language pairs. Comparisons with three different state-of-the-art bilingual word embedding induction models demonstrate that the gains of MM modeling are generally applicable.

As future work, we plan to analyse the ability of multi-view representation learning algorithms to yield fused multi-modal representations in bilingual settings (Lazaridou et al., 2015b; Rastogi et al., 2015; Wang et al., 2015), as well as to apply multi-modal bilingual spaces in other tasks such as zero-short learning (Frome et al., 2013) or cross-lingual MM information search and retrieval following paradigms from monolingual settings (Pereira et al., 2014; Vulić and Moens, 2015).

The inclusion of perceptual data, as this paper reveals, seems especially promising in bilingual settings (Rajendran et al., 2016; Elliott et al., 2016), since the perceptual information demonstrates the ability to transcend linguistic borders.

Acknowledgments

This work is supported by ERC Consolidator Grant LEXICAL (648909) and KU Leuven Grant PDMK/14/117. SC is supported by ERC Starting Grant DisCoTex (306920). We thank the anonymous reviewers for their helpful comments.

References

Rami Al-Rfou, Bryan Perozzi, and Steven Skiena. 2013. Polyglot: Distributed word representations for multilingual NLP. In *CoNLL*, pages 183–192.

Lawrence W. Barsalou and Katja Wiemer-Hastings. 2005. Situating abstract concepts. In D. Pecher and R. Zwaan, editors, *Grounding cognition: The role of perception and action in memory, language, and thought*, pages 129–163.

Shane Bergsma and Benjamin van Durme. 2011. Learning bilingual lexicons using the visual similarity of labeled web images. In *IJCAI*, pages 1764–1769.

Elia Bruni, Nam-Khanh Tran, and Marco Baroni. 2014. Multimodal distributional semantics. *Journal of Artiifical Intelligence Research*, 49:1–47.

Sarath A.P. Chandar, Stanislas Lauly, Hugo Larochelle, Mitesh M. Khapra, Balaraman Ravindran, Vikas C. Raykar, and Amrita Saha. 2014. An autoencoder approach to learning bilingual word representations. In *NIPS*, pages 1853–1861.

Jia Deng, Wei Dong, Richard Socher, Li-Jia Li, Kai Li, and Fei-Fei Li. 2009. ImageNet: A large-scale hierarchical image database. In *CVPR*, pages 248–255.

Thomas Deselaers and Vittorio Ferrari. 2011. Visual and semantic similarity in ImageNet. In *CVPR*, pages 1777–1784.

Georgiana Dinu, Angeliki Lazaridou, and Marco Baroni. 2015. Improving zero-shot learning by mitigating the hubness problem. In *ICLR Workshop Papers*.

D. Elliott, S. Frank, K. Sima'an, and L. Specia. 2016. Multi30K: Multilingual English-German Image Descriptions. *CoRR*, abs/1605.00459.

Manaal Faruqui and Chris Dyer. 2014. Improving vector space word representations using multilingual correlation. In *EACL*, pages 462–471.

Andrea Frome, Gregory S. Corrado, Jonathon Shlens, Samy Bengio, Jeffrey Dean, Marc'Aurelio Ranzato, and Tomas Mikolov. 2013. Devise: A deep visual-semantic embedding model. In *NIPS*, pages 2121–2129.

Éric Gaussier, Jean-Michel Renders, Irina Matveeva, Cyril Goutte, and Hervé Déjean. 2004. A geometric view on bilingual lexicon extraction from comparable corpora. In *ACL*, pages 526–533.

Stephan Gouws, Yoshua Bengio, and Greg Corrado. 2015. BilBOWA: Fast bilingual distributed representations without word alignments. In *ICML*, pages 748–756.

Karl Moritz Hermann and Phil Blunsom. 2014. Multilingual models for compositional distributed semantics. In *ACL*, pages 58–68.

Yangqing Jia, Evan Shelhamer, Jeff Donahue, Sergey Karayev, Jonathan Long, Ross B. Girshick, Sergio Guadarrama, and Trevor Darrell. 2014. Caffe: Convolutional architecture for fast feature embedding. In *ACM Multimedia*, pages 675–678.

Douwe Kiela and Léon Bottou. 2014. Learning image embeddings using convolutional neural networks for improved multi-modal semantics. In *EMNLP*, pages 36–45.

Douwe Kiela, Felix Hill, Anna Korhonen, and Stephen Clark. 2014. Improving multi-modal representations using image dispersion: Why less is sometimes more. In *ACL*, pages 835–841.

Douwe Kiela, Ivan Vulić, and Stephen Clark. 2015. Visual bilingual lexicon induction with transferred ConvNet features. In *EMNLP*, pages 148–158.

Adam Kilgarriff. 1997. Putting frequencies in the dictionary. *International Journal of Lexicography*, 10(2):135–155.

Alex Krizhevsky, Ilya Sutskever, and Geoffrey E. Hinton. 2012. ImageNet classification with deep convolutional neural networks. In *NIPS*, pages 1106–1114.

George Lakoff and Mark Johnson. 1999. *Philosophy in the flesh: The embodied mind and its challenge to Western thought*.

Angeliki Lazaridou, Georgiana Dinu, and Marco Baroni. 2015a. Hubness and pollution: Delving into cross-space mapping for zero-shot learning. In *ACL*, pages 270–280.

Angeliki Lazaridou, Nghia The Pham, and Marco Baroni. 2015b. Combining language and vision with a multimodal skip-gram model. In *NAACL-HLT*, pages 153–163.

Thang Luong, Hieu Pham, and Christopher D. Manning. 2015. Bilingual word representations with monolingual quality in mind. In *Proceedings of the 1st Workshop on Vector Space Modeling for Natural Language Processing*, pages 151–159.

Tomas Mikolov, Quoc V. Le, and Ilya Sutskever. 2013. Exploiting similarities among languages for machine translation. *CoRR*, abs/1309.4168.

Jose Costa Pereira, Emanuele Coviello, Gabriel Doyle, Nikhil Rasiwasia, Gert R. G. Lanckriet, Roger Levy, and Nuno Vasconcelos. 2014. On the role of correlation and abstraction in cross-modal multimedia retrieval. *IEEE Transactions on Pattern Analysis and Machine Intelligence*, 36(3):521–535.

Janarathanan Rajendran, Mitesh M. Kapra, Sarath Chandar, and Balaraman Ravindran. 2016. Bridge correlational neural networks for multilingual multimodal representation learning. In *NAACL*.

Pushpendre Rastogi, Benjamin Van Durme, and Raman Arora. 2015. Multiview LSA: Representation learning via generalized CCA. In *NAACL*, pages 556–566.

Olga Russakovsky, Jia Deng, Hao Su, Jonathan Krause, Sanjeev Satheesh, Sean Ma, Zhiheng Huang, Andrej Karpathy, Aditya Khosla, Michael S. Bernstein, Alexander C. Berg, and Fei-Fei Li. 2015. ImageNet large scale visual recognition challenge. *International Journal of Computer Vision*, 115(3):211–252.

Carina Silberer and Mirella Lapata. 2014. Learning grounded meaning representations with autoencoders. In *ACL*, pages 721–732.

Hubert Soyer, Pontus Stenetorp, and Akiko Aizawa. 2015. Leveraging monolingual data for crosslingual compositional word representations. In *ICLR*.

Jörg Tiedemann. 2012. Parallel data, tools and interfaces in OPUS. In *LREC*, pages 2214–2218.

Ivan Vulić and Marie-Francine Moens. 2013. A study on bootstrapping bilingual vector spaces from nonparallel data (and nothing else). In *EMNLP*, pages 1613–1624.

Ivan Vulić and Marie-Francine Moens. 2015. Monolingual and cross-lingual information retrieval models based on (bilingual) word embeddings. In *SIGIR*, pages 363–372.

Ivan Vulić and Marie-Francine Moens. 2016. Bilingual distributed word representations from document-aligned comparable data. *Journal of Artificial Intelligence Research*, 55:953–994.

Weiran Wang, Raman Arora, Karen Livescu, and Jeff A. Bilmes. 2015. On deep multi-view representation learning. In *ICML*, pages 1083–1092.

Is This Post Persuasive?
Ranking Argumentative Comments in the Online Forum

Zhongyu Wei[12], **Yang Liu**[2] and **Yi Li**[2]
[1]School of Data Science, Fudan University, Shanghai, P.R.China
[2]Computer Science Department, The University of Texas at Dallas
Richardson, Texas 75080, USA
{zywei,yangl,yili}@hlt.utdallas.edu

Abstract

In this paper we study how to identify persuasive posts in the online forum discussions, using data from Change My View sub-Reddit. Our analysis confirms that the users' voting score for a comment is highly correlated with its metadata information such as published time and author reputation. In this work, we propose and evaluate other features to rank comments for their persuasive scores, including textual information in the comments and social interaction related features. Our experiments show that the surface textual features do not perform well compared to the argumentation based features, and the social interaction based features are effective especially when more users participate in the discussion.

1 Introduction

With the popularity of online forums such as idebate[1] and convinceme[2], researchers have been paying increasing attentions to analyzing persuasive content, including identification of arguing expressions in online debates (Trabelsi and Zaiane, 2014), recognition of stance in ideological online debates (Somasundaran and Wiebe, 2010; Hasan and Ng, 2014; Ranade et al., 2013b), and debate summarization (Ranade et al., 2013a). However, how to automatically determine if a text is persuasive is still an unsolved problem.

Text quality and popularity evaluation has been studied in different domains in the past few years (Louis and Nenkova, 2013; Tan et al., 2014; Park et al., 2016; Guerini et al., 2015). However,

quality evaluation of argumentative text in the online forum has some unique characterisitcs. First, persuasive text contains argument that is not common in other genres. Second, beside the text itself, the interplay between a comment and what it responds to is crucial. Third, the community reaction to the comment also needs to be taken into consideration.

In this paper, we propose several sets of features to capture the above mentioned characteristics for persuasive comment identification in the online forum. We constructed a dataset from a sub-forum of Reddit[3], namely *change my view* (CMV)[4] . We first analyze the corpus and show the correlation between the human voting score for an argumentative comment and its entry order and author reputation. Then for the comment ranking task, we propose three sets of features including surface text features, social interaction based features and argumentation based features. Our experimental results show that the argumentation based features work the best in the early stage of the discussion and the effectiveness of social interaction features increases when the number of comments in the discussion grows.

2 Dataset and Task

2.1 Data

On CMV, people initiate a discussion thread with a post expressing their thoughts toward a specific topic and other users reply with arguments from the opposite side in order to change the initiator's mind. The writing quality on CVM is quite good since the discussions are monitored by moderators. Besides commenting, users can vote on different replies to indicate which one is more persuasive than others. The total amount of upvotes

---

[1]http://idebate.org/
[2]http://convinceme.net
[3]https://www.reddit.com
[4]https://www.reddit.com/r/changemyview

Proceedings of the 54th Annual Meeting of the Association for Computational Linguistics, pages 195–200,
Berlin, Germany, August 7-12, 2016. ©2016 Association for Computational Linguistics

Thread #	1,785
Comment #	374,472
Comment # / Thread #	209.79
Author #	32,639
Unique Author # / Thread #	70.67
Delta Awarded Thread #	886 (49.6%)
Delta Awarded Comment #	2,056 (0.5%)

Table 1: Statistics of the CMV dataset.

minus the down votes is called *karma*, indicating the persuasiveness of the reply. Users can also give *delta* to a comment if it changes their original mind about the topic. The comment is then named *delta awarded comment* (DAC), and the thread containing a DAC is noted as *delta awarded thread*.

We use a corpus collected from CMV.[5] The original corpus contains all the threads published between Jan. 2014 and Jan. 2015. We kept the threads with more than 100 comments to form our experimental dataset[6]. The basic statistics of the dataset can be seen in Table 1.

Figure 1a shows the distribution of the karma scores in the dataset. We can see that the karma score is highly skewed, similar to what is reported in (Jaech et al., 2015). 42% of comments obtain a karma score of exactly one (i.e., no votes beyond the author), and around 15% of comments have a score less than one. Figure 1b and 1c show the correlation of the karma score with two metadata features, author reputation[7] and entry order, respectively. We can see the karma score of a comment is highly related to its entry order. In general, the earlier a comment is posted, the higher karma score it obtains. The average score is less than one when it is posted after 30 comments. Figure 1c shows that authors of comments with higher karma scores tend to have higher reputation on average.

2.2 Task

Tan et al. (2016) explored the task of mind change by focusing on delta awarded comments using their CMV data. However, the percentage of delta awarded comments is quite low, as shown in Table 1 (the percentage of comments obtained delta is as low as 0.5%). In addition, a persuasive comment is not necessarily delta awarded. It can be

of high quality but does not change other people's mind. Our research thus uses the karma score of a comment, instead of delta, as the reference to represent the persuasiveness of the comment. Our analysis also shows that delta awarded comments generally have high karma scores (78.7% of DACs obtain a higher karma score than the median value in each delta awarded thread), indicating the karma score is correlated with the delta value.

Using karma scores as ground truth, Jaech et al. (2015) proposed a comment ranking task on several sub-forums of Reddit. In order to reduce the impact of timing, they rank each set of 10 connective comments. However, their setting is not suitable for our task. First, at the later stage of the discussion, comments posted connectively in terms of time can belong to different sub-trees of the discussion, and thus can be viewed or reacted with great difference. Second, as shown in Figure 1b, comments entered in later stage obtain little attention from audience. This makes their karma scores less reliable as the ground-truth of persuasiveness.

To further control the factor of timing, we define the task as ranking the first-N comments in each thread. The final karma scores of these N comments are used to determine their reference rank for evaluation. We study two setups for this ranking task. First we use information until the time point when the thread contains only these N comments. Second we allow the system to access more comments than N. Our goal is to investigate if we can predict whether a comment is persuasive and how the community reacts to a comment in the future.

3 Methods

3.1 Ranking Model

A pair-wise learning-to-rank model (Ranking SVM (Joachims, 2002)) is used in our task. We first construct the training set including pairs of comments. In each pair, the first comment is more persuasive than the second one. Considering that two samples with similar karma scores might not be significantly different in terms of their persuasiveness, we propose to use a modified score to form training pairs in order to improve the learning efficacy. We group comments into 7 buckets based on their karma scores, $[-\infty, 0]$, $(0, 1]$, $(1, 5]$, $(5, 10]$, $(10, 20]$, $(20, 50]$ and $(50, +\infty]$. We then use the bucket number (0 - 6) of each comment

---

[5]The data was shared with us by researchers at the University of Washington.

[6]Please contact authors about sharing the data set.

[7]This is the number of deltas the author has received.

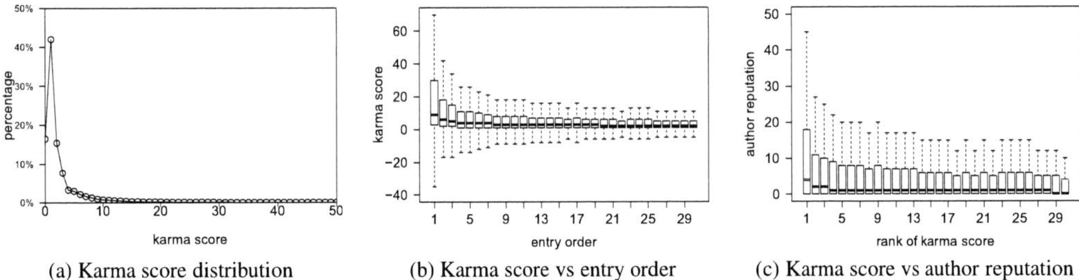

(a) Karma score distribution   (b) Karma score vs entry order   (c) Karma score vs author reputation

Figure 1: Karma value distributions in the CMV dataset.

Feature Category	Feature Name	Feature Description
Surface Text Features	length	# of the words, sentences and paragraphs in c.
	url	# of urls contained in c.
	unique # of words	# of unique words in c.
	punctuation	# of punctuation marks in c.
	unique # of POS	# of unique POS tags in c.
Social Interaction Features	tree_size	The tree size generated by c and rc.
	reply_num	The number of replies obtained by c and rc.
	tree_height	The height of the tree generated by by c and rc.
	Is_root_reply	Is c a root reply of the post?
	Is_leaf	Is c a leaf of the tree generated by rc?
	location	The position of c in the tree generated by rc.
Argumentation Related Features	connective words	Number of connective words in c.
	modal verbs	Number of modal verbs included in c.
	argumentative sentence	Number and percentage of argumentative sentences.
	argument relevance	Similarity with the original post and parent comment.
	argument originality	Maximum similarity with comments published earlier.

Table 2: Feature list (c: the comment; rc: the root comment of c.)

as its modified score. We use all the formed pairs to train our ranker. In order to be consistent, we use the first-N comments in the training threads to construct the training samples to predict the rank for the first-N comments in a test thread.

3.2 Features

We propose several key features that we hypothesize are predictive of persuasive comments. The full feature list is given in Table 2.

- **Surface Text Features**[8]: In order to capture the basic textual information, we use the comment length and content diversity represented as the number of words, POS tags, URLs, and punctuation marks. We also explored unigram features and named entity based features, but they did not improve system performance and are thus not included.

- **Social Interaction Features**: We hypothesize that if a comment attracts more social attention from the community, it is more likely to be persuasive, therefore we propose several social interaction features to capture the community reaction to a comment. Besides the reply tree generated by the comment, we also consider the reply tree generated by the root comment[9] for feature computing. The *tree size* is the number of comments in the reply tree. The position of c is its level in the reply tree (the level of root node is zero).

- **Argumentation Related Features**: We believe a comment's argumentation quality is a good indicator of its persuasiveness. In order to capture the argumentation related information, we propose two sub-groups of features based on the comment itself and the interplay between the comment and other comments in the discussion. **a) Local features:** we trained a binary classifier to classify sentences as argumentative and non-argumentative using features proposed in (Stab and Gurevych, 2014). We then use the number and percentage of argumentative sen-

---

[8]Stanford CoreNLP (Manning et al., 2014) was used to preprocess the text (i.e., comment splitting, sentence tokenization, POS tagging and NER recognition.).

[9]It is a comment that replies to the original post directly.

Approach	NDCG@1	NDCG@5	NDCG@10
random	0.258	0.440	0.564
author	0.382	0.567	0.664
entry-order	0.460	0.600	0.689
LTR_{text}	0.372	0.558	0.658
LTR_{social}	$0.475^{\dagger}$	$0.650^{\dagger}$	$0.718^{\dagger}$
LTR_{arg}	$0.475^{\dagger}$	$0.652^{\dagger}$	$0.725^{\dagger}$
$LTR_{text+social}$	$0.494^{\dagger}$	$0.666^{\dagger}$	$0.733^{\dagger}$
$LTR_{text+arg}$	$0.485^{\dagger}$	$0.654^{\dagger}$	$0.729^{\dagger}$
$LTR_{social+arg}$	$0.502^{\dagger\ddagger}$	$0.674^{\dagger\ddagger}$	$0.740^{\dagger}$
LTR_{T+S+A}	$0.508^{\dagger\ddagger}$	$0.676^{\dagger\ddagger}$	$0.743^{\dagger\ddagger}$
LTR_{all}	$\mathbf{0.521^{\dagger\ddagger}}$	$\mathbf{0.685^{\dagger\ddagger}}$	$\mathbf{0.752^{\dagger\ddagger}}$

Table 3: Performance of first-10 comments ranking ($T+S+A$: the combination of the three sets of features we proposed; *all*: the combination of two meta-data features and our features; **bold**: the best performance in each column; $\dagger$: the approach is significantly better than both metadata baselines (p $<$0.01); $\ddagger$: the approach is significantly better than LTR approaches using a single category of features (p $<$0.01).).

tences predicted by the classifier as features. Besides, we include some features used in the classifier directly (i.e. number of connective words[10] and modal verbs). **b) Interactive features:** for these features, we consider the similarity of a comment and its parent comment, the original post, and all the previously published comments. We use cosine similarity computed based on the term frequency vector representation. Intuitively a comment needs to be relevant to the discussed topic and possibly have some original convincing opinions or arguments to receive a high karma score.

4 Experimental Results

We use 5-fold cross-validation in our experiments. Normalized discounted cumulative gain (NDCG) score (Järvelin and Kekäläinen, 2000) is used as the evaluation metric for our First-N comments ranking task. In this study, N is10.

4.1 Experiment I: Using N Comments for Ranking

Table 3 shows the results for first-10 comments ranking using information from only these 10 comments. As shown in Figure 1, metadata features, entry order and author's reputation are correlated with the karma score of a comment. We

thus use these two values as baselines. We also include the performance of the random baseline for comparison[11]. For our ranking based models (LTR_*), we compare using the three sets of features described in Section. 3.2 (noted as *text*, *social* and *arg* respectively), individually or in combination. We report NDCG scores for position 1, 5 and 10 respectively. The followings are some findings.

- Both metadata based baselines generate significantly[12] better results compared to the random baseline. Baseline *entry-order* performs much better than *author*, suggesting that the entry order is more indicative for the karma score of a comment.

- The surface text features are least effective among the three sets of features, and the performance using them is even worse than the two metadata baselines. This might be because the general writing quality of the comments in CMV is high because of the policy of the forum. Therefore, the surface text features we used are not very discriminative for comment ranking. A further analysis of features in this category shows that *length* is the most effective feature.

- Argumentation based features have the best performance among the three categories. Its performance is significantly better than surface text features, consistent with our expectation that argumentation related features are useful for persuasiveness evaluation. Our additional experiments show that *interactive features* are more effective than *local features*. This might be because the argumentation features and models we use are not perfect. Future research is still needed to better represent argumentation information in the text.

- When combining two categories of features, the performance of the ranker increases consistently. The performance can be further improved by combining all the three categories of features we proposed (the improvement compared to using a single feature category is significant). The best results are achieved by LTR_{all}, i.e., combining two metadata features and features we proposed.

---

[10]We constructed a list of connective words including 55 entries (e.g., because, therefore etc.).

[11]The performance of random baseline is high because of the tie of reference karma scores.

[12]Significance is computed by two tailed t-test.

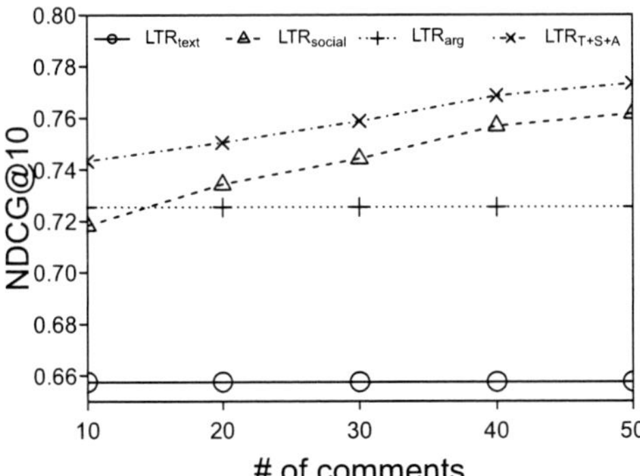

Figure 2: Results using various number of comments in the thread for ranking.

4.2 Experiment II: Using Varying Numbers of Comments for Ranking

With the evolving discussion, there will be more comments joining the thread providing more information for social interaction based features. In order to show the impact of different features at different discussion stage, we conduct another experiment by ranking first-10 comments with varying numbers of comments in the test thread for feature computing. The result of the experiment is shown in Figure 2. The performance of LTR_{text} and LTR_{arg} remain the same since their feature values are not affected by the new coming comments. The performance of LTR_{social} increases consistently when the number of comments grows, and it outperforms LTR_{arg} when the number of comments is more than 20. LTR_{T+S+A} has always the best performance, benefiting from the combination of different types of features.

5 Related Work

Our work is most related to two lines of work, including text quality evaluation and research on Reddit.com.

Text quality: Text quality and popularity evaluation has been studied in different domains in the past few years. Louis and Nenkova (2013) implemented features to capture aspects of great writing in science journalism domain. Tan et al. (2014) looked into the effect of wording while predicting the popularity of social media content. Park et al. (2016) developed an interactive system to assist human moderators to select high quality news. Guerini et al. (2015) modeled a notion of euphony and explored the impact of sounds on different forms of persuasiveness. Their research focused on the phonetic aspect instead of language usage.

Reddit based research: Reddit has been used recently for research on social news analysis and recommendation (e.g., (Buntain and Golbeck, 2014)). Researchers also analyzed the language use on Reddit. Jaech et al. (2015) studied how language use affects community reaction to comments in Reddit. Tan et al. (2016) analyzed the interaction dynamics and persuasion strategies in CMV.

6 Conclusion

In this paper, we studied the impact of different sets of features on the identification of persuasive comments in the online forum. Our experiment results show that argumentation based features work the best in the early stage of the discussion, while the effectiveness of social interaction based features increases when the number of comments in the thread grows.

There are three major future directions for this research. First, the approach for argument modeling in this paper is lexical based, which limits the effectiveness of argumentation related features for our task. It is thus crucial to study more effective ways for argument modeling. Second, we will explore persuasion behavior of the argumentative comments and study the correlation between the strength of the argument and different persuasion behaviors. Third, we plan to automatically construct an argumentation corpus including pairs of arguments from two opposite sides of the topic from CMV, and use this for automatic disputing argument generation.

Acknowledgments

We thank the anonymous reviewers for their detailed and insightful comments on this paper. The work is partially supported by DARPA Contract No. FA8750-13-2-0041 and AFOSR award No. FA9550-15-1-0346. Any opinions, findings, and conclusions or recommendations expressed are those of the authors and do not necessarily reflect the views of the funding agencies. We thank Trang Tran, Hao Fang and Mari Ostendorf at University of Washington for sharing the Reddit data they collected.

References

Cody Buntain and Jennifer Golbeck. 2014. Identifying social roles in reddit using network structure. In *Proceedings of the Companion Publication of the 23rd International Conference on World Wide Web Companion*, pages 615–620.

Marco Guerini, Gözde Özbal, and Carlo Strapparava. 2015. Echoes of persuasion: The effect of euphony in persuasive communication. *arXiv preprint arXiv:1508.05817*.

Kazi Saidul Hasan and Vincent Ng. 2014. Why are you taking this stance? identifying and classifying reasons in ideological debates. In *Proceedings of the Conference on Empirical Methods in Natural Language Processing*, pages 751–762.

Aaron Jaech, Vicky Zayats, Hao Fang, Mari Ostendorf, and Hannaneh Hajishirzi. 2015. Talking to the crowd: What do people react to in online discussions? In *Proceedings of the Conference on Empirical Methods in Natural Language Processing*, pages 2026–2031.

Kalervo Järvelin and Jaana Kekäläinen. 2000. IR evaluation methods for retrieving highly relevant documents. In *Proceedings of the 23rd annual international ACM SIGIR conference on Research and development in information retrieval*, pages 41–48.

Thorsten Joachims. 2002. Optimizing search engines using clickthrough data. In *Proceedings of the Eighth ACM SIGKDD International Conference on Knowledge Discovery and Data Mining*, pages 133–142.

Annie Louis and Ani Nenkova. 2013. What makes writing great? first experiments on article quality prediction in the science journalism domain. *Transactions of the Association for Computational Linguistics*, 1:341–352.

Christopher D. Manning, Mihai Surdeanu, John Bauer, Jenny Finkel, Steven J. Bethard, and David McClosky. 2014. The Stanford CoreNLP natural language processing toolkit. In *Proceedings of the Association for Computational Linguistics System Demonstrations*, pages 55–60.

Deokgun Park, Simranjit Sachar, Nicholas Diakopoulos, and Niklas Elmqvist. 2016. Supporting comment moderators in identifying high quality online news comments. In *Proceedings of the 2016 CHI Conference on Human Factors in Computing Systems*.

Sarvesh Ranade, Jayant Gupta, Vasudeva Varma, and Radhika Mamidi. 2013a. Online debate summarization using topic directed sentiment analysis. In *Proceedings of the Second International Workshop on Issues of Sentiment Discovery and Opinion Mining*, page 7.

Sarvesh Ranade, Rajeev Sangal, and Radhika Mamidi. 2013b. Stance classification in online debates by recognizing users' intentions. In *Proceedings of Special Interest Group on Discourse and Dialogue*, pages 61–69.

Swapna Somasundaran and Janyce Wiebe. 2010. Recognizing stances in ideological on-line debates. In *Proceedings of the NAACL HLT 2010 Workshop on Computational Approaches to Analysis and Generation of Emotion in Text*, pages 116–124.

Christian Stab and Iryna Gurevych. 2014. Identifying argumentative discourse structures in persuasive essays. In *Proceedings of the Conference on Empirical Methods in Natural Language Processing*, pages 46–56.

Chenhao Tan, Lillian Lee, and Bo Pang. 2014. The effect of wording on message propagation: Topic- and author-controlled natural experiments on twitter. *arXiv preprint arXiv:1405.1438*.

Chenhao Tan, Vlad Niculae, Cristian Danescu-Niculescu-Mizil, and Lillian Lee. 2016. Winning arguments: Interaction dynamics and persuasion strategies in good-faith online discussions. *arXiv preprint arXiv:1602.01103*.

Amine Trabelsi and Osmar R Zaıane. 2014. Finding arguing expressions of divergent viewpoints in online debates. In *Proceedings of the 5th Workshop on Language Analysis for Social Media (LASM)@ EACL*, pages 35–43.

The Value of Semantic Parse Labeling for
Knowledge Base Question Answering

Wen-tau Yih   Matthew Richardson   Christopher Meek   Ming-Wei Chang   Jina Suh

Microsoft Research
Redmond, WA 98052, USA
{scottyih,mattri,meek,minchang,jinsuh}@microsoft.com

Abstract

We demonstrate the value of collecting semantic parse labels for knowledge base question answering. In particular, (1) unlike previous studies on small-scale datasets, we show that learning from labeled semantic parses significantly improves overall performance, resulting in absolute 5 point gain compared to learning from answers, (2) we show that with an appropriate user interface, one can obtain semantic parses with high accuracy and at a cost comparable or lower than obtaining just answers, and (3) we have created and shared the largest semantic-parse labeled dataset to date in order to advance research in question answering.

1   Introduction

Semantic parsing is the mapping of text to a meaning representation. Early work on learning to build semantic parsers made use of datasets of questions and their associated semantic parses (Zelle and Mooney, 1996; Zettlemoyer and Collins, 2005; Wong and Mooney, 2007). Recent work on semantic parsing for knowledge base question-answering (KBQA) has called into question the value of collecting such semantic parse labels, with most recent KBQA semantic parsing systems being trained using only question-answer pairs instead of question-parse pairs. In fact, there is evidence that using only question-answer pairs can yield improved performance as compared with approaches based on semantic parse labels (Liang et al., 2013). It is also widely believed that collecting semantic parse labels can be a "difficult, time consuming task" (Clarke et al., 2010) even for domain experts. Furthermore, recent focus has been more on the final task-specific performance of a

system (i.e., did it get the right answer for a question) as opposed to agreement on intermediate representations (Berant et al., 2013; Kwiatkowski et al., 2013), which allows for KBQA datasets to be built with only the answers to each question.

In this work, we re-examine the value of semantic parse labeling and demonstrate that semantic parse labels can provide substantial value for knowledge base question-answering. We focus on the task of question-answering on Freebase, using the WEBQUESTIONS dataset (Berant et al., 2013).

Our first contribution is the construction of the largest semantic parse dataset for KB question-answering to date. In order to evaluate the costs and benefits of gathering semantic parse labels, we created the WEBQUESTIONSSP dataset[1], which contains semantic parses for the questions from WEBQUESTIONS that are answerable using Freebase. In particular, we provide SPARQL queries for 4,737 questions. The remaining 18.5% of the original WEBQUESTIONS questions are labeled as "not answerable". This is due to a number of factors including the use of a more stringent assessment of "answerable", namely that the question be answerable via SPARQL rather than by returning or extracting information from textual descriptions. Compared to the previous semantic parse dataset on Freebase, Free917 (Cai and Yates, 2013), our WEBQUESTIONSSP is not only substantially larger, but also provides the semantic parses in SPARQL with standard Freebase entity identifiers, which are directly executable on Freebase.

Our second contribution is a demonstration that semantic parses can be collected at low cost. We employ a staged labeling paradigm that enables efficient labeling of semantic parses and improves the accuracy, consistency and efficiency of ob-

---

[1]Available at http://aka.ms/WebQSP.

Proceedings of the 54th Annual Meeting of the Association for Computational Linguistics, pages 201–206,
Berlin, Germany, August 7-12, 2016. ©2016 Association for Computational Linguistics

taining answers. In fact, in a simple comparison with using a web browser to extract answers from `freebase.com`, we show that we can collect semantic parse labels at a comparable or even faster rate than simply collecting answers.

Our third contribution is an empirical demonstration that we can leverage the semantic parse labels to increase the accuracy of a state-of-the-art question-answering system. We use a system that currently achieves state-of-the-art performance on KBQA and show that augmenting its training with semantic parse labels leads to an absolute 5-point increase in average F_1.

Our work demonstrates that semantic parse labels can provide additional value over answer labels while, with the right labeling tools, being comparable in cost to collect. Besides accuracy gains, semantic parses also have further benefits in yielding answers that are more accurate and consistent, as well as being updatable if the knowledge base changes (for example, as facts are added or revised).

2   Collecting Semantic Parses

In order to verify the benefits of having labeled semantic parses, we completely re-annotated the WEBQUESTIONS dataset (Berant et al., 2013) such that it contains both semantic parses and the derived answers. We chose to annotate the questions with the full semantic parses in SPARQL, based on the schema and data of the latest and last version of Freebase (2015-08-09).

Labeling interface   Writing SPARQL queries for natural language questions using a text editor is obviously not an efficient way to provide semantic parses even for experts. Therefore, we designed a staged, dialog-like user interface (UI) to improve the labeling efficiency. Our UI breaks the potentially complicated structured-labeling task into separate, but inter-dependent sub-tasks. Given a question, the UI first presents entities detected in the questions using an entity linking system (Yang and Chang, 2015), and asks the user to pick an entity in the question as the *topic entity* that could lead to the answers. The user can also suggest a new entity if none of the candidates returned by the entity linking system is correct. Once the entity is selected, the system then requests the user to pick the Freebase predicate that represents the *relationship* between the answers and this topic entity. Finally, additional *filters* can be added to

further constrain the answers. One key advantage of our UI design is that the annotator only needs to focus on one particular sub-task during each stage. All of the choices made by the labeler are used to automatically construct a coherent semantic parse. Note that the user can easily go back and forth to each of these three stages and change the previous choices, before pressing the final submit button.

Take the question *"who voiced meg on family guy?"* for example. The labeler will be presented with two entity choices: `Meg Griffin` and `Family Guy`, where the former links "meg" to the character's entity and the latter links to the TV show. Depending on the entity selected, legitimate Freebase predicates of the selected entity will be shown, along with the objects (either properties or entities). Suppose the labeler chooses `Meg Griffin` as the topic entity. He should then pick `actor` as the main relationship, meaning the answer should be the persons who have played this role. To accurately describe the question, the labeler should add additional filters like the TV series is `Family Guy` and the performance type is `voice` in the final stage[2].

The design of our UI is inspired by recent work on semantic parsing that has been applied to the WEBQUESTIONS dataset (Bast and Haussmann, 2015; Reddy et al., 2014; Berant and Liang, 2014; Yih et al., 2015), as these approaches use a simpler and yet more restricted semantic representation than first-order logic expressions. Following the notion of *query graph* in (Yih et al., 2015), the semantic parse is *anchored* to one of the entities in the question as the *topic entity* and the core component is to represent the relation between the entity and the answer, referred as the *inferential chain*. *Constraints*, such as properties of the answer or additional conditions the relation needs to hold, are captured as well. Figure 1 shows an example of these annotated semantic parse components and the corresponding SPARQL query. While it is clear that our UI does not cover complicated, highly compositional questions, most questions in WEBQUESTIONS can be covered[3].

Labeling process   In order to ensure the data quality, we recruit five annotators who are familiar with design of Freebase. Our goal is to provide

---

[2]Screenshots are included in the supplementary material.

[3]We manually edited the SPARQL queries for about 3.1% of the questions in WEBQUESTIONS that are not expressible by our UI.

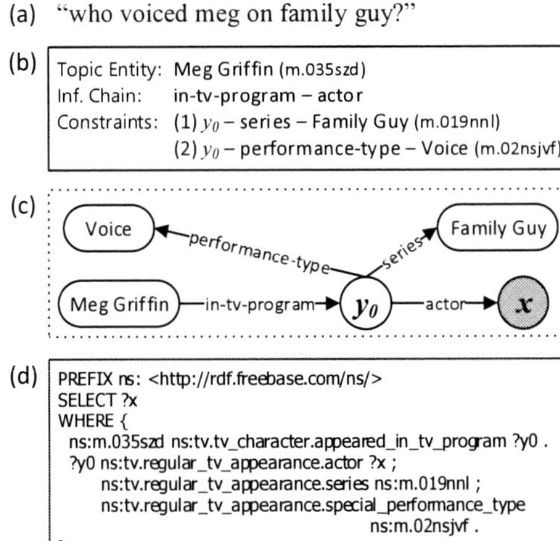

Figure 1: Example semantic parse of the question (a) "who voiced meg on family guy?" The three components in (b) record the labels collected through our dialog-like user interface, and can be mapped deterministically to either the corresponding query graph (c) or the SPARQL query (d).

correct semantic parses for each of the legitimate and unambiguous questions in WEBQUESTIONS. Our labeling instructions (included in the supplementary material) follow several key principles. For instance, the annotators should focus on giving the correct semantic parse of a question, based on the assumption that it will result in correct answers if the KB is *complete* and *correct*.

Among all the 5,810 questions in WEB-QUESTIONS, there are 1,073 questions that the annotators cannot provide the complete parses to find the answers, due to issues with the questions or Freebase. For example, some questions are ambiguous and without clear intent (e.g., *"where did romans go?"*). Others are questions that Freebase is not the appropriate information source (e.g., *"where to watch tv online for free in canada?"*).

3   Using Semantic Parses

In order to compare two training paradigms, learning from *question-answer pairs* and learning from *semantic parses*, we adopt the Staged Query Graph Generation (STAGG) algorithm (Yih et al., 2015), which achieves the highest published answer prediction accuracy on the WEBQUESTIONS dataset. STAGG formulates the output semantic parse in a query graph representation that mimics

the design of a graph knowledge base. It searches over potential query graphs for a question, iteratively growing the query graph by sequentially adding a main *topic entity*, then adding an *inferential chain* and finally adding a set of *constraints*. During the search process, each candidate query graph is judged by a scoring function on how likely the graph is a correct parse, based on features indicating how each individual component matches the original question, as well as some properties of the whole query graph. Example features include the score output by the entity linking system, the match score of the inferential chain to the relation described in the question from a deep neural network model, number of nodes in the candidate query graph, and the number of matching words in constraints. For additional details see (Yih et al., 2015).

When question-answer pairs are available, we create a set of query graphs connecting entities in the question to the answers in the training set, as in (Yih et al., 2015). We score the quality of a query graph by using the F_1 score between the answer derived from the query graph and the answer in the training set. These scores are then used in a learning-to-rank approach to predict high-quality query graphs.

In the case that semantic parses are available, we change the score that we use for evaluating the quality of a query graph. In particular, we assign the query graph score to be zero whenever the query graph is not a subgraph consistent with the semantic parse label and to be the F_1 score described above otherwise. The hope is that by leveraging the semantic parse, we can significantly reduce the number of incorrect query graphs used during training. For instance, the predicate `music.artist.track` was incorrectly predicted as the inferential chain for the question *"what are the songs that justin bieber write?"*, where a correct parse should use the relation `music.composer.compositions`.

4   The Value of Semantic Parses

In this section, we explore the costs of collecting semantic parse labels and the benefits of using them.

4.1   Benefits of Semantic Parses

Leveraging the new dataset, we study whether a semantic parser learned using full parses instead

Training Signals	Prec.	Rec.	Avg. F_1	Acc.
Answers	67.3	73.1	66.8	58.8
Sem. Parses	70.9	80.3	71.7	63.9

Table 1: The results of two different model training settings: answers only vs. semantic parses.

Labeling Methods	Ans.	Ans.	Sem. Parses
Annotator	MTurkers	Experts	Experts
Avg. time/Question	Unknown	82 sec	21 sec
Labeling Correctness	66%	92%	94%

Table 2: Comparing labeling methods on 50 sampled questions.

of just question-answer pairs can answer questions more accurately, using the knowledge base. Below, we describe our basic experimental setting and report the main results.

Experimental setting We followed the same training/testing splits as in the original WEB-QUESTIONS dataset, but only used questions with complete parses and answers for training and evaluation in our experiments. In the end, 3,098 questions are used for model training and 1,639 questions are used for evaluation[4]. Because there can be multiple answers to a question, precision, recall and F_1 are computed for each individual question. The average F_1 score is reported as the main evaluation metric. In addition, we also report the true accuracy – a question is considered answered correctly only when the predicted answers exactly match one of the answer sets.

Results Table 1 shows the results of two different models: learning from question-answer pairs vs. learning from semantic parses. With the labeled parses, the average F_1 score is 4.9-point higher (71.7% vs. 66.8%). The stricter metric, complete answer set accuracy, also reflects the same trend, where the accuracy of training with labeled parses is 5.1% higher than using only the answers (63.9% vs. 58.8%).

While it is expected that training using the annotated parses could result in a better model, it is still interesting to see the performance gap, especially when the evaluation is on the correctness of the answers rather than the parses. We examined the output answers to the questions where the two models differ. Although the setting of using answers only often guesses the correct relations connecting the topic entity and answers, it can be confused by related, but incorrect relations as well. Similar phenomena also occur on constraints, which suggests that subtle differences in the meaning are difficult

to catch if the semantic parses are automatically generated using only the answers.

4.2 Costs of Semantic Parses

Our labeling process is very different from that of the original WEBQUESTIONS dataset, where the question is paired with answers found on the Freebase Website by Amazon MTurk workers. To compare these two annotation methods, we sampled 50 questions and had one expert label them using two schemes: finding answers using the Freebase Website and labeling the semantic parses using our UI. The time needed, as well as the correctness of the answers are summarized in Table 2.

Interestingly, in this study we found that it actually took less time to label these questions with semantic parses using our UI, than to label with only answers. There could be several possible explanations. First, as many questions in this dataset are actually "simple" and do not need complicated compositional structured semantic parses, our UI can help make the labeling process very efficient. By ranking the possible linked entities and likely relations, the annotators are able to pick the correct component labels fairly easily. In contrast, simple questions may have many legitimate answers. Enumerating all of the correct answers can take significantly longer than authoring a semantic parse that computes them.

When we compare the annotation quality between labeling semantic parses and answers, we find that the correctness[5] of the answers are about the same (92% vs 94%). In the original WEB-QUESTIONS dataset, only 66% of the answers are completely correct. This is largely due to the low accuracy (42.9%) of the 14 questions containing multiple answers. This indicates that to ensure data quality, more verification is needed when leveraging crowdsourcing.

5 Discussion

Unlike the work of (Liang et al., 2013; Clarke et al., 2010), we demonstrate that semantic parses

---

[4]The average F_1 score of the original STAGG's output to these 1,639 questions is 60.3%, evaluated using WEB-QUESTIONS. Note that the number is not directly comparable to what we report in Table 1 because many of the labeled answers in WEBQUESTIONS are either incorrect or incomplete.

[5]We considered a label to be correct only if the derived/labeled answer set is completely accurate.

can improve over state-of-the-art knowledge base question answering systems. There are a number of potential differences that are likely to contribute to this finding. Unlike previous work, we compare training with answers and training with semantic parses while making only minimal changes in a state-of-the-art training algorithm. This enables a more direct evaluation of the potential benefits of using semantic parses. Second, and perhaps the more significant difference, is that our evaluation is based on Freebase which is significantly larger than the knowledge bases used in the previous work. We suspect that the gains provided by semantic parse labels are due a significant reduction in the number of paths between candidate entities and answers when we limit to semantically valid paths. However, in domains where the number of potential paths between candidate entities and answers is small, the value of collecting semantic parse labels might also be small.

Semantic parsing labels provide additional benefits. For example, collecting semantic parse labels relative to a knowledge base can ensure that the answers are more faithful to the knowledge base and better captures which questions are answerable by the knowledge base. Moreover, by creating semantic parses using a labeling system based on the target knowledge base, the correctness and completeness of answers can be improved. This is especially true for question that have large answer sets. Finally, semantic labels are more robust to changes in knowledge base facts because answers can be computed via execution of the semantic representation for the question. For instance, the answer to "Who does Chris Hemsworth have a baby with?" might change if the knowledge base is updated with new facts about children but the semantic parse would not need to change.

Notice that besides being used for the full semantic parsing task, our WEBQUESTIONSSP dataset is a good test bed for several important semantic tasks as well. For instance, the topic entity annotations are beneficial to training and testing entity linking systems. The core inferential chains alone are quality annotations for relation extraction and matching. Specific types of constraints are useful too. For example, the temporal semantic labels are valuable for identifying temporal expressions and their time spans. Because our dataset specifically focuses on questions, it complements existing datasets in these individual tasks, as they tend to target at normal corpora of regular sentences.

While our labeling interface design was aimed at supporting labeling experts, it would be valuable to enable crowdsourcing workers to provide semantic parse labels. One promising approach is to use a more dialog-driven interface using natural language (similar to (He et al., 2015)). Such UI design is also crucial for extending our work to handling more complicated questions. For instance, allowing users to traverse longer paths in a sequential manner will increase the expressiveness of the output parses, both in the core relation and constraints. Displaying a small knowledge graph centered at the selected entities and relations may help users explore alternative relations more effectively as well.

Acknowledgments

We thank Andrei Aron for the initial design of the labeling interface.

References

Hannah Bast and Elmar Haussmann. 2015. More accurate question answering on Freebase. In *Proceedings of the 24th ACM International on Conference on Information and Knowledge Management*, pages 1431–1440. ACM.

Jonathan Berant and Percy Liang. 2014. Semantic parsing via paraphrasing. In *Proceedings of the 52nd Annual Meeting of the Association for Computational Linguistics (Volume 1: Long Papers)*, pages 1415–1425, Baltimore, Maryland, June. Association for Computational Linguistics.

Jonathan Berant, Andrew Chou, Roy Frostig, and Percy Liang. 2013. Semantic parsing on Freebase from question-answer pairs. In *Proceedings of the 2013 Conference on Empirical Methods in Natural Language Processing*, pages 1533–1544, Seattle, Washington, USA, October. Association for Computational Linguistics.

Qingqing Cai and Alexander Yates. 2013. Large-scale semantic parsing via schema matching and lexicon extension. In *Proceedings of the 51st Annual Meeting of the Association for Computational Linguistics (Volume 1: Long Papers)*, pages 423–433, Sofia, Bulgaria, August. Association for Computational Linguistics.

James Clarke, Dan Goldwasser, Ming-Wei Chang, and Dan Roth. 2010. Driving semantic parsing from the world's response. In *Proceedings of the Four-teenth Conference on Computational Natural Language Learning*, pages 18–27. Association for Computational Linguistics.

Luheng He, Mike Lewis, and Luke Zettlemoyer. 2015. Question-answer driven semantic role labeling: Using natural language to annotate natural language. In *Proceedings of the 2015 Conference on Empirical Methods in Natural Language Processing*, pages 643–653, Lisbon, Portugal, September. Association for Computational Linguistics.

Tom Kwiatkowski, Eunsol Choi, Yoav Artzi, and Luke Zettlemoyer. 2013. Scaling semantic parsers with on-the-fly ontology matching. In *Proceedings of the 2013 Conference on Empirical Methods in Natural Language Processing*, pages 1545–1556, Seattle, Washington, USA, October. Association for Computational Linguistics.

Percy Liang, Michael I Jordan, and Dan Klein. 2013. Learning dependency-based compositional semantics. *Computational Linguistics*, 39(2):389–446.

Siva Reddy, Mirella Lapata, and Mark Steedman. 2014. Large-scale semantic parsing without question-answer pairs. *Transactions of the Association for Computational Linguistics*, 2:377–392.

Yuk Wah Wong and Raymond J Mooney. 2007. Learning synchronous grammars for semantic parsing with lambda calculus. In *Annual Meeting of the Association for Computational Linguistics (ACL)*.

Yi Yang and Ming-Wei Chang. 2015. S-MART: Novel tree-based structured learning algorithms applied to tweet entity linking. In *Proceedings of the 53rd Annual Meeting of the Association for Computational Linguistics and the 7th International Joint Conference on Natural Language Processing (Volume 1: Long Papers)*, pages 504–513, Beijing, China, July. Association for Computational Linguistics.

Wen-tau Yih, Ming-Wei Chang, Xiaodong He, and Jianfeng Gao. 2015. Semantic parsing via staged query graph generation: Question answering with knowledge base. In *Proceedings of the 53rd Annual Meeting of the Association for Computational Linguistics and the 7th International Joint Conference on Natural Language Processing (Volume 1: Long Papers)*, pages 1321–1331, Beijing, China, July. Association for Computational Linguistics.

John Zelle and Raymond Mooney. 1996. Learning to parse database queries using inductive logic programming. In *Proceedings of the National Conference on Artificial Intelligence*, pages 1050–1055.

Luke S Zettlemoyer and Michael Collins. 2005. Learning to map sentences to logical form: Structured classification with probabilistic categorial grammars. In *Conference on Uncertainty in Artificial Intelligence (UAI)*.

Attention-Based Bidirectional Long Short-Term Memory Networks for Relation Classification

Peng Zhou, Wei Shi, Jun Tian, Zhenyu Qi, Bingchen Li, Hongwei Hao, Bo Xu
Institute of Automation, Chinese Academy of Sciences
{zhoupeng2013, shiwei2013, tianjun2013, zhenyu.qi,
libingchen2013, hongwei.hao, xubo}@ia.ac.cn

Abstract

Relation classification is an important semantic processing task in the field of natural language processing (NLP). State-of-the-art systems still rely on lexical resources such as WordNet or NLP systems like dependency parser and named entity recognizers (NER) to get high-level features. Another challenge is that important information can appear at any position in the sentence. To tackle these problems, we propose Attention-Based Bidirectional Long Short-Term Memory Networks(Att-BLSTM) to capture the most important semantic information in a sentence. The experimental results on the SemEval-2010 relation classification task show that our method outperforms most of the existing methods, with only word vectors.

1 Introduction

Relation classification is the task of finding semantic relations between pairs of nominals, which is useful for many NLP applications, such as information extraction (Wu and Weld, 2010), question answering (Yao and Van Durme, 2014). For instance, the following sentence contains an example of the Entity-Destination relation between the nominals **Flowers** and **chapel**.

$\langle e_1 \rangle$ **Flowers** $\langle /e_1 \rangle$ are carried into the $\langle e_2 \rangle$ **chapel** $\langle /e_2 \rangle$.

$\langle e_1 \rangle$, $\langle /e_1 \rangle$, $\langle e_2 \rangle$, $\langle /e_2 \rangle$ are four position indicators which specify the starting and ending of the nominals (Hendrickx et al., 2009).

Traditional relation classification methods that employ handcrafted features from lexical resources, are usually based on pattern matching, and have achieved high performance (Bunescu

Correspondence author: zhenyu.qi@ia.ac.cn

and Mooney, 2005; Mintz et al., 2009; Rink and Harabagiu, 2010). One downside of these methods is that many traditional NLP systems are utilized to extract high-level features, such as part of speech tags, shortest dependency path and named entities, which consequently results in the increase of computational cost and additional propagation errors. Another downside is that designing features manually is time-consuming, and performing poor on generalization due to the low coverage of different training datasets.

Recently, deep learning methods provide an effective way of reducing the number of handcrafted features (Socher et al., 2012; Zeng et al., 2014). However, these approaches still use lexical resources such as WordNet (Miller, 1995) or NLP systems like dependency parsers and NER to get high-level features.

This paper proposes a novel neural network Att-BLSTM for relation classification. Our model utilizes neural attention mechanism with Bidirectional Long Short-Term Memory Networks(BLSTM) to capture the most important semantic information in a sentence. This model doesn't utilize any features derived from lexical resources or NLP systems.

The contribution of this paper is using BLSTM with attention mechanism, which can automatically focus on the words that have decisive effect on classification, to capture the most important semantic information in a sentence, without using extra knowledge and NLP systems. We conduct experiments on the SemEval-2010 Task 8 dataset, and achieve an $F1$-score of 84.0%, higher than most of the existing methods in the literature.

The remainder of the paper is structured as follows. In Section 2, we review related work about relation classification. Section 3 presents our Att-BLSTM model in detail. In Section 4, we describe details about the setup of experimental evaluation

Proceedings of the 54th Annual Meeting of the Association for Computational Linguistics, pages 207–212,
Berlin, Germany, August 7-12, 2016. ©2016 Association for Computational Linguistics

and the experimental results. Finally, we have our conclusion in Section 5.

2   Related Work

Over the years, various methods have been proposed for relation classification. Most of them are based on pattern matching and apply extra NLP systems to derive lexical features. One related work is proposed by Rink and Harabagiu (2010), which utilizes many features derived from external corpora for a Support Vector Machine(SVM) classifier.

Recently, deep neural networks can learn underlying features automatically and have been used in the literature. Most representative progress was made by Zeng et al. (2014), who utilized convolutional neural networks(CNN) for relation classification. While CNN is not suitable for learning long-distance semantic information, so our approach builds on Recurrent Neural Network(RNN) (Mikolov et al., 2010).

One related work was proposed by Zhang and Wang (2015), which employed bidirectional RNN to learn patterns of relations from raw text data. Although bidirectional RNN has access to both past and future context information, the range of context is limited due to the vanishing gradient problem. To overcome this problem, Long short-Term memory(LSTM) units are introduced by Hochreiter and Schmidhuber (1997).

Another related work is SDP-LSTM model proposed by Yan et al. (2015). This model leverages the shortest dependency path(SDP) between two nominals, then it picks up heterogeneous information along the SDP with LSTM units. While our method regards the raw text as a sequence.

Finally, our work is related to BLSTM model proposed by Zhang et al. (2015). This model utilizing NLP tools and lexical resources to get word, position, POS, NER, dependency parse and hypernym features, together with LSTM units, achieved a comparable result to the state-of-the-art. However, comparing to the complicated features that employed by Zhang et al. (2015), our method regards the four position indicators $\langle e1 \rangle, \langle /e1 \rangle, \langle e2 \rangle, \langle /e2 \rangle$ as single words, and transforms all words to word vectors, forming a simple but competing model.

3   Model

In this section we propose Att-BLSTM model in detail. As shown in Figure 1, the model proposed in this paper contains five components:

(1) Input layer: input sentence to this model;

(2) Embedding layer: map each word into a low dimension vector;

(3) LSTM layer: utilize BLSTM to get high level features from step (2);

(4) Attention layer: produce a weight vector, and merge word-level features from each time step into a sentence-level feature vector, by multiplying the weight vector;

(5) Output layer: the sentence-level feature vector is finally used for relation classification.

These components will be presented in detail in this section.

3.1   Word Embeddings

Given a sentence consisting of T words $S = \{x_1, x_2, \ldots, x_T\}$, every word x_i is converted into a real-valued vector e_i. For each word in S, we first look up the embedding matrix $W^{wrd} \in \mathbb{R}^{d^w |V|}$, where V is a fixed-sized vocabulary, and d^w is the size of word embedding. The matrix W^{wrd} is a parameter to be learned, and d^w is a hyper-parameter to be chosen by user. We transform a word x_i into its word embedding e_i by using the matrix-vector product:

$$e_i = W^{wrd} v^i \qquad (1)$$

where v^i is a vector of size $|V|$ which has value 1 at index e_i and 0 in all other positions. Then the sentence is feed into the next layer as a real-valued vectors $emb_s = \{e_1, e_2, \ldots, e_T\}$.

3.2   Bidirectional Network

LSTM units are firstly proposed by Hochreiter and Schmidhuber (1997) to overcome gradient vanishing problem. The main idea is to introduce an adaptive gating mechanism, which decides the degree to which LSTM units keep the previous state and memorize the extracted features of the current data input. Then lots of LSTM variants have been proposed. We adopt a variant introduced by Graves et al. (2013), which adds weighted peephole connections from the *Constant Error Carousel* (CEC) to the gates of the same memory block. By directly employing the current cell state to generate the gate degrees, the peephole connections allow all gates to *inspect* into the cell (i.e.

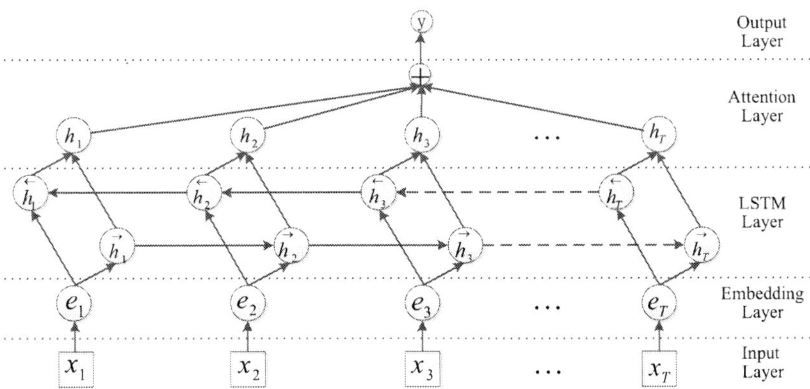

Figure 1: Bidirectional LSTM model with Attention

the current cell state) even when the output gate is closed (Graves, 2013).

Typically, four components composite the LSTM-based recurrent neural networks: one input gate i_t with corresponding weight matrix $W_{xi}, W_{hi}, W_{ci}, b_i$; one forget gate f_t with corresponding weight matrix $W_{xf}, W_{hf}, W_{cf}, b_f$; one output gate o_t with corresponding weight matrix $W_{xo}, W_{ho}, W_{co}, b_o$, all of those gates are set to generate some degrees, using current input x_i, the state h_{i-1} that previous step generated , and current state of this cell c_{i-1} (peephole), for the decisions whether to take the inputs, forget the memory stored before, and output the state generated later. Just as these following equations demonstrate:

$$i_t = \sigma(W_{xi}x_t + W_{hi}h_{t-1} + W_{oi}c_{t-1} + b_i) \quad (2)$$
$$f_t = \sigma(W_{xf}x_t + W_{hf}h_{t-1} + W_{cf}c_{t-1} + b_f) \quad (3)$$
$$g_t = \tanh(W_{xc}x_t + W_{hc}h_{t-1} + W_{cc}c_{t-1} + b_c) \quad (4)$$
$$c_t = i_t g_t + f_t c_{t-1} \quad (5)$$
$$o_t = \sigma(W_{xo}x_t + W_{ho}h_{t-1} + W_{co}c_t + b_o) \quad (6)$$
$$h_t = o_t \tanh(c_t) \quad (7)$$

Hence, current cell state c_t will be generated by calculating the weighted sum using both previous cell state and current information generated by the cell (Graves, 2013).

For many sequence modelling tasks, it is beneficial to have access to future as well as past context. However, standard LSTM networks process sequences in temporal order, they ignore future context. Bidirectional LSTM networks extend the unidirectional LSTM networks by introducing a sec-

ond layer, where the hidden to hidden connections flow in opposite temporal order. The model is therefore able to exploit information both from the past and the future.

In this paper, we use BLSTM. As also shown in Figure 1, the network contains two sub-networks for the left and right sequence context, which are forward and backward pass respectively. The output of the ith word is shown in the following equation:

$$h_i = [\overrightarrow{h_i} \oplus \overleftarrow{h_i}] \quad (8)$$

Here, we use element-wise sum to combine the forward and backward pass outputs.

3.3 Attention

Attentive neural networks have recently demonstrated success in a wide range of tasks ranging from question answering, machine translations, speech recognition, to image captioning (Hermann et al., 2015; Bahdanau et al., 2014; Chorowski et al., 2015; Xu et al., 2015). In this section, we propose the attention mechanism for relation classification tasks. Let H be a matrix consisting of output vectors $[h_1, h_2, \ldots, h_T]$ that the LSTM layer produced, where T is the sentence length. The representation r of the sentence is formed by a weighted sum of these output vectors:

$$M = \tanh(H) \quad (9)$$
$$\alpha = softmax(w^T M) \quad (10)$$
$$r = H\alpha^T \quad (11)$$

Model	Feature Set	F1
SVM (Rink and Harabagiu, 2010)	POS, prefixes, morphological, WordNet, dependency parse, Levin classed, ProBank, FramNet, NomLex-Plus, Google n-gram, paraphrases, TextRunner	82.2
CNN (Zeng et al., 2014)	WV (Turian et al., 2010) (dim=50) + PF + WordNet	69.7 82.7
RNN (Zhang and Wang, 2015)	WV (Turian et al., 2010) (dim=50) + PI WV (Mikolov et al., 2013) (dim=300) + PI	80.0 82.5
SDP-LSTM (Yan et al., 2015)	WV (pretrained by word2vec) (dim=200), syntactic parse + POS + WordNet + grammar relation embeddings	82.4 83.7
BLSTM (Zhang et al., 2015)	WV (Pennington et al., 2014) (dim=100) + PF + POS + NER + WNSYN + DEP	82.7 84.3
BLSTM Att-BLSTM BLSTM Att-BLSTM	WV (Turian et al., 2010) (dim=50) + PI WV (Turian et al., 2010) (dim=50) + PI WV (Pennington et al., 2014) (dim=100) + PI WV (Pennington et al., 2014) (dim=100) + PI	80.7 82.5 82.7 84.0

Table 1: Comparison with previous results. WV, PF, PI stand for word vectors, position features and position indicators respectively.

where $H \in \mathbb{R}^{d^w \times T}$, d^w is the dimension of the word vectors, w is a trained parameter vector and w^{T} is a transpose. The dimension of w, α, r is d^w, T, d^w separately.

We obtain the final sentence-pair representation used for classification from:

$$h^* = \tanh(r) \tag{12}$$

3.4 Classifying

In this setting, we use a softmax classifier to predict label $\hat{y}$ from a discrete set of classes Y for a sentence S. The classifier takes the hidden state h^* as input:

$$\hat{p}(y|S) = softmax\left(W^{(S)}h^* + b^{(S)}\right) \tag{13}$$

$$\hat{y} = \arg\max_y \hat{p}(y|S) \tag{14}$$

The cost function is the negative log-likelihood of the true class labels $\hat{y}$:

$$J(\theta) = -\frac{1}{m}\sum_{i=1}^{m} t_i \log(y_i) + \lambda\|\theta\|_F^2 \tag{15}$$

where $t \in \Re^m$ is the one-hot represented ground truth and $y \in \Re^m$ is the estimated probability for each class by softmax (m is the number of target classes), and λ is an L2 regularization hyperparameter. In this paper, we combine dropout with L2 regularization to alleviate overfitting.

3.5 Regularization

Dropout, proposed by (Hinton et al., 2012), prevents co-adaptation of hidden units by randomly omitting feature detectors from the network during forward propagation. We employ dropout on the embedding layer, LSTM layer and the penultimate layer.

We additionally constrain $L2$-norms of the weight vectors by rescaling w to have $\|w\| = s$, whenever $\|w\| > s$ after a gradient descent step, as shown in equation 15. Training details are further introduced in Section 4.1.

4 Experiments

4.1 Dataset and Experimental Setup

Experiments are conducted on SemEval-2010 Task 8 dataset (Hendrickx et al., 2009). This dataset contains 9 relationships (with two directions) and an undirected Other class. There are 10,717 annotated examples, including 8,000 sentences for training, and 2,717 for testing. We adopt the official evaluation metric to evaluate our systems, which is based on macro-averaged F1-score for the nine actual relations (excluding the Other relation) and takes the directionality into consideration.

In order to compare with the work by Zhang and Wang (2015), we use the same word vectors proposed by Turian et al. (2010) (50-dimensional) to initialize the embedding layer. Additionally, to compare with the work by Zhang et al. (2015), we also use the 100-dimensional word vectors pre-trained by Pennington et al. (2014).

Since there is no official development dataset, we randomly select 800 sentence for validation. The hyper-parameters for our model were tuned on the development set for each task. Our model was trained using AdaDelta (Zeiler, 2012) with a learning rate of 1.0 and a minibatch size 10. The model parameters were regularized with a per-minibatch L2 regularization strength of 10^{-5}. We evaluate the effect of dropout embedding layer, dropout LSTM layer and dropout the penultimate layer, the model has a better performance, when the dropout rate is set as 0.3, 0.3, 0.5 respectively. Other parameters in our model are initialized randomly.

4.2 Experimental Results

Table 1 compares our Att-BLSTM with other state-of-the-art methods of relation classification.

SVM: This is the top performed system in SemEval-2010. Rink and Harabagiu (2010) leveraged a variety of handcrafted features, and use SVM as the classifier. They achieved an F_1-score of 82.2%.

CNN: Zeng et al. (2014) treated a sentences as a sequential data and exploited the convolutional neural network to learn sentence-level features; they also used a special position vector to represent each word. Then the sentence-level and lexical features were concatenated into a single vector and fed into a softmax classifier for prediction. This model achieves an F_1-score of 82.7%.

RNN: Zhang and Wang (2015) employed bidirectional RNN networks with two different dimension word vectors for relation classification. They achieved an F_1-score of 82.8% using 300-dimensional word vectors pre-trained by Mikolov et al. (2013), and an F_1-score of 80.0% using 50-dimensional word vectors pre-trained by Turian et al. (2010). Our model with the same 50-dimensional word vectors achieves an F_1-score of 82.5%, about 2.5 percent more than theirs.

SDP-LSTM: Yan et al. (2015) utilized four different channels to pick up heterogeneous along the SDP, and they achieved an F_1-score of 83.7%. Comparing with their model, our model regarding the raw text as a sequence is simpler.

BLSTM: Zhang et al. (2015) employed many features derived from NLP tools and lexical re-sources with bidirectional LSTM networks to learn the sentence level features, and they achieved state-of-the-art performance on the SemEval-2010 Task 8 dataset. Our model with the same word vectors achieves a very similar result (84.0%), and our model is more simple.

Our proposed Att-BLSTM model yields an F_1-score of 84.0%. It outperforms most of the existing competing approaches, without using lexical resources such as WordNet or NLP systems like dependency parser and NER to get high-level features.

5 Conclusion

In this paper, we propose a novel neural network model, named Att-BLSTM, for relation classification. This model does not rely on NLP tools or lexical resources to get, it uses raw text with position indicators as input. The effectiveness of Att-BLSTM is demonstrated by evaluating the model on SemEval-2010 relation classification task.

Acknowledgments

This research was supported by the National High Technology Research and Development Program of China (No.2015AA015402). We thank the anonymous reviewers for their insightful comments.

References

Dzmitry Bahdanau, Kyunghyun Cho, and Yoshua Bengio. 2014. Neural machine translation by jointly learning to align and translate. *arXiv preprint arXiv:1409.0473*.

Razvan C Bunescu and Raymond J Mooney. 2005. A shortest path dependency kernel for relation extraction. In *Proceedings of the conference on human language technology and empirical methods in natural language processing*, pages 724–731. Association for Computational Linguistics

Jan K Chorowski, Dzmitry Bahdanau, Dmitriy Serdyuk, Kyunghyun Cho, and Yoshua Bengio. 2015. Attention-based models for speech recognition. In *Advances in Neural Information Processing Systems*, pages 577–585.

Alan Graves, Abdel-rahman Mohamed, and Geoffrey Hinton. 2013. Speech recognition with deep recurrent neural networks. In *Acoustics, Speech and Signal Processing (ICASSP), 2013 IEEE International Conference on*, pages 6645–6649. IEEE.

Alex Graves. 2013. Generating sequences with recurrent neural networks. *arXiv preprint arXiv:1308.0850*.

Iris Hendrickx, Su Nam Kim, Zornitsa Kozareva, Preslav Nakov, Diarmuid Ó Séaghdha, Sebastian Padó, Marco Pennacchiotti, Lorenza Romano, and Stan Szpakowicz. 2009. Semeval-2010 task 8: Multi-way classification of semantic relations between pairs of nominals. In *Proceedings of the Workshop on Semantic Evaluations: Recent Achievements and Future Directions*, pages 94–99. Association for Computational Linguistics.

Karl Moritz Hermann, Tomas Kocisky, Edward Grefenstette, Lasse Espeholt, Will Kay, Mustafa Suleyman, and Phil Blunsom. 2015. Teaching machines to read and comprehend. In *Advances in Neural Information Processing Systems*, pages 1684–1692.

Geoffrey E Hinton, Nitish Srivastava, Alex Krizhevsky, Ilya Sutskever, and Ruslan R Salakhutdinov. 2012. Improving neural networks by preventing co-adaptation of feature detectors. *arXiv preprint arXiv:1207.0580*.

Sepp Hochreiter and Jürgen Schmidhuber. 1997. Long short-term memory. *Neural computation*, 9(8):1735–1780.

Tomas Mikolov, Martin Karafiát, Lukas Burget, Jan Cernocký, and Sanjeev Khudanpur. 2010. Recurrent neural network based language model. In *INTERSPEECH 2010, 11th Annual Conference of the International Speech Communication Association, Makuhari, Chiba, Japan, September 26-30, 2010*, pages 1045–1048.

Tomas Mikolov, Ilya Sutskever, Kai Chen, Greg S Corrado, and Jeff Dean. 2013. Distributed representations of words and phrases and their compositionality. In *Advances in neural information processing systems*, pages 3111–3119.

George A Miller. 1995. Wordnet: a lexical database for english. *Communications of the ACM*, 38(11):39–41.

Mike Mintz, Steven Bills, Rion Snow, and Dan Jurafsky. 2009. Distant supervision for relation extraction without labeled data. In *Proceedings of the Joint Conference of the 47th Annual Meeting of the ACL and the 4th International Joint Conference on Natural Language Processing of the AFNLP: Volume 2-Volume 2*, pages 1003–1011. Association for Computational Linguistics.

Jeffrey Pennington, Richard Socher, and Christopher D Manning. 2014. Glove: Global vectors for word representation. In *EMNLP*, volume 14, pages 1532–1543.

Bryan Rink and Sanda Harabagiu. 2010. Utd: Classifying semantic relations by combining lexical and semantic resources. In *Proceedings of the 5th International Workshop on Semantic Evaluation*, pages 256–259. Association for Computational Linguistics.

Richard Socher, Brody Huval, Christopher D Manning, and Andrew Y Ng. 2012. Semantic compositionality through recursive matrix-vector spaces. In *Proceedings of the 2012 Joint Conference on Empirical Methods in Natural Language Processing and Computational Natural Language Learning*, pages 1201–1211. Association for Computational Linguistics.

Joseph Turian, Lev Ratinov, and Yoshua Bengio. 2010. Word representations: a simple and general method for semi-supervised learning. In *Proceedings of the 48th annual meeting of the association for computational linguistics*, pages 384–394. Association for Computational Linguistics.

Fei Wu and Daniel S Weld. 2010. Open information extraction using wikipedia. In *Proceedings of the 48th Annual Meeting of the Association for Computational Linguistics*, pages 118–127. Association for Computational Linguistics.

Kelvin Xu, Jimmy Ba, Ryan Kiros, Aaron Courville, Ruslan Salakhutdinov, Richard Zemel, and Yoshua Bengio. 2015. Show, attend and tell: Neural image caption generation with visual attention. *arXiv preprint arXiv:1502.03044*.

Xu Yan, Lili Mou, Ge Li, Yunchuan Chen, Hao Peng, and Zhi Jin. 2015. Classifying relations via long short term memory networks along shortest dependency path. *arXiv preprint arXiv:1508.03720*.

Xuchen Yao and Benjamin Van Durme. 2014. Information extraction over structured data: Question answering with freebase. In *ACL (1)*, pages 956–966. Citeseer.

Matthew D Zeiler. 2012. Adadelta: An adaptive learning rate method. *arXiv preprint arXiv:1212.5701*.

Daojian Zeng, Kang Liu, Siwei Lai, Guangyou Zhou, and Jun Zhao. 2014. Relation classification via convolutional deep neural network. In *Proceedings of COLING*, pages 2335–2344.

Dongxu Zhang and Dong Wang. 2015. Relation classification via recurrent neural network. *arXiv preprint arXiv:1508.01006*.

Shu Zhang, Dequan Zheng, Xinchen Hu, and Ming Yang. 2015. Bidirectional long short-term memory networks for relation classification.

"The red one!":
On learning to refer to things
based on discriminative properties

Angeliki Lazaridou and **Nghia The Pham** and **Marco Baroni**
University of Trento
{angeliki.lazaridou|thepham.nghia|marco.baroni}@unitn.it

Abstract

As a first step towards agents learning to communicate about their visual environment, we propose a system that, given visual representations of a referent (CAT) and a context (SOFA), identifies their *discriminative attributes*, i.e., properties that distinguish them (has_tail). Moreover, although supervision is only provided in terms of discriminativeness of attributes for pairs, the model learns to assign plausible attributes to specific objects (SOFA-has_cushion). Finally, we present a preliminary experiment confirming the referential success of the predicted discriminative attributes.

1 Introduction

There has recently been renewed interest in developing systems capable of genuine language understanding (Hermann et al., 2015; Hill et al., 2015). In this perspective, it is important to think of an appropriate general framework for teaching language to machines. Since we use language primarily for communication, a reasonable approach is to develop systems within a genuine communicative setup (Steels, 2003; Mikolov et al., 2015). Out long-term goal is thus to develop communities of computational agents that learn how to use language efficiently in order to achieve communicative success (Vogel et al., 2013; Foerster et al., 2016).

Within this general picture, one fundamental aspect of meaning where communication is indeed crucial is the act of *reference* (Searle, 1969; Abbott, 2010), the ability to successfully talk to others about things in the external world. A specific instantiation of reference studied in this paper is that of referring expression generation (Dale and

Figure 1: Discriminative attributes predicted by our model. Can you identify the intended referent? See Section 6 for more information

Reiter, 1995; Mitchell et al., 2010; Kazemzadeh et al., 2014). A *necessary* condition for achieving successful reference is that referring expressions (REs) accurately distinguish the intended referent from any other object in the context (Dale and Haddock, 1991). Along these lines, we present here a model that, given an intended referent and a context object, predicts the attributes that discriminate between the two. Some examples of the behaviour of the model are presented in Figure 1.

Importantly, and distinguishing our work from earlier literature on generating REs (Krahmer and Van Deemter, 2012): (i) the input objects are represented by natural images, so that the agent must learn to extract relevant attributes from realistic data; and (ii) no direct supervision on the attributes of a single object is provided: the training signal concerns their discriminativeness for object pairs (that is, during learning, the agent might be told that has_tail is discriminative for ⟨CAT, SOFA⟩, but not that it is an attribute of cats). We use this "pragmatic" signal since it could later be replaced by a measure of success in actual communication between two agents (e.g., whether a second agent was able to pick the correct referent given a RE).

2 Discriminative Attribute Dataset

We generated the Discriminative Attribute Dataset, consisting of pairs of (intended) *referents* and *contexts*, with respect to which the referents should be identified by their distinctive attributes.

Proceedings of the 54th Annual Meeting of the Association for Computational Linguistics, pages 213–218,
Berlin, Germany, August 7-12, 2016. ©2016 Association for Computational Linguistics

⟨referent, context⟩	visual instances	discriminative attributes
⟨CAT, SOFA⟩	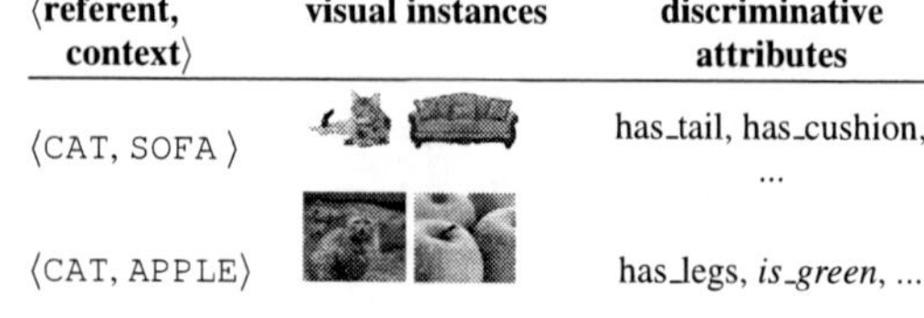	has_tail, has_cushion, ...
⟨CAT, APPLE⟩		has_legs, is_green, ...

Table 1: Example training data

Our starting point is the Visual Attributes for Concepts Dataset (ViSA) (Silberer et al., 2013), which contains *per-concept* (as opposed to *per-image*) attributes for 500 concrete concepts (CAT, SOFA, MILK) spanning across different categories (MAMMALS, FURNITURE), annotated with 636 general attributes. We disregarded ambiguous concepts (e.g., *bat*), thus reducing our working set of concepts C to 462 and the number of attributes V to 573, as we eliminated any attribute that did not occur with concepts in C. We extracted on average 100 images annotated with each of these concepts from ImageNet (Deng et al., 2009). Finally, each image i of concept c was associated to a *visual instance vector*, by feeding the image to the VGG-19 ConvNet (Simonyan and Zisserman, 2014), as implemented in the MatConvNet toolkit (Vedaldi and Lenc, 2015), and extracting the second-to-last fully-connected (fc) layer as its 4096-dimensional visual representation $\mathbf{v}_{c_i}$.

We split the target concepts into *training, validation* and *test* sets, containing 80%, 10% and 10% of the concepts in each category, respectively. This ensures that (i) the intersection between train and test concepts is empty, thus allowing us to test the generalization of the model across different objects, but (ii) there are instances of all categories in each set, so that it is possible to generalize across training and testing objects. Finally we build all possible combinations of concepts in the training split to form pairs of referents and contexts $\langle c_r, c_c \rangle$ and obtain their (binary) attribute vectors $\mathbf{p}_{c_r}$ and $\mathbf{p}_{c_c}$ from ViSA, resulting in 70K training pairs. From the latter, we derive, for each pair, a concept-level "discriminativeness" vector by computing the symmetric difference $\mathbf{d}_{c_r,c_c} = (\mathbf{p}_{c_r} - \mathbf{p}_{c_c}) \cup (\mathbf{p}_{c_c} - \mathbf{p}_{c_r})$. The latter will contain 1s for discriminative attributes, 0s elsewhere. On average, each pair is associated with 20 discriminative attributes. The final training data are triples of the form $\langle c_r, c_c, \mathbf{d}_{c_r,c_c} \rangle$ (the model *never* observes the attribute vectors of specific concepts), to be associated with visual instances of the two concepts. Table 1 presents some examples.

Note that ViSA contain concept-level attributes, but images contain specific instances of concepts for which a general attribute might not hold. This introduces a small amount of noise. For example, is_green would in general be a discriminative attribute for apples and cats, but it is not for the second sample in Table 1. Using datasets with *per-image* attribute annotations would solve this issue. However, those currently available only cover specific classes of concepts (e.g., only clothes, or animals, or scenes, etc.). Thus, taken separately, they are not general enough for our purposes, and we cannot merge them, since their concepts live in different attribute spaces.

3 Discriminative Attribute Network

The proposed *Discriminative Attribute Network* (DAN) learns to predict the discriminative attributes of referent object c_r and context c_c without direct supervision at the attribute level, but relying only on discriminativeness information (e.g., for the objects in the first row of Table 1, the gold vector would contain 1 for has_tail, but 0 for both is_green and has_legs). Still, the model is implicitly encouraged to embed objects into a consistent attribute space, to generalize across the discriminativeness vectors of different training pairs, so it also effectively learns to annotate objects with visual attributes.

Figure 2 presents a schematic view of DAN, focusing on a single attribute. The model is presented with two concepts ⟨CAT, SOFA⟩, and randomly samples a visual instance of each. The instance visual vectors $\mathbf{v}$ (i.e., ConvNet second-to-last fc layers) are mapped into *attribute* vectors of dimensionality $|V|$ (cardinality of all available attributes), using weights $\mathbf{M}^{\mathrm{a}} \in \mathbf{R}^{4096 \times |V|}$ shared between the two concepts. Intuitively, this layer should learn whether an attribute is active for a specific object, as this is crucial for determining whether the attribute is discriminative for an object pair. In Section 5, we present experimental evidence corroborating this hypothesis.

In order to capture the *pairwise* interactions between attribute vectors, the model proceeds by concatenating the two units associated with the *same* visual attribute v across the two objects (e.g., the units encoding information about has_tail) and pass them as input to the *discriminative* layer.

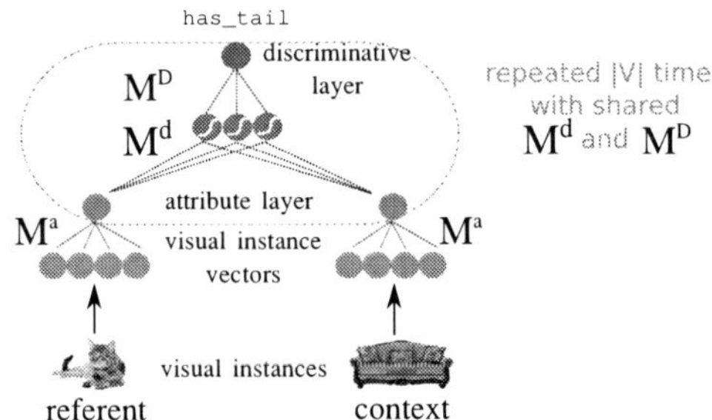

Figure 2: Schematic representation of DAN. For simplicity, the prediction process is only illustrated for `has_tail`

The discriminative layer processes the two units by applying a linear transformation with weights $\mathbf{M^d} \in \mathbf{R}^{2 \times h}$, followed by a sigmoid activation function, finally deriving a single value by another linear transformation with weights $\mathbf{M^D} \in \mathbf{R}^{h \times 1}$. The output $\hat{d}_v$ encodes the predicted degree of discriminativeness of attribute v for the specific reference-context pair. The same process is applied to all attributes $v \in V$, to derive the estimated discriminativeness vector $\hat{\mathbf{d}}$, using the same shared weights $\mathbf{M^d}$ and $\mathbf{M^D}$ for each attribute.

To learn the parameters θ of the model (i.e. $\mathbf{M^a}$, $\mathbf{M^d}$ and $\mathbf{M^D}$), given training data $\langle c_r, c_c, \mathbf{d}_{c_r,c_c} \rangle$, we minimize MSE between the gold vector $\mathbf{d}_{c_r,c_c}$ and model-estimated $\hat{\mathbf{d}}_{c_r,c_c}$. We trained the model with rmsprop and with a batch size of 32. All hyperparameters (including the hidden size h which was set to 60) were tuned to maximize performance on the validation set.

4 Predicting Discriminativeness

We evaluate the ability of the model to predict attributes that discriminate the intended referent from the context. Precisely, we ask the model to return all *discriminative attributes* for a pair, independently of whether they are positive for the referent or for the context (given images of a cat and a building, both $+$`is_furry` and $-$`made_of_bricks` are discriminative of the cat).

Test stimuli We derive our test stimuli from the VisA test split (see Section 2), containing 2000 pairs. Unlike in training, where the model was presented with specific *visual instances* (i.e., single images), for evaluation we use *visual concepts* (`CAT`, `BED`), which we derive by *averaging* the vectors of all images associated to an object (i.e., deriving `CAT` from all images of cats), due to lack

of gold information on *per-image* attributes.

Results We compare DAN against a random baseline based on per-attribute discriminativeness probabilities estimated from the training data and an ablation model without attribute layer. We test moreover a model that is trained with supervision to predict attributes and then deterministically computes the discriminative attributes. Specifically, we implemented a neural network with one hidden layer, which takes as input a visual instance, and it is trained to predict its gold attribute vector, casting the problem as logistic regression, thus relying on supervision at the attribute level. Then, given two paired images, we let the model generate their predicted attribute vectors and compute the discriminative attributes by taking the symmetric difference of the predicted attribute vectors as we do for DAN. For the DAN and its ablation, we use a 0.5 threshold to deem an attribute discriminative, without tuning.

The results in Table 2 confirm that, with appropriate supervision, DAN performs discriminativeness prediction reasonably well – indeed, as well as the model with similar parameter capacity requiring direct supervision on an attribute-by-attribute basis, followed by the symmetric difference calculation. Interestingly, allowing the model to embed visual representations into an intermediate attribute space has a strong positive effect on performance. Intuitively, since DAN is evaluated on novel concepts, the mediating attribute layer provides more high-level semantic information helping generalization, at the expense of extra parameters compared to the ablation without attribute layer.

5 Predicting Attributes

Attribute learning is typically studied in supervised setups (Ferrari and Zisserman, 2007; Farhadi et al., 2009; Russakovsky and Fei-Fei, 2010). Our model learns to embed visual objects in an attribute space through indirect supervision about attribute discriminativeness for specific *<referent, context>* pairs. Attributes are *never*

Model	Precision	Recall	F1
DAN	0.66	0.49	0.56
attribute+sym. difference	0.64	0.48	0.55
no attribute layer	0.63	0.33	0.43
Random baseline	0.16	0.16	0.16

Table 2: Predicting discriminative features

explicitly associated to a specific concept during training. The question arises of whether discriminativeness pushes the model to learn plausible concept attributes. Note that the idea that the semantics of attributes arises from their distinctive function within a communication system is fully in line with the classic structuralist view of linguistic meaning (Geeraerts, 2009).

To test our hypothesis, we feed DAN the same test stimuli (visual concept vectors) as in the previous experiment, but now look at activations in the attribute layer. Since these activations are real numbers whereas gold values (i.e., the visual attributes in the ViSA dataset) are binary, we use the validation set to learn the threshold to deem an attribute active, and set it to 0.5 without tuning. Note that no further training and no extra supervision other than the discriminativeness signal are needed to perform attribute prediction. The resulting binary attribute vector $\hat{\mathbf{p}}_c$ for concept c is compared against the corresponding gold attribute vector $\mathbf{p}_c$.

Results We compare DAN to the random baseline and to an explicit *attribute classifier* similar to the one used in the previous experiment, i.e., a one-hidden-layer neural network trained with logistic regression to predict the attributes. We report moreover the best F1 score of Silberer et al. (2013), who learn a SVM for each visual attribute based on HOG visual features. Unlike in our setup, in theirs, images for the same concept are used both for training and to derive visual attributes (our setup is "zero-shot" at the concept level, i.e., we predict attributes of concepts not seen in training). Thus, despite the fact that they used presumably less accurate pre-CNN visual features, the setup is much easier for them, and we take their performance to be an upper bound on ours.

DAN reaches, and indeed surpasses, the performance of the model with direct supervision at the attribute level, confirming the power of discriminativeness as a driving force in building semantic representations. The comparison with Silberer's model suggests that there is room for improvement, although the noise inherent in concept-level annotation imposes a relatively low bound on realistic performance.

Model	Precision	Recall	F1
DAN	0.58	0.64	0.61
direct supervision	0.56	0.60	0.58
Silberer et. al.	0.70	0.70	0.70
Random baseline	0.13	0.12	0.12

Table 3: Predicting concept attributes

6 Evaluating Referential Success

We finally ran a pilot study testing whether DAN's ability to predict discriminative attributes at the concept level translates into producing features that would be useful in constructing successful referential expressions for specific object instances.

Test stimuli Our starting point is the ReferIt dataset (Kazemzadeh et al., 2014), consisting of REs denoting objects (delimited by bounding boxes) in natural images. We filter out any ⟨RE, bounding box⟩ pair whose RE does not overlap with our attribute set V and annotate the remaining ones with the overlapping attribute, deriving data of the form ⟨RE, bounding box, attribute⟩. For each intended referent of this type, we sample as context another ⟨RE, bounding box⟩ pair such that (i) the context RE does not contain the referent attribute, so that the latter is a likely discriminative feature; (ii) referent and context come from different images, so that their bounding boxes do not accidentally overlap; (iii) there is maximum word overlap between referent and contexts REs, creating a realistic referential ambiguity setup (e.g., two cars, two objects in similar environments). Finally we sample maximally 20 ⟨referent, context⟩ pairs per attribute, resulting in 790 test items. For each referent and context we extract CNN visual vectors from their bounding boxes, and feed them to DAN to obtain their discriminative attributes. Note that we used the ViSA-trained DAN for this experiment as well.

Results For 12% of the test ⟨referent, context⟩ pairs, the discriminative attribute is contained in the set of discriminative attributes predicted by DAN. A random baseline estimated from the distribution of attributes in the ViSA dataset would score 15% recall. This baseline however on average predicts 20 discriminative attributes, whereas DAN activates, only 4. Thus, the baseline has a trivial recall advantage.

In order to evaluate whether in general the discriminative attributes activated by DAN would lead to referential success, we further sampled a subset of 100 ⟨referent, context⟩ test pairs. We presented them separately to two subjects (one a co-author of this study) together with the attribute that the model activated with the largest score (see Figure 1 for examples). Subjects were asked to identify the intended referent based on the attribute. If both agreed on the same referent, we achieved referential success, since the model-predicted attribute sufficed to coherently discriminate between the two images. Encouragingly, the subjects agreed on 78% of the pairs ($p<0.001$ when comparing against chance guessing, according to a 2-tailed binomial test). In cases of disagreement, the predicted attribute was either too generic or very salient in both objects, a behaviour observed especially in same-category pairs (e.g., is_round in Figure 1).

7 Concusion

We presented DAN, a model that, given a referent and a context, learns to predict their discriminative features, while also inferring visual attributes of concepts as a by-product of its training regime. While the predicted discriminative attributes can result in referential success, DAN is currently lacking all other properties of reference (Grice, 1975) (salience, linguistic and pragmatic felicity, etc). We are currently working towards adding communication (thus simulating a speaker-listener scenario (Golland et al., 2010)) and natural language to the picture.

Acknowledgments

This work was supported by ERC 2011 Starting Independent Research Grant n. 283554 (COMPOSES). We gratefully acknowledge the support of NVIDIA Corporation with the donation of the GPUs used for this research.

References

Barbara Abbott. 2010. *Reference*. Oxford University Press, Oxford, UK.

Robert Dale and Nicholas Haddock. 1991. Content determination in the generation of referring expressions. *Computational Intelligence*, 7(4):252–265.

Robert Dale and Ehud Reiter. 1995. Computational interpretations of the gricean maxims in the generation of referring expressions. *Cognitive science*, 19(2):233–263.

Jia Deng, Wei Dong, Richard Socher, Lia-Ji Li, and Li Fei-Fei. 2009. Imagenet: A large-scale hierarchical image database. In *Proceedings of CVPR*, pages 248–255, Miami Beach, FL.

Ali Farhadi, Ian Endres, Derek Hoiem, and David Forsyth. 2009. Describing objects by their attributes. In *Proceedings of CVPR*, pages 1778–1785, Miami Beach, FL.

Vittorio Ferrari and Andrew Zisserman. 2007. Learning visual attributes. In *Proceedings of NIPS*, pages 433–440, Vancouver, Canada.

Jakob N. Foerster, Yannis M. Assael, Nando de Freitas, and Shimon Whiteson. 2016. Learning to communicate to solve riddles with deep distributed recurrent q-networks. Technical Report arXiv:1602.02672.

Dirk Geeraerts. 2009. *Theories of lexical semantics*. Oxford University Press, Oxford, UK.

Dave Golland, Percy Liang, and Dan Klein. 2010. A game-theoretic approach to generating spatial descriptions. In *Proceedings of the 2010 conference on empirical methods in natural language processing*, pages 410–419. Association for Computational Linguistics.

Herbert P Grice. 1975. *Logic and conversation*. Syntax and Semantics.

Karl Moritz Hermann, Tomáš Kočiský, Edward Grefenstette, Lasse Espeholt, Will Kay, Mustafa Suleyman, and Phil Blunsom. 2015. Teaching machines to read and comprehend. In *Advances in Neural Information Processing Systems (NIPS)*.

Felix Hill, Antoine Bordes, Sumit Chopra, and Jason Weston. 2015. The Goldilocks principle: Reading children's books with explicit memory representations. http://arxiv.org/abs/1511.02301.

Sahar Kazemzadeh, Vicente Ordonez, Mark Matten, and Tamara L Berg. 2014. Referitgame: Referring to objects in photographs of natural scenes. In *EMNLP*, pages 787–798.

Emiel Krahmer and Kees Van Deemter. 2012. Computational generation of referring expressions: A survey. *Computational Linguistics*, 38(1):173–218.

Tomas Mikolov, Armand Joulin, and Marco Baroni. 2015. A roadmap towards machine intelligence. *arXiv preprint arXiv:1511.08130*.

Margaret Mitchell, Kees van Deemter, and Ehud Reiter. 2010. Natural reference to objects in a visual domain. In *Proceedings of the 6th international natural language generation conference*, pages 95–104. Association for Computational Linguistics.

Olga Russakovsky and Li Fei-Fei. 2010. Attribute learning in large-scale datasets. In *Proceedings of ECCV*, pages 1–14.

John R. Searle. 1969. *Speech Acts: An Essay in the Philosophy of Language*. Cambridge University Press.

Carina Silberer, Vittorio Ferrari, and Mirella Lapata. 2013. Models of semantic representation with visual attributes. In *Proceedings of ACL*, pages 572–582, Sofia, Bulgaria.

Karen Simonyan and Andrew Zisserman. 2014. Very deep convolutional networks for large-scale image recognition. *arXiv preprint arXiv:1409.1556*.

Luc Steels. 2003. Social language learning. In Mario Tokoro and Luc Steels, editors, *The Future of Learning*, pages 133–162. IOS, Amsterdam.

Andrea Vedaldi and Karel Lenc. 2015. *MatConvNet – Convolutional Neural Networks for MATLAB*. Proceeding of the ACM Int. Conf. on Multimedia.

Adam Vogel, Max Bodoia, Christopher Potts, and Daniel Jurafsky. 2013. Emergence of gricean maxims from multi-agent decision theory. In *HLT-NAACL*, pages 1072–1081.

Don't Count, Predict! An Automatic Approach to Learning Sentiment Lexicons for Short Text

Duy Tin Vo and **Yue Zhang**
Singapore University of Technology and Design
08 Somapah Road, Singapore 487372
`duytin_vo@mymail.sutd.edu.sg` and `yue_zhang@sutd.edu.sg`

Abstract

We describe an efficient neural network method to automatically learn sentiment lexicons without relying on any manual resources. The method takes inspiration from the NRC method, which gives the best results in SemEval13 by leveraging emoticons in large tweets, using the PMI between words and tweet sentiments to define the sentiment attributes of words. We show that better lexicons can be learned by using them to predict the tweet sentiment labels. By using a very simple neural network, our method is fast and can take advantage of the same data volume as the NRC method. Experiments show that our lexicons give significantly better accuracies on multiple languages compared to the current best methods.

1 Introduction

Sentiment lexicons contain the sentiment polarity and/or the strength of words or phrases (Baccianella et al., 2010; Taboada et al., 2011; Tang et al., 2014a; Ren et al., 2016a). They have been used for both rule-based (Taboada et al., 2011) and unsupervised (Turney, 2002; Hu and Liu, 2004; Kiritchenko et al., 2014) or supervised (Mohammad et al., 2013; Tang et al., 2014b; Vo and Zhang, 2015) machine-learning-based sentiment analysis. As a result, constructing sentiment lexicons is one important research task in sentiment analysis.

Many approaches have been proposed to construct sentiment lexicons. Traditional methods manually label the sentiment attributes of words (Hu and Liu, 2004; Wilson et al., 2005; Taboada et al., 2011). One benefit of such lexicons is high quality. On the other hand, the methods are time-consuming, requiring language and domain exper-

tise. Recently, statistical methods have been exploited to learn sentiment lexicons automatically (Esuli and Sebastiani, 2006; Baccianella et al., 2010; Mohammad et al., 2013). Such methods leverage knowledge resources (Bravo-Marquez et al., 2015) or labeled sentiment data (Tang et al., 2014a), giving significantly better coverage compared to manual lexicons.

Among the automatic methods, Mohammad et al. (2013) proposed to use tweets with emoticons or hashtags as training data. The main advantage is that such training data are abundant, and manual annotation can be avoided. Despite that emoticons or hashtags can be noisy in indicating the sentiment of a tweet, existing research (Go et al., 2009; Pak and Paroubek, 2010; Agarwal et al., 2011; Kalchbrenner et al., 2014; Ren et al., 2016b) has shown that effectiveness of such data when used to supervise sentiment classifiers.

Mohammad et al. (2013) collect sentiment lexicons by calculating pointwise mutual information (PMI) between words and emoticons. The resulting lexicons give the best results in a SemEval13 benchmark (Nakov et al., 2013). In this paper, we show that a better lexicon can be learned by directly optimizing the prediction accuracy, taking the lexicon as input and emoticon as the output. The correlation between our method and the method of Mohammad et al. (2013) is analogous to the "predicting" vs "counting" correlation between distributional and distributed word representations (Baroni et al., 2014).

We follow Esuli and Sebastiani (2006) in using two simple attributes to represent each sentiment word, and take inspiration from Mikolov et al. (2013) in using a very simple neural network for sentiment prediction. The method can leverage the same data as Mohammad et al. (2013) and therefore benefits from both scale and annotation independence. Experiments show

Proceedings of the 54th Annual Meeting of the Association for Computational Linguistics, pages 219–224,
Berlin, Germany, August 7-12, 2016. ©2016 Association for Computational Linguistics

that the neural model gives the best results on standard benchmarks across multiple languages. Our code and lexicons are publicly available at *https://github.com/duytinvo/acl2016*.

2   Related work

Existing methods for automatically learning sentiment lexicons can be classified into three main categories. The first category augments existing lexicons with sentiment information. For example, Esuli and Sebastiani (2006) and Baccianella et al. (2010) use a tuple (pos, neg, neu) to represent each word, where pos, neg and neu stand for possibility, negativity and neutrality, respectively, training these attributes by extracting features from WordNet. These methods rely on the taxonomic structure of existing lexicons, which are limited to specific languages.

The second approach expands existing lexicons, which are typically manually labeled. For example, Tang et al. (2014a) apply a neural network to learn sentiment-oriented embeddings from a small amount of annotated tweets, and then expand a set of seed sentiment words by measuring vector space distances between words. Bravo-Marquez et al. (2015) extend an existing lexicon by classifying words using manual features. These methods are also limited to domains and languages with manual resources.

The third line of methods constructs lexicons from scratch by accumulating statistical information over large data. Turney (2002) proposes to estimate the sentiment polarity of words by calculating PMI between seed words and search hits. Mohammad et al. (2013) improve the method by computing sentiment scores using distance-supervised data from emoticon-baring tweets instead of seed words. This approach can be used to automatically extract multilingual sentiment lexicons (Salameh et al., 2015; Mohammad et al., 2015) without using manual resources, which makes it more flexible compared to the first two methods. We consider it as our baseline.

We use the same data source as Mohammad et al. (2013) to train lexicons. However, rather than relying on PMI, we take a machine-learning method in optimizing the prediction accuracy of emoticons using the lexicons. To leverage large data, we use a very simple neural network to train the lexicons.

Figure 1: Our model.

3   Baseline

Mohammad et al. (2013) employ emoticons and relevant hashtags contained in a tweet as the sentiment label of the tweet. Given a set of tweets with their labels, the sentiment score (SS) for a token w was computed as:

$$SS(w) = PMI(w, pos) - PMI(w, neg), \quad (1)$$

where pos represents the positive label and neg represents the negative label. *PMI* stands for pointwise mutual information, which is

$$PMI(w, pos) = \log_2 \frac{freq(w, pos) * N}{freq(w) * freq(pos)} \quad (2)$$

Here $freq(w, pos)$ is the number of times the term w occurs in positive tweets, $freq(w)$ is the total frequency of term w in the corpus, $freq(pos)$ is the total number of tokens in positive tweets, and N is the total number of tokens in the corpus. $PMI(w, neg)$ is calculated in a similar way. Thus, Equation 1 is equal to:

$$SS(w) = \log_2 \frac{freq(w, pos) * freq(neg)}{freq(w, neg) * freq(pos)} \quad (3)$$

4   Model

We follow Esuli and Sebastiani (2006), using positivity and negativity attributes to define lexicons. In particular, each word takes the form $w = (n, p)$, where n denotes negativity and p denotes positivity $(n, p \in \mathbf{R})$. As shown in Figure 1, given a tweet $tw = w_1, w_2, ..., w_n$, a simple neural network is used to predict its two-dimensional sentiment label y, where [1,0] for negative and [0,1] for positive tweets. The predicted sentiment probability y of a tweet is computed as:

$$h = \sum_i (w_i) \quad (4)$$

Language	#pos	#neg	#Tweets
English	4.5M	4.5M	9M
Arabic	400k	400k	800k

Table 1: Emoticon-based training data.

Type		#pos	#neg	#Tweets
Supervised	train	3009	1187	4196
	dev	483	283	766
	test	1313	490	1803
Unsupervised		4805	1960	6765

Table 2: Statistics of the Semeval13.

$$y = softmax(hW) \qquad (5)$$

where W is fixed to the diagonal matrix ($W \in \mathbf{R}^{2 \times 2}$).

We follow Go et al. (2009) in defining the sentiment labels of tweets via emoticons. Each token is first initialized by random negative and positive attribute scores in [-0.25,0.25], and then trained by supervised learning. The cross-entropy error is employed as the objective function:

$$loss(tw) = -\sum \hat{y} . \log(y) \qquad (6)$$

Backpropagation is applied to learn (n, p) for each token. Optimization is done using stochastic gradient descent over shuffled mini-batches, with the AdaDelta update rule (Zeiler, 2012). All models are trained over 5 epochs with a batch size of 50. Due to its simplicity, the method is very fast, training a sentiment lexicon over 9 million tweets within 35 minutes per epoch on an Intel® core™ i7-3770 CPU @ 3.40 GHz.

5 Sentiment Classification

The resulting lexicon can be used in both unsupervised and supervised sentiment classifiers. The former is implemented by summing the sentiment scores of all tokens contained in a given document (Taboada et al., 2011; Kiritchenko et al., 2014). If the total sentiment score is larger than 0, the document is classified as positive. Here only one positivity attribute is required to represent a lexicon, and we use the contrast between the positivity and negativity attributes ($p - n$) as the score.

The supervised method makes use of sentiment lexicons as features for machine learning classification. Given a document D, we follow Zhu et al. (2014) and extract the following features:

- The number of sentiment tokens in D, where sentiment tokens are word tokens whose sentiment scores are not zero in a lexicon;

- The total sentiment score of a document: $\sum_{w_i \in D} SS(w_i)$;

- The maximal score: $max_{w_i \in D} SS(w_i)$;

- The total scores of positive and negative words in D;

- The sentiment score of the last token in D.

Again we use $SS(w_i) = p_{w_i} - n_{w_i}$ as the sentiment score of each word w_i, because the methods are based on a single sentiment score value for each word.

6 Experiments

6.1 Experimental Settings

Training data: To automatically obtain training data, we use the Twitter Developers API[1] to crawl emoticon tweets[2] of English and Arabic from February 2014 to September 2014. We follow Go et al. (2009), removing all emoticons used to collect training data from the tweets, and Tang et al. (2014b), ignoring tweets which are less than 7 tokens. A Twitter tokenizer (Gimpel et al., 2011) is applied to preprocess all tweets. Rare words that occur less than 5 times in the vocabulary are removed. HTTP links and username are replaced by $\langle http \rangle$ and $\langle user \rangle$, respectively. The statistics of training data is shown in Table 1.

Sentiment classifier: We use LibLinear[3] (Fan et al., 2008) as the supervised classifier on benchmark datasets. The parameter c is tuned by making a grid search (Hsu et al., 2003) on the accuracy of development set on the English dataset and five-fold cross validation on the Arabic dataset.

Evaluation: We follow Kiritchenko et al. (2014) in employing precision (P), recall (R) and F1 score (F) to evaluate unsupervised classification. We follow Hsu et al. (2003) and use accuracy (acc), the tuning criterion, to evaluate supervised classification.

Code and lexicons: We make the Python implementation of our models and the resulting sentiment lexicons available at *https://github.com/duytinvo/acl2016*

---

[1] https://dev.twitter.com/
[2] :), :), :-), :D, =) for positive and :(, : (, :-(for negative
[3] https://www.csie.ntu.edu.tw/~cjlin/liblinear/

Lexicons		Unsup			Sup
		P	**R**	**F**	**Acc**
WEKA	ED	61	55.9	55.4	73.8
	STS	66.4	52.5	47.7	73.7
HIT		**75.3**	73.3	74.1	78.5
NRC	Hashtag	70.3	71.4	70.8	77.4
	Emoticon	73.2	74.6	73.8	79.9
nnLexicon		74.4	**77.3**	**75.3**	**81.3**

Table 3: Results on SemEval13 (English).

Labels	Balanced			Unbalanced		
	train	dev	test	train	dev	test
#pos				481	159	159
#neg	481	159	159	1012	336	336
#mix				500	166	166
#obj				4015	1338	1338
#Tweets	1924	636	636	6008	1999	1999

Table 4: Standard splits of ASTD.

6.2 English Lexicons

The Twitter benchmark of SemEval13 (Nakov et al., 2013) is used as the English test set. In order to evaluate both unsupervised and supervised methods, we follow Tang et al. (2014b) and Kiritchenko et al. (2014), removing neutral tweets. The statistics is shown in Table 2. We compare our lexicon with the lexicons of NRC[4] (Mohammad et al., 2013), HIT[5] (Tang et al., 2014a) and WEKA[6] (Bravo-Marquez et al., 2015). As shown in Table 3, using the unsupervised sentiment classification method (unsup) in Section 5, our lexicon gives significantly better result in comparison with count-based lexicons of NRC. Under both settings, our lexicon yields the best results compared to other methods.

6.3 Arabic Lexicons

We employ the standard Arabic Twitter dataset ASTD (Nabil et al., 2015), which consists of about 10,000 tweets with 4 labels: objective (obj), negative (neg), positive (pos) and mixed subjective (mix). The standard splits of ASTD are shown in Table 4. We follow Nabil et al. (2015) by merging training and validating data for learning model. We compare our lexicon with only the lexicons of NRC[7] (Salameh et al., 2015), because the methods of Tang et al. (2014a) and Bravo-Marquez et al. (2015) depend on manual resources, which are

---

[4]http://saifmohammad.com/WebPages/Abstracts/NRC-SentimentAnalysis.htm

[5]http://ir.hit.edu.cn/~dytang/

[6]http://www.cs.waikato.ac.nz/~fjb11/

[7]http://saifmohammad.com/WebPages/ArabicSA.html

Lexicons		Balanced	Unbalanced
NRC	Hashtag	31.9	63.4
	Emoticon	31.4	65.3
nnLexicon		**33.3**	**66.5**

Table 5: Results on ASTD (Arabic).

Words	nnLexicon	NRC
bad	-1.122	-1.295
worse	-1.626	-1.417
worst	-2.256	-1.875
busy	-0.520	-0.003
busier	-0.609	0.106*
busiest	-1.254	-0.712
suitable	0.502	-0.040*
satisfy	0.570	-0.173*
lazy	-0.462	0.224*
scummy	-0.852	0.049*
old wine	0.453	0.552
old meat	-0.172	0.014*
strong memory	0.081	-0.083*
strong snowstorm	-0.554	0.182*

Table 6: Example sentiment scores, where * denotes incorrect polarity.

not available. As shown in Table 5, our lexicon consistently gives the best performance on both the balanced and unbalanced datasets, showing the advantage of "predicting" over "counting".

6.4 Analysis

Table 6 shows examples of our predicting-based lexicon and the counting-based lexicon of Mohammad et al. (2013). First, both lexicons can correctly reflect the strength of emotional words (e.g. *bad, worse, worst*), which demonstrates that our method can learn statistical relevance as effectively as PMI. Second, we find many cases where our lexicon gives the correct polarity (e.g. *suitable, lazy*) but the lexicon of Mohammad et al. (2013) does not. To quantitatively compare the lexicons, we calculated the accuracies of their polarities (i.e. sign) by using the manually-annotated lexicon of Hu and Liu (2004) as the gold standard. We take the intersection between the automatic lexicons and the lexicon of Hu and Liu (2004) as the test set, which contains 3270 words. The polarity accuracy of our lexicon is 78.2%, in contrast to 76.9% by the lexicon of Mohammad et al. (2013), demonstrating the relative strength of our method. Third, by having two attributes (n, p) instead of one, our lexicon is better in compositionality (e.g. $SS(strong\ memory) > 0$, $SS(strong\ snowstorm) < 0$).

7 Conclusion

We constructed a sentiment lexicon for short text automatically using an efficient neural network, showing that prediction-based training is better than counting-based training for learning from large tweets with emoticons. In standard evaluations, the method gave better accuracies across multiple languages compared to the state-of-the-art counting-based method.

References

Apoorv Agarwal, Boyi Xie, Ilia Vovsha, Owen Rambow, and Rebecca Passonneau. 2011. Sentiment analysis of twitter data. In *Proceedings of the Workshop on Languages in Social Media*, LSM '11, pages 30–38.

Stefano Baccianella, Andrea Esuli, and Fabrizio Sebastiani. 2010. Sentiwordnet 3.0: An enhanced lexical resource for sentiment analysis and opinion mining. In *Proceedings of LREC*, volume 10, pages 2200–2204.

Marco Baroni, Georgiana Dinu, and Germán Kruszewski. 2014. Don't count, predict! a systematic comparison of context-counting vs. context-predicting semantic vectors. In *Proceedings of ACL*, pages 238–247.

Felipe Bravo-Marquez, Eibe Frank, and Bernhard Pfahringer. 2015. Positive, negative, or neutral: learning an expanded opinion lexicon from emoticon-annotated tweets. In *Proceedings of IJCAI*, pages 1229–1235.

Andrea Esuli and Fabrizio Sebastiani. 2006. Sentiwordnet: A publicly available lexical resource for opinion mining. In *Proceedings of LREC*, volume 6, pages 417–422.

Rong-En Fan, Kai-Wei Chang, Cho-Jui Hsieh, Xiang-Rui Wang, and Chih-Jen Lin. 2008. Liblinear: A library for large linear classification. *The Journal of Machine Learning Research*, 9:1871–1874.

Kevin Gimpel, Nathan Schneider, Brendan O'Connor, Dipanjan Das, Daniel Mills, Jacob Eisenstein, Michael Heilman, Dani Yogatama, Jeffrey Flanigan, and A. Noah Smith. 2011. Part-of-speech tagging for twitter: Annotation, features, and experiments. In *Proceedings of ACL-HLT*, pages 42–47.

Alec Go, Richa Bhayani, and Lei Huang. 2009. Twitter sentiment classification using distant supervision. *CS224N Project Report, Stanford*, 1:12.

Chih-Wei Hsu, Chih-Chung Chang, Chih-Jen Lin, et al. 2003. A practical guide to support vector classification.

Minqing Hu and Bing Liu. 2004. Mining and summarizing customer reviews. In *Proceedings of KDD*, KDD '04, pages 168–177.

Nal Kalchbrenner, Edward Grefenstette, and Phil Blunsom. 2014. A convolutional neural network for modelling sentences. In *Proceedings of ACL*, pages 655–665.

Svetlana Kiritchenko, Xiaodan Zhu, and Saif M. Mohammad. 2014. Sentiment analysis of short informal texts. *J. Artif. Intell. Res.*, 50:723–762.

Tomas Mikolov, Kai Chen, Greg Corrado, and Jeffrey Dean. 2013. Efficient estimation of word representations in vector space. *arXiv preprint arXiv:1301.3781*.

Saif M. Mohammad, Svetlana Kiritchenko, and Xiaodan Zhu. 2013. Nrc-canada: Building the state-of-the-art in sentiment analysis of tweets. In *Proceedings of SemEval-2013*, June.

Saif M Mohammad, Mohammad Salameh, and Svetlana Kiritchenko. 2015. How translation alters sentiment. *Journal of Artificial Intelligence Research*, 54:1–20.

Mahmoud Nabil, Mohamed Aly, and Amir F Atiya. 2015. Astd: Arabic sentiment tweets dataset. In *Proceedings of EMNLP*, pages 2515–2519.

Preslav Nakov, Sara Rosenthal, Zornitsa Kozareva, Veselin Stoyanov, Alan Ritter, and Theresa Wilson. 2013. Semeval-2013 task 2: Sentiment analysis in twitter. In *Second Joint Conference on Lexical and Computational Semantics (*SEM), Volume 2: Proceedings of SemEval-2013*, pages 312–320.

Alexander Pak and Patrick Paroubek. 2010. Twitter based system: Using twitter for disambiguating sentiment ambiguous adjectives. In *Proceedings of the 5th International Workshop on Semantic Evaluation*, SemEval '10, pages 436–439.

Yafeng Ren, Yue Zhang, Meishan Zhang, and Donghong Ji. 2016a. Context-sensitive twitter sentiment classification using neural network. In *Proceedings of AAAI*.

Yafeng Ren, Yue Zhang, Meishan Zhang, and Donghong Ji. 2016b. Improving twitter sentiment classification using topic-enriched multi-prototype word embeddings. In *Proceedings of AAAI*.

Mohammad Salameh, Saif Mohammad, and Svetlana Kiritchenko. 2015. Sentiment after translation: A case-study on arabic social media posts. In *Proceedings of NAACL-HLT*, pages 767–777, May–June.

Maite Taboada, Julian Brooke, Milan Tofiloski, Kimberly Voll, and Manfred Stede. 2011. Lexicon-based methods for sentiment analysis. *Computational linguistics*, 37(2):267–307.

Duyu Tang, Furu Wei, Bing Qin, Ming Zhou, and Ting Liu. 2014a. Building large-scale twitter-specific sentiment lexicon : A representation learning approach. In *Proceedings of COLING*, pages 172–182, August.

Duyu Tang, Furu Wei, Nan Yang, Ming Zhou, Ting Liu, and Bing Qin. 2014b. Learning sentiment-specific word embedding for twitter sentiment classification. In *Proceedings of ACL*, pages 1555–1565, June.

Peter Turney. 2002. Thumbs up or thumbs down? semantic orientation applied to unsupervised classification of reviews. In *Proceedings of ACL*.

Duy-Tin Vo and Yue Zhang. 2015. Target-dependent twitter sentiment classification with rich automatic features. In *Proceedings of IJCAI*, pages 1347–1353, July.

Theresa Wilson, Janyce Wiebe, and Paul Hoffmann. 2005. Recognizing contextual polarity in phrase-level sentiment analysis. In *Proceedings of HLT-EMNLP*.

Matthew D Zeiler. 2012. Adadelta: an adaptive learning rate method. *arXiv preprint arXiv:1212.5701*.

Xiaodan Zhu, Svetlana Kiritchenko, and Saif Mohammad. 2014. Nrc-canada-2014: Recent improvements in the sentiment analysis of tweets. In *Proceedings of SemEval-2014*, pages 443–447.

Dimensional Sentiment Analysis Using a Regional CNN-LSTM Model

Jin Wang[1,3,4], Liang-Chih Yu[2,4], K. Robert Lai[3,4] and Xuejie Zhang[1]

[1]School of Information Science and Engineering, Yunnan University, Yunnan, P.R. China
[2]Department of Information Management, Yuan Ze University, Taiwan
[3]Department of Computer Science & Engineering, Yuan Ze University, Taiwan
[4]Innovation Center for Big Data and Digital Convergence Yuan Ze University, Taiwan
Contact: lcyu@saturn.yzu.edu.tw

Abstract

Dimensional sentiment analysis aims to recognize continuous numerical values in multiple dimensions such as the valence-arousal (VA) space. Compared to the categorical approach that focuses on sentiment classification such as binary classification (i.e., positive and negative), the dimensional approach can provide more fine-grained sentiment analysis. This study proposes a *regional* CNN-LSTM model consisting of two parts: regional CNN and LSTM to predict the VA ratings of texts. Unlike a conventional CNN which considers a whole text as input, the proposed regional CNN uses an individual sentence as a region, dividing an input text into several regions such that the useful affective information in each region can be extracted and weighted according to their contribution to the VA prediction. Such regional information is sequentially integrated across regions using LSTM for VA prediction. By combining the regional CNN and LSTM, both local (regional) information within sentences and long-distance dependency across sentences can be considered in the prediction process. Experimental results show that the proposed method outperforms lexicon-based, regression-based, and NN-based methods proposed in previous studies.

1 Introduction

Sentiment analysis has been useful in the development of online applications for customer reviews and public opinion analysis (Pang and Lee 2008; Calvo and D'Mello 2010; Liu 2012; Feldman 2013). In sentiment representation, the cate-gorical approach represents emotional states as several discrete classes such as binary (i.e., positive and negative) or as multiple categories such as Ekman's (1992) six basic emotions (anger, happiness, fear, sadness, disgust, and surprise). Classification algorithms can then be used to identify sentiment categories from texts.

The dimensional approach represents emotional states as continuous numerical values in multiple dimensions such as the valence-arousal (VA) space (Russell, 1980). The dimension of valence refers to the degree of positive and negative sentiment, whereas the dimension of arousal refers to the degree of calm and excitement. Both dimensions range from 1 (highly negative or calm) to 9 (highly positive or excited) based on the self-assessment manikin (SAM) annotation scheme (Bradley et al. 1994). For example, the following passage consisting of three sentences is associated with a valence-arousal rating of (2.5, 7.8), which displays a high degree of negativity and arousal.

(r1) *A few days ago I checked into a franchise hotel.*

(r2) *The front desk service was terrible, and they didn't know much about local attrac-tions.*

(r3) *I would not recommend this hotel to a friend.*

Such high-arousal negative (or high-arousal positive) texts are usually of interest and could prioritized in product review systems. Dimensional sentiment analysis can accomplish this by recognizing the VA ratings of texts and rank them accordingly, thus providing more intelligent and fine-grained sentiment applications.

Proceedings of the 54th Annual Meeting of the Association for Computational Linguistics, pages 225–230,
Berlin, Germany, August 7-12, 2016. ©2016 Association for Computational Linguistics

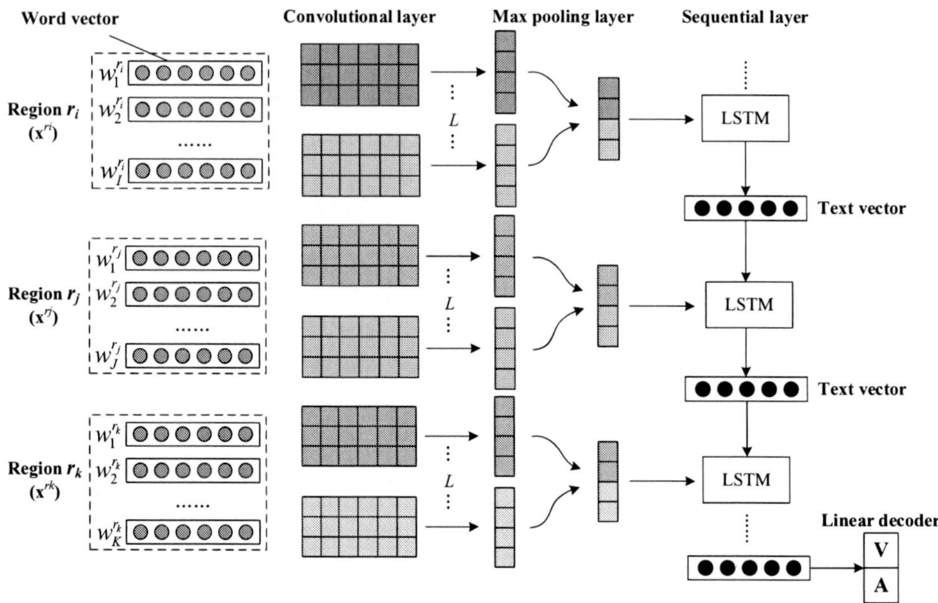

Figure 1: System architecture of the proposed regional CNN-LSTM model.

Research on dimensional sentiment analysis has addressed VA recognition at both the word-level (Wei et al., 2011; Malandrakis et al., 2011; Yu et al., 2015) and the sentence-level (Paltoglou et al., 2013; Malandrakis et al., 2013). At the word-level, Wei et al. (2011) used linear regression to transfer VA ratings from English affective words to Chinese words. Malandrakis et al. (2011) used a kernel function to combine the similarity between words for VA prediction. Yu et al. (2015) used a weighted graph model to iteratively determine the VA ratings of affective words. At the sentence level, Paltoglou et al. (2013) adopted a lexicon-based method to calculate the VA ratings of texts by averaging the VA ratings of affective words in the texts using a weighted arithmetic/geometric mean. Malandrakis et al. (2013) proposed a regression method that extracted n-gram with affective ratings as features to predict VA values for texts.

Recently, word embedding (Mikolov et al., 2013a; Mikolov et al., 2013b) and deep neural networks (NN) such as convolutional neural networks (CNN) (Kim, 2014; Kalchbrenner et al., 2014), recurrent neural networks (RNN) (Graves, 2012; Irsoy and Cardie, 2014) and long short-term memory (LSTM) (Wang et al., 2015; Liu et al., 2015) have been successfully employed for categorical sentiment analysis. In general, CNN is capable of extracting local information but may fail to capture long-distance dependency. LSTM can address this limitation by sequentially modeling texts across sentences. Such NN-based and word embedding methods have not been well explored for dimensional sentiment analysis.

This study proposes a regional CNN-LSTM model consisting of two parts, regional CNN and LSTM, to predict the VA ratings of texts. We first construct word vectors for vocabulary words using word embedding. The regional CNN is then used to build text vectors for the given texts being predicted based on the word vectors. Unlike a conventional CNN which considers a whole text as input, the proposed regional CNN uses individual sentences as regions, dividing an input text into several regions such that the useful affective information in different regions can be extracted and weighted according to their contribution to the VA prediction. For example, in the aforementioned example text, it would be useful for the system to emphasize the two sentences/regions (r2) and (r3) containing negative affective information. Finally, such regional information is sequentially integrated across regions using LSTM for VA prediction. By combining the regional CNN and LSTM, both local (regional) information within sentences and long-distance dependency across sentences can be considered in the prediction process.

The rest of this paper is organized as follows. Section 2 describes the proposed regional CNN-LSTM model. Section 3 reports the evaluation results of the proposed method against lexicon-based, regression-based, and NN-based methods. Conclusions are finally drawn in Section 4.

2 Regional CNN-LSTM Model

Figure 1 shows the overall framework of the proposed regional CNN-LSTM model. First, the word vectors of vocabulary words are trained from a large corpus using the word2vec toolkit. For each given text, the regional CNN model uses a sentence as a region to divide the given text into R regions, i.e. $r_1,\ldots, r_i, r_j, r_k,\ldots, r_R$. In each region, useful affective features can be extracted once the word vectors sequentially pass through a convolutional layer and max pooling layer. Such local (regional) features are then sequentially integrated across regions using LSTM to build a text vector for VA prediction.

2.1 Convolutional Layer

In each region, a convolutional layer is first used to extract local n-gram features. All word embeddings are stacked in a region matrix $M \in \mathbb{R}^{d \times |V|}$, where $|V|$ is the vocabulary size of a region, and d is the dimensionality of word vectors. For example, in Fig.1, the word vectors in the regions $r_i = \{w_1^{r_i}, w_2^{r_i},\ldots,w_I^{r_i}\}$, $r_j = \{w_1^{r_j}, w_2^{r_j},\ldots, w_J^{r_j}\}$ and $r_k = \{w_1^{r_k}, w_2^{r_k},\ldots, w_K^{r_k}\}$ are combined to form the region matrices $\mathbf{x}^{r_i}$, $\mathbf{x}^{r_j}$, and $\mathbf{x}^{r_k}$. In each region, we use L convolutional filters to learn local n-gram features. In a window of ω words $\mathbf{x}_{n:n+\omega-1}$, a filter F_l ($1 \leq l \leq L$) generates the feature map y_n^l as follows,

$$y_n^l = f(W^l \circ \mathbf{x}_{n:n+\omega-1} + b^l) \qquad (1)$$

where $\circ$ is a convolutional operator, $W \in \mathbb{R}^{\omega \times d}$ and b respectively denote the weight matrix and bias, ω is the length of the filter, d is the dimension of the word vector, and f is the ReLU function. When a filter gradually traverses from $\mathbf{x}_{1:\omega-1}$ to $\mathbf{x}_{N+\omega-1:N}$, we get the output feature maps $\mathbf{y}^l = y_1^l, y_2^l,\ldots,y_{N-\omega+1}^l$ of filter F_l. Given varying text lengths in the regions, $\mathbf{y}^l$ may have different dimensions for different texts. Therefore, we define the maximum length of the CNN input in the

corpora as the dimension N. If the input length is shorter than N, then several random vectors with a uniform distribution $U(-0.25, 0.25)$ will be appended.

2.2 Max-pooling Layer

Max-pooling subsamples the output of the convolutional layer. The most common way to do pooling it to apply a max operation to the result of each filter. There are two reasons to use a max-pooling layer here. First, by eliminating non-maximal values, it reduces computation for upper layers. Second, it can extract the local dependency within different regions to keep the most salient information. The obtained region vectors are then fed to a sequential layer.

2.3 Sequential Layer

To capture long-distance dependency across regions, the sequential layer sequentially integrates each region vector into a text vector. Due to the problem of gradients vanishing or exploding in RNN (Bengio et al., 1994), LSTM is introduced in the sequential layer for vector composition. After the LSTM memory cell sequentially traverses through all regions, the last hidden state of the sequential layer is regarded as the text representation for VA prediction.

2.4 Linear Decoder

Since the values in both the valence and arousal dimensions are continuous, the VA prediction task requires a regression. Instead of using a softmax classifier, a linear activation function (also known as a linear decoder) is used in the output layer, defined as,

$$y = W_d \mathbf{x}_t + b_d \qquad (2)$$

where $\mathbf{x}_t$ is the text vector learned from the sequential layer, y is the degree of valence or arousal of the target text, and W_d and b_d respectively denote the weight and bias associated with the linear decoder.

The regional CNN-LSTM model is trained by minimizing the mean squared error between the predicted y and actual y. Given a training set of text matrix $\mathbf{X} = \{\mathbf{x}^{(1)}, \mathbf{x}^{(2)},\ldots, \mathbf{x}^{(m)}\}$, and their VA ratings set $\mathbf{y} = \{y^{(1)}, y^{(2)}, \ldots, y^{(m)}\}$, the loss function is defined as

$$L(\mathbf{X}, \mathbf{y}) = \frac{1}{2m} \sum_{i=1}^{m} \left\| h(\mathbf{x}^{(i)}) - y^{(i)} \right\|^2 \qquad (3)$$

SST (English)			
Valence	RMSE	MAE	r
Lexicon-wAM	2.018	1.709	0.350
Lexicon-wGM	1.985	1.692	0.385
Regression-AVR	1.856	1.542	0.455
Regression-MVR	1.868	1.551	0.448
CNN	1.489	1.184	0.706
RNN	1.976	1.715	0.401
LSTM	1.444	1.151	0.717
Regional CNN-LSTM	**1.341***	**0.987***	**0.778***

* Regional CNN-LSTM vs LSTM significantly different (p<0.05)

Table 1: Comparative results of different methods in SST.

In the training phase, a back propagation (BP) algorithm with stochastic gradient descent (SGD) is used to learn model parameters. Details of the BP algorithm can be found in (LeCun et al., 2012).

3 Experiments

This section evaluates the performance of the proposed regional CNN-LSTM model against lexicon-based, regression-based, and NN-based methods.

Datasets. This experiment used two affective corpora. i) Stanford Sentiment Treebank (SST) (Socher et al., 2013) contains 8,544 training texts, 2,210 test texts, and 1,101 validation texts. Each text was rated with a single dimension (valence) in the range of (0, 1). ii) Chinese Valence-Arousal Texts (CVAT) (Yu et al., 2016) consists of 2,009 texts collected from social forums, manually rated with both valence and arousal dimensions in the range of (1, 9) using the SAM annotation scheme (Bradley et al. 1994). The word vectors for English and Chinese were respectively trained using the Google News and Chinese wiki dumps (zhwiki) datasets. The dimensionality for both word vectors are 300.

Experimental Settings. Two lexicon-based methods were used for comparison: weighted arithmetic mean (wAM) and weighted geometric mean (wGM) (Paltoglou et al., 2013), along with two regression-based methods: average values regression (AVR) and maximum values regression (MVR) (Malandrakis et al., 2013). The valence ratings of English and Chinese words were respectively taken from the Extended ANEW (Warriner et al., 2013) and Chinese Valence-Arousal Words (CVAW) lexicons (Yu et al.,

CVAT (Chinese)			
Valence	RMSE	MAE	r
Lexicon - wAM	1.884	1.632	0.406
Lexicon - wGM	1.843	1.597	0.418
Regression-AVR	1.685	1.374	0.476
Regression-MVR	1.697	1.392	0.468
CNN	1.093	0.880	0.645
RNN	1.424	1.262	0.493
LSTM	1.135	0.939	0.641
Regional CNN-LSTM	**1.026***	**0.842***	**0.781***
Arousal	RMSE	MAE	r
Lexicon-wAM	1.232	0.985	0.268
Lexicon-wGM	1.243	0.996	0.263
Regression-AVR	1.154	0.862	0.286
Regression-MVR	1.128	0.842	0.289
CNN	0.991	0.788	0.453
RNN	1.024	0.816	0.290
LSTM	0.945	0.751	0.472
Regional CNN-LSTM	**0.874***	**0.689***	**0.557***

* Regional CNN-LSTM vs LSTM significantly different (p<0.05)

Table 2. Comparative results of different methods in CVAT.

2016). A conventional CNN, RNN and LSTM were also implemented for comparison.

Metrics. Performance was evaluated using the root mean square error (RMSE), mean absolute error (MAE), and Pearson correlation coefficient (r), defined as

- *Root mean square error* (RMSE)

$$RMSE = \sqrt{\sum_{i=1}^{n} \left(A_i - P_i \right)^2 \Big/ n} \qquad (4)$$

- *Mean absolute error* (MAE)

$$MAE = \frac{1}{n}\sum_{i=1}^{n} | A_i - P_i | \qquad (5)$$

- *Pearson correlation coefficient (r)*

$$r = \frac{1}{n-1}\sum_{i=1}^{n} (\frac{A_i - \overline{A}}{\sigma_A})(\frac{P_i - \overline{P}}{\sigma_P}) \qquad (6)$$

where A_i is the actual value, P_i is the predicted value, n is the number of test samples, $\overline{A}$ and $\overline{P}$ respectively denote the arithmetic mean of A and P, and σ is the standard deviation. A lower RMSE or MAE and a higher r value indicates better prediction performance. A *t-test* was used to determine whether the performance difference was statistically significant.

Comparative Results. Tables 1 and 2 respectively present the comparative results of the regional CNN-LSTM against several methods for VA prediction of texts in both English and Chinese corpora. For the lexicon-based methods, wGM outperformed wAM, which is consistent with the results presented in (Paltoglou et al., 2013). Instead of using the VA ratings of words to directly measure those of texts, the regression-based methods learned the correlations between the VA ratings of words and texts, thus yielding better performance. Once the word embedding and deep learning techniques were introduced, the performance of NN-based methods (except RNN) jumped dramatically. In addition, the proposed regional CNN-LSTM outperformed the other NN-based methods, indicating the effectiveness of sequentially integrating the regional information across regions. Another observation is that the Pearson correlation coefficient of prediction in arousal is lower than that for the valence prediction, indicating that arousal is more difficult to predict.

4   Conclusion

This study presents a regional CNN-LSTM model to predict the VA ratings of texts. By capturing both local (regional) information within sentences and long-distance dependency across sentences, the proposed method outperformed regression- and conventional NN-based methods presented in previous studies. Future work will focus on the use of a parser to identify regions so that the structural information can be further incorporated to improve the prediction performance.

Acknowledgments

This work was supported by the Ministry of Science and Technology, Taiwan, ROC, under Grant No. MOST 102-2221-E-155-029-MY3 and MOST 104-3315-E-155-002. The authors would like to thank the anonymous reviewers and the area chairs for their constructive comments.

References

Yoshua Bengio, Patrice Simard, and Paolo Frasconi. 1994. Learning long-term dependencies with gradient descent is difficult. *IEEE Trans. Neural Networks*, 5(21):57-166.

Margaret M. Bradley, and Peter J. Lang. 1994. Measuring emotion: the self-assessment manikin and the semantic differential. *Journal of Behavior Therapy and Experimental Psychiatry*, 25 (1): 49-59.

Rafael A. Calvo and Sidney D'Mello. 2010. Affect detection: An interdisciplinary re-view of models, methods, and their applications. *IEEE Trans. Affective Computing*, 1(1): 18-37.

Paul Ekman. 1992. An argument for basic emotions. *Cognition and Emotion*, 6:169-200.

Ronen Feldman. 2013. Techniques and applications for sentiment analysis. *Communications of the ACM*, 56(4):82-89.

Alex Graves. 2012. Supervised sequence labelling with recurrent neural networks. Vol. 385, Springer.

Ozan Irsoy and Claire Cardie. 2014. Opinion mining with deep recurrent neural networks. In *Proceedings of the 2014 Conference on Empirical Methods in Natural Language Processing (EMNLP-14)*, pages 720-728.

Yoon Kim. 2014. Convolutional neural networks for sentence classification. In *Proceedings of the 2014 Conference on Empirical Methods on Natural Language Processing (EMNLP-14)*, pages 1746-1751.

Nal Kalchbrenner, Edward Grefenstette, and Phil Blunsom. 2014. A convolutional neural network for modelling sentences. In *Proceedings of the 52nd Annual Meeting of the Association for Computational Linguistics (ACL-14)*, pages 655-665.

Yann LeCun, Leon Bottou, Genevieve B. Orr and Klaus-Robert Muller. 2012. Efficient backprop. Neural networks: Tricks of the trade. Springer Berlin Heidelberg, 2012. 9-48.

Bing Liu. 2012. Sentiment Analysis and Opinion Mining. Morgan & Claypool, Chicago, IL.

Pengfei Liu, Shafiq Joty and Helen Meng. 2015. Fine-grained opinion mining with recurrent neural networks and word embeddings. In *Proceedings of the 2015 Conference on Empirical Methods in Natural Language Processing (EMNLP-15)*, pages 1433-1443.

Nikos Malandrakis, Alexandros Potamianos, Elias Iosif, Shrikanth Narayanan. 2011. Kernel models for affective lexicon creation. In *Proceedings of INTERSPEECH*, pages 2977-2980.

Nikos Malandrakis, Alexandros Potamianos, Elias Iosif, Shrikanth Narayanan. 2013. Distributional semantic models for affective text analysis. *IEEE Trans. Audio, Speech, and Language Processing*, 21(11): 2379-2392.

Tomas Mikolov, Kai Chen, Greg Corrado, and Jeffrey Dean. 2013a. Efficient estimation of word representations in vector space. In *Proceedings of International Conference on Learning Representations (ICLR-13): Workshop Track*.

Tomas Mikolov, Ilya Sutskever, Kai Chen, Greg Corrado, and Jeffrey Dean. 2013b. Distributed representations of words and phrases and their compositionality. In *Advances in Neural Information Processing Systems 26*, pages 3111-3119.

Bo Pang and Lillian Lee. 2008. Opinion mining and sentiment analysis. *Foundations and trends in information retrieval*, 2(1-2):1-135.

Georgios Paltoglou, Mathias Theunis, Arvid Kappas, and Mike Thelwall. 2013. Predicting emotional responses to long informal text. *IEEE Trans. Affective Computing*, 4(1):106-115.

James A. Russell. 1980. A circumplex model of affect. *Journal of Personality and Social Psychology*, 39(6):1161.

Richard Socher, Alex Perelygin, Jean Y. Wu, Jason Chuang, Christopher D. Manning, Andrew Y. Ng and Christopher Potts. 2013. Recursive deep models for semantic compositionality over a sentiment treebank. In *Proceedings of the 2013 Empirical Methods on Natural Language Processing (EMNLP-13)*, pages 1631-1642.

Amy Beth Warriner, Victor Kuperman, and Marc Brysbaert. 2013. Norms of valence, arousal, and dominance for 13,915 English lemmas. *Behavior research methods*, 45(4): 1191-1207.

Xin Wang, Yuanchao Liu, Chengjie Sun, Baoxun Wang and Xiaolong Wang. 2015. Predicting polarities of tweets by composing word embeddings with long short-term memory. In *Proceedings of the 53th Annual Meeting of the Association for Computational Linguistics (ACL-15)*, pages 1343-1353.

Wen-Li Wei, Chung-Hsien Wu, and Jen-Chun Lin. 2011. A regression approach to affective rating of Chinese words from ANEW. In *Proceedings of Affective Computing and Intelligent Interaction (ACII-11)*, pages 121-131.

Liang-Chih Yu, Jin Wang, K. Robert Lai, and Xuejie Zhang. 2015. Predicting valence-arousal ratings of words using a weighted graph method. In *Proceedings of the 53th Annual Meeting of the Association for Computational Linguistics (ACL-15)*, pages 788-793.

Liang-Chih Yu, Lung-Hao Lee, Shuai Hao, Jin Wang, Yunchao He, Jun Hu, K. Robert Lai and Xuejie Zhang. 2016. Building Chinese Affective Resources in Valence-Arousal Dimensions. In *Proceedings of the 15th Annual Conference of the North American Chapter of the Association for Computational Linguistics: Human Language Technologies (NAACL/HLT-16)*.

Deep multi-task learning with low level tasks supervised at lower layers

Anders Søgaard
University of Copenhagen
soegaard@hum.ku.dk

Yoav Goldberg
Bar-Ilan University
yoav.goldberg@gmail.com

Abstract

In all previous work on deep multi-task learning we are aware of, all task supervisions are on the same (outermost) layer. We present a multi-task learning architecture with deep bi-directional RNNs, where different tasks supervision can happen at different layers. We present experiments in syntactic chunking and CCG supertagging, coupled with the additional task of POS-tagging. We show that it is consistently better to have POS supervision at the innermost rather than the outermost layer. We argue that this is because "low-level" tasks are better kept at the lower layers, enabling the higher-level tasks to make use of the shared representation of the lower-level tasks. Finally, we also show how this architecture can be used for domain adaptation.

1 Introduction

We experiment with a multi-task learning (MTL) architecture based on deep bi-directional recurrent neural networks (bi-RNNs) (Schuster and Paliwal, 1997; Irsoy and Cardie, 2014). MTL can be seen as a way of regularizing model induction by sharing representations (hidden layers) with other inductions (Caruana, 1993). We use deep bi-RNNs with task supervision from multiple tasks, sharing one or more bi-RNNs layers among the tasks. Our main contribution is the novel insight that (what has historically been thought of as) low-level tasks are better modeled in the low layers of such an architecture. This is in contrast to previous work on deep MTL (Collobert et al., 2011; Luong et al., 2015) , in which supervision for all tasks happen at the same (outermost) layer. Multiple-tasks supervision at the outermost layer has a strong tradi-

tion in neural net models in vision and elsewhere (Caruana, 1993; Zhang and Zhang, 2014; Yim et al., 2015). However, in NLP it is natural to think of some levels of analysis as feeding into others, typically with low-level tasks feeding into high-level ones; e.g., POS tags as features for syntactic chunking (Sang and Buchholz, 2000) or parsing (Nivre et al., 2007). Our architecture can be seen as a seamless way to combine multi-task and cascaded learning. We also show how the proposed architecture can be applied to domain adaptation, in a scenario in which we have high-level task supervision in the source domain, and lower-level task supervision in the target domain.

As a point of comparison, Collobert et al. (2011) improved deep convolutional neural network models of syntactic chunking by also having task supervision from POS tagging at the outermost level. In our work, we use recurrent instead of convolutional networks, but our main contribution is observing that we obtain better performance by having POS task supervision at a lower layer. While Collobert et al. (2011) also experiment with NER and SRL, they only obtain improvements from MTL with POS and syntactic chunking. We show that similar gains can be obtained for CCG supertagging.

Our contributions   (i) We present a MTL architecture for sequence tagging with deep bi-RNNs; (ii) We show that having task supervision from all tasks at the outermost level is often suboptimal; (iii) we show that this architecture can be used for domain adaptation.

2 Sequence tagging with deep bi-RNNs

Notation   We use $x_{1:n}$ to denote a sequence of n vectors $x_1, \cdots, x_n$. $F_\theta(\cdot)$ is a function parameterized with parameters θ. We write $F_L(\cdot)$ as a shortcut to F_{θ_L} – an instantiation of F with a spe-

Proceedings of the 54th Annual Meeting of the Association for Computational Linguistics, pages 231–235,
Berlin, Germany, August 7-12, 2016. ©2016 Association for Computational Linguistics

cific set of parameters θ_L. We use $\circ$ to denote a vector concatenation operation.

Deep bi-RNNs We use a specific flavor of Recurrent Neural Networks (RNNs) (Elman, 1990) called long short-term memory networks (LSTMs) (Hochreiter and Schmidhuber, 1997). For brevity, we treat RNNs as a black-box abstraction, and LSTMs as an instance of the RNN interface. For further details on RNNs and LSTMs, see (Goldberg, 2015; Cho, 2015). We view RNN as a parameterized function $RNN_\theta(x_{1:n})$ mapping a sequence of n input vectors $x_{1:n}$, $x_i \in \mathbb{R}^{d_{in}}$ to a an output vector $h_n \in \mathbb{R}^{d_{out}}$. The output vector h_n is conditioned on all the input vectors $x_{1:n}$, and can be thought of as a *summary* of $x_{1:n}$. The RNN can be applied to all prefixes $x_{1:i}$, $1 \leq i \leq n$ of $x_{1:n}$, resulting in n output vectors $h_{1:n}$, where $h_{1:i}$ summarizes $x_{1:i}$.

A *deep RNN* (or k-layer RNN) is composed of k RNN functions $RNN_1, \cdots, RNN_k$ that feed into each other: the output $h_{1:n}^\ell$ of RNN_ℓ becomes the input of $RNN_{\ell+1}$. Stacking RNNs in this way was empirically shown to be effective.

A *bidirectional RNN* (Schuster and Paliwal, 1997; Irsoy and Cardie, 2014) is composed of two RNNs, RNN_F and RNN_R, one reading the sequence in its regular order, and the other reading it in reverse. Concretely, given a sequence $x_{1:n}$ and a desired index i, the function $BIRNN_\theta(x_{1:n}, i)$ is defined as:

$$BIRNN_\theta(x_{1:n}, i) = v_i = h_{F,i} \circ h_{R,i}$$
$$h_{F,i} = RNN_F(x_1, x_2, \cdots, x_i)$$
$$h_{R,i} = RNN_R(x_n, x_{n-1}, \cdots, x_i)$$

The vector $v_i = BIRNN(x_{1:n}, i)$ is then a representation of the ith item in $x_{1:n}$, taking into account both the entire history $x_{1:i}$ and the entire future $x_{i:n}$.

Finally, in a *deep bidirectional RNN*, both RNN_F and RNN_R are k-layer RNNs, and $BIRNN^\ell(x_{1:n}, i) = v_i^\ell = h_{F,i}^\ell \circ h_{R,i}^\ell$.

Greedy sequence tagging with deep bi-RNNs In a sequence tagging task, we are given an input $w_1, \cdots, w_n$ and need to predict an output $y_1, \cdots, y_n$, $y_i \in [1, \cdots, |L|]$, where L is a label set of interest; i.e., in a POS tagging task, L is the part-of-speech tagset, and y_i is the pos-tag for word w_i.

If we take the inputs $x_{1:n}$ to correspond to a sequence of sentence words $w_1, \cdots, w_n$, we can think of $v_i = BIRNN(x_{1:n}, i)$ as inducing an infinite window around a focus word w_i. We can then use v_i as an input to a multiclass classification function $f(v_i)$, to assign a tag $\hat{y}_i$ to each input location i. The tagger is greedy: the tagging decisions are independent of each other. However, as shown below and in other recent work using bi-RNNs for sequence tagging, we can still produce competitive tagging accuracies, because of the richness of the representation v_i that takes the entire input sequence into account.

For a k-layer bi-RNN tagger we get:

$$tag(w_{1:n}, i) = \hat{y}_i = f(v_i^k)$$
$$v_i^k = BIRNN^k(x_{1:n}, i)$$
$$x_{1:n} = E(w_1), E(w_2), \cdots, E(w_n)$$

where E as an embedding function mapping each word in the vocabulary into a d_{emb}-dimensional vector, and v_i^k is the output of the kth BIRNN layer as defined above.

All the parameters (the embedding vectors for the different vocabulary items, the parameters of the different RNNs and the parameters of the classification function f) are trained jointly in order to minimize the tagging loss over a sentence. The embedding vectors are often initialized using vectors that were pre-trained in a semi-supervised manner.

This sequence tagging architecture was introduced to NLP by Irsoy and Cardie (2014). A similar architecture (with an RNN instead of bi-RNN) was applied to CCG supertagging by Xu et al (2015).

MTL in deep bi-RNNs In a multi-task learning (MTL) setting, we have several prediction tasks over the same input space. For example, in sequence tagging, the input may be the words in the sentence, and the different tasks can be POS-tagging, named entity recognition, syntactic chunking, or CCG supertagging. Note that the different tasks do not have to be traditional NLP tasks, but also, say, two POS-annotated corpora with slightly different guidelines. Each task has its own output vocabulary (a task specific tagset), but all of them map the length n input sequence into a length n output sequence.

Intuitively, although NLP tasks such as POS tagging, syntactic chunking and CCG supertagging are different than each other, they also share lot of substructure, e.g., knowing that a word is a verb can help in determining its CCG supertag and the syntactic chunk it participate in. We would therefore like for these models to share parameters.

The common approach is to share parameters across most of the network. In the k-layers deep bi-RNN tagger described above this is naturally achieved by sharing the bi-RNN part of the network across tasks, but training a specialized classification tagger $f_t(v_i^k)$ for each task t.

This encourages the deep bi-RNN to learn a representation v_i^k that is useful for prediction of the different tasks, allowing them to share parameters.

Supervising different tasks on different layers Previous work in NLP on cascaded learning such as Shen and Sarkar (2005) suggests there is sometimes a natural order among the different tasks: some tasks may benefit more from other tasks, than the other way around. This suggests having task supervision for low-level tasks at the lower bi-RNN layers. This also enables task-specific deep learning of the high-level tasks.

Instead of conditioning all tasks on the outermost bi-RNN layer, we associate an RNN level $\ell(t)$ with each task t, and let the task specific classifier feed from that layer, e.g., $pos\_tag(w_{1:n}, i) = f_{pos}(v_i^{\ell(pos)})$. This enables a hierarchy a task with cascaded predictions, as well as deep task-specific learning for high-level tasks. This means there will be layers shared by all tasks and layers that are specific to some tasks:

$$pos\_tag(w_{1:n}, i) = f_{pos}(v_i^{\ell(pos)})$$
$$chunk\_tag(w_{1:n}, i) = f_{chunk}(v_i^{\ell(chunk)})$$
$$ccg\_tag(w_{1:n}, i) = f_{ccg}(v_i^{\ell(ccg)})$$
$$v_i^\ell = BIRNN^\ell(x_{1:n}, i)$$
$$x_{1:n} = E(w_1), E(w_2), \cdots, E(w_n)$$

The Multi-task training protocol We assume T different training set, $D_1, \cdots, D_T$, where each D_t contains pairs of input-output sequences $(w_{1:n}, y_{1:n}^t)$, $w_i \in V$, $y_i^t \in L^t$. The input vocabulary V is shared across tasks, but the output vocabularies (tagset) L^t are task dependent.

At each step in the training process we choose a random task t, followed by a random training instance $(w_{1:n}, y_{1:n}^t) \in D_t$. We use the tagger to predict the labels $\hat{y}_i^t$, suffer a loss with respect to the true labels y_i^t and update the model parameters. Notice that a task t is associated

with a bi-RNN level $\ell(t)$. The update for a sample from task t affects the parameters of f_t and $BIRNN^1, \cdots, BIRNN^{\ell(t)}$, but not the parameters of $f_{t' \neq t}$ or $BIRNN^{j > \ell(t)}$.

Implementation details Our implementation is based the CNN library[1] for dynamic neural networks. We use CNN's LSTM implementation as our RNN variant. The classifiers $f_t()$ take the form of a linear transformation followed by a softmax $f_t(v) = \arg\max_i softmax(W^{(t)}v + b^t)[i]$, where the weights matrix $W^{(t)}$ and bias vector $b^{(t)}$ are task-specific parameters. We use a cross-entropy loss summed over the entire sentence. The network is trained using back-propagation and SGD with batch-sizes of size 1, with the default learning rate. Development data is used to determine the number of iterations.

We initialize the embedding layer E with pre-trained word embeddings. We use the Senna embeddings[2] in our domain adaptation experiments, but these embeddings may have been induced from data including the test data of our main experiments, so we use the Polyglot embeddings in these experiments.[3] We use the same dimensionality for the hidden layers as in our pre-trained embeddings.

3 Experiments and Results

We experiment with POS-tagging, syntactic chunking and CCG supertagging. See examples of the different tasks below:

WORDS	Vinken	,	61	years	old
POS	NNP	,	CD	NNS	JJ
CHUNKS	B-NP	I-NP	I-NP	I-NP	I-NP
CCG	N	,	N/N	N	(S[adj]\ NP)\ NP

In-domain MTL In these experiments, POS, Chunking and CCG data are from the English Penn Treebank. We use sections 0–18 for training POS and CCG supertagging, 15–18 for training chunking, 19 for development, 20 for evaluating chunking, and 23 for evaluating CCG supertagging. These splits were motivated by the need for comparability with previous results.[4]

---

[1] http://www.github.com/clab/cnn
[2] http://ronan.collobert.com/senna/
[3] http://polyglot.readthedocs.org
[4] In CCG supertagging, we follow common practice and only evaluate performance with respect to the 425 most frequent labels. For this reason, we also do not calculate any loss from not predicting the other labels during training (but we do suffer a loss for tokens tagged with a different label during evaluation).

	LAYERS		DOMAINS			
	CHUNKS	POS	BROADCAST (6)	BC-NEWS (8)	MAGAZINES (1)	WEBLOGS (6)
BI-LSTM	3	-	88.98	91.84	90.09	90.36
	3	3	88.91	91.84	90.95	90.43
	3	1	**89.48**	**92.03**	**91.53**	**90.78**

Table 1: Domain adaptation results for chunking across four domains (averages over micro-F_1s for individual files). The number in brackets is # files per domain in OntoNotes 4.0. We use the two first files in each folder for POS supervision (for train+dev).

We do MTL training for either (POS+chunking) or (POS+CCG), with POS being the lower-level task. We experiment three architectures: single task training for higher-level tasks (no POS layer), MTL with both tasks feeding off of the outer layer, and MTL where POS feeds off of the inner (1st) layer and the higher-level task on the outer (3rd) layer. OUr main results are below:

	POS	CHUNKS	CCG
BI-LSTM	-	95.28	91.04
	3	95.30	92.94
	1	**95.56**	**93.26**

Our CHUNKS results are competitive with state-of-the-art. Suzuki and Isozaki (2008), for example, reported an F_1-score of 95.15% on the CHUNKS data. Our model also performs considerably better than the MTL model in Collobert et al. (2011) (94.10%). Note that our relative improvements are also bigger than those reported by Collobert et al. (2011). Our CCG super tagging results are also slighly better than a recently reported result in Xu et al. (2015) (93.00%). Our results are significantly better ($p < 0.05$) than our baseline, and POS supervision at the lower layer is consistently better than standard MTL.

Additional tasks? We also experimented with NER (CoNLL 2003), super senses (SemCor), and the Streusle Corpus of texts annotated with MWE brackets and super sense tags. In none of these cases, MTL led to improvements. This suggests that MTL only works when tasks are sufficiently similar, e.g., all of syntactic nature. Collobert et al. (2011) also observed a drop in NER performance and insignificant improvements for SRL. We believe this is an important observation, since previous work on deep MTL often suggests that most tasks benefit from each other.

Domain adaptation We experiment with domain adaptation for syntactic chunking, based on OntoNotes 4.0. We use WSJ newswire as our source domain, and broadcast, broadcasted news, magazines, and weblogs as target domains. We assume main task (syntactic chunking) supervision for the source domain, and lower-level POS supervision for the target domains. The results in Table 1 indicate that the method is effective for domain adaptation when we have POS supervision for the target domain. We believe this result is worth exploring further, as the scenario in which we have target-domain training data for low-level tasks such as POS tagging, but not for the task we are interested in, is common. The method is effective *only when the lower-level POS supervision is applied at the lower layer*, supporting the importance of supervising different tasks at different layers.

Rademacher complexity is the ability of models to fit random noise. We use the procedure in Zhu et al. (2009) to measure Rademacher complexity, i.e., computing the average fit to k random relabelings of the training data. The subtask in our set-up acts like a regularizer, increasing the inductive bias of our model, preventing it from learning random patterns in data. Rademacher complexity measures the decrease in ability to learn such patterns. We use the CHUNKS data in these experiments. A model that does not fit to the random data, will be right in 1/22 cases (with 22 labels). We report the Rademacher complexities relative to this.

LSTM(-3)	LSTM(3-3)	LSTM(1-3)
1.298	1.034	0.990

Our deep single task model increases performance over this baseline by 30%. In contrast, we see that when we predict both POS and the target task at the top layer, Rademacher complexity is lower and close to a random baseline. Interestingly, regularization seems to be even more effective, when the subtask is predicted from a lower layer.

4 Conclusion

MTL and sharing of intermediate representations, allowing supervision signals of different tasks to benefit each other, is an appealing idea. However, in case we suspect the existence of a hierarchy between the different tasks, we show that it is worthwhile to incorporate this knowledge in the MTL architecture's design, by making lower level tasks affect the lower levels of the representation.

Acknowledgments

Anders Søgaard was supported by ERC Starting Grant LOWLANDS No. 313695. Yoav Goldberg was supported by The Israeli Science Foundation grant No. 1555/15 and a Google Research Award.

References

Rich Caruana. 1993. Multitask learning: a knowledge-based source of inductive bias. In *ICML*.

Kyunghyun Cho. 2015. Natural language understanding with distributed representation. *CoRR*, abs/1511.07916.

Ronan Collobert, Jason Weston, Léon Bottou, Michael Karlen, Koray Kavukcuoglu, and Pavel Kuksa. 2011. Natural language processing (almost) from scratch. *The Journal of Machine Learning Research*, 12:2493–2537.

Jeffrey L. Elman. 1990. Finding Structure in Time. *Cognitive Science*, 14(2):179–211, March.

Yoav Goldberg. 2015. A primer on neural network models for natural language processing. *CoRR*, abs/1510.00726.

Sepp Hochreiter and Juergen Schmidhuber. 1997. Long short-term memory. *Neural Computation*, 9:1735–1780.

Ozan Irsoy and Claire Cardie. 2014. Opinion Mining with Deep Recurrent Neural Networks. In *Proceedings of the 2014 Conference on Empirical Methods in Natural Language Processing (EMNLP)*, pages 720–728, Doha, Qatar, October. Association for Computational Linguistics.

M.-T. Luong, Q. V. Le, I. Sutskever, O. Vinyals, and L. Kaiser. 2015. Multi-task Sequence to Sequence Learning. *ArXiv e-prints*, November.

Joakim Nivre, Johan Hall, Sandra Kübler, Ryan McDonald, Jens Nilsson, Sebastian Riedel, and Deniz Yuret. 2007. The CoNLL 2007 shared task on dependency parsing. In *Proceedings of the CoNLL Shared Task Session of EMNLP-CoNLL 2007*, pages 915–932, Prague, Czech Republic, June. Association for Computational Linguistics.

Erik F. Tjong Kim Sang and Sabine Buchholz. 2000. Introduction to the conll-2000 shared task chunking. In *Fourth Conference on Computational Natural Language Learning and of the Second Learning Language in Logic Workshop*, pages 127–132.

M. Schuster and Kuldip K. Paliwal. 1997. Bidirectional recurrent neural networks. *IEEE Transactions on Signal Processing*, 45(11):2673–2681, November.

Hong Shen and Anoop Sarkar. 2005. Voting between multiple data representations for text chunking. In *Proceedings of the 18th Meeting of the Canadian Society for Computational Intelligence*.

Jun Suzuki and Hideki Isozaki. 2008. Semi-supervised sequential labeling and segmentation using gigaword scale unlabeled data. In *ACL*.

Wenduan Xu, Michael Auli, and Stephen Clark. 2015. Ccg supertagging with a recurrent neural network. In *ACL*.

Junho Yim, Heechul Jung, ByungIn Yoo amd Changkyu Choi, Dusik Park, and Junmo Kim. 2015. Rotating Your Face Using Multi-task Deep Neural Network. In *CVPR*.

Cha Zhang and Zhengyou Zhang. 2014. Improving Multiview Face Detection with Multi-Task Deep Convolutional Neural Networks. In *WACV*.

Jerry Zhu, Timothy Rogers, and Bryan Gibson. 2009. Human Rademacher complexity. In *NIPS*.

Domain Specific Named Entity Recognition
Referring to the Real World by Deep Neural Networks

Suzushi Tomori[†] **Takashi Ninomiya**[††] **Shinsuke Mori**[†††]

[†]Graduate School of Informatics, Kyoto University[*]
[††]Graduate School of Science and Engineering, Ehime University
[†††]Academic Center for Computing and Media Studies, Kyoto University

[†]tomori.suzushi.72e@st.kyoto-u.ac.jp
[††]ninomiya@cs.ehime-u.ac.jp
[†††]forest@i.kyoto-u.ac.jp

Abstract

In this paper, we propose a method for referring to the real world to improve named entity recognition (NER) specialized for a domain. Our method adds a stacked auto-encoder to a text-based deep neural network for NER. We first train the stacked auto-encoder only from the real world information, then the entire deep neural network from sentences annotated with NEs and accompanied by real world information. In our experiments, we took Japanese chess as the example. The dataset consists of pairs of a game state and commentary sentences about it annotated with game-specific NE tags. We conducted NER experiments and showed that referring to the real world improves the NER accuracy.

1 Introduction

In recent years there has been a surge of interest in relating natural language to the real world. And more and more language resources accompanied by nonlinguistic data are becoming available. Typical examples are image descriptions (Yang et al., 2011; Ushiku et al., 2011) and video (Hashimoto et al., 2014). Ferraro et al. (2015) summarized many other image and video datasets. These datasets allow us to attempt the task of connecting language expressions to the real world, which is called *symbol grounding* (Harnad, 1990). Bruni et al. (2014) proposed methods for acquiring multimodal representations by applying SVD to distributional semantics and bag-of-visual-words (BoVW). Ngiam et al. (2011) proposed unsupervised multimodal learning based on deep restricted boltzmann machines (RBMs). In the field of natural language processing (NLP) research,

Kiela et al. (2015) proposed to acquire bilingual lexicon based on visual similarity. Ramisa et al. (2015) describe a method for predicting a preposition referring to positions in the image.

In this paper, we propose a method for enhancing a named entity (NE) recognizer referring to the real world. Because of the lack of datasets consisting of sentences annotated with the general NE tags such as names of people, organizations, and times (Sang and Meulder, 2003), with accompanying real world data, we take game states as the counterpart of the language and the NE tag set specialized for game commentaries such as defense formations and opening names (Mori et al., 2016). Similar to bio-medical NEs (Settles, 2004; Tateisi et al., 2002), these NEs are useful for applications in the game domain. Our method could be used to improve automatic game commentary systems (Kameko et al., 2015b; Chen et al., 2010) or to build a state search method that uses natural language queries instead of state notations (Ganguly et al., 2014). In addition to these interesting applications, game states have another advantage for NLP research. They are much easier to recognize than images and video, which allows us to concentrate on the NLP problem.

In order to incorporate the real world, *i.e.* game states, into NE recognition (NER), we propose to use deep neural networks (DNNs), which have been reported to be successful in various NLP tasks such as word embedding (Bengio et al., 2003; Mikolov et al., 2013b; Pennington et al., 2014; Mikolov et al., 2013a), part-of-speech tagging (Tsuboi, 2014), parsing (Socher et al., 2010; Socher et al., 2012; Socher et al., 2013a), parsing (Socher et al., 2013a), NER (Hammerton, 2003), sentiment analysis (Socher et al., 2013b) and machine translation (Neubig et al., 2015). First we build a normal NE recognizer by referring only to the text information based on DNN. Each unit of its output layer corresponds to a BIO tag for

---

[*]This work was done when the first author was at Ehime University.

Proceedings of the 54th Annual Meeting of the Association for Computational Linguistics, pages 236–242,
Berlin, Germany, August 7-12, 2016. ©2016 Association for Computational Linguistics

the word (see Section 3). We use post processing based on the Viterbi algorithm to choose the best tag sequence by discarding inconsistent ones. This design allows us to train the model from partially annotated sentences, in which only some words are annotated with NE tags (Sasada et al., 2015). Next we extend the text-based DNN with a module that refers to game states. This module is a stacked-auto-encoder (SAE) (Bengio et al., 2007) and we first train it only from game states. The pre-training allows the model to learn game state embedding which abstracts game state information. Then we fine-tune the entire DNN for NER, consisting of both text-based DNN and SAE. As we show in later section of this paper, we end up with an NE recognizer that refers to real world information in addition to text information, which increases its accuracy.

2 Related Work

There are several lines of multimodal learning in the fields of pattern recognition and NLP. Most learn multimodal representations by solving unsupervised learning tasks or pseudo-supervised learning tasks, but there were only a few studies that directly learned multimodal representations for target tasks in NLP. Our method incorporates multimodal information in DNNs for NER.

Bruni et al. (2014) proposed methods for acquiring multimodal representations by applying SVD to distributional semantics and BoVW. Lopopolo and van Miltenburg (2015) proposed a similar method for acquiring sound-based distributional semantics. Textual vectors are acquired by using latent semantic analysis (LSA) and auditory vectors are acquired by the bag-of-audio-words (BoAW) method. The multimodal representations are acquired by applying SVD. Ngiam et al. (2011) and Srivastava and Salakhutdinov (2012) proposed unsupervised learning methods based on deep RBMs for learning multimodal representations in hidden layers. Providing paired information such as text-image pairs or audio-video pairs to RBMs, shared representations are learned in their hidden layers. Ngiam et al. (2011) also used deep auto-encoders for learning RBMs. After acquiring multimodal representations, they can be used as inputs for other supervised learning tasks, such as speech recognition and image retrieval, where standard linear classifiers are used for solving the tasks. Silberer and Lapata (2014)

proposed a deep learning method for learning multimodal representations by solving pseudo-supervised tasks to predict the input's object label, such as 'boat,' given textual and visual attribute-based representations for the object. Their objective function is the weighted sum of the auto-encoding error and the classification error. Though their model is for supervised learning, Multimodal representations are learned In their experiments, the acquired multimodal representations were used for evaluating the word similarity task and word clustering task.

Lazaridou et al. (2015) extend word2vec (Mikolov et al., 2013a; Mikolov et al., 2013b) to incorporate visual information for acquiring multimodal representations. Word embedding methods including word2vec are often used for various NLP tasks instead of one hot representations, and were shown to improve the performance of NLP systems. Word embeddings are mappings from a word to a low-dimensional real vectors that represents word meanings and relations between words. Word2vec is a method for acquiring word embeddings from a neural network which solves a pseudo-supervised task to predict surrounding words. Kiela and Clark (2015) extend word2vec to incorporate bag-of-audio-words (BoAW). Gupta et al. (2015) have shown that word embeddings contain much information for predicting attributes. Herbelot and Vecchi (2015) proposed a method for predicting general quantifiers such as *some* for predicate-subject pairs.

Similar to this paper Kameko et al. (2015a) proposed a method for word segmentation using game states and DNNs. The main differences between their method and ours is that i) they use game states to build a term dictionary for word segmentation, but our method directly incorporates a game state to improve NER, and ii) they used manually developed features to extract game states while we automatically acquire game states by using pre-training.

3 Game Commentary Corpus

The game we chose for the experiments is Japanese chess, called *shogi* in Japanese. It is a two-player board game with professional players. The board has 9×9 squares and games are played with 40 pieces of 14 different types. Unlike chess, players can reuse captured pieces. In computer science terms, it is a deterministic perfect informa-

Tag	Meaning
Hu	Human
Tu	Turn
Po	Position
Pi	Piece
Ps	Piece specifier
Mc	Move compliment
Pa	Piece attribute
Pq	Piece quantity
Re	Region
Ph	Phase
St	Strategy
Ca	Castle
Me	Move eval.
Mn	Move name
Ee	Eval. element
Ev	Evaluation
Ti	Time
Ac	Player action
Ap	Piece action
Ao	Other action
Ot	Other notion

Table 1: The named entity tag set.

tion game, so we can completely specify a game state by the positions of the pieces on the board and the captured pieces held by on both sides.

Many matches between professional players have been recorded, and many game states have commentaries made for fans by other professional players.

A game commentary corpus[1] (Mori et al., 2016) defines 21 types of NEs, which are called *shogi*-NEs, as listed in Table 1. The words in the commentary sentences in the corpus are annotated with BIO-style tags. B, I, and O stand for beginning, intermediate, and others, respectively. B or I are used for representing the beginning or intermediate words of an NE as extension like Hu-B. And O is used for representing words that are not part of any NEs. Therefore there are $43 = 21 \times 2 + 1$ BIO tags.

The main idea of this paper is that the game state, *i.e.* the real world, provides information on the texts that describe it. In the next section, we propose a method for utilizing this information in the NER task.

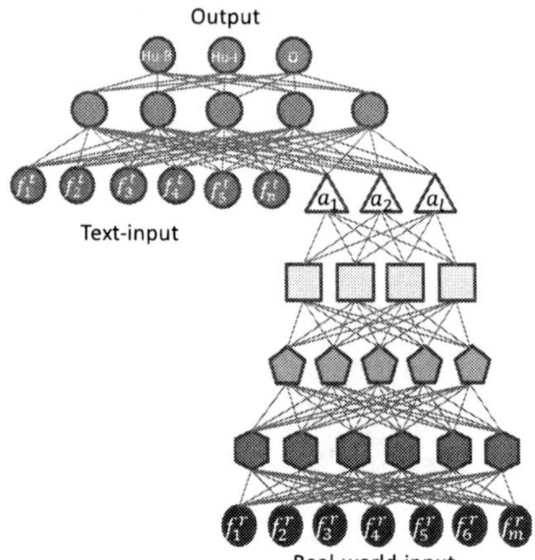

Figure 1: Deep neural networks for *shogi* NER.

Text features
$w_{i-2},\ w_{i-1},\ w_i,\ w_{i+1},\ w_{i+2}$
$w_{i-2}w_{i-1},\ w_{i-1}w_i,\ w_iw_{i+1},\ w_{i+1}w_{i+2}$
$w_{i-2}w_{i-1}w_i,\ w_iw_{i+1}w_{i+2}$
$c(w_{i-2}),\ c(w_{i-1}),\ c(w_i),\ c(w_{i+1}),\ c(w_{i+2})$
$pos(w_{i-2}),\ pos(w_{i-1}),\ pos(w_i),\ pos(w_{i+1}),$
$pos(w_{i+2})$

Table 2: Text features for DNN/CRF NER.

4 Utilizing Real World Information in a Named Entity Recognizer

Figure 1 shows the overall architecture of our DNN for NER. The left part is the DNN for text-based NER and the bottom right part is an additional DNN for referring to the real world.

4.1 Text-based NER

The text-based NER refers to the text only through the standard features for NER (Sang and Meulder, 2003) listed in Table 2. They consist of word n-grams in the window $w_{i-2}^{i+2} = w_{i-2}w_{i-1}w_iw_{i+1}w_{i+2}$, where w_i is the word to be labelled, the part-of-speech tags $pos(w)$ and the character type $c(w)^2$ of a word w in the window w_{i-2}^{i+2}. Each feature corresponds to a unit at the bottom left in Figure 1 ($f_1^t \ldots f_n^t$).

Each unit aligned at the top of Figure 1 corresponds to a BIO tag. Thus there are 43 units in the *shogi* NE case. The last layer is the softmax function and we choose the tag of the highest unit value

---

[1]http://www.ar.media.kyoto-u.ac.jp/data/game/

[2]In the target language in the experiments, Japanese, the types are *hiragana, katakana, kanji*, number, symbol, and combinations of them.

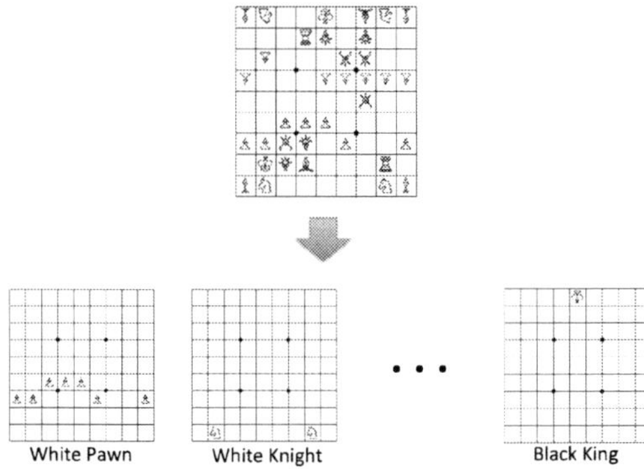

Figure 2: Game state features.

for the input word. As we mentioned in Section 1, this design makes it possible to use partially annotated data.[3] It can, however, generate inconsistent BIO tag sequences, *e.g.*, an NE starting with an I tag. We use a best path search module based on the Viterbi algorithm while limiting the search space into valid tag sequences (Sasada et al., 2015).

4.2 NER Referring to the Real World

To enable our NE recognizer to refer to the real world, we add a network to the DNN for text-based NER as shown in the bottom right in Figure 1. The input layer corresponds to the game state features depicted in Figure 2 ($f_1^r \ldots f_m^r$). For *shogi* they are nine-by-nine binary features which represent the positions of pieces on the board for each piece type and each player. Thus we have $m = 2,268 \ (= 9 \times 9 \times 14 \times 2)$ features for the pieces on the board and $14 \ (= 7 \times 2)$ integer features which represent the number of captured pieces for each type and each player.

To incorporate the game state features we propose using an SAE (Bengio et al., 2007) to abstract the game state information instead of directly adding the units for these features to the text-based NER. To build the SAE, we first prepare a three-layer neural network (with one hidden layer) as depicted on the left side of Figure 3 and train it providing the same game states to both input and output layers. With this process we can obtain the best reduced representations for the game states as the hidden layer that reconstructs the input game state features at the output layer.

---

[3]Tsuboi et al. (2008) extended conditional random fields to be trained from partially annotated data. One can extend sequence labeling DNN (RNN or LSTM) in a similar way. This is, however, clearly out of the scope of this paper.

Usage	#Sentences	#NEs	#Words	#Game states
Pretraining	-	-	-	213,195
Training	1,546	7,922	27,025	391
Test	492	2,365	7,161	156

Table 3: Game commentary corpus specifications.

Layer	0	1	2	3	4	5
Dimension	2,282	1,000	500	200	100	50

Table 4: Dimensions of the SAE layers.

Then we duplicate the hidden layer and put another hidden layer of smaller dimension between them (see the network in the middle of Figure 3) and train it in the same manner. This time the output layer is the duplicated former hidden layer and we train the new hidden layer by minimizing the difference between the duplicated former hidden layers. We repeat this process for a fixed number of times as shown on the right side of Figure 3. This process is called pre-training. Note that during pre-training only game states are used.

After the pre-training, we cut off the top layer to obtain a network with a trapezoid shape whose top layer abstracts game states ($a_1 \ldots a_l$ in Figure 1). Then we join it to the DNN for the text-based NER as shown in Figure 1. Finally, we fine-tune it from both game states and texts annotated with NE tags. Note that we also tune parameters in the pre-trained SAE.

5 Experimental Evaluation

In this section we describe the NER experiments we conducted to evaluate our method.

5.1 Experimental Settings

The corpus we used is the game commentary corpus (Mori et al., 2016) described in Section 3 briefly. Table 3 shows its specifications. Table 4 shows the number of dimensions in each layer for game state embeddings in pre-training. We set the number of layers in the SAE (Subsection 4.2) to four, with which we could maximize the accuracy on the development set held-out from the training data.

5.2 Models for Comparison

The baseline is text-based NER based on DNN as described in Subsection 4.1. In addition, we tested NER based on conditional random fields (CRFs) (Lafferty et al., 2001) with the same text features, because NER is a sequence labeling problem and

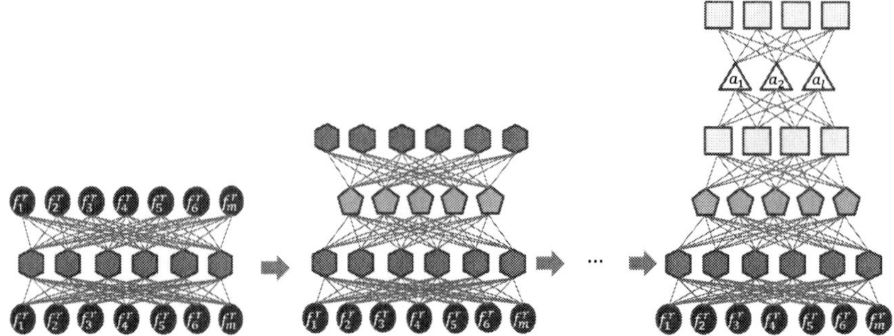

Figure 3: Building stacked-auto-encoder.

Method	BIO Accu.	Prec.	Recall	F-meas.
CRFs	89.76%	**90.58%**	76.87%	83.17
DNN	90.87%	89.27%	79.49%	84.10
DNN + R	**91.30%**	89.13%	**80.76%**	**84.74**

Table 5: NER results.

CRFs are the standard method used to solve it (McCallum and Li, 2003). We compared these baselines and our NER that refers to the real world (*DNN+R*) as described in Subsection 4.2. Its SAE was trained on 213,195 game states.

5.3 Results and Discussion

Table 5 shows the results. From the F-measures we see that *DNN* is better than *CRFs*. This is consistent with many works which apply DNN to NLP problems. A comparison between *DNN* and *DNN+R* tells us that we can achieve a further improvement by referring to real world information. The difference in BIO accuracies between them is statistically significant (McNemar's test, $p < 0.01$). Therefore we can say that our method successfully integrates real world information into text information to build a better solution to the NER problem.

When we take a close look at the precision and recall, *DNN+R* and *DNN* balance them better than *CRFs*. *CRFs* recognized *shogi*-NEs with high precision but with low recall. The NER results tell that *CRFs* tended to output O tags when they were not confident to classify correct *shogi*-NE tags. *DNN+R* and *DNN* can classify BIO tags more accurately than *CRFs* as can be seen in BIO accuracies in Table 5. As a consequence *DNN+R* and *DNN* confidently recognize more *shogi*-NEs, which makes their recall higher than that of *CRFs*.

From Table 5 we see that *DNN+R* is better than *DNN*. Followings are examples of *shogi*-NEs which *DNN+R* successfully recognized but *DNN* failed: Ot tag for "*tataki*," which means dropping a pawn in front of a piece of the opponent, and Mn tag for "*tsumero*" (threatmate). By referring to the game state, *DNN+R* was better at understanding the game situation and resulted better performance than *DNN*, the text-based NER.

6 Conclusion

In this paper, we proposed a method for referring to the real world to improve NER in a specialized domain. Our method adds an SAE to a text-based DNN for NER. We first pre-train the SAE using only real world information, and then we train the entire DNN from sentences annotated with NEs and accompanied by real world information.

In our experiments, we used *shogi* (Japanese chess) as the example. The dataset consists of pairs of a game state and commentary sentences on it annotated with 21 *shogi* NE tags. We conducted NER experiments and showed that referring to the real world improves NER accuracy.

Our method has the potential to be applied to various NER problems, such as general NER with pictures and financial NER with stock charts, by changing the SAE features. An interesting area of future work is preparing datasets in these domains and testing our method on them.

Acknowledgments

This work was supported by JSPS Grants-in-Aid for Scientific Research Grant Numbers 26540190 and 25280084. We are also grateful to Professor Yoshimasa Tsuruoka and Mr. Hirotaka Kameko for their valuable comments.

References

Yoshua Bengio, Rejean Ducharme, Pascal Vincent, and Christian Jauvin. 2003. A neural probabilistic language model. *Journal of Machine Learning Research*, 3:1137–1155.

Yoshua Bengio, Pascal Lamblin, Dan Popovici, and Hugo Larochelle. 2007. Greedy layer-wise training of deep networks. In B. Schölkopf, J. C. Platt, and T. Hoffman, editors, *Advances in Neural Information Processing Systems 19*, pages 153–160. MIT Press.

E. Bruni, N. K. Tran, and M. Baroni. 2014. Multimodal distributional semantics. *Journal of Artificial Intelligence Research*, 49:1–47.

D. L. Chen, J. Kim, and R. J. Mooney. 2010. Training a multilingual sportscaster: Using perceptual context to learn language. *Journal of Artificial Intelligence Research*, 37:397–435.

Francis Ferraro, Nasrin Mostafazadeh, Ting-Hao Huang, Lucy Vanderwende, Jacob Devlin, Michel Galley, and Margaret Mitchell. 2015. A survey of current datasets for vision and language research. In *Proceedings of the 2015 Conference on Empirical Methods in Natural Language Processing*, pages 207–213.

Debasis Ganguly, Johannes Leveling, and Gareth J.F. Jones. 2014. Retrieval of similar chess positions. In *Proceedings of the 37th annual international ACM SIGIR conference*, pages 687–696. ACM.

Abhijeet Gupta, Gemma Boleda, Marco Baroni, and Sebastian Padó. 2015. Distributional vectors encode referential attributes. In *Proceedings of the 2015 Conference on Empirical Methods in Natural Language Processing*, pages 12–21, Lisbon, Portugal, September. Association for Computational Linguistics.

James Hammerton. 2003. Named entity recognition with long short-term memory. In Walter Daelemans and Miles Osborne, editors, *Proceedings of the Seventh Conference on Natural Language Learning at HLT-NAACL 2003*, pages 172–175.

Stevan Harnad. 1990. The symbol grounding problem. *Physica D*, 42:335–346.

Atsushi Hashimoto, Tetsuro Sasada, Yoko Yamakata, Shinsuke Mori, and Michihiko Minoh. 2014. Kusk dataset: Toward a direct understanding of recipe text and human cooking activity. In *Proceedings of the SixthInternational Workshop on Cooking and Eating Activities*.

Aurélie Herbelot and Eva Maria Vecchi. 2015. Building a shared world: mapping distributional to model-theoretic semantic spaces. In *Proceedings of the 2015 Conference on Empirical Methods in Natural Language Processing*, pages 22–32, Lisbon, Portugal, September. Association for Computational Linguistics.

Hirotaka Kameko, Shinsuke Mori, and Yoshimasa Tsuruoka. 2015a. Can symbol grounding improve low-level NLP? word segmentation as a case study. In *Proceedings of the 2015 Conference on Empirical Methods in Natural Language Processing*, pages 2298–2303, Lisbon, Portugal, September. Association for Computational Linguistics.

Hirotaka Kameko, Shinsuke Mori, and Yoshimasa Tsuruoka. 2015b. Learning a game commentary generator with grounded move expressions. In *Proceedings of the 2015 IEEE Conference on Computational Intelligence and Games*.

Douwe Kiela and Stephen Clark. 2015. Multi- and cross-modal semantics beyond vision: Grounding in auditory perception. In *Proceedings of the 2015 Conference on Empirical Methods in Natural Language Processing*, pages 2461–2470, Lisbon, Portugal, September. Association for Computational Linguistics.

Douwe Kiela, Ivan Vulić, and Stephen Clark. 2015. Visual bilingual lexicon induction with transferred convnet features. In *Proceedings of the 2015 Conference on Empirical Methods in Natural Language Processing*, pages 148–158.

John D. Lafferty, Andrew McCallum, and Fernando C. N. Pereira. 2001. Conditional random fields: Probabilistic models for segmenting and labeling sequence data. In *Proceedings of the Eighteenth International Conference on Machine Learning*, ICML '01, pages 282–289, San Francisco, CA, USA. Morgan Kaufmann Publishers Inc.

Angeliki Lazaridou, Nghia The Pham, and Marco Baroni. 2015. Combining language and vision with a multimodal skip-gram model. In *Proceedings of the 2015 Conference of the North American Chapter of the Association for Computational Linguistics: Human Language Technologies*, pages 153–163, Denver, Colorado, May–June. Association for Computational Linguistics.

Alessandro Lopopolo and Emiel van Miltenburg. 2015. Sound-based distributional models. In *Proceedings of the 11th International Conference on Computational Semantics*, pages 70–75, London, UK, April. Association for Computational Linguistics.

Andrew McCallum and Wei Li. 2003. Early results for named entity recognition with conditional random fields, feature induction and web-enhanced lexicons. In *Proceedings of the Seventh Conference on Computational Natural Language Learning*.

Tomas Mikolov, Kai Chen, Greg Corrado, and Jeffrey Dean. 2013a. Efficient estimation of word representations in vector space. In *Proceedings of workshop at the International Conference on Learning Representations (ICLR 2013)*.

Tomas Mikolov, Ilya Sutskever, Kai Chen, Greg S Corrado, and Jeffrey Dean. 2013b. Distributed representations of words and phrases and their compositionality. *Advances in Neural Information Processing Systems*, 26:3111–3119.

Shinsuke Mori, John Richardson, Atsushi Ushiku, Tetsuro Sasada, Hirotaka Kameko, and Yoshimasa Tsuruoka. 2016. A Japanese chess commentary corpus. In *Proceedings of the Tenth International Conference on Language Resources and Evaluation*.

Graham Neubig, Makoto Morishita, and Satoshi Nakamura. 2015. Neural reranking improves subjective quality of machine translation: NAIST at WAT2015. In *Proceedings of the 2nd Workshop on Asian Translation (WAT2015)*, Kyoto, Japan, October.

J. Ngiam, A. Khosla, M. Kim, J. Nam, H. Lee, and A. Ng. 2011. Multimodal deep learning. In *Proceedings of the 28th International Conference on Machine Learning (ICML 2011)*, pages 689–696.

Jeffrey Pennington, Richard Socher, and Christopher Manning. 2014. Glove: Global vectors for word representation. In *Proceedings of the 2014 Conference on Empirical Methods in Natural Language Processing (EMNLP)*, pages 1532–1543, Doha, Qatar, October. Association for Computational Linguistics.

Arnau Ramisa, Josiah Wang, Ying Lu, Emmanuel Dellandrea, Francesc Moreno-Noguer, and Robert Gaizauskas. 2015. Combining geometric, textual and visual features for predicting prepositions in image descriptions. In *Proceedings of the 2015 Conference on Empirical Methods in Natural Language Processing*, pages 214–220.

Erik F. Tjong Kim Sang and Fien De Meulder. 2003. Introduction to the conll-2003 shared task: Language-independent named entity recognition. In *Proceedings of the Seventh Conference on Computational Natural Language Learning*, pages 142–147.

Tetsuro Sasada, Shinsuke Mori, Tatsuya Kawahara, and Yoko Yamakata. 2015. Named entity recognizer trainable from partially annotated data. In *Proceedings of the Eleventh International Conference Pacific Association for Computational Linguistics*.

Burr Settles. 2004. Biomedical named entity recognition using conditional random fields and rich feature sets. In *Proceedings of the International Joint Workshop on Natural Language Processing in Biomedicine and its Applications*, pages 33–38.

Carina Silberer and Mirella Lapata. 2014. Learning grounded meaning representations with autoencoders. In *Proceedings of the 52nd Annual Meeting of the Association for Computational Linguistics (Volume 1: Long Papers)*, pages 721–732, Baltimore, Maryland, June. Association for Computational Linguistics.

Richard Socher, Christopher D. Manning, and Andrew Y. Ng. 2010. Learning continuous phrase representations and syntactic parsing with recursive neural networks. In *Deep Learning and Unsupervised Feature Learning Workshop - NIPS 2010*.

Richard Socher, Brody Huval, Christopher D. Manning, and Andrew Y. Ng. 2012. Semantic compositionality through recursive matrix-vector spaces. In *Proceedings of the 2012 Joint Conference on Empirical Methods in Natural Language Processing and Computational Natural Language Learning*, pages 1201–1211, Jeju Island, Korea, July. Association for Computational Linguistics.

Richard Socher, John Bauer, Christopher D. Manning, and Ng Andrew Y. 2013a. Parsing with compositional vector grammars. In *Proceedings of the 51st Annual Meeting of the Association for Computational Linguistics (Volume 1: Long Papers)*, pages 455–465, Sofia, Bulgaria, August. Association for Computational Linguistics.

Richard Socher, Alex Perelygin, Jean Wu, Jason Chuang, Christopher D. Manning, Andrew Ng, and Christopher Potts. 2013b. Recursive deep models for semantic compositionality over a sentiment treebank. In *Proceedings of the 2013 Conference on Empirical Methods in Natural Language Processing*, pages 1631–1642, Seattle, Washington, USA, October. Association for Computational Linguistics.

Nitish Srivastava and Ruslan R Salakhutdinov. 2012. Multimodal learning with deep boltzmann machines. In F. Pereira, C. J. C. Burges, L. Bottou, and K. Q. Weinberger, editors, *Advances in Neural Information Processing Systems 25*, pages 2222–2230. Curran Associates, Inc.

Yuka Tateisi, Jin-Dong Kim, and Tomoko Ohta. 2002. The genia corpus: an annotated research abstract corpus in molecular biology domain. In *Proceedings of the HLT*, pages 73–77.

Yuta Tsuboi, Hisashi Kashima, Shinsuke Mori, Hiroki Oda, and Yuji Matsumoto. 2008. Training conditional random fields using incomplete annotations. In *Proceedings of the 22nd International Conference on Computational Linguistics*, pages 897–904.

Yuta Tsuboi. 2014. Neural networks leverage corpus-wide information for part-of-speech tagging. In *Proceedings of the 2014 Conference on Empirical Methods in Natural Language Processing (EMNLP)*, pages 938–950, Doha, Qatar, October. Association for Computational Linguistics.

Yoshitaka Ushiku, Tatsuya Harada, and Yasuo Kuniyoshi. 2011. Automatic sentence generation from images. In *Proceedings of the 19th Annual ACM International Conference on Multimedia*, pages 1533–1536.

Yezhou Yang, Ching Lik Teo, Hal Daumé III, and Yiannis Aloimonos. 2011. Corpus-guided sentence generation of natural images. In *Proceedings of the 2011 Conference on Empirical Methods in Natural Language Processing*.

An Entity-Focused Approach to Generating Company Descriptions

Gavin Saldanha*
Columbia University

Or Biran**
Columbia University

Kathleen McKeown**
Columbia University

Alfio Gliozzo†
IBM Watson

*gvs2106@columbia.edu **{orb, kathy}@cs.columbia.edu
†gliozzo@us.ibm.com

Abstract

Finding quality descriptions on the web, such as those found in Wikipedia articles, of newer companies can be difficult: search engines show many pages with varying relevance, while multi-document summarization algorithms find it difficult to distinguish between core facts and other information such as news stories. In this paper, we propose an entity-focused, hybrid generation approach to automatically produce descriptions of previously unseen companies, and show that it outperforms a strong summarization baseline.

1 Introduction

As new companies form and grow, it is important for potential investors, procurement departments, and business partners to have access to a 360-degree view describing them. The number of companies worldwide is very large and, for the vast majority, not much information is available in sources like Wikipedia. Often, only firmographics data (e.g. industry classification, location, size, and so on) is available. This creates a need for cognitive systems able to aggregate and filter the information available on the web and in news, databases, and other sources. Providing good quality natural language descriptions of companies allows for easier access to the data, for example in the context of virtual agents or with text-to-speech applications.

In this paper, we propose an entity-focused system using a combination of targeted (knowledge base driven) and data-driven generation to create company descriptions in the style of Wikipedia descriptions. The system generates sentences from RDF triples, such as those found in DBPedia and Freebase, about a given company and combines these with sentences on the web that match learned expressions of relationships. We evaluate our hybrid approach and compare it with a targeted-only approach and a data-driven-only approach, as well as a strong multi-document summarization baseline. Our results show that the hybrid approach performs significantly better than either approach alone as well as the baseline.

The targeted (TD) approach to company description uses Wikipedia descriptions as a model for generation. It learns how to realize RDF relations that have the company as their subject: each relation contains a company/entity pair and it is these pairs that drive both content and expression of the company description. For each company/entity pair, the system finds all the ways in which similar company/entity pairs are expressed in other Wikipedia company descriptions, clustering together sentences that express the same company/entity relation pairs. It generates templates for the sentences in each cluster, replacing the mentions of companies and entities with typed slots and generates a new description by inserting expressions for the given company and entity in the slots. All possible sentences are generated from the templates in the cluster, the resulting sentences are ranked and the best sentence for each relation selected to produce the final description. Thus, the TD approach is a top-down approach, driven to generate sentences expressing the relations found in the company's RDF data using realizations that are typically used on Wikipedia.

In contrast, the data-driven (DD) approach uses a semi-supervised method to select sentences from descriptions about the given company on the web. Like the TD approach, it also begins with a seed set of relations present in a few companies' DBPedia entries, represented as company/entity pairs, but instead of looking at the corresponding Wikipedia articles, it learns patterns that are typ-

Proceedings of the 54th Annual Meeting of the Association for Computational Linguistics, pages 243–248,
Berlin, Germany, August 7-12, 2016. ©2016 Association for Computational Linguistics

ically used to express the relations on the web. In the process, it uses bootstrapping (Agichtein and Gravano, 2000) to learn new ways of expressing the relations corresponding to each company/entity pair, alternating with learning new pairs that match the learned expression patterns. Since the bootstrapping process is driven only by company/entity pairs and lexical patterns, it has the potential to learn a wider variety of expressions for each pair and to learn new relations that may exist for each pair. Thus, this approach lets data for company descriptions on the web determine the possible relations and patterns for expressing those relations in a bottom-up fashion. It then uses the learned patterns to select matching sentences from the web about a target company.

2   Related Work

The TD approach falls into the generation pipeline paradigm (Reiter and Dale, 1997), with content selection determined by the relation in the company's DBpedia entry while microplanning and realization are carried out through template generation. While some generation systems, particularly in early years, used sophisticated grammars for realization (Matthiessen and Bateman, 1991; Elhadad, 1991; White, 2014), in recent years, template-based generation has shown a resurgence. In some cases, authors focus on document planning and sentences in the domain are stylized enough that templates suffice (Elhadad and Mckeown, 2001; Bouayad-Agha et al., 2011; Gkatzia et al., 2014; Biran and McKeown, 2015). In other cases, learned models that align database records with text snippets and then abstract out specific fields to form templates have proven successful for the generation of various domains (Angeli et al., 2010; Kondadadi et al., 2013). Others, like us, target atomic events (e.g., date of birth, occupation) for inclusion in biographies (Filatova and Prager, 2005) but the templates used in other work are manually encoded.

Sentence selection has also been used for question answering and query-focused summarization. Some approaches focus on selection of relevant sentences using probabilistic approaches (Daumé III and Marcu, 2005; Conroy et al., 2006), semi-supervised learning (Wang et al., 2011) and graph-based methods (Erkan and Radev, 2004; Otterbacher et al., 2005). Yet others use a mixture of targeted and data-driven methods for a pure sen-

tence selection system (Blair-Goldensohn et al., 2003; Weischedel et al., 2004; Schiffman et al., 2001). In our approach, we target both relevance and variety of expression, driving content by selecting sentences that match company/entity pairs and inducing multiple patterns of expression. Sentence selection has also been used in prior work on generating Wikipedia overall articles (Sauper and Barzilay, 2009). Their focus is more on learning domain-specific templates that control the topic structure of an overview, a much longer text than we generate.

3   Targeted Generation

The TD system uses a development set of 100 S&P500 companies along with their Wikipedia articles and DBPedia entries to form templates. For each RDF relation with the company as the subject, it identifies all sentences in the corresponding article containing the entities in the relation. The specific entities are then replaced with their relation to create a template. For example, "Microsoft was founded by Bill Gates and Paul Allen" is converted to "⟨company⟩ was founded by ⟨founder⟩," with conjoined entities collapsed into one slot. Many possible templates are created, some of which contain multiple relations (e.g., "⟨company⟩, located in ⟨location⟩, was founded by ⟨founder⟩"). In this way the system learns how Wikipedia articles express relations between the company and its key entities (founders, headquarters, products, etc).

At generation time, we fill the template slots with the corresponding information from the RDF entries of the target company. Conjunctions are inserted when slots are filled by multiple entities. Continuing with our example, we might now produce the sentence "Palantir was founded by Peter Thiel, Alex Karp, Joe Lonsdale, Stephen Cohen, and Nathan Gettings" for target company Palantir. Preliminary results showed that this method was not adequate - the data for the target company often lacked some of the entities needed to fill the templates. Without those entities the sentence could not be generated. As Wikipedia sentences tend to have multiple relations each (high information density), many sentences containing important, relevant facts were discarded due to phrases that mentioned lesser facts we did not have the data to replace. We therefore added a post-processing step to remove, if possible, any phrases from the sentence that could not be filled; otherwise, the sentence is discarded.

This process yields many potential sentences for each relation, of which we only want to choose the best. We cluster the newly generated sentences by relation and score each cluster. Sentences are scored according to how much information about the target company they contain (number of replaced relations). Shorter sentences are also weighted more as they are less likely to contain extraneous information, and sentences with more post-processing are scored lower. The highest scored sentence for each relation type is added to the description as those sentences are the most informative, relevant, and most likely to be grammatically correct.

4   Data-Driven Generation

The DD method produces descriptions using sentences taken from the web. Like the TD approach, it aims to produce sentences realizing relations between the input company and other entities. It uses a bootstrapping approach (Agichtein and Gravano, 2000) to learn patterns for expressing the relations. It starts with a seed set of company/entity pairs, representing a small subset of the desired relations, but unlike previous approaches, can generate additional relations as it goes.

Patterns are generated by reading text from the web and extracting those sentences which contain pairs in the seed set. The pair's entities are replaced with placeholder tags denoting the type of the entity, while the words around them form the pattern (the words between the tags are selected as well as words to the left and right of the tags). Each pattern thus has the form "$\langle L \rangle \langle T1 \rangle \langle M \rangle \langle T2 \rangle \langle R \rangle$," where L, M, and R are respectively the words to the left of, between, and to the right of the entities. T1 is the type of the first entity, and T2 the type of the second. Like the TD algorithm, this is essentially a template based approach, but the templates in this case are not aligned to a relation between the entity and the company; only the type of entity (person, location, organization, etc) is captured by the tag.

New entity pairs are generated by matching the learned patterns against web text. A sentence is considered to match a pattern if it has the same entity types in the same order and its L, M, and R words fuzzy match the corresponding words in the pattern.[1] The entities are therefore assumed to be related since they are expressed in the same way as the seed pair. Unlike the TD approach, the actual relationship between the entities is unknown (since the only data we use is the web text, not the structured RDF data); all we need to know here is that a relationship exists.

We alternate learning the patterns and generating entity pairs over our development set of 100 companies. We then take all the learned patterns and find matching sentences in the Bing search results for each company in the set of target companies.[2] Sentences that match any of the patterns are selected and ranked by number of matches (more matches means greater probability of strong relation) before being added to the description.

4.1   Pruning and Ordering

After selecting the sentences for the description, we perform a post-processing step that removes noise and redundancy. To address redundancy, we remove those sentences which were conveyed previously in the description using exactly the same wording. Thus, sentences which are equal to or subsets of other sentences are removed. We also remove sentences that come from news stories; analysis of our results on the development set indicated that news stories rarely contain information that is relevant to a typical Wikipedia description. To do this we use regular expressions to capture common newswire patterns (e.g., [CITY, STATE: sentence]). Finally, we remove incomplete sentences ending in "…", which sometimes appear on websites which themselves contain summaries.

We order the selected sentences using a scoring method that rewards sentences based on how they refer to the company. Sentences that begin with the full company name get a starting score of 25, sentences that begin with a partial company name start with a score of 15, and sentences that do not contain the company name at all start at -15 (if they contain the company name in the middle of the sentence, they start at 0). Then, 10 points are added to the score for each *keyword* in the sentence (keywords were selected from the most populous DBPedia predicates where the subject is a company). This scoring algorithm was tuned on the development set. The final output is ordered in

---

[1] We use a threshold on the cosine similarity of the texts to determine whether they match.

[2] We excluded Wikipedia results to better simulate the case of companies which do not have a Wikipedia page

descending order of scores.

5 Hybrid system

In addition to the two approaches separately, we also generated hybrid output from a combination of the two. In this approach, we start with the DD output; if (after pruning) it has fewer than three sentences, we add the TD output and re-order.

The hybrid approach essentially supplements the large, more noisy web content of the DD output with the small, high-quality but less diverse TD output. For companies that are not consumer-facing or are relatively young, and thus have a relatively low web presence - our target population - this can significantly impact the description.

6 Experiments

To evaluate our approach, we compare the three versions of our output - generated by the TD, DD, and hybrid approach - against multi-document summaries generated (from the same search results used by our DD approach) by TextRank (Mihalcea and Tarau, 2004). For each one of the approaches as well as the baseline, we generated descriptions for all companies that were part of the S&P500 as of January 2016. We used our development set of 100 companies for tuning, and the evaluation results are based on the remaining 400.

We conducted two types of experiments. The first is an automated evaluation, where we use the METEOR score (Lavie and Agarwal, 2007) between the description generated by one of our approaches or by the baseline and the first section of the Wikipedia article for the company. In Wikipedia articles, the first section typically serves as an introduction or overview of the most important information about the company. METEOR scores capture the content overlap between the generated description and the Wikipedia text. To avoid bias from different text sizes, we set the same size limit for all descriptions when comparing them. We experimented with three settings: 150 words, 500 words, and no size limit.

In addition, we conducted a crowd-sourced evaluation on the CrowdFlower platform. In this evaluation, we presented human annotators with two descriptions for the same company, one described by our approach and one by the baseline, in random order. The annotators were then asked to choose which of the two descriptions is a better overview of the company in question (they were

	150 words	500 words	no limit
TextRank	13.7	12.8	6.3
DD	15.0	14.5	14.0
TD	11.3	11.3	11.3
Hybrid	15.5	14.6	14.2

Table 1: First experiment results: average METEOR scores for various size limits

	% best	Avg. score
TextRank	25.79	2.82
Hybrid	74.21	3.81

Table 2: Second experiment results: % of companies for which the approach was chosen as best by the human annotators, and average scores given

provided a link to the company's Wikipedia page for reference) and give a score on a 1-5 scale to each description. For quality assurance, each pair of descriptions was processed by three annotators, and we only included in the results instances where all three agreed. Those constituted 44% of the instances. In this evaluation we only used the *hybrid* version, and we limited the length of both the baseline and our output to 150 words to reduce bias from a difference in lengths and keep the descriptions reasonably short for the annotators.

7 Results

The results of the automated evaluation are shown in Table 1. Our DD system achieves higher METEOR scores than the TextRank baseline under all size variations, while TD by itself is worse in most cases. In all cases the combined approach achieves a better result than the DD system by itself.

The results of the human evaluation are shown in Table 2. Here the advantage of our approach becomes much more visible: we clearly beat the baseline both in terms of how often the annotators chose our output to be better (almost 75% of the times) and in terms of the average score given to our descriptions (3.81 on a $1 - 5$ point scale).

All results are statistically significant, but the difference in magnitude between the results of the two experiments are striking: we believe that while the TextRank summarizer extracts sentences which are topically relevant and thus achieve results close to ours in terms of METEOR, the more structured entity-focused approach we present here is able to extract content that seems much more reasonable to humans as a general description. One example is shown in Figure 1.

Right from the start, we see that our system out-

246

performs TextRank. Our first sentence introduces the company and provides a critical piece of history about it, while TextRank does not even immediately name it. The hybrid generation output has a more structured output, going from the origins of the company via merger, to its board, and finally its products. TextRank's output, in comparison, focuses on the employee experience and only mentions products at the very end. Our system is much more suitable for a short description of the company for someone unfamilar with it.

TextRank: The company also emphasizes stretch assignments and on-the-job learning for development, while its formal training programs include a Masters in the Business of Activision(or "MBActivision") program that gives employees a deep look at company operations and how its games are made, from idea to development to store shelves. How easy is it to talk with managers and get the information I need? Will managers listen to my input? At Activision Blizzard, 78 percent of employees say they often or almost always experience a free and transparent exchange of ideas and information within the organization. Gaming is a part of day to day life at Activision Blizzard, and the company often organizes internal tournaments for Call of Duty, Hearthstone: Heroes of Warcraft, Destiny, Skylanders and other titles. What inspires employees' company spirit here Do people stand by their teams' work What impact do people have outside the organization.

Hybrid: Activision Blizzard was formed in 2007 from a merger between Activision and Vivendi Games (as well as Blizzard Entertainment, which had already been a division of Vivendi Games.) Upon merger, Activision Blizzard's board of directors initially formed of eleven members: six directors designated by Vivendi, two Activision management directors and three independent directors who currently serve on Activision's board of directors. It's comprised of Blizzard Entertainment, best known for blockbuster hits including World of Warcraft, Hearthstone: Heroes of Warcraft, and the Warcraft, StarCraft, and Diablo franchises, and Activision Publishing, whose development studios (including Infinity Ward, Toys for Bob, Sledgehammer Games, and Treyarch, to name just a few) create blockbusters like Call of Duty, Skylanders, Guitar Hero, and Destiny.

Figure 1: Descriptions for Activision Blizzard

8   Conclusion

We described two approaches to generating company descriptions as well as a hybrid approach. We showed that our output is overwhelmingly preferred by human readers, and is more similar to Wikipedia introductions, than the output of a state-of-the-art summarization algorithm.

These complementary methods each have their advantages and disadvantages: the TD approach ensures that typical expressions in Wikipedia company descriptions - known to be about the fundamental relations of a company - will occur in the generated output. However, since it modifies them, it risks generating ungrammatical sentences or sentences which contain information about another company. The latter can occur because the sentence is uniquely tied to the original. For instance, the following Wikipedia sentence fragment – "Microsoft is the world's largest software maker by revenue" - is a useful insight about the company, but our system would not be able to correctly modify that to fit any other company.

In contrast, by selecting sentences from the web about the given company, the DD approach ensures that the resulting description will be both grammatical and relevant. It also results in a wider variety of expressions and a greater number of sentences. However, it can include nonessential facts that appear in a variety of different web venues. It is not surprising, therefore, that the hybrid approach performs better than either by itself.

While in this paper we focus on company descriptions, the system can be adapted to generate descriptions for other entities (e.g. Persons, Products) by updating the seed datasets for both approaches (to reflect the important facts for the desired descriptions) and retuning for best accuracy.

Acknowledgment

This research was supported in part by an IBM Shared University Research grant provided to the Computer Science Department of Columbia University.

References

Eugene Agichtein and Luis Gravano. 2000. Snowball: Extracting relations from large plain-text collections. In *Proceedings of the fifth ACM conference on Digital libraries*, pages 85–94. ACM.

Gabor Angeli, Percy Liang, and Dan Klein. 2010. A simple domain-independent probabilistic approach to generation. In *Proceedings of the 2010 Conference on Empirical Methods in Natural Language Processing*, EMNLP '10, pages 502–512, Stroudsburg, PA, USA. Association for Computational Linguistics.

Or Biran and Kathleen McKeown. 2015. Discourse planning with an n-gram model of relations. In *Proceedings of the 2015 Conference on Empirical Methods in Natural Language Processing*, pages 1973–1977, Lisbon, Portugal, September. Association for Computational Linguistics.

Sasha Blair-Goldensohn, Kathleen R. McKeown, and And rew Hazen Schlaikjer. 2003. Defscriber: a hybrid system for definitional qa. In *SIGIR '03: Proceedings of the 26th annual international ACM SIGIR conference on Research and development in informaion retrieval*, pages 462–462.

Nadjet Bouayad-Agha, Gerard Casamayor, and Leo Wanner. 2011. Content selection from an ontology-based knowledge base for the generation of football summaries. In *Proceedings of the 13th European Workshop on Natural Language Generation*, ENLG '11, pages 72–81, Stroudsburg, PA, USA. Association for Computational Linguistics.

John Conroy, Judith Schlesinger, and Dianne O'Leary. 2006. Topic-focused multi-document summarization using an approximate or acle score. In *Proceedings of ACL.*

Hal Daumé III and Daniel Marcu. 2005. Bayesian multi-document summarization at mse. In *Proceedings of the Workshop on Multilingual Summarization Eva luation (MSE)*, Ann Arbor, MI, June 29.

Noemie Elhadad and Kathleen R. Mckeown. 2001. Towards generating patient specific summaries of medical articles. In *In Proceedings of NAACL-2001 Workshop Automatic.*

Michael Elhadad. 1991. *FUF: The Universal Unifier User Manual ; Version 5.0.* Department of Computer Science, Columbia University.

Güneş Erkan and Dragomir R. Radev. 2004. Lexrank: Graph-based centrality as salience in text summarization. *Journal of Artificial Intelligence Research (JAIR).*

Elena Filatova and John Prager. 2005. Tell me what you do and i'll tell you what you are: Learning occupation-related activities for biographies. In *Proceedings of the Conference on Human Language Technology and Empirical Methods in Natural Language Processing*, HLT '05, pages 113–120, Stroudsburg, PA, USA. Association for Computational Linguistics.

Dimitra Gkatzia, Helen F. Hastie, and Oliver Lemon. 2014. Finding middle ground? multi-objective natural language generation from time-series data. In Gosse Bouma and Yannick Parmentier, editors, *Proceedings of the 14th Conference of the European Chapter of the Association for Computational Linguistics, EACL 2014, April 26-30, 2014, Gothenburg, Sweden*, pages 210–214. The Association for Computer Linguistics.

Ravi Kondadadi, Blake Howald, and Frank Schilder. 2013. A statistical nlg framework for aggregated planning and realization. In *ACL (1)*, pages 1406–1415. The Association for Computer Linguistics.

Alon Lavie and Abhaya Agarwal. 2007. Meteor: An automatic metric for mt evaluation with high levels of correlation with human judgments. In *Proceedings of the Second Workshop on Statistical Machine Translation*, StatMT '07, pages 228–231. Association for Computational Linguistics.

Christian M.I.M. Matthiessen and John A. Bateman. 1991. Text generation and systemic-functional linguistics: experiences from english and japanese.

Rada Mihalcea and Paul Tarau. 2004. Textrank: Bringing order into texts. In *Conference on Empirical Methods in Natural Language Processing*, Barcelona, Spain.

Jahna Otterbacher, Gunes Erkan, and Dragomir R. Radev. 2005. Using random walks for question-focused sentence retrieval. In *Proceedings of HLT-EMNLP.*

Ehud Reiter and Robert Dale. 1997. Building applied natural language generation systems. *Nat. Lang. Eng.*, 3(1):57–87, March.

Christina Sauper and Regina Barzilay. 2009. Automatically generating wikipedia articles: A structure-aware approach. In *Proceedings of the Joint Conference of the 47th Annual Meeting of the ACL and the 4th International Joint Conference on Natural Language Processing of the AFNLP: Volume 1 - Volume 1*, ACL '09, pages 208–216, Stroudsburg, PA, USA. Association for Computational Linguistics.

B. Schiffman, Inderjeet. Mani, and K. Concepcion. 2001. Producing biographical summaries: Combining linguistic knowledge with corpus statistics. In *Proceedings of the 39th Annual Meeting of the Association for Computational Linguistics (ACL-EACL 2001)*, Toulouse, France, July.

William Yang Wang, Kapil Thadani, and Kathleen McKeown. 2011. Identifying event descriptions using co-training with online news su mmaries. In *Proceedings of IJNLP*, Chiang-Mai, Thailand, November.

Ralph M. Weischedel, Jinxi Xu, and Ana Licuanan. 2004. A hybrid approach to answering biographical questions. In Mark T. Maybury, editor, *New Directions in Question Answering*, pages 59–70. AAAI Press.

Michael White. 2014. Towards surface realization with ccgs induced from dependencies. In *Proceedings of the 8th International Natural Language Generation Conference (INLG)*, pages 147–151, Philadelphia, Pennsylvania, U.S.A., June. Association for Computational Linguistics.

Annotating Relation Inference in Context via Question Answering

Omer Levy **Ido Dagan**

Computer Science Department

Bar-Ilan University

Ramat-Gan, Israel

{omerlevy,dagan}@cs.biu.ac.il

Abstract

We present a new annotation method for collecting data on relation inference in context. We convert the inference task to one of simple factoid question answering, allowing us to easily scale up to 16,000 high-quality examples. Our method corrects a major bias in previous evaluations, making our dataset much more realistic.

1 Introduction

Recognizing entailment between natural-language relations (predicates) is a key challenge in many semantic tasks. For instance, in question answering (QA), it is often necessary to "bridge the lexical chasm" between the asker's choice of words and those that appear in the answer text. Relation inference can be notoriously difficult to automatically recognize because of semantic phenomena such as polysemy and metaphor:

Q: Which drug treats headaches?

A: Aspirin eliminates headaches.

In this context, "eliminates" implies "treats" and the answer is indeed "aspirin". However, this rule does not always hold for other cases – "eliminates patients" has a very different meaning from "treats patients". Hence, *context-sensitive* methods are required to solve relation inference.

Many methods have tried to address relation inference, from DIRT (Lin and Pantel, 2001) through Sherlock (Schoenmackers et al., 2010) to the more recent work on PPDB (Pavlick et al., 2015b) and RELLY (Grycner et al., 2015). However, the way these methods are evaluated remains largely inconsistent. Some papers that deal with phrasal inference in general (Beltagy et al., 2013; Pavlick et al., 2015a; Kruszewski et al., 2015) use

an extrinsic task, such as a recent recognizing textual entailment (RTE) benchmark (Marelli et al., 2014). By nature, extrinsic tasks incorporate a variety of linguistic phenomena, making it harder to analyze the specific issues of relation inference.

The vast majority of papers that do focus on relation inference perform some form of post-hoc evaluation (Lin and Pantel, 2001; Szpektor et al., 2007; Schoenmackers et al., 2010; Weisman et al., 2012; Lewis and Steedman, 2013; Riedel et al., 2013; Rocktäschel et al., 2015; Grycner and Weikum, 2014; Grycner et al., 2015; Pavlick et al., 2015b). Typically, the proposed algorithm generates several inference rules between two relation templates, which are then evaluated manually. Some studies evaluate the rules out of context (is the rule *"X eliminates Y"→"X treats Y"* true?), while others apply them to textual data and evaluate the validity of the rule in context (given "aspirin *eliminates* headaches", is "aspirin *treats* headaches" true?). Not only are these post-hoc evaluations oblivious to recall, their "human in the loop" approach makes them expensive and virtually impossible to accurately replicate.

Hence, there is a real need for *pre-annotated* datasets for *intrinsic* evaluation of relation inference *in context*. Zeichner et al. (2012) constructed such a dataset by applying DIRT-trained inference rules to sampled texts, and then crowd-annotating whether each original text (premise) entails the text generated from applying the inference rule (hypothesis). However, this process is biased; by using DIRT to generate examples, the dataset is inherently blind to the many cases where relation inference exists, but is not captured by DIRT.

We present a new dataset for evaluating relation inference in context, which is *unbiased* towards one method or another, and *natural* to annotate. To create this dataset, we design a QA setting where annotators are presented with a single ques-

Proceedings of the 54th Annual Meeting of the Association for Computational Linguistics, pages 249–255,
Berlin, Germany, August 7-12, 2016. ©2016 Association for Computational Linguistics

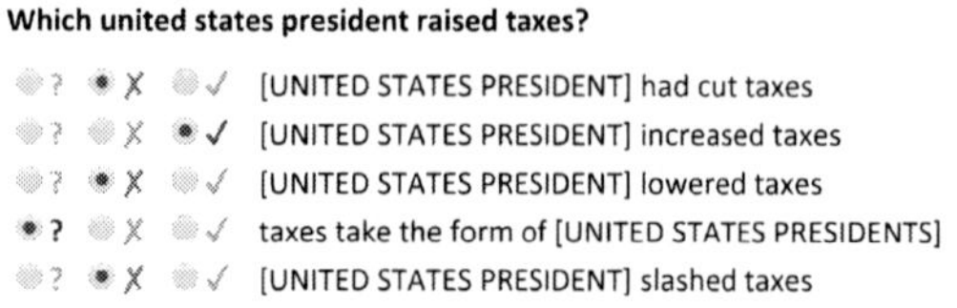

Figure 1: A screenshot from our annotation task.

tion and several automatically-retrieved text fragments. The annotators' goal is to mark which of the text fragments provide a potential answer to the question (see Figure 1). Since the entities in the text fragments are aligned with those in the question, this process implicitly annotates which *relations* entail the one in the question. For example, in Figure 1, if "[US PRESIDENT] increased taxes" provides an answer to "Which US president raised taxes?", then "increased" implies "raised" in that context. Because this task is so easy to annotate, we were able to scale up to 16,371 annotated examples (3,147 positive) with 91.3% precision for only $375 via crowdsourcing.

Finally, we evaluate a collection of existing methods and common practices on our dataset, and observe that even the best combination of methods cannot recall more than 25% of the positive examples without dipping below 80% precision. This places into perspective the huge amount of relevant cases of relation inference inherently ignored by the bias in (Zeichner et al., 2012). Moreover, this result shows that while our annotation task is easy for humans, it is difficult for existing algorithms, making it an appealing challenge for future research on relation inference. Our code[1] and data[2] are publicly available.

2 Relation Inference Datasets

To the best of our knowledge, there are only three pre-annotated datasets for evaluating relation inference in context.[3] Each example in these datasets consists of two binary relations, premise and hypothesis, and a label indicat-

---

[1] http://bitbucket.org/omerlevy/relation_inference_via_qa

[2] http://u.cs.biu.ac.il/~nlp/resources/downloads/relation_inference_via_qa

[3] It is worth noting the lexical substitution datasets (McCarthy and Navigli, 2007; Biemann, 2013; Kremer et al., 2014) also capture instances of relation inference. However, they do not focus on relations and are limited to single-word substitutions. Furthermore, the annotators are tasked with generating substitutions, whereas we are interested in judging (classifying) an existing substitution.

ing whether the hypothesis is inferred from the premise. These relations are essentially Open IE (Banko et al., 2007) assertions, and can be represented as $(subject, relation, object)$ tuples.

Berant et al. (2011) annotated inference between *typed* relations ("[DRUG] *eliminates* [SYMPTOM]"→"[DRUG] *treats* [SYMPTOM]"), restricting the definition of "context". They also used the non-standard type-system from (Schoenmackers et al., 2010), which limits the dataset's applicability to other corpora. Levy et al. (2014) annotated inference between *instantiated* relations sharing at least one argument ("aspirin *eliminates* headaches"→"drugs *treat* headaches"). While this format captures a more natural notion of context, it also conflates the task of relation inference with that of entity inference ("aspirin"→"drug"). Both datasets were annotated by experts.

Zeichner et al. (2012) annotated inference between *instantiated* relations sharing *both* arguments:

aspirin *eliminates* headaches → aspirin *treats* headaches

aspirin *eliminates* headaches ↛ aspirin *murders* headaches

This format provides a broad definition of context on one hand, while isolating the task of relation inference. In addition, methods that can be evaluated on this type of data, can also be directly embedded into downstream applications, motivating subsequent work to use it as a benchmark (Melamud et al., 2013; Abend et al., 2014; Lewis, 2014). We therefore create our own dataset in this format.

The main drawback of Zeichner et al.'s process is that it is biased towards a specific relation inference method, DIRT (Lin and Pantel, 2001). Essentially, Zeichner et al. conducted a post-hoc evaluation of DIRT and recorded the results. While their approach does not suffer from the major disadvantages of post-hoc evaluation – cost and irreplicability – it ignores instances that do not behave according to DIRT's assumptions. These invisible examples amount to an enormous chunk of the inference performed when answering questions, which are covered by our approach (see §4).

3 Collection & Annotation Process

Our data collection and annotation process is designed to achieve two goals: (1) to efficiently sample premise-hypothesis pairs in an *unbiased* manner; (2) to allow for cheap, consistent, and scalable annotations based on an intuitive QA setting.

3.1 Methodology Overview

We start by collecting factoid questions. Each question is captured as a tuple $q = (q_{type}, q_{rel}, q_{arg})$, for example:

$$\text{Which } \underset{q_{type}}{\underline{\text{food}}} \ \underset{q_{rel}}{\underline{\text{is included in}}} \ \underset{q_{arg}}{\underline{\text{chocolate}}} \ ?$$

In addition to "Which?" questions, this template captures other WH-questions such as "Who?" ($q_{type} = $ person).

We then collect a set of candidate answers for each question q. A candidate answer is also represented as a tuple $(a_{answer}, a_{rel}, a_{arg})$ or $(a_{arg}, a_{rel}, a_{answer})$, for example:

$$\underset{a_{arg}}{\underline{\text{chocolate}}} \ \underset{a_{rel}}{\underline{\text{is made from}}} \ \underset{a_{answer}}{\underline{\text{the cocoa bean}}}$$

We collect answer candidates according to the following criteria:

1. $a_{arg} = q_{arg}$
2. a_{answer} is a type of q_{type}
3. $a_{rel} \neq q_{rel}$

These criteria isolate the task of relation inference from additional inference tasks, because they ensure that a's arguments are entailing q's. In addition, the first two criteria ensure that enough candidate answers actually answer the question, while the third discards trivial cases. In contrast to (Zeichner et al., 2012) and post-hoc evaluations, these criteria do not impose any bias on the relation pair a_{rel}, q_{rel}. Furthermore, we show in §3.2 that both a and q are both independent naturally-occurring texts, and are not machine-generated by applying a specific set of inference rules.

For each (a, q) pair, Mechanical Turk annotators are asked whether a provides an answer to q. This natural approach also enables batch annotation; for each question, several candidate answers can be presented at once without shifting the annotator's focus. To make sure that the annotators do not use their world knowledge about a_{answer}, we mask it during the annotation phase and replace it with q_{type} (see Figure 1 and §3.3).

Finally, we instantiate q_{type} with a_{answer}, so that each (a, q) pair fits Zeichner's format: instantiated predicates sharing both arguments.

3.2 Data Collection

We automatically collected 30,703 pairs of questions and candidate answers for annotation. Our process is largely inspired by (Fader et al., 2014).

Questions We collected 573 questions by manually converting questions from TREC (Voorhees and Tice, 2000), WikiAnswers (Fader et al., 2013), WebQuestions (Berant et al., 2013), to our "Which q_{type} q_{rel} q_{arg}?" format. Though many questions did fit our format, a large portion of them were about sports and celebrities, which were not applicable to our choice of corpus (Google books) and taxonomy (WordNet).[4]

Corpus QA requires some body of knowledge from which to retrieve candidate answers. We follow Fader et al. (2013; 2014), and use a collection of Open IE-style assertions (Banko et al., 2007) as our knowledge base. Specifically, we used hand-crafted syntactic rules[5] to extract over 63 million unique subject-relation-object triplets from Google's Syntactic N-grams (Goldberg and Orwant, 2013). The assertions may include multiword phrases as relations or arguments, as illustrated earlier. This process yields some ungrammatical or out-of-context assertions, which are later filtered during annotation (see §3.3).

Answer Candidates In §3.1 we defined three criteria for matching an answer candidate to a question, which we now translate into a retrieval process. We begin by retrieving all assertions where one of the arguments (subject or object) is equal to q_{arg}, ignoring stopwords and inflections. The matching argument is named a_{arg}, while the other (non-matching) argument becomes a_{answer}.

To implement the second criterion (a_{answer} is a type of q_{type}) we require a taxonomy T, as well as a word-sense disambiguation (WSD) algorithm to match natural-language terms to entities in T. In this work, we employ WordNet's hypernymy graph (Fellbaum, 1998) as T and Lesk (Lesk, 1986) for WSD (both via NLTK (Bird et al., 2009)). While automatic WSD is prone to some errors, these cases are usually annotated as nonsensical in the final phase.

Lastly, we remove instances where $a_{rel} = q_{rel}$.[6]

---

[4]This is the only part in our process that might introduce some bias. However, this bias is independent of existing relation inference methods such as DIRT.

[5]See supplementary material for a detailed description.

[6]Several additional filters were applied to prune nongrammatical assertions (see supplementary material).

3.3 Crowdsourced Annotation

Masking Answers We noticed that exposing a_{answer} to the annotator may skew the annotation; rather than annotating whether a_{rel} implies q_{rel} in the given context, the annotator might annotate whether a_{answer} answers q according to her general knowledge. For example:

Q: Which country borders Ethiopia?

A: Eritrea invaded Ethiopia.

An annotator might be misled by knowing in advance that Eritrea borders Ethiopia. Although an invasion typically requires land access, it does not imply a shared border, even in this context; "Italy invaded Ethiopia" also appears in our corpus, but it is not true that "Italy borders Ethiopia".

Effectively, what the annotator might be doing in this case is substituting q_{type} ("country") with a_{answer} ("Eritrea") and asking herself if the assertion $(a_{answer}, q_{rel}, q_{arg})$ is true ("Does Eritrea border Ethiopia?"). As demonstrated, this question may have a different answer from the inference question in which we are interested ("If a country invaded Ethiopia, does that country border Ethiopia?"). We therefore mask a_{answer} during annotation by replacing it with q_{type} as a placeholder:

A: [COUNTRY] invaded Ethiopia.

This forces the annotator to ask herself whether a_{rel} implies q_{rel} in this context, i.e. does invading Ethiopia imply sharing a border with it?

Labels Each annotator was given a single question with several matching candidate answers (20 on average), and asked to mark each candidate answer with one of three labels:

✓ The sentence answers the question.

✗ The sentence does not answer the question.

? The sentence does not make sense,
or is severely non-grammatical.

Figure 1 shows several annotated examples. The third annotation (?) was useful in weeding out noisy assertions (23% of candidate answers).

Aggregation Overall, we created 1,500 questionnaires,[7] spanning a total of 30,703 (a, q) pairs. Each questionnaire was annotated by 5 differ-

ent people, and aggregated using the unanimous-up-to-one (at least 4/5) rule. Examples that did not exhibit this kind of inter-annotator agreement were discarded, and so were examples which were determined as nonsensical/ungrammatical (annotated with ?). After aggregating and filtering, we were left with 3,147 positive (✓) and 13,224 negative (✗) examples.[8]

To evaluate this aggregation rule, we took a random subset of 32 questionnaires (594 (a, q) pairs) and annotated them ourselves (expert annotation). We then compared the aggregated crowdsourced annotation on the same (a, q) pairs to our own. The crowdsourced annotation yielded 91.3% precision on our expert annotations (i.e. only 8.7% of the crowd-annotated positives were expert-annotated as negative), while recalling 86.2% of expert-annotated positives.

4 Performance of Existing Methods

To provide a baseline for future work, we test the performance of two inference-rule resources and two methods of distributional inference on our dataset, as well as a lemma-similarity baseline.[9]

4.1 Baselines

Lemma Baseline We implemented a baseline that takes into account four features from the premise relation (a_{rel}) and the hypothesis relation (q_{rel}) after they have been lemmatized: (1) Does a_{rel} contain all of q_{rel}'s content words? (2) Do the relations share a verb? (3) Does the relations' active/passive voice match their arguments' alignments? (4) Do the relations agree on negation? The baseline will classify the example as positive if all features are true.

PPDB 2.0 We used the largest collection of paraphrases (XXXL) from PPDB (Pavlick et al., 2015b). These paraphrases include argument slots for cases where word order changes (e.g. passive/active).

Entailment Graph We used the publicly-available inference rules derived from Berant et al.'s (2011) entailment graph. These rules contain typed relations and can also be applied in a context-sensitive manner. However, ignoring the

---

[7] Each of our 573 questions had many candidate answers. These were split into smaller chunks (questionnaires) of less than 25 candidate answers each.

[8] This harsh filtering process is mainly a result of poor annotator quality. See supplementary material for a detailed description of the steps we took to improve annotator quality.

[9] To recreate the embeddings, see supplementary material.

types and applying the inference rules out of context worked better on our dataset, perhaps because Berant et al.'s taxonomy was learned from a different corpus.

Relation Embeddings Similar to DIRT (Lin and Pantel, 2001), we create vector representations for relations, which are then used to measure relation similarity. From the set of assertions extracted in §3.2, we create a dataset of relation-argument pairs, and use word2vecf (Levy and Goldberg, 2014) to train the embeddings. We also tried to use the arguments' embeddings to induce a context-sensitive measure of similarity, as suggested by Melamud et al. (2015); however, this method did not improve performance on our dataset.

Word Embeddings Using Google's Syntactic N-grams (Goldberg and Orwant, 2013), from which candidate answers were extracted, we trained dependency-based word embeddings with word2vecf (Levy and Goldberg, 2014). We used the average word vector to represent multi-word relations, and cosine to measure their similarity.

4.2 Results

Under the assumption that collections of inference rules are more precision-oriented, we also try different combinations of rule-based and embedding-based methods by first applying the rules and then calculating the embedding-based similarity only on instances that were not identified as positive by the rules. Since the embeddings produce a similarity score, not a classification, we plot all methods' performance on a single precision-recall curve (Figure 2).

All methods used the lemma baseline as a first step to identify positive examples; without it, performance drops dramatically. This is probably more of a dataset artifact than an observation about the baselines; just like we filtered examples where $a_{rel} \neq q_{rel}$, we could have used a more aggressive policy and removed all pairs that share lemmas.

It seems that most methods provide little value beyond the lemma baseline – the exception being Berant et al.'s (2011) entailment graph. Unifying the entailment graph with PPDB (and, implicitly, the lemma baseline) slightly improves performance, and provides a significantly better starting point for the method based on word embeddings. Even so, performance is still quite poor in absolute terms, with less than 25% recall at 80% precision.

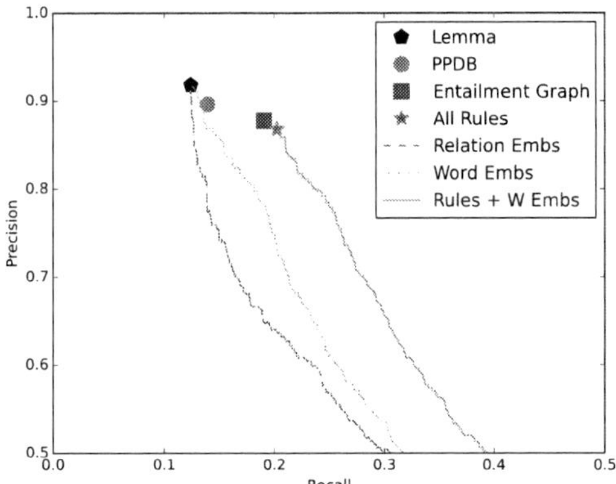

Figure 2: The performance of existing methods on our dataset. All methods are run on top of the lemma baseline. *All Rules* is the union of PPDB and the entailment graph. *Rules + W Embs* is a combination of *All Rules* and our word embeddings.

4.3 The Ramifications of Low Recall

These results emphasize the huge false-negative rate of existing methods. This suggests that a massive amount of inference examples, which are necessary for answering questions, are inherently ignored in (Zeichner et al., 2012) and post-hoc evaluations. Our dataset remedies this bias, and poses a new challenge for future research on relation inference.

Acknowledgements

This work was supported by the German Research Foundation via the German-Israeli Project Cooperation (grant DA 1600/1-1), the Israel Science Foundation grant 880/12, and by grants from the MAGNET program of the Israeli Office of the Chief Scientist (OCS).

References

[Abend et al.2014] Omri Abend, Shay B. Cohen, and Mark Steedman. 2014. Lexical inference over multi-word predicates: A distributional approach. In *Proceedings of the 52nd Annual Meeting of the Association for Computational Linguistics (Volume 1: Long Papers)*, pages 644–654, Baltimore, Maryland, June. Association for Computational Linguistics.

[Banko et al.2007] Michele Banko, Michael J. Cafarella, Stephen Soderland, Matthew Broadhead, and Oren Etzioni. 2007. Open information extraction from the web. In *IJCAI 2007, Proceedings of the 20th International Joint Conference on Artificial*

Intelligence, Hyderabad, India, January 6-12, 2007, pages 2670–2676.

[Beltagy et al.2013] Islam Beltagy, Cuong Chau, Gemma Boleda, Dan Garrette, Katrin Erk, and Raymond Mooney. 2013. Montague meets markov: Deep semantics with probabilistic logical form. In *Second Joint Conference on Lexical and Computational Semantics (*SEM), Volume 1: Proceedings of the Main Conference and the Shared Task: Semantic Textual Similarity*, pages 11–21, Atlanta, Georgia, USA, June. Association for Computational Linguistics.

[Berant et al.2011] Jonathan Berant, Ido Dagan, and Jacob Goldberger. 2011. Global learning of typed entailment rules. In *Proceedings of the 49th Annual Meeting of the Association for Computational Linguistics: Human Language Technologies*, pages 610–619, Portland, Oregon, USA, June. Association for Computational Linguistics.

[Berant et al.2013] Jonathan Berant, Andrew Chou, Roy Frostig, and Percy Liang. 2013. Semantic parsing on Freebase from question-answer pairs. In *Proceedings of the 2013 Conference on Empirical Methods in Natural Language Processing*, pages 1533–1544, Seattle, Washington, USA, October. Association for Computational Linguistics.

[Biemann2013] Chris Biemann. 2013. Creating a system for lexical substitutions from scratch using crowdsourcing. *Language Resources and Evaluation*, 47(1):97–122.

[Bird et al.2009] Steven Bird, Ewan Klein, and Edward Loper. 2009. *Natural Language Processing with Python*. O'Reilly Media.

[Fader et al.2013] Anthony Fader, Luke Zettlemoyer, and Oren Etzioni. 2013. Paraphrase-driven learning for open question answering. In *Proceedings of the 51st Annual Meeting of the Association for Computational Linguistics (Volume 1: Long Papers)*, pages 1608–1618, Sofia, Bulgaria, August. Association for Computational Linguistics.

[Fader et al.2014] Anthony Fader, Luke Zettlemoyer, and Oren Etzioni. 2014. Open question answering over curated and extracted knowledge bases. In *Proceedings of the 20th ACM SIGKDD International Conference on Knowledge Discovery and Data Mining*, pages 1156–1165. ACM.

[Fellbaum1998] Christiane Fellbaum. 1998. *WordNet*. Wiley Online Library.

[Goldberg and Orwant2013] Yoav Goldberg and Jon Orwant. 2013. A dataset of syntactic-ngrams over time from a very large corpus of english books. In *Second Joint Conference on Lexical and Computational Semantics (*SEM), Volume 1: Proceedings of the Main Conference and the Shared Task: Semantic Textual Similarity*, pages 241–247, Atlanta, Georgia, USA, June. Association for Computational Linguistics.

[Grycner and Weikum2014] Adam Grycner and Gerhard Weikum. 2014. Harpy: Hypernyms and alignment of relational paraphrases. In *Proceedings of COLING 2014, the 25th International Conference on Computational Linguistics: Technical Papers*, pages 2195–2204, Dublin, Ireland, August. Dublin City University and Association for Computational Linguistics.

[Grycner et al.2015] Adam Grycner, Gerhard Weikum, Jay Pujara, James Foulds, and Lise Getoor. 2015. Relly: Inferring hypernym relationships between relational phrases. In *Proceedings of the 2015 Conference on Empirical Methods in Natural Language Processing*, pages 971–981, Lisbon, Portugal, September. Association for Computational Linguistics.

[Kremer et al.2014] Gerhard Kremer, Katrin Erk, Sebastian Padó, and Stefan Thater. 2014. What substitutes tell us - analysis of an "all-words" lexical substitution corpus. In *Proceedings of the 14th Conference of the European Chapter of the Association for Computational Linguistics*, pages 540–549, Gothenburg, Sweden, April. Association for Computational Linguistics.

[Kruszewski et al.2015] Germán Kruszewski, Denis Paperno, and Marco Baroni. 2015. Deriving boolean structures from distributional vectors. *Transactions of the Association for Computational Linguistics*, 3:375–388.

[Lesk1986] Michael Lesk. 1986. Automatic sense disambiguation using machine readable dictionaries: How to tell a pine cone from an ice cream cone. In *Proceedings of the 5th Annual International Conference on Systems Documentation*, pages 24–26. ACM.

[Levy and Goldberg2014] Omer Levy and Yoav Goldberg. 2014. Dependency-based word embeddings. In *Proceedings of the 52nd Annual Meeting of the Association for Computational Linguistics (Volume 2: Short Papers)*, pages 302–308, Baltimore, Maryland, June. Association for Computational Linguistics.

[Levy et al.2014] Omer Levy, Ido Dagan, and Jacob Goldberger. 2014. Focused entailment graphs for open ie propositions. In *Proceedings of the Eighteenth Conference on Computational Natural Language Learning*, pages 87–97, Ann Arbor, Michigan, June. Association for Computational Linguistics.

[Lewis and Steedman2013] Mike Lewis and Mark Steedman. 2013. Combining distributional and logical semantics. *Transactions of the Association for Computational Linguistics*, 1:179–192.

[Lewis2014] Mike Lewis. 2014. *Combined Distributional and Logical Semantics*. Ph.D. thesis, University of Edinburgh.

[Lin and Pantel2001] Dekang Lin and Patrick Pantel. 2001. Dirt: Discovery of inference rules from text. In *Proceedings of the seventh ACM SIGKDD international conference on Knowledge discovery and data mining*, pages 323–328. ACM.

[Marelli et al.2014] Marco Marelli, Stefano Menini, Marco Baroni, Luisa Bentivogli, Raffaella bernardi, and Roberto Zamparelli. 2014. A sick cure for the evaluation of compositional distributional semantic models. In Nicoletta Calzolari, Khalid Choukri, Thierry Declerck, Hrafn Loftsson, Bente Maegaard, Joseph Mariani, Asuncion Moreno, Jan Odijk, and Stelios Piperidis, editors, *Proceedings of the Ninth International Conference on Language Resources and Evaluation (LREC'14)*, pages 216–223, Reykjavik, Iceland, May. European Language Resources Association (ELRA). ACL Anthology Identifier: L14-1314.

[McCarthy and Navigli2007] Diana McCarthy and Roberto Navigli. 2007. Semeval-2007 task 10: English lexical substitution task. In *Proceedings of the Fourth International Workshop on Semantic Evaluations (SemEval-2007)*, pages 48–53, Prague, Czech Republic, June. Association for Computational Linguistics.

[Melamud et al.2013] Oren Melamud, Jonathan Berant, Ido Dagan, Jacob Goldberger, and Idan Szpektor. 2013. A two level model for context sensitive inference rules. In *Proceedings of the 51st Annual Meeting of the Association for Computational Linguistics (Volume 1: Long Papers)*, pages 1331–1340, Sofia, Bulgaria, August. Association for Computational Linguistics.

[Melamud et al.2015] Oren Melamud, Omer Levy, and Ido Dagan. 2015. A simple word embedding model for lexical substitution. In *Proceedings of the 1st Workshop on Vector Space Modeling for Natural Language Processing*, pages 1–7, Denver, Colorado, June. Association for Computational Linguistics.

[Pavlick et al.2015a] Ellie Pavlick, Johan Bos, Malvina Nissim, Charley Beller, Benjamin Van Durme, and Chris Callison-Burch. 2015a. Adding semantics to data-driven paraphrasing. In *Proceedings of the 53rd Annual Meeting of the Association for Computational Linguistics and the 7th International Joint Conference on Natural Language Processing (Volume 1: Long Papers)*, pages 1512–1522, Beijing, China, July. Association for Computational Linguistics.

[Pavlick et al.2015b] Ellie Pavlick, Pushpendre Rastogi, Juri Ganitkevitch, Benjamin Van Durme, and Chris Callison-Burch. 2015b. Ppdb 2.0: Better paraphrase ranking, fine-grained entailment relations, word embeddings, and style classification. In *Proceedings of the 53rd Annual Meeting of the Association for Computational Linguistics and the 7th International Joint Conference on Natural Language Processing (Volume 2: Short Papers)*, pages

425–430, Beijing, China, July. Association for Computational Linguistics.

[Riedel et al.2013] Sebastian Riedel, Limin Yao, Andrew McCallum, and Benjamin M. Marlin. 2013. Relation extraction with matrix factorization and universal schemas. In *Proceedings of the 2013 Conference of the North American Chapter of the Association for Computational Linguistics: Human Language Technologies*, pages 74–84, Atlanta, Georgia, June. Association for Computational Linguistics.

[Rocktäschel et al.2015] Tim Rocktäschel, Sameer Singh, and Sebastian Riedel. 2015. Injecting logical background knowledge into embeddings for relation extraction. In *Proceedings of the 2015 Conference of the North American Chapter of the Association for Computational Linguistics: Human Language Technologies*, pages 1119–1129, Denver, Colorado, May–June. Association for Computational Linguistics.

[Schoenmackers et al.2010] Stefan Schoenmackers, Jesse Davis, Oren Etzioni, and Daniel Weld. 2010. Learning first-order horn clauses from web text. In *Proceedings of the 2010 Conference on Empirical Methods in Natural Language Processing*, pages 1088–1098, Cambridge, MA, October. Association for Computational Linguistics.

[Szpektor et al.2007] Idan Szpektor, Eyal Shnarch, and Ido Dagan. 2007. Instance-based evaluation of entailment rule acquisition. In *Proceedings of the 45th Annual Meeting of the Association of Computational Linguistics*, pages 456–463, Prague, Czech Republic, June. Association for Computational Linguistics.

[Voorhees and Tice2000] Ellen M Voorhees and Dawn M Tice. 2000. Building a question answering test collection. In *Proceedings of the 23rd Annual International ACM SIGIR Conference on Research and Development in Information Retrieval*, pages 200–207. ACM.

[Weisman et al.2012] Hila Weisman, Jonathan Berant, Idan Szpektor, and Ido Dagan. 2012. Learning verb inference rules from linguistically-motivated evidence. In *Proceedings of the 2012 Joint Conference on Empirical Methods in Natural Language Processing and Computational Natural Language Learning*, pages 194–204, Jeju Island, Korea, July. Association for Computational Linguistics.

[Zeichner et al.2012] Naomi Zeichner, Jonathan Berant, and Ido Dagan. 2012. Crowdsourcing inference-rule evaluation. In *Proceedings of the 50th Annual Meeting of the Association for Computational Linguistics (Volume 2: Short Papers)*, pages 156–160, Jeju Island, Korea, July. Association for Computational Linguistics.

Automatic Semantic Classification of German Preposition Types: Comparing Hard and Soft Clustering Approaches across Features

Maximilian Köper and **Sabine Schulte im Walde**
Institut für Maschinelle Sprachverarbeitung
Universität Stuttgart, Germany
`{maximilian.koeper,schulte}@ims.uni-stuttgart.de`

Abstract

This paper addresses an automatic classification of preposition types in German, comparing hard and soft clustering approaches and various window- and syntax-based co-occurrence features. We show that (i) the semantically most salient preposition features (i.e., subcategorised nouns) are the most successful, and that (ii) soft clustering approaches are required for the task but reveal quite different attitudes towards predicting ambiguity.

1 Introduction

In the last decades, an impressive number of semantic classifications has been developed, both regarding manual lexicographic and/or cognitive classifications such as *WordNet* (Fellbaum, 1998), *FrameNet* (Fillmore et al., 2003), *VerbNet* (Kipper Schuler, 2006) and *PrepNet/The Preposition Project* (Litkowski and Hargraves, 2005; Saint-Dizier, 2005), as well as regarding computational classifications for *nouns* (Hindle, 1990; Pereira et al., 1993; Snow et al., 2006), *verbs* (Merlo and Stevenson, 2001; Korhonen et al., 2003; Schulte im Walde, 2006) and *adjectives* (Hatzivassiloglou and McKeown, 1993; Boleda et al., 2012).

Semantic classifications are of great interest to computational linguistics, specifically regarding the pervasive problem of data sparseness in the processing of natural language. Such classifications have been used in applications such as *word sense disambiguation* (Dorr and Jones, 1996; Kohomban and Lee, 2005; McCarthy et al., 2007), *parsing* (Carroll et al., 1998; Carroll and Fang, 2004), *machine translation* (Prescher et al., 2000; Koehn and Hoang, 2007; Weller et al., 2014), and *information extraction* (Surdeanu et al., 2003; Venturi et al., 2009).

Regarding prepositions, comparably little effort in computational semantics has gone beyond a specific choice of prepositions (such as spatial prepositions), towards a systematic classification of preposition senses, as in *The Preposition Project* (Litkowski and Hargraves, 2005). Distributional approaches towards preposition meaning and sense distinction have only recently started to explore salient preposition features, but with few exceptions (such as Baldwin (2006)) these approaches focused on token-based classification of preposition senses (Ye and Baldwin, 2006; O'Hara and Wiebe, 2009; Tratz and Hovy, 2009; Hovy et al., 2010; Hovy et al., 2011).

This paper addresses an automatic classification of preposition types in German, comparing various clustering approaches. We aim for an unsupervised setting that does not require predefined expensive resources, such as a token-based annotation of preposition senses. Our task is challenging, because (i) prepositions are notoriously ambiguous, (ii) the interpretation of out-of-context preposition type classification is more difficult than context-embedded token interpretation, (iii) there are no established lexical resources for type-based semantic classification other than for English, and (iv) there are no established evaluation measures for ambiguous linguistic classifications. We accept the challenges, identify salient preposition features, and demonstrate the inevitability to apply soft (rather than hard) clustering in order to explore linguistic ambiguity.

2 Experiments

2.1 Preposition Data

In the absence of any large-scale semantic hierarchical type classification, the German grammar book by Helbig and Buscha (1998) represents our gold standard. We selected those preposition

Proceedings of the 54th Annual Meeting of the Association for Computational Linguistics, pages 256–263,
Berlin, Germany, August 7-12, 2016. ©2016 Association for Computational Linguistics

Class		Size
lokal	'local'	27
modal	'modal'	24
temporal	'temporal'	21
kausal	'causal'	5
distributiv	'distributive'	6
final	'final'	4
urheber	'creator'	3
konditional	'conditional'	3
ersatz	'replacement'	2
restriktiv	'restrictive'	2
partitiv	'partitive'	2
kopulativ	'copulative'	2

Table 1: Preposition classes.

classes that contained more than one preposition, and deleted prepositions that appeared $<$10,000 times in our web corpus containing 880 million words (cf. Section ??). This selection process resulted in 12 semantic classes covering between 2 and 27 prepositions each (cf. Table 1), and a more fine-grained version that sub-divided the three largest classes 'local', 'modal' and 'temporal' into 6/10/7 sub-classes, respectively, and resulted in a total of 32 classes.[1][2] The prepositions in the fine-grained version exhibit ambiguity rates of 1 (monosemous) up to 10. Out of the 49 preposition types, 23 are polysemous (46.9%).

2.2 Preposition Features

The corpus-based features for the German prepositions were induced from the *SdeWaC* corpus (Faaß and Eckart, 2013), a cleaned version of the German web corpus *deWaC* (Baroni et al., 2009) containing approx. 880 million words. We compare three categories of distributional features:

(1) ***bag-of-words window co-occurrence features***: we apply a standard bag-of-words model (*BOW*) relying on a window of 2 words to the left and to the right, and a continuous bag-of-words model (*CBOW*) using negative sampling with K=15 (Mikolov et al., 2013);

(2) ***direct syntactic dependency***: we compare the most salient preposition-related dependencies: preposition subcategorised nouns (*nouns-dep*, e.g., *in Buch* 'in book'), preposition-subcategorising nouns (*nouns-gov*, e.g., *Buch von* 'book by'), and preposition-subcategorising verbs (*verbs-gov*, e.g., *reisen nach* 'to travel to');

(3) ***2nd-order syntactic co-occurrence***: adjectives that modify nouns subcategorised by the prepositions, and adverbs that modify verbs subcategorising the prepositions.

The dependency information was extracted from a parsed version of the SdeWaC using Bohnet's MATE dependency parser (Bohnet, 2010; Scheible et al., 2013). All but the CBOW features were weighted according to positive pointwise mutual information.

2.3 Clustering Approaches

As we wanted to explore hard vs. soft clustering approaches on the same task, we chose *k-Means* as a standard hard clustering approach (relying on WEKA's spherical k-Means implementation), and compared it to various soft clustering approaches.

We transfered the hard k-Means cluster analyses to soft cluster analyses, using two alternative methods. (1) The ***prep-based soft k-Means*** method (Springorum et al., 2013) calculated the mean cosine distance $\bar{d}$ for each preposition p to the centroids z_c of the clusters c, and assigned a preposition to a specific cluster if its distance to the respective cluster centroid was below a threshold t multiplied with the mean distance, with $t = 0.05, 0.1, 0.15, \ldots, 0.95$. Additionally, (2) we propose a hard-to-soft clustering transfer ***prob-based soft k-Means*** that converts the cosine distances between the prepositions and the hard cluster centroids to membership probabilities.

Instead of transferring a hard clustering to a soft clustering we also directly applied soft clustering approaches: (1) The fuzzy ***c-Means*** algorithm extends k-means by a cluster membership function for each preposition, $f_m \in [0, 1]$. (2) We applied ***Latent Semantic Clustering (LSC)***, an instance of the Expectation-Maximisation (EM) algorithm (Baum, 1972) for unsupervised training on unannotated data (Rooth et al., 1999). The cluster analyses define two-dimensional soft clusters (in our case: preposition–feature clusters) with cluster membership probabilities, which are able to generalise over hidden data. (3) We used ***Non-negative matrix factorization (NMF)***, a factorisation approach with an inherent (soft) clustering property (Ding et al., 2005).

All variants of our hard-to-soft clustering approaches and the direct soft clustering approaches (except for k-Means/prep)[3] resulted in a

---

[1] While we also conducted experiments using the coarse-grained class distribution in Table 1, the experiments in this paper focus on the fine-grained inventory.

[2] The gold standard was previously used in Springorum et al. (2013) and in Köper and Schulte im Walde (2014).

[3] *k-Means/prep* directly provides binary membership.

preposition–cluster membership matrix with values $\in [0, 1]$. We transfered the real membership values to binary membership by applying a threshold t to decide about the cluster membership, again with $t = 0.05, 0.1, 0.15, \ldots, 0.95$. For each clustering approach and for each number of clusters k we then identified the best threshold.

2.4 Evaluation

We chose the fuzzy extension of *B-Cubed* (Bagga and Baldwin, 1998) as evaluation measure, because it is (a) a pair-wise evaluation, which is considered as most suitable for soft clustering evaluations, and (b) distinguishes between homogeneity and completeness of a clustering, and thus resembles an evaluation by precision and recall. Amigó et al. (2009) demonstrated the strengths of B-Cubed, and a similar version has been used in SemEval 2013 for Word Sense Induction (Jurgens and Klapaftis, 2013).

Pair-wise precision P determines the homogeneity of a cluster analysis, by calculating for each individual preposition p the amount of prepositions p' in the same cluster c that also belong to the same gold-standard class g, cf. Equation (1). Pair-wise recall R determines the completeness of a cluster analysis, by calculating for each individual preposition p the amount of prepositions p' in the same gold-standard class g that also belong to the same cluster c, cf. Equation (2). The overall B-Cubed precision and recall scores are the averages over all preposition-wise scores. We combined precision and recall by their harmonic mean, the f-score.

$$P(p, p') = \frac{min(|c(p) \cap c(p')|, |g(p) \cap g(p')|)}{|c(p) \cap c(p')|} \quad (1)$$

$$R(p, p') = \frac{min(|c(p) \cap c(p')|, |g(p) \cap g(p')|)}{|g(p) \cap g(p')|} \quad (2)$$

2.5 Baselines

We created two baselines for our preposition clusterings: The **hard baseline** was computed for every number of clusters k=[5, 40]. For each k, each preposition was randomly assigned to one of the k clusters, and the resulting hard cluster analysis was evaluated. The hard cluster assignments were repeated 1,000 times for each k, and the overall evaluation score for k clusters is the average score of the 1,000 runs. The **soft baseline** was also created by random assignment across 1,000 runs for each k, but –integrating the fuzzy component–

each preposition was assigned to n clusters, with n a random number between 1 and the number of gold-standard classes for that specific preposition. Note that this baseline is more informed than an entirely random baseline, because the information about the number of gold-standard classes for each preposition is very helpful. For example, the baseline assigns monosemous prepositions to only one cluster, and prepositions with three senses to a random integer in $[1, 3]$.

3 Results

Figure 1 compares the fuzzy B-Cubed f-score values across the hard and soft clustering approaches, relying on the preposition-subcategorised nouns as one of the best features (cf. Figure 2 below). The plot demonstrates that (i) the hard k-Means clustering approach is the only one resulting in f-scores below the soft baseline, while (ii) the vast majority of soft clustering results lies above the soft baseline. Furthermore, (iii) there is a clear tendency for all soft clustering approaches to provide the best f-scores for similar values of k clusters: $15 \leq k \leq 19$. The overall best result is reached by NMF for a clustering with 17 clusters.

Figure 2 compares the f-scores across feature types, relying on NMF as the best clustering approach. The plot confirms that (i) –across features–, the vast majority of soft clustering results lies above the soft baseline. In addition, (ii) in the previously most successful range for $15 \leq k \leq 19$ clusters, the preposition-subcategorised nouns represent the best features. (iii) The best cluster analyses relying on window vs. syntax features are similarly successful, and outperform 2nd-order co-occurrence features.

We checked the overall best cluster analysis (NMF, $k = 17$, nouns-dep) on the predicted degree of ambiguity (cf. Figure 3): for 23 out of the 26 monosemous prepositions, we *correctly* predicted one preposition sense; for 7 out of the 23 polysemous prepositions, we predicted the *correct* number of senses; for 9 out of the 23 polysemous prepositions, we predicted *less* senses than the gold standard defines; and for 7 out of the 23 polysemous prepositions, we predicted *more* senses than the gold standard defines.

Our best soft-clustering approach to the preposition classification task thus demonstrates its usefulness through quantitative B-Cubed evaluation and through reliable predictions of ambiguity.

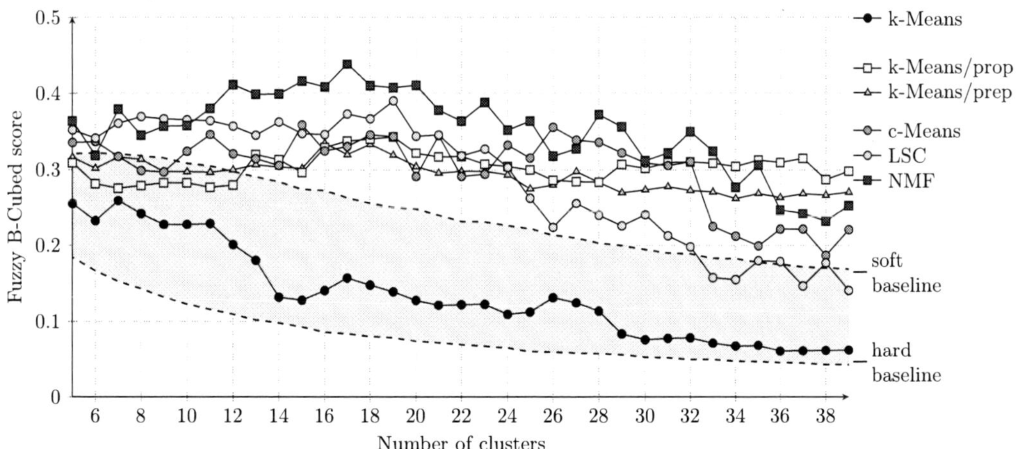

Figure 1: Fuzzy B-Cubed f-score using the subcategorised noun feature set (nouns-dep), across soft clustering approaches.

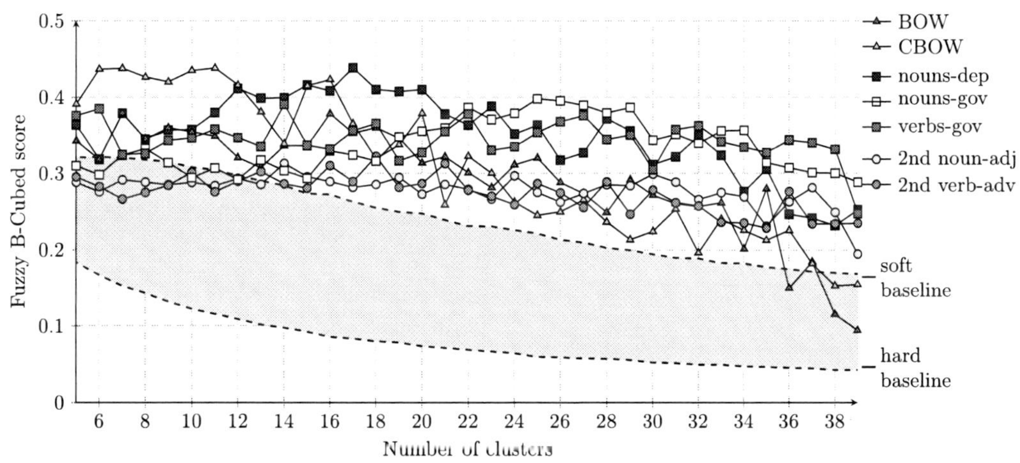

Figure 2: Fuzzy B-Cubed f-score using NMF soft clustering, across feature sets.

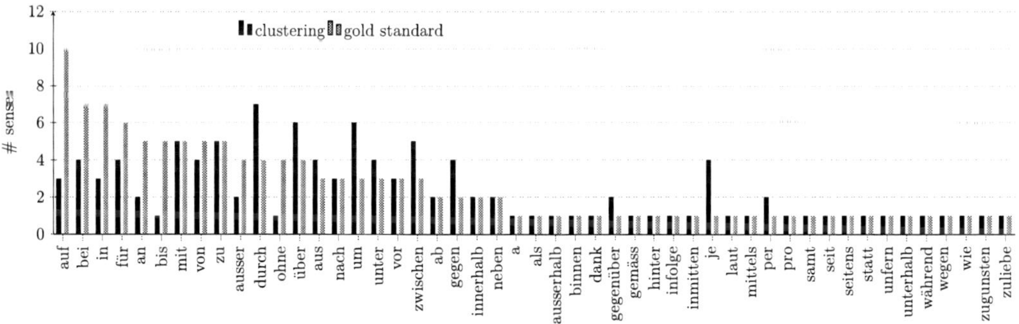

Figure 3: Predicting polysemy across prepositions (NMF, $k = 17$, *nouns-dep*).

4 Discussion

While the results in the previous section demonstrate the success of the type-based clustering, we were interested in two specific questions: (i) Where do the differences in the quality of the cluster analyses come from? (ii) Do the best cluster analyses present linguistically reliable and useful semantic classes?

From a quantitative point of view, both questions have been addressed by the evaluation measure, fuzzy B-Cubed, which we chose for reasons outlined in Section 2.4. One should keep in mind, however, that there is an ongoing discussion about cluster comparison and cluster evaluation (Meila, 2007; Rosenberg and Hirschberg, 2007; Vinh and Bailey, 2010; Utt et al., 2014), which demonstrates uncertainty about an optimal measure, and which concerns us, expecially regarding the linguistic aspects of soft clustering. In the following, we therefore provide qualitative analyses and discussions of the cluster approaches and analyses.

Ambiguity rate of soft-clustering approaches: We looked into the best cluster analysis for each soft-clustering approach, and checked the ambiguities. While the number of preposition types in the cluster analyses is similar across approaches (between 44 and 48), the ambiguity rate (i.e., the number of cluster assignments per preposition type) and the number of ambiguous preposition types (i.e., the number of prepositions assigned to more than one cluster) differ strongly. For example, k-Means/prob and NMF perform an average of 3.1/3.7 assignments for each preposition, in comparison to 2.2–2.4 assignments by the other approaches. On the other hand, while k-Means/prob defines almost all preposition types (43 out of 48) as ambiguous, NMF only defines 28 out of 46 prepositions as ambiguous. NMF (best approach) thus shows a high ambiguity rate, but only 60% of the prepositions are ambiguous.

Cluster sizes: Looking into the actual cluster analyses reveals that the sizes and the structures within the individual clusters differ strongly. The best k-Means/prep and k-Means/prob analyses ($k = 16$, $F = 0.33$, and $k = 19$, $F = 0.34$), for example, each contain 7 large clusters with 10–25 prepositions. All other clusters contain only 1–3 prepositions. In comparison, the best NMF analysis ($k = 17$, $F = 0.43$) contains only one cluster with three prepositions, and all other clusters but one contain ≥ 5 and ≤ 14 prepositions. The cluster sizes of the best NMF analysis are therefore more homogeneous than for other clustering approaches.

Optimal k: While fuzzy B-Cubed determined the numbers of clusters $[15, 19]$ as optimal for the soft-clustering approaches, we also looked into the NMF cluster analysis with $k = 32$, with NMF as the best approach and 32 as the number of gold standard classes. The clusters are, again, very similar in size, including only one singleton and only one cluster with 9 prepositions. All other clusters contain $2 - 6$ prepositions. The smaller cluster sizes allow manual evaluations. We can indeed find reliable semantic clusters, such as $\{$*an, auf, hinter, in, mit, nach, neben, um, vor*$\}$, where 7 out of 9 prepositions belong to the gold-standard class *local: not target-oriented* containing a total of 12 prepositions.

5 Conclusion

We presented variants of hard and soft clustering approaches across several sets of preposition features, to automatically classify preposition types into semantic classes. While type-based classifications for highly ambiguous word classes are a computational challenge, our best approach (NMF-based classification with 17 clusters) reached an f-score of 0.43. The clustering experiments showed that (i) the semantically most salient preposition features are indeed the most successful, and that (ii) the clustering of highly ambiguous words requires soft rather than hard clustering approaches.

Most interestingly, a qualitative analysis zoomed into the assignment behaviour of the soft clustering approaches, and revealed different attitudes towards predicting ambiguity. NMF as the best approach predicted a high ambiguity rate but only for a restricted proportion of 60% of the preposition types. Furthermore, the distribution of cluster sizes was less skewed than for other approaches.

Acknowledgments

The research was supported by the DFG Research Project "Distributional Approaches to Semantic Relatedness" (Maximilian Köper) and the DFG Heisenberg Fellowship SCHU-2580/1 (Sabine Schulte im Walde).

References

Enrique Amigó, Julio Gonzalo, Javier Artiles, and Felisa Verdejo. 2009. A Comparison of Extrinsic Clustering Evaluation Metrics Based on Formal Constraints. *Information Retrieval*, 12(4):461–486.

Amit Bagga and Breck Baldwin. 1998. Entity-based Cross-document Coreferencing Using the Vector Space Model. In *Proceedings of the 36th Annual Meeting of the Association for Computational Linguistics and the 17th International Conference on Computational Linguistics*, pages 79–85, Montréal, Canada.

Timothy Baldwin. 2006. Distributional Similarity and Preposition Semantics. In Patrick Saint-Dizier, editor, *Syntax and Semantics of Prepositions*, chapter 1, pages 197–210. Kluwer Academic Publishers, Dordrecht, The Netherlands.

Marco Baroni, Silvia Bernardini, Adriano Ferraresi, and Eros Zanchetta. 2009. The WaCky Wide Web: A Collection of Very Large Linguistically Processed Web-Crawled Corpora. *Language Resources and Evaluation*, 43(3):209–226.

Leonard E. Baum. 1972. An Inequality and Associated Maximization Technique in Statistical Estimation for Probabilistic Functions of Markov Processes. *Inequalities*, III:1–8.

Bernd Bohnet. 2010. Top Accuracy and Fast Dependency Parsing is not a Contradiction. In *Proceedings of the 23rd International Conference on Computational Linguistics*, pages 89–97, Beijing, China.

Gemma Boleda, Sabine Schulte im Walde, and Toni Badia. 2012. Modelling Regular Polysemy: A Study on the Semantic Classification of Catalan Adjectives. *Computational Linguistics*, 38(3):575–616.

John Carroll and Alex C. Fang. 2004. The Automatic Acquisition of Verb Subcategorisations and their Impact on the Performance of an HPSG Parser. In *Proceedings of the 1st International Joint Conference on Natural Language Processing*, pages 107–114, Sanya City, China.

John Carroll, Guido Minnen, and Ted Briscoe. 1998. Can Subcategorisation Probabilities Help a Statistical Parser? In *Proceedings of the 6th ACL/SIGDAT Workshop on Very Large Corpora*, pages 118–126, Montréal, Canada.

Chris Ding, Xiaofeng He, and Horst D. Simon. 2005. On the Equivalence of Nonnegative Matrix Factorization and Spectral Clustering. In *Proceedings of the SIAM International Conference on Data Mining*, pages 606–610, Newport Beach, CA, USA.

Bonnie J. Dorr and Doug Jones. 1996. Role of Word Sense Disambiguation in Lexical Acquisition: Predicting Semantics from Syntactic Cues. In *Proceedings of the 16th International Conference on Computational Linguistics*, pages 322–327, Copenhagen, Denmark.

Gertrud Faaß and Kerstin Eckart. 2013. SdeWaC – A Corpus of Parsable Sentences from the Web. In *Proceedings of the International Conference of the German Society for Computational Linguistics and Language Technology*, pages 61–68, Darmstadt, Germany.

Christiane Fellbaum, editor. 1998. *WordNet – An Electronic Lexical Database*. Language, Speech, and Communication. MIT Press, Cambridge, MA.

Charles J. Fillmore, Christopher R. Johnson, and Miriam R.L. Petruck. 2003. Background to FrameNet. *International Journal of Lexicography*, 16:235–250.

Vasileios Hatzivassiloglou and Kathleen R. McKeown. 1993. Towards the Automatic Identification of Adjectival Scales: Clustering Adjectives According to Meaning. In *Proceedings of the 31st Annual Meeting of the Association for Computational Linguistics*, pages 172–182, Columbus, OH.

Gerhard Helbig and Joachim Buscha. 1998. *Deutsche Grammatik*. Langenscheidt – Verlag Enzyklopädie, 18th edition.

Donald Hindle. 1990. Noun Classification from Predicate-Argument Structures. In *Proceedings of the 28th Annual Meeting of the Association for Computational Linguistics*, pages 268–275, Pittsburgh, PA.

Dirk Hovy, Stephen Tratz, and Eduard Hovy. 2010. What's in a Preposition? Dimensions of Sense Disambiguation for an Interesting Word Class. In *Proceedings of the 23rd International Conference on Computational Linguistics*, pages 454–462, Beijing, China.

Dirk Hovy, Ashish Vaswani, Stephen Tratz, David Chiang, and Eduard Hovy. 2011. Methods and Training for Unsupervised Preposition Sense Disambiguation. In *Proceedings of the 49th Annual Meeting of the Association for Computational Linguistics*, pages 323–328, Portland, OR.

David Jurgens and Ioannis Klapaftis. 2013. SemEval-2013 Task 13: Word Sense Induction for Graded and Non-Graded Senses. In *Proceedings of the 2nd Joint Conference on Lexical and Computational Semantics*, pages 290–299, Atlanta, Georgia, USA.

Karin Kipper Schuler. 2006. *VerbNet: A Broad-Coverage, Comprehensive Verb Lexicon*. Ph.D. thesis, University of Pennsylvania, Computer and Information Science.

Philipp Koehn and Hieu Hoang. 2007. Factored Translation Models. In *Proceedings of the Joint Conference on Empirical Methods in Natural Language Processing and Computational Natural Language Learning*, pages 868–876, Prague, Czech Republic.

Upali S. Kohomban and Wee Sun Lee. 2005. Learning Semantic Classes for Word Sense Disambiguation. In *Proceedings of the 43rd Annual Meeting on Association for Computational Linguistics*, pages 34–41, Ann Arbor, MI.

Maximilian Köper and Sabine Schulte im Walde. 2014. A Rank-based Distance Measure to Detect Polysemy and to Determine Salient Vector-Space Features for German Prepositions. In *Proceedings of the 9th International Conference on Language Resources and Evaluation*, pages 4459–4466, Reykjavik, Iceland.

Anna Korhonen, Yuval Krymolowski, and Zvika Marx. 2003. Clustering Polysemic Subcategorization Frame Distributions Semantically. In *Proceedings of the 41st Annual Meeting of the Association for Computational Linguistics*, pages 64–71, Sapporo, Japan.

Kenneth C. Litkowski and Orin Hargraves. 2005. The Preposition Project. In *Proceedings of the 2nd ACL-SIGSEM Workshop on The Linguistic Dimensions of Prepositions and their Use in Computational Linguistics Formalisms and Applications*, pages 171–179, Colchester, England.

Diana McCarthy, Rob Koeling, Julie Weeds, and John Carroll. 2007. Unsupervised Acquisition of Predominant Word Senses. *Computational Linguistics*, 33(4):553–590.

Marina Meila. 2007. Comparing Clusterings – An Information-based Distance. *Journal of Multivariate Analysis*, 98(5):873–895.

Paola Merlo and Suzanne Stevenson. 2001. Automatic Verb Classification Based on Statistical Distributions of Argument Structure. *Computational Linguistics*, 27(3):373–408.

Tomas Mikolov, Ilya Sutskever, Kai Chen, Greg S. Corrado, and Jeff Dean. 2013. Distributed Representations of Words and Phrases and their Compositionality. In *Advances in Neural Information Processing Systems 26*, pages 3111–3119.

Tom O'Hara and Janyce Wiebe. 2009. Exploiting Semantic Role Resources for Preposition Disambiguation. *Computational Linguistics*, 35(2):151–184. Special Issue on Prepositions in Applications.

Fernando Pereira, Naftali Tishby, and Lillian Lee. 1993. Distributional Clustering of English Words. In *Proceedings of the 31st Annual Meeting of the Association for Computational Linguistics*, pages 183–190, Columbus, OH.

Detlef Prescher, Stefan Riezler, and Mats Rooth. 2000. Using a Probabilistic Class-Based Lexicon for Lexical Ambiguity Resolution. In *Proceedings of the 18th International Conference on Computational Linguistics*, pages 649–655, Saarbrücken, Germany.

Mats Rooth, Stefan Riezler, Detlef Prescher, Glenn Carroll, and Franz Beil. 1999. Inducing a Semantically Annotated Lexicon via EM-Based Clustering. In *Proceedings of the 37th Annual Meeting of the Association for Computational Linguistics*, pages 104–111, Maryland, MD.

Andrew Rosenberg and Julia Hirschberg. 2007. V-Measure: A Conditional Entropy-based External Cluster Evaluation Measure. In *Proceedings of the joint Conference on Empirical Methods in Natural Language Processing and Computational Natural Language Learning*, pages 410–420, Prague, Czech Republic.

Patrick Saint-Dizier. 2005. An Overview of PrepNet: Abstract Notions, Frame, and Inferential Patterns. In *Proceedings of the 2nd ACL-SIGSEM Workshop on The Linguistic Dimensions of Prepositions and their Use in Computational Linguistics Formalisms and Applications*, Colchester, England.

Silke Scheible, Sabine Schulte im Walde, Marion Weller, and Max Kisselew. 2013. A Compact but Linguistically Detailed Database for German Verb Subcategorisation relying on Dependency Parses from a Web Corpus: Tool, Guidelines and Resource. In *Proceedings of the 8th Web as Corpus Workshop*, pages 63–72, Lancaster, UK.

Sabine Schulte im Walde. 2006. Experiments on the Automatic Induction of German Semantic Verb Classes. *Computational Linguistics*, 32(2):159–194.

Rion Snow, Daniel Jurafsky, and Andrew Y. Ng. 2006. Semantic Taxonomy Induction from Heterogenous Evidence. In *Proceedings of the 45th Annual Meeting of the Association for Computational Linguistics*, pages 801–808, Sydney, Australia.

Sylvia Springorum, Sabine Schulte im Walde, and Jason Utt. 2013. Detecting Polysemy in Hard and Soft Cluster Analyses of German Preposition Vector Spaces. In *Proceedings of the 6th International Joint Conference on Natural Language Processing*, pages 632–640, Nagoya, Japan.

Mihai Surdeanu, Sanda Harabagiu, John Williams, and Paul Aarseth. 2003. Using Predicate-Argument Structures for Information Extraction. In *Proceedings of the 41st Annual Meeting of the Association for Computational Linguistics*, pages 8–15, Sapporo, Japan.

Stephen Tratz and Dirk Hovy. 2009. Disambiguation of Preposition Sense using Linguistically Motivated Features. In *Proceedings of the NAACL-HLT Student Research Workshop and Doctoral Consortium*, pages 96–100, Boulder, CO.

Jason Utt, Sylvia Springorum, Maximilian Köper, and Sabine Schulte im Walde. 2014. Fuzzy V-Measure – An Evaluation Method for Cluster Analyses of

Ambiguous Data. In *Proceedings of the 9th International Conference on Language Resources and Evaluation*, pages 581–587, Reykjavik, Iceland.

Giulia Venturi, Simonetta Montemagni, Simone Marchi, Yutaka Sasaki, Paul Thompson, John McNaught, and Sophia Ananiadou. 2009. Bootstrapping a Verb Lexicon for Biomedical Information Extraction. In Alexander Gelbukh, editor, *Linguistics and Intelligent Text Processing*, pages 137–148. Springer, Heidelberg.

Nguyen Xuan Vinh and James Bailey. 2010. Information Theoretic Measures for Clusterings Comparison: Variants, Properties, Normalization and Correction for Chance. *Journal of Machine Learning Research*, 11:2837–2854.

Marion Weller, Sabine Schulte im Walde, and Alexander Fraser. 2014. Using Noun Class Information to model Selectional Preferences for Translating Prepositions in SMT. In *Proceedings of the 11th Conference of the Association for Machine Translation in the Americas*, pages 275–287, Vancouver, Canada.

Patrick Ye and Timothy Baldwin. 2006. Semantic Role Labelling of Prepositional Phrases. *ACM Transactions on Asian Language Information Processing*, 5(3):228–244.

Natural Language Generation enhances human decision-making with uncertain information

Dimitra Gkatzia
School of Computing
Edinburgh Napier University
Edinburgh, EH10 5DT, UK
d.gkatzia@napier.ac.uk

Oliver Lemon
Interaction Lab
Heriot-Watt University
Edinburgh, EH14 4AS, UK
o.lemon@hw.ac.uk

Verena Rieser
Interaction Lab
Heriot-Watt University
Edinburgh, EH14 4AS, UK
v.t.rieser@hw.ac.uk

Abstract

Decision-making is often dependent on uncertain data, e.g. data associated with confidence scores or probabilities. We present a comparison of different information presentations for uncertain data and, for the first time, measure their effects on human decision-making. We show that the use of Natural Language Generation (NLG) improves decision-making under uncertainty, compared to state-of-the-art graphical-based representation methods. In a task-based study with 442 adults, we found that presentations using NLG lead to 24% better decision-making on average than the graphical presentations, and to 44% better decision-making when NLG is combined with graphics. We also show that women achieve significantly better results when presented with NLG output (an 87% increase on average compared to graphical presentations).

1 Introduction

Natural Language Generation (NLG) technology can achieve comparable results to commonly used data visualisation techniques for supporting accurate human decision-making (Gatt et al., 2009). In this paper, we investigate whether NLG technology can also be used to support decision-making when the underlying data is uncertain. Current data-to-text systems assume that the underlying data is precise and correct – an assumption which is heavily criticised by other disciplines concerned with decision support, such as medicine (Gigerenzer and Muir Gray, 2011), environmental modelling (Beven, 2009), climate change (Manning et al., 2004), or weather forecasting (Kootval, 2008). However, simply presenting numerical expressions of risk and uncertainty is not enough. Psychological studies on decision making have found that a high percentage of people do not understand and can't act upon numerical uncertainty (Cokely et al., 2012; Galesic and Garcia-Retamero, 2010). For example, only 28% of Germans and 25% of Americans are able to answer the question: *"Which of the following numbers represents the biggest risk of getting a disease: 1 in 100, 1 in 1000, 1 in 10?"* (Galesic and Garcia-Retamero, 2010).

So far, the NLG community has investigated the conversion of numbers into language (Power and Williams, 2012) and the use of vague expressions (van Deemter, 2009). In this work, we explore how to convert numerical representations of uncertainty into Natural Language so as to maximise confidence and correct outcomes of human decision-making. We consider the exemplar task of weather forecast generation. We initially present two NLG strategies which present the uncertainty in the input data. The two strategies are based on (1) the World Meteorological Organisation (WMO) (Kootval, 2008) guidelines and (2) commercial forecast presentations (e.g. from BBC presenters). We then evaluate the strategies against a state-of-the-art graphical system (Stephens et al., 2011), which presents the uncertain data in a graphical way. Figure 1 shows an example of this baseline graphical presentation. We use a game-based setup (Gkatzia et al., 2015) to perform task-based evaluation, to investigate the effect that the different information presentation strategies have on human decision-making.

Weather forecast generation is a common topic within the NLG community, e.g. (Konstas and Lapata, 2012; Angeli et al., 2010; Belz and Kow, 2010; Sripada et al., 2005). Previous approaches have not focused on how to communicate uncertain information or the best ways of referring to

Proceedings of the 54th Annual Meeting of the Association for Computational Linguistics, pages 264–268,
Berlin, Germany, August 7-12, 2016. ©2016 Association for Computational Linguistics

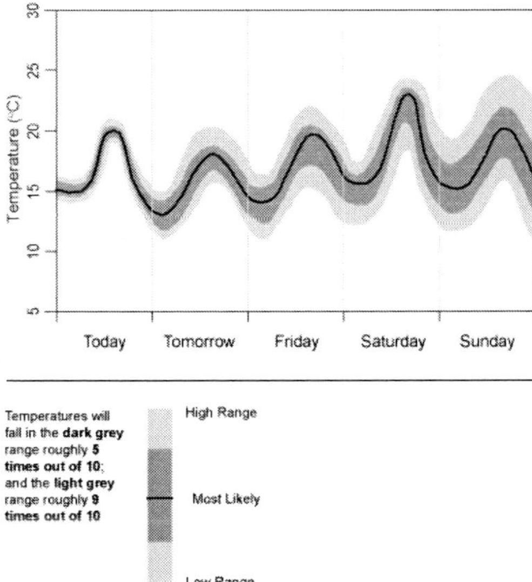

Figure 1: Graphics for temperature data.

Likelihood of oc-currence	Lexicalisation
p >0.99	"extremely likely"
$0.90 \leq p \leq 0.99$	"very likely"
$0.70 \leq p \leq 0.89$	"likely"
$0.55 \leq p \leq 0.69$	"probable - more likely than not"
$0.45 \leq p \leq 0.54$	"equally likely as not"
$0.30 \leq p \leq 0.44$	"possible - less likely than not"
$0.10 \leq p \leq 0.29$	"unlikely"
$0.01 \leq p \leq 0.09$	"very unlikely"
$p<0.01$	"extremely unlikely"

Table 1: WMO-based mapping of likelihoods.

probabilities of meteorological phenomena to occur. In addition, their evaluation is based on user ratings of grammatically, semantic correctness, fluency, coherence or via post-edit evaluation. Although these metrics are indicative of the quality of the text produced, they do not measure the impact the texts might have in people's comprehension of uncertainty or on their ability to make decisions based on the information conveyed.

Our contributions to the field are as follows: (1) We study a principled mapping of uncertainty to Natural Language and provide recommendations and data for future NLG systems; (2) We introduce a game-based data collection environment which extends task-based evaluation by measuring the impact of NLG on decision-making (measuring user confidence and game/task success); and (3) We show that effects of the different representations vary for different user groups, so that user adaptation is necessary when generating multimodal presentations of uncertain information.

2 The Extended Weather Game

In this section, we present our extended version of the MetOffice's Weather Game (Stephens et al., 2011). The player has to choose where to send an ice-cream vendor in order to maximise sales, given weather forecasts for four weeks and two locations. These forecasts describe (1) predicted rainfall (Figure 2) and (2) temperature levels together

with their likelihoods in three ways: (a) through graphical representations (which is the version of the original game), (b) through textual forecasts, and (c) through combined graphical and textual forecasts. We generated the textual format using two rule-based NLG approaches as described in the next section. Users are asked to initially choose the best destination for the ice-cream vendor and then they are asked to state how confident they are with their choice. Based on their decisions and their confidence levels, the participants are finally presented with their "monetary gain". For example, the higher the likelihood of sunshine, the higher the monetary gain if the player has declared that s/he is confident that it is not going to rain and it doesn't actually rain. In the opposite scenario, the player would lose money. The decision on whether rain occurred is estimated by sampling the probability distribution. At the end of the game, users were scored according to their "risk literacy" following the Berlin Numeracy Test (Cokely et al., 2012). Further details are presented in (Gkatzia et al., 2015).

3 Natural Language Generation from Uncertain Information

We developed two NLG systems, WMO-based and NATURAL, using SimpleNLG (Gatt and Reiter, 2009), which both generate textual descriptions of rainfall and temperature data addressing the uncertain nature of forecasts

WMO-based: This is a rule-based system which uses the guidelines recommended by the WMO (Kootval, 2008) for reporting uncertainty, as shown in Table 1. Consider for instance a forecast of sunny intervals with 30% probability of rain. This WMO-based system will generate the following forecast: "Sunny intervals with rain being possible - less likely than not".

NATURAL: This system imitates forecasters and

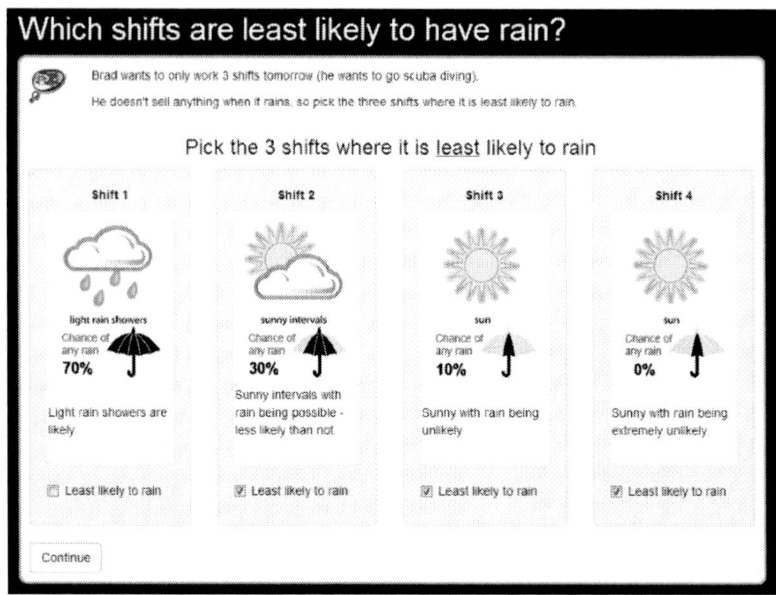

Figure 2: Screenshot of the Extended Weather Game (Rainfall: Graphics and WMO condition).

their natural way of reporting weather. The rules used in this system have been derived by observing the way that experts (e.g. BBC weather reporters) produce forecasts. For the previous example (sunny intervals with 30% probability of rain), this system will generate the following forecast: "Mainly dry with sunny spells".

4 Evaluation

In order to investigate what helps people to better understand and act upon uncertainty in information presentations, we use five conditions within the context of the Extended Weather Game:

1. **Graphics only:** This representation shows the users only the graphical representation of the weather forecasts. For this condition we used the graphs that scored best in terms of human comprehension from (Stephens et al., 2011).

2. **Multi-modal Representations:**
   − **Graphics and NATURAL:** This is a multi-modal representation consisting of graphics (as described in the previous condition) and text produced by the NATURAL system.
   − **Graphics and WMO-based:** This is also a multi-modal representation consisting of graphics and text produced by the WMO-based system.

3. **NLG only:**
   − **NATURAL only:** This is a text-only representation as described above.
   − **WMO-based system only:** This is also a text-only representation.

5 Data

We recruited 442 unique players (197 females[1], 241 males, 4 non-disclosed) using social media. We collected 450 unique game instances (just a few people played the game twice). The anonymised data will be released as part of this submission.

6 Results

In order to investigate which representations assist people in decision-making under uncertainty, we analysed both the players' scores (in terms of monetary gain) and their predictions for rainfall with regard to their confidence scores. As we described in Section 2, the game calculates a monetary gain based on both the decisions and the confidence of the player, i.e. the decision-making ability of the player. Regarding confidence, we asked users to declare how confident they are on a 10-point scale. In our analysis we therefore focus on both confidence and score at the game.

---

[1]Women made up 44.5% of the subjects.

266

	Monetary gains	Confidence
Graphs only	81.15	78.5%
Multi-modal	117.51	83.7%
NLG only	101.33	66%

Table 2: Average Monetary gains and Confidence scores (All Adults).

	Monetary gains	Confidence
Graphs only	60.83	74.6%
Multi-modal	118.41	81.3%
NLG only	113.86	65.8%

Table 3: Average Monetary gains and Confidence scores (Females).

6.1 Results for all adults

Multi-modal vs. Graphics-only: We found that use of multi-modal representations leads to gaining significantly higher game scores (i.e. better decision-making) than the Graphics-only representation ($p = 0.03$, effect = +36.36). This is a 44% average increase in game score.

Multi-modal vs. NLG-only: However, there is no significant difference between the NLG only and the multi-modal representation, for game score.

NLG vs. Graphics-only: We found that the NLG representations resulted in a 24.8% increase in average task score (i.e. better decision-making) compared to the Graphics-only condition, see Table 2: an average score increase of over 20 points. There was no significant difference found between the WMO and NATURAL NLG conditions.

Confidence: For confidence, the multi-modal representation is significantly more effective than NLG only ($p < 0.01$, effect = 17.7%). However, as Table 2 shows, although adults did not feel very confident when presented with NLG only, they were able to make better decisions compared to being presented with graphics only.

Demographic factors: We further found that prior experience on making decisions based on risk, familiarity with weather models, and correct literacy test results are predictors of the players' understanding of uncertainty, which is translated in both confidence and game scores. In contrast, we found that the education level, the gender, or being native speaker of English does not contribute to players' confidence and game scores.

6.2 Results for Females

We found that females score significantly higher at the decision task when exposed to either of the NLG output presentations, when compared to the graphics-only presentation ($p < 0.05$, effect = +53.03). This is an increase of 87%, also see Table 3. In addition, the same group of users scores significantly higher when presented with the multi-modal output as compared to graphics only ($p = 0.05$, effect = 60.74%). Interestingly, for this group, the multi-modal presentation adds little more in effectiveness of decision-making than the NLG-only condition, but the multi-modal presentations do enhance their confidence (+15%). We furthermore found that educated (i.e. holding a BSc or higher degree) females, who also correctly answered the risk literacy test, feel significantly more confident when presented with the multi-modal representations than with NLG only ($p = 0.01$, effect = 16.7%).

6.3 Results for Males

We found that males obtained similar game scores with all the types of representation. This suggests that the overall improved scores (for All Adults) presented above, are largely due to the beneficial effects of NLG for women. In terms of confidence, males are more likely to be more confident if they are presented with graphics only (81% of the time) or a multi-modal representation (85% of the time) ($p = 0.01$).

7 Conclusions and Future Work

We present results from a game-based study on how to generate descriptions of uncertain data – an issue which so far has been unexplored by data-to-text systems. We find that there are significant gender differences between multi-modal, NLG, and graphical versions of the task, where for women, use of NLG results in a 87% increase in task success over graphics. Multimodal presentations lead to a 44% increase for all adults, compared to graphics. People are also more confident of their judgements when using the multimodal representations. These are significant findings, as previous work has not distinguished between genders when comparing different representations of data, e.g. (Gatt et al., 2009). It also confirms research on gender effects in multi-modal systems, as for example reported in (Foster and Oberlander, 2006; Rieser and Lemon, 2008; Weiss et al., 2012). The results are also related to educational research, which shows that women perform better in verbal-logical tasks than visual-spatial tasks

(Zhu, 2007). An interesting investigation for future research is the interplay between uncertainty, risk-taking behaviour and gender, as for example reported in (Sarin and Wieland, 2016).

Acknowledgments

This research received funding from the EPSRC projects GUI (EP/L026775/1), DILiGENt (EP/M005429/1) and MaDrIgAL (EP/N017536/1).

References

Gabor Angeli, Percy Liang, and Dan Klein. 2010. A simple domain-independent probabilistic approach to generation. In *Conference on Empirical Methods in Natural Language Processing (EMNLP)*.

Anja Belz and Eric Kow. 2010. Extracting parallel fragments from comparable corpora for data-to-text generation. In *6th International Natural Language Generation Conference (INLG)*.

Keith Beven. 2009. *Environmental Modelling: An Uncertain Future?* Routledge.

Edward T. Cokely, Mirta Galesic, Eric Schulz, Saima Ghazal, and Rocio Garcia-Retamero. 2012. Measuring risk literacy: The berlin numeracy test. *Judgment and Decision Making*, 7(1):25–47.

Mary Ellen Foster and Jon Oberlander. 2006. Data-driven generation of emphatic facial displays. In *Proc. of the 11th Conference of the European Chapter of the Association for Computational Linguistics (EACL)*.

Mirta Galesic and Rocio Garcia-Retamero. 2010. Statistical numeracy for health: A cross-cultural comparison with probabilistic national samples. *Archives of Internal Medicine*, 170(462–468).

Albert Gatt and Ehud Reiter. 2009. SimpleNLG: A realisation engine for practical applications. In *ENLG*.

Albert Gatt, Francois Portet, Ehud Reiter, James Hunter, Saad Mahamood, Wendy Moncur, and Somayajulu Sripada. 2009. From Data to Text in the Neonatal Intensive Care Unit: Using NLG Technology for Decision Support and Information Management. *AI Communications*, 22: 153-186.

G. Gigerenzer and J. A. Muir Gray, editors. 2011. *Better doctors, better patients, better decisions: Envisioning health care 2020*. Cambridge MIT Press.

Dimitra Gkatzia, Amanda Cercas Curry, Verena Rieser, and Oliver Lemon. 2015. A game-based setup for data collection and task-based evaluation of uncertain information presentation. In *Proceedings of the 15th European Workshop on Natural Language Generation (ENLG)*, pages 112–113, Brighton, UK, September. Association for Computational Linguistics.

Ioannis Konstas and Mirella Lapata. 2012. Unsupervised concept-to-text generation with hypergraphs. In *Conference of the North American Chapter of the Association for Computational Linguistics (NAACL)*.

Haleh Kootval, editor. 2008. *Guidelines on Communicating Forecast Uncertainty*. World Meteorological Organisation.

Martin Manning, Michel Petit, David Easterling, James Murphy, Anand Patwardhan, Hans-Holger Rogner, Rob Swart, and Gary Yohe. 2004. IPCC Workshop on Describing Scientific Uncertainties in Climate Change to Support Analysis of Risk and of Options.

Richard Power and Sandra Williams. 2012. Generating numerical approximations. *Computational Linguistics*, 38(1):113–134, March.

V. Rieser and O. Lemon. 2008. Learning effective multimodal dialogue strategies from wizard-of-oz data: Bootstrapping and evaluation. *Proceedings of ACL*, pages 638–646.

Rakesh Sarin and Alice Wieland. 2016. Risk aversion for decisions under uncertainty: Are there gender differences? *Journal of Behavioral and Experimental Economics*, 60:1 – 8.

Somayajulu G. Sripada, Ehud Reiter, and Lezan Hawizy. 2005. Evaluation of an NLG system using post-edit data. In *International Joint Conference on Artificial Intelligence (IJCAI)*.

Liz Stephens, Ken Mylne, and David Spiegelhalter. 2011. Using an online game to evaluate effective methods of communicating ensemble model output to different audiences. In *American Geophysical Union, Fall Meeting*.

Kees van Deemter. 2009. Utility and language generation: The case of vagueness. *Journal of Philosophical Logic*, 38(6):607–632.

Benjamin Weiss, Sebastian Möller, and Matthias Schulz. 2012. Modality preferences of different user groups. In *The Fifth International Conference on Advances in Computer-Human Interactions (ACHI)*.

Zheng Zhu. 2007. Gender differences in mathematical problem solving patterns: A review of literature. *International Education Journal*, 8(2):187 – 203.

Tweet2Vec: Character-Based Distributed Representations for Social Media

Bhuwan Dhingra[1], Zhong Zhou[2], Dylan Fitzpatrick[1,2]
Michael Muehl[1] and **William W. Cohen[1]**
[1]School of Computer Science, Carnegie Mellon University, Pittsburgh, PA, USA
[2]Heinz College, Carnegie Mellon University, Pittsburgh, PA, USA
{bdhingra,djfitzpa,mmuehl}@andrew.cmu.edu
zhongzhou@cmu.edu   wcohen@cs.cmu.edu

Abstract

Text from social media provides a set of challenges that can cause traditional NLP approaches to fail. Informal language, spelling errors, abbreviations, and special characters are all commonplace in these posts, leading to a prohibitively large vocabulary size for word-level approaches. We propose a character composition model, tweet2vec, which finds vector-space representations of whole tweets by learning complex, non-local dependencies in character sequences. The proposed model outperforms a word-level baseline at predicting user-annotated *hashtags* associated with the posts, doing significantly better when the input contains many out-of-vocabulary words or unusual character sequences. Our *tweet2vec* encoder is publicly available[1].

1 Introduction

We understand from Zipf's Law that in any natural language corpus a majority of the vocabulary word types will either be absent or occur in low frequency. Estimating the statistical properties of these rare word types is naturally a difficult task. This is analogous to the curse of dimensionality when we deal with sequences of tokens - most sequences will occur only once in the training data. Neural network architectures overcome this problem by defining non-linear compositional models over vector space representations of tokens and hence assign non-zero probability even to sequences not seen during training (Bengio et al., 2003; Kiros et al., 2015). In this work, we explore a similar approach to learning distributed representations of social media posts by composing them from their constituent *characters*, with the goal of generalizing to out-of-vocabulary words as well as sequences at test time.

Traditional Neural Network Language Models (NNLMs) treat words as the basic units of language and assign independent vectors to each word type. To constrain memory requirements, the vocabulary size is fixed before-hand; therefore, rare and out-of-vocabulary words are all grouped together under a common type 'UNKNOWN'. This choice is motivated by the assumption of arbitrariness in language, which means that surface forms of words have little to do with their semantic roles. Recently, (Ling et al., 2015) challenge this assumption and present a bidirectional Long Short Term Memory (LSTM) (Hochreiter and Schmidhuber, 1997) for composing word vectors from their constituent characters which can memorize the arbitrary aspects of word orthography as well as generalize to rare and out-of-vocabulary words.

Encouraged by their findings, we extend their approach to a much larger unicode character set, and model long sequences of text as functions of their constituent characters (including whitespace). We focus on social media posts from the website Twitter, which are an excellent testing ground for character based models due to the noisy nature of text. Heavy use of slang and abundant misspellings means that there are many orthographically and semantically similar tokens, and special characters such as emojis are also immensely popular and carry useful semantic information. In our moderately sized training dataset of 2 million tweets, there were about 0.92 million unique word types. It would be expensive to capture all these phenomena in a word based model in terms of both the memory requirement (for the increased vocabulary) and the amount of training data required for effective learning. Additional benefits of the character based approach

---

[1]https://github.com/bdhingra/tweet2vec

Proceedings of the 54th Annual Meeting of the Association for Computational Linguistics, pages 269–274,
Berlin, Germany, August 7-12, 2016. ©2016 Association for Computational Linguistics

include language independence of the methods, and no requirement of NLP preprocessing such as word-segmentation.

A crucial step in learning good text representations is to choose an appropriate objective function to optimize. Unsupervised approaches attempt to reconstruct the original text from its latent representation (Mikolov et al., 2013; Bengio et al., 2003). Social media posts however, come with their own form of supervision annotated by millions of users, in the form of *hashtags* which link posts about the same topic together. A natural assumption is that the posts with the same hashtags should have embeddings which are close to each other. Hence, we formulate our training objective to maximize cross-entropy loss at the task of predicting hashtags for a post from its latent representation.

We propose a Bi-directional Gated Recurrent Unit (Bi-GRU) (Chung et al., 2014) neural network for learning tweet representations. Treating white-space as a special character itself, the model does a forward and backward pass over the entire sequence, and the final GRU states are linearly combined to get the tweet embedding. Posterior probabilities over hashtags are computed by projecting this embedding to a softmax output layer. Compared to a word-level baseline this model shows improved performance at predicting hashtags for a held-out set of posts. Inspired by recent work in learning vector space text representations, we name our model *tweet2vec*.

2   Related Work

Using neural networks to learn distributed representations of words dates back to (Bengio et al., 2003). More recently, (Mikolov et al., 2013) released `word2vec` - a collection of word vectors trained using a recurrent neural network. These word vectors are in widespread use in the NLP community, and the original work has since been extended to sentences (Kiros et al., 2015), documents and paragraphs (Le and Mikolov, 2014), topics (Niu and Dai, 2015) and queries (Grbovic et al., 2015). All these methods require storing an extremely large table of vectors for all word types and cannot be easily generalized to unseen words at test time (Ling et al., 2015). They also require preprocessing to find word boundaries which is non-trivial for a social network domain like Twitter.

In (Ling et al., 2015), the authors present a compositional character model based on bidirectional LSTMs as a potential solution to these problems. A major benefit of this approach is that large word lookup tables can be compacted into character lookup tables and the compositional model scales to large data sets better than other state-of-the-art approaches. While (Ling et al., 2015) generate word embeddings from character representations, we propose to generate vector representations of entire tweets from characters in our `tweet2vec` model.

Our work adds to the growing body of work showing the applicability of character models for a variety of NLP tasks such as Named Entity Recognition (Santos and Guimarães, 2015), POS tagging (Santos and Zadrozny, 2014), text classification (Zhang et al., 2015) and language modeling (Karpathy et al., 2015; Kim et al., 2015).

Previously, (Luong et al., 2013) dealt with the problem of estimating rare word representations by building them from their constituent morphemes. While they show improved performance over word-based models, their approach requires a morpheme parser for preprocessing which may not perform well on noisy text like Twitter. Also the space of all morphemes, though smaller than the space of all words, is still large enough that modelling all morphemes is impractical.

Hashtag prediction for social media has been addressed earlier, for example in (Weston et al., 2014; Godin et al., 2013). (Weston et al., 2014) also use a neural architecture, but compose text embeddings from a lookup table of words. They also show that the learned embeddings can generalize to an unrelated task of document recommendation, justifying the use of hashtags as supervision for learning text representations.

3   Tweet2Vec

Bi-GRU Encoder: Figure 1 shows our model for encoding tweets. It uses a similar structure to the C2W model in (Ling et al., 2015), with LSTM units replaced with GRU units.

The input to the network is defined by an alphabet of characters C (this may include the entire unicode character set). The input tweet is broken into a stream of characters $c_1, c_2, ...c_m$ each of which is represented by a 1-by-$|C|$ encoding. These one-hot vectors are then projected to a character space by multiplying with the matrix $P_C \in$

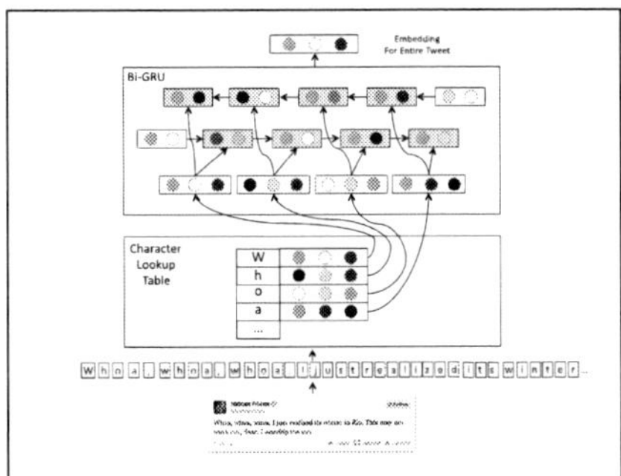

Figure 1: Tweet2Vec encoder for social media text

$\mathbb{R}^{|C| \times d_c}$, where d_c is the dimension of the character vector space. Let $x_1, x_2, ... x_m$ be the sequence of character vectors for the input tweet after the lookup. The encoder consists of a forward-GRU and a backward-GRU. Both have the same architecture, except the backward-GRU processes the sequence in reverse order. Each of the GRU units process these vectors sequentially, and starting with the initial state h_0 compute the sequence $h_1, h_2, ... h_m$ as follows:

$$r_t = \sigma(W_r x_t + U_r h_{t-1} + b_r),$$
$$z_t = \sigma(W_z x_t + U_z h_{t-1} + b_z),$$
$$\tilde{h}_t = tanh(W_h x_t + U_h(r_t \odot h_{t-1}) + b_h),$$
$$h_t = (1 - z_t) \odot h_{t-1} + z_t \odot \tilde{h}_t.$$

Here r_t, z_t are called the *reset* and *update* gates respectively, and $\tilde{h}_t$ is the *candidate* output state which is converted to the actual output state h_t. W_r, W_z, W_h are $d_h \times d_c$ matrices and U_r, U_z, U_h are $d_h \times d_h$ matrices, where d_h is the hidden state dimension of the GRU. The final states h_m^f from the forward-GRU, and h_0^b from the backward-GRU are combined using a fully-connected layer to the give the final tweet embedding e_t:

$$e_t = W^f h_m^f + W^b h_0^b \qquad (1)$$

Here W^f, W^b are $d_t \times d_h$ and b is $d_t \times 1$ bias term, where d_t is the dimension of the final tweet embedding. In our experiments we set $d_t = d_h$. All parameters are learned using gradient descent.

Softmax: Finally, the tweet embedding is passed through a linear layer whose output is the same size as the number of hashtags L in the data set. We use a softmax layer to compute the posterior hashtag probabilities:

$$P(y = j|e) = \frac{exp(w_j^T e + b_j)}{\sum_{i=1}^{L} exp(w_i^T e + b_j)}. \qquad (2)$$

Objective Function: We optimize the categorical cross-entropy loss between predicted and true hashtags:

$$J = \frac{1}{B} \sum_{i=1}^{B} \sum_{j=1}^{L} -t_{i,j} log(p_{i,j}) + \lambda \|\Theta\|^2. \qquad (3)$$

Here B is the batch size, L is the number of classes, $p_{i,j}$ is the predicted probability that the i-th tweet has hashtag j, and $t_{i,j} \in \{0, 1\}$ denotes the ground truth of whether the j-th hashtag is in the i-th tweet. We use L2-regularization weighted by λ.

4 Experiments and Results

4.1 Word Level Baseline

Since our objective is to compare character-based and word-based approaches, we have also implemented a simple word-level encoder for tweets. The input tweet is first split into tokens along white-spaces. A more sophisticated tokenizer may be used, but for a fair comparison we wanted to keep language specific preprocessing to a minimum. The encoder is essentially the same as *tweet2vec*, with the input as words instead of characters. A lookup table stores word vectors for the V (20K here) most common words, and the rest are grouped together under the 'UNK' token.

4.2 Data

Our dataset consists of a large collection of global posts from Twitter[2] between the dates of June 1, 2013 to June 5, 2013. Only English language posts (as detected by the *lang* field in Twitter API) and posts with at least one hashtag are retained. We removed infrequent hashtags (< 500 posts) since they do not have enough data for good generalization. We also removed very frequent tags ($> 19K$ posts) which were almost always from automatically generated posts (ex: #androidgame) which are trivial to predict. The final dataset contains 2 million tweets for training, 10K for validation and 50K for testing, with a total of 2039 distinct hashtags. We use simple regex to preprocess the post text and remove hashtags (since these are to be predicted) and HTML tags, and replace usernames and URLs with special tokens. We also removed *retweets* and convert the text to lower-case.

---

[2]https://twitter.com/

271

Tweets	Word model baseline	*tweet2vec*
`ninety-one degrees. *`♥☺	`#initialsofsomeone..` `#nw #gameofthrones`	`#summer` **`#loveit`** `#sun`
`self-cooked scramble egg.  yum!!  !url`	`#music #cheap` `#cute`	**`#yummy`** `#food` `#foodporn`
`can't sleeeeeeep`	`#gameofthrones` `#heartbreaker`	`#tired` **`#insomnia`**
`oklahoma!!!!!!!!!!!  champions!!!!!`	`#initialsofsomeone..` `#nw #lrt`	**`#wcws`** `#sooners` `#ou`
`7 % of battery .  iphones die too quick .`	`#help #power` `#money #s`	`#fml #apple #bbl` **`#thestruggle`**
`i have the cutest nephew in the world !url`	`#nephew` **`#cute`** `#family`	`#socute` **`#cute`** `#puppy`

Table 1: Examples of top predictions from the models. The correct hashtag(s) if detected are in bold.

	word	*tweet2vec*
d_t, d_h	200	500
Total Parameters	3.91M	3.90M
Training Time / Epoch	**1528s**	9649s

Table 2: Model sizes and training time/epoch

Model	Precision @1	Recall @10	Mean Rank
Full test set (50K)			
word	24.1%	42.8%	133
tweet2vec	**28.4%**	**48.5%**	**104**
Rare words test set (2K)			
word	20.4%	37.2%	167
tweet2vec	**32.9%**	**51.3%**	**104**
Frequent words test set (2K)			
word	20.9%	41.3%	133
tweet2vec	**23.9%**	**44.2%**	**112**

Table 3: Hashtag prediction results. Best numbers for each test set are in bold.

4.3 Implementation Details

Word vectors and character vectors are both set to size $d_L = 150$ for their respective models. There were 2829 unique characters in the training set and we model each of these independently in a character look-up table. Embedding sizes were chosen such that each model had roughly the same number of parameters (Table 2). Training is performed using mini-batch gradient descent with Nesterov's momentum. We use a batch size $B = 64$, initial learning rate $\eta_0 = 0.01$ and momentum parameter $\mu_0 = 0.9$. L2-regularization with $\lambda = 0.001$ was applied to all models. Initial weights were drawn from 0-mean gaussians with $\sigma = 0.1$ and initial biases were set to 0. The hyperparameters were tuned one at a time keeping others fixed, and values with the lowest validation cost were chosen. The resultant combination was used to train the models until performance on validation set stopped increasing. During training, the learning rate is halved everytime the validation set precision increases by less than 0.01 % from one epoch to the next. The models converge in about 20 epochs. Code for training both the models is publicly available on github.

4.4 Results

We test the character and word-level variants by predicting hashtags for a held-out test set of posts. Since there may be more than one correct hashtag per post, we generate a ranked list of tags for each post from the output posteriors, and report average precision@1, recall@10 and mean rank of the correct hashtags. These are listed in Table 3.

To see the performance of each model on posts containing rare words (RW) and frequent words (FW) we selected two test sets each containing 2,000 posts. We populated these sets with posts which had the maximum and minimum number of out-of-vocabulary words respectively, where vocabulary is defined by the 20K most frequent words. Overall, *tweet2vec* outperforms the word model, doing significantly better on RW test set and comparably on FW set. This improved performance comes at the cost of increased training time (see Table 2), since moving from words to characters results in longer input sequences to the GRU.

We also study the effect of model size on the performance of these models. For the word model we set vocabulary size V to 8K, 15K and 20K respectively. For *tweet2vec* we set the GRU hidden state size to 300, 400 and 500 respectively. Figure 2 shows precision 1 of the two models as the number of parameters is increased, for each test

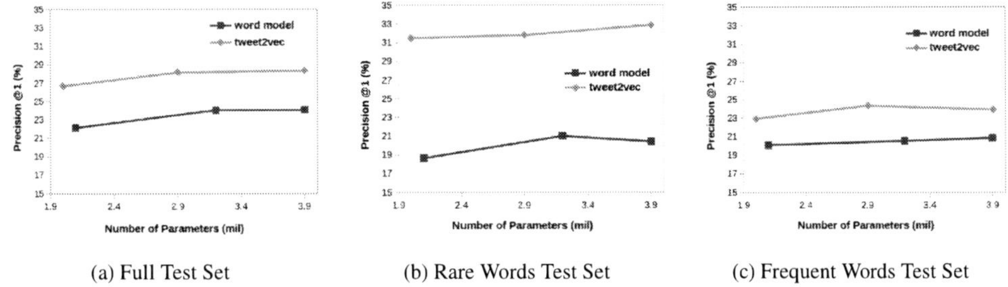

	(a) Full Test Set	(b) Rare Words Test Set	(c) Frequent Words Test Set

Figure 2: Precision @1 v Number of model parameters for word model and *tweet2vec*.

Dataset	# Hashtags	word	*tweet2vec*
small	933	28.0%	**33.1%**
medium	2039	24.1%	**28.4%**
large	5114	20.1%	**24.6%**

Table 4: Precision @1 as training data size and number of output labels is increased. Note that the test set is different for each setting.

set described above. There is not much variation in the performance, and moreover *tweet2vec* always outperforms the word based model for the same number of parameters.

Table 4 compares the models as complexity of the task is increased. We created 3 datasets (small, medium and large) with an increasing number of hashtags to be predicted. This was done by varying the lower threshold of the minimum number of tags per post for it to be included in the dataset. Once again we observe that *tweet2vec* outperforms its word-based counterpart for each of the three settings.

Finally, table 1 shows some predictions from the word level model and *tweet2vec*. We selected these to highlight some strengths of the character based approach - it is robust to word segmentation errors and spelling mistakes, effectively interprets emojis and other special characters to make predictions, and also performs comparably to the word-based approach for in-vocabulary tokens.

5   Conclusion

We have presented *tweet2vec* - a character level encoder for social media posts trained using supervision from associated *hashtags*. Our result shows that *tweet2vec* outperforms the word based approach, doing significantly better when the input post contains many rare words. We have focused only on English language posts, but the character

model requires no language specific preprocessing and can be extended to other languages. For future work, one natural extension would be to use a character-level decoder for predicting the hashtags. This will allow generation of hashtags not seen in the training dataset. Also, it will be interesting to see how our tweet2vec embeddings can be used in domains where there is a need for semantic understanding of social media, such as tracking infectious diseases (Signorini et al., 2011). Hence, we provide an off-the-shelf encoder trained on *medium* dataset described above to compute vector-space representations of tweets along with our code on github.

Acknowledgments

We would like to thank Alex Smola, Yun Fu, Hsiao-Yu Fish Tung, Ruslan Salakhutdinov, and Barnabas Poczos for useful discussions. We would also like to thank Juergen Pfeffer for providing access to the Twitter data, and the reviewers for their comments.

References

Yoshua Bengio, Réjean Ducharme, Pascal Vincent, and Christian Janvin. 2003. A neural probabilistic language model. *The Journal of Machine Learning Research*, 3:1137–1155

Junyoung Chung, Caglar Gulcehre, KyungHyun Cho, and Yoshua Bengio. 2014. Empirical evaluation of gated recurrent neural networks on sequence modeling. *arXiv preprint arXiv:1412.3555*.

Fréderic Godin, Viktor Slavkovikj, Wesley De Neve, Benjamin Schrauwen, and Rik Van de Walle. 2013. Using topic models for twitter hashtag recommendation. In *Proceedings of the 22nd international conference on World Wide Web companion*, pages 593–596. International World Wide Web Conferences Steering Committee.

Mihajlo Grbovic, Nemanja Djuric, Vladan Radosavljevic, Fabrizio Silvestri, and Narayan Bhamidipati. 2015. Context-and content-aware embeddings for query rewriting in sponsored search. In *Proceedings of the 38th International ACM SIGIR Conference on Research and Development in Information Retrieval*, pages 383–392. ACM.

Sepp Hochreiter and Jürgen Schmidhuber. 1997. Long short-term memory. *Neural computation*, 9(8):1735–1780.

Andrej Karpathy, Justin Johnson, and Fei-Fei Li. 2015. Visualizing and understanding recurrent networks. *arXiv preprint arXiv:1506.02078*.

Yoon Kim, Yacine Jernite, David Sontag, and Alexander M Rush. 2015. Character-aware neural language models. *arXiv preprint arXiv:1508.06615*.

Ryan Kiros, Yukun Zhu, Ruslan Salakhutdinov, Richard S Zemel, Antonio Torralba, Raquel Urtasun, and Sanja Fidler. 2015. Skip-thought vectors. *arXiv preprint arXiv:1506.06726*.

Quoc V Le and Tomas Mikolov. 2014. Distributed representations of sentences and documents. *arXiv preprint arXiv:1405.4053*.

Wang Ling, Tiago Luís, Luís Marujo, Ramón Fernandez Astudillo, Silvio Amir, Chris Dyer, Alan W Black, and Isabel Trancoso. 2015. Finding function in form: Compositional character models for open vocabulary word representation. *arXiv preprint arXiv:1508.02096*.

Thang Luong, Richard Socher, and Christopher D Manning. 2013. Better word representations with recursive neural networks for morphology. In *CoNLL*, pages 104–113. Citeseer.

Tomas Mikolov, Kai Chen, Greg Corrado, and Jeffrey Dean. 2013. Efficient estimation of word representations in vector space. *arXiv preprint arXiv:1301.3781*.

Li-Qiang Niu and Xin-Yu Dai. 2015. Topic2vec: Learning distributed representations of topics. *arXiv preprint arXiv:1506.08422*.

Cicero Nogueira dos Santos and Victor Guimarães. 2015. Boosting named entity recognition with neural character embeddings. *arXiv preprint arXiv:1505.05008*.

Cicero D Santos and Bianca Zadrozny. 2014. Learning character-level representations for part-of-speech tagging. In *Proceedings of the 31st International Conference on Machine Learning (ICML-14)*, pages 1818–1826.

Alessio Signorini, Alberto Maria Segre, and Philip M Polgreen. 2011. The use of twitter to track levels of disease activity and public concern in the us during the influenza a h1n1 pandemic. *PloS one*, 6(5):e19467.

Jason Weston, Sumit Chopra, and Keith Adams. 2014. tagspace: Semantic embeddings from hashtags. In *Proceedings of the 2014 Conference on Empirical Methods in Natural Language Processing (EMNLP)*, pages 1822–1827.

Xiang Zhang, Junbo Zhao, and Yann LeCun. 2015. Character-level convolutional networks for text classification. In *Advances in Neural Information Processing Systems*, pages 649–657.

Phrase-Level Combination of SMT and TM
Using Constrained Word Lattice

Liangyou Li and **Andy Way** and **Qun Liu**
ADAPT Centre, School of Computing
Dublin City University
Dublin 9, Ireland
{liangyouli,away,qliu}@computing.dcu.ie

Abstract

Constrained translation has improved statistical machine translation (SMT) by combining it with translation memory (TM) at sentence-level. In this paper, we propose using a *constrained word lattice*, which encodes input phrases and TM constraints together, to combine SMT and TM at phrase-level. Experiments on English–Chinese and English–French show that our approach is significantly better than previous combination methods, including sentence-level constrained translation and a recent phrase-level combination.

1 Introduction

The combination of statistical machine translation (SMT) and translation memory (TM) has proven to be beneficial in improving translation quality and has drawn attention from many researchers (Biçici and Dymetman, 2008; He et al., 2010; Koehn and Senellart, 2010; Ma et al., 2011; Wang et al., 2013; Li et al., 2014). Among various combination approaches, constrained translation (Koehn and Senellart, 2010; Ma et al., 2011) is a simple one and can be readily adopted.

Given an input sentence, constrained translation retrieves similar TM instances and uses matched segments to constrain the translation space of the input by generating a constrained input. Then an SMT engine is used to search for a complete translation of the constrained input.

Despite its effectiveness in improving SMT, previous constrained translation works at the sentence-level, which means that matched segments in a TM instance are either all adopted or all abandoned regardless of their individual quality (Wang et al., 2013). In this paper, we propose a phrase-level constrained translation approach which uses a *constrained word lattice* to encode the input and constraints from the TM together and allows a decoder to directly optimize the selection of constraints towards translation quality (Section 2).

We conduct experiments (Section 3) on English–Chinese (EN–ZH) and English–French (EN–FR) TM data. Results show that our method is significantly better than previous combination approaches, including sentence-level constrained methods and a recent phrase-level combination method. Specifically, it improves the BLEU (Papineni et al., 2002) score by up to +5.5% on EN–ZH and +2.4% on EN–FR over a phrase-based baseline (Koehn et al., 2003) and decreases the TER (Snover et al., 2006) error by up to -4.3%/-2.2%, respectively.

2 Constrained Word Lattice

A word lattice $G = (V, E, \Sigma, \phi, \psi)$ is a directed acyclic graph, where V is a set of nodes, including a start point and an end point, $E \subseteq V \times V$ is a set of edges, Σ is a set of symbols, a label function $\phi : E \to \Sigma$ and a weight function $\psi : E \to \mathbb{R}$.[1] A constrained word lattice is a special case of a word lattice, which extends Σ with extra symbols (i.e. constraints).

A constraint is a target phrase which will appear in the final translation. Constraints can be obtained in two ways: *addition* (Ma et al., 2011) and *subtraction* (Koehn and Senellart, 2010).[2] Figure 1 exemplifies the differences between them.

The construction of a constrained lattice is very similar to that of a word lattice, except that we need to label some edges with constraints. The general process is:

---

[1] In this paper, edge weights are set to 1.

[2] *Addition* means that constraints are added from a TM target to an input, while *subtraction* means that some constraints are removed from the TM target.

Proceedings of the 54th Annual Meeting of the Association for Computational Linguistics, pages 275–280,
Berlin, Germany, August 7-12, 2016. ©2016 Association for Computational Linguistics

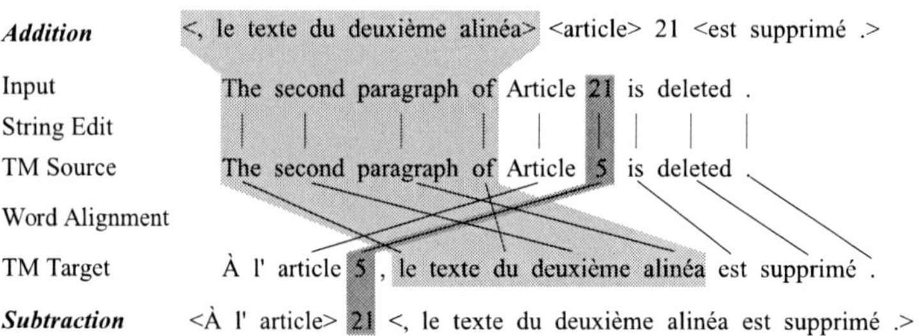

Figure 1: An example of generating a constrained input in two ways: *addition* and *subtraction*. While *addition* replaces an input phrase with a target phrase from a TM instance (an example is marked by lighter gray), *subtraction* removes mismatched target words and inserts mismatched input words (darker gray). Constraints are specified by <>. Sentences are taken from Koehn and Senellart (2010).

1. Building an initial lattice for an input sentence. This produces a chain.

2. Adding phrasal constraints into the lattice which produces extra nodes and edges.

Figure 2 shows an example of a constrained lattice for the sentence in Figure 1.

In the rest of this section, we explain how to use *addition* and *subtraction* to build a constrained lattice and the decoder for translating the lattice. Notations we use in this section are: an input f and a TM instance $\langle f', e', A \rangle$ where f' is the TM source, e' is the TM target and A is a word alignment between f' and e'.

2.1 Addition

In *addition*, matched input words are directly replaced by their translations from a retrieved TM, which means that *addition* follows the word order of an input sentence. This property makes it easy to obtain constraints for an input phrase.

For an input phrase $\overline{f}$, we firstly find its matched phrase $\overline{f'}$ from f' via string edits[3] between f and f', so that $\overline{f} = \overline{f'}$. Then, we extract its translation $\overline{e'}$ from e', which is consistent with the alignment A (Och and Ney, 2004).

To build a lattice using *addition*, we directly add a new edge to the lattice which covers $\overline{f}$ and is labeled by $\overline{e'}$. For example, dash-dotted lines in Figure 2 are labeled by constraints from *addition*.

---

[3]String edits, as used in the Levenshtein distance (Levenshtein, 1966), include match, substitution, deletion, and insertion with a priority in this paper: match > substitution > deletion > insertion.

2.2 Subtraction

In *subtraction*, mismatched input words in f are inserted into e' and mismatched words in e' are removed. The inserted position is determined by A. The advantage of *subtraction* is that it keeps the word order of e'. This is important since the reordering of target words is one of the fundamental problems in SMT, especially for language pairs which have a high degree of syntactic reordering.

However, this property makes it hard to build a lattice from *subtraction*, as – different from the *addition* – *subtraction* does not directly produce a constraint for an input phrase. Thus, for some generated constraints, there is not a specific corresponding phrase in the input. In addition, when adding a constraint to the lattice, we need to consider its context so that the lattice keeps target word order.

To solve this problem, in this paper we propose to segment an input sentence into a sequence of phrases according to information from a matched TM (i.e. the string edit and word alignment) and then create a constrained input for each phrase and add them to the lattice.

Formally, we produce a monotonic segmentation, $\langle \overline{f}_1, \overline{f'}_1, \overline{e'}_1 \rangle \cdots \langle \overline{f}_N, \overline{f'}_N, \overline{e'}_N \rangle$, for each sentence triple: $\langle f, f', e' \rangle$. Each $\langle \overline{f}_i, \overline{f'}_i, \overline{e'}_i \rangle$ tuple is obtained in two phases: (1) According to the alignment A, $\overline{f'}_i$ and $\overline{e'}_i$ are produced. (2) Based on string edits between f and f', $\overline{f}_i$ is recognized. The resulting tuple is subject to several restrictions:

1. Each $< \overline{f'}_i, \overline{e'}_i >$ is consistent with the word alignment A and at least one word in $\overline{f'}_i$ is aligned to words in $\overline{e'}_i$.

276

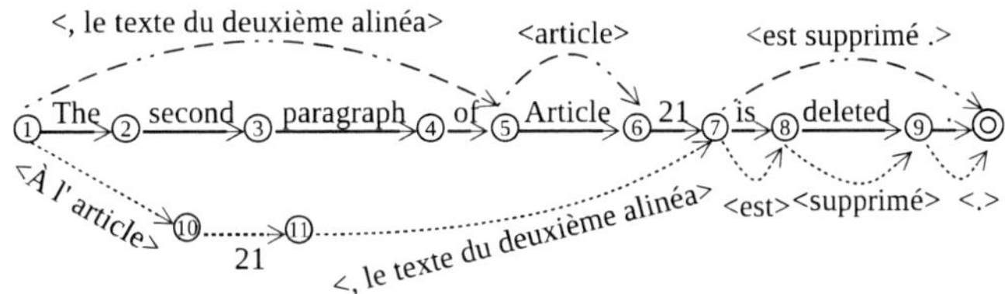

Figure 2: An example of constructing a constrained word lattice for the sentence in Figure 1. Dash-dotted lines are generated by *addition* and dotted lines are generated by *subtraction*. Constraints are specified by <>.

2. Each boundary word in $\overline{f'}_i$ is either the first word or the last word of f' or aligned to at least one word in e', so that mismatched input words in $\overline{f}_i$ which are unaligned can find their position in the current tuple.

3. The string edit for the first word of $\overline{f}_i$, where $i \neq 1$, is not "deletion". That means the first word is not an extra input word. This is because, in *subtraction*, the inserted position of a mismatched unaligned word depends on the alignment of the word before it.

4. No smaller tuples may be extracted without violating restrictions 1–3. This allows us to obtain a unique segmentation where each tuple is minimal.

After obtaining the segmentation, we create a constrained input for each $\overline{f}_i$ using *subtraction* and add it to the lattice by creating a path covering $\overline{f}_i$. The path contains one or more edges, each of which is labeled either by an input word or a constraint in the constrained input.

2.3 Decoding

The decoder for integrating word lattices into the phrase-based model (Koehn et al., 2003) works similarly to the phrase-based decoder, except that it tracks *nodes* instead of words (Dyer et al., 2008): given the topological order of nodes in a lattice, the decoder builds a translation hypothesis from left to right by selecting a range of untranslated nodes.

The decoder for a constrained lattice works similarly except that, for a constrained edge, the decoder can only build its translation directly from the constraint. For example, in Figure 2, the translation of the edge "1 $\rightarrow$ 5" is ", *le texte du deuxième alinéa*".

EN–ZH	Sentences	W/S (EN)	W/S (ZH)
Train	84,871	13.5	13.8
Dev	734	14.3	14.5
Test	943	17.4	17.4

EN–FR	Sentences	W/S (EN)	W/S (FR)
Train	751,548	26.9	29.3
Dev	2,665	26.8	29.2
Test	2,655	27.1	29.4

Table 1: Summary of English–Chinese (EN–ZH) and English–French (EN–FR) datasets

3 Experiment

In our experiments, a baseline system **PB** is built with the phrase-based model in Moses (Koehn et al., 2007). We compare our approach with three other combination methods. **ADD** combines PB with *addition* (Ma et al., 2011), while **SUB** combines PB with *subtraction* (Koehn and Senellart, 2010). **WANG** combines SMT and TM at phrase-level during decoding (Wang et al., 2013; Li et al., 2014). For each phrase pair applied to translate an input phrase, WANG finds its corresponding phrase pairs in a TM instance and then extracts features which are directly added to the log-linear framework (Och and Ney, 2002) as sparse features. We build three systems based on our approach: $\mathbf{CWL}_{\text{add}}$ only uses constraints from *addition*; $\mathbf{CWL}_{\text{sub}}$ only uses constraints from *subtraction*; $\mathbf{CWL}_{\text{both}}$ uses constraints from both.

Table 1 shows a summary of our datasets. The EN–ZH dataset is a translation memory from Symantec. Our EN–FR dataset is from the publicly available JRC-Acquis corpus.[4] Word alignment is performed by GIZA++ (Och and Ney, 2003) with heuristic function *grow-diag-final-and*.

---

[4] http://ipsc.jrc.ec.europa.eu/index.php?id=198

Systems	EN–ZH		EN–FR	
	BLEU↑	TER↓	BLEU↑	TER↓
PB	44.3	40.0	65.7	25.9
Sentence-Level Combination				
ADD	45.6*	39.2*	64.2	27.2
SUB	49.4*	36.3*	64.2	27.3
Phrase-Level Combination				
WANG	44.7*	39.3*	66.1*	25.7*
CWL_{add}	49.8*	35.7*	**68.1***	**23.7***
CWL_{Sub}	**51.4***	**33.7***	68.6*	23.4*
CWL_{both}	**51.2***	33.8*	68.3*	23.6*

Table 2: Experimental results of comparing our approach (CWL_x) with previous work. All scores reported are an average of 3 runs. Scores with * are significantly better than that of the baseline PB at $p < 0.01$. **Bold** scores are significantly better than that of all previous work at $p < 0.01$.

We use SRILM (Stolcke, 2002) to train a 5-gram language model on the target side of our training data with modified Kneser-Ney discounting (Chen and Goodman, 1996). Batch MIRA (Cherry and Foster, 2012) is used to tune weights. Case-insensitive BLEU [%] and TER [%] are used to evaluate translation results.

3.1 Results

Table 2 shows experimental results on EN–ZH and EN–FR. We find that our method (CWL_x) significantly improves the baseline system PB on EN–ZH by up to +5.5% BLEU score and by +2.4% BLEU score on EN–FR. In terms of TER, our system significantly decreases the error by up to -4.3%/-2.2% on EN–ZH and EN–FR, respectively.

Although, compared to the baseline PB, ADD and SUB work well on EN–ZH, they reduce the translation quality on EN–FR. By contrast, their phrase-level countparts (CWL_{add} and CWL_{sub}) bring consistent improvements over the baseline on both language pairs. This suggests that a combination approach based on constrained word lattices is more effective and robust than sentence-level constrained translation. Compared to system WANG, our method produces significantly better translations as well. In addition, our approach is simpler and easier to adopt than WANG.

Compared with CWL_{add}, CWL_{sub} produces better translations. This may suggest that, for a constrained word lattice, *subtraction* generates a better sequence of constraints than *addition* since it keeps target words and the word order. However,

Ranges	Sentence	W/S (EN)
[0.8, 1.0)	198	16.4
[0.6, 0.8)	195	14.7
[0.4, 0.6)	318	16.8
(0.0, 0.4)	223	21.5

(a) English–Chinese

Ranges	Sentences	W/S (EN)
[0.9, 1.0)	313	32.5
[0.8, 0.9)	258	28.3
[0.7, 0.8)	216	28.4
[0.6, 0.7)	156	33.3
[0.5, 0.6)	171	34.1
[0.4, 0.5)	168	34.3
[0.3, 0.4)	277	40.3
(0.0, 0.3)	360	54.7

(b) English–French

Table 3: Composition of test subsets based on fuzzy match scores on English–Chinese and English–French data.

combining them together (i.e. CWL_{both}) does not bring a further improvement. We assume the reason for this is that *addition* and *subtraction* share parts of the constraints generated from the same TM. For example, in Figure 2, the edge "1 → 5" based on *addition* and the edge "11 → 7" based on *subtraction* are labeled by the same constraint.

3.2 Influence of Fuzzy Match Scores

Since a fuzzy match scorer[5] is used to select the best TM instance for an input and thus is an important factor for combining SMT and TM, it is interesting to know what impact it has on the translation quality of various approaches. Table 3 shows statistics of each test subset on EN–ZH and EN–FR where sentences are grouped by their fuzzy match scores.

Figure 3 shows BLEU scores of systems evaluated on these subsets. We find that BLEU scores increasingly grow when match scores become higher. While ADD achieves better BLEU scores than SUB on lower fuzzy ranges, SUB performs better than ADD on higher fuzzy scores. In addition, our approaches (CWL_x) are better than the baseline on all ranges but show much more improvement on ranges with higher fuzzy scores.

---

[5]In this paper, we use a lexical fuzzy match score (Koehn and Senellart, 2010) based on Levenshtein distance to find the best match.

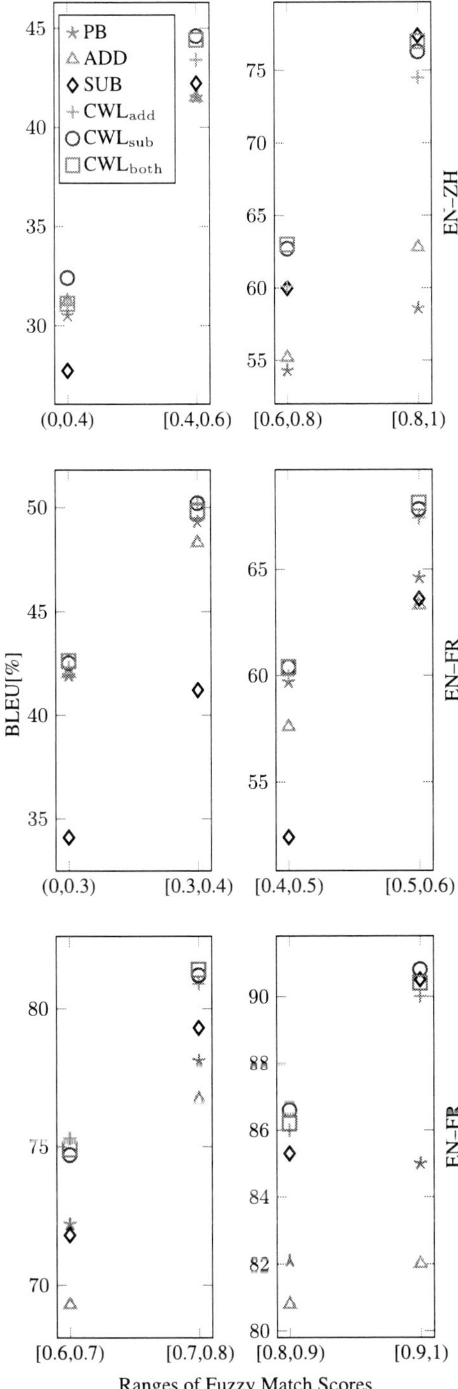

Figure 3: BLEU scores of systems evaluated on sentences which fall into different ranges according to fuzzy match scores on EN–ZH and EN–FR. All scores are averaged over 3 runs.

4 Conclusion

In this paper, we propose a *constrained word lattice* to combine SMT and TM at phrase-level. This method uses a word lattice to encode all possible phrasal constraints together. These constraints come from two sentence-level constrained approaches, including *addition* and *subtraction*. Experiments on English–Chinese and English–French show that compared with previous combination methods, our approach produces significantly better translation results.

In the future, we would like to consider generating constraints from more than one fuzzy match and using fuzzy match scores or a more sophisticated function to weight constraints. It would also be interesting to know if our method will work better when discarding fuzzy matches with very low scores.

Acknowledgments

This research has received funding from the People Programme (Marie Curie Actions) of the European Union's Framework Programme (FP7/2007-2013) under REA grant agreement n° 317471. The ADAPT Centre for Digital Content Technology is funded under the SFI Research Centres Programme (Grant 13/RC/2106) and is co-funded under the European Regional Development Fund. The authors thank all anonymous reviewers for their insightful comments and suggestions.

References

Ergun Biçici and Marc Dymetman. 2008. Dynamic Translation Memory: Using Statistical Machine Translation to Improve Translation Memory Fuzzy Matches. In *Proceedings of the 9th International Conference on Computational Linguistics and Intelligent Text Processing*, pages 454–465, Haifa, Israel, February.

Stanley F. Chen and Joshua Goodman. 1996. An Empirical Study of Smoothing Techniques for Language Modeling. In *Proceedings of the 34th Annual Meeting on Association for Computational Linguistics*, pages 310–318, Santa Cruz, California, June.

Colin Cherry and George Foster. 2012. Batch Tuning Strategies for Statistical Machine Translation. In *Proceedings of the 2012 Conference of the North American Chapter of the Association for Computational Linguistics: Human Language Technologies*, pages 427–436, Montreal, Canada, June.

Christopher Dyer, Smaranda Muresan, and Philip Resnik. 2008. Generalizing Word Lattice Translation. In *Proceedings of the 46th Annual Meeting of the Association for Computational Linguistics: Human Language Technologies*, Columbus, Ohio, June.

Yifan He, Yanjun Ma, Josef van Genabith, and Andy Way. 2010. Bridging SMT and TM with Translation Recommendation. In *Proceedings of the 48th Annual Meeting of the Association for Computational Linguistics*, pages 622–630, Uppsala, Sweden, July.

Philipp Koehn and Jean Senellart. 2010. Convergence of Translation Memory and Statistical Machine Translation. In *Proceedings of AMTA Workshop on MT Research and the Translation Industry*, pages 21–31, Denver, Colorado, USA, November.

Philipp Koehn, Franz Josef Och, and Daniel Marcu. 2003. Statistical Phrase-based Translation. In *Proceedings of the 2003 Conference of the North American Chapter of the Association for Computational Linguistics on Human Language Technology - Volume 1*, pages 48–54, Edmonton, Canada.

Philipp Koehn, Hieu Hoang, Alexandra Birch, Chris Callison-Burch, Marcello Federico, Nicola Bertoldi, Brooke Cowan, Wade Shen, Christine Moran, Richard Zens, Chris Dyer, Ondřej Bojar, Alexandra Constantin, and Evan Herbst. 2007. Moses: Open Source Toolkit for Statistical Machine Translation. In *Proceedings of the 45th Annual Meeting of the ACL on Interactive Poster and Demonstration Sessions*, pages 177–180, Prague, Czech Republic, June.

Vladimir Iosifovich Levenshtein. 1966. Binary Codes Capable of Correcting Deletions, Insertions and Reversals. *Soviet Physics Doklady*, 10:707.

Liangyou Li, Andy Way, and Qun Liu. 2014. A Discriminative Framework of Integrating Translation Memory Features into SMT. In *Proceedings of the 11th Conference of the Association for Machine Translation in the Americas, Vol. 1: MT Researchers Track*, pages 249–260, Vancouver, BC, Canada, October.

Yanjun Ma, Yifan He, Andy Way, and Josef van Genabith. 2011. Consistent Translation using Discriminative Learning - A Translation Memory-Inspired Approach. In *Proceedings of the 49th Annual Meeting of the Association for Computational Linguistics: Human Language Technologies*, pages 1239–1248, Portland, Oregon, USA, June.

Franz Josef Och and Hermann Ney. 2002. Discriminative Training and Maximum Entropy Models for Statistical Machine Translation. In *Proceedings of the 40th Annual Meeting on Association for Computational Linguistics*, pages 295–302, Philadelphia, Pennsylvania, July.

Franz Josef Och and Hermann Ney. 2003. A Systematic Comparison of Various Statistical Alignment Models. *Computational Linguistics*, 29(1):19–51, March.

Franz Josef Och and Hermann Ney. 2004. The Alignment Template Approach to Statistical Machine Translation. *Compututational Linguistics*, 30(4):417–449, December.

Kishore Papineni, Salim Roukos, Todd Ward, and Wei-Jing Zhu. 2002. BLEU: A Method for Automatic Evaluation of Machine Translation. In *Proceedings of the 40th Annual Meeting on Association for Computational Linguistics*, pages 311–318, Philadelphia, Pennsylvania, July.

M. Snover, B. Dorr, R. Schwartz, L. Micciulla, and J. Makhoul. 2006. A Study of Translation Edit Rate with Targeted Human Annotation. In *Proceedings of Association for Machine Translation in the Americas*, pages 223–231, Cambridge, Massachusetts, USA, August.

Andreas Stolcke. 2002. SRILM-an Extensible Language Modeling Toolkit. In *Proceedings of the 7th International Conference on Spoken Language Processing*, pages 257–286, Denver, Colorado, USA, November.

Kun Wang, Chengqing Zong, and Keh-Yih Su. 2013. Integrating Translation Memory into Phrase-Based Machine Translation during Decoding. In *Proceedings of the 51st Annual Meeting of the Association for Computational Linguistics (Volume 1: Long Papers)*, pages 11–21, Sofia, Bulgaria, August.

A Neural Network based Approach to Automatic Post-Editing

Santanu Pal[1], Sudip Kumar Naskar[3], Mihaela Vela[1], Josef van Genabith[1,2]
[1]Saarland University, Saarbrücken, Germany
[2]German Research Center for Artificial Intelligence (DFKI), Germany
[3]Jadavpur University, Kolkata, India
{santanu.pal, josef.vangenabith}@uni-saarland.de
sudip.naskar@cse.jdvu.ac.in, m.vela@mx.uni-saarland.de

Abstract

We present a neural network based automatic post-editing (APE) system to improve raw machine translation (MT) output. Our neural model of APE (NNAPE) is based on a bidirectional recurrent neural network (RNN) model and consists of an encoder that encodes an MT output into a fixed-length vector from which a decoder provides a post-edited (PE) translation. APE translations produced by NNAPE show statistically significant improvements of 3.96, 2.68 and 1.35 BLEU points absolute over the original MT, phrase-based APE and hierarchical APE outputs, respectively. Furthermore, human evaluation shows that the NNAPE generated PE translations are much better than the original MT output.

1 Introduction

For many applications the performance of state-of-the-art MT systems is useful but often far from perfect. MT technologies have gained wide acceptance in the localization industry. Computer aided translation (CAT) has become the de-facto standard in large parts of the translation industry which has resulted in a surge of demand for professional post-editors. This, in turn, has resulted in substantial quantities of PE data which can be used to develop APE systems.

In the context of MT, "post-editing" (PE) is defined as the correction performed by humans over the translations produced by an MT system (Veale and Way, 1997), often with minimal amount of manual effort (TAUS Report, 2010) and as a process of modification rather than revision (Loffler-Laurian, 1985).

MT systems primarily make two types of errors – lexical and reordering errors. However, due to the statistical and probabilistic nature of modelling in statistical MT (SMT), the currently dominant MT technology, it is non-trivial to rectify these errors in the SMT models. Post-edited data are often used in incremental MT frameworks as additional training material. However, often this does not fully exploit the potential of these rich PE data: e.g., PE data may just be drowned out by a large SMT model. An APE system trained on human post-edited data can serve as a MT post-processing module which can improve overall performance. An APE system can be considered as an MT system, translating predictable error patterns in MT output into their corresponding corrections.

APE systems assume the availability of source language input text (SL_{IP}), target language MT output (TL_{MT}) and target language PE data (TL_{PE}). An APE system can be modelled as an MT system between $SL_{IP}\_TL_{MT}$ and TL_{PE}. However, if we do not have access to SL_{IP}, but have sufficiently large amounts of parallel TL_{MT}-TL_{PE} data, we can still build an APE model between TL_{MT} and TL_{PE}.

Translations provided by state-of-the-art MT systems suffer from a number of errors including incorrect lexical choice, word ordering, word insertion, word deletion, etc. The APE work presented in this paper is an effort to improve the MT output by rectifying some of these errors. For this purpose we use a deep neural network (DNN) based approach. Neural MT (NMT) (Kalchbrenner and Blunsom, 2013; Cho et al., 2014a; Cho et al., 2014b) is a newly emerging approach to MT. On the one hand DNNs represent language in a continuous vector space which eases the modelling of semantic similarities (or distance) between phrases or sentences, and on the other hand it can also consider contextual information, e.g.,

Proceedings of the 54th Annual Meeting of the Association for Computational Linguistics, pages 281–286,
Berlin, Germany, August 7-12, 2016. ©2016 Association for Computational Linguistics

utilizing all available history information in deciding the next target word, which is not an easy task to model with standard APE systems.

Unlike phrase-based APE systems (Simard et al., 2007a; Simard et al., 2007b; Pal, 2015; Pal et al., 2015), our NNAPE system builds and trains a single, large neural network that accepts a 'draft' translation (TL_{MT}) and outputs an improved translation (TL_{PE}).

The remainder of the paper is organized as follows. Section 2 gives an overview of relevant related work. The proposed NNAPE system is described in detail in Section 3. We present the experimental setup in Section 4. Section 5 presents the results of automatic and human evaluation together with some analysis. Section 6 concludes the paper and provides avenues for future work.

2 Related Work

APE has proved to be an effective remedy to some of the inaccuracies in raw MT output. APE approaches cover a wide methodological range. Simard et al. (2007a) and Simard et al. (2007b) applied SMT for post-editing, handling the repetitive nature of errors typically made by rule-based MT systems. Lagarda et al. (2009) used statistical information from the trained SMT models for post-editing of rule-based MT output. Rosa et al. (2012) and Mareček et al. (2011) applied a rule-based approach to APE on the morphological level. Denkowski (2015) developed a method for real time integration of post-edited MT output into the translation model by extracting a grammar for each input sentence. Recent studies have even shown that the quality of MT plus PE can exceed the quality of human translation (Fiederer and OBrien, 2009; Koehn, 2009; DePalma and Kelly, 2009) as well as the productivity (Zampieri and Vela, 2014) in some cases.

Recently, a number of papers have presented the application of neural networks in MT (Kalchbrenner and Blunsom, 2013; ?; Cho et al., 2014b; Bahdanau et al., 2014). These approaches typically consist of two components: an **encoder** encodes a source sentence and a **decoder** decodes into a target sentence.

In this paper we present a neural network based approach to automatic PE (NNAPE). Our NNAPE model is inspired by the MT work of Bahdanau et al. (2014) which is based on bidirectional recurrent neural networks (RNN). Unlike Bahdanau et al. (2014), we use LSTMs rather than GRUs as hidden units. RNNs allow processing of arbitrary length sequences, however, they are susceptible to the problem of vanishing and exploding gradients (Bengio et al., 1994). To tackle vanishing gradients in RNNs, two architectures are generally used: gated recurrent units (GRU) (Cho et al., 2014b) and long-short term memory (LSTM) (Hochreiter and Schmidhuber, 1997). According to empirical studies (Chung et al., 2014; Józefowicz et al., 2015) both architectures yield comparable performance. GRUs tend to train faster than LSTMs. On the other hand, given sufficient amounts of training data, LSTMs may lead to better results. Since our task is monolingual and we have more than 200K sentence pairs for training, we use a full LSTM (as the hidden units) to model our NNAPE system.

The model takes TL_{MT} as input and provides TL_{PE} as output. To the best of our knowledge the work presented in this paper is the first approach to APE using neural networks.

3 Neural Network based APE

The NNAPE system is based on a bidirectional (forward-backward) RNN based encoder-decoder.

3.1 A Bidirectional RNN APE Encoder-Decoder

Our NNAPE model encodes a variable-length sequence of TL_{MT} (e.g. $\mathbf{x} = x_1, x_2, x_3...x_m$) into a fixed-length vector representation and then decodes a given fixed-length vector representation back into a variable-length sequence of TL_{PE} (e.g. $\mathbf{y} = y_1, y_2, y_3...y_n$). Input and output sequence lengths, m and n, may differ.

A Bidirectional RNN encoder consists of forward and backward RNNs. The forward RNN encoder reads in each $\mathbf{x}$ sequentially from x_1 to x_m and at each time step t, the hidden state h_t of the RNN is updated by using a non-linear activation function f (Equation 1), an elementwise logistic sigmoid with an LSTM unit.

$$h_t = f(h_{t-1}, x_t) \qquad (1)$$

Similarly, the backward RNN encoder reads the input sequence and calculates hidden states in reverse direction (i.e. x_m to x_1 and h_m to h_1 respectively). After reading the entire input sequence, the hidden state of the RNN is provided a summary c context vector ('C' in Figure 1) of the whole input sequence.

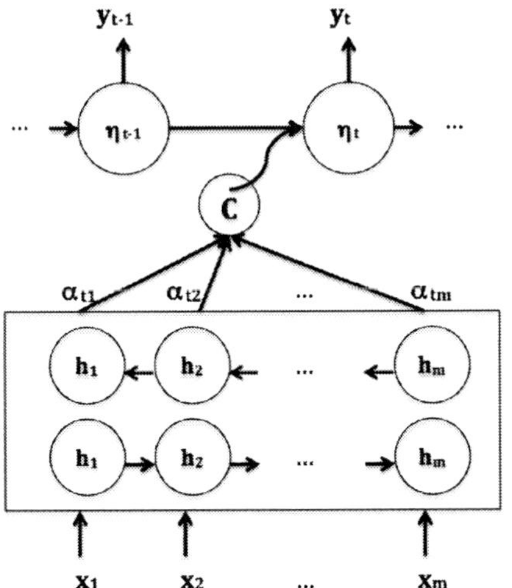

Figure 1: Generating the tth TL_{PE} word y_t for a given TL_{MT} (**x**) by our NNAPE System.

The decoder is another RNN trained to generate the output sequence by predicting the next word y_t given the hidden state η_t and the context vector c_t (c.f., Figure1). The hidden state of the decoder at time t is computed as given below.

$$P(y_t|y_1,...y_{t-1},\mathbf{x}) = f(\eta_t, y_{t-1}, c_t) \quad (2)$$

$$\eta_t = f(\eta_{t-1}, y_{t-1}, c_t) \quad (3)$$

The context vector c_t can be computed as

$$c_t = \sum_{i=1}^{m} \alpha_{ti} h_i \quad (4)$$

Here, α_{ti}, is the weight of each h_i and can be computed as

$$\alpha_{ti} = \frac{exp(e_{ti})}{\sum_{j=1}^{m} exp(e_{tj})} \quad (5)$$

where $e_{ti} = a(\eta_{t-1}, h_i)$ is an alignment model which provides a matching score between the inputs around position i and the output at position t. The alignment score is based on the ith annotation h_i of the input sentence and the RNN hidden state η_{t-1}. The alignment model itself is a feed forward neural network which directly computes a soft alignment that allows the gradient of the cost function to be backpropagated through. The gradient is used to train the alignment model as well as the TL_{MT}–TL_{PE} translation model jointly.

The alignment model is computed $m \times n$ times as follows:

$$a(\eta_{t-1}, h_i) = v_a^T \tanh(W_a \eta_{t-1} + U_a h_i) \quad (6)$$

where $W_a \in \mathbf{R}^{n_h \times n_h}$, $U_a \in \mathbf{R}^{n_h \times 2n_h}$ and $v_a \in \mathbf{R}^{n_h}$ are the weight matrices of n_h hidden units.

4 Experiments

We evaluate the model on an English–Italian APE task, which is detailed in the following subsections.

4.1 Data

The training data used for the experiments was developed in the MateCat[1] project and consists of 312K TL_{MT}–TL_{PE} parallel sentences. The parallel sentences are (English to) Italian MT output and their corresponding (human) post-edited Italian translations. Google Translate (GT) is the MT engine which provided the original Italian TL_{MT} output. The data includes sentences from the Europarl corpus as well as news commentaries. Since the data contains some non-Italian sentences, we applied automatic language identification (Shuyo, 2010) in order to select only Italian sentences. Automatic cleaning and pre-processing of the data was carried out by sorting the entire parallel training corpus based on sentence length, filtering the parallel data on maximum allowable sentence length of 80 and sentence length ratio of 1:2 (either direction), removing duplicates and applying tokenization and punctuation normalization using Moses (Koehn et al., 2007) scripts. After cleaning the corpus we obtained a sentence-aligned TL_{MT}–TL_{PE} parallel corpus containing 213,795 sentence pairs. We randomly extracted 1000 sentence pairs each for the development set and test set from the pre-processed parallel corpus and used the remaining (211,795) as the training corpus. The training data features 57,568 and 61,582 unique word types in TL_{MT} and TL_{PE}, respectively. We chose the 40,000 most frequent words from both TL_{MT} and TL_{PE} to train our NNAPE model. The remaining words which are not among the most frequent words are replaced by a special token ([UNK]). The model was trained for approximately 35 days, which is equivalent to 2,000,000 updates with GPU settings.

4.2 Experimental Settings

Our bidirectional RNN Encoder-Decoder contains 1000 hidden units for the forward backward RNN encoder and 1000 hidden units for the decoder.

---

[1]https://www.matecat.com/

The network is basically a multilateral neural network with a single maxout unit as hidden layer (Goodfellow et al., 2013) to compute the conditional probability of each target word. The word embedding vector dimension is 620 and the size of the maxout hidden layer in the deep output is 500. The number of hidden units in the alignment model is 1000. The model has been trained on a mini-batched stochastic gradient descent (SGD) with 'Adadelta' (Zeiler, 2012). The main reason behind the use of 'Adadelta' is to automatically adapt the learning rate of each parameter ($\epsilon = 10^{-6}$ and $\rho = 0.95$). Each SGD update direction is computed using a mini-batch of 80 sentences.

We compare our NNAPE system with state-of-the-art phrase-based (Simard et al., 2007b) as well as hierarchical phrase-based APE (Pal, 2015) systems. We also compare the output provided by our system against the original GT output. For building the phrase-based and hierarchical phrase-based APE systems, we set maximum phrase length to 7. A 5-gram language model built using KenLM (Heafield, 2011) was used for decoding. System tuning was carried out using both k-best MIRA (Cherry and Foster, 2012) and Minimum Error Rate Training (MERT) (Och, 2003) on the held-out development set (devset). After parameters were tuned, decoding was carried out on the held out test set.

5 Evaluation

The performance of the NNAPE system was evaluated using both automatic and human evaluation methods, as described below.

5.1 Automatic Evaluation

The output of the NNAPE system on the 1000 sentences testset was evaluated using three MT evaluation metrics: BLEU (Papineni et al., 2002), TER (Snover et al., 2006) and Meteor (Denkowski and Lavie, 2011). Table 1 provides a comparison of our neural system performance against the baseline phrase-based APE (S_1), baseline hierarchical phrase-based APE (S_2) and the original GT output. We use a, b, c, and d to indicate statistical significance over GT, S_1, S_2 and our NNAPE system (NN), respectively. For example, the S_2 BLEU score $63.87_{a,b}$ in Table 1 means that the improvement provided by S_2 in BLEU is statistically significant over Google Translator and phrase-based

APE. Table 1 shows that S_1 provides statistically significant ($0.01 < p < 0.04$) improvements over GT across all metrics. Similarly S_2 yields statistically significant ($p < 0.01$) improvements over both GT and S_1 across all metrics. The NN system performs best and results in statistically significant ($p < 0.01$) improvements over all other systems across all metrics. A systematic trend ($NN > S_2 > S_1 > GT$) can be observed in Table 1 and the improvements are consistent across the different metrics. The relative performance gain achieved by NN over GT is highest in TER.

System	BLEU	TER	METEOR
GT (a)	61.26	30.94	72.73
S_1 (b)	62.54_a	29.49_a	73.21_a
S_2 (c)	$63.87_{a,b}$	$28.67_{a,b}$	$73.63_{a,b}$
NN (d)	$\mathbf{65.22}_{a,b,c}$	$\mathbf{27.56}_{a,b,c}$	$\mathbf{74.59}_{a,b,c}$

Table 1: Automatic evaluation.

5.2 Human Evaluation

Human evaluation was carried out by four professional translators, native speakers of Italian, with professional translation experience between one and two years. Since human evaluation is very costly and time consuming, it was carried out on a small portion of the test set consisting of 145 randomly sampled sentences and only compared NN with the original GT output. We used a polling scheme with three different options. Translators choose which of the two (GT or NN) outputs is the better translation or whether there is a tie ('uncertain'). To avoid any bias towards any particular system, the order in which two system outputs are presented is randomized so that the translators do not know which system they are contributing their votes to.

We analyzed the outcome of the voting process (4 translators each giving 145 votes) and found that the winning NN system received 285 (49.13%) votes compared to 99 (17.07%) votes received by the GT system, while the rest of the votes (196, 33.79%) go to the 'uncertain' option. We measured pairwise inter-annotator agreement between the translators by computing Cohen's κ coefficient (Cohen, 1960) reported in Table 2. The overall κ coefficient is 0.330. According to (Landis and Koch, 1977) this correlation coefficient can be interpreted as fair.

Cohen's κ	T1	T2	T3	T4
T1	-	0.141	0.424	0.398
T2	0.141	-	0.232	0.540
T3	0.424	0.232	-	0.248
T4	0.398	0.540	0.248	-

Table 2: Pairwise correlation between translators in the evaluation process.

5.3 Analysis

The results of the automatic evaluation show that NNAPE has advantages over the phrase-based and hierarchical APE approaches. On manual inspection we found that the NNAPE system drastically reduced the preposition insertion and deletion error in Italian GT output and was also able to handle the improper use of prepositions and determiners (e.g. "states" $\rightarrow$ "dei stati", "the states" $\rightarrow$ "gli stati"). The use of a bidirectional RNN neural model makes the model sensitive towards contexts. Moreover, NNAPE captures global reordering by capturing contextual features which helps to reduce word ordering errors to some extent.

6 Conclusion and Future Work

The NNAPE system provides statistically significant improvements over existing state-of-the-art APE models and produces significantly better translations than GT which is very difficult to beat. This enhancement in translation quality through APE should reduce human PE effort. Human evaluation revealed that the NNAPE generated PE translations contain less lexical errors, NNAPE rectifies erroneous word insertions and deletions, and improves word ordering.

In future, we would like to test our system in a real-life translation scenario to analyze productivity gains in a commercial environment. We also want to extend the APE system by incorporating source language knowledge into the network and compare LSTM against GRU hidden units.

Acknowledgments

We would like to thank all the anonymous reviewers for their feedback. We are also thankful to Translated SRL, Rome, Italy. They have shared their data for the experiments and enabled the manual evaluation of our system.

Santanu Pal is supported by the People Programme (Marie Curie Actions) of the European Union's Framework Programme (FP7/2007-2013) under REA grant agreement no 317471.

References

Dzmitry Bahdanau, Kyunghyun Cho, and Yoshua Bengio. 2014. Neural Machine Translation by Jointly Learning to Align and Translate. *arXiv preprint arXiv:1409.0473*.

Yoshua Bengio, Patrice Simard, and Paolo Frasconi. 1994. Learning Long-Term Dependencies with Gradient Descent is Difficult. *IEEE Transactions on Neural Networks*, 5(2):157–166.

Colin Cherry and George Foster. 2012. Batch Tuning Strategies for Statistical Machine Translation. In *Proceedings of the 2012 Conference of the North American Chapter of the Association for Computational Linguistics: Human Language Technologies*, pages 427–436.

KyungHyun Cho, Bart van Merrienboer, Dzmitry Bahdanau, and Yoshua Bengio. 2014a. On the Properties of Neural Machine Translation: Encoder-Decoder Approaches. *CoRR*, abs/1409.1259.

Kyunghyun Cho, Bart Van Merriënboer, Çalar Gülçehre, Dzmitry Bahdanau, Fethi Bougares, Holger Schwenk, and Yoshua Bengio. 2014b. Learning Phrase Representations using RNN Encoder–Decoder for Statistical Machine Translation. In *Proceedings of the 2014 Conference on Empirical Methods in Natural Language Processing (EMNLP)*, pages 1724–1734.

Junyoung Chung, Çalar Gülçehre, Kyunghyun Cho, and Yoshua Bengio. 2014. Empirical Evaluation of Gated Recurrent Neural Networks on Sequence Modeling. Technical Report Arxiv report 1412.3555, Université de Montréal.

Jacob Cohen. 1960. A Coefficient of Agreement for Nominal Scales. *Educational and Psychological Measurement*, 20(1):37–46, April.

Michael Denkowski and Alon Lavie. 2011. Meteor 1.3: Automatic Metric for Reliable Optimization and Evaluation of Machine Translation Systems. In *Proceedings of the EMNLP 2011 Workshop on Statistical Machine Translation*, pages 85–91.

Michael Denkowski. 2015. *Machine Translation for Human Translators*. Ph.D. thesis, Carnegie Mellon University.

Donald A. DePalma and Nataly Kelly. 2009. Project Management for Crowdsourced Translation: How User-Translated Content Projects Work in Real Life. *Translation and Localization Project Management: The Art of the Possible*, pages 379–408.

Rebecca Fiederer and Sharon OBrien. 2009. Quality and Machine Translation: a Realistic Objective. *Journal of Specialised Translation*, 11:52–74.

Ian J Goodfellow, David Warde-Farley, Mehdi Mirza, Aaron Courville, and Yoshua Bengio. 2013. Maxout networks. *arXiv preprint arXiv:1302.4389*.

Kenneth Heafield. 2011. KenLM: Faster and Smaller Language Model Queries. In *Proceedings of the Sixth Workshop on Statistical Machine Translation*, pages 187–197.

Sepp Hochreiter and Jürgen Schmidhuber. 1997. Long Short-Term Memory. *Neural Comput.*, 9(8):1735–1780, November.

Rafal Józefowicz, Wojciech Zaremba, and Ilya Sutskever. 2015. An Empirical Exploration of Recurrent Network Architectures. In *Proceedings of the 32nd International Conference on Machine Learning*, pages 2342–2350.

Nal Kalchbrenner and Phil Blunsom. 2013. Recurrent Continuous Translation Models. In *Proceedings of the 2013 Conference on Empirical Methods in Natural Language Processing*, pages 1700–1709.

Philipp Koehn, Hieu Hoang, Alexandra Birch, Chris Callison-Burch, Marcello Federico, Nicola Bertoldi, Brooke Cowan, Wade Shen, Christine Moran, Richard Zens, Chris Dyer, Ondřej Bojar, Alexandra Constantin, and Evan Herbst. 2007. Moses: Open Source Toolkit for Statistical Machine Translation. In *Proceedings of the 45th Annual Meeting of the ACL on Interactive Poster and Demonstration Sessions*, pages 177–180.

Philipp Koehn. 2009. A Process Study of Computeraided Translation. *Machine Translation*, 23(4):241–263.

Antonio Lagarda, Vicent Alabau, Francisco Casacuberta, Roberto Silva, and Enrique Díaz-de Liaño. 2009. Statistical post-editing of a rule-based machine translation system. In *Proceedings of Human Language Technologies: The 2009 Annual Conference of the North American Chapter of the Association for Computational Linguistics, Companion Volume: Short Papers*, NAACL-Short '09, pages 217–220.

J. Richard Landis and Gary G. Koch. 1977. The Measurement of Observer Agreement for Categorical Data. *Biometrics*, 33(1):159–74.

Anne-Marie Loffler-Laurian. 1985. Traduction Automatique et Style. *Babel*, 31(2):70–76.

David Mareček, Rudolf Rosa, Petra Galuščáková, and Ondřej Bojar. 2011. Two-step Translation with Grammatical Post-processing. In *Proceedings of the Sixth Workshop on Statistical Machine Translation*, pages 426–432.

Franz Josef Och. 2003. Minimum Error Rate Training in Statistical Machine Translation. In *Proceedings of the 41st Annual Meeting on Association for Computational Linguistics - Volume 1*, pages 160–167.

Santanu Pal, Mihaela Vela, Sudip Kumar Naskar, and Josef van Genabith. 2015. USAAR-SAPE: An English–Spanish Statistical Automatic Post-Editing System. In *Proceedings of the Tenth Workshop on Statistical Machine Translation*, pages 216–221.

Santanu Pal. 2015. Statistical Automatic Post Editing. In *The Proceedings of the EXPERT Scientific and Technological workshop*.

Kishore Papineni, Salim Roukos, Todd Ward, and Wei-Jing Zhu. 2002. BLEU: A Method for Automatic Evaluation of Machine Translation. In *Proceedings of the 40th Annual Meeting on Association for Computational Linguistics*, ACL '02, pages 311–318.

Rudolf Rosa, David Mareček, and Ondřej Dušek. 2012. DEPFIX: A System for Automatic Correction of Czech MT Outputs. In *Proceedings of the Seventh Workshop on Statistical Machine Translation*, pages 362–368.

Nakatani Shuyo. 2010. Language Detection Library for Java.

Michel Simard, Cyril Goutte, and Pierre Isabelle. 2007a. Statistical Phrase-Based Post-Editing. In *Human Language Technologies 2007: The Conference of the North American Chapter of the Association for Computational Linguistics; Proceedings of the Main Conference*, pages 508–515.

Michel Simard, Nicola Ueffing, Pierre Isabelle, and Roland Kuhn. 2007b. Rule-Based Translation with Statistical Phrase-Based Post-Editing. In *Proceedings of the Second Workshop on Statistical Machine Translation*, pages 203–206.

Matthew Snover, Bonnie Dorr, Richard Schwartz, Linnea Micciulla, and John Makhoul. 2006. A study of Translation Edit Rate with Targeted Human Annotation. In *Proceedings of association for machine translation in the Americas*, pages 223–231.

TAUS Report. 2010. Post editing in practice. Technical report, TAUS.

Tony Veale and Andy Way. 1997. Gaijin: A Bootstrapping, Template-driven Approach to Example-based MT. In *Proceedings of the Recent Advances in Natural Language Processing*.

Marcos Zampieri and Mihaela Vela. 2014. Quantifying the Influence of MT Output in the Translators Performance: A Case Study in Technical Translation. In *Proceedings of the EACL Workshop on Humans and Computer-assisted Translation (HaCat)*, pages 93–98.

Matthew D. Zeiler. 2012. ADADELTA: An Adaptive Learning Rate Method. *arXiv:1212.5701 [cs.LG]*.

An Unsupervised Method for Automatic Translation Memory Cleaning

Masoud Jalili Sabet[1]**, Matteo Negri**[2]**, Marco Turchi**[2]**, Eduard Barbu**[3]
[1] School of Electrical and Computer Engineering, University of Tehran, Iran
[2] Fondazione Bruno Kessler, Trento, Italy
[3] Translated srl, Rome, Italy
`jalili.masoud@ut.ac.ir`
`{negri,turchi}@fbk.eu`
`eduard@translated.net`

Abstract

We address the problem of automatically cleaning a large-scale Translation Memory (TM) in a fully unsupervised fashion, i.e. without human-labelled data. We approach the task by: *i)* designing a set of features that capture the similarity between two text segments in different languages, *ii)* use them to induce reliable training labels for a subset of the translation units (TUs) contained in the TM, and *iii)* use the automatically labelled data to train an ensemble of binary classifiers. We apply our method to clean a test set composed of 1,000 TUs randomly extracted from the English-Italian version of MyMemory, the world's largest public TM. Our results show competitive performance not only against a strong baseline that exploits machine translation, but also against a state-of-the-art method that relies on human-labelled data.

1 Introduction

Translation Memories (TMs) are one of the main sources of knowledge supporting human translation with the so-called Computer-assisted Translation (CAT) tools. A TM is a database that stores (*source, target*) segments called translation units (TUs). These segments can be sub-sentential fragments, full sentences or even paragraphs in two languages and, ideally, they are perfect translations of each other. Their use in a CAT framework is based on computing a "fuzzy match" score between an input sentence to be translated and the left-hand side (the source) of each TU stored in the TM. If the score is above a certain threshold, the right-hand side (the target) is presented to the user as a translation suggestion. When translating a document with a CAT tool, the user can store each translated (*source, target*) pair in the TM for future use. Each newly added TU contributes to the growth of the TM which, as time goes by, will become more and more useful to the user. Due to such constant growth, in which they evolve incorporating users style and terminology, the so-called private TMs represent an invaluable asset for individual translators and translation companies. Collaboratively-created public TMs grow in a less controlled way (e.g. incorporating potentially noisy TUs supplied by anonymous contributors or automatically extracted from the Web) but still remain a practical resource for the translators' community at large.

Together with the *quantity*, the *quality* of the stored material is a crucial factor that determines the usefulness of the TM and, all in all, its value. For this reason, the growth of the TM should go hand in hand with its continuous maintenance. This problem is usually addressed through manual (hence costly) revision, or by applying simple (hence approximate) automatic filtering routines. Advanced automatic methods for tidying up an existing TM would contribute to reduce management costs, increase its quality, speed-up and simplify the daily work of human translators.

Focusing on TM maintenance, we explore an automatic method to clean a large-scale TM by identifying the TUs in which the target is a poor translation of the source. Its main strength is the reliance on a fully unsupervised approach, which makes it independent from the availability of human-labelled data. As it allows us to avoid the burden of acquiring a (possibly large) set of annotated TUs, our method is cost-effective and highly portable across languages and TMs. This contrasts with supervised strategies like the one presented in (Barbu, 2015) or those applied in closely-related tasks such as cross-lingual seman-

Proceedings of the 54th Annual Meeting of the Association for Computational Linguistics, pages 287–292,
Berlin, Germany, August 7-12, 2016. ©2016 Association for Computational Linguistics

	ENGLISH	ITALIAN *(EN translation)*
a	traditional costumes of Iceland	costumi tradizionali dell'islanda *(traditional costumes of iceland)*
b	Active substances: per dose of 2 ml:	Principi attivi Per ogni dose da 2 ml: *(Active substances Per dose of 2 ml:)*
c	The length of time of ...	La durata delperiodo di ... *(The length oftime of ...)*
d	... 4 weeks after administration ...	... 4 settimane dopo la somministarzione ... *(... 4 weeks after somministarzione ...)*
e	5. ensure the organization of ...	5. *5.*
f	Read package leaflet	Per lo smaltimento leggere il foglio illustrativo *For disposal read the package leaflet*
g	beef chuck roast	chuck carne assada *?chuck meat ?assada*
h	is an integral part of the contract	risultato della stagione *(result of the season)*

Table 1: Examples of problematic translation units mined from the English-Italian version of MyMemory.

tic textual similarity,[1] cross-lingual textual entailment (Negri et al., 2013), and quality estimation (QE) for MT (Specia et al., 2009; Mehdad et al., 2012; C. de Souza et al., 2014; Turchi et al., 2014; C. de Souza et al., 2015). Also most of the previous approaches to bilingual data mining/cleaning for statistical MT rely on supervised learning (Resnik and Smith, 2003; Munteanu and Marcu, 2005; Jiang et al., 2009). Unsupervised solutions, like the one proposed by Cui et al. (2013) usually rely on redundancy-based approaches that reward parallel segments containing phrase pairs that are frequent in a training corpus. This idea is well-motivated in the SMT framework but scarcely applicable in the CAT scenario, in which it is crucial to manage and reward rare phrases as a source of useful suggestions for difficult translations.

2 The problem

We consider as "problematic TUs" those containing translation errors whose correction during the translation process can reduce translators' productivity. Table 1 provides some examples extracted from the English-Italian training data recently released for the NLP4TM 2016 shared task on cleaning translation memories.[2] As can be seen in the table, TU quality can be affected by a variety of problems. These include: *1.* minor formatting errors like the casing issue in example (a), the casing+punctuation issue in (b) and the missing space in (c), *2.* misspelling errors like the one in (d),[3] *3.* missing or extra words in the translation, as in (e)

and (f), *4.* situations in which the translation is awkward (due to mistranslations and/or untranslated terms) like in (g) or it is completely unrelated to the source sentence like in (h).

Especially in the case of collaboratively-created public TMs, these issues are rather frequent. For instance, in the NLP4TM shared task training data (randomly sampled from MyMemory) the instances affected by any of these error types are about 38% of the total.

3 Method

Our unsupervised TM cleaning method exploits the independent views of three groups of similarity-based features. These allow us to infer a binary label for a subset of the TUs stored in a large-scale TM. The inferred labels are used to train an ensemble of binary classifiers, specialized to capture different aspects of the general notion of translation quality. Finally, the ensemble of classifiers is used to label the rest of the TM. To minimize overfitting issues, each base classifier exploits features that are different from those used to infer the label of the training instances.

3.1 General workflow

Given a TM to be cleaned, our approach consists of two main steps: *i)* label inference and *ii)* training of the base classifiers.

Label inference. The first step aims to infer a reliable binary label (1 or 0, respectively for "good" and "bad") for a subset Z of unlabelled TUs randomly selected from the input TM. To this aim, the three groups of features described in §3.2 (say A, B, C) are first organised into combinations of two

---

[1] http://alt.qcri.org/semeval2016/task1/

[2] http://rgcl.wlv.ac.uk/nlp4tm2016/shared-task/

[3] *"somministARzione"* instead of *"somministRAzione"*.

groups (i.e. AB, AC, BC). As the features are different in nature, each combination reflects a particular "view" of the data, which is different from the other combinations.

Then, for each TU in Z, we extract the features belonging to each combination. Being designed and normalized to return a similarity score in the [0-1] interval, the result of feature extraction is a vector of numbers whose average value can be computed to sort each TU from the best (avg. close to 1, indicating a high similarity between source and target) to the worst (avg. close to 0). This is done separately for each feature combination, so that the independent views they provide will produce three different ranked lists for the TUs in Z.

Finally, the three ranked lists are processed to obtain different sets of positive/negative examples, whose variable size depends on the amount of TUs taken from the top and the bottom of the lists.

Training of the base classifiers. Each of the three inferred annotations of Z (say z^1, z^2, z^3) reflects the specific view of the two groups of features used to obtain it (i.e. AB for z^1, AC for z^2, BC for z^3). Based on each view, we train a binary classifier using the third group of features (i.e. C for z^1, B for z^2, A for z^3). This results in three base classifiers: $\hat{A}$, $\hat{B}$ and $\hat{C}$ that, in spite of the same shared purpose, are by construction different from each other. This allows us to create an ensemble of base classifiers and to minimize the risk of overfitting, in which we would have incurred by training one single classifier with the same features (A,B,C) used as labelling criterion.

3.2 Features

Our features capture different aspects of the similarity between the source and the target of a TU. The degree of similarity is mapped into a numeric score in the [0-1] interval. The full set consists of 31 features, which are organized in three groups.[4]

Basic features (8). This group represents a slightly improved variant of those proposed by Barbu (2015). They aim to capture translation quality by looking at surface aspects, such as the possible mismatches in the number of dates, numbers, URLs and XML tags present in the source and target segments.[5] The consistency between the actual source and target languages and those indicated in the TM is also verified. Language identification, carried out with the Langid tool (Lui and Baldwin, 2012), is a highly predictive feature since sometimes the two languages are inverted or even completely different. Other features model the similarity between source and target by computing the direct and inverse ratio between the number of characters and words, as well as the average word length in the two segments. Finally, two features look at the presence of uncommon character or word repetitions.

QE-derived features (18). This group contains features borrowed from the closely-related task of MT quality estimation, in which the complexity of the source, the fluency of the target and the adequacy between source and target are modeled as quality indicators. Focusing on the adequacy aspect, we exploit a subset of the features proposed by Camargo de Souza et al. (2013). They use word alignment information to link source and target words and capture the quantity of meaning preserved by the translation. For each segment of a TU, word alignment information is used to calculate: *i)* the proportion of aligned and unaligned word n-grams (n=1,2), *ii)* the ratio between the longest aligned/unaligned word sequence and the length of the segment, *iii)* the average length of the aligned/unaligned word sequences, and *iv)* the position of the first/last unaligned word, normalized by the length of the segment. Word alignment models were trained on the whole TM, using MGIZA++ (Gao and Vogel, 2008).

Word embeddings (5). This is a newly developed group of features that rely on cross-lingual word embeddings to identify "good" and "bad" TUs. Cross-lingual word embeddings provide a common vector representation for words in different languages and allow us to build features that look at the same time at the source and target segments. Cross-lingual word embeddings are computed using the method proposed in (Søgaard et al., 2015). Differently from the original paper, which takes advantage of bilingual documents as atomic concepts to bridge the two languages, we use the TUs contained in the whole TM to build the embeddings. Given a TU and a 100-dimensional vector representation of each word in the source and target segments, the new features are: *i)* the cosine similarity between source and

---

[4]Implemented in TMop: https://github.com/hlt-mt/TMOP
[5]Being these feature very sparse, we collapsed them into a single one, which is set to 1 if any feature has value 1.

target segment vectors obtained by averaging (or using the median) the source and target word vectors; *ii)* the average embedding alignment score obtained by computing the cosine similarity between each source word and all the target words and averaging over the largest cosine score of each source word; *iii)* the average cosine similarity between source/target word alignments; *iv)* a score that merges features *(ii)* and *(iii)* by complementing word alignments (obtained using MGIZA++) with the alignments obtained from word embedding and averaging all the alignment weights.

4   Experiments

Data. We experiment with the English-Italian version of MyMemory,[6] the world's largest public TM. This collaboratively built TM contains about 11M TUs coming from heterogeneous sources: aggregated private TMs or automatically extracted from the web/corpora, and anonymous contributions of (*source, target*) bi-segments. Being large and free, the TM is of great utility for professional translators. Its uncontrolled sources, however, call for accurate cleaning methods (e.g. to make it more accurate, smaller and manageable). From the TM we randomly extracted: *i)* subsets of variable size to automatically obtain training data for the base classifiers and *ii)* a collection of 2,500 TUs manually annotated with binary labels. Data annotation was done by two Italian native speakers properly trained with the same guidelines prepared by the TM owner for periodic manual revisions. After agreement computation (Cohen's kappa is 0.7838), a reconciliation ended up with about 65% positive and 35% negative examples. This pool is randomly split in two parts. One (1,000 instances) is used as test set for our evaluation. The other (1,500 instances) is used to replicate the approach of Barbu (2015) used as term of comparison.

Learning algorithm. Our base classifiers are trained with the Extremely Randomized Trees algorithm (Geurts et al., 2006), optimized using 10-fold cross-validation in a randomized search process and combined in a majority voting schema.

Evaluation metric. To handle the imbalanced (65%-35%) data distribution, and equally reward the correct classification on both classes, we evaluate performance in terms of balanced accuracy

(BA), computed as the average of the accuracies on the two classes (Brodersen et al., 2010).

Terms of comparison. We evaluate our approach against two terms of comparison, both stronger than the trivial random baseline achieving a BA of 50.0%. The first competitor (MT-based) is a translation-based solution that exploits Bing translator[7] to render the source segment of a TU in the same language of the target. Then, the similarity between the translated source and the target segment is measured in terms of Translation Edit Rate (TER (Snover et al., 2006)). The TU is marked as "good" if the TER is smaller than 0.4 ("bad" otherwise). This value is chosen based on the findings of Turchi et al. (2013), which suggests that only for TER values lower than 0.4 human translators consider MT suggestions as good enough for being post-editable. In our scenario we hence assume that "good" TUs are those featuring a small TER distance between the target and an automatic translation of the source.

The second competitor (Barbu15) is the supervised approach proposed by Barbu (2015), which leverages human-labelled data to train an SVM binary classifier. To the best of our knowledge, it represents the state-of-the-art in this task.

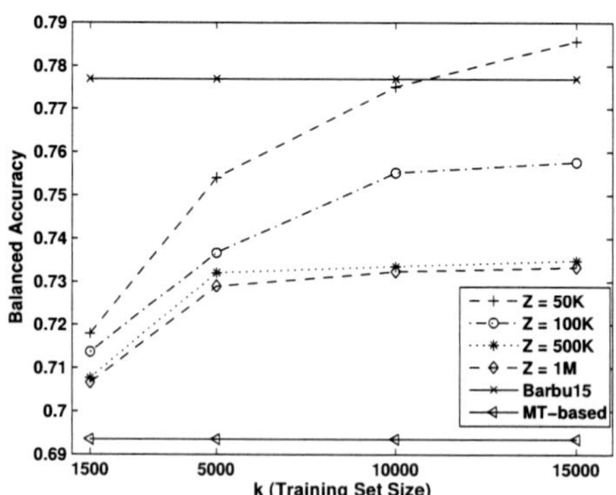

Figure 1: BA results as a function of Z and k.

5   Results and Discussion

The result of the "label inference" step described in §3.1 is a set of automatically labelled TUs to train the base classifiers. Positive and negative examples are respectively the top and the bottom k elements extracted from a list of TUs (of size Z) ranked according to the inferred similarity between source and target. In this process, the size

---

[6]https://mymemory.translated.net/

[7]https://www.bing.com/translator/

of the list and the value of k clearly have influence on the separability between the training instances belonging to the two classes. Long lists and small values of k will result in highly polarized training data, with a very high similarity between the instances assigned to each class and feature values respectively close to 1 and 0. Vice-versa, short lists and large values of k will result in less separable training data, with higher variability in the points assigned to each class and in the respective feature values. In light of this trade-off, we analyse performance variations as a function of: *i)* the amount (Z) of data considered to initialise the label inference step, and *ii)* the amount (k) of training instances used to learn the base classifiers. For the first dimension, we consider four values: 50K (a value compatible with the size of most of the existing TMs), 100K, 500K and 1M units (a value compatible only with a handful of large-scale TMs). For the second dimension we experiment with four balanced training sets, respectively containing: 1.5K (the same amount used in (Barbu, 2015)), 5K, 10K and 15K instances.

Figure 1 illustrates the performance of our TM cleaning method for different values of Z and k. Each of the four dashed learning curves refers to one of the four chosen values of Z. BA variations for the same line are obtained by increasing the number of training instances k and averaging over three random samples of size Z. As can be seen from the figure, the results obtained by our classifiers trained with the inferred data always outperform the `MT-based` system and, in one case (Z=50K, k=15K), also the `Barbu15` classifier trained with human labelled data.[8] Considering that all our training data are collected without any human intervention, hence eliminating the burden and the high costs of the annotation process, this is an interesting result.

Overall, for the same value of k, smaller values of Z consistently show higher performance. At the same time, for the same value of Z, increasing k consistently yields higher results. Such improvements, however, are less evident when the pool of TUs used for the label inference step is larger (Z>100K). These observations confirm the intuition that classifiers' performance is highly influenced by the relation between the amount and the polarization of the training data. Indeed, looking at the average feature values used to infer the positive and negative instances, we noticed that, for the considered values of k, these scores are closer to 0 and 1 for the 1M curve than for the 50K curve. In the former case, highly polarized training data limit the generalisation capability of the base classifiers (and their ability, for instance, to correctly label the borderline test instances), which results in lower BA results.

Nevertheless, it's worth remarking that our larger value of k (15K) represents 30% of the data in the case of Z=50K, but just 1.5% of the data in case of Z=1M. This suggests that for large values of Z, more training points would be probably needed to introduce enough variance in the data and improve over the almost flat curves shown in Figure 1. Exploring this possibility was out of the scope of this initial analysis but would be doable by applying scalable algorithms capable to manage larger quantities of training data (up to 300K, in the case of Z=1M). For the time being, a statistically significant improvement of $\sim$1 BA point over a supervised method in the most normal conditions (Z=50K) is already a promising step.

6 Conclusion

We presented a fully unsupervised method to remove useless TUs from a large-scale TM. Focusing on the identification of wrongly translated segments, we exploited the independent views of different sets of features to: *i)* infer a binary label for a certain amount of TUs, and *ii)* use the automatically labelled units as training data for an ensemble of binary classifiers. Such independent labelling/training routines exploit the "wisdom of the features" to bypass the need of human annotations and obtain competitive performance. Our results are not only better than a strong MT-based baseline, but they also outperform a state-of-the-art approach relying on human-labelled data.

Acknowledgments

This work has been partially supported by the EC-funded projects ModernMT (H2020 grant agreement no. 645487) and EXPERT (FP7 grant agreement no. 317471). The work carried out at FBK by Masoud Jalili Sabet was sponsored by the EAMT Summer internships 2015 program. The authors would like to thank Anders Søgaard for sharing the initial version of the code for computing word embeddings.

---

[8] Improvements are statistically significant with $p < 0.05$, measured by approximate randomization (Noreen, 1989).

References

Eduard Barbu. 2015. Spotting False Translation Segments in Translation Memories. In *Proceedings of the Workshop Natural Language Processing for Translation Memories*, pages 9–16, Hissar, Bulgaria, September.

Kay Henning Brodersen, Cheng Soon Ong, Klaas Enno Stephan, and Joachim M. Buhmann. 2010. The Balanced Accuracy and Its Posterior Distribution. In *Proceedings of the 2010 20th International Conference on Pattern Recognition*, ICPR '10, pages 3121–3124, Istanbul, Turkey, August.

José G. C. de Souza, Jesús González-Rubio, Christian Buck, Marco Turchi, and Matteo Negri. 2014. FBK-UPV-UEdin participation in the WMT14 Quality Estimation shared-task. In *Proceedings of the Ninth Workshop on Statistical Machine Translation*, pages 322–328, Baltimore, Maryland, USA, June.

José G. C. de Souza, Matteo Negri, Elisa Ricci, and Marco Turchi. 2015. Online Multitask Learning for Machine Translation Quality Estimation. In *Proceedings of the 53rd Annual Meeting of the Association for Computational Linguistics (Volume 1: Long Papers)*, pages 219–228, Beijing, China, July.

José Guilherme Camargo de Souza, Christian Buck, Marco Turchi, and Matteo Negri. 2013. FBK-UEdin Participation to the WMT13 Quality Estimation Shared Task. In *Proceedings of the Eighth Workshop on Statistical Machine Translation*, pages 352–358, Sofia, Bulgaria, August.

Lei Cui, Dongdong Zhang, Shujie Liu, Mu Li, and Ming Zhou. 2013. Bilingual data cleaning for smt using graph-based random walk. In *Proceedings of the 51st Annual Meeting of the Association for Computational Linguistics (Volume 2: Short Papers)*, pages 340–345, Sofia, Bulgaria, August.

Qin Gao and Stephan Vogel. 2008. Parallel implementations of word alignment tool. In *In Proceedings of the ACL 2008 Software Engineering, Testing, and Quality Assurance Workshop*, pages 49–57, Columbus, Ohio, USA, June.

Pierre Geurts, Damien Ernst, and Louis Wehenkel. 2006. Extremely randomized trees. *Machine learning*, 63(1):3–42.

Long Jiang, Shiquan Yang, Ming Zhou, Xiaohua Liu, and Qingsheng Zhu. 2009. Mining bilingual data from the web with adaptively learnt patterns. In *Proceedings of the Joint Conference of the 47th Annual Meeting of the ACL and the 4th International Joint Conference on Natural Language Processing of the AFNLP*, pages 870–878, Suntec, Singapore, August.

Marco Lui and Timothy Baldwin. 2012. langid.py: An Off-the-shelf Language Identification Tool. In *Proceedings of the ACL 2012 System Demonstrations*, pages 25–30, Jeju Island, Korea, July.

Yashar Mehdad, Matteo Negri, and Marcello Federico. 2012. Match without a Referee: Evaluating MT Adequacy without Reference Translations. In *Proceedings of the Machine Translation Workshop (WMT2012)*, pages 171–180, Montréal, Canada, June.

Dragos Stefan Munteanu and Daniel Marcu. 2005. Improving machine translation performance by exploiting non-parallel corpora. *Computational Linguistics*, 31(4):477–504, December.

Matteo Negri, Alessandro Marchetti, Yashar Mehdad, Luisa Bentivogli, and Danilo Giampiccolo. 2013. Semeval-2013 Task 8: Crosslingual Textual Entailment for Content Synchronization. In *Proceedings of the 7th International Workshop on Semantic Evaluation (SemEval 2013)*, pages 25–33, Atlanta, Georgia, USA, June.

Erik W. Noreen. 1989. Computer-intensive methods for testing hypotheses: an introduction. *Wiley Interscience*.

Philip Resnik and Noah A. Smith. 2003. The web as a parallel corpus. *Computational Linguistics*, 29(3):349–380.

Matthew Snover, Bonnie Dorr, Richard Schwartz, Linnea Micciulla, and John Makhoul. 2006. A Study of Translation Edit Rate with Targeted Human Annotation. In *Proceedings of Association for Machine Translation in the Americas*, pages 223–231, Cambridge, Massachusetts, USA, August.

Anders Søgaard, Željko Agić, Héctor Martínez Alonso, Barbara Plank, Bernd Bohnet, and Anders Johannsen. 2015. Inverted indexing for cross-lingual NLP. In *Proceedings of the 53rd Annual Meeting of the Association for Computational Linguistics and the 7th International Joint Conference on Natural Language Processing (Volume 1: Long Papers)*, pages 1713–1722, Beijing, China, July.

Lucia Specia, Nicola Cancedda, Marc Dymetman, Marco Turchi, and Nello Cristianini. 2009. Estimating the Sentence-level Quality of Machine Translation Systems. In *Proceedings of the 13th Annual Conference of the European Association for Machine Translation (EAMT-2009)*, pages 28–35, Barcelona, Spain.

Marco Turchi, Matteo Negri, and Marcello Federico. 2013. Coping with the Subjectivity of Human Judgements in MT Quality Estimation. In *Proceedings of the Eighth Workshop on Statistical Machine Translation*, pages 240–251, Sofia, Bulgaria, August.

Marco Turchi, Antonios Anastasopoulos, José G. C. de Souza, and Matteo Negri. 2014. Adaptive Quality Estimation for Machine Translation. In *Proceedings of the 52nd Annual Meeting of the Association for Computational Linguistics (Volume 1: Long Papers)*, pages 710–720, Baltimore, Maryland, USA, June.

Exponentially Decaying Bag-of-Words Input Features for Feed-Forward Neural Network in Statistical Machine Translation

Jan-Thorsten Peter, Weiyue Wang, Hermann Ney
Human Language Technology and Pattern Recognition, Computer Science Department
RWTH Aachen University, 52056 Aachen, Germany
{peter,wwang,ney}@cs.rwth-aachen.de

Abstract

Recently, neural network models have achieved consistent improvements in statistical machine translation. However, most networks only use one-hot encoded input vectors of words as their input. In this work, we investigated the exponentially decaying bag-of-words input features for feed-forward neural network translation models and proposed to train the decay rates along with other weight parameters. This novel bag-of-words model improved our phrase-based state-of-the-art system, which already includes a neural network translation model, by up to 0.5% BLEU and 0.6% TER on three different translation tasks and even achieved a similar performance to the bidirectional LSTM translation model.

1 Introduction

Neural network models have recently gained much attention in research on statistical machine translation. Several groups have reported strong improvements over state-of-the-art baselines when combining phrase-based translation with feed-forward neural network-based models (FFNN) (Schwenk et al., 2006; Vaswani et al., 2013; Schwenk, 2012; Devlin et al., 2014), as well as with recurrent neural network models (RNN) (Sundermeyer et al., 2014). Even in alternative translation systems they showed remarkable performance (Sutskever et al., 2014; Bahdanau et al., 2015).

The main drawback of a feed-forward neural network model compared to a recurrent neural network model is that it can only have a limited context length on source and target sides. Using the *Bag-of-Words* (BoW) model as additional input of a neural network based language model, (Mikolov et al., 2015) have achieved very similar perplexities on automatic speech recognition tasks in comparison to the long short-term memory (LSTM) neural network, whose structure is much more complex. This suggests that the bag-of-words model can effectively store the longer term contextual information, which could show improvements in statistical machine translation as well. Since the bag-of-words representation can cover as many contextual words without further modifying the network structure, the problem of limited context window size of feed-forward neural networks is reduced. Instead of predefining fixed decay rates for the exponentially decaying bag-of-words models, we propose to learn the decay rates from the training data like other weight parameters in the neural network model.

2 The Bag-of-Words Input Features

The bag-of-words model is a simplifying representation applied in natural language processing. In this model, each sentence is represented as the set of its words disregarding the word order. Bag-of-words models are used as additional input features to feed-forward neural networks in addition to the one-hot encoding. Thus, the probability of the feed-forward neural network translation model with an m-word source window can be written as:

$$p(e_1^I \mid f_1^J) \approx \prod_{i=1}^{I} p(e_i \mid f_{b_i-\Delta_m}^{b_i+\Delta_m}, f_{\text{BoW},i}) \quad (1)$$

where $\Delta_m = \frac{m-1}{2}$ and b_i is the index of the single aligned source word to the target word e_i. We applied the *affiliation* technique proposed in (Devlin et al., 2014) for obtaining the one-to-one align-

Proceedings of the 54th Annual Meeting of the Association for Computational Linguistics, pages 293–298,
Berlin, Germany, August 7-12, 2016. ©2016 Association for Computational Linguistics

ments. The bag-of-words input features $f_{\text{BoW},i}$ can be seen as normalized n-of-N vectors as demonstrated in Figure 1, where n is the number of words inside each bag-of-words.

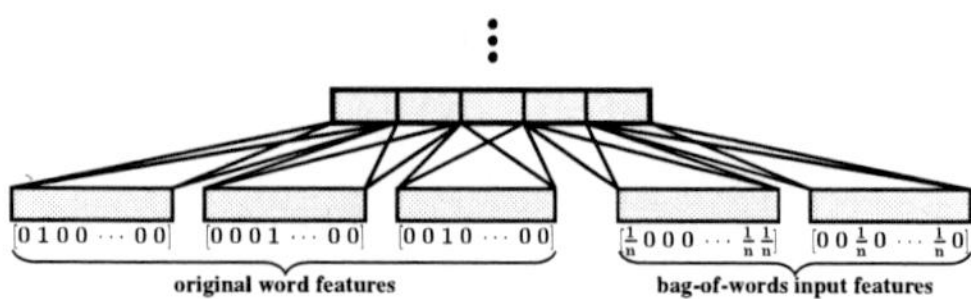

Figure 1: The bag-of-words input features along with the original word features. The input vectors are projected and concatenated at the projection layer. We omit the hidden and output layers for simplification, since they remain unchanged.

2.1 Contents of Bag-of-Words Features

Before utilizing the bag-of-words input features we have to decide which words should be part of it. We tested multiple different variants:

1. Collecting all words of the sentence in one bag-of-words except the currently aligned word.

2. Collecting all preceding words in one bag-of-words and all succeeding words in a second bag-of-words.

3. Collecting all preceding words in one bag-of-words and all succeeding words in a second bag-of-words except those already included in the source window.

All of these variants provide the feed-forward neural network with an unlimited context in both directions. The differences between these setups only varied by 0.2% BLEU and 0.1% TER. We choose to base further experiments on the last variant since it performed best and seemed to be the most logical choice for us.

2.2 Exponentially Decaying Bag-of-Words

Another variant is to weight the words within the bag-of-words model. In the standard bag-of-words representation these weights are equally distributed for all words. This means the bag-of-words input is a vector which marks if a word is given or not and does not encode the word order. To avoid this problem, the *exponential decay* approach proposed in (Clarkson and Robinson, 1997) has been adopted to express the distance of

contextual words from the current word. Therefore the bag-of-words vector with decay weights can be defined as following:

$$\tilde{f}_{\text{BoW},i} = \sum_{k \in S_{\text{BoW}}} d^{|i-k|} \tilde{f}_k \qquad (2)$$

where

i, k Positions of the current word and words within the BoW model respectively.

$\tilde{f}_{\text{BoW},i}$ The value vector of the BoW input feature for the i-th word in the sentence.

$\tilde{f}_k$ One-hot encoded feature vector of the k-th word in the sentence.

S_{BoW} Indices set of the words contained in the BoW. If a word appears more than once in the BoW, the index of the nearest one to the current word will be selected.

d Decay rate with float value ranging from zero to one. It specifies how fast weights of contextual words decay along with distances, which can be learned like other weight parameters of the neural network.

Instead of using fixed decay rate as in (Irie et al., 2015), we propose to train the decay rate like other weight parameters in the neural network. The approach presented by (Mikolov et al., 2015) is comparable to the corpus decay rate shown here, except that their work makes use of a diagonal matrix instead of a scalar as decay rate. In our experiments, three different kinds of decay rates are trained and applied:

1. Corpus decay rate: all words in vocabulary share the same decay rate.

2. Individual decay rate for each bag-of-words: each bag-of-words has its own decay rate given the aligned word.

3. Individual decay rate for each word: each word uses its own decay rate.

We use the English sentence

"friends had been talking about this fish for a long time"

as an example to clarify the differences between these variants. A five words contextual window centered at the current aligned word fish has been applied: {about, this, fish, for, a}. The bag-of-words models are used to collect all other source words outside the context window: {friends, had, been, talking} and {long, time}. Furthermore, there are multiple choices for assigning decay weights to all these words in the bag-of-words feature:

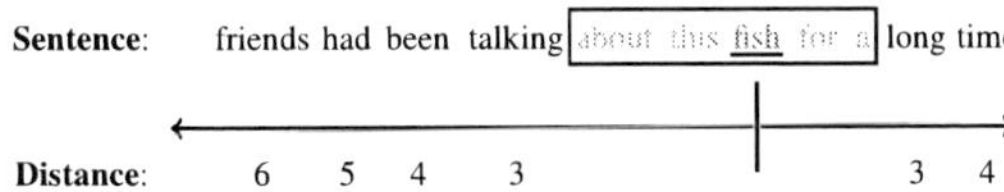

1. Corpus decay rate: d

2. Bag-of-words individual decay rate: $d = d_{\text{fish}}$

3. Word individual decay rate:
$d \in \{d_{\text{friends}}, d_{\text{had}}, d_{\text{been}}, d_{\text{talking}}, d_{\text{long}}, d_{\text{time}}\}$

3 Experiments

3.1 Setup

Experiments are conducted on the IWSLT 2013 German→English, WMT 2015 German→English and DARPA BOLT Chinese→English translation tasks. GIZA++ (Och and Ney, 2003) is applied for aligning the parallel corpus. The translation quality is evaluated by case-insensitive BLEU (Papineni et al., 2002) and TER (Snover et al., 2006) metric. The scaling factors are tuned with MERT (Och, 2003) with BLEU as optimization criterion on the development sets. The systems are evaluated using *MultEval* (Clark et al., 2011). In the experiments the maximum size of the n-best lists applied for reranking is 500. For the translation experiments, the averaged scores are presented on the development set from three optimization runs.

Experiments are performed using the *Jane* toolkit (Vilar et al., 2010; Wuebker et al., 2012) with a log-linear framework containing following feature functions:

- Phrase translation probabilities both directions

- Word lexicon features in both directions

- Enhanced low frequency counts (Chen et al., 2011)

- 4-gram language model

- 7-gram word class language model (Wuebker et al., 2013)

- Word and phrase penalties

- Hierarchical reordering model (Galley and Manning, 2008)

Additionally, a neural network translation model, similar to (Devlin et al., 2014), with following configurations is applied for reranking the n-best lists:

- Projection layer size 100 for each word

- Two non-linear hidden layers with 1000 and 500 nodes respectively

- Short-list size 10000 along with 1000 word classes at the output layer

- 5 one-hot input vectors of words

Unless otherwise stated, the investigations on bag-of-words input features are based on this neural network model. We also integrated our neural network translation model into the decoder as proposed in (Devlin et al., 2014). The relative improvements provided by integrated decoding and reranking are quite similar, which can also be confirmed by (Alkhouli et al., 2015). We therefore decided to only work in reranking for repeated experimentation.

3.2 Exponentially Decaying Bag-of-Words

As shown in Section 2.2, the exponential decay approach is applied to express the distance of contextual words from the current word. Thereby the information of sequence order can be included into bag-of-words models. We demonstrated three different kinds of decay rates for words in the bag-of-words input feature, namely the corpus general decay rate, the bag-of-words individual decay rate and the word individual decay rate.

Table 1 illustrates the experimental results of the neural network translation model with exponentially decaying bag-of-words input features on IWSLT 2013 German→English, WMT 2015 German→English and BOLT Chinese→English

| | IWSLT | | | | WMT | | BOLT | |
| | test | | eval11 | | newstest2013 | | test | |
	$\text{BLEU}^{[\%]}$	$\text{TER}^{[\%]}$	$\text{BLEU}^{[\%]}$	$\text{TER}^{[\%]}$	$\text{BLEU}^{[\%]}$	$\text{TER}^{[\%]}$	$\text{BLEU}^{[\%]}$	$\text{TER}^{[\%]}$
Baseline + NNTM	31.9	47.5	36.7	43.0	28.8	53.8	17.4	67.1
+ BoW Features	32.0	47.3	36.9	42.9	28.8	53.5*	17.5	67.0
+ Fixed DR (0.9)	32.2*	47.3	37.0*	42.6*†	29.0	53.5*	17.7*	66.8*
+ Corpus DR	32.1	47.3	36.9	42.7*	29.1*†	53.5*	17.7*	66.7*†
+ BoW DR	**32.4*†**	**47.0*†**	**37.2*†**	**42.4*†**	**29.2*†**	**53.2*†**	**17.9*†**	**66.6*†**
+ Word DR	32.3*†	**47.0***	37.1*	42.7*	29.1*†	53.4*	17.8*†	66.7*†
Baseline + LSTM	32.2*	47.4	37.1*	42.5*†	29.0	53.3*	17.6	66.8*

Table 1: Experimental results of translations using exponentially decaying bag-of-words models with different kinds of decay rates. Improvements by systems marked by ∗ have a 95% statistical significance from the baseline system, whereas † denotes the 95% statistical significant improvements with respect to the BoW Features system (without decay weights). We experimented with several values for the fixed decay rate (DR) and 0.9 performed best. The applied RNN model is the LSTM bidirectional translation model proposed in (Sundermeyer et al., 2014).

translation tasks. Here we applied two bag-of-words models to separately contain the preceding and succeeding words outside the context window. We can see that the bag-of-words feature without exponential decay weights only provides small improvements. After appending the decay weights, four different kinds of decay rates provide further improvements to varying degrees. The bag-of-words individual decay rate performs the best, which gives us improvements by up to 0.5% on BLEU and up to 0.6% on TER. On these tasks, these improvements even help the feed-forward neural network achieve a similar performance to the popular long short-term memory recurrent neural network model (Sundermeyer et al., 2014), which contains three LSTM layers with 200 nodes each. The results of the word individual decay rate are worse than that of the bag-of-words decay rate. One reason is that in word individual case, the sequence order can still be missing. We initialize all values for the tunable decay rates with 0.9. In the IWSLT 2013 German→English task, the corpus decay rate is tuned to 0.578. When investigating the values of the trained bag-of-words individual decay rate vector, we noticed that the variance of the value for frequent words is much lower than for rare words. We also observed that most function words, such as prepositions and conjunctions, are assigned low decay rates. We could not find a pattern for the trained value vector of the word individual decay rates.

3.3 Comparison between Bag-of-Words and Large Context Window

The main motivation behind the usage of the bag-of-words input features is to provide the model with additional context information. We compared the bag-of-words input features to different source side windows to refute the argument that simply increasing the size of the window could achieve the same results. Our experiments showed that increasing the source side window beyond 11 gave no more improvements while the model that used the bag-of-words input features is able to achieve the best result (Figure 2). A possible explanation for this could be that the feed-forward neural network learns its input position-dependent. If one source word is moved by one position the feed-forward neural network needs to have seen a word with a similar word vector at this position during training to interpret it correctly. The likelihood of precisely getting the position decreases with a larger distance. The bag-of-words model on the other hand will still get the same input only slightly stronger or weaker on the new distance and decay rate.

4 Conclusion

The aim of this work was to investigate the influence of exponentially decaying bag-of-words input features with trained decay rates on the feed-forward neural network translation model. Applying the standard bag-of-words model as an additional input feature in our feed-forward neural network translation model only yields slight im-

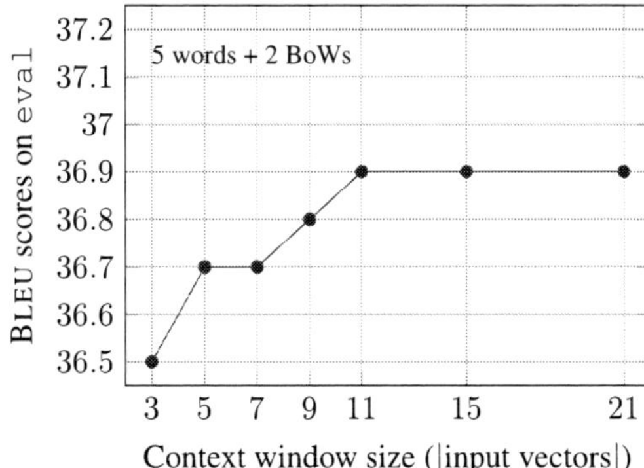

Figure 2: The change of BLEU scores on the `eval11` set of the IWSLT 2013 German→English task along with the source context window size. The source windows are always symmetrical with respect to the aligned word. For instance, window size five denotes that two preceding and two succeeding words along with the aligned word are included in the window. The average sentence length of the corpus is about 18 words. The red line is the result of using a model with bag-of-words input features and a bag-of-words individual decay rate.

provements, since the original bag-of-words representation does not include information about the ordering of each word. To avoid this problem, we applied the exponential decay weight to express the distances between words and propose to train the decay rate as other weight parameters of the network. Three different kinds of decay rates are proposed, the bag-of-words individual decay rate performs best and provides improvements by averagely 0.5% BLEU on three different translation tasks, which is even able to outperform a bidirectional LSTM translation model on the given tasks. By contrast, applying additional one-hot encoded input vectors or enlarging the network structure can not achieve such good performances as bag-of-words features.

Acknowledgments

This paper has received funding from the European Union's Horizon 2020 research and innovation programme under grant agreement n° 645452 (QT21).

References

Tamer Alkhouli, Felix Rietig, and Hermann Ney. 2015. Investigations on phrase-based decoding with recurrent neural network language and translation models. In *EMNLP 2015 Tenth Workshop on Statistical Machine Translation (WMT 2015)*, pages 294–303, Lisbon, Portugal, September.

Dzmitry Bahdanau, Kyunghyun Cho, and Yoshua Bengio. 2015. Neural machine translation by jointly learning to align and translate. In *Proceedings of the 3rd International Conference on Learning Representations*, San Diego, CA, USA, May.

Boxing Chen, Roland Kuhn, George Foster, and Howard Johnson. 2011. Unpacking and Transforming Feature Functions: New Ways to Smooth Phrase Tables. In *Proceedings of MT Summit XIII*, pages 269–275, Xiamen, China, September.

Jonathan H. Clark, Chris Dyer, Alon Lavie, and Noah A. Smith. 2011. Better Hypothesis Testing for Statistical Machine Translation: Controlling for Optimizer Instability. In *Proceedings of the 49th Annual Meeting of the Association for Computational Linguistics: Short Papers*, pages 176–181, Portland, OR, USA, June.

P. Clarkson and A. Robinson. 1997. Language Model Adaptation Using Mixtures and an Exponentially Decaying Cache. In *Proceedings of the 1997 IEEE International Conference on Acoustics, Speech, and Signal Processing*, pages 799–802, Washington, DC, USA, April.

Jacob Devlin, Rabih Zbib, Zhongqiang Huang, Thomas Lamar, Richard Schwartz, and John Makhoul. 2014. Fast and robust neural network joint models for statistical machine translation. In *Proceedings of the 52nd Annual Meeting of the Association for Computational Linguistics*, pages 1370–1380, Baltimore, MD, USA, June.

Michel Galley and Christopher D. Manning. 2008. A simple and effective hierarchical phrase reordering model. In *Proceedings of the 2008 Conference on Empirical Methods in Natural Language Processing*, pages 848–856, Honolulu, HI, USA, October.

Kazuki Irie, Ralf Schlüter, and Hermann Ney. 2015. Bag-of-Words Input for Long History Representation in Neural Network-based Language Models for Speech Recognition. In *Proceedings of the 16th Annual Conference of International Speech Communication Association*, pages 2371–2375, Dresden, Germany, September.

Tomas Mikolov, Armand Joulin, Sumit Chopra, Michael Mathieu, and Marc'Aurelio Ranzato. 2015. Learning longer memory in recurrent neural networks. In *Proceedings of the 3rd International Conference on Learning Representations*, San Diego, CA, USA, May.

Franz Josef Och and Hermann Ney. 2003. A Systematic Comparison of Various Statistical Alignment Models. *Computational Linguistics*, 29:19–51, March.

Franz Josef Och. 2003. Minimum Error Rate Training in Statistical Machine Translation. In *Proceedings of the 41st Annual Meeting on Association for Computational Linguistics*, pages 160–167, Sapporo, Japan, July.

Kishore Papineni, Salim Roukos, Todd Ward, and Wei-Jing Zhu. 2002. BLEU: A Method for Automatic Evaluation of Machine Translation. In *Proceedings of the 40th Annual Meeting on Association for Computational Linguistics*, pages 311–318, Philadelphia, PA, USA, July.

Holger Schwenk, Daniel Déchelotte, and Jean-Luc Gauvain. 2006. Continuous space language models for statistical machine translation. In *Proceedings of the 44th Annual Meeting of the International Committee on Computational Linguistics and the Association for Computational Linguistics*, pages 723–730, Sydney, Australia, July.

Holger Schwenk. 2012. Continuous space translation models for phrase-based statistical machine translation. In *Proceedings of the 24th International Conference on Computational Linguistics*, pages 1071–1080, Mumbai, India, December.

Matthew Snover, Bonnie Dorr, Richard Schwartz, Linnea Micciulla, and John Makhoul. 2006. A study of translation edit rate with targeted human annotation. In *Proceedings of the Conference of the Association for Machine Translation in the Americas*, pages 223–231, Cambridge, MA, USA, August.

Martin Sundermeyer, Tamer Alkhouli, Joern Wuebker, and Hermann Ney. 2014. Translation modeling with bidirectional recurrent neural networks. In *Proceedings of the 2014 Conference on Empirical Methods in Natural Language Processing*, pages 14–25, Doha, Qatar, October.

Ilya Sutskever, Oriol Vinyals, and Quoc V. Le. 2014. Sequence to sequence learning with neural networks. In Z Ghahramani, M Welling, C Cortes, N D Lawrence, and K Q Weinberger, editors, *Advances in Neural Information Processing Systems 27*, pages 3104–3112. Curran Associates, Inc.

Ashish Vaswani, Yinggong Zhao, Victoria Fossum, and David Chiang. 2013. Decoding with large-scale neural language models improves translation. In *Proceedings of the 2013 Conference on Empirical Methods in Natural Language Processing*, pages 1387–1392, Seattle, WA, USA, October.

David Vilar, Daniel Stein, Matthias Huck, and Hermann Ney. 2010. Jane: Open Source Hierarchical Translation, Extended with Reordering and Lexicon Models. In *ACL 2010 Joint Fifth Workshop on Statistical Machine Translation and Metrics MATR*, pages 262–270, Uppsala, Sweden, July.

Joern Wuebker, Matthias Huck, Stephan Peitz, Malte Nuhn, Markus Freitag, Jan-Thorsten Peter, Saab Mansour, and Hermann Ney. 2012. Jane 2: Open Source Phrase-based and Hierarchical Statistical Machine Translation. In *International Conference on Computational Linguistics*, pages 483–491, Mumbai, India, December.

Joern Wuebker, Stephan Peitz, Felix Rietig, and Hermann Ney. 2013. Improving Statistical Machine Translation with Word Class Models. In *Proceedings of the 2013 Conference on Empirical Methods in Natural Language Processing*, pages 1377–1381, Seattle, WA, USA, October.

Syntactically Guided Neural Machine Translation

Felix Stahlberg[†] and **Eva Hasler**[†] and **Aurelien Waite**[‡] and **Bill Byrne**[‡†]

[†]Department of Engineering, University of Cambridge, UK

[‡]SDL Research, Cambridge, UK

Abstract

We investigate the use of hierarchical phrase-based SMT lattices in end-to-end neural machine translation (NMT). Weight pushing transforms the Hiero scores for complete translation hypotheses, with the full translation grammar score and full n-gram language model score, into posteriors compatible with NMT predictive probabilities. With a slightly modified NMT beam-search decoder we find gains over both Hiero and NMT decoding alone, with practical advantages in extending NMT to very large input and output vocabularies.

1 Introduction

We report on investigations motivated by the idea that the structured search spaces defined by syntactic machine translation approaches such as Hiero (Chiang, 2007) can be used to guide Neural Machine Translation (NMT) (Kalchbrenner and Blunsom, 2013; Sutskever et al., 2014; Cho et al., 2014; Bahdanau et al., 2015). NMT and Hiero have complementary strengths and weaknesses and differ markedly in how they define probability distributions over translations and what search procedures they use.

The NMT encoder-decoder formalism provides a probability distribution over translations $\mathbf{y} = y_1^T$ of a source sentence $\mathbf{x}$ as (Bahdanau et al., 2015)

$$P(y_1^T|\mathbf{x}) = \prod_{t=1}^{T} P(y_t|y_1^{t-1}, \mathbf{x}) = \prod_{t=1}^{T} g(y_{t-1}, s_t, c_t) \tag{1}$$

where $s_t = f(s_{t-1}, y_{t-1}, c_t)$ is a decoder state variable and c_t is a context vector depending on the source sentence and the attention mechanism.

This posterior distribution is potentially very powerful, however it does not easily lend itself to sophisticated search procedures. Decoding is done by 'beam search to find a translation that approximately maximizes the conditional probability' (Bahdanau et al., 2015). Search looks only one word ahead and no deeper than the beam.

Hiero defines a synchronous context-free grammar (SCFG) with rules: $X \rightarrow \langle \alpha, \gamma \rangle$, where α and γ are strings of terminals and non-terminals in the source and target languages. A target language sentence $\mathbf{y}$ can be a translation of a source language sentence $\mathbf{x}$ if there is a derivation D in the grammar which yields both $\mathbf{y}$ and $\mathbf{x}$: $\mathbf{y} = \mathbf{y}(D)$, $\mathbf{x} = \mathbf{x}(D)$. This defines a regular language $\mathcal{Y}$ over strings in the target language via a projection of the sentence to be translated: $\mathcal{Y} = \{\mathbf{y}(D) : \mathbf{x}(D) = \mathbf{x}\}$ (Iglesias et al., 2011; Allauzen et al., 2014). Scores are defined over derivations via a log-linear model with features $\{\phi_i\}$ and weights λ. The decoder searches for the translation $\mathbf{y}(D)$ in $\mathcal{Y}$ with the highest derivation score $S(D)$ (Chiang, 2007, Eq. 24) :

$$\hat{\mathbf{y}} = \mathbf{y} \left(\underset{D:\mathbf{x}(D)=\mathbf{x}}{\operatorname{argmax}} \underbrace{P_G(D) P_{LM}(\mathbf{y}(D))^{\lambda_{LM}}}_{S(D)} \right) \tag{2}$$

where P_{LM} is an n-gram language model and $P_G(D) \propto \prod_{(X \rightarrow \langle \gamma, \alpha \rangle) \in D} \prod_i \phi_i(X \rightarrow \langle \gamma, \alpha \rangle)^{\lambda_i}$.

Hiero decoders attempt to avoid search errors when combining the translation and language model for the translation hypotheses (Chiang, 2007; Iglesias et al., 2009). These procedures search over a vast space of translations, much larger than is considered by the NMT beam search. However the Hiero context-free grammars that make efficient search possible are weak models of translation. The basic Hiero formalism can be extended through 'soft syntactic constraints' (Venugopal et al., 2009; Marton and Resnik, 2008) or by

Proceedings of the 54th Annual Meeting of the Association for Computational Linguistics, pages 299–305,
Berlin, Germany, August 7-12, 2016. ©2016 Association for Computational Linguistics

adding very high dimensional features (Chiang et al., 2009), however the translation score assigned by the grammar is still only the product of probabilities of individual rules. From the modelling perspective, this is an overly strong conditional independence assumption. NMT clearly has the potential advantage in incorporating long-term context into translation scores.

NMT and Hiero differ in how they 'consume' source words. Hiero applies the translation rules to the source sentence via the CYK algorithm, with each derivation yielding a complete and unambiguous translation of the source words. The NMT beam decoder does not have an explicit mechanism for tracking source coverage, and there is evidence that may lead to both 'over-translation' and 'under-translation' (Tu et al., 2016).

NMT and Hiero also differ in their internal representations. The NMT continuous representation captures morphological, syntactic and semantic similarity (Collobert and Weston, 2008) across words and phrases. However, extending these representations to the large vocabularies needed for open-domain MT is an open area of research (Jean et al., 2015a; Luong et al., 2015; Sennrich et al., 2015; Chitnis and DeNero, 2015). By contrast, Hiero (and other symbolic systems) can easily use translation grammars and language models with very large vocabularies (Heafield et al., 2013; Lin and Dyer, 2010). Moreover, words and phrases can be easily added to a fully-trained symbolic MT system. This is an important consideration for commercial MT, as customers often wish to customise and personalise SMT systems for their own application domain. Adding new words and phrases to an NMT system is not as straightforward, and it is not clear that the advantages of the continuous representation can be extended to the new additions to the vocabularies.

NMT has the advantage of including long-range context in modelling individual translation hypotheses. Hiero considers a much bigger search space, and can incorporate n-gram language models, but a much weaker translation model. In this paper we try to exploit the strengths of each approach. We propose to guide NMT decoding using Hiero. We show that restricting the search space of the NMT decoder to a subset of $\mathcal{Y}$ spanned by Hiero effectively counteracts NMT modelling errors. This can be implemented by generating translation lattices with Hiero, which are then rescored by the NMT decoder. Our approach addresses the limited vocabulary issue in NMT as we replace NMT OOVs with lattice words from the much larger Hiero vocabulary. We also find good gains from neural and Kneser-Ney n-gram language models.

2 Syntactically Guided NMT (SGNMT)

2.1 Hiero Predictive Posteriors

The Hiero decoder generates translation hypotheses as weighted finite state acceptors (WFSAs), or lattices, with weights in the tropical semiring. For a translation hypothesis $\mathbf{y}(D)$ arising from the Hiero derivation D, the path weight in the WFSA is $-\log S(D)$, after Eq. 2. While this representation is correct with respect to the Hiero translation grammar and language model scores, having Hiero scores at the path level is not convenient for working with the NMT system. What we need are predictive probabilities in the form of Eq. 1.

The Hiero WFSAs are determinised and minimised with epsilon removal under the tropical semiring, and weights are pushed towards the initial state under the log semiring (Mohri and Riley, 2001). The resulting transducer is stochastic in the log semiring, i.e. the log sum of the arc log probabilities leaving a state is 0 ($= \log 1$). In addition, because the WFSA is deterministic, there is a unique path leading to every state, which corresponds to a unique Hiero translation prefix. Suppose a path to a state accepts the translation prefix y_1^{t-1}. An outgoing arc from that state with symbol y has a weight that corresponds to the (negative log of the) conditional probability

$$P_{Hiero}(y_t = y | y_1^{t-1}, \mathbf{x}). \qquad (3)$$

This conditional probability is such that for a Hiero translation $y_1^T = \mathbf{y}(D)$ accepted by the WFSA

$$P_{Hiero}(y_1^T) = \prod_{t=1}^{T} P_{Hiero}(y_t | y_1^{t-1}, \mathbf{x}) \propto S(D).$$
$$(4)$$

The Hiero WFSAs have been transformed so that their arc weights have the negative log of the conditional probabilities defined in Eq. 3. All the probability mass of this distribution is concentrated on the Hiero translation hypotheses. The complete translation and language model scores computed over the entire Hiero translations are pushed as far forward in the WFSAs as possible. This is commonly done for left-to-right decoding in speech recognition (Mohri et al., 2002).

2.2 NMT–Hiero Decoding

As above, suppose a path to a state in the WFSA accepts a Hiero translation prefix y_1^{t-1}, and let y_t be a symbol on an outgoing arc from that state. We define the joint NMT+Hiero score as

$$\log P(y_t|y_1^{t-1}, \mathbf{x}) =$$
$$\lambda_{Hiero} \log P_{Hiero}(y_t|y_1^{t-1}, \mathbf{x}) +$$
$$\lambda_{NMT} \begin{cases} \log P_{NMT}(y_t|y_1^{t-1}, \mathbf{x}) & y_t \in \Sigma_{NMT} \\ \log P_{NMT}(\text{unk}|y_1^{t-1}, \mathbf{x}) & y_t \notin \Sigma_{NMT} \end{cases}$$
$$(5)$$

Note that the NMT-HIERO decoder only considers hypotheses in the Hiero lattice. As discussed earlier, the Hiero vocabulary can be much larger than the NMT output vocabulary Σ_{NMT}. If a Hiero translation contains a word not in the NMT vocabulary, the NMT model provides a score and updates its decoder state as for an unknown word.

Our decoding algorithm is a natural extension of beam search decoding for NMT. Due to the form of Eq. 5 we can build up hypotheses from left-to-right on the target side. Thus, we can represent a partial hypothesis $h = (y_1^t, h_s)$ by a translation prefix y_1^t and an accumulated score h_s. At each iteration we extend the current hypotheses by one target token, until the best scoring hypothesis reaches a final state of the Hiero lattice. We refer to this step as *node expansion*, and in Sec. 3.1 we report the number of node expansions per sentence, as an indication of computational cost.

We can think of the decoding algorithm as breath-first search through the translation lattices with a limited number of active hypotheses (a beam). Rescoring is done on-the-fly: as the decoder traverses an edge in the WFSA, we update its weight by Eq 5 The output-synchronous char-

acteristic of beam search enables us to compute the NMT posteriors only once for each history based on previous calculations.

Alternatively, we can think of the algorithm as NMT decoding with revised posterior probabilities: instead of selecting the most likely symbol y_t according the NMT model, we adjust the NMT posterior with the Hiero posterior scores and delete NMT entries that are not allowed by the lattice. This may result in NMT choosing a different symbol, which is then fed back to the neural network for the next decoding step.

3 Experimental Evaluation

We evaluate SGNMT on the WMT *news-test2014* test sets (the filtered version) for English-German (En-De) and English-French (En-Fr). We also report results on WMT *news-test2015* En-De.

The En-De training set includes *Europarl v7*, *Common Crawl*, and *News Commentary v10*. Sentence pairs with sentences longer than 80 words or length ratios exceeding 2.4:1 were deleted, as were *Common Crawl* sentences from other languages (Shuyo, 2010). The En-Fr NMT system was trained on preprocessed data (Schwenk, 2014) used by previous work (Sutskever et al., 2014; Bahdanau et al., 2015; Jean et al., 2015a), but with truecasing like our Hiero baseline. Following (Jean et al., 2015a), we use *news-test2012* and *news-test2013* as a development set. The NMT vocabulary size is 50k for En-De and 30k for En-Fr, taken as the most frequent words in training (Jean et al., 2015a). Tab. 1 provides statistics and shows the severity of the OOV problem for NMT.

The BASIC NMT system is built using the Blocks framework (van Merriënboer et al., 2015) based on the Theano library (Bastien et al., 2012) with standard hyper-parameters (Bahdanau et al., 2015): the encoder and decoder networks consist of 1000 gated recurrent units (Cho et al., 2014). The decoder uses a single maxout (Goodfellow et al., 2013) output layer with the feed-forward attention model (Bahdanau et al., 2015).

The En-De Hiero system uses rules which encourage verb movement (de Gispert et al., 2010). The rules for En-Fr were extracted from the full data set available at the WMT'15 website using a shallow-1 grammar (de Gispert et al., 2010). 5-gram Kneser-Ney language models (KN-LM) for the Hiero systems were trained on WMT'15 parallel and monolingual data (Heafield et al., 2013).

	Train set		Dev set		Test set	
	en	de	en	de	en	de
# sentences	4.2M		6k		2.7k	
# word tokens	106M	102M	138k	138k	62k	59k
# unique words	647k	1.5M	13k	20k	9k	13k
OOV (Hiero)	0.0%	0.0%	0.8%	1.6%	1.0%	2.0%
OOV (NMT)	1.6%	5.5%	2.5%	7.5%	3.1%	8.8%
	en	fr	en	fr	en	fr
# sentences	12.1M		6k		3k	
# word tokens	305M	348M	138k	155k	71k	81k
# unique words	1.6M	1.7M	14k	17k	10k	11k
OOV (Hiero)	0.0%	0.0%	0.6%	0.6%	0.4%	0.4%
OOV (NMT)	3.5%	3.8%	4.5%	5.3%	5.0%	5.3%

Table 1: Parallel texts and vocabulary coverage on *news-test2014*.

(Jean et al., 2015a, Tab. 2)		SGNMT	
Setup	**BLEU**	**Setup**	**BLEU**
BASIC NMT	16.46	BASIC NMT	16.31
NMT-LV	16.95	HIERO	19.44
+ UNK Replace	18.89	NMT-HIERO	20.69
–	–	+ Tuning	21.43
+ Reshuffle	19.40	+ Reshuffle	21.87
+ Ensemble	21.59		

(a) English-German

(Jean et al., 2015a, Tab. 2)		SGNMT	
Setup	**BLEU**	**Setup**	**BLEU**
BASIC NMT	29.97	BASIC NMT	30.42
NMT-LV	33.36	HIERO	32.86
+ UNK Replace	34.11	NMT-HIERO	35.37
–	–	+ Tuning	36.29
+ Reshuffle	34.60	+ Reshuffle	36.61
+ Ensemble	37.19		

(b) English-French

Table 2: BLEU scores on *news-test2014* calculated with `multi-bleu.perl`. NMT-LV refers to the RNNSEARCH-LV model from (Jean et al., 2015a) for large output vocabularies.

	Search space	Vocab.	NMT scores	Grammar scores	KN-LM scores	NPLM scores	# of node expansions per sen.	BLEU (single)	BLEU (ensemble)
1	Lattice	Hiero		✓	✓		–	21.1 (Hiero)	
2	Lattice	Hiero		✓	✓	✓	–	21.7 (Hiero)	
3	Unrestricted	NMT	✓				254.8	19.5	21.8
4	100-best	Hiero	✓				2,233.6 (DFS: 832.1)	22.8	23.3
5	100-best	Hiero	✓	✓	✓			22.9	23.4
6	100-best	Hiero	✓	✓	✓	✓		22.9	23.3
7	1000-best	Hiero	✓				21,686.2 (DFS: 6,221.8)	23.3	23.8
8	1000-best	Hiero	✓	✓	✓			23.4	23.9
9	1000-best	Hiero	✓	✓	✓	✓		23.5	24.0
10	Lattice	NMT	✓				243.3	20.3	21.4
11	Lattice	Hiero	✓				243.3	23.0	24.2
12	Lattice	Hiero	✓	✓			243.3	23.0	24.2
13	Lattice	Hiero	✓		✓		240.5	23.4	24.5
14	Lattice	Hiero	✓	✓	✓		243.9	23.4	24.4
15	Lattice	Hiero	✓	✓	✓	✓	244.3	24.0	24.4
16	Neural MT – UMontreal-MILA (Jean et al., 2015b)							22.8	25.2

Table 3: BLEU English-German *news-test2015* scores calculated with `mteval-v13a.pl`.

Our SGNMT system[1] is built with the Pyfst interface [2] to OpenFst (Allauzen et al., 2007).

3.1 SGNMT Performance

Tab. 2 compares our combined NMT+Hiero decoding with NMT results in the literature. We use a beam size of 12. In En-De and in En-Fr, we find that our BASIC NMT system performs similarly (within 0.5 BLEU) to previously published results (16.31 vs. 16.46 and 30.42 vs. 29.97).

In NMT-HIERO, decoding is as described in Sec. 2.2, but with $\lambda_{Hiero} = 0$. The decoder searches through the Hiero lattice, ignoring the Hiero scores, but using Hiero word hypotheses in place of any UNKs that might have been produced by NMT. The results show that NMT-HIERO is much more effective in fixing NMT OOVs than the 'UNK Replace' technique (Luong et al., 2015); this holds in both En-De and En-Fr.

For the NMT-HIERO+TUNING systems, lattice MERT (Macherey et al., 2008) is used to optimise λ_{Hiero} and λ_{NMT} on the tuning sets. This yields further gains in both En-Fr and En-De, suggesting that in addition to fixing UNKs, the Hiero predictive posteriors can be used to improve the NMT translation model scores.

Tab. 3 reports results of our En-De system with reshuffling and tuning on *news-test2015*. BLEU scores are directly comparable to WMT'15 results [3]. By comparing row 3 to row 10, we see that constraining NMT to the search space defined by the Hiero lattices yields an improvement of +0.8 BLEU for single NMT. If we allow Hiero to fix NMT UNKs, we see a further +2.7 BLEU gain (row 11). The majority of gains come from fixing UNKs, but there is still improvement from the constrained search space for single NMT.

We next investigate the contribution of the Hiero system scores. We see that, once lattices are generated, the KN-LM contributes more to rescoring than the Hiero grammar scores (rows 12-14). Further gains can be achieved by adding a feed-forward neural language model with NPLM (Vaswani et al., 2013) (row 15). We observe that *n*-best list rescoring with NMT (Neubig et al., 2015) also outperforms both the Hiero and NMT

[1] http://ucam-smt.github.io/sgnmt/html/
[2] https://pyfst.github.io/
[3] http://matrix.statmt.org/matrix/systems_list/1774

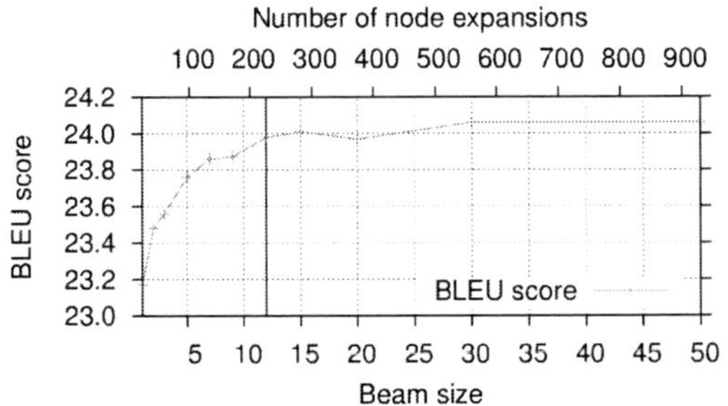

Figure 1: Performance with NPLM over beam size on English-German *news-test2015*. A beam of 12 corresponds to row 15 in Tab. 3.

Determini- sation	Minimi- sation	Weight pushing	Sentences per second
✓			2.51
✓	✓		1.57
✓	✓	✓	1.47

Table 4: Time for lattice preprocessing operations on English-German *news test2015*.

baselines, although lattice rescoring gives the best results (row 9 vs. row 15). Lattice rescoring with SGNMT also uses far fewer node expansions per sentence. We report n-best rescoring speeds for rescoring each hypothesis separately, and a depth-first (DFS) scheme that efficiently traverses the n-best lists. Both these techniques are very slow compared to lattice rescoring. Fig. 1 shows that we can reduce the beam size from 12 to 5 with only a minor drop in BLEU. This is nearly 100 times faster than DFS over the 1000-best list.

Cost of Lattice Preprocessing As described in Sec. 2.1, we applied determinisation, minimisation, and weight pushing to the Hiero lattices in order to work with probabilities. Tab. 4 shows that those operations are generally fast[4].

Lattice Size For previous experiments we set the Hiero pruning parameters such that lattices had 8,510 nodes on average. Fig. 2 plots the BLEU score over the lattice size. We find that SGNMT works well on lattices of moderate or large size, but pruning lattices too heavily has a negative effect as they are then too similar to Hiero first best hypotheses. We note that lattice rescoring involves nearly as many node expansions as unconstrained NMT decoding. This confirms that the lattices at 8,510 nodes are already large enough for SGNMT.

[4]Testing environment: Ubuntu 14.04, Linux 3.13.0, single Intel® Xeon® X5650 CPU at 2.67 GHz

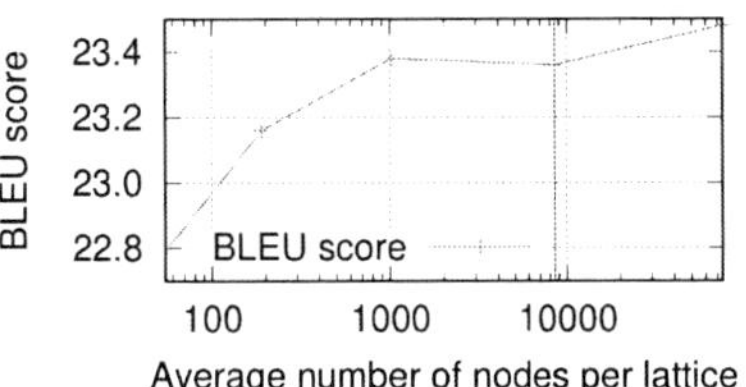

Figure 2: SGNMT performance over lattice size on English-German *news-test2015*. 8,510 nodes per lattice corresponds to row 14 in Tab. 3.

Local Softmax In SGNMT decoding we have the option of normalising the NMT translation probabilities over the words on outgoing words from each state rather than over the full 50,000 words translation vocabulary. There are ~4.5 arcs per state in our En-De'14 lattices, and so avoiding the full softmax could cause significant computational savings. We find this leads to only a modest 0.5 BLEU degradation: 21.45 BLEU in En-De'14, compared to 21.87 BLEU using NMT probabilities computed over the full vocabulary.

Modelling Errors vs. Search Errors In our En-De'14 experiments with $\lambda_{Hiero} = 0$ we find that constraining the NMT decoder to the Hiero lattices yields translation hypotheses with much lower NMT probabilities than unconstrained BASIC NMT decoding: under the NMT model, NMT hypotheses are 8,300 times more likely (median) than NMT-HIERO hypotheses. We conclude (tentatively) that BASIC NMT is not suffering only from search errors, but rather that NMT-HIERO discards some hypotheses ranked highly by the NMT model but lower in the evaluation metric.

4 Conclusion

We have demonstrated a viable approach to Syntactically Guided Neural Machine Translation formulated to exploit the rich, structured search space generated by Hiero and the long-context translation scores of NMT. SGNMT does not suffer from the severe limitation in vocabulary size of basic NMT and avoids any difficulty of extending distributed word representations to new vocabulary items not seen in training data.

Acknowledgements

This work was supported in part by the U.K. Engineering and Physical Sciences Research Council (EPSRC grant EP/L027623/1).

References

Cyril Allauzen, Michael Riley, Johan Schalkwyk, Wojciech Skut, and Mehryar Mohri. 2007. OpenFst: A general and efficient weighted finite-state transducer library. In *Implementation and Application of Automata*, pages 11–23. Springer.

Cyril Allauzen, Bill Byrne, de Adrià Gispert, Gonzalo Iglesias, and Michael Riley. 2014. Pushdown automata in statistical machine translation. *Volume 40, Issue 3 - September 2014*, pages 687–723.

Dzmitry Bahdanau, Kyunghyun Cho, and Yoshua Bengio. 2015. Neural machine translation by jointly learning to align and translate. In *ICLR*.

Frédéric Bastien, Pascal Lamblin, Razvan Pascanu, James Bergstra, Ian Goodfellow, Arnaud Bergeron, Nicolas Bouchard, David Warde-Farley, and Yoshua Bengio. 2012. Theano: new features and speed improvements. In *Deep Learning and Unsupervised Feature Learning NIPS 2012 Workshop*.

David Chiang, Kevin Knight, and Wei Wang. 2009. 11,001 new features for statistical machine translation. In *ACL*, pages 218–226.

David Chiang. 2007. Hierarchical phrase-based translation. *Computational Linguistics*, 33(2):201–228.

Rohan Chitnis and John DeNero. 2015. Variable-length word encodings for neural translation models. In *EMNLP*, pages 2088–2093.

Kyunghyun Cho, Bart van Merrienboer, Caglar Gulcehre, Fethi Bougares, Holger Schwenk, and Yoshua Bengio. 2014. Learning phrase representations using RNN encoder-decoder for statistical machine translation. In *EMNLP*.

Ronan Collobert and Jason Weston. 2008. A unified architecture for natural language processing: Deep neural networks with multitask learning. In *Proceedings of the 25th International Conference on Machine Learning*, pages 160–167. ACM.

Adrià de Gispert, Gonzalo Iglesias, Graeme Blackwood, Eduardo R Banga, and William Byrne. 2010. Hierarchical phrase-based translation with weighted finite-state transducers and shallow-n grammars. *Computational Linguistics*, 36(3):505–533.

Ian Goodfellow, David Warde-farley, Mehdi Mirza, Aaron Courville, and Yoshua Bengio. 2013. Maxout networks. In *ICML*, pages 1319–1327.

Kenneth Heafield, Ivan Pouzyrevsky, Jonathan H. Clark, and Philipp Koehn. 2013. Scalable modified Kneser-Ney language model estimation. In *ACL*, pages 690–696.

Gonzalo Iglesias, Adrià de Gispert, Eduardo R Banga, and William Byrne. 2009. Hierarchical phrase-based translation with weighted finite state transducers. In *NAACL-HLT*, pages 433–441.

Gonzalo Iglesias, Cyril Allauzen, William Byrne, Adrià de Gispert, and Michael Riley. 2011. Hierarchical phrase-based translation representations. In *EMNLP*, pages 1373–1383.

Sébastien Jean, Kyunghyun Cho, Roland Memisevic, and Yoshua Bengio. 2015a. On using very large target vocabulary for neural machine translation. In *ACL*, pages 1–10.

Sébastien Jean, Orhan Firat, Kyunghyun Cho, Roland Memisevic, and Yoshua Bengio. 2015b. Montreal neural machine translation systems for WMT15. In *Proceedings of the Tenth Workshop on Statistical Machine Translation*, pages 134–140.

Nal Kalchbrenner and Phil Blunsom. 2013. Recurrent continuous translation models. In *EMNLP*, page 413.

Jimmy Lin and Chris Dyer. 2010. *Data-intensive text processing with MapReduce*. Morgan &Claypool.

Minh-Thang Luong, Ilya Sutskever, Quoc V Le, Oriol Vinyals, and Wojciech Zaremba. 2015. Addressing the rare word problem in neural machine translation. In *ACL*.

Wolfgang Macherey, Franz Josef Och, Ignacio Thayer, and Jakob Uszkoreit. 2008. Lattice-based minimum error rate training for statistical machine translation. In *EMNLP*, pages 725–734.

Yuval Marton and Philip Resnik. 2008. Soft syntactic constraints for hierarchical phrased-based translation. In *ACL*, pages 1003–1011.

Mehryar Mohri and Michael Riley. 2001. A weight pushing algorithm for large vocabulary speech recognition. In *Interspeech*, pages 1603–1606.

Mehryar Mohri, Fernando Pereira, and Michael Riley. 2002. Weighted finite-state transducers in speech recognition. *Computer Speech and Language*, 16(1).

Graham Neubig, Makoto Morishita, and Satoshi Nakamura. 2015. Neural reranking improves subjective quality of machine translation: NAIST at WAT2015. In *Workshop on Asian Translation*, pages 35–41.

Holger Schwenk. 2014. Universit du Maine. http://www-lium.univ-lemans.fr/~schwenk/nnmt-shared-task/. [Online; accessed 1-March-2016].

Rico Sennrich, Barry Haddow, and Alexandra Birch. 2015. Neural machine translation of rare words with subword units. *arXiv preprint arXiv:1508.07909*.

Nakatani Shuyo. 2010. Language detection library for Java. http://code.google.com/p/language-detection/. [Online; accessed 1-March-2016].

Ilya Sutskever, Oriol Vinyals, and Quoc V Le. 2014.
Sequence to sequence learning with neural networks. In *Advances in Neural Information Processing Systems*, pages 3104–3112.

Zhaopeng Tu, Zhengdong Lu, Yang Liu, Xiaohua Liu,
and Hang Li. 2016. Coverage-based neural machine
translation. *arXiv preprint arXiv:1601.04811*.

Bart van Merriënboer, Dzmitry Bahdanau, Vincent Dumoulin, Dmitriy Serdyuk, David Warde-Farley, Jan
Chorowski, and Yoshua Bengio. 2015. Blocks and
fuel: Frameworks for deep learning. *arXiv preprint
arXiv:1506.00619*.

Ashish Vaswani, Yinggong Zhao, Victoria Fossum, and
David Chiang. 2013. Decoding with large-scale
neural language models improves translation. In
EMNLP, pages 1387–1392.

Ashish Venugopal, Andreas Zollmann, Noah A. Smith,
and Stephan Vogel. 2009. Preference grammars:
Softening syntactic constraints to improve statistical
machine translation. In *NAACL-HLT*, pages 236–
244.

Very quaffable and great fun: Applying NLP to wine reviews

Iris Hendrickx[1]

[1]Centre for Language Studies
Radboud University, P.O. Box 9103
NL6500 HD Nijmegen, Netherlands
`i.hendrickx@let.ru.nl`

Els Lefever[2]

[2]Language and Translation Technology Team
Dep. of Translation, Interpreting and
Communication, Ghent University, Belgium
`els.lefever@ugent.be`

Ilja Croijmans[1]**, Asifa Majid**[1,3] **and Antal van den Bosch**[1]

[3]Max Planck Institute for
Psycholinguistics, P.O. Box 310,
6500 AH Nijmegen, The Netherlands
`{i.croijmans,asifa.majid,a.vandenbosch}@let.ru.nl`

Abstract

We automatically predict properties of wines on the basis of smell and flavor descriptions from experts' wine reviews. We show wine experts are capable of describing their smell and flavor experiences in wine reviews in a sufficiently consistent manner, such that we can use their descriptions to predict properties of a wine based solely on language. The experimental results show promising F-scores when using lexical and semantic information to predict the color, grape variety, country of origin, and price of a wine. This demonstrates, contrary to popular opinion, that wine experts' reviews really are informative.

1 Introduction

Describing smells and flavors is something the average person is not particularly good at. If people are asked to identify familiar smells such as cinnamon and chocolate, they are only able to correctly name the smell around 50% of the time (Cain, 1979; Olofsson and Gottfried, 2015). In comparison to the elaborate vocabulary we have for visual and auditory phenomena, English and other languages spoken in Western societies appear to have few words to describe smells and flavors (Levinson and Majid, 2014; Majid and Burenhult, 2014). Instead, speakers often refer to the source as the name of the smell ('it smells like banana').

Flavor is a complex experience that combines the multisensory sensations of taste, touch and smell. Flavor descriptions contain basic taste descriptors (e.g., sweet, sour, salty, bitter), with metaphorical (e.g., 'elegant') and source-based terminology (e.g., 'it tastes buttery').

The lack of vocabulary for smells and flavors contrasts starkly with the interest people in the West have for flavors and fragrances, and what they are willing to spend on such products. The flavor and fragrance industry is estimated to be worth over $20 billion in 2015[1]. In this context, experts' recommendations are used by the public in order to help them make decisions about purchases. But are the expert recommendations meaningful, given the limitations of language for smells and flavors?

We are interested in the relation between language and sensory information, and how this information is put into words. We focus on descriptions produced by a select group of people who have considerable experience naming smells and flavors, i.e., sommeliers and wine journalists. Through their descriptions, wine experts can influence consumers' purchasing patterns (McCoy, 2006; Horverak, 2009), suggesting their descriptions are written in an informative manner. In this paper we aim to discover whether we can extract the properties of a wine based on the tasting notes written by a wine expert. This should be possible if wine experts are capable of translating their sensory experiences into words in a consistent manner.

Previous experimental studies provide a mixed picture as to whether wine experts' language is consistent. Some studies find similar levels of agreement in smell descriptions generated by wine experts and those generated by novices (Lawless, 1984; Parr et al., 2002), and wine experts use more

---

[1]`http://www.leffingwell.com/top_10.htm`

Proceedings of the 54th Annual Meeting of the Association for Computational Linguistics, pages 306–312,
Berlin, Germany, August 7-12, 2016. ©2016 Association for Computational Linguistics

metaphorical descriptions to describe wine (Caballero and Suárez-Toste, 2010; Paradis and Eeg-Olofsson, 2013), which potentially are not as informative about properties of the wine itself. In contrast, others find wine experts use more specific vocabulary (Zucco et al., 2011; Sezille et al., 2014), and find that wine experts are, in fact, more consistent than non-experts, when they describe wines (Croijmans and Majid, 2016).

We examined the following wine properties and aimed to predict these solely on the basis of the review content: color, grape variety, price, and country of origin. The outcomes of this investigation are interesting for two reasons. First, we test the ability of experts to review wines with consistent language using naturalistic materials. Most previous studies about wine experts and their reviewing consistency are performed in experimental settings and cover some dozens of wine reviews (see for example (Gawel and Godden, 2008; Hopfer and Heymann, 2014)). With automatic analysis we are able to scale up to a much larger and more representative set of reviews.

Second, we gather new insights into the specific vocabulary and type of lexical descriptors used to describe smells and flavors, and what words are most distinctive for different wine characteristics. Market analyses (Vigar-Ellis et al., 2015) show that consumers increasingly select wines based on information provided by experts, for example through expert descriptions and recommender systems, and that wine apps become ever more popular. This is a positive development, as research suggests that informed consumers are able to benefit more from the loose relationship between price and quality in wine (Oczkowski and Doucouliagos, 2014).

In the long run, as we are training automatic systems to predict wine properties, we could use such systems for automatic metadata prediction and error correction in wine review databases. These systems are also a first step towards a recommender system for wines based on review content and flavor descriptions. Current recommender systems such as the mobile apps *Vivino*[2] or *Delectable*[3] work with metadata and user-based filtering, i.e. the principle of 'other users also bought ...'. So there is potential here for content-based recommender systems to be developed.

2   Related work

The relationship between wines and wine reviews has been studied from many different perspectives, aside from those discussed in the previous section. Economically, the relationship between price, wine quality and wine ratings is interesting as a high rating by a famous wine expert can make a substantial difference to product sales (McCoy, 2006). Goldstein and colleagues (2008) investigated whether a jury of wine experts vs non-experts can taste the difference between expensive and cheap wines, and found while wine experts could distinguish the difference, non-experts could not. Lecocq and Visser (2006) investigated what wine properties determine wine prices. They showed wine experts based their overall wine quality ratings on sensory information, and that expert ratings together with features such as region, vintage and designation explained price differences for a subset of French red wines. The relationship between the chemical substances in a wine and wine quality have also been the focus of research (Chen et al., 2009; Cortez et al., 2009).

Brochet and Dubourdieu (2001) conducted a lexical analysis of four corpora of wine reviews from a cognitive linguistic perspective and concluded wine reviews are not only describing sensory properties of the wine, but also include idealistic and hedonistic information from wine prototypes based on previous experiences. Anthropologists have noted that wine experts form their own discourse community with a particular style and vocabulary (Silverstein, 2006). In this research we aim to discover stylistic and lexical patterns with which we can relate wine reviews to wine properties automatically.

3   Data set

The website http://www.winemag.com/, owned by Wine Enthusiast Companies, hosts a substantial catalog of wine descriptions. We downloaded the available reviews[4] and gathered a total of 76,585 wine reviews. The catalog data is structured and contains information about the wine such as the producer, appellation region and country, grape variety, color, alcohol percentage, price, and where to buy it. The expert who writes the wine review also rates the wine by assigning it a score between 80 and 100. The reviews are writ-

---

[2]Vivino: http://www.vivino.com
[3]Delectable: http://www.delectable.com

[4]Downloading took place in February 2015

ten by 33 different experts, and can be considered concise, with an average length of 39 words.

Wine reviews have a distinct style and vocabulary, which tends to focus on smell and flavor descriptions, as shown in example reviews 1 and 2 from our data. As noted previously, wine experts use creative metaphors to characterize the smell and flavor of a wine, as well as source-based descriptions. The metaphors perhaps add variation to otherwise dull or repetitive descriptions (Paradis and Eeg-Olofsson, 2013; Suárez Toste, 2007).

1. *There is not a great deal of dolcetto grown in the Northwest, but this is the best version I've yet seen. Its vivid, spicy fruit core expresses the soil, the plant and the grape in equal proportion. Sappy flavors of spiced plum and wild berry hold the fort; it's built like a race car, sleek and stylish, with a powerful, tannic frame.*

2. *Here's a fragrant and very aromatic Grillo with cheerful notes of peach, passion fruit and mango. The wine has an easy approach and would pair perfectly with appetizers or finger foods.*

4 Methodology

In our classification experiments, we evaluated the viability of predicting the following four wine properties: color, grape variety, price, and country of origin. Wines can be categorized into three different **colors**: white, red and rosé. The database of winemag.com is not complete in all metadata fields. We excluded reviews with missing metadata from our experiments, and performed this selection separately for each metadata field. For instance, we excluded 5,328 wines without a color label in the color labeling experiment.

For **grape variety** we only considered those wines that were produced from a single grape and for which we had at least 200 reviews in the training set, leading to 33 categories. We disregarded all wines with grape blends, as these can have different ratios of different grape varieties. When different names were used for the same grape, we normalized these to the same category; e.g., *Pinot Gris* (French) and *Pinot Grigio* (Italian) were mapped together manually.

The sample contained wines from 47 different **countries**, ranging from South Korea (3 wines) to USA (31,401 wines). Even though **price** itself is an objective value, a division into cheap and expensive prices is a rather subjective choice. We tested two alternatives: a discretization where cheap wine costs less than $10 and expensive wine at least $100; and a more relaxed version

where cheap means less then $15 and expensive at least $50. Wines between these prices were left out in both price experiments.

We pre-processed the data set automatically with the Stanford toolkit (Manning et al., 2014): we tokenized, PoS-tagged and lemmatized the reviews. For the classification experiments, we split the randomized data set into an 80% training and 20% test set. As information sources, we use both lexical and semantic features. A first experimental setup merely uses a bag-of-words (BoW) representation of the wine reviews. To construct these BoW features, we lowercased all lemmas in the review and selected only the content words (PoS-tag *noun*, *verb* or *adjective*) that occurred at least twice in the training set.

As the reviews are short and only contain about 23 content words on average, we decided to also add semantic features to reduce data sparsity. As shown by Kusner and colleagues (2015), semantic representations such as Latent Semantic Indexing and Latent Dirichlet Allocation (LDA) can outperform a BoW representation. For our second experimental setup, we combined our set of BoW features with (1) 100 topics generated with Latent Dirichlet Allocation (Blei, 2012), and (2) 100 clusters based on word embeddings generated with Word2Vec (Mikolov et al., 2013). We ran initial experiments with exemplar-based classification and experimented with different cluster (Word2Vec) and topic (LDA) sizes of 100, 500, 1000, 2000 on the training set. For LDA (McCallum, 2002), we also varied the threshold to assign a topic only to a text when it covered 1%, 2%, or 5% of the text. The best results were obtained with 100 topics and a proportion threshold of 1%. We used these settings throughout our experiments. Two examples of LDA topics are shown here:

LDA42 color rosé strawberry raspberry pink flavor aroma wine light red cherry pale rise dry fresh

LDA49 flavor acidity wine crisp dry clean lime peach citrus lemon fruit pineapple white vanilla

To create the word embeddings we ran Word2Vec on the training corpus, applying the BoW model, a context size of 8, and a word vector dimensionality of 200 features. In a next step, K-means clustering (with $k = 100$) was applied on the resulting word vectors. As an example, we show part of the terms contained by cluster 20, which all have the connotation of "dark/intense":

Property	#test instances	Bag-of-Word features	combined: BoW+LDA+W2V	combined optimised
color	14,213	90.7	94.3	97.6
country	15,317	44.4	58.0	78.2
price big difference	1,135	60.9	61.0	94.6
price small difference	4,922	65.0	80.8	90.6
variety	9,946	30.5	36.6	70.6

Table 1: F-scores per task for Bag-of-Word features, a combination of BoW, LDA and Word2Vec clusters, and combined & optimised LIBSVM parameters.

Word2Vec20 asphalt black-fruit blackness burly dark deep inky masculine muscular purple roasted saturated sun-baked superconcentrated

The Word2Vec clusters were then implemented as binary features, meaning that for each instance containing a word occurring in one of the clusters, the respective cluster is coded by "1" in the feature vector, while the other cluster features are coded as "0".

As a classifier, we used LIBSVM (Chang and Lin, 2011), with the RBF kernel and optimized parameters c and g per prediction task. The parameters for SVM were optimized by means of a Grid search on a randomized subset (5,000 instances) of the training data, resulting in the following parameter settings:

- *color*: $c = 8.0$, $g = 0.0078125$
- *variety*: $c = 8.0$, $g = 0.0078125$
- *country*: $c = 32.0$, $g = 0.00048828125$
- *price big difference*: $c = 8.0$, $g = 0.03125$
- *price small difference*: $c = 8.0$, $g = 0.0078125$

5 Results

Table 1 presents the classification results per wine property for three system flavors: (1) feature vectors including BoW, (2) feature vectors combining BoW features, LDA and Word2Vec clusters, and (3) combined feature vectors trained with an SVM classifier with optimized hyperparameters c and g. The results confirm the initial hypothesis that adding semantic information helps the classifier. In addition, optimizing the c and g parameters for the LIBSVM RBF kernel results in markedly higher classification scores.

To get some insight into what terms are important for these classification results, we computed chi-square feature weights on the training set of examples for the different tasks. The top-10 features with highest chi-square values are shown in Table 2[5].

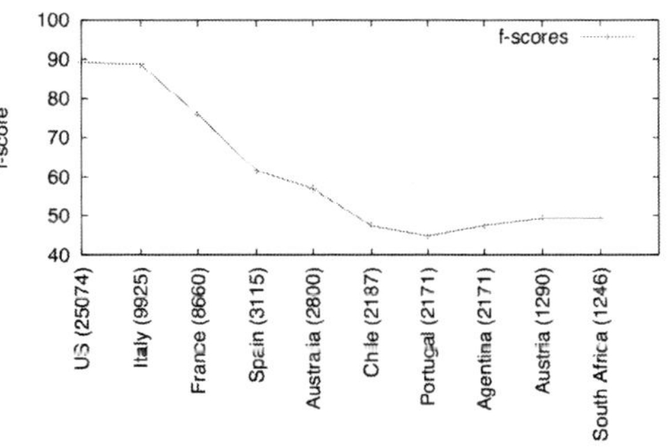

Figure 1: More training material leads to better individual F-scores, as shown for the 10 most frequent country classes.

The classifier for color achieves a rather high F-score, as illustrated in Table 3. The rosé category is the odd one out with a markedly lower F-score. There are two main reasons for this. First, rosé is a low-frequency class compared to the other two classes. Second, rosé wine is made from red grapes, but the grapes are processed in a different way to red wines. Therefore, we expect to find a certain amount of overlap between red and rosé. When we examine the confusion matrix of the classifiers' predictions on the test set, we see that, indeed, most errors are due to misclassifying rosé as red wine.

One could argue color prediction from wine reviews is trivial where the wine color is actually mentioned in the review. Therefore, we also performed an additional experiment with a BoW feature set (with optimized SVM parameters) where the words *red, white,* and *rosé* were removed. This affected the overall F-score by 2.2 points, with the

---

[5] The variety features are all grape names. For the country features: prokubac is a Serbian grape variety, meoru is a Korean grape that grows at mount Jiri. Yves refers to a French producer. Calatrasus is an erroneous lemma form predicted by the Stanford toolkit for the Italian wine producer Calatrasi.

color	rosé, cherry, tannin, apple, peach, citrus, pear, blush, black, pineapple, chardonnay
variety	aglianico, barbera, prosecco, viognier, moscato, malbec, sirah, carmenère, chenin, zin, franc
country	korea, jiri, rose-like, meoru, morocco, serbian, yves, calatrasus, chocolate-cherry, prokupac
price	year, tannin, age, rich, blackberry, black, vineyard, cellar, currant, vintage, simple

Table 2: Top 10 features based on Chi-Square measures on the training set.

class	#number	prec	recall	f-score
red	9296	97.7	99.0	98.4
white	4582	97.6	97.1	97.4
rose	335	94.5	66.3	77.9

Table 3: Results with optimized and combined SVM for color classification on the test set.

decrease due mostly to the performance drop of the rosé class from an F-score of 76.0 to 31.7.

For the property country we see that more training material has a positive effect on the individual scores, as visualized in Figure 1.

For grape varieties we find individual F-scores varying between 82.4 (Chardonnay grape) and 30.8 (Grenache). The Tempranillo grape, for example, is known for its rather neutral profile, and as a consequence it is often used in blends. The classifier could only distinguish the Tempanillo variety at a moderate rate (F-score 47.5), and the confusion matrix showed it is confused with Cabernet Sauvignon, Malbec, Pinot Noir, and Syrah. Varieties that were relatively easy to predict were Grüner Veltliner (F-score 74.3) and Nebbiolo (F-score 78.6). These grapes are rather strictly bound to geographic areas (Nebbiolo is from the region Piemonte, Italy and Grüner Veltliner is a typical Austrian grape). Cabernet Sauvignon (F-score 68.4) and Syrah (F-score 65.2) are common grapes for which we had many training examples, but they were often wrongly predicted as labels, leading to low precision. We are aware the location of wineries can strongly influence the sensory properties of a wine. The higher scores for grape varieties which are clearly tied to a particular region further confirms this.

With regard to the price, the more relaxed version (*price big difference*) does not seem to benefit from adding semantic features. An analysis of the classification output revealed the trained SVM model nearly always predicts the majority class for both the BoW and combined features, whereas the optimised version predicts both classes with an F-score of 94.6%. In future research, we intend to recast the price classification as a regression task.

6 Conclusions

We have demonstrated that wine experts are capable of describing wines in a sufficiently consistent manner that we can use their descriptions to predict the properties of a wine based solely on its review. Using existing NLP tools and techniques, we were able to produce classifiers that could predict the color, grape variety, price and country of origin of thousands of wines with high F-scores.

This study is a first step in a larger investigation into the relationship between expert language and sensory descriptions. We are particularly interested in lexical descriptors used for smells and flavors, and aim to study the specific terminology at the phrase level. It would also be informative to know to what extent the wines were classified on the basis of smell and flavor descriptions per se, as opposed to other information provided in the reviews, such as vineyard or producer descriptions, for example. The present models cannot address this. In addition, it is interesting to investigate questions of genre and style. For example, we could ask to what extent does the writing style of an author, or the wine ratings, affect these results. Finally, we expect there are differences in the way wines are described in different countries and different languages. Ultimately a multilingual, multinational comparison of wine reviews could uncover further insights into the human linguistic potential for describing complex smells and flavors.

Acknowledgments

Part of this work was funded by The Netherlands Organization for Scientific Research: NWO VICI grant "Human olfaction at the intersection of language, culture and biology", project number 277-70-011.

References

Davis M. Blei. 2012. Probabilistic topic models. *Communications of the ACM*, 55(4):77–84.

Frédéric Brochet and Denis Dubourdieu. 2001. Wine descriptive language supports cognitive specificity of chemical senses. *Brain and Language*, 77:187–196.

Rosario Caballero and Ernesto Suárez-Toste. 2010. A genre approach to imagery in winespeak: Issues and prospects. *Researching and applying metaphor in the real world*, 26:265–288.

William S Cain. 1979. To know with the nose: keys to odor identification. *Science*, 203(4379):467–470.

Chih-Chung Chang and Chih-Jen Lin. 2011. LIB-SVM: A library for support vector machines. *ACM Transactions on Intelligent Systems and Technology*, 2:27:1–27:27. Software available at http://www.csie.ntu.edu.tw/~cjlin/libsvm.

Deng-feng Chen, Qi-chun Ji, Liang Zhao, and Hong-cai Zhang. 2009. The classification of wine based on pca and ann. In Bingyuan Cao, Tai-Fu Li, and Cheng-Yi Zhang, editors, *Fuzzy Information and Engineering Volume 2*, volume 62 of *Advances in Intelligent and Soft Computing*, pages 647–655. Springer Berlin Heidelberg.

Paulo Cortez, António Cerdeira, Fernando Almeida, Telmo Matos, and José Reis. 2009. Modeling wine preferences by data mining from physicochemical properties. *Decision Support Systems*, 47(4):547–553.

Ilja Croijmans and Asifa Majid. 2016. Not all flavor expertise is equal: The language of wine and coffee experts. *PLoS ONE*.

Richard Gawel and Peter Godden. 2008. Evaluation of the consistency of wine quality assessments from expert wine tasters. *Australian Journal of Grape and Wine Research*, 14(1):1–8.

Robin Goldstein, Johan Almenberg, Anna Dreber, John W Emerson, Alexis Herschkowitsch, and Jacob Katz. 2008. Do more expensive wines taste better? evidence from a large sample of blind tastings. *Journal of Wine Economics*, 3(01).1–9.

Helene Hopfer and Hildegarde Heymann. 2014. Judging wine quality: Do we need experts, consumers or trained panelists? *Food Quality and Preference*, 32:221–233.

Øyvind Horverak. 2009. Wine journalism—marketing or consumers' guide? *Marketing Science*, 28(3):573–579.

Matt Kusner, Yu Sun, Nicholas Kolkin, and Kilian Q Weinberger. 2015. From word embeddings to document distances. In *Proceedings of the 32nd International Conference on Machine Learning (ICML-15)*, pages 957–966.

Harry T Lawless. 1984. Flavor description of white wine by "expert" and nonexpert wine consumers. *Journal of Food Science*, 49(1):120–123.

Sébastien Lecocq and Michael Visser. 2006. What determines wine prices: Objective vs. sensory characteristics. *Journal of Wine Economics*, 1(01):42–56.

Stephen C Levinson and Asifa Majid. 2014. Differential ineffability and the senses. *Mind & Language*, 29(4):407–427.

Asifa Majid and Niclas Burenhult. 2014. Odors are expressible in language, as long as you speak the right language. *Cognition*, 130(2):266–270.

Christopher D. Manning, Mihai Surdeanu, John Bauer, Jenny Finkel, Steven J. Bethard, and David McClosky. 2014. The Stanford CoreNLP natural language processing toolkit. In *Association for Computational Linguistics (ACL) System Demonstrations*, pages 55–60.

Andrew McCallum. 2002. MALLET: A machine learning for language toolkit. http://mallet.cs.umass.edu.

Elin McCoy. 2006. *The Emperor of Wine: The Rise of Robert M. Parker, Jr., and the Reign of American Taste*. Harper Perennial.

Tomas Mikolov, ILya Sutskever, Kai Chen, Greg Corrado, and Jeff Dean. 2013. Distributed representations of words and phrases and their compositionality. *Advances in Neural Information Processing Systems 26*, pages 3111–3119.

Edward Oczkowski and Hristos Doucouliagos. 2014. Wine prices and quality ratings: A meta-regression analysis. *American Journal of Agricultural Economics*, page aau057.

Jonas K Olofsson and Jay A Gottfried. 2015. The muted sense: neurocognitive limitations of olfactory language. *Trends in cognitive sciences*, 19(6):314–321.

Carita Paradis and Mats Eeg-Olofsson. 2013. Describing sensory experience: The genre of wine reviews. *Metaphor and Symbol*, 28(1):22–40.

Wendy V Parr, David Heatherbell, and K Geoffrey White. 2002. Demystifying wine expertise: olfactory threshold, perceptual skill and semantic memory in expert and novice wine judges. *Chemical Senses*, 27(8):747–755.

Caroline Sezille, Arnaud Fournel, Catherine Rouby, Fanny Rinck, and Moustafa Bensafi. 2014. Hedonic appreciation and verbal description of pleasant and unpleasant odors in untrained, trainee cooks, flavorists, and perfumers. *Front. Psychol*, 5:12.

Michael Silverstein. 2006. Old wine, new ethnographic lexicography. *Annual Review of Anthropology*, 35:481–496.

Ernesto Suárez Toste. 2007. Metaphor inside the wine cellar: On the ubiquity of personification schemas in winespeak. *Metaphorik. de*, 12(1):53–64.

Debbie Vigar-Ellis, Leyland Pitt, and Albert Caruana. 2015. Knowledge effects on the exploratory acquisition of wine. *International Journal of Wine Business Research*, 27(2):84–102.

Gesualdo M. Zucco, Aurelio Carassai, Maria Rosa Baroni, and Richard J. Stevenson. 2011. Labeling, identification, and recognition of wine-relevant odorants in expert sommeliers, intermediates, and untrained wine drinkers. *Perception*, 40(5):598–607.

Exploring Stylistic Variation with Age and Income on Twitter

Lucie Flekova[*]
Ubiquitous Knowledge Processing Lab
Department of Computer Science
Technische Universität Darmstadt
`www.ukp.tu-darmstadt.de`

Lyle Ungar and **Daniel Preoţiuc-Pietro**
Computer & Information Science
University of Pennsylvania
`ungar@cis.upenn.edu`
`danielpr@sas.upenn.edu`

Abstract

Writing style allows NLP tools to adjust to the traits of an author. In this paper, we explore the relation between stylistic and syntactic features and authors' age and income. We confirm our hypothesis that for numerous feature types writing style is predictive of income even beyond age. We analyze the predictive power of writing style features in a regression task on two data sets of around 5,000 Twitter users each. Additionally, we use our validated features to study daily variations in writing style of users from distinct income groups. Temporal stylistic patterns not only provide novel psychological insight into user behavior, but are useful for future research and applications in social media.

1 Introduction

The widespread use of social media enables researchers to examine human behavior at a scale hardly imaginable before. Research in text profiling has recently shown that a diverse set of user traits is predictable from language use. Examples range from demographics such as age (Rao et al., 2010), gender (Burger et al., 2011; Bamman et al., 2014), popularity (Lampos et al., 2014), occupation (Preoţiuc-Pietro et al., 2015a) and location (Eisenstein et al., 2010) to psychological traits such as personality (Schwartz et al., 2013) or mental illness (De Choudhury et al., 2013) and their interplay (Preotiuc-Pietro et al., 2015). To a large extent, the prominent differences captured by text are topical: adolescents post more about school, females about relationships (Sap et al., 2014) and sport fans about their local team (Cheng et al.,

2010). Writing style and readability offer a different insight into who the authors are. This can help applications such as cross-lingual adaptations without direct translation, for text simplification closely matching the reader's age, level of education and income or tailored to the specific moment the document is presented. Recently, Hovy and Søgaard (2015) have shown that the age of the authors should be taken into account when building and using part-of-speech taggers. Likewise, socioeconomic factors have been found to influence language use (Labov, 2006). Understanding these biases and their underlying factors in detail is important to develop NLP tools without socio-demographic bias.

Writing style measures have initially been created to be applied at the document level, where they are often used to assess the quality of a document (Louis and Nenkova, 2013) or a summarization (Louis and Nenkova, 2014) , or even to predict the success of a novel (Ashok et al., 2013). In contrast to these document-level studies, we adopt a user-centric approach to measuring stylistic differences. We examine writing style of users on Twitter in relation to their age and income. Both attributes should be closely related to writing style: users of older age write on average more standard-conform (up to a certain point), and higher income is an indicator of education and conscientiousness (Judge et al., 1999), which determines writing style. Indeed, many features that aim to measure the complexity of the language use have been developed in order to study human cognitive abilities, e.g., cognitive decline (Boyé et al., 2014; Le et al., 2011).

The relationship between age and language has been extensively studied by psychologists, and more recently by computational linguists in various corpora, including social media. Pennebaker et al. (2003) connect language use with style and personality, while Schler et al. (2006) automatically

---

[*] Project carried out during a research stay at the University of Pennsylvania

Proceedings of the 54th Annual Meeting of the Association for Computational Linguistics, pages 313–319,
Berlin, Germany, August 7-12, 2016. ©2016 Association for Computational Linguistics

classified blogs text into three classes based on self-reported age using part-of-speech features. Johannsen et al. (2015) uncover some consistent age patterns in part-of-speech usage across languages, while Rosenthal and McKeown (2011) studies the use of Internet specific phenomena such as slang, acronyms and capitalisation patterns. Preoţiuc-Pietro et al. (2016) study differences in paraphrase choice between older and younger Twitter users as a measure of style. Nguyen et al. (2013) analyzed the relationship between language use and age, modelled as a continuous variable. They found similar language usage trends for both genders, with increasing word and tweet length with age, and an increasing tendency to write more grammatically correct, standardized text. Such findings encourage further research in the area of measuring readability, which not only facilitates adjusting the text to the reader (Danescu-Niculescu-Mizil et al., 2011), but can also play an important role in identifying authorial style (Pitler and Nenkova, 2008). Davenport and DeLine (2014) report negative correlation between tweet readability (i.e., simplicity) and the percentage of people with college degree in the area. Eisenstein et al. (2011) employ language use as a socio-demographic predictor.

In this paper we analyze two data sets of millions of tweets produced by thousands of users annotated with their age and income. We define a set of features ranging from readability and style to syntactic features. We use both linear and non-linear machine learning regression methods to predict and analyze user income and age. We show that writing style measures give large correlations with both age and income, and that writing style is predictive of income even beyond age. Finally, Twitter data allows the unique possibility to study the variation in writing with time. We explore the effects of time of day in user behavior dependent in part on the socio-demographic group.

2 Data

We study two large data sets of tweets. Each data set consists of users and their historical record of tweet content, profile information and trait level features extracted with high precision from their profile information. All data was tokenized using the Trendminer pipeline (Preoţiuc-Pietro et al., 2012), @-mentions and URL's collapsed, automatically filtered for English using the *langid.py* tool (Lui and Baldwin, 2012) and part-of-speech tagged using the ArkTweet POS tagger (Gimpel et al., 2011).

Income ($\mathcal{D}_1$) First, we use a large data set consisting of 5,191 Twitter users mapped to their income through their occupational class. This data set, introduced in (Preoţiuc-Pietro et al., 2015a; Preoţiuc-Pietro et al., 2015b), relies on a standardised job classification taxonomy (the UK Standard Occupational Classification) to extract job-related keywords, search user profile fields for users having those jobs and map them to their mean UK income, independently of user location. The final data set consists of 10,796,836 tweets.

Age ($\mathcal{D}_2$) The age data set consists of 4,279 users mapped to their age from (Volkova and Bachrach, 2015). The final data set consists of 574,095 tweets.

3 Features

We use a variety of features to capture the language behavior of a user. We group these features into:

Surface We measure the length of tweets in words and characters, and the length of words. As shorter words are considered more readable (Gunning, 1969; Pitler and Nenkova, 2008), we also measure the ratio of words longer than five letters. We further calculate the type-token ratio per user, which indicates the lexical density of text and is considered to be a readability predictor (Oakland and Lane, 2004). Additionally we capture the number of positive and negative smileys in the tweet and the number of URLs.

Readability After filtering tweets to contain only words, we use the most prominent readability measures per user: the Automatic Readability Index (Senter and Smith, 1967), the Flesch-Kincaid Grade Level (Kincaid et al., 1975), the Coleman-Liau Index (Coleman and Liau, 1975), the Flesch Reading Ease (Flesch, 1948), the LIX Index (Anderson, 1983), the SMOG grade (McLaughlin, 1969) and the Gunning-Fog Index (Gunning, 1969). The majority of those are computed using the average word and sentence lengths and number of syllables per sentence, combined with weights.

Syntax Researchers argue about longer sentences not necessarily being more complex in terms of syntax (Feng et al., 2009; Pitler and Nenkova, 2008). However, advanced sentence parsing on Twitter remains a challenging task. We thus limit ourselves in this study to the part-of-speech (POS)

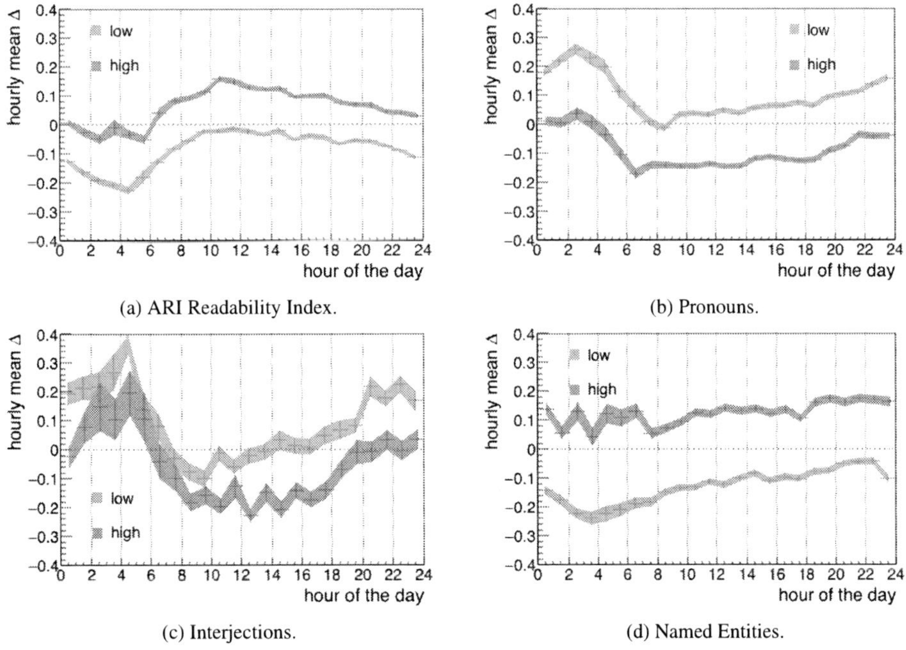

(a) ARI Readability Index.   (b) Pronouns.

(c) Interjections.   (d) Named Entities.

Figure 1: Temporal patterns for groups of lowest (blue) and highest (orange) income users in our data set. X-axis shows the course of 24 hours in normalized time of day. Y-axis shows a normalized difference of the hourly means from the overall mean feature value. Width of a line shows the standard error.

information. In previous work on writing style (Pennebaker et al., 2003; Argamon et al., 2009; Rangel et al., 2014), a text with more nouns and articles as opposed to pronouns and adverbs is considered more formal. We thus measure the ratio of each POS using the universal tagset (Petrov et al., 2012).

Style We implemented a contextuality measure, based on the work of Heylighen and Dewaele (2002), which assesses explicitness of the text based on the POS used and serves as a proxy for formality. Using Stanford Named Entity Recognizer (Finkel et al., 2005), we measure the proportion of named entities (3-classed) to words, as their presence potentially decreases readability (Beinborn et al., 2012), and netspeak aspects such as the proportion of elongations (*wooow*) and words with numbers (*good n8*). We quantify the number of hedges (Hyland, 2005) and abstract words[1] used, and the ratio of standalone numbers stated per user as these are indicators of specificity (Pennebaker et al., 2003; Pitler and Nenkova, 2008). We also capture the ratio of hapax legomena, and of superlatives and plurals using Stanford POS Tagger

---

[1] www.englishbanana.com

(Toutanova et al., 2003) using the Twitter model.

4 Temporal Patterns in Style

Social media data offers the opportunity to interpret the features in a richer context, including time or space. In our income data set, a timestamp is available for each message. Golder and Macy (2011) showed user-level diurnal and seasonal patterns of mood across the world using Twitter data, suggesting that individuals awaken in a good mood that deteriorates as the day progresses. In this work we explore user-level daily temporal trends in style for the 1500 highest- and 1500 lowest-income users (mean income $\geq$ £35,000 vs mean income $\leq$ £25,000). In Figure 1 we present normalized temporal patterns for a selected set of features.

While the difference between groups is most striking, we also observe some consistent daily patterns. These display an increase in readability (Figure 1a) starting in the early hours of the morning, peaking at 10AM and then decreasing constantly throughout the day, which is in accordance with the mood swings reported by Golder and Macy (2011). The proportion of pronouns (Figure 1b) and interjections (Figure 1c) follows the exact opposite pattern, with a peak in frequency during nights. This suggests that the language gets more contextual (Heylighen and Dewaele, 2002) towards the end of the day. Finally, named entities (Figure 1d) display a very distinctive pattern, with a constant increase starting mornings, which increases throughout the day. While the first three patterns mirror the active parts of the day, coinciding with regular working hours, the latter pattern is possibly associated with mentions of venues or news. An increase in usage of named entities in the evening is steeper for low-income users - we hypothesize that this phenomenon could be reasoned by a stronger association of named entities with leisure in this user group. Overall, we notice a similarity between income groups, which, despite strongly separated, follow similar – perhaps universal – patterns.

5 Analysis

We view age and income as continuous variables and model them in a regression setup. This is in contrast to most previous studies on age as a categorical variable (Rangel et al., 2014) to allow for finer grained predictions useful for downstream applications which use exact values of user traits, as opposed to being limited to broad classes such as young vs. old. We apply linear regression with Elastic Net regularization (Zou and Hastie, 2005) and support vector regression with an RBF kernel (as a non-linear counterpart) for comparison (Vapnik, 1998). We report Pearson correlation results on 10-fold cross-validation. We also study if our features are predictive of income above age, by controlling for age assigned by a state-of-the-art model trained on social media data (Sap et al., 2014). Similar results have been obtained with log-scaling the income variable. Table 1 presents our prediction results. The strength of the correlation to the income and age, together with the sign of the correlation coefficient, are visually displayed in Figure 2.

As expected, all features correlate with age and income in the same direction. However, some features and groups are more predictive of one or the other (depicted above or below the principal diagonal in Figure 2). Most individual surface features correlate with age stronger than with income, with the exception of punctuation and, especially, words longer than 5 characters. The correlation of each readability measure is remarkably stronger with high income than with age, despite the fact

Features	Income ($\mathcal{D}_1$)		Age ($\mathcal{D}_2$)		Income-Age ($\mathcal{D}_1$)	
Readability	Lin	RSVM	Lin	RSVM	Lin	RSVM
ARI	.282	.311	.269	**.318**	.230	.263
Flesch-Kincaid	.285	.319	.263	.310	.234	.284
Coleman-Liau	.230	.197	.203	.265	.202	.289
Flesch RE	.277	**.345**	.186	.295	.239	**.318**
FOG	.291	.309	.222	.270	.238	.267
SMOG	.288	.339	.240	.263	.234	.301
LIX	.208	.286	.215	.268	.177	.245
ALL	**.301**	**.380**	**.278**	**.329**	**.249**	**.354**
Syntax	Lin	RSVM	Lin	RSVM	Lin	RSVM
Nouns	.155	.200	.278	**.302**	.078	**.150**
Verbs	.044	.071	(.046)	.104	.093	.114
Pronouns	.264	**.297**	.148	.180	.114	.127
Adverbs	.115	.110	.077	.111	.135	.131
Adjectives	(.030)	.149	.162	.200	(.046)	.139
Determiners	(.040)	.070	.135	.154	.103	.121
Interjections	.123	.188	.084	.122	.059	.139
ALL	**.323**	**.258**	**.319**	**.229**	**.299**	**.267**
Style	Lin	RSVM	Lin	RSVM	Lin	RSVM
Named entities	.241	**.288**	.282	.293	.255	**.281**
Contextuality	(.044)	.204	.287	**.310**	(.030)	.134
Abstract words	.108	.120	.141	.183	.125	.139
Hedging	(.019)	.079	(.015)	.000	.(000)	.083
Specific (num)	.093	.011	.072	.176	.059	.124
Elongations	.097	.160	.072	.073	.056	.114
Hapax legom.	.056	.066	.160	.219	.064	.067
ALL	**.279**	**.347**	**.306**	**.134**	**.296**	**.312**
Surface	Lin	RSVM	Lin	RSVM	Lin	RSVM
# char. / token	.085	.144	.104	.148	.051	.101
# tokens / tweet	.158	.159	.228	.237	.115	.116
# char. / tweet	.214	**.261**	.262	**.278**	.153	**.169**
# words >5 char.	.139	.191	(.009)	.087	.112	.163
Type/token ratio	.099	.132	.090	.180	.100	.126
Punctuation	.218	.123	.093	.086	.057	.084
Smileys	.064	.113	.146	.144	(.030)	.090
URLs	.084	.128	.187	.194	(.040)	.077
ALL	**.379**	**.330**	**.294**	**.307**	**.352**	**.126**

Table 1: Predictive performance (Pearson correlation) for Income, Age and Income controlled for predicted age using linear (Lin) and non-linear (RSVM) learning methods. The last line of each sub-table shows the results for all features from that block together, while individual rows display individual performance for the predictive features. Numbers in bold represent the highest correlations from the specific block of features and data set. All correlations are significant on $p < 0.001$ level except for those in brackets.

these are to a large extent based on the surface features. Notably, Flesch Reading Ease – previously reported to correlate with education levels at a community level (Davenport and DeLine, 2014) and with the usage of pronouns (Štajner et al., 2012) – is highly indicative for income. On the syntactic level we observe that increased use of nouns, determiners and adjectives is correlated higher with age as opposed to income, while a high ratio of pronouns and interjections is a good predictor of lower income but, only to a lesser extent, younger age, with which it is traditionally associated (Schler et al., 2006). From the stylistic features, the contextuality measure stands out as being correlated with increase in age, in line with Heylighen and De-

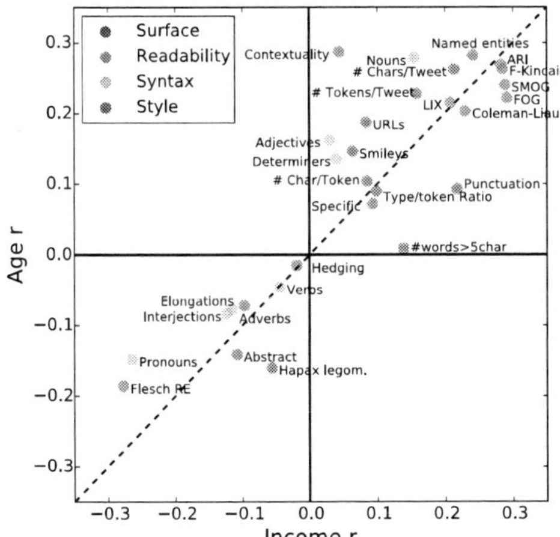

Figure 2: Predictive performance (Pearson correlation) for Income and Age. Individual points display univariate correlations (including sign) of the most predictive features.

waele (2002), but is almost orthogonal to income. Similarly, the frequency of named entities is correlated with higher income, while elongations have stronger association with younger age. Our results show, that based on the desired application, one can exploit these differences to tailor the style of a document without altering the topic to suit either age or income individually.

6 Conclusions and Future Work

Using two large data sets from thousands of users, annotated with their age and income, we presented the first study which analyzes these variables jointly, in relation to writing style. We have shown that the stylistic measures not only obtain significant correlations with both age and income, but are predictive of income beyond age. Moreover, we explored temporal patterns in user behavior on Twitter, discovering intriguing trends in writing style. While the discovery of these patterns provides useful psychosocial insight, it additionally hints to future research and applications that piggyback on author profiling in social media e.g., taking the message timestamp into account for stylistic features may yield improved results in user sociodemographic predictions. Likewise, utilizing additional proxies to control for income and education may lead to improvements in user age prediction.

Acknowledgments

The authors acknowledge the support from Templeton Religion Trust, grant TRT-0048. We also wish to thank Prof. Iryna Gurevych for supporting the collaboration.

References

Jonathan Anderson. 1983. LIX and RIX: Variations on a Little-Known Readability Index. *Journal of Reading*, pages 490–496.

Shlomo Argamon, Moshe Koppel, James W. Pennebaker, and Jonathan Schler. 2009. Automatically Profiling the Author of an Anonymous Text. *Communications of the ACM*, 52(2).

Vikas Ganjigunte Ashok, Song Feng, and Yejin Choi. 2013. Success with style: Using writing style to predict the success of novels. In *Proceedings of the Conference on Empirical Methods in Natural Language Processing*, EMNLP.

David Bamman, Jacob Eisenstein, and Tyler Schnoebelen. 2014. Gender Identity and Lexical Variation in Social Media. *Journal of Sociolinguistics*, 18(2):135–160.

Lisa Beinborn, Torsten Zesch, and Iryna Gurevych. 2012. Towards Fine-Grained Readability Measures for Self-Directed Language Learning. In *Proceedings of the SLTC 2012 workshop on NLP for CALL*.

Maité Boyé, Thi Mai Tran, and Natalia Grabar. 2014. Nlp-oriented contrastive study of linguistic productions of alzheimer and control people. In LNCS 8686 Springer, Advances in Natural Language Processing, editor, *POLTAL*, pages 412–424.

D. John Burger, John Henderson, George Kim, and Guido Zarrella. 2011. Discriminating Gender on Twitter. In *Proceedings of the 2011 Conference on Empirical Methods in Natural Language Processing*, EMNLP.

Zhiyuan Cheng, James Caverlee, and Kyumin Lee. 2010. You are where you Tweet: A Content-based Approach to Geo-locating Twitter Users. In *Proceedings of the 19th ACM Conference on Information and Knowledge Management*, CIKM.

Meri Coleman and TL Liau. 1975. A Computer Readability Formula Designed for Machine Scoring. *Journal of Applied Psychology*, 60(2).

Cristian Danescu-Niculescu-Mizil, Michael Gamon, and Susan Dumais. 2011. Mark my Words!: Linguistic Style Accommodation in Social Media. In *Proceedings of the 20th International Conference on World Wide Web*, WWW.

James RA Davenport and Robert DeLine. 2014. The Readability of Tweets and their Geographic Correlation with Education. *arXiv preprint arXiv:1401.6058*.

Munmun De Choudhury, Michael Gamon, Scott Counts, and Eric Horvitz. 2013. Predicting Depression via Social Media. In *Proceedings of the Seventh International AAAI Conference on Weblogs and Social Media*, ICWSM.

Jacob Eisenstein, Brendan O'Connor, Noah A. Smith, and Eric P. Xing. 2010. A latent variable model for geographic lexical variation. In *Proceedings of the Conference on Empirical Methods in Natural Language Processing*, EMNLP.

Jacob Eisenstein, Noah A Smith, and Eric P Xing. 2011. Discovering Sociolinguistic Associations with Structured Sparsity. In *Proceedings of the 49th annual meeting of the Association for Computational Linguistics: Human Language Technologies*, NAACL.

Lijun Feng, Noémie Elhadad, and Matt Huenerfauth. 2009. Cognitively Motivated Features for Readability Assessment. In *Proceedings of the 12th Conference of the European Chapter of the Association for Computational Linguistics*, EACL.

Jenny Rose Finkel, Trond Grenager, and Christopher Manning. 2005. Incorporating Non-Local Information into Information extraction Systems by Gibbs Sampling. In *Proceedings of the 43rd Annual Meeting of the Association for Computational Linguistics*, ACL.

Rudolf Flesch. 1948. A New Readability Yardstick. *The Journal of Applied Psychology*, 32(3).

Kevin Gimpel, Nathan Schneider, Brendan O'Connor, Dipanjan Das, Daniel Mills, Jacob Eisenstein, Michael Heilman, Dani Yogatama, Jeffrey Flanigan, and Noah A. Smith. 2011. Part-of-Speech Tagging for Twitter: Annotation, Features, and Experiments. In *Proceedings of the 49th annual meeting of the Association for Computational Linguistics*, ACL.

Scott A. Golder and Michael W. Macy. 2011. Diurnal and Seasonal Mood Vary with Work, Sleep, and Daylength Across Diverse Cultures. *Science*, 333.

Robert Gunning. 1969. The Fog index after Twenty Years. *Journal of Business Communication*, 6(2).

Francis Heylighen and Jean-Marc Dewaele. 2002. Variation in the Contextuality of Language: An Empirical Measure. *Foundations of Science*, 7(3).

Dirk Hovy and Anders Søgaard. 2015. Tagging Performance Correlates with Author Age. In *Proceedings of the 53rd Annual Meeting of the Association for Computational Linguistics*, ACL.

Ken Hyland. 2005. Stance and Engagement: A Model of Interaction in Academic Discourse. *Discourse Studies*, 7(2):173–192.

Anders Johannsen, Dirk Hovy, and Anders Sogaard. 2015. Cross-lingual syntactic variation over age and gender. In *CONNL*.

Timothy A. Judge, Chad A. Higgins, Carl J. Thoresen, and Murray R. Barrick. 1999. The big five personality traits, general mental ability, and carreer success across the life span. *Personnel Psychology*, 52.

J Peter Kincaid, Robert P Fishburne Jr, Richard L Rogers, and Brad S Chissom. 1975. Derivation of New Readability Formulas (Automated Readability Index, Fog Count and Flesch Reading Ease Formula) for Navy Enlisted Personnel. Technical report, Naval Technical Training Command Millington TN Research Branch.

William Labov. 2006. *The Social Stratification of English in New York City*. Cambridge University Press.

Vasileios Lampos, Nikolaos Aletras, Daniel Preoţiuc-Pietro, and Trevor Cohn. 2014. Predicting and Characterising User Impact on Twitter. In *Proceedings of the 14th Conference of the European Chapter of the Association for Computational Linguistics*, EACL, pages 405–413.

Xuan Le, Ian Lancashire, Graeme Hirst, and Regina Jokel. 2011. Longitudinal Detection of Dementia through Lexical and Syntactic Changes in Writing: A Case Study of Three British Novelists. *Literary and Linguistic Computing*, 26(4).

Annie Louis and Ani Nenkova. 2013. What makes Writing Great? First Experiments on Article Quality Prediction in the Science Journalism Domain. *Transactions of the Association for Computational Linguistics*.

Annie Louis and Ani Nenkova. 2014. Verbose, Laconic or Just Right: A Simple Computational Model of Content Appropriateness under Length Constraints. In *Proceedings of the 14th Conference of the European Chapter of the Association for Computational Linguistics*, EACL.

Marco Lui and Timothy Baldwin. 2012. langid.py: An Off-the-Shelf Language Identification Tool. In *Proceedings of the 50th Annual Meeting of the Association for Computational Linguistics*, ACL.

G Harry McLaughlin. 1969. SMOG Grading: A New Readability Formula. *Journal of Reading*, 12(8).

Dong Nguyen, Rilana Gravel, Dolf Trieschnigg, and Theo Meder. 2013. 'How Old do you Think I am?'; A Study of Language and Age in Twitter. In *Proceedings of the Seventh International AAAI Conference on Weblogs and Social Media*, ICWSM.

Thomas Oakland and Holly B Lane. 2004. Language, Reading, and Readability Formulas: Implications for Developing and Adapting Tests. *International Journal of Testing*, 4(3):239–252.

J.W. Pennebaker, Matthias R. Mehl, and K.G. Niederhoffer. 2003. Psychological Aspects of Natural Language Use: Our Words, Our Selves. *Annual Review of Psychology*, 54(1).

Slav Petrov, Dipanjan Das, and Ryan T. McDonald. 2012. A Universal Part-of-Speech Tagset. In *Proceedings of the Eighth International Conference on Language Resources and Evaluation*, LREC.

Emily Pitler and Ani Nenkova. 2008. Revisiting Readability: A Unified Framework for Predicting Text Quality. In *Proceedings of the Conference on Empirical Methods in Natural Language Processing*, EMNLP.

Daniel Preoţiuc-Pietro, Sina Samangooei, Trevor Cohn, Nick Gibbins, and Mahesan Niranjan. 2012. Trendminer: An Architecture for Real Time Analysis of Social Media Text. In *Workshop on Real-Time Analysis and Mining of Social Streams*, ICWSM, pages 38–42.

Daniel Preoţiuc-Pietro, Vasileios Lampos, and Nikolaos Aletras. 2015a. An Analysis of the User Occupational Class through Twitter Content. In *Proceedings of the 53rd Annual Meeting of the Association for Computational Linguistics*, ACL.

Daniel Preoţiuc-Pietro, Svitlana Volkova, Vasileios Lampos, Yoram Bachrach, and Nikolaos Aletras. 2015b. Studying user income through language, behaviour and affect in social media. *PLoS ONE*.

Daniel Preoţiuc-Pietro, Wei Xu, and Lyle Ungar. 2016. Discovering User Attribute Stylistic Differences via Paraphrasing. In *Proceedings of the Thirtieth AAAI Conference on Artificial Intelligence*, AAAI.

Daniel Preotiuc-Pietro, Johannes Eichstaedt, Gregory Park, Maarten Sap, Laura Smith, Victoria Tobolsky, H Andrew Schwartz, and Lyle H Ungar. 2015. The Role of Personality, Age and Gender in Tweeting about Mental Illnesses. In *Proceedings of the Workshop on Computational Linguistics and Clinical Psychology: From Linguistic Signal to Clinical Reality*, NAACL.

Francisco Rangel, Paolo Rosso, Irina Chugur, Martin Potthast, Martin Trenkmann, Benno Stein, Ben Verhoeven, and Walter Daelemans. 2014. Overview of the 2nd Author Profiling Task at PAN 2014. In *Proceedings of the Conference and Labs of the Evaluation Forum (Working Notes)*, CLEF.

Delip Rao, David Yarowsky, Abhishek Shreevats, and Manaswi Gupta. 2010. Classifying Latent User Attributes in Twitter. In *Proceedings of the 2nd International Workshop on Search and Mining User-generated Contents*, SMUC.

Sara Rosenthal and Kathleen McKeown. 2011. Age Prediction in Blogs: A Study of Style, Content, and Online Behavior in Pre-and Post-Social Media Generations. In *Proceedings of the 53rd Annual Meeting of the Association for Computational Linguistics*, ACL.

Maarten Sap, Gregory Park, Johannes Eichstaedt, Margaret Kern, David Stillwell, Michal Kosinski, Lyle Ungar, and H Andrew Schwartz. 2014. Developing Age and Gender Predictive Lexica over Social Media. In *Proceedings of the 2014 Conference on Empirical Methods in Natural Language Processing*, EMNLP.

Jonathan Schler, Moshe Koppel, Shlomo Argamon, and James Pennebaker. 2006. Effects of Age and Gender on Blogging. In *Proceedings of 2006 AAAI Spring Symposium on Computational Approaches for Analyzing Weblogs*.

H Andrew Schwartz, Johannes C Eichstaedt, Margaret L Kern, Lukasz Dziurzynski, Stephanie M Ramones, Megha Agrawal, Achal Shah, Michal Kosinski, David Stillwell, Martin EP Seligman, and Lyle H Ungar. 2013. Personality, Gender, and Age in the Language of Social Media: The Open-Vocabulary Approach. *PLoS ONE*.

R.J. Senter and E.A. Smith. 1967. *Automated Readability Index*. Aerospace Medical Research Laboratories.

Sanja Štajner, Richard Evans, Constantin Orasan, and Ruslan Mitkov. 2012. What can readability measures really tell us about text complexity. In *NLP for Improving Textual Accessibility workshop*, pages 14–22.

Kristina Toutanova, Dan Klein, Christopher D. Manning, and Yoram Singer. 2003. Feature-rich Part-of-Speech Tagging with a Cyclic Dependency Network. In *Proceedings of the 2003 Conference of the North American Chapter of the Association for Computational Linguistics*, NAACL.

Vladimir N Vapnik. 1998. *Statistical learning theory*. Wiley.

Svitlana Volkova and Yoram Bachrach. 2015. On predicting socio-demographic traits and emotions in social networks and implications to online self-disclosure. *Cyberpsychology, behavior and social networking*, 18(12):726–736.

Hui Zou and Trevor Hastie. 2005. Regularization and Variable Selection via the Elastic Net. *Journal of the Royal Statistical Society, Series B*, 67.

Finding Optimists and Pessimists on Twitter

Xianzhi Ruan, Steven R. Wilson, and Rada Mihalcea
University of Michigan
Ann Arbor, MI
{rxianzhi, steverw, mihalcea}@umich.edu

Abstract

Optimism is linked to various personality factors as well as both psychological and physical health, but how does it relate to the way a person tweets? We analyze the online activity of a set of Twitter users in order to determine how well machine learning algorithms can detect a person's outlook on life by reading their tweets. A sample of tweets from each user is manually annotated in order to establish ground truth labels, and classifiers are trained to distinguish between optimistic and pessimistic users. Our results suggest that the words in people's tweets provide ample evidence to identify them as optimists, pessimists, or somewhere in between. Additionally, several applications of these trained models are explored.

1 Introduction

Optimists believe that future events are going to work out for the best; pessimists expect the worst (Carver et al., 2010). Research has shown that optimism is correlated with many positive life outcomes including improvements in life expectancy (Diener and Chan, 2011), physical health (Peterson and Bossio, 2001), and mental health (Achat et al., 2000). Previously, it was found that optimism and pessimism are differentiable but related: pessimism was principally associated with neuroticism and negative affect while optimism was primarily associated with extraversion and positive affect (Marshall et al., 1992). Another study found that optimism was correlated with personality factors, including extraversion, emotional stability, conscientiousness, and agreeableness (Sharpe et al., 2011).

It is clear that optimism relates to a wide variety of psychological and social variables, but how might optimism influence the way a person utilizes a social media platform? What features distinguish optimistic users from pessimistic ones? In order to answer these questions, we must first establish a means by which we can measure people's levels of optimism and pessimism. The Life Orientation Test (LOT) is commonly used to assess the degree to which a person is an optimist (Scheier and Carver, 1985). This short survey asks respondents to evaluate their own agreement with a number of short statements using a five-point scale. However, distributing such a survey over a large population requires both time and a form of incentive. Recent work has shown that open-ended text samples can be computationally analyzed to provide a more comprehensive view of a person's personal values than can be achieved using a more constrained, forced choice survey (Boyd et al., 2015). Furthermore, we know that language use is an independent and meaningful way of exploring personality (Pennebaker and King, 1999), and personality is correlated with optimism (Sharpe et al., 2011). Given a large enough text corpus, it may therefore be possible to build computational models that can automatically recognize optimism itself by looking at the words people use. The vast amount of publicly available social media data provides an excellent source of data that can be used to build models of users' psychological traits, as was done in previous studies that trained machines to predict aspects of personality from tweets (Golbeck et al., 2011; Sumner et al., 2012).

A tool that could identify optimists and pessimists by analyzing their text would aid in large scale studies of optimism among social media or other web users by providing a large number of subjects to analyze. This would open the door to

320

Proceedings of the 54th Annual Meeting of the Association for Computational Linguistics, pages 320–325,
Berlin, Germany, August 7-12, 2016. ©2016 Association for Computational Linguistics

massive studies of the relationships between optimism, pessimism, and a range of online behaviors. On the other hand, an optimism classification system could help improve the social platform itself. For example, by learning more about the psychological traits of its users, Twitter could improve its "who to follow" suggestions so that they reflect people who have a similar outlook on life.

2 Data and Method

As a data source, we chose Twitter because it is widely used and is ripe with short pieces of text (i.e., tweets) containing people's everyday thoughts, observations, and conversations. We used Twitter's basic search function to look for users whose tweets include words and phrases that indicate that they might identify as optimistic or pessimistic. Looking for phrases such as "I am optimistic" within a user's tweets to find potentially optimistic users, we identified 714 candidates. Finding pessimistic Twitter users proved more difficult because users would not usually tweet something negative such as "I am pessimistic" and present themselves in an unflattering way. We instead searched for keywords such as "hate," "unfair," and "disgust," which may indicate a pessimistic nature. This led to 640 potential pessimists. For each user, we crawled their 2,000 most recent tweets (or all their tweets if the user had less than 2,000). In order to verify that the accounts identified were owned mostly by individual users (as opposed to organizations), we manually inspected a random sample of 50 accounts and found only one that appeared to be related to an organization

Using the collected data set, which we expected would be more representative of optimistic or pessimistic nature than the norm based on the content of their tweets, we selected a fraction of the users to create a ground truth set for our task. We used Amazon Mechanical Turk (MTurk)[1] to obtain human annotatations for a subset of our corpus. We randomly selected 500 users who were retrieved by the optimistic queries and 500 users found when searching for pessimists. For each user, we randomly selected 15 tweets for a total of 15,000 tweets to be labeled on a scale of -3 (very pessimistic) to 3 (very optimistic) by five independent annotators. Before labeling began, we provided clear definitions of optimism and pessimism to the annotators.

In order to pick the tweets from each user that had a stronger emotional signal, we took advantage of the "positive emotions" and "negative emotions" word categories included in the Linguistic Inquiry and Word Count Tool (Pennebaker et al., 2001).[2] If any of the original 15 tweets did not contain at least one word from either category, the tweet was removed and a new tweet was chosen at random to replace it. This process was repeated until we had a set of 15 tweets per user without skewing that user's true distribution of positive and negative tweets.

During the MTurk annotation, to identify workers who were quickly selecting options without even reading the tweets, we added a "check" question that asked the workers to choose a specific value for that question. All the workers who did not correctly answer this "check" question were removed from the annotation. When a worker's annotations had to be thrown out, the tweets were put back onto MTurk for reannotation. Additionally, we compared the scores of each annotator with the average score and removed workers who deviated significantly from the others. The final agreement (Krippendorf's alpha) between the five annotators was measured at 0.731, assuming an interval scale.

For each individual tweet, we assigned a label of "optimistic," "pessimistic," or "neutral". Any tweet with an average score greater than one (slightly optimistic or higher in the annotation task) was considered an "optimistic" tweet, and those with an average score less than one (slightly pessimistic or lower) were given the "pessimistic" class label. The tweets with average MTurk annotation scores between -1 and 1 were considered to be "neutral."

We also assigned a class label to each user. To accomplish this, we calculated the average of the assigned scores, sorted the Twitter users by their level of optimism, and considered the top 25% of users as optimists, the bottom 25% as pessimists, and the remaining ones as neutral.

Before moving on, we decided to investigate the online behaviors and attributes of the optimistic and pessimistic users in our new data set. A summary of some of the differences between the two groups is shown in Table 1. Interestingly the optimists have more followers and are following more

---

[1] http://www.mturk.com

[2] The 2007 version of LIWC was used

	Optimistic	**Pessimistic**
mean followers	6238	1840
mean following	1898	1156
mean tweets	12156	28190
median followers	972	572
median following	718	443
median tweets	5687	17451
std. dev of tweets	17952	37851
min number of tweets	108	28
max number of tweets	99344	231220
tweet rate	10.24	19.184
favorite count	4314.34	8761.2
listed count	112.62	10.23

Table 1: Statistics for the most extreme 100 optimistic & 100 pessimistic users.

other users than the more pessimistic users. On the other hand, the pessimists tend to tweet much more frequently, with a mean and median number of tweets both more than twice as large as the optimist group. This is not just a factor of the pessimists having been around longer to build up a history of tweets- we also compute the "tweet rate" for each user by dividing their total number of tweets by the total number of days since the activation of their Twitter account. Looking at this variable, we see that the average number of tweets per day is much higher for the pessimists. Optimists are also included in more lists, while pessimists choose to label things as a "favorite" more often.

In order to build computational models to differentiate between the optimistic and pessimistic users, we use five different methods from the scikit-learn python library[3]: Naive Bayes (NB), Nearest Neighbor (NN), Decision Tree (DT), Random Forest Classifier (RFC), Gradient Boosting Classifier (GBC) and Stochastic Gradient Descent (SGD). The default parameters are used for each. The preprocessing method was the same for all different classifiers: the text was preprocessed by removing mentions (@), web links, and the phrase RT. We also used the Emoji unicode tables to replace all Emoji unicodes to their corresponding meanings (e.g., "<smiling-face>"). We tried performing classification both with and without removing stopwords to see what the effect was. For all different classifiers, we tested with different settings: with and without stopwords; and adding a user's profile information as additional features or not.

---

[3]http://scikit-learn.org/stable/

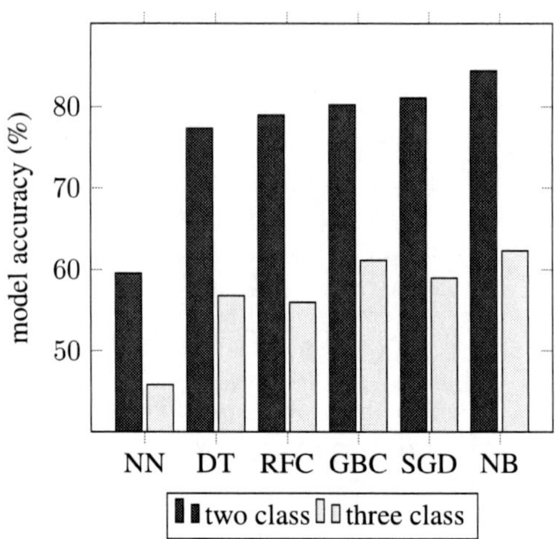

Figure 1: Tweet level classification accuracy for the two-way and three-way classification problems.

3 Results

We first evaluate the ability of our classifiers to distinguish between optimistic and pessimistic tweets (two-way classification) or among optimistic, pessimistic, and neutral tweets (three-way classification). We randomly selected 1,000 tweets from each class. Figure 1 shows the ten-fold cross validation results obtained using the six classifiers. During each classification, we made sure that tweets from the same user were not shared between the training and testing folds. In both cases, the best setting was using the Naive Bayes classifier and not including profile information as features. Stopword removal had no noticeable effect. Note that the majority baseline is a score of 50% in the two-class case, while it is 33% in the three-class case.

For additional insight, Table 2 shows some of the top features for the optimistic and pessimistic class, sorted by the probability of the feature given the class. We can see that, as one might expect, the useful words for detecting optimists are generally very positive, while the pessimistic features are negative and sprinkled with profanity. Since we formulated the problem as a three-way classification, it is reasonable that some words may have high scores for both optimistic and pessimistic classes. These words distinguish optimism/pessimism from the neutral class.

We perform our next evaluation at the user level, which means that we consider all tweets from

Optimism	Pessimism
love, so, that, be	fuck, that, not, so
have, good, am, this	like, am, do, hate
on, your, not, day	have, be, this, just
like, just, do, will	up, life, on, shit
can, get, what, at	no, people, can, what
great, make, up, much	feel, your, about, I'm
best, we, if, go	go, know, get, even
was, from, thing, out	want, at, was, off
look, thank, know,he	out, kill, if, done

Table 2: Most discriminating features collected by the Naive Bayes classifier for the three-class tweet-level prediction setting.

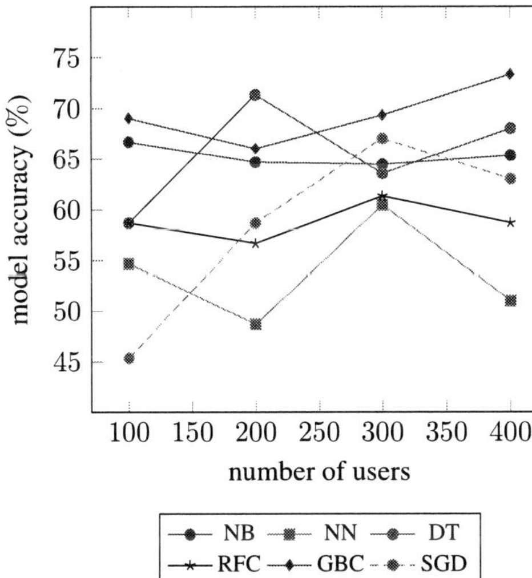

Figure 2: Accuracy on the user-level prediction task for different data sizes.

a user as a single document. The classification is performed using a randomly selected set of 100, 200, 300, and 400 users from the annotated set (each set adds 100 new users to the previous group). In each case, the 25% users with highest annotation score are considered the optimistic group, 25% users with lowest annotation score as pessimist group, and the other 50% of users is the neutral group. The results of the ten fold cross val idation are shown in Figure 2. In this setting, the Gradient Boosting Classifier usually outperforms the others and achieves an accuracy of 73.33% on the 400 user data set.

We also sought to discover how accurate the classifiers would be if the objective was simply to identify the top N optimists or pessimists. For example, if we wanted to find the 10 users out of a group with the greatest number of optimistic tweets, how accurately could this be done? To

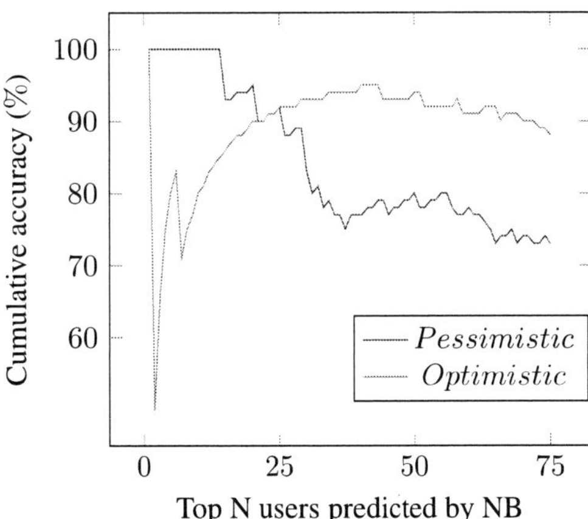

Figure 3: Cumulative classification accuracy on the top N users sorted by Naive Bayes predicted probabilities

City	Neutral Users	Optimists	Pessimists
Chicago	20.65%	39.27%	40.08%
Los Angeles	14.55%	31.87%	53.58%
New York	20.74%	40.63%	38.63%

Table 3: Predicted optimism & pessimism in three major cities

carry out this analysis, we sorted the users by the probabilities that they belonged to either the optimistic class or the pessimistic class as predicted by a Naive Bayes classifier (Figure 3). Then, we compute the accuracy for the top N optimists and pessimists. As we can see, it is possible to predict the most pessimistic 14 users with perfect accuracy. On the other hand, some of the most likely optimistic users actually belonged to another class based on the ground truth labels. With a larger number of users to classify, it becomes easier to correctly label optimists than pessimists.

4 Applications

What kinds of things can we learn with a tool for classifying optimists and pessimists? First, we look at groups of users from three major cities in the United States: Chicago, Los Angeles, and New York. We found users who listed their location as one of these three cities (494 users from Chicago, 433 from Los Angeles, 480 from New York), then collected 2,000 tweets from each user. Using our best models from the user-level experiments, we obtain predictions for the optimism/pessimism of the users. The breakdown of predicted optimists, pessimists, and neutral users is listed in Table 3.

Chicago and New York are fairly balanced with roughly 40% of people falling into each category (leaving 20% as neutral). However, pessimists were predicted much more often than optimists in Los Angeles.

For a second sample application, we went to the official twitter accounts of six presidential candidates: Hillary Clinton, Donald Trump, Marco Rubio, Martin O'Malley, Bernie Sanders and Ben Carson. We randomly picked approximately 500 followers of each of the candidates and predicted the optimism/pessimism of them (Table 4).[4] While these scores are only estimates, we see that O'Malley's followers tend to be the users who posted a greater number of optimistic tweets, while the users who tweeted lots of pessimistic tweets are those keeping up-to-date with Rubio's campaign. Overall, we see that most of the followers of these candidates are optimistic.

Candidate	Neutral Users	Optimists	Pessimists
Clinton	31.52%	49.22%	19.26%
Trump	36.20%	39.46%	24.32%
Rubio	30.00%	49.41%	20.59%
O'Malley	29.22%	64.51%	6.26%
Sanders	44.62%	44.42%	10.96%
Carson	31.54%	49.90%	18.56%

Table 4: Predicted optimism & pessimism of those following some of the candidates for the 2016 Presidential election.

5 Conclusions and Future Work

We have shown that we can use Twitter to collect a data set[5] of optimistic and pessimistic users, and predict the most (top 25%) optimistic/pessimistic users with greater than 70% accuracy. The optimistic users on Twitter tended to have more social connections, but tweet less often than the pessimists. In the future, we hope to explore the social effects of optimism, such as the degree to which optimistic users follow one another and whether or not optimistic comments receive more "favorites" and retweets. Finally, we would like to compare the optimism and pessimism scores that our model predicts with those received when taking the LOT in order to compare the text-based analysis with a widely used tool for measuring optimism.

---

[4]data collected late December, 2015

[5]The data set introduced in this paper is available at http://lit.eecs.umich.edu/research/downloads.

Acknowledgements

We would like to thank Seong Ju Park, Tian Bao, and Yihan Li for their assistance in the initial project that led to this work. This material is based in part upon work supported by the National Science Foundation award #1344257 and by grant #48503 from the John Templeton Foundation. Any opinions, findings, and conclusions or recommendations expressed in this material are those of the authors and do not necessarily reflect the views of the National Science Foundation or the John Templeton Foundation.

References

Helen Achat, Ichiro Kawachi, Avron Spiro, Deborah A DeMolles, and David Sparrow. 2000. Optimism and depression as predictors of physical and mental health functioning: the normative aging study. *Annals of Behavioral Medicine*, 22(2):127–130.

Ryan L Boyd, Steven R Wilson, James W Pennebaker, Michal Kosinski, David J Stillwell, and Rada Mihalcea. 2015. Values in words: Using language to evaluate and understand personal values. In *Ninth International AAAI Conference on Web and Social Media*.

Charles S Carver, Michael F Scheier, and Suzanne C Segerstrom. 2010. Optimism. *Clinical psychology review*, 30(7):879–889.

Ed Diener and Micaela Y Chan. 2011. Happy people live longer: Subjective well-being contributes to health and longevity. *Applied Psychology: Health and Well-Being*, 3(1):1–43.

Jennifer Golbeck, Cristina Robles, Michon Edmondson, and Karen Turner. 2011. Predicting personality from twitter. In *Privacy, Security, Risk and Trust (PASSAT) and 2011 IEEE Third Inernational Conference on Social Computing (SocialCom), 2011 IEEE Third International Conference on*, pages 149–156. IEEE.

Grant N Marshall, Camille B Wortman, Jeffrey W Kusulas, Linda K Hervig, and Ross R Vickers Jr. 1992. Distinguishing optimism from pessimism: Relations to fundamental dimensions of mood and personality. *Journal of personality and social psychology*, 62(6):1067.

James W Pennebaker and Laura A King. 1999. Linguistic styles: language use as an individual difference. *Journal of personality and social psychology*, 77(6):1296.

James W Pennebaker, Martha E Francis, and Roger J Booth. 2001. Linguistic inquiry and word count: Liwc 2001. *Mahway: Lawrence Erlbaum Associates*, 71:2001.

Christopher Peterson and Lisa M. Bossio. 2001. Optimism and physical well-being. In *Optimism & pessimism: Implications for theory, research, and practice.*, pages 127–145. American Psychological Association (APA).

Michael F Scheier and Charles S Carver. 1985. Optimism, coping, and health: assessment and implications of generalized outcome expectancies. *Health psychology*, 4(3):219.

J Patrick Sharpe, Nicholas R Martin, and Kelly A Roth. 2011. Optimism and the big five factors of personality: Beyond neuroticism and extraversion. *Personality and Individual Differences*, 51(8):946–951.

Chris Sumner, Alison Byers, Rachel Boochever, and Gregory J Park. 2012. Predicting dark triad personality traits from twitter usage and a linguistic analysis of tweets. In *Machine Learning and Applications (ICMLA), 2012 11th International Conference on*, volume 2, pages 386–393. IEEE.

Transductive Adaptation of Black Box Predictions

Stéphane Clinchant, Gabriela Csurka and Boris Chidlovskii
Xerox Research Centre Europe
6 chemin Maupertuis, Meylan, France
`Firstname.Lastname@xrce.xerox.com`

Abstract

Access to data is critical to any machine learning component aimed at training an accurate predictive model. In reality, data is often a subject of technical and legal constraints. Data may contain sensitive topics and data owners are often reluctant to share them. Instead of access to data, they make available decision making procedures to enable predictions on new data. Under the *black box classifier constraint*, we build an effective domain adaptation technique which adapts classifier predictions in a transductive setting. We run experiments on text categorization datasets and show that significant gains can be achieved, especially in the unsupervised case where no labels are available in the target domain.

1 Introduction

While huge volumes of unlabeled data are generated and made available in various domains, the cost of acquiring data labels remains high. Domain Adaptation problems arise each time when one leverage labeled data in one or more related *source* domains, to learn a classifier for unseen data in a *target* domain which is related, but not identical. The majority of domain adaptation methods makes an assumption of *largely available* source collections; this allows to measure the discrepancy between distributions and either build representations common to both target and sources, or directly reuse source instances for a better target classification (Xu and Sun, 2012).

Numerous approaches have been proposed to address domain adaptation for statistical machine translation (Koehn and Schroeder, 2007), opinion mining, part of speech tagging and document ranking (Daumé, 2009), (Pan and Yang, 2010), (Zhou and Chang, 2014). Most effective techniques include feature replication (Daumé, 2009), pivot features (Blitzer et al., 2006), (Pan et al., 2010) and finding topic models shared by source and target collections (Chen and Liu, 2014). Domain adaptation has equally received a lot of attention in computer vision (Gopalan et al., 2015) where *domain shift* is a consequence of changing conditions, such as background, location and pose, etc.

More recently, domain adaptation has been tackled with word embedding techniques or deep learning. (Bollegala et al., 2015) proposed an unsupervised method for learning domain-specific word embedding while (Yang and Eisenstein, 2014) relied on *word2vec* models (Mikolov et al., 2013) to compute feature embedding. Deep learning has been considered as a generic solution to domain adaptation (Vincent et al., 2008; Glorot et al., 2011), (Chopra et al., 2013) and transfer learning problems (Long et al., 2015). For instance, denoising autoencoders are successful models which find common features between source and target collection. They are trained to reconstruct input data from partial random corruption and can be stacked into a multi-layered network where the weights are fine-tuned with backpropagation (Vincent et al., 2008) or marginalized out (Chen et al., 2012).

Domain adaptation is also very attractive for service companies operating customer business processes as it can reduce annotation costs. For instance, opinion mining components deployed in a service solution can be customized to a new customer and adapted with few annotations in order to achieve a contractual performance.

But, *in reality*, the simplifying assumption of having access to source data rarely holds and limits therefore the application of existing domain

Proceedings of the 54th Annual Meeting of the Association for Computational Linguistics, pages 326–331,
Berlin, Germany, August 7-12, 2016. ©2016 Association for Computational Linguistics

adaptation methods. Source data are often a subject of legal, technical and contractual constraints between data owners and data customers. Often, customers are reluctant to share their data. Instead, they often put in place *decision making procedures*. This allows to obtain predictions for new data under *a black box scenario*. Note that this scenario is different from the differential privacy setting (Dwork and Roth, 2014) in the sense that no queries to the raw source database are allowed whereas, in our case, only requests for predicting labels of target documents are permitted. This makes privacy preserving machine learning methods inapplicable here (Chaudhuri and Monteleoni, 2008), (Agrawal and Srikant, 2000).

In addition, black boxes systems are frequent in natural language processing applications. For instance, Statistical Machine Translation (SMT) systems are often used as black box to extract features (Specia et al., 2009). Similarly, the problem of adapting SMT systems for cross lingual retrieval has been addressed in (Nikoulina et al., 2012) where target document collections cannot be accessed and the retrieval engine works as a black box.

In this paper we address the problem of adapting classifiers trained on the source data and available as *black boxes*. The case of available source classifiers has been studied by (Duan et al., 2009) to regularize supervised target classifiers, but we consider here a transductive setting, where the source classifiers are used to predict class scores for a set of available target instances.

We then apply the denoising principle (Vincent et al., 2008) and consider these predictions on target instances as corrupted by the domain shift from the source to target. More precisely, we use the stacked Marginalized Denoising Autoencoders (Chen et al., 2012) to *reconstruct* the predictions by exploiting the correlation between the target features and the predicted scores. This method has the advantage of coping with *unsupervised cases* where no labels in the target domain is available. We test the prediction denoising method on two benchmark text classification datasets and demonstrate its capacity to significantly improve the classification accuracy.

2 Transductive Prediction Adaptation

The domain adaptation problem consists of leveraging the source labeled and target unlabeled data to derive a hypothesis performing well on the target domain. To achieve this goal, most DA methods compute correlation between features in source and target domains. With no access to source data, we argue that the above principle can be extended to *the correlation between target features and the source class decisions*. We tune an *adaptation trick* by considering predicted class scores as augmented features for target data. In other words, we use the source classifiers *as a pivot* to transfer knowledge from source to target. In addition, one can exploit relations between the predictions scores and the target feature distribution to provide adapted predictions.

2.1 Marginalized Denoising Autoencoder

The *stacked Marginalized Denoising Autoencoder* (sMDA) is a version of the multi-layer neural network trained to reconstruct input data from partial random corruption (Vincent et al., 2008) proposed by (Chen et al., 2012), where the random corruption is marginalized out yielding the optimal reconstruction weights in the closed form.

The basic building block of the method is a one-layer linear denoising autoencoder where a set of N input documents $\mathbf{x}_n$ are corrupted M times by random feature dropout with the probability p. It is then reconstructed with a linear mapping $\mathbf{W} : \mathbb{R}^d \to \mathbb{R}^d$ by minimizing the squared reconstruction loss[1]:

$$\mathcal{L}(\mathbf{W}) = \sum_{n=1}^{N} \sum_{m=1}^{M} ||\mathbf{x}_n - \mathbf{W}\tilde{\mathbf{x}}_{nm}||^2. \qquad (1)$$

Let $\bar{\mathbf{X}}$ be the concatenation of M replicated version of the original data and $\tilde{\mathbf{X}}$ be the matrix representation of the M corrupted versions.

Then, the solution of (1) can be expressed as the closed-form solution for ordinary least squares $\mathbf{W} = \mathbf{P}\mathbf{Q}^{-1}$ with $\mathbf{Q} = \tilde{\mathbf{X}}\tilde{\mathbf{X}}^\top$ and $P = \bar{\mathbf{X}}\tilde{\mathbf{X}}^\top$, where the solution depends on the re-sampling of $\mathbf{x}_1, \ldots, \mathbf{x}_N$ and which features are randomly corrupted.

It is preferable to consider all possible corruptions of all possible inputs when the denoising transformation $\mathbf{W}$ is computed, i.e. letting $m \to \infty$. By the weak law of large numbers, the matrices $\mathbf{P}$ and $\mathbf{Q}$ converge to their expected values $\mathbb{E}[\mathbf{Q}], \mathbb{E}[\mathbf{P}]$ as more copies of the corrupted data

---

[1] A constant is added to the input, $\mathbf{x}_n = [\mathbf{x}_n; 1]$, and an appropriate bias, never corrupted, is incorporated within $\mathbf{W}$.

are created. In the limit, one can derive their expectations and express the corresponding mapping for $\mathbf{W}$ in a closed form as $\mathbf{W} = \mathbb{E}[\mathbf{P}]\,\mathbb{E}[\mathbf{Q}]^{-1}$, where:

$$\mathbb{E}[\mathbf{Q}]_{ij} = \left[\begin{array}{ll} \mathbf{S}_{ij}q_iq_j, & \text{if } i \neq j, \\ \mathbf{S}_{ij}q_i, & \text{if } i = j, \end{array} \right.$$

and $\mathbb{E}[\mathbf{P}]_{ij} = \mathbf{S}_{ij}q_j$ where $q = [1 - p, \ldots, 1 - p, 1] \in \mathbb{R}^{d+1}$ and $\mathbf{S} = \mathbf{X}\mathbf{X}^\top$ is the covariance matrix of the uncorrupted data. This closed form denoising layer with a unique noise p is referred in the following as *marginalized denoising autoencoder* (MDA).

It was shown by (Chen et al., 2012) that MDA can be applied with success to domain adaptation where the source set $\mathbf{X}_s$ and target set $\mathbf{X}_t$ are concatenated to form $\mathbf{X}$ and the mapping $\mathbf{W}$ can exploit the correlation between source and target features. The case of fully available source and target data is referred as a *dream case* in the evaluation section.

2.2 Prediction Adaptation

Without access to $\mathbf{X}_s$, MDA cannot be directly applied to $[\mathbf{X}_s; \mathbf{X}_t]$. Instead, we augment the feature set $\mathbf{X}_t$ with the class predictions represented as vector $f^s(\mathbf{x}^t)$ of class predictions $P_s(Y = y|\mathbf{x}_n^t), n = 1, \ldots, N$. Let $\mathbf{u}_n^t = [\mathbf{x}_n^t; f^s(\mathbf{x}_n^t)]$ be the target instance augmented with the source classifier predictions and $\mathbf{U} = [\mathbf{u}_1^t \mathbf{u}_2^t \ldots \mathbf{u}_N^t]$ be the input to the MDA. Then we compute the optimal mapping $\mathbf{W}^* = \min_{\mathbf{W}} ||\mathbf{U} - \mathbf{W}\tilde{\mathbf{U}}||^2$ that takes into account the correlation between the target features $\mathbf{x}^t$ and class predictions $f^s(\mathbf{x}^t)$. The reconstructed class predictions can be obtained as $\mathbf{W}^*_{[1:N,d+1:d+C]} \cdot f^s(\mathbf{x}^t)$, where C is the number of classes, and used to label the target data. Algorithm 1 summarizes all steps of the transductive prediction adaptation for a single source domain; the generalization to multiple sources is straightforward[2].

3 Experimental results

We test our approach on two standard domain adaptation datasets: the Amazon reviews (AMT) and the 20Newsgroups (NG). The AMT dataset consists of products reviews with 2 classes (positive and negative) represented by tf-idf normalized

---

Algorithm 1 Transductive prediction adaptation.

Require: Unlabeled target dataset $\mathbf{X}_t \in \mathbb{R}^{N \times d}$.
Require: Class predictions $f^s(\mathbf{x}^t) = [P_s(Y = 1|\mathbf{x}_i^t), \ldots, P_s(Y = C|\mathbf{x}_n^t)] \in \mathbb{R}^C$.
1: Compose $\mathbf{U} \in \mathbb{R}^{N \times (d+C)}$ with $\mathbf{u}_n^t = [\mathbf{x}_n^t; f^s(\mathbf{x}_n^t)]$.
2: Use MDA with noise level p to estimate $\mathbf{W}^* = \min_{\mathbf{W}} ||\mathbf{U} - \mathbf{W}\tilde{\mathbf{U}}||^2$.
3: Get the denoised class predictions for $\mathbf{x}^t$ as $\mathbf{y}^t = \mathbf{W}^*_{[1:N,d+1:d+C]} \cdot f^s(\mathbf{x}^t)$.
4: Label $\mathbf{x}^t$ with $c^* = \mathrm{argmax}_c\{y_c^t|\mathbf{y}^t\}$.
5: **return** Labels for $\mathbf{X}_t$.

---

bag-of-words, used in previous studies on domain adaptation (Blitzer et al., 2011). We consider the 10,000 most frequent features and four domains used in the studies: *kitchen* (k), *dvd* (d), *books* (b) and *electronics* (e) with roughly 5,000 documents per domain. We use all the source dataset as training and test on the whole target dataset. We set the MDA noise level p to high values (*e.g.* 0.9), as document representations are sparse and adding low noise have no effect on the features already equal to zero.

In Table 1, we show the performance of the Transductive Prediction Adaptation (TPA) on 12 adaptation tasks in the AMT dataset. The first column shows the accuracies for *the dream case* where the standard MDA is applied to both source and target data. The second column shows the baseline results ($f^s(\mathbf{X}^t)$) obtained directly as class predictions by the source classifier. The classification model is an l_2 regularized Logistic Regression[3] cross-validated with regularized parameter $C \in [0.0001, 0.001, 0.1, 1, 10, 50, 100]$.

The two last columns show the results obtained with two versions of TPA (results are underlined when improving over the baseline and in bold when yielding the highest values). In the first version, target instances $\mathbf{x}_n^t$ contains only features (words and bigrams) appearing in the source documents and used to make the predictions $f(\mathbf{x}_n^t)$. In the second version, denoted as TPAe, we extend TPA with words unseen in the source documents. If the extension part is denoted $\mathbf{v}_n^t$, we obtain an augmented representation $\mathbf{u}_n^t = [\mathbf{x}_n^t; \mathbf{v}_n^t; f(\mathbf{x}_n^t)]$ as input to MDA.

---

[2] It requires concatenating the class predictions from different sources at step 1 and averaging the reconstructed predictions per class at step 3.

[3] We also experimented with other classifiers, such as SVM , Multinomial Naive Bayes, and obtained similar improvement after applying TPA. Results are not shown due to the space limitation.

Table 1: TPA results on the AMT dataset.

$S \rightarrow T$	MDA*	$f^s(\mathbf{X}^t)$	TPA	TPAe
$d \rightarrow b$	84.59	81.36	82.61	**83.19**
$e \rightarrow b$	78.07	73.87	75.93	**79.95**
$k \rightarrow b$	78.75	73.50	75.02	**78.39**
$b \rightarrow d$	85.07	82.54	83.56	**84.32**
$e \rightarrow d$	79.99	76.46	77.67	**81.60**
$k \rightarrow d$	80.76	77.58	79.16	**81.92**
$b \rightarrow e$	80.32	76.44	78.54	**81.81**
$d \rightarrow e$	83.70	78.65	80.75	**82.89**
$k \rightarrow e$	89.05	87.55	88.38	**88.50**
$b \rightarrow k$	84.00	79.46	81.44	**85.21**
$d \rightarrow k$	86.08	80.83	83.15	**86.14**
$e \rightarrow k$	90.76	89.97	**91.10**	90.86
Avg	83.4	79.85	81.44	**83.73**

As we can see, both TPA and TPAe significantly outperform the baseline $f^s(\mathbf{X}^t)$ obtained with no adaptation. Furthermore, extending TPA with words present in target documents only allows to further improve the classification accuracy in most cases. Finally, TPAe often outperforms the *dream case* and also on average (note however that MDA* uses the features common to source and target documents as input).

To understand the effect of prediction adaptation we analyze the *book* $\rightarrow$ *electronics* adaptation task. In the mapping $\mathbf{W}$, we sort the weights corresponding to the correlation between the positive class and the target features. Features with the highest weights (up-weighted by TPA) are *great, my, sound, easy, excellent, good, easy_to, best, yo, a_great, when, well, the_best*. On contrary, the words that got the smallest weight (down-weighted by TPA) are *no, was, number, don't, after, money, if, work, bad, get, buy*.

As TPA is totally unsupervised, we run additional experiments to understand its practical usefulness. We compare TPA to the case of *weakly annotated* target data, where few target examples are labelled and used for training a target classifier. Trained with 40, 100 and 200 target examples, a logistic regression yields an average accuracy of 64.63%, 68.01% and 75.13% over 12 tasks and a Multinomial Naives Bayes reports 65.82%, 71.49% and 76%, respectively. Even with 200 labeled target documents, the target versus target classification results are significantly below the 79.8% average accuracy of the baseline source classifier.

All these values are therefore significantly below the 83.73% obtained with TPAe. This strongly supports the domain adaptation scenario, when a sentiment analysis classifier trained on a larger source set and adapted to target documents can do better than a classifier trained on a small set of labeled target documents. Furthermore, we have seen that the baseline can be significantly improved by TPA and even more by TPAe without the need of even a small amount of manual labeling of the target set.

The second group of evaluation tests is on the 20Newsgroup dataset. It contains around 20,000 documents of 20 classes and represents a standard testbed for text categorization. For the domain adaptation, we follow the setting described in (Pan et al., 2012). We filter out rare words (appearing less than 3 times) and keep at most 10,000 features for each task with a tf-idf termweighting. As all documents are organized as a hierarchy, the domain adaptation tasks are defined on category pairs with sources and targets corresponding to subcategories. For example, for the *'comp vs sci'* task, subcategories such as *comp.sys.ibm.pc.hardware* and *sci.crypt* are set as source domains and *comp.sys.ibm.mac.hardware* and *sci.med* as targets, respectively.

In our experiments we consider 5 adaptation tasks on category pairs (*'comp vs sci'*, *'rec vs talk'*, *'rec vs sci'*, *'sci vs talk'* and *'comp vs rec'* as in (Pan et al., 2012)), and run the baseline, TPA and TPAe methods. For each category pair, we additionally inverse the source and target roles; this explains two sets of experimental results for each pair. We show the evaluation results in Table 2. It is easy to observe again the significant improvement over the baseline $f^s(\mathbf{x}_n^t)$ and the positive effect of including the unseen words in the TPA.

Table 2: TPA results on the 20Newsgroup dataset.

class pair	$f^s(\mathbf{X}^t)$	TPA	TPAe
'comp vs sci'	71.06	80.24	**80.43**
	65.4	71.6	**71.98**
'rec vs talk'	65.66	68.01	**70.18**
	69.93	75.84	**77.2**
'rec vs sci'	76.02	85.97	**86.42**
	74 17	81.14	**82.71**
'sci vs talk'	76.1	80.22	**81.3**
	74.92	80.07	**80.19**
'comp vs rec'	86.63	91.56	**92.06**
	86.97	92.67	**93.34**
Avg	74.69	80.73	**81.58**

4 Conclusion

In this paper we address the domain adaptation scenario without access to source data and where source classifiers are available as *black boxes*. In the transductive setting, the source classifiers can predict class scores for target instances, and we consider these predictions as corrupted by domain shift. We use the Marginalized Denoising Autoencoders (Chen et al., 2012) to reconstruct the predictions by exploiting the "correlation" between the target features and the predicted scores. We test the transductive prediction adaptation on two known benchmarks and demonstrate that it can significantly improve the classification accuracy, comparing to the baseline and to the case of full access to source data. This is an encouraging result because it demonstrates that domain adaptation can still be effective despite the absence of source data. Lastly, in the future, we would like to explore the adaptation of other language processing components, such as named entity recognition, with our method.

References

[Agrawal and Srikant2000] Rakesh Agrawal and Ramakrishnan Srikant. 2000. Privacy-preserving data mining. In *ACM SIGMOD International Conference on Management of Data (SIGMOD)*, pages 439–450.

[Blitzer et al.2006] John Blitzer, Ryan McDonald, and Fernando Pereira. 2006. Domain adaptation with structural correspondence learning. In *International Conference on Empirical Methods in Natural Language Processing (EMNLP)*, pages 120–128.

[Blitzer et al.2011] John Blitzer, Sham Kakade, and Dean P. Foster. 2011. Domain adaptation with coupled subspaces. In *International Conference on Artificial Intelligence and Statistics (AISTATS)*, pages 173–181.

[Bollegala et al.2015] Danushka Bollegala, Takanori Maehara, and Ken-ichi Kawarabayashi. 2015. Unsupervised cross-domain word representation learning. In *Annual Meeting of the Association for Computational Linguistics(ACL)*, pages 730–740.

[Chaudhuri and Monteleoni2008] Kamalika Chaudhuri and Claire Monteleoni. 2008. Privacy-preserving logistic regression. In *Annual Conference on Neural Information Processing Systems (NIPS)*, pages 289–296.

[Chen and Liu2014] Zhiyuan Chen and Bing Liu. 2014. Topic modeling using topics from many domains, lifelong learning and big data. In *International Conference on Machine Learning (ICML)*, pages 703–711.

[Chen et al.2012] Minmin Chen, Zhixiang Xu, Kilian Q. Weinberger, and Fei Sha. 2012. Marginalized denoising autoencoders for domain adaptation. In *International Conference on Machine Learning (ICML)*, pages 767–774.

[Chopra et al.2013] Sumit Chopra, Suhrid Balakrishnan, and Raghuraman Gopalan. 2013. DLID: Deep learning for domain adaptation by interpolating between domains. In *ICML Workshop on Challenges in Representation Learning (WREPL)*.

[Daumé2009] H. Daumé. 2009. Frustratingly easy domain adaptation. *CoRR*, arXiv:0907.1815.

[Duan et al.2009] Lixin Duan, Ivor W. Tsang, Dong Xu, and Tat-Seng Chua. 2009. Domain adaptation from multiple sources via auxiliary classifiers. In *International Conference on Machine Learning (ICML)*, pages 289–296.

[Dwork and Roth2014] Cynthia Dwork and Aaron Roth. 2014. The algorithmic foundations of differential privacy. *Foundations and Trends in Theoretical Computer Science*, 9:211–407.

[Glorot et al.2011] Xavier Glorot, Antoine Bordes, and Yoshua Bengio. 2011. Domain adaptation for large-scale sentiment classification: A deep learning approach. In *International Conference on Machine Learning (ICML)*, pages 513–520.

[Gopalan et al.2015] Raghuraman Gopalan, Ruonan Li, Vishal M. Patel, and Rama Chellappa. 2015. Domain adaptation for visual recognition. *Foundations and Trends in Computer Graphics and Vision*, 8(4).

[Koehn and Schroeder2007] Philipp Koehn and Josh Schroeder. 2007. Experiments in domain adaptation for statistical machine translation. In *ACL Workshop on Statistical Machine Translation (STAT-MT)*, pages 224–227.

[Long et al.2015] Mingsheng Long, Yue Cao, Jianmin Wang, and Michael I. Jordan. 2015. Learning transferable features with deep adaptation networks. In *International Conference on Machine Learning (ICML)*.

[Mikolov et al.2013] Tomas Mikolov, Kai Chen, Greg Corrado, and Jeffrey Dean. 2013. Efficient estimation of word representations in vector space. *CoRR*, arXiv:1301.3781.

[Nikoulina et al.2012] Vassilina Nikoulina, Bogomil Kovachev, Nikolaos Lagos, and Christof Monz. 2012. Adaptation of statistical machine translation model for cross-lingual information retrieval in a service context. In *Conference of the European Chapter of the Association for Computational Linguistics (EACL)*, pages 109–119.

[Pan and Yang2010] Sinno J. Pan and Qiang Yang. 2010. A survey on transfer learning. *Transactions on Knowledge and Data Engineering*, 22(10):1345–1359.

[Pan et al.2010] Sinno Jialin Pan, Xiaochuan Ni, Jian-Tao Sun, Qiang Yang, and Zheng Chen. 2010. Cross-domain sentiment classification via spectral feature alignment. In *International Conference on World Wide Web (WWW)*.

[Pan et al.2012] Weike Pan, Erheng Zhong, and Yang Qiang. 2012. Transfer learning for text mining. In Charu C. Aggarwal and ChengXiang Zhai, editors, *Mining Text Data*, pages 223–257. Springer.

[Specia et al.2009] Lucia Specia, Marco Turchi, Nicola Cancedda, Marc Dymetman, and Nello N. Cristianini. 2009. Estimating the sentence-level quality of machine translation systems. In *Annual Conference of the European Association for Machine Translation (EAMT)*, pages 28–35.

[Vincent et al.2008] Pascal Vincent, Hugo Larochelle, Yoshua Bengio, and Pierre-Antoine Manzagol. 2008. Extracting and composing robust features with denoising autoencoders. In *International Conference on Machine Learning (ICML)*.

[Xu and Sun2012] Zhijie Xu and Shiliang Sun. 2012. Multi-source transfer learning with multi-view adaboost. In *Annual Conference on Neural Information Processing Systems (NIPS)*, volume LNCS 7665, pages 332–339. Springer.

[Yang and Eisenstein2014] Yi Yang and Jacob Eisenstein. 2014. Unsupervised multi-domain adaptation with feature embeddings. In *Annual Conference of the North American Chapter of the Association for Computational Linguistics: Human Language Technologies (NAACL HLT)*, pages 672–682.

[Zhou and Chang2014] Mianwei Zhou and Kevin C. Chang. 2014. Unifying learning to rank and domain adaptation: Enabling cross-task document scoring. In *ACM SIGKDD Conference on Knowledge Discovery and Data Mining (SIGKDD*, pages 781–790.

Which Tumblr Post Should I Read Next?

Zornitsa Kozareva
Yahoo!
701 First Avenue
Sunnyvale, CA 94089
zornitsa@kozareva.com

Makoto Yamada
Institute of Chemical Research
Kyoto University
Gokasho, Uji, 611-0011, Japan
myamada@kuicr.kyoto-u.ac.jp

Abstract

Microblogging sites have emerged as major platforms for bloggers to create and consume posts as well as to follow other bloggers and get informed of their updates. Due to the large number of users, and the huge amount of posts they create, it becomes extremely difficult to identify relevant and interesting blog posts.

In this paper, we propose a novel convex collective matrix completion (CCMC) method that effectively utilizes user-item matrix and incorporates additional user activity and topic-based signals to recommend relevant content. The key advantage of CCMC over existing methods is that it can obtain a globally optimal solution and can easily scale to large-scale matrices using Hazan's algorithm. To the best of our knowledge, this is the first work which applies and studies CCMC as a recommendation method in social media. We conduct a large scale study and show significant improvement over existing state-of-the-art approaches.

1 Introduction

The usage of social media sites has significantly increased over the years. Every minute people upload thousands of new videos on YouTube, write blogs on Tumblr[1], take pictures on Flickr and Instagram, and send messages on Twitter and Facebook. This has lead to an information overload that makes it hard for people to search and discover relevant information.

Social media sites have attempted to mitigate this problem by allowing users to follow, or subscribe to updates from specific users. However, as the number of followers grows over time, the information overload problem returns. One possible solution to this problem is the usage of recommendation systems, which can display to users items and followers that are related to their interests and past activities.

Over time recommender methods have significantly evolved. By observing the history of user-item interactions, the systems learn the preferences of the users and use this information to accurately filter through vast amount of items and allowing the user to quickly discover new, interesting and relevant items such as movies, clothes, books and posts. There is a substantial body of work on building recommendation systems for discovering new items, following people in social media platforms, predicting what people like (Purushotham et al., 2012; Chua et al., 2013; Kim et al., 2013). However, these models either do not consider the characteristics of user-item adoption behaviors or cannot scale to the magnitude of data.

It is important to note that the problem of recommending blog posts differs from the traditional collaborative filtering settings, such as the Netflix rating prediction problem in two main aspects. First, the interactions between the users and blogs are *binary* in the form of follows and there is no explicit rating information available about the user's preference. The follow information can be represented as an unidirectional unweighted graph and popular proximity measures based on the structural properties of the graph have been applied to the problem (Yin et al., 2011). Second, the blog recommendation inherently has richer *side information* additional to the conventional user-item matrix (i.e. follower graph).

In Tumblr, text data includes a lot of information, since posts have no limitation in length, compared to other microblogging sites such as Twitter. While such user generated content charac-

---

[1] www.tumblr.com

Proceedings of the 54th Annual Meeting of the Association for Computational Linguistics, pages 332–336,
Berlin, Germany, August 7-12, 2016. ©2016 Association for Computational Linguistics

terizes various blogs, user activity is a more direct and informative signal of user preference as users can explicitly express their interests by liking and reblogging a post. This implies that users who liked or reblogged the same posts are likely to follow similar blogs. The challenge is how to combine multiple sources of information (text and activity) at the same time. For the purpose, we propose a novel convex collective matrix completion (CCMC) social media recommender model, which can scale to million by million matrix using Hazan's algorithm (Gunasekar et al., 2015). Our contributions are as follows:

- We propose a novel CCMC based Tumblr blog post recommendation model.
- We represent users and blogs with an extensive set of side information sources such as the user/blog activity and text/tags.
- We conduct extensive experimental evaluations on Tumblr data and show that our approach significantly outperforms existing methods.

2 Convex Collective Matrix Completion

In this section, we formulate the Tumblr blog post recommendation task as collective matrix factorization problem and we describe our large-scale convect collective matrix completion method with Hazan's algorithm (Gunasekar et al., 2015).

2.1 Model Description

Let $X_1 \in \{0, 1\}^{n_{r_1} \times n_{c_1}}$ denote the user-blog (follower) matrix, where n_{r_1} is the number of users and n_{c_1} is the number of blogs. In this matrix, if the user i likes blog j, the (i, j)th element is set to 1. In addition to the user-blog matrix, we have other auxiliary matrices denoted by $X_2 \subset \mathbb{R}^{n_{r_2} \times n_{c_2}}$ and $X_3 \in \mathbb{R}^{n_{r_3} \times n_{c_3}}$. For example, if we have an user activity matrix, we can use it as X_2, where $n_{r_2} = n_{r_1}$ and n_{c_2} is the number of activities. Moreover, if we have the content information of articles, we can use them as X_3. In this case, $n_{c_1} = n_{c_3}$ is the number of blogs, and n_{r_3} is the number of topics in LDA. Note that, X_1 tends to be a sparse matrix, while X_2 and X_3 tend to be denser matrices. The final goal is to factorize X_1 with the help of the auxiliary matrices X_2 and/or X_3. First, we form a large matrix M by concatenating all matrices $[X_v]_{v=1}^V$ and then factorizing M together with the regularizations.

In this paper, we adopt a convex approach (Bouchard et al., 2013; Gunasekar et al., 2015).

For example, for $V = 3$, the matrix M is given as

$$M = \begin{bmatrix} \cdot & X_1 & X_2 & \cdot \\ X_1^\top & \cdot & \cdot & X_3 \\ X_2^\top & \cdot & \cdot & \cdot \\ \cdot & X_3^\top & \cdot & \cdot \end{bmatrix}. \tag{1}$$

This framework is called convex collective matrix completion (CMC) (Singh and Gordon, 2008). The key advantage of the CCMC approach is that the sparse user-blog matrix X_1 is factorized precisely with the help of the dense matrices X_2 and/or X_3. Moreover, it has been recently shown that the sample complexity of the CCMC algorithm can be smaller than that of the simple matrix factorization approach (i.e., only factorize X_1) (Gunasekar et al., 2015). Finally, the CCMC method can easily incorporate multiple sources of information. Over time if Tumblr provides new signals or if we decide to incorporate new features, CCMC can easily adopt them. Therefore, we believe that CCMC is very suitable for solving the Tumblr recommendation task.

2.2 CCMC-Hazan Algorithm

One of the key challenges of CCMC for Tumblr data is the scalability, since Tumblr has more than million users and hundred millions of blog posts. The original CCMC approach adopts Singular Value Thresholding (SVT) to solve the problem, and it works for small scale problems. However, SVT needs to solve $N \times N$ dimensional eigenvalue decomposition on each iteration, and thus it is not feasible to deal directly with the Tumblr data. Recently, Gunasekar et al. proposed an Atomic norm minimization algorithm for CCMC (Gunasekar et al., 2015) using the approximate SDP solver of Hazan (Hazan, 2008; Jaggi and Sulovsky, 2010). The optimization problem is given as

$$\min_{Z \succeq 0} \sum_{v=1}^V \| P_{\Omega_v} (X_v - P_v(Z)) \|_F^2$$
$$\text{s.t.} \quad \text{tr}(Z) \leq \eta, \tag{2}$$

where $\|X\|_F$ is the Frobenius norm of matrix X, P_{Ω_v}, which extracts the elements in the set, Ω_v is the set of non-zero indexes of X_v, $P_v(Z) = Z_v \in \mathbb{R}^{n_{r_v} \times n_{c_v}}$, and $\eta \geq 0$ is a regularization parameter. The Hazan's algorithm for CMF is summarized in Algorithm 1.

Algorithm 1 CCMC with Hazan's Algorithm of (2)

Parameters: T (Number of iterations)
Rescale loss: $\hat{f}_\eta(\boldsymbol{Z}) = \sum_v \|P_{\Omega_v}(\boldsymbol{X}_v - P_v(\eta \boldsymbol{Z}))\|_F^2$
Initialize $\boldsymbol{Z}^{(1)}$
for all $t = 1, 2 \ldots, T = \frac{4}{\epsilon}$ **do**
    Compute $\boldsymbol{u}^{(t)} = \mathrm{approxEV}\big(-\nabla \hat{f}_\eta(\boldsymbol{Z}^{(t)}), \frac{1}{t^2}\big)^2$
    $\alpha_t := \frac{2}{2+t}$
    $\boldsymbol{Z}^{(t+1)} = \boldsymbol{Z}^{(t)} + \alpha_t \boldsymbol{u}^{(t)} \boldsymbol{u}^{(t)\top}$
end forreturn $[P_v(\boldsymbol{Z}^{(T)})]_{v=1}^V$

The advantage of CCMC-Hazan is that it needs to compute only a top eigenvector on each iteration. Practically, on each iteration t in Algorithm 1, we just need to compute an $\frac{1}{t^2}$-approximate largest eigenvalue of the sparse matrix with $|\Omega|$ non-zero elements, which needs $O(\frac{|\Omega|}{t})$ computation using Lanczos algorithm. On the other hand, the original CCMC algorithms adopt Singular Value Thresholding (SVT) method, which converges much faster than CCMC-Hazan. However, the SVT approach has to compute all eigenvalues in each iteration. Thus, CCMC-Hazan is more suited for large-scale dataset than CCMC-SVT. The details of CMC with Hazan's algorithm, please refer to (Gunasekar et al., 2015).

3 Task Definition

We define our task as given a set of users and their Tumblr post adoption behavior over a period of time, the goal is to build a model that can discover and recommend relevant Tumblr posts to the users.

3.1 Evaluation Setup and Data

We set up our Tumblr post evaluation framework by considering the posting or reblogging of an item j by a user i as an adopted item, and otherwise as unadopted. We present each user with top k items sorted by their predicted adoption score and evaluate how many of the recommended items (posts) were actually adopted by the users.

For our post recommendation study, we used Tumblr data from July until September. We used the data from July to August for training, and tested on the data from September. This experimental set up simulates A/B testing.

From the derived data, we sampled $15,000$ active users and $35,000$ posts resulting in 5 million user-item adoptions for training and 8.6 million user-item adoptions for testing.

Topic	Keywords
23	**fashion style** vintage model design photography nature photo street
117	**flickr photo** mirror photograph artist camera **lake sunset island paint**
71	**wear cloth** shirt **hair** dress jean clean top pant short outfit girl **makeup**
148	**hold hand** wound broken pain heart **together** anger stand memory **heal**
84	**feel empty** remember silence remind reason **hard miss friendly vein**
152	**music feat rap** west drake lil bank kanye hiphop audio **remix** rapper
124	video watch **play game** press start made film show happy **tutorial**
124	**teacher class school** told hell high **homework** math late student course

Figure 1: LDA.

In post recommendation our CCMC-Hazan method uses an user-item matrix $\boldsymbol{X}_1 \in \{0,1\}^{15000 \times 35000}$ and an item-topic matrix $\boldsymbol{X}_2 \in \mathbb{R}^{35000 \times 1000}$. To learn the topics we use Latent Dirichlet Allocation (LDA) (Blei et al., 2003). We represent a document as a collection of post description, captions and hashtags. We use 1000 topics for our experiments. Figure 1 shows some examples of the learned topics from the Tumblr posts.

3.2 Evaluation Metrics

To evaluate the performance of our collaborative matrix factorization approach for Tumblr post recommendation, we calculate precision (P), recall (R) and normalized discounted cumulative gain (nDCG) for top-k recommended posts.

-**P@**k as the fraction of adopted items by each user in top-k items in the list. We aveage precision@k across all users.

-**R@**k as the fraction of adopted items that are successfully discovered in top-k ranked list out of all adopted items by each user. We average recall@k across all users.

-**nDCG@**k computes the weighted score of adopted items based on the position in the top-k list. We average nDCG@k of all users.
We set k to 10 since recommending too many posts is unrealistic. While nDCG@k uses the position of correct answer in the top-k ranked list, it does not penalize for unadopted posts or missing adopted posts in the top-k ranked list. Therefore, to judge the performance of the algorithms, one has to consider all three metrics together. Intuitively a good performing model is the one that has high P@k, R@k and nDCG@k.

3.3 Comparison Against State-of-art Models

In addition to evaluating the performance of our algorithm on Tumblr post recommendation, we

---

^{2}approxEV(X, ϵ) computes the approximate top eigen vector of $\boldsymbol{X}$ upto ϵ error.

also conducted a comparative study against existing state-of-the-art models.

Item-based[3] The item-based model recommends items that are similar to what the users have already adopted (Karypis, 2001). The model does not use textual information and only uses adopted items to compute the similarity between the items. The similarity metric is the Tanimoto Coefficient, which is used to handle binary ratings.

User-based The user-based model recommends items that are adopted by other users with similar taste (Herlocker et al., 1999). The model does not use textual information and only uses adopted items to compute the similarity between the users. Similar to the item-based recommendation, we use the Tanimoto Coefficient. We choose top k items using k-Nearest Neighbor of similar users.

MC[4] Alternating least squares (ALS) is matrix completion (MC) based collaborative filtering model, which was originally introduced to model user-movie rating prediction using mean-square loss function with weighted λ regularization (Zhou et al., 2008). The model does not use textual information or signals for adopted items.

PMC[5] Probabilistic Matrix Completion (Salakhutdinov and Mnih, 2008) is a probabilistic linear model with Gaussian observation noise that handles very large data sets and is robust to sparse user-item matrix. Similar to MC, PMC models the user-item adoption as the product of two K-dimensional lower-rank user and item hidden variables. The model does not use textual information, but unlike the previous methods it uses information on unadopted items.

CF Collaborative Filtering model with softmax function (Guadagni and Little, 1983; Manski, 1975; McFadden, 1974) captures the adoption and un-adoption behavior of users on items in social media. The model does not use textual information, but it uses signals on unadopted items. CF allows us to study the gain of performance in post recommendation when softmax function is used instead of the objective functions used in MC and PMC.

CTR Collaborative Topic Regression (Wang and Blei, 2011) was originally introduced to recommend scientific articles. It combines collaborative filtering PMC and probabilistic topic model-

---
[3]https://mahout.apache.org
[4]www.graphlab.org
[5]http://www.cs.cmu.edu/ chongw/citeulike/

Method	PRC@10	RCL@20	AUC
Item-based	0.24	0.08	0.42
User-based	0.32	0.11	0.51
MC	0.31	0.11	0.52
PMC	0.35	0.12	0.55
CF	0.36	0.13	0.56
CTR	0.39	0.14	0.59
CCMC-Hazan	**0.41**	**0.16**	**0.61**

Table 1: Tumblr Post Recommendation Results

ing LDA. It captures two K-dimensional lower-rank user and item hidden variables from user-item adoption matrix and the content of the items. This model uses textual information and signal for unadopted items.

3.4 Results

Table 1 shows the obtained results of the proposed CCMC-Hazan method against the remaining recommendation models. The simple user and item based recommendations have the lowest performance. This shows that for accurate post recommendation using direct post and user information is insufficient and one needs stronger context driven signals. This is shown in the performance of the CF and CTR methods, which model context information with LDA and perform better than the rest of the models.

However, when we compare the performance of our collaborative matrix completion method, we can see that the rest of the models have significantly lower performance. The main reasons are due to the dense information of CCMC-Hazan method and the fact that our method optimizes a convex function whereas the MC, CF and CTR models can get stuck in local optima.

4 Conclusions

Recommending blog posts is one of the major tasks for user engagement and revenue generation in online microblogging sites such as Tumblr. In this paper, we propose a convex collective matrix completion based recommendation method that effectively utilizes the user-item matrix as well as rich side information from users and/or items. We evaluate the proposed method on real-world dataset collected from Tumblr. Extensive experiments demonstrate the effectiveness of the proposed method in comparison to existing state-of-the-art approaches.

Acknowledgement

We would like to thank the anonymous reviewers for their valuable feedback and grant MEXT KAKENHI #16K16114.

References

David Blei, Andrew Ng, and Michael Jordan. 2003. Latent dirichlet allocation. *The Journal of Machine Learning Research*, 3:993–1022.

Guillaume Bouchard, Shengbo Guo, and Dawei Yin. 2013. Convex collective matrix factorization. In *AISTATS*.

Freddy Chong Tat Chua, Hady W. Lauw, and Ee-Peng Lim. 2013. Generative models for item adoptions using social correlation. *IEEE Trans. on Knowl. and Data Eng.*, 25:2036–2048.

Peter M Guadagni and John DC Little. 1983. A logit model of brand choice calibrated on scanner data. *Marketing science*, 2(3):203–238.

Suriya Gunasekar, Makoto Yamada, Dawei Yin, and Yi Chang. 2015. Consistent collective matrix completion under joint low rank structure. In *AISTATS*.

Elad Hazan, 2008. *Sparse Approximate Solutions to Semidefinite Programs*, pages 306–316. Springer Berlin Heidelberg.

Jonathan L. Herlocker, Joseph A. Konstan, Al Borchers, and John Riedl. 1999. An algorithmic framework for performing collaborative filtering. In *SIGIR*.

Martin Jaggi and Marek Sulovsky. 2010. A simple algorithm for nuclear norm regularized problems. In *ICML*.

George Karypis. 2001. Evaluation of item-based top-n recommendation algorithms. In *CIKM*.

Jihie Kim, Jaebong Yoo, Ho Lim, Huida Qiu, Zornitsa Kozareva, and Aram Galstyan. 2013. Sentiment prediction using collaborative filtering. In *ICWSM*.

Charles F Manski. 1975. Maximum score estimation of the stochastic utility model of choice. *Journal of Econometrics*, 3(3):205–228.

Daniel McFadden. 1974. Conditional logit analysis of qualitative choice behavior. In *Frontiers in Econometrics*, pages 105–142.

Sanjay Purushotham, Yan Liu, and C.-C. Jay Kuo. 2012. Collaborative topic regression with social matrix factorization for recommendation systems. *CoRR*.

Ruslan Salakhutdinov and Andriy Mnih. 2008. Bayesian probabilistic matrix factorization using markov chain monte carlo. In *ICML*.

Ajit P. Singh and Geoffrey J. Gordon. 2008. Relational learning via collective matrix factorization. In *KDD*.

Chong Wang and David M. Blei. 2011. Collaborative topic modeling for recommending scientific articles. In *KDD*.

Dawei Yin, Liangjie Hong, and Brian D Davison. 2011. Structural link analysis and prediction in microblogs. In *CIKM*.

Yunhong Zhou, Dennis Wilkinson, Robert Schreiber, and Rong Pan. 2008. Large-scale parallel collaborative filtering for the netflix prize. In *AAIM*.

Text Simplification as Tree Labeling

Joachim Bingel
Centre for Language Technology
University of Copenhagen
bingel@hum.ku.dk

Anders Søgaard
Centre for Language Technology
University of Copenhagen
soegaard@hum.ku.dk

Abstract

We present a new, structured approach to text simplification using conditional random fields over top-down traversals of dependency graphs that jointly predicts possible compressions and paraphrases. Our model reaches readability scores comparable to word-based compression approaches across a range of metrics and human judgements while maintaining more of the important information.

1 Introduction

Sentence-level text simplification is the problem of automatically modifying sentences so that they become easier to read, while maintaining most of the relevant information in them. This can benefit applications as pre-processing for machine translation (Bernth, 1998) and assisting technologies for readers with reduced literacy (Carroll et al., 1999; Watanabe et al., 2009; Rello et al., 2013).

Sentence-level text simplification ignores sentence splitting and reordering, and typically focuses on *compression* (deletion of words) and *paraphrasing* or *lexical substitution* (Cohn and Lapata, 2008). We include paraphrasing and lexical substitution here, while previous work in sentence simplification has often focused exclusively on deletion. Approaches that address compression and paraphrasing (or more tasks) integrally include (Zhu et al., 2010; Narayan and Gardent, 2014; Mandya et al., 2014).

Simplification beyond deletion is motivated by Pitler's (2010) observation that abstractive sentence summaries written by humans often "include paraphrases or synonyms ('said' versus 'stated') and use alternative syntactic constructions ('gave John the book' versus 'gave the book to John')." Such lexical or syntactic alternations may contribute strongly to the readability of a sentence if they replace difficult words with shorter or more familiar ones, in particular for low-literacy readers (Rello et al., 2013). Our joint approach to deletion and paraphrasing works against the limitation that abstractive simplifications "are not capable of being generated by [...] most sentence compression algorithms" (Pitler, 2010).

Furthermore, a central concern in text simplification is to ensure the grammaticality of the output, especially with low-proficiency readers as the target audience. Our approach to this problem is to remove or paraphrase entire syntactic units in the original sentence, thus avoiding to remove phrase heads without removing their arguments or modifiers. Like Filippova and Strube (2008), we rely on dependency structures rather than constituent structures, which promises more robust syntactic analysis and allows us to operate on discontinuous syntactic units.

Contributions We present a sentence simplification model which is, to the best of our knowledge, the first model that uses structured prediction over dependency trees *and* models compression and paraphrasing jointly. Our model uses Viterbi decoding rather than scoring of all candidates and outputs probabilities reflecting model confidence.

2 Data

We use the publicly available Google compression data set,[1] which consists of 10,000 English sentence triples with (1) the original sentence as present in the body of an online news article, (2) a headline based on the original sentence, and (3) a compression that is automatically derived from the original such that it only contains word forms

---

[1] http://storage.googleapis.com/
sentencecomp/compressiondata.json

Proceedings of the 54th Annual Meeting of the Association for Computational Linguistics, pages 337–343,
Berlin, Germany, August 7-12, 2016. ©2016 Association for Computational Linguistics

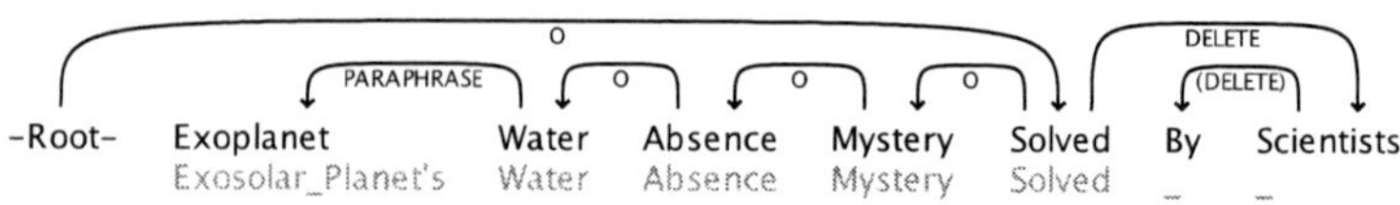

Figure 1: An example simplification tree

present in the original, preserving their order. The following sentence triple exemplifies these different versions:

(1) *In official documents released earlier this month it appears the Queen of England used the wrong name for the Republic of Ireland when writing to president Patrick Hillery.*

(2) *Queen elizabeth ii used wrong name for Republic*

(3) *The Queen of England used the wrong name for the Republic of Ireland.*

The data is pre-processed with the Stanford CoreNLP tools (Manning et al., 2014), retrieving lemmas, parts-of-speech, named entities and dependency trees. We reserve the first 200 sentences from the data set for evaluation, the next 200 for tuning parameters (including the used PPDB versions, see next paragraph), and use the remaining 9,600 sentences for training our model.

Deletion and paraphrase targets As our approach operates on dependency trees, aiming to prune or paraphrase subtrees from the dependency tree of a sentence, we identify deleted or paraphrased subtrees, marking their heads with a corresponding label. A subtree receives a Delete label if none of the words subsumed by this subtree occur in the compressed version of the sentence.

We identify paraphrased subsequences in an original sentence by looking up the subsequence string in the Paraphrase Database (PPDB) (Ganitkevitch et al., 2013) and testing if one of its possible paraphrases occurs in the headline version of the sentence in question. The Paraphrase Database 1.0 is a set of phrasal and lexical pairs that were automatically acquired from bilingual parallel corpora, and thus contain a portion of flawed paraphrase pairs. The database comes in a number of different sizes, where small editions are restricted to high-precision paraphrases with relatively high paraphrase probabilities. As the two smallest editions of PPDB only yield a very low number of paraphrase targets (less than 100 in the

entire Google compression data set), we opt to employ a medium-sized version of the resource (size 'L') and find a total of 510 phrasal and lexical paraphrases in the corpus.

3 Method

We assume that text simplification is a generative process on syntactic dependency graphs with a paraphrase dictionary. A dependency graph $G = (V, A)$ is a labeled directed graph in the standard graph-theoretic sense and consists of nodes, V, and arcs, A, such that for sentence $S = w_0 w_1 \ldots w_n$ and label set R, $V \subseteq \{w_0, w_1, \ldots, w_n\}$, and $A \subseteq V \times R \times V$ hold, and if $(w_i, r, w_j) \in A$ then $(w_i, r', w_j) \neq A$ for all $r' \neq r$. We restrict the dependency graphs to the class of trees, i.e., for $(w_i, r, w_j) \in A$, if $(w_k, r, w_j) \in A$ then $k = i$.

The generative process traverses the tree in a top-down fashion, deleting or paraphrasing subtrees (see Figure 1). Note that elements in subtrees dominated by a deleted node are automatically deleted (analogously for paraphrases).

For each dependency tree $G = (V, A)$ in a training set of T sentences, we derive an input sequence of K-dimensional feature vectors $\mathbf{x} = x_1, \ldots, x_n$ and an output sequence of $\mathbf{y} = y_1, \ldots, y_n$. Our tree-to-string simplification model is a second-order linear-chain conditional random field (CRF)

$$p(\mathbf{y}|\mathbf{x}) = \frac{1}{Z(\mathbf{x})} \prod_{i=1}^{n} \exp\{\sum_{k=1}^{K} \theta_k f_k(y_t, y_{t-1}, x_t)\}$$

with $y_i = $ Delete if and only if x_i represents the least upper bound in G covering a deleted span in the training data, and $y_i = $ Paraphrase if and only if x_i represents the least upper bound in G covering a paraphrased span in the training data. For example, if the entire sentence is deleted, and $(w_0, r, w_i) \in A$, then $y_i = $ Delete (but $y_j = $ Leave for $j \neq i$).

This encoding means that theoretically we can predict to paraphrase a subtree that is dominated by a node which is in turn predicted to be deleted (or vice versa). However, once an operation is carried out on a subtree, none of its dominated nodes are considered in the remainder of the top-down simplification process. Giving preference to operations at higher-level syntactic environments in this manner serves as a mechanism to resolve ambiguities in the decision process by taking a wider context into account.

Furthermore, predicting a node to get paraphrased at the right corner of a deleted subtree can potentially influence labeling decisions outside this subtree as a consequence of the dynamic-program Viterbi decoding. We acknowledge that this is a theoretical drawback of the presented approach, but given that we do not observe any such dependency graphs in our data, we do not expect this to be a serious problem in most cases.

Whenever our model predicts that a subtree be paraphrased, we look up the respective token sequence in PPDB and replace it with the candidate paraphrase (if available) that maximises the product of frequency and translation probability according to PPDB.

Features for CRF model We train a second-order CRF model using MarMoT (Mueller et al., 2013), an efficient higher-order CRF implementation. The model computes its observational probabilities from features based on properties of the subtree root token (incl. POS, language model probability, NE mention, word difficulty), of the internal structure of the subtree (incl. number of children, depth, length of sequence), and of the external grammatical structure (incl. dependency relation, parent POS, distance from parent, position in sentence).

4   Evaluation

Baselines In the following experiments, we compare our approach to state-of-the-art approaches to sentence compression and joint compression/paraphrasing. For the first of these two categories, we consider the LSTM system described in Filippova et al. (2015) as well as the results reported therein for the MIRA system (McDonald, 2006). As a joint approach, we consider Reluctant Trimmer (RT), a simplification system that employs synchronous dependency grammars (Mandya et al., 2014). Since the LSTM system requires great amounts of training data, which were not available to us, we cannot reproduce its out-

		Recall	**Precision**	**F1**
		Reluctant Trimmer		
tokens	Delete	54.60	20.23	29.52
	Paraphrase	01.67	66.67	03.27
	Leave	52.27	78.54	54.60
		Tree Labeling		
subtrees	Delete	43.31	67.54	52.77
	Paraphrase	23.85	50.89	32.48
	Leave	94.29	84.82	89.30
tokens	Delete	49.67	77.16	60.44
	Paraphrase	21.16	51.52	30.00
	Leave	80.33	50.91	62.32

Table 1: Performance on joint deletion and paraphrasing detection for our tree labeling system (evaluating both on entire subtrees and token level) as well as for the RT baseline (tokens only). Note that RT is trained on the (Simple) English Wikipedia, not on the Google compressions, and therefore the results may not be directly comparable.

put and therefore limit our comparison of human rankings to the eleven output examples provided in the paper.

F-Scores We first evaluate our tree labeling model (TL) on its ability to predict subtree deletion and paraphrasing (i.e. whether a subtree should be paraphrased, independent of the actual replacement). The results for this evaluation setup, as well as word-level performance, are listed in Table 1 and compared to RT. Note that for deletion and paraphrasing, our model consistently has higher precision than recall, thus generating more confident simplifications and less ungrammatical output.

Automated Readability Scores Table 2 reports the compression ratio (CR, percentage of retained words) as well as automated readability scores that our model achieves on the test set and compares it to the output of the RT baseline. Our system manages to compress the original texts by more than one third, but the gold simplifications (headlines and compressions) are still considerably shorter.

Our approach improves readability as measured by the Flesch Reading Ease score[2] (Flesch,

---

[2]The negative value that the headlines receive for this met-

Data version	CR$\downarrow$	Flesch$\uparrow$	Dale-C.$\downarrow$
Original	—	49.15	9.55
Headlines	**0.32***	-80.77*	17.61*
Compressions	0.40*	**70.80***	9.56
TL output	0.62*	56.25*	9.30*
RT output	0.86*	60.65*	**9.27***

Table 2: Compression ratios and automatic readability scores for the Google compression data set, compared to the system output. Readability is indicated by a high Flesh Reading Ease score and a low Dale-Chall score. * indicates differences compared to the original sentences that are significant at $p < 10^{-3}$.

System	Readability	Informativeness
MIRA	4.31	3.55
LSTM	**4.51**	3.78
TL	4.14	**4.01**
RT (11)	3.09	4.12
LSTM (11)	**4.23**	3.42
TL (11)	4.21	**4.15**

Table 3: Mean readability and informativeness ratings for the first 200 sentences in the Google data (upper) and for the 11 sample sentences listed in Filippova et al. (2015) (lower).

1948) and the Dale-Chall formula (Dale and Chall, 1948). The former score measures textual difficulty as a function of sentence length and the number of syllables per word, while the latter aims to estimate a US school grade level at which a text can be well understood, based on a vocabulary list. Both metrics deem the output of our system easier to read than the original texts, while the Dale-Chall formula also rates our system better than the gold simplifications.

Human Readability Ratings Following Filippova et al. (2015) in their evaluation setup for the sake of comparability, we ask raters to assign scores on a one-to-five Likert scale to the first 200 sentences from the Google compression data paired with the output of our system. Each pair is rated by three native or near-native speakers of English.

The raters are asked to evaluate the sentence

pairs for *readability* and *informativeness*. The former, following Filippova et al. (2015), "covers the grammatical correctness, comprehensibility and fluency of the output." The latter metric pertains to the relation between the original sentence and the system output as it "measures the amount of important content preserved in the compression."

Table 3 compares the performance of our model to the figures reported in Filippova et al. (2015) for their LSTM model and McDonald's (2006) system (MIRA). For a comparison with the same judges, we repeat the evaluation with the 11 sample output compressions listed in Filippova et al. (2015)as well as the respective output from Reluctant Trimmer; see the lower part of Table 3. The results suggest that, compared to the compression-only LSTMs, our approach yields comparable performance in terms of readability, while maintaining more of the central information in the original sentences. Compared to RT, our system does considerably better in terms of readability and retains slightly more of the important information.

5 Related Work

Several approaches to sentence compression have been presented in the last decade. Knight and Marcu (2002) and Turner and Charniak (2005) apply noisy channel models, using language models to control for grammaticality. McDonald (2006) introduces a different approach, discriminatively training a scoring function, informed by syntactic features, to score all possible subtrees of a sentence. His work was inspired by Riezler et al. (2003) scoring substrings generated from LFG parses. A third approach to sentence compression is sequence labeling, which has been explored by Elming et al. (2013) using linear-chain CRFs with syntactic features, and more recently by Filippova et al. (2015) and Klerke et al. (2016) using recurrent neural networks with LSTM cells.

Most recent approaches to sentence compression make use of syntactic analysis, either by operating directly on trees (Riezler et al., 2003; Nomoto, 2007; Filippova and Strube, 2008; Cohn and Lapata, 2008; Cohn and Lapata, 2009) or by incorporating syntactic information in their model (McDonald, 2006; Clarke and Lapata, 2008). Recently, however, Filippova et al. (2015) presented an approach to sentence compression using

	Original Sentence & *Simplifications*
O	OG&E is warning customers about a prepaid debit card scam that is targeting utility customers across the county.
C	*OG&E is warning customers about a scam.*
R	*OG&E is warning customers about a debit card scam that is targeting utility customers across the country.*
T	*OG&E is warning customers **regarding** a prepaid debit card scam.*
O	The husband of murdered Melbourne woman Jill Meagher will return to Ireland later this month "to clear his head" while fighting for parole board changes.
C	*The husband of murdered woman Jill Meagher will return to Ireland.*
R	*The husband of Melbourne woman Jill Meagher will return to Ireland this month to clear his head fighting for parole board changes.*
T	*The husband of murdered Melbourne woman Jill Meagher will return to Ireland.*
O	A research project has found that taxi drivers often don't know what the speed limit is.
C	*Taxi drivers don't know the speed limit is.*
R	*A research project has found that drivers often **do not** know what the speed limit is.*
T	*A project has found taxi drivers don't know what the speed limit is.*

Table 4: Example output for original sentences (O) as generated by the Reluctant Trimmer baseline (R) and our tree labeling system (T), as well as the headline-generated Google compressions (C).

LSTMs with word embeddings, with no syntactic features. We return to working directly on trees, presenting a tree-to-string model of sentence simplification. Our model has interesting similarities to (Riezler et al., 2003), but uses Viterbi decoding rather than scoring of all candidates. Also, it follows Cohn and Lapata (2008) in going beyond most of these models, modeling compression *and* paraphrasing.

For lexical simplification, most systems typically use pre-compiled dictionaries (Devlin, 1999; Inui et al., 2003) and select the synonym candidate with the highest frequency. More recently, Baeza-Yates et al. (2015) introduced an algorithm for lexical simplification in Spanish that selects the best synonym candidate in a context-sensitive fashion.

Cohn and Lapata (2008), Woodsend and Lapata (2011) and Mandya et al. (2014) present *joint* approaches to compression and paraphrasing that are based on (quasi-) synchronous grammars, and similarly Zhu et al. (2010) take a syntax-based approach, but employ a probabilistic model of various simplification operations. Napoles et al. (2011) do not use syntactic information, but instead employ a character-based metric to compress and paraphrase.

6 Conclusion

We presented a new approach to sentence simplification that uses linear-chain conditional random fields over dependency graphs to jointly predict compression and paraphrasing of entire syntactic units. The objective of our model is to delete or paraphrase entire subtrees in dependency graphs as a strategy to avoid ungrammatical output. Our approach makes innovative use of a three-fold parallel monolingual corpus that features headlines and compressions to learn paraphrases and deletions, respectively. Human evaluation shows that our approach leads to readability figures that are comparable to previous state-of-the-art approaches to the more basic sentence compression task, and better than previous work on joint compression and paraphrasing. While our model does rely on syntactic analysis, it only needs a tiny fraction (less than 0.5%) of the training data used by Filippova et al. (2015).

Acknowledgments

This research was partially funded by the ERC Starting Grant LOWLANDS No. 313695, as well as by Trygfonden.

References

Ricardo Baeza-Yates, Luz Rello, and Julia Dembowski. 2015. Cassa: A context-aware synonym simplification algorithm. *Proceedings of the 2015 Conference of the North American Chapter of the Association for Computational Linguistics on Human Language Technology*, pages 1380–1385.

Arendse Bernth. 1998. EasyEnglish: Preprocessing for MT. In *Proceedings of the Second International Workshop on Controlled Language Applications*, pages 30–41.

John Carroll, Guido Minnen, Darren Pearce, Yvonne Canning, Siobhan Devlin, and John Tait. 1999. Simplifying text for language-impaired readers. In *Proceedings of EACL*, volume 99, pages 269–270.

James Clarke and Mirella Lapata. 2008. Global inference for sentence compression: An integer linear programming approach. *Journal of Artificial Intelligence Research*, pages 399–429.

Trevor Cohn and Mirella Lapata. 2008. Sentence compression beyond word deletion. In *Proceedings of the 22nd International Conference on Computational Linguistics-Volume 1*, pages 137–144. Association for Computational Linguistics.

Trevor Cohn and Mirella Lapata. 2009. Sentence compression as tree transduction. *Journal of Artificial Intelligence Research*, pages 637–674.

Edgar Dale and Jeanne S Chall. 1948. A formula for predicting readability: Instructions. *Educational research bulletin*, pages 37–54.

Siobhan Lucy Devlin. 1999. *Simplifying natural language for aphasic readers.* Ph.D. thesis, University of Sunderland.

Jakob Elming, Anders Johannsen, Sigrid Klerke, Emanuele Lapponi, Hector Martinez Alonso, and Anders Søgaard. 2013. Down-stream effects of tree-to-dependency conversions. In *HLT-NAACL*, pages 617–626.

Katja Filippova and Michael Strube. 2008. Dependency tree based sentence compression. In *Proceedings of the Fifth International Natural Language Generation Conference*, pages 25–32. Association for Computational Linguistics.

Katja Filippova, Enrique Alfonseca, Carlos A Colmenares, Lukasz Kaiser, and Oriol Vinyals. 2015. Sentence compression by deletion with lstms. In *Proceedings of the 2015 Conference on Empirical Methods in Natural Language Processing*, pages 360–368.

Rudolph Flesch. 1948. A new readability yardstick. *Journal of applied psychology*, 32(3):221.

Juri Ganitkevitch, Benjamin Van Durme, and Chris Callison-Burch. 2013. PPDB: The paraphrase database. In *Proceedings of NAACL-HLT*, pages 758–764, Atlanta, Georgia, June. Association for Computational Linguistics.

Kentaro Inui, Atsushi Fujita, Tetsuro Takahashi, Ryu Iida, and Tomoya Iwakura. 2003. Text simplification for reading assistance: a project note. In *Proceedings of the second international workshop on Paraphrasing-Volume 16*, pages 9–16. Association for Computational Linguistics.

Sigrid Klerke, Yoav Goldberg, and Anders Søgaard. 2016. Improving sentence compression by learning to predict gaze. In *Proceedings of ACL 2016 (short)*.

Kevin Knight and Daniel Marcu. 2002. Summarization beyond sentence extraction: A probabilistic approach to sentence compression. *Artificial Intelligence*, 139(1):91–107.

Angrosh A. Mandya, Tadashi Nomoto, and Advaith Siddharthan. 2014. Lexico-syntactic text simplification and compression with typed dependencies. In *COLING*, pages 1996–2006.

Christopher D. Manning, Mihai Surdeanu, John Bauer, Jenny Finkel, Steven J. Bethard, and David McClosky. 2014. The Stanford CoreNLP natural language processing toolkit. In *Proceedings of 52nd Annual Meeting of the Association for Computational Linguistics: System Demonstrations*, pages 55–60.

Ryan T McDonald. 2006. Discriminative sentence compression with soft syntactic evidence. In *EACL*.

Thomas Mueller, Helmut Schmid, and Hinrich Schütze. 2013. Efficient higher-order CRFs for morphological tagging. In *Proceedings of the 2013 Conference on Empirical Methods in Natural Language Processing*, pages 322–332, Seattle, Washington, USA, October. Association for Computational Linguistics.

Courtney Napoles, Chris Callison-Burch, Juri Ganitkevitch, and Benjamin Van Durme. 2011. Paraphrastic sentence compression with a character-based metric: Tightening without deletion. In *Proceedings of the Workshop on Monolingual Text-To-Text Generation*, pages 84–90. Association for Computational Linguistics.

Shashi Narayan and Claire Gardent. 2014. Hybrid simplification using deep semantics and machine translation. In *the 52nd Annual Meeting of the Association for Computational Linguistics*, pages 435–445.

Tadashi Nomoto. 2007. Discriminative sentence compression with conditional random fields. *Information Processing and Management: an International Journal*, 43(6):1571–1587.

Emily Pitler. 2010. Methods for sentence compression. Technical report, Department of Computer and Information Science, University of Pennsylvania.

Luz Rello, Ricardo Baeza-Yates, Laura Dempere-Marco, and Horacio Saggion. 2013. Frequent words improve readability and short words improve understandability for people with dyslexia. In *Human-Computer Interaction–INTERACT 2013*, pages 203–219. Springer.

Stefan Riezler, Tracy H King, Richard Crouch, and Annie Zaenen. 2003. Statistical sentence condensation using ambiguity packing and stochastic disambiguation methods for lexical-functional grammar.

In *Proceedings of the 2003 Conference of the North American Chapter of the Association for Computational Linguistics on Human Language Technology-Volume 1*, pages 118–125. Association for Computational Linguistics.

Jenine Turner and Eugene Charniak. 2005. Supervised and unsupervised learning for sentence compression. In *Proceedings of the 43rd Annual Meeting on Association for Computational Linguistics*, pages 290–297. Association for Computational Linguistics.

Willian Massami Watanabe, Arnaldo Candido Junior, Vinícius Rodriguez Uzêda, Renata Pontin de Mattos Fortes, Thiago Alexandre Salgueiro Pardo, and Sandra Maria Aluísio. 2009. Facilita: reading assistance for low-literacy readers. In *Proceedings of the 27th ACM international conference on Design of communication*, pages 29–36. ACM.

Kristian Woodsend and Mirella Lapata. 2011. Learning to simplify sentences with quasi-synchronous grammar and integer programming. In *Proceedings of the conference on empirical methods in natural language processing*, pages 409–420. Association for Computational Linguistics.

Zhemin Zhu, Delphine Bernhard, and Iryna Gurevych. 2010. A monolingual tree-based translation model for sentence simplification. In *Proceedings of the 23rd international conference on computational linguistics*, pages 1353–1361. Association for Computational Linguistics.

Bootstrapped Text-level Named Entity Recognition for Literature

Julian Brooke   Timothy Baldwin
Computing and Information Systems
The University of Melbourne
jabrooke@unimelb.edu.au
tb@ldwin.net

Adam Hammond
English and Comparative Literature
San Diego State University
ahammond@mail.sdsu.edu

Abstract

We present a named entity recognition (NER) system for tagging fiction: `LitNER`. Relative to more traditional approaches, `LitNER` has two important properties: (1) it makes no use of hand-tagged data or gazetteers, instead it bootstraps a model from term clusters; and (2) it leverages multiple instances of the same name in a text. Our experiments show it to substantially outperform off-the-shelf supervised NER systems.

1 Introduction

Much of the work on applying NLP to the analysis of literature has focused on literary figures/characters in the text, e.g. in the context of social network analysis (Elson et al., 2010; Agarwal et al., 2013; Ardanuy and Sporleder, 2015) or analysis of characterization (Bamman et al., 2014). Named entity recognition (NER) of person names is generally the first step in identifying characters; locations are also a prevalent NE type, and can be useful when tracking different plot threads (Wallace, 2012), or trends in the settings of fiction.

There are not, to our knowledge, any NER systems that are specifically targeted at literature, and most related work has used `Stanford CoreNLP` as an off-the-shelf solution (Bamman et al., 2014; Vala et al., 2015). In this paper, we show that it is possible to take advantage of the properties of fiction texts, in particular the repetition of names, to build a high-performing 3-class NER system which distinguishes people and locations from other capitalized words and phrases. Notably, we do this without any hand-labelled

data whatsoever, bootstrapping a text-level context classifier from a low-dimensional Brown clustering of the Project Gutenberg corpus.

2 Related work

The standard approach to NER is to treat it as a supervised sequential classification problem, typically using conditional random fields or similar models, based on local context features as well as properties of the token itself. Relevant to the present work is the fact that, despite there being some work on enforcing tag consistency across multiple instances of the same token (Finkel et al., 2005) and the use of non-local features (Ratinov and Roth, 2009) to improve supervised sequential models, the consensus seems to be that this non-local information has a relatively modest effect on performance in standard datasets, and as a result off-the-shelf NER systems in practice treat each sentence as a separate document, with multiple instances of the same token in different sentences viewed as entirely independent classification problems. We also note that although supervised NER is the norm, there is a smaller body of work in semi-supervised and unsupervised approaches to NER and semantic lexicon induction, for instance pattern bootstrapping (Nadeau et al., 2006; Thelen and Riloff, 2002; McIntosh et al., 2011) as well as generative approaches (Elsner et al., 2009).

In the context of literature, the most closely related task is character identification (Vala et al., 2015), which is itself an intermediate task for character speech identification (He et al., 2013), analysis of characterization (Bamman et al., 2014), and analysis of social networks (Elson et al., 2010; Agarwal et al., 2013; Ardanuy and Sporleder, 2015). In addition to NER, character identifica-

Proceedings of the 54th Annual Meeting of the Association for Computational Linguistics, pages 344–350,
Berlin, Germany, August 7-12, 2016. ©2016 Association for Computational Linguistics

tion also involves clustering multiple aliases of the same character, and discarding person names that don't correspond to characters. Vala et al. (2015) identify some of the failures of off-the-shelf NER with regards to character identification, and attempt to fix them; their efforts are focused, however, on characters that are referred to by description rather than names or aliases.

3 Method

3.1 Corpus preparation and segmentation

The corpus we use for building and testing our NER system is the 2010 image of the (US) Project Gutenberg corpus,[1] a reasonably comprehensive collection of out-of-copyright English literary texts, to our knowledge the largest that is publicly available in a machine-readable, full-text format. We access the texts via the GutenTag tool (Brooke et al., 2015), which allows both filtering of texts by genre as well as within-text filtering to remove Project Gutenberg copyright information, front and back matter (e.g. table of contents), and headers. We focus here only on fiction texts (i.e. novels and short stories); other kinds of literature (e.g. plays) are rare in the corpus and have very different properties in terms of the distribution of names. The final corpus size is 10844 texts.

GutenTag also provides an initial segmentation of tokens into potential names, using a simple rule-based system which segments contiguous capitalized words, potentially with common intervening function words like *of* as well as leading *the* (e.g. *the King of Westeros*). It largely (but not entirely) overcomes the problem of sentence-initial capitalization in English by generalizing over an entire text; as long as a capitalized word or phrase appears in a non-sentence initial position at least once in a text, it will be tagged in the sentence-initial position as well. To improve precision, the name tagger in the version of GutenTag used for this paper (0.1.3) has lower bounds on token count (at least 10) and an upper bound on the length of names (no longer than 3 words). For this work, however, we remove those restrictions to maximize recall. Though not our primary concern, we return to evaluate the quality of the initial segmentation in Section 5.

3.2 Brown clustering

The next step is to induce Brown clusters (Brown et al., 1992) over the pre-segmented corpus (including potential names), using the tool of Liang (2005). Briefly, Brown clusters are formed using an agglomerative hierarchical cluster of terms based on their immediate context, placing terms into categories to maximize the probability of consecutive terms over the entire corpus. Note that using information from Brown clusters is a well established technique in NER, but more typically as features within a supervised framework (Miller et al., 2004; Liang, 2005; Ritter et al., 2011); we are unaware of any work using them directly as a source of bootstrapped training examples. We used default settings except for the number of clusters (c): 50. The rationale for such a small cluster size—the default is 1000, and NER systems which use Brown clusters as features do better with even more (Derczynski et al., 2015)—is that we want to have clusters that correspond to major noun categories (e.g. PERSON and LOCATION), which we consider the next most fundamental division beyond part-of-speech; 50 was selected because it is roughly comparable to the size of the Penn Treebank tagset (Marcus et al., 1993). We did not tune this number, except to observe that larger numbers (e.g. 100 or 200) resulted in increasingly fragmented clusters for our entities of interest.

To automatically extract a seed list of people and locations, we ranked the clusters by the total (token) count of names (as identified by GutenTag), and took the first cluster to be PERSON, and the second to be LOCATION; all other clusters are considered OTHER, our third, catchall category. Alternatively, we could have set c higher and manually grouped the clusters based on the common words in the clusters, adding a thin layer of supervision to the process; with a low c, however, this was unnecessary since the composition and ranking of the clusters conformed exactly to our expectations. The top-5 clusters by token count of names are given in Table 1.[2] Note the presence of the multiword name *New York* in the second cluster, as a result of the segmentation.

The most common words in the first two clusters are mostly what we would expect, though there is a bit of noise, e.g. *Him* included as a place. The other clusters are messier, but still in-

---

[1]http://www.gutenberg.org

[2]Note that each cluster generally includes large numbers of non-names, which we ignore.

Count	Top-10 name types
17.2M	Tom, Jack, Dick, Mary, John
	Harry, Peter, Frank, George, Jim
2.5M	London, England, Paris, New York, France
	Him, America, Rome, Europe, Boston
1.8M	English, French, Lord, Indian, American
	German, Christian, Indians, King, Italian
0.5M	Sir, Doctor, Colonel, Madam, Major
	Professor, Dieu, Squire, Heavens, Sire
0.5M	Christmas, Spanish, British, Irish, Roman
	Latin, Chinese, European, Dutch, Scotch

Table 1: Top-5 Brown clusters derived from PG corpus, by token count of names

terpretable: e.g. Cluster 4 is a collection of terms of address. Note that although we do not consider an term like *Doctor* to be a person name, *Doctor Smith* or *the Doctor* would be; in many literary contexts characters are referred to by an alias, and failure to deal properly with these situations is a significant problem with off-the-shelf NER systems in literature (Vala et al., 2015). In any case, Brown clustering works fairly well for common names, but for rarer ones, the clustering is haphazard. Fiction, though, has many rare names and locations, since authors will often invent them. Another problem with Brown clustering is that ignores possible sense distinctions: for instance, *Florence* is both a city and a person name. To avoid confusion, authors will generally preserve one-sense-per-document, but this is not true at the corpus level.

3.3 Text-level context classifier

The central element of our NER system is a text-level classifier of names based on context. By text-level, we mean that it assumes one-sense-per-document, classifying a name for an entire document, based on all instances of the name in the document (Gale et al., 1992). It is trained on the (text-level) "instances" of relatively common names (appearing more than 100 times in the corpus) from the 3 NE label types derived based on the Brown clustering. That is, to build a training set, we pass through the corpus and each time we come across a common name in a particular document, we build a feature vector corresponding to all the contexts *in that document*, with the label taken from the clustering. Our rationale here is that the challenging part of NER in literature is names that appear only in one text; by limiting our context for common words to a single text,

we simulate the task for rarer words. *Mary* is a common name, and may be a major character in one text, but a minor one in another; hence, we build a classifier that deals with both context-rich and context-poor situations. The noisy training set thus constructed has about 1 million examples.

Our feature set consists of filtered word features in a 2-word window ($w_{-2}\, w_{-1}\, w_0\, w_{+1}\, w_{+2}$) around the token occurrences w_0 of a target type in a given text, made up of position-indexed unigrams (w_{-2}, w_{-1}, w_{+1} and w_{+2}) and bigrams ($w_{-2}w_{-1}$, $w_{+1}w_{+2}$ and $w_{-1}w_{+1}$), excluding unigrams when a subsuming bigram feature matched (e.g. if we match *trust in*, we do not add *trust* and *in*). For this we used the name-segmented corpus, and when one of the words in the context was also a name, we take the category from the Brown clustering as the word (so w_2 for *London* in *from London to New York* is LOCATION, not *New*). Across multiple tokens of the same type, we count the same context only once, creating a binary feature vector which was normalized by dividing by the count of all non-zero entries once all contexts were collected. To be included as features, the n-grams had to occur with ≥ 10 different w_0 target word types. Note that given our bootstrapping setup, the word type itself cannot be used directly as a feature.

For classification, we use logistic regression from scikit-learn (Pedregosa et al., 2011) trained with SGD using L2 regularization ($C = 1$).[3] The only non-standard setting that we use is the "balanced" option, which weights classes by the inverse of their count in the training set, countering the preference for the majority class; we do this because our bootstrapped distribution is an unreliable reflection of the true distribution, and also because it makes it a fairer comparison to off-the-shelf models with no access to this distribution.

3.4 Improved phrase classification

Relative to (true) supervised models, our bootstrapped model suffers from being able to use only context, and not the identity of the name itself. In the case of names which are phrases, this is troubling because there are many generalizations to be made; for instance names ending with *City* are locations. Our final model addresses this failing somewhat by using more information from our

---

[3]Using cross-validation over the training data, we tested other solvers, L1 regularization, and settings of the C parameter, but saw no appreciable improvement in performance.

Brown clustering: from each of the initial and final words across all names, we extract a set of words W_s that appear at least ten times in position $s \in S, S = \{initial, final\}$ across all phrases. Let $c(w, t, s)$ be the the number of times a word $w \in W_s$ appears in the corpus at position s in phrases which were Brown clustered into the entity type $t \in T$, and $p(t|r)$ be the original probability of phrase r being type t as determined by the logistic regression classifier. For our two homogenous entity types (PERSON and LOCATION), we calculate a new score p':

$$p'(t|r) = p(t|r) + \sum_{s \in S} \left(\frac{c(r_s, t, s)}{\sum_{t' \in T} c(r_s, t', s)} - \frac{\sum_{w' \in W_s} \frac{c(w', t, s)}{\sum_{t' \in T} c(w', t', s)}}{|W_s|} \right) \quad (1)$$

The first term in the outermost summation in Equation 1 is the proportion of occurrences of the given expression in position s which correspond to type t. To avoid applying too much weight to the homogeneous classes, the second term in the summation subtracts the average number of occurrences in the given position for all words in W_s. As such, the total effect on the score can be negative. Note that if $r_s \notin W_s$, no modification is made, and for the OTHER type $p'(t|r) = p(t|r)$. Once we have calculated $p'(t|r)$ for each class, we choose the t with the highest $p'(t|r)$.

4 Evaluation

Our interest is in a general NER system for literature. Though there are a few novels which have been tagged for characters (Vala et al., 2015), we wanted to test our system relative to a much wider range of fiction. To this end, we randomly sampled texts, sentences, and then names within those sentences from our name-segmented Project Gutenberg corpus to produce a set of 1000 examples. These were tagged by a single annotator, an English native speaker with a PhD in English Literature. The annotator was presented with the sentence and the pre-segmented name of interest, and asked (via written instructions) to categorize the indicated name into PERSON, LOCATION, OTHER, UNCERTAIN due to ambiguity, or segmentation error. We ran a separate two-annotator agreement study over 200 examples which yielded a Cohen's Kappa of 0.84, suggesting high enough reliability that a single annotator was sufficient. The class

System	Acc	$\mathcal{F}_{\mathbf{M}}$
All PERSON baseline	.696	—
OpenNLP	.435	.572
LingPipe	.528	.536
Stanford CoreNLP	.786	.751
Brown clusters	.803	.672
LitNER sentence +phrase	.757	.671
LitNER text −phrase	.855	.771
LitNER text +phrase	**.871**	**.792**

Table 2: Performance of NER systems

distribution for the main annotation was 66.9% PERSON, 10.2% LOCATION, 19.0% OTHER, 2.4% UNCERTAIN, and 1.5% segmentation error. For the main evaluation, we excluded both UNCERTAIN examples and segmentation errors, but had our annotator provide correct segmentation for the 15 segmentation errors and carried out a separate comparison on these.

We compare our system to a selection of publicly available, off-the-shelf NER systems: OpenNLP,[4] LingPipe,[5] and Stanford CoreNLP (Finkel et al., 2005), as well as the initial Brown clustering. OpenNLP allowed us to classify only PERSON and LOCATION, but for Stanford CoreNLP and LingPipe we used the existing 3-entity systems, with the ORGANIZATION tag collapsed into OTHER (as it was in our guidelines; instances of ORGANIZATION are rare in literature). Since the exact segmentation guidelines likely varied across these systems—in particular, we found that Stanford CoreNLP often left off the title in names such as *Mr. Smith*—and we didn't want to focus on these issues, we did not require exact matches of our name segmentation; instead, we consider the entire name as PERSON or LOCATION if any of the tokens were tagged as such (names with both tags were considered OTHER). For our system (LitNER), we test a version where only the immediate sentence context is used ("sentence"), and versions based on text context ("text") with or without our phrase improvement ("±phrase").

We evaluate using two standard metrics: accuracy ("Acc"), and macroaveraged F-score ("$\mathcal{F}_{\mathbf{M}}$").

5 Results

The results in Table 2 show that our system easily bests the off-the-shelf systems when it is given

---

[4]https://opennlp.apache.org/
[5]http://alias-i.com/lingpipe

the contextual information from the entire text; the difference is more stark for accuracy (+0.085 absolute), though consistent for $\mathcal{F}_M$ (+0.041 absolute). `Stanford CoreNLP` is the only competitive off-the-shelf system—the other two are far too conservative when encountering names they haven't seen before. `LitNER` is also clearly better than the Brown clusters it was trained on, particularly for $\mathcal{F}_M$ (+0.120 absolute). With regards to different options for `LitNER`, we see a major benefit from considering all occurrences of the name in the texts rather than just the one we are testing on (Section 3.3), and a more modest benefit from using the information on parts of phrases taken from the Brown clustering (Section 3.4).

For the segmentation errors, we compared our corrected segmentations with the segmentation provided by the CRF-based `Stanford CoreNLP` system, our best competitor. Only 2 of the 15 were segmented correctly by `Stanford CoreNLP`. This potential 0.002 improvement is tiny compared to the 0.085 difference in accuracy between the two systems.

6 Discussion

Aspects of the method presented here could theoretically be applied to NER in other genres and other languages, but one important point we wish to make is that our approach clearly takes advantage of specific properties of (English) literature. The initial rule-based segmentation, for instance, depends on reliable capitalization of names, which is often not present in social media, or in most non-European languages. We have found more subtle genre effects as well: for comparison, we applied the preliminary steps of our approach to another corpus of published texts which is of comparable (token) size to the Project Gutenberg corpus, namely the Gigaword newswire corpus (Graff and Cieri, 2003), and noted degraded performance for both segmentation and Brown clustering. With respect to the former, the obvious issue is considerably more complex proper nouns phrases such as governmental organizations and related titles. For the latter, there were several clusters in the top 10 (including the first one) which corresponded to LOCATION, while the first (fairly) clean PERSON cluster was the 15th largest; in general, individual people, organizations, and other groupings of people (e.g. by country of origin) were not well distinguished by Brown clustering in the Gigaword

corpus, at least not with the same low number of clusters that worked well in the Project Gutenberg corpus.

Also less than promising is the potential for using text-level classification in other genres: whereas the average number of token occurrences of distinct name types within a single text in the Project Gutenberg corpus is 5.9, this number is just 1.6 for the much-shorter texts of the Gigaword corpus. Except in cases where it is possible to collapse texts into appropriately-sized groups where the use of a particular name is likely to be both common and consistent—an example might be a collection of texts written by a single author, which in social media such as Twitter seems to obey the classic one-sense-per-discourse rule (Gella et al., 2014)—it's not clear that this approach can be applied successfully in cases where texts are relatively short, which is a far more common situation. We also note that relying primarily on contextual classification while eschewing resources such as gazetteers makes much less sense outside the context of fiction; we would expect relatively few fictitious entities in most genres.

`LitNER` tags names into only two main classes, PERSON and LOCATION, plus a catch-all OTHER. This coarse-grained tag set reflects not only the practical limitations of the method, but also where we believe automatic methods have potential to provide useful information for literary analysis. The other clusters in Table 1 reflect word categories which are relatively closed-class and much less central to the fictional narratives as character and setting; we don't see a compelling case for tagging them. When these and non-entities are excluded from OTHER, what remains is eclectic, including names referring to small groups of people (e.g. families), animals, gods, ships, and titles of other works of literature.

7 Conclusion

In this paper, we have presented `LitNER`, an NER system targeted specifically at fiction. Our results show that a simple classifier, trained only with noisy examples derived in an unsupervised fashion, can easily beat a general-purpose supervised system, provided it has access to the full context of the text. Finally, we note that the NER tagging provided by `LitNER` has been integrated into the GutenTag tool (as of version 0.1.4).[6]

---

[6]See http://www.projectgutentag.org

References

Apoorv Agarwal, Anup Kotalwa, and Owen Rambow. 2013. Automatic extraction of social networks from literary text: A case study on *Alice in Wonderland*. In *The Proceedings of the 6th International Joint Conference on Natural Language Processign (IJC-NLP '13)*.

Mariona Coll Ardanuy and Caroline Sporleder. 2015. Clustering of novels represented as social networks. *Linguistic Issues in Language Technology*, 12(4).

David Bamman, Ted Underwood, and Noah A. Smith. 2014. A Bayesian mixed effects model of literary character. In *Proceedings of the 52st Annual Meeting of the Association for Computational Linguistics (ACL '14)*.

Julian Brooke, Adam Hammond, and Graeme Hirst. 2015. GutenTag: An NLP-driven tool for digital humanities research in the Project Gutenberg corpus. In *Proceedings of the 4nd Workshop on Computational Literature for Literature (CLFL '15)*.

Peter F. Brown, Peter V. deSouza, Robert L. Mercer, Vincent J. Della Pietra, and Jenifer C. Lai. 1992. Class-based n-gram models of natural language. *Computational Linguistics*, 18(4):467–479.

Leon Derczynski, Sean Chester, and Kenneth S. Bgh. 2015. Tune your Brown clustering, please. In *Proceedings of Recent Advances in Natural Language Processing (RANLP 15)*.

Micha Elsner, Eugene Charniak, and Mark Johnson. 2009. Structured generative models for unsupervised named-entity clustering. In *Proceedings of the 2009 Annual Conference of the North American Chapter of the Association for Computational Linguistics: Human Language Technologies (NAACL '09)*.

David K. Elson, Nicholas Dames, and Kathleen R. McKeown. 2010. Extracting social networks from literary fiction. In *Proceedings of the 48th Annual Meeting of the Association for Computational Linguistics (ACL '10)*.

Jenny Rose Finkel, Trond Grenager, and Christopher Manning. 2005. Incorporating non-local information into information extraction systems by gibbs sampling. In *Proceedings of the 43rd Annual Meeting on Association for Computational Linguistics (ACL '05)*.

William A. Gale, Kenneth W. Church, and David Yarowsky. 1992. One sense per discourse. In *Proceedings of the 4th DARPA Speech and Natural Language Workshop*.

Spandana Gella, Paul Cook, and Timothy Baldwin. 2014. One sense per tweeter ... and other lexical semantic tales of twitter. In *Proceedings of the 14th Conference of the European Chapter of the Association for Computational Linguistics*.

David Graff and Christopher Cieri. 2003. *English Gigaword*. Linguistic Data Consortium.

Hua He, Denilson Barbosa, and Grzegorz Kondrak. 2013. Identification of speakers in novels. In *Proceedings of the 51st Annual Meeting of the Association for Computational Linguistics (ACL '13)*.

Percy Liang. 2005. Semi-supervised learning for natural language. Master's thesis, MIT.

Mitchell P. Marcus, Beatrice Santorini, and Mary Ann Marcinkiewicz. 1993. Building a large annotated corpus of English: the Penn treebank. *Computational Linguistics*, 19(2):313–330.

Tara McIntosh, Lars Yencken, James R. Curran, and Timothy Baldwin. 2011. Relation guided bootstrapping of semantic lexicons. In *Proceedings of the 49th Annual Meeting of the Association for Computational Linguistics: Human Language Technologies (ACL HLT 2011)*.

Scott. Miller, Jethran. Guinness, and Alex Zamanian. 2004. Name tagging with word clusters and discriminative training. In *Proceedings of the 2004 Conference of the North American Chapter of the Association for Computational Linguistics: Human Language Technologies (NAACL HLT '13)*.

David Nadeau, Peter D. Turney, and Stan Matwin. 2006. Unsupervised named-entity recognition: Generating gazetteers and resolving ambiguity. In *Proceedings of the 19th International Conference on Advances in Artificial Intelligence: Canadian Society for Computational Studies of Intelligence*, AI'06.

F. Pedregosa, G. Varoquaux, A. Gramfort, V. Michel, B. Thirion, O. Grisel, M. Blondel, P. Prettenhofer, R. Weiss, V. Dubourg, J. Vanderplas, A. Passos, D. Cournapeau, M. Brucher, M. Perrot, and E. Duchesnay. 2011. Scikit-learn: Machine learning in Python. *Journal of Machine Learning Research*, 12:2825–2830.

Lev Ratinov and Dan Roth. 2009. Design challenges and misconceptions in named entity recognition. In *Proceedings of the Thirteenth Conference on Computational Natural Language Learning (CoNLL '09)*.

Alan Ritter, Sam Clark, Mausam, and Oren Etzioni. 2011. Named entity recognition in tweets: An experimental study. In *Proceedings of the 2011 Conference on Empirical Methods in Natural Language Processing (EMNLP 2011)*.

Michael Thelen and Ellen Riloff. 2002. A bootstrapping method for learning semantic lexicons using extraction pattern contexts. In *Proceedings of the 2002 Conference on Empirical Methods in Natural Language Processing (EMNLP 2002)*.

Hardik Vala, David Jurgens, Andrew Piper, and Derek Ruths. 2015. Mr. Bennet, his coachman, and the Archbishop walk into a bar but only one of them gets

recognized: On the difficulty of detecting characters
in literary texts. In *Proceedings of the 2015 Conference on Empirical Methods in Natural Language
Processing (EMNLP '15).*

Byron C. Wallace. 2012. Multiple narrative disentan-
glement: Unraveling *Infinite Jest.* In *Proceedings of
the 2012 Conference of the North American Chapter of the Association for Computational Linguistics:
Human Language Technologies (NAACL-HLT '12).*

The Enemy in Your Own Camp:
How Well Can We Detect Statistically-Generated Fake Reviews – An Adversarial Study

Dirk Hovy
Center for Language Technology
University of Copenhagen
2300 Copenhagen, Denmark
`dirk.hovy@hum.ku.dk`

Abstract

Online reviews are a growing market, but it is struggling with fake reviews. They undermine both the value of reviews to the user, and their trust in the review sites. However, fake positive reviews can boost a business, and so a small industry producing fake reviews has developed. The two sides are facing an arms race that involves more and more natural language processing (NLP). So far, NLP has been used mostly for detection, and works well on human-generated reviews. But what happens if NLP techniques are used to *generate* fake reviews as well? We investigate the question in an adversarial setup, by assessing the detectability of different fake-review generation strategies. We use generative models to produce reviews based on meta-information, and evaluate their effectiveness against deception-detection models and human judges. We find that meta-information helps detection, but that NLP-generated reviews conditioned on such information are also much harder to detect than conventional ones.

1 Introduction

Online reviews written by customers are a booming market. Several companies cater to a wide variety of audiences, supplying—among others—reviews for restaurants (Yelp), travel (TripAdvisor), businesses (Trustpilot), and specialized communities, such as beer (RateBeer). While the revenue of the providers is in the billions of dollars, the currency this industry is built on is consumer trust. The majority of consumers uses such reviews to inform themselves before buying.[1] On-line review companies therefore put considerable effort into maintaining this trust, by addressing the greatest threat to consumer trust (and therefore income)—fake reviews.

Identifying fake reviews is a natural fit for NLP, since they presumably contain linguistic cues that indicate their nature. Indeed, a number of previous works have dealt with the detection of fake reviews (Jindal and Liu, 2007; Badaskar et al., 2008; Mackiewicz, 2008; Jindal et al., 2010; Ott et al., 2011; Fornaciari and Poesio, 2014). However, in those cases, human writers were producing reviews to fool a human audience, not an NLP model. The detection models were therefore able to exploit the regularities resulting from the writers' tendency to follow a pattern to minimize their effort.

Writing fake reviews has become a lucrative business (Streitfeld, 2012), and so there is now an arms race going on between producers and detectors (Roberts, 2012). What if fake review writers become aware of the ways to game a detection algorithm?[2] As NLP technology becomes more common, we should expect to also see fake reviews *generated* by NLP models. This pits technology against technology.

In this paper, we explore the impact fake review generation has on NLP models' ability to detect them, and an ethical challenge in our development of NLP technology: the fact that it can be used for both sides (Hovy and Spruit, 2016).

Our contributions We set up an adversarial evaluation approach inspired by (Smith, 2012), using graphical models to build various language models that generate fake reviews, with and without recurrence to meta-information. We then test

---

[1] `http://www.business2community.com/`
`infographics/impact-online-reviews-`
`customers-buying-decisions-infographic-`
`01280945`

[2] Similarly, some members of the Mechanical Turk community have adapted to the presence of assessment tools.

Proceedings of the 54th Annual Meeting of the Association for Computational Linguistics, pages 351–356,
Berlin, Germany, August 7-12, 2016. ©2016 Association for Computational Linguistics

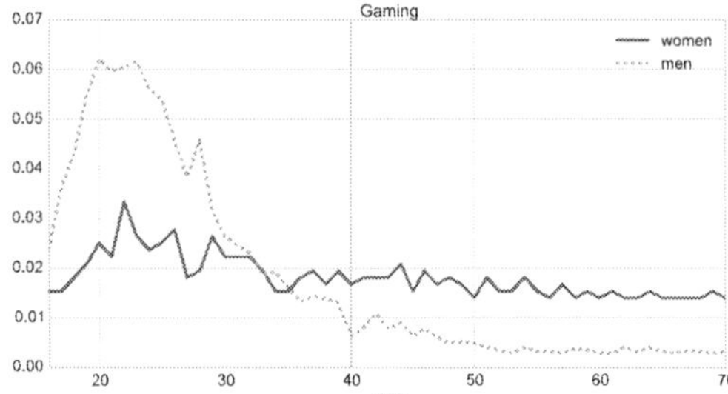

Figure 1: Age distribution of gaming reviews for men and women in the US

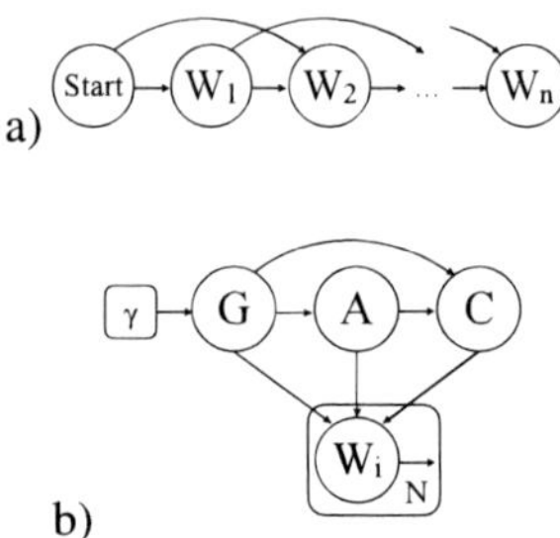

Figure 2: Regular n-gram Markov chain LM (top) and conditioned LM (bottom). γ based on empirically-observed gender distribution in data

how well a logistic regression model can distinguish real from fake reviews from both models under two settings (the model has access to meta-information or not), and how well human judges can detect fake reviews generated by the model with meta-information.

Our results indicate that fake review generation could be a serious problem for detection mechanisms that solely rely on textual features.

2 Data

We use data extracted from the American and British versions of the review site Trustpilot.[3] It comprises reviews for a variety of online businesses, as well as information about users' age and gender.[4] We extracted all reviews that contained the full set of meta-information. We lower-case and tokenize by words, but leave reviews intact, rather than splitting them up into sentences. This results in 120,976 review instances. We reserve 10,000 for evaluation purposes, and use the rest to induce our adversarial generative models, and to derive features for the detection model (see below).

3 Review Generation Models

The basic approach is a simple Markov chain with a sufficiently large horizon to generate fluent reviews. Such an n-gram language model (LM) is a function that assigns probability to any sentence S, where S is a sequence $w_0, w_1, \cdots, w_n$, and

$$P(S) = \prod_i^N P(w_i|w_{i-n:i-1})$$

w_0 is a special (sequence of) start token(s), n is the size of the Markov horizon, and $w_{i-1:i-(n-1)}$

is the sequence of preceding words in context. The model is depicted in Figure 2 a). Since this is a generative model, it can not only be used to assign probability to observed sentences, but also generate new sentences based on the model parameters.

However, extra-linguistic information, if available, can improve classification performance (Volkova et al., 2013; Hovy, 2015), and fake-review detection models often also exploit meta-information about the author and their behavior (Lim et al., 2010), looking for irregularities. We therefore use a generative story that assumes that people of different age and gender review different things, which in turn influences the type of business reviewed, and the choice of words. This assumption is borne out in the data (cf. Figure 1).

We extend this model by conditioning on latent variables age (A), gender (G), and review category (C).[5] In the generative story of this model, we first draw a user from one of the two genders in our data, select an age based on gender-specific age distributions, and choose a review category dependent on the two previous variables. We then then generate a sentence conditioned on all of these settings and the Markov horizon. Our model is depicted as plate diagram in Figure 2 b) (we omit the start token and the Markov horizon for clarity). It can formally be written as:

$$P(S|G, A, C) = P(G) \cdot P(A|G) \cdot P(C|G, A)$$
$$\cdot \prod_i^N P(w_i|w_{i-n:i-1}, C, G, A)$$

---

[3] www.trustpilot.com

[4] For a more detailed description of the data, see Hovy et al. (2015).

[5] These factors could of course be extended to cover other information, including ratings. We do not condition on ratings here, but a commercial system for fake reviews would presumably be restricted to positive scores.

Category	Age group	Sex	Text
Hotels	30–45	F	*i ordered a new toner for our printer and after price matching the best i could find they also honoured a free delivery on top .*
Computer Accessories	45–60	M	*this is a company that takes customer care seriously . we received really impressive service when we contacted the company .*

Table 1: Generated examples from unconditional (top) and conditional (bottom) LM.

We can now use either model to generate fake reviews. In both cases, we use a Markov horizon of 6 words, i.e., a 7-gram model. For the unconditioned LM, meta-information is generated at random. This simulates a fake-review writer who is unaware of the context effects, but knows that companies might take profile information into account. Two examples are shown in Figure 1. Both examples are fluent, but the unconditioned one suffers from two problems: somewhat stream-of-consciousness-like sentences and a for human readers obvious mismatch between the category and the discussed topic.

Conditional LMs, on the other hand, suffer from a certain sparsity: the more meta-information we condition on, the sparser the n-gram counts become. They are therefore more likely to faithfully re-generate the training data. We use interpolation between genders, but this could also be addressed with a wide variety of techniques (Chen and Goodman, 1998).

Even though the classifier does not have access to the training data, we want to make the task as difficult as possible, so we remove all duplicates, as well as any generated reviews that do not end in a punctuation mark, that exceed 200 words, or that have a category not contained in our real-review test set, and select from the rest by lowest entropy.

4 Experiments

In our experiments, we pit an adversary (i.e., the two LMs we experiment with) against a judge (a classifier or human annotator). The goal of the adversary is to produce fake reviews that convince the judge.

4.1 Logistic Regression Model

As classifier, we use a logistic regression model, regularized with L_2 norm, and fit it on a data set of 10,000 true reviews and a varying amount of fake reviews. In one setting, we use 1600 fake reviews , based on current estimates of 16% (Luca

and Zervas, 2015). In a second setting, we use 10,000 fake reviews, a scenario where 50% of all reviews are fake. Given the ease of generating fake reviews with the models presented here, the rate could quickly go up in the future, so this ration gives a bound on how much our detection models could decline.

The base features of the classifier are word n-grams, with n ranging from 1 to 4. Depending on the setting, we also add meta-information features, including combinations of the n-grams with each category (e.g., `category=Hotels & word="soft bed"`), and the average PMI score for the words in the sentence and each category (e.g., `PMI(Hotels, soft bed)`). That way, we hope to capture mismatches between the stated category and the review content.

We measure F1 performance over 5-fold stratified cross-validation.

Initially, we would like to establish whether conditioning LMs on demographic information has any effect on detection. For this purpose, we compare the performance of the logistic regression model on (1) a test set including fake reviews generated by an unconditioned 7-gram LM and (2) a test set whose fake reviews have been conditioned on meta-information. In both cases, the detector has only access to the base features, i.e., ignores demographic information. This is equivalent to a situation where the judge can only see the text, not the meta information.

As mentioned before, though, many companies employ meta-information in order to capture fake reviews, and if a spammer knew this, they could simply generate some meta-information. The question is: *does this meta-information have to follow a coherent generative story?* Intuitively, we expect the answer to be *"yes"*: we would be surprised to see a teenager review retirement homes.

To test this assumption, we compare the performance of the classifier when having access to the base features plus meta-information under two settings: (3) with each piece of meta-information generated independently at random, and (4) with meta-information generated as part of our generative process.

4.2 Human Judges

The first experiment tests the detectability of fake reviews by statistical means. How hard is it for humans, though, to distinguish the fake reviews generated by this model from real reviews, and do they exploit meta-information?

To answer these questions, we also conduct a human judges study on Crowdflower[6]. We select 200 items at random (100 real reviews and 100 from the conditional model, half of each with meta-information), and ask annotators to rate them as real or fake. Judges were not informed about the nature of the reviews, only advised to use their best judgement. The task involved 8 test questions to bar bad annotators from entering. 76 unique judges participated, and rated the task as relatively difficult (3.5/5).

5 Results

Bear in mind that this is an adversarial setup: we are trying to improve the fake reviews to "trick" the judge into producing as many false positives as possible. A low F1-score thus means that the respective LM has managed to fool the classifier. Table 2 shows the results. Note also that the fake reviews are generated independent of the classification model, i.e., the generative LM does not take the classification model into account.

5.1 Logistic Regression Model

In order to assess whether the differences in performance are statistically significant, we conduct a bootstrap sampling test (Efron and Tibshirani, 1993) with 10,000 repetitions on the overall predictions.

The numbers are generally in a high range, which is encouraging, since it means that our models can detect fake reviews fairly reliably. However, we also see that the conditional models introduced here quickly become significantly harder to detect than the regular LM.

Adding meta-information leads to sometimes small, but always significant increases in perfor-

---

[6]https://crowdflower.com

16% FAKE			
JUDGE	COND. LM	REG. LM	$p < 0.01$
words only	88.27	87.89	no
+meta-info	88.92	92.42	yes
$p < 0.01$	yes	yes	
50% FAKE			
words only	75.52	72.78	yes
+meta-info	77.40	88.43	yes
$p < 0.01$	yes	yes	

Table 2: Model performance (F1) with different amounts of information on reviews generated by regular or conditional model under two conditions

mance. This effect is especially pronounced in the regular LMs, since the detection model is able to pick up on the mismatch between category and text content.

As the number of fake reviews grows, though, detection gets more difficult, and the rift between the two generation models becomes more apparent: at 50% fake reviews, the conditional LM is almost twice as hard to detect as the regular LM when using meta-information.

Feature Analysis Finally, we analyze the features (word-based and meta-information) to find the most predictive elements of fake reviews. For each feature, we average over all folds of our cross-validation. Features which are selected frequently, irrespective of the exact training conditions, can be assumed to be robust predictors.

Unsurprisingly, the most predictive features are `PMI(gender, ·)` and `PMI(category, ·)`, followed by gender- and age-specific words (`gender=M & word="delivery"`, `age-group=3 & word="."`), category-specific words (`category=Package Service & word="parcel"`), and individual words (`service, easy, quick`)

For the unconditional models, the PMI-category coefficients dominate other features in a power-law distribution, while for the conditional model, the PMI-age score is only slightly ahead.

5.2 Human Judges

The general tendency among human judges was to assume reviews are real: overall, 87% of the individual answers judged a review to be real. That is, only a minority of judges suspected fraud, irrespective of whether they had access to the meta-information or not. Whatever signal the logistic regression model picks up seems to be more subtle than what the average human can perceive.

This tendency plays out in the F1 scores (see Table 3): human judges have a much lower detection rate than the logistic regression model, even though the availability of meta-information improves performance here as well.

These results hold whether we treat each vote as an individual item or aggregating the five votes for each instance by an item-response model (Hovy et al., 2013). In the latter case, the performance for both conditions and the average increases, more so for the instances without meta-information, but still not reaching the same level.

ACCESS TO	RAW	AGGREGATED
words only	63.90	65.77
+meta-info	65.31	66.66
avg.	64.65	66.22

Table 3: Human performance (F1) with different amounts of information on reviews generated by conditional model

6 Related Work

Reviews are a rich source of studies for NLP, and a variety of recent papers (McAuley et al., 2012; Danescu-Niculescu-Mizil et al., 2013; Reschke et al., 2013; Jurafsky et al., 2014; Hovy et al., 2015) have explored it.

Badaskar et al. (2008) also use real and fake reviews and LMs, but in almost exactly the opposite setup: they select features that have high discriminative power in distinguishing real from fake reviews to include in their LMs. However, they use a review corpus that is more than an order of magnitude smaller, focus on tri- and quad-gram features, and do not take meta-information into account.

The work of Fornaciari and Poesio (2014) is similar in that they also deal with fake review detection. However, they do not use an adversarial setup, but focus on the use of an item-response model to detect fake-review writers. Their corpus is considerably smaller than ours, but the detection rate they report is similar to the one we find when not using meta-information.

To our knowledge, only Lappas (2012) has taken the view from the adversary's point of view,

although the paper does not generate fake reviews, but assesses the presence of several defined measures of meretriciousness.

7 Conclusion

We have investigated the detectability of fake reviews generated with meta-information. We find that (1) using access to meta-information can significantly improve the detection of fake reviews, and (2) generated reviews conditioned on meta-information are considerably harder to detect than the ones generated without. We also see that statistical models fare better than human judges. Our results indicate the viability of an adversarial setup to test detection tasks, but also highlight the fact that NLP techniques can be used for either side. We should therefore be more vigilant and willing to play devil's advocate, pitting potential models as adversaries against our solutions.

Acknowledgments

The author would like to thank the members of the COASTAL group and the anonymous reviewers for their detailed comments and suggestions, and Noah Smith for pointing out a missing reference. This research was funded under the ERC Starting Grant LOWLANDS No. 313695.

References

Sameer Badaskar, Sachin Agarwal, and Shilpa Arora. 2008. Identifying real or fake articles: Towards better language modeling. In *Proceedings of the Third International Joint Conference on Natural Language Processing: Volume-II*.

Stanley Chen and Joshua Goodman. 1998. An empirical study of smoothing techniques for language modeling. Technical Report TR-10-98, Harvard University.

Cristian Danescu-Niculescu-Mizil, Robert West, Dan Jurafsky, Jure Leskovec, and Christopher Potts. 2013. No country for old members: User lifecycle and linguistic change in online communities. In *Proceedings of the 22nd International conference on World Wide Web*, pages 307–318. International World Wide Web Conferences Steering Committee.

Bradley Efron and Robert Tibshirani. 1993. *An introduction to the bootstrap*. Chapman & Hall, Boca Raton, FL.

Tomes Fornaciari and Massimo Poesio. 2014. Identifying fake amazon reviews as learning from crowds. In *Proceedings of the 14th Conference of the European Chapter of the Association for Computational Linguistics*, pages 279–287. Association for Computational Linguistics.

Dirk Hovy and Shannon L. Spruit. 2016. Beyond Privacy: The Social Impact of Natural Language Processing. In *Proceedings of the 54th Annual Meeting of the Association for Computational Linguistics*. ACL, Association for Computational Linguistics.

Dirk Hovy, Taylor Berg-Kirkpatrick, Ashish Vaswani, and Eduard Hovy. 2013. Learning whom to trust with MACE. In *Proceedings of NAACL*.

Dirk Hovy, Anders Johannsen, and Anders Søgaard. 2015. User review-sites as a source for large-scale sociolinguistic studies. In *Proceedings of WWW*.

Dirk Hovy. 2015. Demographic factors improve classification performance. In *Proceedings of the 53rd annual meeting of the ACL*.

Nitin Jindal and Bing Liu. 2007. Review spam detection. In *Proceedings of the 16th international conference on World Wide Web*, pages 1189–1190. ACM.

Nitin Jindal, Bing Liu, and Ee-Peng Lim. 2010. Finding unusual review patterns using unexpected rules. In *Proceedings of the 19th ACM international conference on Information and knowledge management*, pages 1549–1552. ACM.

Dan Jurafsky, Victor Chahuneau, Bryan R Routledge, and Noah A Smith. 2014. Narrative framing of consumer sentiment in online restaurant reviews. *First Monday*, 19(4).

Theodoros Lappas. 2012. Fake reviews: The malicious perspective. In *Natural Language Processing and Information Systems*, pages 23–34. Springer.

Ee-Peng Lim, Viet-An Nguyen, Nitin Jindal, Bing Liu, and Hady Wirawan Lauw. 2010. Detecting product review spammers using rating behaviors. In *Proceedings of the 19th ACM international conference on Information and knowledge management*, pages 939–948. ACM.

Michael Luca and Georgios Zervas. 2015. Fake it till you make it: Reputation, competition, and yelp review fraud. *Harvard Business School NOM Unit Working Paper*, (14-006).

Jo Mackiewicz. 2008. Reviewer motivations, bias, and credibility in online reviews. *Handbook of research on computer mediated communication*, 1:252–266.

Julian McAuley, Jure Leskovec, and Dan Jurafsky. 2012. Learning attitudes and attributes from multi-aspect reviews. In *Data Mining (ICDM), 2012 IEEE 12th International Conference on*, pages 1020–1025. IEEE.

Myle Ott, Yejin Choi, Claire Cardie, and Jeffrey T Hancock. 2011. Finding deceptive opinion spam by any stretch of the imagination. In *Proceedings of the 49th Annual Meeting of the Association for Computational Linguistics: Human Language*

Technologies-Volume 1, pages 309–319. Association for Computational Linguistics.

Kevin Reschke, Adam Vogel, and Dan Jurafsky. 2013. Generating recommendation dialogs by extracting information from user reviews. In *Proceedings of the 51st annual meeting of the ACL*, pages 499–504.

Jeff John Roberts. 2012. Amazon sues people who charge $5 for fake reviews. Fortune, October 19. `http://fortune.com/2015/10/19/amazon-fake-reviews/` Retrieved Feb 27, 2016.

Noah Smith. 2012. Adversarial evaluation for models of natural language. http://arxiv.org/abs/1207.0245.

David Streitfeld. 2012. The Best Book Reviews Money Can Buy. The New York Times, August 25. `http://www.nytimes.com/2012/08/26/business/book-reviewers-for-hire-meet-a-demand-for-online-raves.html` Retrieved Feb 27, 2016.

Svitlana Volkova, Theresa Wilson, and David Yarowsky. 2013. Exploring demographic language variations to improve multilingual sentiment analysis in social media. In *Proceedings of EMNLP*, pages 1815–1827.

Character-based Neural Machine Translation

Marta R. Costa-jussà and **José A. R. Fonollosa**
TALP Research Center
Universitat Politècnica de Catalunya, Barcelona
{marta.ruiz,jose.fonollosa}@upc.edu

Abstract

Neural Machine Translation (MT) has reached state-of-the-art results. However, one of the main challenges that neural MT still faces is dealing with very large vocabularies and morphologically rich languages.

In this paper, we propose a neural MT system using character-based embeddings in combination with convolutional and highway layers to replace the standard lookup-based word representations. The resulting unlimited-vocabulary and affix-aware source word embeddings are tested in a state-of-the-art neural MT based on an attention-based bidirectional recurrent neural network. The proposed MT scheme provides improved results even when the source language is not morphologically rich. Improvements up to 3 BLEU points are obtained in the German-English WMT task.

1 Introduction

Machine Translation (MT) is the set of algorithms that aim at transforming a source language into a target language. For the last 20 years, one of the most popular approaches has been statistical phrase-based MT, which uses a combination of features to maximise the probability of the target sentence given the source sentence (Koehn et al., 2003). Just recently, the neural MT approach has appeared (Kalchbrenner and Blunsom, 2013; Sutskever et al., 2014; Cho et al., 2014; Bahdanau et al., 2015) and obtained state-of-the-art results.

Among its different strengths neural MT does not need to pre-design feature functions beforehand; optimizes the entire system at once because it provides a fully trainable model; uses word embeddings (Sutskever et al., 2014) so that words (or minimal units) are not independent anymore; and is easily extendable to multimodal sources of information (Elliott et al., 2015). As for weaknesses, neural MT has a strong limitation in vocabulary due to its architecture and it is difficult and computationally expensive to tune all parameters in the deep learning structure.

In this paper, we use the neural MT baseline system from (Bahdanau et al., 2015), which follows an encoder-decoder architecture with attention, and introduce elements from the character-based neural language model (Kim et al., 2016). The translation unit continues to be the word, and we continue using word embeddings related to each word as an input vector to the bidirectional recurrent neural network (attention-based mechanism). The difference is that now the embeddings of each word are no longer an independent vector, but are computed from the characters of the corresponding word. The system architecture has changed in that we are using a convolutional neural network (CNN) and a highway network over characters before the attention-based mechanism of the encoder. This is a significant difference from previous work (Sennrich et al., 2015) which uses the neural MT architecture from (Bahdanau et al., 2015) without modification to deal with subword units (but not including unigram characters).

Subword-based representations have already been explored in Natural Language Processing (NLP), e.g. for POS tagging (Santos and Zadrozny, 2014), name entity recognition (Santos and aes, 2015), parsing (Ballesteros et al., 2015), normalization (Chrupala, 2014) or learning word representations (Botha and Blunsom, 2014; Chen et al., 2015). These previous works show different advantages of using character-level information. In our case, with the new character-

357

Proceedings of the 54th Annual Meeting of the Association for Computational Linguistics, pages 357–361,
Berlin, Germany, August 7-12, 2016. ©2016 Association for Computational Linguistics

based neural MT architecture, we take advantage of intra-word information, which is proven to be extremely useful in other NLP applications (Santos and Zadrozny, 2014; Ling et al., 2015a), especially when dealing with morphologically rich languages. When using the character-based source word embeddings in MT, there ceases to be unknown words in the source input, while the size of the target vocabulary remains unchanged. Although the target vocabulary continues with the same limitation as in the standard neural MT system, the fact that there are no unknown words in the source helps to reduce the number of unknowns in the target. Moreover, the remaining unknown target words can now be more successfully replaced with the corresponding source-aligned words. As a consequence, we obtain a significant improvement in terms of translation quality (up to 3 BLEU points).

The rest of the paper is organized as follows. Section 2 briefly explains the architecture of the neural MT that we are using as a baseline system. Section 3 describes the changes introduced in the baseline architecture in order to use character-based embeddings instead of the standard lookup-based word representations. Section 4 reports the experimental framework and the results obtained in the German-English WMT task. Finally, section 5 concludes with the contributions of the paper and further work.

2 Neural Machine Translation

Neural MT uses a neural network approach to compute the conditional probability of the target sentence given the source sentence (Cho et al., 2014; Bahdanau et al., 2015). The approach used in this work (Bahdanau et al., 2015) follows the encoder-decoder architecture.First, the encoder reads the source sentence $s = (s_1, ..s_I)$ and encodes it into a sequence of hidden states $h = (h_1, ..h_I)$. Then, the decoder generates a corresponding translation $t = t_1, ..., t_J$ based on the encoded sequence of hidden states h. Both encoder and decoder are jointly trained to maximize the conditional log-probability of the correct translation.

This baseline autoencoder architecture is improved with a attention-based mechanism (Bahdanau et al., 2015), in which the encoder uses a bi-directional gated recurrent unit (GRU). This GRU allows for a better performance with long sentences. The decoder also becomes a GRU and each word t_j is predicted based on a recurrent hidden state, the previously predicted word t_{j-1}, and a context vector. This context vector is obtained from the weighted sum of the annotations h_k, which in turn, is computed through an alignment model α_{jk} (a feedforward neural network). This neural MT approach has achieved competitive results against the standard phrase-based system in the WMT 2015 evaluation (Jean et al., 2015).

3 Character-based Machine Translation

Word embeddings have been shown to boost the performance in many NLP tasks, including machine translation. However, the standard lookup-based embeddings are limited to a finite-size vocabulary for both computational and sparsity reasons. Moreover, the orthographic representation of the words is completely ignored. The standard learning process is blind to the presence of stems, prefixes, suffixes and any other kind of affixes in words.

As a solution to those drawbacks, new alternative character-based word embeddings have been recently proposed for tasks such as language modeling (Kim et al., 2016; Ling et al., 2015a), parsing (Ballesteros et al., 2015) or POS tagging (Ling et al., 2015a; Santos and Zadrozny, 2014). Even in MT (Ling et al., 2015b), where authors use the character transformation presented in (Ballesteros et al., 2015; Ling et al., 2015a) both in the source and target. However, they do not seem to get clear improvements. Recently, (Luong and Manning, 2016) propose a combination of word and characters in neural MT.

For our experiments in neural MT, we selected the best character-based embedding architecture proposed by Kim et al. (Kim et al., 2016) for language modeling. As the Figure 1 shows, the computation of the representation of each word starts with a character-based embedding layer that associates each word (sequence of characters) with a sequence of vectors. This sequence of vectors is then processed with a set of 1D convolution filters of different lengths (from 1 to 7 characters) followed with a max pooling layer. For each convolutional filter, we keep only the output with the maximum value. The concatenation of these max values already provides us with a representation of each word as a vector with a fixed length equal to the total number of convolutional kernels. However, the addition of two highway layers was shown to improve the quality of the language model in (Kim et al., 2016) so we also kept these additional layers in our case. The output of the second Highway layer will give us the final vector representation of each source word, replacing the standard source word embedding in the neural machine translation system.

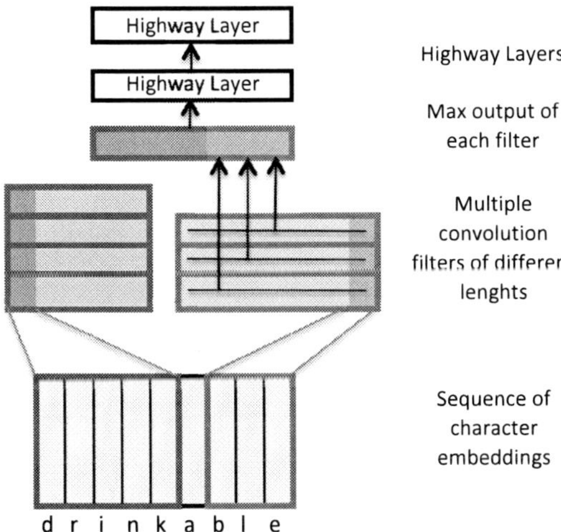

Figure 1: Character-based word embedding

In the target size we are still limited in vocabulary by the softmax layer at the output of the network and we kept the standard target word embeddings in our experiments. However, the results seem to show that the affix-aware representation of the source words has a positive influence on all the components of the network. The global optimization of the integrated model forces the translation model and the internal vector representation of the target words to follow the affix-aware codification of the source words.

4   Experimental framework

This section reports the data used, its preprocessing, baseline details and results with the enhanced character based neural MT system.

4.1   Data

We used the German-English WMT data[1] including the EPPS, NEWS and Commoncrawl. Preprocessing consisted of tokenizing, truecasing, normalizing punctuation and filtering sentences with more than 5% of their words in a language

other than German or English. Statistics are shown in Table 1.

L	Set	S	W	V	OOV
De	Train	3.5M	77.7M	1.6M	-
	Dev	3k	63.1k	13.6k	1.7k
	Test	2.2k	44.1k	9.8k	1.3k
En	Train	3.5M	81.2M	0.8M	-
	Dev	3k	67.6k	10.1k	0.8k
	Test	2.2k	46.8k	7.8k	0.6k

Table 1: Corpus details. Number of sentences (S), words (W), vocabulary (V) and out-of-vocabulary-words (OOV) per set and language (L). M standing for millions, k standing for thousands.

4.2   Baseline systems

The phrase-based system was built using Moses (Koehn et al., 2007), with standard parameters such as grow-final-diag for alignment, Good-Turing smoothing of the relative frequencies, 5-gram language modeling using Kneser-Ney discounting, and lexicalized reordering, among others. The neural-based system was built using the software from DL4MT[2] available in github. We generally used settings from previous work (Jean et al., 2015): networks have an embedding of 620 and a dimension of 1024, a batch size of 32, and no dropout. We used a vocabulary size of 90 thousand words in German-English. Also, as proposed in (Jean et al., 2015) we replaced unknown words (UNKs) with the corresponding source word using the alignment information.

4.3   Results

Table 3 shows the BLEU results for the baseline systems (including phrase and neural-based, NN) and the character-based neural MT (CHAR). We also include the results for the CHAR and NN systems with post-processing of unknown words, which consists in replacing the UNKs with the corresponding source word (+Src), as suggested in (Jean et al., 2015). BLEU results improve by almost 1.5 points in German-to-English and by more than 3 points in English-to-German. The reduction in the number of unknown words (after postprocessing) goes from 1491 (NN) to 1260 (CHAR) in the direction from German-to-English and from 3148 to 2640 in the opposite direction. Note the

---

[1] http://www.statmt.org/wmt15/translation-task.html

[2] http://dl4mt.computing.dcu.ie/

1	SRC	Berichten zufolge hofft Indien darber hinaus auf einen Vertrag zur **Verteidigungszusammenarbeit** zwischen den beiden Nationen .
	Phrase	reportedly hopes India , in addition to a contract for the defence cooperation between the two nations .
	NN	according to reports , India also hopes to establish a contract for the UNK between the two nations .
	CHAR	according to reports , India hopes to see a Treaty of **Defence Cooperation** between the two nations .
	REF	India is also reportedly hoping for a deal on **defence collaboration** between the two nations .
2	SRC	der durchtrainierte Mainzer sagt von sich , dass er ein " ambitionierter **Rennradler** " ist .
	Phrase	the will of Mainz says that he a more ambitious .
	NN	the UNK Mainz says that he is a " ambitious , . "
	CHAR	the UNK in Mainz says that he is a ' **ambitious racer** ' .
	REF	the well-conditioned man from Mainz said he was an " **ambitious racing cyclist** . "
3	SRC	die GDL habe jedoch nicht gesagt , wo sie **streiken** wolle , so dass es schwer sei , die Folgen konkret vorherzusehen .
	Phrase	the GDL have , however , not to say , where they strike , so that it is difficult to predict the consequences of concrete .
	NN	however , the UNK did not tell which they wanted to UNK , so it is difficult to predict the consequences .
	CHAR	however , the UNK did not say where they wanted to **strike** , so it is difficult to predict the consequences .
	REF	the GDL have not said , however , where they will **strike** , making it difficult to predict exactly what the consequences will be .
4	SRC	die Premierminister Indiens und Japans trafen sich in Tokio .
	Phrase	the Prime Minister of India and Japan in Tokyo .
	NN	the Prime Minister of India and Japan met in Tokyo
	CHAR	the Prime **Ministers** of India and Japan met in Tokyo
	REF	India and Japan prime **ministers** meet in Tokyo
5	SRC	wo die Beamten es aus den Augen verloren .
	Phrase	where the officials lost sight of
	NN	where the officials lost it out of the eyes
	CHAR	where officials **lose sight of it**
	REF	causing the officers to **lose sight of it**

Table 2: Translation examples.

	De->En	En->De
Phrase	20.99	17.04
NN	18.83	16.47
NN+Src	20.64	17.15
CHAR	21.40	19.53
CHAR+Src	**22.10**	**20.22**

Table 3: De-En BLEU results.

number of out-of-vocabulary words of the test set is shown in Table 1.

The character-based embedding has an impact in learning a better translation model at various levels, which seems to include better alignment, reordering, morphological generation and disambiguation. Table 2 shows some examples of the kind of improvements that the character-based neural MT system is capable of achieving compared to baseline systems. Examples 1 and 2 show how the reduction of source unknowns improves the adequacy of the translation. Examples 3 and 4 show how the character-based approach is able to handle morphological variations. Finally, example 5 shows an appropriate semantic disambiguation.

5 Conclusions

Neural MT offers a new perspective in the way MT is managed. Its main advantages when compared with previous approaches, e.g. statistical phrase-based, are that the translation is faced with trainable features and optimized in an end-to-end scheme. However, there still remain many challenges left to solve, such as dealing with the limi-tation in vocabulary size.

In this paper we have proposed a modification to the standard encoder/decoder neural MT architecture to use unlimited-vocabulary character-based source word embeddings. The improvement in BLEU is about 1.5 points in German-to-English and more than 3 points in English-to-German.

As further work, we are currently studying different alternatives (Chung et al., 2016) to extend the character-based approach to the target side of the neural MT system.

Acknowledgements

This work is supported by the 7th Framework Program of the European Commission through the International Outgoing Fellowship Marie Curie Action (IMTraP-2011-29951) and also by the Spanish Ministerio de Economía y Competitividad and European Regional Developmend Fund, contract TEC2015-69266-P (MINECO/FEDER, UE).

References

Dimitry Bahdanau, Kyunghyun Cho, and Yoshua Bengio. 2015. Neural machine translation by jointly learning to align and translate. *CoRR*, abs/1409.0473.

Miguel Ballesteros, Chris Dyer, and Noah A. Smith. 2015. Improved transition-based parsing by modeling characters instead of words with lstms. In *Proceedings of the 2015 Conference on Empirical Methods in Natural Language Processing*, pages 349–359, Lisbon, Portugal, September. Association for Computational Linguistics.

Jan A. Botha and Phil Blunsom. 2014. Compositional Morphology for Word Representations and Language Modelling. In *Proceedings of the 31st International Conference on Machine Learning (ICML)*, Beijing, China, jun. *Award for best application paper*.

Xinxiong Chen, Lei Xu, Zhiyuan Liu, Maosong Sun, and Huan-Bo Luan. 2015. Joint learning of character and word embeddings. In Qiang Yang and Michael Wooldridge, editors, *IJCAI*, pages 1236–1242. AAAI Press.

Kyunghyun Cho, Bart van van Merrienboer, Dzmitry Bahdanau, and Yoshua Bengio. 2014. On the properties of neural machine translation: Encoder–decoder approaches. In *Proc. of the Eighth Workshop on Syntax, Semantics and Structure in Statistical Translation*, Doha.

Grzegorz Chrupala. 2014. Normalizing tweets with edit scripts and recurrent neural embeddings. In *Proceedings of the 52nd Annual Meeting of the Association for Computational Linguistics, ACL 2014, June 22-27, 2014, Baltimore, MD, USA, Volume 2: Short Papers*, pages 680–686.

Junyoung Chung, Kyunghyun Cho, and Yoshua Bengio. 2016. A character-level decoder without explicit segmentation for neural machine translation. *CoRR*, abs/1603.06147.

Desmond Elliott, Stella Frank, and Eva Hasler. 2015. Multi-language image description with neural sequence models. *CoRR*, abs/1510.04709.

Sebastien Jean, Orhan Firat, Kyunghun Cho, Roland Memisevic, and Yoshua Bengio. 2015. Montreal neural machine translation systems for wmt15. In *Proc. of the 10th Workshop on Statistical Machine Translation*, Lisbon.

Nal Kalchbrenner and Phil Blunsom. 2013. Recurrent continuous translation models. In *Proc. of the Conference on Empirical Methods in Natural Language Processing*, Seattle.

Yoon Kim, Yacine Jernite, David Sontag, and Alexander M. Rush. 2016. Character-aware neural language models. In *Proceedings of the 30th AAAI Conference on Artificial Intelligence (AAAI'16)*.

Philipp Koehn, Franz Joseph Och, and Daniel Marcu. 2003. Statistical Phrase-Based Translation. In *Proc. of the 41th Annual Meeting of the Association for Computational Linguistics*.

Philipp Koehn, Hieu Hoang, Alexandra Birch, Chris Callison-Burch, Marcello Federico, Nicolas Bertoldi, Brooke Cowan, Wade Shen, Christine Moran, Richard Zens, Chris Dyer, Ondrej Bojar, Alexandra Constantin, and Evan Herbst. 2007. Moses: Open Source Toolkit for Statistical Machine Translation. In *Proc. of the 45th Annual Meeting of the Association for Computational Linguistics*, pages 177–180.

Wang Ling, Chris Dyer, Alan W Black, Isabel Trancoso, Ramon Fermandez, Silvio Amir, Luis Marujo, and Tiago Luis. 2015a. Finding function in form: Compositional character models for open vocabulary word representation. In *Proceedings of the 2015 Conference on Empirical Methods in Natural Language Processing*, pages 1520–1530, Lisbon, Portugal, September. Association for Computational Linguistics.

Wang Ling, Isabel Trancoso, Chris Dyer, and Alan W. Black. 2015b. Character-based neural machine translation. *CoRR*, abs/1511.04586.

Min-Thang Luong and Cristopher D. Manning. 2016. Character-based neural machine translation. *CoRR*, abs/1511.04586.

Cicero D. Santos and Victor Guimar aes. 2015. Boosting named entity recognition with neural character embeddings. In *Proceedings of the Fifth Named Entity Workshop*, pages 25–33, Beijing, China, July. Association for Computational Linguistics.

Cicero D. Santos and Bianca Zadrozny. 2014. Learning character-level representations for part-of-speech tagging. In Tony Jebara and Eric P. Xing, editors, *Proceedings of the 31st International Conference on Machine Learning (ICML-14)*, pages 1818–1826.

Rico Sennrich, Barry Haddow, and Alexandra Birch. 2015. Neural machine translation of rare words with subword units. *CoRR*, abs/1508.07909.

Ilya Sutskever, Oriol Vinyals, and Quoc V. Le. 2014. Sequence to sequence learning with neural networks. In Z. Ghahramani, M. Welling, C. Cortes, N. D. Lawrence, and K. Q. Weinberger, editors, *Advances in Neural Information Processing Systems 27*, pages 3104–3112. Curran Associates, Inc.

Learning Monolingual Compositional Representations via Bilingual Supervision

Ahmed Elgohary and **Marine Carpuat**
Department of Computer Science
University of Maryland
College Park, MD 20742, USA
elgohary@cs.umd.edu, marine@cs.umd.edu

Abstract

Bilingual models that capture the semantics of sentences are typically only evaluated on cross-lingual transfer tasks such as cross-lingual document categorization or machine translation. In this work, we evaluate the quality of the monolingual representations learned with a variant of the bilingual compositional model of Hermann and Blunsom (2014), when viewing translations in a second language as a semantic annotation as the original language text. We show that compositional objectives based on phrase translation pairs outperform compositional objectives based on bilingual sentences and on monolingual paraphrases.

1 Introduction

The effectiveness of new representation learning methods for distributional word representations (Baroni et al., 2014) has brought renewed interest to the question of how to compose semantic representations of words to capture the semantics of phrases and sentences. These representations offer the promise of capturing phrasal or sentential semantics in a general fashion, and could in principle benefit any NLP applications that analyze text beyond the word level, and improve their ability to generalize beyond contexts seen in training.

While most prior work has focused either on composing words into short phrases (Mitchell and Lapata, 2010; Baroni and Zamparelli, 2010; Hermann et al., 2012; Fyshe et al., 2015), or on supervised task-specific composition functions (Socher et al., 2013; Iyyer et al., 2015; Rocktäschel et al., 2015; Iyyer et al., 2014; Tai et al., 2015, inter alia), Wieting et al. (2016) recently showed that

a simple composition architecture (vector averaging) can yield sentence models that consistently perform well in semantic textual similarity tasks in a wide range of domains, and outperform more complex sequence models (Tai et al., 2015). Interestingly, these models are trained using PPDB, the paraphrase database (Ganitkevitch et al., 2013), which was learned from bilingual parallel corpora.

In bilingual settings, there are also a few examples of bilingual sentence models (Zou et al., 2013; Hermann and Blunsom, 2014; Lauly et al., 2014; Gouws et al., 2014). However, they have only been evaluated in cross-lingual transfer settings (e.g., cross-lingual document classification, or machine translation), which do not directly evaluate the quality of the sentence-level semantic representations learned.

In this work, we directly evaluate the usefulness of modeling semantic equivalence using compositional models of translated texts for detecting semantic textual similarity *in a single language*. For instance, in addition to using translated texts to model cross-lingual transfer from English to a foreign language, we can view English translations as a semantic annotation of the foreign text, and evaluate the usefulness of the resulting foreign representations. While learning representations in languages other than English is a pressing practical problem, this paper will focus on evaluating English sentence representations learned on English semantic similarity tasks to facilitate comparison with prior work.

Our results show that sentence representations learned using a bilingual compositional objective outperform representations learned using monolingual evidence, whether compositional or not. In addition, phrasal translations yield better representations than full sentence translations, even when applied to sentence-level tasks.

Proceedings of the 54th Annual Meeting of the Association for Computational Linguistics, pages 362–368,
Berlin, Germany, August 7-12, 2016. ©2016 Association for Computational Linguistics

Table 1: Positive and negative examples for each of the 3 types of supervision considered

Bilingual Sentences	+	thus, in fact, we might say that he hurried ahead of the decision by our fellow member.	as que podramos decir , de hecho, que se adelant a la decisin de nuestro colega.
	-	thus, in fact, we might say that he hurried ahead of the decision by our fellow member.	seor presidente, la votacin sobre sellafield ha sido una novedad en el parlamento europeo .
English paraphrases	+	by our fellow member	by our colleague
	-	by our fellow member	of the committee's work
	+	slowly than anticipated	slowly than expected
Bilingual phrases	+	by our fellow member	de nuestro colega diputado
	-	by our fellow member	miles de personas de todo
	+	book and buy airline tickets	reserva y adquisicin de billetes
	+	the air fare advertised should show	el precio del billete anunciado debera indicar
	+	a book by the american writer noam	un libro del escritor norteamericano noam

2 Models

Inspired by the bilingual model of (Hermann and Blunsom, 2014), and paraphrase model of (Wieting et al., 2016), representations for multi-word segments are built with a simple bag-of-word additive combination of word representations, which are trained to minimize the distance between semantically equivalent segments.

2.1 Three Views of Semantic Equivalence

The different types of semantic equivalence used for training are illustrated in Table 1.

Parallel Sentences occur naturally, and provide training examples that are more consistent with downstream applications. However, they can be noisy due to automatic sentence alignment and one-to-many mappings, and bag-of-word representations of sentence meaning are likely to be increasingly noisier as segments get longer.

Monolingual Paraphrases are invaluable resources, but rarely occur naturally , and creating paraphrase resources therefore requires considerable effort. Ganitkevitch et al. (2013) automatically-created paraphrase resources for many languages using parallel corpora.

Parallel Phrases or phrasal translations might provide a tighter definition of semantic equivalence than longer sentence pairs, but phrase pairs have to be extracted automatically based on word alignments, an automatic and noisy process.

2.2 Models and Learning Objectives

Our main model is based on the bilingual composition model of Hermann and Blunsom (2014), which learns a word embedding matrix W from a training set $\mathcal{X}$ of aligned sentence pairs $\langle x_1, x_2 \rangle$. Each of x_1 and x_2 is represented as a bag-of-words, i.e. a superset of column indices in W. Each aligned pair $\langle x_1, x_2 \rangle$ is augmented with k randomly selected sentences that are not aligned to x_1, and another k that are not aligned to x_2. Given this augmented example $\langle x_1, x_2, \bar{x}_1^1, ..., \bar{x}_1^k, \bar{x}_2^1, ..., \bar{x}_2^k \rangle$, the model training objective is defined as follows:

$$J_{bi}(W) = \frac{\lambda}{2}||W||_F^2 + \sum_{\langle x_1, x_2, \bar{x}_1, \bar{x}_2 \rangle} \sum_{i=1}^{k}$$
$$[\delta + ||g(x_1) - g(x_2)||^2$$
$$- ||g(x_1) - g(\bar{x}_2^i)||^2]_h$$
$$[\delta + ||g(x_1) - g(x_2)||^2$$
$$- ||g(x_2) - g(\bar{x}_1^i)||^2]_h \qquad (1)$$

where $g(x) = \sum_{i \in x} W_{:i}$, $[.]_h$ is the hinge function (i.e. $[v]_h = \max(0, v)$) whose margin is given by δ and λ is a regularization parameter.

The paraphrase-based model of Wieting et al. (2016) shares the same structure as the bilingual model above, but differs in the nature of segments used to define semantic equivalence (sentence pairs vs. paraphrases), the distance function used (Euclidean distance vs. cosine similarity), as well as the negative sampling strategies, and word embeddings initialization and regularization. We

Table 2: Training conditions: three types of semantic equivalence for composed representations.

Condition	# examples	Avg. length	Provenance
Bilingual Sentences	1.9M	28	Europarl-v7 (Koehn, 2005)
Bilingual phrases	3M	5	+ Moses phrase extraction (Koehn et al., 2007)
Monolingual phrases	3M	3	PPDB XL (Ganitkevitch et al., 2013)

provide empirical comparisons with the Wieting et al. (2016) embeddings, and also define a simplified version of that objective, J_{pa}, to allow for controlled comparisons with J_{bi}.

J_{pa} uses random initialization and penalizes large values in W with a $||W||_F^2$ regularization term[1]. The choice of distance function (Euclidean distance or cosine similarity) and of the negative sampling strategy[2] are viewed as tunable hyperparameters.

3 Experiments

3.1 Evaluating Sentence Representations

Following Wieting et al. (2016), the models above are evaluated on the four Semantic Textual Similarity (STS) datasets (Agirre et al., 2012; Agirre et al., 2013; Agirre et al., 2014; Agirre et al., 2015), which provide pairs of English sentences from different domains (e.g., Tweets, news, webforums, image captions), annotated with human judgments of similarity on a 1 to 5 scale. Systems have to output a similarity score for each pair. Systems are evaluated using the Pearson correlation between gold and predicted rankings.

The Sentences Involving Compositional Knowledge (SICK) test set (Marelli et al., 2014) provides a complementary evaluation. It consists of sentence pairs annotated with semantic relatedness scores. While STS examples were simply drawn from existing NLP datasets, SICK examples were constructed to avoid non-compositional phenomena such as multiword expressions, named entities and world knowledge.

3.2 Experimental Conditions

At training time we learn word embeddings for each combination of objective (Section 2.2) and type of training examples (Table 2), using modified implementations of open-source implementations for J_{bi} (Hermann and Blunsom, 2014) and J_{pa} (Wieting et al., 2016). This results in six model configurations. Each was trained for 10 epochs using tuned hyperparameters.

At tuning time we use the SMT-europarl subset of STS-2012. We consider mini-batch sizes of $\{25, 50, 100\}$, $\delta \in \{1, 10, 100\}$ with Euclidean distance, $\delta \in \{0.4, 0.6, 0.8\}$ with cosine similarly, and $\lambda \in \{1, 10^{-3}, 10^{-5}, 10^{-7}, 10^{-9}\}$. In J_{bi}, we consider $k \in \{1, 5, 10, 15\}$, and in J_{pa} we tuned over the sampling strategy $\in \{MIX, MAX\}$ and the distance function used. To speed up tuning for J_{pa}, we follow Wieting et al. (2016), by limiting training to $100k$ pairs, and tuning to 5 epochs.

Tuning results confirmed the importance of negative sampling and distance function in our models: in J_{bi}, increasing k consistently helps the bilingual models, whereas the correlation score for monolingual models degrade for $k > 10$. In J_{pa}, MAX always outperforms MIX. Euclidean distance was consistently chosen for bilingual sentences and monolingual phrases, while cosine similarity was chosen for bilingual phrases.

At test time we construct sentence-level embeddings by averaging the representations of words in each sentence, and compute cosine similarity to capture the similarity between sentences.

4 Findings

Table 3 reports the Pearson correlation scores achieved for each approach and dataset.

Bilingual phrases yield the best models in controlled settings

Overall, the best representations are obtained using bilingual phrase pairs and the J_{bi} objective. They outperform all other compositional models for all tasks, except for one subset of STS-2015.

The best objective for a given type of training example varies: J_{pa} generally yields better

---

[1] In contrast, Wieting et al. (2016) initialize W with high-quality but resource intensive embeddings – they are trained using word-level PPDB paraphrases, tuned on SimLex-999, and regularized to penalize deviations from initial GloVe embeddings (Pennington et al., 2014).

[2] *MAX* (use the unaligned phrase of minimum distance) or *MIX* (use *MAX* with probability 0.5 and sample randomly otherwise)

Table 3: Pearson correlation scores obtained on the English STS sets (with per year averages) and on semantic-relatedness task (SICK). The left columns report results based on new representations learned in this work, while the 2 rightmost columns report reference results from prior work (Wieting et al., 2016).

	Monolingual Phrases		Bilingual Phrases		Bilingual Sentences		Reference Results	
	J_{bi}	J_{pa}	J_{bi}	J_{pa}	J_{bi}	J_{pa}	Paragram	GloVe
MSRpar	0.28	0.42	**0.54**	0.38	**0.54**	0.36	0.44	0.47
MSRvid	0.33	0.55	**0.71**	0.38	0.71	0.19	0.77	0.64
SMT-eur	0.39	0.41	0.49	0.46	0.47	0.47	0.48	0.46
SMT-news	0.40	0.50	**0.59**	0.40	0.58	0.38	0.63	0.50
OnWN	0.52	0.57	**0.64**	0.62	0.46	0.62	0.71	0.55
2012 Avg	0.39	0.49	**0.59**	0.45	0.54	0.41	0.61	0.53
headline	0.56	0.66	**0.70**	0.58	0.66	0.61	0.74	0.64
OnWN	0.55	0.53	**0.75**	0.34	0.48	0.25	0.72	0.63
FNWN	0.35	0.29	**0.41**	0.32	0.25	0.16	0.47	0.34
2013 Avg	0.49	0.49	**0.62**	0.41	0.46	0.34	0.58	0.42
deft forum	0.35	0.47	**0.51**	0.36	0.36	0.33	0.53	0.27
deft news	0.59	0.68	**0.77**	0.59	0.76	0.58	0.75	0.68
headline	0.56	0.63	**0.73**	0.58	0.67	0.58	0.72	0.60
images	0.58	0.73	**0.73**	0.59	0.66	0.49	0.80	0.61
OnWN	0.65	0.62	**0.80**	0.55	0.55	0.47	0.81	0.58
tweet news	0.59	0.66	**0.73**	0.64	0.56	0.69	0.77	0.51
2014 Avg	0.55	0.63	**0.71**	0.55	0.59	0.52	0.73	0.54
forums	0.35	0.42	**0.55**	0.48	0.50	0.45	0.66	0.31
students	0.66	0.66	**0.73**	0.73	0.65	0.69	0.77	0.63
headline	0.64	0.60	**0.79**	0.64	0.73	0.66	0.76	0.62
belief	0.46	**0.71**	0.68	0.67	0.48	0.61	0.77	0.41
images	0.52	0.71	**0.75**	0.62	0.67	0.56	0.82	0.68
2015 Avg	0.53	0.63	**0.70**	0.63	0.59	0.60	0.76	0.53
SICK	0.53	0.62	**0.66**	0.57	0.63	0.54	0.72	0.66

results with monolingual phrases, while J_{bi} performs better with bilingual examples. Bilingual phrases seem to benefit from larger number of randomly selected negative samples and from using the Euclidean distance rather than cosine similarity. The best bilingual compositional representations are better than non-compositional Glove embeddings (Pennington et al., 2014), but worse than compositional Paragram embeddings (Wieting et al., 2016). However, Paragram initialization requires large amounts of text and human word similarity judgments for tuning, while our models were initialized randomly.

Table 4: Undertrained word ratios (tokens seen fewer than 100 times during training) are uncorrelated with performance in Table 3.

Dataset	Monolingual Phrases	Bilingual Phrases	Bilingual Sentences
2012 Avg	0.15	0.17	0.09
2013 Avg	0.16	0.17	0.11
2014 Avg	0.19	0.22	0.11
2015 Avg	0.15	0.19	0.11
SICK	0.2	0.25	0.15

Bilingual sentences vs. bilingual phrases

Why do bilingual phrases outperform the bilingual sentences they are extracted from? In this section, we verify that this is not explained by systematic biases in the distribution of training examples.

First, Table 4 shows that bilingual sentences have the smallest ratios of undertrained words, and are therefore not penalized by rare words more than bilingual phrases[3].

Second, we see that the rankings are not biased due to memorization of the phrases seen during training. Rankings of models does not change when testing on unseen word sequences, as shown by SICK results with models trained using J_{bi} on a filtered training set that contains none of the bigrams observed at test time (Table 5).

Third, the advantage of bilingual phrases over bilingual sentences is not due to the larger number of training examples. $1.9M$ (and even $1M$) bilin-

---

[3]Further, more than 80% of words that appear in both bilingual sentences and bilingual phrases occur in 460 (in average) more bilingual sentences than in bilingual phrases. The remaining 20% were found to be the rare words (e.g. zazvorkova, woldesmayat, yellow-bellies) that hardly occur in test sets.

Table 5: Impact of memorization: Pearson correlation scores on SICK with training sets with and without filtering out training pairs that contain any bigrams that appear in SICK. Number of training pairs (# Pairs) is shown in millions.

	Not Filtered		Filtered	
	# Pairs	Score	# Pairs	Score
Monoling. Phrases	3M	0.52	2.3M	0.54
Bilingual Phrases	3M	**0.67**	2.1M	**0.65**
Bilingual Sentences	1.9M	0.66	0.47M	0.58

Table 6: Impact of training set size: Average Pearson correlation per test set with different numbers (in millions) of bilingual phrase pairs, compared to the full set of bilingual sentences and monolingually pretrained GloVe.

	Bilingual Phrases				Sent.	
	$0.5M$	$1M$	$1.9M$	$3M$	$1.9M$	GloVe
2012	0.55	0.58	0.59	0.59	0.54	0.53
2013	0.59	0.61	0.61	0.62	0.46	0.42
2014	0.69	0.71	0.71	0.71	0.59	0.54
2016	0.68	0.69	0.70	0.70	0.61	0.53
SICK	0.62	0.64	0.65	0.66	0.63	0.66

gual phrase pairs still outperform the $1.9M$ bilingual sentence pairs on all subsets (See Table 6).

Taken together, these additional results support our initial intuition that the main advantage of bilingual phrases over bilingual sentences is that phrase pairs have stronger semantic equivalence than sentence pairs, since phrase pairs are shorter and are constructed by identifying strongly aligned subsets of sentence pairs.

Monolingual vs. bilingual phrases

Based on the analysis thus far, we hypothesize that paraphrase pairs with overlapping tokens make the compositional training objective less useful. Around 40% of the paraphrase training pairs differ only by one token. With Euclidean distance in the training objective, overlapping tokens cancel each other out of the composition term. For example, the pair $\langle healthy\ and\ stable,\ healthy\ and\ steady \rangle$ yields the compositional term

$$||(healthy + and + stable) -$$
$$(healthy + and + steady)||_2$$
$$= ||stable - steady||_2$$

In contrast, overlap cannot occur in the bilingual setting, and all words within bilingual phrases contribute to the compositional objective. Furthermore, bilingual pairs provide a more explicit semantic signal as translations can disambiguate polysemous words (Diab, 2004; Carpuat and Wu, 2007) and help discover synonyms by pivoting (Callison-Burch, 2007; Yao et al., 2012).

All these factors might contribute to the ability of training with bilingual phrases of taking advantage of larger number of negative samples k.

5 Conclusion

We conducted the first evaluation of compositional representations learned using bilingual supervision on monolingual textual similarity tasks.

Phrase and sentence representations are constructed by composing word representations using a simple additive composition function. We considered two training objective that encourage the resulting representations to distinguish English-Spanish segment pairs that are semantically equivalent or not. The resulting English sentence representations consistently outperform compositional models trained to detect monolingual paraphrases on five different English semantic textual similarity tasks from SemEval.

Bilingual phrase pairs are consistently the best evidence of semantic equivalence in our experiments. They yield better results than the sentence pairs they are extracted from, despite the noise introduced by the automatic extraction process.

Furthermore the composed representations outperform non-compositional word representations derived from monolingual co-occurrence statistics. While sizes of monolingual vs. bilingual corpora are not directly comparable, it is remarkable that representations learned with only 500k bilingual phrase pairs outperform GloVe embeddings trained on 840B tokens.

Since our best models still underperform Paragram vectors, which require a more sophisticated initialization process, we will turn to improving our initialization strategies in future work. Nevertheless, current results provide further evidence of the usefulness of compositional text representations, even with a simple bag-of-word additive composition function, and of bilingual translation pairs as a strong signal of semantic equivalence.

References

Eneko Agirre, Mona Diab, Daniel Cer, and Aitor Gonzalez-Agirre. 2012. Semeval-2012 task 6: A pilot on semantic textual similarity. In *Proceedings of the First Joint Conference on Lexical and Computational Semantics-Volume 1: Proceedings of the main conference and the shared task, and Volume 2: Proceedings of the Sixth International Workshop on Semantic Evaluation*, pages 385–393.

Eneko Agirre, Daniel Cer, Mona Diab, Aitor Gonzalez-Agirre, and Weiwei Guo. 2013. sem 2013 shared task: Semantic textual similarity, including a pilot on typed-similarity. In *In* SEM 2013: The Second Joint Conference on Lexical and Computational Semantics.*

Eneko Agirre, Carmen Banea, Claire Cardie, Daniel Cer, Mona Diab, Aitor Gonzalez-Agirre, Weiwei Guo, Rada Mihalcea, German Rigau, and Janyce Wiebe. 2014. Semeval-2014 task 10: Multilingual semantic textual similarity. In *Proceedings of the 8th international workshop on semantic evaluation (SemEval 2014)*, pages 81–91.

Eneko Agirre, Carmen Banea, Claire Cardie, Daniel Cer, Mona Diab, Aitor Gonzalez-Agirre, Weiwei Guo, Inigo Lopez-Gazpioa, Montse Maritxalar, Rada Mihalcea, et al. 2015. Semeval-2015 task 2: Semantic textual similarity, english, spanish and pilot on interpretability. In *Proceedings of the 9th international workshop on semantic evaluation (SemEval 2015)*, pages 252–263.

Marco Baroni and Roberto Zamparelli. 2010. Nouns are vectors, adjectives are matrices: Representing adjective-noun constructions in semantic space. In *Proceedings of the 2010 Conference on Empirical Methods in Natural Language Processing*, pages 1183–1193.

Marco Baroni, Georgiana Dinu, and Germán Kruszewski. 2014. Don't count, predict! a systematic comparison of context-counting vs. context-predicting semantic vectors. In *Proceedings of the ACL.*

Chris Callison-Burch. 2007. *Paraphrasing and Translation*. Ph.D. thesis, University of Edinburgh.

Marine Carpuat and Dekai Wu. 2007. Improving Statistical Machine Translation using Word Sense Disambiguation. In *Proceedings of the 2007 Joint Conference on Empirical Methods in Natural Language Processing and Computational Natural Language Learning (EMNLP-CoNLL 2007)*, pages 61–72, Prague, June.

Mona Diab. 2004. Relieving the data acquisition bottleneck in word sense disambiguation. In *Proceedings of the 42nd Annual Meeting of the Association for Computational Linguistics.*

Alona Fyshe, Leila Wehbe, Partha P Talukdar, Brian Murphy, and Tom M Mitchell. 2015. A compositional and interpretable semantic space. In *Proc. of NAACL.*

Juri Ganitkevitch, Benjamin Van Durme, and Chris Callison-Burch. 2013. Ppdb: The paraphrase database. In *HLT-NAACL*, pages 758–764.

Stephan Gouws, Yoshua Bengio, and Greg Corrado. 2014. Bilbowa: Fast bilingual distributed representations without word alignments. *arXiv preprint arXiv:1410.2455.*

Karl Moritz Hermann and Phil Blunsom. 2014. Multilingual models for compositional distributed semantics. In *Association for Computational Linguistics (ACL), 2014.*

Karl Moritz Hermann, Phil Blunsom, and Stephen Pulman. 2012. An unsupervised ranking model for noun-noun compositionality. In *Proceedings of the First Joint Conference on Lexical and Computational Semantics-Volume 1: Proceedings of the main conference and the shared task, and Volume 2: Proceedings of the Sixth International Workshop on Semantic Evaluation*, pages 132–141.

Mohit Iyyer, Jordan L Boyd-Graber, Leonardo Max Batista Claudino, Richard Socher, and Hal Daumé III. 2014. A neural network for factoid question answering over paragraphs. In *EMNLP*, pages 633–644.

Mohit Iyyer, Varun Manjunatha, Jordan Boyd-Graber, and Hal Daumé III. 2015. Deep unordered composition rivals syntactic methods for text classification. In *Proceedings of the 53rd Annual Meeting of the Association for Computational Linguistics and the 7th International Joint Conference on Natural Language Processing*, volume 1, pages 1681–1691.

Philipp Koehn, Hieu Hoang, Alexandra Birch, Chris Callison-Burch, Marcello Federico, Nicola Bertoldi, Brooke Cowan, Wade Shen, Christine Moran, Richard Zens, et al. 2007. Moses: Open source toolkit for statistical machine translation. In *Proceedings of the 45th annual meeting of the ACL on interactive poster and demonstration sessions*, pages 177–180.

Philipp Koehn. 2005. Europarl: A parallel corpus for statistical machine translation. In *MT summit*, volume 5, pages 79–86.

Stanislas Lauly, Hugo Larochelle, Mitesh Khapra, Balaraman Ravindran, Vikas C Raykar, and Amrita Saha. 2014. An autoencoder approach to learning bilingual word representations. In *Advances in Neural Information Processing Systems*, pages 1853–1861.

Marco Marelli, Luisa Bentivogli, Marco Baroni, Raffaella Bernardi, Stefano Menini, and Roberto Zamparelli. 2014. Semeval-2014 task 1: Evaluation of compositional distributional semantic models on full sentences through semantic relatedness and textual entailment. *SemEval-2014*.

Jeff Mitchell and Mirella Lapata. 2010. Composition in distributional models of semantics. *Cognitive science*, 34(8):1388–1429.

Jeffrey Pennington, Richard Socher, and Christopher D Manning. 2014. Glove: Global vectors for word representation. In *EMNLP*, volume 14, pages 1532–1543.

Tim Rocktäschel, Edward Grefenstette, Karl Moritz Hermann, Tomáš Kočiskỳ, and Phil Blunsom. 2015. Reasoning about entailment with neural attention. *arXiv preprint arXiv:1509.06664*.

Richard Socher, Alex Perelygin, Jean Y Wu, Jason Chuang, Christopher D Manning, Andrew Y Ng, and Christopher Potts. 2013. Recursive deep models for semantic compositionality over a sentiment treebank. In *Proceedings of the conference on empirical methods in natural language processing (EMNLP)*, volume 1631, page 1642.

Kai Sheng Tai, Richard Socher, and Christopher D Manning. 2015. Improved semantic representations from tree-structured long short-term memory networks. *arXiv preprint arXiv:1503.00075*.

John Wieting, Mohit Bansal, Kevin Gimpel, and Karen Livescu. 2016. Towards universal paraphrastic sentence embeddings. In *In International Conference on Learning Representations (ICLR)*.

Xuchen Yao, Benjamin Van Durme, and Chris Callison-Burch. 2012. Expectations of word sense in parallel corpora. In *Proceedings of the 2012 Conference of the North American Chapter of the Association for Computational Linguistics: Human Language Technologies*, pages 621–625, Montréal, Canada, June. Association for Computational Linguistics.

Will Y Zou, Richard Socher, Daniel M Cer, and Christopher D Manning. 2013. Bilingual word embeddings for phrase-based machine translation. In *EMNLP*, pages 1393–1398.

Event Nugget Detection with Forward-Backward Recurrent Neural Networks

Reza Ghaeini, Xiaoli Z. Fern, Liang Huang, Prasad Tadepalli
School of Electrical Engineering and Computer Science, Oregon State University
1148 Kelley Engineering Center, Corvallis, OR 97331-5501, USA
{ghaeinim, xfern, huanlian, tadepall}@eecs.oregonstate.edu

Abstract

Traditional event detection methods heavily rely on manually engineered rich features. Recent deep learning approaches alleviate this problem by automatic feature engineering. But such efforts, like tradition methods, have so far only focused on single-token event mentions, whereas in practice events can also be a phrase. We instead use forward-backward recurrent neural networks (FBRNNs) to detect events that can be either words or phrases. To the best our knowledge, this is one of the first efforts to handle multi-word events and also the first attempt to use RNNs for event detection. Experimental results demonstrate that FBRNN is competitive with the state-of-the-art methods on the ACE 2005 and the Rich ERE 2015 event detection tasks.

1 Introduction

Automatic event extraction from natural text is an important and challenging task for natural language understanding. Given a set of ontologized event types, the goal of event extraction is to identify the mentions of different event types and their arguments from natural texts. In this paper we focus on the problem of extracting event mentions, which can be in the form of a single word or multiple words. In the current literature, events have been annotated in two different forms:

- **Event trigger**: a single token that is considered to signify the occurrence of an event. Here a token is not necessarily a word, for example, in order to capture a death event, the phrase "kick the bucket" is concatenated into a single token "kick_the_bucket". This

scheme has been used in the ACE and Light ERE data and has been followed in most studies on event extraction.

- **Event nugget**: a word or a phrase of multiple words that most clearly expresses the occurrence of an event. This scheme is recently introduced to remove the limitation of single-token event triggers and has been adopted by the rich ERE data for event annotation.

Existing event extraction work often heavily relies on a rich set of hand-designed features and utilizes existing NLP toolkits and resources (Ji and Grishman, 2008; Patwardhan and Riloff, 2009; Liao and Grishman, 2010; McClosky et al., 2011; Huang and Riloff, 2012; Li et al., 2013a; Li et al., 2013b; Li et al., 2014). Consequently, it is often challenging to adapt prior methods to multi-lingual or non-English settings since they require extensive linguistic knowledge for feature engineering and mature NLP toolkits for extracting the features without severe error propagation.

By contrast, deep learning has recently emerged as a compelling solution to avoid the aforementioned problems by automatically extracting meaningful features from raw text without relying on existing NLP toolkits. There have been some limited attempts in using deep learning for event detection (Nguyen and Grishman, 2015; Chen et al., 2015) which apply Convolutional Neural Networks (CNNs) to a window of text around potential triggers to identify events. These efforts outperform traditional methods, but there remain two major limitations:

- So far they have, like traditional methods, only focused on the oversimplified scenario of single-token event detection.

- Such CNN-based approaches require a fixed size window. In practice it is often unclear

Proceedings of the 54th Annual Meeting of the Association for Computational Linguistics, pages 369–373,
Berlin, Germany, August 7-12, 2016. ©2016 Association for Computational Linguistics

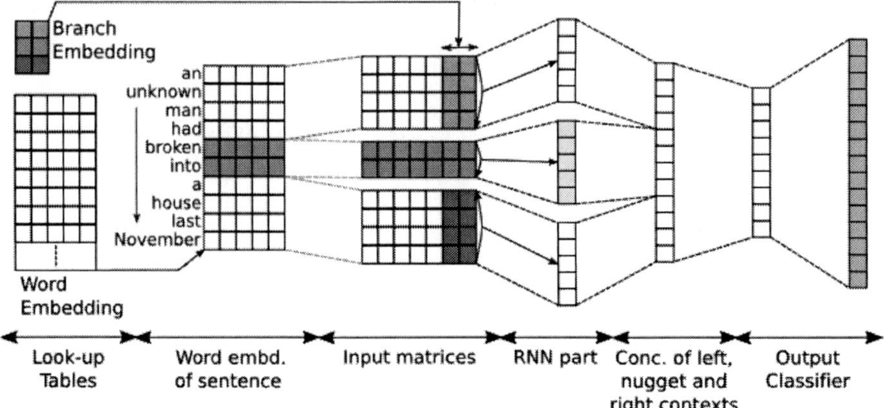

Figure 1: The Proposed Forward-Backward Recurrent Neural Network (FBRNN) Model, with the example sentence "an unknown man had [broken into] a house last November" and event nugget candidate "broken into"

how large this window needs to be in order to capture necessary context to make decision for an event candidate.

Recurrent Neural Networks (RNNs), by contrast, is a natural solution to both problems above because it can be applied to inputs of variable length which eliminates both the requirement of single-token event trigger and the need for a fixed window size. Using recurrent nodes with Long Short Term Memory (LSTM) (Hochreiter and Schmidhuber, 1997) or Gated Recurrent Units (GRU) (Cho et al., 2014), RNN is potentially capable of selectively deciding the relevant context to consider for detecting events.

In this paper we present a forward-backward recurrent neural network (FBRNN) to extract (possibly multi-word) event mentions from raw text. Although RNNs have been studied extensively in other NLP tasks (Cross and Huang, 2016; Tai et al., 2015; Socher et al., 2014; Paulus et al., 2014), to the best of our knowledge, this is the first work to use RNNs for event detection. This is also one of the first efforts to handle multi-word event nuggets. Experimental results confirm that FBRNN is competitive compared to the state-of-the-art on the ACE 2005 dataset and the Rich ERE 2015 event detection task.

2 Proposed Model

Let $x = [w_0, w_1, ..., w_n]$ be a sentence. We first go over each word and phrase and heuristically ex-

tract a set of event candidates. The task is then to predict for each candidate given the sentence whether it is an event and, if so, its type. Figure 1 demonstrates our proposed model for this task.

For each event candidate, which consists of a continuous span of texts $[w_i, ..., w_j]$, we split the sentence into three parts: the left context $[w_0, ..., w_{i-1}]$, the event nugget candidate $[w_i, ..., w_j]$ and the right context $[w_{j+1}, ..., w_n]$. For instance, for event candidate "broken into" and given sentence "an unknown man had broken into a house last November"; [an, unknown, man, had], [broken, into] and [a, house, last, November] are the left context, the event nugget candidate and the right context respectively. For each part, we learn a separate RNN to produce a representation. Before feeding the data into the network, each word is represented as a real-valued vector that is formed by concatenating a word embedding with a branch embedding, which we describe below:

- **Word embedding**: Several studies have investigated methods for representing words as real-valued vectors in order to capture the hidden semantic and syntactic properties of words (Collobert and Weston, 2008; Mikolov et al., 2013). Such embeddings are typically learned from large unlabeled text corpora, consequently can serve as good initializations. In our work, we initialize the word embedding with the pretrained 300-diemension word2vec (Mikolov et al., 2013).

- **Branch embedding**: The relative position of a word to the current event nugget candidate may contain useful information toward how the word should be used or interpreted in identifying events. It is thus a common practice to include an additional embedding for each word that characterizes its relative position to the event nugget candidate. In this work, to reduce the complexity of our model and avoid overfitting, we only learn embeddings for three different positions: the left branch, the nugget branch and the right branch respectively. This is illustrated using three different colors in Figure 1.

Now each word is represented as a real-valued vector, formed by concatenating its word and branch embeddings. The sequence of words in the left, nugget and right branches will each pass through a separate Recurrent Neural Network. For the left and nugget branches, we process the words from left to right, and use the opposite direction (from right to left) for the right context, thus the name Forward-Backward RNN (FBRNN).

The output of each recurrent neural network is a fixed size representation of its input. We concatenate the representations from the three branches and pass it through a fully connected neural network with a softmax output node that classifies each event candidate as an event of specific type or a non-event. Note that in cases where an event candidate can potentially belong to multiple event types, one can replace the softmax output node with a set of binary output nodes or a sigmoid to allow for multi-label prediction for each event candidate.

To avoid overfitting, we use dropout (Hinton et al., 2012; Srivastava et al., 2014) with rate of 0.5 for regularization. The weights of the recurrent neural networks as well as the fully connected neural network are learned by minimizing the log loss on the training data via the Adam optimizer (Kingma and Ba, 2015) which performs better that other optimization methods like AdaDelta (Zeiler, 2012), AdaGrad (Duchi et al., 2011), RMSprop and SGD. During training, the word and branch embeddings are updated to learn effective representations for this specific task.

3 Experiments

In this section, we first empirically examine some design choices for our model and then compare the proposed model to the current state-of-the-art on two different event detection datasets.

3.1 Datasets, candidate generation and hyper-parameters

We experiment on two different corpora, ACE 2005 and Rich ERE 2015.

- **ACE 2005**: The ACE 2005 corpus is annotated with single-token event triggers and has eight event types and 33 event subtypes that, along with the "non-event" class, constitutes a 34-class classification problem. In our experiments we used the same train, development and test sets as the previous studies on this dataset (Nguyen and Grishman, 2015; Li et al., 2013b). Candidate generation for this corpus is based on a list of candidate event trigger words created from the training data and the PPDB paraphrase database. Given a sentence, we go over each token and extract the tokens that appear in this high-recall list as event candidates, which we then classify with our proposed FBRNN model.

- **Rich ERE 2015**: The Rich ERE 2015 corpus was released in the TAC 2015 competition and annotated at the nugget level, thus addressing phrasal event mentions. The Rich ERE 2015 corpus has nine event types and 38 event subtypes, forming a 39-class classification problem (considering "non-event" as an additional class). We utilized the same train and test sets that have been used in the TAC 2015 event nugget detection competition. A subset of the provided train set was set aside as our development set. To generate event nugget candidates, we first followed the same strategy that we used for the ACE 2005 dataset experiment to identify single-token event candidates. We then expand the single-token event candidates using a heuristic rule based on POS tags.

There are a number of hyper-parameters for our model, including the dimension of the branch embedding, the number of recurrent layers in each RNN, the size of the RNN outputs, the dropout rates for training the networks. We tune these parameters using the development set.

3.2 Exploration of different design choices

We first design some experiments to evaluate the impact of the following design choices:

Configurations		P	R	F1
LSTM	+branch	59.82	48.39	53.50
	-branch	58.50	44.82	50.76
GRU	+branch	63.72	47.68	**54.55**
	-branch	64.56	43.93	52.28

Table 1: Performance on the development set with different configurations on Rich ERE 2015.

Methods	P	R	F1
Sentence level in Ji and Grishman (2008)	-	-	59.7
MaxEnt with local features in Li et al. (2013b)	-	-	64.7
Joint beam search with local features in Li et al. (2013b)	-	-	63.7
Joint beam search with local and global features in Li et al. (2013b)	-	-	65.6
CNN (Nguyen, 2015)	71.9	63.8	67.6
FBRNN	66.8	68.0	67.4

Table 2: Comparison with reported performance by event detection systems without using gold entity mentions and types on the ACE 2005 corpus.

i) Different RNN structures: LSTM and GRU are two popular recurrent network structures that are capable of extracting long-term dependencies in different ways. Here we compare their performance for event detection.

ii) The effect of branch embedding: A word can present different role and concept when it is in a nugget branch or other branches. Here we would examine the effect of including branch embedding.

Table 1 shows the results of our model with different design choices on the development set of the Rich ERE 2015 corpus. We note that the performance of GRU is slightly better than that of LSTM. We believe this is because GRU is a less complex structure compared to LSTM, thus less prone to overfitting given the limited training data for our task. From the results we can also see that the branch embedding performs a crucial role for our model, producing significant improvement for both LSTM and GRU.

Based on the results presented above, for the remaining experiments we will focus on GRU structure with branch embeddings.

3.3 Results on ACE 2005

Many prior studies employ gold-standard entity mentions and types from manual annotation,

Methods	P	R	F1
1st	75.23	47.74	58.41
2nd	73.95	46.61	57.18
3th	73.68	44.94	55.83
4th	73.73	44.57	55.56
5th	71.06	43.50	53.97
FBRNN	71.58	48.19	57.61

Table 3: Performance of FBRNN compared with reported top results in TAC competition (Mitamura et al., 2015) on Rich ERE 2015.

which would not be available in reality during testing. Nguyen and Grishman (2015) examined the performance of a number of traditional systems (Li et al., 2013b) in a more realistic setting, where entity mentions and types are acquired from an automatic high-performing name tagger and information extraction system. In Table 2 we compare the performance of our system with these results reported by Nguyen and Grishman (2015).

We first note that the deep learning methods (CNN and FBRNN) achieve significantly better F1 performance compared to traditional methods using manually engineered features (both local and global). Compared to CNN, our FBRNN model achieved better recall but the precision is lower. For the overall F1 measure, our model is comparable with the CNN model.

3.4 Results on Rich ERE 2015

Table 3 reports the test performance of our model and shows that it is competitive with the top-ranked results obtained in the TAC 2015 event nugget detection competition. It is interesting to note that FBRNN is again winning in recall, but losing in precision, a phenomenon that is consistently observed in both corpora and a topic worth a closer look for future work.

Finally, in Rich ERE test data, approximately 9% of the events are actually multi-labeled. Our current model uses softmax output layer and is thus innately incapable of making multi-label predictions. Despite this limitation, FBRNN achieved competitive result on Rich ERE with only 0.8% difference from the best reported system in the TAC 2015 competition.

4 Conclusions

This paper proposes a novel language-independent event detection method based on RNNs which can automatically extract effective features from raw text to detect event nuggets. We conducted two experiments to compare FBRNN with the state-of-the-art event detection systems on the ACE 2005 and Rich ERE 2015 corpora. These experiments demonstrate that FBRNN achieves competitive results compared to the current state-of-the-art.

References

Yubo Chen, Liheng Xu, Kang Liu, Daojian Zeng, and Jun Zhao. 2015. Event Extraction via Dynamic Multi-Pooling Convolutional Neural Networks. *Association for Computational Linguistics*, 1:167–176.

Kyunghyun Cho, Bart van Merrienboer, Çaglar Gülçehre, Dzmitry Bahdanau, Fethi Bougares, Holger Schwenk, and Yoshua Bengio. 2014. Learning Phrase Representations using RNN Encoder-Decoder for Statistical Machine Translation. *Empirical Methods in Natural Language Processing*, pages 1724–1734.

Ronan Collobert and Jason Weston. 2008. A unified architecture for natural language processing: deep neural networks with multitask learning. *ICML*, pages 160–167.

James Cross and Liang Huang. 2016. Incremental Parsing with Minimal Features Using Bi-Directional LSTM. *Association for Computational Linguistics*.

John Duchi, Elad Hazan, and Yoram Singer. 2011. Adaptive subgradient methods for online learning and stochastic optimization. *The Journal of Machine Learning Research*, 12:2121–2159.

Geoffrey E. Hinton, Nitish Srivastava, Alex Krizhevsky, Ilya Sutskever, and Ruslan Salakhutdinov. 2012. Improving neural networks by preventing co-adaptation of feature detectors. *CoRR*, abs/1207.0580.

Sepp Hochreiter and Jürgen Schmidhuber. 1997. Long Short-Term Memory. *Neural Computation*, 9(8):1735–1780.

Ruihong Huang and Ellen Riloff. 2012. Modeling Textual Cohesion for Event Extraction. *AAAI*.

Heng Ji and Ralph Grishman. 2008. Refining Event Extraction through Cross-Document Inference. *Association for Computational Linguistics*, pages 254–262.

Diederik Kingma and Jimmy Ba. 2015. Adam: A method for stochastic optimization. *arXiv:1412.6980*.

Peifeng Li, Qiaoming Zhu, and Guodong Zhou. 2013a. Argument Inference from Relevant Event Mentions in Chinese Argument Extraction. *Association for Computational Linguistics*, 1:1477–1487.

Qi Li, Heng Ji, and Liang Huang. 2013b. Joint Event Extraction via Structured Prediction with Global Features. *Association for Computational Linguistics*, 1:73–82.

Qi Li, Heng Ji, Yu Hong, and Sujian Li. 2014. Constructing Information Networks Using One Single Model. *Empirical Methods in Natural Language Processing*, pages 1846–1851.

Shasha Liao and Ralph Grishman. 2010. Using Document Level Cross-Event Inference to Improve Event Extraction. *Association for Computational Linguistics*, pages 789–797.

David McClosky, Mihai Surdeanu, and Christopher D. Manning. 2011. Event Extraction as Dependency Parsing. *Association for Computational Linguistics*, pages 1626–1635.

Tomas Mikolov, Ilya Sutskever, Kai Chen, Gregory S. Corrado, and Jeffrey Dean. 2013. Distributed Representations of Words and Phrases and their Compositionality. *Neural Information Processing Systems*, pages 3111–3119.

Teruko Mitamura, Zhengzhong Liu, and Eduard Hovy. 2015. Overview of TAC KBP 2015 Event Nugget Track. *Text Analysis Conference*.

Thien Huu Nguyen and Ralph Grishman. 2015. Event Detection and Domain Adaptation with Convolutional Neural Networks. *Association for Computational Linguistics*, 2:365–371.

Siddharth Patwardhan and Ellen Riloff. 2009. A Unified Model of Phrasal and Sentential Evidence for Information Extraction. *Empirical Methods in Natural Language Processing*, pages 151–160.

Romain Paulus, Richard Socher, and Christopher D. Manning. 2014. Global Belief Recursive Neural Networks. *Neural Information Processing Systems*, pages 2888–2896.

Richard Socher, Andrej Karpathy, Quoc V. Le, Christopher D. Manning, and Andrew Y. Ng. 2014. Grounded Compositional Semantics for Finding and Describing Images with Sentences. *Transactions of the Association for Computational Linguistics*, 2:207–218.

Nitish Srivastava, Geoffrey E. Hinton, Alex Krizhevsky, Ilya Sutskever, and Ruslan Salakhutdinov. 2014. Dropout: a simple way to prevent neural networks from overfitting. *Journal of Machine Learning Research*, 15(1):1929–1958.

Kai Sheng Tai, Richard Socher, and Christopher D. Manning. 2015. Improved Semantic Representations From Tree-Structured Long Short-Term Memory Networks. *Association for Computational Linguistics*, 1:1556–1566.

Matthew D Zeiler. 2012. ADADELTA: an adaptive learning rate method. *arXiv preprint arXiv:1212.5701*.

IBC-C: A Dataset for Armed Conflict Event Analysis

Andrej Žukov-Gregorič and **Bartal Veyhe** and **Zhiyuan Luo**
Department of Computer Science
Royal Holloway, University of London
Egham TW20 0EX
{andrej.zukovgregoric.2010, bartal.veyhe.2014}@live.rhul.ac.uk
zhiyuan@cs.rhul.ac.uk

Abstract

We describe the Iraq Body Count Corpus (IBC-C) dataset, the first substantial armed conflict-related dataset which can be used for conflict analysis. IBC-C provides a ground-truth dataset for conflict specific named entity recognition, slot filling, and event de-duplication. IBC-C is constructed using data collected by the Iraq Body Count project which has been recording incidents from the ongoing war in Iraq since 2003. We describe the dataset's creation, how it can be used for the above three tasks and provide initial baseline results for the first task (named entity recognition) using Hidden Markov Models, Conditional Random Fields, and Recursive Neural Networks.

1 Introduction

Many reports about armed conflict related incidents are published every day. However, these reports on the deaths and injuries of civilians and combatants often get forgotten or go unnoticed for long periods of time. Automatically extracting casualty counts from such reports would help better track ongoing conflicts and understand past ones.

One popular approach of discovering incidents is to identify them from textual reports and extract casualty, and other, information from them. This can either be done by hand or automatically. The Iraq Body Count (IBC) project has been directly recording casualties since 2003 for the ongoing conflict in Iraq (IBC, 2016; Hicks et al., 2011). IBC staff collect reports, link them to unique incidents, extract casualty information, and save the information on a per incident basis as can be seen in Table 2.

Direct recording by hand is a slow process and notable efforts to do so have tended to lag behind the present. Information extraction systems capable of automating this process must explicitly or implicitly successfully solve three tasks: (1) find and extract casualty information in reports (2) detect events mentioned in reports (3) deduplicate detected events into unique events which we call *incidents*. The three tasks correspond to named entity recognition, slot filling, and de-duplication.

In this work we introduce the report based IBC-C dataset.[1] Each report can contain one or more sections; each section, one or more sentences; each sentence, one or more words. Each word is tagged with one of nine entity tags in the inside-outside-beginning (IOB) style. A visual representation of the dataset can be seen in Figure 1 and its statistics in Table 1.

To the best of our knowledge apart from the significantly smaller MUC-3 and MUC-4 datasets (which aren't casualty-specific) there are no other publicly available datasets made specifically for tasks (1), (2) or (3). The IBC-C dataset can be used to train supervised models for all three tasks.

We provide baseline results for task (1) which we posit as a sequence-classification problem and solve using an HMM, a CRF, and an RNN.

Since the 1990s the conflict analysis and NLP/IE communities have diverged. With the IBC-C dataset we hope to bring the two communities closer again.

2 Related Work

Extracting information from conflict related reports has been a topic of interest at various times for both the conflict analysis, information extraction, and natural language processing communi-

---

[1] More information about the IBC-C dataset can be found on: http://andrejzg.github.io/ibcc/

Proceedings of the 54th Annual Meeting of the Association for Computational Linguistics, pages 374–379,
Berlin, Germany, August 7-12, 2016. ©2016 Association for Computational Linguistics

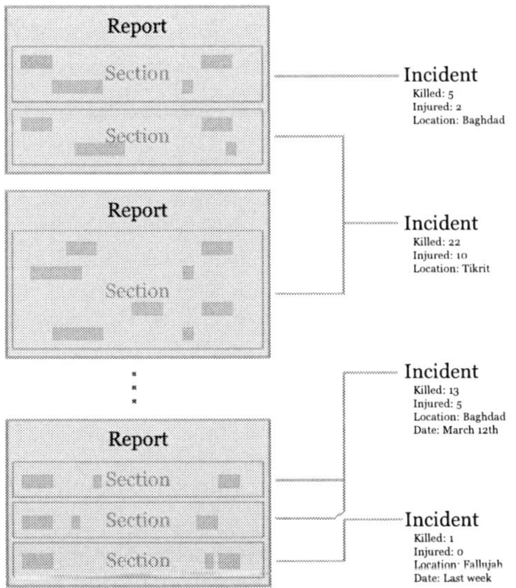

Figure 1: The IBC-C dataset visualised. A report is split into one or more non overlapping sections. A section is comprised of sentences which are comprised of words. Each section is linked to exactly one incident which in turn can be linked to one or more sections.

Element	Count
incidents	9,184
sections	18,379
reports	16,405
sentences	35,295
words	857,465
KNUM	13,597
INUM	6,689
KSUB	14,395
ISUB	1,036
KOTHER	1,192
IOTHER	495
LOCATION	25,251
DATE	4,765
WEAPON	35,617

Table 1: Dataset statistics. Fully capitalised words indicate named entity tags.

ties.

The 1990s saw a series of message understanding conferences (MUCs) of which MUC-3 and MUC-4 are closely related to our work and contain reports of terrorist incidents in Central and South America. MUC data is most often used for slot filling and although MUC-3 and MUC-4 contain more slots than IBC-C they are at the same time much smaller (MUC4 contains 1,700 reports) and cannot be used for incident de-duplication.

Although various ACE, CoNLL, and TAC-KBP tasks contain within them conflict-related reports, none of them are specific to conflict and haven't been studied for conflict-related information extraction specifically.

Studies more directly related to our dataset include work by Tanev and Piskorski (Tanev et al., 2008) who use pattern matching to count casualties. They report a 93% accuracy on counting the wounded. However, they have access to only 29 unique conflict events. Other non-casualty conflict-related work in the domain also suffers from a lack of data, for example, (King and Lowe, 2003) only deal with 711 reports.

Despite work in the NLP and IE communities, the conflict analysis community is still reliant on datasets created by hand. These include IBC (IBC, 2016), ACLED (Raleigh et al., 2010), EDACS (Chojnacki et al., 2012), UCDP (Gleditsch et al., 2002), and GTD (GTD, 2015).

To the best of our knowledge there are no efforts to fully automate casualty counting. However, efforts using NLP/IE tools to automate incident detection do exist but their ability to de-deduplicate incidents has been called into question (Weller and McCubbins, 2014).

Three notable such efforts originating in the conflict analysis community are GDELT (Leetaru and Schrodt, 2013), ICEWS (Obrien, 2010), and OEDA (Schrodt, 2016). All three use pattern matching software such as TABARI (Schrodt, 2001) and to categorise reports using the CAMEO coding scheme (Schrodt et al., 2008).

3 Creating the IBC-C Dataset

3.1 Preprocessing

The Iraq Body Count project (IBC) has been recording conflict-related incidents from the Iraq war since 2003. An incident is a unique event related to war or other forms of violence which led to the death or injury of people. An example can be seen in Table 2.

The recording of incidents by the IBC works as follows: IBC staff first collect relevant *reports* before highlighting *sections* of them which they deem relevant to individual incidents. Parts of the report outside the highlighted sections are discarded. Sections can be seen in Figure 1. Because of the way IBC staff highlight sections there are no overlapping sections in the IBC-C dataset. Events are then recognised from the highlighted sections and de-duplicated into incidents. A final descrip-

Incident ID	Start date	End date
d3473	22 Mar 2003	22 Mar 2003
Min killed	**Max killed**	**Min injured**
2	2	8
Max injured	**Location**	**Cause of death**
9	Khurmal	Suicide car bomb
Sources	**Town**	**Province**
BBC 23 Mar DPA 23 Mar	Khurmal	Sulaymaniyah
Alt. province	**District**	**Alt district**
/	Halabja	/
Killed Subjects		
Person 1, Person 2, ...		
Injured Subjects		
Person 3, Person 4, ...		
Report Sections		
BBC: "On Saturday **Person 1** died in **Khurmal** ..."		
DPA: "**2** people died yesterday afternoon..."		

Table 2: An example of an incident hand coded by IBC staff. Min and max values represent the minimum and maximum figures quoted in report sections linked to the incident.

tion of the incident (e.g. death and injury counts, location and date) is agreed upon after multiple rounds of human checking.

In the preprocessing step we gathered all incidents which occurred between March 20th, 2003 and December 31st, 2013. We removed spurious incidents (e.g. where the minimum number killed is larger than the maximum number killed) and cleaned the section text by removing all formatting and changing all written-out numbers into their numeric form (e.g. 'three' to 3).

3.2 Annotation

Using the information extracted by the IBC (see Table 2) we annotated each section word with one of ten tags: *KNUM* and *INUM* for numbers representing the number killed and injured respectively; *KSUB* and *ISUB* for named individuals were killed or injured; *KOTHER* and *IOTHER* for unnamed people who were killed or injured (for example "The doctor was injured yesterday."); *LOCATION* for the location in which an incident occurred; *WEAPON* for any weapons used in an attack; *DATE* for words which identify when the incident happened; and, *O* for all other words.

Our data generation process can be thought of as a form of *distant supervision* (Mintz et al., 2009) where we use agreed upon knowledge about an incident to label words contained within its sections instead of having hand-labeled individual words. This inevitably introduces errors which we try to mitigate using a filtration step where we remove ambiguous data.

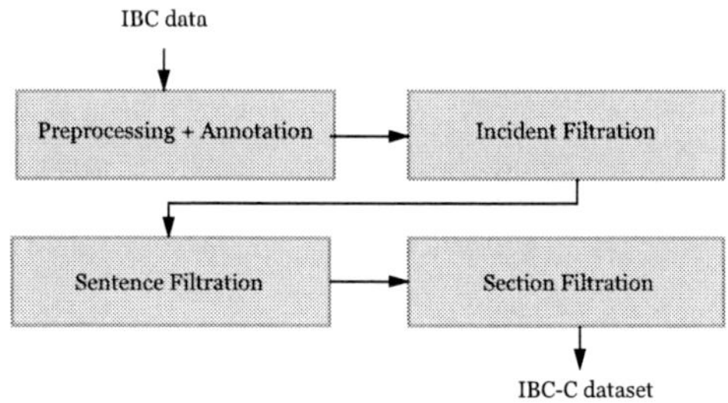

Figure 2: A visualisation of the different steps taken to create the dataset.

3.3 Filtration

Simply annotating words based on the information in Table 2 can lead to wrong annotations. For example, if two people were recorded as having died in an incident, then, if another number two appears in the same sentence, this might lead to a wrong annotation. The sentence, "2 civilians were killed after 2 rockets hit the compound" could lead to the second '2' being annotated as a KNUM. The actual *cardinality* of a number makes little difference to a sequence classifier compared to the difference a *misannotated* number would make. To minimise such misannotations we remove sentences and reports which do not pass all filtration criteria. Our filtration criteria consist of boolean functions over sentences, sections and incidents which return false if a test isn't passed.

The goal of filtration is to remove as much ambiguously labelled data as possible without biasing against any particular set of linguistic forms. There is thus a tradeoff which must be struck between linguistic richness and the quality of annotation.

In our case we found that simple combinations of pattern matching and semantic functions, as in 3, worked well. No syntactic functions were used.

3.3.1 Incident Filtration

Incidents are filtered using a single criterion: if the minimum number of people killed or injured does not equal the maximum number of people killed or injured, respectively, (Table 2) then the incident is removed. We do this so as to minimise any ambiguity in our named entity tagging (the only task for which we provide baseline results). This has the adverse effect of removing any incidents where reports mention different casualty counts. To compile a dataset which disregards this criterion, or considers a permissible window of casual-

hasKNUM	isKillSentence	hasOneTaggedAsKNUM	hasNumber	otherKNUMsInSection	toConsider	#
+	+	+	+	+	-	2,445
+	+	+	+	-	+	7,526
+	+	-	+	+	-	14,624
+	+	-	+	-	+	30,204
+	-	+	+	+	-	2,119
+	-	+	+	-	-	1,498
+	-	-	+	+	-	4,282
+	-	-	+	-	-	4,648
-	+	-	+	+	+	2,757
-	+	-	+	-	-	67,402
-	+	-	-	+	+	3,360
-	+	-	-	-	+	43,006
-	-	-	+	+	+	7,573
-	-	-	+	-	+	47,736
-	-	-	-	+	+	19,749
-	-	-	-	-	+	125,010

Table 3: Filtration criteria. An example of a set of boolean functions (columns one through five) applied to sentences to filter out ambiguous KNUM annotations. Sentences which we wish to allow are identified by a '+' in the *toConsider* column. Sentence counts are given in the last column. Only rows with non-zero counts are shown. Shaded rows indicate sentences which are ambiguous are shaded and identified by a '-'. We show only the KNUM table due to lack of space.

ties, a parameter in our dataset generating program may be changed.

3.3.2 Sentence Filtration

Filtering sentences is by far the hardest step. It is here where we must be careful to not bias against any linguistic forms. A separate set of boolean functions are applied to each sentence for the KNUM and INUM entity tags. An example for the KNUM tag can be seen in Table 3. Every sentence passes through four boolean functions (the first four columns) and is then labeled as either having passed or failed the test (fifth column). The fifth column was decided upon by us in advance.

In the case of Table 3: *hasKNUM* indicates whether the sentence contains a word tagged as KNUM; *isKillSentence* indicates whether any of its words are connected to death or killing (by matching them against a list of predefined words);

hasOneTaggedAsKNUM indicates whether the number '1' is tagged as a KNUM (remember that we convert written out numbers such as 'three' to '3' and that 'one', and thus '1', can also be a pronoun); *hasNumber* indicates whether a sentence has a number; and, *otherKNUMsInSection* indicates whether there are other words tagged as KNUM in the section.

3.3.3 Report Filtration

Report filtering is simple and again done using only one rule. If any sentence a report contains fails to pass a single sentence-level test, then the whole report is removed.

3.4 Tasks

3.4.1 Named Entity Recognition

Each word in the IBC-C dataset is tagged with one of nine (excluding *O*) entity tags as can be seen in Table 1 which can be thought of as subsets of more common named entity tags such as person or location. The dataset can be used to train a supervised NER model for conflict-specific named entity tags. This is important for relationship extraction which relies on good named entity tags.

3.4.2 Slot Filling and Relationship Extraction

Each IBC-C event can be thought of as a 9-slot *event* template where each slot is named after an entity tag. The important thing to keep in mind is that a report may contain more than one section so just correctly recognising the entities isn't enough to solve the slot filling task. Instead, if a report mentions two events then two separate templates must be created and their slots filled.

A common sub-problem of slot filling is relationship extraction. Because we know which incident every section refers to, generating ground-truth relationships is trivial because we may be sure that an entity which appears in one of the sections is related to every other entity in that same section. For example, finding a KSUB and a LOCATION means that we can build a *killed_in(KSUB, LOCATION)* relationship.

3.4.3 Event De-duplication

Since the IBC-C dataset preserves the links between sections and incidents it may be used as a ground-truth training set for training event de-duplication models.

	HMM			CRF 13-window			RNN 13-window		
Tag	Precision	Recall	**F1**	Precision	Recall	**F1**	Precision	Recall	**F1**
KNUM	0.63	0.86	**0.73**	0.91	0.94	**0.92**	0.90	0.85	**0.88**
INUM	0.50	0.39	**0.44**	0.95	0.93	**0.94**	0.87	0.91	**0.89**
KSUB	0.73	0.68	**0.70**	0.82	0.76	**0.79**	0.86	0.53	**0.66**
ISUB	0.00	0.00	**0.00**	0.89	0.24	**0.38**	0.80	0.06	**0.12**
KOTHER	0.39	0.19	**0.25**	0.83	0.54	**0.66**	0.41	0.36	**0.38**
IOTHER	0.00	0.00	**0.00**	0.80	0.61	**0.69**	0.55	0.50	**0.52**
LOCATION	0.75	0.70	**0.73**	0.85	0.77	**0.80**	0.86	0.70	**0.77**
DATE	0.75	0.64	**0.69**	0.75	0.64	**0.69**	0.41	0.30	**0.35**
WEAPON	0.98	0.89	**0.93**	0.98	0.90	**0.94**	0.97	0.87	**0.92**
Overall	0.57	0.53	**0.55**	0.88	0.73	**0.78**	0.74	0.57	**0.61**

Table 4: Results for various models

4 Experiments

Baseline results were computed for the named entity recognition task using an 80:20 tag split across sentences (we ignore report or section boundaries). We compare three different sequence-classification models as seen in Table 4: a Hidden Markov Model (Zhou and Su, 2002), a Conditional Random Field (McCallum and Li, 2003), and a Elman-style Recursive Neural Network similar to the one used in (Mesnil et al., 2013).

For the HMM we use bigram features in combination with the current word and the current base named entity features[2]. We trained the HMM in CRF form using LBFGS.

For the CRF we find that using bigram features and a 13-word window, across words and base named entities, gives us the best result. We train the CRF using LBFGS. All CRF training, including the HMM, was done using CRFSuite (Okazaki, 2007).

For the Elman-style recurrent network we use randomly initialised 100 dimensional word vectors as input, the network has 100 hidden units, and we use a 13-word context window again. The RNN was implemented using Theano (Bastien et al., 2012). We train the RNN using stochastic gradient descent on a single GPU.

4.1 Evaluation

The first thing which strikes us is how low the ISUB scores are. The CRF returns a recall score of 0.24. At the same time, the precision is relatively high at 0.89. Low recall indicates a lot of false negative classifications - i.e. there were many injured people who were mistakingly tagged as uninjured. A high precision rate means a low false positive rate - i.e. most uninjured people were correctly tagged as uninjured. In short, the classifier was too generous with tagging people as having been injured. Looking at the dataset we realise that in contrast to KSUBS, words which we associate with injury such as "wounded" or "injured" are often very far away from an ISUB. Increasing the window size with the CRF didn't help (such large features are often never expressed during the test phase).

Low recall scores across multiple tags indicate that long-distance dependencies determine a word's classification. K/INUM recall is exceptionally high because K/INUMs are usually surrounded by words such as "killed". We were surprised to see the RNN perform relatively poorly and expected it to be able to factor in long-distance dependencies. We believe this has more to do with our hyper-parameter settings than deficiencies in the actual model.

5 Conclusion

We present IBC-C, a new dataset for armed conflict analysis which can be used for entity recognition, slot filling, and incident de-duplication.

6 Acknowledgements

We would like to thank members of the IBC, especially Hamit Dardagan for his help with procuring and helping us understand the data collected by the IBC. We would also like to thank Gregory Chockler, Mike Spagat, and Andrew Evans for their insightful discussions and suggestions. This work was partially supported by EPSRC grant EP/K033344/1 ('Mining the Network Behaviour of Bots').

---

[2]Base named entities such as PERSON and LOCATION were found using Stanford's named entity recogniser (Finkel et al., 2005).

References

Frédéric Bastien, Pascal Lamblin, Razvan Pascanu, James Bergstra, Ian Goodfellow, Arnaud Bergeron, Nicolas Bouchard, David Warde-Farley, and Yoshua Bengio. 2012. Theano: new features and speed improvements. *arXiv preprint arXiv:1211.5590*.

Sven Chojnacki, Christian Ickler, Michael Spies, and John Wiesel. 2012. Event data on armed conflict and security: New perspectives, old challenges, and some solutions. *International Interactions*, 38(4):382–401.

Jenny Rose Finkel, Trond Grenager, and Christopher Manning. 2005. Incorporating non-local information into information extraction systems by gibbs sampling. In *Proceedings of the 43rd Annual Meeting on Association for Computational Linguistics*, pages 363–370. Association for Computational Linguistics.

Nils Petter Gleditsch, Peter Wallensteen, Mikael Eriksson, Margareta Sollenberg, and Håvard Strand. 2002. Armed conflict 1946-2001: A new dataset. *Journal of peace research*, 39(5):615–637.

GTD. 2015. Global terrorism database. `http://www.start.umd.edu/gtd`. (Accessed on 02/23/2016).

Madelyn Hsiao-Rei Hicks, Hamit Dardagan, Gabriela Guerrero Serdán, Peter M Bagnall, John A Sloboda, and Michael Spagat. 2011. Violent deaths of iraqi civilians, 2003–2008: analysis by perpetrator, weapon, time, and location. *PLoS Med*, 8(2):e1000415.

IBC. 2016. Iraq body count. `https://www.iraqbodycount.org/database/`. (Accessed on 02/23/2016).

Gary King and Will Lowe. 2003. An automated information extraction tool for international conflict data with performance as good as human coders. A rare events evaluation design. *International Organization*, 57(03):617–642.

Kalev Leetaru and Philip A Schrodt. 2013. Gdelt: Global data on events, location, and tone, 1979–2012. In *ISA Annual Convention*, volume 2. Citeseer.

Andrew McCallum and Wei Li. 2003. Early results for named entity recognition with conditional random fields, feature induction and web-enhanced lexicons. In *Proceedings of the seventh conference on Natural language learning at HLT-NAACL 2003-Volume 4*, pages 188–191. Association for Computational Linguistics.

Grégoire Mesnil, Xiaodong He, Li Deng, and Yoshua Bengio. 2013. Investigation of recurrent-neural-network architectures and learning methods for spoken language understanding. In *INTERSPEECH*, pages 3771–3775.

Mike Mintz, Steven Bills, Rion Snow, and Dan Jurafsky. 2009. Distant supervision for relation extraction without labeled data. In *Proceedings of the Joint Conference of the 47th Annual Meeting of the ACL and the 4th International Joint Conference on Natural Language Processing of the AFNLP: Volume 2-Volume 2*, pages 1003–1011. Association for Computational Linguistics.

Naoaki Okazaki. 2007. Crfsuite: a fast implementation of conditional random fields (crfs). (Accessed on 02/23/2016).

Sean P Obrien. 2010. Crisis early warning and decision support: Contemporary approaches and thoughts on future research. *International Studies Review*, 12(1):87–104.

Clionadh Raleigh, Andrew Linke, Håvard Hegre, and Joakim Karlsen. 2010. Introducing acled: An armed conflict location and event dataset special data feature. *Journal of peace research*, 47(5):651–660.

Philip A Schrodt, Omür Yilmaz, Deborah J Gerner, and Dennis Hermreck. 2008. The cameo (conflict and mediation event observations) actor coding framework. In *2008 Annual Meeting of the International Studies Association*.

Philip A Schrodt. 2001. Automated coding of international event data using sparse parsing techniques. In *annual meeting of the International Studies Association, Chicago*.

Philip A Schrodt. 2016. Open event data alliance (oeda). (Accessed on 02/23/2016).

Hristo Tanev, Jakub Piskorski, and Martin Atkinson. 2008. Real-time news event extraction for global crisis monitoring. In *Natural Language and Information Systems*, pages 207–218. Springer.

Nicholas Weller and Kenneth McCubbins. 2014. Open event data alliance (oeda)raining on the parade: Some cautions regarding the global database of events, language and tone dataset. (Accessed on 05/18/2016).

GuoDong Zhou and Jian Su. 2002. Named entity recognition using an hmm-based chunk tagger. In *proceedings of the 40th Annual Meeting on Association for Computational Linguistics*, pages 473–480. Association for Computational Linguistics.

A Latent Concept Topic Model for Robust Topic Inference
Using Word Embeddings

Weihua Hu[†] and Jun'ichi Tsujii[‡§]

[†]Department of Computer Science, The University of Tokyo, Japan
[‡]Artificial Intelligence Research Center, AIST, Japan
[§]School of Computer Science, The University of Manchester, UK
{hu, j-tsujii}@ms.k.u-tokyo.ac.jp, @aist.go.jp

Abstract

Uncovering thematic structures of SNS and blog posts is a crucial yet challenging task, because of the severe data sparsity induced by the short length of texts and diverse use of vocabulary. This hinders effective topic inference of traditional LDA because it infers topics based on document-level co-occurrence of words. To robustly infer topics in such contexts, we propose a latent concept topic model (LCTM). Unlike LDA, LCTM reveals topics via co-occurrence of *latent concepts*, which we introduce as latent variables to capture conceptual similarity of words. More specifically, LCTM models each topic as a distribution over the *latent concepts*, where each *latent concept* is a localized Gaussian distribution over the word embedding space. Since the number of unique concepts in a corpus is often much smaller than the number of unique words, LCTM is less susceptible to the data sparsity. Experiments on the 20Newsgroups show the effectiveness of LCTM in dealing with short texts as well as the capability of the model in handling held-out documents with a high degree of OOV words.

1 Introduction

Probabilistic topic models such as Latent Dirichlet allocation (LDA) (Blei et al., 2003), are widely used to uncover hidden topics within a text corpus. LDA models each document as a mixture of topics where each topic is a distribution over words. In essence, LDA reveals latent topics in a corpus by implicitly capturing document-level word co-occurrence patterns (Wang and McCallum, 2006).

In recent years, Social Networking Services and blogs have become increasingly prevalent due to the explosive growth of the Internet. Uncovering the themantic structures of these posts is crucial for tasks like market review, trend estimation (Asur and Huberman, 2010) and so on. However, compared to more conventional documents, such as news articles and academic papers, analyzing the thematic content of blog posts can be challenging, because of their typically short length and the use of diverse vocabulary by various authors. These factors can substantially decrease the chance of topically related words co-occurring in the same post, which in turn hinders effective topic inference in conventional topic models. Additionally, sometimes small corpus size can further exacerbate topic inference, since word co-occurrence statistics becomes more sparse as the number of documents decreases.

Recently, word embedding models, such as word2vec (Mikolov et al., 2013) and GloVe (Pennington et al., 2014) have gained much attention with their ability to form clusters of conceptually similar words in the embedding space. Inspired by this, we propose a latent concept topic model (LCTM) that infers topics based on document-level co-occurrence of references to the same *concept*. More specifically, we introduce a new latent variable, termed a *latent concept* to capture conceptual similarity of words, and redefine each topic as a distribution over the *latent concepts*. Each *latent concept* is then modeled as a localized Gaussian distribution over the embedding space. This is illustrated in Figure 1, where we denote the centers of the Gaussian distributions as *concept vectors*. We see that each *concept vector* captures a representative concept of surrounding words, and the Gaussian distributions model the small variation between the *latent concepts* and the actual use of words. Since the number of unique concepts that are referenced in a corpus is often much smaller than the number of unique

Proceedings of the 54th Annual Meeting of the Association for Computational Linguistics, pages 380–386,
Berlin, Germany, August 7-12, 2016. ©2016 Association for Computational Linguistics

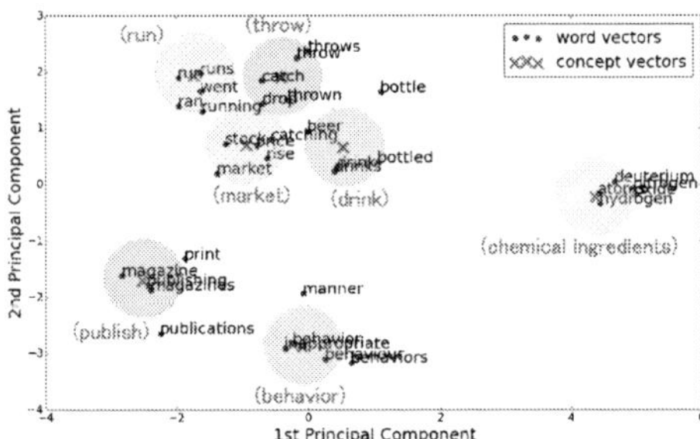

Figure 1: Projected *latent concepts* on the word embedding space. *Concept vectors* are annotated with their representative concepts in parentheses.

words, we expect topically-related *latent concepts* to co-occur many times, even in short texts with diverse usage of words. This in turn promotes topic inference in LCTM.

LCTM further has the advantage of using continuous word embedding. Traditional LDA assumes a fixed vocabulary of word types. This modeling assumption prevents LDA from handling *out of vocabulary* (OOV) words in held-out documents. On the other hands, since our topic model operates on the continuous vector space, it can naturally handle OOV words once their vector representation is provided.

The main contributions of our paper are as follows: We propose LCTM that infers topics via document-level co-occurrence patterns of *latent concepts*, and derive a collapsed Gibbs sampler for approximate inference. We show that LCTM can accurately represent short texts by outperforming conventional topic models in a clustering task. By means of a classification task, we furthermore demonstrate that LCTM achieves superior performance to other state-of-the-art topic models in handling documents with a high degree of OOV words.

The remainder of the paper is organized as follows: related work is summarized in Section 2, while LCTM and its inference algorithm are presented in Section 3. Experiments on the 20News-groups are presented in Section 4, and a conclusion is presented in Section 5.

2 Related Work

There have been a number of previous studies on topic models that incorporate word embeddings. The closest model to LCTM is Gaussian LDA

(Das et al., 2015), which models each topic as a Gaussian distribution over the word embedding space. However, the assumption that topics are unimodal in the embedding space is not appropriate, since topically related words such as 'neural' and 'networks' can occur distantly from each other in the embedding space. Nguyen et al. (2015) proposed topic models that incorporate information of word vectors in modeling topic-word distributions. Similarly, Petterson et al. (Petterson et al., 2010) exploits external word features to improve the Dirichlet prior of the topic-word distributions. However, both of the models cannot handle OOV words, because they assume fixed word types.

Latent concepts in LCTM are closely related to '*constraints*' in interactive topic models (ITM) (Hu et al., 2014). Both *latent concepts* and *constraints* are designed to group conceptually similar words using external knowledge in an attempt to aid topic inference. The difference lies in their modeling assumptions: *latent concepts* in LCTM are modeled as *Gaussian distributions* over the embedding space, while *constraints* in ITM are sets of conceptually similar words that are interactively identified by humans for each topic. Each *constraint* for each topic is then modeled as a *multinomial distribution* over the constrained set of words that were identified as mutually related by humans. In Section 4, we consider a variant of ITM, whose *constraints* are instead inferred using external word embeddings.

As regards short texts, a well-known topic model is Biterm Topic Model (BTM) (Yan et al., 2013). BTM directly models the generation of biterms (pairs of words) in the whole corpus. However, the assumption that pairs of co-occurring words should be assigned to the same topic might be too strong (Chen et al., 2015).

3 Latent Concept Topic Model

3.1 Generative Model

The primary difference between LCTM and the conventional topic models is that LCTM describes the generative process of word vectors in documents, rather than words themselves.

Suppose α and β are parameters for the Dirichlet priors and let $v_{d,i}$ denote the word embedding for a word type $w_{d,i}$. The generative model for LCTM is as follows.

1. For each topic k

    (a) Draw a topic *concept* distribution $\phi_k \sim$ Dirichlet(β).

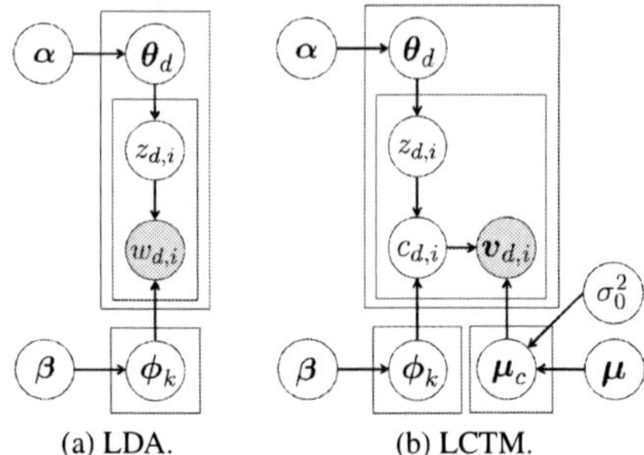

(a) LDA.   (b) LCTM.

Figure 2: Graphical representation.

2. For each *latent concept* c

    (a) Draw a *concept vector* $\boldsymbol{\mu}_c \sim \mathcal{N}(\boldsymbol{\mu}, \sigma_0^2 \boldsymbol{I})$.

3. For each document d

    (a) Draw a document topic distribution $\boldsymbol{\theta}_d \sim \text{Dirichlet}(\boldsymbol{\alpha})$.

    (b) For the i-th word $w_{d,i}$ in document d

        i. Draw its topic assignment $z_{d,i} \sim \text{Categorical}(\boldsymbol{\theta}_d)$.

        ii. Draw its *latent concept assignment* $c_{d,i} \sim \text{Categorical}(\boldsymbol{\phi}_{z_{d,i}})$.

        iii. Draw a word vector $\boldsymbol{v}_{d,i} \sim \mathcal{N}(\boldsymbol{\mu}_{c_{d,i}}, \sigma^2 \boldsymbol{I})$.

The graphical models for LDA and LCTM are shown in Figure 2. Compared to LDA, LCTM adds another layer of latent variables to indicate the conceptual similarity of words.

3.2 Posterior Inference

In our application, we observe documents consisting of word vectors and wish to infer posterior distributions over all the hidden variables. Since there is no analytical solution to the posterior, we derive a collapsed Gibbs sampler to perform approximate inference. During the inference, we sample a *latent concept* assignment as well as a topic assignment for each word in each document as follows:

$$p(z_{d,i} = k \mid c_{d,i} = c, \boldsymbol{z}^{-d,i}, \boldsymbol{c}^{-d,i}, \boldsymbol{v})$$
$$\propto \left(n_{d,k}^{-d,i} + \alpha_k \right) \cdot \frac{n_{k,c}^{-d,i} + \beta_c}{n_{k,\cdot}^{-d,i} + \sum_{c'} \beta_{c'}}, \qquad (1)$$

$$P(c_{d,i} = c \mid z_{d,i} = k, \boldsymbol{v}_{d,i}, \boldsymbol{z}^{-d,i}, \boldsymbol{c}^{-d,i}, \boldsymbol{v}^{-d,i})$$
$$\propto \left(n_{k,c}^{-d,i} + \beta_c \right) \cdot \mathcal{N}(\boldsymbol{v}_{d,i} \mid \overline{\boldsymbol{\mu}}_c, \sigma_c^2 \boldsymbol{I}), \qquad (2)$$

where $n_{d,k}$ is the number of words assigned to topic k in document d, and $n_{k,c}$ is the number of words assigned to both topic k and *latent concept* c. When an index is replaced by '$\cdot$', the number is obtained by summing over the index. The superscript $^{-d,i}$ indicates that the current assignments of $z_{d,i}$ and $c_{d,i}$ are ignored. $\mathcal{N}(\cdot \mid \boldsymbol{\mu}, \boldsymbol{\Sigma})$ is a multivariate Gaussian density function with mean $\boldsymbol{\mu}$ and covariance matrix $\boldsymbol{\Sigma}$. $\overline{\boldsymbol{\mu}}_c$ and σ_c^2 in Eq. (2) are parameters associated with the *latent concept* c and are defined as follows:

$$\overline{\boldsymbol{\mu}}_c = \frac{1}{\sigma^2 + n_{\cdot,c}^{-d,i} \sigma_0^2} \left(\sigma^2 \boldsymbol{\mu} + \sigma_0^2 \cdot \sum_{(d',i') \in A_c^{-d,i}} \boldsymbol{v}_{d',i'} \right), \qquad (3)$$

$$\sigma_c^2 = \left(1 + \frac{\sigma_0^2}{n_{\cdot,c}^{-d,i} \sigma_0^2 + \sigma^2} \right) \sigma^2, \qquad (4)$$

where $A_c^{-d,i} \equiv \{(d', i') \mid c_{d',i'} = c \wedge (d', i') \neq (d, i)\}$ (Murphy, 2012). Eq. (1) is similar to the collapsed Gibbs sampler of LDA (Griffiths and Steyvers, 2004) except that the second term of Eq. (1) is concerned with topic-*concept* distributions. Eq. (2) of sampling *latent concepts* has an intuitive interpretation: the first term encourages *concept* assignments that are consistent with the current topic assignment, while the second term encourages *concept* assignments that are consistent with the observed word. The Gaussian variance parameter σ^2 acts as a trade-off parameter between the two terms via σ_c^2. In Section 4.2, we study the effect of σ^2 on document representation.

3.3 Prediction of Topic Proportions

After the posterior inference, the posterior means of $\{\boldsymbol{\theta}_d\}, \{\boldsymbol{\phi}_k\}$ are straightforward to calculate:

$$\overline{\theta}_{d,k} = \frac{n_{d,k} + \alpha_k}{n_{d,\cdot} + \sum_{k'} \alpha_{k'}}, \quad \overline{\phi}_{k,c} = \frac{n_{k,c} + \beta_c}{n_{k,\cdot} + \sum_{c'} \beta_{c'}}. \qquad (5)$$

Also posterior means for $\{\boldsymbol{\mu}_c\}$ are given by Eq. (3). We can then use these values to predict a topic proportion $\boldsymbol{\theta}_{d_{\text{new}}}$ of an unseen document d_{new} using collapsed Gibbs sampling as follows:

$$p(z_{d_{\text{new}},i} = k \mid \boldsymbol{v}_{d_{\text{new}},i}, \boldsymbol{v}^{-d_{\text{new}},i}, \boldsymbol{z}^{-d_{\text{new}},i}, \overline{\boldsymbol{\phi}}, \overline{\boldsymbol{\mu}})$$
$$\propto \left(n_{d_{\text{new}},k}^{-d_{\text{new}},i} + \alpha_k \right) \cdot \sum_c \overline{\phi}_{k,c} \frac{\mathcal{N}(\boldsymbol{v}_{d_{\text{new}},i} \mid \overline{\boldsymbol{\mu}}_c, \sigma_c^2)}{\sum_{c'} \mathcal{N}(\boldsymbol{v}_{d_{\text{new}},i} \mid \overline{\boldsymbol{\mu}}_{c'}, \sigma_{c'}^2)}. \qquad (6)$$

The second term of Eq. (6) is a weighted average of $\overline{\phi}_{k,c}$ with respect to *latent concepts*. We see that more weight is given to the *concepts* whose corresponding vectors $\overline{\boldsymbol{\mu}}_c$ are closer to the word vector $\boldsymbol{v}_{d_{\text{new}},i}$. This to be expected because statistics of nearby *concepts* should give more information about the word. We also see from Eq. (6) that the

382

topic assignment of a word is determined by its embedding, instead of its word type. Therefore, LCTM can naturally handle OOV words once their embeddings are provided.

3.4 Reducing the Computational Complexity

From Eqs. (1) and (2), we see that the computational complexity of sampling per word is $\mathcal{O}(K + SD)$, where K, S and D are numbers of topics, *latent concepts* and embedding dimensions, respectively. Since $K \ll S$ holds in usual settings, the dominant computation involves the sampling of *latent concept*, which costs $\mathcal{O}(SD)$ computation per word.

However, since LCTM assumes that Gaussian variance σ^2 is relatively small, the chance of a word being assigned to distant *concepts* is negligible. Thus, we can reasonably assume that each word is assigned to one of $M \ll S$ nearest *concepts*. Hence, the computational complexity is reduced to $\mathcal{O}(MD)$. Since *concept vectors* can move slightly in the embedding space during the inference, we periodically update the nearest *concepts* for each word type.

To further reduce the computational complexity, we can apply dimensional reduction algorithms such as PCA and t-SNE (Van der Maaten and Hinton, 2008) to word embeddings to make D smaller. We leave this to future work.

4 Experiments

4.1 Datasets and Models Description

In this section, we study the empirical performance of LCTM on short texts. We used the 20Newsgroups corpus, which consists of discussion posts about various news subjects authored by diverse readers. Each document in the corpus is tagged with one of twenty newsgroups. Only posts with less than 50 words are extracted for training datasets. For external word embeddings, we used 50-dimensional GloVe[1] that were pre-trained on Wikipedia. The datasets are summarized in Table 1. See appendix A for the detail of the dataset preprocessing.

We compare the performance of the LCTM to the following six baselines:

- LFLDA (Nguyen et al., 2015), an extension of Latent Dirichlet Allocation that incorporates word embeddings information.

Dataset	Doc size	Vocab size	Avg len
400short	400	4729	31.87
800short	800	7329	31.78
1561short	1561	10644	31.83
held-out	7235	37944	140.15

Table 1: Summary of datasets.

- LFDMM (Nguyen et al., 2015), an extension of Dirichlet Multinomial Mixtures that incorporates word embeddings information.

- nI-cLDA, non-interactive constrained Latent Dirichlet Allocatoin, a variant of ITM (Hu et al., 2014), where *constraints* are inferred by applying k-means to external word embeddings. Each resulting word cluster is then regarded as a *constraint*. See appendix B for the detail of the model.

- GLDA (Das et al., 2015), Gaussian LDA.

- BTM (Yan et al., 2013), Biterm Topic Model.

- LDA (Blei et al., 2003).

In all the models, we set the number of topics to be 20. For LCTM (resp. nI-ITM), we set the number of *latent concepts* (resp. *constraints*) to be 1000. See appendix C for the detail of hyperparameter settings.

4.2 Document Clustering

To demonstrate that LCTM results in a superior representation of short documents compared to the baselines, we evaluated the performance of each model on a document clustering task. We used a learned topic proportion as a feature for each document and applied k-means to cluster the documents. We then compared the resulting clusters to the actual newsgroup labels. Clustering performance is measured by Adjusted Mutual Information (AMI) (Manning et al., 2008). Higher AMI indicates better clustering performance. Figure 3 illustrates the quality of clustering in terms of Gaussian variance parameter σ^2. We see that setting $\sigma^2 = 0.5$ consistently obtains good clustering performance for all the datasets with varying sizes. We therefore set $\sigma^2 = 0.5$ in the later evaluation. Figure 4 compares AMI on four topic models. We see that LCTM outperforms the topic models without word embeddings. Also, we see that LCTM performs comparable to LFLDA and nI-cLDA, both of which incorporate information of word embeddings to aid topic inference. However, as we will see in the next section, LCTM can

---

[1]Downloaded at
http://nlp.stanford.edu/projects/glove/

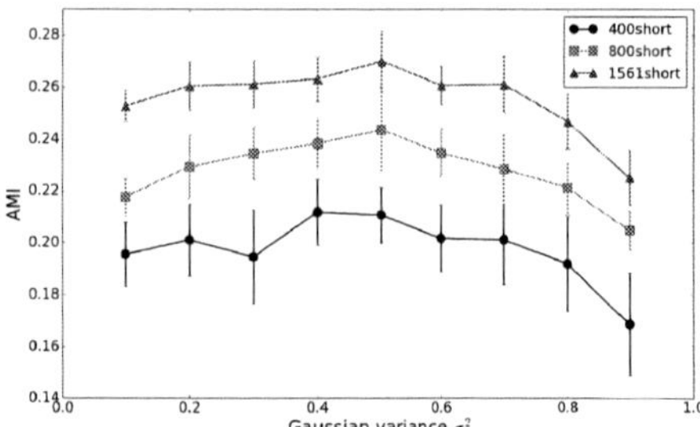

Figure 3: Relationship between σ^2 and AMI.

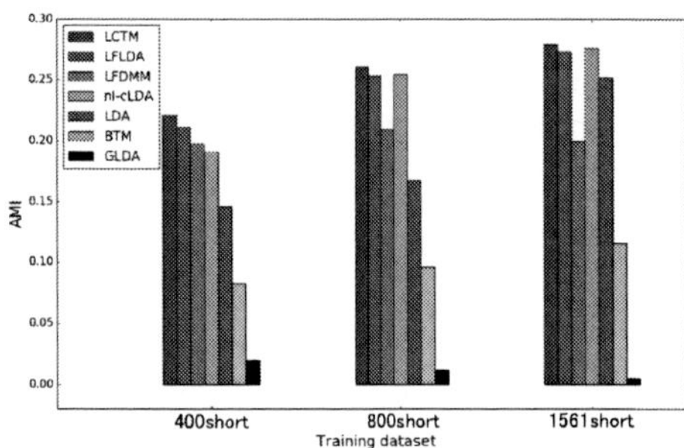

Figure 4: Comparisons on clustering performance of the topic models.

Training Set	400short	800short	1561short
OOV prop	0.348	0.253	0.181
Method	Classification Accuracy		
LCTM	**0.302**	**0.367**	**0.416**
LCTM-UNK	0.262	0.340	0.406
LFLDA	0.253	0.333	0.410
nI-cLDA	0.261	0.333	0.412
LDA	0.215	0.293	0.382
GLDA	0.0527	0.0529	0.0529
Chance Rate	0.0539	0.0539	0.0539

Table 2: Proportions of OOV words and classification accuracy in the held-out documents.

better handle OOV words in held-out documents than LFLDA and nl-cLDA do.

4.3 Representation of Held-out Documents with OOV words

To show that our model can better predict topic proportions of documents containing OOV words than other topic models, we conducted an experiment on a classification task. In particular, we infer topics from the training dataset and predicted topic proportions of held-out documents using collapsed Gibbs sampler. With the inferred topic proportions on both training dataset and held-out documents, we then trained a multi-class classifier (multi-class logistic regression implemented in sklearn[2] python module) on the training dataset and predicted newsgroup labels of the held-out documents.

We compared classification accuracy using LFLDA, nI-cLDA, LDA, GLDA, LCTM and a variant of LCTM (LCTM-UNK) that ignores OOV in the held-out documents. A higher classification accuracy indicates a better representation of unseen documents. Table 2 shows the proportion of OOV words and classification accuracy

[2]See http://scikit-learn.org/stable/.

of the held-out documents. We see that LCTM-UNK outperforms other topic models in almost every setting, demonstrating the superiority of our method, even when OOV words are ignored. However, the fact that LCTM outperforms LCTM-UNK in all cases clearly illustrates that LCTM can effectively make use of information about OOV to further improve the representation of unseen documents. The results show that the level of improvement of LCTM over LCTM-UNK increases as the proportion of OOV becomes greater.

5 Conclusion

In this paper, we have proposed LCTM that is well suited for application to short texts with diverse vocabulary. LCTM infers topics according to document-level co-occurrence patterns of *latent concepts*, and thus is robust to diverse vocabulary usage and data sparsity in short texts. We showed experimentally that LCTM can produce a superior representation of short documents, compared to conventional topic models. We additionally demonstrated that LCTM can exploit OOV to improve the representation of unseen documents. Although our paper has focused on improving performance of LDA by introducing the *latent concept* for each word, the same idea can be readily applied to other topic models that extend LDA.

Acknowledgments

We thank anonymous reviewers for their constructive feedback. We also thank Hideki Mima for helpful discussions and Paul Thompson for insightful reviews on the paper. This paper is based on results obtained from a project commissioned by the New Energy and Industrial Technology Development Organization (NEDO).

References

Sitaram Asur and Bernardo A Huberman. 2010. Predicting the future with social media. In *Web Intelligence and Intelligent Agent Technology (WI-IAT), 2010 IEEE/WIC/ACM International Conference on*, volume 1, pages 492–499. IEEE.

David M Blei, Andrew Y Ng, and Michael I Jordan. 2003. Latent Dirichlet allocation. *the Journal of machine Learning research*, 3:993–1022.

Weizheng Chen, Jinpeng Wang, Yan Zhang, Hongfei Yan, and Xiaoming Li. 2015. User based aggregation for biterm topic model. *Proceedings of the 53rd Annual Meeting of the Association for Computational Linguistics*, 2:489–494.

Rajarshi Das, Manzil Zaheer, and Chris Dyer. 2015. Gaussian LDA for topic models with word embeddings. In *Proceedings of the 53nd Annual Meeting of the Association for Computational Linguistics*, pages 795–804.

Thomas L Griffiths and Mark Steyvers. 2004. Finding scientific topics. *Proceedings of the National Academy of Sciences*, 101(suppl 1):5228–5235.

Yuening Hu, Jordan L. Boyd-Graber, Brianna Satinoff, and Alison Smith. 2014. Interactive topic modeling. *Machine Learning*, 95(3):423–469.

Christopher D Manning, Prabhakar Raghavan, Hinrich Schütze, et al. 2008. *Introduction to information retrieval*, volume 1. Cambridge university press Cambridge.

Tomas Mikolov, Kai Chen, Greg Corrado, and Jeffrey Dean. 2013. Efficient estimation of word representations in vector space. *arXiv preprint arXiv:1301.3781*.

Kevin P Murphy. 2012. *Machine learning: a probabilistic perspective*. MIT press.

Dat Quoc Nguyen, Richard Billingsley, Lan Du, and Mark Johnson. 2015. Improving topic models with latent feature word representations. *Transactions of the Association for Computational Linguistics*, 3:299–313.

Jeffrey Pennington, Richard Socher, and Christopher D Manning. 2014. GloVe: Global vectors for word representation. In *EMNLP*, volume 14, pages 1532–1543.

James Petterson, Wray Buntine, Shravan M Narayanamurthy, Tibério S Caetano, and Alex J Smola. 2010. Word features for latent Dirichlet allocation. In *Advances in Neural Information Processing Systems*, pages 1921–1929.

Laurens Van der Maaten and Geoffrey Hinton. 2008. Visualizing data using t-SNE. *Journal of Machine Learning Research*, 9(2579-2605):85.

Xuerui Wang and Andrew McCallum. 2006. Topics over time: a non-Markov continuous-time model of topical trends. In *Proceedings of the 12th ACM SIGKDD international conference on Knowledge discovery and data mining*, pages 424–433. ACM.

Xiaohui Yan, Jiafeng Guo, Yanyan Lan, and Xueqi Cheng. 2013. A biterm topic model for short texts. In *Proceedings of the 22nd international conference on World Wide Web*, pages 1445–1456. International World Wide Web Conferences Steering Committee.

A Dataset Preprocessing

We preprocessed the 20Newsgroups as follows: We downloaded bag-of-words representation of the corpus available online[3]. Stop words[4] and words that were not covered in the GloVe were both removed. After the preprocessing, we extracted short texts containing less than 50 words for training datasets. We created three training datasets with varying numbers of documents, and one held-out dataset. Each dataset was balanced in terms of the proportion of documents belonging to each newsgroup.

B Non-Interactive Contained LDA (nI-cLDA)

We describe nI-cLDA, a variant of interactive topic model (Hu et al., 2014). nI-cLDA is non-interactive in the sense that *constraints* are inferred from the word embeddings instead of being interactively identified by humans. In particular, we apply k-means to word embeddings to cluster words. Each resulting cluster is then regarded as a *constraint*. In general, *constraints* can be different from topic to topic. Let $r_{k,w}$ be a *constraint* of topic k which word w belongs to. The generative process of nI-cLDA is as follows. It is essentially the same as (Hu et al., 2014)

1. For each topic k
   (a) Draw a topic *constraint* distribution $\phi_k \sim \text{Dirichlet}(\beta)$.
   (b) For each *constraint* s of topic k
       i. Draw a *constraint* word distribution $\pi_{k,s} \sim \text{Dirichlet}(\gamma)$.
2. For each document d
   (a) Draw a document topic distribution $\theta_d \sim \text{Dirichlet}(\alpha)$.
   (b) For the i-th word $w_{d,i}$ in document d
       i. Draw its topic assignment $z_{d,i} \sim \text{Categorical}(\theta_d)$.

---

[3] http://qwone.com/~jason/20Newsgroups/
[4] Available at http://www.nltk.org/

    ii. Draw its *constraint* $l_{d,i}$ $\sim$ Categorical$(\phi_{z_{d,i}})$.

    iii. Draw a word $w_{d,i}$ $\sim$ Categorical$(\pi_{z_{d,i},l_{d,i}})$.

Let V be the set of vocabulary. We note that $\pi_{k,s}$ is a multinomial distribution over $W_{k,s}$, which is a subset of V, defined as $W_{k,s} \equiv \{w \in V \mid r_{k,w} = s\}$. $W_{k,s}$ represents a constrained set of words that are conceptually related to each other under topic k.

In our application, we observe documents and *constraints* for each topic, and wish to infer posterior distributions over all the hidden variables. We apply collapsed Gibbs sampling for the approximate inference. For the detail of the inference, see (Hu et al., 2014).

C Hyperparameter Settings

For all the topic models, we used symmetric Dirichlet priors. The hyperparameters were set as follows: for our model (LCTM and LCTM-UNK), nl-cLDA and LDA, we set $\alpha = 0.1$ and $\beta = 0.01$. For nl-cLDA, we set the parameter of Dirichlet prior for *constraint*-word distribution (γ in appendix B) as 0.1. Also for our model, we set, $\sigma_0^2 = 1.0$ and μ to be the average of word vectors. We randomly initialized the topic assignments in all the models. Also, we initialized the *latent concept* assignments using k-means clustering on the word embeddings. The k-means clustering was implemented using sklearn[5] python module. We set M (number of nearest *concepts* to sample from) to be 300, and updated the nearest *concepts* every 5 iterations. For LFLDA, LFDMM, BTM and Gaussian LDA, we used the original implementations available online[6] and retained the default hyperparameters.

We ran all the topic models for 1500 iterations for training, and 500 iterations for predicting held-out documents.

---

[5] See http://scikit-learn.org/stable/.

[6] **LFTM**: https://github.com/datquocnguyen/LFTM
BTM: https://github.com/xiaohuiyan/BTM
GLDA: https://github.com/rajarshd/Gaussian_LDA

Word Embeddings with Limited Memory

Shaoshi Ling[1] **and Yangqiu Song**[2] **and Dan Roth**[1]
[1]Department of Computer Science, University of Illinois at Urbana-Champaign
[2]Department of Computer Science and Engineering, HKUST
[1]{sling3,danr}@illinois.edu, [2]yqsong@gmail.com

Abstract

This paper studies the effect of limited precision data representation and computation on word embeddings. We present a systematic evaluation of word embeddings with limited memory and discuss methods that directly train the limited precision representation with limited memory. Our results show that it is possible to use and train an 8-bit fixed-point value for word embedding without loss of performance in word/phrase similarity and dependency parsing tasks.

1 Introduction

There is an accumulation of evidence that the use of dense distributional lexical representations, known as *word embeddings*, often supports better performance on a range of NLP tasks (Bengio et al., 2003; Turian et al., 2010; Collobert et al., 2011; Mikolov et al., 2013a; Mikolov et al., 2013b; Levy et al., 2015). Consequently, word embeddings have been commonly used in the last few years for lexical similarity tasks and as features in multiple, syntactic and semantic, NLP applications.

However, keeping embedding vectors for hundreds of thousands of words for repeated use could take its toll both on storing the word vectors on disk and, even more so, on loading them into memory. For example, for 1 million words, loading 200 dimensional vectors takes up to 1.6 GB memory on a 64-bit system. Considering applications that make use of billions of tokens and multiple languages, size issues impose significant limitations on the practical use of word embeddings.

This paper presents the question of whether it is possible to significantly reduce the memory needs for the use and training of word embeddings.

Specifically, we ask "what is the impact of representing each dimension of a dense representation with significantly fewer bits than the standard 64 bits?" Moreover, we investigate the possibility of directly *training* dense embedding vectors using significantly fewer bits than typically used.

The results we present are quite surprising. We show that it is possible to reduce the memory consumption by an order of magnitude both when word embeddings are being used and in training. In the first case, as we show, simply truncating the resulting representations after training and using a smaller number of bits (as low as 4 bits per dimension) results in comparable performance to the use of 64 bits. Moreover, we provide two ways to train existing algorithms (Mikolov et al., 2013a; Mikolov et al., 2013b) when the memory is limited during training and show that, here, too, an order of magnitude saving in memory is possible without degrading performance. We conduct comprehensive experiments on existing word and phrase similarity and relatedness datasets as well as on dependency parsing, to evaluate these results. Our experiments show that, in all cases and without loss in performance, 8 bits can be used when the current standard is 64 and, in some cases, only 4 bits per dimension are sufficient, reducing the amount of space required by a factor of 16. The truncated word embeddings are available from the papers web page at https://cogcomp.cs.illinois.edu/page/publication_view/790.

2 Related Work

If we consider traditional cluster encoded word representation, e.g., Brown clusters (Brown et al., 1992), it only uses a small number of bits to track the path on a hierarchical tree of word clusters to represent each word. In fact, word embedding

Proceedings of the 54th Annual Meeting of the Association for Computational Linguistics, pages 387–392,
Berlin, Germany, August 7-12, 2016. ©2016 Association for Computational Linguistics

generalized the idea of discrete clustering representation to continuous vector representation in language models, with the goal of improving the continuous word analogy prediction and generalization ability (Bengio et al., 2003; Mikolov et al., 2013a; Mikolov et al., 2013b). However, it has been proven that Brown clusters as discrete features are even better than continuous word embedding as features for named entity recognition tasks (Ratinov and Roth, 2009). Guo et al. (Guo et al., 2014) further tried to binarize embeddings using a threshold tuned for each dimension, and essentially used less than two bits to represent each dimension. They have shown that binarization can be comparable to or even better than the original word embeddings when used as features for named entity recognition tasks. Moreover, Faruqui et al. (Faruqui et al., 2015) showed that imposing sparsity constraints over the embedding vectors can further improve the representation interpretability and performance on several word similarity and text classification benchmark datasets. These works indicate that, for some tasks, we do not need all the information encoded in "standard" word embeddings. Nonetheless, it is clear that binarization loses a lot of information, and this calls for a systematic comparison of how many bits are needed to maintain the expressivity needed from word embeddings for different tasks.

3 Value Truncation

In this section, we introduce approaches for word embedding when the memory is limited. We truncate any value x in the word embedding into an n bit representation.

3.1 Post-processing Rounding

When the word embedding vectors are given, the most intuitive and simple way is to round the numbers to their n-bit precision. Then we can use the truncated values as features for any tasks that word embedding can be used for. For example, if we want to round x to be in the range of $[-r, r]$, a simple function can be applied as follows.

$$R_d(x, n) = \begin{cases} \lfloor x \rfloor & \text{if } \lfloor x \rfloor \le x \le \lfloor x \rfloor + \frac{\epsilon}{2} \\ \lfloor x \rfloor + \epsilon & \text{if } \lfloor x \rfloor + \frac{\epsilon}{2} < x \le \lfloor x \rfloor + \epsilon \end{cases}$$
$$(1)$$

where $\epsilon = 2^{1-n}r$. For example, if we want to use 8 bits to represent any value in the vectors, then we only have 256 numbers ranging from -128 to 127

for each value. In practice, we first scale all the values and then round them to the 256 numbers.

3.2 Training with Limited Memory

When the memory for training word embedding is also limited, we need to modify the training algorithms by introducing new data structures to reduce the bits used to encode the values. In practice, we found that in the stochastic gradient descent (SGD) iteration in word2vec algorithms (Mikolov et al., 2013a; Mikolov et al., 2013b), the updating vector's values are often very small numbers (e.g., $< 10^{-5}$). In this case, if we directly apply the rounding method to certain precisions (e.g., 8 bits), the update of word vectors will always be zero. For example, the 8-bit precision is $2^{-7} = 0.0078$, so 10^{-5} is not significant enough to update the vector with 8-bit values. Therefore, we consider the following two ways to improve this.

Stochastic Rounding. We first consider using stochastic rounding (Gupta et al., 2015) to train word embedding. Stochastic rounding introduces some randomness into the rounding mechanism, which has been proven to be helpful when there are many parameters in the learning system, such as deep learning systems (Gupta et al., 2015). Here we also introduce this approach to update word embedding vectors in SGD. The probability of rounding x to $\lfloor x \rfloor$ is proportional to the proximity of x to $\lfloor x \rfloor$:

$$R_s(x, n) = \begin{cases} \lfloor x \rfloor & \text{w.p. } 1 - \frac{x - \lfloor x \rfloor}{\epsilon} \\ \lfloor x \rfloor + \epsilon & \text{w.p. } \frac{x - \lfloor x \rfloor}{\epsilon} \end{cases} .$$
$$(2)$$

In this case, even though the update values are not significant enough to update the word embedding vectors, we randomly choose some of the values being updated proportional to the value of how close the update value is to the rounding precision.

Auxiliary Update Vectors. In addition to the method of directly applying rounding to the values, we also provide a method using auxiliary update vectors to trade precision for more space. Suppose we know the range of update value in SGD as $[-r', r']$, and we use additional m bits to store all the values less than the limited numerical precision ϵ. Here r' can be easily estimated by running SGD for several examples. Then the real precision is $\epsilon' = 2^{1-m}r'$. For example, if $r' = 10^{-4}$ and $m = 8$, then the numerical precision is $7.8 \cdot 10^{-7}$ which can capture much higher precision than the SGD update values have. When

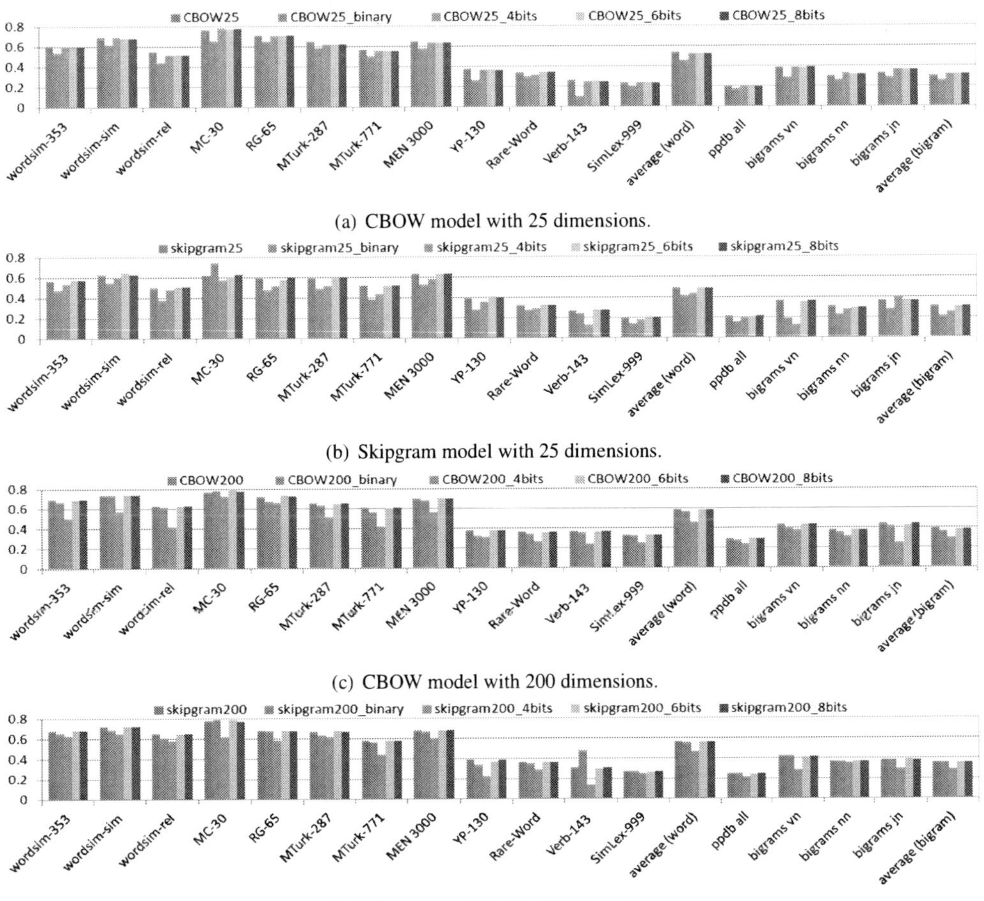

(a) CBOW model with 25 dimensions.

(b) Skipgram model with 25 dimensions.

(c) CBOW model with 200 dimensions.

(d) Skipgram model with 200 dimensions.

Figure 1: **Comparing performance on multiple similarity tasks, with different values of truncation**. The y-axis represents the Spearman's rank correlation coefficient for word similarity datasets, and the cosine value for paraphrase (bigram) datasets (see Sec. 4.2).

the cumulated values in the auxiliary update vectors are greater than the original numerical precision ϵ, e.g., $\epsilon = 2^{-7}$ for 8 bits, we update the original vector and clear the value in the auxiliary vector. In this case, we can have final n-bit values in word embedding vectors as good as the method presented in Section 3.1.

4 Experiments on Word/Phrase Similarity

In this section, we describe a comprehensive study on tasks that have been used for evaluating word embeddings. We train the word embedding algorithms, word2vec (Mikolov et al., 2013a; Mikolov et al., 2013b), based on the Oct. 2013 Wikipedi-

a dump.[1] We first compare levels of truncation of word2vec embeddings, and then evaluate the stochastic rounding and the auxiliary vectors based methods for training word2vec vectors.

4.1 Datasets

We use multiple test datasets as follows.

Word Similarity. Word similarity datasets have been widely used to evaluate word embedding results. We use the datasets summarized by Faruqui and Dyer (Faruqui and Dyer, 2014): wordsim-353, wordsim-sim, wordsim-rel, MC-30, RG-65, MTurk-287, MTurk-771, MEN 3000, YP-130, Rare-Word, Verb-143, and SimLex-999.[2] We compute the similarities between pairs of words

[1] https://dumps.wikimedia.org/
[2] http://www.wordvectors.org/

Table 1: **The detailed average results for word similarity and paraphrases of Fig. 1.**

Average	CBOW					Skipgram				
	Original	Binary	4-bits	6-bits	8-bits	Original	Binary	4-bits	6-bits	8-bits
wordsim (25)	0.5331	0.4534	0.5223	0.5235	0.5242	0.4894	0.4128	0.4333	0.4877	0.4906
wordsim (200)	0.5818	0.5598	0.4542	0.5805	0.5825	0.5642	0.5588	0.4681	0.5621	0.5637
bigram (25)	0.3023	0.2553	0.3164	0.3160	0.3153	0.3110	0.2146	0.2498	0.3050	0.3082
bigram (200)	0.3864	0.3614	0.2954	0.3802	0.3858	0.3565	0.3562	0.2868	0.3529	0.3548

and check the Spearman's rank correlation coefficient (Myers and Well., 1995) between the computer and the human labeled ranks.

Paraphrases (bigrams). We use the paraphrase (bigram) datasets used in (Wieting et al., 2015), ppdb_all, bigrams_vn, bigrams_nn, and bigrams_jnn, to test whether the truncation affects phrase level embedding. Our phrase level embedding is based on the average of the words inside each phrase. Note that it is also easy to incorporate our truncation methods into existing phrase embedding algorithms. We follow (Wieting et al., 2015) in using cosine similarity to evaluate the correlation between the computed similarity and annotated similarity between paraphrases.

4.2 Analysis of Bits Needed

We ran both CBOW and skipgram with negative sampling (Mikolov et al., 2013a; Mikolov et al., 2013b) on the Wikipedia dump data, and set the window size of context to be five. Then we performed value truncation with 4 bits, 6 bits, and 8 bits. The results are shown in Fig. 1, and the numbers of the averaged results are shown in Table 1. We also used the binarization algorithm (Guo et al., 2014) to truncate each dimension to three values; these experiments are is denoted using the suffix "binary" in the figure. For both CBOW and skipgram models, we train the vectors with 25 and 200 dimensions respectively.

The representations used in our experiments were trained using the whole Wikipedia dump. A first observation is that, in general, CBOW performs better than the skipgram model. When using the truncation method, the memory required to store the embedding is significantly reduced, while the performance on the test datasets remains almost the same until we truncate down to 4 bits. When comparing CBOW and skipgram models, we again see that the drop in performance with 4-bit values for the skipgram model is greater than the one for the CBOW model. For the CBOW model, the drop in performance with 4-bit values is greater when using 200 dimensions than it is when using 25 dimensions. However, when using skipgram, this drop is slightly greater when using 25 dimensions than 200.

We also evaluated the binarization approach (Guo et al., 2014). This model uses three values, represented using two bits. We observe that, when the dimension is 25, the binarization is worse than truncation. One possible explanation has to do merely with the size of the space; while 3^{25} is much larger than the size of the word space, it does not provide enough redundancy to exploit similarity as needed in the tasks. Consequently, the binarization approach results in worse performance. However, when the dimension is 200, this approach works much better, and outperforms the 4-bit truncation. In particular, binarization works better for skipgram than for CBOW with 200 dimensions. One possible explanation is that the binarization algorithm computes, for each dimension of the word vectors, the positive and negative means of the values and uses it to split the original values in that dimension, thus behaving like a model that clusters the values in each dimension. The success of the binarization then indicates that skipgram embeddings might be more discriminative than CBOW embeddings.

4.3 Comparing Training Methods

We compare the training methods for the CBOW model in Table 2. For stochastic rounding, we scale the probability of rounding up to make sure that small gradient values will still update the values. Both stochastic rounding and truncation with auxiliary update vectors (shown in Sec. 3.2) require 16 bits for each value in the training phase. Truncation with auxiliary update vectors finally produces 8-bit-value based vectors while stochastic rounding produces 16-bit-value based vectors. Even though our auxiliary update algorithm uses smaller memory/disk to store vectors, its performance is still better than that of stochastic rounding. This is simply because the update values in SGD are too small to allow the stochastic round-

Table 2: **Comparing the training CBOW models**: We set the average value of the original word2vec embeddings to be 1, and the values in the table are relative to the original embeddings baselines. "avg. (w.)" represents the average values of all word similarity datasets. "avg. (b.)" represents the average values of all bigram phrase similarity datasets. "Stoch. (16 b.)" represents the method using stochastic rounding applied to 16-bit precision. "Trunc. (8 b.)" represents the method using truncation with 8-bit auxiliary update vectors applied to 8-bit precision.

		Stoch. (16 b.)	Trunc. (8 b.)
25	avg. (w.)	0.990	0.997
dim	avg. (b.)	0.966	0.992
200	avg. (w.)	0.994	1.001
dim	avg. (b.)	0.991	0.999

ing method to converge. Auxiliary update vectors achieve very similar results to the original vectors, and, in fact, result in almost the same vectors as produced by the original truncation method.

5   Experiments on Dependency Parsing

We also incorporate word embedding results into a downstream task, dependency parsing, to evaluate whether the truncated embedding results are still good features compared to the original features. We follow the setup of (Guo et al., 2015) in a monolingual setting[3]. We train the parser with 5,000 iterations using different truncation settings for word2vec embedding. The data used to train and evaluate the parser is the English data in the CoNLL-X shared task (Buchholz and Marsi, 2006). We follow (Guo et al., 2015) in using the labeled attachment score (LAS) to evaluate the different parsing results. Here we only show the word embedding results for 200 dimensions, since empirically we found 25-dimension results were not as stable as 200 dimensions.

The results shown in Table 3 for dependency parsing are consistent with word similarity and paraphrasing. First, we see that binarization for CBOW and skipgram is again better than the truncation approach. Second, for truncation results, more bits leads to better results. With 8-bits, we can again obtain results similar to those obtained

---

[3] https://github.com/jiangfeng1124/acl15-clnndep

Table 3: **Evaluation results for dependency parsing (in LAS).**

Bits	CBOW	Skipgram
Original	88.58%	88.15%
Binary	89.25%	88.41%
4-bits	87.56%	86.46%
6-bits	88.62%	87.98%
8-bits	88.63%	88.16%

from the original word2vec embedding.

6   Conclusion

We systematically evaluated how small can the representation size of dense word embedding be before it starts to impact the performance of NLP tasks that use them. We considered both the final size of the size we provide it while learning it. Our study considers both the CBOW and the skipgram models at 25 and 200 dimensions and showed that 8 bits per dimension (and sometimes even less) are sufficient to represent each value and maintain performance on a range of lexical tasks. We also provided two ways to train the embeddings with reduced memory use. The natural future step is to extend these experiments and study the impact of the representation size on more advanced tasks.

Acknowledgment

The authors thank Shyam Upadhyay for his help with the dependency parser embeddings results, and Eric Horn for his help with this write-up. This work was supported by DARPA under agreement numbers HR0011-15-2-0025 and FA8750-13-2-0008. The U.S. Government is authorized to reproduce and distribute reprints for Governmental purposes notwithstanding any copyright notation thereon. The views and conclusions contained herein are those of the authors and should not be interpreted as necessarily representing the official policies or endorsements, either expressed or implied, of any of the organizations that supported the work.

References

Yoshua Bengio, Réjean Ducharme, Pascal Vincent, and Christian Janvin. 2003. A neural probabilistic language model. *Journal of Machine Learning Researc*, 3:1137–1155.

Peter F. Brown, Vincent J. Della Pietra, Peter V. de Souza, Jennifer C. Lai, and Robert L. Mercer.

1992. Class-based n-gram models of natural language. *Computational Linguistics*, 18(4):467–479.

Sabine Buchholz and Erwin Marsi. 2006. Conll-x shared task on multilingual dependency parsing. In *CoNLL*, pages 149–164.

Ronan Collobert, Jason Weston, Léon Bottou, Michael Karlen, Koray Kavukcuoglu, and Pavel P. Kuksa. 2011. Natural language processing (almost) from scratch. *Journal of Machine Learning Research*, 12:2493–2537.

Manaal Faruqui and Chris Dyer. 2014. Improving vector space word representations using multilingual correlation. In *EACL*, pages 462–471.

Manaal Faruqui, Yulia Tsvetkov, Dani Yogatama, Chris Dyer, and Noah A. Smith. 2015. Sparse overcomplete word vector representations. In *ACL*, pages 1491–1500.

Jiang Guo, Wanxiang Che, Haifeng Wang, and Ting Liu. 2014. Revisiting embedding features for simple semi-supervised learning. In *EMNLP*, pages 110–120.

Jiang Guo, Wanxiang Che, David Yarowsky, Haifeng Wang, and Ting Liu. 2015. Cross-lingual dependency parsing based on distributed representations. In *ACL*, pages 1234–1244.

Suyog Gupta, Ankur Agrawal, Kailash Gopalakrishnan, and Pritish Narayanan. 2015. Deep learning with limited numerical precision. In *ICML*, pages 1737–1746.

Omer Levy, Yoav Goldberg, and Ido Dagan. 2015. Improving distributional similarity with lessons learned from word embeddings. *TACL*, 3:211–225.

Tomas Mikolov, Ilya Sutskever, Kai Chen, Greg S. Corrado, and Jeff Dean. 2013a. Distributed representations of words and phrases and their compositionality. In *NIPS*, pages 3111–3119.

Tomas Mikolov, Wen-tau Yih, and Geoffrey Zweig. 2013b. Linguistic regularities in continuous space word representations. In *NAACL-HLT*, pages 746–751.

Jerome L. Myers and Arnold D. Well. 1995. *Research Design & Statistical Analysisn*. Routledge.

Lev Ratinov and Dan Roth. 2009. Design challenges and misconceptions in named entity recognition. In *Proceedings of CoNLL-09*, pages 147–155.

Joseph Turian, Lev-Arie Ratinov, and Yoshua Bengio. 2010. Word representations: A simple and general method for semi-supervised learning. In *ACL*, pages 384–394.

John Wieting, Mohit Bansal, Kevin Gimpel, and Karen Livescu. 2015. From paraphrase database to compositional paraphrase model and back. *TACL*, 3:345–358.

Hawkes Processes for Continuous Time Sequence Classification: an Application to Rumour Stance Classification in Twitter

Michal Lukasik,[1] P.K. Srijith,[1] Duy Vu,[2]
Kalina Bontcheva,[1] Arkaitz Zubiaga[3] and Trevor Cohn[2]
[1]Department of Computer Science, The University of Sheffield
[2]Department of Computing and Information Systems, The University of Melbourne
[3]Department of Computer Science, The University of Warwick
{m.lukasik, pk.srijith, k.bontcheva}@shef.ac.uk
{duy.vu, t.cohn}@unimelb.edu.au a.zubiaga@warwick.ac.uk

Abstract

Classification of temporal textual data sequences is a common task in various domains such as social media and the Web. In this paper we propose to use Hawkes Processes for classifying sequences of temporal textual data, which exploit both temporal and textual information. Our experiments on rumour stance classification on four Twitter datasets show the importance of using the temporal information of tweets along with the textual content.

1 Introduction

Sequence classification tasks are often associated with temporal information, where the timestamp is available for each of the data instances. For instance, in sentiment classification of reviews in forums, opinions of users are associated with a timestamp, indicating the time at which they were posted. Similarly, in an event detection task in Twitter, tweets being posted on a continuous basis need to be analysed and classified in order to detect the occurrence of some event. Nevertheless, traditional sequence classification approaches (Song et al., 2014; Gorrell and Bontcheva, 2016) ignore the time information in these textual data sequences. In this paper, we aim to consider the continuous time information along with the textual information for classifying sequences of temporal textual data. In particular, we consider the problem of rumour stance classification in Twitter, where tweets provide temporal information associated with the textual tweet content.

Rumours spread rapidly through social media, creating widespread chaos, increasing anxiety in society and in some cases even leading to riots. For instance, during an earthquake in Chile in 2010, rumours circulating on Twitter stated that a volcano had become active and there was a tsunami warning, which were later proven false. Denials and corrections of these viral pieces of information might often come late and without the sufficient effect to prevent the harm that the rumours can produce (Lewandowsky et al., 2012). This posits the importance of carefully analysing tweets associated with rumours and the stance expressed in them to prevent the spread of malicious rumours. Determining the stance of rumour tweets can in turn be effectively used for early detection of the spread of rumours, as well as for flagging rumours as being potentially false when a large number of people are found to be countering them. The rumour stance classification task has been previously defined as that in which a classifier needs to determine whether each of the tweets is *supporting*, *denying* or *questioning* a rumour (Qazvinian et al., 2011). Here we add a fourth label, *commenting*, which is assigned to tweets that do not add anything to the veracity of a rumour.

In this paper, we propose to use Hawkes Processes (Hawkes, 1971), commonly used for modelling information diffusion in social media (Yang and Zha, 2013; De et al., 2015), for the task of rumour stance classification. Hawkes Processes (HP) are a self-exciting temporal point process ideal for modelling the occurrence of tweets in Twitter (Zhao et al., 2015). The model assumes that the occurrence of a tweet will influence the rate at which future tweets will arrive. Figure 1 shows the behaviour of the intensity functions associated with a multivariate Hawkes Process. Note the intensity spikes at the points of tweet occurrences. In applications such as stance classification, different labels can influence one another. This can be modelled effectively using the mutually exciting behaviour of Hawkes Processes. In the end, we demonstrate how the information gar-

Proceedings of the 54th Annual Meeting of the Association for Computational Linguistics, pages 393–398,
Berlin, Germany, August 7-12, 2016. ©2016 Association for Computational Linguistics

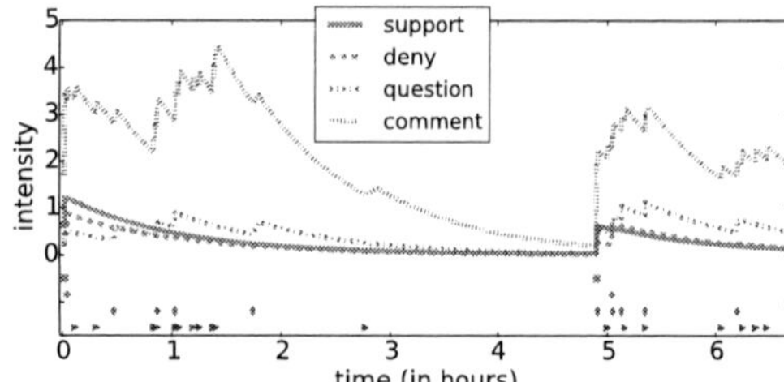

Figure 1: Intensities of the Hawkes Process for an example Ferguson rumour. Tweet occurrences over time are denoted at the bottom of the figure by different symbols. Intensity for comments is high throughout the rumour lifespan.

nered from rumour dynamics can be beneficial to stance classification of tweets around rumours.

Little work has been done on stance classification of rumour tweets. Qazvinian et al. (2011) introduced a system for classifying rumour tweets and Lukasik et al. (2015a) considered this problem in a setting where the tweets associated with a new emerging rumour is the target for classification. Both works ignored the temporal information. On the other hand, research has been done on modeling dynamics of rumour propagation (Lukasik et al., 2015b). Here, we show how using information about dynamics of rumour propagation is important to the problem of rumour stance classification.

The novel contributions of this paper are: 1. Developing a Hawkes Process model for time sensitive sequence classification. 2. Demonstrating on real world data how temporal dynamics conveys important information for stance classification. 3. Establishing the new state of the art method for rumour stance classification. 4. Broadening the set of labels considered in previous work to include a new label *commenting*.

Software used for experiments can be found at `https://github.com/mlukasik/seqhawkes`.

2 Problem definition

We consider a collection D of rumours, $D = \{R_1, \cdots, R_{|D|}\}$. Each rumour R_i contains a set of tweets discussing it, $R_i = \{d_1, \cdots, d_{n_i}\}$. Each tweet is represented as a tuple $d_j = (t_j, W_j, m_j, y_j)$, which includes the following information: t_j is the posting time of the tweet, W_j is the text message, m_j is the rumour category and y_j is the label, $y_j \in Y = \{supporting, denying, questioning, commenting\}$.

We define the stance classification task as that in which each tweet d_j needs to be classified into one of the four categories, $y_j \in Y$, which represents the stance of the tweet d_j with respect to the rumour R_i it belongs to.

We consider the Leave One Out (LOO) setting, introduced by Lukasik et al. (2015a), where for each rumour $R_i \in D$ we construct the test set equal to R_i and the training set equal to $D \setminus R_i$. The final performance scores we report in the paper are averaged across all rumours. This represents a realistic scenario where a classifier has to deal with a new, unseen rumour.

3 Data

We consider four Twitter rumour datasets with tweets annotated for stance (Zubiaga et al., 2016).[1] The authors relied on a slightly different scheme for the annotation, given that they annotated tree-structured conversation threads where a source tweet initiates a rumour and a number of replies follow responding to it. Given this structure, the source tweet of a Twitter conversation is annotated as *supporting*, *denying* or *underspecified*, and each subsequent tweet is annotated as *agreed*, *disagreed*, *appeal for more information* (*questioning*) or *commenting* with respect to the source tweet. We convert these labels into our set of four including *supporting*, *denying*, *questioning* and *commenting*, which extends the set of three labels used before in the literature (Qazvinian et al., 2011; Lukasik et al., 2015a) adding the new label *commenting*. To perform this conversion, we first remove rumours where the source tweet is annotated as *underspecified*, keeping the rest of source tweets as *supporting* or *denying*. For the subsequent tweets, we keep their label as is for the tweets that are *questioning* or *commenting*. To convert those tweets that agree or disagree into *supporting* or *denying*, we apply the following set of rules: (1) if a tweet agrees to a supporting source tweet, we label it *supporting*, (2) if a tweet agrees to a denying source tweet, we label it *denying*, (3) if a tweet disagrees to a supporting source tweet, we label it *denying* and (4) if a tweet disagrees to a denying tweet, we label it *supporting*. The latter enables to infer stance with respect to the rumour from the original annotations that instead refer to agreement with respect to the source.

---

[1] While the authors annotated and released 9 datasets, here we make use of 4 sufficiently large datasets.

Dataset	Rumours	Tweets	Supporting	Denying	Questioning	Commenting
Ottawa shooting	58	782	161	76	64	481
Ferguson riots	46	1017	161	82	94	680
Charlie Hebdo	74	1053	236	56	51	710
Sydney siege	71	1124	89	223	99	713

Table 1: Statistics and distribution of labels for the four datasets used in our experiments. Each dataset consists of multiple rumours, and the rest of the columns offer the aggregated counts for all rumours within that dataset.

Figure 2 shows examples of tweets taken from the dataset along with our inferred annotations.

We summarise the statistics of the resulting dataset in Table 1. Note that the *commenting* label accounts for the majority of the tweets.

4 Model

Hawkes Processes are a probabilistic framework for modelling self-exciting phenomena, which has been used for modelling memes and their spread across social networks (Yang and Zha, 2013). They have been used to model the generation of tweets over a continuous time domain (Zhao et al., 2015). The frequency of tweets generated by them is determined by an underlying intensity function which considers the influence from past tweets. The intensity function models the self-exciting nature by adding up the influence from past tweets. We use a multi-variate Hawkes process for modelling the mutually exciting phenomena between the tweet labels. In this section we describe how we apply the Hawkes Process framework for rumour stance classification.

Intensity Function In the intensity function formulation, we assume that all previous tweets associated with a rumour influence the occurrence of a new tweet. This allows to use information on all the other tweets that have been posted about a rumour. We consider the intensity function to be summation of base intensity and the intensities associated with all the previous tweets,

$$\lambda_{y,m}(t) = \mu_y + \sum_{t_\ell < t} \mathbb{I}(m_\ell = m)\alpha_{y_\ell,y}\kappa(t - t_\ell), \quad (1)$$

where the first term represents the constant base intensity of generating label y. The second term represents the influence from the tweets that happen prior to time of interest. The influence from each tweet decays over time and is modelled using an exponential decay term $\kappa(t - t_\ell) =$

$\omega \exp(-\omega(t - t_\ell))$. The matrix α of size $|Y| \times |Y|$ encodes the degrees of influence between pairs of labels assigned to the tweets, e.g. a *questioning* label may influence the occurrence of a *rejecting* label in future tweets differently from how it would influence a *commenting* label.

Likelihood function The parameters governing the intensity function are learnt by maximizing the likelihood of generating the tweets. The complete likelihood function is given by

$$L(t, y, m, W) = \quad (2)$$

$$\prod_{n=1}^{N} p(W_n|y_n) \times \left[\prod_{n=1}^{N} \lambda_{y_n,m_n}(t_n)\right] \times p(E_T),$$

where the first term provides the likelihood of generating text given the label and is modelled as a multinomial distribution conditioned on the label,

$$p(W_n|y_n) = \prod_{v=1}^{V} \beta_{y_n v}^{W_{nv}}, \quad (3)$$

where V is the vocabulary size and β is the matrix of size $|Y| \times V$ specifying the language model for each label. The second term provides the likelihood of occurrence of tweets at times $t_1, \ldots, t_n$ and the third term provides the likelihood that no tweets happen in the interval $[0, T]$ except at times $t_1, \ldots, t_n$. We estimate the parameters of the model by maximizing the log-likelihood,

$$l(t, y, m, W) = -\sum_{y=1}^{|Y|} \sum_{m=1}^{|D|} \int_0^T \lambda_{y,m}(s)ds +$$

$$\sum_{n=1}^{N} \log \lambda_{y_n,m_n}(t_n) + \sum_{n=1}^{N} \sum_{v=1}^{V} W_{nv} \log \beta_{y_n v}. \quad (4)$$

The integral term in Equation (4) is easily computed for the intensity function since the exponential decay function and the constant function are easily integrable.

Rumour 1 - u1: We understand there are two gunmen and up to a dozen hostages inside the cafe under siege at Sydney.. ISIS flags remain on display #7News [supporting]
Rumour 1 - u2: @u1 sorry - how do you know it's an ISIS flag? Can you actually confirm that? [questioning]
Rumour 2 - u1: These are not timid colours; soldiers back guarding Tomb of Unknown Soldier after today's shooting #StandforCanada –PICTURE– [supporting]
Rumour 2 - u2: @u1 This photo was taken this morning, before the shooting. [denying]
Rumour 2 - u3: @u1 More on situation at Martin Place in Sydney, AU –LINK– [commenting]

Figure 2: Examples of rumour tweets associated with two different rumours.

Note that β is independent from the dynamics part, and a closed form solution after applying Laplacian smoothing takes form

$$\beta_{yv} = \frac{\sum_{n=1}^{N} \mathbb{I}(y_n = y)W_{nv} + 1}{\sum_{n=1}^{N} \sum_{v=1}^{V} \mathbb{I}(y_n = y)W_{nv} + V}.$$

In one approach to μ and α optimization (*HP Approx.*) we approximate the log term in Equation (4) by taking the log inside the summation terms in Equation (1). This approximation leads to closed form updates for μ and α,

$$\mu_y = \frac{\sum_{n=1}^{N} \mathbb{I}(y_n = y)}{T|D|},$$

$$\alpha_{ij} = \frac{\sum_{n=1}^{N} \sum_{l=1}^{n} \mathbb{I}(m_l = m_n)\mathbb{I}(y_l = i)\mathbb{I}(y_n = j)}{\sum_{k=1}^{N} \mathbb{I}(y_k = i)K(T - t_k)},$$

where $K(T - t_k) = 1 - \exp(-\omega(T - t_k))$ arises from the integration of $\kappa(t - t_k)$.

In a different approach (*HP Grad.*) we find parameters using joint gradient based optimization over μ and α, using derivatives of log-likelihood $\frac{dl}{d\mu}$ and $\frac{dl}{d\alpha}$. In optimization, we operate in the log-space of the parameters in order to ensure positivity, and employ L-BFGS approach to gradient search. Moreover, we initialize parameters with those found by the *HP Approx.* method.

Similar to Yang and Zha (2013), we fix the decay parameter ω, in our case to 0.1.

Prediction We predict the most likely label for each test tweet as the label which maximises the likelihood of occurrence of the tweet from Equation (2), or the approximated likelihood in case of *HP Approx.* The likelihood considers both the textual information and the temporal dynamics in predicting the label for the tweet. The predicted labels are then considered while predicting the labels for next tweets in the test data. Thus, we follow a greedy sequence classification approach.

5 Experiments

We conduct experiments using the rumour datasets described in Table 1. We consider our Hawkes Process model described in Section 4 as well as a set of baseline and benchmark approaches.

5.1 Baselines

We compare our model against baselines:

Language Model considers only the textual information through multinomial distribution defined in Equation (3).

Majority vote classifier based on the training label distribution.

Naive Bayes models the text using a multinomial likelihood and a prior over label frequencies (Manning et al., 2008).

Note that Multinomial, Majority vote and Naive Bayes approaches are special cases of our Hawkes Process model for classification, where a particular subset of parameters is fixed to 0.

5.2 Benchmark models

We compare our model against the following competitive benchmark models:

SVM Support Vector Machines with the cost coefficient selected via nested cross-validation.

GP Gaussian Processes have been shown by Lukasik et al. (2015a) to work well, particularly in supervised settings where a multi-task learning kernel has been used to learn correlations across different rumours. Here we use a single task kernel (linear) as we consider the fully unsupervised setting.

CRF Conditional Random Field (Lafferty et al., 2001) over temporally ordered sequences using both text and neighbouring label features. The model is trained using ℓ_2 penalized log-likelihood where the regularisation parame-

	Ottawa		Ferguson		Charlie Hebdo		Sydney Siege	
	Acc	F_1	Acc	F_1	Acc	F_1	Acc	F_1
Majority vote	61.51	19.04	66.86	20.04	67.53	20.15	63.43	19.41
SVM	64.58	35.39	66.86	20.04	69.90	35.11	67.26	37.74
GP	62.28	42.41	64.31	32.90	70.66	**44.09**	65.04	**42.24**
Lang. model	53.20	**42.66**	49.56	**34.35**	63.44	42.84	51.60	41.51
NB	61.76	40.64	62.05	31.29	70.18	39.69	62.01	38.56
CRF	64.58	33.07	67.35	28.11	71.89	40.12	67.44	35.74
HP Approx.	**67.77**	32.29	**68.44**	25.99	**72.93**	32.56	**68.59**	32.49
HP Grad.	63.43	42.40	63.23	33.14	71.79	41.91	62.99	39.45

Table 2: Accuracy and F_1 scores for different methods across datasets. HP Approx. is the best method according to accuracy, whereas Language model and GP are both strong methods according to F_1.

ters are chosen using cross-validation.

5.3 Results

The results are shown in Table 2. We report accuracy (Acc) and macro average of F_1 scores across all labels (F_1). Each metric is calculated over combined sequences of labels from all rumours, thus conducting a micro average over rumours.

We can observe that in terms of accuracy, *HP Approx.* beats all other methods. Notice that Language model is the worst model for this metric. On the other hand, in terms of F_1 score, Language model and GP become the best methods, with *HP Approx.* method not performing as well anymore. Overall, different metrics yield very different rankings of methods. Nevertheless, we can notice that *HP Grad.* outperforms NB under all metrics on all datasets. This is the case also for GP baseline, which turns out to be very competitive according to F_1 score. As we mentioned before, HP can be viewed as a NB classifier with a time-dependent prior. This shows, that the temporal dynamics based prior provided by HP is more helpful than the simple frequency based prior from NB according to all considered metrics.

In Figure 1 we show an illustration of the intensity function of the *HP Grad.* model for rumour #1 from the Ferguson dataset. Notice the self-exciting property, with spikes in the intensity functions for different labels at times when tweets occur. Moreover, spikes occur even when a tweet from a different label is posted, for example around 1 hour and 50 minutes into the rumour lifespan a *questioning* tweet is posted which causes a spike in intensity for *commenting* tweets.

Another issue is the approximation used in *HP*

Approx. which might lead to violation of the Hawkes Process mutual-excitation property. In particular, we noticed that in some scenarios occurrences of tweets cause decrease in the intensity value rather than spikes. However, the accuracy metric which has been used in previous work for this task (Lukasik et al., 2015a) yielded by this method turns out to be the best, although when measuring F_1 the relative ordering changes with the GP performing best (Lukasik et al., 2015a) closely followed by other techniques including *HP Grad.* which is competitive on all datasets.

6 Conclusions

We proposed a novel model based on Hawkes Processes for sequence classification of stances in Twitter which takes into account temporal information in addition to text. Using four Twitter datasets and experimenting on rumour stance classification of tweets, we have shown that HP is a competitive approach, which outperforms a range of strong benchmark methods by providing the multinomial language model with an informative prior based on temporal dynamics. Our experiments posit the importance of making use of temporal information available in tweets, which along with the textual content provide valuable information for the model to perform well on the task.

Acknowledgments

The work was supported by the European Union under grant agreement No. 611233 PHEME. Cohn was supported by an ARC Future Fellowship scheme (project number FT130101105).

References

Abir De, Isabel Valera, Niloy Ganguly, Sourang-shu Bhattacharya, and Manuel Gomez-Rodriguez. 2015. Modeling opinion dynamics in diffusion networks. *CoRR*, abs/1506.05474.

Genevieve Gorrell and Kalina Bontcheva. 2016. Classifying twitter favorites: Like, bookmark, or thanks? *Journal of the Association for Information Science and Technology*, 67(1):17–25.

Alan G. Hawkes. 1971. Spectra of Some Self-Exciting and Mutually Exciting Point Processes. *Biometrika*, 58(1):83–90.

John D. Lafferty, Andrew McCallum, and Fernando C. N. Pereira. 2001. Conditional Random Fields: Probabilistic Models for Segmenting and Labeling Sequence Data. In *Proc. of International Conference on Machine Learning (ICML)*, pages 282–289.

Stephan Lewandowsky, Ullrich KH Ecker, Colleen M Seifert, Norbert Schwarz, and John Cook. 2012. Misinformation and its correction continued influence and successful debiasing. *Psychological Science in the Public Interest*, 13(3):106–131.

Michal Lukasik, Trevor Cohn, and Kalina Bontcheva. 2015a. Classifying Tweet Level Judgements of Rumours in Social Media. In *Proc. of Empirical Methods in Natural Language Processing (EMNLP)*, pages 2590–2595.

Michal Lukasik, Trevor Cohn, and Kalina Bontcheva. 2015b. Point process modelling of rumour dynamics in social media. In *Proc. of the 53rd ACL, vol. 2*, pages 518–523.

Christopher D. Manning, Prabhakar Raghavan, and Hinrich Schütze. 2008. *Introduction to Information Retrieval*. Cambridge University Press.

Vahed Qazvinian, Emily Rosengren, Dragomir R. Radev, and Qiaozhu Mei. 2011. Rumor has it: Identifying misinformation in microblogs. In *Proc. of Empirical Methods in Natural Language Processing (EMNLP)*, pages 1589–1599.

Ge Song, Yunming Ye, Xiaolin Du, Xiaohui Huang, and Shifu Bie. 2014. Short text classification: A survey. *Journal of Multimedia*, 9(5).

Shuang-Hong Yang and Hongyuan Zha. 2013. Mixture of mutually exciting processes for viral diffusion. In *Proc. of International Conference on Machine Learning (ICML)*, volume 28, pages 1–9.

Qingyuan Zhao, Murat A. Erdogdu, Hera Y. He, Anand Rajaraman, and Jure Leskovec. 2015. Seismic: A self-exciting point process model for predicting tweet popularity. In *Proc. of International Conference on Knowledge Discovery and Data Mining (KDD)*, pages 1513–1522.

Arkaitz Zubiaga, Maria Liakata, Rob Procter, Geraldine Wong Sak Hoi, and Peter Tolmie. 2016. Analysing how people orient to and spread rumours in social media by looking at conversational threads. *PLoS ONE*, 11(3):1–29, 03.

Hunting for Troll Comments in News Community Forums

Todor Mihaylov
Institute for Computational Linguistics*
Heidelberg University
Heidelberg, Germany
mihaylov@cl.uni-heidelberg.de

Preslav Nakov
Qatar Computing Research Institute
Hamad bin Khalifa University
P.O. box 5825, Doha, Qatar
pnakov@qf.org.qa

Abstract

There are different definitions of what a troll is. Certainly, a troll can be somebody who teases people to make them angry, or somebody who offends people, or somebody who wants to dominate any single discussion, or somebody who tries to manipulate people's opinion (sometimes for money), etc. The last definition is the one that dominates the public discourse in Bulgaria and Eastern Europe, and this is our focus in this paper.

In our work, we examine two types of opinion manipulation trolls: paid trolls that have been revealed from leaked "reputation management contracts" and "mentioned trolls" that have been called such by several different people. We show that these definitions are sensible: we build two classifiers that can distinguish a post by such a *paid troll* from one by a *non-troll* with 81-82% accuracy; the same classifier achieves 81-82% accuracy on so called *mentioned troll* vs. *non-troll* posts.

1 Introduction

The practice of using Internet trolls for opinion manipulation has been reality since the rise of Internet and community forums. It has been shown that user opinions about products, companies and politics can be influenced by opinions posted by other online users in online forums and social networks (Dellarocas, 2006). This makes it easy for companies and political parties to gain popularity by paying for "reputation management" to people that write in discussion forums and social networks fake opinions from fake profiles.

Opinion manipulation campaigns are often launched using "personal management software" that allows a user to open multiple accounts and to appear like several different people. Over time, some forum users developed sensitivity about trolls, and started publicly exposing them. Yet, it is hard for forum administrators to block them as trolls try formally not to violate the forum rules. In our work, we examine two types of opinion manipulation trolls: paid trolls that have been revealed from leaked "reputation management contracts"[1] and "mentioned trolls" that have been called such by several different people.

2 Related Work

Troll detection was addressed using analysis of the semantics in posts (Cambria et al., 2010) and domain-adapting sentiment analysis (Seah et al., 2015). There are also studies on general troll behavior (Herring et al., 2002; Buckels et al., 2014).

Astroturfing and misinformation have been addressed in the context of political elections using mapping and classification of massive streams of microblogging data (Ratkiewicz et al., 2011). *Fake profile detection* has been studied in the context of cyber-bullying (Galán-García et al., 2014).

A related research line is on *offensive language* use (Xu and Zhu, 2010). This is related to *cyber-bullying*, which has been detected using sentiment analysis (Xu et al., 2012), graph-based approaches over signed social networks (Ortega et al., 2012; Kumar et al., 2014), and lexico-syntactic features about user's writing style (Chen et al., 2012).

---

*This research started in the Sofia University.

[1]The independent Bulgarian media Bivol published a leaked contract described the following services in favor of the government: *"Monthly posting online of 250 comments by virtual users with varied, typical and evolving profiles from different (non-recurring) IP addresses to inform, promote, balance or counteract. The intensity of the provided online presence will be adequately distributed and will correspond to the political situation in the country."* See `https://bivol.bg/en/category/b-files-en/b-files-trolls-en`

Proceedings of the 54th Annual Meeting of the Association for Computational Linguistics, pages 399–405,
Berlin, Germany, August 7-12, 2016. ©2016 Association for Computational Linguistics

Object	Count
Publications	34,514
Comments	1,930,818
-of which replies	897,806
User profiles	14,598
Topics	232
Tags	13,575

Table 1: Statistics about our dataset.

Label	Comments
Paid troll comments	650
Mentioned troll comments	578
Non-troll comments	650+578

Table 2: Comments selected for experiments.

Trustworthiness of statements on the Web is another relevant research direction (Rowe and Butters, 2009). Detecting untruthful and deceptive information has been studied using both psychology and computational linguistics (Ott et al., 2011).

A related problem is *Web spam detection*, which has been addressed using spam keyword spotting (Dave et al., 2003), lexical affinity of arbitrary words to spam content (Hu and Liu, 2004), frequency of punctuation and word co-occurrence (Li et al., 2006). See (Castillo and Davison, 2011) for an overview on adversarial web search.

In our previous work, we focused on finding opinion manipulation troll *users* (Mihaylov et al., 2015a) and on modeling the behavior of exposed vs. paid trolls (Mihaylov et al., 2015b). Here, we go beyond user profile and we try to detect individual troll vs. non-troll *comments* in a news community forum based on both text and metadata.

3 Data

We crawled the largest community forum in Bulgaria, that of Dnevnik.bg, a daily newspaper (in Bulgarian) that requires users to be signed in order to read and comment. The platform allows users to comment on news, to reply to other users' comments and to vote on them with thumbs up/down. We crawled the *Bulgaria*, *Europe*, and *World* categories for the period 01-Jan-2013 to 01-Apr-2015, together with comments and user profiles: 34,514 publications on 232 topics with 13,575 tags and 1,930,818 comments (897,806 of them replies) by 14,598 users; see Table 1. We then extracted comments by *paid trolls* vs. *mentioned trolls* vs. *non-trolls*; see Table 2.

Paid troll comments: We collected them from the leaked reputation management documents, which included 10,150 paid troll comments: 2,000 in Facebook, and 8,150 in news community forums. The latter included 650 posted in the forum of Dnevnik.bg, which we used in our experiments.

Mentioned troll comments: We further collected 1,140 comments that have been replied to with an accusation of being troll comments. We considered a comment as a potential accusation if (*i*) it was a reply to a comment, and (*ii*) it contained words such as *troll* or *murzi(lka)*.[2] Two annotators checked these comments and found 578 actual accusations. The inter-annotator agreement was substantial: Cohen's Kappa of 0.82. Moreover, a simple bag-of-words classifier could find these 578 accusations with an F_1-score of 0.85. Here are some examples (translated):

Accusation: *"To comment from "Prorok Ilia": I can see that you are a red troll by the words that you are using"*

Accused troll's comment: *This Boyko[3] is always in your mind! You only think of him. We like Boko the Potato (the favorite of the Lamb), the way we like the Karlies.*

Paid troll's comment: *in the previous protests, the entire country participated, but now we only see the paid fans of GERB.[4] These are not true protests, but chaotic happenings.*

Non-troll comments are those posted by users that have at least 100 comments in the forum and have never been accused of being trolls. We selected 650 non-troll comments for the paid trolls, and other 578 for the mentioned trolls as follows: for each paid or mentioned troll comment, we selected a non-troll comment at random *from the same thread.* Thus, we have two separate non-troll sets of 650 and of 578 comments.

4 Features

We train a classifier to distinguish *troll* (*paid* or *mentioned*) vs. *non-troll* comments using the following features:

Bag of words. We use words and their frequencies as features, after stopword filtering.[5]

Bag of stems. We further experiment with bag of stems, where we stem the words with the Bul-Stem stemmer (Nakov, 2003a; Nakov, 2003b).

Word n-grams. We also experiment with 2- and 3-word n-grams.

---

[2]Commonly believed in Bulgaria to mean *troll* in Russian (which it does not).

[3]The Bulgarian Prime Minister Mr. Boyko Borisov.

[4]Boyko Borisov's party GERB had fallen down due to protests and here is being accused of organizing protests in turn against the new Socialist government that replaced it.

[5]`http://members.unine.ch/jacques.savoy/clef/bulgarianST.txt`

Char n-grams. We further use character n-grams, where for each word token we extract all n consecutive characters. We use n-grams of length 3 and 4 only as other values did not help.

Word prefix. For each word token, we extract the first 3 or 4 consecutive characters.

Word suffix. For each word token, we take the last 3 or 4 consecutive characters.

Emoticons. We extract the standard HTML-based emoticons used in the forum of Dnevnik.bg.

Punctuation count. We count the number of exclamation marks, dots, and question marks, both single and elongated, the number of words, and the number of ALL CAPS words.

Metadata. We use the time of comment posting (worktime: 9:00-19:00h vs. night: 21:00-6:00h), part of the week (workdays: Mon-Fri vs. weekend: Sat-Sun), and the rank of the comment divided by the number of comments in the thread.

Word2Vec clusters. We trained word2vec on 80M words from 34,514 publications and 1,930,818 comments in our forum, obtaining 268,617 word vectors, which we grouped into 5,372 clusters using K-Means clustering, and then we use these clusters as features.

Sentiment. We use features derived from MPQA Subjectivity Lexicon (Wilson et al., 2005) and NRC Emotion Lexicon (Mohammad and Turney, 2013) and the lexicon of Hu and Liu (2004). Originally these lexicons were built for English, but we translated them to Bulgarian using Google Translate. Then, we reused the sentiment analysis pipeline from (Velichkov et al., 2014), which we adapted for Bulgarian.

Bad words. We use the number of bad words in the comment as a feature. The words come from the *Bad words list v2.0*, which contains 458 bad words collected for a filter of forum or IRC channels in English.[6] We translated this list to Bulgarian using Google Translate and we removed duplicates to obtain *Bad_Words_Bg_1*. We further used the above word2vec model to find the three most similar words for each bad word in *Bad_Words_Bg_1*, and we constructed another lexicon: *Bad_Words_Bg_3*.[7] Finally, we generate two features: one for each lexicon.

Mentions. We noted that trolls use diminutive names or humiliating nicknames when referring to politicians that they do not like, but use full or family names for people that they respect. Based on these observations, we constructed several lexicons with Bulgarian politician names, their variations and nicknames (see footnote 7), and we generated a mention count feature for each lexicon.

POS tag distribution. We also use features based on part of speech (POS). We tag using GATE (Cunningham et al., 2011) with a simplified model trained on a transformed version of the BulTreeBank-DP (Simov et al., 2002). For each POS tag type, we take the number of occurrences in the text divided by the total number of tokens. We use both fine-grained and course-grained POS tags, e.g., from the POS tag *Npmsi*, we generate three tags: *Npmsi*, *N* and *Np*.

Named entities. We also use the occurrence of named entities as features. For extracting named entities such as *location*, *country*, *person_name*, *date_unit*, etc., we use the lexicons that come with Gate's ANNIE (Cunningham et al., 2002) pipeline, which we translated to Bulgarian. In future work, we plan to use a better named entity recognizer based on CRF (Georgiev et al., 2009).

5 Experiments and Evaluation

We train and evaluate an L2-regularized Logistic Regression with LIBLINEAR (Fan et al., 2008) as implemented in SCIKIT-LEARN (Pedregosa et al., 2011), using scaled and normalized features to the [0;1] interval. As we have perfectly balanced sets of 650 positive and 650 negative examples for *paid troll* vs. *non-trolls* and 578 positive and 578 negative examples for *mentioned troll* vs. *non-trolls*, the baseline accuracy is 50%. Below, we report F-score and accuracy with cross-validation.

Table 3, shows the results for experiments to distinguish comments by mentioned trolls vs. such by non-trolls, using all features, as well as when excluding individual feature groups. We can see that excluding character n-grams, word suffixes and word prefixes from the features, as well as excluding bag of words with stems or stop words, yields performance gains; the most sizable gain is when excluding char n-grams, which yields one point of improvement. Excluding bad words usage and emoticons also improves the performance but insignificantly, which might be because they are covered by the bag of words features.

[6] http://urbanoalvarez.es/blog/2008/04/04/bad-words-list/

[7] https://github.com/tbmihailov/gate-lang-bulgarian-gazetteers/ - GATE resources for Bulgarian, including sentiment lexicons, bad words lexicons, politicians' names, etc.

Features	F	Acc
All − char n-grams	79.24	78.54
All − word suff	78.58	78.20
All − word preff	78.51	78.02
All − bow stems	78.32	77.85
All − bow with stop	78.25	77.77
All − bad words	78.10	77.68
All − emoticons	78.08	77.76
All − mentions	78.06	77.68
All	78.06	77.68
All − (bow, no stop)	78.04	77.68
All − NE	77.98	77.59
All − sentiment	77.95	77.51
All − POS	77.80	77.33
All − w2v clusters	77.79	77.25
All − word 3-grams	77.69	77.33
All − word 2-grams	77.62	77.25
All − punct	77.29	76.90
All − metadata	70.77	70.94
Baseline	50.00	50.00

Table 3: **Mentioned troll vs. non-troll comments.** Ablation excluding feature groups.

Features	F	Acc
All − char n-grams	81.08	81.77
All − word suff	81.00	81.77
All − word preff	80.83	81.62
All − bow with stop	80.67	81.54
All − sentiment	80.63	81.46
All − word 2-grams	80.62	81.46
All − w2v clusters	80.54	81.38
All − word 3-grams	80.46	81.38
All − punct	80.40	81.23
All − mentions	80.40	81.31
All	80.40	81.31
All − bow stems	80.37	81.31
All − emoticons	80.33	81.15
All − bad words	80.09	81.00
All − NE	80.00	80.92
All − POS	79.77	80.69
All − (bow, no stop)	79.46	80.38
All − metadata	75.37	76.62
Baseline	50.00	50.00

Table 4: **Paid troll vs. non-troll comments.** Ablation excluding feature groups.

Excluding any of the other features hurts performance, the two most important features to keep being metadata (as it allows us to see the time of posting), and bag of words without stopwords (which looks at the vocabulary choice that mentioned trolls use differently from regular users).

Table 4 shows the results for telling apart comments by paid trolls vs. such by non-trolls, using cross-validation and ablation with the same features as for the mentioned trolls. There are several interesting observations we can make. First, we can see that the overall accuracy for finding paid trolls is slightly higher, namely 81.02, vs. 79.24 for mentioned trolls. The most helpful feature again is metadata, but this time it is less helpful (excluding it yields a drop of 5 points vs. 8 points before). The least helpful feature again are character n-grams. The remaining features fall in between, and most of them yield better performance when excluded, which suggests that there is a lot of redundancy in the features.

Next, we look at individual feature groups. Table 5 shows the results for comments by mentioned trolls vs. such by non-trolls. We can see that the metadata features are by far the most important: using them alone outperforms the results when using all features by 3.5 points.

The reason could be that most troll comments are replies to other comments, while those by non-trolls are mostly not replies. Adding other features such as sentiment-based features, bad words, POS, and punctuation hurts the performance significantly. Features such as bad words are at the very bottom: they do not apply to all comments and thus are of little use alone; similarly for mentions and sentiment features, which are also quite weak in isolation. These results suggest that mentioned trolls are not that different from non-trolls in terms of language use, but have mainly different behavior in terms of replying to other users.

Table 6 shows a bit different picture for comments by paid trolls vs. such by non-trolls. The biggest difference is that metadata features are not so useful. Also, the strongest feature set is the combination of sentiment, bad words distribution, POS, metadata, and punctuation. This suggests that paid trolls are smart to post during time intervals and days of the week as non-trolls, but they use comments with slightly different sentiment and bad word use than non-trolls. Features based on words are also very helpful because paid trolls have to defend pre-specified key points, which limits their vocabulary use, while non-trolls are free to express themselves as they wish.

Features	F	Acc
All	78.06	77.68
Only metadata	84.14	81.14
Sent,bad,pos,NE,meta,punct	77.79	76.73
Only bow, no stop	73.41	73.79
Only bow with stop	73.41	73.44
Only bow stems	72.43	72.49
Only word preff	71.11	71.62
Only w2v clusters	69.85	70.50
Only word suff	69.17	68.95
Only word 2-grams	68.96	69.29
Only char n-grams	68.44	68.94
Only word 3-grams	64.74	67.21
Only POS	64.60	65.31
Sent,bad,pos,NE	63.68	64.10
Only sent,bad	63.66	64.44
Only emoticons	63.30	64.96
Sent,bad,ment,NE	63.11	64.01
Only punct	63.09	64.79
Only sentiment	62.50	63.66
Only NE	62.45	64.27
Only mentions	62.41	64.10
Only bad words	62.27	64.01
Baseline	50.00	50.00

Table 5: **Mentioned troll comments vs. non-troll comments.** Results for individual feature groups.

Features	F	Acc
All	80.40	81.31
Sent,bad,pos,NE,meta,punct	78.04	78.15
Only bow, no stop	75.95	76.46
Only word 2-grams	75.55	74.92
Only bow with stop	75.27	75.62
Only bow stems	75.25	76.08
Only w2v clusters	74.20	74.00
Only word preff	74.01	74.77
Sent,bad,pos,NE	73.89	73.85
Only metadata	73.79	72.54
Only char n-grams	73.02	74.23
Only POS	72.94	72.69
Only word suff	72.03	72.69
Only word 3-grams	69.20	68.00
Only punct	66.80	65.00
Only NE	66.54	64.77
Sent,bad,ment,NE	66.04	64.92
Only sentiment	64.28	62.62
Only mentions	63.28	61.46
Only sent,bad	63.14	61.54
Only emoticons	62.95	61.00
Only bad words	62.22	60.85
Baseline	50.00	50.00

Table 6: **Paid troll vs. non-troll comments.** Results for individual feature groups.

	5	10	15	20
Acc	80.70	81.08	83.41	85.59
Diff	+8.46	+18.51	+30.81	+32.26

Table 7: **Mentioned troll vs. non-troll *users (not comments!)*.** Experiments with different number of minimum mentions for January, 2015. 'Diff' is the difference from the majority class baseline.

6 Discussion

Overall, we have seen that our classifier for telling apart comments by mentioned trolls vs. such by non-trolls performs almost equally well for paid trolls vs. non-trolls, where the non-troll comments are sampled from the same threads that the troll comments come from. Moreover, the most and the least important features ablated from all are also similar. This suggests that mentioned trolls are very similar to paid trolls (except for their reply rate, time and day of posting patterns).

However, using just mentions might be a "witch hunt": some users could have been accused of being "trolls" unfairly. One way to test this is to look not at comments, but at users and to see which users were called trolls by several different other users. Table 7 shows the results for distinguishing users with a given number of alleged troll comments from non-troll users; the classification is based on all comments by the corresponding users. We can see that finding users who have been called trolls more often is easier, which suggests they might be trolls indeed.

7 Conclusion and Future Work

We have presented experiments in predicting whether a comment is written by a troll or not, where we define troll as somebody who was called such by other people. We have shown that this is a useful definition and that comments by mentioned trolls are similar to such by confirmed paid trolls.

Acknowledgments. This research is part of the Interactive sYstems for Answer Search (Iyas) project, which is developed by the Arabic Language Technologies (ALT) group at the Qatar Computing Research Institute (QCRI), Hamad bin Khalifa University (HBKU), part of Qatar Foundation in collaboration with MIT-CSAIL.

References

Erin E Buckels, Paul D Trapnell, and Delroy L Paulhus. 2014. Trolls just want to have fun. *Personality and individual Differences*, 67:97–102.

Erik Cambria, Praphul Chandra, Avinash Sharma, and Amir Hussain. 2010. Do not feel the trolls. In *Proceedings of the 3rd International Workshop on Social Data on the Web*, SDoW '10, Shanghai, China.

Carlos Castillo and Brian D. Davison. 2011. Adversarial web search. *Found. Trends Inf. Retr.*, 4(5):377–486, May.

Ying Chen, Yilu Zhou, Sencun Zhu, and Heng Xu. 2012. Detecting offensive language in social media to protect adolescent online safety. In *Proceedings of the 2012 International Conference on Privacy, Security, Risk and Trust and of the 2012 International Conference on Social Computing*, PASSAT/SocialCom '12, pages 71–80, Amsterdam, Netherlands.

Hamish Cunningham, Diana Maynard, Kalina Bontcheva, and Valentin Tablan. 2002. GATE: an architecture for development of robust HLT applications. In *Proceedings of 40th Annual Meeting of the Association for Computational Linguistics*, ACL '02, pages 168–175, Philadelphia, Pennsylvania, USA.

Hamish Cunningham, Diana Maynard, and Kalina Bontcheva. 2011. *Text Processing with GATE*. Gateway Press CA.

Kushal Dave, Steve Lawrence, and David M Pennock. 2003. Mining the peanut gallery: Opinion extraction and semantic classification of product reviews. In *Proceedings of the 12th International World Wide Web conference*, WWW '03, pages 519–528, Budapest, Hungary.

Chrysanthos Dellarocas. 2006. Strategic manipulation of internet opinion forums: Implications for consumers and firms. *Management Science*, 52(10):1577–1593.

Rong-En Fan, Kai-Wei Chang, Cho-Jui Hsieh, Xiang-Rui Wang, and Chih-Jen Lin. 2008. Liblinear: A library for large linear classification. *J. Mach. Learn. Res.*, 9:1871–1874, June.

Patxi Galán-García, José Gaviria de la Puerta, Carlos Laorden Gómez, Igor Santos, and Pablo García Bringas. 2014. Supervised machine learning for the detection of troll profiles in Twitter social network: Application to a real case of cyberbullying. In *Proceedings of the International Joint Conference SOCO13-CISIS13-ICEUTE13*, Advances in Intelligent Systems and Computing, pages 419–428. Springer International Publishing.

Georgi Georgiev, Preslav Nakov, Kuzman Ganchev, Petya Osenova, and Kiril Simov. 2009. Feature-rich named entity recognition for Bulgarian using conditional random fields. In *Proceedings of the International Conference Recent Advances in Natural Language Processing*, RANLP '09, pages 113–117, Borovets, Bulgaria.

Susan Herring, Kirk Job-Sluder, Rebecca Scheckler, and Sasha Barab. 2002. Searching for safety online: Managing "trolling" in a feminist forum. *The Information Society*, 18(5):371–384.

Minqing Hu and Bing Liu. 2004. Mining and summarizing customer reviews. In *Proceedings of the 10th ACM SIGKDD International Conference on Knowledge Discovery and Data Mining*, KDD '04, pages 168–177, Seattle, Washington, USA.

Srijan Kumar, Francesca Spezzano, and VS Subrahmanian. 2014. Accurately detecting trolls in slashdot zoo via decluttering. In *Proceedings of the 2014 IEEE/ACM International Conference on Advances in Social Network Analysis and Mining*, ASONAM '14, pages 188–195, Beijing, China.

Wenbin Li, Ning Zhong, and Chunnian Liu. 2006. Combining multiple email filters based on multivariate statistical analysis. In *Foundations of Intelligent Systems*, pages 729–738. Springer.

Todor Mihaylov, Georgi Georgiev, and Preslav Nakov. 2015a. Finding opinion manipulation trolls in news community forums. In *Proceedings of the Nineteenth Conference on Computational Natural Language Learning*, CoNLL '15, pages 310–314, Beijing, China.

Todor Mihaylov, Ivan Koychev, Georgi Georgiev, and Preslav Nakov. 2015b. Exposing paid opinion manipulation trolls. In *Proceedings of the International Conference Recent Advances in Natural Language Processing*, RANLP '15, pages 443–450, Hissar, Bulgaria.

Saif M. Mohammad and Peter D. Turney. 2013. Crowdsourcing a word-emotion association lexicon. *Computational Intelligence*, 29(3):436–465.

Preslav Nakov. 2003a. Building an inflectional stemmer for Bulgarian. In *Proceedings of the 4th International Conference on Computer Systems and Technologies: E-Learning*, CompSysTech '03, pages 419–424, Rousse, Bulgaria.

Preslav Nakov. 2003b. BulStem: Design and evaluation of inflectional stemmer for Bulgarian. In *Proceedings of Workshop on Balkan Language Resources and Tools (1st Balkan Conference in Informatics)*, Thessaloniki, Greece, November, 2003.

F. Javier Ortega, Jos A. Troyano, Fermn L. Cruz, Carlos G. Vallejo, and Fernando Enrquez. 2012. Propagation of trust and distrust for the detection of trolls in a social network. *Computer Networks*, 56(12):2884 – 2895.

Myle Ott, Yejin Choi, Claire Cardie, and Jeffrey T. Hancock. 2011. Finding deceptive opinion spam by any stretch of the imagination. In *Proceedings of the 49th Annual Meeting of the Association for Computational Linguistics: Human Language Technologies - Volume 1*, HLT '11, pages 309–319, Portland, Oregon.

F. Pedregosa, G. Varoquaux, A. Gramfort, V. Michel, B. Thirion, O. Grisel, M. Blondel, P. Prettenhofer, R. Weiss, V. Dubourg, J. Vanderplas, A. Passos, D. Cournapeau, M. Brucher, M. Perrot, and E. Duchesnay. 2011. Scikit-learn: Machine learning in Python. *Journal of Machine Learning Research*, 12:2825–2830.

Jacob Ratkiewicz, Michael Conover, Mark Meiss, Bruno Gonçalves, Snehal Patil, Alessandro Flammini, and Filippo Menczer. 2011. Truthy: Mapping the spread of astroturf in microblog streams. In *Proceedings of the 20th International Conference Companion on World Wide Web*, WWW '11, pages 249–252, Hyderabad, India.

Matthew Rowe and Jonathan Butters. 2009. Assessing Trust: Contextual Accountability. In *Proceedings of the First Workshop on Trust and Privacy on the Social and Semantic Web*, SPOT '09, Heraklion, Greece.

Chun-Wei Seah, Hai Leong Chieu, Kian Ming Adam Chai, Loo-Nin Teow, and Lee Wei Yeong. 2015. Troll detection by domain-adapting sentiment analysis. In *Proceedings of the 18th International Conference on Information Fusion*, FUSION '15, pages 792–799, Washington, DC, USA.

Kiril Simov, Petya Osenova, Milena Slavcheva, Sia Kolkovska, Elisaveta Balabanova, Dimitar Doikoff, Krassimira Ivanova, Er Simov, and Milen Kouylekov. 2002. Building a linguistically interpreted corpus of Bulgarian: the BulTreeBank. In *Proceedings of the Third International Conference on Language Resources and Evaluation*, LREC '02, Canary Islands, Spain.

Boris Velichkov, Borislav Kapukaranov, Ivan Grozev, Jeni Karanesheva, Todor Mihaylov, Yasen Kiprov, Preslav Nakov, Ivan Koychev, and Georgi Georgiev. 2014. SU-FMI: System description for SemEval-2014 task 9 on sentiment analysis in Twitter. In *Proceedings of the 8th International Workshop on Semantic Evaluation*, SemEval '14, pages 590–595, Dublin, Ireland.

Theresa Wilson, Janyce Wiebe, and Paul Hoffmann. 2005. Recognizing contextual polarity in phrase-level sentiment analysis. In *Proceedings of the Conference on Human Language Technology and Empirical Methods in Natural Language Processing*, HLT '05, pages 347–354, Vancouver, British Columbia, Canada.

Zhi Xu and Sencun Zhu. 2010. Filtering offensive language in online communities using grammatical relations. In *Proceedings of the Seventh Annual Collaboration, Electronic Messaging, Anti-Abuse and Spam Conference*, CEAS '10, Redmond, Washington, USA.

Jun-Ming Xu, Xiaojin Zhu, and Amy Bellmore. 2012. Fast learning for sentiment analysis on bullying. In *Proceedings of the First International Workshop on Issues of Sentiment Discovery and Opinion Mining*, WISDOM '12, pages 10:1–10:6, Beijing, China.

Phrase Table Pruning via Submodular Function Maximization

Masaaki Nishino and **Jun Suzuki** and **Masaaki Nagata**
NTT Communication Science Laboratories, NTT Corporation
2-4 Hikaridai, Seika-cho, Soraku-gun, Kyoto, 619-0237, Japan
{nishino.masaaki,suzuki.jun,nagata.masaaki}@lab.ntt.co.jp

Abstract

Phrase table pruning is the act of re-moving phrase pairs from a phrase table to make it smaller, ideally removing the least useful phrases first. We propose a phrase table pruning method that formu-lates the task as a submodular function maximization problem, and solves it by using a greedy heuristic algorithm. The proposed method can scale with input size and long phrases, and experiments show that it achieves higher BLEU scores than state-of-the-art pruning methods.

1 Introduction

A phrase table, a key component of phrase-based statistical machine translation (PBMT) systems, consists of a set of phrase pairs. A phrase pair is a pair of source and target language phrases, and is used as the atomic translation unit. Today's PBMT systems have to store and process large phrase ta-bles that contain more than 100M phrase pairs, and their sheer size prevents PBMT systems for running in resource-limited environments such as mobile phones. Even if a computer has enough resources, the large phrase tables increase turn-around time and prevent the rapid development of MT systems.

Phrase table pruning is the technique of remov-ing ineffective phrase pairs from a phrase table to make it smaller while minimizing the perfor-mance degradation. Existing phrase table pruning methods use different metrics to rank the phrase pairs contained in the table, and then remove low-ranked pairs. Metrics used in previous work are frequency, conditional probability, and Fisher's exact test score (Johnson et al., 2007). Zens et al. (2012) evaluated many phrase table pruning methods, and concluded that entropy-based prun-ing method (Ling et al., 2012; Zens et al., 2012) offers the best performance. The entropy-based pruning method uses entropy to measure the re-dundancy of a phrase pair, where we say a phrase pair is redundant if it can be replaced by other phrase pairs. The entropy-based pruning method runs in time linear to the number of phrase-pairs. Unfortunately, its running time is also exponential to the length of phrases contained in the phrase pairs, since it contains the problem of finding an optimal phrase alignment, which is known to be NP-hard (DeNero and Klein, 2008). Therefore, the method can be impractical if the phrase pairs consist of longer phrases.

In this paper, we introduce a novel phrase ta-ble pruning method that formulates and solves the phrase table pruning problem as a submodu-lar function maximization problem. A submodular function is a kind of set function that satisfies the submodularity property. Generally, the submod-ular function maximization problem is NP-hard, however, it is known that $(1 - 1/e)$ optimal solu-tions can be obtained by using a simple greedy al-gorithm (Nemhauser et al., 1978). Since a greedy algorithm scales with large inputs, our method can be applicable to large phrase tables.

One key factor of the proposed method is its carefully designed objective function that evalu-ates the quality of a given phrase table. In this pa-per, we use a simple monotone submodular func-tion that evaluates the quality of a given phrase table by its coverage of a training corpus. Our method is simple, parameter free, and does not cause exponential explosion of the computation time with longer phrases. We conduct experiments with two different language pairs, and show that the proposed method shows higher BLEU scores than state-of-the-art pruning methods.

Proceedings of the 54th Annual Meeting of the Association for Computational Linguistics, pages 406–411,
Berlin, Germany, August 7-12, 2016. ©2016 Association for Computational Linguistics

2 Submodular Function Maximization

Let Ω be a base set consisting of M elements, and $g : 2^\Omega \mapsto \mathbb{R}$ be a set function that upon the input of $X \subseteq \Omega$ returns a real value. If g is a submodular function, then it satisfies the condition

$$g(X \cup \{x\}) - g(X) \geq g(Y \cup \{x\}) - g(Y),$$

where $X, Y \in 2^\Omega$, $X \subseteq Y$, and $x \in \Omega \setminus Y$. This condition represents the diminishing return property of a submodular function, i.e., the increase in the value of the function due to the addition of item x to Y is always smaller than that obtained by adding x to any subset $X \subseteq Y$. We say a submodular function is *monotone* if $g(Y) \geq g(X)$ for any $X, Y \in 2^\Omega$ satisfying $X \subseteq Y$. Since a submodular function has many useful properties, it appears in a wide range of applications (Kempe et al., 2003; Lin and Bilmes, 2010; Kirchhoff and Bilmes, 2014).

The maximization problem of a monotone submodular function under cardinality constraints is formulated as

$$\text{Maximize } g(X)$$

$$\text{Subject to } X \in 2^\Omega \text{ and } |X| \leq K,$$

where $g(X)$ is a monotone submodular function and K is the parameter that defines maximum cardinality. This problem is known to be NP-hard, but a greedy algorithm can find an approximate solution whose score is certified to be $(1 - 1/e)$ optimal (Nemhauser et al., 1978). Algorithm 1 shows a greedy approximation method the can solve the submodular function maximization problem under cardinality constraints. This algorithm first sets $X \leftarrow \emptyset$, and adds item $x^* \in \Omega \setminus X$ that maximizes $g(X \cup \{x^*\}) - g(X)$ to X until $|X| = K$.

Assuming that the evaluation of $g(X)$ can be performed in constant time, the running time of the greedy algorithm is $O(MK)$ because we need $O(M)$ evaluations of $g(X)$ for selecting x^* that maximizes $g(X \cup \{x^*\}) - g(X)$, and these evaluations are repeated K times. If we naively apply the algorithm to situations where M is very large, then the algorithm may not work in reasonable running time. However, an accelerated greedy algorithm can work with large inputs (Minoux, 1978; Leskovec et al., 2007), since it can drastically reduce the number of function evaluations from MK. We applied the accelerated greedy algorithm in the following experiments, and found it

---

Algorithm 1 Greedy algorithm for maximizing a submodular function

Input: Base set Ω, cardinality K

Output: $X \in 2^\Omega$ satisfying $|X| = K$.

1: $X \leftarrow \emptyset$
2: **while** $|X| < K$ **do**
3:     $x^* \leftarrow \arg\max\limits_{x \in \Omega \setminus X} g(X \cup \{x\}) - g(X)$
4:     $X \leftarrow X \cup \{x^*\}$
5: **output** X

---

could solve the problems in 24 hours. Moreover, further enhancement can be achieved by applying distributed algorithms (Mirzasoleiman et al., 2013) and stochastic greedy algorithms (Mirzasoleiman et al., 2015).

3 Phrase Table Pruning

We first define some notations. Let $\Omega = \{x_1, \ldots, x_M\}$ be a phrase table that has M phrase pairs. Each phrase pair, x_i, consists of a source language phrase, p_i, and a target language phrase, q_i, and is written as $x_i = \langle p_i, q_i \rangle$. Phrases p_i and q_i are sequences of words $p_i = (p_{i1}, \ldots, p_{i|p_i|})$ and $q_i = (q_{i1}, \ldots, q_{i|q_i|})$, where p_{ij} represents the j-th word of p_i and q_{ij} represents the j-th word of q_i. Let t_i be the i-th translation pair contained in the training corpus, namely $t_i = \langle f_i, e_i \rangle$, where f_i and e_i are source and target sentences, respectively. Let N be the number of translation pairs contained in the corpus. f_i and e_i are represented as sequences of words $f_i = (f_{i1}, \ldots, f_{i|f_i|})$ and $e_i = (e_{i1}, \ldots, e_{i|e_i|})$, where f_{ij} is the j-th word of sentence f_i and e_{ij} is the j-th word of sentence e_i.

Definition 1. Let $x_j = \langle p_j, q_j \rangle$ be a phrase pair and $t_i = \langle f_i, e_i \rangle$ be a translation pair. We say x_j *appears* in t_i if p_j is contained in f_i as a subsequence and q_j is contained in e_i as a subsequence. We say phrase pair x_j *covers* word f_{ik} if x_j appears in $\langle f_i, e_i \rangle$ and f_{ik} is contained in the subsequence that equals p_j. Similarly, we say x_j covers e_{ik} if x_j appears in $\langle f_i, e_i \rangle$ and e_{ik} is contained in the subsequence that equals q_j.

Using the above definitions, we describe here our phrase-table pruning algorithm; it formulates the task as a combinatorial optimization problem. Since phrase table pruning is the problem of finding a subset of Ω, we formulate the problem as a submodular function maximization problem under cardinality constraints, i.e., the problem is finding

$X \subseteq \Omega$ that maximizes objective function $g(X)$ while satisfying the condition $|X| = K$, where K is the size of pruned phrase table. If $g(X)$ is a monotone submodular function, we can apply Algorithm 1 to obtain an $(1 - 1/e)$ approximate solution. We use the following objective function.

$$g(X) = \sum_{i=1}^{N} \sum_{k=1}^{|f_i|} \log\left[c(X, f_{ik}) + 1\right]$$
$$+ \sum_{i=1}^{N} \sum_{k=1}^{|e_i|} \log\left[c(X, e_{ik}) + 1\right],$$

where $c(X, f_{ik})$ is the number of phrase pairs contained in X that cover f_{ik}, the k-th word of the i-th source sentence f_i. Similarly, $c(X, e_{ik})$ is the number of phrase pairs that cover e_{ik}.

Example 1. Consider phrase table X holding phrase pairs $x_1 = \langle(\text{das Haus}), (\text{the house})\rangle$, $x_2 = \langle(\text{Haus}), (\text{house})\rangle$, and $x_3 = \langle(\text{das Haus}), (\text{the building})\rangle$. If a corpus consists of a pair of sentences $f_1 = $ "das Haus ist klein" and $e_1 = $ "this house is small", then x_1 and x_2 appear in $\langle f_1, e_1 \rangle$ and word $f_{12} = $ "Haus" is covered by x_1 and x_2. Hence $c(X, f_{12}) = 2$.

This objective function basically gives high scores to X if it contains many words of the training corpus. However, since we take the logarithm of cover counts $c(X, f_{ik})$ and $c(X, e_{ik})$, $g(X)$ becomes high when X covers many different words. This objective function prefers to select phrase pairs that frequently appear in the training corpus but with low redundantly. This objective function prefers pruned phrase table X that contains phrase pairs that frequently appear in the training corpus, with no redundant phrase pairs. We prove the submodularity of the objective function below.

Proposition 1. $g(X)$ *is a monotone submodular function.*

Proof. Apparently, every $c(X, f_{ik})$ and $c(X, e_{ik})$ is a monotone function of X, and it satisfies the diminishing return property since $c(X \cup \{x\}, f_{ik}) - c(X, f_{ik}) = c(Y \cup \{x\}, f_{ik}) - c(Y, f_{ik})$ for any $X \subseteq Y$ and $x \notin Y$. If function $h(X)$ is monotone and submodular, then $\phi(h(X))$ is also monotone and submodular for any concave function $\phi : \mathbb{R} \mapsto \mathbb{R}$. Since $\log(X)$ is concave, every $\log[c(X, f_{ik}) + 1]$ and $\log[c(X, e_{ik}) + 1]$ is a monotone submodular function. Finally, if $h_1, \ldots, h_n$ are monotone and submodular, then $\sum_i h_i$ is also

monotone and submodular. Thus $g(X)$ is monotone and submodular. $\qquad\square$

Computation costs If we know all counts $c(X, f_{ik})$ and $c(X, e_{ik})$ for all f_{ik}, e_{ik}, then $g(X \cup \{x\})$ can be evaluated in time linear with the number of words contained in the training corpus[1]. Thus our algorithm does not cause exponential explosion of the computation time with longer phrases.

4 Evaluation

4.1 Settings

We conducted experiments on the Chinese-English and Arabic-English datasets used in NIST OpenMT 2012. In each experiment, English was set as the target language. We used Moses (Koehn et al., 2007) as the phrase-based machine translation system. We used the 5-gram Kneser-Ney language model trained separately using the English GigaWord V5 corpus (LDC2011T07), a monolingual corpus distributed at WMT 2012, and Google Web 1T 5-gram data (LDC2006T13). Word alignments are obtained by running giza++ (Och and Ney, 2003) included in the Moses system. As the test data, we used 1378 segments for the Arabic-English dataset and 2190 segments for the Chinese-English dataset, where all test segments have 4 references (LDC2013T07, LDC2013T03). The tuning set consists of about 5000 segments gathered from MT02 to MT06 evaluation sets (LDC2010T10, LDC2010T11, LDC2010T12, LDC2010T14, LDC2010T17). We set the maximum length of extracted phrases to 7. Table 1 shows the sizes of phrase tables. Following the settings used in (Zens et al., 2012), we reduce the effects of other components by using the same feature weights obtained by running the MERT training algorithm (Och, 2003) on full size phrase tables and tuning data to all pruned tables. We run MERT for 10 times to obtain 10 different feature weights. The BLEU scores reported in the following experiments are the averages of the results obtained by using these different feature weights.

We adopt the entropy-based pruning method used in (Ling et al., 2012; Zens et al., 2012) as the baseline method, since it shows best BLEU

---

[1]Running time can be further reduced if we compute the set of words covered by each phrase pair x_i before executing the greedy algorithm.

Language Pair	Number of phrase pairs
Arabic-English	234M
Chinese-English	169M

Table 1: Phrase table sizes.

scores as per (Zens et al., 2012). We used the parameter value of the entropy-based method suggested in (Zens et al., 2012). We also compared with the significance-based method (Johnson et al., 2007), which uses Fisher's exact test to calculate significance scores of phrase pairs and prunes less-significant phrase pairs.

4.2 Results

Figure 1 and Figure 2 show the BLEU scores of pruned tables. The horizontal axis is the number of phrase pairs contained in a table, and the vertical axis is the BLEU score. The values in the figure are difference of BLEU scores between the proposed method and the baseline method that shows higher score. In the experiment with the Arabic-English dataset, both methods can remove 80% of phrase pairs without losing 1 BLEU point, and the proposed method shows better performance than the baseline methods for all table sizes. The difference in BLEU scores becomes larger when table sizes are small. In the experiment on the Chinese-English dataset, both methods can remove 80% of phrase pairs without losing 1 BLEU point, and the proposed method also shows comparable or better performance. The difference in BLEU scores also becomes larger when table sizes are small.

Figure 3 shows phrase table sizes in the binarized and compressed phrase table format used in Moses (Junczys-Dowmunt, 2012). The horizontal axis is the number of phrase pairs contained in the table, and the vertical axis is phrase table size. We can see that there is a linear relationship between phrase table sizes and the number of phrase pairs. The original phrase table requires 2.8GB memory. In contrast, the 90% pruned table only requires 350MB of memory. This result shows the effectiveness of phrase table pruning on reducing resource requirements in practical situations.

5 Related Work

Previous phrase table pruning methods fall into two groups. Self-contained methods only use resources already used in the MT system, e.g., training corpus and phrase tables. Entropy-based

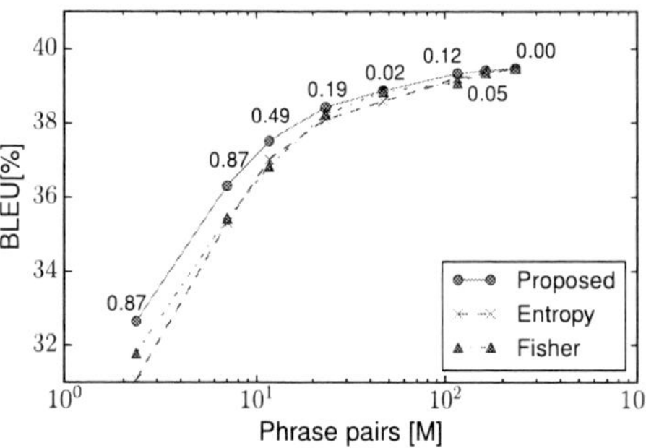

Figure 1: BLEU score as a function of the number of phrase pairs (Arabic-English).

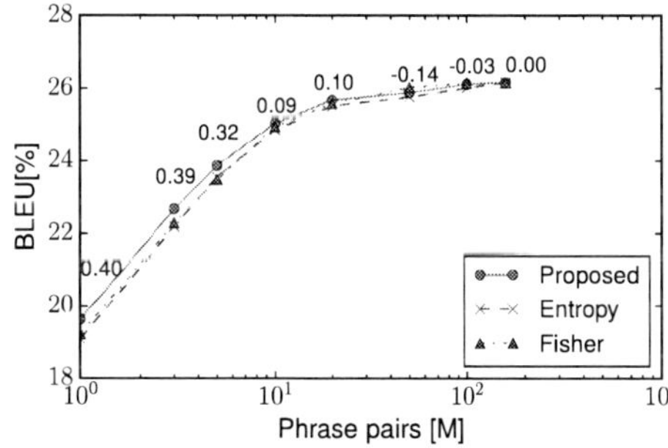

Figure 2: BLEU score as a function of the number of phrase pairs (Chinese-English).

methods (Ling et al., 2012; Zens et al., 2012), a significance-based method (Johnson et al., 2007), and our method are self-contained methods. Non self-contained methods exploit usage statistics for phrase pairs (Eck et al., 2007) and additional bilingual corpora (Chen et al., 2009). Since self-contained methods require additional resources, it is easy to apply to existing MT systems.

Effectiveness of the submodular functions maximization formulation is confirmed in various NLP applications including text summarization (Lin and Bilmes, 2010; Lin and Bilmes, 2011) and training data selection for machine translation (Kirchhoff and Bilmes, 2014). These methods are used for selecting a subset that contains important items but not redundant items. This paper can be seen as applying the subset selection formulation to the phrase table pruning problem.

6 Conclusion

We have introduced a method that solves the phrase table pruning problem as a submodular function maximization problem under cardinal-

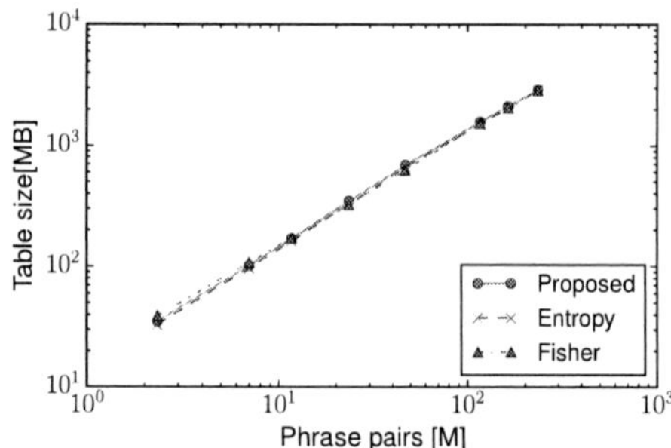

Figure 3: Moses compact phrase table size as a function of the number of phrase pairs (Arabic-English).

ity constraints. Finding an optimal solution of the problem is NP-hard, so we apply a scalable greedy heuristic to find $(1 - 1/e)$ optimal solutions. Experiments showed that our greedy algorithm, which uses a relatively simple objective function, can achieve better performance than state-of-the-art pruning methods.

Our proposed method can be easily extended by using other types of submodular functions. The objective function used in this paper is a simple one, but it is easily enhanced by the addition of metrics used in existing phrase table pruning techniques, such as Fisher's exact test scores and entropy scores. Testing such kinds of objective function enhancements is an important future task.

References

Yu Chen, Martin Kay, and Andreas Eisele. 2009. Intersecting multilingual data for faster and better statistical translations. In *Proceedings of Human Language Technologies: The 2009 Annual Conference of the North American Chapter of the Association for Computational Linguistics (NAACL-HLT)*, pages 128–136.

John DeNero and Dan Klein. 2008. The complexity of phrase alignment problems. In *Proceedings of the 46th Annual Meeting of the Association for Computational Linguistics: Human Language Technologies (ACL-HLT)*, pages 25–28.

Matthias Eck, Stephan Vogel, and Alex Waibel. 2007. Translation model pruning via usage statistics for statistical machine translation. In *Human Language Technologies 2007: The Conference of the North American Chapter of the Association for Computational Linguistics (NAACL-HLT)*, pages 21–24.

Howard Johnson, Joel Martin, George Foster, and Roland Kuhn. 2007. Improving translation quality by discarding most of the phrasetable. In *Proceedings of the 2007 Joint Conference on Empirical Methods in Natural Language Processing and Computational Natural Language Learning (EMNLP-CoNLL)*, pages 967–975.

Marcin Junczys-Dowmunt. 2012. Phrasal rank-encoding: Exploiting phrase redundancy and translational relations for phrase table compression. *The Prague Bulletin of Mathematical Linguistics*, 98:63–74.

David Kempe, Jon Kleinberg, and Éva Tardos. 2003. Maximizing the spread of influence through a social network. In *Proceedings of the 9th ACM SIGKDD international conference on Knowledge discovery and data mining (KDD)*, pages 137–146.

Katrin Kirchhoff and Jeff Bilmes. 2014. Submodularity for data selection in machine translation. In *Proceedings of the 2014 Conference on Empirical Methods in Natural Language Processing (EMNLP)*, pages 131–141.

Philipp Koehn, Hieu Hoang, Alexandra Birch, Chris Callison-Burch, Marcello Federico, Nicola Bertoldi, Brooke Cowan, Wade Shen, Christine Moran, Richard Zens, Chris Dyer, Ondrej Bojar, Alexandra Constantin, and Evan Herbst. 2007. Moses: Open source toolkit for statistical machine translation. In *Proceedings of the 45th Annual Meeting of the Association for Computational Linguistics Companion Volume Proceedings of the Demo and Poster Sessions*, pages 177–180.

Jure Leskovec, Andreas Krause, Carlos Guestrin, Christos Faloutsos, Jeanne VanBriesen, and Natalie Glance. 2007. Cost-effective outbreak detection in networks. In *Proceedings of the 13th ACM SIGKDD International Conference on Knowledge Discovery and Data Mining (KDD)*, pages 420–429.

Hui Lin and Jeff Bilmes. 2010. Multi-document summarization via budgeted maximization of submodular functions. In *Human Language Technologies: The 2010 Annual Conference of the North American Chapter of the Association for Computational Linguistics (NAACL-HLT)*, pages 912–920.

Hui Lin and Jeff Bilmes. 2011. A class of submodular functions for document summarization. In *Proceedings of the 49th Annual Meeting of the Association for Computational Linguistics: Human Language Technologies (ACL-HLT)*, pages 510–520.

Wang Ling, João Graça, Isabel Trancoso, and Alan Black. 2012. Entropy-based pruning for phrase-based machine translation. In *Proceedings of the 2012 Joint Conference on Empirical Methods in Natural Language Processing and Computational Natural Language Learning (EMNLP-CoNLL)*, pages 962–971.

Michel Minoux. 1978. Accelerated greedy algorithms for maximizing submodular set functions. In *Proceedings of the 8th IFIP Conference on Optimization Techniques*, pages 234–243.

Baharan Mirzasoleiman, Amin Karbasi, Rik Sarkar, and Andreas Krause. 2013. Distributed submodular maximization: Identifying representative elements in massive data. In *Advances in Neural Information Processing Systems (NIPS)*, pages 2049–2057.

Baharan Mirzasoleiman, Ashwinkumar Badanidiyuru, Amin Karbasi, Jan Vondrák, and Andreas Krause. 2015. Lazier than lazy greedy. In *Proceedings of the 29th AAAI Conference on Artificial Intelligence (AAAI)*, pages 1812–1818.

George L Nemhauser, Laurence A Wolsey, and Marshall L Fisher. 1978. An analysis of approximations for maximizing submodular set functionsi. *Mathematical Programming*, 14(1):265–294.

Franz Josef Och and Hermann Ney. 2003. A systematic comparison of various statistical alignment models. *Computational Linguistics*, 29(1):19–51.

Franz Josef Och. 2003. Minimum error rate training in statistical machine translation. In *Proceedings of the 41st Annual Meeting of the Association for Computational Linguistics (ACL)*, pages 160–167.

Richard Zens, Daisy Stanton, and Peng Xu. 2012. A systematic comparison of phrase table pruning techniques. In *Proceedings of the 2012 Joint Conference on Empirical Methods in Natural Language Processing and Computational Natural Language Learning (EMNLP-CoNLL)*, pages 972–983.

Multilingual Part-of-Speech Tagging with
Bidirectional Long Short-Term Memory Models and Auxiliary Loss

Barbara Plank
University of Groningen
The Netherlands
b.plank@rug.nl

Anders Søgaard
University of Copenhagen
Denmark
soegaard@hum.ku.dk

Yoav Goldberg
Bar-Ilan University
Israel
yoav.goldberg@gmail.com

Abstract

Bidirectional long short-term memory (bi-LSTM) networks have recently proven successful for various NLP sequence modeling tasks, but little is known about their reliance to input representations, target languages, data set size, and label noise. We address these issues and evaluate bi-LSTMs with word, character, and unicode byte embeddings for POS tagging. We compare bi-LSTMs to traditional POS taggers across languages and data sizes. We also present a novel bi-LSTM model, which combines the POS tagging loss function with an auxiliary loss function that accounts for rare words. The model obtains state-of-the-art performance across 22 languages, and works especially well for morphologically complex languages. Our analysis suggests that bi-LSTMs are less sensitive to training data size and label corruptions (at small noise levels) than previously assumed.

1 Introduction

Recently, bidirectional long short-term memory networks (bi-LSTM) (Graves and Schmidhuber, 2005; Hochreiter and Schmidhuber, 1997) have been used for language modelling (Ling et al., 2015), POS tagging (Ling et al., 2015; Wang et al., 2015), transition-based dependency parsing (Ballesteros et al., 2015; Kiperwasser and Goldberg, 2016), fine-grained sentiment analysis (Liu et al., 2015), syntactic chunking (Huang et al., 2015), and semantic role labeling (Zhou and Xu, 2015). LSTMs are recurrent neural networks (RNNs) in which layers are designed to prevent vanishing gradients. Bidirectional LSTMs make a backward and forward pass through the sequence before passing on to the next layer. For further details, see (Goldberg, 2015; Cho, 2015).

We consider using bi-LSTMs for POS tagging. Previous work on using deep learning-based methods for POS tagging has focused either on a single language (Collobert et al., 2011; Wang et al., 2015) or a small set of languages (Ling et al., 2015; Santos and Zadrozny, 2014). Instead we evaluate our models across 22 languages. In addition, we compare performance with representations at different levels of granularity (words, characters, and bytes). These levels of representation were previously introduced in different efforts (Chrupała, 2013; Zhang et al., 2015; Ling et al., 2015; Santos and Zadrozny, 2014; Gillick et al., 2016; Kim et al., 2015), but a comparative evaluation was missing.

Moreover, deep networks are often said to require large volumes of training data. We investigate to what extent bi-LSTMs are more sensitive to the amount of training data and label noise than standard POS taggers.

Finally, we introduce a novel model, a bi-LSTM trained with auxiliary loss. The model jointly predicts the POS and the log frequency of the next word. The intuition behind this model is that the auxiliary loss, being predictive of word frequency, helps to differentiate the representations of rare and common words. We indeed observe performance gains on rare and out-of-vocabulary words. These performance gains transfer into general improvements for morphologically rich languages.

Contributions In this paper, we a) evaluate the effectiveness of different representations in bi-LSTMs, b) compare these models across a large set of languages and under varying conditions (data size, label noise) and c) propose a novel bi-LSTM model with auxiliary loss (LOGFREQ).

412

Proceedings of the 54th Annual Meeting of the Association for Computational Linguistics, pages 412–418,
Berlin, Germany, August 7-12, 2016. ©2016 Association for Computational Linguistics

2 Tagging with bi-LSTMs

Recurrent neural networks (RNNs) (Elman, 1990) allow the computation of fixed-size vector representations for word sequences of arbitrary length. An RNN is a function that reads in n vectors $x_1, ..., x_n$ and produces an output vector h_n, that depends on the entire sequence $x_1, ..., x_n$. The vector h_n is then fed as an input to some classifier, or higher-level RNNs in stacked/hierarchical models. The entire network is trained jointly such that the hidden representation captures the important information from the sequence for the prediction task.

A bidirectional recurrent neural network (bi-RNN) (Graves and Schmidhuber, 2005) is an extension of an RNN that reads the input sequence twice, from left to right and right to left, and the encodings are concatenated. The literature uses the term bi-RNN to refer to two related architectures, which we refer to here as "context bi-RNN" and "sequence bi-RNN". In a sequence bi-RNN (bi-RNN$_{\text{seq}}$), the input is a sequence of vectors $x_{1:n}$ and the output is a concatenation ($\circ$) of a forward (f) and reverse (r) RNN each reading the sequence in a different directions:

$$v = \text{bi-RNN}_{\text{seq}}(x_{1:n}) = \text{RNN}_f(x_{1:n}) \circ \text{RNN}_r(x_{n:1})$$

In a context bi-RNN (bi-RNN$_{\text{ctx}}$), we get an additional input i indicating a sequence position, and the resulting vectors v_i result from concatenating the RNN encodings up to i:

$$v_i = \text{bi-RNN}_{\text{ctx}}(x_{1:n}, i) = \text{RNN}_f(x_{1:i}) \circ \text{RNN}_r(x_{n:i})$$

Thus, the state vector v_i in this bi-RNN encodes information at position i and its entire sequential context. Another view of the context bi-RNN is of taking a sequence $x_{1:n}$ and returning the corresponding sequence of state vectors $v_{1:n}$.

LSTMs (Hochreiter and Schmidhuber, 1997) are a variant of RNNs that replace the cells of RNNs with LSTM cells that were designed to prevent vanishing gradients. Bidirectional LSTMs are the bi-RNN counterpart based on LSTMs.

Our basic bi-LSTM tagging model is a context bi-LSTM taking as input word embeddings $\vec{w}$. We incorporate subtoken information using an hierarchical bi-LSTM architecture (Ling et al., 2015; Ballesteros et al., 2015). We compute subtoken-level (either characters $\vec{c}$ or unicode byte $\vec{b}$) embeddings of words using a sequence bi-LSTM at the lower level. This representation is then concatenated with the (learned) word embeddings vector $\vec{w}$ which forms the input to the context bi-LSTM at the next layer. This model, illustrated in Figure 1 (lower part in left figure), is inspired by Ballesteros et al. (2015). We also test models in which we only keep sub-token information, e.g., either both byte and character embeddings (Figure 1, right) or a single (sub-)token representation alone.

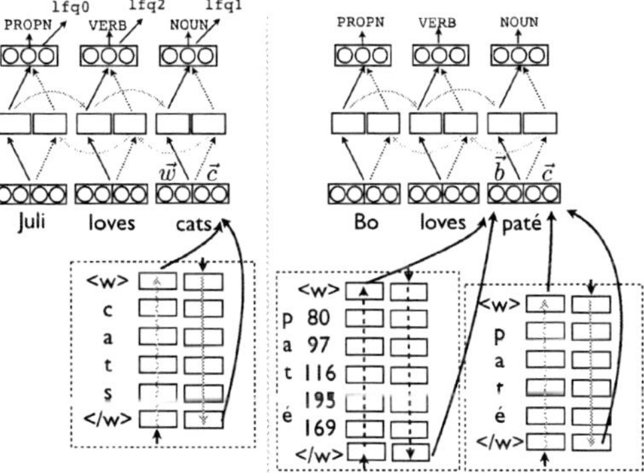

Figure 1: Right: bi-LSTM, illustrated with $\vec{b} + \vec{c}$ (bytes and characters), for $\vec{w} + \vec{c}$ replace $\vec{b}$ with words $\vec{w}$. Left: FREQBIN, our multi-task bi-LSTM that predicts at every time step the tag and the frequency class for the next token.

In our novel model, cf. Figure 1 left, we train the bi-LSTM tagger to predict both the tags of the sequence, as well as a label that represents the log frequency of the next token as estimated from the training data. Our combined cross-entropy loss is now: $L(\hat{y}_t, y_t) + L(\hat{y}_a, y_a)$, where t stands for a POS tag and a is the log frequency label, i.e., $a = int(log(freq_{train}(w)))$. Combining this log frequency objective with the tagging task can be seen as an instance of multi-task learning in which the labels are predicted jointly. The idea behind this model is to make the representation predictive for frequency, which encourages the model to not share representations between common and rare words, thus benefiting the handling of rare tokens.

3 Experiments

All bi-LSTM models were implemented in CNN/pycnn,[1] a flexible neural network library. For all models we use the same hyperparameters, which were set on English dev, i.e., SGD training with cross-entropy loss, no mini-batches, 20

[1] https://github.com/clab/cnn

epochs, default learning rate (0.1), 128 dimensions for word embeddings, 100 for character and byte embeddings, 100 hidden states and Gaussian noise with σ=0.2. As training is stochastic in nature, we use a fixed seed throughout. Embeddings are not initialized with pre-trained embeddings, except when reported otherwise. In that case we use off-the-shelf `polyglot` embeddings (Al-Rfou et al., 2013).[2] No further unlabeled data is considered in this paper. The code is released at: `https://github.com/bplank/bilstm-aux`

Taggers We want to compare POS taggers under varying conditions. We hence use three different types of taggers: our implementation of a bi-LSTM; TNT (Brants, 2000)—a second order HMM with suffix trie handling for OOVs. We use TNT as it was among the best performing taggers evaluated in Horsmann et al. (2015).[3] We complement the NN-based and HMM-based tagger with a CRF tagger, using a freely available implementation (Plank et al., 2014) based on `crfsuite`.

3.1 Datasets

For the multilingual experiments, we use the data from the Universal Dependencies project v1.2 (Nivre et al., 2015) (17 POS) with the canonical data splits. For languages with token segmentation ambiguity we use the provided gold segmentation. If there is more than one treebank per language, we use the treebank that has the canonical language name (e.g., *Finnish* instead of *Finnish-FTB*). We consider all languages that have at least 60k tokens and are distributed with word forms, resulting in 22 languages. We also report accuracies on WSJ (45 POS) using the standard splits (Collins, 2002; Manning, 2011). The overview of languages is provided in Table 1.

3.2 Results

Our results are given in Table 2. First of all, notice that TNT performs remarkably well across the 22 languages, closely followed by CRF. The bi-LSTM tagger ($\vec{w}$) without lower-level bi-LSTM for subtokens falls short, outperforms the traditional taggers only on 3 languages. The bi-LSTM

	COARSE	FINE		COARSE	FINE
ar	non-IE	Semitic	he	non-IE	Semitic
bg	Indoeuropean	Slavic	hi	Indoeuropean	Indo-Iranian
cs	Indoeuropean	Slavic	hr	Indoeuropean	Slavic
da	Indoeuropean	Germanic	id	non-IE	Austronesian
de	Indoeuropean	Germanic	it	Indoeuropean	Romance
en	Indoeuropean	Germanic	nl	Indoeuropean	Germanic
es	Indoeuropean	Romance	no	Indoeuropean	Germanic
eu	Language isolate		pl	Indoeuropean	Slavic
fa	Indoeuropean	Indo-Iranian	pt	Indoeuropean	Romance
fi	non-IE	Uralic	sl	Indoeuropean	Slavic
fr	Indoeuropean	Romance	sv	Indoeuropean	Germanic

Table 1: Grouping of languages.

model clearly benefits from character representations. The model using characters alone ($\vec{c}$) works remarkably well, it improves over TNT on 9 languages (incl. Slavic and Nordic languages). The combined word+character representation model is the best representation, outperforming the baseline on all except one language (Indonesian), providing strong results already without pre-trained embeddings. This model ($\vec{w} + \vec{c}$) reaches the biggest improvement (more than +2% accuracy) on Hebrew and Slovene. Initializing the word embeddings (+POLYGLOT) with off-the-shelf language-specific embeddings further improves accuracy. The only system we are aware of that evaluates on UD is Gillick et al. (2016) (last column). However, note that these results are not strictly comparable as they use the earlier UD v1.1 version.

The overall best system is the multi-task bi-LSTM FREQBIN (it uses $\vec{w} + \vec{c}$ and POLYGLOT initialization for $\vec{w}$). While on macro average it is on par with bi-LSTM $\vec{w} + \vec{c}$, it obtains the best results on 12/22 languages, and it is successful in predicting POS for OOV tokens (cf. Table 2 OOV ACC columns), especially for languages like Arabic, Farsi, Hebrew, Finnish.

We examined simple RNNs and confirm the finding of Ling et al. (2015) that they performed worse than their LSTM counterparts. Finally, the bi-LSTM tagger is competitive on WSJ, cf. Table 3.

Rare words In order to evaluate the effect of modeling sub-token information, we examine accuracy rates at different frequency rates. Figure 2 shows absolute improvements in accuracy of bi-LSTM $\vec{w} + \vec{c}$ over mean log frequency, for different language families. We see that especially for Slavic and non-Indoeuropean languages, having high morphologic complexity, most of the improvement is obtained in the Zipfian tail. Rare tokens benefit from the sub-token representations.

---

[2]`https://sites.google.com/site/rmyeid/projects/polyglot`

[3]They found TreeTagger was closely followed by HunPos, a re-implementation of TnT, and Stanford and ClearNLP were lower ranked. In an initial investigation, we compared Tnt, HunPos and TreeTagger and found Tnt to be consistently better than Treetagger, Hunpos followed closely but crashed on some languages (e.g., Arabic).

	BASELINES		bi-LSTM using:				$\vec{w}+\vec{c}$ +POLYGLOT		OOV ACC		BTS
	TNT	CRF	$\vec{w}$	$\vec{c}$	$\vec{c}+\vec{b}$	$\vec{w}+\vec{c}$	bi-LSTM	FREQBIN	bi-LSTM	FREQBIN	
avg	94.61	94.27	92.37	94.29	94.01	96.08†	**96.50**	**96.50**	87.80	87.98	95.70
Indoeur.	94.70	94.58	92.72	94.58	94.28	96.24†	**96.63**	96.61	87.47	87.63	–
non-Indo.	94.57	93.62	91.97	93.51	93.16	95.70†	96.21	**96.28**	90.26	90.39	–
Germanic	93.27	93.21	91.18	92.89	92.59	94.97†	**95.55**	95.49	85.58	85.45	–
Romance	95.37	95.53	94.71	94.76	94.49	95.63†	**96.93**	**96.93**	85.84	86.07	–
Slavic	95.64	94.96	91.79	96.45	96.26	97.23†	97.42	**97.43**	91.48	91.69	–
ar	97.82	97.56	95.48	98.68	98.43	98.89	98.87	**98.91**	95.90	96.21	–
bg	96.84	96.36	95.12	97.89	97.78	**98.25**	98.23	90.06	90.06	90.56	97.84
cs	96.82	96.56	93.77	96.38	96.08	97.93	**98.02**	97.89	91.65	91.30	98.50
da	94.29	93.83	91.96	95.12	94.88	95.94	96.16	**96.35**	86.13	86.35	95.52
de	92.64	91.38	90.33	90.02	90.11	93.11	**93.51**	93.38	85.37	86.77	92.87
en	92.66	93.35	92.10	91.62	91.57	94.61	**95.17**	95.16	80.28	80.11	93.87
es	94.55	94.23	93.60	93.06	92.29	95.34	95.67	**95.74**	79.26	79.27	95.80
eu	93.35	91.63	88.00	92.48	92.72	94.91	95.38	**95.51**	83.55	84.30	–
fa	95.98	95.65	95.31	95.82	95.03	96.89	**97.60**	97.49	88.82	89.05	96.82
fi	93.59	90.32	87.95	90.25	89.15	95.18	95.74	**95.85**	88.35	88.85	95.48
fr	94.51	95.14	94.44	94.39	93.69	96.04	**96.20**	96.11	82.79	83.54	95.75
he	93.71	93.63	93.97	93.74	93.58	95.92	96.92	**96.96**	88.75	88.83	–
hi	94.53	96.00	95.99	93.40	92.99	96.64	96.97	**97.10**	83.98	85.27	–
hr	94.06	93.16	89.24	95.32	94.47	95.59	96.27	**96.82**	90.50	92.71	–
id	93.16	92.96	90.48	91.37	91.46	92.79	93.32	**93.41**	88.03	87.67	92.85
it	96.16	96.43	96.57	95.62	95.77	97.64	97.90	**97.95**	89.15	89.15	97.56
nl	88.54	90.03	84.96	89.11	87.74	92.07	92.82	**93.30**	78.61	75.95	–
no	96.31	96.21	94.39	95.87	95.75	97.77	**98.06**	98.03	93.56	93.75	–
pl	95.57	93.96	89.73	95.80	96.19	96.62	**97.63**	97.62	95.00	94.94	–
pt	96.27	96.32	94.24	95.96	96.2	97.48	**97.94**	97.90	92.16	92.33	–
sl	94.92	94.77	91.09	96.87	96.77	97.78	**96.97**	96.84	90.19	88.94	–
sv	95.19	94.45	93.32	95.57	95.5	96.30	96.60	**96.69**	89.53	89.80	95.57

Table 2: Tagging accuracies on UD 1.2 test sets. $\vec{w}$: words, $\vec{c}$: characters, $\vec{b}$: bytes. Bold/†: best accuracy/representation; +POLYGLOT: using pre-trained embeddings. FREQBIN: our multi-task model. OOV ACC: accuracies on OOVs. BTS: best results in Gillick et al. (2016) (not strictly comparable).

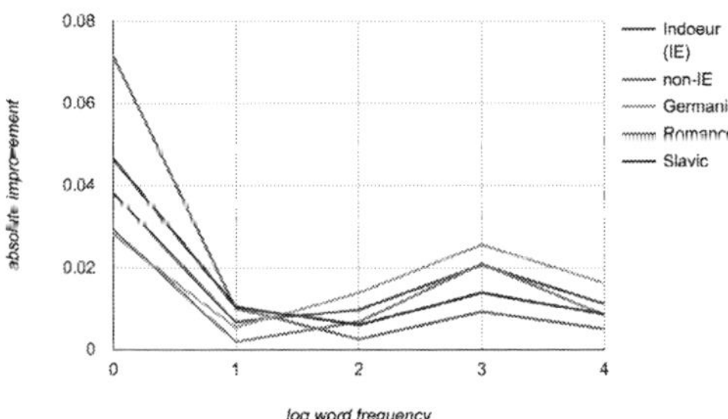

Figure 2: Absolute improvements of bi-LSTM ($\vec{w}+\vec{c}$) over TNT vs mean log frequency.

WSJ	Accuracy
Convnet (Santos and Zadrozny, 2014)	97.32
Convnet reimplementation (Ling et al., 2015)	96.80
Bi-RNN (Ling et al., 2015)	95.93
Bi-LSTM (Ling et al., 2015)	97.36
Our bi-LSTM $_{\vec{w}+\vec{c}}$	97.22

Table 3: Comparison POS accuracy on WSJ; bi-LSTM: 30 epochs, σ=0.3, no POLYGLOT.

Data set size Prior work mostly used large data sets when applying neural network based approaches (Zhang et al., 2015). We evaluate how brittle such models are with respect to their more traditional counterparts by training bi-LSTM ($\vec{w}+\vec{c}$ without Polyglot embeddings) for increas-ing amounts of training instances (number of sentences). The learning curves in Figure 3 show similar trends across language families.[4] TNT is better with little data, bi-LSTM is better with more data, and bi-LSTM always wins over CRF. The bi-LSTM model performs already surprisingly well after only 500 training sentences. For non-Indoeuropean languages it is on par and above

---

[4]We observe the same pattern with more, 40, iterations.

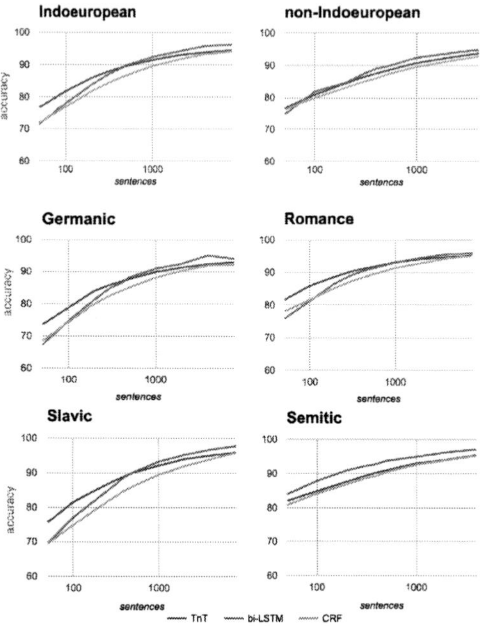

Figure 3: Amount of training data (number of sentences) vs tagging accuracy.

the other taggers with even less data (100 sentences). This shows that the bi-LSTMs often needs more data than the generative markovian model, but this is definitely less than what we expected.

Label Noise We investigated the susceptibility of the models to noise, by artificially corrupting training labels. Our initial results show that at low noise rates, bi-LSTMs and TNT are affected similarly, their accuracies drop to a similar degree. Only at higher noise levels (more than 30% corrupted labels), bi-LSTMs are less robust, showing higher drops in accuracy compared to TNT. This is the case for all investigated language families.

4 Related Work

Character embeddings were first introduced by Sutskever et al. (2011) for language modeling. Early applications include text classification (Chrupała, 2013; Zhang et al., 2015). Recently, these representations were successfully applied to a range of structured prediction tasks. For POS tagging, Santos and Zadrozny (2014) were the first to propose character-based models. They use a convolutional neural network (CNN; or convnet) and evaluated their model on English (PTB) and Portuguese, showing that the model achieves

state-of-the-art performance close to taggers using carefully designed feature templates. Ling et al. (2015) extend this line and compare a novel bi-LSTM model, learning word representations through character embeddings. They evaluate their model on a language modeling and POS tagging setup, and show that bi-LSTMs outperform the CNN approach of Santos and Zadrozny (2014). Similarly, Labeau et al. (2015) evaluate character embeddings for German. Bi-LSTMs for POS tagging are also reported in Wang et al. (2015), however, they only explore word embeddings, orthographic information and evaluate on WSJ only. A related study is Cheng et al. (2015) who propose a multi-task RNN for named entity recognition by jointly predicting the next token and current token's name label. Our model is simpler, it uses a very coarse set of labels rather then integrating an entire language modeling task which is computationally more expensive. An interesting recent study is Gillick et al. (2016), they build a single byte-to-span model for multiple languages based on a sequence-to-sequence RNN (Sutskever et al., 2014) achieving impressive results. We would like to extend this work in their direction.

5 Conclusions

We evaluated token and subtoken-level representations for neural network-based part-of-speech tagging across 22 languages and proposed a novel multi-task bi-LSTM with auxiliary loss. The auxiliary loss is effective at improving the accuracy of rare words.

Subtoken representations are necessary to obtain a state-of-the-art POS tagger, and character embeddings are particularly helpful for non-Indoeuropean and Slavic languages.

Combining them with word embeddings in a hierarchical network provides the best representation. The bi-LSTM tagger is as effective as the CRF and HMM taggers with already as little as 500 training sentences, but is less robust to label noise (at higher noise rates).

Acknowledgments

We thank the anonymous reviewers for their feedback. AS is funded by the ERC Starting Grant LOWLANDS No. 313695. YG is supported by The Israeli Science Foundation (grant number 1555/15) and a Google Research Award.

References

Rami Al-Rfou, Bryan Perozzi, and Steven Skiena. 2013. Polyglot: Distributed Word Representations for Multilingual NLP. In *CoNLL*.

Miguel Ballesteros, Chris Dyer, and Noah A. Smith. 2015. Improved Transition-based Parsing by Modeling Characters instead of Words with LSTMs. In *EMNLP*.

Thorsten Brants. 2000. Tnt: a statistical part-of-speech tagger. In *Proceedings of the sixth conference on Applied natural language processing*.

Hao Cheng, Hao Fang, and Mari Ostendorf. 2015. Open-Domain Name Error Detection using a Multi-Task RNN. In *EMNLP*.

Kyunghyun Cho. 2015. Natural language understanding with distributed representation. *ArXiv*, abs/1511.07916.

Grzegorz Chrupała. 2013. Text segmentation with character-level text embeddings. In *Workshop on Deep Learning for Audio, Speech and Language Processing, ICML*.

Michael Collins. 2002. Discriminative training methods for Hidden Markov Models. In *EMNLP*.

Ronan Collobert, Jason Weston, Léon Bottou, Michael Karlen, Koray Kavukcuoglu, and Pavel Kuksa. 2011. Natural language processing (almost) from scratch. *The Journal of Machine Learning Research*, 12:2493–2537.

Jeffrey L Elman. 1990. Finding structure in time. *Cognitive science*, 14(2):179–211.

Dan Gillick, Cliff Brunk, Oriol Vinyals, and Amarnag Subramanya. 2016. Multilingual language processing from bytes. In *NAACL*.

Yoav Goldberg. 2015. A primer on neural network models for natural language processing. *ArXiv*, abs/1510.00726.

Alex Graves and Jürgen Schmidhuber. 2005. Framewise phoneme classification with bidirectional lstm and other neural network architectures. *Neural Networks*, 18(5):602–610.

Sepp Hochreiter and Jürgen Schmidhuber. 1997. Long short-term memory. *Neural computation*, 9(8):1735–1780.

Tobias Horsmann, Nicolai Erbs, and Torsten Zesch. 2015. Fast or accurate?–a comparative evaluation of pos tagging models. In *Proceedings of the International Conference of the German Society for Computational Linguistics and Language Technology*.

Zhiheng Huang, Wei Xu, and Kai Yu. 2015. Bidirectional LSTM-CRF models for sequence tagging. *arXiv preprint arXiv:1508.01991*.

Yoon Kim, Yacine Jernite, David Sontag, and Alexander M Rush. 2015. Character-aware neural language models. *arXiv preprint arXiv:1508.06615*.

E. Kiperwasser and Y. Goldberg. 2016. Simple and Accurate Dependency Parsing Using Bidirectional LSTM Feature Representations. *ArXiv e-prints*.

Matthieu Labeau, Kevin Löser, and Alexandre Allauzen. 2015. Non-lexical neural architecture for fine-grained pos tagging. In *EMNLP*.

Wang Ling, Chris Dyer, Alan W Black, Isabel Trancoso, Ramon Fermandez, Silvio Amir, Luis Marujo, and Tiago Luis. 2015. Finding function in form: Compositional character models for open vocabulary word representation. In *EMNLP*.

Pengfei Liu, Shafiq Joty, and Helen Meng. 2015. Fine-grained opinion mining with recurrent neural networks and word embeddings. In *EMNLP*.

Christopher D Manning. 2011. Part-of-speech tagging from 97% to 100%: is it time for some linguistics? In *Computational Linguistics and Intelligent Text Processing*. Springer.

Joakim Nivre, Željko Agić, Maria Jesus Aranzabe, Masayuki Asahara, Aitziber Atutxa, Miguel Ballesteros, John Bauer, Kepa Bengoetxea, Riyaz Ahmad Bhat, Cristina Bosco, Sam Bowman, Giuseppe G. A. Celano, Miriam Connor, Marie-Catherine de Marneffe, Arantza Diaz de Ilarraza, Kaja Dobrovoljc, Timothy Dozat, Tomaž Erjavec, Richárd Farkas, Jennifer Foster, Daniel Galbraith, Filip Ginter, Iakes Goenaga, Koldo Gojenola, Yoav Goldberg, Berta Gonzales, Bruno Guillaume, Jan Hajič, Dag Haug, Radu Ion, Elena Irimia, Anders Johannsen, Hiroshi Kanayama, Jenna Kanerva, Simon Krek, Veronika Laippala, Alessandro Lenci, Nikola Ljubešić, Teresa Lynn, Christopher Manning, Ctlina Mrnduc, David Mareček, Héctor Martínez Alonso, Jan Mašek, Yuji Matsumoto, Ryan McDonald, Anna Missilä, Verginica Mititelu, Yusuke Miyao, Simonetta Montemagni, Shunsuke Mori, Hanna Nurmi, Petya Osenova, Lilja Øvrelid, Elena Pascual, Marco Passarotti, Cenel-Augusto Perez, Slav Petrov, Jussi Piitulainen, Barbara Plank, Martin Popel, Prokopis Prokopidis, Sampo Pyysalo, Loganathan Ramasamy, Rudolf Rosa, Shadi Saleh, Sebastian Schuster, Wolfgang Seeker, Mojgan Seraji, Natalia Silveira, Maria Simi, Radu Simionescu, Katalin Simkó, Kiril Simov, Aaron Smith, Jan Štěpánek, Alane Suhr, Zsolt Szántó, Takaaki Tanaka, Reut Tsarfaty, Sumire Uematsu, Larraitz Uria, Viktor Varga, Veronika Vincze, Zdeněk Žabokrtský, Daniel Zeman, and Hanzhi Zhu. 2015. Universal dependencies 1.2. LINDAT/CLARIN digital library at Institute of Formal and Applied Linguistics, Charles University in Prague.

Barbara Plank, Dirk Hovy, Ryan McDonald, and Anders Søgaard. 2014. Adapting taggers to twitter using not-so-distant supervision. In *COLING*.

Cicero D Santos and Bianca Zadrozny. 2014. Learning character-level representations for part-of-speech tagging. In *ICML*.

Ilya Sutskever, James Martens, and Geoffrey E Hinton. 2011. Generating text with recurrent neural networks. In *ICML*.

Ilya Sutskever, Oriol Vinyals, and Quoc V Le. 2014. Sequence to sequence learning with neural networks. In *NIPS*.

Peilu Wang, Yao Qian, Frank K. Soong, Lei He, and Hai Zhao. 2015. Part-of-speech tagging with bidirectional long short-term memory recurrent neural network. *pre-print*, abs/1510.06168.

Xiang Zhang, Junbo Zhao, and Yann LeCun. 2015. Character-level convolutional networks for text classification. In *Advances in Neural Information Processing Systems*, pages 649–657.

Jie Zhou and Wei Xu. 2015. End-to-end learning of semantic role labeling using recurrent neural networks. In *ACL*.

Matrix Factorization using Window Sampling and Negative Sampling for Improved Word Representations

Alexandre Salle[1]   Marco Idiart[2]   Aline Villavicencio[1]

[1] Institute of Informatics
[2] Physics Department
Universidade Federal do Rio Grande do Sul
Porto Alegre, Brazil
{atsalle,avillavicencio}@inf.ufrgs.br, idiart@if.ufrgs.br

Abstract

In this paper, we propose LexVec, a new method for generating distributed word representations that uses low-rank, weighted factorization of the Positive Point-wise Mutual Information matrix via stochastic gradient descent, employing a weighting scheme that assigns heavier penalties for errors on frequent co-occurrences while still accounting for negative co-occurrence. Evaluation on word similarity and analogy tasks shows that LexVec matches and often outperforms state-of-the-art methods on many of these tasks.

1 Introduction

Distributed word representations, or word embeddings, have been successfully used in many NLP applications (Turian et al., 2010; Collobert et al., 2011; Socher et al., 2013). Traditionally, word representations have been obtained using *count-based* methods (Baroni et al., 2014), where the co-occurrence matrix is derived directly from corpus counts (Lin, 1998) or using association measures like Point-wise Mutual Information (PMI) (Church and Hanks, 1990) and Positive PMI (PPMI) (Bullinaria and Levy, 2007; Levy et al., 2014).

Techniques for generating lower-rank representations have also been employed, such as PPMI-SVD (Levy et al., 2015) and GloVe (Pennington et al., 2014), both achieving state-of-the-art performance on a variety of tasks.

Alternatively, vector-space models can be generated with *predictive* methods, which generally outperform the count-based methods (Baroni et al., 2014), the most notable of which is Skip-gram with Negative Sampling (SGNS, Mikolov

et al. (2013b)), which uses a neural network to generate embeddings. It implicitly factorizes a shifted PMI matrix, and its performance has been linked to the weighting of positive and negative co-occurrences (Levy and Goldberg, 2014).

In this paper, we present Lexical Vectors (LexVec), a method for factorizing PPMI matrices that combines characteristics of all these methods. On the one hand, it uses SGNS window sampling, negative sampling, and stochastic gradient descent (SGD) to minimize a loss function that weights frequent co-occurrences heavily but also takes into account negative co-occurrence. However, since PPMI generally outperforms PMI on semantic similarity tasks (Bullinaria and Levy, 2007), rather than implicitly factorize a shifted PMI matrix (like SGNS), LexVec explicitly factorizes the PPMI matrix.

This paper is organized as follows: First, we describe PPMI-SVD, GloVe, and SGNS (§2) before introducing the proposed method, LexVec (§3), and evaluating it on word similarity and analogy tasks (§4). We conclude with an analysis of results and discussion of future work.

We provide source code for the model at `https://github.com/alexandres/lexvec`.

2 Related Work

2.1 PPMI-SVD

Given a word w and a symmetric window of *win* context words to the left and *win* to the right, the co-occurrence matrix of elements M_{wc} is defined as the number of times a target word w and the context word c co-occurred in the corpus within the window. The PMI matrix is defined as

$$PMI_{wc} = \log \frac{M_{wc} \, M_{**}}{M_{w*} \, M_{*c}} \qquad (1)$$

Proceedings of the 54th Annual Meeting of the Association for Computational Linguistics, pages 419–424,
Berlin, Germany, August 7-12, 2016. ©2016 Association for Computational Linguistics

where '*' represents the summation of the corresponding index. As this matrix is unbounded in the inferior limit, in most applications it is replaced by its positive definite version, PPMI, where negative values are set to zero. The performance of the PPMI matrix on word similarity tasks can be further improved by using *context-distribution smoothing* (Levy et al., 2015) and *subsampling* the corpus (Mikolov et al., 2013b). As word embeddings with lower dimensionality may improve efficiency and generalization (Levy et al., 2015), the improved PPMI* matrix can be factorized as a product of two lower rank matrices.

$$PPMI^*_{wc} \simeq W_w \tilde{W}_c^\top \qquad (2)$$

where W_w and $\tilde{W}_c$ are d-dimensional row vectors corresponding to vector embeddings for the target and context words. Using the truncated SVD of size d yields the factorization $U\Sigma T^\top$ with the lowest possible L_2 error (Eckert and Young, 1936).

Levy et al. (2015) recommend using $W = U\Sigma^p$ as the word representations, as suggested by Bullinaria and Levy (2012), who borrowed the idea of weighting singular values from the work of Caron (2001) on Latent Semantic Analysis. Although the optimal value of p is highly task-dependent (Österlund et al., 2015), we set $p = 0.5$ as it has been shown to perform well on the word similarity and analogy tasks we use in our experiments (Levy et al., 2015).

2.2 GloVe

GloVe (Pennington et al., 2014) factors the logarithm of the co-occurrence matrix $\hat{M}$ that considers the position of the context words in the window. The loss function for factorization is

$$L_{wc}^{GloVe} = \frac{1}{2} f(\hat{M}_{wc})(W_w \tilde{W}_c^\top + b_w + \tilde{b}_c - \log \hat{M}_{wc})^2 \qquad (3)$$

where b_w and $\tilde{b}_c$ are bias terms, and f is a weighting function defined as

$$f(x) = \begin{cases} (x/x_{max})^\beta & if \ x < x_{max} \\ 1 & otherwise \end{cases} \qquad (4)$$

W and $\tilde{W}$ are obtained by iterating over all non-zero (w, c) cells in the co-occurrence matrix and minimizing eq. (3) through SGD.

The weighting function (in eq. (3)) penalizes more heavily reconstruction error of frequent co-occurrences, improving on PPMI-SVD's L_2 loss, which weights all reconstruction errors equally. However, as it does not penalize reconstruction errors for pairs with zero counts in the co-occurrence matrix, no effort is made to scatter the vectors for these pairs.

2.3 Skip-gram with Negative Sampling (SGNS)

SGNS (Mikolov et al., 2013b) trains a neural network to predict the probability of observing a context word c given a target word w, sliding a symmetric window over a subsampled training corpus with the window size being sampled uniformly from the range $[1, win]$. Each observed (w, c) pair is combined with k randomly sampled noise pairs (w, w_i) and used to calculate the loss function

$$L_{wc}^{SGNS} = \log \sigma(W_w \tilde{W}_c^\top) + \\ \sum_{i=1}^{k} \mathbf{E}_{w_i \sim P_n(w)} \log \sigma(-W_w \tilde{W}_{w_i}^\top) \qquad (5)$$

where $P_n(w)$ is the distribution from which noise words w_i are sampled.[1] We refer to this routine which SGNS uses for selecting (w, c) pairs by sliding a context window over the corpus for loss calculation and SGD as *window sampling*.

SGNS is implicitly performing the weighted factorization of a shifted PMI matrix (Levy and Goldberg, 2014). Window sampling ensures the factorization weights frequent co-occurrences heavily, but also takes into account negative co-occurrences, thanks to negative sampling.

3 LexVec

LexVec is based on the idea of factorizing the PPMI matrix using a reconstruction loss function that does not weight all errors equally, unlike SVD, but instead penalizes errors of frequent co-occurrences more heavily, while still treating negative co-occurrences, unlike GloVe. Moreover, given that using PPMI results in better performance than PMI on semantic tasks, we propose keeping the SGNS weighting scheme by using window sampling and negative sampling, but explicitly factorizing the PPMI matrix rather than implicitly factorizing the shifted PMI matrix. The LexVec loss function has two terms

---

[1] Following Mikolov et al. (2013b) it is the unigram distribution raised to the 3/4 power.

$$L_{wc}^{LexVec} = \frac{1}{2}(W_w \tilde{W}_c{}^\top - PPMI_{wc}^*)^2 \tag{6}$$

$$L_w^{LexVec} = \frac{1}{2}\sum_{i=1}^k \mathbf{E}_{w_i \sim P_n(w)}(W_w \tilde{W}_{w_i}{}^\top - PPMI_{ww_i}^*)^2 \tag{7}$$

We minimize eqs. (6) and (7) using two alternative approaches:

Mini-Batch (MB): This variant executes gradient descent in exactly the same way as SGNS. Every time a pair (w, c) is observed by window sampling and pairs $(w, w_{1...k})$ drawn by negative sampling, W_w, $\tilde{W}_c$, and $\tilde{W}_{w_{1...k}}$ are updated by gradient descent on the sum of eq.(6) and eq.(7). The global loss for this approach is

$$L^{LexVec} = \sum_{(w,c)} \#(w, c)\, (L_{wc}^{LexVec} + L_w^{LexVec}) \tag{8}$$

where $\#(w, c)$ is the number of times (w, c) is observed in the subsampled corpus.

Stochastic (St): Every context window is extended with k negative samples $w_{1...k}$. Iterative gradient descent of eq. (6) is then run on pairs (w, c_j), for $j = 1, .., 2*win$ and (w, c_i), $j = 1, .., k$ for each window. The global loss for this approach is

$$L^{LexVec'} = \sum_{(w,c)} \#(w, c) L_{wc}^{LexVec} + \sum_w \#(w) L_w^{LexVec} \tag{9}$$

where $\#(w)$ is the number of times w is observed in the subsampled corpus.

If a pair (w, c) co-occurs frequently, $\#(w, c)$ will weigh heavily in both eqs. (8) and (9), giving the desired weighting for frequent co-occurrences. The noise term, on the other hand, has corrections proportional to $\#(w)$ and $\#(w_i)$, for each pair (w, w_i). It produces corrections in pairs that due to frequency should be in the corpus but are not observed, therefore accounting automatically for negative co-occurrences.

4 Materials

All models were trained on a dump of Wikipedia from June 2015, split into sentences, with punctuation removed, numbers converted to words, and lower-cased. Words with less than 100 counts were removed, resulting in a vocabulary of 302,203 words. All models generate embeddings of 300 dimensions.

The PPMI* matrix used by both PPMI-SVD and LexVec was constructed using smoothing of $\alpha = 3/4$ suggested in (Levy et al., 2015) and an unweighted window of size 2. A dirty subsampling of the corpus is adopted for PPMI* and SGNS with threshold of $t = 10^{-5}$ (Mikolov et al., 2013b).[2] Additionally, SGNS uses 5 negative samples (Mikolov et al., 2013b), a window of size 10 (Levy et al., 2015), for 5 iterations with initial learning rate set to the default 0.025. GloVe is run with a window of size 10, $x_{max} = 100$, $\beta = 3/4$, for 50 iterations and initial learning rate of 0.05 (Pennington et al., 2014).

In LexVec two window sampling alternatives are compared: WS_{PPMI}, which keeps the same fixed size $win = 2$ as used to create the $PPMI^*$ matrix; or WS_{SGNS}, which adopts identical SGNS settings ($win = 10$ with size randomization). We run LexVec for 5 iterations over the training corpus.

All methods generate both word and context matrices (W and $\tilde{W}$): W is used for SGNS, PPMI-SVD and $W + \tilde{W}$ for GloVe (following Levy et al. (2015), and W and $W + \tilde{W}$ for LexVec.

For evaluation, we use standard word similarity and analogy tasks (Mikolov et al., 2013b; Levy et al., 2014; Pennington et al., 2014; Levy et al., 2015). We examine, in particular, if LexVec weighted PPMI* factorization outperforms SVD, GloVe (weighted factorization of $\log \hat{M}$) and Skip-gram (implicit factorization of the shifted PMI matrix), and compare the stochastic and mini-batch approaches.

Word similarity tasks are:[3] WS-353 Similarity (WSim) and Relatedness (WRel) (Finkelstein et al., 2001), MEN (Bruni et al., 2012), MTurk (Radinsky et al., 2011), RW (Luong et al., 2013), SimLex-999 (Hill et al., 2015), MC (Miller and Charles, 1991), RG (Rubenstein and Goodenough, 1965), and SCWS (Huang et al., 2012), calculated using cosine. Word analogy tasks are: Google semantic (GSem) and syntactic (GSyn) (Mikolov et al., 2013a) and MSR syntactic analogy dataset (Mikolov et al., 2013c), using $3CosAdd$ and $3CosMul$ (Levy et al., 2014).

---

[2] Words with unigram relative frequency $f > t$ are discarded from the training corpus with probability $p_w = 1 - \sqrt{t/f}$.

[3] http://www.cs.cmu.edu/ mfaruqui/suite.html

Method	WSim	WRel	MEN	MTurk	RW	SimLex-999	MC	RG	SCWS
PPMI-SVD	.731	.617	.731	.627	.427	.303	.770	.756	.615
GloVe	.719	.607	.736	.643	.400	.338	.725	.774	.573
SGNS	.770	.670	**.763**	**.675**	.465	**.339**	.823	.793	**.643**
LexVec + MB + $WS_{PPMI} + (W + \tilde{W})$	.770	.671	.755	.650	.455	.322	.824	.830	.623
LexVec + St. + $WS_{PPMI} + (W + \tilde{W})$	.763	.671	.760	.655	.458	.336	.816	.827	.630
LexVec + MB + $WS_{PPMI} + W$	.748	.635	.741	.636	.456	.320	.827	.820	.632
LexVec + St. + $WS_{PPMI} + W$	.741	.622	.733	.628	.457	.338	.820	.808	.638
LexVec + MB + $WS_{SGNS} + (W + \tilde{W})$	.768	**.675**	.755	.654	.448	.312	.824	.827	.626
LexVec + St. + $WS_{SGNS} + (W + \tilde{W})$	**.775**	.673	.762	.654	**.468**	**.339**	**.838**	**.848**	.628
LexVec + MB + $WS_{SGNS} + W$	.745	.640	.734	.645	.447	.311	.814	.802	.624
LexVec + St. + $WS_{SGNS} + W$	.740	.628	.728	.640	.459	**.339**	.821	.818	.638

Table 1: Spearman rank correlation on word similarity tasks.

Method	GSem 3CosAdd / 3CosMul	GSyn 3CosAdd / 3CosMul	MSR 3CosAdd / 3CosMul
PPMI-SVD	.460 / .498	.445 / .455	.303 / .313
GloVe	**.818** / .813	.630 / .626	.539 / **.547**
SGNS	.773 / .777	.642 / **.644**	.481 / .505
LexVec + MB + $WS_{PPMI} + (W + \tilde{W})$	.775 / .792	.520 / .539	.371 / .413
LexVec + St + $WS_{PPMI} + (W + \tilde{W})$	.794 / .807	.543 / .555	.378 / .408
LexVec + MB + $WS_{PPMI} + W$	.800 / .805	.584 / .597	.421 / .457
LexVec + St. + $WS_{PPMI} + W$	.787 / .782	.597 / .613	.445 / .475
LexVec + MB + $WS_{SGNS} + (W + \tilde{W})$	.762 / .785	.520 / .534	.349 / .386
LexVec + St. + $WS_{SGNS} + (W + \tilde{W})$	.792 / .809	.536 / .553	.362 / .396
LexVec + MB + $WS_{SGNS} + W$	.798 / .807	.573 / .580	.399 / .435
LexVec + St. + $WS_{SGNS} + W$	.779 / .778	.600 / .614	.434 / .463

Table 2: Results on word analogy tasks, given as percent accuracy.

5 Results

Results for word similarity and for the analogy tasks are in tables 1 and 2, respectively. Compared with PPMI-SVD, LexVec performs better in all tasks. As they factorize the same $PPMI^*$ matrix, it is the loss weighting from window sampling that is an improvement over L_2 loss. As expected, due to PPMI, LexVec performs better than SGNS in several word similarity tasks, but in addition it also does so on the semantic analogy task, nearly approaching GloVe. LexVec generally outperforms GloVe on word similarity tasks, possibly due to the factorization of the PPMI matrix and to window sampling's weighting of negative co-occurrences.

We believe LexVec fares well on semantic analogies because its vector-space does a good job of preserving semantics, as evidenced by its performance on word similarity tasks. We believe the poor syntactic performance is a result of the PPMI measure. PPMI-SVD also struggled with syntactic analogies more than any other task. Levy et al. (2015) obtained similar results, and suggest that using positional contexts as done by Levy et al. (2014) might help in recovering syntactic analogies.

In terms of configurations, WS_{SGNS} performed marginally better than WS_{PPMI}. We hypothesize it is simply because of the additional computation. While W and $(W + \tilde{W})$ are roughly equivalent on word similarity tasks, W is better for analogies. This is inline with results for PPMI-SVD and SGNS models (Levy et al., 2015). Both mini-batch and stochastic approaches result in similar scores for all tasks. For the same parameter k of negative samples, the mini-batch approach uses $2 * win_{WS_{PPMI}}$ times more negative samples than stochastic when using WS_{PPMI}, and $win_{WS_{SGNS}}$ times more samples when using WS_{SGNS}. Therefore, the stochastic approach is more computationally efficient while delivering similar performance.

6 Conclusion and Future Work

In this paper, we introduced LexVec, a method for low-rank, weighted factorization of the PPMI matrix that generates distributed word representations, favoring low reconstruction error on frequent co-occurrences, whilst accounting for negative co-occurrences as well. This is in contrast with PPMI-SVD, which does no weighting, and GloVe, which only considers positive co-occurrences. Finally, its PPMI factorization seems to better capture semantics when compared to the shifted PMI factorization of SGNS. As a result, it outperforms PPMI-SVD and SGNS in a variety of word similarity and semantic analogy tasks, and generally outperforms GloVe on similarity tasks.

Future work will examine the use of positional contexts for improving performance on syntactic analogy tasks. Moreover, we will explore further the hyper-parameter space to find globally optimal values for LexVec, and will experiment with the factorization of other matrices for developing alternative word representations.

Acknowledgments

This work has been partly funded by CAPES and by projects AIM-WEST (FAPERGS-INRIA 1706- 2551/13-7), CNPq 482520/2012-4, 312114/2015-0, "Simplificação Textual de Expressões Complexas", sponsored by Samsung Eletrônica da Amazônia Ltda. under the terms of Brazilian federal law No. 8.248/91.

References

Marco Baroni, Georgiana Dinu, and Germán Kruszewski. 2014. Don't count, predict! a systematic comparison of context-counting vs. context-predicting semantic vectors. In *Proceedings of the 52nd Annual Meeting of the Association for Computational Linguistics*. volume 1, pages 238–247.

Elia Bruni, Gemma Boleda, Marco Baroni, and Nam-Khanh Tran. 2012. Distributional semantics in technicolor. In *Proceedings of the 50th Annual Meeting of the Association for Computational Linguistics: Long Papers-Volume 1*. Association for Computational Linguistics, pages 136–145.

John A. Bullinaria and Joseph P. Levy. 2007. Extracting semantic representations from word co-occurrence statistics: A computational study. *Behavior research methods* 39(3):510–526.

John A Bullinaria and Joseph P Levy. 2012. Extracting semantic representations from word co-occurrence statistics: stop-lists, stemming, and svd. *Behavior research methods* 44(3):890–907.

John Caron. 2001. Experiments with lsa scoring: Optimal rank and basis. In *Proceedings of the SIAM Computational Information Retrieval Workshop*. pages 157–169.

Kenneth W. Church and Patrick Hanks. 1990. Word association norms, mutual information, and lexicography. *Computational Linguistics* 16(1):22–29.

Ronan Collobert, Jason Weston, Léon Bottou, Michael Karlen, Koray Kavukcuoglu, and Pavel Kuksa. 2011. Natural language processing (almost) from scratch. *The Journal of Machine Learning Research* 12:2493–2537.

C. Eckert and G. Young. 1936. The approximation of one matrix by another of lower rank. *Psych.* 1:211–218.

Lev Finkelstein, Evgeniy Gabrilovich, Yossi Matias, Ehud Rivlin, Zach Solan, Gadi Wolfman, and Eytan Ruppin. 2001. Placing search in context: The concept revisited. In *Proceedings of the 10th international conference on World Wide Web*. ACM, pages 406–414.

Felix Hill, Roi Reichart, and Anna Korhonen. 2015. Simlex-999: Evaluating semantic models with (genuine) similarity estimation. *Computational Linguistics* .

Eric H. Huang, Richard Socher, Christopher D. Manning, and Andrew Y. Ng. 2012. Improving word representations via global context and multiple word prototypes. In *Proceedings of the 50th Annual Meeting of the Association for Computational Linguistics: Long Papers-Volume 1*. Association for Computational Linguistics, pages 873–882.

Omer Levy and Yoav Goldberg. 2014. Neural word embedding as implicit matrix factorization. In *Advances in Neural Information Processing Systems*. pages 2177–2185.

Omer Levy, Yoav Goldberg, and Ido Dagan. 2015. Improving distributional similarity with lessons learned from word embeddings. *Transactions of the Association for Computational Linguistics* pages 211–225.

Omer Levy, Yoav Goldberg, and Israel Ramat-Gan. 2014. Linguistic regularities in sparse and explicit word representations. *CoNLL-2014* page 171.

Dekang Lin. 1998. Automatic retrieval and clustering of similar words. In *of the 36th and 17th , Volume 2*. Montreal, Quebec, Canada, pages 768–774.

Minh-Thang Luong, Richard Socher, and Christopher D. Manning. 2013. Better word representations with recursive neural networks for morphology. *CoNLL-2013* 104.

Tomas Mikolov, Kai Chen, Greg Corrado, and Jeffrey Dean. 2013a. Efficient estimation of word representations in vector space. *arXiv preprint arXiv:1301.3781* .

Tomas Mikolov, Ilya Sutskever, Kai Chen, Greg S. Corrado, and Jeff Dean. 2013b. Distributed representations of words and phrases and their compositionality. In *Advances in Neural Information Processing Systems*. pages 3111–3119.

Tomas Mikolov, Wen-tau Yih, and Geoffrey Zweig. 2013c. Linguistic regularities in continuous space word representations. In *HLT-NAACL*. pages 746–751.

George A. Miller and Walter G. Charles. 1991. Contextual correlates of semantic similarity. *Language and cognitive processes* 6(1):1–28.

Arvid Österlund, David Ödling, and Magnus Sahlgren. 2015. Factorization of latent variables in distributional semantic models. In *Proceedings of the 2015 Conference on Empirical Methods in Natural Language Processing*. Association for Computational Linguistics, Lisbon, Portugal, pages 227–231.

Jeffrey Pennington, Richard Socher, and Christopher D. Manning. 2014. Glove: Global vectors for word representation. *Proceedings of the Empiricial Methods in Natural Language Processing (EMNLP 2014)* 12.

Kira Radinsky, Eugene Agichtein, Evgeniy Gabrilovich, and Shaul Markovitch. 2011. A word at a time: computing word relatedness using temporal semantic analysis. In *Proceedings of the 20th international conference on World wide web*. ACM, pages 337–346.

Herbert Rubenstein and John B. Goodenough. 1965. Contextual correlates of synonymy. *Communications of the ACM* 8(10):627–633.

Richard Socher, John Bauer, Christopher D Manning, and Andrew Y Ng. 2013. Parsing with compositional vector grammars. In *ACL (1)*. pages 455–465.

Joseph Turian, Lev Ratinov, and Yoshua Bengio. 2010. Word representations: a simple and general method for semi-supervised learning. In *Proceedings of the 48th annual meeting of the association for computational linguistics*. Association for Computational Linguistics, pages 384–394.

One model, two languages: training bilingual parsers with harmonized treebanks

David Vilares, Carlos Gómez-Rodríguez and Miguel A. Alonso
Grupo LyS, Departamento de Computación, Universidade da Coruña
Campus de A Coruña s/n, 15071, A Coruña, Spain
{david.vilares, carlos.gomez, miguel.alonso}@udc.es

Abstract

We introduce an approach to train lexicalized parsers using bilingual corpora obtained by merging harmonized treebanks of different languages, producing parsers that can analyze sentences in either of the learned languages, or even sentences that mix both. We test the approach on the Universal Dependency Treebanks, training with MaltParser and MaltOptimizer. The results show that these bilingual parsers are more than competitive, as most combinations not only preserve accuracy, but some even achieve significant improvements over the corresponding monolingual parsers. Preliminary experiments also show the approach to be promising on texts with code-switching and when more languages are added.

1 Introduction

The need of frameworks for analyzing content in different languages has been discussed recently (Dang et al., 2014), and multilingual dependency parsing is no stranger to this challenge. Data-driven parsing models (Nivre, 2006) can be trained for any language, given enough annotated data.

On languages where treebanks are not available, cross-lingual transfer can be used to train parsers for a target language with data from one or more source languages. Data transfer approaches (e.g. Yarowsky et al. (2001), Tiedemann (2014)) map linguistic annotations across languages through parallel corpora. Instead, model transfer approaches (e.g. Naseem et al. (2012)) rely on cross-linguistic syntactic regularities to learn aspects of the source language that help parse an unseen language, without parallel corpora.

Model transfer approaches have benefitted from the development of multilingual resources that harmonize annotations. Petrov et al. (2011) proposed a universal tagset, and McDonald et al. (2011) employed it to transfer delexicalized parsers (Zeman and Resnik, 2008). More recently, several projects have presented treebank collections of multiple languages with their annotations standardized at the syntactic level, including HamleDT (Zeman et al., 2012) and the Universal Dependency Treebanks (McDonald et al., 2013).

In this paper we also rely on these resources, but with a different goal: we use universal annotations to train bilingual dependency parsers that effectively analyze unseen sentences in any of the learned languages. Unlike delexicalized approaches for model transfer, our parsers exploit lexical features. The results are encouraging: our experiments show that, starting with a monolingual parser, we can "teach" it an additional language for free in terms of accuracy (i.e., without significant accuracy loss on the original language, in spite of learning a more complex task) in the vast majority of cases.

2 Bilingual training

Universal Dependency Treebanks v2.0 (McDonald et al., 2013) is a set of CoNLL-formatted treebanks for ten languages, annotated with common criteria. They include two versions of PoS tags: universal tags (Petrov et al., 2011) in the CPOSTAG column, and a refined annotation with treebank-specific information in the POSTAG column. Some of the latter tags are not part of the core universal set, and they can denote linguistic phenomena that are language-specific, or phenomena that not all the corpora have annotated in the same way.

To train monolingual parsers (our baseline), we used the official training-dev-set splits provided

425

Proceedings of the 54th Annual Meeting of the Association for Computational Linguistics, pages 425–431,
Berlin, Germany, August 7-12, 2016. ©2016 Association for Computational Linguistics

with the corpora. For the bilingual models, for each pair of languages L_1, L_2; we simply merged their training sets into a single file acting as a training set for $L_1 \cup L_2$, and we did the same for the development sets. The test sets were not merged because comparing the bilingual parsers to monolingual ones requires evaluating each bilingual parser on the two corresponding monolingual test sets.

To build the models, we relied on MaltParser (Nivre et al., 2007). Due to the large number of language pairs that complicates manual optimization, and to ensure a fair comparison, we used MaltOptimizer (Ballesteros and Nivre, 2012), an automatic optimizer for MaltParser models. This system works in three phases: *Phase 1* and *2* choose a parsing algorithm by analyzing the training set, and performing experiments with default features. *Phase 3* tunes the feature model and algorithm parameters. We hypothesize that the bilingual models will learn a set of features that fits both languages, and check this hypothesis by evaluating on the test sets.

We propose two training configurations: (1) a *treebank-dependent tags* configuration where we include the information in the POSTAG column and (2) a *universal tags only* configuration, where we do not use this information, relying only on the CPOSTAG column. Information that could be present in FEATS or LEMMA columns is not used in any case. This methodology plans to answer two research questions: (1) can we train bilingual parsers with good accuracy by merging harmonized training sets?, and (2) is it essential that the tagsets for both languages are the same, or can we still get accuracy gains from fine-grained PoS tags (as in the monolingual case) even if some of them are treebank-specific?

All models are freely available.[1]

3 Evaluation

To ensure a fair comparison between monolingual and bilingual models, we chose to optimize the models from scratch with MaltOptimizer, expecting it to choose the parsing algorithm and feature model which is most likely to obtain good results. We observed that the selection of a bilingual parsing algorithm was not necessarily related with the algorithms selected for the monolingual models. The system sometimes chose an algorithm for a bilingual model that was not selected for any of

the corresponding monolingual models.

In view of this, and as it is known that different parsing algorithms can be more or less competitive depending on the language (Nivre, 2008), we ran a control experiment to evaluate the models setting the same parsing algorithm for all cases, executing only *phase 3* of MaltOptimizer. We chose the arc-eager parser for this experiment, as it was the algorithm that MaltOptimizer chose most frequently for the monolingual models in the previous configuration. The aim was to compare the accuracy of the bilingual models with respect to the monolingual ones, when there is no variation on the parsing algorithm between them. The results of this control experiment are not shown for space reasons, but they were very similar to those of the original experiment.

3.1 Results on the Universal Treebanks

Table 1 compares the accuracy of bilingual models to that of monolingual ones, under the *treebank-dependent tags* configuration. Each table cell shows the accuracy of a model, in terms of LAS and UAS. Cells in the diagonal correspond to monolingual models (the baseline), with the cell located at row i and column i representing the result obtained by training a monolingual parser on the training set of language L_i, and evaluating it on the test set of the same language L_i. Each cell outside the diagonal (at row i and column j, with $j \neq i$) shows the results of training a bilingual model on the training set for $L_i \cup L_j$, evaluated on the test set of L_i.

As we can see, in a large majority of cases, bilingual parsers learn to parse two languages with no statistically significant accuracy loss with respect to the corresponding monolingual parsers ($p < 0.05$ with Bikel's randomized parsing evaluation comparator). This happened in 74 out of 90 cases when measuring UAS, or 69 out of 90 in terms of LAS. Therefore, in most cases where we are applying a parser to texts in a given language, adding a second language comes for free in terms of accuracy.

More strikingly, there are many cases where bilingual parsers outperform monolingual ones, even in this evaluation on purely monolingual datasets. In particular, there are 12 cases where a bilingual parser obtains statistically significant gains in LAS over the monolingual baseline, and 9 cases with significant gains in UAS. This clearly

---

[1] http://grupolys.org/software/PARSERS/

	de	en	es	fr	id	it	ja	ko	pt-br	sv
de	78.27	78.01^{-}	77.82^{-}	77.83^{-}	77.84^{-}	78.10^{-}	77.86^{-}	77.94^{-}	78.13^{-}	78.60^{+}
	84.03	84.08^{+}	83.82^{-}	83.55^{--}	83.85^{-}	84.12^{+}	83.88^{-}	83.63^{-}	83.87^{-}	84.38^{+}
en	89.37^{+}	89.36	89.46^{+}	89.38^{+}	89.69^{++}	89.82^{++}	89.43^{+}	89.63^{++}	89.60^{++}	89.11
	91.02^{+}	91.02	91.09^{+}	91.06^{+}	91.32^{++}	91.47^{++}	91.10^{+}	91.32^{++}	91.24^{+}	90.79^{--}
es	80.85^{+}	81.08^{++}	80.60	80.95^{+}	81.16^{+}	80.92^{+}	81.41^{++}	81.49^{++}	79.96^{-}	81.26^{++}
	85.17^{+}	85.27^{++}	84.75	85.15^{+}	85.00^{+}	85.13^{+}	85.52^{++}	85.39^{++}	84.70^{-}	85.42^{++}
fr	79.01^{-}	79.39^{+}	79.36^{+}	79.29	79.61^{+}	79.34^{+}	79.16^{-}	79.36^{+}	79.09^{-}	79.66^{+}
	84.17^{-}	84.49^{+}	84.56^{+}	84.47	84.32^{-}	84.41^{-}	84.34^{-}	84.72^{+}	83.98^{-}	84.84^{+}
id	75.72^{--}	77.19^{-}	77.12^{-}	77.15^{-}	77.69	78.29^{+}	77.60^{-}	76.68^{--}	77.45^{-}	77.01^{--}
	81.73^{-}	82.66^{-}	82.72^{-}	82.66^{-}	83.38	84.09^{+}	83.18^{-}	82.16^{-}	82.96^{-}	82.59^{-}
it	82.62^{--}	83.17^{--}	83.12^{--}	83.10^{--}	83.74^{-}	84.40	84.62^{+}	84.79^{+}	83.70^{-}	84.55^{+}
	86.14^{--}	86.46^{--}	86.78^{-}	86.69^{-}	86.73^{--}	87.54	87.48^{-}	87.46^{-}	87.39^{-}	87.23^{-}
ja	76.53^{--}	76.24^{--}	76.61^{--}	76.32^{--}	75.18^{--}	77.05^{-}	77.46	76.89^{-}	76.69^{-}	76.89^{-}
	83.77^{-}	83.89^{-}	84.26^{-}	84.05^{--}	83.08^{--}	83.97^{-}	84.34	83.65^{-}	83.97^{-}	84.17^{-}
ko	86.13^{--}	88.30^{+}	87.91^{+}	88.49^{+}	85.86^{--}	88.72^{++}	87.14^{--}	87.83	86.75^{--}	88.68^{-}
	90.61^{--}	92.16^{+}	92.00^{-}	92.35^{+}	90.19^{--}	92.55^{+}	91.89^{-}	92.12	91.39^{--}	92.39^{-}
pt-br	84.83^{-}	85.06^{+}	84.99^{+}	84.97^{+}	85.10^{+}	85.43^{++}	84.95^{+}	85.12^{+}	84.88	85.25^{++}
	87.18^{-}	87.19^{-}	87.27^{+}	87.17^{-}	87.35^{-}	87.68^{++}	87.13^{-}	87.35^{-}	87.39	87.43^{++}
sv	81.71^{--}	82.01^{--}	82.03^{-}	81.92^{--}	82.34^{-}	82.63^{+}	82.81^{+}	82.94^{++}	82.19^{-}	82.48
	86.01^{--}	86.39^{-}	86.55^{-}	86.28^{--}	86.69^{-}	86.55^{-}	86.92^{+}	86.83^{-}	86.39^{-}	86.92

Table 1: Performance on the Universal Dependency Treebanks test sets using the gold POSTAG information. For each cell, its (row,column) pair indicates the language(s) with which the model was trained, with the row corresponding to the language where it was evaluated. ' ++ ' and ' + ' indicate that the improvement in performance obtained by the bilingual model is statistically significant or not, respectively. ' -- ' and ' - ' correspond to significant and not significant *decreases* in accuracy.

	de	en	es	fr	id	it	ja	ko	pt-br	sv
de	74.07	72.04^{--}	74.51^{+}	74.44^{+}	73.68^{-}	73.76^{-}	73.90^{-}	74.30^{+}	74.29^{+}	74.76^{++}
	79.77	77.52^{--}	79.95^{+}	79.83^{+}	79.24^{-}	79.44^{--}	79.83^{+}	79.76^{-}	79.71^{-}	80.25^{+}
en	88.46^{+}	88.35	88.65^{++}	88.39^{+}	88.61^{++}	88.68^{++}	88.65^{++}	88.61^{++}	88.65^{++}	88.50^{+}
	90.35^{+}	90.27	90.54^{++}	90.26^{-}	90.47^{++}	90.53^{++}	90.49^{++}	90.43^{++}	90.55^{++}	90.43^{++}
es	79.66^{-}	78.78^{-}	80.54	79.59^{-}	78.98^{-}	79.84^{-}	79.59^{-}	79.80^{-}	79.74^{-}	79.09^{-}
	83.81^{--}	82.94^{--}	84.35	83.26^{--}	82.79^{--}	83.79^{--}	83.53^{--}	83.57^{-}	83.76^{--}	83.28^{--}
fr	78.43^{+}	78.10^{-}	78.63^{+}	78.40	77.79^{-}	78.60^{+}	79.11^{+}	78.22^{-}	78.56^{+}	78.83^{+}
	83.26^{-}	82.77^{-}	83.38^{-}	83.40	82.85^{-}	83.50^{+}	84.03^{+}	83.05^{-}	83.45^{+}	83.73^{+}
id	74.46^{--}	74.65^{--}	77.09^{--}	76.23^{--}	78.31	77.86^{-}	77.10^{--}	75.58^{--}	76.90^{--}	78.34^{+}
	80.87^{--}	80.21^{--}	82.81^{--}	81.78^{--}	83.81	83.52^{-}	82.68^{--}	81.20^{--}	82.50^{--}	83.83^{+}
it	82.27^{--}	82.13^{--}	82.24^{--}	82.75^{--}	82.65^{--}	83.88	83.04^{--}	83.77^{-}	83.07^{--}	83.47^{-}
	85.40^{--}	85.38^{--}	85.36^{--}	86.31^{--}	85.45^{--}	86.68	85.83^{--}	86.30^{-}	86.21^{-}	86.33^{-}
ja	69.41^{--}	68.88^{--}	69.28^{--}	69.24^{--}	69.73^{--}	70.22^{--}	70.87	69.73^{--}	69.24^{--}	70.02^{-}
	79.62^{--}	79.21^{--}	79.45^{--}	80.11^{--}	79.58^{--}	79.58^{--}	81.16	80.23^{-}	79.37^{--}	80.47^{--}
ko	84.40^{--}	84.82^{--}	85.40^{--}	84.59^{--}	84.74^{--}	86.79^{-}	86.21^{--}	87.52	86.29^{--}	86.40^{--}
	89.61^{--}	90.00^{--}	90.77^{--}	89.88^{--}	90.00^{--}	91.39^{-}	91.46^{--}	92.00	90.92^{--}	91.19^{--}
pt-br	83.40^{-}	82.76^{--}	83.56^{-}	83.72^{-}	83.08^{--}	83.95^{+}	83.80^{-}	84.16++	83.83	84.28++
	85.78^{-}	85.01^{--}	85.82^{-}	85.85^{-}	85.38^{--}	86.15^{+}	85.93^{-}	86.33^{+}	86.11	86.41++
sv	79.65^{--}	79.61^{--}	79.75^{--}	80.46^{-}	80.94^{+}	81.06^{+}	81.19^{+}	81.11^{+}	80.89^{-}	80.93
	84.14^{--}	84.42^{--}	84.46^{--}	84.88^{-}	85.14^{-}	85.51^{+}	85.29^{-}	85.14^{-}	85.05^{-}	85.32

Table 2: Performance on the Universal Dependency Treebanks test sets using the gold CPOSTAG information. The table is laid out like Table 1.

surpasses the amount of significant gains to be expected by chance, and applying the Benjamini-Hochberg procedure (Benjamini and Hochberg, 1995) to correct for multiple comparisons with a maximum false discovery rate of 20% yields 8 significant improvements in LAS and UAS. Therefore, it is clear that there is synergy between datasets: in some cases, adding annotated data in a different language to our training set can actually improve the accuracy that we obtain in the *original* language. This opens up interesting research potential in using confidence criteria to select the data that can help parsing in this way, akin to what is done in self-training approaches (Chen et al., 2008; Goutam and Ambati, 2011).

Comparing the results by language, we note that the accuracy on the English and Spanish datasets almost always improves when adding a second treebank for training. Other languages that tend to get improvements in this way are French and Portuguese. There seems to be a rough trend towards the languages with the largest training corpora benefiting from adding a second language, and those with the smallest corpora (e.g. Indonesian, Italian or Japanese) suffering accuracy loss, likely because the training gets biased towards the second language.

Training bilingual models containing a significant number of non-overlapping treebank-dependent tags tends to have a positive effect. English and Spanish are two of the clearest examples of this. As shown in Table 3, which shows a complete report of shared PoS tags for each pair of languages under the *treebank-dependent* tags configuration, English only shares 1 PoS tag with the rest of the corpora under the said configuration, except for Swedish, with up to 5 tags in common; and the *en-sv* model is the only one suffering a significant loss on the English test set. Similar behavior is observed on Spanish: *sv* (0), *en* (1), *ja* (10) and *ko* (12) are the four languages with fewest shared PoS tags, and those are the four that obtained a significant improvement on the Spanish evaluation; while with *pt-br*, with 15 shared PoS tags, we lose accuracy. The validity of this hypothesis is reinforced by an experiment where we differentiate the universal tags by language by appending a language code to them (e.g. EN_NOUN for an English noun). An overall improvement was observed with respect to the bilingual parsers with non-disjoint sets of features.

	de	*en*	*es*	*fr*	*id*	*it*	*ja*	*ko*	*pt-br*	*sv*
de	16	1	14	14	14	13	10	12	14	0
en		45	1	1	1	1	1	1	1	5
es			24	14	14	13	10	12	15	0
fr				14	14	13	10	12	14	0
id					14	13	10	12	14	0
it						13	10	12	13	0
ja							763	10	10	0
ko								20	12	0
pt-br									15	0
sv										25

Table 3: Shared language-specific tags between pairs of languages

While all these experiments have been performed on sentences with gold PoS tags, preliminary experiments assuming predicted tags instead show analogous results: the absolute values of LAS and UAS are slightly smaller across the board, but the behavior in relative terms is the same, and the bilingual models that improved over the monolingual baseline in the gold experiments keep doing so under this setting.

On the other hand, Table 2 shows the performance of the monolingual and bilingual models under the *universal tags only* configuration. The bilingual parsers are also able to keep an acceptable accuracy with respect to the monolingual models, but significant losses are much more prevalent than under the *treebank-dependent tags* configuration.

Putting both tables together, our experiments clearly suggest that not only treebank-specific tags do not impair the training of bilingual models, but they are even beneficial, supporting the idea that using partially treebank-dependent tagsets helps multilingual parsing. We hypothesize that this may be because complementing the universal information at the syntactic level with language-specific information at the lower levels (lexical and morphological) may help the parser identify specific constructions of one language that would not benefit from the knowledge learned from the other, preventing it from trying to exploit spurious similarities between languages. This explanation is coherent with work on delexicalized parser transfer (Lynn et al., 2014) showing that better results can be obtained using disparate languages than closely-related languages, as long as they have common syntactic constructions. Thus, using universal PoS tags to train multilingual parsers can be, surprisingly, counterproductive.

3.2 Parsing code-switched sentences

Our bilingual parsers also show robustness on texts exhibiting code-switching. Unfortunately, there are no syntactically annotated code-switching corpora, so we could not perform a formal evaluation. We did perform informal tests, by running the Spanish-English bilingual parsers on some such sentences. We observed that they were able to parse the English and Spanish parts of the sentences much better than monolingual models. This required training a bilingual tagger, which we did with the free distribution of the Stanford tagger (Toutanova and Manning, 2000); merging the Spanish and English corpora to train a combined bilingual tagger. Under the *universal tags only* configuration, the multilingual tagger obtained 98.00% and 95.88% over the monolingual test sets. Using treebank-dependent tags instead, it obtained 97.19% and 93.88% over the monolingual test sets. Figure 1 shows an interesting example on how using bilingual parsers (and taggers) affects the parsing accuracy.

Table 4 shows the performance on a tiny code-switching treebank built on top of ten normalized tweets.[2] This confirms that monolingual pipelines perform poorly. Using a bilingual tagger helps improve the performance, thanks to accurate tags for both languages, but a bilingual parser is needed to

---

[2]The code-switching treebank follows the Universal Treebank v2.0 annotations. It can be obtained by asking any of the authors.

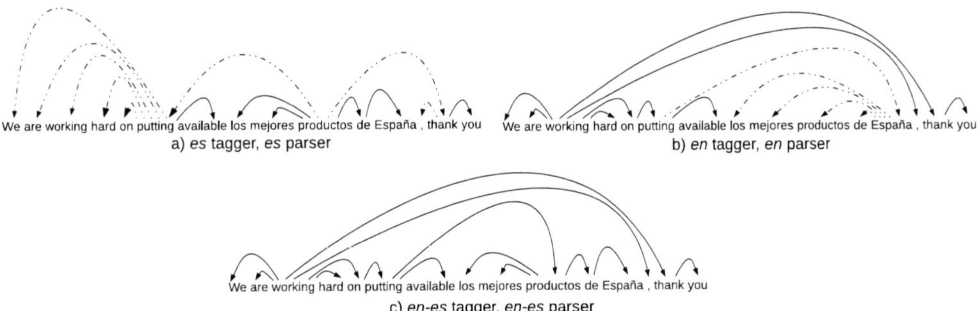

Figure 1: Example with the *en*, *es*, *en-es* models. Dotted lines represent incorrectly-parsed dependencies. The corresponding English sentence is: *'We are working hard on putting available the best products of Spain, thank you'*

Tagger	Parser	LAS	UAS
en	*en*	37.82	44.23
es	*es*	27.56	41.03
en-es	*en*	66.03	78.85
en-es	*es*	67.95	77.56
en-es	*en-es*	**87.18**	**92.31**

Table 4: Performance on a code-switching treebank composed of 10 sentences.

push both LAS and UAS up to state-of-the-art levels.

3.3 Adding more languages

To show that our approach works when more languages are added, we created a quadrilingual parser using the romanic languages and the fine PoS tag set. The results (LAS/UAS) on the monolingual sets were: 80.18/84.64 (*es*), 79.11/84.29 (*fr*), 82.16/86.15 (*it*) and 84.45/86.80 (*pt*). In all cases, the performance is almost equivalent to the monolingual parser.

Noah's ARK group (Ammar et al., 2016) has shown that this idea can be also adapted to universal parsing. Our models are a collection of weights learned from mixing harmonized treebanks, that accurately analyze sentences in any of the learned languages and where it is possible to take advantage of linguistic universals, but they are still dependent on language-specific word forms. Instead, Ammar et al. (2016) rely on multilingual word clusters and multilingual word embeddings, learning a universal representation. They also support incorporating language-specific information (e.g. PoS tags) to keep learning language-specific behavior. To address syntactic differences between languages (e.g. noun-adjective vs adjective-noun structure) they can inform the parser about the input language.

4 Conclusions and future work

To our knowledge, this is the first attempt to train purely bilingual parsers to analyze sentences irrespective of which of the two languages they are written in; as existing work on training a parser on two languages (Smith and Smith, 2004) focused on using parallel corpora to transfer linguistic knowledge between languages.

Our results reflect that bilingual parsers do not lose accuracy with respect to monolingual parsers on their corresponding language, and can even outperform them, especially if fine-grained tags are used. This shows that, thanks to universal dependencies and shared syntactic structures across different languages, using treebank-dependent tag sets is not a drawback, but even an advantage.

The applications include parsing sentences of different languages with a single model, improving the accuracy of monolingual parsing with training sets from other languages, and successfully parsing sentences exhibiting code-switching.

As future work, our approach could benefit from simple domain adaptation techniques (Daumé III, 2009), to enrich the training set for a target language by incorporating data from a source language.

5 Acknowledgments

This research is supported by the Ministerio de Economía y Competitividad (FFI2014-51978-C2). David Vilares is funded by the Ministerio de Educación, Cultura y Deporte (FPU13/01180). Carlos Gómez-Rodríguez is funded by an Oportunius program grant (Xunta de Galicia). We thank Marcos Garcia for helping with the code-switching treebank. We also thank the reviewers for their comments and suggestions.

References

W. Ammar, G. Mulcaire, M. Ballesteros, C. Dyer, and N. A. Smith. 2016. Many languages, one parser. *arXiv preprint arXiv:1602.01595*.

M. Ballesteros and J. Nivre. 2012. MaltOptimizer: an optimization tool for MaltParser. In *Proceedings of the Demonstrations at the 13th Conference of the European Chapter of the Association for Computational Linguistics*, pages 58–62. Association for Computational Linguistics.

Y. Benjamini and Y. Hochberg. 1995. Controlling the false discovery rate: a practical and powerful approach to multiple testing. *Journal of the Royal Statistical Society. Series B (Methodological)*, pages 289–300.

W. Chen, Y. Wu, and H. Isahara. 2008. Learning reliable information for dependency parsing adaptation. In *Proceedings of the 22Nd International Conference on Computational Linguistics - Volume 1*, COLING '08, pages 113–120, Stroudsburg, PA, USA. Association for Computational Linguistics.

Y. Dang, Y. Zhang, Paul J. Hu, S. A. Brown, Y. Ku, J. Wang, and H. Chen. 2014. An integrated framework for analyzing multilingual content in Web 2.0 social media. *Decision Support Systems*, 61:126–135.

H. Daumé III. 2009. Frustratingly easy domain adaptation. *arXiv preprint arXiv:0907.1815*.

R. Goutam and B. R. Ambati. 2011. Exploring self training for Hindi dependency parsing. In *Proceedings of 5th International Joint Conference on Natural Language Processing*, pages 1452–1456, Chiang Mai, Thailand, November. Asian Federation of Natural Language Processing.

T. Lynn, J. Foster, M. Dras, and L. Tounsi. 2014. Cross-lingual transfer parsing for low-resourced languages: An Irish case study. In *CLTW 2014. The First Celtic Language Technology Workshop. Proceedings of the Workshop*, pages 41–49, Dublin, Ireland.

R. McDonald, S. Petrov, and K. Hall. 2011. Multi-source transfer of delexicalized dependency parsers. In *Proceedings of the Conference on Empirical Methods in Natural Language Processing*, pages 62–72. Association for Computational Linguistics.

R. McDonald, J. Nivre, Y. Quirmbach-brundage, Y. Goldberg, D. Das, K. Ganchev, K. Hall, S. Petrov, Hao Zhang, O. Täckström, C. Bedini, N. Castelló, and J. Lee. 2013. Universal dependency annotation for multilingual parsing. In *Proceedings of the 51st Annual Meeting of the Association for Computational Linguistics*, pages 92–97. Association for Computational Linguistics.

T. Naseem, R. Barzilay, and A. Globerson. 2012. Selective sharing for multilingual dependency parsing. In *Proceedings of the 50th Annual Meeting of the Association for Computational Linguistics*, pages 629–637.

J. Nivre, J. Hall, J. Nilsson, A. Chanev, G. Eryigit, S. Kübler, S. Marinov, and E. Marsi. 2007. MaltParser: A language-independent system for data-driven dependency parsing. *Natural Language Engineering*, 13(2):95–135.

J. Nivre. 2006. Two strategies for text parsing. In Mickael Suominen, Antti Arppe, Anu Airola, Orvoki Heinämäki, Matti Miestamo, Urho Määttä, Jussi Niemi, Kari K. Pitkänen, and Kaius Sinnemäki, editors, *A Man of Measure: Festschrift in Honour of Fred Karlsson on his 60th Birthday*, pages 440–448. A special supplement to SKY Journal of Linguistics 19.

J. Nivre. 2008. Algorithms for deterministic incremental dependency parsing. *Computational Linguistics*, 34(4):513–553.

S. Petrov, D. Das, and R. McDonald. 2011. A universal part-of-speech tagset. *arXiv preprint arXiv:1104.2086*.

D. A. Smith and N. A. Smith. 2004. Bilingual Parsing with Factored Estimation: Using English to Parse Korean. In Dekang Lin and Dekai Wu, editors, *Proceedings of EMNLP 2004*, pages 49–56, Barcelona, Spain, July. Association for Computational Linguistics.

J. Tiedemann. 2014. Rediscovering annotation projection for cross-lingual parser induction. In *Proceedings of COLING 2014: 25th International Conference on Computational Linguistics*, pages 1854–1864.

K. Toutanova and C. D Manning. 2000. Enriching the knowledge sources used in a maximum entropy part-of-speech tagger. In *Proceedings of the 2000 Joint SIGDAT conference on Empirical methods in natural language processing and very large corpora: held in conjunction with the 38th Annual Meeting of the Association for Computational Linguistics-Volume 13*, pages 63–70.

D. Yarowsky, G. Ngai, and R. Wicentowski. 2001. Inducing multilingual text analysis tools via robust projection across aligned corpora. In *Proceedings of the 1st International Conference on Human Language Technology Research*, pages 1–8. Association for Computational Linguistics.

D. Zeman and P. Resnik. 2008. Cross-language parser adaptation between related languages. In *IJCNLP 2008 Workshop on NLP for Less Privileged Languages*, pages 35–42, Hyderabad, India. International Institute of Information Technology.

D. Zeman, D. Mareček, M. Popel, L. Ramasamy, J. Štěpánek, Z. Žabokrtský, and J. Hajič. 2012. HamleDT: To Parse or Not to Parse? In Nicoletta Calzolari (Conference Chair), Khalid Choukri,

Thierry Declerck, Mehmet Uğur Doğan, Bente Maegaard, Joseph Mariani, Asuncion Moreno, Jan Odijk, and Stelios Piperidis, editors, *Proceedings of the Eight International Conference on Language Resources and Evaluation (LREC'12)*, Istanbul, Turkey, May. European Language Resources Association (ELRA).

Using Mention Accessibility to Improve Coreference Resolution

Kellie Webster and Joel Nothman
School of Information Technologies
University of Sydney
NSW 2006, Australia
{kellie.webster, jnothman}@sydney.edu.au

Abstract

Modern coreference resolution systems require linguistic and general knowledge typically sourced from costly, manually curated resources. Despite their intuitive appeal, results have been mixed. In this work, we instead implement fine-grained surface-level features motivated by cognitive theory. Our novel fine-grained feature specialisation approach significantly improves the performance of a strong baseline, achieving state-of-the-art results of 65.29 and 61.13% on CoNLL-2012 using gold and automatic preprocessing, with system extracted mentions.

1 Introduction

Coreference resolution (Pradhan et al., 2011, 2012) is the task of clustering mentions in a document according to their referent. For instance, we need to resolve Ehud Barak, his, and he as coreferential to understand the meaning of the excerpt:

Israeli Prime Minister Ehud Barak called **his** cabinet into special session late Wednesday , to discuss what **he** called a grave escalation of the level of violence ...

While knowledge-poor approaches establish a reasonable baseline, they perform poorly when positional and surface form heuristics break down. To address this, research has extracted world knowledge from manually curated resources including Wikipedia, Yago, Freebase, and FrameNet (e.g. Uryupina et al., 2011; Rahman and Ng, 2011; Ratinov and Roth, 2012; Hajishirzi et al., 2013; Durrett and Klein, 2014). Despite their intuitive appeal, results have been mixed. We instead focus on linguistic knowledge which can be extracted completely automatically, guided by insights from

Accessibility theory (Ariel, 2001). This result is consistent with Wiseman et al. (2015) which similarly finds performance gains above state-of-the-art from extending simple, surface-level features.

We implement a mention classification scheme based on the Accessibility hierarchy and use this for feature specialisation, yielding state-of-the-art results of 65.29 and 61.13% on CoNLL-2012 on gold and automatic preprocessing, with system extracted mentions. Our approach is simple and effective, contributing to arguments for incorporating cognitive insights in computational modelling.

2 Accessibility Hierarchy

Accessibility theory (Ariel, 2001) builds on a body of cognitively motivated theories of discourse processing, notably Centering Theory (Grosz et al., 1995). Where Centering describes pronoun interpretation in terms of relative discourse entity salience, Accessibility theory expands from this, describing discourse entities as having corresponding human memory nodes which fluctuate in their degree of activation as the entity features in a discourse. The surface form of a reference indicates to the hearer how activated its corresponding node is expected to be. That is, surface form is an instruction for how to retrieve suitable referents, guiding the resolution of coreference. Relative degree of activation is captured in the theory's hierarchy of reference expression types, reproduced in Figure 1. Section 4 proposes a mapping of this hierarchy (derived for spoken Hebrew) to written English.

The hierarchy encodes and expands the widely-used rule of thumb that full names introduce an entity (their referent has low accessibility; it has not yet been discussed) and pronouns are anaphoric (their referent is a highly accessible, active dis-

Proceedings of the 54th Annual Meeting of the Association for Computational Linguistics, pages 432–437,
Berlin, Germany, August 7-12, 2016. ©2016 Association for Computational Linguistics

Full name + modifier < Full name < Long definite description < Short definite description < Last name < First name < Distal demonstrative + modifier < Proximate demonstrative + modifier < Distal demonstrative + NP < Proximate demonstrative + NP < Distal demonstrative < Proximate demonstrative < Stressed pronoun + gesture < Stressed pronoun < Unstressed pronoun < Cliticised pronoun < Verbal inflections < Zero

Figure 1: Accessibility hierarchy from Ariel (2001)

course entity); the accessibility of definite descriptions is intermediate. In this work, we show that the fine-grained categorisation in the Accessibility hierarchy can be leveraged to improve the discriminative power of a strong system, compared to coarser-grained typologies from previous work. That is, this work contributes valuable empirical support for the psycholinguistic theory.

3 Related Work

A particularly successful way to leverage mention classification has been to specialise modelling by mention type. Denis and Baldridge (2008) learn five different models, one each for proper name, definite nominal, indefinite nominal, third person pronoun, and non-third person pronoun. Bengtson and Roth (2008) and Durrett and Klein (2013) implement specialisation at the level of features within a model, rather than explicitly learning separate models. Bengtson and Roth (2008) prefix each base feature generated with the type of the current mention, one of proper name, nominal, or pronoun, for instance `nominal-head_match:true`. Durrett and Klein (2013) extend from this by learning a model over three versions of each base feature: unprefixed, conjoined with the type of the current mention, and conjoined with concatenation of the types of the current mention and candidate antecedent mention: `nominal+nominal-head_match=true`.

The success of Durrett and Klein is possible due to the large training dataset provided by OntoNotes (Pradhan et al., 2007). In this work, we successfully extend data-driven specialisation still further: Section 4 shows how we can discover fine-grained patterns in reference expression usage, and Section 5 how these patterns can be used to significantly improve the performance of a strong coreference system.

4 Accessibility Transitions in OntoNotes

In this section, we propose an implementation of the Accessibility hierarchy for written English and how this can be used to encode fine-grained discourse transitions. We discover trends in OntoNotes, over mentions automatically extracted from the DEV portion of English CoNLL-2012 (Pradhan et al., 2011).

AR	Description	%
1	Multi-word name + modifier	7.7
2	Multi-word name	8.7
3	Long indefinite description	18.9
4	Short indefinite description	16.3
5	Long definite description	10.2
6	Short definite description	5.0
7	Single-word name	8.8
8	Distal demonstrative + modifier	0.2
9	Proximate demonstrative + modifier	0.0
10	Distal demonstrative + NP	0.7
11	Proximate demonstrative + NP	1.2
12	Distal demonstrative	0.8
13	Proximate demonstrative	0.5
14	Pronoun	21.0
-	Zero	-

Table 1: Accessibility rank values used in our experiments, with their base distribution over extracted NPs.

4.1 Mention classification

Our experiments start by classifying a mention's Accessibility rank value, AR. Table 1 gives the schema we propose for written English, along with the base distribution over extracted mentions. This mapping is a simple ordinal numbering of Figure 1 with the following refinements.

We have generalised last name and first name to single-word name (AR = 7) and full name to multi-word name (AR = 2) to handle non-person entities. Name modifiers are tokens without the head NER label, excluding determiners, possessive markers, and punctuation. We have introduced indefinite descriptions above definite descriptions since they are more likely to introduce discourse entities than definite descriptions are. We label any nominal started by the or a possessive pronoun as a definite; otherwise it is indefinite. Long descriptions comprise more than one token when possessive markers, punctuation, and articles are excluded. Distals start with those or that while

AR(antecedent)			AR(anaphor)												
			1	2	3	4	5	6	7	8	10	11	12	13	14
Name + modifier	1	0.12	0.22	0.06					0.15						0.48
Multi-word name	2	0.12		0.31				0.06	0.14						0.40
Long indefinite description	3	0.21			0.07		0.09	0.14							0.52
Short indefinite description	4	0.06				0.05		0.12	0.05						0.65
Long definite description	5	0.14					0.21	0.15	0.09						0.41
Short definite description	6	0.08					0.07	0.37	0.07						0.39
Single-word name	7	0.15							0.49						0.42
Distal demonstrative + modifier	8	0.01			0.05			0.05		0.05					0.79
Distal demonstrative + NP	10	0.01					0.07	0.10			0.13				0.54
Proximate demonstrative + NP	11	0.02					0.05	0.10	0.11			0.12			0.54
Distal demonstrative	12	0.00						0.05	0.05				0.34		0.43
Proximate demonstrative	13	0.00							0.08			0.05		0.05	0.71
Pronoun	14	0.08							0.09						0.82

Table 2: Accessibility transitions (>0.05) CoNLL-2012 DEV.

proximates start with these or this.

4.2 Discourse Transitions

Discourse transitions are then AR tuples whose values come from mentions aligned to the same gold cluster. We chose 2-tuples, whose values come from mention-antecedent pairs, since mention-pair models have dominated the research space. However, we generate up to three pairs per mention since antecedents are latent at the entity level. That is, for he in the following, we generate pairs (1, 14) and (14, 14).

Israeli Prime Minister Ehud Barak$_{AR=1}$ called **his**$_{AR=14}$ cabinet into special session late Wednesday , to discuss what **he**$_{AR=14}$ called a grave escalation of the level of violence ...

The aggregated counts for each pair type are represented in Table 2, with $AR(antecedent)$ on the vertical and $AR(anaphor)$ on the horizontal. The first column gives the proportion of cluster-initial mentions of each AR type (e.g. 21% of gold clusters have a long indefinite description as their first mention). Each row is normalised to sum to 1 so each row indicates the probability distribution for the expected next mention of a cluster. For clarity, only values 0.05 and higher are shown.

We can see that commonly used rules of thumb are borne out in this data, though with some extra granularity. Modified and multi-word names reduce to single-word names, and both reduce to pronouns. Single word names retain their mention form and reduce to pronouns with roughly equal probability. All mention types reduce to be pronouns and, once reference has reduced to be pronominal, there is a high likelihood (82%) that this form will be retained.

Encouragingly, we can also see transitions in

AR	Description	
1	Name + modifier	0.56
2	Multi-word name	0.65
3	Long indefinite description	0.89
4	Short indefinite description	0.92
5	Long definite description	0.75
6	Short definite description	0.54
7	Single-word name	0.44
8	Distal demonstrative + modifier	0.69
9	Proximate demonstrative + modifier	1.00
10	Distal demonstrative + NP	0.43
11	Proximate demonstrative + NP	0.41
12	Distal demonstrative	0.43
13	Proximate demonstrative	0.60
14	Pronoun	0.21

Table 3: Proportion of singletons by AR.

Table 2 can not be expressed with the coarser-grained typologies of prior work. Firstly, mention article is important. Long indefinite descriptions are more likely to start coreference clusters than long definite descriptions (21% vs. 14%), which are in turn much more likely to start clusters than demonstratives. Mention length is also important: short indefinite descriptions are more likely to reduce to pronouns than long definite descriptions and short definite descriptions have a higher chance of being retained throughout the discourse than long definite descriptions. Exploring further, of coreferential pairs where both mentions are short definite descriptions, 86% are head matched, compared to 60% of long definite descriptions; 60% of short definite descriptions are string matched, compared to 27% of long.

4.3 Anaphoricity

Table 3 gives the proportion of extracted mentions which can not be aligned to gold mentions, by AR value. Modelling these discourse singletons is important for models jointly learning coreference and anaphoricity (Webster and Curran, 2014).

	Gold				Auto			
	MUC	B^3	CEAFE	CoNLL	MUC	B^3	CEAFE	CoNLL
Fernandes et al. (2012)	72.18	59.17	55.72	62.36	70.51	57.58	53.86	60.65
Björkelund and Kuhn (2014)	73.80	62.00	59.06	64.95	70.72	58.58	55.61	61.63
LIMERIC Baseline	74.07	60.91	58.57	64.52	70.36	56.60	54.42	60.46
+ Fine-Grained Specialisation	*74.73*	*61.72*	*59.43*	**65.29**	70.72	*57.40*	*55.26*	**61.13**

Table 4: Performance on CoNLL-2012 TEST evaluated with gold and automatic annotations and system extracted mentions.

After pronouns, demonstratives and proper names have low proportion of singletons. Single word names are less likely to be singletons than modified and multi-word names. We highlight two contributing factors. The first is that certain names, particularly the children of an apposition, are not markable in OntoNotes. The second is that the burden of supplying disambiguation will be more worthwhile for important entities.

Consistent with Recasens et al. (2013), indefinites are more likely to be singletons than definites, and long definites are more likely than short definites. Since length and article are the key factors for AR typing, this is good evidence in favour of using the hierarchy's fine-grained classification.

5 Experiments

In this section, we show how fine-grained feature specialisation can significantly improve the performance of LIMERIC, a competitive coreference resolution system. This strength demonstrates that simple surface-form features have yet to be fully utilised in current modelling, and that cognitive theory can guide their development.

5.1 LIMERIC

The system we base our work on is LIMERIC (Webster and Curran, 2014). We choose this system due to its cognitive motivation and strong performance. Importantly, this system already uses the coarse-grained featurisation of Durrett and Klein (2013), allowing us to directly measure the impact of our proposed fine-grained featurisation.

We, however, improve it in a number of ways. The biggest performance boosts came from using MIRA (Margin Infused Relaxation Algorithm) updates in place of standard perceptron updates and implementing the full range of common features from the literature. We also fix a number of bug fixes and improve mention extraction. This im-

proved system forms our LIMERIC baseline in Table 4.

5.2 Fine-Grained Feature Specialisation

We build on work in discourse transition prefixing (particularly Durrett and Klein, 2013), which expands the feature space of a learner by including multiple versions of each generated feature. LIMERIC previously used three versions of each feature: one unprefixed, one prefixed with the current mention's type (one of name, nominal, or pronoun), and one prefixed with the concatenation of the types of the current and candidate antecedents. In this work, we introduce a fourth prefix, formed by concatenating the AR of the current mention with that of the closest mention in the candidate antecedent cluster.

The power of such transition features is that they allow us to learn, for instance, that pronoun to name transitions are preferred when the anaphor is distant from its antecedent and the name mention is one token, or that head match is a particularly strong indicator of coreferentiality between short definite nominals: `6+6-head_match=true`.

5.3 Results

Table 4 tabulates system performance on CoNLL-2012 TEST using system extracted mentions and v8.01 of the official scorer (Pradhan et al., 2014).

Comparing feature specialisation against the LIMERIC baseline, we can see that it yields substantial performance gains on all metrics and both evaluation settings. Performance gains indicated in bold are statistically significant for the conservative p = 0.01 using bootstrap re-sampling[1]. Performance gains indicated in italics are significant at the standard threshold of p = 0.05.

We benchmark against the state-of-the-art by

---

[1] Since Specialisation is a development of LIMERIC, the two models are not independent which means we would expect to see relatively high confidence values for relatively small gains in score (see Berg-Kirkpatrick et al., 2012).

comparing performance to the winner of the shared task (Fernandes et al., 2012), as well as the best documented system at the time of this work (Björkelund and Kuhn, 2014). Fine-grained feature specialisation improves LIMERIC's performance to push past that of Björkelund and Kuhn (2014) when using gold preprocessing. Furthermore, on the difficult automatic setting, we outperform Fernandes et al. (2012) and are not significantly worse than Björkelund and Kuhn (2014).

On the link-based MUC and B^3 metrics, our recall gains are larger than our precision gains. That is, specialisation enables coreference indicators to accrue sufficient weight so as to promote new coreference links, a known problem case for modern systems. We found particularly enhanced weight on features for relaxed string matching.

6 Conclusion

In this paper, we have found fine-grained patterns in reference expression usage based on the Accessibility hierarchy and shown how these can be used to significantly improve the performance of a strong system, LIMERIC. Despite being simple to implement, we achieve comparable or improved performance than the best reported results, furthering arguments for incorporating cognitive insights in computational modelling.

7 Acknowledgements

The authors thank their anonymous reviewers and members of the Schwa Lab at the University of Sydney for their insightful and helpful feedback. The first author was supported by an Australian Postgraduate Award scholarship.

References

Mira Ariel. 2001. Accessibility theory: An overview. *Text representation: Linguistic and psycholinguistic aspects*, pages 29–87.

Eric Bengtson and Dan Roth. 2008. Understanding the value of features for coreference resolution. In *Proceedings of the Conference on Empirical Methods in Natural Language Processing*, pages 294–303. Association for Computational Linguistics.

Taylor Berg-Kirkpatrick, David Burkett, and Dan Klein. 2012. An empirical investigation of statistical significance in nlp. In *Proceedings of the 2012 Joint Conference on Empirical Methods in Natural Language Processing and Computational Natural Language Learning*, pages 995–1005. Association for Computational Linguistics, Jeju Island, Korea.

Anders Björkelund and Jonas Kuhn. 2014. Learning structured perceptrons for coreference resolution with latent antecedents and non-local features. *ACL, Baltimore, MD, USA, June*.

Pascal Denis and Jason Baldridge. 2008. Specialized models and ranking for coreference resolution. In *Proceedings of the Conference on Empirical Methods in Natural Language Processing*, pages 660–669. Association for Computational Linguistics.

Greg Durrett and Dan Klein. 2013. Easy victories and uphill battles in coreference resolution. In *Proceedings of the Conference on Empirical Methods in Natural Language Processing*.

Greg Durrett and Dan Klein. 2014. A joint model for entity analysis: Coreference, typing, and linking. In *Proceedings of the Transactions of the Association for Computational Linguistics*.

Eraldo Fernandes, Cícero dos Santos, and Ruy Milidiú. 2012. Latent structure perceptron with feature induction for unrestricted coreference resolution. In *Joint Conference on EMNLP and CoNLL - Shared Task*, pages 41–48. Association for Computational Linguistics, Jeju Island, Korea.

Barbara J Grosz, Scott Weinstein, and Aravind K Joshi. 1995. Centering: A framework for modeling the local coherence of discourse. *Computational Linguistics*, 21(2):203–225.

Hannaneh Hajishirzi, Leila Zilles, Daniel S Weld, and Luke Zettlemoyer. 2013. Joint coreference resolution and named-entity linking with multi-pass sieves. pages 289–299.

Sameer Pradhan, Xiaoqiang Luo, Marta Recasens, Eduard Hovy, Vincent Ng, and Michael Strube. 2014. Scoring coreference partitions of predicted mentions: A reference implementation.

Sameer Pradhan, Alessandro Moschitti, Nianwen Xue, Olga Uryupina, and Yuchen Zhang. 2012. Conll-2012 shared task: Modeling multilingual unrestricted coreference in ontonotes. In *Joint Conference on EMNLP and CoNLL - Shared Task*, pages 1–40. Association for Computational Linguistics, Jeju Island, Korea.

Sameer Pradhan, Lance Ramshaw, Mitchell Marcus, Martha Palmer, Ralph Weischedel, and Nianwen Xue. 2011. Conll-2011 shared task: Modeling unrestricted coreference in ontonotes. In *Proceedings of the Fifteenth Conference on Computational Natural Language Learning: Shared Task*, pages 1–27. Association for Computational Linguistics, Portland, Oregon, USA.

Sameer S. Pradhan, Eduard H. Hovy, Mitchell P. Marcus, Martha Palmer, Lance A. Ramshaw, and Ralph M. Weischedel. 2007. Ontonotes: a unified relational semantic representation. *Int. J. Semantic Computing*, 1(4):405–419.

Altaf Rahman and Vincent Ng. 2011. Coreference resolution with world knowledge. In *Proceedings of the 49th Annual Meeting of the Association for Computational Linguistics: Human Language Technologies*, volume 1, pages 814–824.

Lev Ratinov and Dan Roth. 2012. Learning-based multi-sieve co-reference resolution with knowledge. In *EMNLP*.

Marta Recasens, Marie-Catherine de Marneffe, and Christopher Potts. 2013. The life and death of discourse entities: Identifying singleton mentions. In *Proceedings of the 2013 Conference of the North American Chapter of the Association for Computational Linguistics: Human Language Technologies*, pages 627–633. Association for Computational Linguistics, Atlanta, Georgia.

Olga Uryupina, Massimo Poesio, Claudio Giuliano, and Kateryna Tymoshenko. 2011. Disambiguation and filtering methods in using web knowledge for coreference resolution. In *Proceedings of the 24th International Florida Artificial Intelligence Research Society Conference*, pages 317–322.

Kellie Webster and James R Curran. 2014. Limited memory incremental coreference resolution. In *Proceedings of COLING 2014, the 25th International Conference on Computational Linguistics: Technical Papers*, pages 2129–2139. Dublin,Ireland.

Sam Wiseman, Alexander M Rush, Stuart M Shieber, Jason Weston, Heather Pon-Barry, Stuart M Shieber, Nicholas Longenbaugh, Sam Wiseman, Stuart M Shieber, Elif Yamangil, et al. 2015. Learning anaphoricity and antecedent ranking features for coreference resolution. In *Proceedings of the 53rd Annual Meeting of the Association for Computational Linguistics*, volume 1, pages 92–100. Association for Computational Linguistics.

Exploiting Linguistic Features for Sentence Completion

Aubrie M. Woods
Carnegie Mellon University
5000 Forbes Avenue
Pittsburgh, PA 15213, USA
amwoods@cmu.edu

Abstract

This paper presents a novel approach to automated sentence completion based on pointwise mutual information (PMI). Feature sets are created by fusing the various types of input provided to other classes of language models, ultimately allowing multiple sources of both local and distant information to be considered. Furthermore, it is shown that additional precision gains may be achieved by incorporating feature sets of higher-order n-grams. Experimental results demonstrate that the PMI model outperforms all prior models and establishes a new state-of-the-art result on the Microsoft Research Sentence Completion Challenge.

1 Introduction

Skilled reading is a complex cognitive process that requires constant interpretation and evaluation of written content. To develop a coherent picture, one must reason from the material encountered to construct a mental representation of meaning. As new information becomes available, this representation is continually refined to produce a globally consistent understanding. Sentence completion questions, such as those previously featured on the Scholastic Aptitude Test (SAT), were designed to assess this type of verbal reasoning ability. Specifically, given a sentence containing 1-2 blanks, the test taker was asked to select the correct answer choice(s) from the provided list of options (College Board, 2014). A sample sentence completion question is illustrated in Figure 1.

To date, relatively few publications have focused on automatic methods for solving sentence completion questions. This scarcity is likely attributable to the difficult nature of the task, which

Certain clear patterns in the metamorphosis of a butterfly indicate that the process is

———-.

(A) systematic
(B) voluntary
(C) spontaneous
(D) experimental
(E) clinical

Figure 1: An example sentence completion question (The Princeton Review, 2007).

occasionally involves logical reasoning in addition to both general and semantic knowledge (Zweig et al., 2012b). Fundamentally, text completion is a challenging semantic modeling problem, and solutions require models that can evaluate the global coherence of sentences (Gubbins and Vlachos, 2013). Thus, in many ways, text completion epitomizes the goals of natural language understanding, as superficial encodings of meaning will be insufficient to determine which responses are accurate.

In this paper, a model based on pointwise mutual information (PMI) is proposed to measure the degree of association between answer options and other sentence tokens. The PMI model considers multiple sources of information present in a sentence prior to selecting the most likely alternative.

The remainder of this report is organized as follows. Section 2 describes the high-level characteristics of existing models designed to perform automated sentence completion. This prior work provides direct motivation for the PMI model, introduced in Section 3. In Section 4, the model's performance on the Microsoft Research (MSR) Sentence Completion Challenge and a data set comprised of SAT questions are juxtaposed. Finally, Section 5 offers concluding remarks on this topic.

Proceedings of the 54th Annual Meeting of the Association for Computational Linguistics, pages 438–442,
Berlin, Germany, August 7-12, 2016. ©2016 Association for Computational Linguistics

2 Background

Previous research expounds on various architectures and techniques applied to sentence completion. Below, models are roughly categorized on the basis of complexity and type of input analyzed.

2.1 N-gram Models

Advantages of n-gram models include their ability to estimate the likelihood of particular token sequences and automatically encode word ordering. While relatively simple and efficient to train on large, unlabeled text corpora, n-gram models are nonetheless limited by their dependence on local context. In fact, such models are likely to overvalue sentences that are locally coherent, yet improbable due to distant semantic dependencies.

2.2 Dependency Models

Dependency models circumvent the sequentiality limitation of n-gram models by representing each word as a node in a multi-child dependency tree. Unlabeled dependency language models assume that each word is (1) conditionally independent of the words outside its ancestor sequence, and (2) generated independently from the grammatical relations. To account for valuable information ignored by this model, e.g., two sentences that differ only in a reordering between a verb and its arguments, the labeled dependency language model instead treats each word as conditionally independent of the words and labels outside its ancestor path (Gubbins and Vlachos, 2013).

In addition to offering performance superior to n-gram models, advantages of this representation include relative ease of training and estimation, as well as the ability to leverage standard smoothing methods. However, the models' reliance on output from automatic dependency extraction methods and vulnerability to data sparsity detract from their real-world practicality.

2.3 Continuous Space Models

Neural networks mitigate issues with data sparsity by learning distributed representations of words, which have been shown to excel at preserving linear regularities among tokens. Despite drawbacks that include functional opacity, propensity toward overfitting, and elevated computational demands, neural language models are capable of outperforming n-gram and dependency models (Gubbins and Vlachos, 2013; Mikolov et al., 2013; Mnih and Kavukcuoglu, 2013).

Log-linear model architectures have been proposed to address the computational cost associated with neural networks (Mikolov et al., 2013; Mnih and Kavukcuoglu, 2013). The continuous bag-of-words model attempts to predict the current word using n future and n historical words as context. In contrast, the continuous skip-gram model uses the current word as input to predict surrounding words. Utilizing an ensemble architecture comprised of the skip-gram model and recurrent neural networks, Mikolov et al. (2013) achieved prior state-of-the-art performance on the MSR Sentence Completion Challenge.

3 PMI Model

This section describes an approach to sentence completion based on pointwise mutual information. The PMI model was designed to account for both local and distant sources of information when evaluating overall sentence coherence.

Pointwise mutual information is an information-theoretic measure used to discover collocations (Church and Hanks, 1990; Turney and Pantel, 2010). Informally, PMI represents the association between two words, i and j, by comparing the probability of observing them in the same context with the probabilities of observing each independently.

The first step toward applying PMI to the sentence completion task involved constructing a word-context frequency matrix from the training corpus. The context was specified to include all words appearing in a single sentence, which is consistent with the hypothesis that it is necessary to examine word co-occurrences at the sentence level to achieve appropriate granularity. During development/test set processing, all words were converted to lowercase and stop words were removed based on their part-of-speech tags (Toutanova et al., 2003). To determine whether a particular part-of-speech tag type did, in fact, signal the presence of uninformative words, tokens assigned a hypothetically irrelevant tag were removed if their omission positively affected performance on the development portion of the MSR data set. This non-traditional approach, selected to increase specificity and eliminate dependence on a non-universal stop word list, led to the removal of determiners, coordinating conjunctions,

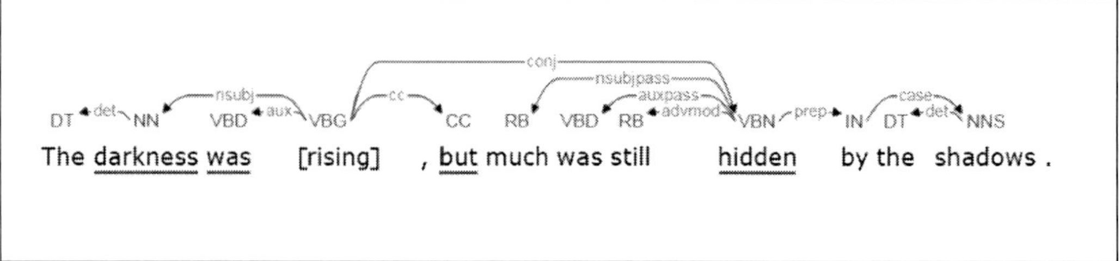

Figure 2: The dependency parse tree for Question 17 in the MSR data set. Words that share a grammatical relationship with the missing word *rising* are underscored. Following stop word removal, the feature set for this question is [*darkness, was, hidden*].

pronouns, and proper nouns.[1] Next, feature sets were defined to capture the various sources of information available in a sentence. While feature set number and type is configurable, composition varies, as sets are dynamically generated for each sentence at run time. Enumerated below are the three feature sets utilized by the PMI model.

1. **Reduced Context.** This feature set consists of words that remain following the pre-processing steps described above.

2. **Dependencies.** Sentence words that share a semantic dependency with the candidate word(s) are included in this set (Chen and Manning, 2014). Absent from the set of dependencies are words removed during the pre-processing phase. Figure 2 depicts an example dependency parse tree along with features provided to the PMI model.

3. **Keywords.** Providing the model with a collection of salient tokens effectively increases the tokens' associated weights. An analogous approach to the one described for stop word identification was applied to discover that common nouns consistently hold greater significance than other words assigned hypothetically informative part-of-speech tags.

Let X represent a word-context matrix with n rows and m columns. Row $x_{i:}$ corresponds to word i and column $x_{:j}$ refers to context j. The term $x(i,j)$ indicates how many times word i occurs in context j. Applying PMI to X results in the n x m matrix Y, where term $y(i,j)$ is defined by (1). To avoid overly penalizing words that are unrelated to the context,

---

[1] Perhaps counterintuitively, most proper nouns are uninformative for sentence completion, since they refer to specific named entities (e.g. people, locations, organizations, etc.).

the positive variant of PMI is considered, in which negative scores are replaced with zero (4).

$$P(i,j) = \frac{x(i,j)}{\sum_{i=1}^{n} \sum_{j=1}^{m} x(i,j)} \tag{1}$$

$$P(i*) = \frac{\sum_{j=1}^{m} x(i,j)}{\sum_{i=1}^{n} \sum_{j=1}^{m} x(i,j)} \tag{2}$$

$$P(*j) = \frac{\sum_{i=1}^{n} x(i,j)}{\sum_{i=1}^{n} \sum_{j=1}^{m} x(i,j)} \tag{3}$$

$$pmi(i,j) = max \left\{ 0, log \left(\frac{P(i,j)}{P(i*)P(*j)} \right) \right\} \tag{4}$$

In addition, the discounting factor described by Pantel and Lin (2002) is applied to reduce bias toward infrequent words (7).

$$mincontext = min(\sum_{k=1}^{n} x(k,j), \sum_{k=1}^{m} x(i,k)) \tag{5}$$

$$\delta(i,j) = \frac{x(i,j)}{x(i,j) + 1} \cdot \frac{mincontext}{mincontext + 1} \tag{6}$$

$$dpmi(i,j) = pmi(i,j) \cdot \delta(i,j) \tag{7}$$

$$similarity(i,S) = \sum_{j \in S} dpmi(i,j) \cdot \gamma \tag{8}$$

The PMI model evaluates each possible response to a sentence completion question by substituting each candidate answer, i, in place of the blank and scoring the option according to (8). This equation measures the semantic similarity between each candidate answer and all other words in the sentence, S. Prior to being summed, individual PMI values associated with a particular word i

and context word j are multiplied by γ, which reflects the number of feature sets containing j. Ultimately, the candidate option with the highest similarity score is selected as the most likely answer.

Using the procedure described above, additional feature sets of bigrams and trigrams were created and subsequently incorporated into the semantic similarity assessment. This extended model accounts for both word- and phrase-level information by considering windowed co-occurrence statistics.

4 Experimental Evaluation

4.1 Data Sets

Since its introduction, the Microsoft Research Sentence Completion Challenge (Zweig and Burges, 2012a) has become a commonly used benchmark for evaluating semantic models. The data is comprised of material from nineteenth-century novels featured on Project Gutenberg. Each of the 1,040 test sentences contains a single blank that must be filled with one of five candidate words. Associated candidates consist of the correct word and decoys with similar distributional statistics.

To further validate the proposed method, 285 sentence completion problems were collected from SAT practice examinations given from 2000-2014 (College Board, 2014). While the MSR data set includes a list of specified training texts, there is no comparable material for SAT questions. Therefore, the requisite word-context matrices were constructed by computing token co-occurrence frequencies from the New York Times portion of the English Gigaword corpus (Parker et al., 2009).

4.2 Results

The overall accuracy achieved on the MSR and SAT data sets reveals that the PMI model is able to outperform prior models applied to sentence completion. Table 1 provides a comparison of the accuracy values attained by various architectures, while Table 2 summarizes the PMI model's performance given feature sets of context words, dependencies, and keywords. Recall that the n-gram variant reflects how features are partitioned.

It appears that while introducing phrase-level information obtained from higher-order n-grams leads to gains in precision on the MSR data set, the same cannot be stated for the set of SAT ques-

Language Model	MSR
Random chance	20.00
N-gram [Zweig (2012b)]	39.00
Skip-gram [Mikolov (2013)]	48.00
LSA [Zweig (2012b)]	49.00
Labeled Dependency [Gubbins (2013)]	50.00
Dependency RNN [Mirowski (2015)]	53.50
RNNs [Mikolov (2013)]	55.40
Log-bilinear [Mnih (2013)]	55.50
Skip-gram + RNNs [Mikolov (2013)]	58.90
PMI	**61.44**

Table 1: Best performance of various models on the MSR Sentence Completion Challenge. Values reflect overall accuracy (%).

Features	MSR	SAT
Unigrams	58.46	**58.95**
Unigrams + Bigrams	60.87	58.95
Unigrams + Bigrams + Trigrams	**61.44**	58.95

Table 2: PMI model performance improvements (% accurate) from incorporating feature sets of higher-order n-grams.

tions. The most probable explanation for this is twofold. First, informative context words are much less likely to occur within 2-3 tokens of the target word. Second, missing words, which are selected to test knowledge of vocabulary, are rarely found in the training corpus. Bigrams and trigrams containing these infrequent terms are extremely uncommon. Regardless of sentence structure, the sparsity associated with higher-order n-grams guarantees diminishing returns for larger values of n. When deciding whether or not to incorporate this information, it is also important to consider the significant trade-off with respect to information storage requirements.

5 Conclusion

This paper described a novel approach to answering sentence completion questions based on pointwise mutual information. To capture unique information stemming from multiple sources, several features sets were defined to encode both local and distant sentence tokens. It was shown that while precision gains can be achieved by augmenting these feature sets with higher-order n-grams, a significant cost is incurred as a result of the increased data storage requirements. Finally, the superiority of the PMI model is demonstrated by its performance on the Microsoft Research Sentence Completion Challenge, during which a new state-of-the-art result was established.

References

Danqi Chen and Christopher Manning. 2014. A fast and accurate dependency parser using neural networks. In *Proceedings of the 2014 Conference on Empirical Methods in Natural Language Processing*, pages 740–750.

Kenneth Ward Church and Patrick Hanks. 1990. Word association norms, mutual information, and lexicography. *Computational Linguistics*, 16(1):22–29.

The College Board. 2014. Sat reading practice questions: Sentence completion. Retrieved from https://sat.collegeboard.org/practice/sat-practice-questions-reading/sentence-completion.

Joseph Gubbins and Andreas Vlachos. 2013. Dependency language models for sentence completion. In *Proceedings of the 2013 Conference on Empirical Methods in Natural Language Processing*, pages 1405–1410.

Tomas Mikolov, Kai Chen, Greg Corrado, and Jeffrey Dean. 2013. Efficient estimation of word representations in vector space. In *Workshop Proceedings of the International Conference on Learning Representations*.

Piotr Mirowski and Andreas Vlachos. 2015. Dependency recurrent neural language models for sentence completion. In *Proceedings of the 53rd Annual Meeting of the Association for Computational Linguistics and the 7th International Joint Conference on Natural Language Processing*, pages 511–517. Association for Computational Linguistics.

Andriy Mnih and Koray Kavukcuoglu. 2013. Learning word embeddings efficiently with noise-contrastive estimation. In *Advances in Neural Information Processing Systems 26*, pages 2265–2273. Curran Associates, Inc.

Patrick Pantel and Dekang Lin. 2002. Discovering word senses from text. In *Proceedings of the Eighth ACM SIGKDD International Conference on Knowledge Discovery and Data Mining*, pages 613–619. Association for Computing Machinery.

Robert Parker, David Graff, Junbo Kong, Ke Chen, and Kazuaki Maeda. 2009. English gigaword fourth edition ldc2009t13.

The Princeton Review. 2007. *11 Practice Tests for the SAT and PSAT, 2008 Edition*. Random House, Inc., New York City, NY.

Kristina Toutanova, Dan Klein, Christopher Manning, and Yoram Singer. 2003. Feature-rich part-of-speech tagging with a cyclic dependency network. In *Proceedings of the Human Language Technology Conference of the North American Chapter of the Association for Computational Linguistics*, volume 1, pages 252–259. Association for Computational Linguistics.

Peter D. Turney and Patrick Pantel. 2010. From frequency to meaning: Vector space models of semantics. *Journal of Artificial Intelligence Research*, 37(1):141–188.

Geoffrey Zweig and Christopher J.C. Burges. 2012a. A challenge set for advancing language modeling. In *Proceedings of the NAACL-HLT 2012 Workshop: Will We Ever Really Replace the N-gram Model? On the Future of Language Modeling for HLT*, pages 29–36. Association for Computational Linguistics.

Geoffrey Zweig, John C. Platt, Christopher Meek, Christopher J.C. Burges, Ainur Yessenalina, and Qiang Liu. 2012b. Computational approaches to sentence completion. In *Proceedings of the 50th Annual Meeting of the Association for Computational Linguistics*, volume 1, pages 601–610. Association for Computational Linguistics.

Convergence of Syntactic Complexity in Conversation

Yang Xu and **David Reitter**
College of Information Sciences and Technology
The Pennsylvania State University
University Park, PA 16802, USA
`yang.xu@psu.edu, reitter@psu.edu`

Abstract

Using corpus data of spoken dialogue, we examine the convergence of syntactic complexity levels between interlocutors in natural conversations, as it occurs within spans of topic episodes. The findings of general convergence in the Switchboard and BNC corpora are compatible with an information-theoretic model of dialogue and with Interactive Alignment Theory.

1 Introduction

According to *Interactive Alignment* theory (Pickering and Garrod, 2004), mutual understanding in dialogue is helped by a variety of interconnected adaptation processes. Over the course of a conversation, interlocutors' linguistic productions assimilate at multiple levels, such as phonemes (Pardo, 2006), lexical choice (Garrod and Anderson, 1987), syntactic structures (Pickering and Branigan, 1998; Branigan et al., 2000; Reitter et al., 2006) and so on. The alignment at these levels contributes to the establishment of aligned *situation models* between speakers, which is the ultimate goal of a successful conversation (Pickering and Garrod, 2004; Reitter and Moore, 2007, 2014).

Alignment does not only refer to the mimicking and repetition of particular linguistic structures; it also includes the convergence at the statistical and ensemble level, which is known as *distributional matching* (Abney et al., 2014). Speech rates (Webb, 1969), probability distributions over syntactic forms (Jaeger and Snider, 2008), power law distributions of acoustic onset events (Abney et al., 2014), and social intent of the speech act (Wang et al., 2015) were all found to match between interlocutors.

An aspect of accommodation that presumably very much helps dialogue partners understand each other's language is *syntactic complexity*. Despite rich investigation of alignment in conversation, this property has been largely overlooked in the analysis of dialogue.

The general concept of syntactic complexity has, of course, been addressed in various ways. In educational psychology and applied linguistics, it is often defined as the degree of sophistication of language forms. It has broad application in the assessment of second language acquisition (Ortega, 2003; Lu, 2010, 2011), the readability test (MacGinitie and Tretiak, 1971), and elementary education (Abedi and Lord, 2001). In computational linguistics, previous studies have shown that the syntactic complexity of a sentence is closely related to the amount of information being transmitted (Genzel and Charniak, 2002, 2003; Jaeger and Levy, 2006; Jaeger, 2010). However, as far as we know, syntactic complexity as a high level feature of language production has not been investigated under the theoretical lens of the Interactive Alignment Model (Pickering and Garrod, 2004).

Therefore, the focus of this study is to track the syntactic complexity of different interlocutors as the conversation develops. A convergence of sentence complexity between interlocutors would be compatible with two pertinent theories. The first is the Interactive Alignment Model. The second is the Uniform Information Density hypothesis (Jaeger and Levy, 2006; Jaeger, 2010), as it applies to syntactic structure. It postulates that speakers will strive to keep information density approximately constant. In other words, if one interlocutor decreased their rate of information transmission, the other one would increase it in response. As far as syntactic complexity is proportional to the amount of information, this would imply that if one interlocutor changes their syntactic complex-

443

Proceedings of the 54th Annual Meeting of the Association for Computational Linguistics, pages 443–448,
Berlin, Germany, August 7-12, 2016. ©2016 Association for Computational Linguistics

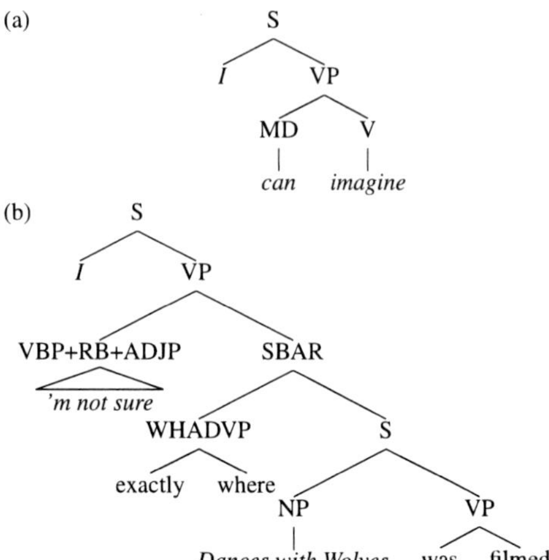

Figure 1: Contrast the syntactic complexity of a simple sentence (a) vs. a complex sentence (b). The tree depth of (a) is 4, while the value of (b) is 7. The branching factor of (a) is 1.38, while the value of (b) is 1.48

ity, their dialogue partner is likely to make the opposite change.

2   Methods

2.1   Corpus data

We use the Switchboard corpus (Godfrey et al., 1992) and the British National Corpus (BNC) (BNC, 2007) in this study. Switchboard contains 1126 conversations over the telephone, where each conversation features exactly two native American English speakers. From the BNC, we use only a subset of the data that contains spoken conversations with exactly two participants so that the dialogue structures are consistent with Switchboard.

2.2   Metrics of syntactic complexity

We consider three candidate statistics to measure the syntactic complexity of a sentence: *sentence length* (number of words in a sentence), *tree depth*, and *branching factor*. The first two are straightforward: syntactically complex sentences are typically used to express complex meanings, and thus are more likely to contain more words than simple ones. More complex syntactic structures, such as relative clauses and noun clauses, also have deeper parse trees (see Figure 1).

The third statistic, branching factor, is defined as the average number of children of all non-leaf nodes in the parse tree of a sentence. In contrast

to tree depth, it measures the *width* of a tree structure, thus a sentence with a larger branching factor looks flatter.

These three statistics are inter-correlated. For instance, tree depth has an almost linear correlation with sentence length. To come up with a measure that solely characterizes the complexity of a sentence in terms of its tree structure, we normalize tree depth and branching factor by excluding the effect of sentence length. We adopt the method proposed by Genzel and Charniak (2002). Let f be a complexity measure of a sentence (tree depth or branching factor). We compute the average measure $\bar{f}(n)$ for sentences of the same length n ($n = 1, 2, \ldots$):

$$\bar{f}(n) = 1/|S(n)| \sum_{s \in S(n)} f(s) \qquad (1)$$

where s denotes a sentence, and $S(n) = \{s | l(s) = n\}$ is the set of sentences of length n. The normalized complexity measure is:

$$f'(s) = \frac{f(s)}{\bar{f}(n)} \qquad (2)$$

This normalized measure f' is not sensitive to sentence length. This gives us five metrics of complexity: *sentence length* (SL), *tree depth* (TD), *branching factor* (BF), *normalized tree depth* (NTD), and *normalized branching factor* (NBF).

2.3   Topic segmentation and speaker role assignment

To verify the hypothesized convergence of a certain statistic between two speakers in dialogue, one possible method is to measure whether the difference in that statistic becomes smaller as the conversation progresses. However, this design is overly simplistic in this case for several reasons. For instance, previous studies have found that sentence complexity in written text increases with its position (Genzel and Charniak, 2003); thus even if we observed that the difference of complexity becomes smaller, a ceiling effect could be a simpler explanation.

Additionally, the syntactic complexity of a sentence largely depends on the amount of meaning that is conveyed. Intuitively, when a speaker has a large amount of information to express, she tends to use more sophisticated syntactic constructions Linking this consideration to another very common scenario in dialogue: one interlocutor *leads* the conversation by steering the on-going topics,

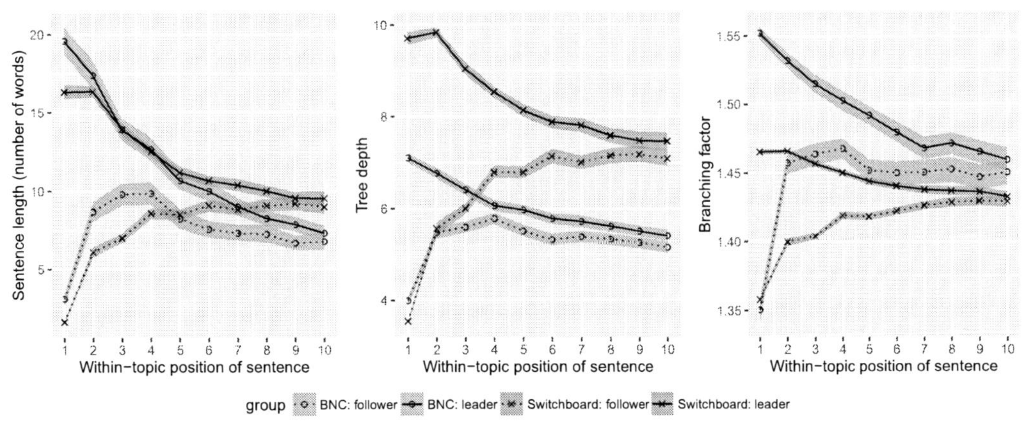

Figure 2: *Sentence length* (SL), *tree depth* (TD) and *branching factor* (BF) against within-topic sentence position (the relative position of a sentence from the beginning of the topic episode), grouped by speaker role, *leader* vs. *follower*. Shaded areas: bootstrapped 95% confidence intervals.

while the other participant *follows* along. Here, we are not talking about the *turn-taking* mechanism in dialogue, which describes the shift at the utterance level. Rather, we are describing the shift at a higher level in conversation, the *topic* level, which is formally referred to as *topic shift* in Conversation Analysis (Ng and Bradac, 1993; Linell, 1998). According to these related theories, a complete conversation consists of several *topic episodes*. Some speakers play a more active role in *leading* the unfolding of new topic episodes, while others play a more passive role by *following* the topic shift. Beginning a new topic means bringing in new information, thus it is reasonable to infer that the interlocutor's syntactic complexity would partially depend on whether he is playing the *leader* or the *follower*. Considering the fact that the leader vs. follower roles are not fixed among interlocutors (a previous leader could be a follower later and vise versa), we should not examine the convergence of syntactic complexity within the whole conversation. Rather, we want to zoom in to the finer scale of topic episodes, in which the interlocutors' roles are relatively stable.

Based on these considerations, we use the Text-Tiling algorithm (Hearst, 1997) to segment the conversation into several topic episodes. This is a sufficient topic segmentation method for our research questions, though it is less sophisticated compared to Bayesian models (Eisenstein and Barzilay, 2008) or Hidden Markov Models (Blei and Moreno, 2001).

Within each topic episode that resulted from the segmentation operation, we assign roles to the two speakers. This is based on which of the interlocutors is leading this topic episode, as previously explained. We use two rules to determine this *leader* and *follower* differentiation:

Rule I: If the topic episode starts in the middle of the speaking turn of speaker A, then let A be the *leader* of this topic.

Rule II: If the topic episode starts with a complete speaking turn, then let the first speaker who contributes a sentence greater than N words in length in this episode be the *leader*.

Note that the purpose of Rule II is to select the most *probable* topic leader, based on the intuition that longer sentences are more *likely* to initiate a new topic. Thus the determination of the N words threshold here is totally empirical. We use $N = 5$ as the final threshold, because for $N \geq 5$ our experiments draw similar results.

3 Results

For each sentence in conversation, we compute the five earlier-discussed metrics of syntactic complexity: SL, TD, BF, NTD, and NBF.

For the first three metrics, SL, TD and BF, we observe convergence between topic leaders and followers, for both corpora (Fig. 2). Basically, topic leaders have higher syntactic complexity measures at the early stage of a topic episode, which drops gradually as the topic develops. The converse holds for topic followers. We fit 12 linear

Table 1: β coefficients of the fixed effect (within-topic position) of the linear mixed models.

group	SL	TD	BF
Switchboard leader	0.363***	-0.129***	-1.82×10^{-3}***
Switchboard follower	0.188***	0.104***	2.141×10^{-3}***
BNC leader	-0.166***	-0.030***	-1.88×10^{-3}***
BNC follower	0.012	9.45×10^{-3}***	5.51×10^{-4}***

***$p < 0.001$

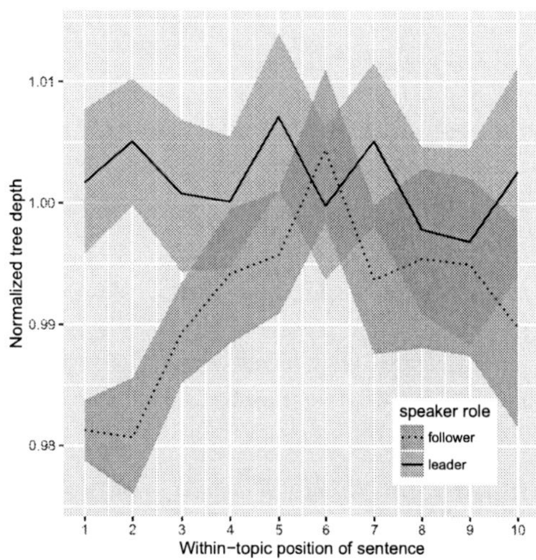

(a) NTD

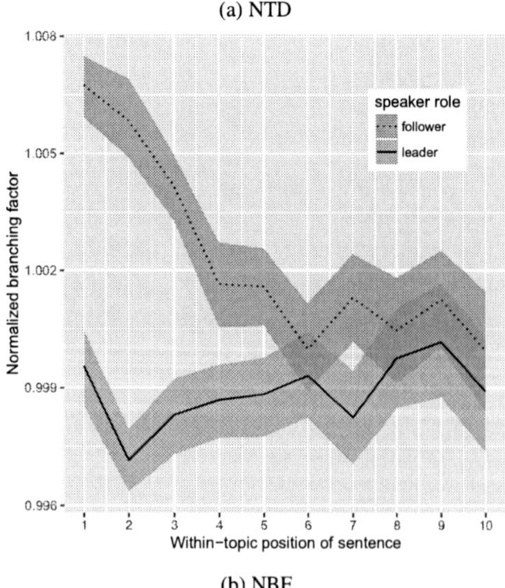

(b) NBF

Figure 3: Two normalized metrics of syntactic complexity, tree depth (NTD) (a) and branching factor (NBF) (b), vs. within-topic position of sentences in Switchboard. Shaded areas: bootstrapped 95% confidence intervals.

mixed models (3 metrics $\times$ 2 roles $\times$ 2 corpora) using metrics as the respective response variables, the within-topic position as a fixed effect, and a random intercept grouped by individual speakers. We find a positive effect of within-topic position for leaders, and a reliably negative effect for followers (except SL of BNC follower), which confirms the observation of convergence trend (See Table 1).

For NTD and NBF, we observe convergence patterns in Switchboard, but not reliably in BNC (Figure 3). Linear mixed models are fit in similar ways, and the β coefficients are: for NTD, $\beta_{\text{leader}} = -2.2 \times 10^{-5}$, $\beta_{\text{follower}} = 9.7 \times 10^{-4***}$; for NBF, $\beta_{\text{leader}} = 6.8 \times 10^{-5*}$, $\beta_{\text{follower}} = -2.9 \times 10^{-4***}$ (*** indicates $p < 0.001$, and * indicates $p < 0.05$). Thus, a general trend seems supported. As NBF is the only metric that is lower in leaders and higher in followers, it could actually be an index for syntactic *simplicity*.

4 Discussion and Conclusion

By segmenting a conversation into several topic episodes, and then differentiating the interlocutors in terms of their roles in initiating the topic, leader or follower, we show that the syntactic complexity of the two interlocutors converges within topic episodes. The syntactic complexity of the topic leader decreases, while the complexity of the topic follower increases.

From an information-theoretical point of view, the syntactic complexity of a sentence is closely related to its amount of lexical information or negative entropy (Genzel and Charniak, 2002, 2003). By starting a new topic in conversation, the leading speaker brings novelty to the existing context, which often involves relatively long and complex utterances. On the other hand, the following speaker has to accommodate this change of context, by first producing short acknowledging phrases at the early stage, and gradually increase his contribution as the topic develops. Therefore, the convergence of syntactic complexity within a topic episode is a reflection of the process in which two interlocutors contribute jointly to build up common ground (Clark and Brennan, 1991) with respect to a certain topic.

We find our results explained the theoretical frameworks of common ground (Clark, 1996) and the Interactive Alignment Model (IAM, Pickering and Garrod, 2004), models which are sometimes characterized as opposing accounts of coordination in dialogue. From the common-ground perspective of language-as-activity, interlocutors play different roles in dialogue, and the coordination between these roles facilitates the successful unfolding of dialogue. Our account identifies two such macro-level roles: topic *leader* vs *follower*. From the perspective of Interactive Alignment, interactions between interlocutors in a dialogue are accompanied by the alignment of linguistic elements at multiple levels, including syntactic rules. Thus, the micro-level convergence of syntactic complexity is predicted by the IAM. Therefore, our findings point to the possibility of a unified perspective that combines the two theories.

It is worth pointing out that we present some novel ideas about the scope of convergence. Existing studies focus on the alignment effect that is observable throughout the whole conversation. In our case, the convergence of syntactic complexity occurs within smaller scope: the topic episodes. Note that the direction of convergence is dynamic: a speaker of higher complexity in one episode might be of lower complexity in the next episode, depending on her role. The next questions arising from these patterns mirror those asked of other types of alignment: is complexity alignment purposeful, is it controlled by individual differences or situational goals, and can it predict task success? We leave these questions for future work.

Acknowledgments

This work has been funded by the National Science Foundation under CRII IIS grant 1459300.

References

Jamal Abedi and Carol Lord. 2001. The language factor in mathematics tests. *Applied Measurement in Education* 14(3):219–234.

Drew H Abney, Alexandra Paxton, Rick Dale, and Christopher T Kello. 2014. Complexity matching in dyadic conversation. *Journal of Experimental Psychology: General* 143(6):2304–2315.

David M Blei and Pedro J Moreno. 2001. Topic segmentation with an aspect hidden Markov model. In *Proceedings of the 24th Annual International ACM SIGIR Conference on Research and Development in Information Retrieval*. ACM, pages 343–348.

BNC. 2007. The British National Corpus, version 3 (BNC XML Edition).

Holly P Branigan, Martin J Pickering, and Alexandra A Cleland. 2000. Syntactic co-ordination in dialogue. *Cognition* 75(2):B13–B25.

Herbert H Clark. 1996. *Using language*. Cambridge University Press.

Herbert H Clark and Susan F. Brennan. 1991. Grounding in communication. *Perspectives on socially shared cognition* 13(1991):127–149.

Jacob Eisenstein and Regina Barzilay. 2008. Bayesian unsupervised topic segmentation. In *Proceedings of the Conference on Empirical Methods in Natural Language Processing*. Association for Computational Linguistics, pages 334–343.

Simon Garrod and Anthony Anderson. 1987. Saying what you mean in dialogue: A study in conceptual and semantic co-ordination. *Cognition* 27(2):181–218.

Dmitriy Genzel and Eugene Charniak. 2002. Entropy rate constancy in text. In *Proc. 40th Annual Meeting of the Association for Computational Linguistics*. Association for Computational Linguistics, pages 199–206.

Dmitriy Genzel and Eugene Charniak. 2003. Variation of entropy and parse trees of sentences as a function of the sentence number In *Proc. 2003 Conference on Empirical Methods in Natural Language Processing*. Association for Computational Linguistics, pages 65–72.

John J Godfrey, Edward C Holliman, and Jane McDaniel. 1992. Switchboard: Telephone speech corpus for research and development. In *Acoustics, Speech, and Signal Processing, 1992. ICASSP-92., 1992 IEEE International Conference on*. IEEE, volume 1, pages 517–520.

Marti A Hearst. 1997. Texttiling: Segmenting text

into multi-paragraph subtopic passages. *Computational Linguistics* 23(1):33–64.

T Florian Jaeger. 2010. Redundancy and reduction: Speakers manage syntactic information density. *Cognitive Psychology* 61(1):23–62.

T Florian Jaeger and Roger P Levy. 2006. Speakers optimize information density through syntactic reduction. In *Advances in Neural Information Processing Systems*. pages 849–856.

T Florian Jaeger and Neal Snider. 2008. Implicit learning and syntactic persistence: Surprisal and cumulativity. In *Proc. 30th Annual Meeting of the Cognitive Science Society*. pages 1061–1066.

Per Linell. 1998. *Approaching dialogue: Talk, interaction and contexts in dialogical perspectives*, volume 3. John Benjamins Publishing.

Xiaofei Lu. 2010. Automatic analysis of syntactic complexity in second language writing. *International Journal of Corpus Linguistics* 15(4):474–496.

Xiaofei Lu. 2011. A corpus-based evaluation of syntactic complexity measures as indices of college-level ESL writers' language development. *Tesol Quarterly* 45(1):36–62.

Walter H MacGinitie and Richard Tretiak. 1971. Sentence depth measures as predictors of reading difficulty. *Reading Research Quarterly* pages 364–377.

Sik Hung Ng and James J Bradac. 1993. *Power in language: Verbal communication and social influence*. Sage Publications, Inc.

Lourdes Ortega. 2003. Syntactic complexity measures and their relationship to L2 proficiency: A research synthesis of college-level L2 writing. *Applied Linguistics* 24(4):492–518.

Jennifer S Pardo. 2006. On phonetic convergence during conversational interaction. *The Journal of the Acoustical Society of America* 119(4):2382–2393.

Martin J Pickering and Holly P Branigan. 1998. The representation of verbs: Evidence from syntactic priming in language production. *Journal of Memory and Language* 39(4):633–651.

Martin J Pickering and Simon Garrod. 2004. Toward a mechanistic psychology of dialogue. *Behavioral and Brain Sciences* 27(02):169–190.

David Reitter and Johanna D. Moore. 2007. Predicting success in dialogue. In *Proc. 45th Annual Meeting of the Association of Computational Linguistics*. Prague, Czech Republic, pages 808–815.

David Reitter and Johanna D. Moore. 2014. Alignment and task success in spoken dialogue. *Journal of Memory and Language* 76:29–46.

David Reitter, Johanna D. Moore, and Frank Keller. 2006. Priming of syntactic rules in task-oriented dialogue and spontaneous conversation. In *Proceedings of the 28th Annual Conference of the Cognitive Science Society (CogSci)*. Cognitive Science Society, Vancouver, Canada, pages 685–690.

Yafei Wang, John Yen, and David Reitter. 2015. Pragmatic alignment on social support type in health forum conversations. In *Proc. Cognitive Modeling and Computational Linguistics (CMCL)*. Association for Computational Linguistics, Denver, CO, pages 9–18.

James T Webb. 1969. Subject speech rates as a function of interviewer behaviour. *Language and Speech* 12(1):54–67.

User Embedding for Scholarly Microblog Recommendation

Yang Yu, Xiaojun Wan and Xinjie Zhou

Institute of Computer Science and Technology, The MOE Key Laboratory of Computational
Linguistics, Peking University, Beijing 100871, China
{yu.yang, wanxiaojun, xinjiezhou}@pku.edu.cn

Abstract

Nowadays, many scholarly messages are posted on Chinese microblogs and more and more researchers tend to find scholarly information on microblogs. In order to exploit microblogging to benefit scientific research, we propose a scholarly microblog recommendation system in this study. It automatically collects and mines scholarly information from Chinese microblogs, and makes personalized recommendations to researchers. We propose two different neural network models which learn the vector representations for both users and microblog texts. Then the recommendation is accomplished based on the similarity between a user's vector and a microblog text's vector. We also build a dataset for this task. The two embedding models are evaluated on the dataset and show good results compared to several baselines.

1 Introduction

Online social networks such as microblogs have drawn growing attention in recent years, and more and more researchers are involved in microblogging websites. Besides expressing their own emotions and exchanging their life experiences just like other users, these researchers also write from time to time about their latest findings or recommend useful research resources on their microblogs, which may be insightful to other researchers in the same field. We call such microblog texts scholarly microblog texts. The volume of scholarly microblog texts is huge, which makes it time-consuming for a researcher to browse and find the ones that he or she is interested in.

In this study, we aim to build a personalized recommendation system for recommending scholarly microblogs. With such a system a re-searcher can easily obtain the scholarly microblogs he or she has interests in. The system first collects the latest scholarly microblogs by crawling from manually selected microblog users or by applying scholarly microblog classification methods, as introduced in (Yu and Wan, 2016). Second, the system models the relevance of each scholarly microblog to a researcher and make personalized recommendation. In this study, we focus on the second step of the system and aim to model the interest and preference of a researcher by embedding the researcher into a dense vector. We also embed each scholarly microblog into a dense vector, and thus the relevance of a scholarly microblog to a researcher can be estimated based on their vector representations.

In this paper, we propose two neural embedding algorithms for learning the vector representations for both users (researchers) and microblog texts. By extending the paragraph vector representation method proposed by (Le and Mikolov, 2014), the vector representations are jointly learned in a single framework. By modeling the user preferences into the same vector space with the words and texts, we can obtain the similarity between them in a straightforward way, and use this relevance for microblog recommendation. We build a real evaluation dataset from Sina Weibo. Evaluation results on the dataset show the efficacy of our proposed methods.

2 Related Work

There have been a few previous studies focusing on microblog recommendation. Chen et al. (2012) proposed a collaborative ranking model. Their approach takes advantage of collaborative filtering based recommendation by collecting preference information from many users. Their approach takes into account the content of the tweet, user's social relations and certain other explicitly defined features. Ma et al. (2011) generated recommendations by adding additional social regularization terms in MF to constrain the user latent feature vectors to be similar to his or her friends' average latent features. Bhattacharya et al. (2014)

Proceedings of the 54th Annual Meeting of the Association for Computational Linguistics, pages 449–453,
Berlin, Germany, August 7-12, 2016. ©2016 Association for Computational Linguistics

proposed a method benefiting from knowing the user's topics of interest, inferring the topics of interest for an individual user. Their idea is to infer them from the topical expertise of the users whom the user follows. Khater and Elmongu (2015) proposed a dynamic personalized tweet recommendation system capturing the user's interests, which change over the time. Their system shows the messages that correspond to such dynamic interests. Kuang et al. (2016) considered three major aspects in their proposed tweet recommending model, including the popularity of a tweet itself, the intimacy between the user and the tweet publisher, and the interest fields of the user. They also divided the users into three types by analyzing their behaviors, using different weights for the three aspects when recommending tweets for different types of users.

Most of the above studies make use of the relationships between users, while in this study, we focus on leveraging only the microblog texts for addressing the task.

3　Our Approach

3.1　Task Definition

We denote a set of users by $u = \{u_1, u_2, \ldots, u_m\}$, and a set of microblog texts by $d = \{d_1, d_2, \ldots, d_n\}$. We assume that a user tweeting, retweeting or commenting on a microblog text reflects that the user is interested in that microblog. Given $u_t \in u$, we denote the set of microblogs that u_t is interested in by $d(u_t)$. In our task, the entire sets of d and u are given, while given a user $u_t \in u$, only a subset of $d(u_t)$ is known. This subset is used as the training set, denoted as $\tilde{d}(u_t)$. Our task aims to retrieve a subset d' of d, that d' is as similar to $d(u_t) - \tilde{d}(u_t)$ as possible.

In this section, we introduce one baseline method and then propose two different neural network methods for user and microblog embedding. The baseline averages the vector representation of microblog texts into a user vector representation. Our proposed two methods learn user vector representations jointly with word and text vectors, either indirectly or directly from word vectors.

3.2　Paragraph Vector

As our methods are mainly based on the Paragraph Vector model proposed by (Le and

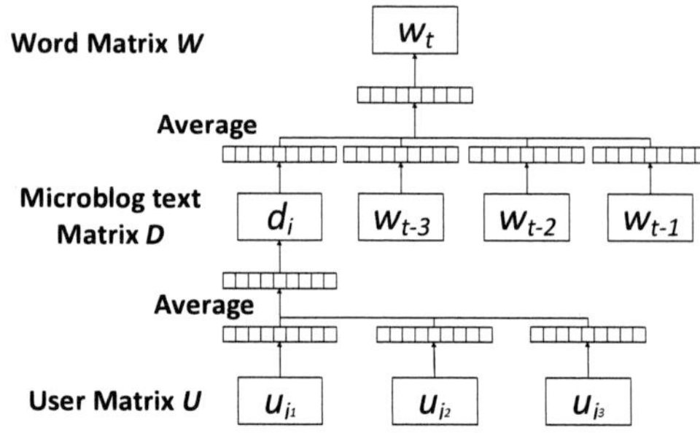

Figure 1. The proposed User2Vec#1 framework for learning user vector representation. In this framework, the word vectors do not directly contribute to the user vectors.

Mikolov, 2014), we start by introducing this framework first.

Paragraph Vector is an unsupervised framework that learns continuous distributed vector representations for pieces of texts. In this approach, every paragraph is mapped to a unique vector, represented by a column in matrix D and every word is also mapped to a unique vector, represented by a column in matrix W. This approach is similar to the Word2Vec approach proposed in (Mikolov et al., 2013), except that a paragraph token is added to the paragraph and is treated as a special word. The paragraph vector is asked to contribute to the prediction work in addition to the word vectors in the context of the word to be predicted. The paragraph vector and word vectors are averaged to predict the next word in a context.

Formally speaking, given a paragraph $\{d_i, w_1, w_2, \ldots, w_T\}$ with d_i as the paragraph token, k as the window size, the Paragraph Vector model applies hierarchical softmax to maximize the average log probability

$$\frac{1}{T}\sum_t \log p(w_t \mid d_i, w_{t-k}, \ldots, w_{t+k})$$

3.3　Averaging Microblog Text Vectors as User Vector

An intuitive baseline approach to map a microblog user into a vector space is to build such representation from the vector representations of the microblogs he or she likes.

We treat microblog texts as paragraphs, and then apply the Paragraph Vector model introduced in Section 3.2 to learn vector representations of the microblog texts. After learning all vector representations of microblog texts, for each user, we average all vectors of microblog texts he or she likes in the training set as the user vector.

3.4 Learning User Vectors Indirectly From Word Vectors

Besides the above-mentioned baseline approach we further consider to jointly learn the vectors of users and microblog texts. In this framework, every user is mapped to a vector represented in a column in matrix U, in addition to the microblog text matrix D and the word matrix W. Given a microblog text $\{d_i, w_1, w_2, ..., w_T\}$, besides predicting words in the microblog texts using the microblog token d_i and words in the sliding window, we also try to predict d_i using the users related to it. Denoting the set of all users related to d_i in the training set as $\tilde{u}(d_i) = \{u_{i_1}, u_{i_2}..., u_{i_k}\}$, we maximize the average log probability

$$\frac{1}{T}\sum_t [\log p(w_t \mid d_i, w_{t-k}, ..., w_{t+k}) + \log p(d_i \mid u_{i_1}, ..., u_{i_k})]$$

The structure of this framework is shown in Figure 1. We name this framework User2Vec#1.

3.5 Learning User Vectors Directly From Word Vectors

In the above framework, the user vectors are learned only from microblog text vectors, not directly from word vectors. Another framework we proposed for learning user vector representation is to put user vectors and microblog vectors in the same layer. Unlike User2Vec#1, we do not use user vectors to predict microblog text vector. Instead, we directly add user vectors into the input layer of word vector prediction task, along with the microblog text vector.

In this framework, the average log probability we want to maximize is

$$\frac{1}{T}\left(\sum_t \log p(w_t \mid d_i, w_{t-k}, ..., w_{t+k}, u_{i_1}, ..., u_{i_k})\right)$$

In practical tasks, we modify the dataset by copying each microblog once for each user in $\tilde{u}(d_i)$, and make each copied microblog text only relate to one user. All copies of the same microblog text share a same vector representation.

The structure of the framework is shown in Figure 2. We name this framework User2Vec#2.

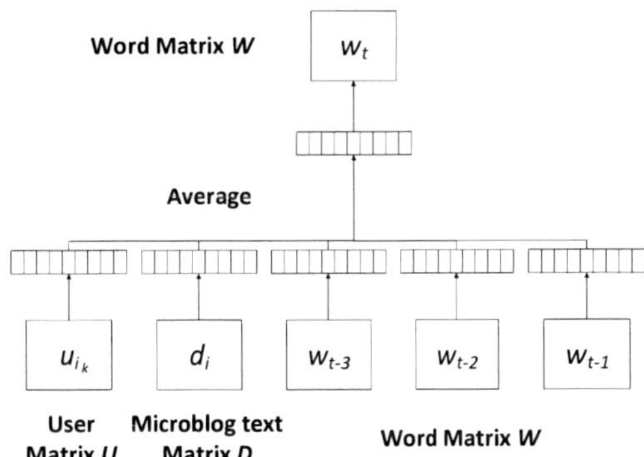

Figure 2. The proposed User2Vec#2 framework for learning user vector representation. In this framework, the word vectors contribute directly to the user vectors, along with the microblog text vectors.

3.6 Recommending Microblogs

When recommending microblogs, given a microblog d_j and a user u_k, we compute the cosine distance between their vector representations, and use the cosine distance to determine whether d_j should be recommended to u_k or not.

4 Evaluation

4.1 Data Preparation

To evaluate our proposed user embedding methods in a scholarly microblog recommending system, we built a dataset by crawling from the website Machine Learning Daily[1].

The Machine Learning Daily is a Chinese website which focuses on collecting and labeling scholarly microblogs related to machine learning, natural language processing, information retrieval and data mining on Sina Weibo. These microblog texts were collected by a combination of manual and automatic methods, and each microblog text is annotated with multiple tags by experts, yielding an excellent dataset for our experiment. The microblog texts in our dataset can be written in a mixture of both Chinese and English. We removed stop words from the raw texts, leaving 16,797 words in our corpus. The texts were then segmented with the Jieba Chinese text segmentation tool[2].

---

[1] http://ml.memect.com/
[2] https://github.com/fxsjy/jieba

451

	$k=10$			$k=20$			$k=50$			$k=100$		
	Precision	Recall	MRR	Precision	Recall	MRR	Precision	Recall	MRR	Precision	Recall	MRR
Bag-of-Words	0.5036	0.0504	0.0153	0.4917	0.0983	0.0185	0.4461	0.2231	0.0223	0.3204	0.3204	0.0246
SVM on BoW	0.5774	0.0577	0.0172	0.5662	0.1132	0.0212	0.5122	0.2561	0.0256	0.3675	0.3675	0.0282
Average Embedding	0.5963	0.0596	0.0183	0.5824	0.1165	0.0219	0.5266	0.2633	0.0264	0.3793	0.3793	0.0291
User2Vec#1	0.6246	0.0625	0.0189	0.6055	0.1211	0.0228	0.5511	0.2756	0.0275	0.3953	0.3953	0.0304
User2Vec#2	**0.6652**	**0.0665**	**0.0201**	**0.6498**	**0.1300**	**0.0244**	**0.5883**	**0.2942**	**0.0295**	**0.4231**	**0.4231**	**0.0325**

Table 1. Overview of results.

After crawling the microblogs from the Machine Learning Daily, we used Sina Weibo API to retrieve the list of users who retweeted or commented on those microblogs. These retweeting and commenting actions indicated that those users have interests in the microblogs they retweeted or commented, and such microblogs were considered the gold-standard (positive) microblogs for the users in the recommendation system. Then we filtered out the users who have less than two hundred positive samples to avoid the data sparseness problem. This left us with 711 users and 10,620 microblog texts in our corpus. Each user was associated with 282.3 positive microblogs on average.

4.2 Evaluation Setup

Because there is no API that can directly grant us the access to the follower and followee list for each user without authorization on Sina Weibo, when evaluating the effectiveness of our methods, we randomly choose one hundred positive samples and another four hundred negative samples randomly selected from the crawled microblogs, to simulate the timeline of a user, and use this simulated timeline as the test dataset. The remaining positive samples are used for training.

We adopt two additional baselines: Bag-of-Words and SVM on Bag-of-Words. For the Bag-of-Words baseline, we use the Bag-of-Words vector of each microblog text as the microblog text vector, and average them to obtain user vectors. For the SVM on Bag-of-Words baseline, we randomly choose the same amount of negative samples as that of positive samples for training. We use the Bag-of-Words vector of each microblog text as the features, and run the SVM algorithm implemented in LibSVM[3] once for every user. Note that the Average Embedding

---

[3] https://www.csie.ntu.edu.tw/~cjlin/libsvm/

Figure 3. Precision/Recall@k=100 w.r.t. vector dimension.

method introduced in Section 3.3 is considered a strong baseline for comparison.

For each method and each user, we sort the microblog texts according to their similarity with the user and select the top k microblog texts as recommendation results, where k varies from 10 to 100.

Besides precision and recall values, we also compute mean reciprocal rank (MRR) to measure the recommendation results in our experiments, which is the average of the multiplicative inverse of the rank of the positive samples in the output of the recommending system, and then averaged again across all users. Note that when k is set to 100, the precision and recall value will be equal to each other.

4.3 Evaluation Results

The comparison results with respect to different k are shown in Table 1. As we can see, the two proposed joint learning methods outperform the simple average embedding method and the two other baselines, indicating the effectiveness of the proposed methods. Moreover, User2Vec#2 yields better results than User2Vec#1.We believe this is because in User2Vec#2, the word vectors have a direct contribution to the user vectors, which improves the learning effect of the user

452

vectors learnt in the framework. Furthermore, the precision/recall scores of the embedding methods (k=100) with respect to different vector dimensions are shown in Figure 3. We can see that the dimension size has little impact on the recommendation performance, and our proposed two methods always outperform the strong baseline.

5   Conclusion

In this paper, we proposed two neural embedding methods for learning the vector representations for both the users and the microblog texts. We tested their performance by applying them to recommending scholarly microblogs. In future work, we will investigate leveraging user relationships and temporal information to further improve the recommendation performance.

Acknowledgments

The work was supported by National Natural Science Foundation of China (61331011), National Hi-Tech Research and Development Program (863 Program) of China (2015AA015403) and IBM Global Faculty Award Program. We thank the anonymous reviewers and mentor for their helpful comments. Xiaojun Wan is the corresponding author.

References

Michal Barla. 2011. Towards social-based user modeling and personalization. *Information Sciences and Technologies Bulletin of the ACM Slovakia*, 3(1).

Parantapa Bhattacharya, Muhammad Bilal Zafar, Niloy Ganguly, Saptarshi Ghosh, and Krishna P. Gummadi. 2014. Inferring user interests in the twitter social network. In *Proceedings of the 8th ACM Conference on Recommender systems*. ACM.

Kailong Chen, Tianqi Chen, Guoqing Zheng, Ou Jin, Enpeng Yao, and Yong Yu. 2012. Collaborative personalized tweet recommendation. In *Proceedings of the 35th international ACM SIGIR conference on Research and development in information retrieval*. ACM.

Shaymaa Khater and Hicham G. Elmongui. 2015. Tweets You Like: Personalized Tweets Recommendation based on Dynamic Users Interests. In *2014 ASE Conference.*

Li Kuang, Xiang Tang, Meiqi Yu, Yujian Huang and Kehua Guo. 2016. A comprehensive ranking model for tweets big data in online social network. *EURASIP Journal on Wireless Communications and Networking, 2016(1).*

Quoc V. Le and Tomas Mikolov. 2014. Distributed representations of sentences and documents. *arXiv preprint arXiv:1405.4053.*

Hao Ma, Dengyong Zhou, Chao Liu, Michael R. Lyu and Irwin King. 2011. Recommender systems with social regularization. In *Proceedings of the fourth ACM international conference on Web search and data mining.* ACM.

Tomas Mikolov, Kai Chen, Greg Corrado, and Jeffrey Dean. 2013. Efficient estimation of word representations in vector space. *arXiv preprint arXiv:1301.3781.*

Tomas Mikolov, Ilya Sutskever, Kai Chen, Greg S. Corrado and Jeff Dean. 2013. Distributed representations of words and phrases and their compositionality. In *Advances in neural information processing systems.*

Hongzhi Yin, Bin Cui, Ling Chen, Zhiting Hu and Xiaofang Zhou. 2015. Dynamic user modeling in social media systems. *ACM Transactions on Information Systems (TOIS)*, 33(3).

Jianjun Yu, Yi Shen and Zhenglu Yang. 2014. Topic-STG: Extending the session-based temporal graph approach for personalized tweet recommendation. In *Proceedings of the companion publication of the 23rd international conference on World Wide Web companion.* International World Wide Web Conferences Steering Committee.

Yang Yu and Xiaojun Wan. 2016. MicroScholar: Mining Scholarly Information from Chinese Microblogs. In *Thirtieth AAAI Conference on Artificial Intelligence.*

Integrating Distributional Lexical Contrast into Word Embeddings for Antonym–Synonym Distinction

Kim Anh Nguyen and **Sabine Schulte im Walde** and **Ngoc Thang Vu**
Institut für Maschinelle Sprachverarbeitung
Universität Stuttgart
Pfaffenwaldring 5B, 70569 Stuttgart, Germany
{nguyenkh, schulte, thangvu}@ims.uni-stuttgart.de

Abstract

We propose a novel vector representation that integrates lexical contrast into distributional vectors and strengthens the most salient features for determining degrees of word similarity. The improved vectors significantly outperform standard models and distinguish antonyms from synonyms with an average precision of 0.66–0.76 across word classes (adjectives, nouns, verbs). Moreover, we integrate the lexical contrast vectors into the objective function of a skip-gram model. The novel embedding outperforms state-of-the-art models on predicting word similarities in SimLex-999, and on distinguishing antonyms from synonyms.

1 Introduction

Antonymy and synonymy represent lexical semantic relations that are central to the organization of the mental lexicon (Miller and Fellbaum, 1991). While antonymy is defined as the oppositeness between words, synonymy refers to words that are similar in meaning (Deese, 1965; Lyons, 1977). From a computational point of view, distinguishing between antonymy and synonymy is important for NLP applications such as Machine Translation and Textual Entailment, which go beyond a general notion of semantic relatedness and require to identify specific semantic relations. However, due to interchangeable substitution, antonyms and synonyms often occur in similar contexts, which makes it challenging to automatically distinguish between them.

Distributional semantic models (DSMs) offer a means to represent meaning vectors of words and to determine their semantic "relatedness" (Budanitsky and Hirst, 2006; Turney and Pantel, 2010).

They rely on the *distributional hypothesis* (Harris, 1954; Firth, 1957), in which words with similar distributions have related meaning. For computation, each word is represented by a weighted feature vector, where features typically correspond to words that co-occur in a particular context. However, DSMs tend to retrieve both synonyms (such as *formal–conventional*) and antonyms (such as *formal–informal*) as related words and cannot sufficiently distinguish between the two relations.

In recent years, a number of distributional approaches have accepted the challenge to distinguish antonyms from synonyms, often in combination with lexical resources such as thesauruses or taxonomies. For example, Lin et al. (2003) used dependency triples to extract distributionally similar words, and then in a post-processing step filtered out words that appeared with the patterns 'from X to Y' or 'either X or Y' significantly often. Mohammad et al. (2013) assumed that word pairs that occur in the same thesaurus category are close in meaning and marked as synonyms, while word pairs occurring in contrasting thesaurus categories or paragraphs are marked as opposites. Scheible et al. (2013) showed that the distributional difference between antonyms and synonyms can be identified via a simple word space model by using appropriate features. Santus et al. (2014a) and Santus et al. (2014b) aimed to identify the most salient dimensions of meaning in vector representations and reported a new average-precision-based distributional measure and an entropy-based measure to discriminate antonyms from synonyms (and further paradigmatic semantic relations).

Lately, antonym–synonym distinction has also been a focus of word embedding models. For example, Adel and Schütze (2014) integrated coreference chains extracted from large corpora into a skip-gram model to create word embeddings that identified antonyms. Ono et al. (2015) pro-

Proceedings of the 54th Annual Meeting of the Association for Computational Linguistics, pages 454–459,
Berlin, Germany, August 7-12, 2016. ©2016 Association for Computational Linguistics

posed thesaurus-based word embeddings to capture antonyms. They proposed two models: the WE-T model that trains word embeddings on thesaurus information; and the WE-TD model that incorporated distributional information into the WE-T model. Pham et al. (2015) introduced the multi-task lexical contrast model (mLCM) by incorporating WordNet into a skip-gram model to optimize semantic vectors to predict contexts. Their model outperformed standard skip-gram models with negative sampling on both general semantic tasks and distinguishing antonyms from synonyms.

In this paper, we propose two approaches that make use of lexical contrast information in distributional semantic space and word embeddings for antonym–synonym distinction. Firstly, we incorporate lexical contrast into distributional vectors and strengthen those word features that are most salient for determining word similarities, assuming that feature overlap in synonyms is stronger than feature overlap in antonyms. Secondly, we propose a novel extension of a skip-gram model with negative sampling (Mikolov et al., 2013b) that integrates the lexical contrast information into the objective function. The proposed model optimizes the semantic vectors to predict degrees of word similarity and also to distinguish antonyms from synonyms. The improved word embeddings outperform state-of-the-art models on antonym–synonym distinction and a word similarity task.

2 Our Approach

In this section, we present the two contributions of this paper: a new vector representation that improves the quality of weighted features to distinguish between antonyms and synonyms (Section 2.1), and a novel extension of skip-gram models that integrates the improved vector representations into the objective function, in order to predict similarities between words and to identify antonyms (Section 2.2).

2.1 Improving the weights of feature vectors

We aim to improve the quality of weighted feature vectors by strengthening those features that are most salient in the vectors and by putting less emphasis on those that are of minor importance, when distinguishing degrees of similarity between words. We start out with standard corpus co-occurrence frequencies and apply *local mutual*

information (LMI) (Evert, 2005) to determine the original strengths of the word features. Our score $weight^{SA}(w, f)$ subsequently defines the weights of a target word w and a feature f:

$$weight^{SA}(w, f) = \frac{1}{\#(w,u)} \sum_{u \in W(f) \cap S(w)} sim(w, u) - \frac{1}{\#(w',v)} \sum_{w' \in A(w)} \sum_{v \in W(f) \cap S(w')} sim(w', v)$$

$$(1)$$

The new $weight^{SA}$ scores of a target word w and a feature f exploit the differences between the average similarities of synonyms to the target word ($sim(w, u)$, with $u \in S(w)$), and the average similarities between antonyms of the target word ($sim(w', v)$, with $w' \in A(w)$ and $v \in S(w')$). Only those words u and v are included in the calculation that have a positive original LMI score for the feature f: $W(f)$. To calculate the similarity sim between two word vectors, we rely on cosine distances. If a word w is not associated with any synonyms or antonyms in our resources (cf. Section 3.1), or if a feature does not co-occur with a word w, we define $weight^{SA}(w, f) = 0$.

The intuition behind the *lexical contrast information* in our new $weight^{SA}$ is as follows. The strongest features of a word also tend to represent strong features of its synonyms, but weaker features of its antonyms. For example, the feature *conception* only occurs with synonyms of the adjective *formal* but not with the antonym *informal*, or with synonyms of the antonym *informal*. $weight^{SA}(formal, conception)$, which is calculated as the average similarity between *formal* and its synonyms minus the average similarity between *informal* and its synonyms, should thus return a high positive value. In contrast, a feature such as *issue* that occurs with many different adjectives, would enforce a feature score near zero for $weight^{SA}(formal, issue)$, because the similarity scores between *formal* and its synonyms and *informal* and its synonyms should not differ strongly. Last but not least, a feature such as *rumor* that only occurs with *informal* and its synonyms, but not with the original target adjective *formal* and its synonyms, should invoke a very low value for $weight^{SA}(formal, rumor)$. Figure 1 provides a schematic visualization for computing the new $weight^{SA}$ scores for the target *formal*.

Since the number of antonyms is usually much smaller than the number of synonyms, we enrich the number of antonyms: Instead of using the

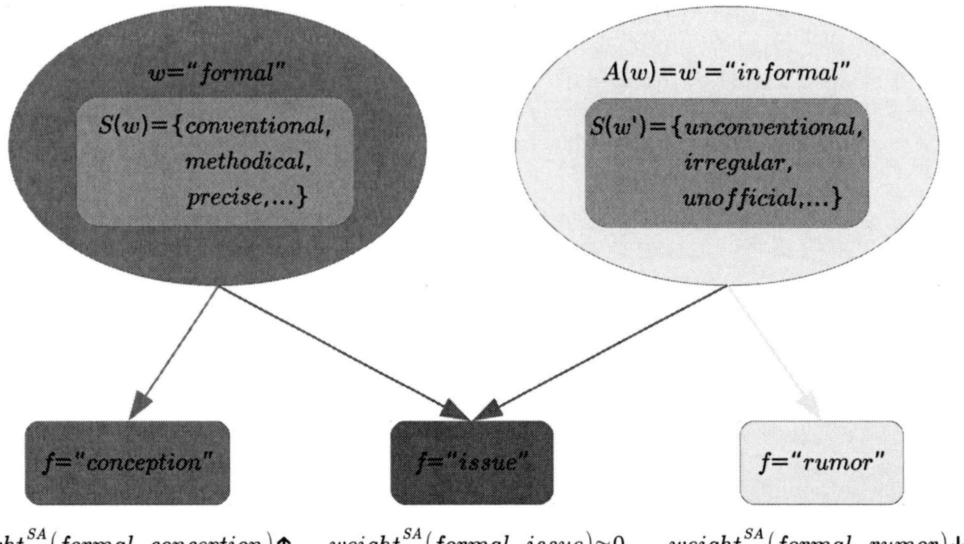

Figure 1: Illustration of the $weight^{SA}$ scores for the adjective target *formal*. The feature *conception* only occurs with *formal* and synonyms of *formal*, so $weight^{SA}(formal, conception)$ should return a positive value; the feature *rumor* only occurs with the antonym *informal* and with synonyms of *informal*, so $weight^{SA}(formal, rumor)$ should return a negative value; the feature *issue* occurs with both *formal* and *informal* and also with synonyms of these two adjectives, so $weight^{SA}(formal, issue)$ should return a feature score near zero.

direct antonym links, we consider all synonyms of an antonym $w' \in A(w)$ as antonyms of w. For example, the target word *good* has only two antonyms in WordNet (*bad* and *evil*), in comparison to 31 synonyms. Thus, we also exploit the synonyms of *bad* and *evil* as antonyms for *good*.

2.2 Integrating the distributional lexical contrast into a skip-gram model

Our model relies on Levy and Goldberg (2014) who showed that the objective function for a skip-gram model with negative sampling (SGNS) can be defined as follows:

$$\sum_{w \in V} \sum_{c \in V} \{ \#(w,c) \log \sigma(sim(w,c)) + k\#(w)P_0(c) \log \sigma(-sim(w,c)) \} \quad (2)$$

The first term in Equation (2) represents the co-occurrence between a target word w and a context c within a context window. The number of appearances of the target word and that context is defined as $\#(w,c)$. The second term refers to the negative sampling where k is the number of negatively sampled words, and $\#(w)$ is the number of appearances of w as a target word in the unigram distribution P_0 of its negative context c.

To incorporate our lexical contrast information into the SGNS model, we propose the objective function in Equation (3) to add distributional contrast followed by all contexts of the target word. V is the vocabulary; $\sigma(x) = \frac{1}{1+e^{-x}}$ is the sigmoid function; and $sim(w_1, w_2)$ is the cosine similarity between the two embedded vectors of the corresponding two words w_1 and w_2. We refer to our distributional lexical-contrast embedding model as *dLCE*.

$$\sum_{w \in V} \sum_{c \in V} \{ (\#(w,c) \log \sigma(sim(w,c)) + k\#(w)P_0(c) \log \sigma(-sim(w,c))) + (\frac{1}{\#(w,u)} \sum_{u \in W(c) \cap S(w)} sim(w,u)) - \frac{1}{\#(w,v)} \sum_{v \in W(c) \cap A(w)} sim(w,v)) \} \quad (3)$$

Equation (3) integrates the lexical contrast information in a slightly different way compared to Equation (1): For each of the target words w, we only rely on its antonyms $A(w)$ instead of using the synonyms of its antonyms $S(w')$. This makes the word embeddings training more efficient in running time, especially since we are using a large amount of training data.

The dLCE model is similar to the WE-TD model (Ono et al., 2015) and the mLCM model (Pham et al., 2015); however, while the WE-TD and mLCM models only apply the lexical contrast information from WordNet to each of the target words, dLCE applies lexical contrast to every single context of a target word in order to better capture and classify semantic contrast.

3 Experiments

3.1 Experimental Settings

The corpus resource for our vector representations is one of the currently largest web corpora: *ENCOW14A* (Schäfer and Bildhauer, 2012; Schäfer, 2015), containing approximately 14.5 billion tokens and 561K distinct word types. As distributional information, we used a window size of 5 tokens for both the original vector representation and the word embeddings models. For word embeddings models, we trained word vectors with 500 dimensions; k negative sampling was set to 15; the threshold for sub-sampling was set to 10^{-5}; and we ignored all words that occurred < 100 times in the corpus. The parameters of the models were estimated by backpropagation of error via stochastic gradient descent. The learning rate strategy was similar to Mikolov et al. (2013a) in which the initial learning rate was set to 0.025. For the lexical contrast information, we used WordNet (Miller, 1995) and Wordnik[1] to collect antonyms and synonyms, obtaining a total of 363,309 synonym and 38,423 antonym pairs.

3.2 Distinguishing antonyms from synonyms

The first experiment evaluates our lexical contrast vectors by applying the vector representations with the improved $weight^{SA}$ scores to the task of distinguishing antonyms from synonyms. As gold standard resource, we used the English dataset described in (Roth and Schulte im Walde, 2014), containing 600 adjective pairs (300 antonymous pairs and 300 synonymous pairs), 700 noun pairs (350 antonymous pairs and 350 synonymous pairs) and 800 verb pairs (400 antonymous pairs and 400 synonymous pairs). For evaluation, we applied Average Precision (AP) (Voorhees and Harman, 1999), a common metric in information retrieval previously used by Kotlerman et al.

(2010) and Santus et al. (2014a), among others.

Table 1 presents the results of the first experiment, comparing our improved vector representations with the original LMI representations across word classes, without/with applying singular-value decomposition (SVD), respectively. In order to evaluate the distribution of word pairs with AP, we sorted the synonymous and antonymous pairs by their cosine scores. A synonymous pair was considered correct if it belonged to the first half; and an antonymous pairs was considered correct if it was in the second half. The optimal results would thus achieve an AP score of 1 for SYN and 0 for ANT. The results in the tables demonstrate that $weight^{SA}$ significantly[2] outperforms the original vector representations across word classes.

In addition, Figure 2 compares the medians of cosine similarities between antonymous pairs (red) vs. synonymous pairs (green) across word classes, and for the four conditions (1) LMI, (2) $weight^{SA}$, (3) SVD on LMI, and (4) SVD on $weight^{SA}$. The plots show that the cosine similarities of the two relations differ more strongly with our improved vector representations in comparison to the original LMI representations, and even more so after applying SVD.

3.3 Effects of distributional lexical contrast on word embeddings

The second experiment evaluates the performance of our dLCE model on both antonym–synonym distinction and a word similarity task. The similarity task requires to predict the degree of similarity for word pairs, and the ranked list of predictions is evaluated against a gold standard of human ratings, relying on the Spearman rank-order correlation coefficient ρ (Siegel and Castellan, 1988).

In this paper, we use the *SimLex-999* dataset (Hill et al., 2015) to evaluate word embedding models on predicting similarities. The resource contains 999 word pairs (666 noun, 222 verb and 111 adjective pairs) and was explicitly built to test models on capturing similarity rather than relatedness or association. Table 2 shows that our dLCE model outperforms both SGNS and mLCM, proving that the lexical contrast information has a positive effect on predicting similarity.

---

[2] χ^2, *** $p < .001$, ** $p < .005$, * $p < .05$

	Adjectives		Nouns		Verbs	
	ANT	SYN	ANT	SYN	ANT	SYN
LMI	0.46	0.56	0.42	0.60	0.42	0.62
$weight^{SA}$	**0.36****	**0.75****	**0.40**	**0.66**	**0.38***	**0.71***
LMI + SVD	0.46	0.55	0.46	0.55	0.44	0.58
$weight^{SA}$ + SVD	**0.36*****	**0.76*****	**0.40***	**0.66***	**0.38*****	**0.70*****

Table 1: AP evaluation on DSMs.

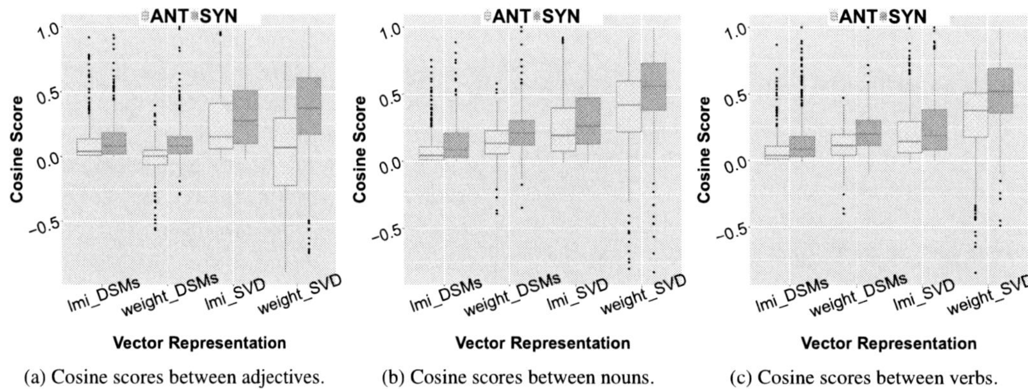

(a) Cosine scores between adjectives.   (b) Cosine scores between nouns.   (c) Cosine scores between verbs.

Figure 2: Differences between cosine scores for antonymous vs. synonymous word pairs.

SGNS	mLCM	dLCE
0.38	0.51	**0.59**

Table 2: Spearman's ρ on SimLex-999.

	Adjectives	Nouns	Verbs
SGNS	0.64	0.66	0.65
mLCM	0.85	0.69	0.71
dLCE	**0.90**	**0.72**	**0.81**

Table 3: AUC scores for identifying antonyms.

Therefore, the improved distinction between synonyms (strongly similar words) and antonyms (often strongly related but highly dissimilar words) in the dLCE model also supports the distinction between degrees of similarity.

For distinguishing between antonyms and synonyms, we computed the cosine similarities between word pairs on the dataset described in Section 3.2, and then used the area under the ROC curve (AUC) to evaluate the performance of dLCE compared to SGNS and mLCM. The results in Table 3 report that dLCE outperforms SGNS and mLCM also on this task.

4 Conclusion

This paper proposed a novel vector representation which enhanced the prediction of word similarity, both for a traditional distributional semantics model and word embeddings. Firstly, we significantly improved the quality of weighted features to distinguish antonyms from synonyms by using lexical contrast information. Secondly, we incorporated the lexical contrast information into a skip-gram model to successfully predict degrees of similarity and also to identify antonyms.

References

Heike Adel and Hinrich Schütze. 2014. Using mined coreference chains as a resource for a semantic task. In *Proceedings of the 2014 Conference on Empirical Methods in Natural Language Processing*, pages 1447–1452, Doha, Qatar.

Alexander Budanitsky and Graeme Hirst. 2006. Evaluating WordNet-based measures of lexical semantic relatedness. *Computational Linguistics*, 32(1):13–47.

James Deese. 1965. *The Structure of Associations in Language and Thought*. The John Hopkins Press, Baltimore, MD.

Stefan Evert. 2005. *The Statistics of Word Cooccurrences*. Ph.D. thesis, Stuttgart University.

John R. Firth. 1957. *Papers in Linguistics 1934-51*. Longmans, London, UK.

Zellig S. Harris. 1954. Distributional structure. *Word*, 10(23):146–162.

Felix Hill, Roi Reichart, and Anna Korhonen. 2015. Simlex-999: Evaluating semantic models with (genuine) similarity estimation. *Computational Linguistics*, 41(4):665–695.

Lili Kotlerman, Ido Dagan, Idan Szpektor, and Maayan Zhitomirsky-Geffet. 2010. Directional distributional similarity for lexical inference. *Natural Language Processing*, 16(4):359–389.

Omer Levy and Yoav Goldberg. 2014. Neural word embedding as implicit matrix factorization. In Z. Ghahramani, M. Welling, C. Cortes, N.D. Lawrence, and K.Q. Weinberger, editors, *Advances in Neural Information Processing Systems 27*, pages 2177–2185.

Dekang Lin, Shaojun Zhao, Lijuan Qin, and Ming Zhou. 2003. Identifying synonyms among distributionally similar words. In *Proceedings of the 18th International Joint Conference on Artificial Intelligence*, pages 1492–1493, Acapulco, Mexico.

John Lyons. 1977. *Semantics*, volume 1. Cambridge University Press.

Tomas Mikolov, Kai Chen, Greg Corrado, and Jeffrey Dean. 2013a. Efficient estimation of word representations in vector space. *Computing Research Repository*, abs/1301.3781.

Tomas Mikolov, Wen-tau Yih, and Geoffrey Zweig. 2013b. Linguistic regularities in continuous space word representations. In *Proceedings of the Conference of the North American Chapter of the Association for Computational Linguistics: Human Language Technologies*, pages 746–751, Atlanta, Georgia.

George A. Miller and Christiane Fellbaum. 1991. Semantic networks of English. *Cognition*, 41:197–229.

George A. Miller. 1995. WordNet: A lexical database for English *Communications of the ACM*, 38(11):39–41.

Saif M. Mohammad, Bonnie J. Dorr, Graeme Hirst, and Peter D. Turney. 2013. Computing lexical contrast. *Computational Linguistics*, 39(3):555–590.

Masataka Ono, Makoto Miwa, and Yutaka Sasaki. 2015. Word embedding-based antonym detection using thesauri and distributional information. In *Proceedings of the Conference of the North American Chapter of the Association for Computational Linguistics: Human Language Technologies*, pages 984–989, Denver, Colorado.

Nghia The Pham, Angeliki Lazaridou, and Marco Baroni. 2015. A multitask objective to inject lexical contrast into distributional semantics. In *Proceedings of the 53rd Annual Meeting of the Association for Computational Linguistics and the 7th International Joint Conference on Natural Language Processing*, pages 21–26, Beijing, China.

Michael Roth and Sabine Schulte im Walde. 2014. Combining word patterns and discourse markers for paradigmatic relation classification. In *Proceedings of the 52nd Annual Meeting of the Association for Computational Linguistics*, pages 524–530, Baltimore, MD.

Enrico Santus, Alessandro Lenci, Qin Lu, and Sabine Schulte im Walde. 2014a. Chasing hypernyms in vector spaces with entropy. In *Proceedings of the 14th Conference of the European Chapter of the Association for Computational Linguistics*, pages 38–42, Gothenburg, Sweden.

Enrico Santus, Qin Lu, Alessandro Lenci, and Chu-Ren Huang. 2014b. Taking antonymy mask off in vector space. In *Proceedings of the 28th Pacific Asia Conference on Language, Information and Computation*, pages 135–144.

Roland Schäfer and Felix Bildhauer. 2012. Building large corpora from the web using a new efficient tool chain. In *Proceedings of the 8th International Conference on Language Resources and Evaluation*, pages 486–493, Istanbul, Turkey.

Roland Schäfer. 2015. Processing and querying large web corpora with the COW14 architecture. In *Proceedings of the 3rd Workshop on Challenges in the Management of Large Corpora*, pages 28–34.

Silke Scheible, Sabine Schulte im Walde, and Sylvia Springorum. 2013. Uncovering distributional differences between synonyms and antonyms in a word space model. In *Proceedings of the 6th International Joint Conference on Natural Language Processing*, pages 489–497, Nagoya, Japan.

Sidney Siegel and N. John Castellan. 1988. *Nonparametric Statistics for the Behavioral Sciences*. McGraw-Hill, Boston, MA.

Peter D. Turney and Patrick Pantel. 2010. From frequency to meaning: Vector space models of semantics. *Journal of Artificial Intelligence Research*, 37:141–188.

Ellen M. Voorhees and Donna K. Harman. 1999. The 7th Text REtrieval Conference (trec-7). *National Institute of Standards and Technology, NIST*.

Machine Translation Evaluation Meets Community Question Answering

Francisco Guzmán, **Lluís Màrquez** and **Preslav Nakov**
Arabic Language Technologies Research Group
Qatar Computing Research Institute, HBKU
{fguzman,lmarquez,pnakov}@qf.org.qa

Abstract

We explore the applicability of machine translation evaluation (MTE) methods to a very different problem: answer ranking in community Question Answering. In particular, we adopt a pairwise neural network (NN) architecture, which incorporates MTE features, as well as rich syntactic and semantic embeddings, and which efficiently models complex non-linear interactions. The evaluation results show state-of-the-art performance, with sizeable contribution from both the MTE features and from the pairwise NN architecture.

1 Introduction and Motivation

In a community Question Answering (cQA) task, we are given a question from a community forum and a thread of associated text comments intended to answer the given question; and the goal is to rank the comments according to their appropriateness to the question. Since cQA forum threads are noisy (e.g., because over time people tend to engage in discussion and to deviate from the original question), as many comments are not answers to the question, the challenge lies in learning to rank all *good* comments above all *bad* ones.

Here, we adopt the definition and the datasets from SemEval–2016 Task 3 (Nakov et al., 2016) on "Community Question Answering", focusing on subtask A (Question-Comment Similarity) only.[1] See the task description paper and the task website[2] for more detail. An annotated example is shown in Figure 1.

[1] SemEval-2016 Task 3 had two more subtasks: subtask B on Question-Question Similarity, and subtask C on Question-External Comment Similarity, which are out of our scope. However, they could be potentially addressed within our general MTE-NN framework, with minor variations.

[2] http://alt.qcri.org/semeval2016/task3/

In this paper, we tackle the task from a novel perspective: by using ideas from machine translation evaluation (MTE) to decide on the *quality* of a comment. In particular, we extend our MTE neural network framework from (Guzmán et al., 2015), showing that it is applicable to the cQA task as well. We believe that this neural network is interesting for the cQA problem because: (*i*) it works in a pairwise fashion, i.e., given two translation hypotheses and a reference translation to compare to, the network decides which translation hypothesis is better, which is appropriate for a ranking problem; (*ii*) it allows for an easy incorporation of rich syntactic and semantic embedded representations of the input texts, and it efficiently models complex non-linear relationships between them; (*iii*) it uses a number of machine translation evaluation measures that have not been explored for the cQA task before, e.g., TER (Snover et al., 2006), METEOR (Lavie and Denkowski, 2009), and BLEU (Papineni et al., 2002).

The analogy we apply to adapt the neural MTE architecture to the cQA problem is the following: given two comments c_1 and c_2 from the question thread—which play the role of the two competing translation hypotheses—we have to decide whether c_1 is a better answer than c_2 to question q—which plays the role of the translation reference. If we have a function $f(q, c_1, c_2)$ to make this decision, then we can rank the finite list of comments in the thread by comparing all possible pairs and by accumulating for each comment the scores for it given by f.

From a general point of view, MTE and the cQA task addressed in this paper seem similar: both reason about the similarity of two competing texts against a reference text in order to decide which one is better. However, there are some profound differences, which have implications on how each task is solved.

Proceedings of the 54th Annual Meeting of the Association for Computational Linguistics, pages 460–466,
Berlin, Germany, August 7-12, 2016. ©2016 Association for Computational Linguistics

```xml
<OrgQuestion ORGQ_ID="Q1">
  <OrgQSubject>Massage oil</OrgQSubject>
  <OrgQBody>Where I can buy good oil for massage?</OrgQBody>

  <Thread THREAD_SEQUENCE="Q1_R1">
    <RelQuestion RELQ_ID="Q1_R1" RELQ_RANKING_ORDER="1" RELQ_CATEGORY="Qatar Living Lounge"
    RELQ_DATE="2010-08-27 01:38:59" RELQ_USERID="U1" RELQ_USERNAME="sognabodl"
    RELQ_PELEVANCE2ORGQ="PerfectMatch">
      <RelQSubject>massage oil</RelQSubject>
      <RelQBody>is there any place i can find scented massage oils in qatar?</RelQBody>
    </RelQuestion>

    <RelComment RELC_ID="Q1_R1_C1" RELC_DATE="2010-08-27 01:40:05" RELC_USERID="U2"
    RELC_USERNAME="anonymous" RELC_RELEVANCE2ORGQ="Good" RELC_RELEVANCE2RELQ="Good">
      <RelCText>Yes. It is right behind Kahrama in the National area.</RelCText>
    </RelComment>

    <RelComment RELC_ID="Q1_R1_C2" RELC_DATE="2010-08-27 01:42:59" RELC_USERID="U1"
    RELC_USERNAME="sognabodl" RELC_PELEVANCE2ORGQ="Bad" RELC_RELEVANCE2RELQ="Bad">
      <RelCText>whats the name of the shop?</RelCText>
    </RelComment>
```

Figure 1: Annotated English question from the CQA-QL corpus. Shown are the first two comments only.

In MTE, the goal is to decide whether a hypothesis translation conveys the same meaning as the reference translation. In cQA, it is to determine whether the comment is an appropriate answer to the question. Furthermore, in MTE we can expect shorter texts, which are typically much more similar. In contrast, in cQA, the question and the intended answers might differ significantly both in terms of length and in lexical content. Thus, it is not clear a priori whether the MTE network can work well to address the cQA problem. Here, we show that the analogy is not only convenient, but also that using it can yield state-of-the-art results for the cQA task.

To validate our intuition, we present series of experiments using the publicly available SemEval-2016 Task 3 datasets, with focus on subtask A. We show that a naïve application of the MTE architecture and features on the cQA task already yields results that are largely above the task baselines. Furthermore, by adapting the models with in-domain data, and adding lightweight task-specific features, we are able to boost our system to reach state-of-the-art performance.

More interestingly, we analyze the contribution of several features and parts of the NN architecture by performing an ablation study. We observe that every single piece contributes important information to achieve the final performance. While task-specific features are crucial, other aspects of the framework are relevant as well: syntactic embeddings, machine translation evaluation measures, and pairwise training of the network.

The rest of the paper is organized as follows: Section 2 introduces some related work. Section 3 presents the overall architecture of our MTE-inspired NN framework for cQA. Section 4 summarizes the features we use in our experiments. Section 5 describes the experimenal settings and presents the results. Finally, Section 6 offers further discussion and presents the main conclusions.

2 Related Work

Recently, many neural network (NN) models have been applied to cQA tasks: e.g., *question-question similarity* (Zhou et al., 2015; dos Santos et al., 2015; Lei et al., 2016) and *answer selection* (Severyn and Moschitti, 2015; Wang and Nyberg, 2015; Shen et al., 2015; Feng et al., 2015; Tan et al., 2015). Most of these papers concentrate on providing advanced neural architectures in order to better model the problem at hand. However, our goal here is different: we extend and reuse an existing pairwise NN framework from a different but related problem.

There is also work that uses machine translation models as a features for cQA (Berger et al., 2000; Echihabi and Marcu, 2003; Jeon et al., 2005; Soricut and Brill, 2006; Riezler et al., 2007; Li and Manandhar, 2011; Surdeanu et al., 2011; Tran et al., 2015) e.g., a variation of IBM model 1, to compute the probability that the question is a possible "translation" of the candidate answer. Unlike that work, here we port an entire MTE framework to the cQA problem. A preliminary version of this work was presented in (Guzmán et al., 2016).

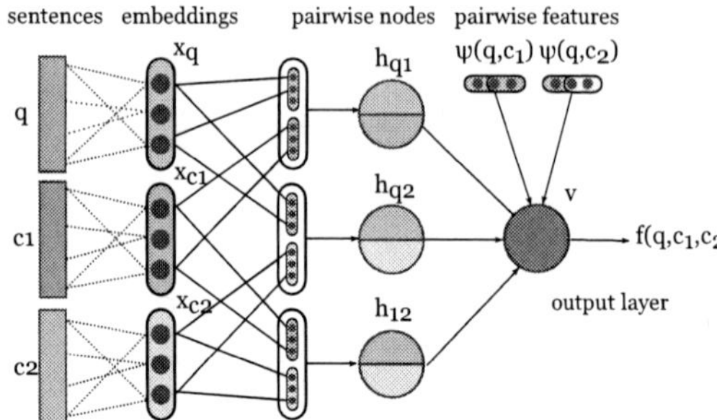

Figure 2: Overall architecture of the NN.

3 Neural Model for Answer Ranking

The NN model we use for answer ranking is de-picted in Figure 2. It is a direct adaptation of our feed-forward NN for MTE (Guzmán et al., 2015). Technically, we have a binary classification task with input (q, c_1, c_2), which should output 1 if c_1 is a better answer to q than c_2, and 0 other-wise. The network computes a sigmoid function $f(q, c_1, c_2) = \text{sig}(\mathbf{w_v^T}\phi(q, c_1, c_2) + b_v)$, where $\phi(x)$ transforms the input x through the hidden layer, $\mathbf{w_v}$ are the weights from the hidden layer to the output layer, and b_v is a bias term.

We first map the question and the comments to a fixed-length vector $[\mathbf{x}_q, \mathbf{x}_{c_1}, \mathbf{x}_{c_2}]$ using syntactic and semantic embeddings. Then, we feed this vec-tor as input to the neural network, which models three types of interactions, using different groups of nodes in the hidden layer. There are two *eval-uation* groups $\mathbf{h_{q1}}$ and $\mathbf{h_{q2}}$ that model how good each comment c_i is to the question q. The input to these groups are the concatenations $[\mathbf{x}_q, \mathbf{x}_{c_1}]$ and $[\mathbf{x}_q, \mathbf{x}_{c_2}]$, respectively. The third group of hidden nodes $\mathbf{h_{12}}$, which we call *similarity* group, models how close c_1 and c_2 are. Its input is $[\mathbf{x}_{c_1}, \mathbf{x}_{c_2}]$. This might be useful as highly similar comments are likely to be comparable in appropriateness, irre-spective of whether they are good or bad answers in absolute terms.

In summary, the transformation $\phi(q, c_1, c_2) = [\mathbf{h_{q1}}, \mathbf{h_{q2}}, \mathbf{h_{12}}]$ can be written as

$$\mathbf{h_{qi}} = g(\mathbf{W_{qi}}[\mathbf{x_q}, \mathbf{x_{c_i}}] + \mathbf{b_{qi}}), \; i = 1, 2$$
$$\mathbf{h_{12}} = g(\mathbf{W_{12}}[\mathbf{x_{c_1}}, \mathbf{x_{c_2}}] + \mathbf{b_{12}}),$$

where $g(.)$ is a non-linear activation function (ap-plied component-wise), $\mathbf{W} \in \mathbb{R}^{H \times N}$ are the asso-ciated weights between the input layer and the hid-den layer, and $\mathbf{b}$ are the corresponding bias terms.

We use tanh as an activation function, rather than sig, to be consistent with how the word em-bedding vectors we use were generated.

The model further allows to incorporate exter-nal sources of information in the form of *skip arcs* that go directly from the input to the output, skip-ping the hidden layer. These arcs represent pair-wise *similarity* feature vectors between q and ei-ther c_1 or c_2. In these feature vectors, we en-code MT evaluation measures (e.g., TER, ME-TEOR, and BLEU), cQA task-specific features, etc. See Section 4 for detail about the features im-plemented as skip arcs. In the figure, we indi-cate these pairwise external feature sets as $\psi(q, c_1)$ and $\psi(q, c_2)$. When including the external fea-tures, the activation at the output is $f(q, c_1, c_2) = \text{sig}(\mathbf{w_v^T}[\phi(q, c_1, c_2), \psi(q, c_1), \psi(q, c_2)] + b_v)$.

4 Features

We experiment with three kinds of features: (*i*) in-put embeddings, (*ii*) features from MTE (Guzmán et al., 2015) and (*iii*) task-specific features from SemEval-2015 Task 3 (Nicosia et al., 2015).

A. Embedding Features We used two types of vector-based embeddings to encode the input texts q, c_1 and c_2: (1) GOOGLE_VECTORS: 300-dimensional embedding vectors, trained on 100 billion words from Google News (Mikolov et al., 2013). The encoding of the full text is just the average of the word embeddings. (2) SYNTAX: We parse the entire question/comment using the Stanford neural parser (Socher et al., 2013), and we use the final 25-dimensional vector that is pro-duced internally as a by-product of parsing.

Also, we compute cosine similarity features with the above vectors: $\cos(q, c_1)$ and $\cos(q, c_2)$.

B. MTE features We use the following MTE metrics (**MTFEATS**), which compare the similar-ity between the question and a candidate answer: (1) BLEU (Papineni et al., 2002); (2) NIST (Dod-dington, 2002); (3) TER v0.7.25 (Snover et al., 2006). (4) METEOR v1.4 (Lavie and Denkowski, 2009) with paraphrases; (5) Unigram PRECISION; (6) Unigram RECALL.

BLEUCOMP. We further use as features var-ious components involved in the computation of BLEU: n-gram precisions, n-gram matches, total number of n-grams (n=1,2,3,4), lengths of the hy-potheses and of the reference, length ratio between them, and BLEU's brevity penalty.

C. Task-specific features First, we train domain-specific vectors using WORD2VEC on all available QatarLiving data, both annotated and raw (**QL_VECTORS**).

Second, we compute various easy task-specific features (**TASK_FEATURES**), most of them proposed for the 2015 edition of the task (Nicosia et al., 2015). This includes some comment-specific features: (1) number of URLs/images/emails/phone numbers; (2) number of occurrences of the string "thank";[3] (3) number of tokens/sentences; (4) average number of tokens; (5) type/token ratio; (6) number of nouns/verbs/adjectives/adverbs/pronouns; (7) number of positive/negative smileys; (8) number of single/double/triple exclamation/interrogation symbols; (9) number of interrogative sentences (based on parsing); (10) number of words that are not in WORD2VEC's Google News vocabulary.[4] Also some question-comment pair features: (1) question to comment count ratio in terms of sentences/tokens/nouns/verbs/adjectives/adverbs/pronouns; (2) question to comment count ratio of words that are not in WORD2VEC's Google News vocabulary. Finally, we also have two meta features: (1) is the person answering the question the one who asked it; (2) reciprocal rank of the comment in the thread.

5 Experiments and Results

We experiment with the data from SemEval-2016 Task 3. The task offers a higher quality training dataset TRAIN-PART1, which includes 1,412 questions and 14,110 answers, and a lower-quality TRAIN-PART2 with 382 questions and 3,790 answers. We train our model on TRAIN-PART1 with hidden layers of size 3 for 100 epochs with mini-batches of size 30, regularization of 0.005, and a decay of 0.0001, using stochastic gradient descent with adagrad (Duchi et al., 2011); we use Theano (Bergstra et al., 2010) for learning. We normalize the input feature values to the $[-1; 1]$ interval using minmax, and we initialize the network weights by sampling from a uniform distribution as in (Bengio and Glorot, 2010). We train the model using all pairs of good vs. bad comments, in both orders, ignoring ties.

System	MAP	AvgRec	MRR
MTE-CQA$_{pairwise}$	**78.20**	**88.01**	**86.93**
MTE-CQA$_{classification}$	77.62	87.85	85.79
MTE$_{vanilla}$	70.17	81.84	78.60
Baseline$_{time}$	59.53	72.60	67.83
Baseline$_{rand}$	52.80	66.52	58.71

Table 1: Main results on the ranking task.

At test time, we get the full ranking by scoring all possible pairs, and we accumulate the scores at the comment level.

We evaluate the model on TRAIN-PART2 after each epoch, and ultimately we keep the model that achieves the highest accuracy;[5] in case of a tie, we prefer the parameters from an earlier epoch. We selected the above parameter values on the DEV dataset (244 questions and 2,440 answers) using the full model, and we used them for all experiments below, where we evaluate on the official TEST dataset (329 questions and 3,270 answers). We report mean average precision (MAP), which is the official evaluation measure, and also average recall (AvgRec) and mean reciprocal rank (MRR).

5.1 Results

Table 1 shows the evaluation results for three configurations of our MTE-based cQA system. We can see that the vanilla MTE system (MTE$_{vanilla}$), which only uses features from our original MTE model, i.e., it does not have any task-specific features (TASK_FEATURES and QL_VECTORS), performs surprisingly well despite the differences in the MTE and cQA tasks. It outperforms a random baseline (Baseline$_{rand}$) and a chronological baseline that assumes that early comments are better than later ones (Baseline$_{time}$) by large margins: by about 11 and 17 MAP points absolute, respectively. For the other two measures the results are similar.

We can further see that adding the task-specific features in MTE-CQA$_{pairwise}$ improves the results by another 8 MAP points absolute. Finally, the second line shows that adapting the network to do classification (MTE-CQA$_{classification}$), giving it a question and a single comment as input, yields a performance drop of 0.6 MAP points absolute compared to the proposed pairwise learning model. Thus, the pairwise training strategy is confirmed to be better for the ranking task, although not by a large margin.

---

[3]When an author thanks somebody, this post is typically a bad answer to the original question.

[4]Can detect slang, foreign language, etc., which would indicate a bad answer.

[5]We also tried Kendall's Tau (τ), but it performed worse.

System	MAP	AvgRec	MRR	Δ_{MAP}
MTE-CQA	**78.20**	**88.01**	**86.93**	
−BLEUCOMP	77.83	87.85	86.32	-0.37
−MTFEATS	77.75	87.76	86.01	-0.45
−SYNTAX	77.65	87.65	85.85	-0.55
−GOOGLE_VECT.	76.96	87.66	84.72	-1.24
−QL_VECTORS	75.83	86.57	83.90	-2.37
−TASK_FEATS.	72.91	84.06	78.73	-5.29

Table 2: Results of the ablation study.

System	MAP	AvgRec	MRR
1st (Filice et al., 2016)	79.19	88.82	86.42
MTE-CQA	*78.20*	*88.01*	*86.93*
2nd (Barrón-Cedeño et al., 2016)	77.66	88.05	84.93
3rd (Mihaylov and Nakov, 2016)	77.58	88.14	85.21
. . .	. . .	. . .	. . .
Average	73.54	84.61	81.54
. . .	. . .	. . .	. . .
12th (Worst)	62.24	75.41	70.58

Table 3: Comparative results with the best SemEval-2016 Task 3, subtask A systems.

Table 2 presents the results of an ablation study, where we analyze the contribution of various features and feature groups to the performance of the overall system. For the purpose, we study Δ_{MAP}, i.e., the absolute drop in MAP when the feature group is excluded from the full system.

Not surprisingly, the most important turn out to be the TASK_FEATURES (contributing over five MAP points) as they handle important information sources that are not available to the system from other feature groups, e.g., the reciprocal rank alone contributes about two points.

Next in terms of importance come word embeddings, QL_VECTORS (contributing over 2 MAP points), trained on text from the target forum, QatarLiving. Then come the GOOGLE_VECTORS (contributing over one MAP point), which are trained on 100 billion words, and thus are still useful even in the presence of the domain-specific QL_VECTORS, which are in turn trained on four orders of magnitude less data.

Interestingly, the MTE-motivated SYNTAX vectors contribute half a MAP point, which shows the importance of modeling syntax for this task. The other two MTE features, MTFEATS and BLEU-COMP, together contribute 0.8 MAP points. It is interesting that the BLEU components manage to contribute on top of the MTFEATS, which already contain several state-of-the-art MTE measures, including BLEU itself. This is probably because the other features we have do not model n-gram matches directly.

Finally, Table 3 puts the results in perspective. We can see that our system MTE-CQA would rank first on MRR, second on MAP, and fourth on AvgRec in SemEval-2016 Task 3 competition.[6] These results are also 5 and 16 points above the average and the worst systems, respectively.

This is remarkable given the lightweight task-specific features we use, and confirms the validity of the proposed neural approach to produce state-of-the-art systems for this particular cQA task.

6 Conclusion

We have explored the applicability of machine translation evaluation methods to answer ranking in community Question Answering, a seemingly very different task, where the goal is to rank the comments in a question-answer thread according to their appropriateness to the question, placing all good comments above all bad ones.

In particular, we have adopted a pairwise neural network architecture, which incorporates MTE features, as well as rich syntactic and semantic embeddings of the input texts that are non-linearly combined in the hidden layer. The evaluation results on benchmark datasets have shown state-of-the-art performance, with sizeable contribution from both the MTE features and from the network architecture. This is an interesting and encouraging result, as given the difference in the tasks, it was not a-priori clear that an MTE approach would work well for cQA.

In future work, we plan to incorporate other similarity measures and better task-specific features into the model. We further want to explore the application of this architecture to other semantic similarity problems such as question-question similarity, and textual entailment.

Acknowledgments

This research was performed by the Arabic Language Technologies (ALT) group at the Qatar Computing Research Institute (QCRI), Hamad bin Khalifa University, part of Qatar Foundation. It is part of the Interactive sYstems for Answer Search (Iyas) project, which is developed in collaboration with MIT-CSAIL.

---

[6]The full results can be found on the task website: http://alt.qcri.org/semeval2016/task3/index.php?id=results

References

Alberto Barrón-Cedeño, Giovanni Da San Martino, Shafiq Joty, Alessandro Moschitti, Fahad A. Al Obaidli, Salvatore Romeo, Kateryna Tymoshenko, and Antonio Uva. 2016. ConvKN at SemEval-2016 Task 3: Answer and question selection for question answering on Arabic and English fora. In *Proceedings of the 10th International Workshop on Semantic Evaluation*, SemEval '16, San Diego, CA.

Yoshua Bengio and Xavier Glorot. 2010. Understanding the difficulty of training deep feedforward neural networks. In *Proceedings of the 13th International Conference on Artificial Intelligence and Statistics*, AISTATS '10, pages 249–256, Sardinia, Italy.

Adam Berger, Rich Caruana, David Cohn, Dayne Freitag, and Vibhu Mittal. 2000. Bridging the lexical chasm: Statistical approaches to answer-finding. In *Proceedings of the 23rd Annual International ACM Conference on Research and Development in Information Retrieval*, SIGIR '00, pages 192–199, Athens, Greece.

James Bergstra, Olivier Breuleux, Frédéric Bastien, Pascal Lamblin, Razvan Pascanu, Guillaume Desjardins, Joseph Turian, David Warde-Farley, and Yoshua Bengio. 2010. Theano: a CPU and GPU math expression compiler. In *Proceedings of the Python for Scientific Computing Conference*, SciPy '10, Austin, Texas, USA.

George Doddington. 2002. Automatic evaluation of machine translation quality using n-gram co-occurrence statistics. In *Proceedings of the Second International Conference on Human Language Technology Research*, HLT '02, pages 138–145, San Diego, California, USA.

Cicero dos Santos, Luciano Barbosa, Dasha Bogdanova, and Bianca Zadrozny. 2015. Learning hybrid representations to retrieve semantically equivalent questions. In *Proceedings of the 53rd Annual Meeting of the Association for Computational Linguistics and the 7th International Joint Conference on Natural Language Processing*, ACL-IJCNLP '15, pages 694–699, Beijing, China.

John Duchi, Elad Hazan, and Yoram Singer. 2011. Adaptive subgradient methods for online learning and stochastic optimization. *Journal of Machine Learning Research*, 12:2121–2159.

Abdessamad Echihabi and Daniel Marcu. 2003. A noisy-channel approach to question answering. In *Proceedings of the 41st Annual Meeting of the Association for Computational Linguistics*, ACL '03, pages 16–23, Sapporo, Japan.

Minwei Feng, Bing Xiang, Michael R Glass, Lidan Wang, and Bowen Zhou. 2015. Applying deep learning to answer selection: A study and an open task. In *Proceedings of the 2015 IEEE Automatic Speech Recognition and Understanding Workshop*, ASRU '15, Scottsdale, Arizona, USA.

Simone Filice, Danilo Croce, Alessandro Moschitti, and Roberto Basili. 2016. KeLP at SemEval-2016 Task 3: Learning semantic relations between questions and answers. In *Proceedings of the 10th International Workshop on Semantic Evaluation*, SemEval '16, San Diego, California, USA.

Francisco Guzmán, Shafiq Joty, Lluís Màrquez, and Preslav Nakov. 2015. Pairwise neural machine translation evaluation. In *Proceedings of the 53rd Annual Meeting of the Association for Computational Linguistics and the 7th International Joint Conference on Natural Language Processing*, ACL-IJCNLP '15, pages 805–814, Beijing, China.

Francisco Guzmán, Lluís Màrquez, and Preslav Nakov. 2016. MTE-NN at SemEval-2016 Task 3: Can machine translation evaluation help community question answering? In *Proceedings of the 10th International Workshop on Semantic Evaluation*, SemEval '16, San Diego, California, USA.

Jiwoon Jeon, W. Bruce Croft, and Joon Ho Lee. 2005. Finding similar questions in large question and answer archives. In *Proceedings of the 14th ACM International Conference on Information and Knowledge Management*, CIKM '05, pages 84–90, Bremen, Germany.

Alon Lavie and Michael Denkowski. 2009. The METEOR metric for automatic evaluation of machine translation. *Machine Translation*, 23(2–3):105–115.

Tao Lei, Hrishikesh Joshi, Regina Barzilay, Tommi S. Jaakkola, Kateryna Tymoshenko, Alessandro Moschitti, and Lluís Màrquez. 2016. Semi-supervised question retrieval with gated convolutions. In *Proceedings of the 15th Annual Conference of the North American Chapter of the Association for Computational Linguistics: Human Language Technologies*, NAACL-HLT '16, San Diego, California, USA.

Shuguang Li and Suresh Manandhar. 2011. Improving question recommendation by exploiting information need. In *Proceedings of the 49th Annual Meeting of the Association for Computational Linguistics: Human Language Technologies*, HLT '11, pages 1425–1434, Portland, Oregon, USA.

Todor Mihaylov and Preslav Nakov. 2016. SemanticZ at SemEval-2016 Task 3: Ranking relevant answers in community question answering using semantic similarity based on fine-tuned word embeddings. In *Proceedings of the 10th International Workshop on Semantic Evaluation*, SemEval '16, San Diego, California, USA.

Tomas Mikolov, Wen-tau Yih, and Geoffrey Zweig. 2013. Linguistic regularities in continuous space word representations. In *Proceedings of the 2013 Conference of the North American Chapter of the Association for Computational Linguistics: Human Language Technologies*, NAACL-HLT '13, pages 746–751, Atlanta, Georgia, USA.

Preslav Nakov, Lluís Màrquez, Alessandro Moschitti, Walid Magdy, Hamdy Mubarak, Abed Alhakim Freihat, Jim Glass, and Bilal Randeree. 2016. SemEval-2016 task 3: Community question answering. In *Proceedings of the 10th International Workshop on Semantic Evaluation*, SemEval '16, San Diego, California, USA.

Massimo Nicosia, Simone Filice, Alberto Barrón-Cedeño, Iman Saleh, Hamdy Mubarak, Wei Gao, Preslav Nakov, Giovanni Da San Martino, Alessandro Moschitti, Kareem Darwish, Lluís Màrquez, Shafiq Joty, and Walid Magdy. 2015. QCRI: Answer selection for community question answering - experiments for Arabic and English. In *Proceedings of the 9th International Workshop on Semantic Evaluation*, SemEval '15, pages 203–209, Denver, Colorado, USA.

Kishore Papineni, Salim Roukos, Todd Ward, and Wei-Jing Zhu. 2002. BLEU: a method for automatic evaluation of machine translation. In *Proceedings of 40th Annual Meting of the Association for Computational Linguistics*, ACL '02, pages 311–318, Philadelphia, Pennsylvania, USA.

Stefan Riezler, Alexander Vasserman, Ioannis Tsochantaridis, Vibhu Mittal, and Yi Liu. 2007. Statistical machine translation for query expansion in answer retrieval. In *Proceedings of the 45th Annual Meeting of the Association of Computational Linguistics*, ACL '07, pages 464–471, Prague, Czech Republic.

Aliaksei Severyn and Alessandro Moschitti. 2015. Learning to rank short text pairs with convolutional deep neural networks. In *Proceedings of the 38th International ACM SIGIR Conference on Research and Development in Information Retrieval*, SIGIR '15, pages 373–382, Santiago, Chile.

Yikang Shen, Wenge Rong, Nan Jiang, Baolin Peng, Jie Tang, and Zhang Xiong. 2015. Word embedding based correlation model for question/answer matching. *arXiv preprint arXiv:1511.04646*.

Matthew Snover, Bonnie Dorr, Richard Schwartz, Linnea Micciulla, and John Makhoul. 2006. A study of translation edit rate with targeted human annotation. In *Proceedings of the 7th Biennial Conference of the Association for Machine Translation in the Americas*, AMTA '06, pages 223–231, Cambridge, Massachusetts, USA.

Richard Socher, John Bauer, Christopher D. Manning, and Ng Andrew Y. 2013. Parsing with compositional vector grammars. In *Proceedings of the 51st Annual Meeting of the Association for Computational Linguistics*, ACL '13, pages 455–465, Sofia, Bulgaria.

Radu Soricut and Eric Brill. 2006. Automatic question answering using the web: Beyond the factoid. *Inf. Retr.*, 9(2):191–206, March.

Mihai Surdeanu, Massimiliano Ciaramita, and Hugo Zaragoza. 2011. Learning to rank answers to non-factoid questions from web collections. *Comput. Linguist.*, 37(2):351–383, June.

Ming Tan, Bing Xiang, and Bowen Zhou. 2015. LSTM-based deep learning models for non-factoid answer selection. *arXiv preprint arXiv:1511.04108*.

Quan Hung Tran, Vu Tran, Tu Vu, Minh Nguyen, and Son Bao Pham. 2015. JAIST: Combining multiple features for answer selection in community question answering. In *Proceedings of the 9th International Workshop on Semantic Evaluation*, SemEval '15, pages 215–219, Denver, Colorado, USA.

Di Wang and Eric Nyberg. 2015. A long short-term memory model for answer sentence selection in question answering. In *Proceedings of the 53rd Annual Meeting of the Association for Computational Linguistics and the 7th International Joint Conference on Natural Language Processing*, ACL-IJCNLP '15, pages 707–712, Beijing, China.

Guangyou Zhou, Tingting He, Jun Zhao, and Po Hu. 2015. Learning continuous word embedding with metadata for question retrieval in community question answering. In *Proceedings of the 53rd Annual Meeting of the Association for Computational Linguistics and the 7th International Joint Conference on Natural Language Processing*, ACL-IJCNLP '15, pages 250–259, Beijing, China.

Science Question Answering using Instructional Materials

Mrinmaya Sachan   **Avinava Dubey**   **Eric P. Xing**

School of Computer Science
Carnegie Mellon University
{mrinmays, akdubey, epxing}@cs.cmu.edu

Abstract

We provide a solution for elementary science tests using instructional materials. We posit that there is a hidden structure that explains the correctness of an answer given the question and instructional materials and present a unified max-margin framework that learns to find these hidden structures (given a corpus of question-answer pairs and instructional materials), and uses what it learns to answer novel elementary science questions. Our evaluation shows that our framework outperforms several strong baselines.

1   Introduction

We propose an approach for answering multiple-choice elementary science tests (Clark, 2015) using the science curriculum of the student and other domain specific knowledge resources. Our approach learns latent *answer-entailing structures* that align question-answers with appropriate snippets in the curriculum. The student curriculum usually comprises of a set of textbooks. Each textbook, in-turn comprises of a set of chapters, each chapter is further divided into sections – each discussing a particular science concept. Hence, the answer-entailing structure consists of selecting a particular textbook from the curriculum, picking a chapter in the textbook, picking a section in the chapter, picking a few sentences in the section and then aligning words/multi-word expressions (mwe's) in the hypothesis (formed by combining the question and an answer candidate) to words/mwe's in the picked sentences. The answer-entailing structures are further refined using external domain-specific knowledge resources such as science dictionaries, study guides and semi-structured tables (see Figure 1). These domain-specific knowledge resources can be very useful forms of knowledge representation as shown in previous works (Clark et al., 2016).

Alignment is a common technique in many NLP applications such as MT (Blunsom and Cohn, 2006), RTE (Sammons et al., 2009; MacCartney et al., 2008; Yao et al., 2013; Sultan et al., 2014), QA (Berant et al., 2013; Yih et al., 2013; Yao and Van Durme, 2014; Sachan et al., 2015), etc. Yet, there are three key differences between our approach and alignment based approaches for QA in the literature: (i) We incorporate the curriculum hierarchy (i.e. the book, chapter, section bifurcation) into the latent structure. This helps us jointly learn the retrieval and answer selection modules of a QA system. Retrieval and answer selection are usually designed as isolated or loosely connected components in QA systems (Ferrucci, 2012) leading to loss in performance – our approach mitigates this shortcoming. (ii) Modern textbooks typically provide a set of review questions after each section to help students understand the material better. We make use of these review problems to further improve our model. These review problems have additional value as part of the latent structure is known for these questions. (ii) We utilize domain-specific knowledge sources such as study guides, science dictionaries or semi-structured knowledge tables within our model.

The joint model is trained in max-margin fashion using a latent structural SVM (LSSVM) where the answer-entailing structures are latent. We train and evaluate our models on a set of 8th grade science problems, science textbooks and multiple domain-specific knowledge resources. We achieve superior performance vs. a number of baselines.

2   Method

Science QA as Textual Entailment: First, we

Proceedings of the 54th Annual Meeting of the Association for Computational Linguistics, pages 467–473,
Berlin, Germany, August 7-12, 2016. ©2016 Association for Computational Linguistics

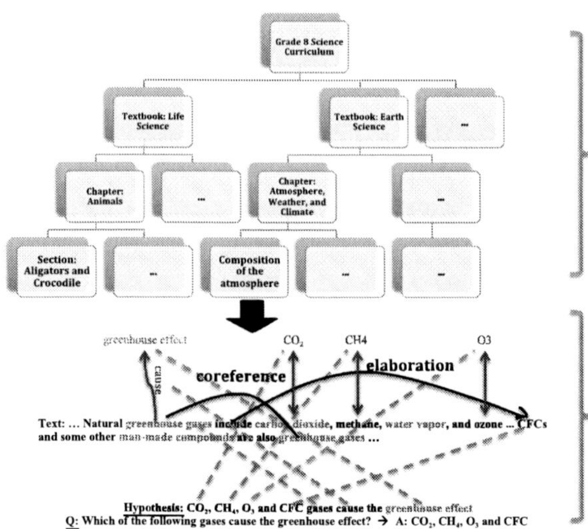

Figure 1: An example *answer-entailing structure*. The answer-entailing structure consists of selecting a particular textbook from the curriculum, picking a chapter in the textbook, picking a section in the chapter, picking sentences in the section and then aligning words/mwe's in the hypothesis (formed by combining the question and an answer candidate) to words/mwe's in the picked sentences or some related "knowledge" appropriately chosen from additional knowledge stores. In this case, the relation (greenhouse gases, cause, greenhouse effect) and the equivalences (e.g. carbon dioxide = CO_2) – shown in violet – are hypothesized using external knowledge resources. The dashed red lines show the word/mwe alignments from the hypothesis to the sentences (some word/mwe are not aligned, in which case the alignments are not shown), the solid black lines show coreference links in the text and the RST relation (elaboration) between the two sentences. The picked sentences do not have to be contiguous sentences in the text. All mwe's are shown in green.

consider the case when review questions are not used. For each question $q_i \in Q$, let $A_i = \{a_{i1}, \ldots, a_{im}\}$ be the set of candidate answers to the question [1]. We cast the science QA problem as a textual entailment problem by converting each question-answer candidate pair $(q_i, a_{i,j})$ into a hypothesis statement h_{ij} (see Figure 1)[2]. For each question q_i, the science QA task thereby reduces to picking the hypothesis $\hat{h}_i$ that has the highest likelihood of being entailed by the curriculum among the set of hypotheses $\mathbf{h}_i = \{h_{i1}, \ldots, h_{im}\}$ generated for that question. Let $h_i^* \in \mathbf{h}_i$ be the correct hypothesis corresponding to the correct answer.

Latent Answer-Entailing Structures help the model in providing evidence for the correct hypothesis. As described before, the structure depends on: (a) snippet from the curriculum hierarchy chosen to be aligned to the hypothesis, (b) external knowledge relevant for this entailment, and (c) the word/mwe alignment. The snippet from the curriculum to be aligned to the hypothesis is determined by walking down the curriculum hierarchy and then picking a set of sentences from the section chosen. Then, a subset of relevant external knowledge in the form of triples and equivalences (called knowledge bits) is selected from our reservoir of external knowledge (science dictionaries, cheat sheets, semi-structured tables, etc). Finally, words/mwe's in the hypothesis are aligned to words/mwe's in the snippet or knowledge bits. Learning these alignment edges helps the model determine which semantic constituents should be compared to each other. These alignments are also used to generate more effective features. The choice of snippets, choice of the relevant external knowledge and the alignments in conjunction form the latent answer-entailing structure. Let $\mathbf{z}_{ij}$ represent the latent structure for the question-answer candidate pair $(q_i, a_{i,j})$.

Max-Margin Approach: We treat science QA as a structured prediction problem of ranking the hypothesis set $\mathbf{h}_i$ such that the correct hypothesis is at the top of this ranking. We learn a scoring function $S_{\mathbf{w}}(h, \mathbf{z})$ with parameter $\mathbf{w}$ such that the score of the correct hypothesis h_i^* and the corresponding best latent structure $\mathbf{z}_i^*$ is higher than the score of the other hypotheses and their corresponding best latent structures. In fact, in a max-margin fashion, we want that $S_{\mathbf{w}}(h_i^*, \mathbf{z}_i^*) > S(h_{ij}, \mathbf{z}_{ij}) + 1 - \xi_i$ for all $h_j \in \mathbf{h} \setminus h^*$ for some slack ξ_i. Writing the relaxed max margin formulation:

$$\min_{\|\mathbf{w}\|} \frac{1}{2}\|\mathbf{w}\|_2^2 + C\sum_i \max_{\mathbf{z}_{ij}, h_{ij} \in \mathbf{h}_i \setminus h_i^*} S_{\mathbf{w}}(h_{ij}, \mathbf{z}_{ij}) + \Delta(h_i^*, h_{ij})$$
$$-C\sum_i S_{\mathbf{w}}(h_i^*, \mathbf{z}_i^*) \qquad (1)$$

We use 0-1 cost, i.e. $\Delta(h_i^*, h_{ij}) = \mathbb{1}(h_i^* \neq h_{ij})$ If the scoring function is convex then this objective is in concave-convex form and hence can be

---

[1]Candidate answers may be pre-defined, as in multiple-choice QA, or may be undefined but easy to extract with a degree of confidence (e.g., by using a pre-existing system)

[2]We use a set of question matching/rewriting rules to achieve this transformation. The rules match each question into one of a large set of pre-defined templates and applies a unique transformation to the question & answer candidate to achieve the hypothesis. Code provided in the supplementary.

solved by the concave-convex programming procedure (CCCP) (Yuille and Rangarajan, 2003). We assume the scoring function to be linear:$S_{\mathbf{w}}(h, \mathbf{z}) = \mathbf{w}^T \psi(h, \mathbf{z})$. Here, $\psi(h, \mathbf{z})$ is a feature map discussed later. The CCCP algorithm essentially alternates between solving for $\mathbf{z}_i^*$, $\mathbf{z}_{ij} \ \forall j$ s.t. $h_{ij} \in \mathbf{h}_i \setminus h_i^*$ and $\mathbf{w}$ to achieve a local minima. In the absence of information regarding the latent structure $\mathbf{z}$ we pick the structure that gives the best score for a given hypothesis i.e. $\arg\max_z S_{\mathbf{w}}(h, z)$. The complete procedure is given in the supplementary.

Inference and knowledge selection: We use beam search with a fixed beam size (5) for inference. We infer the textbook, chapter, section, snippet and alignments one by one in this order. In each step, we only expand the five most promising (given by the current score) substructure candidates so far. During inference, we select top 5 knowledge bits (triples, equivalences, etc.) from the knowledge resources that could be relevant for this question-answer. This is done heuristically by picking knowledge bits that explain parts of the hypothesis not explained by the chosen snippets.

Incorporating partially known structures: Now, we describe how review questions can be incorporated. As described earlier, modern textbooks often provide review problems at the end of each section. These review problems have value as part of the answer-entailing structure (textbook, chapter and section) is known for these problems. In this case, we use the formulation (equation 1) except that the max over $\mathbf{z}$ for the review questions is only taken over the unknown part of the latent structure.

Multi-task Learning: Question analysis is a key component of QA systems. Incoming questions are often of different types (counting, negation, entity queries, descriptive questions, etc.). Different types of questions usually require different processing strategies. Hence, we also extend of our LSSVM model to a multi-task setting where each question q_i now also has a pre-defined associated type t_i and each question-type is treated as a separate task. Yet, parameters are shared across tasks,which allows the model to exploit the commonality among tasks when required. We use the MTLSSVM formulation from Evgeniou and Pontil (2004) which was also used in a reading comprehension setting by Sachan et al. (2015). In a nutshell, the approach redefines the LSSVM feature map and shows that the MTLSSVM objective takes the same form as equation 1 with a kernel corresponding to the feature map. Hence, one can simply redefine the feature map and reuse LSSVM algorithm to solve the *MTLSSVM*.

Features: Our feature vector $\psi(h, \mathbf{z})$ decomposes into five parts, where each part corresponds to a part of the answer-entailing structure. For the first part, we index all the textbooks and score the top retrieved textbook by querying the hypothesis statement. We use tf-idf and BM25 scorers resulting in two features. Then, we find the jaccard similarity of bigrams and trigrams in the hypothesis and the textbook to get two more features for the first part. Similarly, for the second part we index all the textbook chapters and compute the tf idf, BM25 and bigram, trigram features. For the third part we index all the sections instead. The fourth part has features based on the text snippet part of the answer entailing structure. Here we do a deeper linguistic analysis and include features for matching local neighborhoods in the snippet and the hypothesis: features for matching bigrams, trigrams, dependencies, semantic roles, predicate-argument structure as well as the global syntactic structure: a tree kernel for matching dependency parse trees of entire sentences (Srivastava and Hovy, 2013). If a text snippet contains the answer to the question, it should intuitively be similar to the question as well as to the answer. Hence, we add features that are the element-wise product of features for the text-question match and text-answer match. Finally, we also have features corresponding to the RST (Mann and Thompson, 1988) and coreference links to enable inference across sentences. RST tells us that sentences with discourse relations are related to each other and can help us answer certain kinds of questions (Jansen et al., 2014). For example, the "cause" relation between sentences in the text can often give cues that can help us answer "why" or "how" questions. Hence, we add additional features - conjunction of the rhetorical structure label from a RST parser and the question word - to our feature vector. Similarly, the entity and event co-reference relations allow us to reason about repeating entities or events. Hence, we replace an entity/event mention with their first mentions if that results into a greater score. For the alignment part, we induce features based on word/mwe level similarity of aligned words:

(a) Surface-form match (Edit-distance), and (b) Semantic word match (cosine similarity using SENNA word vectors (Collobert et al., 2011) and "Antonymy" 'Class-Inclusion' or 'Is-A' relations using Wordnet). Distributional vectors for mwe's are obtained by adding the vector representations of comprising words (Mitchell and Lapata, 2008). To account for the hypothesized knowledge bits, whenever we have the case that a word/mwe in the hypothesis can be aligned to a word/mwe in a hypothesized knowledge bit to produce a greater score, then we keep the features for the alignment with the knowledge bit instead.

Negation Negation is a concern for our approach as facts usually align well with their negated versions. To overcome this, we use a simple heuristic. During training, if we detect negation using a set of simple rules that test for the presence of negation words ("not", "n't", etc.), we flip the partial order adding constraints that require that the correct hypothesis to be ranked below all the incorrect ones. During test phase if we detect negation, we predict the answer corresponding to the hypothesis with the lowest score.

3 Experiments

Dataset: We used a set of 8th grade science questions released as the training set in the Allen AI Science Challenge[3] for training and evaluating our model. The dataset comprises of 2500 questions. Each question has 4 answer candidates, of which exactly one is correct. We used questions 1-1500 for training, questions 1500-2000 for development and questions 2000-2500 for testing. We also used publicly available 8th grade science textbooks available through $ck12.org$. The science curriculum consists of seven textbooks on Physics, Chemistry, Biology, Earth Science and Life Science. Each textbook on an average has 18 chapters, and each chapter in turn is divided into 12 sections on an average. Also, as described before, each section, on an average, is followed by 3-4 multiple choice review questions (total 1369 review questions). We collected a number of domain specific science dictionaries, study guides, flash cards and semi-structured tables (Simple English Wiktionary and Aristo Tablestore) available online and create triples and equivalences used as external knowledge.

---

[3]https://www.kaggle.com/c/the-allen-ai-science-challenge/

Question Category	Example
Questions without context:	Which example describes a learned behavior in a dog?
Questions with context:	When athletes begin to exercise, their heart rates and respiration rates increase. At what level of organization does the human body coordinate these functions?
Negation Questions:	A teacher builds a model of a hydrogen atom. A red golf ball is used for a proton, and a green golf ball is used for an electron. Which is not accurate concerning the model?

Table 1: Example questions for *Qtype* classification

Baselines: We compare our framework with ten baselines. The first two baselines (*Lucene and PMI*) are taken from Clark et al. (2016). The *Lucene* baseline scores each answer candidate a_i by searching for the combination of the question q and answer candidate a_i in a lucene-based search engine and returns the highest scoring answer candidate. The *PMI* baseline similarly scores each answer candidate a_i by computing the pointwise mutual information to measure the strength of the association between parts of the question-answer candidate combine and parts of the CK12 curriculum. The next three baselines, inspired from Richardson et al. (2013), retrieve the top two CK12 sections querying $q+a_i$ in *Lucene* and score the answer candidates using these documents. The *SW* and *SW+D* baselines match bag of words constructed from the question and the answer answer candidate to the retrieved document. The *RTE* baseline uses textual entailment (Stern and Dagan, 2012) to score answer candidates as the likelihood of being entailed by the retrieved document. Then we also tried other approaches such as the *RNN* approach described in Clark et al. (2016), *Jacana aligner* (Yao et al., 2013) and two neural network approaches, *LSTM* (Hochreiter and Schmidhuber, 1997) and *QANTA* (Iyyer et al., 2014) They form our next four baselines. To test if our approach indeed benefits from jointly learning the retrieval and the answer selection modules, our final baseline *Lucene+LSSVM Alignment* retrieves the top section by querying $q + a_i$ in *Lucene* and then learns the remaining answer-entailment structure (alignment part of the answer-entailing structure in Figure 1) using a LSSVM.

Task Classification for Multitask Learning: We explore two simple question classification schemes. The first classification scheme classifies questions based on the question word (what, why, etc.). We call this *Qword* classification. The second scheme is based on the type of the question asked and classifies questions into three coarser categories: (a) questions without context,

(b) questions with context and (c) negation questions. This classification is based on the observation that many questions lay down some context and then ask a science concept based on this context. However, other questions are framed without any context and directly ask for the science concept itself. Then there is a smaller, yet, important subset of questions that involve negation that also needs to be handled separately. Table 1 gives examples of this classification. We call this classification *Qtype* classification[4].

Results: We compare variants of our method[5] where we consider our modification for negation or not and multi-task LSSVMs. We consider both kinds of task classification strategies and joint training (JT). Finally, we compare our methods against the baselines described above. We report accuracy (proportion of questions correctly answered) in our results. Figure 2 shows the results. First, we can immediately observe that all the LSSVM models have a better performance than all the baselines. We also found an improvement when we handle negation using the heuristic described above[6]. MTLSSVMs showed a boost over single task LSSVM. *Qtype* classification scheme was found to work better than *Qword* classification which simply classifies questions based on the question word. The multi-task learner could benefit even more if we can learn a better separation between the various strategies needed to answer science questions. We found that joint training with review questions helped improve accuracy as well.

Feature Ablation: As described before, our feature set comprises of five parts, where each part corresponds to a part of the answer-entailing structure – textbook (z_1), chapter (z_2), section (z_3), snippets (z_4), and alignment (z_5). It is interesting to know the relative importance of these parts in our model. Hence, we perform feature ablation on our best performing model - *MTLSSVM(QWord, JT)* where we remove the five feature parts one by one and measure the loss in accuracy. Figure

<hr>

[4]We wrote a set of question matching rules (similar to the rules used to convert question answer pairs to hypotheses) to achieve this classification

[5]We tune the SVM regularization parameter C on the development set. We use Stanford CoreNLP, the HILDA parser (Feng and Hirst, 2014), and jMWE (Kulkarni and Finlayson, 2011) for linguistic preprocessing

[6]We found that the accuracy over test questions tagged by our heuristic as negation questions went up from 33.64 percent to 42.52 percent and the accuracy over test questions not tagged as negation did not decrease significantly

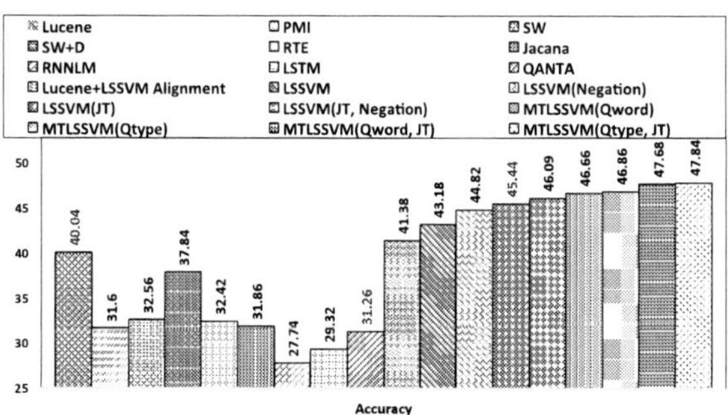

Figure 2: Variations of our method vs several baselines on the Science QA dataset. Differences between the baselines and LSSVMs, the improvement due to negation, the improvements due to multi-task learning and joint-learning are significant ($p < 0.05$) using the two-tailed paired T-test.

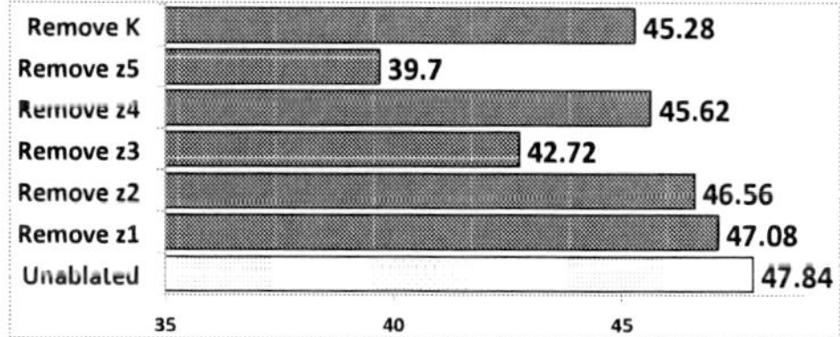

Figure 3: Ablation on *MTLSSVM(Qword, JT) model*

3 shows that the choice of section and alignment are important components of our model. Yet, all components are important and removing any of them will result in a loss of accuracy. Finally, in order to understand the value of external knowledge resources (K), we removed the component that induces and aligns the hypothesis with knowledge bits. This results in significant loss in performance, establishing the efficacy of adding in external knowledge via our approach.

4 Conclusion

We addressed the problem of answering 8th grade science questions using textbooks, domain specific dictionaries and semi-structured tables. We posed the task as an extension to textual entailment and proposed a solution that learns latent structures that align question answer pairs with appropriate snippets in the textbooks. Using domain specific dictionaries and semi-structured tables, we further refined the structures. The task required handling a variety of question types so we extended our technique to multi-task setting. Our technique showed improvements over a number of baselines. Finally, we also used a set of associated review questions, which were used to gain further improvements.

References

[Berant et al.2013] Jonathan Berant, Andrew Chou, Roy Frostig, and Percy Liang. 2013. Semantic parsing on freebase from question-answer pairs. In *Proceedings of Empirical Methods in Natural Language Processing*, pages 1533–1544.

[Blunsom and Cohn2006] Phil Blunsom and Trevor Cohn. 2006. Discriminative word alignment with conditional random fields. In *Proceedings of the 21st International Conference on Computational Linguistics and the 44th annual meeting of the Association for Computational Linguistics*, pages 65–72. Association for Computational Linguistics.

[Clark et al.2016] Peter Clark, Oren Etzioni, Daniel Khashabi, Tushar Khot, Ashish Sabharwal, Oyvind Tafjord, and Peter Turney. 2016. Combining retrieval, statistics, and inference to answer elementary science questions. In *Proceedings of AAAI*.

[Clark2015] Peter Clark. 2015. Elementary School Science and Math Tests as a Driver for AI:Take the Aristo Challenge! In *Proceedings of IAAI*.

[Collobert et al.2011] Ronan Collobert, Jason Weston, Léon Bottou, Michael Karlen, Koray Kavukcuoglu, and Pavel Kuksa. 2011. Natural language processing (almost) from scratch. *The Journal of Machine Learning Research*, 12:2493–2537.

[Evgeniou and Pontil2004] Theodoros Evgeniou and Massimiliano Pontil. 2004. Regularized multi–task learning. In *Proceedings of the Tenth ACM SIGKDD International Conference on Knowledge Discovery and Data Mining*, pages 109–117.

[Feng and Hirst2014] Vanessa Wei Feng and Graeme Hirst. 2014. A linear-time bottom-up discourse parser with constraints and post-editing. In *Proceedings of the 52nd Annual Meeting of the Association for Computational Linguistics (Volume 1: Long Papers)*, pages 511–521.

[Ferrucci2012] David A Ferrucci. 2012. Introduction to "this is watson". *IBM Journal of Research and Development*, 56(3.4):1–1.

[Hochreiter and Schmidhuber1997] Sepp Hochreiter and Jürgen Schmidhuber. 1997. Long short-term memory. *Neural computation*, 9(8):1735–1780.

[Iyyer et al.2014] Mohit Iyyer, Jordan Boyd-Graber, Leonardo Claudino, Richard Socher, and Hal Daumé III. 2014. A neural network for factoid question answering over paragraphs. In *Proceedings of Empirical Methods in Natural Language Processing*.

[Jansen et al.2014] Peter Jansen, Mihai Surdeanu, and Peter Clark. 2014. Discourse complements lexical semantics for non-factoid answer reranking. In *Proceedings of the 52nd Annual Meeting of the Association for Computational Linguistics, ACL 2014, June 22-27, 2014, Baltimore, MD, USA, Volume 1: Long Papers*, pages 977–986.

[Kulkarni and Finlayson2011] Nidhi Kulkarni and Mark Alan Finlayson. 2011. jmwe: A java toolkit for detecting multi-word expressions. In *Proceedings of the Workshop on Multiword Expressions: from Parsing and Generation to the Real World*, pages 122–124. Association for Computational Linguistics.

[MacCartney et al.2008] Bill MacCartney, Michel Galley, and Christopher D Manning. 2008. A phrase-based alignment model for natural language inference. In *Proceedings of the conference on empirical methods in natural language processing*, pages 802–811.

[Mann and Thompson1988] William C Mann and Sandra A Thompson. 1988. {Rhetorical Structure Theory: Toward a functional theory of text organisation}. *Text*, 3(8):234–281.

[Mitchell and Lapata2008] Jeff Mitchell and Mirella Lapata. 2008. Vector-based models of semantic composition. In *ACL 2008, Proceedings of the 46th Annual Meeting of the Association for Computational Linguistics, June 15-20, 2008, Columbus, Ohio, USA*, pages 236–244.

[Richardson et al.2013] Matthew Richardson, Christopher JC Burges, and Erin Renshaw. 2013. Mctest: A challenge dataset for the open-domain machine comprehension of text. In *Proceedings of Empirical Methods in Natural Language Processing (EMNLP)*.

[Sachan et al.2015] Mrinmaya Sachan, Avinava Dubey, Eric P Xing, and Matthew Richardson. 2015. Learning answer-entailing structures for machine comprehension. In *Proceedings of the Annual Meeting of the Association for Computational Linguistics*.

[Sammons et al.2009] M. Sammons, V. Vydiswaran, T. Vieira, N. Johri, M. Chang, D. Goldwasser, V. Srikumar, G. Kundu, Y. Tu, K. Small, J. Rule, Q. Do, and D. Roth. 2009. Relation alignment for textual entailment recognition. In *TAC*.

[Srivastava and Hovy2013] Shashank Srivastava and Dirk Hovy. 2013. A walk-based semantically enriched tree kernel over distributed word representations. In *Proceedings of Empirical Methods in Natural Language Processing*, pages 1411–1416.

[Stern and Dagan2012] Asher Stern and Ido Dagan. 2012. Biutee: A modular open-source system for recognizing textual entailment. In *Proceedings of the ACL 2012 System Demonstrations*, pages 73–78.

[Sultan et al.2014] Arafat Md Sultan, Steven Bethard, and Tamara Sumner. 2014. Back to basics for monolingual alignment: Exploiting word similarity and contextual evidence. *Transactions of the Association of Computational Linguistics – Volume 2, Issue 1*, pages 219–230.

[Yao and Van Durme2014] Xuchen Yao and Benjamin Van Durme. 2014. Information extraction over structured data: Question answering with freebase. In *Proceedings of the 52nd Annual Meeting of the Association for Computational Linguistics (Volume 1: Long Papers)*, pages 956–966. Association for Computational Linguistics.

[Yao et al.2013] Xuchen Yao, Benjamin Van Durme, Chris Callison-Burch, and Peter Clark. 2013. A lightweight and high performance monolingual word aligner. In *ACL (2)*, pages 702–707.

[Yih et al.2013] Wentau Yih, Ming-Wei Chang, Christopher Meek, and Andrzej Pastusiak. 2013. Question answering using enhanced lexical semantic models. In *Proceedings of the 51st Annual Meeting of the Association for Computational Linguistics*.

[Yuille and Rangarajan2003] A. L. Yuille and Anand Rangarajan. 2003. The concave-convex procedure. *Neural Comput.*

Specifying and Annotating Reduced Argument Span
Via QA-SRL

Gabriel Stanovsky   Meni Adler   Ido Dagan
Computer Science Department, Bar-Ilan University
{gabriel.satanovsky,meni.adler}@gmail.com
dagan@cs.biu.ac.il

Abstract

Prominent semantic annotations take an inclusive approach to argument span annotation, marking arguments as full constituency subtrees. Some works, however, showed that identifying a reduced argument span can be beneficial for various semantic tasks. While certain practical methods do extract reduced argument spans, such as in Open-IE , these solutions are often ad-hoc and system-dependent, with no commonly accepted standards. In this paper we propose a generic argument reduction criterion, along with an annotation procedure, and show that it can be consistently and intuitively annotated using the recent QA-SRL paradigm.

1 Introduction

Representations of predicate-argument structure need to determine the span of predicates and their corresponding arguments. Surprisingly, there are no accepted NLP-standards which specify what the "right" span of an argument should be.

Semantic representations typically take an inclusive (or maximal) approach: PropBank annotation (Palmer et al., 2005), for example, marks arguments as full constituency subtrees. From an application perspective, this maximal approach ensures that all arguments are indeed embedded within the annotated span, yet it is often not trivial how to accurately recover them.

In contrast to this maximal-span approach, Open-IE systems (Etzioni et al., 2008; Fader et al., 2011) put emphasis on extracting readable stand-alone propositions, typically producing shorter arguments (see examples in Section 2.1). Several recent works have exploited this property, using Open-IE extractions as an intermediate representation within a larger framework.

Angeli et al. (2015) built an Open-IE system which focuses on shorter argument spans. They hypothesize that "shorter arguments [are] more likely to be useful for downstream applications", and demonstrate this by using their system to extract facts about predefined entities in a state-of-the-art Knowledge Base Population system.

Further, Stanovsky et al. (2015) compared the performance of several off-the-shelf parsers in different semantic tasks. Most relevant to this work is the comparison between Open-IE and SRL. Specifically, they suggest that SRL's longer arguments introduce noise which hurts performance for downstream tasks. This is sustained empirically by showing that extractions from Open-IE4[1] significantly outperform ClearNLP's SRL (Choi, 2012) in textual similarity, analogies, and reading comprehension tasks.[2]

While Open-IE extractors do provide a reduction of argument span, they lack consistency and principled rigor – there is no clear definition for the desired argument span, which is defined de-facto by the different implementations. This lack of a common system-independent definition, let alone an annotation methodology, hinders the creation of gold standard argument-span annotation.

In this work we propose a concrete argument span reduction criterion and an accompanying annotation procedure, based on the recent QA-SRL paradigm (He et al., 2015). We show that this criterion can be consistently annotated with high agreement, and that it is intuitive enough to be obtained through crowd-sourcing.

As future work, we intend to apply the reduction criterion to other types of predicates (e.g., nomi-

---

[1] http://knowitall.github.io/openie
[2] Open IE-4 is based on ClearNLPs SRL, allowing for a direct comparison.

474

Proceedings of the 54th Annual Meeting of the Association for Computational Linguistics, pages 474–478,
Berlin, Germany, August 7-12, 2016. ©2016 Association for Computational Linguistics

nal and adjectival predication). Subsequently, we would like to create a comprehensive annotated resource, as a benchmark for the detection of reduced argument spans.

2 Background

2.1 Argument Span

As discussed in the Introduction, PropBank takes an inclusive approach to annotating arguments, by marking them as full constituency subtrees. For example, given the sentence "*Obama, the newly elected president, flew to Russia*", PropBank will mark "Obama, the newly elected president" as ARG0 of the predicate *flew*.

However, in certain applications, such as question answering or abstractive summarization, a reduced argument is preferred (i.e., "Obama"). Notably, different implementations of Open-IE provide an applicable generic way to reduce argument span. Since there are no common guidelines for this task, each Open-IE extractor produces different argument spans. We cover briefly some of the main differences in a few prominent Open-IE systems.

ReVerb (Fader et al., 2011) uses part-of-speech-based regular expressions to decide whether a word should be included within an argument span. For example, they move certain light verb compliments and prepositions from the argument to the predicate slot (e.g., "***gave a talk at***"). OLLIE (Mausam et al., 2012) learns lexical-syntactic patterns and splits extractions across certain prepositions. For example, given "*I flew from Paris to Berlin*", OLLIE yields (I; **flew**; from Paris) and (I; **flew**; to Berlin). More recently, (Angell et al., 2015) used natural logic to remove non-integral parts of arguments (e.g., removing the underlined non-restrictive prepositional phrase in "*Heinz Fischer of Austria*").

2.2 QA-SRL

SRL is typically perceived as answering **argument role questions**, such as *who, what, to whom, when*, or *where*, regarding a target predicate. For instance, PropBank's ARG0 for the predicate *say* answers the question "*who said something?*".

QA-SRL (He et al., 2015) follows this perspective, and suggests that answering explicit role questions is an intuitive means to solicit predicate-argument structures from non-expert annotators. Annotators are presented with a sentence in which a target predicate[3] was marked, and are requested to annotate argument role questions (from a restricted grammar) and corresponding answers.

For example, given the previous sentence and the target predicate *flew*, an annotator can intuitively provide the following QA pairs: (1) *Who flew somewhere?* **Obama**, and (2) *Where did someone fly?* **Russia**.

The annotation guidelines further solicit multiple shorter answers, each typically embedded in the span of a maximal PropBank-style argument, while providing a different answer to the (same) argument role question.

In Section 4 we make use of QA-SRL's framework in order to produce annotations by our reduction argument criterion, which is defined in the next section.

3 Argument Reduction

In this section, we propose annotation criteria and process for obtaining minimal argument spans. Given an original, non-reduced argument, we aim to reduce it to a set of (one or more) smaller arguments, which jointly specify the same answer to the argument's role question.

Formally, given a non-reduced argument $a = \{w_1, ..., w_n\}$, along with its role question $Q(a)$ with respect to predicate p in sentence s, we seek to find a set of minimally-scoped arguments, $M(a)$, such that:

(1) Each $m \in M(a)$ is a proper subset of a.

(2) Each $m \in M(a)$ provides a different, independently interpreted answer to $Q(a)$.

(3) $M(a)$ is *equivalent* to a, in the sense that when taken jointly, $M(a)$ specifies the same answers as a does for $Q(a)$.

(4) Each $m \in M(a)$ is *minimal*, meaning it cannot be further reduced without violating the equivalence criterion (3).

Note that this definition relies on human judgments, which are used to decide whether two arguments provide the same or different answers.

Generally speaking, a non-minimal argument a can be reduced in one of two ways:

(a) *Removal* of tokens from a, forming a smaller argument.

---

[3] Currently these consist of automatically annotated verbs.

(b) *Splitting* a, yielding multiple arguments.

In our context, we would like to apply these two operations as long as they maintain the equivalence criterion (3). We empirically observe that the first case (removal) corresponds to the omission of non-restrictive modifiers, that is, modifiers for which the content of the modifier presents a separate, parenthetical unit of information about the NP (Huddleston et al., 2002). For example, revisiting the sentence: *"Obama, the newly elected president, flew to Russia."*, the non-reduced argument "Obama, the newly elected president" can be reduced to the minimal argument "Obama", as both specify the same answer to the role question *"who flew to Russia?"*.

In contrast, a restrictive modifier is an integral part of the meaning of the containing NP, and hence should not be removed, as in *"She wore the necklace **that her mother gave her**"*.

The second reduction operation (splitting) corresponds to decoupling distributive coordinations, that is, cases in which a predicate applies separately to all of the elements in the coordination. For example, in: *"Obama and Clinton were born in America."*, the non-reduced PropBank-style argument "Obama and Clinton" can be reduced to two arguments {"Obama", "Clinton"}. Each of these arguments independently answers the role question *"Who was born in America?"*, while jointly they correspond to the longer, non-reduced argument.

Note that splitting a shorter distributive argument does not necessarily produce disjoint arguments. For example, consider: *"The tall boys and girls were born in America."*, in which "The tall boys and girls" would reduce to two overlapping arguments: {"The tall boys", "The tall girls"}.

In contrast, non-distributive conjuncts cannot be split. These are cases in which the predicate applies to the conjuncts taken together, while applying it separately to each element changes the interpretation of the clause. Consider for example the reciprocal structure of: *"Obama and Putin met in Moscow"*, in which we cannot split the argument "Obama and Putin" since the predicate *met* implies that Obama and Putin met with each other, which will be lost if we split the argument to two independent answers.

Based on these two operations, a set of minimal arguments, $M(a)$, can be obtained from a in a top-down manner: first apply *removal*, if possi-

ble; then *splitting*, if possible.[4] Next, apply recursively to each of the smaller arguments, stopping when none of the two reduction operations can be applied.

This annotation process might yield different sets of minimal arguments by different annotators, depending on their decisions regarding the reduction steps. As we show empirically in the next section, high agreement levels can be obtained, supporting the validity of our proposed criterion.

4 Annotation Experiment

In this section we describe the compilation and analysis of a small-scale expert annotation corpus. Creating such corpus serves 3 goals: (1) It allows us to test the applicability of the argument reducing procedure, (2) By comparing it with Propbank we can examine how often, and in which cases, we reduce arguments (Section 4.1), and (3) We can assess the plausibility of crowd-sourcing argument span annotation (Sections 4.2 and 4.3).

In order to achieve these goals, we sample 100 predicates of the Propbank corpus, which covered 260 arguments. To allow comparisons, we sample predicates which were annotated by QA-SRL and whose arguments were aligned by (He et al., 2015) with a matching Propbank argument.[5]

Two expert annotators used the QA-SRL's interface to re-answer the original QA-SRL annotated questions with minimally-scoped arguments, according to the procedure described in Section 3. Prior to annotating the expert dataset, the annotators discussed the process and resolved conflicts on a separate development set of 20 predicates.

Annotator agreement From an argument perspective, the annotators fully agreed on the span of 94.6% of the arguments.

Looking into the word token level, we found that for a given PropBank argument $a = (w_1, ..., w_n)$, the respective reduced arguments always constitute a subset of a. This allows us to look at the annotation process as a list of n mapping decisions – for each w_i, an annotator decides whether he (1) Maps it to one or more of the argu-

---

[4] This order is arbitrary, chosen solely to provide a deterministic process. Alternating the steps would yield an identical set.

[5] An annotated answer is judged to match the PropBank argument if either (1) the gold argument head is within the annotated answer span, or (2) the gold argument head is a preposition and at least one of its children is within the answer span.

ments of $M(a)$, or (2) Deletes it. The complete annotation required each annotator to make 985 such mappings decisions. Word level agreement between the annotators was calculated as the percent of the decisions on which they agreed, and found to be 97.1%.

Overall, the annotators achieved a high level of agreement, suggesting that the reduction criterion can be consistently applied by trained annotators. An analysis of the few disagreements revealed that the deviations between the annotators stem from semantic ambiguities, where two legitimate readings of the sentence led to different span annotations.[6]

Finally, we compose the expert annotation dataset from 247 arguments on which both annotators fully agreed.

4.1 Comparison with Propbank

Comparing our annotation with PropBank showed that we reduced roughly 24% of the arguments: 19% of the arguments were reduced by omitting non-restrictive modifications and 5% of the arguments were split across distributive co-ordinations (see discussion on both types of reductions in Section 3).

The average reduced argument shrunk by roughly 58%. In general, these numbers suggest that our annotation scheme targets commonly recurring phenomena, and significantly deviates from PropBank's annotation of arguments.

4.2 Crowdsourcing

We created an Amazon Mechanical Turk[7] project to investigate the possible scalability of our annotation using non-trained annotators.

Similarly to the setting used by the expert annotators, turkers were presented with a sentence, followed by a list of questions regarding a target predicate. The sentences, predicates and questions were taken from the expert corpus, which aligns between QA SRL and Propbank.[8]

The guidelines for annotators refined those of He et al. (2015), soliciting answers which follow

---

Annotation	Argument	Word
Expert - IAA	94.6%	97.1%
QA-SRL - Expert	80%	88.5%
Our Crowdsourcing - Expert	**89.1%**	**93.5%**

Table 1: Agreement levels between the different annotations: (1) IAA - Inter-Annotator agreement between the expert annotators (2) Agreement of QA-SRL corpus with our expert annotation and (3) Our Crowdsourcing - agreement of the Amazon Mechanical Turk annotations with our expert annotation. See Section 4.

our formal criterion. In cases of multiple answers referring to the same entity, annotators are asked to provide the most specific answer, otherwise (if the answers refer to different entities), the annotators are asked to list all of the answers. Furthermore, the annotators are requested to provide the shortest answer they can, while preserving its correctness.

We chose annotations which were agreed upon by at least two annotators. In cases where the three annotators gave different answers (26% of the time), we used a fourth annotator to arbitrate, and calculated agreement using the same metrics discussed above. Cases where annotators disagreed were mostly semantically ambigouos. For example, given the sentence *"Our pilot simply laughed, fired up the burner and with another blast of flame lifted us, oh, a good 12 - inches above the water level."* and the question *"how much did someone lift someone?"*, one annotator replied **12 - inches** while another replied *a good* **12 - inches**.

We found that the crowdsourcing annotations to be of high quality, reaching 89.1% argument agreement and 93.5% word agreement with our expert annotation. These results suggest that the annotation of argument span is efficiently and accurately attainable using crowd-sourcing techniques, with only subtle refinements over the original QA-SRL guidelines.

4.3 Comparison with QA-SRL

Finally, we want to compare our crowdsourcing annotation versus that of QA-SRL, with respect to argument span. Using the previously mentioned agreement metric, we find that QA-SRL agrees with our expert dataset on 80% of the arguments and 88.5% of the word-level decisions. Although it is outperformed by our crowdsourcing annota-

---

⁶For example, in *"The American Stock Exchange said a seat was sold for $ 160,000, down $ 5,000 from the previous sale last Friday."*, one annotator did not reduce ARG1, while the second annotator chose to restrict the span of the argument to *"a seat was sold for $ 160,00"*, interpreting the remaining part of the clause as an addition by the author.

⁷https://www.mturk.com

⁸To be clear, the annotators saw only the raw text and questions from QA-SRL and were not exposed to the Prop-Bank annotations.

tion project, QA-SRL still manages to capture significant amounts of the minimally-reduced arguments. This is interesting, as the QA-SRL guidelines did not address this issue specifically, but instead solicited annotators to provide "as many answers as possible". This suggests that the question answering format intuitively prompts human annotators to reduce the span of their answers.

To conclude this section, the entire comparison measurements are summarized in Table 1.

5 Conclusion and Future Work

In this work we proposed a concrete criterion for specifying minimally-scoped arguments. While this issue was applicably addressed by previous work, it was not consistently defined or annotated. Following this definition, we created an expert annotation dataset over texts from Prop-Bank, using the QA-SRL paradigm. This annotation achieved high levels of inter-annotator agreement, and was shown to be intuitive enough so that it can be scaled to crowdsourcing annotation. As future work, we plan to extend this annotation project to larger volumes of text, and to additional types of (non-verbal) predications, which will allow to develop learning-based methods that identify minimally-reduced argument span.

Acknowledgments

We would like to thank Luheng He and Luke Zettlemoyer for the fruitful discussions, and the anonymous reviewers for their helpful comments.

This work was supported in part by grants from the MAGNET program of the Israeli Office of the Chief Scientist (OCS), the Israel Science Foundation grant 880/12, and the German Research Foundation through the German-Israeli Project Cooperation (DIP, grant DA 1600/1-1).

References

Gabor Angeli, Melvin Johnson Premkumar, and Christopher D. Manning. 2015. Leveraging linguistic structure for open domain information extraction. In *Proceedings of the 53rd Annual Meeting of the Association for Computational Linguistics (ACL 2015)*.

Jinho D. Choi. 2012. *Optimization of Natural Language Processing Components for Robustness and Scalability*. Ph.D. thesis, Boulder, CO, USA. AAI3549172.

Oren Etzioni, Michele Banko, Stephen Soderland, and Daniel S Weld. 2008. Open information extraction from the Web. *Communications of the ACM*, 51(12):68–74.

Anthony Fader, Stephen Soderland, and Oren Etzioni. 2011. Identifying relations for open information extraction. In *Proceedings of the Conference on Empirical Methods in Natural Language Processing*, pages 1535–1545. Association for Computational Linguistics.

Luheng He, Mike Lewis, and Luke Zettlemoyer. 2015. Question-answer driven semantic role labeling: Using natural language to annotate natural language. In *the Conference on Empirical Methods in Natural Language Processing (EMNLP)*.

Rodney Huddleston, Geoffrey K Pullum, et al. 2002. The cambridge grammar of english. *Language. Cambridge: Cambridge University Press*.

Mausam, Michael Schmitz, Stephen Soderland, Robert Bart, and Oren Etzioni. 2012. Open language learning for information extraction. In *Proceedings of the 2012 Joint Conference on Empirical Methods in Natural Language Processing and Computational Natural Language Learning*, pages 523–534, Jeju Island, Korea, July. Association for Computational Linguistics.

Martha Palmer, Daniel Gildea, and Paul Kingsbury. 2005. The proposition bank: An annotated corpus of semantic roles. *Computational linguistics*, 31(1):71–106.

Gabriel Stanovsky, Ido Dagan, and Mausam. 2015. Open IE as an intermediate structure for semantic tasks. In *Proceedings of the 53rd Annual Meeting of the Association for Computational Linguistics (ACL 2015)*.

Improving Argument Overlap for Proposition-Based Summarisation

Yimai Fang and **Simone Teufel**
University of Cambridge Computer Laboratory
15 JJ Thomson Avenue
Cambridge CB3 0FD, United Kingdom
`{yf261,sht25}@cam.ac.uk`

Abstract

We present improvements to our incremental proposition-based summariser, which is inspired by Kintsch and van Dijk's (1978) text comprehension model. Argument overlap is a central concept in this summariser. Our new model replaces the old overlap method based on distributional similarity with one based on lexical chains. We evaluate on a new corpus of 124 summaries of educational texts, and show that our new system outperforms the old method and several state-of-the-art non-proposition-based summarisers. The experiment also verifies that the incremental nature of memory cycles is beneficial in itself, by comparing it to a non-incremental algorithm using the same underlying information.

1 Introduction

Automatic summarisation is one of the big artificial intelligence challenges in a world of information overload. Many summarisers, mostly extractive, have been developed in recent years (Radev et al., 2004; Mihalcea and Tarau, 2004; Wong et al., 2008; Celikyilmaz and Hakkani-Tür, 2011). Research is moving beyond extraction in various directions: One could perform text manipulation such as compression as a separate step after extraction (Knight and Marcu, 2000; Cohn and Lapata, 2008), or alternatively, one could base a summary on an internal semantic representation such as the proposition (Lehnert, 1981; McKeown and Radev, 1995).

One summarisation model that allows manipulation of semantic structures of texts was proposed by Kintsch and van Dijk (1978, henceforth KvD). It is a model of human text processing, where the text is turned into propositions and processed incrementally, sentence by sentence. The final summary is based on those propositions whose semantic participants (arguments) are well-connected to others in the text and hence likely to be remembered by a human reading the text, under the assumption of memory limitations.

Such a deep model is attractive because it provides the theoretical possibility of performing inference and generalisation over propositions, even if current NLP technology only supports shallow versions of such manipulations. This gives it a clear theoretical advantage over non-propositional extraction systems whose information units are individual words and their connections, e.g. centroids or random-walk models.

We present in this paper a new KvD-based summariser that is word sense-aware, unlike our earlier implementation (Fang and Teufel, 2014). §2 explains the KvD model with respect to summarisation. §3 and §4 explain why and how we use lexical chains to model argument overlap, a phenomenon which is central to KvD-style summarisation. §6 presents experimental evidence that our model of argument overlap is superior to the earlier one. Our summariser additionally beats several extractive state-of-the-art summarisers. We show that this advantage does not come from our use of lexical chains alone, but also from KvD's incremental processing.

Our second contribution concerns a new corpus of educational texts, presented in §5. Part of the reason why we prefer a genre other than news is the vexingly good performance of the lead baseline in the news genre. Traditionally, many summarisers struggled to beat this baseline (Lin and Hovy, 2003). We believe that the problem is partly due to the journalistic style, which calls for an abstract-like lead. If we want to measure the content selection ability of summarisers, alternat-

Proceedings of the 54th Annual Meeting of the Association for Computational Linguistics, pages 479–485,
Berlin, Germany, August 7-12, 2016. ©2016 Association for Computational Linguistics

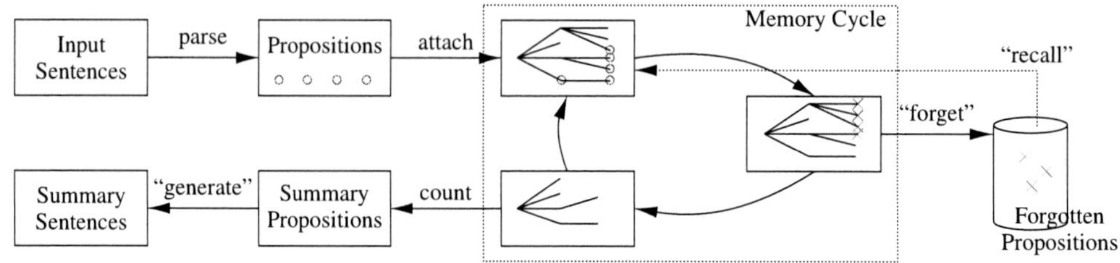

Figure 1: The KvD-inspired incremental summarisation model.

ive data sets are needed. Satisfyingly, we find that on our corpus the lead baseline is surpassable by intelligent summarisers.

2 The KvD Model

The KvD model is a cognitive account of human text comprehension. In our KvD-inspired model (Figure 1), the summariser constructs a list of propositions as a meaning representation from a syntactic parse of the input text. A batch of new propositions ($\circ$ in the figure) are processed for each sentence. At the beginning of a memory cycle, these new propositions are added to a *coherence tree*, which represents the working memory. They attach to the existing propositions on the tree with which they have the strongest overlap in arguments. At the end of a cycle, as a simulation of limited memory, only a few important propositions are carried over to the next cycle, while the others are "forgotten" (represented by $\times$). This selection is based on the location of propositions in the tree, using the so-called *leading edge strategy*; propositions that are on more recent edges, or that are attached higher, are more likely to be retained. The model attempts all future attachments using only the propositions in working memory, and allows to reuse forgotten ones only if this strategy runs into problems (when a new proposition could not otherwise be attached).

KvD suggest that the decision whether a proposition should be included in the final summary depends on three factors: a) the number of cycles where it was retained in working memory, b) whether it is a generalisation, and c) whether it is a meta-statement (or macro-proposition).

For its explanatory power and simplicity, the model has been well-received not only in the fields of cognitive psychology (Paivio, 1990; Lave, 1988) and education (Gay et al., 1976), but also in the summarisation community (Moens et al., 2003; Uyttendaele et al., 1998; Hahn and Reimer,

1984).

We presented the first computational prototype of the model that follows the proposition-centric processing closely (Fang and Teufel, 2014). Of the factors mentioned above, only the first is modelled in this summariser (called FT14). That is, we use the frequency of a proposition being retained in memory as the only indicator of its summary-worthiness. This is a simplification due to the fact that robust inference is beyond current NLP capability. Additionally, macro-propositions depend on domain-specific schema, whereas our system aims to be domain-independent.

Zhang et al. (2016) presented a summariser based on a later cognitive model by Kintsch (1998). Instead of modelling importance of propositions directly, their summariser computes the importance of words by spreading activation cyclically, but extracts at proposition level.

Although the summariser presented in the current paper, a newer version of FT14, is capable of sub-sentential content selection, we present its output in the form of extracted sentences that contain the most summary-worthy propositions. This is different from FT14, where we used a token-based extraction method. A better output would of course be an abstract based on the selected propositions, but we currently do not have a language generation module and can therefore evaluate only the content selection ability of our summariser.

3 Argument Overlap

The central mechanism of the KvD model is *argument overlap* of propositions, and it is key to successful content selection. This is because there are often multiple propositions on the tree where a new proposition could attach, of varying attractiveness. The task therefore boils down to ranking attachments, for instance by the strength of overlap, and the position in the tree.

Figure 2 is an example of competing attachment

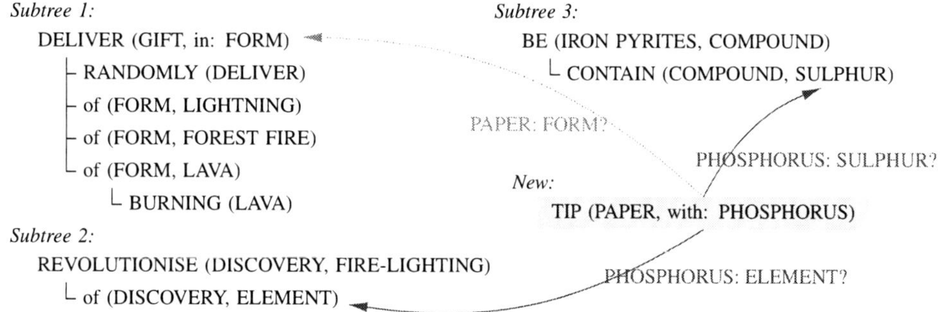

Figure 2: Possible attachments of a new proposition.

sites. Three subtrees in the working memory are shown, containing propositions that correspond to the text pieces 1) *[fire was] a gift randomly delivered in the form of lightning, forest fire or burning lava*, 2) *fire-lighting was revolutionised by the discovery of the element*, and 3) *iron pyrites, a compound that contains sulphur*, respectively. The new proposition corresponds to the text *paper tipped with phosphorus*. It can attach in subtree 2, because *phosphorus* is a kind of *element*; it can also attach in subtree 3, because both *phosphorus* and *sulphur* are chemicals.

The definition of argument overlap is conceptually simple, namely reference of the arguments to the same concept, which can be an entity, an event, or a class of things. In KvD's manual demonstration of the algorithm, the resolution of textual expressions to concepts relies on human intelligence. A "perfect" coreference resolver is arguably all we need, but coreference as currently defined excludes generics, abstract concepts, paraphrases, bridging connections (Weischedel et al., 2007) and several other relevant linguistic phenomena. This means an insufficient number of possible overlaps are found by current coreference systems, if no further information is used. How exactly to model argument overlap for a KvD summariser is therefore open to exploration.

We use other sources of information that addresses topicality and semantic relatedness, in combination with coreference resolution. In FT14, that source was the distributional similarity of words, normalised with respect to their distractors in context to achieve numerically comparable overlap scores. In this paper, we argue that using the shared membership in lexical chains as the other source provides a better basis for ranking argument overlap.

FT14's overlap detection runs into problems in the situation above (Figure 2). Under FT14's definition of argument overlap as distributional semantic distance, the link between *paper* and *form* is as strong as the other possibilities, which leads to the attachment of the new proposition as a child node of the root proposition of subtree 1 due to higher tree level. This attachment uses the wrong sense of the polysemous word *form* ("form/8 – a printed document with spaces in which to write"). In our new ranking of attachment sites, lexical chains enable us to reject the spurious attachment, as we will now explain.

4 Our Lexical Chain-Based System

In our new model, argument overlap is computed using lexical chains (Barzilay and Elhadad, 1997), a construct that combines the ideas of topicality and word sense clusters. A lexical chain is an equivalence class of expressions found in the text whose presumed senses in context are related to the same concept or topic. For the example in the last section, in our system *form* is correctly resolved to sense 2, not sense 8, and as form/2 and paper/1 are not members of the same lexical chain, the wrong attachment is prevented.

Lexical chain algorithms typically use Word-Net (Miller, 1995) to provide the lexical relations needed, whereby each synset (synonym set) represents a concept. Hypernyms and hyponyms are related to the same topic, and they may be in a coreference relationship with the concept. To a lesser extent, the potential for coreference also holds for siblings of a concept. WordNet relations therefore give information about concept identity and topical relatedness, both of which are aspects of argument overlap.

We implemented Galley and McKeown's (2003, henceforth GM03) chaining algorithm, which improves over Barzilay and Elhadad's and Silber and McCoy's (2002) chain definition by introducing the limitation of "one sense per discourse", i.e. by enforcing that all occurrences of the same word take the same sense in one document. Initially designed to improve word sense disambiguation accuracy, GM03's method has been shown to improve summarisation quality as well (Ercan and Cicekli, 2008).

In GM03, the edge weight between possible word senses of two word occurrences depends on the lexical relation and the textual distance between them. Each word is disambiguated by choosing the sense that maximises the sum of weights of the edges leaving all its occurrences. Edges that are based on non-selected senses are then discarded. Once the entire text has been processed, each connected component of the graph represents a lexical chain.

As far as nouns[1] are concerned, we follow GM03's edge weights, but unlike GM03, we also allow verbs to enter into chains. We do this in order to model nominalised event references, and to provide a sufficient number of possible connections. Table 1 provides the distance of relations; weights of verb and derivation relations equal to the weights of noun relations on the same row. Instead of assigning an overlap value of 1 to all pairs of words in the same chain, the extent of overlap is given as $a^{\Sigma_{e \in E} d_e}$, where E is the set of edges in the shortest path between the two words in the graph of lexical relations, d_e the distance of the lexical relation of e, and a an attenuation factor we set at 0.7. This models the transition from concept sameness to broader relatedness. We found empirically that the introduction of verbs and the graded overlap value using relation distance improves the performance of our KvD summariser.

Lexical coverage of this algorithm is good: WordNet covers 98.3% of all word occurrences allowed into our lexical chains in the experiment in §6, excluding those POS-tagged as proper nouns. For unknown words, the system's backoff strategy is to form overlap only if the surface strings match.

The structuring of information in a memory tree and the incremental addition of information, including the concept of "forgetting", are key claims of the KvD model. But do these manipulations actually add any value beyond the information con-

Distance	Noun	Verb	Derivation
0	synonymy		
1	hypernymy	synonymy	noun-to-verb
2	sibling	hypernymy	

Table 1: Distance of lexical relations.

tained in a global network representing *all* connections between all propositions in the text? In such a network without forgetting or discourse structure, standard graph algorithms could be used to determine central propositions. This hypothesis is tested in §6.

5 New Corpus of Texts and Summaries

We introduce new evaluation materials, created from the reading sections of Academic Tests of the *Official IELTS Practice Materials* (British Council et al., 2012).

The IELTS is a standardised test of English proficiency for non-native speakers. The texts cover various general topics, and resemble popular science or educational articles. They are carefully chosen to be of the same difficulty level, and understandable by people of any cultural background. Unlike news text, they also presuppose less external knowledge, such as US politics, which makes it easier to demonstrate the essence of proposition-based summarisation.

Out of all 108 texts of volumes 1–9, we randomly sampled 31. We then elicited 4 summaries summary for each, written by 14 members of our university, i.e., a total of 124 summaries.[2] We asked the summarisers to create natural-sounding text, keeping the length strictly to 100 ± 2 words. They were allowed but not encouraged to paraphrase text.

6 Experiment

6.1 Systems and Baselines

We test 7 automatic summarisers against each other on this evaluation corpus. Our summariser (O) runs the KvD memory cycles and uses lexical chains to determine argument overlap. It is not directly comparable to FT14 due to the difference in generation method, described in §2. In order to be able to compare to FT14 nevertheless, we created a version that uses our new sentence extraction module together with an argument over-

---

[1]Following Silber and McCoy (2002), we create an additional chain for each named entity, in addition to those chains defined by WordNet synsets.

[2]Max number of summaries per person 31, min number 2. The summaries are available for download at http://www.cl.cam.ac.uk/~sht25.

	O	D	C	M	LR	TR	L
1	**.376**	.349	.351	.343	.341	.343	.341
2	**.122**	.094	.088	.092	.100	.094	.100
L	**.345**	.320	.318	.308	.314	.309	.314
SU4	**.154**	.131	.129	.128	.132	.130	.132

Table 2: ROUGE F-scores by four metrics.

lap module very similar to FT14 but with an even stronger model for semantic similarity, the cosine similarity of word embeddings pre-trained using word2vec (Mikolov et al., 2013) on part of the Google News dataset (~ 100 billion words), and we call this system D.

Another variant, C, tests the hypothesis that the recurrent KvD processing is not superior than simpler network analysis. Summariser C constructs only one graph, where every two propositions are connected by an edge whose length is the reciprocal of their argument overlap, and uses betweenness centrality to determine proposition importance. We choose betweenness centrality because we found it to outperform other graph algorithms, including closeness centrality and eigenvector centrality.

We also test against the lead baseline (L) and three well-known lexical similarity-based single document summarisers: MEAD (Radev et al., 2004, M), TextRank (Mihalcea and Tarau, 2004, TR), and LexRank (Erkan and Radev, 2004, LR).

Because the evaluation tool we use is sensitive to text length, fair evaluation demands equal length of all summaries tested. We obtain output of exactly 100 ± 2 words from each summariser by iteratively requesting longer summaries, and unless this results in a sentence break within 2 tokens of the 100-word limit, we cut the immediately longer output to exactly 100 words.

6.2 Results

For automated evaluation, we use ROUGE (Lin, 2004), which evaluates a summary by comparing it against several gold standard summaries. Table 2 shows our results in terms of ROUGE-1, 2, L and SU4.[3] The metrics are based on the co-occurrence of unigrams, bigrams, longest common subsequences, and skip-bigrams (within distance of 4 and including unigrams), respectively. Our summariser outperforms all other summarisers,[4] and is the only summariser that beats the lead baseline.

The fact that our summariser beats D, our KvD summariser using FT14-style distributional semantics for argument overlap, is clear evidence that our method of lexical chaining provides a superior model of argument overlap. On this genre, D performs indistinguishably from the other summarisers. This is in line with our earlier findings for FT14 on DUC (Over and Liggett, 2002) news texts, where the token extraction-based summariser was comparable to extractive summarisers but was outperformed by MEAD. In a qualitative analysis, we found that a main source of error in FT14's system was that it favoured related but semantically and pragmatically incompatible terms over compatible paraphrases. This is a side-effect of the use of co-occurrence, which relies on syntagmatic rather than paradigmatic similarities, and which is insensitive to word senses. As a result, context unaware distributional semantics allows too many spurious overlaps.

The fact that summariser C is significantly worse than our summariser shows that the idea of incrementally maintaining a KvD-style structured memory is effective for summarisation, despite the simplifications we had to make. This naturally points to the direction of modelling incremental memory updates for summarisation, which also makes modelling with a recurrent neural network plausible in the future.

The current experiment can be seen as a demonstration of the superiority of KvD proposition-based *content selection* on a genre of commonsense, naturally occurring texts. This was the case even with a inferior "generation" method, namely sentence extraction. Reading through the propositions, we had the impression that they manage to capture relevant information about the text in a much shorter and more modular form than extracted sentences, although this cannot be demonstrated with a surface-based methodology such as ROUGE. Content selection is of course only the first step of summarisation; we are currently working on a grammar-based re-generation from the selected propositions.

Acknowledgments

The CSC Cambridge International Scholarship for the first author is gratefully acknowledged.

---

[3]The scores of L and LR are very close, but not identical.

[4]We use the paired Wilcoxon test (two-tailed). Differences between O and each other summariser at $p < 0.01$. All differences between all summarisers other than O are insignificant ($p > 0.05$).

References

Regina Barzilay and Michael Elhadad. 1997. Using lexical chains for text summarization. *Proceedings of the ACL Workshop on Intelligent Scalable Text Summarization.*

British Council, IDP Education Australia, and University of Cambridge Local Examinations Syndicate. 2012. *Official IELTS Practice Materials Volume 1. Paperback with CD.* Klett Ernst /Schulbuch.

Asli Celikyilmaz and Dilek Hakkani-Tür. 2011. Discovery of topically coherent sentences for extractive summarization. In *Proceedings of the 49th Annual Meeting of the Association for Computational Linguistics: Human Language Technologies-Volume 1,* pages 491–499. Association for Computational Linguistics.

Trevor Cohn and Mirella Lapata. 2008. Sentence compression beyond word deletion. In *Proceedings of the 22nd International Conference on Computational Linguistics-Volume 1,* pages 137–144. Association for Computational Linguistics.

Gonenc Ercan and Ilyas Cicekli. 2008. Lexical cohesion based topic modeling for summarization. In *Computational Linguistics and Intelligent Text Processing,* pages 582–592. Springer.

Günes Erkan and Dragomir R Radev. 2004. Lexrank: Graph-based lexical centrality as salience in text summarization. *Journal of Artificial Intelligence Research,* pages 457–479.

Yimai Fang and Simone Teufel. 2014. A summariser based on human memory limitations and lexical competition. *EACL 2014,* page 732.

Michel Galley and Kathleen McKeown. 2003. Improving Word Sense Disambiguation in Lexical Chaining. In *IJCAI,* pages 1486–1488.

Lorraine R Gay, Geoffrey E Mills, and Peter W Airasian. 1976. *Educational research: Competencies for analysis and application.* Merrill Columbus, OH.

Udo Hahn and Ulrich Reimer. 1984. Computing text constituency: An algorithmic approach to the generation of text graphs. In *Proceedings of the 7th Annual International ACM SIGIR Conference on Research and Development in Information Retrieval,* SIGIR '84, pages 343–368, Swinton, UK. British Computer Society.

Walter Kintsch and Teun A. van Dijk. 1978. Toward a model of text comprehension and production. *Psychological review,* 85(5):363–394.

Walter Kintsch. 1998. *Comprehension: A paradigm for cognition.* Cambridge university press.

Kevin Knight and Daniel Marcu. 2000. Statistics-based summarization-step one: Sentence compression. In *AAAI/IAAI,* pages 703–710.

Jean Lave. 1988. *Cognition in practice: Mind, mathematics and culture in everyday life.* Cambridge University Press.

Wendy G Lehnert. 1981. Plot units and narrative summarization. *Cognitive Science,* 5(4):293–331.

Chin-Yew Lin and Eduard Hovy. 2003. The potential and limitations of automatic sentence extraction for summarization. In *Proceedings of the HLT-NAACL 03 on Text summarization workshop-Volume 5,* pages 73–80. Association for Computational Linguistics.

Chin-Yew Lin. 2004. ROUGE: A package for automatic evaluation of summaries. In *Text Summarization Branches Out: Proceedings of the ACL-04 Workshop,* pages 74–81.

Kathleen McKeown and Dragomir R Radev. 1995. Generating summaries of multiple news articles. In *Proceedings of the 18th annual international ACM SIGIR conference on Research and development in information retrieval,* pages 74–82. ACM.

Rada Mihalcea and Paul Tarau. 2004. Textrank: Bringing order into texts. In *EMNLP 2004.* Association for Computational Linguistics.

Tomas Mikolov, Kai Chen, Greg Corrado, and Jeffrey Dean. 2013. Efficient estimation of word representations in vector space. *arXiv preprint arXiv:1301.3781.*

George A Miller. 1995. WordNet: a lexical database for English. *Communications of the ACM,* 38(11):39–41.

Marie-Francine Moens, Roxana Angheluta, and Rik De Busser. 2003. Summarization of texts found on the world wide web. In *Knowledge-Based Information Retrieval and Filtering from the Web,* pages 101–120. Springer.

Paul Over and W Liggett. 2002. Introduction to duc: an intrinsic evaluation of generic news text summarization systems. *Proc. DUC. http://wwwnlpir. nist. gov/projects/duc/guidelines/2002. html.*

Allan Paivio. 1990. *Mental representations.* Oxford University Press.

Dragomir Radev, Timothy Allison, Sasha Blair-Goldensohn, John Blitzer, Arda Celebi, Stanko Dimitrov, Elliott Drabek, Ali Hakim, Wai Lam, Danyu Liu, et al. 2004. MEAD – a platform for multidocument multilingual text summarization. In *Proceedings of LREC.*

H. Gregory Silber and Kathleen F. McCoy. 2002. Efficiently Computed Lexical Chains as an Intermediate Representation for Automatic Text Summarization. *Computational Linguistics,* 28(4):487–496, December.

Caroline Uyttendaele, Marie-Francine Moens, and Jos Dumortier. 1998. Salomon: automatic abstracting of legal cases for effective access to court decisions. *Artificial Intelligence and Law*, 6(1):59–79.

Ralph Weischedel, Sameer Pradhan, Lance Ramshaw, Michelle Franchini, Mohammed El-bachouti, Martha Palmer, Mitchell Marcus, Ann Taylor, Craig Greenberg, Eduard Hovy, Robert Belvin, and Ann Houston. 2007. Co-reference Guidelines for English OntoNotes. Technical report, Linguistic Data Consortium.

Kam-Fai Wong, Mingli Wu, and Wenjie Li. 2008. Extractive summarization using supervised and semi-supervised learning. In *Proceedings of the 22nd International Conference on Computational Linguistics-Volume 1*, pages 985–992. Association for Computational Linguistics.

Renxian Zhang, Wenjie Li, Naishi Liu, and Dehong Gao. 2016. Coherent narrative summarization with a cognitive model. *Computer Speech & Language*, 35:134–160.

Machine Comprehension using Rich Semantic Representations

Mrinmaya Sachan   **Eric P. Xing**
School of Computer Science
Carnegie Mellon University
{mrinmays, epxing}@cs.cmu.edu

Abstract

Machine comprehension tests the system's ability to understand a piece of text through a reading comprehension task. For this task, we propose an approach using the Abstract Meaning Representation (AMR) formalism. We construct meaning representation graphs for the given text and for each question-answer pair by merging the AMRs of comprising sentences using cross-sentential phenomena such as coreference and rhetorical structures. Then, we reduce machine comprehension to a graph containment problem. We posit that there is a latent mapping of the question-answer meaning representation graph onto the text meaning representation graph that explains the answer. We present a unified max-margin framework that learns to find this mapping (given a corpus of texts and question-answer pairs), and uses what it learns to answer questions on novel texts. We show that this approach leads to state of the art results on the task.

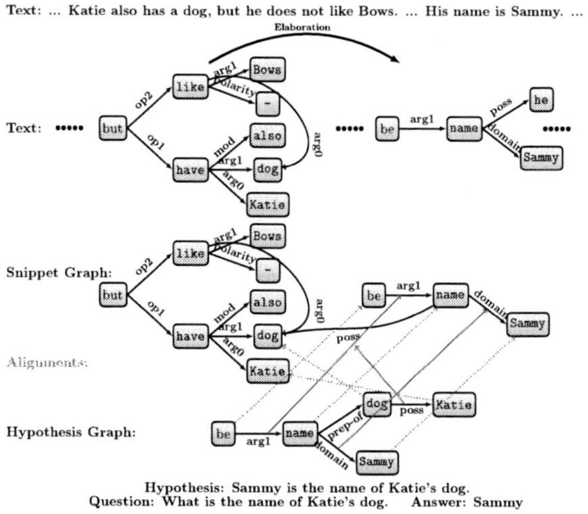

1   Introduction

Learning to efficiently represent and reason with natural language is a fundamental yet long-standing goal in NLP. This has led to a series of efforts in broad-coverage semantic representation (or "sembanking"). Recently, AMR, a new semantic representation in standard neo-Davidsonian (Davidson, 1969; Parsons, 1990) framework has been proposed. AMRs are rooted, labeled graphs which incorporate PropBank style semantic roles, within-sentence coreference, named entities and the notion of types, modality, negation, quantification, etc. in one framework.

In this paper, we describe an approach to use

Hypothesis: Sammy is the name of Katie's dog.
Question: What is the name of Katie's dog.   Answer: Sammy

Figure 1: Example latent *answer-entailing* structure from the MCTest dataset. The question and answer candidate are combined to generate a hypothesis. This hypothesis is AMR parsed to construct a hypothesis meaning representation graph after some post-processing (§ 2.1). Similar processing is done for each sentence in the passage as well. Then, a subset (not necessarily contiguous) of these sentence meaning representation graphs is found. These representation subgraphs are further merged using coreference information, resulting into a structure called the relevant text snippet graph. Finally, the hypothesis meaning representation graph is aligned to the snippet graph. The dashed red lines show node alignments, solid red lines show edge alignments, and thick solid black arrow shows the rhetorical structure label (elaboration).

AMR for the task of machine comprehension. Machine comprehension (Richardson et al., 2013) evaluates a machine's *understanding* by posing a series of multiple choice reading comprehension tests. The tests are unique as the answer to each question can be found only in its associated texts, requiring us to go beyond simple lexical solutions. Our approach models machine comprehension as an extension to textual entailment, learning to output an answer that is best *entailed* by the passage. It works in two stages. First, we construct a meaning representation graph for the entire passage (§ 2.1) from the AMR graphs of comprising sentences. To do this, we account for cross-sentence linguistic phenomena such as entity and

Proceedings of the 54th Annual Meeting of the Association for Computational Linguistics, pages 486–492,
Berlin, Germany, August 7-12, 2016. ©2016 Association for Computational Linguistics

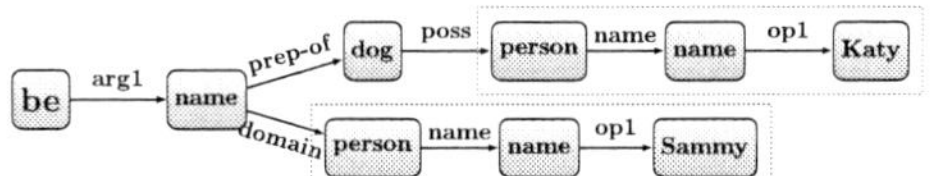

Figure 2: The AMR parse for the hypothesis in Figure 1. The person nodes are merged to achieve the hypothesis meaning representation graph.

event coreference, and rhetorical structures. A similar meaning representation graph is also constructed for each question-answer pair. Once we have these graphs, the comprehension task henceforth can be reduced to a graph containment problem. We posit that there is a latent subgraph of the text meaning representation graph (called snippet graph) and a latent alignment of the question-answer graph onto this snippet graph that *entails* the answer (see Figure 1 for an example). Then, we propose a unified max-margin approach (§ 2.2) that jointly learns the latent structure (subgraph selection and alignment) and the QA model. We evaluate our approach on the MCTest dataset and achieve competitive or better results than a number of previous proposals for this task.

2 The Approach

2.1 The Meaning Representation Graphs

We construct the meaning representation graph using individual sentences AMR graphs and merging identical concepts (using entity and event coreference). First, for each sentence AMR, we merge nodes corresponding to multi-word expressions and nodes headed by a date entity ("date-entity"), or a named entity ("name") or a person entity ("person"). For example, the hypothesis meaning representation graph in Figure 1 was achieved by merging the AMR parse shown in Figure 2.

Next, we select the subset of sentence AMRs corresponding to sentences needed to answer the question. This step uses cross-sentential phenomena such as rhetorical structures[1] and entities/event coreference. The coreferent entities/event mentions are further merged into one node resulting in a graph called the relevant text snippet graph. A similar process is also per-

formed with the hypothesis sentences (generated by combining the question and answer candidate) as shown in Figure 1.

2.2 Max-Margin Solution

For each question $q_i \in Q$, let $\mathbf{t}_i$ be the corresponding passage text and $A_i = \{a_{i1}, \ldots, a_{im}\}$ be the set of candidate answers to the question. Our solution casts the machine comprehension task as a textual entailment task by converting each question-answer candidate pair (q_i, a_{ij}) into a hypothesis statement h_{ij}. We use the question matching/rewriting rules described in Cucerzan and Agichtein (2005) to get the hypothesis statements. For each question q_i, the machine comprehension task reduces to picking the hypothesis $\hat{h}_i$ that has the highest likelihood of being entailed by the text $\mathbf{t}_i$ among the set of hypotheses $\mathbf{h}_i = \{h_{i1}, \ldots, h_{im}\}$ generated for the question q_i. Let $h_i^* \in \mathbf{h}_i$ be the hypothesis corresponding to the correct answer.

As described, we use subgraph matching to help us model the inference. We assume that the selection of sentences to generate the relevant text snippet graph and the mapping of the hypothesis meaning representation graph onto the passage meaning representation graph is latent and infer it jointly along with the answer. We treat it as a structured prediction problem of ranking the hypothesis set $\mathbf{h}_i$ such that the correct hypothesis h_i^* is at the top of this ranking. We learn a scoring function $S_{\mathbf{w}}(\mathbf{t}, h, \mathbf{z})$ with parameter $\mathbf{w}$ such that the score of the correct hypothesis h_i^* and corresponding best latent structure $\mathbf{z}_i^*$ is higher than the score of the other hypotheses and corresponding best latent structures. In a max-margin fashion, we want that $S_{\mathbf{w}}(\mathbf{t}_i, h_i^*, \mathbf{z}_i^*) > S(\mathbf{t}_i, h_{ij}, \mathbf{z}_{ij}) + 1 - \xi_i$ for all $h_j \in \mathbf{h} \setminus h^*$ for some slack ξ_i. Writing the relaxed max margin formulation:

$$\min_{\|\mathbf{w}\|} \frac{1}{2}\|\mathbf{w}\|_2^2 + C \sum_i \max_{\mathbf{z}_{ij}, h_{ij} \in \mathbf{h}_i \setminus h_i^*} S_{\mathbf{w}}(\mathbf{t}_i, h_{ij}, \mathbf{z}_{ij}) + \Delta(h_i^*, h_{ij})$$
$$- C \sum_i S_{\mathbf{w}}(\mathbf{t}_i, h_i^*, \mathbf{z}_i^*) \qquad (1)$$

We use 0-1 cost, i.e. $\Delta(h_i^*, h_{ij}) = \mathbb{1}(h_i^* \neq h_{ij})$. If the scoring function is convex then this objective is in concave-convex form and hence can be solved by the concave-convex programming procedure (CCCP) (Yuille and Rangarajan, 2003). We assume the scoring function to be linear: $S_{\mathbf{w}}(\mathbf{t}, h, \mathbf{z}) = \mathbf{w}^T \psi(\mathbf{t}, h, \mathbf{z})$. Here,

---

[1] Rhetorical structure theory (Mann and Thompson, 1988) tells us that sentences with discourse relations are related to each other. Previous works in QA (Jansen et al., 2014) have shown that these relations can help us answer certain kinds of questions. As an example, the "cause" relation between sentences in the text can often give cues that can help us answer "why" or "how" questions. Hence, the passage meaning representation also remembers RST relations between sentences.

$\psi(\mathbf{t}, h, \mathbf{z})$ is a feature map discussed later. The CCCP algorithm essentially alternates between solving for $\mathbf{z}_i^*$, $\mathbf{z}_{ij}$ $\forall j$ s.t. $h_{ij} \in \mathbf{h}_i \setminus h_i^*$ and $\mathbf{w}$ to achieve a local minima. In the absence of information regarding the latent structure $\mathbf{z}$ we pick the structure that gives the best score for a given hypothesis i.e. $\arg\max_z S_{\mathbf{w}}(\mathbf{t}, h, z)$.

2.3 Scoring Function and Inference

Now, we define the scoring function $S_{\mathbf{w}}(\mathbf{t}, h, \mathbf{z})$. Let the hypothesis meaning representation graph be $G' = (V', E')$. Our latent structure $\mathbf{z}$ decomposes into the selection ($\mathbf{z}_s$) of relevant sentences that lead to the text snippet graph G, and the mapping ($\mathbf{z}_m$) of every node and edge in G' onto G. We define the score such that it factorizes over the nodes and edges in G'. The weight vector $\mathbf{w}$ also has three components $\mathbf{w}_s$, $\mathbf{w}_v$ and $\mathbf{w}_e$ corresponding to the relevant sentences selection, node matches and edge matches respectively. An edge in the graph is represented as a triple (v^1, r, v^2) consisting of the enpoint vertices and relation r.

$$S_{\mathbf{w}}(\mathbf{t}, h, \mathbf{z}) = \mathbf{w}_s^T \mathbf{f}(G', G, \mathbf{t}, h, \mathbf{z}_s)$$
$$+ \sum_{v' \in V'} \mathbf{w}_v^T \mathbf{f}(v', z_m(v')) + \sum_{e' \in E'} \mathbf{w}_e^T \mathbf{f}(e', z_m(e'))$$

Here, $\mathbf{t}$ is the text corresponding to the hypothesis h, and $\mathbf{f}$ are parts of the feature map ψ to be described later. $z(v')$ maps a node $v' \in V'$ to a node in V. Similarly, $z(e')$ maps an edge $e' \in E'$ to an edge in E.

Next, we describe the inference procedure i.e. how to select the structure that gives the best score for a given hypothesis. The inference is performed in two steps: The first step selects the relevant sentences from the text. This is done by simply maximizing the first part of the score: $\mathbf{z}_s = \arg\max_{\mathbf{z}_s} \mathbf{w}_s^T \mathbf{f}(G', G, \mathbf{t}, h, \mathbf{z}_s)$. Here, we only consider subsets of 1, 2 and 3 sentences as most questions can be answered by 3 sentences in the passage. The second step is formulated as an integer linear program by rewriting the scoring function. The ILP objective is:

$$\sum_{v' \in V'} \sum_{v \in V} z_{v',v} \mathbf{w}_v^T \mathbf{f}(v', v) + \sum_{e' \in E'} \sum_{e \in E} z_{e',e} \mathbf{w}_e^T \mathbf{f}(e', e)$$

Here, with some abuse of notation, $z_{v',v}$ and $z_{e',e}$ are binary integers such that $z_{v',v} = 1$ iff $\mathbf{z}$ maps v' onto v else $z_{v',v} = 0$. Similarly, $z_{e',e} = 1$ iff $\mathbf{z}$ maps e' onto e else $z_{e',e} = 0$. Additionally, we have the following constrains to our ILP:

- Each node $v' \in V'$ (or each edge $e' \in E'$) is mapped to exactly one node $v \in V$ (or one edge $e \in E$). Hence: $\sum_{v \in V} z_{v',v} = 1$ $\forall v'$ and $\sum_{e \in E} z_{e',e} = 1$ $\forall e'$

- If an edge $e' \in E'$ is mapped to an edge $e \in E$, then vertices $(v_{e'}^1, v_{e'}^2)$ that form the end points of e' must also be aligned to vertices (v_e^1, v_e^2) that form the end points of e. Here, we note that AMR parses also have inverse relations such as "arg0-of". Hence, we resolve this with a slight modification. If neither or both relations (corresponding to edges e' and e) are inverse relations (case 1), we enforce that $v_{e'}^1$ align with v_e^1 and $v_{e'}^2$ align with v_e^2. If exactly one of the relations is an inverse relation (case 2), we enforce that $v_{e'}^1$ align with v_e^2 and $v_{e'}^2$ align with v_e^1. Hence, we introduce the following constraints:

$$z_{e'e} \leq z_{v_{e'}^1, v_e^1} \text{ and } z_{e'e} \leq z_{v_{e'}^2, v_e^2} \quad \forall e'.e \text{ in case 1}$$
$$z_{e'e} \leq z_{v_{e'}^1, v_e^2} \text{ and } z_{e'e} \leq z_{v_{e'}^2, v_e^1} \quad \forall e'.e \text{ in case 2}$$

2.4 Features

Our feature function $\psi(\mathbf{t}, h, \mathbf{z})$ decomposes into three parts, each corresponding to a part of the latent structure.

The first part corresponds to relevant sentence selection. Here, we include features for matching local neighborhoods in the sentence subset and the hypothesis: features for matching bigrams, trigrams, dependencies, semantic roles, predicate-argument structure as well as the global syntactic structure: a graph kernel for matching AMR graphs of entire sentences (Srivastava and Hovy, 2013). Before computing the graph kernel, we reverse all inverse relation edges in the AMR graph. Note that if a sentence subset contains the answer to the question, it should intuitively be similar to the question as well as to the answer. Hence, we add features that are the element-wise product of features for the subset-question match and subset-answer match. In addition to features for the exact word/phrase match of the snippet and the hypothesis, we also add features using two paraphrase databases: ParaPara (Chan et al., 2011) and DIRT (Lin and Pantel, 2001). These databases contain paraphrase rules of the form $string_1 \rightarrow string_2$. ParaPara rules were extracted through bilingual pivoting and DIRT rules were extracted using the distributional hypothesis. Whenever we have a substring in the text snippet that can be transformed into another using any of these two databases, we keep match features for the substring with a higher score (according to the current $\mathbf{w}$) and ignore the other substring. Finally, we also have features corresponding to the RST (Mann and Thompson, 1988) links to enable inference across sentences. RST tells us that sentences with discourse relations are related to each other and can help us answer certain kinds of questions (Jansen et al., 2014). For example, the "cause" relation between sentences in the text can often give cues that can help us answer "why" or "how" questions. Hence, we have additional features - conjunction of the rhetorical structure label from a RST parser and the question word as well.

The second part corresponds to node matches. Here, we have features for (a) Surface-form match (Edit-distance), and (b) Semantic word match (cosine similarity using SENNA word vectors (Collobert et al., 2011) and "Antonymy" 'Class-Inclusion' or 'Is-A' relations using Wordnet).

The third part corresponds to edge matches. Let the edges be $e = (v^1, r, v^2)$ and $e' = (v'^1, r', v'^2)$ for notational convenience. Here, we introduce two features based on the relations - indicator that the two relations are the same or inverse of each other, indicator that the two relations are in the same relation category – categories as described in Banarescu et al. (2013). Then, we introduce a number of features based on distributional representation of the node pairs. We compute three vertex vector compositions (sum, difference and product) of the nodes for each edge proposed in recent representation learning literature in NLP (Mitchell and Lapata, 2008; Mikolov et al., 2013) i.e. $v^1 \odot v^2$ and $v'^1 \odot v'^2$ for $\odot = \{+, -, \times\}$. Then, we compute the cosine similarities of the resulting compositions producing three features. Finally we introduce features based on the structured distributional semantic representation (Erk and Padó, 2008; Baroni and Lenci, 2010; Goyal et al., 2013) which takes the relations into account while performing the composition. Here, we use a large text corpora (in our experiments, the English Wikipedia) and construct a representation matrix $M^{(r)} \subset V \times V$ for every relation r (V is the vocabulary) where, the ij^{th} element $M_{ij}^{(r)}$ has the value $\log(1+x)$ where x is the frequency for the ith and j^{th} vocabulary items being in relation r in the corpora. This allows us to compose the node and relation representations and compare them. Here we compute the cosine similarity of the compositions $(v^1)^T M^{(r)}$ and $(v'^1)^T M^{(r')}$, the compositions $M^{(r)} v^2$ and $M^{(r')} v'^2$ and their repective sums $(v^1)^T M^{(r)} + M^{(r)} v^2$ and $(v'^1)^T M^{(r')} + M^{(r')} v'^2$ to get three more features.

2.5 Negation and Multi-task Learning

Next, we borrow two ideas from Sachan et al. (2015) namely, negation and multi-task learning, treating different question types in the machine comprehension setup as different tasks.

Handling negation is important for our model as facts align well with their negated versions. We use a simple heuristic. During training, if we detect negation (using a set of simple rules that test for presence of negation words ("not", "n't", etc.)), we flip the corresponding constraint, now requiring that the correct hypothesis to be ranked below all the incorrect ones. During test phase if we detect negation, we predict the answer corresponding to the hypothesis with the lowest score.

QA systems often include a question classification component that divides the questions into semantic categories based on the type of the question or answers expected. This allows the model to learn question type specific parameters when needed. We experiment with three task classifications proposed by Sachan et al. (2015). First is QClassification, which classifies the question, based on the question word (what, why, what, etc.). Next is the QAClassification scheme, which classifies questions into different semantic classes based on the possible semantic types of the answers sought. The third scheme, TaskClassification classifies the questions into one of 20 subtasks for Machine Comprehension proposed in Weston et al. (2015). We point the reader to Sachan et al. (2015) for details on the multi-task model.

3 Experiments

Datasets: We use MCTest-500 dataset (Richardson et al., 2013), a freely available set of 500 stories (300 train, 50 dev and 150 test) and associated questions to evaluate our model. Each story in MCTest has four multiple-choice questions, each with four answer choices. Each question has exactly one correct answer. Each question is also annotated as 'single' or 'multiple'. The questions annotated 'single' require just one sentence in the passage to answer them. For 'multiple' questions it should not be possible to find the answer to the question with just one sentence of the passage. In a sense, 'multiple' questions are harder than 'single' questions as they require more complex inference. We will present the results breakdown for 'single' or 'multiple' category questions as well.

Baselines: We compare our approach to the following baselines: (1-3) The first three baselines are taken from Richardson et al. (2013). *SW* and *SW+D* use a sliding window and match a bag of words constructed from the question and the candidate answer to the text. *RTE* uses textual entailment by selecting the hypothesis that has the highest likelihood of being entailed by the passage. (4) *LEX++*, taken from Smith et al. (2015) is another lexical matching method that takes into account multiple context windows, question types and coreference. (5) *JACANA* uses an off the shelf aligner and aligns the hypothesis statement with the passage. (6-7) *LSTM* and *QANTA*, taken from Sachan et al. (2015), use neural networks (LTSMs and Recursive NNs, respectively). (8) *ATTENTION*, taken from Yin et al. (2016), uses an attention-based convolutional neural network. (9) *DISCOURSE*, taken from Narasimhan and Barzilay (2015), proposes a discourse based model. (10-14) *LSSVM*, *LSSVM+Negation*, *LSSVM+Negation (MultiTask)*, taken from Sachan et al. (2015) are all discourse aware latent structural svm models. *LSSVM+Negation* accounts for negation. *LSSVM+Negation+MTL* further incoporates multi-task learning based on question types. Here, we have three variants of multitask learners based on the three question classification strategies. (15) Finally, *SYN+FRM+SEM*, taken from Wang et al. (2015) proposes a framework with features based on syntax, frame semantics, coreference and word embeddings.

Results: We compare our AMR subgraph containment approach[2] where we consider our modifications for negation and multi-task learning as well in Table 1. We can observe that our models have a comparable performance to all the baselines including the neural network approaches and all previous approaches proposed for this task. Further, when we incorporate multi-task learning, our approach achieves the state of the art. Also, our approaches have a considerable improvement over the baselines for 'multiple' questions. This shows

---

[2]We tune the SVM parameter C on the dev set. We use Stanford CoreNLP, HILDA parser (Feng and Hirst, 2014) and JAMR (Flanigan et al., 2014) for preprocessing.

			Single	Multiple	All
AMR		Subgraph	67.28	65.24	66.16
		Subgraph+Negation	69.48	66.46	67.83
	+MTL	QClassification	70.59	67.99	69.17
		QAClassification	71.32	68.29	69.67
		TaskClassification	**72.05**	**68.90**	**70.33**
Baselines		SW	54.56	54.04	54.28
		SW+D	62.99	58.00	60.26
		RTE	69.85	42.71	55.01
		LEX++	69.12	63.34	65.96
		JACANA Aligner	58.82	54.88	56.67
		LSTM	62.13	58.84	60.33
		QANTA	63.23	59.45	61.00
		ATTENTION	54.20	51.70	52.90
		DISCOURSE	68.38	59.90	63.75
		LSSVM	61.12	66.67	64.15
		LSSVM+Negation	63.24	66.15	64.83
	+MTL	QClassification	64.34	66.46	65.50
		QAClassification	66.18	67.37	66.83
		TaskClassification	67.65	67.99	67.83
		SYN+FRM+SEM	72.05	67.94	69.94

Table 1: Comparison of variations of our method against several baselines on the MCTest-500 dataset. The table shows accuracy on the test set of MCTest-500. All differences between the baselines (except *SYN+FRM+SEM*) and our approaches, and the improvements due to negation and multi-task learning are significant ($p < 0.05$) using the two-tailed paired T-test.

the benefit of our latent structure that allows us to combine evidence from multiple sentences. The negation heuristic helps significantly, especially for 'single' questions (majority of negation cases in the *MCTest* dataset are for the "single" questions). The multi-task method which performs a classification based on the subtasks for machine comprehension defined in Weston et al. (2015) does better than QAClassification that learns the question answer classification. QAClassification in turn performs better than QClassification that learns the question classification only.

These results, together, provide validation for our approach of subgraph matching over meaning representation graphs, and the incorporation of negation and multi-task learning.

4 Conclusion

We proposed a solution for reading comprehension tests using AMR. Our solution builds intermediate meaning representations for passage and question-answers. Then it poses the comprehension task as a subgraph matching task by learning latent alignments from one meaning representation to another. Our approach achieves competitive or better performance than other approaches proposed for this task. Incorporation of negation and multi-task learning leads to further improvements establishing it as the new state-of-the-art.

References

[Banarescu et al.2013] Laura Banarescu, Claire Bonial, Shu Cai, Madalina Georgescu, Kira Griffitt, Ulf Hermjakob, Kevin Knight, Philipp Koehn, Martha Palmer, and Nathan Schneider. 2013. Abstract meaning representation for sembanking. In *Proceedings of the 7th Linguistic Annotation Workshop and Interoperability with Discourse*, pages 178–186, Sofia, Bulgaria, August. Association for Computational Linguistics.

[Baroni and Lenci2010] Marco Baroni and Alessandro Lenci. 2010. Distributional memory: A general framework for corpus-based semantics. *Computational Linguistics*, 36(4):673–721.

[Chan et al.2011] Tsz Ping Chan, Chris Callison-Burch, and Benjamin Van Durme. 2011. Reranking bilingually extracted paraphrases using monolingual distributional similarity. In *Proceedings of the GEMS 2011 Workshop on GEometrical Models of Natural Language Semantics*, pages 33–42.

[Collobert et al.2011] Ronan Collobert, Jason Weston, Léon Bottou, Michael Karlen, Koray Kavukcuoglu, and Pavel Kuksa. 2011. Natural language processing (almost) from scratch. *The Journal of Machine Learning Research*, 12:2493–2537.

[Cucerzan and Agichtein2005] S. Cucerzan and E. Agichtein. 2005. Factoid question answering over unstructured and structured content on the web. In *Proceedings of TREC 2005*.

[Davidson1969] Donald Davidson. 1969. *The individuation of events*. Springer.

[Erk and Padó2008] Katrin Erk and Sebastian Padó. 2008. A structured vector space model for word meaning in context. In *Proceedings of the Conference on Empirical Methods in Natural Language Processing*, EMNLP '08, pages 897–906, Stroudsburg, PA, USA. Association for Computational Linguistics.

[Feng and Hirst2014] Vanessa Wei Feng and Graeme Hirst. 2014. A linear-time bottom-up discourse parser with constraints and post-editing. In *Proceedings of the 52nd Annual Meeting of the Association for Computational Linguistics (Volume 1: Long Papers)*, pages 511–521.

[Flanigan et al.2014] Jeffrey Flanigan, Sam Thomson, Jaime G. Carbonell, Chris Dyer, and Noah A. Smith. 2014. A discriminative graph-based parser for the abstract meaning representation. In *Proceedings of the 52nd Annual Meeting of the Association for Computational Linguistics, ACL 2014, June 22-27, 2014, Baltimore, MD, USA, Volume 1: Long Papers*, pages 1426–1436.

[Goyal et al.2013] Kartik Goyal, Sujay Kumar Jauhar, Huiying Li, Mrinmaya Sachan, Shashank Srivastava, and Eduard H. Hovy. 2013. A structured distributional semantic model for event co-reference.

In *Proceedings of the 51st Annual Meeting of the Association for Computational Linguistics, ACL 2013, 4-9 August 2013, Sofia, Bulgaria, Volume 2: Short Papers*, pages 467–473.

[Jansen et al.2014] Peter Jansen, Mihai Surdeanu, and Peter Clark. 2014. Discourse complements lexical semantics for non-factoid answer reranking. In *Proceedings of the 52nd Annual Meeting of the Association for Computational Linguistics (Volume 1: Long Papers)*, pages 977–986.

[Lin and Pantel2001] Dekang Lin and Patrick Pantel. 2001. Dirt@ sbt@ discovery of inference rules from text. In *Proceedings of the seventh ACM SIGKDD international conference on Knowledge discovery and data mining*, pages 323–328.

[Mann and Thompson1988] William C Mann and Sandra A Thompson. 1988. {Rhetorical Structure Theory: Toward a functional theory of text organisation}. *Text*, 3(8):234–281.

[Mikolov et al.2013] Tomas Mikolov, Wen-tau Yih, and Geoffrey Zweig. 2013. Linguistic regularities in continuous space word representations. In *Proceedings of the 2013 Conference of the North American Chapter of the Association for Computational Linguistics: Human Language Technologies*, pages 746–751, Atlanta, Georgia, June. Association for Computational Linguistics.

[Mitchell and Lapata2008] Jeff Mitchell and Mirella Lapata. 2008. Vector-based models of semantic composition. In *ACL 2008, Proceedings of the 46th Annual Meeting of the Association for Computational Linguistics, June 15-20, 2008, Columbus, Ohio, USA*, pages 236–244.

[Narasimhan and Barzilay2015] Karthik Narasimhan and Regina Barzilay. 2015. Machine comprehension with discourse relations. In *Proceedings of the 53rd Annual Meeting of the Association for Computational Linguistics and the 7th International Joint Conference on Natural Language Processing of the Asian Federation of Natural Language Processing, ACL 2015, July 26-31, 2015, Beijing, China, Volume 1: Long Papers*, pages 1253–1262.

[Parsons1990] Terence Parsons. 1990. *Events in the Semantics of English*, volume 5. In MIT Press.

[Richardson et al.2013] Matthew Richardson, Christopher JC Burges, and Erin Renshaw. 2013. Mctest: A challenge dataset for the open-domain machine comprehension of text. In *Proceedings of Empirical Methods in Natural Language Processing (EMNLP)*.

[Sachan et al.2015] Mrinmaya Sachan, Avinava Dubey, Eric P Xing, and Matthew Richardson. 2015. Learning answer-entailing structures for machine comprehension. In *Proceedings of the Annual Meeting of the Association for Computational Linguistics*.

[Smith et al.2015] Ellery Smith, Nicola Greco, Matko Bosnjak, and Andreas Vlachos. 2015. A strong lexical matching method for the machine comprehension test. In *Proceedings of the 2015 Conference on Empirical Methods in Natural Language Processing, EMNLP 2015, Lisbon, Portugal, September 17-21, 2015*, pages 1693–1698.

[Srivastava and Hovy2013] Shashank Srivastava and Dirk Hovy. 2013. A walk-based semantically enriched tree kernel over distributed word representations. In *Proceedings of Empirical Methods in Natural Language Processing*, pages 1411–1416.

[Wang et al.2015] Hai Wang, Mohit Bansal, Kevin Gimpel, and David A. McAllester. 2015. Machine comprehension with syntax, frames, and semantics. In *Proceedings of the 53rd Annual Meeting of the Association for Computational Linguistics and the 7th International Joint Conference on Natural Language Processing of the Asian Federation of Natural Language Processing, ACL 2015, July 26-31, 2015, Beijing, China, Volume 2: Short Papers*, pages 700–706.

[Weston et al.2015] Jason Weston, Antoine Bordes, Sumit Chopra, and Tomas Mikolov. 2015. Towards ai-complete question answering: A set of prerequisite toy tasks. *arXiv preprint arXiv:1502.05698*.

[Yin et al.2016] Wenpeng Yin, Sebastian Ebert, and Hinrich Schtze. 2016. Attention-based convolutional neural network for machine comprehension. *arXiv preprint arXiv:1602.04341*.

[Yuille and Rangarajan2003] A. L. Yuille and Anand Rangarajan. 2003. The concave-convex procedure. *Neural Comput.*

Cross-Lingual Word Representations via Spectral Graph Embeddings

Takamasa Oshikiri, Kazuki Fukui, Hidetoshi Shimodaira
Division of Mathematical Science, Graduate School of Engineering Science
Osaka University, Japan
1-3 Machikaneyama-cho, Toyonaka, Osaka
{oshikiri, fukui, shimo}@sigmath.es.osaka-u.ac.jp

Abstract

Cross-lingual word embeddings are used for cross-lingual information retrieval or domain adaptations. In this paper, we extend Eigenwords, spectral monolingual word embeddings based on canonical correlation analysis (CCA), to cross-lingual settings with sentence-alignment. For incorporating cross-lingual information, CCA is replaced with its generalization based on the spectral graph embeddings. The proposed method, which we refer to as Cross-Lingual Eigenwords (CL-Eigenwords), is fast and scalable for computing distributed representations of words via eigenvalue decomposition. Numerical experiments of English-Spanish word translation tasks show that CL-Eigenwords is competitive with state-of-the-art cross-lingual word embedding methods.

1 Introduction

There have been many methods proposed for word embeddings. Neural network based models are popular, and one of the most major approaches is the skip-gram model (Mikolov et al., 2013b), and some extended methods have also been developed (Levy and Goldberg, 2014a; Lazaridou et al., 2015). The skip-gram model has many interesting syntactic and semantic properties, and it can be seen as the factorization of a word-context matrix whose elements represent pointwise mutual information (Levy and Goldberg, 2014b). However, word embeddings based on neural networks (without neat implementation) can be very slow in general, and it is sometimes difficult to understand how they work. Recently, a simple spectral method, called Eigenwords, for word embeddings

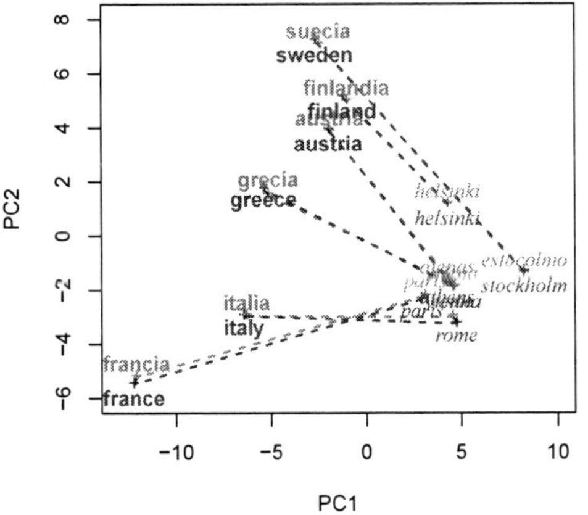

Figure 1: PCA projections (PC1 and PC2) of CL-Eigenwords of countries (bold) and its capitals (italic) in Spanish (red) and English (blue). Word vectors of the two languages match quite well, although they are computed using sentence-level alignment without knowing word-level alignment. 100-dim word representations are used for PCA computation.

is proposed (Dhillon et al., 2012; Dhillon et al., 2015). It is based on canonical correlation analysis (CCA) for computing word vectors by maximizing correlations between words and their contexts. Eigenword algorithms are fast and scalable, yet giving good performance comparable to neural network approaches for capturing the meaning of words from their context.

The skip-gram model, originally proposed for monolingual corpora, has been extended to cross-lingual settings. Given two vector representations of two languages, a linear transformation between the two spaces is trained from a set of word pairs for translation task (Mikolov et al., 2013a), while other researchers use CCA for learning linear projections to a common vector space where

Proceedings of the 54th Annual Meeting of the Association for Computational Linguistics, pages 493–498,
Berlin, Germany, August 7-12, 2016. ©2016 Association for Computational Linguistics

translation pairs are strongly correlated (Faruqui and Dyer, 2014). These methods require word-alignment in the training data, while some multilingual corpora have only coarse information such as a set of sentence pairs or paragraph pairs. Recently, extensions of the skip-gram model requiring only sentence-alignment have been developed by introducing cross-lingual losses in the objective of the original models (Gouws et al., 2015; Coulmance et al., 2015; Shi et al., 2015).

In this paper, instead of the skip-gram model, we extend Eigenwords (Dhillon et al., 2015) to cross-lingual settings with sentence-alignment. Our main idea is to replace CCA, which is applicable to only two different kinds of data, with a generalized method (Nori et al., 2012; Shimodaira, 2016) based on spectral graph embeddings (Yan et al., 2007) so that the Eigenwords can deal with two or more languages for cross-lingual word embeddings. Our proposed method, referred to as Cross-Lingual Eigenwords (CL-Eigenwords), requires only sentence-alignment for capturing cross-lingual relationships. The method is very simple in mathematics as well as computation; it involves a generalized eigenvalue problem, which can be solved by fast and scalable algorithms such as the randomized eigenvalue decomposition (Halko et al., 2011).

Fig. 1 shows an illustrative example of cross-lingual word vectors obtained by CL-Eigenwords. Although only sentence-alignment is available in the corpus, word-level translation is automatically captured in the vector representations; the same words (countries and capitals) in the two languages are placed in close proximity to each other; *greece* is close to *grecia* and *rome* is close to *roma*. In addition, the same kinds of relationships between word pairs share similar directions in the vector space; the direction from *sweden* to *stockholm* is nearly parallel to the direction from *finland* to *helsinki*.

We evaluate the word vectors obtained by our method on the English-Spanish cross-lingual translation task and compare the results with those of state-of-the-art methods, showing that our proposed method is competitive with those existing methods. We use Europarl corpus for learning the vector representation of words. Although the experiments in this paper are conducted using bilingual corpus, our method can be easily applied to three or more languages.

2 Eigenwords (One Step CCA)

CCA (Hotelling, 1936) is a multivariate analysis method for finding optimal projections of two sets of data vectors by maximizing the correlations. Applying CCA to pairs of raw word vector and raw context vector, Eigenword algorithms attempt to find low dimensional vector representations of words (Dhillon et al., 2012). Here we explain the simplest version of Eigenwords called One Step CCA (OSCCA).

We have monolingual corpus consisting of T tokens; $(t_i)_{i=1,\ldots,T}$, and the vocabulary consisting of V word types; $\{v_i\}_{i=1,\ldots,V}$. Each token t_i is drawn from this vocabulary. We define word matrix $\mathbf{V} \in \{0,1\}^{T \times V}$ whose i-th row encodes token t_i by 1-of-V representation; the j-th element is 1 if the word type of t_i is v_j, 0 otherwise.

Let h be the size of context window. We define context matrix $\mathbf{C} \in \{0,1\}^{T \times 2hV}$ whose i-th row represents the surrounding context of token t_i with concatenated 1-of-V encoded vectors of $(t_{i-h}, \ldots, t_{i-1}, t_{i+1}, \ldots, t_{i+h})$.

We apply CCA to T pairs of row vectors of $\mathbf{V}$ and $\mathbf{C}$. The objective function of CCA is constructed using $\mathbf{V}^\top \mathbf{V}$, $\mathbf{V}^\top \mathbf{C}$, $\mathbf{C}^\top \mathbf{C}$ which represent occurrence and co-occurrence counts of words and contexts. In Eigenwords, however, we use $\boldsymbol{\mathcal{C}}_{VV} \in \mathbb{R}_+^{V \times V}$, $\boldsymbol{\mathcal{C}}_{VC} \in \mathbb{R}_+^{V \times 2hV}$, $\boldsymbol{\mathcal{C}}_{CC} \in \mathbb{R}_+^{2hV \times 2hV}$ with the following preprocessing of these matrices before constructing the objective function. First, centering-process of $\mathbf{V}$ and $\mathbf{C}$ is omitted, and off-diagonal elements of $\mathbf{C}^\top \mathbf{C}$ are ignored for simplifying the computation of inverse matrices. Second, we take the square root of the elements of these matrices for "squashing" the heavy-tailed word count distributions. Finally, we obtain vector representations of words as $\boldsymbol{\mathcal{C}}_{VV}^{-1/2}(\boldsymbol{u}_1, \ldots, \boldsymbol{u}_K)$, where $\boldsymbol{u}_1, \ldots, \boldsymbol{u}_K \in \mathbb{R}^V$ are left singular vectors of $\boldsymbol{\mathcal{C}}_{VV}^{-1/2} \boldsymbol{\mathcal{C}}_{VC} \boldsymbol{\mathcal{C}}_{CC}^{-1/2}$ corresponding to the K largest singular values. The computation of SVD is fast and scalable using recent idea of random projections (Halko et al., 2011).

3 Cross-Lingual Eigenwords

In this section, we introduce **Cross-Lingual Eigenwords (CL-Eigenwords)**, a novel method for cross-lingual word embeddings. Suppose that we have parallel corpora that contain L languages. Schematic diagrams of Eigenwords and

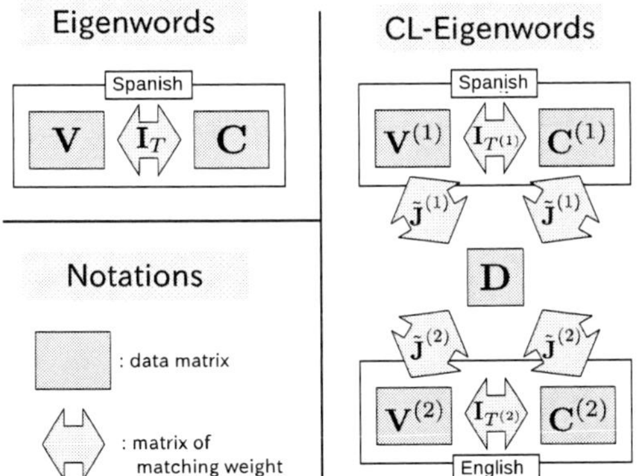

Figure 2: Eigenwords are CCA-based spectral monolingual word embeddings. CL-Eigenwords are CDMCA-based spectral cross-lingual word embeddings, where the two (or more) languages are linked by sentence-alignment.

CL-Eigenwords (with $L = 2$) are shown in Fig. 2.

In the same way as the monolingual Eigenwords, we denote the word matrix and the context matrix for ℓ-th language by $\mathbf{V}^{(\ell)} \in \mathbb{R}_+^{T^{(\ell)} \times V^{(\ell)}}$ and $\mathbf{C}^{(\ell)} \in \mathbb{R}_+^{T^{(\ell)} \times 2h^{(\ell)} V^{(\ell)}}$ respectively, where $V^{(\ell)}$ is the size of vocabulary, $T^{(\ell)}$ is the number of tokens, and $h^{(\ell)}$ is the size of context window. There are D sentences (or paragraphs) in the multilingual corpora, and each token is included in one of the sentences. The sentence-alignment is represented in the matrix $\mathbf{J}^{(\ell)} \in \mathbb{R}_+^{T^{(\ell)} \times D}$ whose (i, j)-element $J_{i,j}^{(\ell)}$ is set to 1 if the i-th token $t_i^{(\ell)}$ of ℓ-th language corpus comes from the j-th sentence or 0 otherwise. We also define document matrix $\mathbf{D}$ whose j-th row encodes j-th sentence by 1-of-D representation; $\mathbf{D} = \mathbf{I}_D$, where $\mathbf{I}_D$ represents D-dimensional identity matrix.

The goal of CL-Eigenwords is to construct vector representations of words of two (or more) languages from multilingual corpora at the same time. This problem is formulated as an example of Cross Domain Matching Correlation Analysis (CDMCA) (Shimodaira, 2016), which deals with many-to-many relationships between data vectors from multiple sources. CDMCA is based on the spectral graph embeddings (Yan et al., 2007), and attempts to find optimal linear projections of data vectors so that associated transformed vectors are placed in close proximity to each other. The strength of association between two vectors is specified by a nonnegative real value called *matching weight*. Since CDMCA includes CCA

and a variant of Latent Semantic Indexing (LSI) (Deerwester et al., 1990) as special cases, CL-Eigenwords can be interpreted as LSI-equipped Eigenwords (See Appendix).

In CL-Eigenwords, the data vectors are given as $v_i^{(\ell)}, c_i^{(\ell)}, d_i$, namely, the i-th row vectors of $\mathbf{V}^{(\ell)}, \mathbf{C}^{(\ell)}, \mathbf{D}$, respectively. The matching weights between row vectors of $\mathbf{V}^{(\ell)}$ and $\mathbf{C}^{(\ell)}$ are specified by the identity matrix $\mathbf{I}_{T^{(\ell)}}$ because the data vectors are in one-to-one correspondence. On the other hand, the matching weights between row vectors of $\mathbf{V}^{(\ell)}$ and $\mathbf{D}$ as well as those between $\mathbf{C}^{(\ell)}$ and $\mathbf{D}$ are specified by $\tilde{\mathbf{J}}^{(\ell)} = b^{(\ell)} \mathbf{J}^{(\ell)}$, the sentence-alignment matrix multiplied by a constant $b^{(\ell)}$. Then we will find linear transformation matrices $\mathbf{A}_V^{(\ell)}, \mathbf{A}_C^{(\ell)}, \mathbf{A}_D, (\ell = 1, 2, \ldots, L)$ to K-dimensional vector space by minimizing the objective function

$$\sum_{\ell=1}^{L} \sum_{i=1}^{T^{(\ell)}} \|v_i^{(\ell)} \mathbf{A}_V^{(\ell)} - c_i^{(\ell)} \mathbf{A}_C^{(\ell)}\|_2^2$$

$$+ \sum_{\ell=1}^{L} \sum_{i=1}^{T^{(\ell)}} \sum_{j=1}^{D} \tilde{J}_{i,j}^{(\ell)} \|v_i^{(\ell)} \mathbf{A}_V^{(\ell)} - d_j \mathbf{A}_D\|_2^2$$

$$+ \sum_{\ell=1}^{L} \sum_{i=1}^{T^{(\ell)}} \sum_{j=1}^{D} \tilde{J}_{i,j}^{(\ell)} \|c_i^{(\ell)} \mathbf{A}_C^{(\ell)} - d_j \mathbf{A}_D\|_2^2 \quad (1)$$

with a scale constraint for projection matrices. Note that the first term in (1) is equivalent to that of CCA between words and contexts, namely the objective of monolingual Eigenwords, and therefore word vectors of two languages are obtained as row vectors of $\mathbf{A}_V^{(\ell)} (\ell = 1, 2, \ldots, L)$.

Hereafter, we assume $L = 2$ for notational simplicity. A generalization to the case $L > 2$ is straightforward: redefine $\mathbf{X}$, $\mathbf{W}$, $\mathbf{A}$ below by repeating the submatrices, such as $\mathbf{V}^{(\ell)}$ and $\mathbf{C}^{(\ell)}$, for L times. For solving the optimization problem, we define

$$\mathbf{X} = \begin{pmatrix} \mathbf{V}^{(1)} & \mathbf{O} & \mathbf{O} & \mathbf{O} & \mathbf{O} \\ \mathbf{O} & \mathbf{C}^{(1)} & \mathbf{O} & \mathbf{O} & \mathbf{O} \\ \mathbf{O} & \mathbf{O} & \mathbf{V}^{(2)} & \mathbf{O} & \mathbf{O} \\ \mathbf{O} & \mathbf{O} & \mathbf{O} & \mathbf{C}^{(2)} & \mathbf{O} \\ \mathbf{O} & \mathbf{O} & \mathbf{O} & \mathbf{O} & \mathbf{D} \end{pmatrix},$$

$$\mathbf{W} = \begin{pmatrix} \mathbf{O} & \mathbf{I}_{T^{(1)}} & \mathbf{O} & \mathbf{O} & \tilde{\mathbf{J}}^{(1)} \\ \mathbf{I}_{T^{(1)}} & \mathbf{O} & \mathbf{O} & \mathbf{O} & \tilde{\mathbf{J}}^{(1)} \\ \mathbf{O} & \mathbf{O} & \mathbf{O} & \mathbf{I}_{T^{(2)}} & \tilde{\mathbf{J}}^{(2)} \\ \mathbf{O} & \mathbf{O} & \mathbf{I}_{T^{(2)}} & \mathbf{O} & \tilde{\mathbf{J}}^{(2)} \\ \tilde{\mathbf{J}}^{(1)\top} & \tilde{\mathbf{J}}^{(1)\top} & \tilde{\mathbf{J}}^{(2)\top} & \tilde{\mathbf{J}}^{(2)\top} & \mathbf{O} \end{pmatrix},$$

$$\mathbf{A}^\top = (\mathbf{A}_V^{(1)\top}, \mathbf{A}_C^{(1)\top}, \mathbf{A}_V^{(2)\top}, \mathbf{A}_C^{(2)\top}, \mathbf{A}_D^\top).$$

Method	Time [min]	$1-1000$ es $\rightarrow$ en		$1-1000$ en $\rightarrow$ es		$5001-6000$ es $\rightarrow$ en		$5001-6000$ en $\rightarrow$ es	
		P@1	P@5	P@1	P@5	P@1	P@5	P@1	P@5
Edit distance	-	29.1	37.8	20.6	34.4	28.5	40.0	26.4	33.5
BilBOWA (40 dim.)	* 4.6	46.7	59.6	43.6	56.4	44.6	53.6	49.4	**58.7**
BilBOWA (100 dim.)	* 7.5	43.3	55.9	36.8	49.0	43.6	53.3	48.6	57.9
BilBOWA (200 dim.)	* 11.6	38.8	52.2	29.7	43.2	43.3	52.0	47.3	57.2
CL-LSI (40 dim.)	1.4	45.9	54.8	46.9	55.8	31.6	38.5	40.7	45.1
CL-LSI (100 dim.)	2.4	51.7	62.9	48.5	61.8	41.6	49.8	42.8	49.1
CL-LSI (200 dim.)	5.1	55.2	66.5	50.7	65.5	45.5	54.7	45.6	51.9
CL-Eigenwords (40 dim.)	9.5	54.7	66.2	53.3	65.7	40.3	49.2	44.7	50.0
CL-Eigenwords (100 dim.)	19.6	57.7	71.3	54.9	70.3	47.9	59.0	49.3	54.6
CL-Eigenwords (200 dim.)	37.5	**58.7**	**72.4**	**56.2**	**72.2**	**51.6**	**62.4**	**50.6**	55.7

Table 1: Computational times (in minutes) and word translation accuracies (in percent, higher is better) evaluated by Precision@n using the 1,000 test words (the 1st to 1,000th most frequent words or the 5,001st to 6,000th most frequent words). Shown are for Spanish (es) to English (en) translation and for English (en) to Spanish (es) translation. * BilBOWA is executed on 3 threads, while CL-LSI and CL-Eigenwords are executed on a single thread.

Also define $\mathbf{H} = \mathbf{X}^\top \mathbf{W} \mathbf{X}$, $\mathbf{G} = \mathbf{X}^\top \mathbf{M} \mathbf{X}$, $\mathbf{M} = \mathrm{diag}(\mathbf{W}\mathbf{1})$. Then the optimization problem (1) is equivalent to maximizing $\mathrm{Tr}(\mathbf{A}^\top \mathbf{H} \mathbf{A})$ with a scale constraint $\mathbf{A}^\top \mathbf{G} \mathbf{A} = \mathbf{I}_K$. Following the Eigenwords implementation (Dhillon et al., 2015), we replace $\mathbf{H}, \mathbf{G}$ with $\mathcal{H}, \mathcal{G}$ by ignoring the non-diagonal elements of $\mathbf{G}$ and taking the square root of elements in $\mathbf{H}, \mathbf{G}$. The optimization problem is solved as a generalized eigenvalue problem, and the word representations, as well as those for contexts and sentences, are obtained as row vectors of $\hat{\mathbf{A}} = \mathcal{G}^{-1/2}(\boldsymbol{u}_1, \ldots, \boldsymbol{u}_K)$, where $\boldsymbol{u}_1, \ldots, \boldsymbol{u}_K$ are eigenvectors of $(\mathcal{G}^{-1/2})^\top \mathcal{H} \mathcal{G}^{-1/2}$ for the K largest eigenvalues. We choose K so that all the K eigenvalues are positive. As in the case of monolingual Eigenwords, we can exploit fast implementations such as the randomized eigenvalue decomposition (Halko et al., 2011); our computation in the experiments is only approximation based on the low-rank factorization with rank $2K$.

For measuring similarities between two word vectors $\boldsymbol{x}, \boldsymbol{y} \in \mathbb{R}^K$, we use the weighted cosine similarity

$$\mathrm{sim}(\boldsymbol{x}, \boldsymbol{y}) = (\|\boldsymbol{x}\|_2 \cdot \|\boldsymbol{y}\|_2)^{-1} \sum_{i=1}^{K} \lambda_i x_i y_i,$$

where λ_i is the i-th largest eigenvalue.

4 Experiments

The implementation of our method is available on GitHub[1]. Following the previous works (Mikolov et al., 2013a; Gouws et al., 2015), we use only

[1] https://github.com/shimo-lab/kadingir

the first 500K lines of English-Spanish sentence-aligned parallel corpus of Europarl (Koehn, 2005) for numerical experiments.

4.1 Word Translation Tasks

Experiments are performed in similar settings as the previous works based on the skip-gram model (Mikolov et al., 2013a; Gouws et al., 2015). We extract 1,000 test words with frequency rank 1–1000 or 5001–6000 from the source language, and translate these words to the target language using Google Translate, assuming they are the correct translations. Then, we evaluate the translation accuracies of each method with precision@n as the fraction of correct translations for the test words being in the top-n words of the target language returned by each method.

4.2 Baseline Systems

We compare CL-Eigenwords with the following three methods.

Edit distance Finding the nearest words measured by Levenshtein distance.

CL-LSI Cross-Language LSI (CL-LSI) (Littman et al., 1998) is not originally for word embeddings. However, since this method can be used for cross-lingual information retrieval, we select it as one of our baselines. For each language, we construct the term-document matrix of size $V^{(\ell)} \times D$ whose (i, j)-element represents the frequency of i-th word in j-th sentence. Then LSI is applied to the concatenated matrix of size $(V^{(1)} + V^{(2)}) \times D$.

BilBOWA BilBOWA (Gouws et al., 2015) is one of the state-of-the-art methods for cross-lingual word embeddings based on the skip-gram model. We obtain vector representations of words using publicly available implementation.[2]

4.3 Results

In CL-Eigenwords, vocabulary size $V^{(1)} = V^{(2)} = 10^4$, window size $h^{(1)} = h^{(2)} = 2$, the constant $b^{(1)} = b^{(2)} = 10^3$. The dimensionality of vector representations is $K = 40, 100$, or 200. Similarities of two vector representations are measured by the unweighted cosine similarity in CL-LSI and BilBOWA. Our experiments were performed on a CentOS 7.2 server with Intel Xeon E5-2680 v3 CPU, 256GB of RAM and gcc 4.8.5. The computation times and the result accuracies of word translation tasks are shown in Table 1. We observe that CL-Eigenwords is competitive with BilBOWA and CL-LSI. In particular, CL-Eigenwords performed very well for the most frequent words (ranks 1–1000) in this particular parameter setting. Furthermore, the computation times of CL-Eigenwords are as short as those of BilBOWA for achieving similar accuracies. Preliminary experiments also suggest that CL-Eigenwords works well for semi-supervised learning where sentence-alignment is specified only partially; the word translation accuracies are maintained well with aligned 240K lines and unaligned 260K lines.

5 Conclusion

We proposed CL-Eigenwords for incorporating cross-lingual information into the monolingual Eigenwords. Although our method is simple, experimental results of English-Spanish word translation tasks show that the proposed method is competitive with other state-of-the-art cross-lingual methods.

Acknowledgments

This work was partially supported by grants from Japan Society for the Promotion of Science KAKENHI (24300106, 16H01547 and 16H02789) to HS.

Appendix

In this Appendix, we discuss the relationships between CL-LSI and CL-Eigenwords.

[2]`https://github.com/gouwsmeister/bilbowa`

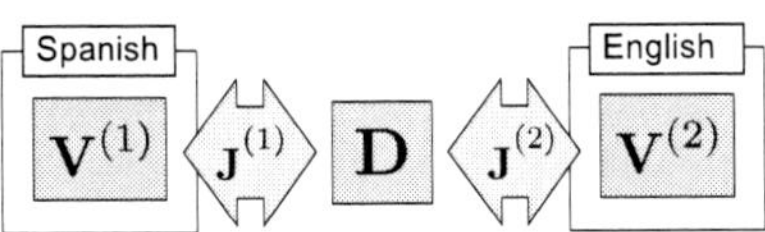

Figure 3: Cross-Language Latent Semantic Indexing (CL-LSI) does not use the context information.

Let $\mathbf{V}^{(1)}, \mathbf{V}^{(2)}, \mathbf{D}, \mathbf{J}^{(1)}, \mathbf{J}^{(2)}$ be those defined in Section 3. In CL-LSI, we consider the truncated singular value decomposition of a word-document matrix

$$\mathbf{B} = \begin{pmatrix} \mathbf{V}^{(1)\top}\mathbf{J}^{(1)} \\ \mathbf{V}^{(2)\top}\mathbf{J}^{(2)} \end{pmatrix} \approx \mathbf{A}_V \mathbf{\Lambda}_K \mathbf{A}_D^\top$$

using the largest K singular values. Then row vectors of $\mathbf{A}_V$ are the vector representations of words of CL-LSI.

CL-LSI can also be interpreted as an eigenvalue decomposition of $\mathbf{H} = \mathbf{X}^\top \mathbf{W} \mathbf{X}$ where

$$\mathbf{X} = \begin{pmatrix} \mathbf{V}^{(1)} & \mathbf{O} & \mathbf{O} \\ \mathbf{O} & \mathbf{V}^{(2)} & \mathbf{O} \\ \mathbf{O} & \mathbf{O} & \mathbf{D} \end{pmatrix},$$

$$\mathbf{W} = \begin{pmatrix} \mathbf{O} & \mathbf{O} & \mathbf{J}^{(1)} \\ \mathbf{O} & \mathbf{O} & \mathbf{J}^{(2)} \\ \mathbf{J}^{(1)\top} & \mathbf{J}^{(2)\top} & \mathbf{O} \end{pmatrix}$$

are redefined from those in Section 3 by removing submatrices related to contexts. The structure of $\mathbf{X}$ and $\mathbf{W}$ is illustrated in Fig. 3. Similarly to CL-Eigenwords of Section 3, but ignoring $\mathbf{G}$, we define $\mathbf{A} = (\boldsymbol{u}_1, \ldots, \boldsymbol{u}_K)$ with the eigenvectors of $\mathbf{H}$ for the largest K eigenvalues $\lambda_1, \ldots, \lambda_K$. It then follows from

$$\mathbf{H} = \begin{pmatrix} \mathbf{O} & \mathbf{B} \\ \mathbf{B}^\top & \mathbf{O} \end{pmatrix}$$

that $\mathbf{A}^\top = 2^{-1/2}(\mathbf{A}_V^\top, \mathbf{A}_D^\top)$ with the same $\mathbf{A}_V$ and $\mathbf{A}_D$ obtained by the truncated singular value decomposition. The eigenvalues are the same as the singular values: $\operatorname{diag}(\lambda_1, \ldots, \lambda_K) = \mathbf{\Lambda}_K$. Therefore CL-LSI is interpreted as a variant of CL-Eigenwords without the context information.

References

Jocelyn Coulmance, Jean-Marc Marty, Guillaume Wenzek, and Amine Benhalloum. 2015. Transgram, fast cross-lingual word-embeddings. In *Proceedings of the 2015 Conference on Empirical Methods in Natural Language Processing*, pages 1109–1113, Lisbon, Portugal, September. Association for Computational Linguistics.

Scott Deerwester, Susan T. Dumais, George W. Furnas, Thomas K. Landauer, and Richard Harshman. 1990. Indexing by latent semantic analysis. *Journal of the American society for information science*, 41(6):391.

Paramveer S. Dhillon, Jordan Rodu, Dean P. Foster, and Lyle H. Ungar. 2012. Two step cca: A new spectral method for estimating vector models of words. In John Langford and Joelle Pineau, editors, *Proceedings of the 29th International Conference on Machine Learning (ICML-12)*, ICML '12, pages 1551–1558, New York, NY, USA, July. Omnipress.

Paramveer S. Dhillon, Dean P. Foster, and Lyle H. Ungar. 2015. Eigenwords: Spectral word embeddings. *Journal of Machine Learning Research*, 16:3035–3078.

Manaal Faruqui and Chris Dyer. 2014. Improving vector space word representations using multilingual correlation. In *Proceedings of the 14th Conference of the European Chapter of the Association for Computational Linguistics*, pages 462–471, Gothenburg, Sweden, April. Association for Computational Linguistics.

Stephan Gouws, Yoshua Bengio, and Greg Corrado. 2015. Bilbowa: Fast bilingual distributed representations without word alignments. In *Proceedings of the 32nd International Conference on Machine Learning, ICML 2015, Lille, France, 6-11 July 2015*, pages 748–756.

Nathan Halko, Per-Gunnar Martinsson, and Joel A. Tropp. 2011. Finding structure with randomness: Probabilistic algorithms for constructing approximate matrix decompositions. *SIAM review*, 53(2):217–288.

Harold Hotelling. 1936. Relations between two sets of variates. *Biometrika*, 28(3/4):321–377.

Philipp Koehn. 2005. Europarl: A Parallel Corpus for Statistical Machine Translation. In *Conference Proceedings: the tenth Machine Translation Summit*, pages 79–86, Phuket, Thailand. AAMT.

Angeliki Lazaridou, The Nghia Pham, and Marco Baroni. 2015. Combining language and vision with a multimodal skip-gram model. In *Proceedings of the 2015 Conference of the North American Chapter of the Association for Computational Linguistics: Human Language Technologies*, pages 153–163. Association for Computational Linguistics.

Omer Levy and Yoav Goldberg. 2014a. Dependency-based word embeddings. In *Proceedings of the 52nd Annual Meeting of the Association for Computational Linguistics (Volume 2: Short Papers)*, pages 302–308. Association for Computational Linguistics.

Omer Levy and Yoav Goldberg. 2014b. Neural word embedding as implicit matrix factorization. In *Advances in Neural Information Processing Systems*, pages 2177–2185.

Michael L. Littman, Susan T. Dumais, and Thomas K. Landauer. 1998. Automatic cross-language information retrieval using latent semantic indexing. In *Cross-language information retrieval*, pages 51–62. Springer.

Tomas Mikolov, Quoc V. Le, and Ilya Sutskever. 2013a. Exploiting similarities among languages for machine translation. *arXiv preprint arXiv:1309.4168*.

Tomas Mikolov, Ilya Sutskever, Kai Chen, Greg Corrado, and Jeff Dean. 2013b. Distributed representations of words and phrases and their compositionality. In *Advances in neural information processing systems*, pages 3111–3119.

Nozomi Nori, Danushka Bollegala, and Hisashi Kashima. 2012. Multinomial relation prediction in social data: A dimension reduction approach. In *AAAI*, volume 12, pages 115–121.

Tianze Shi, Zhiyuan Liu, Yang Liu, and Maosong Sun. 2015. Learning cross-lingual word embeddings via matrix co-factorization. In *Proceedings of the 53rd Annual Meeting of the Association for Computational Linguistics and the 7th International Joint Conference on Natural Language Processing (Volume 2: Short Papers)*, pages 567–572, Beijing, China, July. Association for Computational Linguistics.

Hidetoshi Shimodaira. 2016. Cross-validation of matching correlation analysis by resampling matching weights. *Neural Networks*, 75:126–140.

Shuicheng Yan, Dong Xu, Benyu Zhang, Hong-Jiang Zhang, Qiang Yang, and Stephen Lin. 2007. Graph embedding and extensions: A general framework for dimensionality reduction. *Pattern Analysis and Machine Intelligence, IEEE Transactions on*, 29(1):40–51, Jan.

Semantics-Driven Recognition of Collocations Using Word Embeddings

Sara Rodríguez-Fernández[1], Luis Espinosa-Anke[1], Roberto Carlini[1], and Leo Wanner[1,2]
[1]NLP Group, Department of Information and Communication Technologies, Pompeu Fabra University
C/ Roc Boronat, 138, 08018 Barcelona (Spain)
[2]Catalan Institute for Research and Advanced Studies (ICREA)
sara.rodriguez.fernandez|luis.espinosa|roberto.carlini|leo.wanner@upf.edu

Abstract

L2 learners often produce "ungrammatical" word combinations such as, e.g., *give a suggestion or *make a walk. This is because of the "collocationality" of one of their items (the *base*) that limits the acceptance of *collocates* to express a specific meaning ('perform' above). We propose an algorithm that delivers, for a given base and the intended meaning of a collocate, the actual collocate lexeme(s) (*make / take* above). The algorithm exploits the linear mapping between bases and collocates from examples and generates a collocation transformation matrix which is then applied to novel unseen cases. The evaluation shows a promising line of research in collocation discovery.

1 Introduction

Collocations of the kind *make [a] suggestion, attend [a] lecture, heavy rain, deep thought, strong tea*, etc., are restricted lexical co-occurrences of two syntactically bound lexical elements (Kilgarriff, 2006). The central role of collocations for second language (henceforth, L2) learning has been discussed in a series of theoretical and empirical studies (Hausmann, 1984; Bahns and Eldaw, 1993; Granger, 1998; Lewis and Conzett, 2000; Nesselhauf, 2005; Alonso Ramos et al., 2010) and is widely reflected in (especially English) learner dictionaries. In computational lexicography, several statistical measures have been used to retrieve collocations from corpora, among them, *mutual information* (Church and Hanks, 1989; Lin, 1999), *entropy* (Kilgarriff, 2006), *pointwise mutual information* (Bouma, 2010), and *weighted pointwise*

mutual information (Carlini et al., 2014).[1] However, the needs of language learners go beyond mere lists of collocations: the cited studies reveal that language learners often build "miscollocations" (as, e.g., *give a suggestion or *have the curiosity*) to express the intended meaning. In other words, they fail to observe, in Kilgarriff's terms, the "collocationality" restrictions of L2, which imply that in language production, one of the elements of a collocation (the *base*) is freely chosen, while the choice of the other (the *collocate*) depends on the base (Hausmann, 1989; Cowie, 1994). For instance, to express the *meaning* of 'do' or 'perform', the base *suggestion* prompts for the choice of *make* as collocate: *make [a] suggestion*, while *advice* prompts for *give*: *give [an] advice*; to express the meaning of 'participate in', *lecture* prompts for *attend*: *attend [a] lecture*, while *operation* prompts for *assist*: *assist [an] operation*; to express the meaning of 'intense' in connection with *rain*, the right collocate is *heavy*, while 'intense wind' is *strong wind*. And so on. The idiosyncrasy of collocations makes them also language-specific. Thus, in English, you *take [a] walk*, in Spanish you 'give' it (*dar [un] paseo*), and in German and French you 'make' it (*[einen] Spaziergang machen, faire [une] promenade*); in English, *rain* is *heavy*, while in Spanish and German it is 'strong' (*fuerte lluvia/starker Regen*).

In order to effectively support L2 learners, techniques are thus needed that are able not only to retrieve collocations, but also provide for a given base (or headword) and a given semantic gloss of a collocate meaning, the actual collocate lexeme. In what follows, we present such a technique, which is grounded in Mikolov et al. (2013c)'s word embeddings, and which leverages the fact that semantically related words in two different

---

[1]See (Pecina, 2008) for a detailed survey of such measures.

Proceedings of the 54th Annual Meeting of the Association for Computational Linguistics, pages 499–505,
Berlin, Germany, August 7-12, 2016. ©2016 Association for Computational Linguistics

vector representations are related by linear transformation (Mikolov et al., 2013b). This property has been exploited for word-based translation Mikolov et al. (2013b), learning semantic hierarchies (hyponym-hypernym relations) in Chinese (Fu et al., 2014), and modeling linguistic similarities between standard (Wikipedia) and nonstandard language (Twitter) (Tan et al., 2015). In our task, we learn a *transition matrix* over a small number of collocation examples, where collocates share the same semantic gloss, to apply then this matrix to discover new collocates for any previously unseen collocation base. We discuss the outcome of the experiments with ten different collocate glosses (including 'do' / 'perform', 'increase', 'decrease', etc.), and show that for most glosses, an approach that combines a stage of the application of a gloss-specific transition matrix with a pruning stage that is based on statistical evidence outperforms approaches that exploit only one of these stages as well as a baseline that is based on collocation retrieval exploiting the embeddings property for drawing analogies, such as, e.g., $x \sim applause \equiv heavy \sim rain$ (implying $x=thunderous$) (Rodríguez-Fernández et al., 2016).

2 Theoretical model

The semantic glosses of collocates across collocations can be generalized into a generic semantic typology modeled, e.g., by Mel'čuk (1996)'s *Lexical Functions*. For instance, *absolute, deep, strong, heavy* in *absolute certainty, deep thought, strong wind*, and *heavy storm* can all be glossed as 'intense'; *make, take, give, carry out* in *make [a] proposal, take [a] step, give [a] hint, carry out [an] operation* can be glossed as 'do'/'perform'; etc. Our goal is to capture the relation that holds between the training bases and the collocates with the same gloss, such that given a new base and a gloss, we can retrieve its corresponding collocate(s) with this gloss. Thus, given *absolute certainty, deep thought*, and *strong wind* as training examples, *storm* as input base and 'intense' as gloss, we aim at retrieving the collocate *heavy*. As already mentioned above, our approach is based on Mikolov et al. (2013b)'s linear transformation model, which associates word vector representations between two analogous spaces. In Mikolov et al.'s original work, one space captures words in language L_1 and the other space words in language L_2, such that the found relations are between translation equivalents. In our case, we define a base space $\mathcal{B}$ and a collocate space $\mathcal{C}$ in order to relate bases with their collocates that have the same meaning, in the same language. To obtain the word vector representations in $\mathcal{B}$ and $\mathcal{C}$, we use Mikolov et al. (2013c)'s *word2vec*.[2]

The linear transformation model is constructed as follows. Let $\mathbf{T}$ be a set of collocations whose collocates share the semantic gloss τ, and let b_{t_i} and c_{t_i} be the collocate respectively base of the collocation $t_i \in \mathbf{T}$. The base matrix $B_\tau = [b_{t_1}, b_{t_2} \dots b_{t_n}]$ and the collocate matrix $C_\tau = [c_{t_1}, c_{t_2} \dots c_{t_n}]$ are given by their corresponding vector representations. Together, they constitute a set of training examples Φ_τ, composed by vector pairs $\{b_{t_i}, c_{t_i}\}_{i=1}^n$.

Φ_τ is used to learn a linear transformation matrix $\Psi_\tau \in \mathbb{R}^{\mathcal{B} \times \mathcal{C}}$. Following the notation in (Tan et al., 2015), this transformation can be depicted as:

$$B_\tau \Psi_\tau = C_\tau$$

We follow Mikolov et al.'s original approach and compute Ψ_τ as follows:

$$\min_{\Psi_\tau} \sum_{i=1}^{|\Phi_\tau|} \|\Psi_\tau b_{t_i} - c_{t_i}\|^2$$

Hence, for any given novel base b_{j_τ}, we obtain a novel list of ranked collocates by applying $\Psi_\tau b_{j_\tau}$ and filtering the resulting candidates by part of speech and $NPMI$, an association measure that is based on the pointwise mutual information, but takes into account the asymmetry of the lexical dependencies between a base and its collocate (Carlini et al., 2014):

$$NPMI = \frac{PMI(collocate, base)}{-log(p(collocate))}$$

3 Experiments

3.1 Setup of the Experiments

We carried out experiments with 10 of the most frequent semantic collocate glosses (listed in the first column of Table 1). As is common in previous work on semantic collocation classification (Moreno et al., 2013; Wanner et al., 2016), our training set consists of a list of manually annotated correct collocations. For this purpose, we

----

[2]https://code.google.com/archive/p/word2vec/

Semantic gloss	Example	# instances
'intense'	*absolute certainty*	586
'weak'	*remote chance*	70
'perform'	*give chase*	393
'begin to perform'	*take up a chase*	79
'stop performing'	*abandon a chase*	12
'increase'	*improve concentration*	73
'decrease'	*limit [a] choice*	73
'create', 'cause'	*pose [a] challenge*	195
'put an end'	*break [the] calm*	79
'show'	*exhibit [a] characteristic*	49

Table 1: Semantic glosses and size of training set

randomly selected nouns from the Macmillan Dictionary and manually classified their corresponding collocates with respect to the glosses.[3] Note that there may be more than one collocate for each base. Since collocations with different collocate meanings are not evenly distributed in language (e.g., speakers use more often collocations conveying the idea of 'intense' and 'perform' than 'stop performing'), the number of instances per gloss in our training data also varies significantly (see Table 1).

Due to the asymmetric nature of collocations, not all corpora may be equally suitable for the derivation of word embedding representations for both bases and collocates. Thus, we may hypothesize that for modeling (nominal) bases, which keep in collocations their literal meaning, a standard register corpus with a small percentage of figurative meanings will be more adequate, while for modeling collocates, a corpus which is potentially rich in collocations is likely to be more appropriate. In order to verify this hypothesis, we carried out two different experiments. In the first experiment, we used for both bases and collocates vectors pre-trained on the Google News corpus (*GoogleVecs*), which is available at *word2vec*'s website. In the second experiment, the bases were modeled by training their word vectors over a 2014 dump of the English Wikipedia, while for modeling collocates, again, *GoogleVecs* has been used. In other words, we assumed that Wikipedia is a standard register corpus and thus better for modeling $\mathcal{B}$, while *GoogleVecs* is more suitable for modeling $\mathcal{C}$. The figures in Section 3.2 below will give us a hint whether this assumption is correct.

For the calculation of $NPMI$ during postprocessing, the British National Corpus (BNC) was used.[4]

3.2 Evaluation

The outcome of each experiment was assessed by verifying the correctness of each retrieved candidate from the top-10 candidates obtained for each test base. A total of 10 bases was evaluated for each gloss. The ground truth test set was created in a similar fashion as the training set: nouns from the Macmillan Dictionary were randomly chosen, and their collocates manually classified in terms of the different glosses, until a set of ten unseen base–collocate pairs was obtained for each gloss.

For the outcome of each experiment, we computed both *precision* (p) as the ratio of retrieved collocates that match the targeted glosses to the overall number of obtained collocates for each base, and *Mean Reciprocal Rank* (MRR), which rewards the position of the first correct result in a ranked list of outcomes:

$$\text{MRR} = \frac{1}{|Q|} \sum_{i=1}^{|Q|} \frac{1}{rank_i}$$

where Q is a sample of experiment runs and $rank_i$ refers to the rank position of the *first* relevant outcome for the *i*th run. MRR is commonly used in Information Retrieval and Question Answering, but has also shown to be well suited for collocation discovery; see, e.g., (Wu et al., 2010).

We evaluated four different configurations of our technique against two baselines. The first baseline (**S1**) is based on the regularities in word embeddings, with the $vec(\text{king}) - vec(\text{man}) + vec(\text{woman}) = vec(\text{queen})$ example as paramount case. In this context, we manually selected one representative example for each semantic gloss to discover collocates for novel bases following the same schema; cf., e.g., for the gloss 'perform' $vec(\text{take}) - vec(\text{walk}) + vec(\text{suggestion}) = vec(\text{make})$ (where *make* is the collocate to be discovered); see (Rodríguez-Fernández et al., 2016) for details. The second baseline (**S2**) is an extension of S1 in that its output

---

[3]At this stage of our work, we considered only collocations that involve single word tokens for both the base and the collocate. In other words, we did not take into account, e.g., phrasal verb collocates such as *stand up*, *give up* or *calm down*. We also left aside the problem of subcategorization in collocations; cf., e.g., *into* in *take [into] consideration*.

[4]As one of the reviewers pointed out, BNC might not be optimal as a collocation reference corpus. On the one hand, it does not capture collocations that might be idiosyncratic to American English, and, on the other hand, it might be outdated (and thus not contain more recent collocations). It is subject of future work to verify whether another representative corpus of English serves better.

Semantic gloss	Precision (p)						Mean Reciprocal Rank (MRR)					
	S1	S2	S3	S4	S5	S6	S1	S2	S3	S4	S5	S6
'intense'	0.08	0.43	0.04	0.50	0.24	**0.72**	0.18	0.35	0.35	0.15	0.66	**0.82**
'weak'	0.09	0.11	0.23	**0.45**	0.27	0.39	0.31	0.15	**0.69**	0.64	0.61	0.47
'perform'	0.05	0.17	0.01	0.06	0.13	**0.40**	0.22	0.32	0.01	0.35	0.70	**0.79**
'begin to perform'	0.03	0.08	0.24	0.30	0.22	**0.38**	0.17	0.05	0.61	0.64	0.70	**0.71**
'stop performing'	0.00	0.00	0.11	0.15	0.12	**0.20**	0.01	0.00	**0.90**	0.66	0.71	0.65
'increase'	0.16	**0.53**	0.31	0.43	0.35	**0.53**	0.47	0.72	0.78	0.86	0.86	**0.90**
'decrease'	0.07	0.05	**0.28**	0.25	0.27	**0.28**	0.18	0.04	**0.57**	0.38	0.37	0.30
'create', 'cause'	0.10	0.16	0.01	0.15	0.14	**0.53**	0.41	0.23	0.11	0.11	0.48	**0.58**
'put an end'	0.05	0.09	0.15	0.20	0.08	**0.25**	0.28	0.10	**0.38**	0.36	0.33	**0.38**
'show'	0.10	0.55	0.24	0.49	0.49	**0.70**	0.44	0.54	**0.87**	0.82	0.73	0.81

Table 2: Precision and MRR

Semantic gloss	Base	Retrieved candidates
'intense'	*caution*	*extreme*
'weak'	*change*	*slight, little, modest, minor, noticeable, minimal, sharp, definite, small, big*
'perform'	*calculation*	*produce, carry*
'begin to perform'	*cold*	*catch, get, run, keep*
'stop performing'	*career*	*abandon, destroy, ruin, terminate, threaten, interrupt*
'increase'	*capability*	*enhance, increase, strengthen, maintain, extend, develop, upgrade, build, provide*
'decrease'	*congestion*	*reduce, relieve, cut, ease, combat*
'create', 'cause'	*challenge*	*pose*
'put an end'	*ceasefire*	*break*
'show'	*complexity*	*demonstrate, reveal, illustrate, indicate, reflect, highlight, recognize, explain*

Table 3: Examples of retrieved collocations

is filtered with respect to the valid POS-patterns of targeted collocations and $NPMI$.[5]

The four configurations of our technique that we tested were: **S3**, which is based on the transition matrix for which *GoogleVecs* is used as reference vector space representation for both bases and collocates; **S4**, which applies POS-pattern and $NPMI$ filters to the output of S3; **S5**, which is equivalent to S3, but relies on a vector space representation derived from Wikipedia for learning bases projections and on a vector space representation from *GoogleVecs* for collocate projections; and, finally, **S6**, where the S5 output is, again, filtered by POS collocation patterns and $NPMI$.

4 Discussion

The results of the experiments are displayed in Table 2. In general, the configurations S3 – S6 largely outperform the baselines, with the exception of the gloss 'increase', for which S2 equals S6 as far as p is concerned. However, in this case too MRR is considerably higher for S6, which achieves the highest MMR scores for 6 and the highest precision scores for 7 out of 10 glosses

(see the S6 columns in Table 2). In other words, the full pipeline promotes good collocate candidates to the first positions of the ranked result lists and is also best in terms of accuracy.

Comparing S1, S3, S5 to S2, S4, and S6 , we may conclude that the inclusion of a filtering module (and, in particular, of an $NPMI$ filtering module) contributes substantially to the overall precision in nearly all cases ('decrease' being the only exception). The comparison of the precision obtained for configurations S3 and S5 also reveals that for 7 glosses the strategy to model $\mathcal{C}$ and $\mathcal{B}$ on different corpora paid off. This is different as far as MRR is concerned. Further investigation is needed for the examination of this discrepancy.

We can observe that certain glosses seem to exhibit less linguistic variation, requiring a less populated transformation function from bases to collocates. Consider the case of 'show', which generates with only 49 training pairs the second best transition matrix, with p=0.70. It is also informative to contrast the performance on pairs of glosses with opposite meanings, such as e.g., 'begin to perform' vs. 'stop performing'; 'increase' vs. 'decrease'; 'intense' vs. 'weak'; and finally 'create, cause' vs. 'put an end'. Better performance is achieved consistently on the *positive* counterparts (e.g. 'begin to perform' over 'stop performing'). A closer look at the output reveals that in these

---

[5]At the first glan ce, a state-of-the-art approach on correction of collocation errors by suggesting alternative co-occurrences, such, as, e.g., (Dahlmeier and Ng, 2011; Park et al., 2008; Futagi et al., 2008), might appear as a suitable baseline. We discarded this option given that none of them uses explicit fine-grained semantics.

Semantic gloss	S6
'intense'	0.82
'weak'	0.45
'perform'	0.40
'begin to perform'	0.42
'stop performing'	0.22
'increase'	0.55
'decrease'	0.37
'create', 'cause'	0.59
'put an end'	0.43
'show'	0.85

Table 4: Precision of the coarse-grained evaluation of the S6 configuration

cases positive glosses are persistently classified as negative. Further research is needed to first understand why this is the case and then to come up with an improvement of the technique in particular on the *negative* glosses.

The fact that for some of the glosses precision is rather low may be taken as a hint that the proposed technique is not suitable for the task of semantics-oriented recognition of collocations. However, it should be also stressed that our evaluation was very strict: a retrieved collocate candidate was considered as correct only if it formed a collocation with the base, and if it belonged to the target semantic gloss. In particular the first condition might be too rigorous, given that, in some cases, there is a margin of doubt whether a combination is a free co-occurrence or a collocation; cf., e.g., *huge challenge* or *reflect [a] concern*, which were rejected as collocations in our evaluation. Since for L2 learners such co-occurrences may be also useful, we carried out a second evaluation in which all the suggested collocate candidates that belonged to a target semantic gloss were considered as correct, even if they did not form a collocation.[6] Cf. Table 4 for the outcome of this evaluation for the S6 configuration. Only for 'perform' the precision remained the same as before. This is because collocates assigned to this gloss are support verbs (and thus void of own lexical semantic content).

5 Conclusions

As already pointed out in Section 1, a substantial amount of work has been carried out to automatically retrieve collocations from corpora (Choueka, 1988; Church and Hanks, 1989; Smadja, 1993;

Lin, 1999; Kilgarriff, 2006; Evert, 2007; Pecina, 2008; Bouma, 2010; Futagi et al., 2008; Gao, 2013). Most of this work is based on statistical measures that indicate how likely the elements of a possible collocation are to co-occur, while ignoring the semantics of the collocations. Semantic classification of collocations has been addressed, for instance, in (Wanner et al., 2006; Gelbukh and Kolesnikova., 2012; Moreno et al., 2013; Wanner et al., 2016). However, to the best of our knowledge, our work is the first to automatically retrieve and typify collocations simultaneously. We have illustrated our approach with 10 semantic collocation glosses. We believe that this approach is also valid for the coverage of the remaining glosses (Mel'čuk (1996) lists in his typology 64 glosses in total).

Distributed vector representations (or word embeddings) (Mikolov et al., 2013c; Mikolov et al., 2013a), which we use, have proven useful in a plethora of NLP tasks, including semantic similarity and relatedness (Huang et al., 2012; Faruqui et al., 2015; Camacho-Collados et al., 2015; Iacobacci et al., 2015), dependency parsing (Duong et al., 2015), and Named Entity Recognition (Tang et al., 2014). We show that they also work for semantic retrieval of collocations. Only a small amount of collocations and big unannotated corpora have been necessary to perform the experiments. This makes our approach highly scalable and portable. Given the lack of semantically tagged collocation resources for most languages, our work has the potential to become influential in the context of second language learning. The datasets on which we performed the experiments as well as the details concerning the code and its use can be found at http://www.taln.upf.edu/content/resources/765.

6 Acknowledgements

The present work has been partially funded by the Spanish Ministry of Economy and Competitiveness (MINECO), through a predoctoral grant (BES-2012-057036) in the framework of the project HARenES (FFI2011-30219-C02-02), and by the European Commission under the grant number H2020–645012–RIA. We also acknowledge support from the Maria de Maeztu Excellence Program (MDM-2015-0502). Many thanks to the three anonymous reviewers for insightful comments and suggestions.

---

[6]Obviously, collocate candidates were considered as incorrect if they formed incorrect collocations with the base. Examples of such incorrect collocations are *stop [the] calm* and *develop [a] calculation*.

References

M. Alonso Ramos, L. Wanner, O. Vincze, G. Casamayor, N. Vázquez, E. Mosqueira, and S. Prieto. 2010. Towards a Motivated Annotation Schema of Collocation Errors in Learner Corpora. In *Proceedings of the 7th International Conference on Language Resources and Evaluation (LREC)*, pages 3209–3214, La Valetta, Malta.

J. Bahns and M. Eldaw. 1993. Should we Teach EFL Students Collocations? *System*, 21(1):101–114.

G. Bouma. 2010. Collocation Extraction beyond the Independence Assumption. In *Proceedings of the ACL 2010, Short paper track*, Uppsala.

J. Camacho-Collados, M.T. Pilehvar, and R. Navigli. 2015. NASARI: a Novel Approach to a Semantically-Aware Representation of Items. In *Proceedings of NAACL*, pages 567–577.

R. Carlini, J. Codina-Filba, and L. Wanner. 2014. Improving Collocation Correction by Ranking Suggestions Using Linguistic Knowledge. In *Proceedings of the 3rd Workshop on NLP for Computer-Assisted Language Learning*, Uppsala, Sweden.

Y. Choueka. 1988. Looking for Needles in a Haystack or Locating Interesting Collocational Expressions in Large Textual Databases. In *Proceedings of the RIAO*, pages 34–38.

K. Church and P. Hanks. 1989. Word Association Norms, Mutual Information, and Lexicography. In *Proceedings of the 27th Annual Meeting of the ACL*, pages 76–83.

A. Cowie. 1994. Phraseology. In R.E. Asher and J.M.Y. Simpson, editors, *The Encyclopedia of Language and Linguistics, Vol. 6*, pages 3168–3171. Pergamon, Oxford.

D. Dahlmeier and H.T. Ng. 2011. Correcting Semantic Collocation Errors with L1-Induced Paraphrases. In *Proceedings of the Conference on Empirical Methods in Natural Language Processing*, pages 107–117. Association for Computational Linguistics.

L. Duong, T. Cohn, S. Bird, and P. Cook. 2015. A Neural Network Model for Low-Resource Universal Dependency Parsing. In *Proceedings of the 2015 Conference on Empirical Methods in Natural Language Processing, EMNLP 2015, Lisbon, Portugal, September 17-21, 2015*, pages 339–348.

S. Evert. 2007. Corpora and Collocations. In A. Lüdeling and M. Kytö, editors, *Corpus Linguistics. An International Handbook*. Mouton de Gruyter, Berlin.

M. Faruqui, J. Dodge, Jauhar. S.K., C. Dyer, E.H. Hovy, and N.A. Smith. 2015. Retrofitting Word Vectors to Semantic Lexicons. In *NAACL HLT 2015, The 2015 Conference of the North American Chapter of the Association for Computational Linguistics: Human Language Technologies, Denver, Colorado, USA, May 31 - June 5, 2015*, pages 1606–1615.

R. Fu, J. Guo, B. Qin, W. Che, H. Wang, and T. Liu. 2014. Learning Semantic Hierarchies via Word Embeddings. In *Proceedings of the 52th Annual Meeting of the Association for Computational Linguistics: Long Papers*, volume 1.

Y. Futagi, P. Deane, M. Chodorow, and J. Tetreault. 2008. A Computational Approach to Detecting Collocation Errors in the Writing of Non-Native Speakers of English. *Computer Assisted Language Learning*, 21(1):353–367.

Z.M. Gao. 2013. Automatic Identification of English Collocation Errors based on Dependency Relations. *Sponsors: National Science Council, Executive Yuan, ROC Institute of Linguistics, Academia Sinica NCCU Office of Research and Development*, page 550.

A. Gelbukh and O. Kolesnikova. 2012. *Semantic Analysis of Verbal Collocations with Lexical Functions*. Springer, Heidelberg.

S. Granger. 1998. Prefabricated Patterns in Advanced EFL Writing: Collocations and Formulae. In A. Cowie, editor, *Phraseology: Theory, Analysis and Applications*, pages 145–160. Oxford University Press, Oxford.

F.J. Hausmann. 1984. Wortschatzlernen ist Kollokationslernen. Zum Lehren und Lernen französischer Wortwendungen. *Praxis des neusprachlichen Unterrichts*, 31(1):395–406.

F.J. Hausmann. 1989. Le dictionnaire de collocations. In F.J. Hausmann, O. Reichmann, H.E. Wiegand, and L. Zgusta, editors, *Wörterbücher, Dictionaries, Dictionnaires: An international Handbook of Lexicography*, pages 1010–1019. De Gruyter, Berlin/New-York.

E.H. Huang, R. Socher, C.D. Manning, and A.Y. Ng. 2012. Improving Word Representations via Global Context and Multiple Word Prototypes. In *Proceedings of the 50th Annual Meeting of the Association for Computational Linguistics: Long Papers-Volume 1*, pages 873–882. Association for Computational Linguistics.

I. Iacobacci, M.T. Pilehvar, and R. Navigli. 2015. SENSEMBED: Enhancing Word Embeddings for Semantic Similarity and Relatedness. In *Proceedings of ACL*, Beijing, China, July. Association for Computational Linguistics.

A. Kilgarriff. 2006. Collocationality (and How to Measure it). In *Proceedings of the Euralex Conference*, pages 997–1004, Turin, Italy. Springer-Verlag.

M. Lewis and J. Conzett. 2000. *Teaching Collocation. Further Developments in the Lexical Approach*. LTP, London.

D. Lin. 1999. Automatic Identification of Non-Compositional Phrases. In *Proceedings of the 37th annual meeting of the Association for Computational Linguistics on Computational Linguistics*, pages 317–324. Association for Computational Linguistics.

I.A. Mel'čuk. 1996. Lexical functions: A Tool for the Description of Lexical Relations in the Lexicon. In L. Wanner, editor, *Lexical Functions in Lexicography and Natural Language Processing*, pages 37–102. Benjamins Academic Publishers, Amsterdam.

T. Mikolov, K. Chen, G. Corrado, and J. Dean. 2013a. Efficient Estimation of Word Representations in Vector Space. *arXiv preprint arXiv:1301.3781*.

T. Mikolov, Q.V. Le, and I. Sutskever. 2013b. Exploiting Similarities among Languages for Machine Translation. *arXiv preprint arXiv:1309.4168*.

T. Mikolov, W. Yih, and G. Zweig. 2013c. Linguistic Regularities in Continuous Space Word Representations. In *HLT-NAACL*, pages 746–751.

P. Moreno, G. Ferraro, and L. Wanner. 2013. Can we Determine the Semantics of Collocations without using Semantics?. In I. Kosem, J. Kallas, P. Gantar, S. Krek, M. Langemets, and M. Tuulik, editors, *Proceedings of the eLex 2013 conference*, Tallinn & Ljubljana. Trojina, Institute for Applied Slovene Studies & Eesti Keele Instituut.

N. Nesselhauf. 2005. *Collocations in a Learner Corpus*. Benjamins Academic Publishers, Amsterdam.

T. Park, E. Lank, P. Poupart, and M. Terry. 2008. Is the Sky Pure Today? awkchecker: an Assistive Tool for Detecting and Correcting Collocation Errors. In *Proceedings of the 21st annual ACM symposium on User interface software and technology*, pages 121–130. ACM.

P. Pecina. 2008. A Machine Learning Approach to Multiword Expression Extraction. In *Proceedings of the LREC 2008 Workshop Towards a Shared Task for Multiword Expressions (MWE 2008)*, pages 54–57, Marrakech.

S. Rodríguez-Fernández, R. Carlini, L. Espinosa-Anke, and L. Wanner. 2016. Example-based Acquisition of Fine-grained Collocation Resources. In *Proceedings of LREC*, Portorož, Slovenia.

F. Smadja. 1993. Retrieving Collocations from Text: X-Tract. *Computational Linguistics*, 19(1):143–177.

L. Tan, H. Zhang, C. Clarke, and M. Smucker. 2015. Lexical Comparison Between Wikipedia and Twitter Corpora by Using Word Embeddings. In *Proceedings of the 53rd Annual Meeting of the Association for Computational Linguistics and the 7th International Joint Conference on Natural Language Processing (Volume 2: Short Papers)*, pages 657–661, Beijing, China, July. Association for Computational Linguistics.

B. Tang, H. Cao, X. Wang, Q. Chen, and H. Xu. 2014. Evaluating Word Representation Features in Biomedical Named Entity Recognition Tasks. *BioMed research international*, 2014.

L. Wanner, B. Bohnet, and M. Giereth. 2006. Making Sense of Collocations. *Computer Speech and Language*, 20(4):609–624.

L. Wanner, G. Ferraro, and P. Moreno. 2016. Towards Distributional Semantics-based Classification of Collocations for Collocation Dictionaries. *International Journal of Lexicography, doi:10.1093/ijl/ecw002*.

J.C. Wu, Y.C. Chang, T. Mitamura, and J.S. Chang. 2010. Automatic Collocation Suggestion in Academic Writing. In *Proceedings of the ACL Conference, Short paper track*, Uppsala.

Incorporating Relational Knowledge into Word Representations using Subspace Regularization

Abhishek Kumar
IBM Research
Yorktown Heights, NY 10598, USA
abhishk@us.ibm.com

Jun Araki
Carnegie Mellon University
Pittsburgh, PA 15213, USA
junaraki@cs.cmu.edu

Abstract

Incorporating lexical knowledge from semantic resources (e.g., WordNet) has been shown to improve the quality of distributed word representations. This knowledge often comes in the form of relational triplets (x, r, y) where words x and y are connected by a relation type r. Existing methods either ignore the relation types, essentially treating the word pairs as generic related words, or employ rather restrictive assumptions to model the relational knowledge. We propose a novel approach to model relational knowledge based on low-rank subspace regularization, and conduct experiments on standard tasks to evaluate its effectiveness.

1 Introduction

Distributed word representations, also known as *word embeddings*, are low-dimensional vector representations for words that capture semantic aspects (Bengio et al., 2003; Pennington et al., 2014; Mikolov et al., 2013a). The algorithms for learning the word embeddings rely on *distributional hypothesis* (Harris, 1954) that words occurring in similar contexts tend to have similar meanings. Word embeddings have been shown to capture interesting linguistic regularities by simple vector arithmetic (e.g., *v(king)-v(man)+v(woman)*≈ *v(queen)*) (Mikolov et al., 2013c). They have also been used to derive downstream features for various NLP tasks, such as named entity recognition, chunking, dependency parsing, sentiment analysis, paraphrase detection and machine translation (Turian et al., 2010; Dhillon et al., 2011; Bansal et al., 2014; Maas et al., 2011; Socher et al., 2011; Zou et al., 2013). Their promise as semantic word representations has led to increasing research efforts on improving their quality.

To this end, researchers have attempted to incorporate lexical knowledge into word embeddings by using additional regularization or loss terms in the learning objective. This lexical knowledge is often available in the form of triplets $\{(w_i, r, w_j)\}$, where the words w_i and w_j are connected by relation type r. These methods can be broadly classified into two categories. First family of methods use a (over-)generalized notion of similarity between words and ignore the type of relations, essentially treating the two words as generic similar words (Yu and Dredze, 2014; Faruqui et al., 2015; Liu et al., 2015). This places an implicit restriction on the types of relations that can be used with these methods. Second family of methods model each relation type by a distinct operator. Bordes et al. (2013) assumed a distinct *relation vector* **r** for every relation and minimize the distance between the translated first word and the second word, i.e., $d(\mathbf{w}_i + \mathbf{r}, \mathbf{w}_j)$ for every triplet (w_i, r, w_j). Socher et al. (2013) proposed a neural tensor network which uses a distinct tensor operator for every relation. These methods were used to learn entity and relation embeddings from a large collection of relation triplets for the task of knowledge base completion. Since these methods did not use any co-occurrence information from a text corpus, all entities were required to appear at least once in the training data, ruling out generalization to unseen entities[1]. More recently, Xu et al. (2014) combined the training objective of SKIP-GRAM (Mikolov et al., 2013a) with the training objective of (Bordes et al., 2013) to incorporate lexical

---

[1] There exists work on relation extraction and knowledge-base completion that combines structured relation triplets and logical rules with unstructured text using various forms of latent variable models (Riedel et al., 2013; Chang et al., 2014; Toutanova et al., 2015; Rocktäschel et al., 2015).

Proceedings of the 54th Annual Meeting of the Association for Computational Linguistics, pages 506–511,
Berlin, Germany, August 7-12, 2016. ©2016 Association for Computational Linguistics

knowledge into word embeddings. Fried and Duh (2014) combine the training objective of (Bordes et al., 2013) with that of neural language model (Collobert et al., 2011) using *alternating direction method of multipliers* (Boyd et al., 2011).

Constant translation model (Bordes et al., 2013; Xu et al., 2014; Fried and Duh, 2014) (referred as CTM from now on), although an important step in modeling relational knowledge, makes a rather restrictive assumption requiring all triplets (w_i, r, w_j) pertaining to a relation type r to satisfy $\mathbf{w}_i + \mathbf{r} \approx \mathbf{w}_j, \forall(i,j)$. This restriction can be severe when learning from a large text corpus since vector representation of a word also needs to respect a huge set of co-occurrence instances with other words. CTM is also not suitable for (i) modeling symmetric relations (e.g., synonyms, antonyms), and (ii) modeling transitive relations (e.g., synonyms, hypernyms). In this paper, we propose a novel formulation for modeling the relational knowledge which addresses these issues by relaxing the constant translation assumption and modeling each relation by a low-rank subspace, i.e., all the word pairs pertaining to a relation are assumed to lie in a low-rank subspace. We demonstrate effectiveness of the learned word representations on the tasks of knowledge-base completion and word analogy.

2 Subspace-regularized word embedding

Although our proposed framework for relational modeling is general enough to use with any existing word embedding method, we work with Word2Vec model (Mikolov et al., 2013a) in this paper for illustrating our ideas and later for empirical evaluations. Word2Vec is a neural network model trained on sequence of words and its hidden layer activations can be read out as the word representations. Two variants were proposed in (Mikolov et al., 2013a) – SKIP-GRAM, which maximizes the log likelihood of the local context words given the target word, and CBOW, which maximizes the log likelihood of the target word given its local context. More specifically, CBOW maximizes the objective

$$\frac{1}{T}\sum_{t=1}^{T}\log p(w_t|w_{t-c}^{t+c}) = \frac{1}{T}\sum_{t=1}^{T}\frac{\exp(\mathbf{w}_t'^{\top}\mathbf{v}_t)}{\sum_{w\in V}\exp(\mathbf{w}'^{\top}\mathbf{v}_t)} \tag{1}$$

where w_{t-c}^{t+c} represents the words (or tokens) in the local context window around the t'th word

(or token) and $\mathbf{v}_t = \sum_{-c\leq i\leq c, i\neq 0}\mathbf{w}_{t+i}$ can be seen as the average context vector. The vectors $\mathbf{w}, \mathbf{w}' \in \mathbb{R}^d$ denote the *input* and *output* embeddings for word w, respectively. The *input embeddings* are taken as the final word representations. Negative sampling was proposed to efficiently optimize Eq. 1 (Mikolov et al., 2013b). We report empirical results with CBOW since it was computationally faster than SKIP-GRAM while giving similar results in our early explorations.

We assume access to relational knowledge in the form of triplets $R_k = \{(w_i, r_k, w_j)\} \forall 1 \leq k \leq m$, where words w_i and w_j are connected by relation r_k and R_k is the set of all triplets corresponding to relation r_k with $|R_k| = n_k$. This form of knowledge is commonly available from Knowledge Bases like WordNet (Fellbaum, 1998). Our framework is suitable for both symmetric relations where words can be interchanged (e.g., synonyms) and asymmetric relations which have a directional nature (e.g., hypernyms).

Let $\mathbf{d}_{ij} = (\mathbf{w}_j - \mathbf{w}_i) \in \mathbb{R}^d$ denote the *difference vector* for the triplet (w_i, r_k, w_j) which points from the vector of word w_i to that of word w_j. Let us construct a matrix $\mathbf{D}_k \in \mathbb{R}^{d\times n_k}$ by stacking the *difference vectors* corresponding to all the triplets in relation r_k, i.e.,

$$\mathbf{D}_k = [\cdots \mathbf{d}_{ij} \cdots] \forall \{(i,j) : (w_i, r_k, w_j) \in R_k\}. \tag{2}$$

To incorporate this relational knowledge into word embeddings, we enforce an approximate low-rank constraint on $\mathbf{D}_k$ assuming

$$\mathbf{D}_k \sim \mathbf{U}_k \mathbf{\Lambda}_k^{\top}, \tag{3}$$

where $\mathbf{U}_k \in \mathbb{R}^{d\times p}, p \ll d$ is the relation basis whose linear span contains all the difference vectors pertaining to relation r_k. For $p = 2$, this assumption implies that all the difference vectors pertaining to a relation lie in a 2-D plane. For $p = 1$, it reduces to $\mathbf{D}_k \approx \mathbf{u}_k \alpha_k^{T}, \mathbf{u}_k \in \mathbb{R}^d, \alpha_k \in \mathbb{R}^{n_k}$, implying that all the difference vectors for a relation are collinear. In this paper, we mainly study the rank-1 model (p=1) since it seems to be a natural starting point for evaluating the idea of subspace-regularized relational modeling. The study of higher rank models will potentially require a careful exploration of various structural regularizers for reconstruction matrix $\mathbf{A}_k$ as well as a different evaluation scheme. We leave this study for future work.

Rank-1 subspace regularization can also be motivated from the fact that word embeddings are able to capture some linguistic regularities (Mikolov et al., 2013c) along certain directions in the vector space. For example, the *difference vector* for word pair *(king, queen)* is approximately aligned with the difference vector for *(man,woman)*, encoding the *gender* relation. The direction of the difference vectors carries significant information for these regularities which is evident from the success of *cosine* similarity metrics in the word analogy problems (Levy et al., 2014). CTM that assumes $\mathbf{w}_i + \mathbf{u}_k = \mathbf{w}_j \, \forall (w_i, r_k, w_j) \in R$ enforces an additional equal length constraint on the *difference vectors*, which may be rather restrictive, especially when the word vectors are also influenced by co-occurrence statistics (apart from relational knowledge). Moreover, it may face following challenges in relational modeling:

- It does not have a natural interpretation for modeling symmetric relations (e.g., synonyms, antonyms) that allow interchangeability of words in a given relation triplet (i.e., $(w_i, r_k, w_j) \iff (w_j, r_k, w_i)$). Having a constant translation of $\mathbf{u}_k \in \mathbb{R}^d$ from the first word to the second word leads to contradiction.

- It is also not natural for modeling relations with transitive property (i.e., $(w_i, r_k, w_j) \wedge (w_j, r_k, w_l) \implies (w_i, r_k, w_l)$), again leading to contradictions. Common examples of such relations are synonyms and hypernyms.

The proposed rank-1 subspace relation model naturally allows for modeling such relations by doing away with the constant length restriction on the difference vectors. Our empirical evaluations verify that this relaxation indeed leads to improved quality of word vectors with respect to capturing linguistic regularities.

We incorporate the proposed relational model into the learning objective for word vectors by regularizing the matrix of *difference vectors* towards a rank-1 matrix. We impose a nonnegativity constraint on the reconstruction coefficients α_k if relation r_k is asymmetric. This respects the unidirectional nature of asymmetric relations. To ensure uniqueness of solution for $\mathbf{u}_k$ and α_k, we constrain $\|\mathbf{u}_k\|_2 = 1$. Leaving α_k completely free can end up creating spurious relations between any two words that are arbitrarily far but whose difference vector is directionally aligned with any of the relation basis vectors $\{\mathbf{u}_k\}_{k=1}^m$. To avoid this, we further impose a upper limit of c on the absolute value of elements of α_k. We minimize the following joint objective for word vectors $\{\mathbf{w}_i\}_{i=1}^{|V|}$ and relation parameters $\{\mathbf{u}_k, \alpha_k\}_{k=1}^m$:

$$-\frac{1}{T}\sum_{t=1}^{T} \log p(w_t|w_{t-c}^{t+c}) + \frac{\lambda}{2|R|}\sum_{k=1}^{m}\left\|\mathbf{D}_k - \mathbf{u}_k\alpha_k^{\top}\right\|_F^2$$
$$\text{s.t. } \alpha_k \geq 0 \,\forall \text{ asymmetric } r_k, \|\mathbf{u}_k\|_2 = 1, |(\alpha_k)_l| \leq c. \tag{4}$$

where $\mathbf{D}_k$ is the matrix of *difference vectors* as defined earlier and λ is the regularization parameter. The first term in the objective takes into account the co-occurrence information text corpus while the second term incorporates the relational knowledge.

Optimizing for word vectors: We adopt parallel asynchronous stochastic gradient descent (SGD) with negative sampling approach of (Mikolov et al., 2013b). The model parameters for optimization are input embeddings (weights connecting input and hidden layer) and output embeddings (weights connecting hidden and output layer). Input embeddings are taken as the final word embeddings. Each computing thread works with a predefined segment of the text corpus and updates parameters that are stored in a shared memory. In each gradient step of CBOW, a thread samples a target word and its local context window and updates the parameters of the neural network. It can be seen as sampling one of the $f_t(\cdot)$, $t = 1, 2, \ldots, T$ and taking a gradient step with it. A small number of random target words are also sampled for the same context, treating them as negative examples for the gradient update. In the CBOW architecture, representations for context words are directly encoded as columns of the linear weight matrix $\mathbf{W} \in \mathbb{R}^{d \times |V|}$ that maps input bag-of-words layer to the hidden layer. The columns of $\mathbf{W}$ are taken as the word embeddings for the corresponding words in the vocabulary V. The reader is referred to (Mikolov et al., 2013b; Goldberg and Levy, 2014) for more details on the optimization procedure for CBOW. If a word appears in the set of relation triplets R, our regularization term gets activated. Since we place the regularizer only on input embeddings, the following gradient updates due to the regularization term act only on input embeddings.

$$\mathbf{w}_i \longleftarrow \mathbf{w}_i - \eta \frac{\lambda}{|R|} \left[\sum_{j:(w_i,r_k,w_j)\in R} \left(\mathbf{w}_i - \mathbf{w}_j + \mathbf{u}_k \alpha_{k_{ij}}\right) \right.$$
$$\left. + \sum_{j:(w_j,r_k,w_i)\in R} \left(\mathbf{w}_i - \mathbf{w}_j - \mathbf{u}_k \alpha_{k_{ji}}\right) \right],$$
$$(5)$$

where η is the learning rate, and $\alpha_{k_{ij}}$ denotes the element of α_k corresponding to the column of matrix $\mathbf{D}_k$ which contains *difference vector* $(\mathbf{w}_j - \mathbf{w}_i)$ (and similarly for $\alpha_{k_{ji}}$). The modifications in the learning rate as the SGD progresses are kept same as in the original implementation of CBOW[2].

Optimization for $\mathbf{u}_k$ and α_k: Instead of having stochastic gradient updates, we adopt an asynchronous batch update strategy for relation basis $\{\mathbf{u}_k\}_{k=1}^m$ and reconstruction coefficients $\{\alpha_k\}_{k=1}^m$. We launch one compute thread that keeps solving the batch optimization problem for $\{\mathbf{u}_k\}_{k=1}^m$ and $\{\alpha_k\}_{k=1}^m$ in an infinite loop until the optimization for word embeddings finishes. The batch optimization problem for a symmetric relation r_k is:

$$\min_{\mathbf{u}_k,\alpha_k} \left\| \mathbf{D}_k - \mathbf{u}_k \alpha_k^\top \right\|_F^2, \text{ s.t. } \|\mathbf{u}_k\|_2 = 1, |\alpha_k| \leq c.$$
$$(6)$$

where $\mathbf{D}_k \in \mathbb{R}^{d \times n_k}$ is the matrix of difference vectors for all triplets corresponding to relation r_k as defined in Eq. 2. Without the absolute value constraint on α_k, this problem can be exactly solved by SVD. We follow an alternating optimization procedure for solving this problem. We initialize $\mathbf{u}_k$ to the top left singular vector of $\mathbf{D}_k$ and then alternate between solving two least-squares sub-problems for $\mathbf{u}_k$ and α_k respectively with the corresponding constraints. For asymmetric relations, there is an additional nonnegativity constraint on α_k. We use projected gradient descent to solve these constrained least-squares problems.

3 Empirical Observations

We report preliminary evaluations of the proposed model (termed as RELSUB) on the tasks of word analogy and knowledge base completion. We use

Relation-type	RELCONST	RELSUB
capital-cities	48.15	**59.26**
currency	**58.33**	50.00
city-in-state	17.88	**18.94**
gender	44.44	**50.00**
similar-to	5.44	**7.26**
made-of	0	0
has-context	**10.00**	8.26
is-a	1.35	**1.83**
part-of	17.50	**19.00**
instance-of	8.40	**12.98**
derived-from	9.14	**10.27**
antonym	20.00	**20.62**
entails	0	**4.35**
causes	0	0
member-of	13.43	**26.87**
related-to	0	0
attribute	**11.76**	8.82
SEMANTIC	7.47	**8.44**
adjective-to-adverb	10.14	**47.83**
plural-verbs	61.25	**71.77**
plural-nouns	66.70	**71.89**
comparative	70.00	**75.00**
superlative	66.67	**77.78**
nationality	**85.71**	85.71
past-tense	42.20	**66.84**
present-participle	45.76	**47.62**
SYNTACTIC	54.88	**65.38**
TOTAL	24.61	**29.03**

Table 1: WordRep data: Accuracy on knowledge-base completion

English Wikipedia for training which contains approximately 4.8 million articles and 2 billion tokens. We lowercase all the text and and tokenize using Stanford NLP tokenizer.

We use two datasets for evaluating the proposed method. **Google word analogy data** (Mikolov et al., 2013a) contains 19544 analogy relations (14 relation types – 5 semantic, 9 syntactic) of the form *a:b::c:d* constructed from 550 unique relation triplets. We use this data only for evaluation (test phase). **WordRep** (Gao et al., 2014) contains a large collection of relation triplets (44584 triplets in total, 25 relation types – 18 semantic, 7 syntactic) extracted from WordNet, Wikipedia and Dictionary. For each relation type, we randomly split the triplets in 4 : 1 ratio with larger split used for training and smaller split used for test. We make sure that there is no word overlap between training and test triplets. We also remove triplets containing words from Google Analogy data from the training set.

We compare the proposed RELSUB model with two methods: (i) **CBOW** (Mikolov et al., 2013a), and (ii) **RELCONST** which is based on constant translation model for relations which was originally proposed in (Bordes et al., 2013) for embedding knowledge-bases and was recently used by

[2] https://code.google.com/p/word2vec/

Relation-type	CBOW	RELCONST	RELSUB
SEMANTIC	68.37	69.85	**70.96**
SYNTACTIC	**66.69**	65.42	65.96
TOTAL	67.48	67.43	**68.22**

Table 2: Google analogy data: Accuracy on word analogy task

(Xu et al., 2014) for learning word embeddings. Our objective for RELCONST is same as Eq. 4 except that $\{\alpha_k\}_{k=1}^m$ are set equal to the vector of all 1's and norm constraint on $\mathbf{u}_k$ are removed. This enables us to directly test the merit of the proposed rank-1 subspace relational model over that of constant translational model in the same regularization framework. Note that this objective is similar in spirit to (Xu et al., 2014) in the sense that it also uses a constant translation model for relations. However, Xu et al. (Xu et al., 2014) employ a maximum margin objective on the relation triplets as originally proposed in (Bordes et al., 2013). It encourages the loss (measured in terms of ℓ_2 distance) for true relation triplets to be smaller than the loss for randomly corrupted relation triplets. Instead of a maximum margin objective for relational knowledge, our model uses a simpler regularization based objective. We could not obtain the implementation of RC-NET (Xu et al., 2014) due to copyright issues cited by its authors. We also cannot compare with approaches that use only knowledge-base for training (Faruqui et al., 2015) since they do not learn or modify the embeddings of unseen words and our evaluation triplets do not overlap with training triplets.

We use the CBOW implementation in publicly available Word2Vec code[3] for our experiments. Our vocabulary has $400k$ words and we use a dimensionality of 300 for embeddings. For all other parameters, we use default values that the Word2Vec code comes with including a context window size of 5 tokens to each side, 5 negative samples per positive sample for negative sampling technique, etc. For both RELSUB and RELCONST, we set the regularization parameter to $\frac{\lambda}{|R|} = 1e^{-4}$ in all our experiments. We set the upper limit c in Eq. 4 to 1. The parameters were not fine tuned rigorously but these values seemed to work reasonably well for us. We do total 5 epochs of SGD over the text corpus for all methods.

In knowledge-base completion task, we want to predict the missing word of a relation triplet. For a triplet (x, r, y), we assume that x (first word) and

r (relation type) are observed and the task is to predict the missing word y. We restrict the search for the missing word to the most frequent $300k$ words (75% of the vocabulary). The missing word is predicted to be the closest word along the rank-1 subspace spanned by the relation vector (restricted by c in Eq. 4). For RELCONST, the missing word is predicted by translating the first word by the relation vector and then searching for nearest word. The accuracy results on WordRep data are shown in Table 1. Relaxing the constant translation to rank-1 subspace assumption results in significant improvements on this task.

In the analogy task, we want to predict the missing word in an analogy tuple a:b::c:?. We use the Google word-analogy data (Mikolov et al., 2013a) for this evaluation. We observe considerable gains with RELSUB over CBOW for semantic categories. The accuracy of knowledge regularized methods on syntactic categories is a little worse than CBOW and only slightly better than RELCONST, which is contrary to our observation on the knowledge-base completion task. This is due to the fact that analogy task uses the difference vector $(\mathbf{b} - \mathbf{a})$ instead of the learned relation vector which is assumed to be unknown.

4   Concluding Remarks

We proposed a novel framework for modeling relational knowledge in word embeddings using rank-1 subspace regularization. Our model can be seen as a generalization of the constant translational model for relations (Bordes et al., 2013; Xu et al., 2014). In the future, we would like to study the interplay between word frequencies and the strength of regularization, and perform an exhaustive empirical evaluation. The study of higher rank subspaces for relation modeling is also an important future direction.

References

Mohit Bansal, Kevin Gimpel, and Karen Livescu. 2014. Tailoring continuous word representations for dependency parsing. In *Proceedings of ACL 2014*, pages 809–815.

Yoshua Bengio, Réjean Ducharme, Pascal Vincent, and Christian Janvin. 2003. A neural probabilistic language model. *The Journal of Machine Learning Research*, 3:1137–1155.

Antoine Bordes, Nicolas Usunier, Alberto Garcia-Duran, Jason Weston, and Oksana Yakhnenko.

---

[3] https://code.google.com/p/word2vec/

2013. Translating embeddings for modeling multi-relational data. In *Proceedings of NIPS 2013*, pages 2787–2795.

Stephen Boyd, Neal Parikh, Eric Chu, Borja Peleato, and Jonathan Eckstein. 2011. Distributed optimization and statistical learning via the alternating direction method of multipliers. *Foundations and Trends® in Machine Learning*, 3(1):1–122.

Kai-Wei Chang, Wen-tau Yih, Bishan Yang, and Christopher Meek. 2014. Typed tensor decomposition of knowledge bases for relation extraction. In *EMNLP*.

Paramveer S. Dhillon, Dean Foster, and Lyle Ungar. 2011. Multi-view learning of word embeddings via CCA. In *Proceedings of NIPS 2011*, pages 199–207.

Manaal Faruqui, Jesse Dodge, Sujay K. Jauhar, Chris Dyer, Eduard Hovy, and Noah A. Smith. 2015. Retrofitting word vectors to semantic lexicons. In *Proceedings of NAACL-HLT 2015*, pages 1606–1615.

Christiane Fellbaum, editor. 1998. *WordNet: An Electronic Lexical Database*. MIT Press.

Daniel Fried and Kevin Duh. 2014. Incorporating both distributional and relational semantics in word representations. *arXiv preprint arXiv:1412.4369*.

Bin Gao, Jiang Bian, and Tie-Yan Liu. 2014. Wordrep: A benchmark for research on learning word representations. *arXiv preprint arXiv:1407.1640*.

Yoav Goldberg and Omer Levy. 2014. word2vec explained: deriving mikolov et al.'s negative-sampling word-embedding method. *arXiv preprint arXiv:1402.3722*.

Zellig S. Harris. 1954. Distributional structure. *Word*, 10(23):146–162.

Omer Levy, Yoav Goldberg, and Israel Ramat-Gan. 2014. Linguistic regularities in sparse and explicit word representations. *CoNLL-2014*, page 171.

Quan Liu, Hui Jiang, Si Wei, Zhen-Hua Ling, and Yu Hu. 2015. Learning semantic word embeddings based on ordinal knowledge constraints. *Proceedings of ACL 2015*.

Andrew L. Maas, Raymond E. Daly, Peter T. Pham, Dan Huang, Andrew Y. Ng, and Christopher Potts. 2011. Learning word vectors for sentiment analysis. In *Proceedings of ACL 2011*, pages 142–150.

Tomas Mikolov, Kai Chen, Greg Corrado, and Jeffrey Dean. 2013a. Efficient estimation of word representations in vector space. In *Proceedings of ICLR 2013*.

Tomas Mikolov, Ilya Sutskever, Kai Chen, Greg S Corrado, and Jeff Dean. 2013b. Distributed representations of words and phrases and their compositionality. In *Advances in neural information processing systems*, pages 3111–3119.

Tomas Mikolov, Wen-tau Yih, and Geoffrey Zweig. 2013c. Linguistic regularities in continuous space word representations. In *Proceedings of HLT-NAACL*, pages 746–751.

Jeffrey Pennington, Richard Socher, and Christopher D. Manning. 2014. GloVe: Global vectors for word representation. In *Proceedings of EMNLP 2014*, pages 1532–1543.

Sebastian Riedel, Limin Yao, Benjamin M. Marlin, and Andrew McCallum. 2013. Relation extraction with matrix factorization and universal schemas. In *HLT-NAACL*.

Tim Rocktäschel, Sameer Singh, and Sebastian Riedel. 2015. Injecting logical background knowledge into embeddings for relation extraction. In *HLT-NAALC*.

Richard Socher, Eric H. Huang, Jeffrey Pennington, Andrew Y. Ng, and Christopher D. Manning. 2011. Dynamic pooling and unfolding recursive autoencoders for paraphrase detection. In *Proceedings of NIPS 2011*, pages 801–809.

Kristina Toutanova, Danqi Chen, Patrick Pantel, Pallavi Choudhury, and Michael Gamon. 2015. Representing text for joint embedding of text and knowledge bases. *Proceedings of ACL*.

Joseph Turian, Lev Ratinov, and Yoshua Bengio. 2010. Word representations: A simple and general method for semi-supervised learning. In *Proceedings of ACL 2010*, pages 384–394.

Chang Xu, Yalong Bai, Jiang Bian, Bin Gao, Gang Wang, Xiaoguang Liu, and Tie-Yan Liu. 2014. RC-NET: A general framework for incorporating knowledge into word representations. In *Proceedings of CIKM 2014*, pages 1219–1228.

Mo Yu and Mark Dredze. 2014. Improving lexical embeddings with semantic knowledge. In *Proceedings of ACL 2014*, pages 545–550.

Will Y. Zou, Richard Socher, Daniel Cer, and Christopher D. Manning. 2013. Bilingual word embeddings for phrase-based machine translation. In *Proceedings of EMNLP 2013*, pages 1393–1398.

Word Embedding Calculus in Meaningful Ultradense Subspaces

Sascha Rothe and **Hinrich Schütze**
Center for Information and Language Processing
LMU Munich, Germany
sascha@cis.lmu.de

Abstract

We decompose a standard embedding space into interpretable orthogonal subspaces and a "remainder" subspace. We consider four interpretable subspaces in this paper: polarity, concreteness, frequency and part-of-speech (POS) subspaces. We introduce a new calculus for subspaces that supports operations like "$-1 \times hate = love$" and "give me a neutral word for *greasy*" (i.e., *oleaginous*). This calculus extends analogy computations like "$king - man + woman = queen$". For the tasks of Antonym Classification and POS Tagging our method outperforms the state of the art. We create test sets for Morphological Analogies and for the new task of Polarity Spectrum Creation.

1 Introduction

Word embeddings are usually trained on an objective that ensures that words occurring in similar contexts have similar embeddings. This makes them useful for many tasks, but has drawbacks for others; e.g., antonyms are often interchangeable in context and thus have similar word embeddings even though they denote opposites. If we think of word embeddings as members of a (commutative or Abelian) group, then antonyms should be *inverses* of (as opposed to *similar* to) each other. In this paper, we use DENSIFIER (Rothe et al., 2016) to decompose a standard embedding space into interpretable orthogonal subspaces, including a one-dimensional polarity subspace as well as concreteness, frequency and POS subspaces. We introduce a new calculus for subspaces in which antonyms are inverses, e.g., "$-1 \times hate = love$". The formula shows what happens in the polarity subspace; the orthogonal complement (all the re-

maining subspaces) is kept fixed. We show below that we can predict an entire polarity spectrum based on the subspace, e.g., the four-word spectrum *hate, dislike, like, love*. Similar to polarity, we explore other interpretable subspaces and do operations such as: given a concrete word like *friend* find the abstract word *friendship* (concreteness); given the frequent word *friend* find a less frequent synonym like *comrade* (frequency); and given the noun *friend* find the verb *befriend* (POS).

2 Word Embedding Transformation

We now give an overview of DENSIFIER; see Rothe et al. (2016) for details. Let $Q \in \mathbb{R}^{d \times d}$ be an orthogonal matrix that transforms the original word embedding space into a space in which certain types of information are represented by a small number of dimensions. The orthogonality can be seen as a hard regularization of the transformation. We choose this because we do not want to add or remove any information from the original embeddings space. This ensures that the transformed word embeddings behave differently only when looking at subspaces, but behave identically when looking at the entire space. By choosing an orthogonal and thus linear transformation we also assume that the information is already encoded linearly in the original word embedding. This is a frequent assumption, as we generally use the vector addition for word embeddings.

Concretely, we learn Q such that the dimensions $D^p \subset \{1, \ldots, d\}$ of the resulting space correspond to a word's polarity information and the $\{1, \ldots, d\} \setminus D^p$ remaining dimensions correspond to non-polarity information. Analogously, the sets of dimensions D^c, D^f and D^m correspond to a word's concreteness, frequency and POS (or morphological) information, respectively. In this paper, we assume that these properties do not corre-

Proceedings of the 54th Annual Meeting of the Association for Computational Linguistics, pages 512–517,
Berlin, Germany, August 7-12, 2016. ©2016 Association for Computational Linguistics

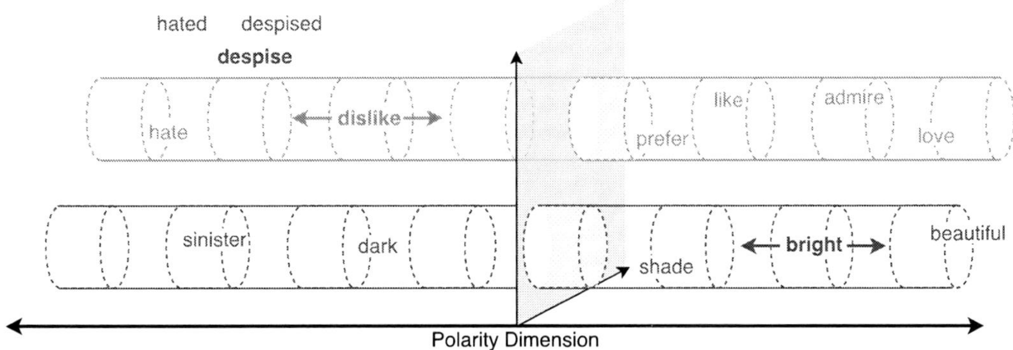

Figure 1: Illustration of the transformed embeddings. The horizontal axis is the polarity subspace. All non-polarity information, including concreteness, frequency and POS, is projected into a two dimensional subspace for visualization (gray plane). A query word (bold) specifies a line parallel to the horizontal axis. We then construct a cylinder around this line. Words in this cylinder are considered to be part of the word spectrum.

late and therefore the ultradense subspaces do not overlap. E.g., $D^p \cap D^c = \emptyset$. This might not be true for other settings, e.g., sentiment and semantic information. As we are using only four properties there is also a subspace which is in the orthogonal complement of all trained subspaces. This subspace includes the not classified information, e.g., genre information in our case (e.g., "clunker" is a colloquial word for "automobile").

If $e_v \in \mathbb{R}^d$ is the original embedding of word v, the transformed representation is $u_v = Qe_v$. We use $*$ as a placeholder for polarity (p), concreteness (c), frequency (f) and POS/morphology (m) and call $d^* = |D^*|$ the dimensionality of the ultradense subspace of property $*$. For each ultradense subspace, we create $P^* \in \mathbb{R}^{d^* \times d}$, an identity matrix for the dimensions in D^*. Thus, the ultradense (UD) representation $u_v^* \in \mathbb{R}^{d^*}$ of word v is defined as:

$$u_v^* := P^* Q e_v \qquad (1)$$

For notational simplicity, u_v^* will either refer to a vector in $\mathbb{R}^{d^*}$ or to a vector in $\mathbb{R}^d$ where all dimensions $\not\in D^*$ are set to zero.

For training, the orthogonal transformation Q we assume we have a lexicon resource. Let $L_{\not\sim}^*$ be a set of word index pairs (v, w) with different labels, e.g., positive/negative, concrete/abstract or noun/verb. We want to maximize the distance for pairs in this group. Thus, our objective is:

$$\operatorname*{argmin}_Q \sum_{*\in\{p,c,f,m\}} \sum_{(v,w)\in L_{\not\sim}^*} -\|P^*Q(e_v - e_w)\| \qquad (2)$$

subject to Q being an orthogonal matrix. Another goal is to minimize the distance of two words with identical labels. Let $L_\sim^*$ be a set of word index pairs (v, w) with identical labels. In contrast to Eq. 2, we now want to minimize each distance. Thus, the objective is given by:

$$\operatorname*{argmin}_Q \sum_{*\in\{p,c,f,m\}} \sum_{(v,w)\in L_\sim^*} \|P^*Q(e_v - e_w)\| \qquad (3)$$

subject to Q being an orthogonal matrix. For training Eq. 2 is weighted with α^* and Eq. 3 with $1 - \alpha^*$. We do a batch gradient descent where each batch contains the same number of positive and negative examples. This means the number of examples in the lexica – which give rise to more negative than positive examples – does not influence the training.

3 Setup and Method

Eqs. 2/3 can be combined to train an orthogonal transformation matrix. We use pretrained 300-dimensional English word embeddings (Mikolov et al., 2013) (W2V). To train the transformation matrix, we use a combination of MPQA (Wilson et al., 2005), Opinion Lexicon (Hu and Liu, 2004) and NRC Emotion lexicons (Mohammad and Turney, 2013) for polarity; BWK, a lexicon of 40,000 English words (Brysbaert et al., 2014), for concreteness; the order in the word embedding file for frequency; and the training set of the FLORS tagger (Schnabel and Schütze, 2014) for POS. The application of the transformation matrix to the word embeddings gives us four subspaces for polarity, concreteness, frequency and POS. These subspaces and their orthogonal complements are the basis for an embedding calculus that supports certain operations. Here, we investigate four such operations. The first operation computes the antonym of word v:

$$\text{antonym}(v) = \text{nn}(u_v - 2u_v^p) \qquad (4)$$

where $\text{nn} : \mathbb{R}^d \to V$ returns the word whose embedding is the nearest neighbor to the input. Thus, our hypothesis is that antonyms are usually very similar in semantics except that they differ on a single "semantic axis," the polarity axis.[1] The second operation is "neutral version of word v":

$$\text{neutral}(v) = \text{nn}(u_v - u_v^p) \qquad (5)$$

Thus, our hypothesis is that neutral words are words with a value close to zero in the polarity subspace. The third operation produces the polarity spectrum of v:

$$\text{spectrum}(v) = \{\text{nn}(u_v + xu_v^p) \mid \forall x \in \mathbb{R}\} \qquad (6)$$

This means that we keep the semantics of the query word fixed, while walking along the polarity axis, thus retrieving different shades of polarity. Figure 1 shows two example spectra. The fourth operation is "word v with POS of word w":

$$\text{POS}_w(v) = \text{nn}(u_v - u_v^m + u_w^m) \qquad (7)$$

This is similar to analogies like *king* − *man* + *woman*, except that the analogy is *inferred by the subspace relevant for the analogy*.

We create word spectra for some manually chosen words using the Google News corpus (W2V) and a Twitter corpus. As the transformation was orthogonal and therefore did not change the length of a dimension, we multiply the polarity dimension with 30 to give it a high weight, i.e., paying more attention to it. We then use Eq. 6 with a sufficiently small step size for x, i.e., further reducing the step size does not increase the spectrum. We also discard words that have a cosine distance of more than .6 in the non-polarity space. Table 1 shows examples. The results are highly domain dependent, with Twitter's spectrum indicating more negative views of politicians than news. While *fall* has negative associations, *autumn*'s are positive – probably because *autumn* is of a higher register in American English.

<hr>

[1] See discussion/experiments below for exceptions

Corpus, Type	Spectrum
News, Polarity	hypocrite, **politician**, legislator, businessman, reformer, statesman, thinker
	fall, winter, summer, **spring**, autumn
	drunks, booze, liquor, lager, **beer**, beers, wine, beverages, wines, tastings
Twitter, Polarity	corrupt, coward, **politician**, journalist, citizen, musician, representative
	stalker, neighbour, gf, bf, cousin, frnd, **friend**, mentor
	#stupid, #problems, #homework, #mylife, #reality, **#life**, #happiness
News, Concreteness	imperialist, conflict, **war**, Iraq, Vietnam War, battlefields, soldiers
	love, friendship, dear friend, friends, **friend**, girlfriend
News, Frequency	redesigned, newer, revamped, **new**
	intellect, insights, familiarity, skills, **knowledge**, experience

Table 1: Example word spectra for polarity, concreteness and frequency on two different corpora. Queries are bold.

	dev set			test set		
	P	R	F_1	P	R	F_1
Adel, 2014	.79	.65	.72	.75	.58	.66
our work	.81	.90	.85	.76	.88	.82

Table 2: Results for Antonym Classification

4 Evaluation

4.1 Antonym Classification.

We evaluate on Adel and Schütze (2014)'s data; the task is to decide for a pair of words whether they are antonyms or synonyms. The set has 2,337 positive and negative pairs each and is split into 80% training, 10% dev and 10% test. Adel and Schütze (2014) collected positive/negative examples from the nearest neighbors of the word embeddings to make it hard to solve the task using word embeddings. We train an SVM (RBF kernel) on three features that are based on the intuition depicted in Figure 1: the three cosine distances in: the polarity subspace; the orthogonal complement; and the entire space. Table 2 shows that improvement of precision is minor (.76 vs. .75), but recall and F_1 improve by a lot (+.30 and +.16).

4.2 Polarity Spectrum Creation

consists of two subtasks. PSC-SET: Given a query word how well can we predict a spectrum? PSC-ORD: How good is the order in the spectrum? Our gold standard is Word Spectrum, included in the Oxford American Writer's Thesaurus (OAWT) and therefore also in MacOS. For each query word

	newsgroups		reviews		weblogs		answers		emails		wsj	
	ALL	OOV	ALL	OOV	ALL	OOV	ALL	OOV	ALL	OOV	ALL	OOV
1 LSJU	$89.11^\dagger$	$56.02^\dagger$	$91.43^\dagger$	$58.66^\dagger$	$94.15^\dagger$	$77.13^\dagger$	$88.92^\dagger$	$49.30^\dagger$	$88.68^\dagger$	$58.42^\dagger$	96.83	90.25
2 SVM	$89.14^\dagger$	$53.82^\dagger$	$91.30^\dagger$	$54.20^\dagger$	$94.21^\dagger$	$76.44^\dagger$	$88.96^\dagger$	$47.25^\dagger$	$88.64^\dagger$	$56.37^\dagger$	96.63	$87.96^\dagger$
3 F	**90.86**	$66.42^\dagger$	**92.95**	$75.29^\dagger$	94.71	$83.64^\dagger$	90.30	$62.15^\dagger$	89.44	$62.61^\dagger$	96.59	90.37
4 F+W2V	90.51	**72.26**	$92.46^\dagger$	78.03	94.70	86.05	90.34	65.16	89.26	$63.70^\dagger$	96.44	91.36
5 F+UD	90.79	72.20	92.84	**78.80**	**94.84**	**86.47**	**90.60**	**65.48**	**89.68**	**66.24**	**96.61**	**92.36**

Table 3: Results for POS tagging. LSJU = Stanford. SVM = SVMTool. F=FLORS. We show three state-of-the-art taggers (lines 1-3), FLORS extended with 300-dimensional embeddings (4) and extended with UD embeddings (5). $\dagger$: significantly better than the best result in the same column ($\alpha = .05$, one-tailed Z-test).

this dictionary returns a list of up to 80 words of shades of meaning between two polar opposites. We look for words that are also present in Adel and Schütze (2014)'s Antonym Classification data and retrieve 35 spectra. Each word in a spectrum can be used as a query word; after intersecting the spectra with our vocabulary, we end up with 1301 test cases.

To evaluate PSC-SET, we calculate the 10 nearest neighbors of the m words in the spectrum and rank the $10m$ neighbors by the distance to our spectrum, i.e., the cosine distance in the orthogonal complement of the polarity subspace. We report mean average precision (MAP) and weighted MAP where each MAP is weighted by the number of words in the spectrum. As shown in Table 4 there is no big difference between both numbers, meaning that our algorithm does not work better or worse on smaller or larger spectra.

To evaluate PSC-ORD, we calculate Spearman's ρ of the ranks in OAWT and the values on the polarity dimension. Again, there is no significant difference between average and weighted average of ρ. Table 4 also shows that the variance of the measures is low for PSC-SET and high for PSC-ORD; thus, we do well on certain spectra and worse on others. The best one, *beautiful* $\leftrightarrow$ *ugly*, is given as an example. The worst performing spectrum is *fat* $\leftrightarrow$ *skinny* ($\rho = .13$) – presumably because both extremes are negative, contradicting our modeling assumption that spectra go from positive to negative. We test this hypothesis by separating the spectrum into two subspectra. We then report the weighted average correlation of the optimal separation. For *fat* $\leftrightarrow$ *skinny*, this improves ρ to .67.

	PSC-SET: MAP	PSC-ORD: ρ	avg(ρ_1, ρ_2)
average	.48	.59	.70
weighted avg.	.47	.59	.70
variance	.004	.048	.014
beautiful/ugly	.48	.84	.84
fat/skinny	.56	.13	.67
absent/present	.43	.72	.76

Table 4: Results for Polarity Spectrum Creation: MAP, Spearman's ρ (one spectrum) and average ρ (two subspectra)

4.3 Morphological Analogy.

The previous two subspaces were one-dimensional. Now we consider a POS subspace, because POS is not one-dimensional and cannot be modeled as a single scalar quantity. We create a word analogy benchmark by extracting derivational forms from WordNet (Fellbaum, 1998). We discard words with ≥ 2 derivational forms of the same POS and words not in the most frequent 30,000. We then randomly select 26 pairs for every POS combination for the dev set and 26 pairs for the test set.[2] An example of the type of equation we solve here is *prediction* $-$ *predict* $+$ *symbolize* $=$ *symbol* (from the dev set). W2V embeddings are our baseline.

We can also rewrite the left side of the equation as POS(*prediction*) $+$ Semantics(*symbolize*); note that this cannot be done using standard word embeddings. In contrast, our method can use meaningful UD embeddings and Eq. 7 with POS(v) being u_v^m and Semantics(v) being $u_v - u_v^m$. The dev set indicates that a 8-dimensional POS subspace is optimal and Table 5 shows that this method out-

---

[2] This results in an even number of $25 * 26 = 650$ questions per POS combination, $4*2*650 = 5200$ in total (4 POS combinations, where each POS can be used as query POS).

	W2V		UD	
	A→B	B→A	A→B	B→A
noun-verb	35.69	6.62	59.69[†]	50.46[†]
adj-noun	30.77	27.38	53.85[†]	43.85[†]
adj-verb	20.62	3.08	32.15[†]	24.77[†]
adj-adverb	45.38	35.54	46.46	43.08[†]
all	25.63		44.29[†]	

Table 5: Accuracy @1 on test for Morphological Analogy. †: significantly better than the corresponding result in the same row ($\alpha = .05$, one-tailed Z-test).

performs the baseline.

4.4 POS Tagging

Our final evaluation is extrinsic. We use FLORS (Schnabel and Schütze, 2014), a state-of-the-art POS tagger which was extended by Yin et al. (2015) with word embeddings as additional features. W2V gives us a consistent improvement on OOVs (Table 3, line 4). However, training this model requires about 500GB of RAM. When we use the 8-dimensional UD embeddings (the same as for Morphological Analogy), we outperform W2V except for a virtual tie on news (Table 3, line 5). So we perform better even though we only use 8 of 300 dimensions! However, the greatest advantage of UD is that we only need 100GB of RAM, 80% less than W2V.

5 Related Work

Yih et al. (2012) also tackled the problem of antonyms having similar embeddings. In their model, the antonym is the inverse of the entire vector whereas in our work the antonym is only the inverse in an ultradense subspace. Our model is more intuitive since antonyms invert only part of the meaning, not the entire meaning. Schwartz et al. (2015) present a method that switches an antonym parameter on or off (depending on whether a high antonym-synonym similarity is useful for an application) and learn *multiple* embedding spaces. We only need a *single* space, but consider different subspaces of this space.

An unsupervised approach using linguistic patterns that ranks adjectives according to their intensity was presented by de Melo and Bansal (2013). Sharma et al. (2015) present a corpus-independent approach for the same problem. Our results (Table 1) suggest that polarity should not be consid-

ered to be corpus-independent.

There is also much work on incorporating the additional information into the original word embedding training. Examples include (Botha and Blunsom, 2014) and (Cotterell and Schütze, 2015). However, postprocessing has several advantages. DENSIFIER can be trained on a normal work station without access to the original training corpus. This makes the method more flexible, e.g., when new training data or desired properties are available.

On a general level, our method bears some resemblance with (Weinberger and Saul, 2009) in that we perform supervised learning on a set of desired (dis)similarities and that we can think of our method as learning specialized metrics for particular subtypes of linguistic information or particular tasks. Using the method of Weinberger and Saul (2009), one could learn k metrics for k subtypes of information and then simply represent a word w as the concatenation of (i) the original embedding and (ii) k representations corresponding to the k metrics.[3] In case of a simple one-dimensional type of information, the corresponding representation could simply be a scalar. We would expect this approach to have similar advantages for practical applications, but we view our orthogonal transformation of the original space as more elegant and it gives rise to a more compact representation.

6 Conclusion

We presented a new word embedding calculus based on meaningful ultradense subspaces. We applied the operations of the calculus to Antonym Classification, Polarity Spectrum Creation, Morphological Analogy and POS Tagging. Our evaluation shows that our method outperforms previous work and is applicable to different types of information. We have published test sets and word embeddings at `http://www.cis.lmu.de/~sascha/Ultradense/`.

Acknowledgments

This research was supported by Deutsche Forschungsgemeinschaft (DFG, grant 2246/10-1).

---

[3]We would like to thank an anonymous reviewer for suggesting this alternative approach.

References

Heike Adel and Hinrich Schütze. 2014. Using mined coreference chains as a resource for a semantic task. In *Proceedings of EMNLP*.

Jan A Botha and Phil Blunsom. 2014. Compositional morphology for word representations and language modelling. *arXiv preprint arXiv:1405.4273*.

Marc Brysbaert, Amy Beth Warriner, and Victor Kuperman. 2014. Concreteness ratings for 40 thousand generally known english word lemmas. *Behavior research methods*, 46(3):904–911.

Ryan Cotterell and Hinrich Schütze. 2015. Morphological word-embeddings. In *Proceedings of the 2015 Conference of the North American Chapter of the Association for Computational Linguistics: Human Language Technologies*, pages 1287–1292, Denver, Colorado, May–June. Association for Computational Linguistics.

Gerard de Melo and Mohit Bansal. 2013. Good, great, excellent: Global inference of semantic intensities. *Transactions of the Association for Computational Linguistics*, 1:279–290.

Christiane Fellbaum. 1998. *WordNet: An Electronic Lexical Database*. Bradford Books.

Minqing Hu and Bing Liu. 2004. Mining and Summarizing Customer Reviews. In *KDD*.

Tomas Mikolov, Kai Chen, Greg Corrado, and Jeffrey Dean. 2013. Efficient estimation of word representations in vector space. *arXiv preprint arXiv:1301.3781*.

Saif M. Mohammad and Peter D. Turney. 2013. Crowdsourcing a Word-Emotion Association Lexicon. *Computational Intelligence*, 29(3).

Sascha Rothe, Sebastian Ebert, and Hinrich Schütze. 2016. Ultradense word embeddings by orthogonal transformation. *arXiv preprint arXiv:1602.07572*.

Tobias Schnabel and Hinrich Schütze. 2014. Flors: Fast and simple domain adaptation for part-of-speech tagging. *Transactions of the Association for Computational Linguistics*, 2:15–26.

Roy Schwartz, Roi Reichart, and Ari Rappoport. 2015. Symmetric pattern based word embeddings for improved word similarity prediction. In *Proceedings of CoNLL*.

Raksha Sharma, Mohit Gupta, Astha Agarwal, and Pushpak Bhattacharyya. 2015. Adjective intensity and sentiment analysis. In *Proceedings of EMNLP*.

Kilian Q. Weinberger and Lawrence K. Saul. 2009. Distance metric learning for large margin nearest neighbor classification. *J. Mach. Learn. Res.*, 10:207–244.

Theresa Wilson, Janyce Wiebe, and Paul Hoffmann. 2005. Recognizing contextual polarity in phrase-level sentiment analysis. In *Proceedings of HLT/EMNLP*.

Wen-tau Yih, Geoffrey Zweig, and John C Platt. 2012. Polarity inducing latent semantic analysis. In *Proceedings of EMNLP*.

Wenpeng Yin, Tobias Schnabel, and Hinrich Schütze. 2015. Online updating of word representations for part-of-speech tagging. In *Proceedings of EMNLP*.

Is "Universal Syntax" Universally Useful for Learning Distributed Word Representations?

Ivan Vulić and **Anna Korhonen**
Language Technology Lab
DTAL, University of Cambridge
{iv250, alk23}@cam.ac.uk

Abstract

Recent comparative studies have demonstrated the usefulness of dependency-based contexts (DEPS) for learning distributed word representations for similarity tasks. In English, DEPS tend to perform better than the more common, less informed bag-of-words contexts (BOW). In this paper, we present the first cross-linguistic comparison of different context types for three different languages. DEPS are extracted from "universal parses" without any language-specific optimization. Our results suggest that the universal DEPS (UDEPS) are useful for detecting functional similarity (e.g., verb similarity, solving syntactic analogies) among languages, but their advantage over BOW is not as prominent as previously reported on English. We also show that simple "post-parsing" filtering of useful UDEPS contexts leads to consistent improvements across languages.

1 Introduction

Dense real-valued distributed representations of words known as word embeddings (WEs) have become ubiquitous in NLP, serving as invaluable features in a broad range of NLP tasks, e.g., (Turian et al., 2010; Collobert et al., 2011; Chen and Manning, 2014). The omnipresent word2vec skip-gram model with negative sampling (SGNS) (Mikolov et al., 2013b) is still considered the state-of-the-art word representation model, due to its simplicity, fast training, as well as its solid and robust performance across a wide variety of semantic tasks (Baroni et al., 2014; Levy et al., 2015).

The original implementation of SGNS learns word representations from local bag-of-words contexts (BOW). However, the underlying SGNS model is equally applicable to other context types.

Recent comparative studies have demonstrated the usefulness of *dependency-based contexts (DEPS)* (Padó and Lapata, 2007) for the task. In comparison with BOW, syntactic contexts steer the induced semantic spaces towards functional similarity (e.g., *tiger:cat*) rather than towards topical similarity/relatedness (e.g., *tiger:jungle*). DEPS-based embeddings outperform the less informed BOW-based embeddings in a variety of similarity tasks (Bansal et al., 2014; Levy and Goldberg, 2014a; Hill et al., 2015; Melamud et al., 2016). However, these studies have all focused solely on English. A comparison extending to additional languages is required before any cross-lingual generalisations can be drawn.

Following recent initiatives on language-agnostic and cross-linguistically consistent *universal natural language processing* (i.e., universal POS (UPOS) tagging and dependency (UD) parsing) (Nivre et al., 2015), this paper is concerned with two important questions:

(Q1) Can one usefully replace the DEPS extraction pipeline optimised for tools developed for English with a pipeline that relies on language-universal syntactic processing (UDEPS)?

(Q2) Are UDEPS universally better than BOW for learning distributed word representations in other languages?

Regarding Q1, the results show that it is possible to replace original DEPS with UDEPS for English and to obtain benchmarking results with only a slight drop in performance. As for Q2, the framework is not equally effective in other languages, as suggested by the performance in Italian and German, which sheds new light on the usefulness of BOW and dependency-based contexts. Further, the results reveal that even a simple preliminary "post-parsing" selection of use-

Proceedings of the 54th Annual Meeting of the Association for Computational Linguistics, pages 518–524,
Berlin, Germany, August 7-12, 2016. ©2016 Association for Computational Linguistics

ful UDEPS contexts leads to consistent improvements across languages, especially in detecting functional similarity.

This focused contribution is the first cross-linguistic comparison of different context types for learning word representations in three languages, reaching beyond English. It also constitutes a first completely language-universal and widely applicable framework for UDEPS extraction.

2 Methodology

Universal Multilingual Resources The departure point in our experiments is the Universal Dependencies project (McDonald et al., 2013; Nivre et al., 2015) which develops cross-linguistically consistent treebank annotation.[1] The annotation scheme leans on the universal Stanford dependencies (de Marneffe et al., 2014) complemented with the Google universal POS tagset (Petrov et al., 2012) and the Interset interlingua for morphological tagsets (Zeman and Resnik, 2008). It provides a universal and consistent inventory of categories for similar syntactic constructions across languages.

The main aim of the "universal initiative" is to facilitate cross-lingual and multilingual learning (e.g., multilingual parser development, typologies) by capturing structural similarities across languages and by exploiting connections that exist naturally between them (Berg-Kirkpatrick and Klein, 2010; McDonald et al., 2011; Cohen et al., 2011; Naseem et al., 2012). Here, we test the ability of such a universal annotation scheme to encode potentially useful semantic knowledge cross-linguistically; in this case, to yield more informed UDEPS contexts for improved word embeddings.

The extraction of UDEPS as the new variant of dependency-based contexts is completely language-agnostic on purpose: exactly the same procedure is followed for each language in comparison in order to make the representation learning framework completely universal.

2.1 Context Types

Prequel: Representation Model For all the context types, we opt for the standard and robust choice in vector space modeling: SGNS (Mikolov et al., 2013b; Levy et al., 2015). In all our experiments we use `word2vecf`, a reimplementa-

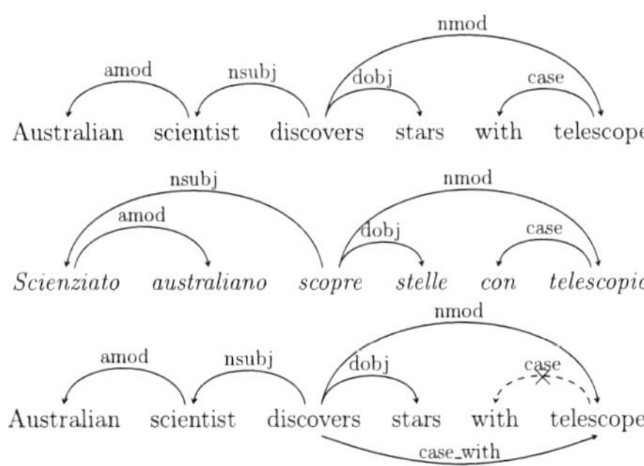

Figure 1: An example of extracting dependency-based contexts from UD parses (UDEPS) in English and Italian. **Top**: the example sentence in English taken from (Levy and Goldberg, 2014a), now UD-parsed. **Middle**: the same sentence in Italian, UD-parsed. Note the very similar structure of the two parses. **Bottom**: the intuition behind UDEPS-ARC. The uninformative short-range *case* arc between *with* and *telescope* is removed, and another "pseudo-arc" now specifying the exact link type (i.e., *case_with*) between *discovers* and *telescope* is added.

tion of `word2vec` which is capable of learning from arbitrary $(word, context)$ pairs.[2] Keeping the representation model fixed across experiments and varying only the context type allows us to attribute any differences in results to a sole factor: the context type.

BOW The English sentence from Fig. 1 is used as the running example for all context types. Given the target word w and the window size k, the BOW context simply comprises all $2k$ word pairs (w, v), where v is found in the window of k words preceding w or k words following w, e.g., BOW with $k = 2$ extracts the following contexts v for the word *discovers* from Fig. 1: *Australian, scientist, stars, with*. Note that BOW may miss valid longer-range contexts (e.g., *telescope*) while including some accidental (e.g., *Australian*) or uninformative ones (e.g., *with*).

POSIT A more informed variant of BOW is *positional contexts*. It includes extra information on the actual sequential position of each context word (Levy and Goldberg, 2014b). Given the same example, POSIT with $k = 2$ extracts the following contexts for *discovers*: *Australian_-2, scientist_-*

---

[1]We use the latest Version 1.2 UD treebanks: http://universaldependencies.org/

[2]https://bitbucket.org/yoavgo/word2vecf
For details concerning the implementation and learning, we refer the interested reader to (Goldberg and Levy, 2014; Levy and Goldberg, 2014a).

1, stars_+2, with_+1. This context type has not been studied systematically in relation to learning WEs. POSIT suffers from the same issues with locality as BOW, but its shallow positional annotations may capture additional shallow syntactic phenomena in the data. Therefore, POSIT may be considered a link from BOW towards DEPS.[3]

UDEPS-NAIVE Given a corpus of parsed sentences, for each target w with modifiers $m_1, \ldots, m_k$ and head h, w is paired with context elements $m_1\_r_1, \ldots, m_k\_r_k, h\_r_h^{-1}$, where r is the type of the UD relation between the head and the modifier (e.g., *amod*), and r^{-1} denotes an inverse relation. A *naive* version of the UD-based model extracts contexts from the parsed corpus without any post-processing. The UDEPS-NAIVE contexts of *discovers* are now: *scientist_nsubj, stars_dobj, telescope_nmod*. They capture longer-range relations (e.g., *telescope*) and filter "accidental contexts" (e.g., *Australian*). In addition, the typed dependencies reveal more than POSIT and BOW about the nature of the relation in context.

UDEPS-ARC However, UDEPS-NAIVE also produces uninformative context pairs such as *(telescope, with_case)*, and it does not specify the type of e.g. the *nmod* relation between *discovers* and *telescope* which are linked through the preposition *with*. Our intuition is that a simple post-hoc intervention into the UDEPS context extraction may yield even more focused contexts. UDEPS-ARC leans on the idea of *arc collapsing* from prior work (Levy and Goldberg, 2014a; Melamud et al., 2016) that we now adjust to the UD annotation scheme. The difference to UDEPS-NAIVE is as follows: For each pair of words linked through *case* (e.g., *discovers* and *telescope*), we introduce a new "pseudo-arc" which is typed by the actual *case*/preposition. This results in a new context for *discovers*: *telescope_case_with* and also for *telescope*: *discovers_case_with*$^{-1}$ (Fig. 1). In addition, we remove the uninformative *case* arc and its associated contexts: *(with, telescope_case*$^{-1}$), *(telescope, with_case)* from the training pairs.

---

[3]Results with another context type relying on substitute vectors (Yatbaz et al., 2012; Melamud et al., 2015) are omitted due to its subpar performance in our experiments as well as across a variety of semantic tasks in a recent English-focused study (Melamud et al., 2016).

Language	Tagging Acc.	LAS [UAS]
English (EN)	0.952	0.852 [0.875]
German (DE)	0.923	0.802 [0.850]
Italian (IT)	0.970	0.884 [0.907]

Table 1: Universal POS tagging accuracy scores and labeled (LAS) vs unlabeled (UAS) attachment scores of universal dependency parsing.

3 Experimental Setup

Evaluation Our cross-linguistic study is made possible not only thanks to the "universal NLP" initiative but also owing to the benchmarking evaluation sets for other languages beyond English (i.e., IT, DE) that have very recently become available, e.g., (Leviant and Reichart, 2015). We evaluate SGNS with different context types from sect. 2.1 across the three languages on two benchmarking tasks and datasets: (1) semantic similarity on SimLex-999 (Hill et al., 2015) translated and re-scored by native speakers in EN, DE, and IT (Leviant and Reichart, 2015), and (2) word analogies on the Google dataset (Mikolov et al., 2013a) made available in IT (Berardi et al., 2015) and DE (Köper et al., 2015) only recently.

WE Induction: Data All the word representations in comparison are induced from the Polyglot Wikipedia data (Al-Rfou et al., 2013).[4]

UPOS Tagging and UD Parsing The Wikipedia corpora were UPOS-tagged using a state-of-the art system TurboTagger (Martins et al., 2013).[5] TurboTagger was trained using suggested settings without any further parameter fine-tuning (SVM MIRA with 20 iterations) on the TRAIN+DEV portion of the UD treebank annotated with UPOS tags. Following that, the Wikipedia data were UD-parsed[6] using the graph-based Mate parser v3.61 (Bohnet, 2010)[7] and the same regime: suggested settings on the TRAIN+DEV UD treebank portion.[8] The performance of the models measured on the TEST portion of the UD treebanks is reported in Tab. 1.

---

[4]https://sites.google.com/site/rmyeid/projects/polyglot
[5]http://www.cs.cmu.edu/ ark/TurboParser/

[6]Besides EN, DE, and IT, we also UPOS-tagged and UD-parsed Wikipedias in NL, ES, and HR. We believe that the full UPOS-tagged and UD-parsed Wikipedias in six languages are a valuable asset for future research and we plan to make the resource publicly available at:
http://ltl.mml.cam.ac.uk/resources/
[7]https://code.google.com/archive/p/mate-tools/

[8]We opted for the Mate parser due to its speed, simplicity, and state-of-the-art performance according to very recent parser evaluations (Choi et al., 2015).

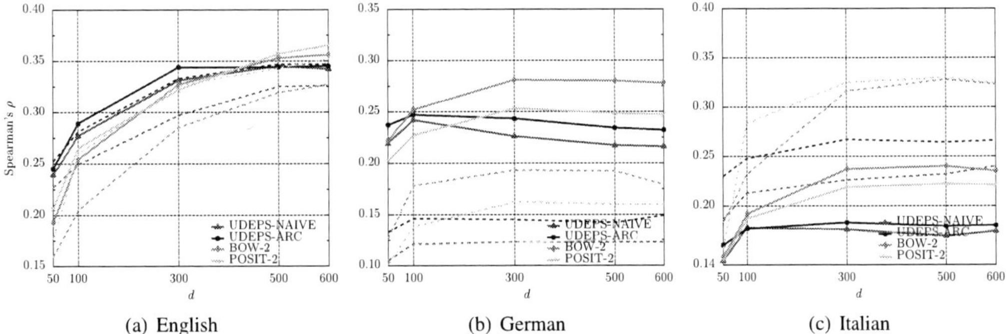

(a) English   (b) German   (c) Italian

Figure 2: Results in the semantic similarity task on SimLex-999 for three languages using different context types in the SGNS model. Solid lines denote the results on all words from SimLex-999, while thinner dashed lines show results on the verb portion of SimLex-999 (222 verb pairs).

Language:	English			German			Italian		
	TOT	SEM	SYN	TOT	SEM	SYN	TOT	SEM	SYN
UDEPS-NAIVE	0.351	0.231	0.446	0.183	0.101	0.276	0.169	0.033	0.282
UDEPS-ARC	0.376	0.247	0.478	0.199	0.091	0.319	0.177	0.033	0.296
DEPS-LEVY	0.390	0.183	0.548	-	-	-	-	-	-
BOW-2	0.581	0.543	0.610	0.334	0.341	0.326	0.225	0.078	0.339
POSIT-2	0.485	0.336	0.607	0.219	0.173	0.271	0.208	0.052	0.330

Table 2: $Acc@1$ scores in the analogy solving task over semantic (SEM), syntactic (SYN) and all analogies (TOT). SGNS with $d = 300$ for all context types. Similar trends are observed with other d-s. DEPS-LEVY refers to pre-trained 300-dimensional EN WEs from (Levy and Goldberg, 2014a).

The results are consistent with prior work on the UD treebanks, e.g., (Tiedemann, 2015).

Training Setup The SGNS preprocessing scheme for English was replicated from (Levy and Goldberg, 2014a) and extended to the other two languages: all tokens were converted to lowercase, and words and contexts that appeared less than 100 times were filtered. Exactly the same vocabularies were used with all context types (approx. 185K distinct EN words, 163K DE words, and 83K IT words). The `word2vecf` SGNS was trained using standard settings: 15 epochs, 15 negative samples, global learning rate 0.025, subsampling rate $1e - 4$. All WEs were trained with $d = 50, 100, 300, 500, 600$. BOW-based WEs were trained with $k = 2$ (BOW-2), proven to be the (near-)optimal choice across various semantic tasks in related work (Levy and Goldberg, 2014a; Melamud et al., 2016). The same k was used for POSIT-based WEs (POSIT-2).

4 Results and Discussion

Fig. 2(a)-2(c) show the results on SimLex-999 (Spearman's ρ) for WEs with different d-s, while Tab. 2 displays the $Acc@1$ scores in the anal-

ogy solving task. English DEPS with arc collapsing from prior work (Levy and Goldberg, 2014a) (DEPS-LEVY, $d = 300$) obtain ρ of 0.372 on all SimLex pairs, and 0.378 on verb pairs.[9] A comparison with UDEPS-ARC reveals only a slight drop in performance when switching to language-agnostic UDEPS (see Fig. 2(a), Q1).[10]

However, the results are heavily dependent on the actual language: the claims made for English (i.e., DEPS $\geq$ BOW) do not extend to other languages (Q2). A comparison of results from Tab. 1 with the task evaluation also shows that excellent tagging and parsing results do not guarantee a strong task performance.

The results over the verb subset of SimLex also reveal that claims established with English are not necessarily general and true with other languages. For instance, while it has been noted that modeling verb similarity is indeed a difficult problem in English as evidenced by lower correlation scores on SimLex (see Fig. 2(a) and e.g. (Schwartz et al., 2015)), verbs are apparently easier to model in Italian (Fig. 2(c)), and a real challenge in German,

---

[9]Note that the correlation scores for all models on the re-annotated version of SimLex-999 (Leviant and Reichart, 2015) are lower than those on the original SimLex-999.

[10]The comparison is valid since DEPS-LEVY were trained on exactly the same data with the same vocabulary.

521

Syntactic Relation	English	German	Italian
gram1-adjective-to-adverb	P>B>A>N	-	P>B>A>N
gram2-opposite	A>N>P>B	A>B>P>N	A>B>P>N
gram3-comparative	P>B>A>N	A>B>P>N	P>A>N>B
gram4-superlative	P>B>A>N	A>N>B>P	P>B>A>N
gram5-present-participle	P>A>B>N	A>N>P>B	P>B>A>N
gram6-nationality-adjective	B>P>A>N	B>P>A>N	B>P>A>N
gram7-past-tense	A>P>N>B	A>B>N>P	A>B>P>N
gram8-plural	B>P>A>N	A>B>P>N	A>P>N>B
gram9-plural-verbs	P>A>B>N	A>N>B>P	A>N>P>B

Table 3: Rankings based on Acc_1 scores over syntactic analogy groups (from the Google dataset). A=UDEPS-ARC, N=UDEPS-NAIVE, B=BOW-2, P=POSIT-2. $d = 300$.

with extremely low correlation scores (Fig. 2(b)).

The results on the analogy task from Tab. 2 suggest the evident advantage of more abundant (but less informed) BOW contexts across all languages. This finding is completely in line with the analyses from prior work on English, e.g., Levy and Goldberg (2014a) report that "DEPS perform dramatically worse than BOW contexts on analogy tasks", but without providing any exact numbers.

Nonetheless, the relative ranking of context types over syntactic analogy sets as highlighted in Tab. 3 marks the evident advantage of the more-informed POSIT and UDEPS-ARC on analogies referring to functional similarity. UDEPS-ARC in German outperforms all other context types on all syntactic analogies, except for the *nationality-adjective* relation. The strongest performance of UDEPS is detected with syntactic analogies where two words in the analogy pair are perfectly replaceable in the given context (e.g., past-tense: *dancing-danced, sleeping-slept* or opposite: *sure-unsure, honest-dishonest*).

We can also see that POSIT displays a strong performance in detecting functional similarity across all three languages in both tasks (e.g., see the results in Tab. 3 where they outperform BOW). This finding reveals that POSIT should be included as a strong baseline in any follow-up work.

We also analysed the influence of the training data size by learning EN WEs from the EN Wikipedia comprising roughly 13M sentences (same size as the IT Wikipedia). As Tab. 4 shows, the absolute scores are naturally lower with less training data, and we observe a decrease in the performance of UDEPS. However, the decrease is small: these results demonstrate that the reduced performance of UDEPS in IT and DE cannot be attributed solely to smaller training datasets and sparsity of $(word, context)$ pairs.

Finally, the consistent improvements of

Set/Model	BOW-2	POSIT-2	NAIVE	ARC
SimLex-all	0.286	0.289	0.271	0.279
SimLex-verbs	0.259	0.286	0.260	0.288

Table 4: Results on SimLex in English with SGNS trained on a reduced EN training set containing the same number of sentences as the entire IT training set ($\approx$ 13M sentences). $d = 300$.

UDEPS-ARC over UDEPS-NAIVE for all three languages on both tasks show the importance of a careful post-hoc selection of informative contexts. Future work will delve deeper into the informative context selection for the WE learning.

5   Conclusion and Future Work

We have presented the first comparison of different context types for learning word embeddings for multiple languages. Dependency-based contexts in different languages are for the first time extracted from "universal" parses made possible by the Universal Dependencies initiative, without any language-specific optimisation.

In sum, our comparison provides no clear answer to the question posed by the title of this paper. However, it shows conclusively that different context types yield semantic spaces with different properties, and that the optimal context type depends on the actual application and language. The usefulness of universal dependency-based contexts is evident with a simple post-parsing context extraction scheme in tasks oriented towards syntactic/functional similarity.

This first cross-linguistic analysis covering only a small set of languages from the same (Indo-European) phylum also reveals that training word embeddings in languages other than English is not trivial, suggesting Anglo-centric assumptions that do not extend to other languages (Bender, 2011). It is therefore essential not to generalise results on English to other languages without clear empirical evidence. Yet, a broader cross-linguistic study involving more languages from other families (with UD treebanks available) and additional experimentation is warranted in order to better guide research on "universal NLP" and language-independent word representation learning.

Acknowledgments

This work is supported by ERC Consolidator Grant LEXICAL (648909). The authors are grateful to Roi Reichart and the anonymous reviewers for their helpful comments and suggestions.

References

Rami Al-Rfou, Bryan Perozzi, and Steven Skiena. 2013. Polyglot: Distributed word representations for multilingual NLP. In *CoNLL*, pages 183–192.

Mohit Bansal, Kevin Gimpel, and Karen Livescu. 2014. Tailoring continuous word representations for dependency parsing. In *ACL*, pages 809–815.

Marco Baroni, Georgiana Dinu, and Germán Kruszewski. 2014. Don't count, predict! A systematic comparison of context-counting vs. context-predicting semantic vectors. In *ACL*, pages 238–247.

Emily M. Bender. 2011. On achieving and evaluating language-independence in NLP. *Linguistic Issues in Language Technology*, 6(3):1–28.

Giacomo Berardi, Andrea Esuli, and Diego Marcheggiani. 2015. Word embeddings go to Italy: A comparison of models and training datasets. In *Italian Information Retrieval Workshop*.

Taylor Berg-Kirkpatrick and Dan Klein. 2010. Phylogenetic grammar induction. In *ACL*, pages 1288–1297.

Bernd Bohnet. 2010. Top accuracy and fast dependency parsing is not a contradiction. In *COLING*, pages 89–97.

Danqi Chen and Christopher D. Manning. 2014. A fast and accurate dependency parser using neural networks. In *EMNLP*, pages 740–750.

Jinho D. Choi, Joel Tetreault, and Amanda Stent. 2015. It depends: Dependency parser comparison using a Web-based evaluation tool. In *ACL*, pages 387–396.

Shay B. Cohen, Dipanjan Das, and Noah A. Smith. 2011. Unsupervised structure prediction with non-parallel multilingual guidance. In *EMNLP*, pages 50–61.

Ronan Collobert, Jason Weston, Léon Bottou, Michael Karlen, Koray Kavukcuoglu, and Pavel P. Kuksa. 2011. Natural language processing (almost) from scratch. *Journal of Machine Learning Research*, 12:2493–2537.

Marie-Catherine de Marneffe, Timothy Dozat, Natalia Silveira, Katri Haverinen, Filip Ginter, Joakim Nivre, and Christopher D. Manning. 2014. Universal Stanford dependencies: A cross-linguistic typology. In *LREC*, pages 4585–4592.

Yoav Goldberg and Omer Levy. 2014. Word2vec explained: Deriving Mikolov et al.'s negative-sampling word-embedding method. *CoRR*, abs/1402.3722.

Felix Hill, Roi Reichart, and Anna Korhonen. 2015. SimLex-999: Evaluating semantic models with (genuine) similarity estimation. *Computational Linguistics*, 41(4):665–695.

Maximilian Köper, Christian Scheible, and Sabine Schulte im Walde. 2015. Multilingual reliability and "semantic" structure of continuous word spaces. In *IWCS*, pages 40–45.

Ira Leviant and Roi Reichart. 2015. Separated by an un-common language: Towards judgment language informed vector space modeling. *CoRR*, abs/1508.00106.

Omer Levy and Yoav Goldberg. 2014a. Dependency-based word embeddings. In *ACL*, pages 302–308.

Omer Levy and Yoav Goldberg. 2014b. Linguistic regularities in sparse and explicit word representations. In *CoNLL*, pages 171–180.

Omer Levy, Yoav Goldberg, and Ido Dagan. 2015. Improving distributional similarity with lessons learned from word embeddings. *Transactions of the ACL*, 3:211–225.

André F. T. Martins, Miguel B. Almeida, and Noah A. Smith. 2013. Turning on the turbo: Fast third-order non-projective turbo parsers. In *ACL*, pages 617–622.

Ryan McDonald, Slav Petrov, and Keith Hall. 2011. Multi-source transfer of delexicalized dependency parsers. In *EMNLP*, pages 62–72.

Ryan T. McDonald, Joakim Nivre, Yvonne Quirmbach-Brundage, Yoav Goldberg, Dipanjan Das, Kuzman Ganchev, Keith B. Hall, Slav Petrov, Hao Zhang, Oscar Täckström, Claudia Bedini, Núria Bertomeu Castelló, and Jungmee Lee. 2013. Universal dependency annotation for multilingual parsing. In *ACL*, pages 92–97.

Oren Melamud, Ido Dagan, and Jacob Goldberger. 2015. Modeling word meaning in context with substitute vectors. In *NAACL-HLT*, pages 472–482.

Oren Melamud, David McClosky, Siddharth Patwardhan, and Mohit Bansal. 2016. The role of context types and dimensionality in learning word embeddings. In *NAACL-HLT*.

Tomas Mikolov, Kai Chen, Gregory S. Corrado, and Jeffrey Dean. 2013a. Efficient estimation of word representations in vector space. In *ICLR Workshop Papers*.

Tomas Mikolov, Ilya Sutskever, Kai Chen, Gregory S. Corrado, and Jeffrey Dean. 2013b. Distributed representations of words and phrases and their compositionality. In *NIPS*, pages 3111–3119.

Tahira Naseem, Regina Barzilay, and Amir Globerson. 2012. Selective sharing for multilingual dependency parsing. In *ACL*, pages 629–637.

Joakim Nivre et al. 2015. Universal Dependencies 1.2. LINDAT/CLARIN digital library at Institute of Formal and Applied Linguistics, Charles University in Prague.

Sebastian Padó and Mirella Lapata. 2007. Dependency-based construction of semantic space models. *Computational Linguistics*, 33(2):161–199.

Slav Petrov, Dipanjan Das, and Ryan T. McDonald. 2012. A universal part-of-speech tagset. In *LREC*, pages 2089–2096.

Roy Schwartz, Roi Reichart, and Ari Rappoport. 2015. Symmetric pattern based word embeddings for improved word similarity prediction. In *CoNLL*, pages 258–267.

Jörg Tiedemann. 2015. Cross-lingual dependency parsing with universal dependencies and predicted PoS labels. In *DepLing*, pages 340–349.

Joseph P. Turian, Lev-Arie Ratinov, and Yoshua Bengio. 2010. Word representations: A simple and general method for semi-supervised learning. In *ACL*, pages 384–394.

Mehmet Ali Yatbaz, Enis Sert, and Deniz Yuret. 2012. Learning syntactic categories using paradigmatic representations of word context. In *EMNLP*, pages 940–951.

Daniel Zeman and Philip Resnik. 2008. Cross-language parser adaptation between related languages. In *IJCNLP*, pages 35–42.

Claim Synthesis via Predicate Recycling

Yonatan Bilu
IBM Haifa Research Lab
Mount Carmel, Haifa, 31905
Israel
yonatanb@il.ibm.com

Noam Slonim
IBM Haifa Research Lab
Mount Carmel, Haifa, 31905
Israel
noams@il.ibm.com

Abstract

Computational Argumentation has two main goals - the detection and analysis of arguments on the one hand, and the synthesis of arguments on the other. Much attention has been given to the former, but considerably less to the latter.

A key component in synthesizing arguments is the synthesis of claims. One way to do so is by employing argumentation mining to detect claims within an appropriate corpus. In general, this appears to be a hard problem. Thus, it is interesting to explore if - for the sake of synthesis - there may be other ways to generate claims.

Here we explore such a method: we extract the predicate of simple, manually-detected, claims, and attempt to generate novel claims from them. Surprisingly, this simple method yields fairly good results.

1 Introduction

When people argue, how do they come up with the arguments they present, and can a machine emulate this? The motivation for this work comes from this second question, for which the relevant field of study is Computational Argumentation, an emerging field with roots in Computer Science, Mathematics, Philosophy and Rhetorics. However, while much attention is given in the field to the modeling and analysis of arguments, automatic synthesis of arguments receives considerably less.

So, how do people come up with arguments? One way is to read-up on the topic and present the arguments you find in the literature. Another - if the topic at hand is within your field of expertise - is to communicate your opinion. Yet a third way is to "recycle" arguments you are familiar with and apply them to new domains. For example, someone who's concerned about the free speech might use an argument like "it's a violation of free speech" when discussing any one of these topics: whether violent video games should be banned, whether some Internet content should be censored, or whether certain types of advertisement should be restricted.

Argumentation Mining (Mochales Palau and Moens, 2011) is analogous to the first option: Given a corpus, it aims to detect arguments therein (and the relations among them). Thus, it can be used to suggest claims when a relevant corpus is available. The second option is analogous to Natural Language Generation (NLG; (Reiter and Dale, 2000)), where applications such as recommender systems synthesize arguments to explain their recommendations, as done for example in (Carenini and Moore, 2006) .

These approaches yield good results when applied to specific domains. In an NLG application, there is commonly a specific knowledge base which the system communicates. The form and content of arguments are derived and determined by it and are thus limited to the knowledge therein. Similarly, argument mining works well when an argument-rich and topic-related corpus is available - e.g. (Wyner et al., 2010) - but in general seems to be hard (Levy et al., 2014). Thus, it is interesting and challenging to synthesize arguments in an open domain. To the best of our knowledge, this is the first work that directly attempts to address this task

Modeling of arguments goes back to the ancient Greeks and Aristotle, and more modern work starting perhaps most famously with the Toulmin argument model (Toulmin, 1958). A common element in all such models is the *claim* (or *conclusion*) being forwarded by the argument. Thus, a natural first step in synthesizing arguments in a general setting is being able to synthesize claims in such a setting.

We suggest here a simple way for doing so,

525

Proceedings of the 54th Annual Meeting of the Association for Computational Linguistics, pages 525–530,
Berlin, Germany, August 7-12, 2016. ©2016 Association for Computational Linguistics

based on the aforementioned notion of argument "recycling". Specifically, that the *predicate* of a claim - what it says on the topic at hand - may be applicable to other topics as well. For example, if we are familiar with the claim "banning violent video games *is a violation of free speech*" in the context of the topic "banning violent video games", we could synthesize the claim "Internet censorship *is a violation of free speech*" when presented with the topic "Internet Censorship". The challenge is then to determine whether the synthesized claim is actually coherent and relevant to the new topic, which we do using statistical Machine Learning techniques, as described in Section 2.1.

This two-stages framework - generating text and then selecting whether or not it is appropriate - is reminiscent of Statistical NLG (SNLG; (Langklide and Knight, 1998)). In an SNLG system, after the macro-planning and micro-planning stages (see (Reiter and Dale, 2000)) are executed, and the message to be communicated is determined, multiple candidate realizations are produced, and then statistical methods are used to determine which of these realizations is the best (based on a reference corpus).

Our work differs from SNLG in that there are no pre-determined messages. The generation stage produces candidate *content*. Each candidate claim is a different message, and the selection stage attempts to identify those which are coherent and relevant, rather than best realized. In other words, while the classical NLG paradigm is to first select the content and then realize it in a natural language, here our building blocks from the onset are natural language elements, and statistical methods are used to determine which content selections - implied by combining them - are valid.

Finally, the notion that predicates of claims regarding one topic may be applicable to another is reminiscent of the motivation for the work of (Card et al., 2015), who observe that there are commonalities (so called "framing dimensions") among the way different topics are framed in news articles.

2 Algorithm

The claim synthesis algorithm is composed of three components. The first is a pre-processing component, in which the Predicate Lexicon is constructed. The second is the Generation Component - the input to this component is a topic (and the Predicate Lexicon), and the output is a list of candidate claims. The final component is the Selection Component, in which a classifier is used to determine which (if any) of the candidate claims are coherent and relevant for the topic. In what follows we describe these three steps in greater detail.

The Predicate Lexicon (PL) was constructed by parsing manually-detected claims (Aharoni et al., 2014) using the Watson ESG parser (McCord et al., 2012), and considering those which have exactly one verb. Then the verb and a concatenation of its right-modifiers, termed here the *predicate*, were extracted from each claim and added to the PL if they contained at least one sentiment word from the sentiment lexicon of (Hu and Liu, 2004). The sentiment criterion was added to select for predicates which have a clear stance with respect to the topic. All in all, there are 1203 entries in the PL used here.[1]

A key feature in filtering and selecting candidate claims is text similarity. The similarity between text segments was defined based on the constituent words' word2vec embedding (Mikolov et al., 2013): Consider two list of words, $l = w_1, \ldots, w_n$ and $l' = w'_1, \ldots, w'_{n'}$. Denote by $w2v(w, w')$ the word2vec similarity between w and w' - the cosine of the angle between the embeddings of w and w'. Then the similarity between l and l' is defined : $sim(l, l') = \frac{1}{n} \sum_{i=1,\ldots,n} \max_{j=1,\ldots,n'} w2v(w_i, w'_j) + \frac{1}{n'} \sum_{j=1,\ldots,n'} \max_{i=1,\ldots,n} w2v(w'_j, w_i)$ (words without embeddings are ignored). Additionally, if S is a set of text segments, define: $sim(l, S) = max_{l' \in S} sim(l, l')$.

Given a new topic t, the Generation Component sorts the predicates p in the PL according to $sim(t, p)$, and takes the top k. It then constructs k claim candidate sentences by setting the subject of the sentence to be the topic t, and the predicate to be one of these k. This may require some manipulation, as the plurality of the topic determines the appropriate surface realization of the predicate verb. We determine the topic's plurality using the Watson parser (McCord et al., 2012), and do the surface realization with SimpleNLG (Gatt and Reiter, 2009) and the NIH lexicon[2].

---

[1] data is avaiable at https://www.research.ibm.com/haifa/dept/vst/mlta_data.shtml.

[2] UMLS Reference Manual [Internet]. Bethesda (MD): National Library of Medicine (US); 2009 Sep-. 6, SPECIALIST Lexicon and Lexical Tools. Available from:

The Selection Component uses a logistic regression classifier to first predict which of the candidate claims generated by the Generation Component are valid, and then to rank the valid candidates according to the classifier's score. It receives two parameters, κ and τ. If the fraction of valid candidates (according to the classifier) is less than τ, then it selects none of them. This is designed to allow the algorithm not to synthesize claims for topics where the PL does not seem to yield a substantial number of valid claims. If the number of valid candidates is at least τ, the top κ valid candidates are returned (or all of them, if there are less than κ).

2.1 Classification Features

To describe the classification features used, we need to define - given a topic - the topic's n-gram Lexicon (n-TL). This is a list of n-grams which are presumably related to the topic. Specifically, given an n-gram, we assume its appearance in Wikipedia articles follows a hyper-geometric distribution, and estimate the distribution's parameters by counting the n-gram's appearance in a large set of Wikipedia articles. With these parameters, the p-value for its appearances in topic-related articles is calculated. The n-TL is the list of n-grams with Bonferroni-corrected p-value at most 0.05. The topic-related articles were identified manually (see (Aharoni et al., 2014)).

For a candidate claim c, denote its words by $w_1, \ldots, w_m$. Recall that c is composed of the given topic, t, and a predicate $p \in PL$. Recall also that p was extracted from a manually-detected claim c_p. Denote by t_p the topic for which c_p was detected, and by s_p the subject of the claim sentence c_p. Denote by m_t the number of words in t.

For example, consider the second candidate claim in Table 1, c = *Truth and reconciliation commissions are a source of conflict* There t = *truth and reconciliation commissions* and p = *are a source of conflict*. p was extracted from the claim c_p = *religion is a source of conflict* in the labeled data, which is associated with the topic *atheism* (and the debatabase motion *atheism is the only way*). Hence, t_p = *atheism* and s_p = *religion*.

The classification features we used are of three types: One aims to identify predicates which are inherently amenable to generation of claims, that is, which state something fairly general about their subject, and which are not very specific to the topic in which the predicate was originally found (e.g., low $sim(p, t_p)$). The second aims to find predicates which are relevant for the new topic for which claims are synthesized (e.g., high $sim(p,\text{n-TL})$). Finally, we'd like the claim to be a valid and plausible sentence, and so look for the frequency of its words, and sub-phrases of it, in Wikipedia.

All in all 15 features were defined: m, the number of words in c; Number of Lucene hits for $w_1, \ldots, w_m$ (as a bag of words); Number of Wikipedia sentences containing all $w_1, \ldots, w_m$; Largest k, such that the k-gram $w_1 \ldots w_k$ appears in Wikipedia; Number of times the 3-gram $w_{m_t} w_{m_t+1} w_{m_t+2}$ appears in Wikipedia; Number of times p appears in a claim candidate labeled positive, and the number of times in one labeled negative (claim candidates generated for t are excluded, see Section 3 for labeling details); Inclusion of p's verb in a manually-crafted list of "causation verbs"; $sim(p,\text{n-TL})$, for $n = 1, 2, 3$; $sim(p, t)$; $sim(p, t_p)$; $sim(s_p, t_p)$; $sim(s_p, t)$.

3 Experimental Setup

We generated claims for 67 topics, extracted from debatabase motions (http://idebate.org) for which we have previously annotated relevant Wikipedia articles (for the benefit of the n-TLs construction; see Section 2.1). Importantly, when generating candidate claims for a topic, predicates which originated from this topic were *not used*.

For each topic 28 candidate claims were generated, and in addition one manually-detected claim (as per (Aharoni et al., 2014)) and one mock claim were included for control. The mock claim was constructed by setting the topic as the subject of a sentence, and selecting a mock predicate at random from a hand-crafted list.

These 67×30 candidate claims were annotated using Amazon's Mechanical Turk (AMT). In each HIT (Human Intelligence Task) we presented the annotators with a debatabase motion and 10 candidate claims, and asked which of the claims is appropriate for the motion (10 annotators per HIT).

After filtering out the less reliable annotators based on mutual agreement and control questions, a reasonable agreement was apparent (average $\kappa = 0.73$). After this filtering 45 of the initial 82 annotators remained, as well as 955 of the initial 2010 annotated candidate claims (discard-

---

http://www.ncbi.nlm.nih.gov/books/NBK9680/

Claim	Original Subject	Label
Democratization **contributes to stability**.	Nuclear weapons	1
Truth and reconciliation commissions **are a source of conflict**.	Religion	1
Graduated response **lacks moral legitimacy**.	The State	1
Nuclear weapons **cause lung cancer**.	Smoking	0
A global language **leads to great exhaustion**.	Great anarchy	0

Table 1: Examples of candidate claims (topics in italics, predicates in bold), the subject of the claim sentence which originated their predicate, and their label.

ing claims with less than 5 valid annotators, those without a clear majority decision, as well as the control claims). See Table 1 for some examples.

We note that annotation tasks like this are inherently subjective ((Aharoni et al., 2014) report $\kappa = 0.4$), so discarding candidates without a clear majority decision can be seen as discarding those for which the true label is not well defined. Nonetheless, the reason for discarding most of the candidate claims was annotator's (lack of) reliability, not ambiguity of the true label.

4   Experimental Results

Initially we thought to label a candidate claim as either positive or negative examples, based on the majority vote of the annotators. This lead to a seemingly 52% of the candidates being "good". However, anecdotal examination of this majority labeling suggested that the many annotators were biased toward answering "good" - even on some of the control questions which contained nonsensical sentences. This, along side relatively low mean agreement, raised the need for filtering mentioned above. After filtering, 40% of the candidate claims were taken to be positive examples. The accuracy of the Selection Component was assessed using a leave-one-out methodology, leaving out one topic at each iteration. The overall accuracy achieved by the classifier was 0.75 (Table 2 depicts the confusion matrix).

We also examined the trade-off between the number of selected candidate claims and the fraction of them which are valid. Figure 1 depicts the

Predict /Label	Pos	Neg
Pos	288 (30%)	145 (15%)
Neg	96 (10%)	426 (45%)

Table 2: Confusion Matrix: Number of claim candidates according to AMT annotation (x-axis) and predicted label (y-axis)

average precision when varying the two Selection Component parameters, κ and τ. For example, at the most conservative setting, where the component outputs at most one claim per topic, and only for a topic for which at least half the candidate claims were predicted to be valid (31 of the 67 topics), the precision is 0.94. Recall that in the entire dataset, 40% of the examples are positive.

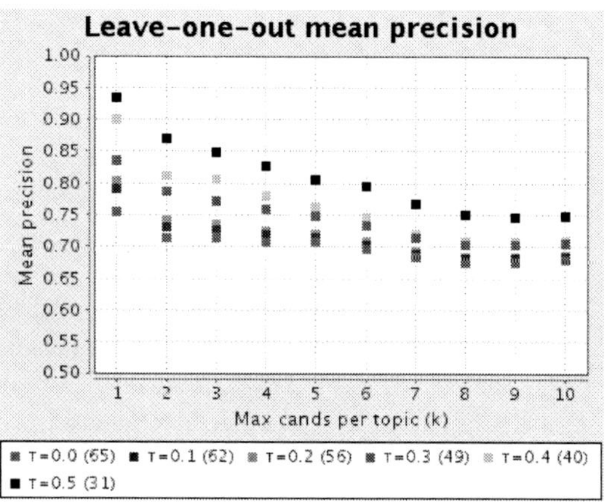

Figure 1: Mean Precision (micro average): Colors indicate different values of τ. In parenthesis is the number of topics for which claims were selected.

We note that this precision is significantly higher than reported for claim detection (Levy et al., 2014), where, for example, mean precision at 5 is 0.28 (in our case it is $0.7 - 0.8$). One should note, however, that this is not a fair comparison. First, we permit the algorithm to discard some topics. Second, here the definition of a valid claim is less strict than in (Levy et al., 2014).

Examining the impact of individual features, we first looked which of them, on their own, are most correlated with the labels. These turned out to be the number of times p appears in a claim candidate labeled positive and negative (Pearson's correlation 0.33 and -0.34 resp.). We then examined which features received the most weight in the logistic regression classifier (trained over all data; features were scaled to a $[0, 1]$). The top feature was the number of sentences in which all words appear, and following it were the aforementioned appearance counts in negative and positive examples.

5 Discussion and Work in Progress

The Generation Component can be thought of as constructing sentences by using pre-defined templates, of the form "<topic-slot> <extracted predicate>". These "generation templates" are created by "mining" a corpus of manually-detected claims and extracting the predicate from them. They are then filled in during run-time, by inserting a new topic in that slot. There are several ways which we have started exploring to extend this paradigm - automatically identifying the grammatical position of a "topic slot" in a corpus claim rather than assuming it is the subject; using unsupervised methods for mining the predicates directly from Wikipedia; and generating candidate claims by using several variants for the subject and object, rather than just the topic and the PL entry. Initial results are promising, but more work is required to achieve reasonable accuracy.

Another interesting alternative is to construct the PL manually, rather than automatically. This can be seen as analogous to Argumentation Schemes (Walton et. al, 2008). Argumentation Schemes can be thought of as templates for modeling arguments - defining a slot for a premise or two (which may be implicit), a slot for a conclusion or claim, and some fixed connecting text. While Argumentation Schemes are used for detecting (Walton, 2012) and analyzing argumentative structures, in principle they can also be used to synthesize them. In this sense, our work here can be seen as applying the same concept at finer granularity - at the claim level instead of the argument.

While at the onset we presented claim synthesis as an alternative to argumentation mining for the purpose of generating arguments, it is interesting how the two augment each other. Specifically, we have started looking at whether claim synthesis can generate claims which do not appear in our corpus (Aharoni et al., 2014), and whether matching Evidence to claims (Rinott et. al, 2015) can improve claim synthesis. Regarding the novelty of synthesized claims, we looked at 18 synthesized claims, labeled as valid for 3 topics - criminalization of blasphemy, building high-rise for housing and making physical education compulsory - and compared them to the 94 manually detected claims

for these topics (each topic separately). Of the 18 claims, 5 appear to be novel.

A more circumvent method to assess novelty is as follows - for each candidate claim we looked for the most similar claim (for the same topic) in our annotated data. We then computed Pearson's correlation between these similarity scores and the labels of the candidate claim, getting a coefficient of 0.29 (p-value=10^{-27}). This is similar to the correlation between for the strongest classification features, suggesting again that many of the generated claims are not novel, yet similarity to annotated claims on its own is not enough to determine a candidate-claim's validity.

Similarly, we examined whether having a matching evidence in the annotated corpus (matches were determined using the algorithm of (Rinott et. al, 2015)), is indicative of a candidate-claim's validity. Computing correlation (over the 51 topic for which annotated evidence was available) gave a Pearson's coefficient of 0.23. This suggests that matching Evidence can be a powerful feature in improving our current classification model.

6 Acknowledgements

We thank Liat Ein-Dor for her contibution to this work, and especially for the development of the Topic Lexicons. We thank Uri Zakai, Ran Levy and Daniel Hershcovich for insightful discussions.

References

Ehud Aharoni, Anatoly Polnarov, Tamar Lavee, Daniel Hershcovich, Ran Levy, Ruty Rinott, Dan Gutfreund, Noam Slonim. A Benchmark Dataset for Automatic Detection of Claims and Evidence in the Context of Controversial Topics 2014. *Workshop on Argumentation Mining, ACL*

Ngo Xuan Bach, Nguyen Le Minh, Tran Thi Oanh, and Akira Shimazu. A Two-Phase Framework for Learning Logical Structures of Paragraphs in Legal Articles. 2013. *In ACM Transactions on Asian Language Information Processing (TALIP)*. 12(1):3

Dallas Card, Amber E. Boydstun, Justin H. Gross, Philip Resnik and Noah A. Smith. The Media Frames Corpus: Annotations of Frames Across Issues. 2015. *Association for Computational Linguistics Conference (ACL)*.

Carenini, Giuseppe, and Johanna D. Moore. Generating and evaluating evaluative arguments. *Artificial Intelligence 170, no. 11*: 925-952.

A Gatt and E Reiter (2009). SimpleNLG: A realisation engine for practical applications. 2009. *Proceedings of ENLG-2009.*

Minqing Hu and Bing Liu. 2004. Mining and summarizing customer reviews. 2004. *In Knowledge Discovery and Data Mining*: 168-177.

J.R. Landis and G.G. Kock. The measurement of observer agreement for categorical data". 1977. *Biometrics* 33 (1): 159174.

Irene Langkilde and Kevin Knight. Generation that exploits corpus-based statistical knowledge. 1998. *In Proceedings of the 36th Annual Meeting of the Association for Computational Linguistics and 17th International Conference on Computational Linguistics - Volume 1 (ACL '98), Vol. 1. Association for Computational Linguistics, Stroudsburg, PA, USA* 704-710.

Ran Levy, Yonatan Bilu, Daniel Hershcovich, Ehud Aharoni and Noam Slonim. Context Dependent Claim Detection 2014. *In The 25th International Conference on Computational Linguistics*

McCord, Michael C., J. William Murdock, and Branimir K. Boguraev. Deep parsing in Watson. 2012 *IBM Journal of Research and Development 56*, no. 3.4: 3-1.

Mikolov, Tomas, Ilya Sutskever, Kai Chen, Greg S. Corrado, and Jeff Dean. Distributed representations of words and phrases and their compositionality. 2013 *In Advances in neural information processing systems,* pp. 3111-3119.

Mochales Palau, Raquel and Moens, Marie-Francine. Argumentation mining. 2011. *In Artificial Intelligence and Law*, 19(1): 1-22.

Ehud Reiter and Robert Dale. Building Natural Language Generation Systems. 2000. Cambridge University Press, New York, NY, USA.

Rinott, Ruty, Lena Dankin, Carlos Alzate, Mitesh M. Khapra, Ehud Aharoni, and Noam Slonim. Show Me Your Evidencean Automatic Method for Context Dependent Evidence Detection. 2015 *In Proceedings of the 2015 Conference on Empirical Methods in NLP (EMNLP), Lisbon, Portugal,* pp. 17-21.

Stephen Toulmin. The Uses of Argument. 1958. Cambridge University Press, Cambridge.

Douglas Walton, Argument Mining by Applying Argumentation Schemes 2012. *In Studies in Logic* 4(1):38-64

Walton, Douglas, Christopher Reed, and Fabrizio Macagno. Argumentation schemes. 2008. *Cambridge University Press.*

Adam Wyner, Raquel Mochales-Palau, Marie-Francine Moens, and David Milward. Approaches to text mining arguments from legal cases. 2010. *In Semantic processing of legal texts* 60-79.

Modeling the Interpretation of Discourse Connectives
by Bayesian Pragmatics

Frances Yung
Nara Institute of Science and Technology
8916-5 Takayama, Ikoma,
Nara, 630-0101, Japan
`pikyufrances-y@is.naist.jp`

Kevin Duh
John Hopkins University
810 Wyman Park Drive,
Baltimore, MD 21211-2840, USA
`kevinduh@cs.jhu.edu`

Taku Komura
University of Edinburgh
10 Crichton Street,
Edinburgh, EH8 9AB, United Kingdom
`tkomura@inf.ed.ac.uk`

Yuji Matsumoto
Nara Institute of Science and Technology
8916-5 Takayama, Ikoma,
Nara, 630-0101, Japan
`matsu@is.naist.jp`

Abstract

We propose a framework to model human comprehension of discourse connectives. Following the Bayesian pragmatic paradigm, we advocate that discourse connectives are interpreted based on a simulation of the production process by the speaker, who, in turn, considers the ease of interpretation for the listener when choosing connectives. Evaluation against the sense annotation of the Penn Discourse Treebank confirms the superiority of the model over literal comprehension. A further experiment demonstrates that the proposed model also improves automatic discourse parsing.

1 Introduction

A growing body of evidence shows that human interpretation and production of natural language are inter-related (Clark, 1996; Pickering and Garrod, 2007; Zeevat, 2011; Zeevat, 2015). In particular, evidence shows that during interpretation, listeners simulate how the utterance is produced; and during language production, speakers simulate how the utterance will be perceived. One explanation is that the human brain reasons by *Bayesian inference* (Doya, 2007; Kilner et al., 2007), which is, at the same time, a popular formulation used in language technology.

In this work, we model how humans interpret the sense of a discourse relation based on the Bayesian pragmatic framework. Discourse relations are relations between units of texts that make a document coherent. These relations are either marked by discourse connectives (DCs), such as *'but'*, *'as a result'*, or implied implicitly, as in the following examples:

1. He came late. *In fact*, he came at noon.

2. It is late. I will go to bed.

The explicit DC *'in fact'* in Example (1) marks a *Specification* relation. On the other hand, a *Result* relation can be inferred between the two sentences in Example (2) although there are not any explicit markers. We say the two sentences (called *arguments*) are connected by an implicit DC.

Discourse relations have a mixture of semantic and pragmatic properties (Van Dijk, 1980; Lewis, 2006). For example, the sense of a discourse relation is encoded in the semantics of a DC (Example (1)), yet the interpretation of polysemic DCs (such as *'since'*, *'as'*) and implicit DCs relies on the pragmatic context (Example (2)).

This work seeks to find out if Bayesian pragmatic approaches are applicable to human comprehension of discourse relations. Our contribution includes: (i) an adaptation of the Bayesian *Rational Speech Acts* model to DC interpretation using a discourse-annotated corpus, the Penn Discourse Treebank; (ii) integration of the proposed model with a state-of-the-art automatic discourse parser to improve discourse sense classification.

2 Related work

There is increasing literature arguing that the human motor control and sensory systems make estimations based on a Bayesian perspective (Doya, 2007; Oaksford and Chater, 2009). For example, it is proposed that the brain's mirror neuron system

Proceedings of the 54th Annual Meeting of the Association for Computational Linguistics, pages 531–536,
Berlin, Germany, August 7-12, 2016. ©2016 Association for Computational Linguistics

recognizes a perceptual input by Bayesian inference (Kilner et al., 2007). Similarly, behavioural, physiological and neurocognitive evidences support that the human brain reasons about the uncertainty in natural languages comprehension by emulating the language production processes (Galantucci et al., 2006; Pickering and Garrod, 2013).

Analogous to this principle of Bayesian language perception, a series of studies have developed the Grice's Maxims (Grice, 1975) based on game-theoretic approaches (Jäger, 2012; Frank and Goodman, 2012; Goodman and Stuhlmüller, 2013; Goodman and Lassiter, 2014; Benz et al., 2016). These proposals argue that the speaker and the listener cooperate in a conversation by recursively inferring the reasoning of each other in a Bayesian manner. The proposed framework successfully explains existing psycholinguistic theories and predict experimental results at various linguistic levels, such as the perception of scalar implicatures (e.g. *some* meaning *not all* in pragmatic usage) and the production of referring expressions (Lassiter and Goodman, 2013; Bergen et al., 2014; Kao et al., 2014; Potts et al., 2015; Lassiter and Goodman, 2015). Recent efforts also acquire and evaluate the models using corpus data (Orita et al., 2015; Monroe and Potts, 2015).

Production and interpretation of discourse relations is also a kind of cooperative communication between speakers and listeners (or authors and readers). We hypothesize that the game-theoretic account of Bayesian pragmatics also applies to human comprehension of the meaning of a DC, which can be ambiguous or even dropped.

3 Method

This section explains how we model the interpretation of discourse relations by Bayesian pragmatics. The model is based on the formal framework known as *Rational Speech Acts* model (Frank and Goodman, 2012; Lassiter and Goodman, 2015). Section 3.1 explains the key elements of the RSA model, and Section 3.2 illustrates how it is adapted for discourse interpretation.

3.1 The Rational Speech Acts model

The Rational Speech Acts (RSA) model describes the speaker and listener as rational agents who cooperate towards efficient communication. It is composed of a speaker model and a listener model.

In the speaker model, the *utility* function U de-fines the effectiveness for the speaker to use utterance d to express the meaning s in context C.

$$U(d; s, C) = \ln P_L(s|d, C) - cost(u) \quad (1)$$

$P_L(s|d, C)$ is the probability that the *listener* can interpret speaker's intended meaning s. The speaker selects an utterance which, s/he thinks, is informative to the listener. The utility of d is thus defined by its informativeness towards the intended interpretation, which is quantified by *negative surprisal* ($\ln P_L(s|d, C)$), according to Information Theory (Shannon, 1948). The utility is modified by production cost ($cost(d)$), which is related to articulation and retrieval difficulties, etc.

$P_S(d|s, C)$ is the probability for the *speaker* to use utterance d for meaning s. It is proportional to the soft-max of the *utility* of d.

$$P_S(d|s, C) \propto \exp(\alpha \cdot U(d; s, C)) \quad (2)$$

where α, the decision noise parameter, is set to 1.

On the other hand, the probability for the listener to infer meaning s from utterance d is defined by Bayes' rule.

$$P_L(s|d, C) \propto P_S(d|s, C)P_L(s) \quad (3)$$

The listener infers the speaker's intended meaning by considering how likely, s/he thinks, the speaker uses that utterance ($P_S(d|s, C)$). The inference is also related to the *salience* of the meaning ($P_L(s)$), a private preference of the listener.

To summarize, the speaker and listener emulate the language processing of each other. However, instead of unlimitted iterations (i.e. the speaker thinks the listener thinks the speaker thinks..), the inference is grounded on literal interpretation of the utterance. Figure 1 illustrates the direction of pragmatic inference between the speaker and listener *in their minds*.

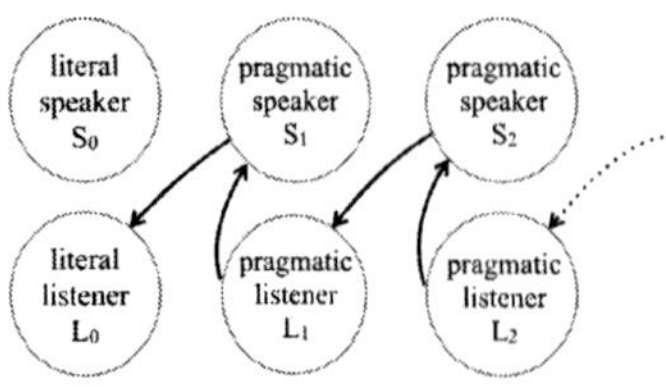

Figure 1: Pragmatic listeners/speakers reason for 1 or more levels, but not the literal listener/speaker.

Our experiment compares the predictions of the literal listener (L_0), the pragmatic listener who reasons for one level (L_1), and the pragmatic listener who reasons for two levels (L_2). Previous works demonstrate that one level of reasoning is robust in modeling human's interpretation of scalar implicatures (Lassiter and Goodman, 2013; Goodman and Stuhlmüller, 2013).

3.2 Applying the RSA model on discourse relation interpretation

We use the listener model of RSA to model how listeners interpret the sense a DC. Given the DC d and context C in a text, the listener's interpreted relation sense s_i is the sense that maximizes $P_L(s|d, C)$. s_i is specifically defined as

$$s_i = \arg\max_{s \in S} P_L(s|d, C) \qquad (4)$$

where S is the set of defined relation senses.

The literal listener, L_0, interprets a DC directly by its most likely sense in the context. The probability is estimated by counting the co-occurrences in corpus data, the Penn Discourse Treebank, in which explicit and implicit DCs are labelled with discourse relation senses.

$$P_{L_0}(s|d, C) = \frac{count(s, d, C)}{count(d, C)} \qquad (5)$$

More details about the annotation of PDTB will be explained in Section 4.1.

As shown in Figure 1, the pragmatic speaker S_1 estimates the utility of a DC by emulating the comprehension of the literal listener L_0 (Eq. 1, 2). The probability for the pragmatic speaker S_n to use DC d to express meaning s is estimated as:

$$P_{S_n}(d|s, C)$$
$$= \frac{\exp(\ln P_{L_{n-1}}(s|d, C) - cost(d))}{\sum_{d' \in D} \exp(\ln P_{L_{n-1}}(s|d', C) - cost(d'))} \qquad (6)$$

where $n \geq 1$. D is the set of annotated DCs, including 'null', which stands for an implicit DC.

The cost function in Equation 6, $cost(d)$, measures the production effort of the DC. As DCs are mostly short words, we simply define the cost of producing *any explicit DC* by a constant positive value, which is tuned manually in the experiments. On the other hand, the production cost for an implicit DC is 0, since no word is produced .

In turn, the pragmatic listener L_1 emulates the DC production of the pragmatic speaker S_1 (Eq.

3). The probability for the pragmatic listener L_n to assign meaning s to DC d is estimated as:

$$P_{L_n}(s|d, C) = \frac{P_{S_n}(d|s, C) P_L(s)}{\sum_{s' \in S} P_{S_n}(d|s', C) P_L(s')} \qquad (7)$$

where $n \geq 1$ and S is the set of defined sense. The salience of a relation sense in Equation 7, $P_L(s)$, is defined by the frequency of the sense in the corpus.

$$P_L(s) = \frac{count(s)}{\sum_{s' \in S} count(s')} \qquad (8)$$

Lastly, we propose to define the context variable C by the the immediately previous discourse relation to resemble incremental processing. We hypothesize that certain patterns of relation transitions are more expected and predictable. Discourse context in terms of relation sense, relation form (explicit DC or not), and the sense-form pair are compared in the experiments.

4 Experiment

This section describes experiments that evaluate the model against discourse-annotated corpus. We seek to answer the following questions: (1) Can the proposed model explain the sense interpretation (annotation) of the DCs in the corpus? (2) Is the DC interpretation refined by the context in terms of previous discourse structure? (3) Does the proposed model help automatic discourse parsing? We first briefly introduce the corpus resource we use, the Penn Discourse Treebank.

4.1 Penn Discourse Treebank

The Penn Discourse Treebank (PDTB) (Prasad et al., 2008) is the largest available discourse-annotated resource in English. The raw text are collected from news articles of the Wall Street Journals. On the PDTB, all explicit DCs are annotated with discourse senses, while implicit discourse senses are annotated between two adjacent sentences. Other forms of discourse relations, such as 'entity relations', are also labeled. In total, there are 5 form labels and 42 distinct sense labels, some of which only occur very sparsely.

We thus use a simplified version of the annotation, which has 2 form labels (*Explicit* and *Non-explicit* DC) and 15 sense labels (first column of Table 3), following the mapping convention of the CONLL shallow discourse parsing shared task (Xue et al., 2015). Sections 2-22 are used as the training set and the rest of the corpus, Sections 0, 1, 23 and 24, are combined as the test set. Sizes of the data sets are summarized in Table 1.

	Train	Test	Total
Explicit	15,402	3,057	18,459
Non-Exp	18,569	3,318	21,887
Total	33,971	6,375	40,346

Table 1: Sample count per data set

4.2 Does RSA explain DC interpretation?

The RSA model argues that a rational listener does not just stick to the literal meaning of an utterance. S/he should reason about how likely the speaker will use that utterance, in the current context, based on the informativeness and production effort of the utterance. If the RSA model explains DC interpretation as well, discourse sense predictions made by the pragmatic listeners should outperform predictions by the literal listener.

In this experiment, we compare the DC interpretation by the literal listener L_0, and pragmatic listeners L_1 and L_2. Given a DC d and the discourse context C for each test instance, the relation sense is deduced by maximizing the probability estimate $P_L(s|d, C)$. $P_{L_0}(s|d, C)$ is simply based on co-occurrences in the training data (Eq. 5). $P_{L_1}(s|d, C)$ and $P_{L_2}(s|d, C)$ are calculated by Eq. 6 and 7, in which the salience of each sense is also extracted from the training data (Eq. 8).

	context C	Explicit	Non-Explicit
L_0	**constant (BL)**	.8767	.2616
	prev. form	.8754	.2616
	prev. sense	.8727	.2507
	form-sense	.8684	.2692
L_1	constant	**.8853***	.2616
	prev. form	**.8830**	.2616
	prev. sense	.8671	**.2698***
	form-sense	.8621	**.2671**
L_2	constant	**.8853***	.2616
	prev. form	**.8830**	.2616
	prev. sense	.8671	.2616
	form-sense	.8621	.2616

Table 2: Accuracy of prediction by L_0, L_1 and L_2. Improvements above the baseline are bolded. * means significant at $p < 0.02$ by McNemar Test.

Table 2 shows the accuracy of discourse sense prediction by listeners L_0, L_1 and L_2, when provided with various discourse contexts. Predictions by L_1, when they are differ from the predictions by L_0 under 'constant' context, are more accurate than expected by chance. This provides support that the RSA framework models DC interpretation. Overall, predictions of non-implicit senses hardly differ among different models, since an implicit DC is much less informative than an explicit DC. Moreover, previous relation senses or forms do not improve the accuracy, suggesting that a more generalized formulation of contextual information is required to refine discourse understanding. It is also observed that predictions by L_2 are mostly the same as L_1. This implies that the listener is unlikely to emulate speaker's production iteratively at deeper levels.

4.3 Insights on automatic discourse parsing

Next, we investigate if the proposed method helps automatic discourse sense classification. A full discourse parser typically consists of a pipeline of classifiers: explicit and implicit DCs are first classified and then processed separately by 2 classifiers (Xue et al., 2015). On the contrary, the pragmatic listener of the RSA model considers if the speaker would prefer a particular DC, explicit or implicit, when expressing the intended sense.

In this experiment, we integrate the output of an automatic discourse parser with the probability prediction by the pragmatic listener L_1. We employ the winning parser of the CONLL shared task (Wang and Lan, 2015). The parser is also trained on Sections 2-22 of PDTB, and thus does not overlap with our test set. The sense classification of the parser is based on a pool of lexicosyntactic features drawn from gold standard arguments, DCs and automatic parsed trees produced by CoreNLP (Manning et al., 2014).

For each test sample, the parser outputs a probability estimate for each sense. We use these estimates to replace the *salience* measure ($P_L(s)$) (in Eq. 8) and deduce $P'_{L_1}(s|d, C)$, where C is the previous relation form.

$$P'_{L_1}(s|d, C) = \frac{P_{S_1}(d|s, C)P_{parser}(s)}{\sum_{s' \in S} P_{S_1}(d|s', C)P_{parser}(s')} \quad (9)$$

Table 3 compares the performance of the original parser output and the prediction based on P'_{L_1}.

[1]This does not match with Table 1 as samples labeled with 2 senses are double counted. Multi-sense training samples are splitted into multiple samples, each labelled with one of the senses. In testing, a prediction is considered correct if it matches with one of the multiple senses.

discourse relation sense tags	parser output	P'_{L_1} output	test counts
Conjunction	.7022	**.7079**	1479
Contrast	**.7382**	.7152	1152
Entity	.5174	**.5249**	862
Reason	.4844	**.5105**	661
Restatement	.2773	**.2871**	567
Result	.4019	**.4150**	405
Instantiation	.4346	**.4357**	282
Synchrony	.6553	**.7007**	264
Condition	.9087	**.9302**	238
Succession	.7022	**.7210**	204
Precedence	.7523	**.7762**	200
Concession	.3048	**.4382**	146
Chosen alternative	.5000	**.5200**	36
Alternative	.8421	**.8929**	28
Exception	1.00	1.00	1
Accuracy / Total	.5833	**.5916**	6525

Table 3: F1 scores of original parser output vs parser output modified with P'_{L_1}. Higher scores are bolded. The improvement in accuracy is significant at $p < 0.05$ by McNemar Test.

Significant improvement in classification accuracy is achieved and the F1 scores for most senses are improved. This confirms the applicational potential of our model on automatic discourse parsing.

5 Conclusion

We propose a new framework to model the interpretation of discourse relations based on Bayesian pragmatics. Experimental results support the applicability of the model on human DC comprehension and automatic discourse parsing. As future work, we plan to deduce a more general abstraction of the context governing DC interpretation. A larger picture is to design a full, incremental discourse parsing algorithm that is motivated by the psycholinguistic reality of human discourse processing.

References

Anton Benz, Gerhard Jäger, Robert Van Rooij, and Robert Van Rooij. 2016. *Game theory and pragmatics*. Springer.

Leon Bergen, Roger Levy, and Noah D. Goodman. 2014. Pragmatic reasoning through semantic inference.

Herbert H Clark. 1996. *Using language*. Cambridge university press.

Kenji Doya. 2007. *Bayesian brain: Probabilistic approaches to neural coding*. MIT press.

Michael C. Frank and Noah D. Goodman. 2012. Predicting pragmatic reasoning in lanuage games. *Science*, 336(6084):998.

Bruno Galantucci, Carol A Fowler, and Michael T Turvey. 2006. The motor theory of speech perception reviewed. *Psychonomic bulletin & review*, 13(3):361–377.

Noah D Goodman and Daniel Lassiter. 2014. Probabilistic semantics and pragmatics: Uncertainty in language and thought. *Handbook of Contemporary Semantic Theory. Wiley-Blackwell*.

Noah D Goodman and Andreas Stuhlmüller. 2013. Knowledge and implicature: modeling language understanding as social cognition. *Topics in cognitive science*, 5(1):173–184.

HP Grice. 1975. Logic and conversation in p. cole and j. morgan (eds.) syntax and semantics volume 3: Speech acts.

Gerhard Jäger. 2012. Game theory in semantics and pragmatics. In Claudia Maienborn, Klaus von Heusinger, and Paul Portner, editors, *Semantics: An International Handbook of Natural Language Meaning*, volume 3, pages 2487–2425. Mouton de Gruyter.

Justine T Kao, Jean Y Wu, Leon Bergen, and Noah D Goodman. 2014. Nonliteral understanding of number words. *Proceedings of the National Academy of Sciences*, 111(33):12002–12007.

James M Kilner, Karl J Friston, and Chris D Frith. 2007. Predictive coding: an account of the mirror neuron system. *Cognitive processing*, 8(3):159–166.

Daniel Lassiter and Noah D Goodman. 2013. Context, scale structure, and statistics in the interpretation of positive-form adjectives. In *Semantics and Linguistic Theory*, volume 23, pages 587–610.

Daniel Lassiter and Noah D Goodman. 2015. Adjectival vagueness in a bayesian model of interpretation. *Synthese*, pages 1–36.

Diana Lewis. 2006. Discourse markers in english: a discourse-pragmatic view. *Approaches to discourse particles*, pages 43–59.

Christopher Manning, Mihai Surdeanu, John Bauer, Jenny Finkey, Steven J. Bethard, and David McClosky. 2014. The standord corenlp natural language processing toolkit. *Proceedings of the Annual Meeting of the Association for Computational Linguistics: System Demonstrations*, pages 55–60.

Will Monroe and Christopher Potts. 2015. Learning in the rational speech acts model. *arXiv preprint arXiv:1510.06807*.

Mike Oaksford and Nick Chater. 2009. Prcis of bayesian rationality: The probabilistic approach to human reasoning. *Behavioral and Brain Sciences*, 32:69–84, 2.

Naho Orita, Eliana Vornov, Naomi H. Feldman, and Hal Daumé III. 2015. Why discourse affects speakers' choice of refering expressions. *Proceedings of the Annual Meeting of the Association for Computational Linguistics*.

Martin J Pickering and Simon Garrod. 2007. Do people use language production to make predictions during comprehension? *Trends in cognitive sciences*, 11(3):105–110.

Martin J Pickering and Simon Garrod. 2013. An integrated theory of language production and comprehension. *Behavioral and Brain Sciences*, 36(04):329–347.

Christopher Potts, Daniel Lassiter, Roger Levy, and Michael C. Frank. 2015. Embedded implicatures as pragmatic inferences under compositional lexical uncertainty. Manuscript.

Rashmi Prasad, Nikhit Dinesh, Alan Lee, Eleni Miltsakaki, Livio Robaldo, Aravind Joshi, and Bonnie Webber. 2008. The penn discourse treebank 2.0. *Proceedings of the Language Resource and Evaluation Conference*.

C.E. Shannon. 1948. A mathematical theory of communication. *The Bell System Technical Journal*, 27(379-423; 623-656).

Teun A Van Dijk. 1980. The semantics and pragmatics of functional coherence in discourse. *Speech act theory: Ten years later*, pages 49–66.

Jianxiang Wang and Man Lan. 2015. A refined end-to-end discourse parser. *CoNLL 2015*, page 17.

Nianwen Xue, Hwee Tou Ng, Sameer Pradhan, Rashmi PrasadO Christopher Bryant, and Attapol T Rutherford. 2015. The conll-2015 shared task on shallow discourse parsing. *CoNLL 2015*, page 1.

Henk Zeevat. 2011. Bayesian interpretation and optimality theory. *Bidirectional Optimality Theory. Palgrave Macmillan, Amsterdam*, pages 191–220.

Henk Zeevat. 2015. Perspectives on bayesian natural language semantics and pragmatics. In *Bayesian Natural Language Semantics and Pragmatics*, pages 1–24. Springer.

Nonparametric Spherical Topic Modeling with Word Embeddings

Nematollah Kayhan Batmanghelich* Ardavan Saeedi*
CSAIL, MIT
kayhan@mit.edu

CSAIL, MIT
ardavans@mit.edu

Karthik R. Narasimhan
CSAIL, MIT
karthikn@mit.edu

Samuel J. Gershman
Department of Psychology
Harvard University
gershman@fas.harvard.edu

Abstract

Traditional topic models do not account for semantic regularities in language. Recent distributional representations of words exhibit semantic consistency over directional metrics such as cosine similarity. However, neither categorical nor Gaussian observational distributions used in existing topic models are appropriate to leverage such correlations. In this paper, we propose to use the von Mises-Fisher distribution to model the density of words over a unit sphere. Such a representation is well-suited for directional data. We use a Hierarchical Dirichlet Process for our base topic model and propose an efficient inference algorithm based on Stochastic Variational Inference. This model enables us to naturally exploit the semantic structures of word embeddings while flexibly discovering the number of topics. Experiments demonstrate that our method outperforms competitive approaches in terms of topic coherence on two different text corpora while offering efficient inference.[1]

1 Introduction

Prior work on topic modeling has mostly involved the use of categorical likelihoods (Blei et al., 2003; Blei and Lafferty, 2006; Rosen-Zvi et al., 2004). Applications of topic models in the textual domain treat words as discrete observations, ignoring the semantics of the language. Recent developments in distributional representations of words (Mikolov et al., 2013; Pennington et al.,

---

*Authors contributed equally and listed alphabetically.
[1] Code is available at https://github.com/Ardavans/sHDP.

2014) have succeeded in capturing certain semantic regularities, but have not been explored extensively in the context of topic modeling. In this paper, we propose a probabilistic topic model with a novel observational distribution that integrates well with directional similarity metrics.

One way to employ semantic similarity is to use the Euclidean distance between word vectors, which reduces to a Gaussian observational distribution for topic modeling (Das et al., 2015). The *cosine distance* between word embeddings is another popular choice and has been shown to be a good measure of semantic relatedness (Mikolov et al., 2013; Pennington et al., 2014). The von Mises-Fisher (vMF) distribution is well-suited to model such directional data (Dhillon and Sra, 2003; Banerjee et al., 2005) but has not been previously applied to topic models.

In this work, we use vMF as the observational distribution. Each word can be viewed as a point on a unit sphere with topics being canonical directions. More specifically, we use a Hierarchical Dirichlet Process (HDP) (Teh et al., 2006), a Bayesian nonparametric variant of Latent Dirichlet Allocation (LDA), to automatically infer the number of topics. We implement an efficient inference scheme based on Stochastic Variational Inference (SVI) (Hoffman et al., 2013).

We perform experiments on two different English text corpora: 20 NEWSGROUPS and NIPS and compare against two baselines - HDP and Gaussian LDA. Our model, spherical HDP (sHDP), outperforms all three systems on the measure of *topic coherence*. For instance, sHDP obtains gains over Gaussian LDA of 97.5% on the NIPS dataset and 65.5% on the 20 NEWSGROUPS dataset. Qualitative inspection reveals consistent topics produced by sHDP. We also empirically demonstrate that employing SVI leads to efficient

537

Proceedings of the 54th Annual Meeting of the Association for Computational Linguistics, pages 537–542,
Berlin, Germany, August 7-12, 2016. ©2016 Association for Computational Linguistics

topic inference.

2 Related Work

Topic modeling and word embeddings Das et al. (2015) proposed a topic model which uses a Gaussian distribution over word embeddings. By performing inference over the vector representations of the words, their model is encouraged to group words that are semantically similar, leading to more coherent topics. In contrast, we propose to utilize von Mises-Fisher (vMF) distributions which rely on the cosine similarity between the word vectors instead of euclidean distance.

vMF in topic models The vMF distribution has been used to model directional data by placing points on a unit sphere (Dhillon and Sra, 2003). Reisinger et al. (2010) propose an admixture model that uses vMF to model documents represented as vector of normalized word frequencies. This does not account for word level semantic similarities. Unlike their method, we use vMF over word embeddings. In addition, our model is nonparametric.

Nonparametric topic models HDP and its variants have been successfully applied to topic modeling (Paisley et al., 2015; Blei, 2012; He et al., 2013); however, all these models assume a categorical likelihood in which the words are encoded as one-hot representation.

3 Model

In this section, we describe the generative process for documents. Rather than one-hot representation of words, we employ normalized word embeddings (Mikolov et al., 2013) to capture semantic meanings of associated words. Word n from document d is represented by a normalized M-dimensional vector x_{dn} and the similarity between words is quantified by the cosine of angle between the corresponding word vectors.

Our model is based on the Hierarchical Dirichlet Process (HDP). The model assumes a collection of "topics" that are shared across documents in the corpus. The topics are represented by the topic centers $\mu_k \in \mathbb{R}^M$. Since word vectors are normalized, the μ_k can be viewed as a direction on unit sphere. Von Mises−Fisher (vMF) is a distribution that is commonly used to model directional data. The likelihood of the topic k for word x_{dn}

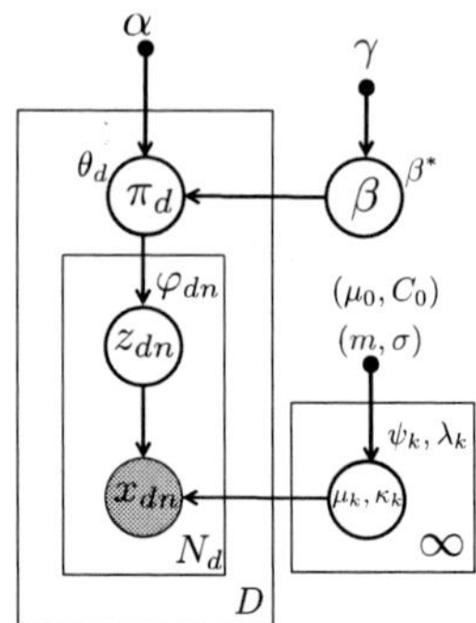

Figure 1: Graphical representation of our spherical HDP (sHDP) model. The symbol next to each random variable denotes the parameter of its variational distribution. We assume D documents in the corpus, each document contains N_d words and there are countably infinite topics represented by (μ_k, κ_k).

is:

$$f(x_{dn}; \mu_k; \kappa_k) = \exp\left(\kappa_k \mu_k^T x_{dn}\right) C_M(\kappa_k)$$

where κ_k is the concentration of the topic k, the $C_M(\kappa_k) := \kappa_k^{M/2-1}/\left((2\pi)^{M/2} I_{M/2-1}(\kappa_k)\right)$ is the normalization constant, and $I_\nu(\cdot)$ is the modified Bessel function of the first kind at order ν. Interestingly, the log-likelihood of the vMF is proportional to $\mu_k^T x_{dn}$ (up to a constant), which is equal to the cosine distance between two vectors. This distance metric is also used in Mikolov et al. (2013) to measure semantic proximity.

When sampling a new document, a subset of topics determine the distribution over words. We let z_{dn} denote the topic selected for the word n of document d. Hence, z_{dn} is drawn from a categorical distribution: $z_{dn} \sim \text{Mult}(\pi_d)$, where π_d is the proportion of topics for document d. We draw π_d from a Dirichlet Process which enables us to estimate the the number of topics from the data. The generative process for the generation of new document is as follows:

$$\beta \sim \text{GEM}(\gamma) \qquad \pi_d \sim \text{DP}(\alpha, \beta)$$
$$\kappa_k \sim \text{log-Normal}(m, \sigma^2) \qquad \mu_k \sim \text{vMF}(\mu_0, C_0)$$
$$z_{dn} \sim \text{Mult}(\pi_d) \qquad x_{dn} \sim \text{vMF}(\mu_k, \kappa_k)$$

where $\text{GEM}(\gamma)$ is the stick-breaking distribution with concentration parameter γ, $\text{DP}(\alpha, \beta)$ is a Dirichlet process with concentration parameter α and stick proportions β (Teh et al., 2012). We use log-normal and vMF as hyper-prior distributions for the concentrations (κ_k) and centers of the topics (μ_k) respectively. Figure 1 provides a graphical illustration of the model.

Stochastic variational inference In the rest of the paper, we use bold symbols to denote the variables of the same kind (*e.g.*, $\boldsymbol{x}_d = \{x_{dn}\}_n$, $\boldsymbol{z} := \{z_{dn}\}_{d,n}$). We employ stochastic variational mean-field inference (SVI) (Hoffman et al., 2013) to estimate the posterior distributions of the latent variables. SVI enables us to sequentially process batches of documents which makes it appropriate in large-scale settings.

To approximate the posterior distribution of the latent variables, the mean-field approach finds the optimal parameters of the fully factorizable q (*i.e.*, $q(\boldsymbol{z}, \beta, \boldsymbol{\pi}, \boldsymbol{\mu}, \boldsymbol{\kappa}) := q(\boldsymbol{z})q(\beta)q(\boldsymbol{\pi})q(\boldsymbol{\mu})q(\boldsymbol{\kappa}))$ by maximizing the Evidence Lower Bound (ELBO),

$$\mathcal{L}(q) = \mathbb{E}_q\left[\log p(\boldsymbol{X}, \boldsymbol{z}, \beta, \boldsymbol{\pi}, \boldsymbol{\mu}, \boldsymbol{\kappa})\right] - \mathbb{F}_q\left[\log q\right]$$

where $\mathbb{E}_q[\cdot]$ is expectation with respect to q, $p(\boldsymbol{X}, \boldsymbol{z}, \beta, \boldsymbol{\pi}, \boldsymbol{\mu}, \boldsymbol{\kappa})$ is the joint likelihood of the model specified by the HDP model.

The variational distributions for $\boldsymbol{z}, \boldsymbol{\pi}, \boldsymbol{\mu}$ have the following parametric forms,

$$q(\boldsymbol{z}) = \text{Mult}(\boldsymbol{z}|\boldsymbol{\varphi})$$
$$q(\boldsymbol{\pi}) = \text{Dir}(\boldsymbol{\pi}|\boldsymbol{\theta})$$
$$q(\boldsymbol{\mu}) = \text{vMF}(\boldsymbol{\mu}|\boldsymbol{\psi}, \boldsymbol{\lambda}),$$

where Dir denotes the Dirichlet distribution and $\boldsymbol{\varphi}, \boldsymbol{\theta}, \boldsymbol{\psi}$ and $\boldsymbol{\lambda}$ are the parameters we need to optimize the ELBO. Similar to (Bryant and Sudderth, 2012), we view β as a parameter; hence, $q(\beta) = \delta_{\beta^*}(\beta)$. The prior distribution κ does not follow a conjugate distribution; hence, its posterior docs not have a closed-form. Since κ is only one dimensional variable, we use importance sampling to approximate its posterior. For a batch size of one (*i.e.*, processing one document at time), the update equations for the parameters are:

$$\varphi_{dwk} \propto \exp\{\mathbb{E}_q[\log \text{vMF}(x_{dw}|\psi_k, \lambda_k)] + \mathbb{E}_q[\log \pi_{dk}]\}$$

$$\theta_{dk} \leftarrow (1-\rho)\theta_{dk} + \rho(\alpha\beta_k + D\sum_{n=1}^{W}\omega_{wj}\varphi_{dwk})$$

$$t \leftarrow (1-\rho)t + \rho s(\boldsymbol{x}_d, \varphi_{dk})$$

$$\psi \leftarrow t/\|t\|_2, \quad \lambda \leftarrow \|t\|_2$$

where D, ω_{wj}, W, ρ are the total number of documents, number of word w in document j, the total

number of words in the dictionary, and the step size, respectively. t is a natural parameter for vMF and $s(\boldsymbol{x}_d, \varphi_{dk})$ is a function computing the sufficient statistics of vMF distribution of the topic k. We use numerical gradient ascent to optimize for β^*. For exact forms of $\mathbb{E}_q \log[\text{vMF}(x_{dw}|\psi_k, \lambda_k)]$ and $\mathbb{E}_q[\log \pi_{dk}]$, see Appendix.

4 Experiments

Setup We perform experiments on two different text corpora: 11266 documents from 20 NEWS-GROUPS[2] and 1566 documents from the NIPS corpus[3]. We utilize 50-dimensional word embeddings trained on text from Wikipedia using *word2vec*[4]. The vectors are normalized to have unit ℓ^2-norm, which has been shown to provide superior performance (Levy et al., 2015)).

We evaluate our model using the measure of topic coherence (Newman et al., 2010), which has been shown to effectively correlate with human judgement (Lau et al., 2014). For this, we compute the Pointwise Mutual Information (PMI) using a reference corpus of 300k documents from Wikipedia. The PMI is calculated using co-occurence statistics over pairs of words (u_i, u_j) in 20-word sliding windows:

$$\text{PMI}(u_i, u_j) = \log \frac{p(u_i, u_j)}{p(u_i) \cdot p(u_j)}$$

Additionally, we also use the metric of normalized PMI (NPMI) to evaluate the models in a similar fashion:

$$\text{NPMI}(u_i, u_j) = \frac{\log \frac{p(u_i, u_j)}{p(u_i) \cdot p(u_j)}}{-\log p(u_i, u_j)}$$

We compare our model with two baselines: HDP and the Gaussian LDA model. We ran G-LDA with various number of topics (k).

Results Table 2 details the topic coherence averaged over all topics produced by each model. We observe that our sHDP model outperforms G-LDA by 0.08 points on 20 NEWSGROUPS and by 0.17 points in terms of PMI on the NIPS dataset. The NPMI scores also show a similar trend with sHDP obtaining the best scores on both datasets. We can also see that the individual topics inferred

<hr>

[2] http://qwone.com/~jason/20Newsgroups/
[3] http://www.cs.nyu.edu/~roweis/data.html
[4] https://code.google.com/p/word2vec/

Gaussian LDA							
vector	shows	network	hidden	performance	net	figure	size
image	feature	learning	term	work	references	shown	average
gaussian	show	model	rule	press	introduction	neurons	present
equation	motion	neural	word	tion	statistical	point	family
generalization	action	input	means	ing	related	large	versus
images	spike	data	words	eq	comparison	neuron	spread
gradient	series	function	approximate	performed	source	small	median
theory	final	time	derived	em	statistics	fig	physiology
dimensional	robot	set	describe	vol	free	cells	children
1.16	0.4	0.35	0.29	0.25	0.25	0.21	0.2
Spherical HDP							
neural	function	analysis	press	pattern	problem	noise	algorithm
layer	linear	theory	cambridge	fig	process	gradient	error
neurons	functions	computational	journal	temporal	method	propagation	parameters
neuron	vector	statistical	vol	shape	optimal	signals	computation
activation	random	field	eds	smooth	solution	frequency	algorithms
brain	probability	simulations	trans	surface	complexity	feedback	compute
cells	parameter	simulation	springer	horizontal	estimation	electrical	binary
cell	dimensional	nonlinear	volume	vertical	prediction	filter	mapping
synaptic	equation	dynamics	review	posterior	solve	detection	optimization
1.87	1.73	1.51	1.44	1.41	1.19	1.12	1.03

Table 1: Examples of top words for the most coherent topics (column-wise) inferred on the NIPS dataset by Gaussian LDA (k=40) and Spherical HDP. The last row for each model is the topic coherence (PMI) computed using Wikipedia documents as reference.

Model	Topic Coherence			
	20 NEWS		NIPS	
	pmi	npmi	pmi	npmi
HDP	0.037	0.014	0.270	0.062
G-LDA (k=10)	-0.061	-0.006	0.214	0.055
G-LDA (k=20)	-0.017	0.001	0.215	0.052
G-LDA (k=40)	0.052	0.015	0.248	0.057
G-LDA (k=60)	0.082	0.021	0.137	0.034
sHDP	**0.162**	**0.046**	**0.442**	**0.102**

Table 2: Average topic coherence for various baselines (HDP, Gaussian LDA (G-LDA)) and sHDP. k=number of topics. Best scores are shown in bold.

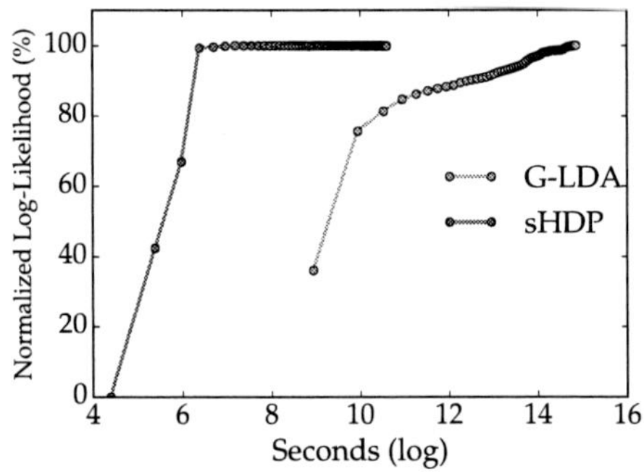

Figure 2: Normalized log-likelihood (in percentage) over a training set of size 1566 documents from the NIPS corpus. Since the log-likelihood values are not comparable for the Gaussian LDA and the sHDP, we normalize them to demonstrate the convergence speed of the two inference schemes for these models.

by sHDP make sense qualitatively and have higher coherence scores than G-LDA (Table 1). This supports our hypothesis that using the vMF likelihood helps in producing more coherent topics. sHDP produces 16 topics for the 20 NEWSGROUPS and 92 topics on the NIPS dataset.

Figure 2 shows a plot of normalized log-likelihood against the runtime of sHDP and G-LDA.[5] We calculate the normalized value of log-likelihood by subtracting the minimum value from it and dividing it by the difference of maximum and minimum values. We can see that sHDP converges faster than G-LDA, requiring only around five iterations while G-LDA takes longer to converge.

5 Conclusion

Classical topic models do not account for semantic regularities in language. Recently, distributional

---

[5]Our sHDP implementation is in Python and the G-LDA code is in Java.

representations of words have emerged that exhibit semantic consistency over directional metrics like cosine similarity. Neither categorical nor Gaussian observational distributions used in existing topic models are appropriate to leverage such correlations. In this work, we demonstrate the use of the von Mises-Fisher distribution to model words as points over a unit sphere. We use HDP as the base topic model and propose an efficient algorithm based on Stochastic Variational Inference. Our model naturally exploits the semantic structures of word embeddings while flexibly inferring the number of topics. We show that our method outperforms three competitive approaches in terms of topic coherence on two different datasets.

Acknowledgments

Thanks to Rajarshi Das for helping with the Gaussian LDA experiments and Matthew Johnson for his help with the HDP code.

References

Arindam Banerjee, Inderjit S Dhillon, Joydeep Ghosh, and Suvrit Sra. 2005. Clustering on the unit hypersphere using von mises-fisher distributions. In *Journal of Machine Learning Research*, pages 1345–1382.

David M Blei and John D Lafferty. 2006. Dynamic topic models. In *Proceedings of the 23rd international conference on Machine learning*, pages 113–120. ACM.

David M Blei, Andrew Y Ng, and Michael I Jordan. 2003. Latent dirichlet allocation. *the Journal of machine Learning research*, 3:993–1022.

David M Blei. 2012. Probabilistic topic models. *Communications of the ACM*, 55(4):77–84.

Michael Bryant and Erik B Sudderth. 2012. Truly nonparametric online variational inference for hierarchical dirichlet processes. In *Advances in Neural Information Processing Systems*, pages 2699–2707.

Rajarshi Das, Manzil Zaheer, and Chris Dyer. 2015. Gaussian LDA for topic models with word embeddings. In *Proceedings of the 53nd Annual Meeting of the Association for Computational Linguistics*.

Inderjit S Dhillon and Suvrit Sra. 2003. Modeling data using directional distributions. Technical report, Technical Report TR-03-06, Department of Computer Sciences, The University of Texas at Austin. URL ftp://ftp. cs. utexas. edu/pub/techreports/tr03-06. ps. gz.

Siddarth Gopal and Yiming Yang. 2014. Von mises-fisher clustering models.

Yulan He, Chenghua Lin, Wei Gao, and Kam-Fai Wong. 2013. Dynamic joint sentiment-topic model. *ACM Transactions on Intelligent Systems and Technology (TIST)*, 5(1):6.

Matthew D Hoffman, David M Blei, Chong Wang, and John Paisley. 2013. Stochastic variational inference. *The Journal of Machine Learning Research*, 14(1):1303–1347.

Matthew Johnson and Alan Willsky. 2014. Stochastic variational inference for bayesian time series models. In *Proceedings of the 31st International Conference on Machine Learning (ICML-14)*, pages 1854–1862.

Jey Han Lau, David Newman, and Timothy Baldwin. 2014. Machine reading tea leaves: Automatically evaluating topic coherence and topic model quality. In *EACL*, pages 530–539.

Omer Levy, Yoav Goldberg, and Ido Dagan. 2015. Improving distributional similarity with lessons learned from word embeddings. *Transactions of the Association for Computational Linguistics*, 3:211–225.

Tomas Mikolov, Ilya Sutskever, Kai Chen, Greg S Corrado, and Jeff Dean. 2013. Distributed representations of words and phrases and their compositionality. In *Advances in neural information processing systems*, pages 3111–3119.

David Newman, Jey Han Lau, Karl Grieser, and Timothy Baldwin. 2010. Automatic evaluation of topic coherence. In *Human Language Technologies: The 2010 Annual Conference of the North American Chapter of the Association for Computational Linguistics*, pages 100–108. Association for Computational Linguistics.

John Paisley, Chingyue Wang, David M Blei, and Michael I Jordan. 2015. Nested hierarchical dirichlet processes. *Pattern Analysis and Machine Intelligence, IEEE Transactions on*, 37(2):256–270.

Jeffrey Pennington, Richard Socher, and Christopher D. Manning. 2014. Glove: Global vectors for word representation. In *Empirical Methods in Natural Language Processing (EMNLP)*, pages 1532–1543.

Joseph Reisinger, Austin Waters, Bryan Silverthorn, and Raymond J Mooney. 2010. Spherical topic models. In *Proceedings of the 27th International Conference on Machine Learning (ICML-10)*, pages 903–910.

Michal Rosen-Zvi, Thomas Griffiths, Mark Steyvers, and Padhraic Smyth. 2004. The author-topic model for authors and documents. In *Proceedings of the 20th conference on Uncertainty in artificial intelligence*, pages 487–494. AUAI Press.

Yee Whye Teh, Michael I Jordan, Matthew J Beal, and David M Blei. 2006. Hierarchical dirichlet processes. *Journal of the American Statistical Association*, 101:1566–1581.

Yee Whye Teh, Michael I Jordan, Matthew J Beal, and David M Blei. 2012. Hierarchical dirichlet processes. *Journal of the american statistical association*.

Appendinx

Mean field update equations

In this section, we provide the mean field update equations. The SVI update equations can be derived from the mean field update (Hoffman et al., 2013).

The following term is computed for the update equations:

$$\mathbb{E}_q[\log \text{vMF}(x_{dn}|\mu_k, \kappa_k)] = \mathbb{E}_q[\log C_M(\kappa_k)] +$$
$$\mathbb{E}_q[\kappa_k] x_{dn}^T \mathbb{E}_q[\mu_k]$$

where $C_M(\cdot)$ is explained in Section 3. The difficulty here lies in computing $\mathbb{E}_q[\kappa_k]$ and $\mathbb{E}_q[C_M(\kappa_k)]$. However, κ is a scalar value. Hence, to compute $\mathbb{E}_q[\kappa_k]$, we divide a reasonable interval of κ_k into grids and compute the weight for each grid point as suggested by Gopal and Yang (2014):

$$p(\kappa_k|\cdots) \propto \exp\left(n_k \log C_M(\kappa_k) + \right.$$
$$\left. \kappa_k \left(\sum_{d=1}^{D}\sum_{n=1}^{N_d} [\varphi_{dn}]_k \langle x_{dn}, \mathbb{E}_q[\mu_k]\rangle\right)\right) \times$$
$$\text{logNormal}(\kappa_k|m, \sigma^2)$$

where $n_k = \sum_{d=1}^{D}\sum_{d=1}^{N_d} [\varphi_{dn}]_k$ and $[a]_k$ denotes the k'th element of vector a. After computing the normalized weights, we can compute $\mathbb{E}_q[\kappa_k]$ or expectation of any other function of κ_k (e.g., $\mathbb{E}_q[C_M(\kappa_k)]$). The rest of the terms can be computed as follows:

$$\mathbb{E}_q[\mu_k] = \mathbb{E}_q\left[\frac{I_{M/2}(\kappa_k)}{I_{M/2-1}(\kappa_k)}\right]\psi_k,$$

$$\psi_k = \mathbb{E}_q[\kappa_k]\left(\sum_{d=1}^{D}\sum_{n=1}^{N_d}[\varphi_{dn}]_k x_{dn}\right) + C_0\mu_0$$

$$\psi_k \leftarrow \frac{\psi_k}{\|\psi_k\|_2},$$

$$[\mathbb{E}_q[\log(\pi_d)]]_k = \Psi([\theta_d]_k) - \Psi\left(\sum_k [\theta_d]_k\right),$$

$$[\varphi_{dn}]_k \propto \exp\left(\mathbb{E}_q[\log \text{vMF}(x_{dn}|\mu_k, \kappa_k)] + \mathbb{E}_q[\log([\pi_d]_k)]\right),$$

$$[\theta_d]_k = \alpha + \sum_{n=1}^{N_d}[\varphi_{dn}]_k$$

$\Psi(\cdot)$ is the digamma function.

To find β^*, similar to Johnson and Willsky (2014), we use the gradient expression of ELBO with respect to β and take a truncated gradient step on β ensuring $\beta^* \geq 0$.

A Novel Measure for Coherence in Statistical Topic Models

Fred Morstatter and Huan Liu
Arizona State University
Tempe, Arizona, USA
{fred.morstatter, huan.liu}@asu.edu

Abstract

Big data presents new challenges for understanding large text corpora. Topic modeling algorithms help understand the underlying patterns, or "topics", in data. Researchersauthor often read these topics in order to gain an understanding of the underlying corpus. It is important to evaluate the interpretability of these automatically generated topics. Methods have previously been designed to use crowdsourcing platforms to measure interpretability. In this paper, we demonstrate the necessity of a key concept, coherence, when assessing the topics and propose an effective method for its measurement. We show that the proposed measure of coherence captures a different aspect of the topics than existing measures. We further study the automation of these topic measures for scalability and reproducibility, showing that these measures can be automated.

1 Introduction

Big data poses new challenges in analyzing text corpora. Topic modeling algorithms have recently grown to popularity for their ability to help discover the underlying topics in a corpus. Topic words are the words selected to represent a topic. They have been shown to be useful in the areas of machine learning, text analysis (Grimmer and Stewart, 2013), and social media analysis (O'Connor et al., 2010), among others. Topic models can be used as predictive models to classify new documents in the context of the training corpus. They are evaluated by measuring their predictive performance on a held-out set of documents. Topic models can also be inspected manually by a human to understand the themes of the underlying corpus. A widely adopted way is suggested by (Chang et al., 2009): it measures the quality of a topic by inspecting how far topic words are from some random words. The idea is that the quality of a topic can be measured by how far topic words are from some random words. In other words, if human evaluators can consistently separate random words from topic words, these topics are good, otherwise, they are not good. An advantage of this measure is that it can be easily implemented to deploy on a crowd-sourcing platform like Amazon's Mechanical Turk.

Assuming that random words represent random topics, we can name the above method "between-topic" measure. In this paper, we hypothesize that this measure considers just one important aspect in assessing the quality of statistical topics. Specifically, we investigate the topic interpretability by examining the "coherence" of a topic generated by topic modeling algorithms, i.e., how close topic words are within a topic. Thus, this measure is a "within-topic" measure. Two immediate challenging questions are: (1) without knowing ground truth of topic coherence, how can we design an equally effective method like "between-topic" measure for crowd-sourcing evaluation? and (2) how different is this "within-topic" coherence measure from the existing "between-topic" measure? We elaborate how we answer these two challenges by starting with some related work, showing how the "between-topic" measure faces difficulty in measuring coherence, and presenting our proposal of a coherence measure.

2 Related Work

Topic modeling is pervasive, and has been widely accepted across many communities such as machine learning and social sciences (Ramage et al., 2009; Schmidt, 2012; Yang et al., 2011). One of

543

Proceedings of the 54th Annual Meeting of the Association for Computational Linguistics, pages 543–548,
Berlin, Germany, August 7-12, 2016. ©2016 Association for Computational Linguistics

the reasons for the wide appreciation of these algorithms is their ability to find underlying topics in enormous sets of data (Blei, 2012). More recently topic modeling has been widely applied to social media data (Kireyev et al., 2009; Joseph et al., 2012; Morstatter et al., 2013), *e.g.* (Yin et al., 2011; Hong et al., 2012; Pozdnoukhov and Kaiser, 2011) focus on identifying topics in geographical Twitter datasets. In (Kumar et al., 2013; Mimno et al., 2011), the authors had to employ subject-matter experts to assess topic quality. These manual topic labels can be supplemented with automatic labeling algorithms (Maiya et al., 2013). While these works attempt to ensure topic quality by employing domain experts, these are highly domain-specific cases. The measures we discuss going forward are more general, and can be applied to topic models trained with text data.

The most important point of comparison between our work and others lies in the Model Precision measure proposed in (Chang et al., 2009). The insight of this measure is that a good topic is one whose top few words are distant, or highly separate, from randomly-selected words. Their task works by showing several human participants, or Turker, the top 5 words from a topic and one randomly-chosen, low-ranking "intruded" word. The humans are then asked to select the word that they think was intruded. The measure then estimates the topic's quality by calculating the number of times the humans correctly guessed the intruded word. While Word Intrusion provides insight into a topic's interpretability, the key assumption is that topic goodness comes only from the top words being separate from a randomly-selected word. This measure does not offer any insight about the coherence of the top words. We propose a new measure which complements Word Intrusion by measuring distance *within* a topic.

(Lau et al., 2014) built a machine learning algorithm to automatically detect the intruded word in a topic. Methods for evaluating topic models were proposed in (Wallach et al., 2009). We investigate the applicability of this measure in our work.

3 Model Precision Quandary

Model Precision works by asking the user to choose the word that does not fit within the rest of the set. We are measuring the top words in the topic by comparing them to an outlier. While this method has merit, it does not help us understand

the coherence *within* the top words for the topic.

A diagram illustrating this phenomenon is shown in Figure 1. In Figure 1(a), we see a coherent topic. This topic is coherent because all 5 of the top words are close together, while the intruded word is far away. In Figure 1(b) we see a topic that is less coherent because the fifth word lies at a distance from the first four. In both cases, Model Precision gives us the intruder word in the topic, as seen in Figures 1(c), and 1(d). While this is the desired performance of Model Precision, it leaves us with no understanding of the coherence of the top words of the topic. Results are masked by the outlier, and do not give information about the intra-cluster distance, or coherence of the topic.

In light of this, we look for a way to separate topics not just by their distance from an outlier, but also by the distance within the top words in the topic. The next section of this paper investigates a method which can measure not just the intruder word, but also the coherence of the top words in the topic. In this way we separate topics such as those shown in Figure 1 based on the coherence of their top words.

4 Word Intrusion Choose Two

In this section we propose a new experiment that measures the interpretability of the top words of a topic. This experiment sets up the task as before: we select the top five words from a topic, and inject one low-probability word. The key difference is that we ask the Turker to select *two* intruded words among the six.

The intuition behind this experiment is that the Turkers' first choice will be the intruded word, just as in Model Precision. However, their second choice is what makes the topic's quality clear. In a coherent topic the Turkers won't be able to distinguish a second word as all of the words will seem similar. A graphical representation of this phenomenon is shown in Figure 1(e). In the case of an incoherent, a strong "second-place" contender will emerge as the Turkers identify a 2nd intruder word, as in Figure 1(f).

4.1 Experimental Setup

To perform this experiment, we inject *one* low-probability word for each topic, and we ask the Turkers to select *two* words that do not fit within the group. We show the six words to the Turker in random order with the following prompt:

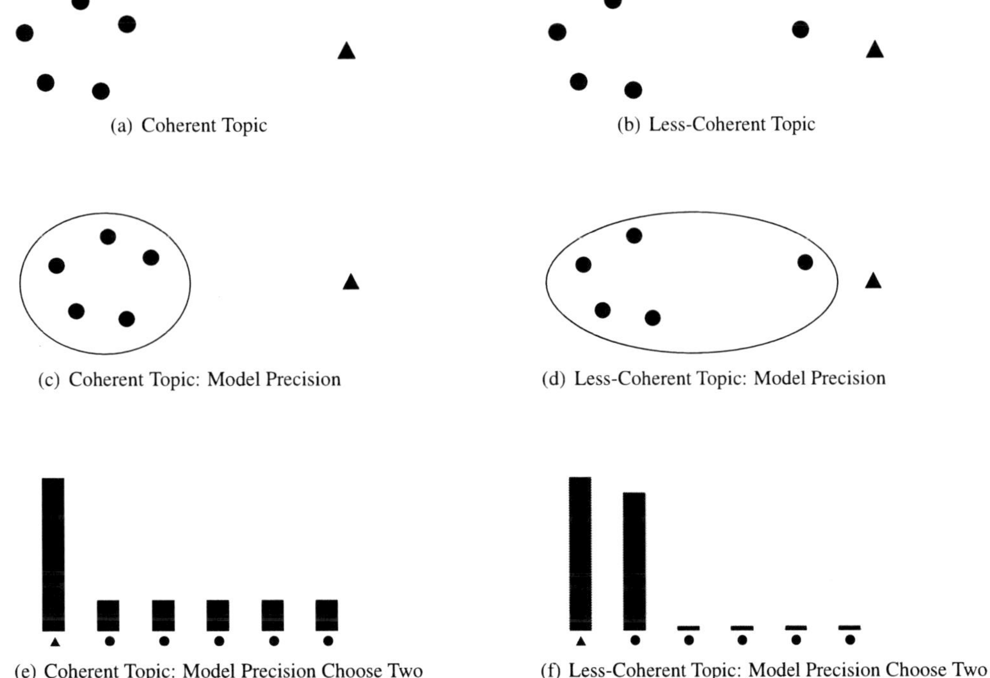

(a) Coherent Topic   (b) Less-Coherent Topic

(c) Coherent Topic: Model Precision   (d) Less-Coherent Topic: Model Precision

(e) Coherent Topic: Model Precision Choose Two   (f) Less-Coherent Topic: Model Precision Choose Two

Figure 1: Comparison between Model Precision, and Model Precision Choose Two for a toy topic. Circles represent the top words and triangles represent intruded words. Model Precision Choose Two can distinguish the less-coherent topic.

> You will be shown six words. Four words belong together, and two of them do not. Choose two words that do **not** belong in the group.

Coherent topics will cause the Turkers' responses regarding the second intruded word to be unpredictable. Thus, our measure of the goodness of the topic should be the predictability of the Turkers' second choice. We propose a new measure called "Model Precision Choose Two" to measure this. Model Precision Choose Two (MPCT) measures this spread as the peakedness of the probability distribution. We define $MPCT_k^m$ for topic k on model m as:

$$MPCT_k^m = H(p_{turk}(\mathbf{w}_{k,1}^m), ..., p_{turk}(\mathbf{w}_{k,5}^m)), \tag{1}$$

where $H(\cdot)$ is the Shannon entropy (Cover and Thomas, 2006), $\mathbf{w}_k^m$ is the vector of the top words in topic k generated by model m, and $p_{turk}(\mathbf{w}_{k,i}^m)$ is the probability that a Turker selects $\mathbf{w}_{k,i}^m$. This measures the strength of the second-place candidate, with higher values indicating a smoother, more even distribution, and lower values indicat-

ing Turkers gravitation towards a second word.

The intuition behind choosing entropy is that it will measure the unpredictability in the Turker selections. That is, if the Turkers are confused about which second word to choose, then their answers will be scattered amongst the remaining five words. As a result, the entropy will be *high*. Conversely, if the second word is obvious, the Turkers will begin to congregate around that second choice, meaning that their answers will be focused. As a result, the entropy will be *low*. Because entropy is able to measure the confusion of the Turkers responses about the second word, we use it directly in the design of our measure.

4.2 Data

The data used in this study consists of articles from English Wikipedia. We sample 10,000 articles uniformly at random from across the dataset. We selected articles containing more than 50 words. In preprocessing we stripped case, removed punctuation, stopwords, and words consisting entirely of numbers. This process yields a corpus containing 10,000 documents, 4,200,174 tokens, and

Table 1: Example topics showing the variance of $MPCT$ when $MP = 1.0$.

MPCT	Top Five Words	Intruded Word
0.202	canada, canadian, north, ontario, http	shipping
0.373	language, century, word, english, greek	drew
0.407	river, highway, road, north, route	berea
0.569	born, children, family, life, father	boatsman
0.795	design, engine, model, power, system	resynthesized
0.946	railway, station, road, line, route	anagarika
1.000	film, series, show, television, films	bubblegrunge

196,219 types.

The topic modeling algorithm used is latent Dirichlet allocation (LDA) (Blei et al., 2003). To build the models used in the experiments, we run LDA on the Wikipedia corpus using values of $K = \{10, 25, 50, 100\}$ with the Mallet package (McCallum, 2002). This yields 4 models and 185 total topics. The model generated by each value of K is denoted by m in the equations.

4.3 Experimental Results

The results of this experiment, aggregated by model, are shown in Figure 2. We see that as the value of K increases, the median score for MPCT stays roughly the same. We compute the Spearman's ρ correlation coefficient (Spearman, 1904) between the MP and $MPCT$ measures, and find that the measures have $\rho = 0.09$. This lack of correlation indicates that this measure is assessing a different dimension of the topics.

To help explain these results, we provide some examples of topics that received different MPCT scores with a perfect separateness (MP) score in Table 1. We see that although all of the topics have perfect scores along this dimension, their cohesiveness score varies. This is due to the Turkers' agreement about the second intruded word.

5 Automating Model Precision Choose Two

The crowdsourced experiments carried out in this paper provide a complementary understanding of how humans understand the topics that are generated using statistical topic models. One drawback of these methods lies in the difficulty of reproducing these experiments. This difficulty comes from two sources: 1) the monetary cost of employing the Turkers to solve the HITs, and 2) the time cost to build the surveys and to collect the results. To overcome these issues, we propose automated methods that can estimate the topics' performance

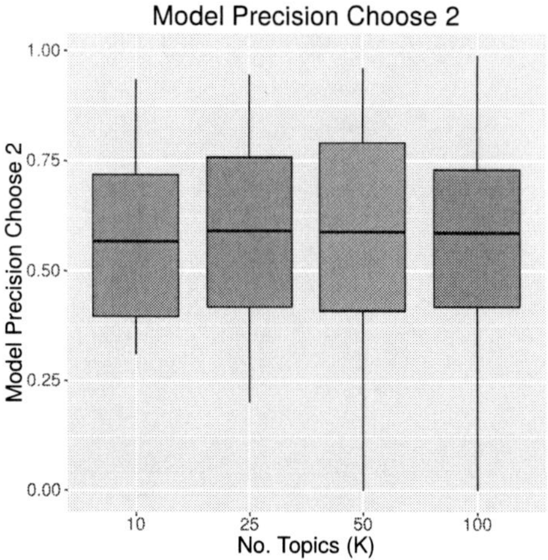

Figure 2: Model Precision Choose Two across the four models used in this work. Higher scores are better. We see that as K increases, the median score does not improve noticeably.

along these different dimensions. These measures can be used by future researchers to automatically gauge their topics.

We test several automated measures for their ability to predict the outcome of the crowdsourced measures. To test these measures, we calculate the Spearman's ρ between the automated measure of the topic and the crowdsourced measure. The automated measures we propose are as follows:

1. **Topic Size:** LDA assigns a topic label to each *token* in the dataset. Topic size measures the number of tokens assigned to the topic by the LDA model, where more tokens indicates a larger topic. This has been tested in (Mimno et al., 2011).

2. **Topic Entropy:** The entropy of the entire probability distribution for the topic. High entropy indicates a flat distribution of probabilities, while low entropy indicates a peaked distribution around the first few words.

3. **Mimno Co-Occurrence:** Measures the frequency of the top words co-occurring within the same document. Proposed in (Mimno et al., 2011), and measured as:

$$MCO(\mathbf{w}) = \sum_{j=2}^{|\mathbf{w}|} \sum_{k=1}^{j-1} log \frac{D(\mathbf{w}_j, \mathbf{w}_k) + 1}{D(\mathbf{w}_k)},$$

$$(2)$$

Table 2: Performance of automated measures in approximating the crowdsourced experiments. All values are Spearman's ρ correlation coefficients with the crowdsourced measure.

	Automated Measure	MPCT
1.	**Topic Size**	-0.572
2.	**Topic Entropy**	-0.539
3.	**Mimno**	-0.438
4.	**No. Word Senses**	-0.456
5.	**Avg. Pairwise JCD**	**-0.844**
6.	**Mean-Link JCD**	-0.434
7.	**NPMI**	-0.582

where **w** is the vector of the top 20 words in the topic, and $D(\cdot)$ returns the number of times the words co-occur in any document in the corpus.

4. **No. Word Senses:** The total number of word senses, according to WordNet, of the top five words in the topic. This varies slightly from the measure proposed in (Chang et al., 2009), where the authors also consider the intruded word. Because the intruded word is generally far away, we exclude it from our calculation.

5. **Avg. Pairwise Jiang-Conrath Distance:** The Jiang-Conrath (Jiang and Conrath, 1997) distance (JCD) is a measure of *semantic similarity*, or coherence, that considers the lowest common subsumer according to Word-Net. Here we compute the average JCD of all $\binom{5}{2} = 10$ pairs of the top five words of the topic. This approach was introduced by (Chang et al., 2009), however we modify it slightly to only consider the top five words in the topic.

6. **Mean-Link JCD:** Using the JCD measure as before, we compute the average distance from the intruded word to each of the top 5 words from the topic.

7. **Normalized Pointwise Mutual Information (NPMI):** NPMI measures the association between the top words in a topic. It is normalized to yield a score of 1 in the case of perfect association. This measure was first introduced by (Bouma, 2009). We use the calculation adapted for the problem of estimating a topic's performance introduced in (Lau et al., 2014).

We calculate the correlation between all automated methods and MPCT, shown in Table 2. MPCT is best predicted using the Avg. Pairwise JCD measure. The implications of this result are important: MPCT is best predicted by JCD, a measure that approximates the *coherence* of topics. Furthermore the correlations are negative, indicating that a low average distance (and thus, a high semantic similarity) indicates a high performance along this automated measure.

6 Conclusion and Future Work

In this work we define a new measure for the performance of statistical topic models. We show that this measure gauges a different aspect of the topics than the traditional model precision measure. Finally, we identify automated measures that can approximate the crowdsourced measures for both interpretability and coherence. This measure can be used by future researchers to complement their analysis of statistical topics. The results from our experiments indicate that Word Intrusion Choose Two is different from Word Intrusion, with almost no correlation between the two measures.

Furthermore, we propose automatic measures that can replace the crowdsourced measures. This is important as it allows for both scalability and reproducibility, as experiments using crowdsourcing are costly in terms of both time and money. We find that measures based on the interpretability of topics can best approximate the Model Precision Choose Two measure, indicating that this measure favors topics whose top words are more semantically similar, furthering our claim that this measure is assessing the coherence of the topic. Code and data to reproduce Model Precision Choose Two can be found at `http://bit.ly/mpchoose2`.

While model precision choose two offers a new way to understand topics, there may be others that could help to reveal other dimensions of topic quality. Future work is to find other measures for the semantic properties of topic modeling algorithms. Furthermore, the automated measures we discover to approximate the crowdsourced ones may be incorporated into a topic modeling algorithm that can better produce interpretable topics.

Acknowledgments

This work is sponsored, in part, by Office of Naval Research (ONR) grant N000141410095.

References

D. M. Blei, A. Y. Ng, and M. I. Jordan. 2003. Latent Dirichlet Allocation. *The Journal of Machine Learning Research*, 3:993–1022.

David Blei. 2012. Topic modeling and digital humanities. *Journal of Digital Humanities*, 2(1):8–11.

Gerlof Bouma. 2009. Normalized (pointwise) mutual information in collocation extraction. *Proceedings of GSCL*, pages 31–40.

Jonathan Chang, Jordan L. Boyd-Graber, Sean Gerrish, Chong Wang, and David M Blei. 2009. Reading tea leaves: How humans interpret topic models. In *NIPS*, pages 288–296.

T. M. Cover and J. A. Thomas. 2006. *Elements of Information Theory*. Wiley InterScience, Hoboken, New Jersey.

Justin Grimmer and Brandon M Stewart. 2013. Text as data: The promise and pitfalls of automatic content analysis methods for political texts. *Political Analysis*.

Liangjie Hong, Amr Ahmed, Siva Gurumurthy, Alexander J. Smola, and Kostas Tsioutsiouliklis. 2012. Discovering geographical topics in the twitter stream. In *Proceedings of the 21st international conference on World Wide Web*, WWW '12, pages 769–778, New York, NY, USA. ACM.

Jay J Jiang and David W Conrath. 1997. Semantic similarity based on corpus statistics and lexical taxonomy. *arXiv preprint cmp-lg/9709008*.

Kenneth Joseph, Chun How Tan, and Kathleen M. Carley. 2012. Beyond "local", "categories" and "friends": clustering foursquare users with latent "topics". In *Proceedings of the 2012 ACM Conference on Ubiquitous Computing*, UbiComp '12, pages 919–926, New York, NY, USA. ACM.

K Kireyev, L Palen, and K Anderson. 2009. Applications of Topics Models to Analysis of Disaster-Related Twitter Data. In *NIPS Workshop on Applications for Topic Models: Text and Beyond*, volume 1.

Shamanth Kumar, Fred Morstatter, Reza Zafarani, and Huan Liu. 2013. Whom Should I Follow?: Identifying Relevant Users During Crises. In *Proceedings of the 24th ACM Conference on Hypertext and Social Media*, HT '13, pages 139–147, New York, NY, USA. ACM.

Jey Han Lau, David Newman, and Timothy Baldwin. 2014. Machine reading tea leaves: Automatically evaluating topic coherence and topic model quality. In *Proceedings of the European Chapter of the Association for Computational Linguistics*.

Arun S Maiya, John P Thompson, Francisco Loaiza-Lemos, and Robert M Rolfe. 2013. Exploratory analysis of highly heterogeneous document collections. In *Proceedings of the 19th ACM SIGKDD international conference on Knowledge discovery and data mining*, pages 1375–1383. ACM.

Andrew McCallum. 2002. Mallet: A machine learning for language toolkit. http://mallet.cs.umass.edu.

David Mimno, Hanna M. Wallach, Edmund Talley, Miriam Leenders, and Andrew McCallum. 2011. Optimizing semantic coherence in topic models. In *Proceedings of the Conference on Empirical Methods in Natural Language Processing*, EMNLP '11, pages 262–272, Stroudsburg, PA, USA. Association for Computational Linguistics.

Fred Morstatter, Jürgen Pfeffer, Huan Liu, and Kathleen M. Carley. 2013. Is the Sample Good Enough? Comparing Data from Twitters Streaming API with Twitters Firehose. *Proceedings of ICWSM*.

Brendan O'Connor, Michel Krieger, and David Ahn. 2010. Tweetmotif: Exploratory search and topic summarization for twitter. In *ICWSM*.

Alexei Pozdnoukhov and Christian Kaiser. 2011. Space-time dynamics of topics in streaming text. In *Proc. of the 3rd ACM SIGSPATIAL Int'l Workshop on Location-Based Social Networks*, LBSN '11, pages 1–8, New York, NY, USA. ACM.

Daniel Ramage, Evan Rosen, Jason Chuang, Christopher D Manning, and Daniel A McFarland. 2009. Topic modeling for the social sciences. In *NIPS 2009 Workshop on Applications for Topic Models: Text and Beyond*, volume 5.

Benjamin M Schmidt. 2012. Words alone: Dismantling topic models in the humanities. *Journal of Digital Humanities*, 2(1):49–65.

Charles Spearman. 1904. The proof and measurement of association between two things. *The American journal of psychology*, 15(1):72–101.

Hanna M Wallach, Iain Murray, Ruslan Salakhutdinov, and David Mimno. 2009. Evaluation methods for topic models. In *ICML*, pages 1105–1112. ACM.

Tze-I Yang, Andrew J Torget, and Rada Mihalcea. 2011. Topic modeling on historical newspapers. In *Proceedings of the 5th ACL-HLT Workshop on Language Technology for Cultural Heritage, Social Sciences, and Humanities*, pages 96–104. Association for Computational Linguistics.

Zhijun Yin, Liangliang Cao, Jiawei Han, Chengxiang Zhai, and Thomas Huang. 2011. Geographical topic discovery and comparison. In *Proceedings of the 20th international conference on World wide web*, WWW '11, pages 247–256, New York, NY, USA. ACM.

Coarse-grained Argumentation Features for Scoring Persuasive Essays

Debanjan Ghosh[§]**, Aquila Khanam**[†]**, Yubo Han**[†] **and Smaranda Muresan**[‡]
[§]School of Communication and Information, Rutgers University, NJ, USA
[†]Department of Computer Science, Columbia University, NY, USA
[‡]Center for Computational Learning Systems, Columbia University, NY, USA
debanjan.ghosh@rutgers.edu, {ak3654,yh2635,smara@columbia.edu}

Abstract

Scoring the quality of persuasive essays is an important goal of discourse analysis, addressed most recently with high-level persuasion-related features such as thesis clarity, or opinions and their targets. We investigate whether argumentation features derived from a coarse-grained argumentative structure of essays can help predict essays scores. We introduce a set of argumentation features related to argument components (e.g., the number of claims and premises), argument relations (e.g., the number of supported claims) and typology of argumentative structure (chains, trees). We show that these features are good predictors of human scores for TOEFL essays, both when the coarse-grained argumentative structure is manually annotated and automatically predicted.

1 Introduction

Persuasive essays are frequently used to assess students' understanding of subject matter and to evaluate their argumentation skills and language proficiency. For instance, the prompt for a TOEFL (Test of English as a Foreign Language) persuasive writing task is:

> *Do you agree or disagree with the following statement? It is better to have broad knowledge of many academic subjects than to specialize in one specific subject. Use specific reasons and examples to support your answer.*

Automatic essay scoring systems generally use features based on grammar usage, spelling, style, and content (e.g., topics, discourse) (Attali and Burstein, 2006; Burstein, 2003). However, recent work has begun to explore the impact of high-level persuasion-related features, such as opinions and their targets, thesis clarity and argumentation schemes (Farra et al., 2015; Song et al., 2014; Ong et al., 2014; Persing and Ng, 2015). In this paper, we investigate whether argumentation features derived from a coarse-grained, general argumentative structure of essays are good predictors of holistic essay scores. We use the argumentative structure proposed by Stab and Gurevych (2014a): *argument components* (major claims, claims, premises) and *argument relations* (support, attack). Figure 1(i) shows an extract from an essay written in response to the above prompt, labeled with a claim and two premises. The advantage of having a simple annotation scheme is two-fold: it allows for more reliable human annotations and it enables better performance for argumentation mining systems designed to automatically identify the argumentative structure (Stab and Gurevych, 2014b).

The paper has two main contributions. First, we introduce a set of argumentation features related to three main dimensions of argumentative structure: 1) features related to *argument components* such as the number of claims in an essay, number of premises, fraction of sentences containing argument components; 2) features related to *argument relations* such as the number and percentage of supported and unsupported claims; and 3) features related to the *typology of argumentative structure* such as number of chains (see Figure 1(ii) for and example of chain) and trees (Section 3). On a dataset of 107 TOEFL essays manually annotated with the argumentative structure proposed by Stab and Gurevych (2014a) (Section 2), we show that using all the argumentation features predicts essay scores that are highly correlated with human scores (Section 3). We discuss what features are correlated with high scoring es-

549

Proceedings of the 54th Annual Meeting of the Association for Computational Linguistics, pages 549–554,
Berlin, Germany, August 7-12, 2016. ©2016 Association for Computational Linguistics

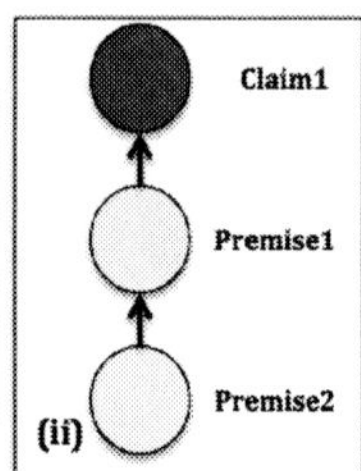

Figure 1: (i) Essay extract showing a claim and two premises and (ii) the corresponding argumentative structure (i.e., chain).

says vs. low scoring essays. Second, we show that the argumentation features extracted based on argumentative structures automatically predicted by a state-of-the-art argumentation mining system (Stab and Gurevych, 2014b) are also good predictors of essays scores (Section 4).[1]

2 Data and Annotation

We use a set of 107 essays from TOEFL11 corpus that was proposed for the first shared task of Native Language Identification (Blanchard et al., 2013). The essays are sampled from 2 prompts: P1 (shown in the Introduction) and P3:

> *Do you agree or disagree with the following statement? Young people nowadays do not give enough time to helping their communities. Use specific reasons and examples to support your answer.*

Each essay is associated with a score: high, medium, or low. From prompt P1, we selected 25 high, 21 medium, and 16 low essays, while for prompt P3 we selected 15 essays for each of the three scores.

For annotation, we used the coarse-grained argumentative structure proposed by Stab and Gurevych (2014a): argument components (major claim, claim, premises) and argument relations (support/attack). The unit of annotation is a clause. Our annotated dataset, $TOEFL_{arg}$, includes 107 major claims, 468 claims, 603 premises, and 641 number of sentences that do not contain any argument component. To measure the inter-annotator agreement we calculated P/R/F1 measures, which are used to account for fuzzy boundaries (Wiebe et al., 2005). The F1

measure for overlap matches (between two annotators) for argument components is 73.98% and for argument relation is 67.56%.

3 Argumentation Features for Predicting Essays Scores

A major contribution of this paper is a thorough analysis of the key features derived from a coarse-grained argumentative structure that are correlated with essay scores. Based on our annotations, we propose three groups of features (Table 1). The first group consists of features related to *argument components* (AC) such as the number of claims, number of premises, fraction of sentences containing argument components. One hypothesis is that an essay with a higher percentage of argumentative sentences will have a higher score. The second group consists of features related to *argument relations* (AR), such as the number and percentage of supported claims (i.e., claims that are supported by at least one premise) and the number and percentage of dangling claims (i.e., claims with no supporting premises). In low scoring essays, test takers often fail to justify their claims with proper premises and this phenomenon is captured by the dangling claims feature. In contrary, in high scoring essays, it is common to find many claims that are justified by premises. We also consider the number of attack relations and attacks against the major claim. Finally, the third group consists of features related to the *typology of argument structures* (TS) such as the number of argument chains ($Chain$), number of argument trees of height $= 1$ ($Tree_{h=1}$) and the number of argument trees of height > 1 ($Tree_{h>1}$). We define an argument chain when a *claim* is supported by a chain of premises. We define $Tree_{h=1}$ as a tree structure of height 1 with more than one leaves, where *the root is a claim* and the leaves are premises

---

[1]The annotated dataset, $TOEFL_{arg}$, is available at https://github.com/debanjanghosh/argessay_ACL2016/

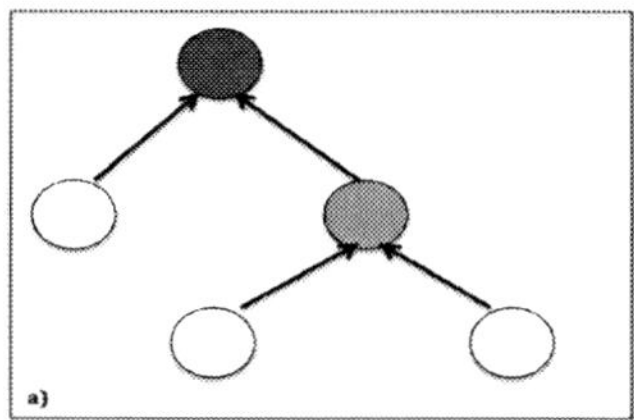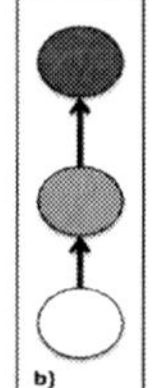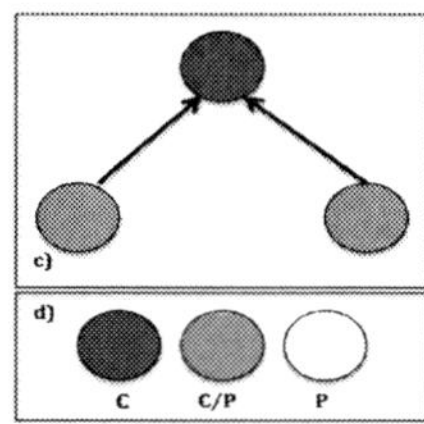

Figure 2: Typology of Argumentative Structure: Examples of (i) $Tree_{h>1}$; (ii) Chain; (iii) $Tree_{h=1}$

Feature Group	Id	Argumentation Feature Description
	1	# of Claims
AC	2	# of Premises
	3,4	# and fraction of sentences containing argument components
	5, 6	# and % of supported Claims
AR	7, 8	# and % of dangling Claims
	9	# of Claims supporting Major Claim
	10, 11	# of total Attacks and Attacks against Major Claim
	12	# of Argument $Chains$
TS	13	# of Argument $Tree_{h=1}$
	14	# of Argument $Tree_{h>1}$

Table 1: Argumentation Features

Features	Correlations
bl	0.535
AC	0.758
AR	0.671
TS	0.691
bl + AC	0.770
bl + AR	0.743
bl + TS	0.735
AC + AR + TS	**0.784**
bl + AC + AR + TS	**0.803**

Table 2: Correlation of LR (10 fold CV) with human scores.

or claims. Finally, $Tree_{h>1}$ is a tree structure of height > 1, where *the root is a claim* and the internal nodes and leaves are either supporting claims or supporting premises. Figure 2 shows examples of a $Tree_{h>1}$ structure, a $Chain$ structure, and a $Tree_{h=1}$ structure. The dark nodes represent claims (C), lighter nodes can be either claims or premises (C/P) and white nodes are premises (P). Figure 1 shows an extract from an essays and the corresponding $Chain$ structure.

To measure the effectiveness of the above features in predicting the holistic essay scores (high/medium/low) we use Logistic Regression (LR) learners and evaluate the learners using quadratic-weighted kappa (QWK) against the human scores, a methodology generally used for essay scoring (Farra et al., 2015). QWK corrects for chance agreement between the system prediction and the human prediction, and it takes into account the extent of the disagreement between labels. Table 2 reports the performance for the three feature groups as well as their combination. Our baseline feature (bl) is the number of sentences in the essay, since essay length has been shown to be generally highly correlated with essay scores (Chodorow and Burstein, 2004). We found that all three feature groups individually are strongly correlated with the human scores, much better than

the baseline feature, and the AC features have the highest correlation. We also see that although the number of claims and premises can affect the score of an essay, the argumentative structures (i.e., how the claims and premises are connected in an essay) are also important. Combining all features gives the highest QWK score (0.803).

We also looked at what features are associated with high scoring essays vs. low scoring essays. Based on the regression coefficients, we observe that the high "number and % of dangling claims" are strong features for low scoring essays, whereas the "fraction of sentences containing argument components" (AC feature), "number of supported claims" (AR feature), and "number of $Tree_{h=1}$ structures" and "number of $Tree_{h>1}$ structures" (TS features) have the highest correlation with high scoring essays. For example, in a good persuasive essay, test takers are inclined to use multiple premises (e.g., reasons or examples) to support a claim, which is captured by the TS and AR features. In addition, we notice that attack relations are sparse, as was the case in Stab and Gurevych (2014b) dataset and thus the coefficients for attack relations features (#10, #11 in Table 1) are negligible.

In summary, our findings contribute to research on essay scoring, showing that argumentation features are good predictors of essay scores, besides spelling, grammar, and stylistic properties of text.

4 Automatic Extraction of Argumentation Features for Predicting Essay Scores

To automatically generate the argumentation features (Table 1), we first need to identify the argumentative structures: argument components (major claim, claim, and premise) and relations (support/attack). We use the approach proposed by Stab and Gurevych (2014b).[2] For argument component identification, we categorize clauses to one of the four classes (major claim (MC), claim (C), premise (P), and $None$). For argument relation identification, given a pair of argument clauses Arg_1 and Arg_2 the classifier decides whether the pair holds a support (S) or non-support (NS) relation (binary classification). For each essay, we extract all possible combinations of Arg_1 and Arg_2 from each paragraph as training data (654 S and 2503 NS instances; attack relations are few and included in NS). We do not consider relations that may span over multiple paragraphs to reduce number of non-support instances. For both tasks we use $Lexical$ features (e.g., unigrams, bigrams, trigrams, modal verbs, adverbs, word-pairs for relation identification), $Structural$ features (e.g., number of tokens/punctuations in argument, as well as in the sentence containing the argument, argument position in essay, paragraph position (paragraph that contains the argument)), $Syntactic$ features (e.g., production rules from parse trees, number of clauses in the argument), and $Indicators$ (discourse markers selected from the three top-level Penn Discourse Tree Bank (PDTB) relation senses: Comparison, Contingency, and Expansion (Prasad et al., 2008)).

We use two settings for the classification experiments using libSVM (Chang and Lin, 2011) for both argument component and relation identification. In the first setting, we used the dataset of 90 high quality persuasive essays from (Stab and Gurevych, 2014b) (S&G) as training and use $TOEFL_{arg}$ for testing (out-of-domain setting). In the second setting (in-domain), we randomly split the $TOEFL_{arg}$ into 80% training and 20% for testing (sampled equally from each category (MC, C, P, and $None$ for argument components; S and NS for relations)). Table 3 and 4 present the classification results for identifying ar-

---

[2]In future work, we plan to use the authors' improved approach and larger dataset released after the acceptance of this paper (Stab and Gurevych, 2016).

Feature Type	MC	C	P	$None$
All features	50.0	44.3	48.6	97.7
top100	60.8	36.2	54.1	97.7

Table 3: F1 for argument components (out-of-domain setting)

Feature Type	MC	C	P	$None$
All features	78.6	53.2	64.0	96.1
top100	53.8	64.5	69.2	96.2

Table 4: F1 for argument components (in-domain setting)

gument components in the first and second setting, respectively. We ran experiments for all different features groups and observe that with the exception of the P class, the F1 scores for all the other classes is comparable to the results reported by Stab and Gurevych (2014b). One explanation of having lower performance on the P (premise) category is that the S&G dataset used for training has higher quality essays, while 2/3 of our $TOEFL_{arg}$ dataset consists of medium and low scoring essays (the writing style for providing reasons or example can differ between high and low scoring essays). When we select the top 100 features ("top100") using Information Gain (Hall et al., 2009) the F1 scores for the P class improves. The results in Table 4 show that when training and testing on same type of essays the results are better for all categories except for MC when using the "top100" setup.

Table 5 shows the results for relation identification in the first setting (out-of-domain). The F1 score of identifying support relations is 84.3% (or 89% using top100), much higher than reported by Stab and Gurevych (2014b). We obtain similar results when training and testing on $TOEFL_{arg}$. We observe that two specific feature groups, $Structural$ and $Lexical$, individually achieve high F1 scores and when combined with other features, they assist the classifier in reaching F1 scores in high 80s%. There can be two explanations for this: 1) essays in $TOEFL_{arg}$ have multiple short paragraphs where the position features such as position of the arguments in the essay and paragraph ($Structural$ group) are strong indicators for argument relations; and 2) due to short paragraphs, the percentage of NS instances are less than in the S&G dataset, hence the $Lexical$ features (i.e., word-pairs between Arg_1 and Arg_2) perform very well.

Feature Type	S	NS
All features	84.3	95.0
top100	89.0	97.1

Table 5: F1 for argument relations (out-of-domain setting)

Features	Correlations
AC	0.669
AR	0.460
TS	0.311
AC + AR + TS	0.728
All features	**0.737**

Table 6: Correlation of LR (10 fold CV) with predicted results.

Based on the automatic identification of the argument components and relations, we generate the argumentation features to see whether they still predict essays scores that are highly correlated with human scores. Since our goal is to compare with the manual annotation setup, we use the first setting, where we train on the S&G dataset and test on our $TOEFL_{arg}$ dataset. We select the best system setup (top100 for both tasks; Table 3 and 5). We ran Logistic Regression learners and evaluated their performance using QWK scores. Table 6 shows that the argumentative features related to argument relations (AR) and the typology of argument structures (TS) extracted based on the automatically predicated argumentative structure perform worse compared to the scores based on manual annotations (Table 2). Our error analysis shows that this is due to the wrong prediction of argument components, specifically wrongly labeling claims as premises (Table 3). AR and TS features rely on correctly identifying the *claims*, and thus a wrong prediction affects the features in these two groups, even if the accuracy of supports relations is high. This also explains why the argument components (AC) features still have a high correlation with human scores (0.669). When we extracted the argumentation features using *gold-standard* argument components and *predicted* argument relations, the correlation of AR and TS features improved to 0.576 and 0.504, respectively and the correlation of all features reached 0.769.

5 Related Work

Researchers have begun to study the impact of features specific to persuasive construct on student essay scores (Farra et al., 2015; Song et al., 2014; Ong et al., 2014; Persing and Ng, 2013; Persing and Ng, 2015). Farra et al. (2015) investigate the impact of opinion and target features on TOEFL essays scores. Our work looks a step further by exploring argumentation features. Song et al. (2014) show that adding features related to argumentation schemes (from manual annotation) as part of an automatic scoring system increases the correlation with human scores. We show that argumentation features are good predictors of human scores for TOEFL essays, both when the coarse-grained argumentative structure is manually annotated and automatically predicted. Persing and Ng (2015) proposed a feature-rich approach for modeling argument strength in student essays, where the features are related to argument components. Our work explores features related to argument components, relations and typology of argument structures, showing that argument relation features show best correlation with human scores (based on manual annotation).

6 Conclusion

We show that argumentation features derived from a coarse-grained, argumentative structure of essays are helpful in predicting essays scores that have a high correlation with human scores. Our manual annotation study shows that features related to argument relations are particularly useful. Our experiments using current methods for the automatic identification of argumentative structure confirms that distinguishing between claim and premises is a particularly hard task. This led to lower performance in predicting the essays scores using automatically generate argumentation features, especially for features related to argument relations and typology of structure. As future work we plan to improve the automatic methods for identifying argument components similar to Stab and Gurevych (2016), and to use the dataset introduced by Persing and Ng (2015) to investigate how our argumentation features impact the argument strength score rather than the holistic essay score.

Acknowledgements

This paper is based on work supported by the DARPA-DEFT program. The views expressed are those of the authors and do not reflect the official policy or position of the Department of Defense or the U.S. Government. The authors thank the anonymous reviewers for helpful comments.

References

Yigal Attali and Jill Burstein. 2006. Automated essay scoring with e-rater® v. 2. *The Journal of Technology, Learning and Assessment*, 4(3).

Daniel Blanchard, Joel Tetreault, Derrick Higgins, Aoife Cahill, and Martin Chodorow. 2013. Toefl11: A corpus of non-native english. *ETS Research Report Series*, 2013(2):i–15.

Jill Burstein. 2003. The e-rater® scoring engine: Automated essay scoring with natural language processing.

Chih-Chung Chang and Chih-Jen Lin. 2011. LIB-SVM: A library for support vector machines. *ACM Transactions on Intelligent Systems and Technology*, 2:27:1–27:27.

Martin Chodorow and Jill Burstein. 2004. Beyond essay length: Evaluating e-rater®'s performance on toefl® essays. *ETS Research Report Series*, 2004(1):i–38.

Noura Farra, Swapna Somasundaran, and Jill Burstein. 2015. Scoring persuasive essays using opinions and their targets. In *Proceedings of the Tenth Workshop on Innovative Use of NLP for Building Educational Applications*, pages 64–74, Denver, Colorado, June. Association for Computational Linguistics.

Mark Hall, Eibe Frank, Geoffrey Holmes, Bernhard Pfahringer, Peter Reutemann, and Ian H Witten. 2009. The weka data mining software: an update. *ACM SIGKDD explorations newsletter*, 11(1):10–18.

Nathan Ong, Diane Litman, and Alexandra Brusilovsky. 2014. Ontology-based argument mining and automatic essay scoring. *ACL 2014*, page 24.

Isaac Persing and Vincent Ng. 2013. Modeling thesis clarity in student essays. In *Proceedings of the 51st Annual Meeting of the Association for Computational Linguistics (Volume 1: Long Papers)*, pages 260–269.

Isaac Persing and Vincent Ng. 2015. Modeling argument strength in student essays. In *Proceedings of the 53rd Annual Meeting of the Association for Computational Linguistics and the 7th International Joint Conference on Natural Language Processing (Volume 1: Long Papers)*, pages 543–552.

Rashmi Prasad, Nikhil Dinesh, Alan Lee, Eleni Miltsakaki, Livio Robaldo, Aravind K Joshi, and Bonnie L Webber. 2008. The penn discourse treebank 2.0. In *LREC*. Citeseer.

Yi Song, Michael Heilman, Beata Beigman Klebanov, and Paul Deane. 2014. Applying argumentation schemes for essay scoring. In *Proceedings of the First Workshop on Argumentation Mining*, pages 69–78.

Christian Stab and Iryna Gurevych. 2014a. Annotating argument components and relations in persuasive essays. In *Proceedings of the 25th International Conference on Computational Linguistics (COLING 2014)*, pages 1501–1510.

Christian Stab and Iryna Gurevych. 2014b. Identifying argumentative discourse structures in persuasive essays. In *Conference on Empirical Methods in Natural Language Processing (EMNLP 2014)(Oct. 2014), Association for Computational Linguistics, p.(to appear)*.

Christian Stab and Iryna Gurevych. 2016. Parsing argumentation structure in persuasive essays. *arXiv preprint, arxiv.org/abs/1604.07370*.

Janyce Wiebe, Theresa Wilson, and Claire Cardie. 2005. Annotating expressions of opinions and emotions in language. *Language resources and evaluation*, 39(2-3):165–210.

Single-Model Encoder-Decoder with Explicit Morphological Representation for Reinflection

Katharina Kann and Hinrich Schütze
Center for Information & Language Processing
LMU Munich, Germany
`kann@cis.lmu.de`

Abstract

Morphological reinflection is the task of generating a target form given a source form, a source tag and a target tag. We propose a new way of modeling this task with neural encoder-decoder models. Our approach reduces the amount of required training data for this architecture and achieves state-of-the-art results, making encoder-decoder models applicable to morphological reinflection even for low-resource languages. We further present a new automatic correction method for the outputs based on edit trees.

1 Introduction

Morphological analysis and generation of previously unseen word forms is a fundamental problem in many areas of natural language processing (NLP). Its accuracy is crucial for the success of downstream tasks like machine translation and question answering. Accordingly, learning morphological inflection patterns from labeled data is an important challenge.

The task of morphological reinflection (MRI) consists of producing an inflected form for a given source form, source tag and target tag. A special case is morphological inflection (MI), the task of finding an inflected form for a given lemma and target tag. An English example is "tree"+PLURAL → "trees". Prior work on MI and MRI includes machine learning models and models that exploit the paradigm structure of the language (Ahlberg et al., 2015; Dreyer, 2011; Nicolai et al., 2015).

In this work, we propose the neural encoder-decoder MED – Morphological Encoder-Decoder – a character-level sequence-to-sequence attention model that is a language-independent solution for MRI. In contrast to prior work, we train a *single* model that is trained on all source to target mappings of the language that are attested in the training set. This radically reduces the amount of training data needed for the encoder-decoder because most MRI patterns occur in many source-target tag pairs. In our model design, what is learned for one pair can be transferred to others.

The key enabler for this single-model approach is a novel representation we use for MRI. We encode the input as a single sequence of (i) the morphological tags of the source form, (ii) the morphological tags of the target form and (iii) the sequence of letters of the source form. The output is the sequence of letters of the target form. As the decoder produces each letter, the attention mechanism can focus on *the input letter sequence* for parts of the output that simply copy the input. For other parts of the output, e.g., an inflectional ending that is predicted using the target tags, the attention mechanism can focus on *the target morphological tags*. In more complex cases, *simultaneous attention can be paid to subsequences of all three input types* – source tags, target tags and input letter sequence. We can train a single generic encoder-decoder per language on this representation that can handle all tag pairs, thus making it possible to make efficient use of the available training data. MED outperformed other systems on the SIGMORPHON16 shared task[1] for all ten languages that were covered (Kann and Schütze, 2016; Cotterell et al., 2016).

We also present POET – Prefer Observed Edit Trees – a new generic method for correcting the output of an MRI system. The combination of MED and POET is state-of-the-art or close to it on a CELEX-based evaluation of MRI even though this evaluation makes it difficult to exploit gener-

---

[1] `ryancotterell.github.io/`
`sigmorphon2016/`

555

Proceedings of the 54th Annual Meeting of the Association for Computational Linguistics, pages 555–560,
Berlin, Germany, August 7-12, 2016. ©2016 Association for Computational Linguistics

alizations across tag pairs.

2 Model Description

Neural network model. Our model is based on the network architecture proposed by Bahdanau et al. (2014) for machine translation.[2] They describe the model in detail; unless we explicitly say so in the description of our model below, we use the same network configuration as Bahdanau et al. (2014).

Bahdanau et al. (2014)'s model is an extension of the recurrent neural network (RNN) encoder-decoder developed by Cho et al. (2014) and Sutskever et al. (2014). The encoder of the latter consists of an RNN that reads an input sequence of vectors x and encodes it into a fixed-length context vector c, computing hidden states h_t and c by

$$h_t = f(x_t, h_{t-1}), \quad c = q(h_1, ..., h_{T_x}) \quad (1)$$

with nonlinear functions f and q. The decoder is trained to predict each output y_t dependent on c and previous predictions $y_1, ..., y_{t-1}$:

$$p(y) = \prod_{t=1}^{T_y} p(y_t|\{y_1, ..., y_{t-1}\}, c) \quad (2)$$

with $y = (y_1, ..., y_{T_y})$ and each conditional probability being modeled with an RNN as

$$p(y_t|\{y_1, ..., y_{t-1}\}, c) = g(y_{t-1}, s_t, c) \quad (3)$$

where g is a nonlinear function and s_t is the hidden state of the RNN.

Bahdanau et al. (2014) proposed an attention-based extension of this model that allows different vectors c_t for each step by automatic learning of an alignment model. Additionally, they made the encoder bidirectional: each hidden state h_j at time step j does not only depend on the preceding, but also on the following input:

$$h_j = \left[\overrightarrow{h_j^T}; \overleftarrow{h_j^T} \right]^T \quad (4)$$

The formula for $p(y)$ changes as follows:

$$p(y) = \prod_{t=1}^{T_y} p(y_t|\{y_1, ..., y_{t-1}\}, x) \quad (5)$$

$$= \prod_{t=1}^{T_y} g(y_{t-1}, s_t, c_t) \quad (6)$$

---

[2]Our implementation of MED is based on `github.com/mila-udem/blocks-examples/tree/master/machine_translation`.

with s_t being an RNN hidden state for time t and c_t being the weighted sum of the annotations $(h_1, ..., h_{T_x})$ produced by the encoder, using the attention weights. Further descriptions can be found in (Bahdanau et al., 2014).

The final model is a multilayer network with a single maxout (Goodfellow et al., 2013) hidden layer that computes the conditional probability of each element in the output sequence (a letter in our case, (Pascanu et al., 2014)). As MRI is less complex than machine translation, we reduce the number of hidden units and embedding size. After initial experiments, we fixed the hyperparameters of our system and did not further adapt them to a specific task or language. Encoder and decoder RNNs have 100 hidden units each. For training, we use stochastic gradient descent, Adadelta (Zeiler, 2012) and a minibatch size of 20. We initialize all weights in the encoder, decoder and the embeddings except for the GRU weights in the decoder with the identity matrix as well as all biases with zero (Le et al., 2015). We train all models for 20,000 iterations. We settled on this number in early experimentation because training usually converged before that limit.

MED is an ensemble of five RNN encoder-decoders. The final decision is made by majority voting. In case of a tie, the answer is chosen randomly among the most frequent predictions.

Input and output format. We define the alphabet Σ_{lang} as the set of characters used in the application language. As each morphological tag consists of one or more subtags, e.g. "number" or "case", we further define Σ_{src} and Σ_{trg} as the set of morphological subtags seen during training as part of the source tag and target tag, respectively. Let S_{start} and S_{end} be predefined start and end symbols. Then each input of our system is of the format $S_{\text{start}}\Sigma_{\text{src}}^+\Sigma_{\text{trg}}^+\Sigma_{\text{lang}}^+S_{\text{end}}$. In the same way, we define the output format as $S_{\text{start}}\Sigma_{\text{lang}}^+S_{\text{end}}$.

A sample input for German is *<w> IN=pos=ADJ IN=case=GEN IN=num=PL OUT=pos=ADJ OUT=case=ACC OUT=num=PL i s o l i e r t e r </w>*. The system should produce the corresponding output *<w> i s o l i e r t e </w>*. The high-level structure of MED can be seen in Figure 1.

POET. We now describe POET (Prefer Observed Edit Trees), a new generic method for correcting the output of an MRI system. We use it in combination with MED in this paper, but it can in

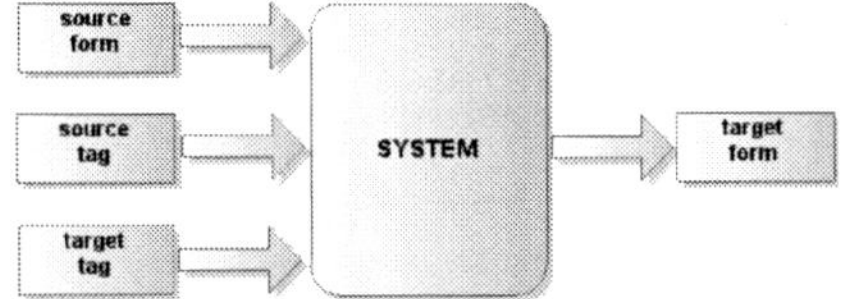

Figure 1: Overview of MED

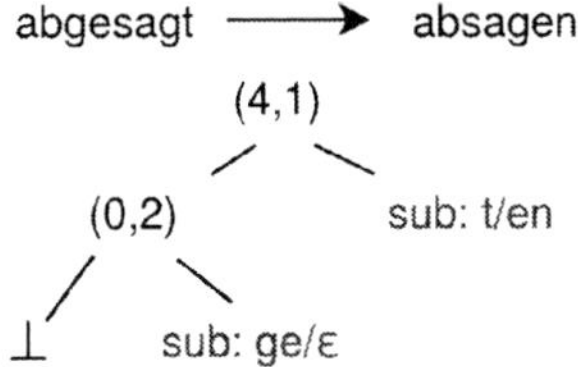

Figure 2: Edit tree for the inflected form *abgesagt* "canceled" and its lemma *absagen* "to cancel". The highest node contains the length of the parts before and after the LCS. The left node in the second row contains the length of the parts before and after the LCS of *abge* and *ab*. The prefix *sub* indicates that the node is a substitution operation.

principle be applied to any MRI system.

An edit tree $e(\sigma, \tau)$ specifies a transformation from a source string σ to a target string τ (Chrupała, 2008). To compute $e(\sigma, \tau)$, we first determine the longest common substring (LCS) (Gusfield, 1997) between σ and τ and then recursively model the prefix and suffix pairs of the LCS. If the length of LCS is zero for (σ, τ), then $e(\sigma, \tau)$ is simply the substitution operation that replaces σ with τ. Figure 2 shows an example.

Let X be a training set for MRI. For each pair (s, t) of tags, we define:

$$E_{s,t} = \{e' | \exists x \in X : e' = e(x), s = S(x), t = T(x)\}$$

where $S(x)$ and $T(x)$ are source and target tags of x and $e(x)$ is $e(\sigma(x), \tau(x))$, the edit tree that transforms the source form into the target form.

Let ρ be a target form predicted by the MRI system for the source form σ and let s and t be source and target tags. POET does not change ρ if $e(\sigma, \rho) \in E_{s,t}$. Otherwise it replaces ρ with τ:

$$\tau := \begin{cases} \tau' & \text{if } e(\sigma, \tau') \in E_{s,t}, |\rho, \tau'| = 1 \\ \rho & \text{else} \end{cases}$$

where $|\rho, \tau'|$ is the Levenshtein distance. If there are several forms τ' with edit distance 1, we select the one with the most frequent edit tree. Ties are broken randomly.

We observed that MED sometimes makes errors that are close to the target, but differ by one edit operation. Those errors are often not covered by edit trees that are observed in the training data whereas the correct form is. Thus, substituting a form not supported by an observed edit tree with a close one that is supported promises to reduce the error rate.

The effectiveness of POET depends on a training set that is large enough to cover the possible edit trees that can occur in reinflection in a language. Thus, if the training set is not large enough in this respect, then POET will not be beneficial.

3 Experiments

We compare MED with the three models of Dreyer et al. (2008) as well as with two recently proposed models: (i) discriminative string transduction (Durrett and DeNero, 2013; Nicolai et al., 2015), the SIGMORPHON16 baseline, and (ii) Faruqui et al. (2015)'s encoder-decoder model.[3] We call the latter MODEL*TAG as it requires training as many models as there are target tags.

We evaluate MED on two MRI tasks: CELEX and SIGMORPHON16.

CELEX. This task is based on complete inflection tables for German extracted from CELEX. For this experiment we follow Dreyer et al. (2008). We use four pairs of morphological tags and corresponding word forms from the German part of the CELEX morphological database. The 4 different transduction tasks are: 13SIA → 13SKE, 2PIE → 13PKE, 2PKE → z and rP → pA.[4] An example for this task would be to produce the output *gesteuert* (target tag *pA*) for the source *steuert* (source tag *rP*). To do so, the system has to learn that the prefix *ge-*, which is used for many participles in German, has to be added to the beginning of the original word form.

We use the same data splits as Dreyer et al. (2008), dividing the original 2500 samples for each tag into five folds, each consisting of 500 training and 1000 development and 1000 test samples. We train a separate model for each fold and report exact match accuracy, averaged over the five folds, as our final result.

[3]For our experiments we ran the code available at github.com/mfaruqui/morph-trans. We used the *enc-dec-attn* model as overall results for the CELEX task were better than with the *sep-morph* model.

[4]13SIA=1st/3rd sg. ind. past; 13SKE=1st/3rd sg. subjunct. pres.; 2PIE=2nd pl. ind. pres.; 13PKE=1st/3rd pl. subjunct. pres.; 2PKE=2nd pl. subjunct. pres.; z=infinitive; rP=imperative pl.; pA=past part.

	model	13SIA	2PIE	2PKE	rP
Dreyer	backoff	82.8	88.7	74.7	69.9
	lat-class	84.8	93.6	75.7	81.8
	lat-region	**87.5**	93.4	87.4	**84.9**
	baseline	77.6	**95.1**	82.5	69.6
	MODEL*TAG	76.4	92.1	83.4	81.8
	MED	82.3	94.4	86.8	83.9
	MED+POET	83.9	95.0	**87.6**	84.0

Table 1: Exact match accuracy of MRI on CELEX. Results of (Dreyer et al., 2008)'s model are from their paper; backoff: *ngrams+x* model; lat-class: *ngrams+x+latent class* model; lat-region: *ngrams+x+latent class+latent region* model; baseline: SIGMORPHON16 baseline.

	MED		
	baseline	average	ensemble
Arabic	58.8	83.1 (0.4)	**88.8**
Finnish	64.6	92.5 (0.8)	**95.6**
Georgian	91.5	95.7 (0.3)	**97.3**
German	87.7	92.1 (0.5)	**95.1**
Navajo	60.9	85.0 (1.1)	**91.1**
Russian	85.6	84.2 (0.3)	**88.4**
Spanish	95.6	96.3 (0.3)	**97.5**
Turkish	54.9	94.7 (1.3)	**97.6**

Table 2: Exact match accuracy of MRI on SIGMORPHON16; baseline: SIGMORPHON16 baseline; MED/average: average of five MED models (standard deviation in parentheses); MED/ensemble: majority voting of five MED models.

SIGMORPHON16. This task covers eight languages and does not provide complete paradigms, but only a set of quadruples, each consisting of word form, source tag, target tag and target form. The main difference to CELEX is that the number of tag pairs is large, resulting in much less training data per tag pair. The number of tag pairs varies by language with Georgian being an extreme case; it has 28 tag pairs in dev that appear less than 10 times in train. For each language, we have around 12,800 training and 1600 development samples. We report exact match accuracy on the development set, as the final test data of the shared task is not publically available yet.

4 Results

Table 1 gives CELEX results. MED+POET is better than prior work on one task, close in performance on two and worse by a small amount on the third. Unlike Dreyer et al. (2008)'s models, MED does not use any hand-crafted features. MED's results are weakest on 13SIA. Typical errors on this task include epenthesis (e.g., *zirkle* vs. *zirkele*) and irregular verbs (e.g., *abhing* vs. *abhängte*).

For SIGMORPHON16, Table 2 shows that MED outperforms the baseline for all eight languages. Absolute performance and variance is probably influenced by type of morphology (e.g., templatic vs. agglutinative), regularity of the language, number of different tag pairs and other factors. MED performs well even for complex and diverse languages like Arabic, Finnish, Navajo and Turkish, suggesting that the type of attention-based encoder-decoder we use – single-model, using an explicit morphological representation – is a good choice for MRI.

We do not compare to MODEL*TAG here because it requires training a large number of individual networks. This is a disadvantage compared to MED both in terms of the number of models that need to be trained and in terms of the effective use of the small number of training examples that are available per tag pair.

POET improves the results for all tag pairs for CELEX. However, initial experiments indicated that it is not effective for SIGMORPHON16 because its training sets are not large enough.

5 Analysis

The main innovation of our work is that MED learns a single model of all MRI patterns of a language and thus can transfer what it has learned from one tag pair to another tag pair. Using CELEX, we now analyze how much our design contributes to better performance by conducting two experiments in which we gradually decrease the training set in two different ways. (i) Large general training set. We only reduce the number of training examples available for a tag pair (s, t) and retain all other training examples. (ii) Small training set. We reduce the number of training examples available for all tag pairs, not just for one.

A typical example of the large general training set scenario is that familiar second person forms are rare in genres like encyclopedia and news. So a training set derived from these genres will be large, but it will have very few tag pairs whose target tag is familiar second person.

A typical example of the small training set scenario is that we are dealing with a low-resource language.

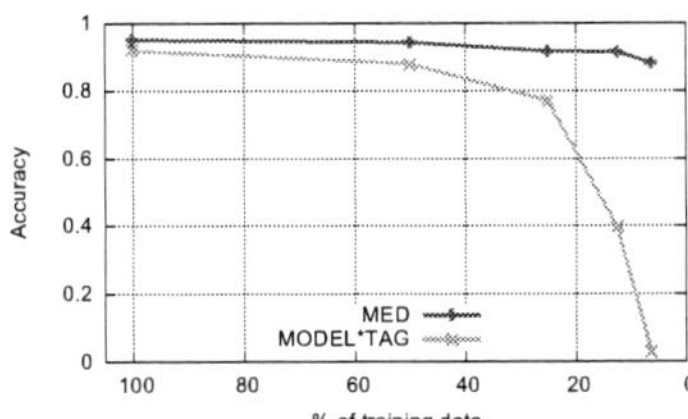

Figure 3: Results for the large general training set experiment: effect of reducing the training set *for only 2PIE → 13PKE* on the accuracy for 2PIE → 13PKE for MED and MODEL*TAG.

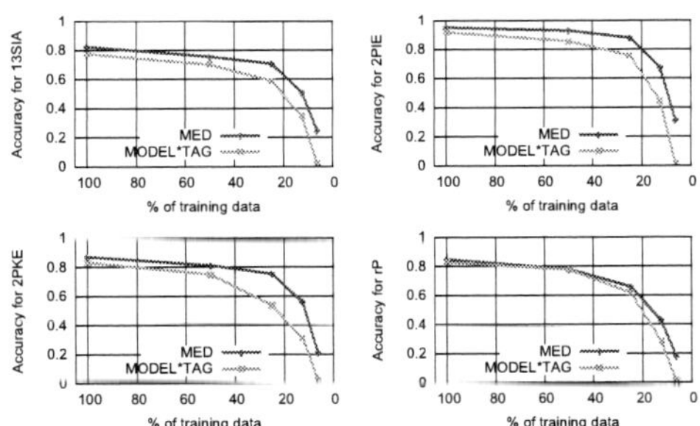

Figure 4: Results for the small training set experiment: effect of reducing the training set *for all tag pairs* on accuracy for MED and MODEL*TAG.

In the following two experiments, we only reduce the training set and do not change the test set.

Large general training set. We iteratively halve the training data for 2PIE → 13PKE until only 6.25% or 32 samples are left. Figure 3 shows that MED performs well even if only 6.25% of the training examples for the tag pair remain. In contrast, MODEL*TAG struggles to generalize correctly. This is due to the fact that we train one single model for all tags, so it can learn from other tags and transfer what it has learned to the tag pair that has a small training set.

Small training set. Figure 4 shows results for reducing the training data equally for all tags. MED performs much better than the baseline for less than 50% of the training data. This can be explained by the fact that MED learns from all given data at once and thus is able to learn common patterns that apply across different tag pairs.

6 Related Work

Earlier work on morphology includes morphological segmentation (Harris, 1955; Hafer and Weiss, 1974; Déjean, 1998) and different approaches for MRI (Ahlberg et al., 2014; Durrett and DeNero,

2013; Eskander et al., 2013; Nicolai et al., 2015). Chrupała (2008) defined edit trees and Chrupała (2008) and Müller et al. (2015) use them for morphological tagging and lemmatization.

In the last years, RNN encoder-decoder models and RNNs in general were applied to several NLP tasks. For example, they proved to be useful for machine translation (Cho et al., 2014; Sutskever et al., 2014; Bahdanau et al., 2014), parsing (Vinyals et al., 2015) and speech recognition (Graves and Schmidhuber, 2005; Graves et al., 2013).

MED bears some resemblance to Faruqui et al. (2015)'s work. However, they train one network for every tag pair; this can negatively impact performance for low-resource languages and in general when training data are limited. In contrast, we train a single model for each language. This radically reduces the amount of training data needed for the encoder-decoder because most MRI patterns occur in many tag pairs, so what is learned for one can be transferred to others. To be able to model all tag pairs of the language together, we introduce an explicit morphological representation that enables the attention mechanism of the encoder-decoder to generalize MRI patterns across tag pairs.

7 Conclusion and Future Work

We have presented MED, a language independent neural sequence-to-sequence mapping approach, and POET, a method based on edit trees for correcting the output of an MRI system. MED obtains results comparable to state-of-the-art systems for CELEX and establishes the state-of-the-art for SIGMORPHON16. POET improves results further for large training sets. Our analysis showed that MED outperforms a neural encoder-decoder baseline system by a large margin, especially for small training sets.

In future work, we would like to make POET less dependent on the source tag and thus increase its accuracy for small training sets. Second, we will look into ways of taking advantage of additional information sources including unlabeled corpora.

Acknowledgments

We gratefully acknowledge the financial support of Siemens for this research.

References

Malin Ahlberg, Markus Forsberg, and Mans Hulden. 2014. Semi-supervised learning of morphological paradigms and lexicons. In *Proc. of EACL*.

Malin Ahlberg, Markus Forsberg, and Mans Hulden. 2015. Paradigm classification in supervised learning of morphology. In *Proc. of NAACL*.

Dzmitry Bahdanau, Kyunghyun Cho, and Yoshua Bengio. 2014. Neural machine translation by jointly learning to align and translate. *arXiv preprint arXiv:1409.0473*.

Kyunghyun Cho, Bart van Merriënboer, Dzmitry Bahdanau, and Yoshua Bengio. 2014. On the properties of neural machine translation: Encoder-decoder approaches. *arXiv preprint arXiv:1409.1259*.

Grzegorz Chrupała. 2008. *Towards a machine-learning architecture for lexical functional grammar parsing*. Ph.D. thesis, Dublin City University.

Ryan Cotterell, Christo Kirov, John Sylak-Glassman, David Yarowsky, Jason Eisner, and Mans Hulden. 2016. The SIGMORPHON 2016 shared task—morphological reinflection. In *Proc. of the 2016 Meeting of SIGMORPHON*.

Hervé Déjean. 1998. Morphemes as necessary concept for structures discovery from untagged corpora. In *Proc. of the Joint Conferences on New Methods in Language Processing and CoNLL*.

Markus Dreyer, Jason R Smith, and Jason Eisner. 2008. Latent-variable modeling of string transductions with finite-state methods. In *Proc. of EMNLP*.

Markus Dreyer. 2011. *A non-parametric model for the discovery of inflectional paradigms from plain text using graphical models over strings*. Ph.D. thesis, Johns Hopkins University, Baltimore, MD.

Greg Durrett and John DeNero. 2013. Supervised learning of complete morphological paradigms. In *Proc. of HLT-NAACL*.

Ramy Eskander, Nizar Habash, and Owen Rambow. 2013. Automatic extraction of morphological lexicons from morphologically annotated corpora. In *Proc. of EMNLP*.

Manaal Faruqui, Yulia Tsvetkov, Graham Neubig, and Chris Dyer. 2015. Morphological inflection generation using character sequence to sequence learning. *arXiv preprint arXiv:1512.06110*.

Ian Goodfellow, David Warde-farley, Mehdi Mirza, Aaron Courville, and Yoshua Bengio. 2013. Maxout networks. In *Proc. of ICML*.

Alex Graves and Jürgen Schmidhuber. 2005. Framewise phoneme classification with bidirectional lstm and other neural network architectures. *Neural Networks*, 18(5):602–610.

Alan Graves, Abdel-rahman Mohamed, and Geoffrey Hinton. 2013. Speech recognition with deep recurrent neural networks. In *Proc of. ICASSP*.

Dan Gusfield. 1997. *Algorithms on strings, trees and sequences: computer science and computational biology*. Cambridge university press.

Margaret A Hafer and Stephen F Weiss. 1974. Word segmentation by letter successor varieties. *Information storage and retrieval*, 10(11):371–385.

Zellig S Harris. 1955. From phoneme to morpheme. *Language*, 31(2):190–222.

Katharina Kann and Hinrich Schütze. 2016. MED: The LMU system for the SIGMORPHON 2016 shared task on morphological reinflection. In *Proc. of the 2016 Meeting of SIGMORPHON*.

Quoc V Le, Navdeep Jaitly, and Geoffrey E Hinton. 2015. A simple way to initialize recurrent networks of rectified linear units. *arXiv preprint arXiv:1504.00941*.

Thomas Müller, Ryan Cotterell, and Alexander Fraser. 2015. Joint lemmatization and morphological tagging with lemming. In *Proc. of EMNLP*.

Garrett Nicolai, Colin Cherry, and Grzegorz Kondrak. 2015. Inflection generation as discriminative string transduction. In *Proc. of NAACL*.

Razvan Pascanu, Caglar Gulcehre, Kyunghyun Cho, and Yoshua Bengio. 2014. How to construct deep recurrent neural networks. In *Proc. of ICLR*.

Ilya Sutskever, Oriol Vinyals, and Quoc V Le. 2014. Sequence to sequence learning with neural networks. In *Proc. of NIPS*.

Oriol Vinyals, Łukasz Kaiser, Terry Koo, Slav Petrov, Ilya Sutskever, and Geoffrey Hinton. 2015. Grammar as a foreign language. In *Proc. of NIPS*.

Matthew D Zeiler. 2012. Adadelta: an adaptive learning rate method. *arXiv preprint arXiv:1212.5701*.

Joint part-of-speech and dependency projection from multiple sources

Anders Johannsen   **Željko Agić**   **Anders Søgaard**
Center for Language Technology, University of Copenhagen, Denmark
anders@johannsen.com

Abstract

Most previous work on annotation projection has been limited to a subset of Indo-European languages, using only a single source language, and projecting annotation for one task at a time. In contrast, we present an Integer Linear Programming (ILP) algorithm that simultaneously projects annotation for multiple tasks from multiple source languages, relying on parallel corpora available for hundreds of languages. When training POS taggers and dependency parsers on jointly projected POS tags and syntactic dependencies using our algorithm, we obtain better performance than a standard approach on 20/23 languages using one parallel corpus; and 18/27 languages using another.

1 Introduction

Cross-language annotation projection for unsupervised POS tagging and syntactic parsing was introduced fifteen years ago (Yarowsky et al., 2001; Hwa et al., 2005), and the best unsupervised dependency parsers today rely on annotation projection (Rasooli and Collins, 2015).

Despite the maturity of the field, there is an inherent language bias in previous work on cross-language annotation projection. Cross-language annotation projection experiments require training data in m source languages, a parallel corpus of translations from the m source languages into the target language of interest, as well as evaluation data for the target language.[1] Since the canonical resource for parallel text is the Europarl Corpus (Koehn, 2005), which covers languages spoken in the European parliament, annotation projection is

typically limited to the subset of Indo-European languages that have treebanks.

Previous work is also limited in another respect. While treebanks typically contain multiple layers of annotation, previous work has focused on projecting data for a single task.

We go significantly beyond previous work in two ways: 1) by considering multi-source projection across languages in parallel corpora that are available for hundreds of languages, including many non-Indo-European languages; and 2) by *jointly* projecting annotation for two mutually dependent tasks, namely POS tagging and dependency parsing. Using multiple source languages makes our projections denser. In single source projection, the source language may not contain all syntactic phenomena of the target language; we combat this by transferring syntactic information from multiple source languages. Our work also differs from previous work on annotation projection in projecting soft rather than hard constraints, i.e., scores rather than labels and edges.

Contributions   We present a novel ILP-based algorithm for jointly projecting POS labels and dependency annotations across word-aligned parallel corpora. The performance of our algorithm compares favorably to that of a state-of-the-art projection algorithm, as well as to multi-source delexicalized transfer. Our experiments include between 23 and 27 languages using two parallel corpora that are available for hundreds of languages, namely a collection of Bibles and Watchtower periodicals. Finally, we make both the parallel corpora and the code publicly available.[2]

2 Projection algorithm

The projection algorithm is divided into two distinct steps. First, we *project* potential syntactic

---

[1] All previous work that we are aware of—with the possible exception of McDonald et al. (2011); but see Sections 2 and 5—uses only a single source ($m = 1$), but in our experiments, we use multiple source languages.

[2] https://bitbucket.org/lowlands/release

Proceedings of the 54th Annual Meeting of the Association for Computational Linguistics, pages 561–566,
Berlin, Germany, August 7-12, 2016. ©2016 Association for Computational Linguistics

edges and POS tags from all source languages into an intermediate target graph, which is left deliberately ambiguous. In the second step, we *decode* the target graph by solving a constrained optimisation problem, which simultaneously resolves all ambiguities and produces a single dependency tree with a fixed set of POS tags. Below we describe both steps in more detail.

2.1 Cross-language sentence

The input to our projection algorithm is a *cross-language sentence*, a data structure that ties together a collection of aligned sentences from a parallel corpus, i.e., sentences in many different languages that are determined to be translation equivalents. One sentence of the set is designated as the target while the rest are sources. We project syntactic information from the sources to the target.

All source sentences are automatically parsed with a graph-based dependency parser and labeled with parts of speech. Instead of using the single best dependency tree output by the parser, we extract its scoring matrix, an ambiguous structure that assigns a numeric score to each potential dependency edge. The target sentence is not parsed or POS-tagged. In fact, our approach is explicitly designed to work for target languages where no such resources are available. Only unsupervised word alignments couple the target sentence with each source sentence.

More formally, a cross-language sentence may be represented as a graph $G = (V, E)$, where each vertex is a POS-tagged token of a sentence in some language. With one target and n source languages, the total set of tagged word vertices V can be written as the union of sentence vertices: $V = V_0 \cup \ldots \cup V_n$. The target sentence is $V_t = V_0$, while source sentences are $V_s = V_1 \cup \ldots \cup V_n$.

Two kinds of weighted edges connect the graph. Edges that go between tagged tokens of a sentence V_i represent potential dependency edges. Thus, for the sentence i, the induced subgraph $G[V_i]$ is the (ambiguous) dependency graph. Edges connecting a source vertex to target vertex represent word alignments. The set of alignment edges is $A \subseteq V_s \times V_t$.

To account for POS we introduce a vertex labeling function $l : V \mapsto \Sigma$, where Σ is the POS vocabulary. The source sentences are automatically tagged, and for any source vertex the label function simply returns this tag. For the target sentence

the POS labels are unknown, which is to say that every target token is ambiguous between $|\Sigma|$ POS tags. We represent this ambiguity in the graph by creating a vertex for each possible combination of target word and POS. Concretely, if a source sentence i has n tokens, and the target sentence has m tokens, then $|V_i| = n$, and $|V_s| = m|\Sigma|$.

Alignments are constrained such that an alignment $(u, v) \in V_s \times V_t$ only exists if the source and target token were linked by the automatic aligner and $l(u) = l(v)$, i.e., the POS tags match. This filters out potential source relations with dissimilar syntax, a luxury that we are allowed in a multiple source language setup.

2.2 Projecting to ambiguous target graph

The target graph $G[V_t]$ starts out empty and is populated with edges in the following way. We go through the source sentences, looking for potential dependency edges where both endpoints are aligned to the target sentence, and transferring the edge whenever we find one. Technically, for every source sentence i and for each edge in the source graph $(u_s, v_s) \in G[V_i]$, we create an edge (u_t, v_t) in the target iff both (u_s, u_t) and $(v_s, v_t) \in A$. The edge weight is the source edge score (as determined by an automatic parser) weighted by the joint alignment probability of (u_s, u_t) and (v_s, v_t):

$$d(u_t, v_t) = \max_{u_s, v_s} a(u_s, v_s)\ a(u_s, u_t)\ d(v_s, v_t).$$

For clarity, d refers to weights of dependency edges, and a to alignment edge weights. Multiple source sentences may project the same edge to the target graph. When this happens we update the target edge weight only if the new weight is larger than the existing. The weight then reflects the strongest evidence found for a given syntactic relation across all source languages.

2.3 Decoding the target graph

We are now ready to decode the target graph. The result of decoding is a dependency tree as well as a labeling of the target sentences with POS tags. Labeling with POS corresponds to selecting a subset of the vertices $\tilde{V} \subset V_t$, such that exactly one vertex is chosen for each token. Similarly the decoded dependency tree is a subset of the projected target edges with the constraint that it must form a tree over the vertices of $\tilde{V}$. The joint optimization objective is to simultaneously select a set of vertices $\tilde{V}$ and edges $\tilde{E}$ to maximize the score of the decoded tree. We solve this constrained optimization problem by casting it as an integer linear programming (ILP) problem.

The full specification of the ILP model is displayed as Figure 1. The model is optimized over two types of binary decision variables mapping directly to the target graph representation discussed in the previous section, plus additional *flow* variables that enforce tree structure. An edge variable $e_{i,k,j,l}$ represents a target edge (i, j) where the POS of i is k and the POS of j is l. For instance, the variable $e_{2,V,1,N}$ represents a directed edge from the second token (a verb) to the first (a noun). An active vertex variable $v_{i,k}$ indicates that the POS of token i is chosen as k.

Following Martins (2012), we constrain the search space to spanning trees by using a single-commodity-flow construction. In the commodity-flow analogy, we imagine the root as a factory that produces n commodities (for an n token sentence) which are distributed along the edges of the tree. Each token is a consumer that must receive and pass on all except one commodity to its dependents, i.e., the difference between incoming and outgoing flow should be 1. Since all commodities must be consumed, the outgoing flow for a leaf node will be zero. Together with the requirement that each token must have exactly one head, this ensures all tokens are connected to the root in the tree structure.

The last two constraint groups enforce edge and POS consistency, and the selection of single POS per token. Both are new to this work.

3   Data sources

Our projection requires parallel text, ideally spanning a large number of languages, and dependency treebanks for the sources.

Treebanks   To train the source-side taggers and dependency parsers, and to evaluate the cross-lingual taggers and parsers, we use the Universal Dependencies (UD) version 1.2 treebanks with the corresponding test sets.[3]

Parallel texts   We exploit two sources of parallel text: the Edinburgh Multilingual Bible corpus (EBC) (Christodouloupoulos and Steedman, 2014), and our own collection of online texts published by the Wathctower Society (WTC).[4] While

---

ILP model

$$\begin{array}{lll} \text{Edges} & e_{i,k,j,l} & \in \{0, 1\} \\ \text{Vertices} & v_{i,k} & \in \{0, 1\} \\ \text{Flow} & \phi_{i,k,j,l} & \in \mathbb{R}^+ \end{array}$$

$$\text{Maximize} \quad \sum_{i,k,j,l} e_{i,k,j,l}\, w_{i,k,j,l}$$

One parent per token

$$\sum_{i,k,l} e_{i,k,j,l} = 1 \qquad \forall j \neq 0$$

The root token (index 0) sends n flow

$$\sum_{j,l} \phi_{0,0,j,l} = n$$

Each token consumes one unit of flow

$$\sum_{i,k,l} \phi_{i,k,x,l} - \sum_{k,j,l} \phi_{x,k,j,l} = 1 \qquad \forall x \neq 0$$

One POS per token

$$\sum_{k} v_{i,k} = 1 \qquad \forall i \neq 0$$

Active edges choose token POS

$$v_{i,k} \geq e_{i,k,j,l} \qquad \forall i \neq 0, j, k, l$$

$$v_{i,l} \geq e_{i,k,j,l} \qquad \forall i, j, k, l$$

Above, i, j, and x are token indices, while k and l refer to POS. Quantification over these symbols in the equations are always with respect to a given target graph.

Figure 1: Specification of the ILP model. We list, in order, the decision variables, the objective, and the five groups of constraint templates.

the two collections span more than 100 languages, we focus on the subsets that overlap with the UD languages to facilitate evaluation. For EBC, that amounts to 27 languages, and 23 for WTC.

Preprocessing   We use simple sentence splitting and tokenization models to segment the parallel corpora.[5] To sentence- and word-align the individual language pairs, we use a Gibbs sampling-based IBM1 alignment model called `efmaral` (Östling, 2015). IBM1 has been shown to lead to more robust alignments across typologically distant language pairs (Östling, 2015). We modify

---

[3]`http://hdl.handle.net/11234/1-1548`
[4]`https://www.jw.org/`

[5]`https://github.com/bplank/`
`multilingualtokenizer`

the aligner to output alignment probabilities. All the source-side texts are POS-tagged and dependency parsed using TnT (Brants, 2000) and TurboParser (Martins et al., 2013). We use our own fork of the arc-factored TurboParser to output the edge weight matrices.[6]

4 Experiments

4.1 Setup

In our experiments, as in the preprocessing, we use the TnT tagger and the arc-factored TurboParser, which we train on the EBC and WTC texts with projected and decoded annotations. We randomly sample up to 20k sentences per training file in both tagging and parsing. This 20k sampling limit applies to all systems.

We compare two cross-lingual projection-based parsing systems, and one baseline system.

ILP The ILP-based joint projection algorithm we presented in Section 2.

DCA Our implementation of the *de facto* standard annotation projection algorithm of Hwa et al. (2005), as refined by Tiedemann (2014). In contrast to our ILP approach, it uses heuristics to ensure dependency tree constraints on a source-target sentence pair basis. We gather all the pairwise projections into a target sentence graph and then perform maximum spanning tree decoding following Sagae and Lavie (2006).

DELEX The multi-source direct delexicalized transfer baseline of McDonald et al. (2011). Each source is represented by an approximately equal number of sentences.

4.2 Results

Table 1 provides a summary of dependency parsing scores. We report UAS scores over predicted and gold POS. The predicted tags come from our cross-lingual taggers. Our ILP approach consistently outperforms DCA on both by a large margin of 3-5 points UAS using predicted POS, and 5-10 points on gold POS. Note that DELEX is trained on gold POS and therefore has an advantage in this

---

	Approach		
Predicted POS	ILP	DCA	DELEX
EBC	**51.62** (18)	48.39 (8)	42.44 (1)
WTC	**53.58** (20)	48.40 (0)	47.35 (3)
Gold POS			
EBC	**65.43** (25)	59.94 (2)	64.13 (–)
WTC	**66.51** (23)	55.73 (0)	66.68 (–)

Table 1: Macro-averaged UAS scores summarizing our evaluation. EBC: Edinburgh Bible corpus, WTC: Watchtower corpus. Numbers of languages with top performance per system are reported in brackets. All parsers use their respective EBC or WTC taggers.[8]

setting. Relying on predicted POS and WTC data, our ILP approach beats DCA for *all* the test languages. With EBC, we outperform DCA on 19 out of 27 languages.

In Table 2, we split the scores across the test languages and parallel data sources, and we also report the POS tagging accuracies. Our WTC taggers are on average 3.5 points better than EBC taggers, yielding the top score for 16/23 languages from the overlap. Notably, on several non-Indo-European languages, we observe significant improvements. For example, on Indonesian, DCA improves over DELEX by 12 points UAS, while ILP adds 6 more points on top. We observe a similar pattern for Arabic and Estonian. We note that DELEX tops ILP and DCA on only 1 EBC and 3 WTC languages, and by a narrow margin.

Analysis A projected parse is allowed to be a composite of edges from many source languages. To find out to what degree this actually happens, we analyze all projections into English and German on the WTC corpus.

For German the top four source languages are Czech, Norwegian, French, and English, contributing between 16% and 7% of all edges. For English the top languages are Norwegian, Italian, Indonesian, and Swedish. Here, the top language Norwegian is responsible for 42% of the edges, while Swedish accounts for 13%. Only the language projecting the highest scoring edge is counted. On average, a German sentence has edges from 4.1 source languages. The same number for English is slightly higher, at 4.5.

Manually annotated data We annotate a small number of sentences in English from EBC and

---

[6]`https://github.com/andersjo/ TurboParser`

[8]We do not include DELEX in the comparison *for the gold POS scenario only*. In this particular scenario, DELEX is also trained on gold POS, and thus biased: the cross-lingual taggers do not have gold POS available for training, and the same holds for DELEX and projected POS.

	POS tagging		Dependency parsing					
			EBC			WTC		
Language	EBC	WTC	ILP	DCA	DELEX	ILP	DCA	DELEX
Arabic	39.54	53.91	36.59	37.70	13.17	37.41	32.14	21.15
Basque	43.43	–	22.77	17.38	27.85	–	–	–
Bulgarian	76.45	68.27	50.6	60.03	57.83	49.68	37.18	48.37
Croatian	72.83	76.18	54.19	45.08	42.34	55.16	50.56	45.49
Czech	70.81	78.49	52.67	41.44	40.99	53.09	44.36	47.99
Danish	76.43	86.36	61.14	53.22	49.65	61.78	58.64	55.96
English	71.90	79.2	55.76	50.64	48.04	58.70	57.12	53.87
* Estonian	75.55	73.98	62.9	56.95	49.32	63.85	58.41	48.48
Farsi	64.94	25.67	23.53	42.37	28.93	20.34	12.26	19.48
Finnish	70.41	67.44	43.66	44.51	41.18	42.59	35.6	41.52
French	74.25	79.23	53.52	53.11	48.97	55.69	51.47	51.53
German	74.36	68.36	45.02	50.21	49.36	43.99	36.7	45.79
* Greek	56.52	75.75	62.59	37.73	37.11	62.43	52.95	54.90
Hebrew	43.65	–	30.25	39.76	19.06	–	–	–
Hindi	59.99	48.86	18.26	35.59	21.03	15.95	10.77	21.04
* Hungarian	71.57	71.42	49.74	44.97	43.07	44.17	42.33	46.66
Indonesian	63.30	75.61	51.99	23.53	31.18	58.01	52.29	39.67
Italian	79.28	83.82	63.13	58.66	53.94	64.88	63.57	58.06
* Latin	83.41	–	68.65	68.45	41.42	–	–	–
Norwegian	77.00	85.31	65.04	58.32	53.46	66.54	64.37	60.11
Polish	73.36	73.68	62.94	59.27	53.33	63.74	55.4	54.87
Portuguese	78.41	83.67	63.75	60.45	52.91	64.62	63.16	56.99
* Romanian	71.56	76.34	57.74	56.73	45.73	58.76	54.78	51.23
* Serbian	74.07	–	49.15	49.38	47.06	–	–	–
Slovene	75.68	78.11	59.17	53.66	50.55	59.79	54.8	52.53
Spanish	76.72	85.69	63.63	52.20	47.6	64.93	61.90	55.87
Swedish	78.26	84.80	65.24	55.21	50.85	66.15	62.45	57.48
Average	69.40	73.05	51.62	48.39	42.44	53.58	48.40	47.35
Best for	7	16	18	8	1	20	0	3

Table 2: Tagging and parsing (UAS) accuracy. Scores are macro-averaged, and all parsers use predicted POS from respective EBC or WTC taggers. *: True target languages, not used as sources.

WTC, which gives us a way to directly evaluate the projections without training parsers. On this small test set of 2×50 sentences, we obtain UAS scores of 68% (WTC) and 62% (EBC). The POS accuracies are 79% and 80%. All figures are comparable to the results from the indirect projection evaluation.

5 Related work

In recent years, we note an increased interest for work in cross-lingual processing, and particularly in POS tagging and dependency parsing of low-resource languages.

Yarowsky et al. (2001) proposed the idea of inducing NLP tools via parallel corpora. Their contribution started a line of work in annotation projection. Das and Petrov (2011) used graph-based label propagation to yield competitive POS taggers, while Hwa et al. (2005) introduced the projection of dependency trees. Tiedemann (2014) further improved this approach to single-source projection in the context of synthesizing dependency treebanks (Tiedemann and Agić, 2016). The current state of the art in cross-lingual dependency parsing also involves exploiting large parallel corpora (Ma and Xia, 2014; Rasooli and Collins, 2015).

Transferring models by training parsers without lexical features was first introduced by Zeman and Resnik (2008). McDonald et al. (2011) and Søgaard (2011) coupled delexicalization with contributions from multiple sources, while McDonald et al. (2013) were the first to leverage uniform representations of POS and syntactic dependencies in cross-lingual parsing.

Even more recently, Agić et al. (2015) exposed a bias towards closely related Indo-European languages shared by most previous work on annotation projection, while introducing a bias-free projection algorithm for learning 100 POS taggers from multiple sources. Their line of work is non-trivially extended to multilingual dependency parsing by Agić et al. (2016).

The work in annotation projection for cross-lingual NLP invariably treats mutually dependent layers of annotation separately. Our contribution is distinct from these works by implementing the first approach to joint projection of POS and dependencies, while maintaining the outlook on processing truly low-resource languages.

6 Conclusion

In our contribution, we addressed tagging and parsing for low-resource languages through joint cross-lingual projection of POS tags and syntactic dependencies from multiple source languages. Our novel approach to transferring the annotations via word alignments is based on integer linear programming, more specifically on a commodity-flow formalization for spanning trees.

In our experiments with 27 treebanks from the Universal Dependencies (UD) project, our approach compared very favorably to two competitive cross-lingual systems: we provided the best cross-lingual taggers and parsers for 18/27 and 20/23 languages, depending on the parallel corpora used. We made no unrealistic assumptions as to the availability of parallel texts and preprocessing tools for the target languages. Our code and data is freely available.[9]

Acknowledgements This research is partially funded by the ERC Starting Grant LOWLANDS (#313695).

---

[9]`https://bitbucket.org/lowlands/release`

References

Željko Agić, Dirk Hovy, and Anders Søgaard. 2015. If All You Have is a Bit of the Bible: Learning POS Taggers for Truly Low-Resource Languages. In *ACL*.

Željko Agić, Anders Johannsen, Barbara Plank, Héctor Martínez Alonso, Natalie Schluter, and Anders Søgaard. 2016. Multilingual Projection for Parsing Truly Low-Resource Languages. *TACL*, 4.

Thorsten Brants. 2000. TnT – A Statistical Part-of-Speech Tagger. In *ANLP*.

Christos Christodouloupoulos and Mark Steedman. 2014. A Massively Parallel Corpus: The Bible in 100 Languages. *Language Resources and Evaluation*, 49(2).

Dipanjan Das and Slav Petrov. 2011. Unsupervised Part-of-Speech Tagging with Bilingual Graph-Based Projections. In *ACL*.

Rebecca Hwa, Philip Resnik, Amy Weinberg, Clara Cabezas, and Okan Kolak. 2005. Bootstrapping Parsers via Syntactic Projection Across Parallel Texts. *Natural Language Engineering*, 11(3).

Philipp Koehn. 2005. Europarl: A Parallel Corpus for Statistical Machine Translation. In *MT Summit*.

Xuezhe Ma and Fei Xia. 2014. Unsupervised Dependency Parsing with Transferring Distribution via Parallel Guidance and Entropy Regularization. In *ACL*.

André F. T. Martins, Miguel Almeida, and Noah A. Smith. 2013. Turning on the Turbo: Fast Third-Order Non-Projective Turbo Parsers. In *ACL*.

André F. T. Martins. 2012. *The Geometry of Constrained Structured Prediction: Applications to Inference and Learning of Natural Language Syntax.* Ph.D. thesis, Carnegie Mellon University and Instituto Superior Tecnico.

Ryan McDonald, Slav Petrov, and Keith Hall. 2011. Multi-Source Transfer of Delexicalized Dependency Parsers. In *EMNLP*.

Ryan McDonald, Joakim Nivre, Yvonne Quirmbach-Brundage, Yoav Goldberg, Dipanjan Das, Kuzman Ganchev, Keith Hall, Slav Petrov, Hao Zhang, Oscar Täckström, Claudia Bedini, Núria Bertomeu Castelló, and Jungmee Lee. 2013. Universal Dependency Annotation for Multilingual Parsing. In *ACL*.

Robert Östling. 2015. Word Order Typology through Multilingual Word Alignment. In *ACL*.

Mohammad Sadegh Rasooli and Michael Collins. 2015. Density-Driven Cross-Lingual Transfer of Dependency Parsers. In *EMNLP*.

Kenji Sagae and Alon Lavie. 2006. Parser Combination by Reparsing. In *NAACL*.

Anders Søgaard. 2011. Data Point Selection for Cross-Language Adaptation of Dependency Parsers. In *ACL*.

Jörg Tiedemann and Željko Agić. 2016. Synthetic Treebanking for Cross-Lingual Dependency Parsing. *Journal of Artificial Intelligence Research*, 55.

Jörg Tiedemann. 2014. Rediscovering Annotation Projection for Cross-Lingual Parser Induction. In *COLING*.

David Yarowsky, Grace Ngai, and Richard Wicentowski. 2001. Inducing Multilingual Text Analysis Tools via Robust Projection Across Aligned Corpora. In *NAACL*.

Daniel Zeman and Philip Resnik. 2008. Cross-Language Parser Adaptation between Related Languages. In *IJCNLP Workshop on NLP for Less Privileged Languages*.

Dependency-based Gated Recursive Neural Network
for Chinese Word Segmentation

Jingjing Xu and **Xu Sun**
MOE Key Laboratory of Computational Linguistics, Peking University
School of Electronics Engineering and Computer Science, Peking University
{xujingjing, xusun}@pku.edu.cn

Abstract

Recently, many neural network models have been applied to Chinese word segmentation. However, such models focus more on collecting local information while long distance dependencies are not well learned. To integrate local features with long distance dependencies, we propose a dependency-based gated recursive neural network. Local features are first collected by bi-directional long short term memory network, then combined and refined to long distance dependencies via gated recursive neural network. Experimental results show that our model is a competitive model for Chinese word segmentation.

1 Introduction

Word segmentation is an important pre-process step in Chinese language processing. Most widely used approaches treat Chinese word segmentation (CWS) task as a sequence labeling problem in which each character in the input sequence is assigned with a tag. Many previous approaches have been effectively applied to CWS problem (Lafferty et al., 2001; Xue and Shen, 2003; Sun et al., 2012; Sun, 2014; Sun et al., 2013; Cheng et al., 2015). However, these approaches incorporated many handcrafted features, thus restricting the generalization ability of these models. Neural network models have the advantage of minimizing the effort in feature engineering. Collobert et al. (2011) developed a general neural network architecture for sequence labeling tasks. Following this work, neural network approaches have been well studied and widely applied to CWS task with good results (Zheng et al., 2013; Pei et al., 2014; Ma and Hinrichs, 2015; Chen et al., 2015).

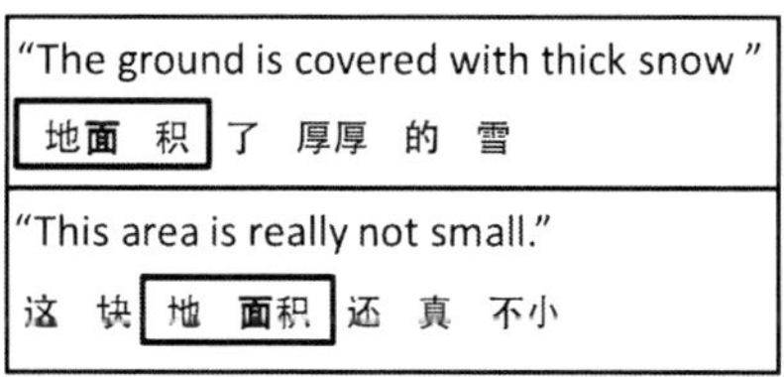

Figure 1: An illustration for the segmentation ambiguity. The character "面" is labeled as "E" (end of word) in the top sentence while labeled as "B" (begin of word) in the bottom one even though "面" has the same adjacent characters, "地" and "积".

However, these models focus more on collecting local features while long distance dependencies are not well learned. In fact, relying on the information of adjacent words is not enough for CWS task. An example is shown in Figure 1. The character "面" has different tags in two sentences, even with the same adjacent characters, " 地" and " 积". Only long distance dependencies can help the model recognize tag correctly in this example. Thus, long distance information is an important factor for CWS task.

The main limitation of chain structure for sequence labeling is that long distance dependencies decay inevitably. Though forget gate mechanism is added, it is difficult for bi-directional long short term memory network (Bi-LSTM), a kind of chain structure, to avoid this problem. In general, tree structure works better than chain structure to model long term information. Therefore, we use gated recursive neural network (GRNN) (Chen et al., 2015) which is a kind of tree structure to capture long distance dependencies.

Motivated by the fact, we propose the dependency-based gated recursive neural network (DGRNN) to integrate local features with long dis-

Proceedings of the 54th Annual Meeting of the Association for Computational Linguistics, pages 567–572,
Berlin, Germany, August 7-12, 2016. ©2016 Association for Computational Linguistics

tance dependencies. Figure 2 shows the structure of DGRNN. First of all, local features are collected by Bi-LSTM. Secondly, GRNN recursively combines and refines local features to capture long distance dependencies. Finally, with the help of local features and long distance dependencies, our model generates the probability of the tag of word.

The main contributions of the paper are as follows:

- We present the dependency-based gated recursive neural network to combine local features with long distance dependencies.

- To verify the effectiveness of the proposed approach, we conduct experiments on three widely used datasets. Our proposed model achieves the best performance compared with other state-of-the-art approaches.

2 Dependency-based Gated Recursive Neural Network

In order to capture local features and long distance dependencies, we propose dependency-based gated recursive neural network. Figure 2 illustrates the structure of the model.

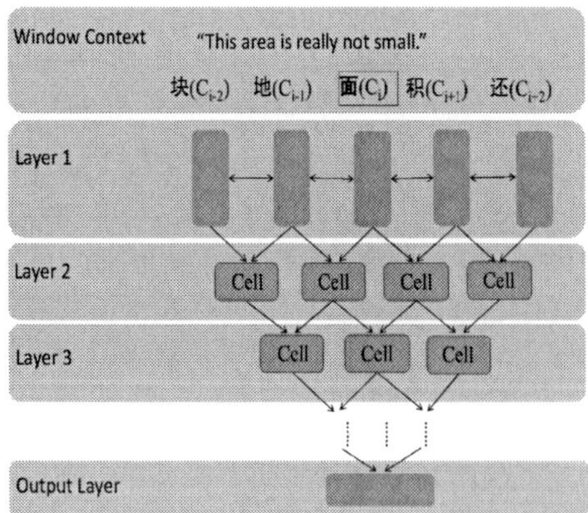

Figure 2: Architecture of DGRNN for Chinese Word Segmentation. Cell is the basic unit of GRNN.

2.1 Collect Local Features

We use bi-directional long short term memory (Bi-LSTM) with single layer to collect local features. Bi-LSTM is composed of two directional

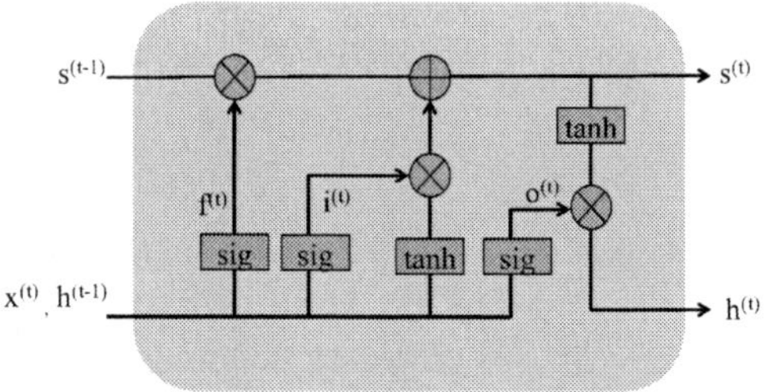

Figure 3: Structure of LSTM unit. The behavior of the LSTM cell is controlled by three "gates", namely input gate $i^{(t)}$, forget gate $f^{(t)}$ and output gate $o^{(t)}$.

long short term memory networks with single layer, which can model word representation with context information. Figure 3 shows the calculation process of LSTM. The behavior of LSTM cell is controlled by three "gates", namely input gate $i^{(t)}$, forget gate $f^{(t)}$ and output gate $o^{(t)}$. The input of LSTM cell are $x^{(t)}$, $s^{(t-1)}$ and $h^{(t-1)}$. $x^{(t)}$ is the character embeddings of input sentence. $s^{(t-1)}$ and $h^{(t-1)}$ stand for the state and output of the former LSTM cell, respectively. The core of the LSTM model is $s^{(t)}$, which is computed using the former state of cell and two gates, $i^{(t)}$ and $f^{(t)}$. In the end, the output of LSTM cell $h^{(t)}$ is calculated making use of $s^{(t)}$ and $o^{(t)}$.

2.2 Refine Long Distance Dependencies

GRNN recursively combines and refines local features to capture long distance dependencies. The structure of GRNN is like a binary tree, where every two continuous vectors in a sentence is combined to form a new vector. For a sequence s with length n, there are n layers in total. Figure 4 shows the calculation process of GRNN cell. The core of GRNN cell are two kinds of gates, reset gates, r_L, r_R, and update gates z. Reset gates control how to adjust the proportion of the input h_{i-1} and h_i, which results to the current new activation h'. By the update gates, the activation of an output neuron can be regarded as a choice among the current new activation h', the left child h_{i-1} and the right child h_i.

2.3 Loss Function

Following the work of Pei et al. (2014), we adopt the max-margin criterion as loss function. For an input sentence $c_{[1:n]}$ with a tag sequence $t_{[1:n]}$, a sentence-level score is given by the sum of net-

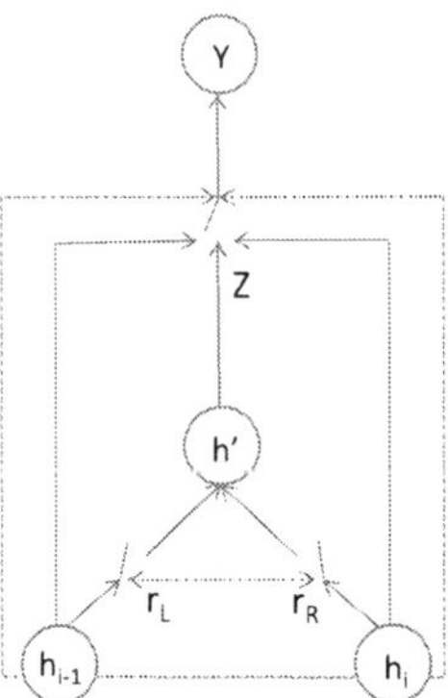

Figure 4: The structure of GRNN cell.

work scores:

$$s(c_{[1:n]}, t_{[1:n]}, \theta) = \sum_{i=1}^{n} f_\theta(t_i | c_{[i-2:i+2]}) \qquad (1)$$

where $s(c_{[1:n]}, t_{[1:n]}, \theta)$ is the sentence-level score. n is the length of $c_{[1:n]}$. $f_\theta(t_i | c_{[i-2:i+2]})$ is the s-core output for tag t_i at the i_{th} character by the network with parameters θ.

We define a structured margin loss $\Delta(y_i, \widehat{y})$ for predicting a tag sequence $\widehat{y}$ and a given correct tag sequence y_i:

$$\Delta(y_i, \widehat{y}) = \sum_{j=1}^{n} \kappa \mathbf{1}\{y_{i,j} \neq y_i\} \qquad (2)$$

where κ is a discount parameter. This leads to the regularized objective function for m training examples:

$$J(\theta) = \frac{1}{m} \sum_{i=1}^{m} l_i(\theta) + \frac{\lambda}{2} \|\theta\|^2 \qquad (3)$$

$$l_i(\theta) = \max_{\widehat{y} \subseteq Y(x_i)} ((s(x_i, \widehat{y}, \theta) \\ + \Delta(y_i, \widehat{y})) - s(x_i, y_i, \theta)) \qquad (4)$$

where $J(\theta)$ is a loss function with parameters θ. λ is regularization factor. By minimizing this object, the score of the correct tag sequence y_i is increased and score of the highest scoring incorrect tag sequence $\widehat{y}$ is decreased.

2.4 Amplification Gate and Training

A direct adaptive method for faster backpropagation learning method (RPROP) (Riedmiller and Braun, 1993) was a practical adaptive learning method to train large neural networks. We use mini-batch version RPROP (RMSPROP) (Hinton, 2012) to minimize the loss function.

Intuitively, extra hidden layers are able to improve accuracy performance. However, it is common that extra hidden layers decrease classification accuracy. This is mainly because extra hidden layers lead to the inadequate training of later layers due to the vanishing gradient problem. This problem will decline the utilization of local and long distance information in our model. To overcome this problem, we propose a simple amplification gate mechanism which appropriately expands the value of gradient while not changing the direction.

Higher amplification may not always perform better while lower value may bring about the unsatisfied result. Therefore, the amplification gate must be carefully selected. Large magnification will cause expanding gradient problem. On the contrary, small amplification gate will hardly reach the desired effect. Thus, we introduce the threshold mechanism to guarantee the robustness of the algorithm, where gradient which is greater than threshold will not be expanded. Amplification gate of difference layer is distinct. For every sample, the training procedure is as follows.

First, recursively calculate m_t and v_t which depend on the gradient of time $t - 1$ or the square of gradient respectively. β_1 and β_2 aim to control the impact of last state.

$$m_t = \beta_1 \cdot m_{t-1} + (1 - \beta_1) \cdot g_t \qquad (5)$$

$$v_t = \beta_2 \cdot v_{t-1} + (1 - \beta_2) \cdot g_t^2 \qquad (6)$$

Second, calculate $\Delta W(t)$ based on v_t and square of m_t. ϵ and μ are smooth parameters.

$$M(w, t) = v_t - m_t^2 \qquad (7)$$

$$\Delta W(t) = \frac{\epsilon g_{t,i}}{\sqrt{M(w, t)} + \mu} \qquad (8)$$

Third, update weight based on the amplification gate and $\Delta W(t)$. The parameter update for the i_{th} parameter for the $\Theta_{t,i}$ at time step t with amplification gate γ is as follows:

$$\Theta_{t,i} = \Theta_{t,i} - \gamma \Delta W(t) \qquad (9)$$

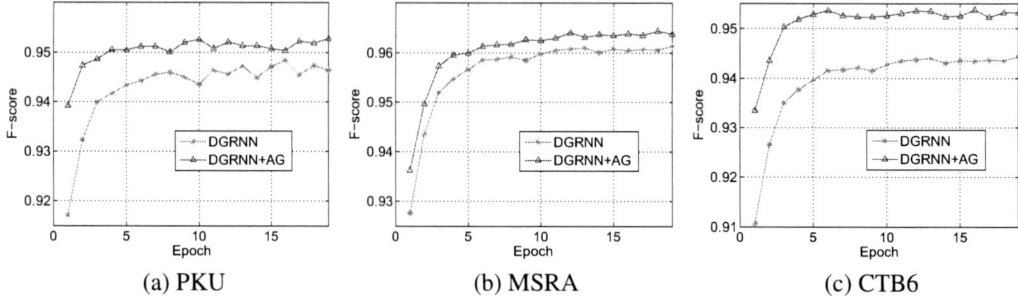

(a) PKU   (b) MSRA   (c) CTB6

Figure 5: Results for DGRNN with amplification gate (AG) on three development datasets.

3 Experiments

3.1 Data and Settings

We evaluate our proposed approach on three datasets, PKU, MSRA and CTB6. The PKU and MSRA data both are provided by the second International Chinese Word Segmentation Bakeoff (Emerson, 2005) and CTB6 is from Chinese TreeBank 6.0[1] (Xue et al., 2005). We randomly divide the whole training data into the 90% sentences as training set and the rest 10% sentences as development set. All datasets are preprocessed by replacing the Chinese idioms and the continuous English characters. The character embeddings are pre-trained on unlabeled data, Chinese Gigaword corpus[2]. We use MSRA dataset to preprocess model weights before training on CTB6 and PKU datasets.

Following previous work and our experimental results, hyper parameters configurations are set as follows: minibatch size $n = 16$, window size $w = 5$, character embedding size $d_1 = 100$, amplification gate range $\gamma = [0, 4]$ and margin loss discount $\kappa = 0.2$. All weight matrixes are diagonal matrixes and randomly initialized by normal distribution.

3.2 Experimental Results and Discussions

We first compare our model with baseline methods, Bi-LSTM and GRNN on three datasets. The results evaluated by F-score (F_1 score) are reported in Table 1.

- **Bi-LSTM**. First, the output of Bi-LSTM is concatenated to a vector. Second, softmax layer takes the vector as input and generates each tag probability.

---

[1]https://catalog.ldc.upenn.edu/LDC2007T36
[2]https://catalog.ldc.upenn.edu/LDC2003T09

Model (Unigram)	PKU	MSRA	CTB6
Bi-LSTM	95.0	95.8	95.2
GRNN	95.8	96.2	95.5
Pei et al. (2014)	94.0	94.9	*
Chen et al. (2015)	**96.1**	96.2	95.6
DGRNN	**96.1**	**96.3**	**95.8**

Table 1: Comparisons for DGRNN and other neural approaches based on traditional unigram embeddings.

Model	PKU	MSRA	CTB6
Zhang et al. (2006)	95.1	97.1	*
Zhang et al. (2007)	94.5	97.2	*
Sun et al. (2009)	95.2	97.3	*
Sun et al. (2012)	95.4	**97.4**	*
Zhang et al. (2013)	**96.1**	**97.4**	*
DGRNN	**96.1**	96.3	**95.8**

Table 2: Comparisons for DGRNN and state-of-the-art non-neural network approaches on F-score.

- **GRNN**. The structure of GRNN is recursive. GRNN combines adjacent word vectors to the more abstract representation in bottom-up way.

Furthermore, we conduct experiments with amplification gate on three development datasets. Figure 5 shows that amplification gate significantly increases F-score on three datasets. Amplification even achieves 0.9% improvement on CTB6 dataset. It is demonstrated that amplification gate is an effective mechanism.

We compare our proposed model with previous neural approaches on PKU, MSRA and CTB6 test datasets. Experimental results are reported in Table 1. It can be clearly seen that our approach achieves the best results compared with

Dataset	Model	Result
MSRA	Bi-LSTM	$t = 5.94, p < 1 \times 10^{-4}$
	GRNN	$t = 1.22, p = 0.22$
PKU	Bi-LSTM	$t = 15.54, p < 1 \times 10^{-4}$
	GRNN	$t = 4.43, p < 1 \times 10^{-4}$
CTB6	Bi-LSTM	$t = 5.01, p < 1 \times 10^{-4}$
	GRNN	$t = 2.55, p = 2.48 \times 10^{-2}$

Table 3: The t-test results for DGRNN and baselines.

other neural networks on traditional unigram embeddings. It is possible that bigram embeddings may achieve better results. With the help of bigram embeddings, Pei et al. (2014) can achieve 95.2% and 97.2% F-scores on PKU and MSRA datasets and Chen et al. (2015) can achieve 96.4%, 97.6% and 95.8% F-scores on PKU, MSRA and CTB6 datasets. However, performance varies among these bigram models since they have different ways of involving bigram embeddings. Besides, the training speed would be very slow after adding bigram embeddings. Therefore, we only compare our model on traditional unigram embeddings.

We also compare DGRNN with other state-of-the-art non-neural networks, as shown in Table 2. Chen et al. (2015) implements the work of Sun and Xu (2011) on CTB6 dataset and achieves 95.7% F-score. We achieve the best result on P-KU dataset only with unigram embeddings. The experimental results show that our model is a competitive model for Chinese word segmentation.

3.3 Statistical Significance Tests

We use the t-test to intuitively show the improvement of DGRNN over baselines. According to the results shown in Table 3, we can draw a conclusion that, by conventional criteria, this improvement is considered to be statistically significant between DGRNN with baselines, except for GRN-N approach on MSRA dataset.

4 Conclusions

In this work, we propose dependency-based recursive neural network to combine local features with long distance dependencies, which achieves substantial improvement over the state-of-the-art approaches. Our work indicates that long distance dependencies can improve the performance of local segmenter. In the future, we will study alternative ways of modeling long distance dependencies.

5 Acknowledgments

We thank Xiaoyan Cai for her valuable suggestions. This work was supported in part by National Natural Science Foundation of China (No. 61300063), National High Technology Research and Development Program of China (863 Program, No. 2015AA015404), and Doctoral Fund of Ministry of Education of China (No. 20130001120004). Xu Sun is the corresponding author.

References

Xinchi Chen, Xipeng Qiu, Chenxi Zhu, and Xuanjing Huang. 2015. Gated recursive neural network for chinese word segmentation. In *ACL (1)*, pages 1744–1753. The Association for Computer Linguistics.

Fei Cheng, Kevin Duh, and Yuji Matsumoto. 2015. Synthetic word parsing improves chinese word segmentation. In *Proceedings of the 53rd Annual Meeting of the Association for Computational Linguistics and the 7th International Joint Conference on Natural Language Processing (Volume 2: Short Papers)*, pages 262–267, Beijing, China, July. Association for Computational Linguistics.

Ronan Collobert, Jason Weston, Léon Bottou, Michael Karlen, Koray Kavukcuoglu, and Pavel Kuksa. 2011. Natural language processing (almost) from scratch. *J. Mach. Learn. Res.*, 12:2493–2537, November.

Thomas Emerson. 2005. The second international chinese word segmentation bakeoff. In *Proceedings of the Fourth SIGHAN Workshop on Chinese Language Processing*, pages 123–133.

G. Hinton. 2012. Lecture 6.5: rmsprop: divide the gradient by a running average of its recent magnitude. coursera: Neural networks for machine learning.

John D. Lafferty, Andrew McCallum, and Fernando C. N. Pereira. 2001. Conditional random fields: Probabilistic models for segmenting and labeling sequence data. In *Proceedings of the Eighteenth International Conference on Machine Learning*, number 8 in ICML '01, pages 282–289, San Francisco, CA, USA. Morgan Kaufmann Publishers Inc.

Jianqiang Ma and Erhard Hinrichs. 2015. Accurate linear-time chinese word segmentation via embedding matching. In *Proceedings of the 53rd Annual Meeting of the Association for Computational Linguistics and the 7th International Joint Conference on Natural Language Processing (Volume 1: Long Papers)*, pages 1733–1743, Beijing, China, July. Association for Computational Linguistics.

Wenzhe Pei, Tao Ge, and Baobao Chang. 2014. Max-margin tensor neural network for chinese word segmentation. In *Proceedings of the 52nd Annual Meeting of the Association for Computational Linguistics (Volume 1: Long Papers)*, pages 293–303, Baltimore, Maryland, June. Association for Computational Linguistics.

Martin Riedmiller and Heinrich Braun. 1993. A direct adaptive method for faster backpropagation learning: The rprop algorithm. In *IEEE INTERNATIONAL CONFERENCE ON NEURAL NETWORKS*, pages 586–591.

Weiwei Sun and Jia Xu. 2011. Enhancing chinese word segmentation using unlabeled data. In *Conference on Empirical Methods in Natural Language Processing, EMNLP 2011, 27-31 July 2011, John Mcintyre Conference Centre, Edinburgh, Uk, A Meeting of Sigdat, A Special Interest Group of the ACL*, pages 970–979.

Xu Sun, Yaozhong Zhang, Takuya Matsuzaki, Yoshimasa Tsuruoka, and Jun'ichi Tsujii. 2009. A discriminative latent variable chinese segmenter with hybrid word/character information. In *Proceedings of Human Language Technologies: The 2009 Annual Conference of the North American Chapter of the Association for Computational Linguistics*, pages 56–64, Boulder, Colorado, June. Association for Computational Linguistics.

Xu Sun, Houfeng Wang, and Wenjie Li. 2012. Fast online training with frequency-adaptive learning rates for chinese word segmentation and new word detection. In *Proceedings of the 50th Annual Meeting of the Association for Computational Linguistics (Volume 1: Long Papers)*, pages 253–262, Jeju Island, Korea, July. Association for Computational Linguistics.

Xu Sun, Yao zhong Zhang, Takuya Matsuzaki, Yoshimasa Tsuruoka, and Jun'ichi Tsujii. 2013. Probabilistic chinese word segmentation with non-local information and stochastic training. *Inf. Process. Manage.*, 49(3):626–636.

Xu Sun. 2014. Structure regularization for structured prediction. In *Advances in Neural Information Processing Systems 27*, pages 2402–2410.

N. Xue and L. Shen. 2003. Chinese Word Segmentation as LMR Tagging. In *Proceedings of the 2nd SIGHAN Workshop on Chinese Language Processing*.

Naiwen Xue, Fei Xia, Fu-dong Chiou, and Marta Palmer. 2005. The Penn Chinese TreeBank: Phrase structure annotation of a large corpus. *Natural Language Engineering*, 11(2):207–238, June.

Yue Zhang and Stephen Clark. 2007. Chinese segmentation with a word-based perceptron algorithm. In *Proceedings of the 45th Annual Meeting of the Association of Computational Linguistics*, pages 840–847, Prague, Czech Republic, June. Association for Computational Linguistics.

Ruiqiang Zhang, Genichiro Kikui, and Eiichiro Sumita. 2006. Subword-based tagging by conditional random fields for chinese word segmentation. In *Proceedings of the Human Language Technology Conference of the NAACL, Companion Volume: Short Papers*, NAACL-Short '06, pages 193–196, Stroudsburg, PA, USA. Association for Computational Linguistics.

Longkai Zhang, Houfeng Wang, Xu Sun, and Mairgup Mansur. 2013. Exploring representations from unlabeled data with co-training for chinese word segmentation. In *EMNLP*, pages 311–321. ACL.

Xiaoqing Zheng, Hanyang Chen, and Tianyu Xu. 2013. Deep learning for chinese word segmentation and pos tagging. In *EMNLP*, pages 647–657. ACL.

Deep Neural Networks for Syntactic Parsing of Morphologically Rich Languages

Joël Legrand[1,2] and **Ronan Collobert**[*3,1]

[1] Idiap Research Institute, Martigny, Switzerland

[2] Ecole Polytechnique Fédérale de Lausanne (EPFL), Lausanne, Switzerland

[3] Facebook AI Research, Menlo Park (CA), USA

Abstract

Morphologically rich languages (MRL) are languages in which much of the structural information is contained at the word-level, leading to high level word-form variation. Historically, syntactic parsing has been mainly tackled using generative models. These models assume input features to be conditionally independent, making difficult to incorporate arbitrary features. In this paper, we investigate the greedy discriminative parser described in (Legrand and Collobert, 2015), which relies on word embeddings, in the context of MRL. We propose to learn morphological embeddings and propagate morphological information through the tree using a recursive composition procedure. Experiments show that such embeddings can dramatically improve the average performance on different languages. Moreover, it yields state-of-the art performance for a majority of languages.

1 Introduction

Morphologically rich languages (MRL) are languages for which important information concerning the syntactic structure is expressed through word formation, rather than constituent-order patterns. Unlike English, they can have complex word structure as well as flexible word order. A common practice when dealing with such languages is to incorporate morphological information explicitly (Tsarfaty et al., 2013). However this poses two problems to the classical generative models: they assume input features to be conditionally independent which makes the incorpora-

tion of arbitrary features difficult. Moreover, refining input features leads to a data sparsity issue.

In the other hand, neural network-based models using continuous word representations as input have been able to overcome the data sparsity problem inherent in NLP (Huang and Yates, 2009). Furthermore, neural networks allow to incorporate arbitrary features and learn complex non-linear relations between them. Legrand and Collobert (2015) introduced a greedy syntactic parser, based on neural networks which relies on word embeddings. This model maintains a history of the previous node predictions, in the form of vector representations, by leveraging a recursive composition procedure.

In this paper, we propose to enhance this model for syntactic parsing of MRL, by learning morphological embeddings. We take advantage of a recursive composition procedure similar to the one used in (Legrand and Collobert, 2015) to propagate morphological information during the parsing process. We evaluate our approach on the SPMRL (Syntactic Parsing of MRL) Shared Task 2014 (Seddah et al., 2013) on nine different languages. Each of them comes with a set of morphological features allowing to augment words with information such as their grammatical functions, relation with other words in the sentence, prefixes, affixes and lemmas. We show that integrating morphological features allows to increase dramatically the average performance and yields state-of-the-art performance for a majority of languages.

1.1 Related work

Both the baseline (Berkeley parser) and the current state-of-the-art model on the SPMRL Shared Task 2014 (Björkelund et al., 2014) rely on probabilistic context free grammar (PCFG)-based features. The latter uses a product of PCFG with latent annotation based models (Petrov, 2010), with a coarse-to-

*All research was conducted at the Idiap Research Institute, before Ronan Collobert joined Facebook AI Research

Proceedings of the 54th Annual Meeting of the Association for Computational Linguistics, pages 573–578,
Berlin, Germany, August 7-12, 2016. ©2016 Association for Computational Linguistics

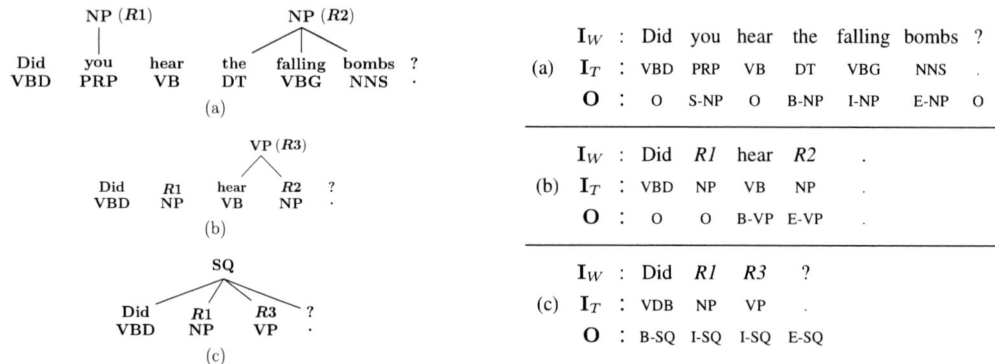

Figure 1: Greedy parsing algorithm (3 iterations), on the sentence "Did you hear the falling bombs ?". $\mathbf{I}_W$, $\mathbf{I}_T$ and $\mathbf{O}$ stand for input words (or composed word representations R_i), input syntactic tags (parsing or part-of-speech) and output tags (parsing), respectively. The tree produced after 3 greedy iterations can be reconstructed as the following: `(SQ (VBD Did) (NP (PRP you)) (VP (VB hear) (NP (DT the) (VBG falling) (NNS bombs))) (. ?))`.

fine decoding strategy. The output is then discriminatively reranked (Charniak and Johnson, 2005) to select the best analysis. In contrast, the parser used in this paper constructs the parse tree in a greedy manner and relies only on word, POS tags and morphological embeddings.

Several other papers have reported results for the SPMRL Shared Task 2014. (Hall et al., 2014) introduced an approach where, instead of propagating contextual information from the leaves of the tree to internal nodes in order to refine the grammar, the structural complexity of the grammar is minimized. This is done by moving as much context as possible onto local surface features. This work was refined in (Durrett and Klein, 2015), taking advantage of continuous word representations. The system used in this paper also leverages words embeddings but has two major differences. First, it proceeds step-by-step in a greedy manner (Durrett and Klein, 2015) by using structured inference (CKY). Second, it leverages a compositional node feature which propagates information from the leaves to internal nodes, which is exactly what is claimed not to be done.

(Fernández-González and Martins, 2015) proposed a procedure to turn a dependency tree into a constituency tree. They showed that encoding order information in the dependency tree make it isomorphic to the constituent tree, allowing any dependency parser to produce constituents. Like the parser we used, their parser do not need to binarize the treebank as most of the others constituency parsers. Unlike this system, we do not use the dependency structure as an intermediate representation and directly perform constituency parsing over raw words.

2   Recurrent greedy parsing

In this paper, we used the model presented in (Legrand and Collobert, 2015). It is a NN-based model which performs parsing in a greedy recurrent way. It follows a bottom-up iterative procedure: the tree is built starting from the terminal nodes (sentence words), as shown in Figure 1. Each step can be seen as a sequence tagging task. A BIOES[1] prefixing scheme is used to rewrite this chunk (here node) prediction problem into a word tagging problem. Each iteration of the procedure merges input constituents into new nodes by applying the following steps:

- **Node tagger:** a neural network sliding window is applied over the input sequence of constituents (leaves or heads of trees predicted so far). This procedure (see Figure 2) outputs for each constituent a score s_i for each BIOES-prefixed parsing tag $t \in \mathcal{T}$ ($\mathcal{T}$ being the parsing tags ensemble).

- **Dynamic programming:** a coherent path of BIOES tags is retrieved by decoding over a constrained graph. This insures (for instance) that a $B\text{-}A$ can be followed only by a $I\text{-}A$ or a $E\text{-}A$ (for all parsing tag A).

---

[1] (*Begin*, *Intermediate*, *Other*, *End*, *Single*)

- **Compositional procedure:** new nodes are
  created, merging input constituents, according to the dynamic programming predictions.
  A neural network composition module is then
  used to compute vector representations for
  the new nodes, according to the representations of the merged constituents, as well as
  their corresponding tags (POS or parsing).

The procedure ends when the top node is produced.

3 Parsing Morphologically Rich Languages

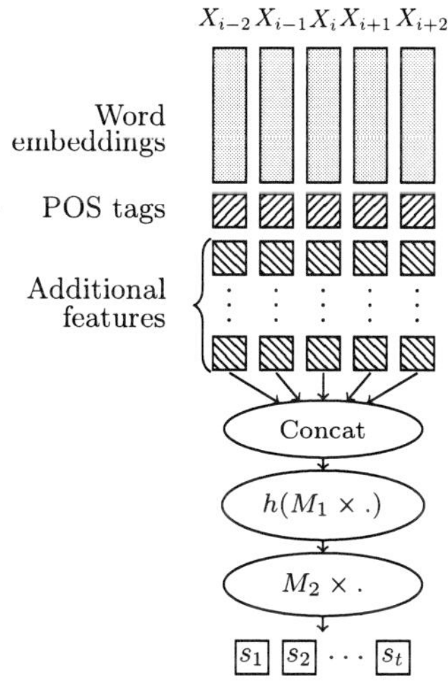

Figure 2: A constituent X_i (word or node previously predicted) is tagged by considering a fixed
size context window of size K (here $K = 5$). The
concatenated output of the compositional history
and constituent tags is fed as input to the tagger.
A standard two-layers neural network outputs a
score s_i for each BIOES-prefixed parsing tag. Additional features can be easily fed to the network.
Each category is assigned a new lookup table containing a vector of feature for every possible tag.

3.1 Morphological features

Morphological features enable the augmentation
of input tokens with information expressed at a
word level, such as grammatical function or relation to other words. For parsing MRL, they have
proven to be very helpful (Cowan and Collins,
2005). The SMPRL corpus provides a different
set of morphological features associated to the

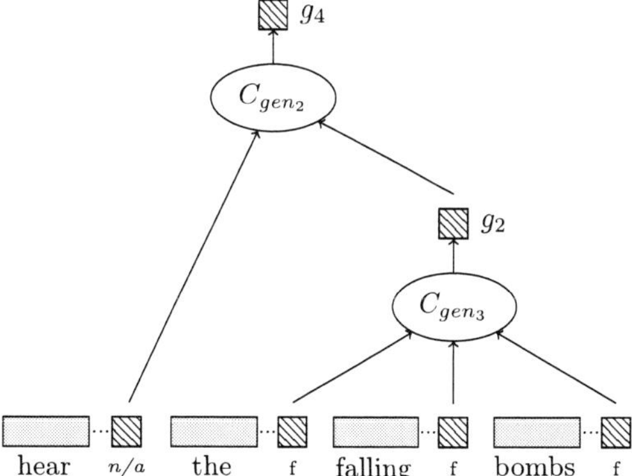

Figure 3: Recursive composition of the morphological feature *gender* (male (m) / female (f) /
not applicable (n/a)). C_{gen_i} are the corresponding composition modules. The representation g_2
is first computed using the 3-inputs module C_{gen_3}.
g_4 is obtained by using the 2-inputs module C_{gen_2}.

tree terminals (tokens) for every language. These
features include morphosyntactic features such as
case, number, gender, person and type, as well as
specific morphological information such as verbal
mood, proper/common noun distinction, lemma,
grammatical function. They also include many
language-specific features. For more details about
the morphological features available, the reader
can refer to (Seddah et al., 2013).

3.2 Morphological Embeddings

The parser from (Legrand and Collobert, 2015) relies only on word and tag embeddings. Besides
these features, our model takes advantage of additional morphological features. As illustrated in
Figure 2, each additional feature m is assigned
a different lookup table containing morphological
feature vectors of size d_m. The output vectors of
the different morphological lookup-tables are simply concatenated to form the input of the next neural network layer.

3.3 Morphological composition

Morphological features are available only for
leaves. To propagate morphological information
to the nodes, we take advantage of a composition procedure similar to the one used in (Legrand
and Collobert, 2015) for words and POS. As illustrated in Figure 3, every morphological feature
m is assigned a set on composition modules C_{m_i}
which take as input i morphological embeddings

Model	Ara.	Bas.	Fre.	Ger.	Heb.	Hun.	Kor.	Pol.	Swe.	AVG
Berkeley+POS	80.8	76.2	81.8	80.3	**92.2**	87.6	82.9	88.1	82.9	83.7
Berkeley RAW	79.1	69.8	80.4	79.0	87.3	81.4	73.3	79.5	78.9	78.7
(Björkelund et al., 2014)	82.2	90.0	84.0	82.1	91.6	**92.6**	86.5	88.6	**85.1**	87.0
Proposed approach	**84.1**	**91.0**	**85.7**	**84.6**	91.7	91.2	**87.8**	**94.1**	82.5	**88.1**

Table 1: Results for all languages in terms of F1-score, using gold POS and morphological tags. Berkeley+POS and Berkeley RAW are the two baseline system results provided by the organizers of the shared task. Our experiments used an ensemble of 5 models, trained starting from different random initializations.

of dimension d_m. Each composition module perform a matrix-vector operation followed by a nonlinearity

$$C_{m_i}(x) = h(M_m^i.x)$$

where $M_m^i \in \mathbb{R}^{d_m \times id_m}$ is a matrix of parameters to be trained and h a pointwise non-linearity function. $x = [x_1...x_i]$ is the concatenation of the corresponding input morphological embeddings. Note that given a morphological feature we have a different matrix of weight for every possible size i. In practice most tree nodes do not merge more than a few constituents and we only consider composition sizes < 5.

4 Experiments

4.1 Corpus

Experiments were conducted on the SPMRL corpus provided for the Shared Task 2014 (Seddah et al., 2013). It provides sentences and tree annotations for 9 different languages (Arabic, Basque, French, German, Hebrew, Hungarian, Korean, Polish and Swedish) coming from various sources. For each language, *gold* part-of-speech and morphological tags are provided. Results for two baseline baseline system are provided in order to evaluate our models.

4.2 Setup

The model was trained using a stochastic gradient descent over the available training data. Hyperparameters were tuned on the provided validation sets. The word embedding size and POS/parsing tag size were set to $D_W = 100$ and $D_T = 30$, respectively. The morphological tag embedding size was set to 10. The window size of the tagger was set to $K = 7$ and its number of hidden units to 300. All parameters were initialized randomly (including the words embeddings). As suggested in

(Plaut and Hinton, 1987), the learning rate was divided by the size of the input vector of each layer. We applied the same dropout regularization as in (Legrand and Collobert, 2015).

4.3 Results

Table 2 presents the influence of adding morphological features to the model. We observe significant improvement for every languages except for Hebrew. On average, morphological features allowed to overcome the original model by 2 F1-score.

language	Words + POS	+ morph
Arabic	80.7	82.9
Basque	82.7	90.6
French	81.1	85.0
German	81.5	83.1
Hebrew	91.6	91.5
Hungarian	89.6	90.3
Korean	86.1	86.7
Polish	93.2	93.7
Swedish	81.1	81.5
AVG	85.3	87.3

Table 2: Influence of the additional morphological embeddings in terms of F1-score

Table 1 compares the performance in F1-score (obtained with the provided EVALB_SPMRL tool) of different systems, using the provided gold POS and morphological features. We compare our results with the two baselines provided with the task: (1) Berkeley parser with provided POS Tags (Berkeley+POS). (2) Berkeley Parser in raw mode where the parser do its own POS tagging (Berkeley RAW). We also report the results of the current state-of-the art model for this task (Björkelund et al., 2014). We included the same voting procedure as in citelegrand:2015, using 5 models trained starting from different random initializations. At

Model	Ara.	Bas.	Fre.	Ger.	Heb.	Hun.	Kor.	Pol.	Swe.	AVG
Berkeley+POS	78.7	74.7	79.8	78.3	85.4	85.2	78.6	86.7	80.6	80.9
Berkeley RAW	79.2	70.5	80.4	78.3	87.0	81.6	71.4	79.2	79.2	78.5
(Durrett and Klein, 2015)	80.2	85.4	81.2	80.9	88.6	90.7	82.2	93.0	83.4	85.1
(Fernández and Martins, 2015)	*n/a*	85.9	78.7	78.7	89.0	88.2	79.3	91.2	82.8	84.2
(Björkelund et al., 2014)	**81.3**	**87.9**	**81.8**	81.3	89.5	**91.8**	84.3	87.5	**84.0**	85.5
Proposed approach	80.4	87.5	80.8	**82.0**	**91.6**	90.0	**84.8**	93.0	80.5	**85.6**

Table 3: Results for all languages in terms of F1-score using predicted POS and morphological tags. Berkeley+POS and Berkeley RAW are the two baseline system results provided by the organizers of the shared task. Our experiments used an ensemble of 5 models, trained starting from different random initializations.

each iteration of the greedy parsing procedure, the BIOES-tag scores are averaged and the new node representations (words+POS and morphological composition) are computed for each model by composing the sub-tree representations corresponding to the given model, using its own compositional network. One can observe that the proposed model outperforms the best model by 1.1 F1-score on average. Moreover, it yields state-of-the art performance for 6 among the 9 available languages.

Finally, Table 3 compares the performance of different systems for a more realistic parsing scenario where the gold POS and morphological tags are unknown. For these experiments, we use the same tags as in (Björkelund et al., 2014)[2] obtained using the freely available tool MarMoT (Mueller et al., 2013). We compare our results with the same model as for the the gold tags experiences. Additionnaly, we compare our results with two recent models reporting results for the SPMRL Shared Task 2014. We see that the proposed model yields state-of-the art performance for 4 out of 9 available languages.

5   Conclusion

In this paper, we proposed to extend the parser introduced in (Legrand and Collobert, 2015) by learning morphological embeddings. We take advantage of a recursive procedure to propagate morphological information through the tree during the parsing process. We showed that using the morphological embeddings boosts the F1-score and allows to outperform the current state-of-the-art model on the SPMRL Shared Task 2014 corpus. Moreover, our approach yields state-of-the art performance for a majority of languages.

[2]The tags used are available here: `http://cistern.cis.lmu.de/marmot/models/CURRENT/`

Acknoledgments

This work was supported by NEC Laboratories America. We would like to thank Dimitri Palaz for our fruitful discussions and Marc Ferras for proofreading this paper.

References

Anders Björkelund, Ozlem Cetinoglu, Agnieszka Falenska, Richárd Farkas, Thomas Mueller, Wolfgang Seeker, and Zsolt Szántó. 2014. Introducing the ims-wrocław-szeged-cis entry at the SPMRL 2014 shared task: Reranking and morpho-syntax meet unlabeled data. *Proceedings of the First Joint Workshop on Statistical Parsing of Morphologically Rich Languages and Syntactic Analysis of Non-Canonical Languages.*

Eugene Charniak and Mark Johnson. 2005. Coarse-to-fine N-best parsing and MaxEnt discriminative reranking. In *Proceedings of the 43rd Annual Meeting on Association for Computational Linguistics.*

Brooke Cowan and Michael Collins. 2005. Morphology and reranking for the statistical parsing of spanish. In *Proceedings of Human Language Technology Conference and Conference on Empirical Methods in Natural Language Processing.*

Greg Durrett and Dan Klein. 2015. Neural CRF parsing. In *Proceedings of the Association for Computational Linguistics.*

Daniel Fernández-González and Andri F. T. Martins. 2015. Parsing as reduction. In *Annual Meeting of the Association for Computational Linguistics ACL.*

David Hall, Greg Durrett, and Dan Klein. 2014. Less grammar, more features. In *Proceedings of the 52nd Annual Meeting of the Association for Computational Linguistics.*

Fei Huang and Alexander Yates. 2009. Distributional representations for handling sparsity in supervised sequence-labeling. In *Proceedings of the Joint Conference of the 47th Annual Meeting of the ACL and the 4th International Joint Conference on Natural*

Language Processing of the AFNLP: Volume 1 - Volume 1.

Joël Legrand and Ronan Collobert. 2015. Joint RNN-based greedy parsing and word composition. In *Proceedings of ICLR.*

T. Mueller, H. Schmid, and H. Schütze. 2013. Efficient higher-order CRFs for morphological tagging. In *Proceedings of the 2013 Conference on Empirical Methods in Natural Language Processing.*

Slav Petrov. 2010. Products of random latent variable grammars. In *NAACL-HLT.*

David C. Plaut and Geoffrey E. Hinton. 1987. Learning sets of filters using back-propagation. *Computer Speech and Language.*

Djamé Seddah, Reut Tsarfaty, Sandra Kübler, Marie Candito, Jinho D. Choi, Richárd Farkas, Jennifer Foster, Iakes Goenaga, Koldo Gojenola, Yoav Goldberg, Spence Green, Nizar Habash, Marco Kuhlmann, Wolfgang Maier, Joakim Nivre, Adam Przepiórkowski, Ryan Roth, Wolfgang Seeker, Yannick Versley, Veronika Vincze, Marcin Wolińsk, Alina Wróblewska, and Éric Villemonte De La Clergerie. 2013. Overview of the SPMRL 2013 shared task: A cross-framework evaluation of parsing morphologically rich languages. In *Proceedings of the 4th Workshop on Statistical Parsing of Morphologically Rich Languages: Shared Task.*

Reut Tsarfaty, Djamé Seddah, Sandra Kbler, and Joakim Nivre. 2013. Parsing morphologically rich languages: Introduction to the special issue. *Computational Linguistics.*

Weakly Supervised Part-of-speech Tagging Using Eye-tracking Data

Maria Barrett[†] **Joachim Bingel**[†] **Frank Keller**[*] **Anders Søgaard**[†]
[†]Centre for Language Technology, University of Copenhagen
Njalsgade 140, 2300 Copenhagen S, Denmark
{barrett, bingel, soegaard}@hum.ku.dk
[*]School of Informatics, University of Edinburgh
10 Crichton Street, Edinburgh EH8 9AB, UK
keller@inf.ed.ac.uk

Abstract

For many of the world's languages, there are no or very few linguistically annotated resources. On the other hand, raw text, and often also dictionaries, can be harvested from the web for many of these languages, and part-of-speech taggers can be trained with these resources. At the same time, previous research shows that eye-tracking data, which can be obtained without explicit annotation, contains clues to part-of-speech information. In this work, we bring these two ideas together and show that given raw text, a dictionary, and eye-tracking data obtained from naive participants reading text, we can train a weakly supervised PoS tagger using a second-order HMM with maximum entropy emissions. The best model use type-level aggregates of eye-tracking data and significantly outperforms a baseline that does not have access to eye-tracking data.

1 Introduction

According to Ethnologue, there are around 7,000 languages in the world.[1] For most of these languages, no or very little linguistically annotated resources are available. This is why over the past decade or so, NLP researchers have focused on developing unsupervised algorithms that learn from raw text, which for many languages is widely available on the web. An example is part-of-speech (PoS) tagging, in which unsupervised approaches have been increasingly successful (see Christodoulopoulos et al. (2010) for an overview). The performance of unsupervised PoS taggers can be improved further if dictionary information is available, making it possible to constrain the PoS

tagging process. Again, dictionary information can be harvested readily from the web for many languages (Li et al., 2012).

In this paper, we show that PoS tagging performance can be improved further by using a weakly supervised model which exploits eye-tracking data in addition to raw text and dictionary information. Eye-tracking data can be obtained by getting native speakers of the target language to read text while their gaze behavior is recorded. Reading is substantially faster than manual annotation, and competent readers are available for languages where trained annotators are hard to find or non-existent. While high quality eye-tracking equipment is still expensive, $100 eye-trackers such as the EyeTribe are already on the market, and cheap eye-tracking equipment is likely to be widely available in the near future, including eye-tracking by smartphone or webcam (Skovsgaard et al., 2013; Xu et al., 2015).

Gaze patterns during reading are strongly influenced by the parts of speech of the words being read. Psycholinguistic experiments show that readers are less likely to fixate on closed-class words that are predictable from context. Readers also fixate longer on rare words, on words that are semantically ambiguous, and on words that are morphologically complex (Rayner, 1998). These findings indicate that eye-tracking data should be useful for classifying words by part of speech, and indeed Barrett and Søgaard (2015) show that word-type-level aggregate statistics collected from eye-tracking corpora can be used as features for supervised PoS tagging, leading to substantial gains in accuracy across domains. This leads us to hypothesize that gaze data should also improve weakly supervised PoS tagging.

In this paper, we test this hypothesis by experimenting with a PoS tagging model that uses raw text, dictionary information, and eye-tracking

---

[1]http://www.ethnologue.com/world

Proceedings of the 54th Annual Meeting of the Association for Computational Linguistics, pages 579–584,
Berlin, Germany, August 7-12, 2016. ©2016 Association for Computational Linguistics

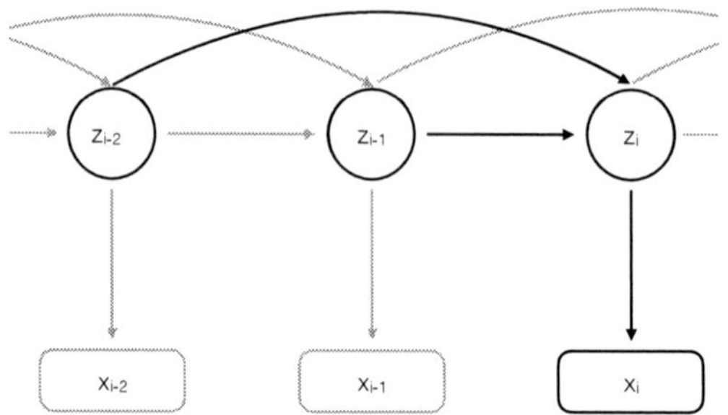

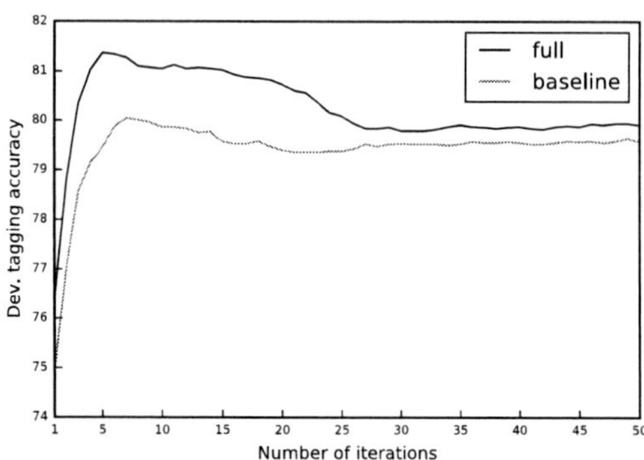

Figure 1: Second-order HMM. In addition to the transitional probabilities of the antecedent state z_{i-1} in first-order HMMs, second-order models incorporate transitional probabilities from the second-order antecedent state z_{i-2}.

Figure 2: Tagging accuracy on development data (token-level) as a function of number of iterations on baseline and full model.

data, but requires no explicit annotation. We start with a state-of-the-art unsupervised PoS tagging model, the second-order hidden Markov model with maximum entropy emissions of Li et al. (2012), which uses only textual features. We augment this model with a wide range of features derived from an eye-tracking corpus at training time (type-level gaze features). We also experiment with token-level gaze features; the use of these features implies that eye-tracking is available both at training time and at test time. We find that eye-tracking features lead to a significant increase in PoS tagging accuracy, and that type-level aggregates work better than token-level features.

2 The Dundee Treebank

The Dundee Treebank (Barrett et al., 2015) is a Universal Dependency annotation layer that has recently been added to the world's largest eye-tracking corpus, the Dundee Corpus (Kennedy et al., 2003). The English portion of the corpus contains 51,502 tokens and 9,776 types in 2,368 sentences. The Dundee Corpus is a well-known and widely used resource in psycholinguistic research. The corpus enables researchers to study the reading of contextualized, running text obtained under relatively naturalistic conditions. The eye-movements in the Dundee Corpus were recorded with a high-end eye-tracker, sampling at 1000 Hz. The corpus contains the eye-movements of ten native English speakers as they read the same twenty newspaper articles from *The Independent*. The

corpus was augmented with Penn Treebank PoS annotation by Frank (2009). When constructing the Dundee Treebank, this PoS annotation was checked and corrected if necessary. In the present paper, we use Universal PoS tags (Petrov et al., 2011), which were obtained by automatically mapping the original Penn Treebank annotation of the Dundee Treebank to Universal tags.

3 Type-constrained second-order HMM PoS tagging

We build on the type-constrained second-order hidden Markov model with maximum entropy emissions (SHMM-ME) proposed by Li et al. (2012). This model is an extension of the first-order max-ent HMM introduced by Berg-Kirkpatrick et al. (2010). Li et al. (2012) derive type constraints from crowd-sourced tag dictionaries obtained from Wiktionary. Using type constraints means confining the emissions for a given word to the tags specified by the Wiktionary for that word. Li et al. (2012) report a considerable improvement over state-of-the-art unsupervised PoS tagging models by using type constraints. In our experiments, we use the tag dictionaries they made available[2] to facilitate comparison. Li et al.'s model was evaluated across nine languages and outperformed a model trained on the Penn Treebank tagset, as well as a models that use parallel text. We follow Li et al.'s approach, including the mapping of the Penn Treebank tags to

---

[2]`https://code.google.com/archive/p/`
`wikily-supervised-pos-tagger/`

	Features
EARLY	First fixation duration w-1 fixation probability w-1 fixation duration First pass duration
LATE	Total regression-to duration n long regressions to w n refixations Re-read probability n regressions to w
BASIC	Total fixation duration Mean fixation duration n fixations Fixation probability
REGFR.	n regressions from w n long regressions from w Total regression-from duration
CONTEXT	w+1 fixation probability w+1 fixation duration w+2 fixation probability w+2 fixation duration w-2 fixation probability w-2 fixation probability
NOGAZEB.	Word length BNC log frequency w-1 BNC log frequency BNC forward transitional log probability BNC backward transitional log probability
NOGAZED.	Word length Dundee log frequency w-1 Dundee log frequency Dundee forward transitional log probability Dundee backward transitional log probability

Table 1: Features in feature selection groups.

Features	TA
NOGAZEDUN	81.03
NOGAZEBNC	80.69
BASIC	80.30
EARLY	79.96
LATE	79.87
REGFROM	79.62
CONTEXT	79.53
Best Group Comb (All)	81.37
Best Gaze-Only Comb (BASIC-LATE)	80.45

Table 2: Tagging accuracy on the development set (token-level) for all individual feature groups, for the best combination of groups and for the best gaze-only combination of groups.

the Universal PoS tags (Petrov et al., 2011). Figure 1 shows a graphical representation of a second-order hidden Markov model.

Li et al. explore two aspects of type-constrained HMMs for unsupervised PoS tagging: the use of a second-order Markov model, and the use of textual features modeled by maximum entropy emissions. They find that both aspects improve tagging accuracy and report the following results for English using Universal PoS tags on the Penn Treebank: first-order HMM 85.4, first-order HMM with max-ent emissions 86.1, second-order HMM 85.0, and second-order HMM with max-ent emissions 87.1. Li et al. employ a set of basic textual features for the max-ent versions, which encode word identity, presence of a hyphen, a capital letter, or a digit, and word suffixes of two to three letters.

4 Experiments

Features Based on the eye-movement data in the Dundee Corpus, we compute token-level values for 22 features pertaining to gaze and comple-

ment them with another nine non-gaze features. Word length and word frequency are known to correlate and interact with gaze features. We use frequency counts from both a large corpus (the British National Corpus, BNC) and the Dundee Corpus itself. From these corpora, we also obtain forward and backward transitional probabilities, i.e., the conditional probabilities of a word given the previous or next word.

All gaze features are averaged over the ten readers and normalized linearly to a scale between 0 and 1. We divide the set of 31 features, which we list in Table 1, into the following seven groups in order to examine for their individual contribution:

1. EARLY measures of processing such as first-pass fixation duration. Fixations on previous words are included in this group due to preview benefits. Early measures capture lexical access and early syntactic processing.

2. LATE measures of processing such as number of regressions to a word and re-fixation probability. These measures reflect late syntactic processing and disambiguation in general.

3. BASIC word-level features, e.g., mean fixation duration and fixation probability. These metrics do not belong explicitly to early or late processing measures.

4. REGFROM includes a small selection of measures based on regressions departing from a token. It also includes counts of long regressions[3]. The token of departure of a regression

---

[3] defined as saccades going further back than w_{i-2}

System	TA
Baseline (Li et al., 2012)	79.77
NoTextFeats	74.61
NoTextFeats + Best Group Comb (token)	79.56
NoTextFeats + Best Group Comb (type)	81.94*
Token-level features	
Best Gaze Group (BASIC)	80.42*
Best Gaze-Only Comb (BASIC+LATE)	80.45*
Best Single Group (NOGAZEDUN)	80.61*
Best Group Comb (All)	81.00*
Type-averaged features	
Best Gaze Group (BASIC)	81.28*
Best Gaze-Only Comb (BASIC+LATE)	81.38*
Best Group (NOGAZEDUN)	81.52*
Best Group Comb (All)	82.44*

Table 3: Tagging accuracy for the baseline, for models with no text features and for our gaze-enriched models using type and token gaze features. Significant improvements over the baseline marked by * ($p < 10^{-3}$, McNemar's test).

Feature groups	Accuracy	Δ
All groups	81.00	
−NOGAZEBNC	80.80	−0.20
−NOGAZEDUN	80.28	−0.52*
−BASIC	80.20	−0.08
−EARLY	79.78	−0.42*
−LATE	79.53	−0.25
−REGFROM	79.24	−0.29*
−CONTEXT (Baseline)	79.77	+0.53*

Table 4: Results of an ablation study over feature groups on the test set on token-level features. Significant differences with previous model are marked by * ($p < 0.05$, McNemar's test).

can have syntactic relevance, e.g., in garden path sentences.

5. CONTEXT features of the surrounding tokens. This group contains features relating to the fixations of the words in near proximity of the token. The eye can only recognize words a few characters to the left, and seven to eight characters to the right of the fixation (Rayner, 1998). Therefore it is useful to know the fixation pattern around the token.

6. NOGAZEBNC includes word length and word frequency obtained from the British National Corpus, as well as forward and backward transitional probabilities. These were computed using the KenLM language modeling toolkit (Heafield, 2011) with Kneser-Ney smoothing for unseen bigrams.

7. NOGAZEDUN includes the same features as NOGAZEBNC, but computed on the Dundee Corpus. They were extracted using CMU-Cambridge language modeling toolkit.[4]

Setup The Dundee Corpus does not include a standard train-development-test split, so we di-

[4] http://www.speech.cs.cmu.edu/SLM/toolkit.html

vided it into a training set containing 46,879 tokens/1,896 sentences, a development set containing 5,868 tokens/230 sentences, and a test set of 5,832 tokens/241 sentences.

To tune the number of EM iterations required for the SHMM-ME model, we ran several experiments on the development set using 1 through 50 iterations. The result is fairly consistent for both the baseline (the original model of Li et al. (2012)) and the full model (which includes all feature groups in Table 1). Tagging accuracy as a function of number of iterations is graphed in Figure 2. The best number of iterations on the full model is five, which we will use for the remaining experiments.

We perform a grid search over all combinations of the seven feature groups, using five EM iterations for training, evaluating the resulting models on token-level features of the development set. We observe that the best single feature group is NOGAZEDUN, the best single group of gaze features is BASIC, the best gaze-only group combination is BASIC-LATE and the best group combination is obtained by including all seven feature groups. Using all feature groups outperforms any individual feature group on development data. The performance of all the individual groups and of the best group combinations can be seen in Table 2. We run experiments on the test set and report results using the best single group (NOGAZEDUN), the best single gaze group (BASIC), the best gaze-only group combination (BASIC-LATE) and the best group combination (all features).

Following Barrett and Søgaard (2015), we contrast the token-level gaze features with features aggregated at the type level. Type-level aggregation was used by Barrett and Søgaard (2015) for supervised PoS tagging: A lexicon of word types was created and the features values were averaged over all occurrences of each type in the training data.

As our baseline, we train and evaluate the original model proposed by Li et al. (2012) on the train-test split described above, and compare it to the models that make use of eye-tracking measures.

To get an estimate of the effect of the textual features of Li et al., we train a model without these features, labeled NOTEXTFEATS. We also augment this model with the best combination of feature groups.

Results   The main results are presented in Table 3. We first of all observe that both type- and token-level gaze features lead to significant improvements over Li et al. (2012), but type-level features perform better than token-level. We observe that the best individual feature group, NOGAZEDUN, performs better than the best individual gaze feature group, BASIC and the best gaze-only feature group, BASIC+LATE. This is true on both type and token-level. Using the best combination of feature groups (All features) works best for both type- and token-level features. Also when excluding the textual feature model gaze helps and type-level features also work better than token-level here.

A feature ablation study (see Table 4) supports the hierarchical ordering of the features based on the development set results (see Table 1).

5   Related Work

The proposed approach continues the work of Barrett and Søgaard (2015) by augmenting an unsupervised baseline PoS tagging model instead of a supervised model. Our work also explores the potentials of token-level features. Zelenina (2014) is the only work we are aware of that uses gaze features for unsupervised PoS tagging. Zelenina (2014) employs gaze features to re-rank the output of a standard unsupervised tagger. She reports a small improvement with gaze features when evaluating on the Universal PoS tagset, but finds no improvement when using the Penn Treebank tagset.

6   Discussion

The best individual feature group is NOGAZE-DUN, indicating that just using word length and word frequency, as well as transitional probabilities, leads to a significant improvement in tagging accuracy. However, performance increases further when we add gaze features, which supports our claim that gaze data is useful for weakly supervising PoS induction.

Type-level features work noticeably better than token-level features, suggesting that access to eye-tracking data at test time is not necessary. On the contrary, our results support the more resource-efficient set-up of just having eye-tracking data available at training time. We assume that this finding is due to the fact that eye-movement data is typically quite noisy; averaging over all tokens of a type reduces the noise more than just averaging over the ten participants that read each token. Thus token-level aggregation leads to more reliable feature values.

Our finding that the best model includes all groups of gaze features, and that the best gaze-only group combination works better than the best individual gaze group suggest that different eye-tracking features contain complementary information. A broad selection of eye-movement features is necessary for reliably identifying PoS classes.

7   Conclusions

We presented the first study of weakly supervised part-of-speech tagging with eye-tracking data, using a type-constrained second-order hidden Markov model with max-ent emissions. We performed experiments adding a broad selection of eye-tracking features at training time (type-level features) and at test time (token-level features). We found significant improvements over the baseline in both cases, but type averaging worked better than token-level features. Our results indicate that using traces of human cognitive processing, such as the eye-movements made during reading, can be used to augment NLP models. This could enable us to bootstrap better PoS taggers for domains and languages for which manually annotated corpora are not available, in particular once eye-trackers become widely available through smartphones or webcams (Skovsgaard et al., 2013; Xu et al., 2015).

Acknowledgments

This research was partially funded by the ERC Starting Grant LOWLANDS No. 313695, as well as by Trygfonden.

References

Maria Barrett and Anders Søgaard. 2015. Reading behavior predicts syntactic categories. *CoNLL 2015*, pages 345–349.

Maria Barrett, Željko Agić, and Anders Søgaard. 2015. The dundee treebank. In *The 14th International Workshop on Treebanks and Linguistic Theories (TLT 14)*, pages 242–248.

Taylor Berg-Kirkpatrick, Alexandre Bouchard-Cote, John DeNero, , and Dan Klein. 2010. Painless unsupervised learning with features. In *Proceedings of NAACL*, pages 582–590.

Christos Christodoulopoulos, Sharon Goldwater, and Mark Steedman. 2010. Two decades of unsupervised POS induction: How far have we come? In *Proceedings of EMNLP*, pages 575–584.

Stefan L. Frank. 2009. Surprisal-based comparison between a symbolic and a connectionist model of sentence processing. In *Proceedings of the 31st annual Conference of the Cognitive Science Society*, pages 1139–1144.

Kenneth Heafield. 2011. KenLM: faster and smaller language model queries. In *Proceedings of the EMNLP 2011 Sixth Workshop on Statistical Machine Translation*, pages 187–197.

Alan Kennedy, Robin Hill, and Joël Pynte. 2003. The dundee corpus. In *Proceedings of the 12th European conference on eye movement*.

Shen Li, João Graça, and Ben Taskar. 2012. Wikily supervised part-of-speech tagging. In *EMNLP*, pages 1389–1398.

Slav Petrov, Dipanjan Das, and Ryan McDonald. 2011. A universal part-of-speech tagset. *CoRR* abs/1104.2086.

Keith Rayner. 1998. Eye movements in reading and information processing: 20 years of research. *Psychological bulletin*, 124(3):372–422.

Henrik Skovsgaard, John Paulin Hansen, and Emilie Møllenbach. 2013. Gaze tracking through smartphones. In *Gaze Interaction in the Post-WIMP World CHI 2013 One-day Workshop*.

P. Xu, K. A. Ehinger, Y. Zhang, A. Finkelstein, S. R. Kulkarni, , and J. Xiao. 2015. TurkerGaze: Crowdsourcing saliency with webcam based eye tracking. arXiv:1504.06755.

Maria Zelenina. 2014. Part of speech induction with gaze features. Master's thesis, University of Edinburgh, United Kingdom.

Metrics for Evaluation of Word-Level Machine Translation Quality Estimation

Varvara Logacheva, Michal Lukasik and **Lucia Specia**
Department of Computer Science
University of Sheffield, UK
{v.logacheva, m.lukasik, l.specia}@sheffield.ac.uk

Abstract

The aim of this paper is to investigate suitable evaluation strategies for the task of word-level quality estimation of machine translation. We suggest various metrics to replace F_1-score for the "BAD" class, which is currently used as main metric. We compare the metrics' performance on real system outputs and synthetically generated datasets and suggest a reliable alternative to the F_1-BAD score — the multiplication of F_1-scores for different classes. Other metrics have lower discriminative power and are biased by unfair labellings.

1 Introduction

Quality estimation (QE) of machine translation (MT) is a task of determining the quality of an automatically translated text without any oracle (reference) translation. This task has lately been receiving significant attention: from confidence estimation (i.e. estimation of how confident a particular MT system is on a word or a phrase (Gandrabur and Foster, 2003)) it evolved to system-independent QE and is performed at the word level (Luong et al., 2014), sentence level (Shah et al., 2013) and document level (Scarton et al., 2015).

The emergence of a large variety of approaches to QE led to need for reliable ways to compare them. The evaluation metrics that have been used to compare the performance of systems participating in QE shared tasks[1] have received some criticisms. Graham (2015) shows that Pearson correlation better suits for the evaluation of sentence-level QE systems than mean absolute error (MAE), often used for this purpose. Pearson correlation evaluates how well a system captures

the regularities in the data, whereas MAE essentially measures the difference between the true and the predicted scores and in many cases can be minimised by always predicting the average score as given by the training set labels.

Word-level QE is commonly framed as a binary task, i.e., the classification of every translated word as "OK" or "BAD". This task has been evaluated in terms of F_1-score for the "BAD" class, a metric that favours 'pessimistic' systems — i.e. systems that tend to assign the "BAD" label to most words. A trivial baseline strategy that assigns the label "BAD" to all words can thus receive a high score while being completely uninformative (Bojar et al., 2014). However, no analysis of the word-level metrics' performance has been done and no alternative metrics have been proposed that are more reliable than the F_1-BAD score.

In this paper we compare existing evaluation metrics for word-level QE, suggest a number of alternatives, and show that one of these alternatives leads to more objective and reliable results.

2 Metrics

One of the reasons word-level QE is a challenging problem is the fact that "OK" and "BAD" labels are not equally important: we are generally more interested in finding incorrect words than in assigning a suitable category to every single word. An ideal metric should be oriented towards the recall for the "BAD" class. However, the case of F_1-BAD score shows that this is not the only requirement: in order to be useful the metric should not favour pessimistic labellings, i.e., all or most words labelled as "BAD". Below we describe possible alternatives to the F_1-BAD score.

2.1 F_1-score variants

Word-level F_1-scores. Since F_1-BAD score is too pessimistic, an obvious solution would be to

---

[1] http://statmt.org/wmt15/
quality-estimation-task.html

Proceedings of the 54th Annual Meeting of the Association for Computational Linguistics, pages 585–590,
Berlin, Germany, August 7-12, 2016. ©2016 Association for Computational Linguistics

balance it with F_1-score for the "OK" class. However, the widely used weighted average of F_1-scores for the two classes is not suitable as it will be dominated by F_1-OK due to labels imbalance. Any reasonable MT system will nowadays generate texts where most words are correct, so the label distribution is very skewed towards the "OK" class. Therefore, we suggest instead the **multiplication of F_1-scores** for individual classes: it is equal to zero if one of the components is zero, and since both are in the [0,1] range, the overall result will not exceed the value of any of the multipliers.

Phrase-level F_1-scores. One of the features of MT errors is their phrase-level nature. Errors are not independent: one incorrect word can influence the classification of its neighbours. If several adjacent words are tagged as "BAD", they are likely to be part of an error which spans over a phrase.

Therefore, we also evaluate word-level F_1-scores and alternative metrics which are based on correctly identified erroneous or error-free spans of words. The phrase-level F_1-score we suggest is similar to the one used for the evaluation of named entity recognition (NER) systems (Tjong Kim Sang and De Meulder, 2003). There, precision is the percentage of named entities found by a system that are correct, recall is the percentage of named entities present in the corpus that are found by a system. For the QE task, instead of named entities we have spans of erroneous (or correct) words. Precision is the percentage of correctly identified spans among all the spans found by a system, recall is the percentage of correctly identified spans among the spans in the test data.

However, in NER the correct borders of a named entity are of big importance, because failure to identify them results in an incorrect entity. On the other hand, the actual borders of an error span in QE are not as important: the primary goal is to identify the erroneous region in the sentence, the task of finding the exact borders of an error cannot be solved unambiguously even by human annotators (Wisniewski et al., 2013). In order to take into account partially correct phrases (e.g. a 4-word "BAD" phrase where the first word was tagged as "OK" by a system and the remaining words were correctly tagged as "BAD"), we compute the number of true positives as the sum of percentages of words with correctly predicted tags for every "OK" phrase. The number of true negatives is defined analogously.

2.2 Other metrics

Matthews correlation coefficient. MCC (Powers, 2011) was used as a secondary metric in WMT14 word-level QE shared task (Bojar et al., 2014). It is determined as follows:

$$MCC = \frac{TP \times TN + FP \times FN}{\sqrt{(TP+FP)(TP+FN)(TN+FP)(TN+FN)}}$$

where TP, TN, FP and FN are true positive, true negative, false positive and false negative values, respectively.

This coefficient results in values in the [-1, 1] range. If the reference and hypothesis labellings agree on the majority of the examples, the final figure is dominated by the $TP \times TN$ quantity, which gets close to the value of the denominator. The more false positives and false negatives the predictor produces, the lower the value of the numerator.

Sequence correlation. The sequence correlation score was used as a secondary evaluation metric in the QE shared task at WMT15 (Bojar et al., 2015). Analogously to the phrase-level F_1-score, it is based on the intersection of spans of correct and incorrect words. It also weights the phrases to give them equal importance and penalises the difference in the number of phrases between the reference and the hypothesis.

3 Metrics comparison

One of the most reliable ways of comparing metrics is to measure their correlation with human judgements. However, for the word-level QE task, asking humans to rate a system labelling or to compare the outputs of two or more QE systems is a very expensive process. A practical way of getting the human judgements is the use of quality labels in downstream human tasks — i.e. tasks where quality labels can be used as additional information and where they can influence human accuracy or speed. One such a downstream task can be computer-assisted translation, where the user translates a sentence having automatic translation as a draft, and word-level quality labels can highlight incorrect parts in a sentence. Improvements in productivity could show the degree of usefulness of the quality labels in this case. However, such an experiment is also very expensive to be performed. Therefore, we consider indirect ways of comparing the metrics' reliability based on pre-labelled gold-standard test sets.

3.1 Comparison on real systems

One of the purposes of system comparison is to identify the best-performing system. Therefore, we expect a good metric to be able to distinguish between systems as well as possible. One of the quality criteria for a metric will thus be the number of significantly different groups of systems the metric can identify. Another criterion to evaluate metrics is to compare the real systems' performance with synthetic datasets for which we know the desirable behaviour of the metrics. If a metric gives the expected scores to all artificially generated datasets, it detects some properties of the data which are relevant to us, so we can expect it to work adequately also on real datasets.

Here we compare the performance of six metrics:

- F_1-**BAD** — F_1-score for the "BAD" class.
- F_1-**mult** — multiplication of F_1-scores for "BAD" and "OK" classes.
- **phr** F_1-**BAD** — phrase-level F_1-score for the "BAD" class.
- **phr** F_1-**mult** — multiplication of phrase-level F_1-scores.
- **MCC** — Matthews Correlation Coefficient.
- **SeqCor** — Sequence Correlation.

We used these metrics to rank all systems submitted to the WMT15 QE shared task 2 (word-level QE).[2] In addition to that, we test the performance of the metrics on a number of synthetically created labellings that should be **ranked low** in comparison to real system labellings:

- **all-bad** — all words are tagged as "BAD".
- **all-good** — all words are tagged as "OK".
- **optimistic** 98% words are tagged as "OK", with only a small number of "BAD" labels generated: this system should have high precision (0.9) and low recall (0.1) for the "BAD" label.
- **pessimistic** — 90% words are tagged as "BAD": this system should have high recall (0.9) for the "BAD" label, but low recall (0.1) for the "OK" label.
- **random** — labels are drawn randomly from the label probability distribution.

We rank the systems according to all the metrics and compute the level of significance for every

pair of systems with **randomisation tests** (Yeh, 2000) **with Bonferroni correction** (Abdi, 2007). In order to evaluate the metrics' performance we compute the system distinction coefficient d — the probability of two systems being significantly different, which is defined as the ratio between the number of significantly different pairs of systems and all pairs of systems. We also compute d for the top half and for the bottom half of the ranked systems list separately in order to check how well each metric can discriminate between better performing and worse performing systems.[3]

The results are shown in Table 1. For every synthetic dataset we show the number of real system outputs that were rated lower than this dataset, with the rightmost column showing the sum of this figure across all the synthetic sets.

We can see that three metrics are better at distinguishing synthetic results from real systems: SeqCor and both multiplied F_1 scores. In the case of SeqCor this result is explained by the fact that it favours longer spans of "OK" and "BAD" labels and thus penalises arbitrary labellings. The multiplications of F_1-scores have two components which penalise different labellings and balance each other. This assumption is confirmed by the fact that F_1-BAD scores become too pessimistic without the "OK" component: they both favour synthetic systems with prevailing "BAD" labels. Phrase-F_1-BAD ranks these systems the highest: **all-bad** and **pessimistic** outperform 16 out of 17 systems according to this metric.

MCC is, in contrast, too 'optimistic': the **optimistic** dataset is rated higher than most of system outputs. In addition to that, it is not good at distinguishing different systems: its system distinction coefficient is the lowest among all metric. SeqCor and phrase-F_1-multiplied, despite identifying artificial datasets, cannot discriminate between real systems: SeqCor fails with the top half systems, phrase-F_1-multiplied is bad at finding differences in the bottom half of the list.

Overall, F_1-multiplied is the only metric that performs well both in the task of distinguishing

---

[2]Systems that took part in the shared task are listed and described in (Bojar et al., 2015).

[3]d_{bottom} is always greater than d_{top} in our experiments because better performing systems tend to have closer scores under all metrics and more often are not significantly different from one another. When comparing two metrics, greater d does not imply greater d_{top} and d_{bottom}: we use Bonferroni correction for which the significance level depends on the number of compared values, so a difference which is significant when comparing eight systems, for example, can become insignificant when comparing 16 systems.

	d	d_{top}	d_{bottom}	all-bad	all-good	optimistic	pessimistic	random	total
F_1-BAD	0.79	**0.61**	**0.81**	4	-	1	4	1	10
F_1-mult	0.81	0.57	0.75	-	-	2	-	2	4
phr F_1-BAD	**0.86**	**0.61**	0.78	16	-	1	16	-	33
phr F_1-mult	0.75	0.54	0.47	-	-	1	-	-	1
MCC	0.63	**0.61**	0.34	-	-	15	-	-	15
SeqCor	0.77	0.39	0.75	-	-	1	1	2	4

Table 1: Results for all metrics. Numbers in synthetic dataset columns denote the number of system submissions that were rated lower than the corresponding synthetic dataset.

synthetic systems from real ones and in the task of discriminating among real systems, despite the fact that its d scores are not the best. However, F_1-BAD is not far behind: it has high values for d scores and can identify synthetic datasets quite often.

3.2 Comparison on synthetic datasets

The experiment described above has a notable drawback: we evaluated metrics on the outputs of systems which had been tuned to maximise the F_1-BAD score. This means that the system rankings produced by other metrics may be unfairly considered inaccurate.

Therefore, we suggest a more objective metric evaluation procedure which uses only synthetic datasets. We generate datasets with different proportion of errors, compute the metrics' values and their statistical significance and then compare the metrics' discriminative power. This procedure is further referred to as **repeated sampling**, because we sample artificial datasets multiple times.

Our goal is for the synthetic datasets to simulate real systems' output. We achieve this by using the following procedure for synthetic data generation:

- Choose the proportion of errors to introduce in the synthetic data.
- Collect all sequences that contain incorrect labels from the outputs of real systems.
- Randomly choose the sequences from this set until the overall number of errors reaches the chosen threshold.
- Take the rest of segments from the gold-standard labelling (so that they contain no errors).

Thus our artificial datasets contain a specific number of errors, and all of them come from real systems. We can generate datasets with very small differences in quality and identify metrics according to which this difference is more significant.

Let us compare the discriminative power of metrics m_1 and m_2. We choose two error thresholds e_1 and e_2. Then we sample a relatively small number (e.g. 100) of random datasets with e_1 errors. Then — 100 random datasets with e_2 errors. We compute the values for both metrics on the two sets of random samples and for each metric we test if the difference between the results for the two sets is significant (we compute the statistic significance using **non-paired t-test with Bonferroni correction**). Since we sampled the synthetic datasets a small number of times it is likely that the metrics will not detect any significant differences between them. In this case we repeat the process with a larger (e.g. 200) number of samples and compare the p-values for two metrics again. By gradually increasing the number of samples at some point we will find that one of the metrics recognises the differences in scores as statistically significant, while another one does not. This means that this metric has higher discriminative power: it needs less samples to determine that the systems they are different. The procedure is outlined in Algorithm 1.

In our experiments in order to make p-values more stable we repeat each sampling round (sampling of a set with e_i errors 100, 200, etc. times) 1,000 times and use the average of p-values. We used fixed sets of sample numbers: [100, 200, 500, 1000, 2000, 5000, 10,000] and error thresholds: [30%, 30.01%, 30.05%, 30.1%, 30.2%]. The significance level α is 0.05.

Since we compare all six metrics on five error thresholds, we have 10 p-values for each metric at every sampling round. We analyse the results in the following way: for every difference in the percentage of errors (e.g. thresholds of 30% and 30.01% give 0.01% difference, thresholds of 30% and 30.2% — 0.2% difference), we define the minimum number of samplings that a metric

	0.01	0.04	0.05	0.1	0.15	0.2
F_1-mult	10000	**2000**	**2000**	**500**	**200**	**100**
MCC	10000	**2000**	**2000**	**500**	**200**	**100**
F_1-BAD	10000	5000	**2000**	1000	500	200
phr F_1-mult	10000	5000	5000	1000	500	200
SeqCor	10000	5000	5000	1000	500	500
phr F_1-BAD	10000	10000	5000	1000	500	500

Table 2: Repeated sampling: the minimum number of samplings required to discriminate between samples with a different proportions of errors.

Result: $m_x \in \{\mathrm{m}_1, m_2\}$, where m_x — metric with the highest discriminative power on error thresholds e_1 and e_2

$N \leftarrow 100$

$\alpha \leftarrow$ significance level

while $p\text{-}val_{m_1} \geqslant \alpha$ and $p\text{-}val_{m_2} \geqslant \alpha$ **do**
  $s_1 \leftarrow$ N random samples with e_1 errors
  $s_2 \leftarrow$ N random samples with e_2 errors
  $p\text{-}val_{m_1} \leftarrow t\text{-}test(m_1(s_1), m_1(s_2))$
  $p\text{-}val_{m_2} \leftarrow t\text{-}test(m_2(s_1), m_2(s_2))$
  if $p\text{-}val_{m_1} < \alpha$ and $p\text{-}val_{m_2} \geqslant \alpha$ **then**
    | **return** m_1
  else if $p\text{-}val_{m_1} \geqslant \alpha$ and $p\text{-}val_{m_2} < \alpha$
  then
    | **return** m_2
  else
    | $N \leftarrow N + 100$
end

Algorithm 1: Repeated sampling for metrics m_1, m_2 and error thresholds e_1, e_2.

needs to observe significant differences between datasets which differ in this number of errors. Table 2 shows the results. Numbers in cells are minimum numbers of samplings. We do not show error differences greater than 0.2 because all metrics identify them well. All metrics are sorted by discriminative power from best to worst, i.e. metrics at the top of the table require less samplings to tell one synthetic dataset from another.

As in the previous experiment, here the discriminative power of the multiplication of F_1-scores is the highest. Surprisingly, MCC performs equally well. Similarly to the experiment with real systems, the F_1-BAD metric performs worse than the F_1-multiply metric, but here their difference is more salient. All phrase-motivated metrics show worse results.

4 Conclusions

The aim of this paper was to compare evaluation metrics for word and phrase-level quality estimation and find an alternative for F_1-BAD score, which has been used as primary metric in recent research but has a number of drawbacks, in particular tendency to overrate labellings with predominantly "BAD" instances.

We found that the multiplication of F_1-BAD and F_1-OK scores is more stable against "pessimistic" labellings and has bigger discriminative power when comparing synthetic datasets. However, other tested metrics, including advanced phrase-based scores, could not outperform F_1-BAD.

This work should be seen as a proxy for real user evaluation of word-level QE metrics, which could be done on downstream tasks (e.g. computer-assisted translation).

References

Hervé Abdi. 2007. The bonferroni and šidák corrections for multiple comparisons. *Encyclopedia of measurement and statistics*, 3:103 107.

Ondrej Bojar, Christian Buck, Christian Federmann, Barry Haddow, Philipp Koehn, Johannes Leveling, Christof Monz, Pavel Pecina, Matt Post, Herve Saint-Amand, Radu Soricut, Lucia Specia, and Aleš Tamchyna. 2014. Findings of the 2014 workshop on statistical machine translation. In *Proceedings of the Ninth Workshop on Statistical Machine Translation*, pages 12 58, Baltimore, Maryland, USA, June. Association for Computational Linguistics.

Ondřej Bojar, Rajen Chatterjee, Christian Federmann, Barry Haddow, Matthias Huck, Chris Hokamp, Philipp Koehn, Varvara Logacheva, Christof Monz, Matteo Negri, Matt Post, Carolina Scarton, Lucia Specia, and Marco Turchi. 2015. Findings of the 2015 workshop on statistical machine translation. In *Proceedings of the Tenth Workshop on Statistical Machine Translation*, pages 1–46, Lisbon, Portugal.

Simona Gandrabur and George Foster. 2003. Confidence estimation for translation prediction. In *HLT-NAACL-2003*, pages 95–102, Edmonton, Canada.

Yvette Graham. 2015. Improving evaluation of machine translation quality estimation. In *Proceedings of the 53rd Annual Meeting of the Association for Computational Linguistics and the 7th International Joint Conference on Natural Language Processing (Volume 1: Long Papers)*, pages 1804–1813.

Ngoc Quang Luong, Laurent Besacier, and Benjamin Lecouteux. 2014. Lig system for word level qe task at wmt14. In *WMT-2014*, pages 335–341, Baltimore, USA, June.

David M.W. Powers. 2011. Evaluation: from precision, recall and F-measure to ROC, informedness, markedness and correlation. *Journal of Machine Learning Technologies*, 2(1):37–63.

Carolina Scarton, Liling Tan, and Lucia Specia. 2015. Ushef and usaar-ushef participation in the wmt15 qe shared task. In *Proceedings of the Tenth Workshop on Statistical Machine Translation*, pages 336–341, Lisbon, Portugal, September.

Kashif Shah, Trevor Cohn, and Lucia Specia. 2013. An investigation on the effectiveness of features for translation quality estimation. In *MT Summit XIV*, pages 167–174, Nice, France.

Erik F. Tjong Kim Sang and Fien De Meulder. 2003. Introduction to the conll-2003 shared task: Language-independent named entity recognition. In *Proceedings of CoNLL-2003*, pages 142–147.

Guillaume Wisniewski, Anil Kumar Singh, Natalia Segal, and François Yvon. 2013. Design and Analysis of a Large Corpus of Post-Edited Translations: Quality Estimation, Failure Analysis and the Variability of Post-Edition. In *MT Summit XIV: 14th Machine Translation Summit*, pages 117–124, Nice, France.

Alexander Yeh. 2000. More accurate tests for the statistical significance of result differences. In *Coling-2000: the 18th Conference on Computational Linguistics*, pages 947–953, Saarbrücken, Germany.

The Social Impact of Natural Language Processing

Dirk Hovy
Center for Language Technology
University of Copenhagen
Copenhagen, Denmark
dirk.hovy@hum.ku.dk

Shannon L. Spruit
Ethics & Philosophy of Technology
Delft University of Technology
Delft, The Netherlands
s.l.spruit@tudelft.nl

Abstract

Medical sciences have long since established an ethics code for experiments, to minimize the risk of harm to subjects. Natural language processing (NLP) used to involve mostly anonymous corpora, with the goal of enriching linguistic analysis, and was therefore unlikely to raise ethical concerns. As NLP becomes increasingly wide-spread and uses more data from social media, however, the situation has changed: the outcome of NLP experiments and applications *can* now have a direct effect on individual users' lives. Until now, the discourse on this topic in the field has not followed the technological development, while public discourse was often focused on exaggerated dangers. This position paper tries to take back the initiative and start a discussion. We identify a number of social implications of NLP and discuss their ethical significance, as well as ways to address them.

1 Introduction

After the Nuremberg trials revealed the atrocities conducted in medical research by the Nazis, medical sciences established a set of rules to determine whether an experiment is ethical. This involved incorporating the principles of biomedical ethics as a *lingua franca* of medical ethics (Beauchamp and Childress, 2001).

These guidelines were designed to balance the potential value of conducting an experiment while preventing the exploitation of human subjects. Today, any responsible research institution uses these—or comparable—criteria to approve or reject experiments before any research can be conducted. The administrative body governing these decisions is the Institutional Review Board (IRB).

IRBs mostly pertain to experiments that directly involve human subjects, though, and so NLP and other data sciences have not employed such guidelines. Work on existing corpora is unlikely to raise any flags that would require an IRB approval.[1]

Data sciences have therefore traditionally been less engaged in ethical debates of their subject, even though this seems to be shifting, see for instance Wallach (2014), Galaz et al. (2015), or O'Neil (2016). The public outcry over the "emotional contagion" experiment on Facebook (Kramer et al., 2014) further suggests that data sciences now affect human subjects in real time, and that we might have to reconsider the application of ethical considerations to our research (Puschmann and Bozdag, 2014). NLP research not only involves similar data sets, but also works with their content, so it is time to start a discussion of the ethical issues specific to our field.

Much of the ethical discussion in data sciences to date, however, has centered around privacy concerns (Tse et al., 2015). We do not deny the reality and importance of those concerns, but they involve aspects of digital rights management/access control, policy making, and security, which are not specific to NLP, but need to be addressed in the data sciences community as a whole. Steps towards this have been taken by Russell et al. (2015).

Instead, we want to move beyond privacy in our ethical analysis and look at the wider **social impact** NLP may have. In particular, we want to explore the impact of NLP on social justice, i.e., equal opportunities for individuals and groups (such as minorities) within society to access resources, get their voice heard, and be represented in society.

---

[1] With few exceptions, such as dialogue research (Joel Tetreault, pers. comm.)

Proceedings of the 54th Annual Meeting of the Association for Computational Linguistics, pages 591–598,
Berlin, Germany, August 7-12, 2016. ©2016 Association for Computational Linguistics

Our contributions We believe ethical discussions are more constructive if led by practitioners, since the public discussion of ethical aspects of IT and data sciences is often loaded with fear of the unknown and unrealistic expectations. For example, in the public discourse about AI (Hsu, 2012; Eadicicco, 2015; Khatchadourian, 2015), people either dismiss the entire approach, or exaggerate the potential dangers (see Etzioni (2014) for a practioner's view point). This paper is an attempt to take back the initiative for NLP.

At the same time, we believe that the field of ethics can contribute a more general framework, and so this paper is an interdisciplinary collaboration between NLP and ethics researchers.

To facilitate the discussion, we also provide some of the relevant **terminology** from the literature on ethics of technology, namely the concepts of *exclusion, overgeneralization, bias confirmation, topic under- and overexposure*, and *dual use*.

2 Does NLP need an ethics discussion?

As discussed above, the makeup of most NLP experiments so far has not obviated a need for ethical considerations, and so, while we are aware of individual discussions (Strube, 2015), there is little discourse in the community yet. A search for *"ethic*"* in the ACL anthology only yields three results. One of the papers (McEnery, 2002) turns out to be a panel discussion, another is a book review, leaving only Couillault et al. (2014), who devote most of the discussion to legal and quality issues of data sets. We know social implications have been addressed in some NLP curricula,[2] but until now, no discipline-wide discussion seems to take place.

The most likely reason is that NLP research has not directly involved human subjects.[3] Historically, most NLP applications focused on further enriching existing text which was not strongly linked to any particular author (newswire), was usually published publicly, and often with some temporal distance (novels). All these factors created a distance between text and author, which prevented the research from directly affecting the authors' situation.

---

²Héctor Martínez Alonso, personal communication

³Except for annotation: there are a number of papers on the status of crowdsource workers (Fort et al., 2011; Pavlick et al., 2014).Couillault et al. (2014) also briefly discuss annotators, but mainly in the context of quality control.

This situation has changed lately due to the increased use of social media data, where authors are current individuals, who can be directly affected by the results of NLP applications. Couillault et al. (2014) touch upon these issues under "traceability" (i.e., whether individuals can be identified): this is undesirable for experimental subjects, but might be useful in the case of annotators.

Most importantly, though: the subject of NLP—language—is a *proxy for human behavior*, and a strong signal of individual characteristics. People use this signal consciously, to portray themselves in a certain way, but can also be identified as members of specific groups by their use of subconscious traits (Silverstein, 2003; Agha, 2005; Johannsen et al., 2015; Hovy and Johannsen, 2016).

Language is always *situated* (Bamman et al., 2014), i.e., it is uttered in a specific situation at a particular place and time, and by an individual speaker with all the characteristics outlined above. All of these factors can therefore leave an imprint on the utterance, i.e., the texts we use in NLP carry *latent* information about the author and situation, albeit to varying degrees.

This information can be used to predict author characteristics from text (Rosenthal and McKeown, 2011; Nguyen et al., 2011; Alowibdi et al., 2013; Ciot et al., 2013; Liu and Ruths, 2013; Volkova et al., 2014; Volkova et al., 2015; Plank and Hovy, 2015; Preotiuc-Pietro et al., 2015a; Preoţiuc-Pietro et al., 2015b), and the characteristics in turn can be detected by and influence the performance of our models (Mandel et al., 2012; Volkova et al., 2013; Hovy, 2015).

As more and more language-based technologies are becoming available, the ethical implications of NLP research become more important. What research is carried out, and its quality, directly affect the functionality and impact of those technologies.

The following is meant to start a discussion addressing ethical issues that can emerge in (and from) NLP research.

3 The social impact of NLP research

We have outlined the relation between language and individual traits above. Language is also a political instrument, though, and an instrument of power. This influence stretches into politics and everyday competition, for example for turn-taking (Laskowski, 2010; Bracewell and Tomlinson, 2012; Prabhakaran and Rambow, 2013; Prabhakaran et al., 2014; Tsur et al., 2015; Khouzami et al., 2015, inter alia), .

The mutual relationships between language, society, and the individual are also the source for the societal impact factors of NLP: failing to recognize group membership (Section 3.1), implying the wrong group membership (see Section 3.2), and overexposure (Section 3.3). In the following, we discuss sources of these problems in the data, modeling, and research design, and suggest possible solutions to address them.

3.1 Exclusion

As a result of the situatedness of language, any data set carries a **demographic bias**, i.e., latent information about the demographics in it. Overfitting to these factors can have have severe effects on the applicability of findings. In psychology, where most studies are based on western, educated, industrialized, rich, and democratic research participants (so-called WEIRD, Henrich et al. (2010)), the tacit assumption that human nature is so universal that findings on this group would translate to other demographics has led to a heavily biased corpus of psychological data. In NLP, overfitting to the demographic bias in the training data is due to the *i.i.d.* assumption. I.e., models implicitly assume all language to be identical to the training sample. They therefore perform worse or even fail on data from other demographics.

Potential consequences are **exclusion** or demographic misrepresentation. This in itself already represents an ethical problem for research purposes, threatening the universality and objectivity of scientific knowledge (Merton, 1973). These problems exacerbate, though, once they are applied to products. For instance, standard language technology may be easier to use for white males from California (as these are taken into account while developing it) rather than women or citizens of Latino or Arabic descent. This will reinforce already existing demographic differences, and makes technology less user friendly for such groups, cf. authors like Bourdieu and Passeron (1990) have shown how restricted language, like class specific language or scientific jargon, can hinder the expression of outsiders' voices from certain practices. A lack of awareness or decreased attention for demographic differences in research stages can therefore lead to issues of exclusion of people along the way.

Concretely, the consequences of exclusion for NLP research have recently been pointed out by Hovy and Søgaard (2015) and Jørgensen et al. (2015): current state-of-the-art NLP models score a significantly lower accuracy for young people and ethnic minorities vis-à-vis the modeled demographics.

Better awareness of these mechanism in NLP research and development can help prevent problems further on. Potential counter-measures to demographic bias can be as simple as downsampling the over-represented group in the training data to even out the distribution. The work by Mohammady and Culotta (2014) shows another approach, by using existing demographic statistics as supervision. In general, measures to address overfitting or imbalanced data can be used to correct for demographic bias in data.

3.2 Overgeneralization

Exclusion is a side-effect of the data. **Overgeneralization** is a modeling side-effect.

As an example, we consider automatic inference of user attributes, a common and interesting NLP task, whose solution also holds promise for many useful applications, such as recommendation engines and fraud or deception detection (Badaskar et al., 2008; Fornaciari and Poesio, 2014; Ott et al., 2011; Banerjee et al., 2014).

The cost of false positives seems low: we might be puzzled or amused when receiving an email addressing us with the wrong gender, or congratulating us to our retirement on our 30th birthday.

In practice, though, relying on models that produce false positives may lead to bias confirmation and overgeneralization. Would we accept the same error rates if the system was used to predict sexual orientation or religious views, rather than age or gender? Given the right training data, this is just a matter of changing the target variable.

To address overgeneralization, the guiding question should be "would a false answer be worse than no answer?" We can use dummy variables, rather than take a *tertium non datur* approach to classification, and employ measures such as error weighting and model regularization, as well as confidence thresholds.

3.3 The problem of exposure

Topic overexposure creates biases Both exclusion and overgeneralization can be addressed algo-

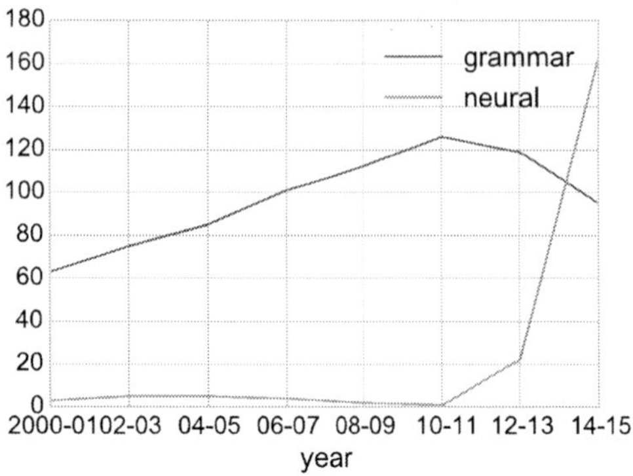

Figure 1: ACL title keywords over time

rithmically, while **topic overexposure** originates from research design.

In research, we can observe this effect in waves of research topics that receive increased mainstream attention, often to fall out of fashion or become more specialized, cf. ACL papers with "grammars" vs. "neural" in the title (Figure 1).

Such topic overexposure may lead to a psychological effect called **availability heuristic** (Tversky and Kahneman, 1973): if people can recall a certain event, or have knowledge about specific things, they infer it must be more important. For instance, people estimate the size of cities they recognize to be larger than that of unknown cities (Goldstein and Gigerenzer, 2002).

However, the same holds for individuals/groups/characteristics we research. The heuristics become ethically charged when characteristics such as violence or negative emotions are more strongly associated with certain groups or ethnicities (Slovic et al., 2007). If research repeatedly found that the language of a certain demographic group was harder to process, it could create a situation where this group was perceived to be difficult, or abnormal, especially in the presence of existing biases. The confirmation of biases through the gendered use of language, for example, has also been at the core of second and third wave feminism (Mills, 2012).

Overexposure thus creates biases which can lead to discrimination. To some extent, the frantic public discussion on the dangers of AI can be seen as a result of overexposure (Sunstein, 2004).

There are no easy solutions to this problem, which might only become apparent in hindsight. It can help to assess whether the research direction of a project feeds into existing biases, or whether it overexposes certain groups.

Underexposure can negatively impact evaluation. Similar to the WEIRD-situation in psychology, NLP tends to focus on Indo-European data/text sources, rather than small languages from other language groups, for example in Asia or Africa. This focus creates an imbalance in the available amounts of labeled data. Most of the exisitng labeled data covers only a small set of languages. When analyzing a random sample of Twitter data from 2013, we found that there were no treebanks for 11 of the 31 most frequent languages, and even fewer semantically annotated resources (the ACE corpus covers only English, Arabic, Chinese, and Spanish).[4]

Even if there is a potential wealth of data available from other languages, most NLP tools are geared towards English (Schnoebelen, 2013; Munro, 2013). The prevalence of resources for English has created an **underexposure** to typological variety: both morphology and syntax of English are global outliers. Would we have focused on n-gram models to the same extent if English was as morhpologically complex as, say, Finnish?

While there are many approaches to develop multi-lingual and cross-lingual NLP tools for linguistic outliers (Yarowsky and Ngai, 2001; Das and Petrov, 2011; Søgaard, 2011; Søgaard et al., 2015; Agić et al., 2015), there simply are more commercial incentives to overexpose English, rather than other languages. Even if other languages are equally (or more) interesting from a linguistic and cultural point of view, English is one of the most widely spoken language and therefore opens up the biggest market for NLP tools. This focus on English may be self-reinforcing: the existence of off-the-shelf tools for English makes it easy to try new ideas, while to start exploring other languages requires a higher startup cost in terms of basic models, so researchers are less likely to work on them.

4 Dual-use problems

Even if we address all of the above concerns and do not intend any harm in our experiments, they can still have unintended consequences that negatively affect people's lives (Jonas, 1984).

Advanced analysis techniques can vastly improve search and educational applications

---

[4]Thanks to Barbara Plank for the analysis!

(Tetreault et al., 2015), but can re-enforce pre-scriptive linguistic norms when degrading on non-standard language. Stylometric analysis can shed light on the provenance of historic texts (Mosteller and Wallace, 1963), but also endanger the anonymity of political dissenters. Text classification approaches help decode slang and hidden messages (Huang et al., 2013), but have the potential to be used for censorship. At the same time, NLP can also help uncovering such restrictions (Bamman et al., 2012). As recently shown by Hovy (2016), NLP techniques can be used to detect fake reviews, but also to generate them in the first place.

All these examples indicate that we should become more aware of the way other people appropriate NLP technology for their own purposes. The unprecedented scale and availability can make the consequences of NLP technologies hard to gauge.

The unintended consequences of research are also linked to the incentives associated with funding sources. The topic of government and military involvement in the field deserves special attention in this respect. On the one hand, Anderson et al. (2012) show how a series of DARPA-funded workshops have been formative for ACL as a field in the 1990s. On the other hand, there are scholars who refuse military-related funding for moral reasons.[5]

While this decision is up to the individual researcher, the examples show that moral considerations go beyond the immediate research projects. We may not directly be held responsible for the unintended consequences of our research, but we can acknowledge the ways in which NLP can enable morally questionable/sensitive practices, raise awareness, and lead the discourse on it in an informed manner. The role of the researcher in such ethical discussions has recently been pointed out by Rogaway (2015).

5 Conclusion

In this position paper, we outlined the potential social impact of NLP, and discussed ways for the practitioner to address this. We also introduced *exclusion, overgeneralization, bias confirmation, topic overexposure*, and *dual use*. Countermeasures for exclusion include bias control techniques

like downsampling or priors; for overgeneralization: dummy labels, error weighting, or confidence thresholds. Exposure problems can only be addressed by careful research design, and dual-use problems seem hardly addressable on the level of the individual researcher, but require the concerted effort of our community.

We hope this paper can point out ethical considerations for collecting our data, designing the experimental setup, and assessing the potential application of our systems, and help start an open discussion in the field about the limitations and problems of our methodology.

Acknowledgements

The authors would like to thank Joel Tetrault, Rachel Tatman, Joel C. Wallenberg, the members of the COASTAL group, and the anonymous reviewers for their detailed and invaluable feedback. The first author was funded under the ERC Starting Grant LOWLANDS No. 313695. The second author was funded by the Netherlands Organization for Scientific Research under grant number 016.114.625.

References

Asif Agha. 2005. Voice, footing, enregisterment. *Journal of linguistic anthropology*, pages 38–59.

Željko Agić, Dirk Hovy, and Anders Søgaard. 2015. If all you have is a bit of the Bible: Learning POS taggers for truly low-resource languages. In *Proceedings of the 53rd annual meeting of the ACL*.

Jalal S Alowibdi, Ugo A Buy, and Philip Yu. 2013. Empirical evaluation of profile characteristics for gender classification on twitter. In *Machine Learning and Applications (ICMLA), 2013 12th International Conference on*, volume 1, pages 365–369. IEEE.

Ashton Anderson, Dan McFarland, and Dan Jurafsky. 2012. Towards a computational history of the ACL: 1980-2008. In *Proceedings of the ACL-2012 Special Workshop on Rediscovering 50 Years of Discoveries*, pages 13–21. Association for Computational Linguistics.

Sameer Badaskar, Sachin Agarwal, and Shilpa Arora. 2008. Identifying real or fake articles: Towards better language modeling. In *Proceedings of the Third International Joint Conference on Natural Language Processing: Volume-II*.

David Bamman, Brendan O'Connor, and Noah Smith. 2012. Censorship and deletion practices in Chinese social media. *First Monday*, 17(3).

---

[5] For a perspective in a related field see `https://web.eecs.umich.edu/~kuipers/opinions/no-military-funding.html`

David Bamman, Chris Dyer, and Noah A. Smith. 2014. Distributed representations of geographically situated language. In *Proceedings of the 52nd Annual Meeting of the Association for Computational Linguistics*, pages 828–834. Proceedings of ACL.

Ritwik Banerjee, Song Feng, Seok Jun Kang, and Yejin Choi. 2014. Keystroke patterns as prosody in digital writings: A case study with deceptive reviews and essays. In *Proceedings of the 2014 Conference on Empirical Methods in Natural Language Processing (EMNLP)*, pages 1469–1473. Association for Computational Linguistics.

Tom L Beauchamp and James F Childress. 2001. *Principles of biomedical ethics*. Oxford University Press, USA.

Pierre Bourdieu and Jean-Claude Passeron. 1990. *Reproduction in education, society and culture*, volume 4. Sage.

David Bracewell and Marc Tomlinson. 2012. The language of power and its cultural influence. In *Proceedings of COLING 2012: Posters*, pages 155–164. The COLING 2012 Organizing Committee.

Morgane Ciot, Morgan Sonderegger, and Derek Ruths. 2013. Gender Inference of Twitter Users in Non-English Contexts. In *Proceedings of the 2013 Conference on Empirical Methods in Natural Language Processing, Seattle, Wash*, pages 18–21.

Alain Couillault, Karën Fort, Gilles Adda, and Hugues Mazancourt (de). 2014. Evaluating corpora documentation with regards to the Ethics and Big Data Charter. In *Proceedings of the Ninth International Conference on Language Resources and Evaluation (LREC-2014)*. European Language Resources Association (ELRA).

Dipanjan Das and Slav Petrov. 2011. Unsupervised part-of-speech tagging with bilingual graph-based projections. In *Proceedings of the 49th annual meeting of the ACL*.

Lisa Eadicicco. 2015. Bill Gates: Elon Musk Is Right, We Should All Be Scared Of Artificial Intelligence Wiping Out Humanity. Business Insider, January 28. http://www.businessinsider.com/bill-gates-artificial-intelligence-2015-1 Retrieved Feb 24, 2016.

Oren Etzioni. 2014. Its Time to Intelligently Discuss Artificial Intelligence. Backchannel, December 9 https://backchannel.com/ai-wont-exterminate-us-it-will-empower-us-5b7224735bf3#.eia6vtimy Retrieved Feb 24, 2016.

Tommaso Fornaciari and Massimo Poesio. 2014. Identifying fake amazon reviews as learning from crowds. In *Proceedings of the 14th Conference of the European Chapter of the Association for Computational Linguistics*, pages 279–287. Association for Computational Linguistics.

Karën Fort, Gilles Adda, and K Bretonnel Cohen. 2011. Amazon mechanical turk: Gold mine or coal mine? *Computational Linguistics*, 37(2):413–420.

Victor Galaz, Fredrik Moberg, and Fernanda Torre. 2015. The Biosphere Code Manifesto. http://thebiospherecode.com/index.php/manifesto Retrieved Feb 24, 2016.

Daniel G Goldstein and Gerd Gigerenzer. 2002. Models of ecological rationality: the recognition heuristic. *Psychological review*, 109(1):75.

Joseph Henrich, Steven J Heine, and Ara Norenzayan. 2010. The weirdest people in the world? *Behavioral and brain sciences*, 33(2-3):61–83.

Dirk Hovy and Anders Johannsen. 2016. Exploring Language Variation Across Europe - A Web-based Tool for Computational Sociolinguistics. In *Proceedings of LREC*.

Dirk Hovy and Anders Søgaard. 2015. Tagging performance correlates with author age. In *Proceedings of the 53rd Annual Meeting of the Association for Computational Linguistics*.

Dirk Hovy. 2015. Demographic factors improve classification performance. In *Proceedings of the 53rd Annual Meeting of the Association for Computational Linguistics*.

Dirk Hovy. 2016. The Enemy in Your Own Camp: How Well Can We Detect Statistically-Generated Fake Reviews–An Adversarial Study. In *Proceedings of the 54th Annual Meeting of the Association for Computational Linguistics*. Association for Computational Linguistics.

Jeremy Hsu. 2012. Control dangerous AI before it controls us, one expert says. NBC News, March 1. http://www.nbcnews.com/id/46590591/ns/technology_and_science-innovation Retrieved Feb 24, 2016.

Hongzhao Huang, Zhen Wen, Dian Yu, Heng Ji, Yizhou Sun, Jiawei Han, and He Li. 2013. Resolving entity morphs in censored data. In *Proceedings of the 51st Annual Meeting of the Association for Computational Linguistics (Volume 1: Long Papers)*, pages 1083–1093. Association for Computational Linguistics.

Anders Johannsen, Dirk Hovy, and Anders Søgaard. 2015. Cross-lingual syntactic variation over age and gender. In *Proceedings of CoNLL*.

Hans Jonas. 1984. *The Imperative of Responsibility: Foundations of an Ethics for the Technological Age*. Original in German: Prinzip Verantwortung.) Chicago: University of Chicago Press.

Anna Jørgensen, Dirk Hovy, and Anders Søgaard. 2015. Challenges of studying and processing dialects in social media. In *Workshop on Noisy User-generated Text (W-NUT)*.

Raffi Khatchadourian. 2015. The Doomsday Invention: Will artificial intelligence bring us utopia or destruction? The New Yorker (magazine), November 23. http://www.newyorker.com/magazine/2015/11/23/doomsday-invention-artificial-intelligence-nick-bostrom Retrieved Feb 24, 2016.

Hatim Khouzami, Romain Laroche, and Fabrice Lefevre, 2015. *Proceedings of the 16th Annual Meeting of the Special Interest Group on Discourse and Dialogue*, chapter Optimising Turn-Taking Strategies With Reinforcement Learning, pages 315–324. Association for Computational Linguistics.

Adam DI Kramer, Jamie E Guillory, and Jeffrey T Hancock. 2014. Experimental evidence of massive-scale emotional contagion through social networks. *Proceedings of the National Academy of Sciences*, 111(24):8788–8790.

Kornel Laskowski. 2010. Modeling norms of turn-taking in multi-party conversation. In *Proceedings of the 48th Annual Meeting of the Association for Computational Linguistics*, pages 999–1008. Association for Computational Linguistics.

Wendy Liu and Derek Ruths. 2013. What's in a name? using first names as features for gender inference in twitter. In *Analyzing Microtext: 2013 AAAI Spring Symposium*.

Benjamin Mandel, Aron Culotta, John Boulahanis, Danielle Stark, Bonnie Lewis, and Jeremy Rodrigue, 2012. *Proceedings of the Second Workshop on Language in Social Media*, chapter A Demographic Analysis of Online Sentiment during Hurricane Irene, pages 27–36. Association for Computational Linguistics.

Tony McEnery. 2002. Ethical and legal issues in corpus construction. In *Proceedings of the Third International Conference on Language Resources and Evaluation (LREC'02)*. European Language Resources Association (ELRA).

Robert K Merton. 1973. The normative structure of science. *The sociology of science: Theoretical and empirical investigations*, 267.

Sara Mills. 2012. *Gender matters: Feminist linguistic analysis*. Equinox Pub

Ehsan Mohammady and Aron Culotta, 2014. *Proceedings of the Joint Workshop on Social Dynamics and Personal Attributes in Social Media*, chapter Using County Demographics to Infer Attributes of Twitter Users, pages 7–16. Association for Computational Linguistics.

Frederick Mosteller and David L Wallace. 1963. Inference in an authorship problem: A comparative study of discrimination methods applied to the authorship of the disputed federalist papers. *Journal of the American Statistical Association*, 58(302):275–309.

Robert Munro. 2013. NLP for all languages. Idibon Blog, May 22 http://idibon.com/nlp-for-all Retrieved May 17, 2016.

Dong Nguyen, Noah A Smith, and Carolyn P Rosé. 2011. Author age prediction from text using linear regression. In *Proceedings of the 5th ACL-HLT Workshop on Language Technology for Cultural Heritage, Social Sciences, and Humanities*, pages 115–123. Association for Computational Linguistics.

Cathy O'Neil. 2016. The Ethical Data Scientist. Slate, February 4 http://www.slate.com/articles/technology/future_tense/2016/02/how_to_bring_better_ethics_to_data_science.html Retrieved Feb 24, 2016.

Myle Ott, Yejin Choi, Claire Cardie, and T. Jeffrey Hancock. 2011. Finding deceptive opinion spam by any stretch of the imagination. In *Proceedings of the 49th Annual Meeting of the Association for Computational Linguistics: Human Language Technologies*, pages 309–319. Association for Computational Linguistics.

Ellie Pavlick, Matt Post, Ann Irvine, Dmitry Kachaev, and Chris Callison-Burch. 2014. The language demographics of amazon mechanical turk. *Transactions of the Association of Computational Linguistics – Volume 2, Issue 1*, pages 79–92.

Barbara Plank and Dirk Hovy. 2015. Personality traits on twitterorhow to get 1,500 personality tests in a week. In *Proceedings of the 6th Workshop on Computational Approaches to Subjectivity, Sentiment and Social Media Analysis*, pages 92–98.

Vinodkumar Prabhakaran and Owen Rambow. 2013. Written dialog and social power: Manifestations of different types of power in dialog behavior. In *Proceedings of the Sixth International Joint Conference on Natural Language Processing*, pages 216–224. Asian Federation of Natural Language Processing.

Vinodkumar Prabhakaran, Ashima Arora, and Owen Rambow. 2014. Staying on topic: An indicator of power in political debates. In *Proceedings of the 2014 Conference on Empirical Methods in Natural Language Processing (EMNLP)*, pages 1481–1486. Association for Computational Linguistics.

Daniel Preotiuc-Pietro, Vasileios Lampos, and Nikolaos Aletras. 2015a. An analysis of the user occupational class through twitter content. In *ACL*.

Daniel Preoţiuc-Pietro, Svitlana Volkova, Vasileios Lampos, Yoram Bachrach, and Nikolaos Aletras. 2015b. Studying user income through language, behaviour and affect in social media. *PloS one*, 10(9):e0138717.

Cornelius Puschmann and Engin Bozdag. 2014. Staking out the unclear ethical terrain of online social experiments. *Internet Policy Review*, 3(4).

Phillip Rogaway. 2015. The moral character of cryptographic work. Technical report, IACR-Cryptology ePrint Archive.

Sara Rosenthal and Kathleen McKeown. 2011. Age prediction in blogs: A study of style, content, and online behavior in pre-and post-social media generations. In *Proceedings of the 49th Annual Meeting of the Association for Computational Linguistics: Human Language Technologies-Volume 1*, pages 763–772. Association for Computational Linguistics.

Stuart Russell, Daniel Dewey, Max Tegmark, Janos Kramar, and Richard Mallah. 2015. Research priorities for robust and beneficial artificial intelligence. Technical report, Future of Life Institute.

Tyler Schnoebelen. 2013. The weirdest languages. Idibon Blog, June 21 `http://idibon.com/the-weirdest-languages` Retrieved May 17, 2016.

Michael Silverstein. 2003. Indexical order and the dialectics of sociolinguistic life. *Language & Communication*, 23(3):193–229.

Paul Slovic, Melissa L. Finucane, Ellen Peters, and Donald G. MacGregor. 2007. The affect heuristic. *European Journal of Operational Research*, 177(3):1333 – 1352.

Anders Søgaard, Željko Agić, Héctor Martínez Alonso, Barbara Plank, Bernd Bohnet, and Anders Johannsen. 2015. Inverted indexing for cross-lingual nlp. In *Proceedings of the 53rd annual meeting of the ACL*.

Anders Søgaard. 2011. Data point selection for cross-language adaptation of dependency parsers. In *Proceedings of ACL*.

Michael Strube. 2015. It is never as simple as it seems: The wide-ranging impacts of ethics violations. *Ethical Challenges in the Behavioral and Brain Sciences*, page 126.

Cass R Sunstein. 2004. Precautions against what? the availability heuristic and cross-cultural risk perceptions. *U Chicago Law & Economics, Olin Working Paper*, (220):04–22.

Joel Tetreault, Jill Burstein, and Claudia Leacock, 2015. *Proceedings of the Tenth Workshop on Innovative Use of NLP for Building Educational Applications*, chapter Proceedings of the Tenth Workshop on Innovative Use of NLP for Building Educational Applications. Association for Computational Linguistics.

Jonathan Tse, Dawn E Schrader, Dipayan Ghosh, Tony Liao, and David Lundie. 2015. A bibliometric analysis of privacy and ethics in ieee security and privacy. *Ethics and Information Technology*, 17(2):153–163.

Oren Tsur, Dan Calacci, and David Lazer. 2015. A frame of mind: Using statistical models for detection of framing and agenda setting campaigns. In *Proceedings of the 53rd Annual Meeting of the Association for Computational Linguistics and the 7th International Joint Conference on Natural Language Processing (Volume 1: Long Papers)*, pages 1629–1638. Association for Computational Linguistics.

Amos Tversky and Daniel Kahneman. 1973. Availability: A heuristic for judging frequency and probability. *Cognitive psychology*, 5(2):207–232.

Svitlana Volkova, Theresa Wilson, and David Yarowsky. 2013. Exploring demographic language variations to improve multilingual sentiment analysis in social media. In *Proceedings of EMNLP*, pages 1815–1827.

Svitlana Volkova, Glen Coppersmith, and Benjamin Van Durme. 2014. Inferring user political preferences from streaming communications. In *Proceedings of the 52nd annual meeting of the ACL*, pages 186–196.

Svitlana Volkova, Yoram Bachrach, Michael Armstrong, and Vijay Sharma. 2015. Inferring latent user properties from texts published in social media (demo). In *Proceedings of the Twenty-Ninth Conference on Artificial Intelligence (AAAI)*, Austin, TX, January.

Hanna Wallach. 2014. Big Data, Machine Learning, and the Social Sciences: Fairness, Accountability, and Transparency. `https://medium.com/@hannawallach/big-data-machine-learning-and-the-social-sciences-927a8e20460d#.uhbcr4wa0` Retrieved Feb 24, 2016.

David Yarowsky and Grace Ngai. 2001. Inducing multilingual POS taggers and NP bracketers via robust projection across aligned corpora. In *Proceedings of NAACL*.

Using Sequence Similarity Networks to Identify Partial Cognates in Multilingual Wordlists

Johann-Mattis List
CRLAO/UPMC
2 rue de Lille
75007 Paris
mattis.list@lingpy.org

Philippe Lopez
UPMC
9 quai de Bernard
75005 Paris
philippe.lopez@upmc.fr

Eric Bapteste
UPMC
9 quai de Bernard
75005 Paris
eric.bapteste@upmc.fr

Abstract

Increasing amounts of digital data in historical linguistics necessitate the development of automatic methods for the detection of cognate words across languages. Recently developed methods work well on language families with moderate time depths, but they are not capable of identifying cognate morphemes in words which are only partially related. Partial cognacy, however, is a frequently recurring phenomenon, especially in language families with productive derivational morphology. This paper presents a pilot approach for partial cognate detection in which networks are used to represent similarities between word parts and cognate morphemes are identified with help of state-of-the-art algorithms for network partitioning. The approach is tested on a newly created benchmark dataset with data from three sub-branches of Sino-Tibetan and yields very promising results, outperforming all algorithms which are not sensible to partial cognacy.

1 Introduction

In a very general notion, cognacy is similar to the concept of *homology* in biology (Haggerty et al. 2014), denoting a relation between words which share a common history (List 2014b). In classical linguistics, borrowings are often excluded from this notion (Trask 2000). Quantitative approaches additionally distinguish cognates which have retained, and cognates which have shifted their meaning (Starostin 2013b). Further aspects of cognacy are rarely distinguished, although they are obvious and common. Words which go back to the same ancestor form can for example have been morphologically modified, such as French *soleil* which does not go directly back to Latin *sōl* `sun' but to *sōliculus* `small sun' which is itself a derivation of *sōl* (Meyer-Lübke 1911).

Variety	Form	Character	Cognacy
Fúzhōu	ŋuoʔ^5	月	1
Měixiàn	ŋiat^5 kuoŋ^{44}	月光	1 2
Wēnzhōu	ny^{31} kuɔ^{35} vai^{13}	月光佛	1 2 3
Běijīng	yɛ^{51} liaŋ$^?$	月亮	1 4

Table 1: Partial cognacy in Chinese dialects.

Another problem are words which have been created from two or more morphemes via processes of *compounding*. While these cases are rather rare in the core vocabulary of Indo-European languages, they are very frequent in South-East Asian language families like Sino-Tibetan or Austro-Asiatic. In 200 basic words across 23 Chinese dialects (Ben Hamed and Wang 2006), for example, almost 50% of the nouns and more than 30% of all words consist of two or more morphemes (see the Sup. Material for details).

The presence of words consisting of more than one morpheme challenges the notion that words can either be cognate or not. It poses problems for phylogenetic approaches which require binary presence-absence matrices as input and model language evolution as cognate gain and cognate loss (Atkinson and Gray 2006). This is illustrated in Table 1 where words for `moon' in four Chinese dialects (Hóu 2004) are compared, with cognate elements being given the same color. If we assign cognacy *strictly*, only matching those words which are identical in all their elements (Ben Hamed and Wang 2006), we would have to label all words as being not cognate. If we assign cognacy *loosely* (Satterthwaite-Phillips 2011), labeling all words as cognate when only they share a common morpheme, we would have to label all

Proceedings of the 54th Annual Meeting of the Association for Computational Linguistics, pages 599–605,
Berlin, Germany, August 7-12, 2016. ©2016 Association for Computational Linguistics

words as cognate. No matter how we code in phylogenetic analyses, as long as we use binary states, we will loose information (List 2016).

Partial cognacy is also a problem for current cognate detection algorithms which compare words in their entirety (List 2014b, Turchin et al. 2010). Given the frequency of compound words in South-East Asian languages, it is not surprising that the algorithms perform much worse on diverse South-East Asian language families, than they perform on other language families where compounding is less frequent (List 2014b:197f).

This paper presents a new algorithm for cognate detection which does not identify cognate *words* but instead searches for cognate *elements* in words. The algorithm takes multilingual word lists as input and outputs statements regarding the cognacy of morphemes, just as the ones shown in the last column of Table 1, where identical numerical IDs are given for all morphemes identified as cognate.

Dataset	Bai	Chinese	Tujia
Languages	9	18	5
Words	1028	3653	513
Concepts	110	180	109
Strict Cogn.	285	1231	247
Partial Cogn.	309	1408	348
Sounds	94	122	57
Source	Wang, 2006	Běijīng Dàxué, 1964	Starostin, 2013b

Table 2: Partial cognate detection gold standard

2 Materials

Three gold standard datasets from different branches of Sino-Tibetan with different degrees of diversity were prepared, including Bai dialects, Chinese dialects, and Tujia dialects. All datasets were taken from existing datasets with cognate codings provided independently. To facilitate further use of the data, all languages were linked to Glottolog (Hammarström et al. 2015) and all concepts were linked to the Concepticon (List et al. 2016a). Furthermore, phonetic transcriptions were cleaned by segmenting phonetic entries into meaningful sound units and unifying phonetic variants representing the same pronunciation. Morphological segmentation was not required, since all languages in our sample (and the majority of all South-East Asian languages) have a morpheme-syllabic structure in which each syllable denotes one morpheme. Partial cognate judgments are displayed with help of multiple integer IDs assigned to a word in the order of its morphemes, as displayed above in Table 1. For the Chinese dataset, partial cognate information was provided in the source itself, for Bai and Tujia, it was manually derived from the cognate judgments in the sources. Detailed information regarding the datasets is given in Table 2, and the full dataset along with further information is given in the Sup. Material.

3 Methods

The workflow for partial cognate detection consists of three major steps. (1) In a first step, pairwise sequence similarities are determined between all morphemes of all words in the same meaning slot in a word list. (2) These similarities are then used to create a similarity network in which nodes represent morphemes and edges between the nodes represent similarities between the morphemes. (3) In a third step, an algorithm for network partitioning is used to cluster the nodes of the network into groups of cognate morphemes.

3.1 Sequence Similarity

There are various ways to determine the similarity or distance between words and morphemes. A general distinction can be made between *language-independent* and *language-specific* approaches. The former determine the word similarity independently of the languages to which the words belong. As a result, the scores only depend on the substantial and structural differences between words. Examples for language-independent similarity measures are SCA distances, as produced by the Sound-Class-Based Phonetic Alignment algorithm (List 2012b), or PMI similarities as produced by the Weighted String Alignment algorithm (Jäger 2013). Language-specific approaches, on the other hand, are based on previously identified recurring correspondences between the languages from which the words are taken (List 2014b: 48-50) and may differ across languages.[1] An example for language-specific similarity measures is the LexStat algorithm, first proposed in List (2012a) and later refined in List

---

[1]Comparing, for example, German *Kuckuck* with French *coucou* and English *cuckoo* may yield quite different scores, although the English and the French words are almost identical in pronunciation.

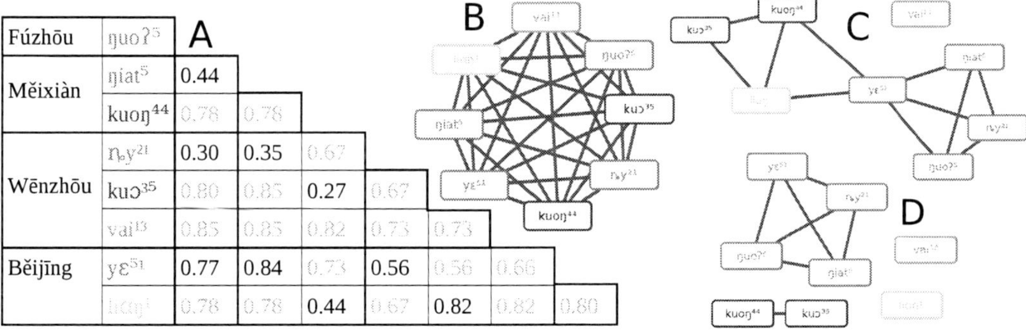

		ŋuoʔ⁵	ŋiat⁵	kuoŋ⁴⁴	n̠y²¹	kuɔ³⁵	vai¹³	yɛ⁵¹
Fúzhōu	ŋuoʔ⁵							
Měixiàn	ŋiat⁵	0.44						
	kuoŋ⁴⁴	0.78	0.78					
Wēnzhōu	n̠y²¹	0.30	0.35	0.67				
	kuɔ³⁵	0.80	0.85	0.27	0.67			
	vai¹³	0.85	0.85	0.82	0.73	0.73		
Běijīng	yɛ⁵¹	0.77	0.84	0.73	0.56	0.56	0.66	
	luɛŋ¹	0.78	0.78	0.44	0.67	0.82	0.82	0.80

Figure 1: Similarity networks for partial cognate detection. A shows pairwise SCA distances computed between all morphemes of Chinese dialect words for `moon'. Values shaded in gray are excluded following filtering rules 1 and 2 (see text). B shows the initial similarity network with all nodes connected. C shows the network after filtering, and D shows the network after applying the partitioning algorithm.

(2014b). As a general rule, language-specific approaches outperform language-independent ones, provided the sample size is large enough (List 2014a).

Two similarity measures are used in this paper, one language-independent, and one language-specific one. The above-mentioned SCA method for phonetic alignments (List 2012b, 2014b) reduces the phonetic space of sound sequences to 28 sound classes. Based on a scoring function which defines transition scores between the sound classes, phonetic sequences are aligned and similarity and distance scores can be determined. The LexStat approach List (2012a, 2014b) also uses sound classes, but instead of using a pre-defined scoring function, transition scores between sound classes are determined with help of a permutation test. In this test, words drawn from a randomized sample are repeatedly aligned with each other in order to create a distribution of sound transitions for unrelated languages. This distribution is then compared with the actual distribution retrieved from aligned words in the word list, and a language-specific scoring function is created List (2014b). SCA is very fast in computation, but LexStat has a much higher accuracy. Both approaches are freely available as part of the LingPy software package (List and Forkel 2016).

3.2 Sequence Similarity Networks

Sequence similarity networks are tools for exploratory data analysis. In evolutionary biology they are used to study complex evolutionary processes (Méheust et al. 2016, Corel et al. 2016). They represent sequences as nodes and connec-

tions between nodes represent similarities which are usually determined from similarity scores exceeding a certain threshold (Alvarez-Ponce et al. 2013). Since evolutionary processes leave specific traces in the network topology, they can be identified by applying techniques for network analysis. In linguistics, sequence similarity networks have been rarely applied (Lopez et al. 2013), although they are applicable, provided that one uses informed measures for phonetic similarity.

For the application of sequence similarity networks it is essential to decide when to draw an edge between two nodes and when not. For the new approach to partial cognate detection, three filtering criteria are applied. (1) No edges are drawn between morphemes which occur in the same word. (2) No morpheme in one word is linked to two morphemes in another word, with the preference given to morpheme pairs with the lowest phonetic distance applying a greedy strategy. (3) Edges are only drawn when the phonetic distance between the morphemes is beyond a certain threshold. The application of the filtering criteria is illustrated in Fig. 1 for the exemplary words shown in Table 1.

3.3 Network Partitioning

Cognate morphemes in a similarity network can be found by partitioning the network into groups. Many algorithms are available for this purpose, as can be seen from evolutionary biology, where homology detection is frequently approached from a network perspective (Vlasblom and Wodak 2009). Three different algorithms were tested for this purpose. A flat version of the UPGMA algorithm for hierarchical clustering (Sokal and Michener 1958), which terminates when a certain user-defined threshold is reached is originally underlying the LexStat algorithm and was therefore also included in this study. Markov Clustering (van Dongen 2000) uses techniques for matrix multiplication to inflate and expand the edge weights in a given network until weak edges have disappeared and a few clusters of connected nodes remain. Markov Clustering is very popular in biology and was shown to outperform the popular Affinity Propagation algorithm (Frey and Dueck 2007) in the task of homolog detection in biology (Vlasblom and Wodak 2009). As a third method, we follow List et al. (2016b) in testing Infomap (Rosvall and Bergstrom 2008), a method that was originally designed to detect *communities* in complex networks. Communities are groups that share more links with each other than outside the group (Newman and Girvan 2004). Infomap uses random walks to find the best partition of a network into communities. Infomap is not a classical partitioning algorithm, and we do not know of any studies which tested its suitability for the task of homolog detection in evolutionary biology, but according to List et al. (2016b), Infomap shows a better performance than UPGMA in automatic cognate detection.

3.4 Analyses and Evaluation

All methods, be it classical or partial cognate detection, require a user-defined threshold. Since our gold standard data was too small to split it into training and tests sets, we carried out an exhaustive comparison of all methods on different thresholds varying between 0.05 and 0.95 in steps of 0.05. B-cubed scores were chosen as an evaluation measure for cognate detection (Bagga and Baldwin 1998), since they have been shown to yield sensible results (Hauer and Kondrak 2011).

With SCA and LexStat, two classical methods for cognate detection were tested List (2014b), and their underlying models for phonetic similarity (see Sec. 3.1) were used as basis for the partial cognate detection algorithm. All in all, this yielded four different methods: LexStat, LexStat-Partial, SCA, and SCA-Partial. Since our new algorithms yield partial cognates, while LexStat and SCA yield ``complete" cognates, it is not possible to compare them directly. In order to allow for a direct comparison, partial cognate sets were converted into ``complete" cognate sets using the above-mentioned strict coding approach

proposed by Ben Hamed and Wang (2006): only those words in which *all* morphemes are cognate were assigned to the cognate same set. With a total of three different clustering algorithms (UPGMA, Markov Clustering, and Infomap), we thus carried out twelve tests on complete cognacy (three for each of our four approaches), and six additional tests on pure partial cognate detection, in which we compared the suitability of SCA and LexStat as string similarity measures.

LexStat				
Cluster-Method	**T**	**P**	**R**	**FS**
UPGMA	0.60	0.9030	0.8743	0.8878
Markov	0.50	0.9123	0.8752	0.8933
Infomap	0.50	0.9131	0.8866	0.8995
SCA				
Cluster-Method	**T**	**P**	**R**	**FS**
UPGMA	0.45	0.8595	0.8707	0.8648
Markov	0.45	0.8049	0.8097	0.8031
Infomap	0.35	0.8901	0.8573	0.8734
LexStat-Partial Complete Cognacy				
Cluster-Method	**T**	**P**	**R**	**FS**
UPGMA	0.90	0.9193	0.9638	0.9399
Markov	0.70	0.9275	0.9342	0.9298
Infomap	0.65	0.9453	0.9363	0.9404
SCA-Partial Complete Cognacy				
Cluster-Method	**T**	**P**	**R**	**FS**
UPGMA	0.60	0.9304	0.9045	0.9172
Markov	0.95	0.8153	0.8949	0.8446
Infomap	0.55	0.9104	0.9366	0.9223
LexStat-Partial Partial Cognacy				
Cluster-Method	**T**	**P**	**R**	**FS**
UPGMA	0.75	0.8920	0.8820	0.8867
Markov	0.60	0.8858	0.8724	0.8782
Infomap	0.60	0.8876	0.8844	0.8856
SCA-Partial Partial Cognacy				
Cluster-Method	**T**	**P**	**R**	**FS**
UPGMA	0.50	0.8597	0.8509	0.8552
Markov	0.50	0.8074	0.7621	0.7755
Infomap	0.35	0.8676	0.8439	0.8553

Table 3: General performance of the algorithms on all datasets. The table shows for each of the 18 different methods the threshold (T) for which the best B-Cubed F-Score was determined, as well as the B-Cubed precision (P), recall (R), and F-score (FS). The best result in each block is shaded in gray.

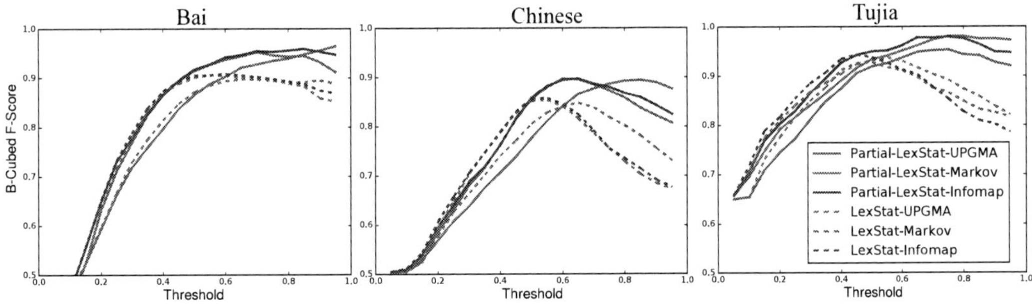

Figure 2: Comparing the results for the LexStat sequences similarities

3.5 Implementation

The code was implemented in Python, as part of the LingPy library (Version 2.5, List and Forkel (2016), `http://lingpy.org`). The Igraph software package (Csárdi and Nepusz 2006) is needed to apply the Infomap algorithm.

4 Results

The aggregated results of the test (thresholds, precision, recall, and F-scores) are given in Table 3, specific results for the comparison of LexStat with LexStat-Partial are given in Table 3. In general, one can clearly see that the partial cognate detection algorithms outperform their non-partial counterparts when applying the complete cognacy measure. The differences are very striking, with LexStat-Partial outperforming its non-partial counterpart by up to four points, and SCA-Partial outperforming the classical SCA variant by almost five points.[2] In contrast, we do not find strong differences in the performance of the cluster algorithms. Infomap outperforms the other cluster algorithms in almost all tests (all other aspects being equal), but the differences are not high enough to make any further conclusions at this point.

When comparing the aggregated results for the true evaluation of partial cognate detection (the last two blocks in Figure 2), the scores are less high than in the complete cognate analyses. Given that we cannot detect any striking tendency, like a drastic drop of precision or recall, this suggests that the algorithms generally loose accuracy in the task of ``true" partial cognate detection. This is surely not surprising, since the task of detecting exactly which morphemes in the data are historically related is much more complex than the task of detecting which words are completely cognate.

In Figure 2, detailed analyses for the LexStat analyses with complete cognate evaluation (the first and the third block in Table 3) are shown for each of the datasets, and throughout all thresholds we tested. The superior performance of the partial cognate detection variants is reflected in all datasets. That the internal diversity of the Chinese languages largely exceeds Bai and Tujia can be seen from the generally lower scores which all algorithms achieve for the datasets.

5 Discussion

This paper has presented a pilot approach for the detection of partial cognates in multilingual word lists. Although the results are very promising at this stage, we can think of many points where improvement is needed, and further studies are needed to fully assess the potential of the current approach. First, it should be tested on additional datasets, and ideally also on language families other than Sino-Tibetan. Second, since our approach is very general, it can easily be adjusted to employ different string similarity measures or different partitioning algorithms, and it would be interesting to see whether alternative measures can improve upon our current version.

Acknowledgments

This research was supported by the DFG research fellowship grant 261553824 *Vertical and lateral aspects of Chinese dialect history* (JML). ED is supported by by the ERC under the European Community's Seventh Framework Programme, FP7/2007-2013 Grant Agreement # 615274.

Supplementary Material

The Sup. Material contains results, benchmark datasets, and code, downloadable at: `https://zenodo.org/record/51328`.

---

[2]By one point, we mean 0.01 on the B-Cube scale.

References

David Alvarez-Ponce, Philippe Lopez, Eric Bapteste, and James O. McInerney. 2013. Gene similarity networks provide tools for understanding eukaryote origins and evolution. *Proceedings of the National Academy of Sciences of the United States of America* 110(17):E1594--1603.

Quentin D. Atkinson and Russell D. Gray. 2006. How old is the Indo-European language family? Illumination or more moths to the flame? In Peter Forster and Colin Renfrew, editors, *Phylogenetic methods and the prehistory of languages*, McDonald Institute for Archaeological Research, Cambridge, pages 91--109.

Amit Bagga and Breck Baldwin. 1998. Entity-based cross-document coreferencing using the vector space model. In *Proceedings of the 36th Annual Meeting of the ACL*. pages 79--85.

Mahe Ben Hamed and Feng Wang. 2006. Stuck in the forest: Trees, networks and Chinese dialects. *Diachronica* 23:29--60.

Běijīng Dàxué 北京大学, editor. 1964. *Hànyǔ fāngyán cíhuì* 汉语方言词汇[Chinese dialect vocabularies]. Wénzì Gǎigé 文字改革, Běijing 北京.

Eduardo Corel, Philippe Lopez, Raphaël Méheust, and Eric Bapteste. 2016. Network-thinking: Graphs to analyze microbial complexity and evolution. *Trends Microbiology* 24(3):224--237.

Gábor Csárdi and Tamás Nepusz. 2006. The igraph software package for complex network research. *InterJournal Complex Systems* page 1695.

Brendan J. Frey and Delbert Dueck. 2007. Clustering by passing messages between data points. *Science* 315:972--976.

Leanne S. Haggerty, Pierre-Alain A. Jachiet, William P. Hanage, David A. Fitzpatrick, Philippe Lopez, Mary J. O'Connell, Davide Pisani, Mark Wilkinson, Eric Bapteste, and James O. McInerney. 2014. A pluralistic account of homology: adapting the models to the data. *Mol. Biol. Evol.* 31(3):501--516.

Harald Hammarström, Robert Forkel, Martin Haspelmath, and Sebastian Bank. 2015. *Glottolog*. Max Planck Institute for Evolutionary Anthropology, Leipzig.

Bradley Hauer and Grzegorz Kondrak. 2011. Clustering semantically equivalent words into cognate sets in multilingual lists. In *Proceedings of the 5th International Joint NLP conference.* pages 865--873.

Hóu, Jīngyī 侯精一, editor. 2004. *Xiàndài Hànyǔ fāngyán yīnkù* 现代汉语方言音库[Phonological database of Chinese dialects]. Shànghǎi Jiàoyù 上海教育, Shànghǎi 上海.

Gerhard Jäger. 2013. Phylogenetic inference from word lists using weighted alignment with empirical determined weights. *Language Dynamics and Change* 3(2):245--291.

Johann-Mattis List. 2012a. Lexstat. automatic detection of cognates in multilingual wordlists. In *Proceedings of the EACL 2012 Joint Workshop of LINGVIS and UNCLH*. Stroudsburg, pages 117--125.

Johann-Mattis List. 2012b. SCA. phonetic alignment based on sound classes. In Marija Slavkovik and Dan Lassiter, editors, *New directions in logic, language, and computation*, Springer, Berlin and Heidelberg, pages 32--51.

Johann-Mattis List. 2014a. Investigating the impact of sample size on cognate detection. *Journal of Language Relationship* 11:91--101.

Johann-Mattis List. 2014b. *Sequence comparison in historical linguistics*. Düsseldorf University Press, Düsseldorf. URL: http://sequencecomparison.github.io.

Johann-Mattis List. 2016. Beyond cognacy: Historical relations between words and their implication for phylogenetic reconstruction. *Journal of Language Evolution* 1(2). Published online before print.

Johann-Mattis List, Michael Cysouw, and Robert Forkel. 2016a. *Concepticon: A resource for the linking of concept lists*. Max Planck Institute for the Science of Human History, Jena. Version: 1.0, URL: http://concepticon.clld.org.

Johann-Mattis List and Robert Forkel. 2016. *LingPy. A Python library for historical linguistics*. Max Planck Institute for the Science of Human History, Jena. Version 2.5. URL: http://lingpy.org. With contributions by Steven Moran, Peter Bouda, Johannes Dellert, Taraka Rama, Frank Nagel, and Simon Greenhill.

Johann-Mattis List, Simon Greenhill, and Russell Gray. 2016b. The potential of automatic cognate detection for historical linguistics. Manuscript in preparation.

Philippe Lopez, Johann-Mattis List, and Eric Bapteste. 2013. A preliminary case for exploratory networks in biology and linguistics. In Heiner Fangerau, Hans Geisler, Thorsten Halling, and William Martin, editors, *Classification and evolution in biology, linguistics and the history of science*, Franz Steiner Verlag, Stuttgart, pages 181--196.

Wilhelm Meyer-Lübke. 1911. *Romanisches etymologisches Wörterbuch*. Winter, Heidelberg.

Raphaël Méheust, Ehud Zelzion, Debashish Bhattacharya, Philippe Lopez, and Eric Bapteste. 2016. Protein networks identify novel symbiogenetic genes resulting from plastid endosymbiosis. *Proceedings of the National Academy of Sciences of the United States of America* 113(3): 3579--3584.

M. E. J. Newman and M. Girvan. 2004. Finding and evaluating community structure in networks. *Physical Review E* 69(2):026113+.

Martin Rosvall and Carl T. Bergstrom. 2008. Maps of random walks on complex networks reveal community structure. *Proceedings of the National Academy of Sciences of the United States of America* 105(4):1118--1123.

Damian Satterthwaite-Phillips. 2011. *Phylogenetic inference of the Tibeto-Burman languages*. PhD Thesis, Stanford University, Stanford.

Robert. R. Sokal and Charles. D. Michener. 1958. A statistical method for evaluating systematic relationships. *University of Kansas Scientific Bulletin* 28:1409--1438.

George S. Starostin. 2013a. Annotated Swadesh wordlists for the Tujia group. In George Starostin, editor, *The Global Lexicostatistical Database*, RGGU, Moscow. URL: `http://starling.rinet.ru/new100/tuj.xls`.

George S. Starostin. 2013b. Lexicostatistics as a basis for language classification. In Heiner Fangerau, Hans Geisler, Thorsten Halling, and William Martin, editors, *Classification and evolution in biology, linguistics and the history of science*, Franz Steiner Verlag, Stuttgart, pages 125--146.

Robert L. Trask. 2000. *The dictionary of historical and comparative linguistics*. Edinburgh University Press, Edinburgh.

Peter Turchin, Ilja Peiros, and Murray Gell-Mann. 2010. Analyzing genetic connections between languages by matching consonant classes. *Journal of Language Relationship* 3:117--126.

Stijn M. van Dongen. 2000. *Graph clustering by flow simulation*. PhD Thesis, University of Utrecht.

James Vlasblom and Shoshana J. Wodak. 2009. Markov clustering versus affinity propagation for the partitioning of protein interaction graphs. *BMC Bioinformatics* 10:99.

Feng Wang. 2006. *Comparison of languages in contact*. Academia Sinica, Taipei.

Author Index

Adler, Meni, 474
Agić, Željko, 561
Alonso, Miguel A., 425
Antetomaso, Stephanie, 59
Araki, Jun, 506
Arora, Raman, 14
Aziz, Wilker, 169

Baldwin, Timothy, 344
Bánréti, Zoltán, 181
Bapteste, Eric, 599
Barbu, Eduard, 287
Baroni, Marco, 213
Barrett, Maria, 579
Batmanghelich, Kayhan, 537
Beigman Klebanov, Beata, 101
Benton, Adrian, 14
Bilu, Yonatan, 525
Bingel, Joachim, 337, 579
Biran, Or, 243
Bontcheva, Kalina, 393
Bouillon, Pierrette, 162
Brooke, Julian, 344
Byrne, Bill, 299

Callison-Burch, Chris, 143
Carlini, Roberto, 499
Carpuat, Marine, 362
Chang, Ming-Wei, 201
Chen, Hsin-Hsi, 20
Chen, Huan-Yuan, 20
Cheung, Jackie Chi Kit, 112
Chidlovskii, Boris, 26, 326
Clark, Stephen, 188
Clinchant, Stephane, 26, 326
Cohen, William, 269
Cohn, Trevor, 393
Collobert, Ronan, 573
Cordeiro, Silvio, 156
Costa-jussà, Marta R., 357
Croijmans, Ilja, 306
Cross, James, 32
Csurka, Gabriela, 26, 326

Dagan, Ido, 249, 474

Dakwale, Praveen, 38
de Kok, Daniël, 1
Dhingra, Bhuwan, 269
Dredze, Mark, 14, 149
Dubey, Kumar, 467
Duh, Kevin, 531
Dušek, Ondřej, 45

Ebling, Sarah, 162
Eger, Steffen, 52
Elgohary, Ahmed, 362
Elsner, Micha, 59
Espinosa Anke, Luis, 499

Fang, Yimai, 479
Feldman, Naomi, 59
Feng, Xiaocheng, 66
Fern, Xiaoli, 369
Ficler, Jessica, 72
Fitzpatrick, Dylan, 269
Flekova, Lucie, 313
Flor, Michael, 101
Fomicheva, Marina, 77
Fonollosa, José A. R., 357
Fukui, Kazuki, 493

Gerlach, Johanna, 162
Gershman, Sam, 537
Gfeller, Beat, 83
Ghaeini, Reza, 369
Ghosh, Debanjan, 549
Gkatzia, Dimitra, 264
Gliozzo, Alfio, 243
Goldberg, Yoav, 72, 231, 412
Gómez-Rodríguez, Carlos, 425
Gosztolya, Gábor, 181
Gu, Yanhui, 89
Guo, Weiwei, 107
Gutierrez, E. Dario, 101
Guzmán, Francisco, 460

Hajishirzi, Hannaneh, 118
Hall, Keith, 83
Hammond, Adam, 344
Han, Yubo, 549

Hao, Hongwei, 207
Hasler, Eva, 299
Hayashi, Katsuhiko, 95
Hendrickx, Iris, 306
Hinrichs, Erhard, 1
Hoffmann, Ildikó, 181
Hovy, Dirk, 351, 591
Hu, Weihua, 380
Huang, Liang, 32, 369
Huang, Lifu, 66

Idiart, Marco, 156, 419
Ittycheriah, Abe, 124

Jalili Sabet, Masoud, 287
Ji, Heng, 66
Ji, Yangfeng, 118
Jin, Zhi, 130
Johannsen, Anders, 561
Jurcicek, Filip, 45

Kálmán, János, 181
Kann, Katharina, 555
Keller, Frank, 579
Khanam, Aquila, 549
Kiela, Douwe, 188
Kim, Young-Bum, 8
Klakow, Dietrich, 175
Komura, Taku, 531
Köper, Maximilian, 256
Korhonen, Anna, 518
Kozareva, Zornitsa, 107, 332
Kumar, Abhishek, 506

Lai, K. Robert, 225
Lazaridou, Angeliki, 213
Lefever, Els, 306
Legrand, Joël, 573
Lemon, Oliver, 264
Leong, Chee Wee, 101
Levy, Omer, 249
Li, Bingchen, 207
Li, Boyang, 118
Li, Ge, 130
Li, Liangyou, 275
Li, Qi, 107
Li, Yi, 195
Ling, Shaoshi, 387
List, Johann-Mattis, 599
Liu, Huan, 543
Liu, Qun, 275
Liu, Ting, 66
Liu, Yang, 195

Logacheva, Varvara, 585
Long, Teng, 112
Lopez, Philippe, 599
Lowe, Ryan, 112
Luan, Yi, 118
Lukasik, Michal, 393, 585
Luo, Zhiyuan, 374

Majid, Asifa, 306
Màrquez, Lluís, 460
Matsumoto, Yuji, 531
McKeown, Kathleen, 243
Meek, Chris, 201
Mehler, Alexander, 52
Men, Rui, 130
Mi, Haitao, 124
Mihalcea, Rada, 320
Mihaylov, Todor, 399
Moens, Marie-Francine, 188
Monz, Christof, 38
Mori, Shinsuke, 236
Morstatter, Fred, 543
Mou, Lili, 130
Muehl, Michael, 269
Muresan, Smaranda, 549

Nagata, Masaaki, 95, 406
Nakov, Preslav, 399, 460
Narasimhan, Karthik, 537
Naskar, Sudip Kumar, 281
Negri, Matteo, 287
Ney, Hermann, 293
Nguyen, Kim Anh, 454
Ninomiya, Takashi, 236
Nishino, Masaaki, 406
Nothman, Joel, 432

Onrust, Louis, 137
Oshikiri, Takamasa, 493

Pákáski, Magdolna, 181
Pal, Santanu, 281
Pavlick, Ellie, 143
Peng, Nanyun, 149
Peter, Jan-Thorsten, 293
Pham, Nghia The, 213
Plank, Barbara, 412
Precup, Doina, 112
Preoţiuc-Pietro, Daniel, 313

Qi, Zhenyu, 207
Qin, Bing, 66
Qu, Weiguang, 89

Ramisch, Carlos, 156
Rayner, Manny, 162
Reitter, David, 443
Richardson, Matthew, 201
Rieser, Verena, 264
Rodríguez-Fernández, Sara, 499
Roth, Dan, 387
Rothe, Sascha, 512
Ruan, Xianzhi, 320

Sachan, Mrinmaya, 467, 486
Saeedi, Ardavan, 537
Saldanha, Gavin, 243
Salle, Alexandre, 419
Sarikaya, Ruhi, 8
Schogol, Vlad, 83
Schulte im Walde, Sabine, 256, 454
Schulz, Philip, 169
Schütze, Hinrich, 512, 555
Søgaard, Anders, 231, 337, 412, 561, 579
Shi, Wei, 207
Shi, Xingtian, 89
Shimodaira, Hidetoshi, 493
Shutova, Ekaterina, 101
Sima'an, Khalil, 169
Slonim, Noam, 525
Song, Yangqiu, 387
Specia, Lucia, 77, 585
Spruit, Shannon L., 591
Srijith, P. K., 393
Stahlberg, Felix, 299
Stanovsky, Gabriel, 474
Strasly, Irene, 162
Stratos, Karl, 8
Suh, Jina, 201
Sun, Xu, 567
Suzuki, Jun, 406
Szatlóczki, Gréta, 181

Tadepalli, Prasad, 369
Tang, Duyu, 66
Teufel, Simone, 479
Tian, Jun, 207
Tomori, Suzushi, 236
Tóth, László, 181
Tsourakis, Nikos, 162
Tsujii, Jun'ichi, 380
Turchi, Marco, 287

Ungar, Lyle, 313

van den Bosch, Antal, 137, 306
van Genabith, Josef, 281

Van hamme, Hugo, 137
Varjokallio, Matti, 175
Vela, Mihaela, 281
Veyhe, Bartal, 374
Vilares, David, 425
Villavicencio, Aline, 156, 419
Vincze, Veronika, 181
Vo, Duy Tin, 219
Vu, Duy, 393
Vu, Ngoc Thang, 454
Vulić, Ivan, 188, 518

Waite, Aurelien, 299
Wan, Xiaojun, 449
Wang, Jin, 225
Wang, Weiyue, 293
Wang, Zhiguo, 124
Wanner, Leo, 499
Way, Andy, 275
Webster, Kellie, 432
Wei, Jinmao, 89
Wei, Zhongyu, 195
Wilson, Steven, 320
Woods, Aubrie, 438

Xing, Eric, 467, 486
Xu, Bo, 207
Xu, Jingjing, 567
Xu, Yan, 130
Xu, Yang, 443

Yamada, Makoto, 332
Yan, Rui, 130
Yang, Zhenglu, 89
Yih, Wen-tau, 201
Yu, Liang-Chih, 225
Yu, Yang, 449
Yung, Frances, 531

Zhai, Ke, 107
Zhang, Lu, 130
Zhang, Xuejie, 225
Zhang, Yue, 219
Zhou, Junsheng, 89
Zhou, Peng, 207
Zhou, Xinjie, 449
Zhou, Zhong, 269
Zilio, Leonardo, 156
Zubiaga, Arkaitz, 393
Zukov Gregoric, Andrej, 374